Commentary

HANDBOOK ON USSR MILITARY FORCES

This is a PRINT REPLICA of TM 30-340, Handbook on USSR Militar
in installments to expedite dissemination to the field starting in 1945 until 1946. Unfortunately,
after an exhaustive search, we were unable to locate Chapter 9, EQUIPMENT. Chapters 8 and
10 were planned, but never published. Most of the text is legible, but some is very small. If
anyone can send us a copy of Chapter 9, we will be happy to update the book.

1. NATIONAL DEFENSE SYSTEM
2. PERSONNEL ADMINISTRATION
3. FIELD ORGANIZATIONS
4. SEMI MILITARY ORGANIZATIONS
5. TACTICS
6. FORTIFICATIONS
7. LOGISTICS
8. Planned but never published.
9. ************* MISSING ************ (EQUIPMENT)
10. Planned but never published.
11. AIR FORCE
12. MAPS AND SYMB0LS

Why buy a book you can download for free? We print this book so you don't have to.

First you gotta find a good clean (legible) copy and make sure it's the latest version (not always
easy). If you find a good copy, you could print it using a network printer you share with 100
other people (typically its either out of paper or toner). If it's just a 10-page document, no
problem, but if it's 250-pages, you will need to punch 3 holes in all those pages and put it in a 3-
ring binder. Takes at least an hour.

It's much more cost-effective to just order the latest version from Amazon.com

Why buy an eBook when you can access data on a website for free? HYPERLINKS

Anyone that has worked with large scientific documents knows how difficult it is to search to
find that one bit of critical information. Yes, the book is available as a PDF file, but do you
really want to search a PDF document manually? (Unfortunately, downloading the free sample
file at Amazon.com does not include this feature. You have to buy a copy to get that
functionality, but as inexpensive as this is, it's worth it.) Kindle allows you to do word search
and Page Flip (temporary place holder takes you back when you want to go back and check
something). Load this copy onto your Kindle, PC, iPad, Android Tablet, Nook, or iPhone
(download the FREE kindle App from the APP Store) and you have an easily searchable copy.
We recommend the Kindle Paperwhite. It's inexpensive, has long battery life (weeks) and can
hold a lot of documents. https://usgovpub.com

Other books we print that are available on Amazon.com:

Russia Military Power – Building a Military to Support Great Power Aspirations 2017

2019 Missile Defense Review

Chinese Military Dictionary   May 1944

China Military Power   Jan 2019

Hard Power   Jan 2019

Chairman Xi Remakes the PLA   Feb 2019

China Military Power   Jan 2019

China's Strategic Support Force: A Force for a New Era   Oct 2018

China's Evolving Surface Fleet   Jul 2017

Contingency Planning in China   2015

The Chinese People's Liberation Army In 2025   Jul 2015

China Cruise Missile A Low-Visibility Force Multiplier   Apr 2014

The Science of Military Strategy   Jun 2013

The Chinese Air Force   Aug 2012

Chinese Lessons from Other Peoples' Wars No 2011

The Science of Campaigns   Feb 2006

A Comparative English – Chinese Dictionary of Military Terms 1986

DOD Dictionary of Military and Associated Terms

Foreign Military Organization Charts

FM 1-04   Legal Support to the Operational Army

FM 3-12   Cyberspace and Electronic Warfare (EW) Operations

FM 3-90-1   Offense and Defense

FM 3-90-2   Reconnaissance, Security, and Tactical Enabling Tasks Volume 2

FM 3-0   Operations

FM 3-04   Army Aviation

FM 3-13   Information Operations

TECHNICAL MANUAL

HANDBOOK ON U. S. S. R. MILITARY FORCES

TM 30–430 is being published in installaments to expedite dissemination to the field. These chapters should be inserted in the loose-leaf binder furnished with Chapter V, November 1945.

WAR DEPARTMENT
WASHINGTON 25, D. C., 1 March 1946

TM 30–430, Handbook on U. S. S. R. Military Forces, is published for the information and guidance of all concerned.

[AG 300.7 (8 Oct 45)]

BY ORDER OF THE SECRETARY OF WAR:

OFFICIAL:

EDWARD F. WITSELL
Major General
The Adjutant General

DWIGHT D. EISENHOWER
Chief of Staff

DISTRIBUTION:

AGF (80); ASF (2); T (10); Arm & Sv Bd (1); S Div ASF (1).

Refer to FM 21–6 for explanation of distribution formula.

CHAPTER I

NATIONAL DEFENSE SYSTEM

TABLE OF CONTENTS

List of Illustrations

CHAPTER II
PERSONNEL ADMINISTRATION

TABLE OF CONTENTS

List of Illustrations

iv

CHAPTER III

FIELD ORGANIZATIONS

TABLE OF CONTENTS

List of Illustrations

CHAPTER IV

SEMI-MILITARY ORGANIZATIONS

TABLE OF CONTENTS

List of Illustrations

CHAPTER V

TACTICS

TABLE OF CONTENTS

List of Illustrations

CHAPTER VI

FORTIFICATIONS

TABLE OF CONTENTS

List of Illustrations

CHAPTER VII

LOGISTICS

TABLE OF CONTENTS

List of Illustrations

Chapter VIII - Never Released
Chapter IX - Not Found
Chapter X - Never Released

CHAPTER XI

AIR FORCES

TABLE OF CONTENTS

List of Illustrations

xiv

CHAPTER XII

MAPS, CONVENTIONAL SIGNS, AND SYMBOLS

TABLE OF CONTENTS

List of Illustrations

xvi

CHAPTER I

NATIONAL DEFENSE SYSTEM

Note: The Peoples' Commissariat of Defense re-absorbed the Red Navy and was renamed "The Peoples' Commissariat of the Armed Forces" in February 1946, and in March 1946 again renamed "Ministry of Armed Forces."

INTRODUCTION

1. GENERAL

The most essential element in the national defense system of the U. S. S. R. springs from the very nature of the totalitarian state. The political, government, economic, and military systems of such a state are so closely integrated that the same machinery and basic processes operate equally well in war and peace. In time of war, it is necessary only to shift the already totalized effort of the nation from civil development to the prosecution of the war. Control of national defense derives both advantages and disadvantages from centralization of control. Centralization of control permits quick changes in policies. It ties industrial production to defense requirements. It assures adequate financial support for necessary defense projects. Because military requirements are given priority over property rights or individual claims, it enables maximum utilization of new inventions, scientific discoveries, etc.

On the other hand, administrative difficulties arise in the regulation of the entire life of a nation through a huge bureaucracy. Valuable time is lost when the approval of many officials is needed for even the most minor projects. Great numbers of personnel are diverted from productive activity to checking, filing, and recording. It is difficult to train executives professionally when higher control revolves on political rather than professional questions. Inertia is inherent in the large bureaus. They tend to resist change, improvement, and general progress.

2. COMMUNIST PARTY SUPREMACY

Another fundamental feature of the national defense system of the U. S. S. R. is the supremacy of the Communist Party, which never has included more than 5 percent of the population, over all aspects

of national life. The constitutional structure of the Soviet Union permits absolute control of essential executive and legislative machinery through the control of a limited number of key positions at each governmental level. Political supervision of the army and the navy as well as civil commissariats ensures Party domination of these organizations and gives the Party a voice in operational and administrative decisions, particularly in matters of loyalty and appointment of personnel.

Although the Party, itself, maintains no armed forces, it has at its disposal two reliable organizations for the suppression of individual dissidence or collective rebellion. They are the troops and agents of the Peoples' Commissariats of Internal Affairs and State Security.

The flexibility of the Communist Party also has been a major factor in its continued strength. Party members generally are entrusted with all the major state offices. The Party constantly reinforces its control by extending membership to nearly all persons who distinguish themselves in any field.

Although the dominence of the Communist Party has continued throughout the history of the Soviet Union, many of its relationships with the Soviet state and the armed forces have changed and fluctuated since 1917. Basic political and propaganda doctrines have shifted from an early emphasis on international proletarian revolution to a more recent emphasis on intense national patriotism.

Lenin and Stalin have retained their eminent position, but Marx and Engels now compete with Peter the Great, Catherine, and even Ivan the Terrible for doctrinary prestige. A parallel change has taken place in the role of the armed forces. Although the armed forces were once a political instrument selected only from the proletariat, they have become, since 1939, increasingly an instrument of national policy selected from all classes. This development of the armed forces as cohesive nonpolitical organizations with increasing autonomy has been subject to considerable fluctuations and reverses.

The contrast between officers of 1918, who were military technicians under the thumb of political commissars, and present officers, who are members of a corps with exceptional authority, is outstanding. However, interim reversals and repressions, such as the Great Purge of 1937 and the restoration of political commissars in 1941 and 1942, also must be considered.

3. DEVELOPMENT OF COORDINATION

The coordination of national defense and the internal structure of the Red Army have been developed by a trial-and-error process which began even before World War I. The authority and degree of independence of the various arms demonstrate that, in some respects, the national defense system is conservative. In other respects, the system has reverted to earlier practice after periods of radical experimentation.

For example, a combined commissariat of defense with co-equal divisions for ground, naval, air, and supply forces, in existence since early revolutionary days, was abandoned as unsuccessful in 1937 when the U. S. S. R. returned to its pre-revolutionary organization of separate army (including air forces) and navy (including naval aviation and coastal defenses). In February 1946, the U. S. S. R. reverted to combined armed forces. The navy was re-absorbed into the Commissariat of Defense, renamed Commissariat of the Armed Forces.

Many successful innovations of World War I were revived during World War II. They include a unified GHQ for control over both land and sea operations and an inter-commissariat council controlling production, supply, transportation, etc.

Experience in World War II has fostered further advances, such as the creation of unified command control over rear services and the replacement system. The present national defense system of the U. S. S. R. combines the lesson of two wars. It appears, in general, to be an effective system.

In a cursory comparison of the Soviet and the late German national defense system, a number of parallels appear. Among these are the unified General Headquarters, the organized replacement army, full separation between the administration of officer and enlisted personnel, special armed organizations outside the armed forces for state security (the Soviet NKVD and NKGB are comparable to the German *SS*), and the delegation of major service functions to civil organizations (the Soviet Commissariats for Rail Transport and Signal Communications, etc., are comparable to the German *Todt* and *Reichsarbeitsdienst*). However, in purpose and in actual operation, these parallel organizations have been profoundly different in the two countries.

4. HISTORICAL DEVELOPMENT

An understanding of the present structure and functioning of the national defense system of the U. S. S. R. requires consideration of the historical development of a number of major factors. These include the coordination of defense, the Supreme Command, the professionalization of the Red Army, and political control over the Red Army.

a. Development of the high command and administration. The concepts of a coordinated direction of civil and military problems in war and of a unified Supreme Command have developed in Tsarist Russia and the U. S. S. R. since 1912. At that time a GHQ (the Imperial Defense Council) was formed to conduct the operations of all land and sea forces. The Army General Staff was removed from the War Office at the same time and placed under the jurisdiction of the GHQ. The War Office thus was left free to concentrate on administrative matters.

In 1915, the War Office strengthened its control over production, transport, and communications with the formation of a Council of Defense, headed by the Minister of War and vested with almost unlimited powers. This council included representatives of industry, the important public bodies, and the military, naval, and other departments. Special committees were organized for transportation, fuel, and supplies.

The October Revolution of 1917 disrupted these organizations. By 1918, however, the new Soviet state had re-instituted a comparable structure. The Council of Workers' and Peasants' Defense, headed by Lenin, provided central control of policy and economic resources. Subordinate to it was the new GHQ, or Revolutionary Military Council, headed by Trotsky as Commander in Chief and Commissar of the Army and Navy. Administrative unification of the armed forces other than the security troops also followed. By 1924, the Commissariat of the Army and Navy presented the following structure:

2

General Staff of the Ground Forces.
Main Administration of Army Personnel and
    Military Schools.
Main Naval Department.
Main Department of the Air Forces.
Main Department of Supply.
Main Sanitary and Veterinary Department.
Political Administration of the Armed Forces.

Between 1934 and 1938, a series of sweeping changes promoted military preparedness. In 1937, the Council of Labor and Defense, which had succeeded the Council of Workers' and Peasant's Defense, was relieved of economic functions by the Supreme Economic Council, and in over-all military policies by the War Council in 1938. To permit more effective technical development of the Navy and the specialized arms and to reduce the concentration of authority under military command after the Purge, the Commissariat of the Army and the Navy was split in 1937, both divisions undergoing further internal organizational changes. The Revolutionary Military Council, abolished in 1934, was replaced in 1937 by the Supreme Military Council and the Supreme Naval Council.

Thus, between 1937 and 1941, the Commissariat of Defense emphasized specialization and autonomy within its structure. It included the Commissar, 14 assistant commissars, and the following divisions:

    Affairs Administration (legal and internal ad-
        ministrative affairs).
    General Staff (operations, intelligence, signal
        communications, organization and training,
        air defense, rear areas, mobilization, fuels,
        topographic, historical, and administrative
        divisions).
    Air Forces Administration.
    Artillery Administration.
    Engineer Administration.
    Signal Administration.
    Antiaircraft Defense Administration.
    Chemical Defense Administration.
    Military Schools Administration.
    Combat Training Administration.
    Personnel Administration.
    Armament Administration.
    Moto-Mechanized Matériel Administration.
    Quartermaster Supplies Administration.
    Military Construction Administration.
    Central Military Cooperative Administration.
    Recreation Administration.

    Sanitary Administration.
    Veterinary Administration.
    Finance Administration.

During the first year of the war with Germany, it became evident that decentralization had been too extensive and that the defense machinery had become too sprawling for efficient operation. Consequently, by 1942, changes were effected which virtually reverted the defense organization to that of World War I. A GHQ to determine strategy and conduct operations was formed directly under the State Defense Committee. It consisted of the key personnel of all the armed forces.

The General Staff was relieved of such administrative functions as mobilization and rear services, was removed from the control of the Commissariat of Defense and operationally was placed directly under the GHQ. A special organization within the Commissariat was formed to administer mobilization and replacement. The combat arms absorbed the development and supply functions peculiar to them. Artillery took over all ammunition and all ordnance, except armored. Miscellaneous service functions, such as quartermaster supply, cooperatives, recreation, and the medical, veterinary, and finance services, were merged under the Chief of the Rear Services of the Red Army. And finally, the appointment of a number of key individuals to two, three, and even four separate positions of authority guaranteed close cooperation between related agencies and helped to minimize the tendency toward administrative inefficiency often characteristic of a bureaucratic structure. This organization has remained fundamentally unchanged up to the present time, except for the reabsorption of the Navy.

b. Changes in status of armed forces. The development of the professional and political status of the armed forces, particularly of the Red Army, has developed along two basic lines. They are the growth of a cohesive, centralized standing army in opposition to attempted formation of localized forces (National Guard), and the gradual reduction of direct political control over the army.

During the Revolution and the Civil War, all professional army men were regarded with suspicion by the new Soviet regime. Former officers operated as "military technicians" under the strict control of political commissars. Trotsky, particularly, favored the ultimate abandonment of a standing army and the substitution of a militia from the proletariat. Frunze, on the other hand, constantly emphasized

3

the necessity for professional training and the immediate inauguration of a pyramidal program for training officers.

In 1924, a compromise had been reached. The strength of the Red Army and Navy was stabilized at 562,000. In addition, 150,000 security troops and 100,000 Frontier Guards were maintained. The rest of the available manpower was trained in territorial units, serving from 8 to 10 months over a period of 5 years. The entire army, standing and territorial, was increasingly placed on a republican basis, with separate forces for the Ukraine, White Russia, Transcaucasia and, ultimately, other republics.

No permanent status was accorded army personnel. At the same time, however, the training of the army developed gradually along the lines advocated by Frunze. As early as 1921, the first class of Soviet General Staff officers was graduated from the War College.

This situation continued until 1934, although one major change took place in 1928. At that time, participation in the armed forces of the U. S. S. R. was restricted to members of the working class, others being relegated to auxiliary service only. Army service became a life-time profession. Concurrently, maximum ages in grade were drastically reduced to eliminate older and less reliable personnel and to provide opportunity for younger Soviet officers.

From 1935 on, an increasingly tense situation forced gradual abandonment of the territorial system. All territorial units were placed on a full standing status by 1939. Increasing demands for manpower in the army led to the widening of conscription.

In 1939, the principle of armed service by all citizens, as embodied in the constitution of 1936, was promulgated in the universal service regulations. The need for mobility and flexibility of the army also led to the merging of all republican units into a single force.

The separate status and prestige of officer personnel increased with the growth of the army. In 1935, officer ranks were re-introduced, including the new title of "Marshal of the Soviet Union." In 1940, even the formerly hated title of "General" was resumed.

This trend was accelerated during the war with Germany. In 1943, officers' epaulets were authorized and the term "officer," itself, returned. Even in the official military press, comparisons were made with the Czarist officer corps. Increasing emphasis was placed on the military, social, and political leadership of the Soviet officer and on military life as a permanent profession. At the same time, responsibility for the loyalty of its members and for the internal security of the army was transferred in its entirety to the Red Army. Thus, with the conclusion of World War II, the Red Army reached the peak of its prestige as a professional permanent group.

The history of political control over the armed forces has varied with changes in their status and prestige. In general, tight political control has coincided with periods of disaster and uncertainty; loosening of control with confidence and victory.

From the Revolution of 1917 until about 1923, the high command of the Red Army was vested in a group of Communist Party leaders. The heterogeneous units and formations which constituted the Red Army were commanded by "Party men." These political leaders were called War Commissars. The military officers, then termed "military specialists," played only a subordinate role. Credit was given the War Commissars for the successes of the Red Army in dealing with counterrevolutionary forces and general unrest. Lenin said, "Without the War Commissars, we should never have had a Red Army."

After 1923, when calm had been restored in Soviet Russia, it was decided to hand control of the Red Army over to the military to create an efficient and well-trained force. The high command was composed of military officers of political reliability. In those units and formations in which the senior army officer was considered politically reliable, the commissars were abolished. The test of political reliability was Party membership or, at the least, sympathy with the Communist Party. Such officers became commanders, and assistants responsible for political work in the unit or formation were assigned to them. War Commissars, who were considered to have acquired sufficient military experience during the revolutionary wars, in some cases became commanders. By about 1936, every unit and formation of the Red Army had a military commander.

All units and formations of the Red Army again were allotted specially selected political commissars following the treason trials of 1936–1938. This was carried out in all cases, regardless of the political reliability of the commander in question. The newly appointed commissars countersigned all orders of the commander and thus had veto power on all decisions.

During the Finnish Campaign of 1939–1940, it was found that considerable difference of opinion existed between commanders and commissars. The

4

commissars used their powers to interfere with purely tactical decisions, about which they had insufficient knowledge. Reverses in the field resulted. Accordingly, in 1940, commissars were abolished for the second time and were reduced to the status of assistant commanders for political matters. Among military commanders, no distinction was made on the basis of Party membership.

The Political Administration of the Red Army was renamed the Main Political Administration. Former Commissars of Red Army and Party members were required not only to disseminate propaganda and instruction inside the army, but also to help to increase Red Army prestige among the civilian population.

The major reverses which followed the initial German offensive against the Soviet Union (1941–1942) led to the reinstitution of the commissars to restore the morale, discipline, and patriotism of the Army. The commander remained the head of the unit or formation and the commissar became, to quote the official directive, its "Father and Soul."

The commissar was required to suppress any trace of treasonable or counterrevolutionary activities, to maintain the morale and patriotism of the troops, to supervise propaganda and political work, and to support the commander in carrying out operational plans. He was responsible, equally with the commander, for maintaining the "fighting strength of the troops." The power of veto, previously mentioned, was revived. This special position of the commissars, most of whom had no military experience, caused serious personal friction between them and the professional military commanders.

In October 1942, when the military situation was critical, Stalin decided that all other considerations should give way to purely military interests. Accordingly, for the third time, the abolition of commissars was ordered. They reverted to the status of assistant commanders for political matters, or chiefs of political administrations and departments of armies and fronts. They were given appropriate military ranks. These were equivalent, in divisions and lower commands, to that of the chief of staff.

Commissars were, in most cases, required to attend courses in basic military subjects. They were not expected to be able to command the units or formations to which they belonged. Although they assisted with military training, they did not share tactical responsibility with the commanders. Polit-

ical control of military command within the armed forces has continued on this basis to the present.

5. FUTURE TRENDS

A number of major changes have occurred and will occur during the transition of the U. S. S. R. from war to peace. The State Defense Committee was dissolved in September 1945. It may be that this will be followed by the dissolution of the GHQ and that the General Staff will be returned to a status of full subordination to the Peoples' Commissariat of Defense. Responsibility for mobilization and replacement probably will revert to the General Staff as it becomes more of a planning and less of an administrative function. The unification of rear services and the extensive functions of the arms probably will continue.

All evidence indicates retention of independent status by the security forces (NKVD and NKGB). It is to be expected that there will be greater independence for the air arm. It is a distinct possibility that the growing importance of the air forces and the expansion of their proportionate strength may lead to the emergence of a separate commissariat for air. Of all the arms, air is certain to witness the most sweeping revisions in organization, equipment, and techniques. A trend that is worthy of note is the diminishing frequency of subordination of supporting air units to lower echelon command headquarters in favor of army or army group control of ever greater masses of tactical air power.

Tighter political control will unquestionably be reestablished over the Red Army, both through intensive indoctrination of its members and through complete elimination of possible unreliable elements.

Another measure designed to lessen the concerted power of army leadership is the constitutional change of 1944 which transforms the Peoples' Commissariat of Defense from an All-Union to a Union-Republican commissariat, with subordinate commissariats for each of the republics. There is little evidence that this change is taking place, except for the organization of Republican Commissariats of Defense by the Ukrainian and White Russian S. S. R's. In fact, the latest organization of the military districts (1946), which cuts across republic boundaries, may be considered a negative indication.

Correspondingly, possible reintroduction of a territorial system is not to be anticipated when consideration is given to the mass drive, at the end of the war, to re-enlist the maximum number of noncommissioned officers in the Red Army.

PART I. THE STATE, THE PARTY, AND THE ARMED FORCES

Section I. U. S. S. R. CONSTITUTIONAL STRUCTURE

The constitution of the U. S. S. R. (1936) vests the highest legislative and executive powers of the nation in the Supreme Soviet, a representative body of two chambers. Representation in one chamber, the Soviet of the Union, is based on one deputy per each 300,000 population. The other chamber, the Soviet of Nationalities, draws its representation on the basis of 25 deputies from each of the Union Republics, 11 from each Autonomous Republic, 5 from each Autonomous *Oblast*, and 1 from each national *Okrug*.

In peacetime, the Supreme Soviet meets biannually, each session lasting approximately 1 week. Between sessions, the powers of the Supreme Soviet are delegated to the Presidium, which is elected by both chambers sitting in joint session. The Supreme Soviet or the Presidium appoints the commissars of the All-Union and Union-Republican commissariats. These collectively form the Soviet or Council of Peoples' Commissars, the chief executive and administrative body of the state.

The Council of Peoples' Commissars consists of the heads of 24 All-Union commissariats which have no counterpart within the republics, 22 Union-Republican commissariats which have counterparts within the republics and operate, at least theoretically, through them, and approximately 15 main administrations and committee chiefs of commissariat importance.

For more efficient operation, this unwieldly body delegates its powers to a smaller number of councils and committees. Especially are they delegated to the Supreme Economic Council and its subordinate organizations for defense industries, such as metallurgy and chemistry, machinery production, fuel and electricity, agricultural procurement, and consumer goods.

Between 1941 and its dissolution at the end of World War II, the State Defense Committee of the Council of Peoples' Commissars was the highest operating committee, and constituted a virtually all-powerful body under the direction of Stalin, Chairman of the Council of Peoples' Commissars, Commissar of Defense, and Commander in Chief of the Armed Forces (fig. 1).

The administration of justice is vested in the Supreme Court as the highest judicial organ of the U. S. S. R. It supervises all courts of the U. S. S. R. Courts are established by the Supreme Soviet for all political divisions of the nation. The Supreme Court and special courts with All-Union jurisdiction are staffed by appointees of the Supreme Soviet. The Military Collegium of the Supreme Court is especially charged with the administration of justice within the armed forces. It supervises the entire system of military courts through the Chief Procurator of the Commissariat of Defense.

Section II. THE COMMUNIST PARTY

More important than the formal governmental structure is the Communist Party. The existence of the Party is specifically authorized in the 1936 Constitution as essential to the preservation and protection of the foundations of the state. Although the formation of trade unions, cooperative associations, youth organizations, and cultural, technical, and scientific societies is an ensured right of the people and such organizations may nominate candidates for election to the Supreme Soviet and other bodies, "the most active and politically conscious citizens in the ranks of the working class and other strata of the workers unite in the Communist Party of the U. S. S. R." These provisions guarantee an unchallengeable position for the Communist Party, and render opposition to it illegal.

Because the Communist Party is the only organized political entity in the U. S. S. R., it alone can provide the trained personnel for key government positions. Domination by the Party is further assured by the fact that the Supreme Soviet and the comparable local legislative bodies are very large and meet but infrequently for brief periods. Consequently, not only is interim power delegated to the corresponding Presidia, but so is the actual review and control of executive activities. Additional concentration of power is facilitated by the Soviet practice of assigning multiple correlated positions to the same individual.

Internally, the Communist Party consists of a centrally-controlled hierarchy which is ultimately based on small semi-secret "cells" in every part and organization of the U. S. S. R. This network maintains its own direct communications, independent of the state. Discipline within the Party is strict, and deviation from authorized doctrine or policy is followed by immediate expulsion or other punishment.

Every possible measure is applied to give the Com-

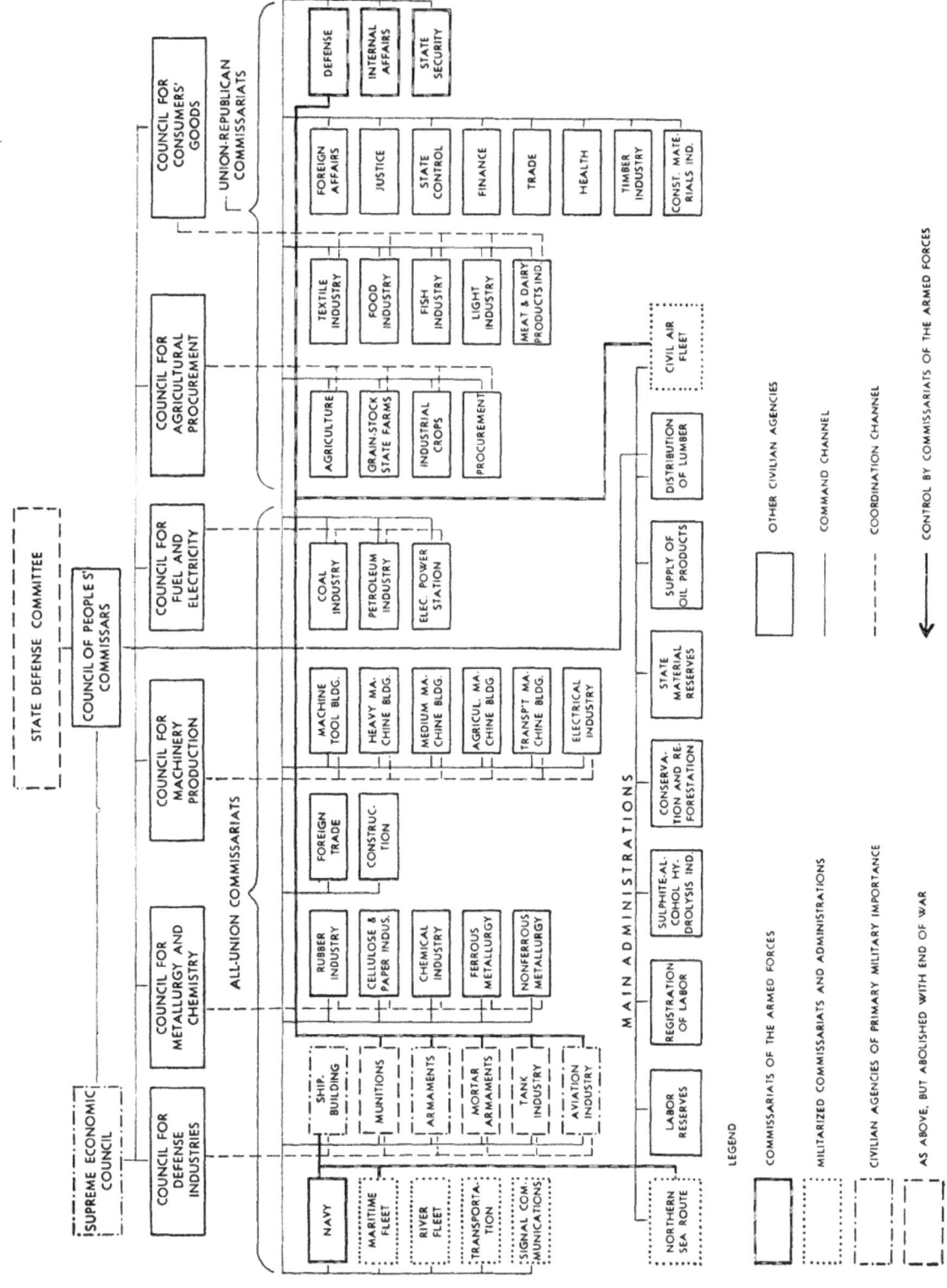

Figure 1. The state administrative structure and the armed forces.

7

munist Party maximum political, social, and economic prestige. It is given credit for every type of successful national achievement. Persons in the U. S. S. R. who distinguish themselves in any way are solicited for membership. The Party is permitted to criticize inefficiency or political deviations. In short, the Communist Party attempts to maintain itself as an elite ruling class directing the state, but apart from and above it.

Another vital source of power of the Communist Party is its legally-sanctioned political tutelage of the armed forces. Its control over the security forces (NKVD and NKGB) and the Navy has been markedly effective at all times. Party control over the Red Army, although subject to major fluctuations in the past, still is pronounced. Supervision of the effectiveness and loyalty of individuals, of their training status, and of their morale, are functions of the Main Political Administration of the Red Army. The Main Political Administration of the Red Army reports directly to the Communist Party. During World War II, the Communist Party was in complete charge of all partisan operations.

A final source of power is the control by the Communist Party of the youth of the U. S. S. R. The *Komsomols*, or League of Communist Youth, the Pioneers, and the *Octobrists* cover even the youngest age groups and provide the major outlet for their constructive play and social activities.

Section III. ARMED AND AUXILIARY FORCES

1. GENERAL

The armed and auxiliary forces of the Soviet Union are of three types: military, semi-military and civil (militarized in time of war). The military forces include the Red Army and its air forces, and the Red Navy and its air component. The semi-military armed forces are the troops of the Peoples' Commissariats of Internal and State Security. These include frontier and internal guards, local police, and other armed components for the security of the nation in time of peace or war.

The entire strength of certain other organizations is mobilized in direct support of military operations in time of war. Militarized during World War II were the Peoples' Commissariats of Transportation, Maritime Fleet, River Transport, and Signal Communications, as well as the Main Administrations of the Civil Air Fleet and the Northern Sea Route and their operating and maintenance personnel.

Their authority and operations extended not only throughout the Soviet Union, but well into the zone of operations. Uniformed personnel of these civil organizations were subject to military law and discipline but, in all areas, remained under the direct control only of their respective commissariats or main administrations. (For these and other civilian organizations which were armed or mobilized for World War II, see Chapter IV.) It is important to note in this connection that the Soviet concept is that all citizens are equally liable for service in the militia, if not in the regular military forces.

No one of these forces can be called a special instrument of the Communist Party. In striking contrast to the methods of the National Socialist Party in Germany during the period of its development and greatest success, the Soviet Communist Party has never been an armed force in itself. Nor has the Communist Party ever permitted one of the armed forces of the Soviet Union to come into conflict with another as a specially favored instrument of the Party.

A carefully exact division of responsibility and authority between the troops of the Commissariat of Internal Affairs (NKVD) and the troops (Red Army) of the Commissariat of Defense (NKO) has been firmly established and jealously protected by the Soviet government. The Great Purge of the Red Army and its command in 1937 was inspired by the NKVD, as Party custodian of the internal security of the state. It is significant, however. that the Purge was conducted by due process of law involving the entire governmental structure, rather than by the troops of the NKVD alone.

2. COMPONENTS OF HIGH COMMAND

Throughout the Red Army and Navy, a distinct division exists between command channels and agencies and administrative channels and agencies. (For administrative channels and agencies, see Part III.)

The "high command" of the armed forces embraces all agencies in the chain of operational command for all elements of the army and the navy. It includes, under the State Defense Committee, the Commander in Chief of the Armed Forces and his General Headquarters, the Chief of the General Staff of the Red Army, the Supreme Naval Council, the Commissariat of the Navy, and the Naval Staff.

Army command stems from the General Headquarters. It extends through the Chief of the General Staff of the Red Army to army groups and other field forces. (See Part II.)

8

Naval command also stems from the General Headquarters. It extends through the Supreme Naval Council, the Commissariat of the Navy, and the Naval Staff to the active naval units. The four commissariats of the Armed Forces (Defense, Navy, Internal Affairs [NKVD], and State Security [NKGB] maintain administrative and technical control, but were subordinated in varying degree in policy questions to the GHQ during World War II.

With the end of the war and the dissolution of the State Defense Committee, it is believed that the respective commissariats have again become dominant and increasingly autonomous. It is not certain whether GHQ for all the armed forces will be continued or whether the independent Supreme Military Council of the Army will be revived as the individual components of the armed forces regain their independence.

3. THE RED ARMY

The chief components of the Red Army are the military districts and the field forces (active army).

a. Military districts. The military districts comprise the basic zones of the interior organization of the U. S. S. R. They are responsible directly to the Peoples' Commissariat of Defense. For replacement purposes, they are controlled by the Main Administration for the Formation and Equipment of Units.

In the last 20 years, the number of military districts has increased steadily while their average area has decreased steadily. A more simple and efficient organization has thus become possible. There now are 30 military districts (figs. 2 and 3).

Each district is directed by a commander and a military council. Each is capable, on the average, of raising an infantry army in the first echelon of mobilization.

Territorially, the military districts coincide with the *Oblasts* of the U. S. S. R. Although military districts may include more than one *Oblast*, their boundaries do not cross those of the *Oblast*. No relation with the Union-Republics exists (fig. 4). The basic operating element of the military districts is the county (*rayon*), although the more densely populated districts may have intermediate (sub-district) control organizations.

The responsibilities of the military districts are as follows:

Conduct combat and political training.
Ensure mobilization readiness of troops, transport, and signal communications.
Conduct the replacement program.

Study and select command and administrative officers, other than general officers or officers of front-line units.
Maintain constant check over the loyalty of all personnel.
Conduct counterintelligence.
Ensure the requisition, procurement, storage, and movement of supplies, and of medical and veterinary facilities.
Supervise antiaircraft defense, including passive measures of the civil population.
Supervise pre-military training and draft board activities.
Guide defense construction work.
Ensure proper civil-military coordination within the district.

b. Field forces. In the field forces of the Red Army, the basic division is not so much a separation of the ground and air components as a separation of tactical from strategic forces.

The tactical forces of the Red Army are composed of army groups (fronts), each embracing a number of air and ground armies and other components The number and size of army groups varies. In 1943, for example, there were 17, but the number had been reduced to 7 shortly after the close of the war with Japan. The seven were as follows in January 1946:

Group	Location
In Europe:	
Northern Group	Old and new Poland.
Central Group	Austria, Hungary.
Southern Group	Bulgaria, Rumania.
Occupation Group, Germany	Germany.
In the Far East:	
Trans-Baikal Front	Trans-Baikal Military District, Outer Mongolia, Eastern Manchuria.
Second Far Eastern Front	Khaborovsk Krai, Northern Manchuria.
First Far Eastern Front	Maritime Krai, Western Manchuria, Northern Korea.

An army group (front) consists basically of two or more infantry armies, one to two air armies, a tank corps, a mechanized corps, and artillery, mortar, rocket, and antiaircraft divisions. (For detailed organization of army groups, see Chapter III).

The strategic forces of the Red Army also are ground and air formations. The principal ground components are tank armies, artillery corps, and fortified areas. Certain of the fortified areas are under

Figure 2. Military districts of the U. S. S. R. (Western area).

10

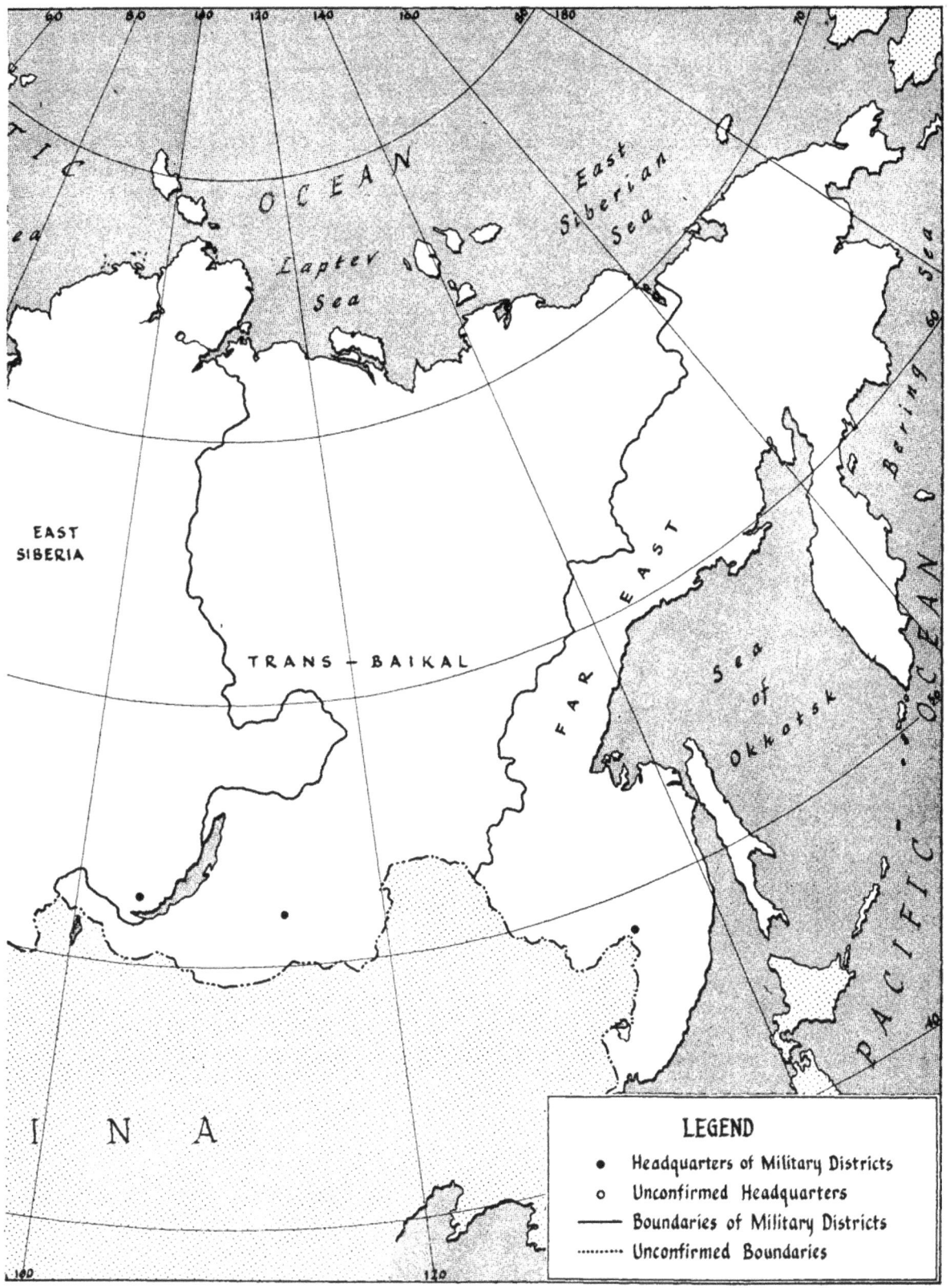

Figure 3. *Military districts of the U. S. S. R. (Eastern area).*

11

Military districts	Headquarters	Political components
White Sea	Kemi (?)	Petsamo (?), Murmansk Ob., Karelian A. S. S. R., Archangel Ob., Komi A. S. S. R., Nentso Nat'l. Ok.
Leningrad	Leningrad	Leningrad Ob., Vologoda Ob.
Baltic	Riga	Estonian S. S. R., Latvian S. S. R.
Special	Koeningsberg (?)	Lithuanian S. S. R., Koeningsberg area (?)
Minsk	Minsk	Belorussian S. S. R., Vitebsk Ob., Minsk Ob., Mogilev Ob., Polesye Ob., Gomel Ob.
Lvov	Lvov	Lvov Area (?).
Carpathian	(?)	Moldavia.
Kiev	Kiev	Zhitomir Ob., Kiev Ob., Chernigov Ob., Kamenets-Podolsk Ob., Vinnitsa Ob.
Odessa	Odessa	Odessa Ob., Kirovograd Ob.
Moscow	Moscow	Kalinin Ob., Yaroslavl Ob., Smolensk Ob., Moscow Ob., Tula Ob., Ryazan Ob.
Gorkii	Gorkii	Ivanovo Ob., Gorkii Ob.
Voronezh	Voronezh	Voronezh Ob., Tambov Ob.
Orel	Orel	Orel Ob., Kursk Ob.
Kharkov	Kharkov	Sumy Ob., Dnepropetrovsk Ob., Poltava Ob., Kharkov Ob., Stalino Ob., Voroshilovgrad Ob.
Tauric	Simferopol	Nicolayev Ob., Zaporozhiye Ob.
Kazan	Kazan	Kirov Ob., Tatar A. S. S. R., Churvas A. S. S. R., Mari A. S. S. R., Udmurt A. S. S. R.
Volga	Kuibyshev	Penza Ob., Kuibyshev Ob., Saratov Ob., German-Volga A. S. S. R., Mordva A. S. S. R.
Steppe	Stalingrad	Stalingrad Ob., Kalmyk A. S. S. R.
Don	Rostov	Rostov Ob.
Kuban	Krasnodar	Krasnodar Krai (containing Adyghey Aut. Ob.).
Stavropol	Voroshilov	Ordzhonikidze Krai, North Ossetian A. S. S. R., Karachayev Aut. Ob., Chechen-Ingushian A. S. S. R., Kabardino—Balkar A. S. S. R., Circassian Aut. Ob.
Tiflis	Tiflis	South Ossetian, Aut. Ob., Nakhichevan A. S. S. R., Adzharian A. S. S. R., Armenian S. S. R., Abkhazian A. S. S. R., Georgian S. S. R.
Baku	Baku	Kaghistan A. S. S. R., Azerbaidzhan S. S. R., (containing Nagarno-Karabakh).
Ural	Sverdlovsk (?)	Komipermyak Ob., Perm Ob., Sverdlovsk Ob., Chelyabinsk Ob.
South Ural	Chkalov	Bashkir A. S. S. R., Chkalov Ob., West Kazakhstan., Aktyubinsk Ob., Guryev Ob.
Central Asia (?)	(?)	North Kazakhstan Ob., Kustanay Ob., Akmolinsk Ob., Pavlodar Ob., East Kazakhstan Ob., Semipalatinsk Ob., Karaganda Ob., Alma-Ata Ob.
Turkestan	Tashkent	Kara-Kalpak A. S. S. R., Kzyl-Orda Ob., South Kazakhstan Ob., Kirghiz S. S. R., Osh Ob., Dzhalal-Abad Ob., Frunze Ob., Tyanshan Ob., Issyk-Kul Ob., Uzbek S. S. R., Samarkand Ob., Tashkent Ob., Fergana Ob., Tadzhik S. S. R., Leninabad Ob., Stalinabad Ob., Kulyab Ob., Gorm Ob., Gorno-Budakhshan Aut. Ob., Krasnovodsk Ob., Turkmen S. S. R., Tashauz Ob., Khorezm Ob., Mary Ob., Chardzhou Ob., Bukhara Ob.
West Siberia	Novosibirsk	Omsk Ob., Yamalo-Nentso Nat'l. Ok., Ostyako-Vogul Nat'l. Ok., Novosibirsk Ob., Altai Krai Oirot Aut. Ob.
East Siberia	Irkutsk	Krasnoyarsk Krai, Taimyr Nat'l Ok., Evenki Nat'l Ok., Irkutsk Ob., Ustordo-Buryant Mongolian Nat'l Ok., Khakass Aut. Ob., Tannu Tuva.
Trans-Baikal	Chita	Chita Ob., Aghinskaye-Buryat Mongolian Nat'l. Ok., Buryat Mongolian A. S. S. R., Yakutsk A. S. S. R.
Far East	Khabarovsk	Chukotsk Nat'l Ok., Koryak Nat'l Ok., Kamchatka Ob., Khabarovsk Krai., Lower Amur Ob., Amur Ob., Jewish Aut. Ob., Ussuri Ob., Primorsk Krai.

Abbreviations used in above list:
A. S. S. R.—Autonomous Soviet Socialist Republic.
Aut. Ob.—Autonomous *Oblast*.
Nat'l O'.—National *Okrug*.
Ob.—*Oblast*.
S. S. R.—Soviet Socialist Republic (Union-Republic).

Note.—The boundaries, names, and headquarters of most of the military districts are well established. However, the existence of the Orel and Central Asia Military Districts is uncertain, and the boundaries of the Tauric, Leningrad, Baltic, and South Ural Military Districts are unconfirmed. It is possible that Estonia is a part of the Leningrad Military District, and Lithuania is a part of the Baltic. Thus the Special Military District includes only East Prussia.

Figure 4. Political components of military districts of the U. S. S. R.

12

naval rather than army command. Other strategic forces are the Civil Air Fleet, the Long-Range Bomber Force (an air army), and the PVO, or Air Defense Force.

The PVO is a separate part of the Red Army only in its operating elements. Its headquarters is charged with coordination of the administrative supervision, by the Commissariat of Internal Affairs (NKVD), over passive civil defense measures and the administrative supervision of the antiaircraft, fighter, and air-warning systems. The latter administration is accomplished by the appropriate main administrations of the Commissariat of Defense.

In combat zones, PVO forces are organized into the defense fronts, consisting of antiaircraft and fighter armies, for the protection of major targets. PVO fronts have direct command of the air observation, signal intercept, early warning, and signal communications systems and operations in their zones.

Elsewhere in the U. S. S. R., PVO operations are controlled on the basis of military districts. In each district, this is accomplished by an Air Defense Force Staff.

4. THE RED NAVY

a. High command. The high command of the Soviet Naval Forces differs from that of the Red Army in that the Commissariat of the Navy (NKVMF) has remained a link in the operational chain of command. Under the command of the General Headquarters, the Supreme Naval Council is the highest authority over naval operations and affairs and is comparable to the Military Council of an army or army group. The Commissariat of the Navy is directly subordinate to the Supreme Naval Council.

The chief agencies within and subordinate to the Commissariat are: the Naval Staff, with divisions similar to those of the Army General Staff, but including a Hydrographic Division; the Coastal Defense Force; and various service and administrative offices comparable to those in the Commissariat of Defense. Included are an Administration for Naval Education, a Main Political Administration, a Signal Communications Administration, and the Office of the Surgeon General.

b. Forces under command. In time of war, the naval high command controls, in addition to naval forces, the Peoples' Commissariat for the Shipbuilding Industry, the Chief Administration of the Northern Sea Route, and the Maritime Fleet.

The Soviet Navy is organized into fleets and flotillas as follows:

> The Northern Fleet.
> The Black Sea Fleet.
> The Pacific Fleet.
> The North Pacific Fleet.
> The Azov Flotilla.
> The Dnieper Flotilla.
> The Amur River Flotilla.
> The Sungari River Flotilla.
> The Danube Flotilla.

A number of fortified areas along the coasts of the U. S. S. R. are under exclusive control of the naval command. Examples are the White Sea Defense Area and the Vladivostok Defense Area.

Section IV. CIVIL–MILITARY RELATIONSHIPS

1. GENERAL

The readiness of a totalitarian state for total mobilization and the extent to which it became a reality in the U. S. S. R. during World War II has already

Commissariat of Defense	Civil Government
Main Administration of the Air Forces	Commissariat of Aviation Industry.
Main Administration of Artillery Troops	Commissariat of Armaments. / Commissariat of Mortar Armaments. / Commissariat of Munitions.
Main Administration of Tank and Mechanized Troops	Commissariat of the Tank Industry.
Main Administration of Signal Troops	Commissariat of Signal Communications.
Main Administration of Chemical Warfare Troops	Commissariat of the Chemical Industry.
Main Administration for Antiaircraft Defense	Commissariat of Internal Affairs (NKVD).
Main Administration of Railway Transport	Commissariat of Transportation.
Main Administration for Intendance Service	Council for Consumers Goods.
Main Administration for Supply of Rations	Council for Agricultural Procurement.
Main Administration for Road Construction	Commissariat of Internal Affairs (NKVD).
Main Administration for Medical Services	Commissariat of Health.
Main Administration for Personnel / Main Administration for the Formation and Equipment of Units.	Central Administration for Labor Reserves. / Central Administration for Registration and Distribution of Labor Forces.
Main Administration for Counterintelligence	Commissariat of Internal Affairs (NKVD). / Commissariat of State Security (NKGB).

Figure 5. Parallel agencies, military and civil, to promote close coordination.

been discussed. The closest cooperation between the armed forces, and their control agencies, and the entire structure of the civil economy was provided and enforced by the central government (fig. 5).

2. MILITARIZATION

The wartime position of such semi-military organizations as the troops of the Commissariats of Internal Affairs and State Security and of such civil organizations as those of the Commissariats of Transportation and Signal Communications also has been discussed. (For further detail concerning them, see Chapter IV.) These organs of the state and their rank and file became auxiliary forces to the field armies and fleets in the fullest sense of the word. Yet they did not lose their nation-wide functions and responsibilities.

It is worth noting that, in these and other commissariats, military ranks were conferred during World War II on a number of key personnel and, in some cases, well down into the ranks of the commissariat and subordinate personnel. Military rank was given the Commissar of the Armaments Industry, for example, and to many members of the State Medical Service. Conversely, many of the outstanding military personalities of World War II were elected to the Supreme Soviet. One, Marshal Budenny, was a member of the Presidium as well.

3. ECONOMIC MOBILIZATION

In World War II, the numerous commissariats which direct the national economy were brought into direct services to the armed forces nearly as closely as the formally militarized commissariats. The recommendations of the General Staff, as the chief agency for the planning and evaluation of field operations, and of the technical arms and services of the Red Army became the basis for State Defense Committee directives issued to those responsible for planning and administering all phases of war production.

The mobilization sections, created with the first Five Year Plan of 1928, in the plants, factories, and installations of the economic commissariats, put their plans for conversion to war production into effect. They remained in close contact with the appropriate arm through specialized liaison officers. Horses and motor transport had been selected in all parts of the U. S. S. R. during peacetime for consignment to the armed forces in the event of war. These were checked every 6 months to determine their readiness for transfer to the armed forces.

Coordination between commissariats was put on a more efficient footing through the institution of economic councils with extensive power over groups of industries and national resources. Six such economic councils were formed, each generally composed of the commissars of a number of related industries or trusts. The chairmen sit together as the Supreme Economic Council.

The decisions of the Supreme Economic Council superseded those of the State Planning Committee, which had produced the Five Year Plans. (This change was instituted because no plan of comparable scope in time, or requiring as much time in preparation as the Five Year Plan, can be appropriate in the pressing years of a war for national survival.) The creation of the Supreme Economic Council, both a planning committee and a body representative of the chief industries and trusts, further guaranteed full-scale efficient management of the resources and production capacity of the nation toward the needs of the armed forces.

Further evidence of the Soviet realization of total war within the peacetime framework of the state is to be found in the system of universal pre-induction military training of the populace, whether subject to the draft or exempt. Within every organized unit of Soviet society, whether industrial, political, cultural, or educational, there were representatives of the Red Army who were attached as instructors in military science. Instruction was graded appropriately to the age, sex, and occupation of the people involved. Spare time, within very strict limits, was devoted entirely to such training in all parts of the U. S. S. R.

Training programs were prescribed and administered by the Red Army through its representatives. Over-all control of the various programs rested in the Commissariat of Defense, where the plans of the State Defense Committee, General Headquarters, and General Staff could best be applied to the military training of the populace.

The absolute legal hegemony of the Red Army and Navy in their zones of operations in time of war also deserves mention. As a right established by Soviet law, the armed forces may, given a state of sufficient urgency, draft for their use any or all of the equipment and populace of any area of the U. S. S. R. This may be done without regard to existing laws, decrees, or directives.

Close coordination also has characterized other relationships between the armed forces and the civil economy. This is true of such affairs as the construction of military facilities, the development of new weapons and equipment, and the handling of discharged soldiers and of pensions for veterans and the families of the dead and wounded.

It can be said without exaggeration that every element in the national economy and every person old enough to do his share is included within the national defense system of the Soviet Union in time of war.

PART II. ARMED FORCES HIGH COMMAND, EARLY 1945

Section I. THE STATE DEFENSE COMMITTEE

1. POSITION AND FUNCTIONS

The State Defense Committee, created 1 July 1941 and dissolved in September 1945, is the supreme governmental body in time of war. In effect, it assumes the functions of both the Presidium of the Supreme Soviet and of the Council of Peoples' Commissars. Thus it has final authority over the armed forces and all the commissariats of the Soviet Union.

The relationship of the State Defense Committee with the Supreme Economic Council, with other special councils and committees of the government, and with the commissariats does not differ from that of the Council of Peoples' Commissars in normal times.

For over-all control of the conduct of a war, however, the State Defense Committee issues directives on major issues of strategy directly to the General Headquarters, which controls the armed forces engaged with the enemy. Thus the State Defense Committee bypasses the administrative machinery of military commissariats in matters of operational strategy.

2. COMPOSITION AND SIGNIFICANCE

The enormous range of powers vested in the State Defense Committee by virtue of its membership is clearly indicated by the titles of the following members composing the committee:

STALIN, Generalissimo: Commander in Chief of the Armed Forces, Chief of the General Headquarters, Chairman of the Council of Peoples' Commissars, Commissar of Defense, Chairman of the *Politburo* of the Central Committee of the Communist Party.

BULGANIN, *General Armii* (General, U. S.): Deputy Commissar of Defense, Vice Chairman of the Council of Peoples' Commissars, Chairman of the Council of Metallurgical and Chemical Industries, member of the *Politburo* of the Central Committee of the Communist Party.

MOLOTOV: Commissar of Foreign Affairs, Chairman of the Supreme Economic Council, Deputy Chairman of the Council of Peoples' Commissars, member of the *Politburo* of the Central Committee of the Communist Party.

BERIYA, Marshal of the Soviet Union: Commissar of Internal Affairs and Chief of Troops of the NKVD, member of the Council of Peoples' Commissars, member of the *Politburo* of the Central Committee of the Communist Party.

MALENKOV: Member of the Presidium of the the Supreme Soviet, member of the *Politburo* and *Orgburo*, Secretary of the Central Committee of the Communist Party, head of the Central Administration for Personnel of the Central Committee of the Communist Party, President of the Committee for the Restoration of Liberated Areas, member of the Council of Peoples' Commissars.

KAGANOVICH: Member of the Council of Peoples' Commissars, member of the *Politburo* of the Central Committee of the Communist Party, former Commissar of Transportation, member of the All-Union Committee on Transportation.

MIKOYAN: Commissar of Foreign Trade, member of the Council of Peoples' Commissars, member of the *Politburo* of the Central Committee of the Communist Party.

VOZNESENSKI: Member of the Council of Peoples' Commissars, members of the *Politburo* of the Central Committee of the Communist Party, Chairman of the Council for Defense Industry.

It will be noted that all members of the State Defense Committee are members of the Council of Peoples' Commissars and of the *Politburo* of the Central Committee of the Communist Party.

The State Defense Committee is not equipped with a large staff. It relies upon the numerous committees, councils, commissariats, and the General Headquarters for expert advice, for preparation of detailed plans, for recommendations, and for the implementation of its policy decisions. It may thus properly be called a "committee," a small group of key leaders responsible for decisions of policy and affairs of state.

Section II. GENERAL HEADQUARTERS

1. POSITION AND FUNCTIONS

The personal Staff of Stalin, Commander-in-Chief of the Armed Forces, is known as the *Stavka* or General Headquarters of the Armed Forces. The General Headquarters of the Armed Forces translates the policy decisions of the State Defense Committee into military action and directs the prosecution of the war through the Chief of Staff of the Army and through the Commissariat and Staff of the Navy.

The General Headquarters of the Armed Forces was formed to replace the Supreme Military and Naval Councils of earlier years in the joint and coordinated command of the Army and Navy. It looks to the General Staffs of the Army and Navy and to their commissariats for plans and recommendations for carrying out major strategic operations and in questions of administration.

The General Headquarters is not equipped with special staffs, nor is it divided into sections. The majority of its members are major chiefs of the armed forces command and administration. Thus the major staffs of the armed forces function as working staffs of the General Headquarters.

Constitutionally, the Commissariats of Defense and Navy are subordinate only to the State Defense Committee. The General Headquarters has no direct authority over them. However, the members of the Headquarters exercise effective control over the administrative affairs of the armed forces by virtue of their appointments as deputy commissars. This dual appointment of key personnel assures close coordination of field command with administration.

The GHQ is not a headquarters in the usual sense of the term. It is, like the State Defense Committee, a periodic meeting of the chief military leaders of the high command structure for the consideration of major strategic plans.

2. COMPOSITION AND SIGNIFICANCE

The General Headquarters consists of 12 to 14 of the top military leaders. They are selected so as to represent the chief branches, arms, and services.

The composition of the GHQ in early 1945 amply illustrates its power and scope and the technical qualifications of its members. It is important to note that all members of the GHQ are members of the Communist Party.

STALIN, Generalissimo: Commander in Chief of the Armed Forces, Commissar of Defense, etc.

ZHUKOV (Chief of GHQ), Marshal of the Soviet Union: First Deputy Commissar of Defense, Commander of the First Belorussian Army Group.

VASILEVSKI, Marshal of the Soviet Union: Chief of Staff of the Red Army, Deputy Commissar of Defense.

KUZNETSOV, Admiral of the Fleet: Peoples' Commissar of the Navy, member of the Central Committee of the Communist Party.

NOVIKOV, Chief Marshal of Air Forces: Chief of the Red Army Forces, Deputy Commissar of Defense.

TIMOSHENKO, Marshal of the Soviet Union: Deputy Commissar of Defense (formerly Commissar, then First Deputy Commissar), Inspector of Infantry, GHQ Coordinator of the Second and Third Ukrainian Army Groups.

VOROSHILOV, Marshal of the Soviet Union: Member of the Council of Peoples' Commissars and of the *Politburo* of the Central Committee of the Communist Party, former member of the State Defense Committee and Deputy Commissar of Defense, Commander in Chief of Partisans.

SHAPOSHNIKOV, Marshal of the Soviet Union: Member of the Central Committee of the Communist Party, formerly Chief of Staff of the Red Army, Deputy Commissar of Defense, Chief of the Historical Division of the General Staff.

KHRULEV, *General Armii* (General, U. S.): Chief of Rear Services of the Red Army, Deputy Commissar of Defense.

VORONOV, Chief Marshal of Artillery: Chief of Artillery Troops of the Red Army, Deputy Commissar of Defense.

FEDORENKO, Chief Marshal of Tanks and Mechanized Troops: Chief of Tank and Mechanized Troops of the Red Army, Deputy Commissar of Defense.

BUDENNY, Marshal of Soviet Union: Member of the Presidium of the Supreme Soviet, Chief of Cavalry Troops of the Red Army, Deputy Commissar of Defense.

VOROBEV, Chief Marshal of Engineer Troops: Chief of Engineer Troops of the Red Army, Deputy Commissar of Defense.

SHCHERBAKOV, *General Polkovnik* (Lieutenant General, U. S.) : Head of the Main Political Administration of the Red Army, Deputy Commissar of Defense, Member of the *Politburo* of the Central Committee of the Communist Party, Secretary of the Moscow Committee of the Communist Party.

3. SPECIAL ACTIVITIES

Elements of the General Headquarters frequently are detached to supervise the conduct of major field operations. A member of the General Headquarters may assume command of an army group (front), as when Zhukov was made Commander of the First White Russian (Belorussian) Front for the concluding phases of the assault on Germany while still chief of the General Headquarters.

Several of the members of the General Headquarters have been appointed as coordinators of the joint operations of two or more army groups (fronts). Notable among these was Timoshenko, who supervised the advance of the Second and Third Ukrainian Fronts in the last months of the war. Groups of officers of the General Headquarters have, on occasion, even been detailed to supervise joint operations of two or more fronts in the field. Thus, they become an advance echelon of the General Headquarters, itself.

The purpose of this detached service is the supervision of operations in order not only to assure execution of the plans of the Headquarters, but also to assure rapid, continuous, and objective reporting of the progress of campaigns.

Another important factor is the authority over the Commissariats of Internal Affairs (NKVD) and State Security (NKGB) that is granted the general Headquarters. Although these units are not constitutionally subordinate, the GHQ may issue direct orders to them in special cases which require immediate action and are closely related to the conduct of operations. Neither commissariat is represented in the General Headquarters.

Section III. CHIEF OF STAFF AND THE GENERAL STAFF OF THE RED ARMY

1. THE CHIEF OF STAFF

In issuing the commands and directives of the General Headquarters to units of the army in the field, the Chief of the General Staff of the Red Army is chief executive officer for the Commander in Chief of the Armed Forces.

The Chief of Staff is the command link between the General Headquarters and the Red Army in the zone of operations. The Chief of Staff also commands all divisions of the General Staff and is responsible for the preparation of operational plans by the staff and for reconnaissance operations ordered by the staff.

A special responsibility of the Chief of the General Staff, of particular importance in time of peace, is the publication of the "Journal of Military Thought." This publication, probably the most influential of all Soviet military journals, is directed to present analyses of problems of military theory and ideology, of basic problems of organization of the armed forces, of strategy, and of operating techniques. It also is directed to cover the analyses and discussion of coordination of arms, of the training of commanders for all arms, and of practical combat lessons. It also is to include extensive critiques of the accomplishments of the armed forces of other nations.

The Chief of the General Staff also is responsible for supervision of policy of the two highest military academies, the Frunze Academy (Command and General Staff School) and the Academy of the General Staff (War College).

2. THE GENERAL STAFF

a. Position. The General Staff of the Red Army is the highest advisory body to the Chief of Staff of the Red Army, to the Commander in Chief of the Armed Forces, and to his personal staff, the General Headquarters. Subordinated operationally only to the General Headquarters in time of war, it remains subordinate to the Commissariat of Defense for its own internal administration. Although the interests of the General Staff are primarily operational, it also exerts considerable influence upon the administration of the Red Army.

b. Functions. The General Staff, in cooperation with the staffs of the arms and rear services, is responsible for the preparation in detail of all operational plans for the Red Army. It also is specifically charged with ensuring effective coordination between arms and services at all levels.

In common with the staffs of lower headquarters, the General Staff maintains operations, intelligence, signal, and topographical divisions. It also maintains three divisions which are peculiar to the General Staff. They are the Formations Division, which corresponds to the statistical control sections of lower staffs, but which appears to have much broader functions than the later in problems of organizational policy; the Fortified Areas Division; and the Historical Division, which is charged with the preparation of critiques of operations and of recommendations based upon them.

c. Organization. The General Staff is organized into divisions as follows:

The *First* (Operations) *Division* of the General Staff includes representatives of all the combat arms and the rear services. It is charged with the final preparation of operational plans for submission to the General Headquarters. The Operations Division is responsible for the initial deployment of field forces in any area which is expected to become a zone of operations.

The Operations Division also is charged with the immediate command of field units not subordinated to army groups or other field headquarters, i. e., GHQ units, certain units in transit from their military districts to the combat zone, and a pool of officers with General Staff qualifications.

As the need arises, the Operations Division is divided geographically into sections for each theater of operations or areas for which General Staff plans are being prepared. Toward the close of World War II, there were at least five sections. These were designated "North," "Center," "South," "Far East," and "Partisans." There also are sections representing the artillery, mechanized, air and engineer arms, the rear services, and the personnel administration of officers of the General Staff.

A branch of this division is believed to control the selection and use of ciphers, codes, and cover names, and to be charged with the preparation and execution of deception operations.

The *Second* (Intelligence) *Division* of the General Staff is the highest agency for the collection, collation, and evaluation of positive information concerning the enemy. Counterintelligence is handled by the Main Administration for Counterintelligence in the Commissariat of Defense (see Part III).

The Intelligence Division also is charged with command responsibility for reconnaissance plans and may prepare direct orders to the arms, services, and field commanders for execution of the plans. Prisoner-of-war and document exploitation is controlled by the Intelligence Division. The employment of secret agents is a joint responsibility of the

Intelligence Division and the Commissariat of State Security (NKGB).

The Intelligence Division also is responsible for the employment of signal intelligence, a responsibility that is shared by the Main Administration for Signal Troops and by the signal security services of the NKVD. The exact delineation of functions and responsibilities among the three agencies is not known.

The Intelligence Division works closely with the Topographic Division on terrain intelligence and with the intelligence branches of the arms on intelligence appropriate to each.

The Intelligence Division is believed to be divided into five branches: information, operations (sabotage, etc.), espionage, cadres (training), and internal administration. The information section consists of at least six subsections: Western, Balkan, German, Far Eastern, Near Eastern, and Publications. The espionage branch includes sections for espionage equipment, for signal intelligence, and for operations in each of the various areas of the world.

The *Third* (Signal Communications) *Division* of the General Staff is charged with planning the signal facilities required for operations under consideration by the General Staff. Its plans are believed not to extend to the detailed requirements worked out by the Main Administration for Signal Troops of the Commissariat of Defense (see Part III). Nor are the plans believed to cover the close coordination of the Main Administration for Signal Troops of the Commissariat of Defense with the Commissariat of Signal Communications. The General Staff lacks command function in this field.

The *Fourth* (Formations) *Division* of the General Staff is believed to perform the functions of the statistical control sections of lower staffs and to analyze current and proposed Tables of Organization.

The internal organization is not known, but the division deals with questions concerning the requirements and systems of mobilization and replacement and with the process of selection and appointment of officers.

In this connection, stress must be laid upon the fact that Soviet Tables of Organization, especially for infantry, are modified in accordance with basic changes in the strategic situation.

During the 1942 defensive stage of the war with Germany, infantry formations were provided with additional weapons, especially mortars. Their transportation allocations were reduced radically. With the resumption of offensive operations, the organization of infantry units again was changed. The planning of these changes is believed to have been the function of the Formations Division.

The Formations Division does not, however, administer such changes. The actual administration of the mobilization and replacement processes has been transferred to the Main Administration for Personnel (officers) and to the Main Administration for the Formation and Equipment of Units (enlisted men) of the Commissariat of Defense.

The *Topographic Division* of the General Staff is responsible for the study of terrain, defense data, and for the preparation of maps and charts in cooperation with the Intelligence Division. It supervises the topographic and mapping services of the Red Army. It also coordinates the survey work of the artillery, engineer, and air arms. The Topographic Division is charged with the production and supply of all types of maps to the Red Army in the field.

The *Fortified Areas Division* of the General Staff plans the development of fixed defenses for strongpoints, strategic bases, cities, frontier passes, and certain larger border areas not under naval command. It also supports the Chief of Staff and the Operations Division in the command control of such areas not under the command of army groups or other lower headquarters.

The *Historical Division* of the General Staff is one of the most important of General Staff divisions. Its organization is not known, but it draws upon the most expert opinion available, including high representatives of each arm and service, and maintains, under its exclusive control, field offices attached to Army Group and Army Headquarters.

The Historical Division transcends the function indicated by its title. Its duties include the accumulation and processing of field reports on strategy, tactics, and the employment of arms, weapons, and equipment. The recommendations of the Historical Division become the chief basis for changes in Red Army operational doctrines, Tables of Organization, equipment, and matériel specifications. Division recommendations also affected the appointment and removal of major field commanders.

Application of the Historical Division's critques, covering every aspect of strategy, tactics, logistics, etc., emerged during World War II as a definitely established function of the General Staff, in which it achieved its greatest prestige and influence. Its influence in this respect is expected to remain as great in peace as it was during war.

During World War II approved modifications of Red Army practices repeatedly were executed within a few months after the critique and recommendations were prepared. The continuous study and rapid application of combat lessons has been one of the greatest assets of the Red Army.

PART III. COMMISSARIAT OF DEFENSE AND RED ARMY ADMINISTRATION

Section I. COMMISSARIAT OF DEFENSE

1. POSITION

The Peoples' Commissariat of Defense, now renamed the Peoples' Commissariat of the Armed Forces, is a Union-Republican Commissariat, directly subordinate to the State Defense Committee in time of war, and to the Council of Peoples' Commissars in time of peace. (There is little evidence that the "Union-Republican" title is based on fact. Only two republics are known to have organized Commissariats of Defense.)

The Commissariat relies upon the General Headquarters for direction in affairs directly bearing upon the prosecution of war. This is not, however, a command subordination. It is based upon the fact that the Commissar, First Deputy Commissar, and certain of the other Deputy Commissars hold the majority of positions in the General Headquarters.

In technical and administrative policies, a third agency exerts a large measure of indirect control over the Commissariat during war. The recommendations of the General Staff, based on evaluation of battle experiences, become directives to the Commissariat or its component administrations when approved by the General Headquarters and adjusted to suit the capabilities of the administrations involved.

Other agencies, such as the Supreme Court and Communist Party, also exert direct control over administrations which are charged with functions within the Commissariat.

2. COMPOSITION AND ORGANIZATION

The Commissariat proper consists of the Commissar of Defense (Stalin), the First Deputy Commissar of

Defense (Zhukov), and 10 or more deputy commissars. The majority of the deputy commissars are heads of the arms or of other main administrations of the Red Army. In January 1945, 8 of the 12 members of the Commissariat were members also of the General Headquarters, held not less than the rank of *General Polkovnik* (lieutenant general), and were officers of long standing in the Red Army.

Directly subordinate to the Commissar and Deputy Commissars are the Inspectorate of Infantry and 18 "bureaus" for Red Army affairs. The "bureaus" are called "main administrations" and "administrations." In addition, there are a number of main administrations which are subordinate to the air, artillery, and rear services.

Of the 18 main administrations and administrations, 1 administration is concerned with the internal affairs of the Commissariat itself; 9 main administrations control Red Army arms and technical services; 4 main administrations supervise personnel, conscription, and training; 3 main administrations are responsible for political and legal supervision of Red Army personnel; and the Main Administration of the Chief of the Rear Services controls supply, maintenance, evacuation, and transportation.

The heads of administrations generally are known as the chiefs of their respective arms or services. For example, the head of the Main Administration of Signal Troops is known as the Chief Marshal of Signal Troops of the Red Army.

3. FUNCTIONS

The deputy commissars are charged with the promulgation of basic regulations and administrative policies for the Red Army. As heads of administrations, they are responsible for the coordination of the activities of their administration with the other administrations, particularly with those for training and political supervision. They also are charged with the close liaison which each administration must maintain with its corresponding commissariat of the civil economy and with the General Staff (fig. 6).

The academies and schools which prepare officers for duty in each arm or service are important responsibilities of the chief of the respective administration. In addition, the publications of the arms and services, which carry the power of directives, are particularly important responsibilities of the chiefs.

It will be noted that there is no main administration for the infantry arm. Responsibility for this arm belongs to the Commissariat as a whole. The infantry arm is supervised only by the Inspector of Infantry, who is a deputy commissar. The Red Army considers the infantry a basic arm and the direct responsibility, at all levels, of the commander rather than of a subordinate chief of an arm. All strategy, tactics, and administration of the entire Red Army spring from, or are added to, basic infantry regulations.

The Inspectorate of Infantry, although not an administrative agency, performs important functions. They are illustrated by the specific subject matter of the "Military Bulletin," published by the Inspector. The mission of the Bulletin is to present "analyses, from current war experience, of the theory and practice of combat; analyses of combat training, especially in the fields of tactics and fire control; and discussion and instruction concerning organization, tactics, techniques, and military experience."

The Affairs Administration handles all internal problems of the Commissariat. It is charged particularly with "housekeeping" and personnel duties. Known divisions of the Affairs Administration include the following:

Inventions Division. Guides research and coordinates the needs of the arms and their inspection of new equipment.

Regulation Division. Prepares regulations applicable to the entire Red Army.

Foreign Liaison Division. Provides liaison with representatives of other nations conducting business with the Commissariat.

Finance Division. Administers the finances of the Commissariat and of the personnel of its administrations.

Economics Division. Administers the internal "housekeeping" affairs of the Commissariat and administrations.

Publications Division. Prints and distributes all publications of the Commissariat and administrations.

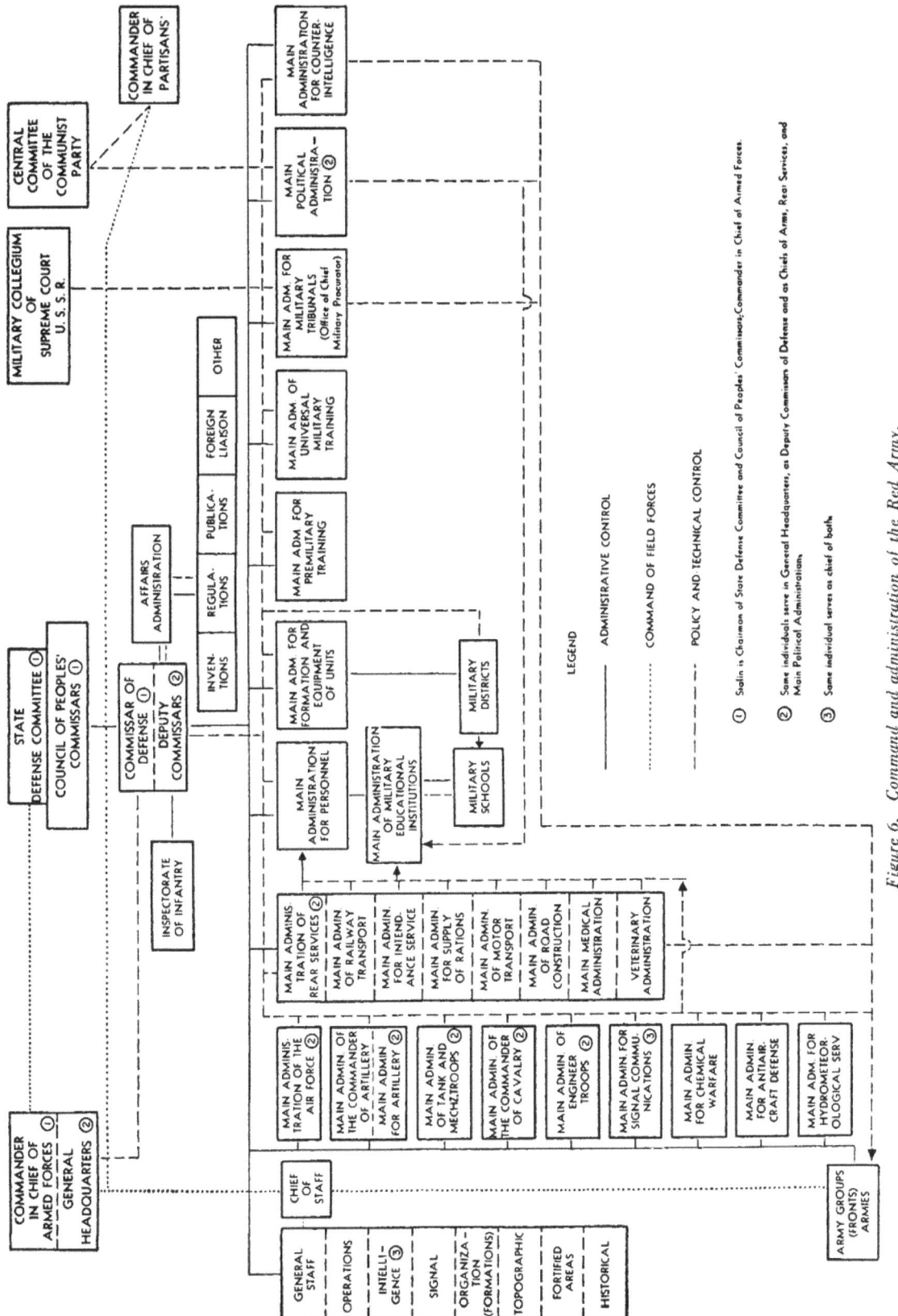

Figure 6. Command and administration of the Red Army.

Section II. MAIN ADMINISTRATIONS OF ARMS AND TECHNICAL SERVICES

1. GENERAL

The main administrations of the nine arms and technical services are organized, under their chiefs, into staff sections and administrations which vary in number according to need.

The staff sections of each main administration form the staff of its respective Chief as commander of the arm or service.

The chiefs of the artillery, air, tank and mechanized, engineer, and cavalry arms are also members of the General Headquarters. Occasionally, they have direct control of the operation or deployment of units of their arm in the field. The staffs also assist the chiefs in these latter capacities.

The staff sections appear to correspond to those of the General Staff and work in close cooperation with them. In most cases, the staffs include sections for operations, intelligence, signal, communications, and statistical control organization.

There are at least three administrations (in some cases, main administrations) within each of the main administrations of the arms and technical services. They administer the supply, combat training, and personnel affairs of their respective arms.

Another element of a main administration is believed to be its Military Council, consisting of the chief (Commander), the chief of staff or head of the operations section, the head of the supply administration, and a political representative who is responsible to the Main Political Administration. The Military Council is a directive body with somewhat wider powers than are vested in the chief of the arm or service, alone.

2. ARTILLERY

a. General. Of all the specialized branches of the Red Army, none has been more highly developed nor has been surrounded with a greater tradition of emphasis and prestige than the artillery arm.

The functions of the artillery arm embrace, in addition to those found in the other armies of the world, responsibility for the development and supply of all weapons and ammunition for every arm. Of necessity, they also include direction of training in the use and maintenance of everything that shoots, the preparation of pertinent technical and training manuals and materials, and a large share of the planning phase of all major operations. It is not unusual to find an artillery officer, usually the Chief of Artillery of an appropriate staff echelon, placed in over-all command of all troops for an operation in which artillery is the major arm employed.

The great weight of responsibility falling to the Commissariat of Defense concerned with artillery affairs and the complexity of administration involved are such that two main administrations have been formed to handle the arm. One of them is concerned with staff structure and the other with administrative structure.

The two administrations perform the following functions:

> Coordination with the air forces of the development of fire plans for major operations.
>
> Technical control and direction of the tactical employment, training of personnel, and supply activities associated with artillery, mortars, and rockets, with the exception of self-propelled artillery.
>
> Coordination with appropriate Commissariats of the development and supply of all weapons, including infantry and aircraft armament, and of all ammunition. Special engineer and chemical weapons and explosives, and aircraft bombs do not fall within this jurisdiction.
>
> All development and dissemination of survey and meteorological data for artillery and cooperating arms. These functions are carried on in conjunction with the Topographic Division of the General Staff, the Meteorological Administration of the Main Administration of the Air Forces, and the Main Administration for the Hydro-Meteorological Services.
>
> Planning of artillery observation aircraft operations in conjunction with the air forces.

b. Commander of artillery. The Chief Marshal of Artillery, ranking artillery officer of the Red Army, is head of the Main Administration of the Commander of Artillery, and probably is assisted by a Military Council. The office is separated both in command and in functions from the Main Administration of Artillery Troops.

The Chief Marshal of Artillery, or "Commander of Artillery," is assisted by deputies for antiaircraft artillery, rockets, and probably for artillery observation aircraft. He is provided with a staff, including the usual branches for operations, intelligence, etc. The artillery Commander is charged with full responsibility for the artillery academies, for the influential

"Artillery Journal," and for all institutions for research and development of the artillery arm.

c. Artillery troops. Most of the routine activities of the administration of the arm are delegated to the Main Administration of Artillery Troops. Organization is believed to include the following:

> Office of the Chief of Artillery Supply.
> Personnel Administration (officers).
> Combat Training Administration (enlisted men).
> Special Administrations:
> > Field Artillery Administration.
> > Tank Destroyer Artillery Administration.
> > Antiaircraft Artillery Administration.
> > Mortar Administration.
> > Rocket Administration.
> > Artillery Topographic Service Administration.

3. AIR FORCES

The Commander of the Air Forces of the Red Army is assisted by a Military Council and deputies for engineers, navigation, aerial gunnery, political affairs, and probably others, including airborne troops. The Main Administration of the Air Forces, under his command, is responsible for:

> Development of fire plans in conjunction with the staff of the Chief of Artillery.
> Control over all the Red Army Air Forces.
> All aircraft development and supply matters, in cooperation with appropriate economic commissariats.
> All artillery spotting units and operations, including photo-reconnaissance, photo-interpretation, and topography, in conjunction with the staff of the Chief of Artillery.
> Publication of the "Air Force Journal."
> Direction and administration of the air academies.
> All air transport and evacuation, especially of the wounded, in cooperation with the Chief of the Rear Services. This includes operational control over the Civil Air Fleet.
> The training and operations of airborne troops, in conjunction with the Inspector of Infantry.

These responsibilities are divided among staff sections, inspectorates, main administrations, and administrations of which the following are known:

> The Air Staff:
> > Operations Section.
> > Intelligence Section.
> > Ciphers Section.
> > Statistical Control (organization) Section.
> > Air Transport Section.
> > Meteorological Section.
> General Inspectorate:
> > Inspector of Fighters.
> > Inspector of Ground-Attack Aircraft.
> > Inspector of Bombers.
> > Inspector of *Sturman* (Navigation, etc.)
> > Inspector of Technical Affairs.
> > Miscellaneous others.
> Administrations:
> > Main Administration of Airborne Troops (probable).
> > Main Administration of the Civil Air Fleet.
> > Main Administration of Rear Services and Supply.
> > Main Administration of Engineer Services.
> > Main Administration for Formation and Training of Units.
> > Personnel Administration (officers).
> > *Sturman* (navigation, etc.) Administration.
> > Aerial Gunnery Service Administration.
> > Administration of Signal Services.
> > Administration of Medical Services (subordinate to the Main Administration of Medical Services under the Chief of the Rear Services).
> > Internal Affairs Administration.
> > Administration of Air Academies.

(For further details, see Chapter XI.)

4. TANK AND MECHANIZED TROOPS

The Main Administration of Tank and Mechanized Troops is charged with control over the tank, self-propelled artillery, and motorized infantry forces of the Red Army; with the development and supply of tanks and armored equipment, in cooperation with the appropriate commissariat; and with coordination of the employment and supply of motor transport for motorized troops, in cooperation with the Chief of the Rear Services. It also is responsible for the publication of the periodical, "Journal of Tank and Mechanized Troops," and for the academy of the arm.

Little is known of the internal structure of this administration. However, it does include the following:

> Office of the Chief.
> Technical Deputy to the Chief (Mechanical Engineer).

23

Military Council.
Staff (probable).
Administrations:
    Tanks.
    Self-propelled artillery.
    Motorized infantry.
    Supply.
    Mechanical engineering.
    Personnel (officers).
    Training (enlisted men).

5. CAVALRY

The Main Administration of Cavalry is concerned with horse cavalry only. It works in close conjunction with the Inspector of Infantry. The periodical of the latter is its only published organ. Organization of the Main Administration of Cavalry is believed to be comparable to that of other arms.

6. ENGINEERS

Only a few subdivisions of the Main Administration of Engineers are known. These include the administrations for combat engineers, ponton engineers, construction engineers, geological services, and construction of fortifications. Staff sections and administrations probably are similar to those of the other arms, but fewer in number.

This administration controls the Engineer Academy and publishes the "Military Engineer Journal." It performs, as do the others, all the training, supply, and development functions peculiar to the arm, including the following:

> Planning of engineer support for major operations, including sieges and river crossings in particular.
> Training of engineers.
> Supply (mines and demolition, construction and fortifications equipment).
> Ponton and bridge construction and supply.
> Geological surveys in conjunction with the Topographic Division of the General Staff and the topographic service of the artillery arm.

7. SIGNAL TROOPS

The Main Administration of Signal troops is charged with all phases of the radio, telephone, telegraph, and postal services of the Red Army. It closely coordinates with the same services of the Commissariat of Signal Communications.

Research and development are charged to the Commissariat. The Administration is largely an operating agency for the sustaining of communications between the General Headquarters and the field forces, and in the zone of operations. In the zone of the interior, all such responsibility is vested in the Commissariat alone.

The Chief Marshal of Signal Troops also is, at the present time, Chief of the Signal Division of the General Staff. He formerly was concurrently Peoples' Commissar of Signal Communications.

The exact channels for coordination of the operations controlled by this administration with those of the Navy and of the Commissariat of Internal Affairs (NKVD), including the signal security operations of the latter, are not known.

Internal organization is little known, but five administrations have been identified. They include telephone and telegraph, radio, postal services, engineers, and signal supply. A small staff and other administrations are presumed to exist.

8. HYDRO-METEOROLOGICAL SERVICES

The Main Administration of Hydro-Meteorological Services was formerly a civil organization directly subordinate to the Council of Peoples' Commissars. During war, this service and the meteorological services of the Navy and of the Red Army have been coordinated under the control of the Main Administration of Hydro-Meteorological Services. It is possible that the civil service may revert to its former status.

The Main Administration is charged with all aspects of procurement and dissemination of meteorological data to military and other agencies. It is organized basically into a Main Administration and an Administration. The Main Administration coordinates all the services involved with the demands of the agencies served, trains all personnel of the services, controls the manufacture of equipment through appropriate Commissariats, and controls the distribution of equipment to military units and to civil units in the military districts. An administration supervises the activities of stations in the military districts.

Internal organization is as follows:

Main Administration.
    Chief of the Service.
    Military Council (probable).
    Staff.
    Deputy for Air Forces.
    Deputy for the Navy.
    Deputy for the Ground Forces.
        Artillery Section.

Chemical Section.
Hydrological Section.
Deputy for Civil Commissariats (probable).
Central Forecasting, Hydrological, and other Institutes.
Central Aerological and other observatories.
Publications Section (periodicals).
Central Bureau of Standards.
Personnel Administration.
Supply Administration.
Administration of Regional Services and Sections.
Supervises and administers stations under the controls of the military districts.

9. ANTIAIRCRAFT DEFENSE FORCES

Little is known about the internal structure of the Main Administration of Antiaircraft Defense Forces (GUPVO). (For the position, functions, and components of the Air Defense Force, see Part I.)

The following agencies are believed to exist in the GUPVO:

Office of the Chief.
Military Council.
Staff Sections.
Deputies for:
Antiaircraft Artillery.
Fighter Forces.
VNOS (early warning service).
NKVD (passive and incendiary defenses under control of the Commissariat of Internal Affairs, [NKVD]).
Chemical Warfare Services.
Administrations for:
Personnel.
Combat Training.
Supply (special supply and coordination of supply from other arms).
Publications:
"Chemistry and Defense."
"Antiaircraft Defense Bulletin."
Administration for coordination of Air Defense Force Headquarters in the military districts.

10. CHEMICAL WARFARE TROOPS

Very little is known about the Main Administration of Chemical Warfare Troops. The activities of the service were neither extensive nor worthy of particular note during World War II. Only in the employment of smoke did the troops of the Chemical Warfare Service perform an important part in operations.

Section III. REAR SERVICES

1. CHIEF OF REAR SERVICES

For the functions of the Chiefs of the Rear Services and their specialized divisions at all echelons in the Red Army, see Chapter VII, Logistics. At commissariat level, these supply and service functions are assigned to the main administrations and the administrations under command of the Chief of the Rear Services.

The Chief of the Rear Services, with the rank of General of the Army, is a Deputy Commissar of Defense. He has a personal staff in addition to the specialized administrations under his control. The staff assists in the coordination of the various supply services and their administrations. It also handles broad problems of supply and assists the Chief of the Rear Services with his duties as a member of the General Headquarters.

2. ADMINISTRATIONS OF REAR SERVICES

The Chief of the Rear Services and the main administrations and administrations under his control are charged with all phases of Red Army logistics, except those specifically allotted to the arms and technical services.

The Main Administrations and Administrations under his control are as follows:

Central Administration of Army Transportation (rail).
Main Administration of Motor Transport.
Main Administration of Roads (construction and maintenance).
Main Administration of Intendance (clothing, etc.).
Main Administration of Subsistence (rations).
Main Administration of the Medical Service.
Administration of the Veterinary Service.
Administration of Motor Fuel and Lubricant Supply.
Administration of Finance.
Administration of Personnel Losses of Noncommissioned Officers and Enlisted Men and for Relief of their Families.
Office for publication of the journal, "Rear Area and Supply of the Red Army."

(For further information, see Chapter VII.)

25

Section IV. POLITICAL, PENAL, AND COUNTERINTELLIGENCE SUPERVISION

1. GENERAL

Three main administrations, constitutionally subordinate to the Peoples' Commissariat of Defense, are concerned with supervision of the loyalty and legal discipline of the Red Army. They are the Main Administration of Counterintelligence, the Main Administration of Military Tribunals, and the Main Political Administration. The basic lines of policy of all three of these administrations are prescribed, not by the Commissariat, but by other agencies of the state.

2. COUNTERINTELLIGENCE

In the establishment of the Main Administration of Counterintelligence, the Red Army is made responsible for the loyalty of all its personnel; for the security of the zone of operations, exclusive of rear areas, against penetration by enemy agents; and for the required personnel and organization.

Close cooperation with the Commissariats of Internal Affairs (NKVD) and State Security (NKGB) is mandatory, but the Administration is not operationally subordinate to either.

Agencies subject to the control of this Administration exist at all echelons of command in the field army, down to and including companies.

3. MAIN POLITICAL ADMINISTRATION

The Main Political Administration of the Red Army, subordinate to the Commissariat, is the chief agency of the Communist Party for control of the Red Army. It occupies a position of great power and influence. The Administration is best considered as the military branch of the Central Committee of the Communist Party, from which it receives its basic directives.

Headed by a senior member of the Central Committee, it issues directives covering all political activities in the combat zone and within the Army structure in all areas. Perhaps the most important function of the Administration is its supervisory control over all Party members in the Red Army and its reporting of their activities.

The Main Political Administration is charged with strengthening the Party and *Komsomol* (Communist Youth or pre-Party) organizations in the Red Army, with psychological warfare and propaganda conducted by the army in the field, and with political indoctrination of Red Army troops, partisans, and the civil population of occupied areas. It also is responsible for a number of educational institutions, including the Lenin Political War Academy and the Engels Military-Political School.

The training of political assistants to commanders, members of the Military Councils, at all echelons and of political commissars (when the political commissar system is operative) is the exclusive responsibility of the Administration.

The Main Political Administration is organized into a number of component administrations. Chief among these are those for organization and training, political propaganda, information, *Komsomol*, and Party members.

4. MILITARY TRIBUNALS

The activities of military tribunals at all echelons down to divisions, excluding only corps, are supervised, coordinated, and administered by the Main Administration of Military Tribunals. The head of this administration is a Chief Procurator of the U. S. S. R., titled the Chief Procurator of Military Tribunals. All procurators (attorney-generals) of subordinate military tribunals are appointed by the Chief Procurator, with the advice and approval of the Commissariat of Defense.

The Chief Procurator is responsible to the Military Collegium of the Supreme Soviet for the application of Soviet law to military affairs and personnel. The members of the Collegium are appointed by the Chairman of the Presidium of the Supreme Soviet.

The jurisdiction of the Military Tribunals extends only to offenses against the laws of the Soviet Union as interpreted or applied to military affairs. Military regulations and discipline which do not stem from the civil law and which apply only to Red Army personnel, are not within the sphere of the tribunals or of the Main Administration of Military Tribunals.

Section V. ADMINISTRATIONS FOR PERSONNEL AND TRAINING

1. GENERAL

The administration of personnel affairs, conscription, training centers, schools and academies, the selection of officers and noncommissioned officers, and the administration of organizations for the military training of civilians is shared by a large number of agencies at commissariat level. (For further details of this system, see Chapter II.)

However, four main administrations (with a fifth subordinated to one of the four) are especially charged with closely related responsibilities in this field. They are the Main Administration of Personnel and its subordinate, the Main Administration of Military Educational Institutions; the Main Administration for the Formation and Equipment of Units; the Main Administration for Universal Compulsory Military Training; and the Main Administration for Pre-Military Training. These administrations are directly responsible for all but the purely technical aspects of the activities of the military districts. The latter are controlled by the arms and services.

2. PERSONNEL

The Main Administration of Personnel is concerned exclusively with officer personnel. It is charged with the maintenance of complete records on all officers in the Red Army, including their assignments, military occupational specialties, schooling, and qualifications. It assigns and promotes all officers up to and including the grade of lieutenant colonel, except where such authority is partially delegated to the army group (front) Commander.

The Main Administration of Personnel also is responsible for the activities of the Main Administration for Military Educational Institutions, because the latter is concerned primarily with officer replacements.

3. MILITARY EDUCATIONAL INSTITUTIONS

The Main Administration for Military Educational Institutions (GUVUZ), already mentioned as being subordinate to the Main Administration of Personnel, is charged with over-all responsibility for all schools of the Red Army. Technical aspects of training in the arms are the responsibility of the appropriate main administrations. Administrative problems are handled by the military districts in which the institutions are located.

Rates and standards for matriculation and graduation of officers are set by the Main Administration of Personnel on the basis of directives from the General Headquarters, or, for minor adjustments, from the Commissariat.

4. FORMATION AND EQUIPMENT OF UNITS

The Main Administration for the Formation and Equipment of Units (GUFUV) is concerned primarily with the formation of units and formations from available personnel or by conscription in ac-

cordance with the directives of the Commissariat.

Tables of Organization and Equipment, worked out by the Formations Division of the General Staff and approved by the General Headquarters and the Commissariat (and the appropriate main administration if a unit of an arm is involved), are the basic directives for the GUFUV. Directives concerning the rate of formation are developed by this Main Administration in conjunction with the Chief Administration for Military Educational Institutions, which supplies officer personnel.

In addition to the processes of mobilization and expansion of the Red Army, GUFUV is charged with the recruiting and equipping of trained replacements for field units. Both the formation and replacement processes are handled locally by the military districts, under the direct supervision of the Main Administration for the Formation and Equipment of Units.

5. UNIVERSAL COMPULSORY MILITARY TRAINING

The Main Administration for Universal Compulsory Military Training of the Citizens of the U. S. S. R. (Vsevobuch) is charged with enforcement of the State Defense Committee decree requiring military training for the duration of World War II for all citizens between the ages of 16 and 50.

The decree applies to all persons not members of the armed forces. All civil organizations, such as factories, cultural societies, and agricultural communities, are instruments for the application of the decree.

This organization may have been dissolved at the end of World War II.

6. PRE-MILITARY TRAINING

The Main Administration for Pre-Military Training (literally, "for the Military Training of School Children") was organized during World War II to administer a program of universal physical and military training through the primary and secondary schools for children in the first 10 grades (7 to 16 years of age).

Although the proportion of military training has been reduced since the end of the war, all school children of both sexes receive as much military training as is commensurate with their individual capabilities. Recruits with this training are prepared to continue full-scale army training immediately after induction.

CHAPTER II

PERSONNEL ADMINISTRATION

INTRODUCTION

1. DISADVANTAGES OF RED ARMY PERSONNEL ADMINISTRATION

In addition to conscription, classification, assignment, promotion, and separation, Red Army personnel administration agencies also are charged with supervision of morale and loyalty to the state and to the Communist Party and with all types of military and political training.

One of the principal weaknesses of Red Army personnel administration is the excessive number of agencies with similar or overlapping functions and responsibilities. This characteristic is especially prominent in the supervision of loyalty, in which the Main Administration of Counterintelligence, agencies of the Commissariat of Internal Affairs (NKVD), agents of the Commissariat of State Security (NKGB), and the Main Political Administration share responsibility with Red Army counterintelligence personnel.

Weaknesses are strikingly apparent in the handling of administrative paper work. There appear to be no machine records units or high-speed facilities to expedite the handling of personnel information. The lack of records on enlisted men, except in their units or home countries, impedes the effectiveness of personnel administration at all higher echelons. Systems for objective classification, such as aptitude tests and analytical recording, are notably absent. Preconscription skills are employed only when directly analogous to army requirements.

Provisions for the promoting of the welfare of enlisted men are singularly weak. Although clubs, motion pictures, reading matter, and other forms of entertainment are provided, their quantity and distribution are inadequate in comparison with the facilities of other armies.

2. ADVANTAGES OF RED ARMY PERSONNEL ADMINISTRATION

One of the advantages of the Soviet military system is the continuous maintenance of detailed mobilization plans. They are prepared in great detail and are revised periodically with meticulous care. In addition to specific plans for the utilization of all U. S. S. R. resources, mobilization plans include detailed personnel requirements.

All persons liable to call for active duty in event of mobilization are given specific instructions as to their individual assignment or reporting station. Instructions include the day and hour to report. The assignment of individuals after they report is governed largely by plans based on careful evaluation of anticipated requirements.

Lessons learned in combat are evaluated rapidly and integrated into Red Army training and tactical doctrine with marked facility. The use of technical journals and army newspapers as training vehicles has proved successful. In general, the training films and instructional methods of the Red Army are of high quality.

The Red Army has outdone other armies in political indoctrination and the development of combat morale on the basis of over-all political objectives. Considerable emphasis always is placed on sustaining the cultivated convictions of military personnel. The administrative apparatus for this task, the materials used, and the planning of indoctrination are extensive and appear to be effective.

Systematic use of awards, decorations, and commendations for the building of troop morale also has been highly developed.

The system of officer selection is one of the outstanding advantages of Red Army personnel administration. Commissions and promotions in officer grades are distributed so as to insure a steady flow of new officers, adequate training and experience, and close correlation with the training courses of schools and academies.

Finally, close cooperation between the Red Army and the civil agencies and meticulous coordination of the requirements of both in peace and in war extend into the field of personal administration, as into all other fields. Application of the conscription law, release of personnel from active duty, and detached service provisions all are managed to provide maximum use of available manpower.

3. OTHER DISTINCTIVE CHARACTERISTICS

The personnel practices of the Red Army include other distinctive features which are neither disadvantageous nor advantageous. One of these is the sharp distinction in training, in assignments, and in responsibility between command or staff officers and troop officers of each of the arms and services. Another is the use of identical machinery for conscription, mobilization planning, mobilization, the replacement system, and demobilization. Available trained personnel is considered only as potential manpower for the expansion of the standing army. No organizations comparable to the National Guard and Organized Reserves of the United States have existed in the U. S. S. R. since 1937.

Another peculiarity of Red Army personnel administration is found in the military penal system. Army disciplinary regulations include only such requirements as do not spring directly from the basic penal code of the U. S. S. R. Although commanders alone have authority to try and sentence offenders against military regulations, violations of the basic penal code of the U. S. S. R. are handled by a system of Military Tribunals subordinate to the Supreme Court of the U. S. S. R.

4. RECENT DEVELOPMENTS

Progressive development and the expansion of a corps of professional career officers before and during World War II have affected Red Army personnel administration. Although the granting of special privileges and separate treatment for officers,

especially in the replacement and mobilization systems, have complicated the processes of personnel administration, they also have made possible a greater degree of reliance on individual officers.

The change from an army of workers and peasants to an army drawn from all classes has furthered the development of a professional status for army personnel. The change also has helped to raise the general educational level of the army.

Instead of the former four individual forces, the standing army, its reserves, the Territorial Forces, and their reserves, there now is only a single, centrally-controlled army with closely integrated reserves. The effects of the change are apparent in the greater standardization of training techniques and in the length and frequency of training periods for reserve personnel.

The gradual, but frequently interrupted, increase in the freedom of the Red Army from interference from other agencies has increased the responsibility of the Red Army for administration of its personnel. Although the authority of the political apparatus within the army has not been diminished, it has been confined to the purely political field. Thus, purely military aspects of personnel policy are left entirely in the hands of military personnel.

Counterintelligence machinery of the Red Army has been removed from NKVD control and subordinated to the Main Administration of Counterintelligence of the Peoples' Commissariat of Defense.

5. PROBABLE FUTURE TRENDS

Efforts to overcome some of the disadvantages of Red Army personnel administration certainly are to be expected in the future. Early efforts to introduce modern record systems, equipment, selection systems, and classification methods are anticipated.

PART I. BASIC CONCEPTS OF MILITARY SERVICE

Section I. LIABILITY FOR MILITARY SERVICE

1. UNIVERSAL SERVICE LIABILITY

Personnel administration in the Red Army is based fundamentally on the definitions of military service included in the Constitution of 1936 and in subsequent laws stemming from the Constitution. The Constitution states that "universal military service is law . . . military service in the workers' and

peasants' Red Army is an honorable duty . . . defense of the Fatherland is the sacred duty of every citizen of the U. S. S. R."

The selection of personnel and the terms of service and duty in the Red Army are determined by the "Universal Military Service Law" of September 1939, and by subsequent amendments and decrees. This law and the decrees are expansions of the constitutional principle of a universal liability for military service. They establish and define the groups of citizens liable to conscription. They define the various categories and classes of military personnel in terms of active duty liabilities and the periods of service during which personnel are subject to military penal law.

2. CONSCRIPTION LIABILITY

Under the terms of the 1939 Law of Compulsory Military Service, all able-bodied males who reach their nineteenth birthday in any given calendar year are subject to conscription under the quotas set for that year. Citizens more than 50 years of age automatically are exempted. Students who graduate from secondary schools after their eighteenth birthday but before their nineteenth birthday, are not eligible for conscription on the basis of age, but they may be inducted. In 1940, the minimum age of conscription was reduced to 17. This adjustment may have been cancelled with the end of other special war legislation.

Certain classes of especially qualified women, such as nurses and veterinary specialists, within the conscription age group, are registered as liable for service in the Red Army in time of war or emergency. These classes are conscriptioned only in time of war or emergency and serve the same periods of active and reserve duty as do male officers or enlisted men of similar grade or rank.

Unless they possess special qualifications, all conscripts are inducted for active service as privates.

Persons wholly unfit for military service because of physical defects are exempted from conscription into active service.

Persons under arrest, exiled, deported, or deprived of their suffrage rights by the courts are excluded from conscription while under sentence. Citizens of other nations also are excluded and may not volunteer for service in the Red Army.

Large numbers are deferred from among those called up for service in the Red Army. Persons who are too ill for service and those who are less than 20 years of age and still in secondary school may be deferred three times. Deferments must be not less than 3 months and not more than 12 months apart. Certain other classes, such as scientists, rural school teachers, workers in distant and isolated regions, relocated farmers, and specially qualified workers in essential civilian work and services, may be deferred until 30 years old. In time of war, the legal provisions for deferment may be cancelled by decree.

3. FULFILLMENT OF SERVICE OBLIGATIONS

After conscription, three forms of military service in the Red Army are accepted as fulfillment of the universal obligation in the defense of the U. S. S. R. They are active duty, extended leave or furlough, and reserve status. Active duty and extended leave or furlough together are referred to as "active service."

Active duty includes periods of active assignment to units or formations of the Red Army and detached duty of a military nature with civil agencies. Extended leaves are granted to officers, and extended furloughs to enlisted men, after completion of the periods of active duty required of them. Personnel on leave or furlough are carried as active members of the Red Army, but are free to accept employment and to live at home as civilians. Officers and enlisted men of the reserve are members of the Red Army, but are subject to military regulations and military penal law only during the required active training periods.

The reserve component of the Red Army is divided into two categories for the determination of the priority of mobilization. Categories are based on the origin of the personnel.

Reserve Category I, composed of officers and enlisted men who have completed the periods of active service (duty and leave or furlough) required by law, has first priority for call-up into active service in time of mobilization.

Reserve Category II is called into active service after Category I. Category II includes:

> New conscripts, fit only for limited service and not needed in the active or standing army.
>
> Conscripts supporting two parents, if both parents are invalided or if the father is over 60 and the mother is over 55.
>
> Conscripts surplus to the current need of the Red Army, but otherwise eligible for active service.
>
> Personnel whose political reliability or disciplinary record make their inclusion in the first waves of mobilization inadvisable.

The reserve components of the Red Army also are divided into classes.

Reserves of the 1st Class are personnel of Categories I and II who are not more than 35 years of age, and who need, because of their specialty, the schedule of reserve training periods presenting the most training at the most frequent intervals. All training programs for reserve personnel must include not less than 3 months' training, with not more than 1 month in any 1 year. Maximum training is required of a soldier placed in the 1st Class of the Reserve at the age of 24. He receives 1 month of training per year until he reaches the age of 34, a total of from 10 to 11 months of training.

Reserves of the 2d Class are personnel in Categories I and II who are not more than 45 years of age. Such personnel may be of any lower age. They are required to attend shorter or less frequent training periods than those of the 1st Class.

Reserves of the 3d Class generally are in Category II and may be of any age up to the retirement age of 50 years. The retirement age was raised to 60 years, by decree, during World War II. These reserves attend the minimum course of training periods.

Section II. ACTIVE SERVICE

1. REQUIRED ACTIVE SERVICE

The periods of service required in the various types of military service that are accepted in fulfillment of the law are prescribed separately for officers and for enlisted men.

a. Enlisted men. All conscripted enlisted men who are not assigned immediately to the reserve are liable for 5 years of active service, comprising active duty and extended furlough periods. Privates in the ground forces are released to 3 years of furlough after 2 years of active duty, if they have not been promoted. Privates and noncommissioned officers in the air forces go on furlough for 1 year after completing 4 years of active duty. Noncommissioned officers in the ground forces are released on extended furlough only after they have completed a total of at least 3 years of active duty.

At the end of 5 years of active service in the Red Army, all enlisted men usually are placed in a reserve category. In time of war or other national emergency, however, all or most of these time limitations on active service are overridden by powers of decree granted to the executive of the U. S. S. R.

Any number of women specialists between 19 and 50 years of age, who are registered for conscription, may be conscripted. They then are liable to active service on the same basis as enlisted men, or may be assigned to Reserve Category II.

b. Officers. Commissions generally are granted only to graduates of army or cadet schools, although some civilians receive direct commissions in special cases without basic military schooling. Upon completion of secondary school and the pre-conscription training which accompanies the schooling, selected students and approved applicants are admitted to officer schools. Other officers are graduates of cadet schools, which they attend throughout the secondary school grades and a subsequent period equivalent to the period of officer candidate training. Beyond secondary school level, candidates in both types of schools are subject to military regulations and penal law and are exempted from conscription for active service. The period spent in such schools is not considered to be in fulfillment of military service liabilities.

Officers are required to perform active service and to remain in the reserve for a period of 2 years or, in some cases, 1½ years for each year spent in army schools. The average length of such compulsory service is 5 years.

Officers who elect to make an army career, as do most graduates of cadet schools, may remain on active service until age or length of service authorizes retirement. Officers who are promoted to field grade or who have been selected in competitive examinations are considered career officers. All officers are liable to active service for not less than the duration of war or national emergency. Officers who are detached from army units and placed on special duty with civilian agencies generally are career officers.

Civilians who have been commissioned directly for special duties are required to serve not less than 2 years of active duty.

c. Extended active service. In case of need, the Commissariat of Defense is empowered by law to retain any member of the Red Army 2 months beyond his date of eligibility for release from active service. In time of war, this power is not limited to any period less than the duration of the emergency.

Upon completion of the required period of active service, all personnel may volunteer for extended active service beyond the normal limit of liability.

They then are committed once more to the standard periods of required service.

2. VOLUNTARY ACTIVE SERVICE

Provisions for voluntary active service or active duty were suspended during World War II. All persons qualified for active duty, whether in active service, reserve status, or deferred, were required to perform active duty in the Red Army, unless required by the more urgent demands of the civil economy or government. The law, however, provides that certain groups may volunteer for active service, in addition to those electing to volunteer for extended active service. This legal provision is applicable in time of peace.

In peacetime, all qualified males, not less than 18 years of age but not of conscription age, all personnel in any category or class of the reserve, and all registered women specialists may volunteer for active duty.

PART II. ADMINISTRATIVE AGENCIES AND PROCEDURES

Section I. PERSONNEL ADMINISTRATION AGENCIES

1. GENERAL

Personnel administration comprehends all control and recording of the individual affairs of all members of the Red Army. It embraces formation of policy, collation of statistics, supply of personnel, conscription, selection, assignment, promotion, training, pay and allowances, decoration and awards, discipline, morale, and supervision of personnel loyalty to country and to regime. Each aspect of personnel administration is the specific responsibility of an agency at each level of Red Army command (figs. 1 and 2).

In the discussion of personnel agencies, the administration of infantry troops is assumed unless another arm or service is cited specifically.

2. POLICY

The development of basic and long-term policies, as distince from actual administration of personnel, is first a legislative function, and therefore concerns the Supreme Soviet. The basic service laws are translated into broad policies for administration of the Red Army by the Commissariat of Defense. In time of war, the emergency governmental powers conferred on the State Defense Committee make it the most important agency in policy matters affecting Red Army personnel.

Below the level of the high command, the formation of personnel policies within the policies handed down by the Commissariat of Defense is a command function of Military Councils, together with the commanders at each echelon. Thus, for example, the Military Council (of which the Commanding General is the chief member) of each military district and the officer in command of a tank brigade each exercise limited policy-making power in personnel administration.

3. CONSCRIPTION AND SEPARATION

a. High command level. Basic policies of conscription and separation are determined by the laws promulgated by the Supreme Soviet. In time of war, the State Defense Committee coordinate military and civil requirements for personnel in application of the law, and the Main Administration for the Formation and Equipment of Units administers the actual conscription and separation process according to its directives. In peacetime, the directives of the Council of Peoples' Commissars govern the execution of the conscription laws by the military districts.

b. Military districts. The Military Council of each military district is responsible for the conscription and separation within its district (fig. 3). In each *Oblast* of the military district, the Second (conscription) Department of the staff of the *Oblast* Military Commissar directly supervises the actual processes as carried out by the *Rayon* Military Commissar in each of the component *Rayons*. A Deputy of the *Rayon* Military Commissar is assisted by a Conscription Board in each of the Conscription Areas of the *Rayon*. The Conscription Board consists of a *Rayon* Deputy Military Commissar, a representative of the local NKVD, a representative of the .*Rayon* Soviet (local government), and two physicians selected by the *Rayon* Military Commissar.

Normal peacetime conscription and conscription for mobilization and wartime replacement requirements of the formation or unit in each Manning Zone are supervised by the Second Department

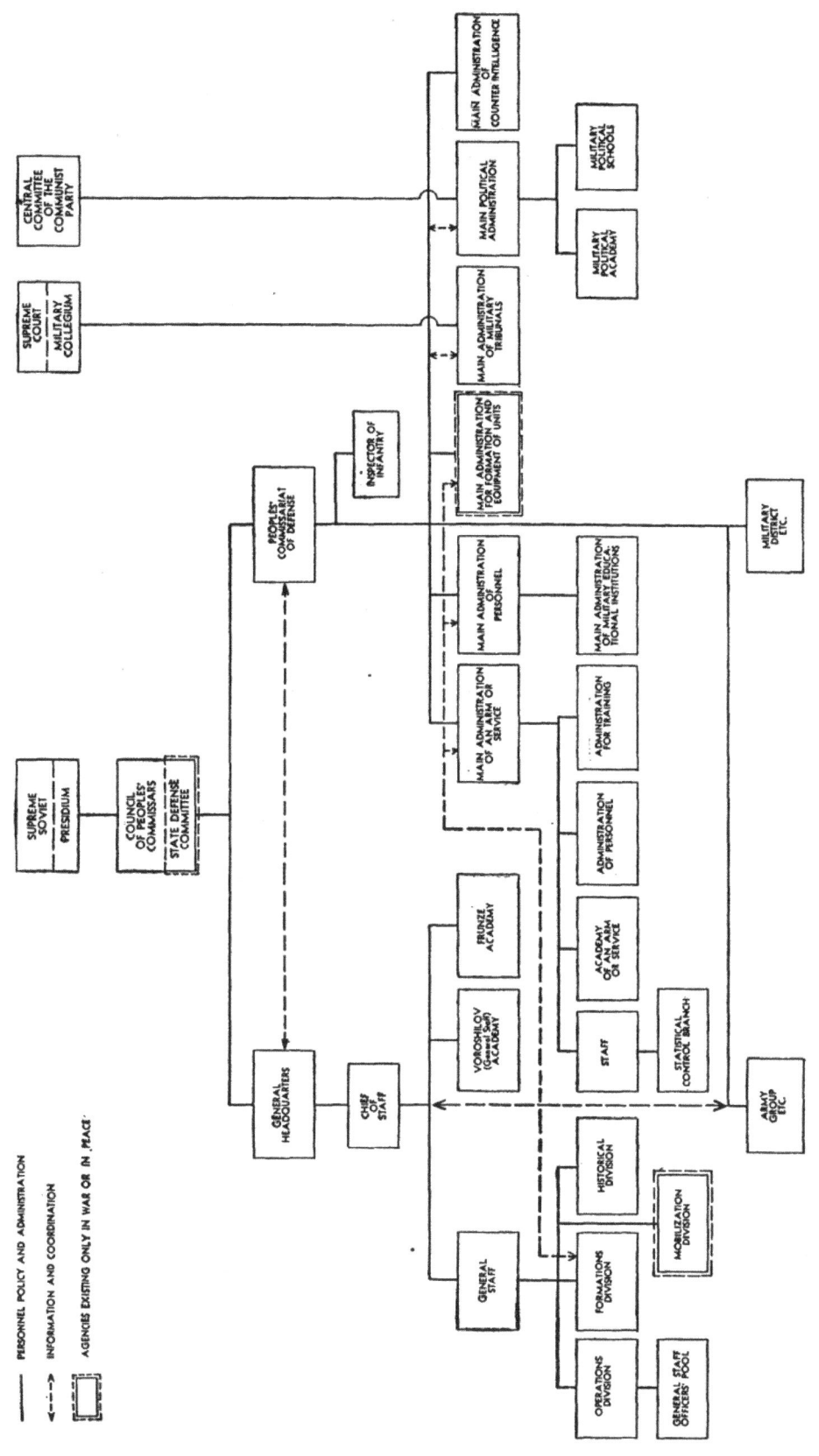

Figure 1. *Central agencies for personnel policy and administration.*

33

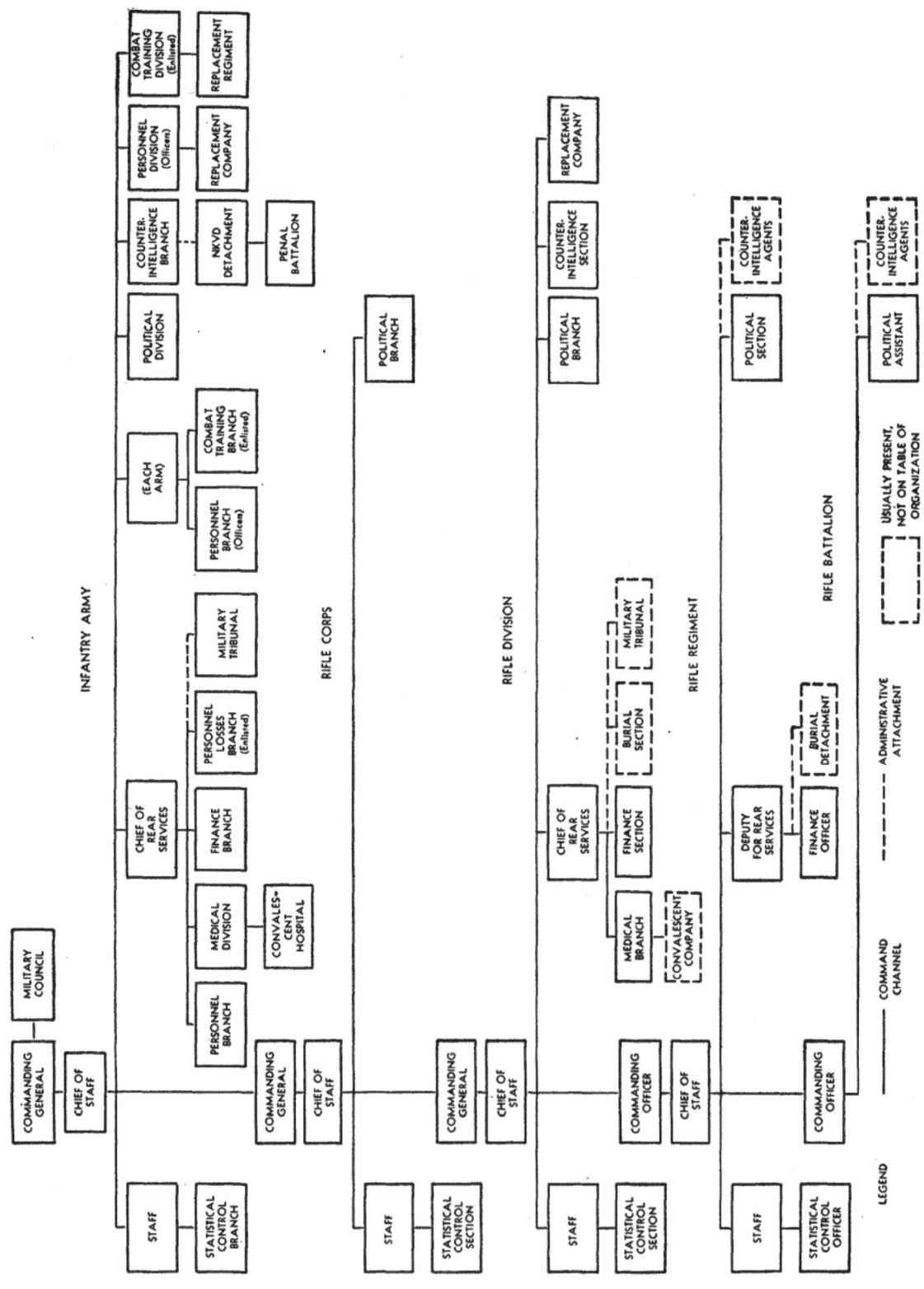

Figure 2. Personnel and training agencies in the field forces.

34

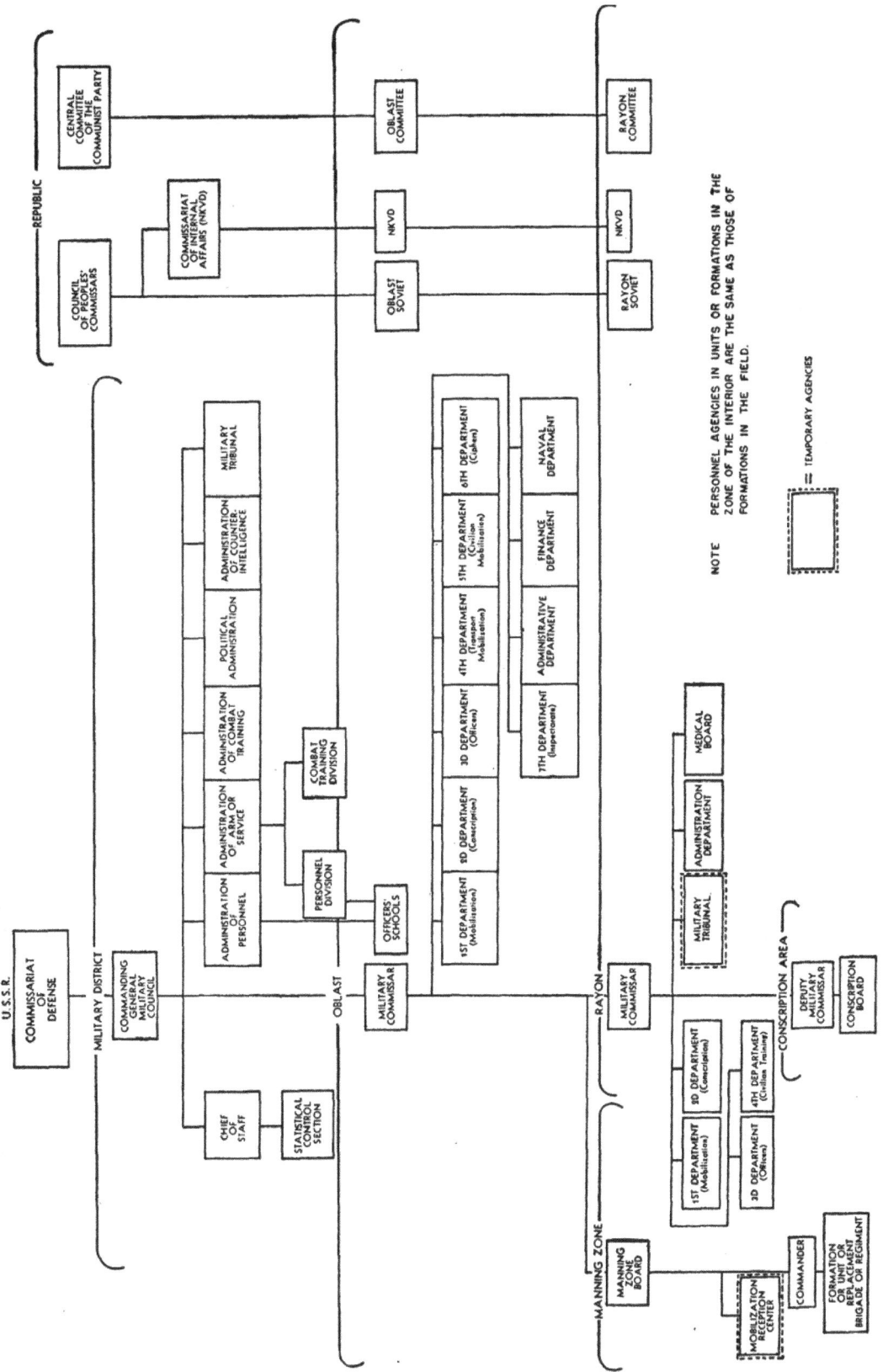

Figure 3. Personnel and training agencies in the zone of interior.

35

of the staff of the Manning Zone (or unit) Commander.

c. Field forces. Conscription and separation normally are not administered by the forces in the field. But, the Military Councils and Commanders of army groups are empowered to set up Military *Rayons* in areas of the U. S. S. R. from which invading forces have been driven. Administration of the conscription laws in such areas, so long as they remain in the Army Group area, is handled as in *Rayons* of the zone of the interior.

4. SELECTION, ASSIGNMENT, AND PROMOTION OF OFFICERS

a. High command level. Administration of officer personnel on the basis of individual records is a responsibility, at the highest level, of the Main Administration of Personnel of the Commissariat of Defense. This main administration maintains complete records of individual officers, approves all new commissions, and supervises the assignment of officers in general and of officers of the higher grades in particular. This office, may, however, promote officers only up to the grade of lieutenant colonel. Promotions above that grade and up to Marshal require the approval of the Council of Peoples' Commissars. Promotions to Marshal and higher require approval of the Supreme Soviet or its Presidium.

The Chief of the General Staff has a measure of control over the assignment of career officers of field grade. Graduates of the Voroshilov (General Staff) Academy and other field grade officers of equal qualifications by reason of experience, but not assigned to attend the Voroshilov, form a pool under the control of the Operations Division of the General Staff. This pool is equivalent to a General Staff Officers' Reserve, such as is found in other armies. The extent of General Staff Administration of such officers after assignment to General Staff positions is not known, and the separate existence of a category of "General Staff Officers" is not accepted.

The Administration for Personnel of each of the Main Administrations of Arms and Services maintains complete individual records and administers the affairs of officers of each particular arm or service.

b. Field forces. The selection, promotion, and assignment of officers are handled at the various echelon levels by the agencies following:

At army group level, by the Military Council, by the Personnel Administration and, for each arm or service, by the Personnel Branch of the Administration of the arm or service.

At army level, by the Military Council, by the Personnel Division and, for each arm and service, by the Personnel Section of the Division of the arm or service.

At all lower echelon levels, by the Commander, who has very limited authority in these matters.

c. Military districts. In the military districts, officer affairs are handled by the Personal Administration of the district headquarters. At *Oblast* level, the Third (officers) Department of the Staff of the Military Commissar is responsible for promotion and assignment, while the Second Department supervises the selection of officer candidates in connection with its conscription responsibility.

The *Rayon* Military Commissar, assisted by the Second and Third Departments of his staff and by his deputies in the Conscription Areas, are responsible for selection of officer prospects from among those conscripted. Promotion and assignment of reserve officers in the *Rayon* is the concern of Commanders of formations or units that are stationed or are to be formed there in time of mobilization. Manning Zones and Manning Zone Boards are created only to supply enlisted men to such formations and units. Officers residing in one *Rayon* are assigned to units in another *Rayon* by the Third Department of the staff of the *Oblast* Military Commissar, or, if necessary, by the Personnel Administration of the military district.

5. ASSIGNMENT AND PROMOTION OF ENLISTED MEN

a. General. Assignment and promotion of enlisted men is handled by agencies other than those involved in the assignment and promotion of officers. Individual records and personnel administration of enlisted men does not concern agencies higher than their units in the field, or the *Rayon* Military Commissar in the zone of the interior. Responsibility in the higher echelons for the affairs of enlisted men is purely statistical. Thus, the higher echelons are concerned only with such matters as setting standards for promotion, the proportionate assignment of enlisted men by arm, and the proportionate granting of promotions according to requirement.

b. High command level. Basic policy for the assignment of enlisted men is determined by the Commissariat of Defense in accordance with the mobilization plans, inclusive of the tables of organization and the statistical demands for the manning of planned units and formations. In time of peace, these plans, in broad scope, are developed by the Mobilization Division of the General Staff, and, in time of war, by the Main Administration for the Formation and Equipment of Units in the Commissariat of Defense. This Main Administration is responsible for the carrying out of the assignment process by the subordinate agencies of the military districts.

c. Military districts. The Statistical Control Section of the Staff of the military district is responsible for the assignment and promotion process as carried out by the subordinate agencies. No individual records are involved, except in special cases where enlisted men of special qualifications must be assigned to units in areas other than in their own Manning Zone, *Oblast*, or *Rayon* in order to fill tables of organization.

The First (mobilization) Department of the *Oblast* Military Commissar's staff has exactly similar responsibilities in the *Oblast*.

The First Department of the Staff of the *Rayon* Military Commissar has similar responsibilities, but also assigns individual enlisted men to formations and units for active duty and, in anticipation of mobilization, to reserve status. This department is not informed as to reassignments, promotions, and other changes in individual status of those on active duty until the return of the individual. This processing is implemented locally by the Deputy Military Commissars and the Conscription Boards of which they are members. Promotions are granted by Commanders of Units with which enlisted men perform active duty.

d. Field forces. Individual assignment and promotion of enlisted men are the responsibilities of unit commanders only. The interest of all higher echelons in the assignment and promotion of enlisted men in this respect are purely statistical.

6. STATISTICAL CONTROL

a. General. The statistical control functions of staffs at all echelons of Red Army command includes the following:

Analysis of problems of organization and manning of all subordinate components.

Complete statistics, including individual records, of all officers under command, giving their status and availability as replacements.

Complete statistical records of personnel losses in all grades, ranks, and arms of service.

The preparation of requisitions for personnel as the need arises.

Statistical control is primarily a reporting and a requisitioning function. Requisitions originate at the lowest level of command and are consolidated at the next higher level. They finally are consolidated by the appropriate divisions of the General Staff. This process applies equally in personnel administration of the forces in the field and in the military districts. The supply of personnel in response to requisition is handled by the agencies responsible for assignment of officers and of enlisted men.

b. High command. In peacetime, statistical control at the highest level is performed by the Mobilization Division of the General Staff. With the dissolution of the Mobilization Division in time of war, two of its chief functions, statistical control and the planning of new formations, are taken over by the Formations Division. The other functions of the Mobilization Division are taken over by the Main Administration for the Formation and Equipment of Units, since mobilization planning is succeeded at that time by actual mobilization and the processes of replacement and formation of new units and formations.

c. Field forces. In the staffs of units and formations in the field, at all echelons down to and including regiments, statistical control is handled by statistical control sections. All reports are channeled upward in the chain of command, as are all requisitions which cannot be satisfied by the replacement units of the unit itself.

d. Military districts. At military district levels, statistical control is handled by the First (mobilization) Department, and, finally, by the Statistical Control Section of the staff of the unit or formation which is stationed in the *Rayon* or Manning Zone. During the actual period of mobilization, statistical control reporting is charged to the Mobilization Reception Centers of the Manning Zones, and to the commanders of all units below regiment, down to and including companies.

7. PAY AND ALLOWANCES

a. State and high command level. The finances of the Red Army are handled by the State Bank, the chief central agency for all U. S. S. R. finances. Within the Commissariat of Defense, the pay and allowances of Red Army personnel and the administration of finance distribution are controlled by the Administration of Finance of the Main Administration of the Chief of Rear Services. Pay and allowances in the field forces are administered by finance offices at all echelons, down to and including regiments.

b. Military districts. Pay and allowances are handled by finance offices in all echelons under command of the military districts, including the finance offices of units and formations within the zone of the interior.

c. Allotments and pensions. Monetary benefits to the dependents of Red Army personnel are not a part of the pay of army personnel, and are disbursed by local civil authorities, who are not under army control. Benefits are granted to dependents of all grades and ranks below captain. Special payments also are granted to survivors of those killed or listed as missing in action. In the case of survivors benefits, the chain of command of the rear services is responsible for the reporting of necessary information regarding enlisted men. At army level, the Section of Enlisted Personnel Losses of the Chief of Rear Services collects such information from lower formations and units and forwards it to the Administration for Personnel Losses of Enlisted Men and Relief (pensions) for their Families of the Chief of Rear Services in the Commissariat of Defense.

Information on officer losses probably is handled by the Main Administration of Personnel, on the basis of reports from the officer personnel agencies of the field forces.

Ordinary allotments are affected by changes in status, such as promotions, awards, and classification changes, only when such changes are reported directly to the local disbursing authority by the person concerned. An individual's claims must be supported by a certificate from his unit.

8. OFFICER TRAINING

a. General. The agencies concerned with the development of training doctrines and regulations have been indicated in Chapter I, National Defense System, and in this chapter. The agencies listed here are concerned directly with the training process only.

b. High command level. The Chief of the General Staff is responsible for all training in the Voroshilov (General Staff) Academy and in the Frunze (Commanders and staffs of combined arms) Academy, and for the publication of the *Voyennaya Mysil* (Military Thought), a periodical combining the features of a training manual and a service journal.

The Main Administrations of the arms and services are responsible for training carried on in the academies of each arm and service, and, in most cases, for the journal of the arm or service. The journals are similar to that charged to the Chief of the General Staff in that they are, in effect, technical and training manuals as well as periodicals.

The Main Political Administration, also in the Commissariat of Defense, directly controls all training in the Military Political Academy and Schools. The Military Political Academy and Schools graduate political officers for assignment, at all echelons, to political administrations, sections, branches, etc. The Main Political Administration also publishes *Red Star*, which includes not only training material for political officers and indoctrination material for all ranks and grades, but also training material that is applicable to all arms, infantry in particular.

c. Field forces. At army group (front) level, officer training is carried on in the replacement regiment, which consists of company and field grade officers only, and is controlled by the Personnel Administration. Training of officers also is supervised by the administrations of arms and services, whether the training takes place in the replacement regiment of the army group, in separate replacement regiments, or in replacement battalions for the arms and services.

Officer training, at army level, takes place in the replacement battalion or company, made up of company grade officers only. The divisions of the arms and services also supervise appropriate aspects of the training at this level.

At all echelons, training courses in special fields, such as reconnaissance, may be instituted by the army group or army at the discretion of the Commander. Such training involves both officers and enlisted men.

d. Military districts. The Personnel Administration of each military district headquarters is responsible for over-all supervision of officer training in the district.

Extension courses for graduates of the Frunze Academy and officers having equivalent experience are instituted by the Chief of Staff of the military district. These courses are known as *Kuks*, "courses for the improvement of command personnel."

The Chiefs of arms and services conduct extension courses for graduates of the academies of the arms and services. Their Personnel Divisions control officer training in the schools of the arms and services. The schools graduate junior lieutenants.

Within the *Oblast* and *Rayon*, the Military Commissars are responsible for the training periods for reserve officers with units in the areas under command. In each case, this function is handled by the Third (officers) Department of the staff. The actual training is supervised, finally, by the Commander of the unit.

9. TRAINING OF ENLISTED MEN

a. High command level. Within the Commissariat of Defense, the Main Administration for the Formation and Equipment of Units is responsible for over-all supervision of the military districts and field forces in the training of enlisted men. Specialized training in all arms and services, other than infantry, is supervised by the various training administrations of the Main Administrations of arms and services. The Main Administrations of the arms and services prescribe training processes and materials and appoint the faculties of replacement regiments in the zone of the interior during time of war. In time of peace, they supply instructors for the noncommissioned officer schools established with formations and units of the arms in the military districts. These schools are not separated from the units in question, but consist of assigned personnel and reserve personnel in training periods. The recipient.

The Main Political Administration also is actively concerned with enlisted training.

b. Field forces. At army group (front) level, the Combat Training Administration supervises training in the enlisted replacement divisions or regiments. The Combat Training Divisions of the Administrations of arms and services supervise the training in the replacement regiments of the arms and services.

At army level, the same functions are performed by the Combat Training Division and by the Combat Training Branches of the arms and services in the respective replacement regiments and battalions.

Mobile corps (tank, cavalry, and mechanized) have replacement battalions attached to them. Training in these replacement battalions is supervised by a single officer.

Each rifle division supervises enlisted training in its attached replacement company through a single officer, as in the mobile corps.

c. Military districts. The Combat Training Administration of each military district supervises training in all formations and units in peacetime, and, in time of war, the training in all unit replacement regiments or brigades stationed in the district.

At *Oblast* level, the Second (conscription) Department of the Military Commissar's Staff, and the same agency at *Rayon* level, supervise training of reserves during active duty periods and all training in units or formations in their respective areas.

Within units and formations, training is conducted as in equivalent components of the field forces.

10. DECORATIONS AND AWARDS

a. General. Throughout the Red Army, personnel may be recommended for decorations and awards by Commanders (and their military councils where relevant) at all echelons, and by the chiefs of arms and services. Decorations and awards are confirmed and awarded only by agencies above specified levels of command. The lowest echelon of command entitled to present recommendations for each award is shown below. In each case, the agency cited may confer all decorations and awards listed for lower levels. The level of command authorized to confer particular awards also varies according to the rank of the recipient. Such variations are not indicated, but it may be assumed that authority is not granted to Commanders less than two echelons removed from the recipient.

Lowest agency or commander conferring awards	Order or medal	Lowest rank or position of recipient
Supreme Soviet..................	Marshal's Star...................	Marshal.
	Hero of the Soviet Union, Orders of Lenin and the Golden Star (combined).	Private.
	Order of Victory..................	General Armii.
	Order of Glory, Class I...........	Enlisted men and air force junior lieutenants only.
	Order of Suvorov, Class I.........	Commander of arm or service at army level.
	Order of Suvorov, Class II........	Chief of staff, brigade.
	Order of Kutuzov, Class I.........	Chief of staff, army.
	Order of Kutuzov, Class II........	Chief of staff, brigade.
	Order of Bogdan Khmelnitsky, Class I.	Commanders, brigade.
	Order of Bogdan Khmelnitsky, Class II.	Chief of staff, brigade.
	Medal for 20 years in the Red Army..	Private.
Commissariat of Defense or Chiefs of Artillery and Tank and Mechanized Troops.	Order of Suvorov, Class III.......	Commanders, company.
	Order of Kutuzov, Class III.......	Commanders, platoon.
Army Group Commander and Military Council.	Order of Lenin...................	Private.
	Order of Bogdan Khmelnitsky, Class III (?).	Enlisted men and officers up to Commanders, battalion.
Commander of an Arm (army group level).	Order of the Red Banner..........	Private.
Army Commander................	Order of Glory, Class II..........	Enlisted men and junior lieutenants only.
Commander of an Arm (army level).	Order of Alexander Nevsky........	Commanders, platoon to regiment only.
	Order of the Fatherland War, Classes I and II.	Private.
Commander of an Arm (army level) and Corps Commander.	Order of the Red Star............	Private.
Commander of an Arm (army level) and Division Commander.	Medal for Valor.................	Private.
	Medal for War Service............	Private.
Commander, Division or Brigade...	Medal for Distinguished Service (by specialty).	Enlisted men.

Figure 4. Agencies authorized to confer awards and decorations.

b. Other medals. Medals for defense of specific areas (Leningrad, Odessa, Sevastopol, Stalingrad, the Caucasus, Moscow, the Soviet Arctic), for victory over Germany and over Japan, for the capture of specific places (Budapest, Koenigsberg, Vienna, Berlin, Belgrade, Warsaw, Prague), and for wounds are awarded by Commanders to all personnel included within the definition given by the Supreme Soviet.

Orders and medals for Partisans and other civilians have been omitted from this tabulation.

11. ADMINISTRATION OF JUSTICE

The discipline and conduct of officers and enlisted men is a command responsibility at all echelons. The Commanders of all formations, units, and military districts, as well as the Commanders of arms, are assisted by their Military Councils, where these exist, in the supervision of all personnel, in the imposition of penalties for infringement of army regulations, and for misconduct in general.

In lesser matters, particularly concerning social behavior, Officers Courts of Honor, independent of higher authority, are formed by the personnel of all formations for the trial of offending officers, and for the determination of standards of conduct and the application of these standards to cases involving officers. Similar courts are formed in all units by enlisted men for their own self-discipline in similar matters. These are known as Comrades' Courts.

a. High command level. The application of the laws of the Soviet Union to personnel of the Red Army is defined by the Military Collegium of the Supreme Court of the U. S. S. R. In the Commissariat of Defense, the system of Tribunals for trial of offenses against the state is supervised by the Main Administration of Military Tribunals.

b. Field forces. Military Tribunals are found at army group, army, mobile corps, and division

40

headquarters. Also attached to army group and army headquarters are NKVD representatives, who command and guard the attached penal units. Penal units for officers and for enlisted men are found at army group level. Penal units for enlisted men are attached only at army levels.

c. Military districts. Military Tribunals are established at all military district headquarters and probably are attached to *Oblast* and *Rayon* Military Commissariats in the absence of formations which ordinarily would have them.

12. MORALE, INDOCTRINATION, AND POLITICAL SUPERVISION

a. High Command level. The morale of the Red Army and the indoctrination of all Red Army personnel are the responsibilities of the agencies of the system of political supervision, operated by the Main Political Administration of the Commissariat of Defense. Basic policies for the building of morale, for indoctrination of troops with concepts of the purpose of their military service, and for increasing the patriotism and loyalty of the Red Army to the regime, are formulated by the Council of Peoples' Commissars, or, in time of war, by the State Defense Committee. The affairs of the Communist Party also are administered in the ranks of the Red Army by the same system of supervision. The political officers and agencies are charged with responsibility for Party and youth organization (*Komsomol*) members, and for the expansion of Party and *Komsomol* membership.

Basic policies for Communist Party work and indoctrination are formulated by the Central Committee of the Communist Party, of which the Main Political Administration can be considered the military branch, as well as an agency within the Commissariat of Defense. All the affairs of the political administration are encompassed in the expression "political work."

b. Field forces. At all echelons where a Military Council exists, the chief of the political office of the headquarters is a council member. The Military Councils are, in part, agencies for political work.

Political work is the responsibility of the Political Administration at army group level, of the Political Division at army level, of the Political Branch at corps level, of the Political Section at division and regimental level, and of the Political Assistant to the Commander at battalion level.

c. Military districts. Political work is carried on in the zone of the interior by the Political Administration at Military District headquarters, and by formation and unit divisions, branches, sections, and assistants, as in the field army.

The personnel for all political agencies are trained in the Military-Political Academy and the Military-Political Schools operated by the Main Political Administration.

13. COUNTERINTELLIGENCE

a. High command level. All the agencies so far described are concerned, in a limited sense, with the apprehension of Red Army personnel whose reliability is questionable or who, while holding Party or *Komsomol* membership, fall below the Party standard of unimpaired loyalty to the state and regime. The greater part of the counterintelligence supervision of Red Army personnel is borne, however, by counterintelligence agencies at all echelons, under the over-all control of the Main Administration for Counterintelligence of the Commissariat of Defense.

The Commissariat of Internal Affairs (NKVD) and the Commissariat of State Security (NKGB) have no direct control over Red Army personnel. But, elements of both services assist in the screening of personnel liable to military service or active duty. They thus play an active part in assuring the security and loyalty of personnel on active duty in the Red Army.

b. Field forces. Counterintelligence Administrations are found at army group level, Divisions at army level, Sections at mobile corps and at division and brigade headquarters, and agents in all the lower components down to and including the company.

In the Field Military *Rayons*, set up in reoccupied areas by army group headquarters, the NKVD takes an active part in the screening of unreliable elements from among persons liable for active duty and conscripted or called up by the Conscription Board of the *Rayon*. The presence of NKVD representatives on all such boards is mandatory.

c. Military districts. Each military district headquarters includes an Administration for Counterintelligence. All formations and units stationed in the zone of the interior are provided with counterintelligence offices appropriate to their size, as in the field forces.

For counterintelligence purposes, representatives of the local Party and NKVD bodies are included on all Conscription Boards and on mobilization Manning Zone Boards. They assure exclusion of unreliable personnel and assignment of less reliable persons to the proper class of the reserve after completion of active duty.

Section II. CLASSIFICATION

1. GENERAL

In handling the large numbers of Red Army personnel, the administrative structure is forced to rely heavily on statistical control methods, generally without individual records for enlisted men and without a highly ramified classification system. A large measure of responsibility necessarily rests with subordinate offices and officers. Personnel administration is controlled by means of sweeping directives, which include broad classification regulations. The importance of individual papers carried by personnel in civilian life, on active duty, and on reserve status is apparent. The lack of centralized personnel records and administration is evident.

Red Army personnel are first classified according to service status and physical fitness. These classifications provide basic data on the availability of personnel for active duty in varying degrees of national emergency. All army personnel also are classified according to arm or service, rank or grade, and military occupational specialty.

2. DUTY STATUS

The three categories of duty status in the Red Army include active duty (including detached service), leave or furlough, and reserve status.

Those on active duty either are assigned to elements of the Red Army, or are placed on detached service, i. e., released from assignment to units of the Red Army and attached for work of a military character in civil agencies and enterprises. Personnel liable for active duty, but not on active duty or on leave or furlough, are members of the Red Army in one of two reserve categories. Reserve Category I includes men who have completed the required period of active service; Reserve Category II includes all newly conscripted persons surplus to the current needs of the armed forces and those granted exemption from active duty because of family circumstances. Persons on limited service in war-

time and enlisted women between the ages of 19 and 50, when not on active duty or detached service, also fall into Category II.

All enlisted reserves in Categories I and II are divided into classes, within maximum age limits as follows:

> First Class—up to 35 years of age.
> Second Class—35 to 45 years of age.
> Third Class—45 to 50 years of age.

Officers of the Red Army and of the NKVD and other semi-military organizations normally remain on active service or in the reserve up to the age limits listed in Figure 5.

Grade	Age limits			
	Active service	Reserves 1st class	Reserves 2d class	Reserves 3d class
Junior lieutenants, lieutenants........	30	40	50	55
Senior lieutenants....	35	45	55	60
Captains...........	40	50	55	60
Lieutenant colonels, colonels..........	45	50	55	60
Brigade commanders..	55	60	..	65
Division commanders and others of equal or higher rank.....	60	60	..	65

Figure 5. Age limits for Red Army officers in service.

3. FITNESS CLASSIFICATIONS

The Universal Military Service Law of 1939 distinguishes between personnel fit for combat service in wartime, personnel declared fit for limited service in wartime, and personnel declared unfit for active military service and excluded from military rosters. These distinctions are based upon medical examinations at the time of call-up for service or conscription.

4. CLASSIFICATION BY ARM OR SERVICE

The personnel of the Red Army are classified on the basis of the arm or service with which they serve. The combat arms of the Red Army are infantry, cavalry, air forces, artillery, armored and mechanized forces, engineers, signal communications, and chemical warfare. The services of the Red Army include transportation, motor transport, road construction and maintenance, intendance, rations and fodder, fuels and lubricants, medical, finance, graves registration, captured weapons, field post office, State Bank, Military Tribunal, topographic, and hydro-meteorological services. Special services include technical engineering, technical air force, artillery engineering, technical armored, veterinary, and administrative services.

5. CLASSIFICATIONS BY RANK AND GRADE

The following table gives the ranks of the Red Army personnel in transliteration of the Russian terminology, standard abbreviations, translation, and equivalent U. S. army ranks.

Transliteration	Standard Abbreviation	Translation	U. S. Equivalent
Generalissimus	Generalissimo	Generalissimo	Commander in Chief.
Marshal Sovetskovo Soyuza.	Marshal SU	Marshal of the Soviet Union.	General of the Army.
Glavnyi Marshal	Chief Marshal (of an arm)	Chief Marshal (of an arm)	(No comparable rank).
Marshal	Marshal (of an arm)	Marshal (of an arm)	(No comparable rank).
General Armii	Genarmy	Army general	General.
General Polkovnik	Genpolk	Colonel general	Lieutenant general.
General Leitenant	Genleit	Lieutenant general	Major general.
General Maior	Genmaior	Major general	Brigadier general.
Polkovnik	Col	Colonel	Colonel.
Podpolkovnik	Lt Col	Lieutenant colonel	Lieutenant colonel.
Maior	Maj	Major	Major.
Kapitan	Capt	Captain	Captain.
Starshii Leitenant	Sr Lt	Senior lieutenant	(No comparable rank)
Leitenant	Lt	Lieutenant	First lieutenant.
Mladshii Leitenant	Jr Lt	Junior lieutenant	Second lieutenant.
Kursant	Kursant	"Student"	Officer cadet.
Starshina	M Sgt	Master sergeant	Master or first sergeant.
Starshii Serzhant	Sr Sgt	Senior sergeant	Staff sergeant.
Serzhant	Sgt	Sergeant	Sergeant.
Mladshii Serzhant	Jr Sgt	Junior sergeant	Corporal.
Yefreitor	Cpl	Corporal	Private first class.
Krasnoarmeets	Pvt	Red Army man	Private.

Figure 6. Ranks of Red Army personnel.

6. CLASSIFICATION NUMBERS

Classification numbers for Red Army personnel are more inclusive than the simple military occupational specialty numbers used in the U. S. Army. Soviet classification numbers include a letter designation for the broad category of duty for which qualified, a military occupational specialty number, and a number indicating the highest echelon of command for which qualified. Roman numerals are used to indicate the highest echelons of command for which an officer is qualified. Arabic numerals are used for noncommissioned officers.

Letters used to designate broad categories of:
Duty officers:

К Command personnel
П Political personnel
Т Technical personnel
А Administrative personnel
М Medical personnel
В Veterinary personnel
Ю Judicial personnel
КА Command personnel (air force)
ТА Technical personnel (air force)

Noncommissioned officers:

МК Command personnel
МТ Technical personnel
ММ Medical personnel
МВ Veterinary personnel

Numbers used within broad categories to designate military occupational specialties:

Category	MOS Number
К	Line arms: 1, 2, 2a, 4, 5, 9, 9a, 10, 11
	Technical service: 17, 18
	Supporting arms: 19, 27, 28, 34, 43, 45, 47, 58
	Technical: 2d Echelon: 66
П	1, 3, 6
Т	1, 4, 11, 21, 22, 23
А	1, 4, 5, 6, 25, 55
М	1, 50, 53
В	1, 2, 6, 8
Ю	Unknown
КА	Unknown
ТА	Unknown
МК	Line arms: 1, 2, 3, 5, 5a, 6, 7, 10, 21, 30
	Technical service: 34, 44, 45, 48, 50, 88, 91
МТ	14, 43, 45, 48, 68, 83, 109, 119

Category	MOS number
MA	15, 123, 124, 126, 128
MM	121
MB	120

There is only one category for privates and privates first class. It has no letter designation.

Line arms: 1, 2, 3, 4, 5, 5a, 6, 7, 10, 11, 67
Technical specialties: 17, 20, 21, 23, 26, 27, 29, 35, 40, 41, 80, 88, 91, 92, 93, 94, 95, 96
Signal: 44, 45, 46, 47, 48, 49, 50, 52, 58, 62, 68
Air: 73, 74, 75, 79
Ordnance specialties: 109, 113
Craft: 114, 115, 116, 118, 119, 123, 124, 125, 126, 127, 128, 131, 132
Medical services: 120, 121
Basic: 133, 133a, 134, 134a

Similar functions are defined by the same Military Occupational Specialty number in different categories. Thus, the numeral "4" is used for officers and NCOs of combat and rear services staffs for Command, Technical, Administrative personnel, and for privates and first class privates assigned to combat and rear services staffs. The numeral "10" designates personnel for fire control of direct-fire weapons and reconnaissance; "11", personnel for horse-drawn artillery.

MOS number "133" designates a physically-fit recruit, "133a" a physically-fit enlisted man with preliminary training, "134" a physically-fit trained enlisted man, and "134a" serviceman assigned to limited service.

Mobilization plans provide for the substitution of one specific MOS number for another in case of necessity; e. g., "89" may be substituted for "88", "4" for "2", and "133" (a basic recruit) for "128" (driver or clerk).

Numbers used to indicate highest echelon of command for which qualified:

Officers:

I	Platoon
III	Company
IV	Battalion
V	Regiment
VI	Brigade or division
VII	Corps
VIII	Army
IX	Army group (front)

Noncommissioned officers:

1	Squad
2	Platoon
3	Company
4	Battalion
5	Regiment
6	Brigade or division
7	Corps
8	Army
9	Army group (front)

Thus, an officer with a classification number K-4-VI would be qualified to perform command duties, further amplified by the military occupational specialty number "4," at any echelon of command up to a rifle division or a tank brigade.

Line officers are considered senior to noncombatant officers. Commanders of combined arms, officers similarly qualified, and cavalry officers are considered senior to those of other arms and services.

The word "Guards" is added to the title of rank of all personnel in units which have been designated officially as "Guards" units in recognition of especially hazardous initial assignment or of superior combat performance.

Section III. PERSONNEL RECORDS

1. GENERAL

Documents carried by members of the Red Army are of considerable importance not only as protection from suspicion and arrest but frequently as the only complete and readily available personnel record. They are essential to the processes of personnel administration, including conscription, mobilization, separation, assignment, promotion, and frequently pay, allowances, and travel.

The basic personal documents of Red Army men are the Civilian Passport, Political Cards (Communist Party, Party Applicant, *Komsomol*), Military Pass, Mobilization Instructions, Red Army Pass, Identification cards, and Deferment and Discharge Certificates.

2. ENLISTED RESERVES

At the time of registration (prior to conscription), when transferred to reserve status from active service, or directly after conscription, all personnel are issued Military Passes.

The Military Pass contains the following:

Photograph	Party status
Name	*Komsomol* status
Father's name	Nationality
Issuing agency	Native tongue
Date of issue	Other languages
Year of birth	Social group
Class of reserve	Education
Registration group	Place of birth
Military specialty	Brief of military service
Military assignment	Training periods completed
Rank or grade	Date of military oath
Dates of issue and with-drawal of Mobilization Instructions	Registrations (if subject moves)
	Record of medical examination
Blood group	
Civilian specialty	

The Military Pass also includes general instructions regarding the Military Service Law, special notes and information as necessary, and space for attachment of Mobilization Instructions, when these are surrendered by personnel mobilized and reporting for duty.

Enlisted reserves must also carry Party and *Komsomol* Membership or Candidate Cards (if appropriate), Civilian Passports (carried by all citizens except soldiers on active duty), and Mobilization Instructions.

3. OFFICER RESERVES

Upon assignment or transfer to the reserve, all officers are issued or re-issued their Military Passes. The reserve officer's Military Pass differs from that of the reserve enlisted men in that it is for Red Army officers only and contains more complete information.

In addition to the information contained in the enlisted reserve Military Pass, the officer's pass contains the following:

Command group (junior, intermediate, senior, higher)
Arm or service
Date of termination of service liability
Service record in White Armies
Exemption from reserve
Training periods
Record of cancellation of registration
Awards and decorations

The officer's Military Pass contains no reference to native tongue or other languages, presumably because all officers must know Russian prior to selection for officer candidate schools. Knowledge of other languages is noted carefully by the Red Army, but does not appear on the officer's Military Pass.

Reserve officers also carry Mobilization Instructions, which give either the full title of the unit to which they are to report or the name of the *Rayon* which will assign them and the place and time (M plus 4, 1700 hours) of reporting. If the Mobilization Instruction includes only the *Rayon* designation, a supplementary Mobilization Instruction is issued at time of call-up to complete the information. Mobilization Instructions also are prepared by the *Rayon* Military Commissariats for distribution to reserve officers only in case of secret mobilization.

Reserve officers also carry, as do reserve enlisted men, Political Cards and Civilian Passports.

4. ENLISTED MEN ON ACTIVE DUTY

When assigned to active duty, reserve enlisted men or conscripts surrender their military passes and civilian passports. They receive in their stead Red Army Passes. These and their Political Cards are carried at all times by active service personnel.

The Red Army Pass contains the following:

Photograph	Education
Name	Nationality
Father's name	Year of birth
Rank	Year of conscription
Assignment	Military Commissariat by which conscripted
Unit	
Serial number	Civilian specialty
Signature	Place of birth
Company commander	Residence
Date of issue	Name of wife
Blood group	Height
Service record	Clothing sizes
Battles, etc.	Awards, etc.
Clothing issued	Weapons and equipment issued
Military specialty	

The Red Army Pass thus is quite similar to the Military Pass with the absence of political information and of mobilization records. Changes in assignment are recorded on Red Army Passes, but the military occupational specialty numbers are not changed, even when personnel are transferred from one arm to another.

5. OFFICERS ON ACTIVE DUTY

Upon surrender of their Military Passes and Civilian Passports, reserve officers called into active service are issued Identification Books, somewhat similar to the Red Army Passes of enlisted men. All officers on active duty carry Identification Books. The officer's Identification Book contains the following:

Photograph	Date of birth
Signature of unit commander	Place of birth
	Marital status
Serial number of book	Dependents
Name	Permission to carry arms
Father's name	Signature
Unit	Regulations concerning use of book
Rank and promotions	
Assignment	Awards and decorations

Identification Books specifically replace civilian passports. They are collected from officers transferring to the reserve or retiring from the Red Army.

Officers also carry Pay Books when on active duty. These are issued by the unit to which an officer first is assigned. They contain records of pay, allowances and allotments due, deductions for allotments, loans, and fines. The Pay Book also contains control tickets, detached as receipts at each time of payment.

Each officer also carries a Clothing Book during his tour of duty. Clothing Books are issued by the supply officer of the unit of initial assignment. They contain a detailed list of items issued, dates of issue, and records of the return, loss, or destruction of issued items. A number of pages of detachable receipts are included for specific items of equipment.

Officers having savings accounts also carry Savings Account Books.

6. ACTIVE DUTY PERSONNEL WOUNDED OR TRAVELING

In addition to papers normally required, personnel traveling or wounded are issued additional papers.

First Aid Cards are issued to wounded officers and enlisted men. They specify by detachable colored edges the type of immediate treatment required. The cards include name, rank, diagnosis, date and hour of injury, date and hour of tourniquet application, prescribed method of evacuation, record of first aid administered at designated company, battalion, regimental, and division medical aid points, record of tetanus and anti-gangrene treatments, and manner of evacuation from the battlefields (walking, sitting, lying). Subsequent history of the patient also is recorded including return to his unit, assignment to convalescent unit, leave or furlough, release from the Red Army, or death, with cause of death and date of interment.

Upon recovery from wounds, personnel are issued Wound Certificates stating the nature of injury. Upon recovery from wounds or illness and release from hospital, convalescents are issued either Hospitalization Certificates, which state the nature of the wounds or illness and the unit to which to report, or Certificates of Release from Military Service, when appropriate.

When traveling, Red Army personnel carry travel orders and free military railroad tickets issued to them on the basis of their unit commander's requisition.

7. RATION CERTIFICATES

Ration Certificates are issued for periods of travel. They contain the rank and name of bearer, name of the unit to which he is transferred, the number and date of the travel order, designation of unit issuing the travel rations, ration category, dates until which the bearer is to be issued rations, record of ration and travel money, if any, cash allowance in lieu of subsistence, if any, date when taken off of the issuing unit's ration list, date of expiration of certificate, and the signature and seal of unit's Assistant Commander for Supply.

8. PAY CERTIFICATES

Pay Certificates carried by traveling personnel contain the designation of the issuing agency or unit, rank and name of bearer, pay category, year of service, base pay, record of last payment, record of payments, and name of the loan to which subscription has been made, date of last payment, amount paid to date, balance due and bonds issued, and the signature and seal of the unit's Chief of Finance.

9. DEFERRED RESERVE PERSONNEL

Personnel of the reserves engaged in important civil work are entitled by law or decree, particularly in time of war, to deferment from mobilization. Such officers and enlisted men are issued Mobilization Deferment Certificates by special selection commissions. Information is supplied and entered on the certificates by the enterprises employing deferred personnel, and the certificate requires the signature of the *Rayon* Military Commissar. Two types of Mobilization Deferment Certificate are used. One is used for special civil deferments. The other is used for deferment of personnel of organizations militarized in time of war, such as the Commissariat of

Transportation or the Commissariat of Signal Communications.

The special certificate is composed of three detachable sections, a stub retained by the enterprise, a notification retained by the *Rayon* Commissariat and a certificate for use with the Military Pass. This certificate is carried by deferred personnel and contains only the dates of the deferment period and administrative information. It is valid only in conjunction with a Military Pass and is surrendered upon expiration.

For personnel deferred for service in militarized organizations, the Mobilization Deferment Certificate is issued to replace the Military Pass, which is surrendered to the *Rayon* Commissariat. Railroad Mobilization Deferment Certificates are issued to all railroad personnel in time of war. The mobilization agencies of the railroad administrations prepare complete military registration lists of railroad personnel, separate from those of the *Rayon* Military Commissariat, and issue the necessary Mobilization Deferment Certificates through their own registration points.

Railroad personnel carry Identification Cards at all times. Their deferment from active military service in the Red Army is guaranteed only while they carry both the Identification Card and Certificate. Reserve personnel entering service with the railroad surrender their Military Passes, but again must carry them if relieved of railroad service.

10. PHYSICALLY DISABLED

Persons liable to military service by virtue of age but exempted from active service or conscription because of physical disability and Red Army men discharged for physical disability before completion of required tours of service are issued Certificates of Release from Military Service. They contain the name of the issuing *Rayon* Military Commissariat, subject's name, photograph, place of birth, date and record of physical examination, reference to the decree or order of the Commissariat of Defense authorizing release, signature and seal of the *Rayon* Military Commissar, and date of issue.

11. *RAYON* PERSONNEL RECORDS

The personnel records known to be kept by the *Rayon* are more detailed than those of any other agency, and are presented as an illustration of the administrative methods of Red Army personnel agencies.

The typical *Rayon* may be considered as an area including between 30,000 and 200,000 population, the average population being 55,000. Of this population, a record of one in every four inhabitants is kept by the *Rayon* Military Commissariat. There is a record of every male citizen over 17 years of age and of all women registered for military service on the basis of specialized skills.

The records kept by the *Rayon* Military Commissariat are as follows:

> File of all persons registered for conscription.
> File of Military Passes of all enlisted men in active service.
> File of all Military Passes of personnel of the reserve deferred for active service with semi-militarized organizations.
> File of Red Army Passes of enlisted men released or retired from military service.
> File of Identification Books of officers released or retired from military service.
> File of Red Army Passes of enlisted men released to the reserve.
> File of Identification Books of officers of the reserve.
> Card file of officers of the reserve, giving their assignment for mobilization or their deferment record.
> Card file of enlisted men of the reserve, giving their assignments for mobilization or their deferment record.
> Card file, by unit, of all reserve personnel having mobilization assignments to units.
> Lists, by unit, of mobilization assignments of officers of the reserve.
> Alphabetical lists filed in chronological order of officers who have reported to units at time of mobilization.
> Lists, filed in chronological order, of enlisted men who have reported to units at time of mobilization.
> Current mobilization plan.
> File of prepared Mobilization Instructions for some of those personnel of the reserve whose Mobilization Instructions do not specify unit assignments.
> Dead file of superseded or fulfilled Mobilization Instructions.

File, by unit, of copies of Mobilization Instructions issued assigned reserve personnel.

File, by unit, of Mobilization Instructions for secret mobilization only.

Section IV. ASSIGNMENT, PROMOTION, AND SEPARATION

1. ASSIGNMENT

Vacancies are filled from qualification lists. Normally, appointment to a higher assignment follows promotion. In exceptional cases, however, officers are appointed to a higher assignment prior to promotion, or retain their old assignment after promotion until a vacancy exists.

Assignment of enlisted personnel to the various arms and services is based initially on their abilities and later on their military occupational specialties.

2. PROMOTION

a. Officers. Eligibility for promotion is closely defined for officers only. Promotion is based on time in grade and favorable efficiency.

Time in grade required for promotion of command officers is believed to be as follows:

Grade	Period of Service
Junior lieutenant	2 years
Lieutenant	2 years
Senior lieutenant	3 years
Captain	3 years
Major	4 years
Lieutenant colonel	4 years

For colonels and above, there are no specific provisions, such promotions being made by high command agencies on a basis of merit and demand. Graduation from the Frunze Academy generally coincides with promotion to colonel. In the case of lower grade officers, graduation from academies of the arms and services guarantees promotion to field grade and graduation from the Voroshilov (General Staff) Academy, promotion to general grades. These are not, however, the only means of promotion to such grades.

Efforts were made during World War II, but with little success, to provide all officers with some degree of appropriate training before or after promotion. Correspondence courses and brief courses within units were the chief means, other than attendance at an academy.

Promotions in units and formations are based on qualifications and seniority lists which include, in order of seniority, the names of all officers of each grade who have completed the required time in grade. The majority of promotions are made, among personnel assigned to regiments, by regimental authority. If the needs of a regiment cannot be filled by its own qualified personnel, selection is made from the divisional lists, and if these are inadequate, from those of the corps, etc.

The rapid expansion and heavy losses of World War II forced a reduction in the time in grade requirements. Promotions were made largely on the basis of proved ability, personal bravery, and leadership. Such reductions were applied less frequently in the zone of the interior and among senior staff officers than among lower grades in the field.

Political reliability always has played an important part in promotion of officers. Before October 1942, the Political Commissars had at least as much influence in promotion of officers as did Commanders. With the abolition of the system of political commissars, their successors, the officers of the political apparatus, as members of Military Councils continued to exert influence second only to that of the Commander. At no level of command are all officers members of the Communist Party, but it is clear that Party membership is not an insignificant factor in promotion. Higher troop commanders and recipients of high decorations and awards generally are subjected to persuasive efforts to bring them into the Party. The percentage of Party members among junior officers has increased steadily since the prewar years. Approximately 75 percent of company grade officers were Party members in 1943.

Demotion of officers is effected only by special orders of the Commissar of Defense in cases of an unusual character. Assignment to penal battalions is the more common practice, and provides penal units with officers of appropriate ranks at the same time. Demotions of division Commanders and above can be effected only by decree of the Council of Peoples' Commissars or by the State Defense Committee in time of war.

b. Enlisted men. Promotion of enlisted men is effected by Commanders of units and formations in the field on the basis of merit, vacancies, and tables of organization and by the noncommissioned officers schools of units and formations which graduate privates into noncommissioned ranks. There are no fixed length of service requirements.

An effort was made during World War II to make promotion to noncommissioned officer rank dependent upon the completion of a short course conducted by replacement units of army groups and armies. But this was not possible always, and in the field army, men often were promoted without taking any course. The most suitable recruits after basic training were transferred to noncommissioned officer training regiments and battalions in the zone of the interior, where most of them served from 8 to 12 months to gain their rating. In the case of less suitable recruits, promotion was made dependent on performance in battle.

3. SEPARATION

Separation from the Red Army follows upon expiration of the period of liability to military service or physical disability. Separation of individual command personnel may be ordered to reduce the strength of the armed forces, because of reorganization, and because of unsatisfactory efficiency ratings. Separation may be requested by an individual. Separation often follows a court sentence or arrest by a judicial or investigation agency. Individuals sentenced to confinement generally are dropped entirely from Red Army rosters.

Section V. MOBILIZATION SYSTEM

1. GENERAL

Military districts administer the universal service law in time of peace, the mobilization and replacement plans in time of war, and the demobilization process at the end of hostilities. The Plan of Development and the Operative Plan comprise the mobilization plans.

The same machinery is used to effect mobilization, the replacement system, and demobilization. This machinery consists of peacetime staffs of the military, civil, and political agencies which prepare their parts of the mobilization plans, of reception centers which are activated during mobilization, and of peacetime army units. This machinery is modified to meet the requirements of three phases; activation of mobilization plan and of reception centers, activation of replacement training centers and replacement units at peacetime installations, and changing the

reception centers into separation centers after the end of hostilities. The Plan of Development includes the first two phases. The Operative Plan is put into effect when mobilization is accomplished in the units.

2. SCOPE OF MOBILIZATION PLANS

In the U. S. S. R. mobilization may be general or partial, open or secret. It embraces all civil and military resources of the country. Actual mobilization of personnel, horses, horse-drawn vehicles, and motor vehicles is accompanied by a simultaneous reorganization of civilian effort and economy. Extreme care in the preparation of mobilization lists of personnel and equipment is demanded from all responsible agencies. These lists are inspected periodically, reviewed, and brought up to date. Rigid security control is exercised over the documents and personnel connected with mobilization plans and lists.

In order to provide for personnel, animal, and equipment shortages which may occur through illness or wear, the following overstrengths above the prescribed wartime tables of organization of units are authorized: officers, 5 percent for the *Oblast* and 10 percent for troop units; technical officers, 3 percent for the *Oblast*; enlisted men, 5 percent for the *Oblast*; horses, 25 percent, for the *Oblast* and up to 35 percent for troop units; horse-drawn and mechanical transport, 40 to 50 percent for the *Oblast*.

Mobilization plans provide for total mobilization of the first echelon in M plus 30 days, and mobilization of the first priority units of the Armed Forces in M plus 5 days. Continuous maintenance of military, civil, and political mobilization staffs and installations and of a standing army in the interior of the U. S. S. R. is essential to these plans. The standing army must be sufficiently large to bring rapidly to war strength a sizeable striking force by M plus 5 days, to expand the remaining units by M plus 30 days, and to leave a sufficient nucleus in training centers to administer and train the second and following echelons of mobilization.

Mobilization plans are prepared in detail. The mobilization lists for each unit, and consolidated lists at all levels of command, include the number of officers and enlisted men for each military occupational specialty. Each category is further broken down into the number available in the particular military districts affected by the mobilization, the number assigned from other military districts, and the authorized overstrength for each. Officers are assigned individually and enlisted men are assigned numerically to specific units or replacement pools. The mobilization lists for horses (cavalry, artillery, and draft) and motor transport (artillery tractors, supply trucks, tractors, and other motor and horse-drawn vehicles) include assignments to specific collection points. Each mobilization plan is accompanied by a calendar schedule, and each plan constantly is kept up to date.

The mobilization plans, whether general or partial, open or secret, provide for wartime expansion of the following types of units:

> Field headquarters.
> Mobilization machinery in the interior.
> GHQ reserve artillery, engineer, chemical warfare, and veterinary units.
> Base and field depots, air bases, and postal service units.
> Fighter or interceptor defense forces, civilian antiaircraft, anti-chemical warfare, and fire fighting units.
> Reserve depots and units.

3. PLAN FOR EXPANSION AND ACTIVATION

Provisions for mobilization of the Red Army in time of national emergency are designed to transform every military unit, formation, administrative organ, and institution into war strength organizations within established time limits.

An over-all mobilization plan is prepared and maintained by the staff of each military district. It includes plans for the organizational development, the preparation for combat, and the formation of new units for each peacetime unit in the Red Army. Appropriate excerpts of this plan are sent to the unit Commanders concerned, through the *Oblast* or *Rayon* Military Commissar.

Units may be expanded from peacetime strength to full mobilization strength by one of four methods. A peacetime military unit or formation may retain its basic organization, lose part of its peacetime complement as cadre to other units, and expand to wartime strength. A peacetime unit or formation may expand into a next higher unit or formation. A unit may be formed at wartime strength by cadres detached from peacetime units and reservists. A peacetime military unit or formation may, on mobilization, be divided into several independent units, which are then brought up to wartime strength. (Service units also are formed by civilian Peoples' Commissariats.)

The immediate responsibility for the development and preparedness of units to be activated on mobilization rests with the Commander of the unit or formation under whose supervision the new unit is manned.

a. First priority units. First priority units are brought up to war strength by M plus 5 days. The mobilization plan for such units provides for the dispatch of a definite number of enlisted men and officers from the unit to a cadre pool. The vacancies resulting from this dispatch of cadres and from the difference between peacetime and wartime tables of organization are filled largely with men on extended leave or furlough and with some officers and enlisted men who have been individually assigned according to the Plan of Development. Armament, equipment, horses, and motor vehicles generally are assigned to these units from depots. All key personnel report for duty on M minus 2 days.

Sub-units and formations constitute the first wave of reinforcements to units stationed in critical border areas and form the strategic forces of antiaircraft artillery and units for the manning of fortified areas.

b. Second priority units. The second priority units are brought to wartime strength by M plus 30 days. These and the first priority units comprise the first echelon of mobilization. They are formed by expanding existing peacetime units to the next higher unit or formation. A rifle regiment, for example, is expanded into a rifle division, and a tank brigade is expanded into a tank corps.

The mobilization plan for these units provides for the transfer of officers and enlisted men individually within the unit to specific new assignments. The reserve officers and enlisted men who complete the wartime table of organization of the expanded unit are secured from two sources. Some reserve officers and enlisted men are assigned individually in advance to specific duties. Others are drawn from the mobilization reception center for unassigned reserve officers and enlisted men of the *Rayon*. Reserve personnel who are called up for second priority units and formations are generally those of the 1st Class and of Category I of the Reserve.

Armament, equipment, horses, and transport vehicles for these units are drawn from the *Rayon* collection center. The responsibility for proper and timely reorganization of second priority units rests with the commander of the parent unit or formation.

c. Third priority units. Third priority units are mobilized between M plus 30 and M plus 120 days. They constitute the second echelon of mobilization, exhaust the supply of personnel of less than 35 years of age, and draw also on the 2d and 3d Classes and both Categories of the Reserve. The key personnel of the cadre for these units are drawn from the cadres provided by first priority units and from other existing peacetime units which are divided on mobilization. As in the mobilization plans for other units, the key personnel are assigned individually to specific duties. The remainder of the officers and enlisted men are drawn from the reception centers. Equipment and transport are drawn from collection centers or directly from factories. Horses are drawn from collection centers.

Third priority units may be mobilized at home, but generally are sent as march regiments or battalions to the zone of operations, where some may be organized into field units and others used to supply replacement pools.

The semi-military units that are mobilized concurrently by the civilian commissariats include militarized technical personnel, such as railroad, signal communications, road construction, road maintenance engineer, medical, and veterinary personnel. Such units are primarily employed in the zone of the interior.

4. FLOW OF PERSONNEL ON MOBILIZATION

The Presidium of the Supreme Soviet of the U. S. S. R. orders mobilization in time of emergency. The call for mobilization is issued by the Peoples' Commissar of Defense on the basis of decrees of the Council of Peoples' Commissars. Upon declaration of mobilization, all who are on active duty in the Army or Navy must remain on duty. Individuals subject to military service and those liable to active duty and enrolled in military units must appear at the assigned stations at the time specified in the mobilization order (fig. 7).

Upon receipt of mobilization orders, officers on active duty report to first, second, or third priority units as prescribed in their orders. Reserve officers either are assigned to a specific or deferred unit, or to a specific *Rayon*. Reserve officers who are assigned to a first or second priority unit report according to their assignment. In first priority units, they may be held in an overstrength pool, from which they may be sent to a reception center for assignment, or they may remain with the unit. Reserve officers who are assigned to a specific *Rayon* report to the reception center of that *Rayon*. From there, they are sent to the second or third priority units or to the *Rayon* overstrength pool.

Reserve officers who are not assigned to specific *Rayons* report to the Conscription Board and are assigned to a reception center. At the reception center, they are processed in the same manner as officers assigned to the *Rayon* pool but not to units.

Enlisted men on active duty either are kept in their units or are sent as cadre to second or third priority units. The assigned reserve enlisted men are assigned either to a specific first or second priority unit or to a specific *Rayon* reception center. If assigned to a first priority unit, they may be used to bring it to wartime strength or may be kept in the unit overstrength pool. The enlisted reserve personnel who are assigned to a reception center are sent to the second or third priority units or kept in the *Rayon* overstrength pool. Enlisted men without assignment to a specific *Rayon* report to the local conscription board and are sent to a reception center, where they are processed in the same manner as the reserve personnel who are assigned only to the *Rayon* in general.

5. FLOW OF HORSES AND TRANSPORT ON MOBILIZATION

A single plan for the supplying of each unit with horses and carts is worked out by the Assistant Chief of Staff, together with the senior veterinary of the unit. The plan indicates mobilization requirements for horses, carts, harnesses, and motor transport. It also provides for reception at time of mobilization, and for the periodic examination and shoeing of horses, and for the repair of carts and harnesses. Officers are detached from the unit to assist the *Rayon* Military Commissariat in the

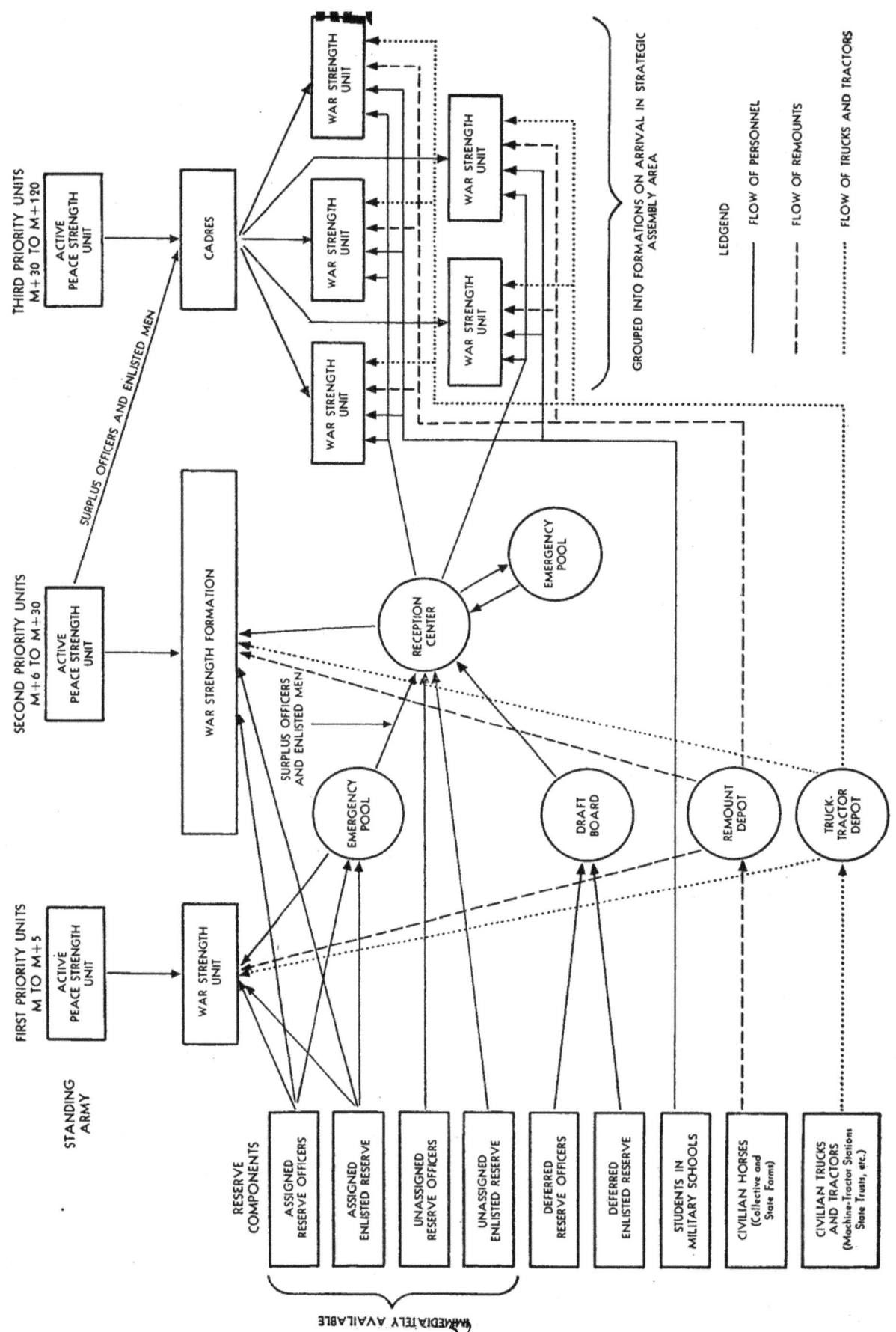

Figure 7. Flow of personnel, remounts, and equipment on mobilization.

52

selection of horses and carts and to aid in the instruction of the heads of farms and enterprises in the proper care of animals and equipment. The condition and quantity of these items are checked not less than twice a year.

The unit Manning Zone for horses and transport coincides with that for personnel. In peacetime, the *Rayon* Military Commissariats distribute requisitions to the village Soviets and local farms and enterprises. On mobilization, the *Rayon* Military Commissariats establish collection centers for horses and transport. A collection center for horses and horse-drawn transport may handle from 800 to 1,000 horses and from 600 to 800 vehicles daily.

A similar plan exists for the collection of motor transport. Collection centers for trucks, tractors, and other motor vehicles are located near industrial centers or at *Rayon* maintenance shops of collective farms. Such a collection center may handle 60 trucks, 40 tractors, and 120 motorcycles, or 200 bicycles and 150 barrels of fuel daily.

6. RECEPTION CENTERS

Each reception center for personnel is designed to process from 1,200 to 1,500 men in a 10-hour working day. Processing of personnel includes six steps:

Reception of arriving groups, check of arrival, separation of those assigned to other centers, assignment to quarters, and political work.

Assignment to companies according to mobilization lists.

Check of mobilization lists of the companies with the number of assigned personnel, examination of Military Passports, and check of the number of persons in each military specialty with the authorized number for each company.

Medical examination, dispatch of sick to hospitals.

Examination and evaluation of personal property.

Bath, issue of uniforms and equipment, shipment of personal property home, collection of Party cards and valuables for safe keeping, and collection of Military Passports.

Section VI. REPLACEMENT SYSTEM

1. GENERAL

The agencies in charge of mobilization also are responsible for the operation of the replacement system. At the end of the mobilization phase, the agencies and installations which directed and administered it are modified so as to receive, train, and dispatch the necessary replacements to the field forces.

At high command level, this modification can be seen in the transfer of the functions of the Mobilization Division of the General Staff to the Main Administration for the Formation and Equipment of Units in the Commissariat of Defense. The reception centers of the military districts are deactivated, and replacement regiments and brigades are activated. In the field, replacement regiments, battalions, and companies are maintained for officers and enlisted men.

2. REPLACEMENT UNITS AND FORMATIONS

In time of war, the forces in the field are supplied with replacement personnel by home and field replacement regiments, brigades, battalions, and companies.

Each formation, on moving from the zone of the interior, leaves behind a replacement regiment. The replacement regiment is administered by the military district, and, in theory, supplies replacements to the formation. In practice, however, under stress of losses, any military district may be ordered to send troops to any sector of the front.

The home replacement regiments are responsible for issue of uniforms, medical examination, and training. The trained replacements are formed into march units (companies and battalions) and are sent to the front, or kept in a pool until needed.

In military districts, when conscription is conducted on a large scale, or in areas well suited for training (Turkestan, Caucasus, and Siberia, for example), several replacement regiments are formed into a replacement brigade. Such a brigade generally includes three rifle regiments, one artillery regiment, and one each mortar, antitank, engineer, and signal communications battalion.

Theoretically, training courses in the replacement regiments last for 3 months. In practice, however, the older recruits often are given only a few weeks of training, and the younger classes sent to Siberia or Turkestan for a more complete course.

At least one artillery, signal, and cavalry replacement unit exists in each military *Rayon*. Training for the more technical arms and services is more extensive than for the infantry. From 1943, a more highly educated class of recruits was assigned to these units. The replacement system for signal personnel follows the replacement theory more closely than the replacement systems for the other arms and services, in that each military *Rayon* furnishes signal replacements to its own particular section of the front.

Field replacement regiments are activated by each army group (front) and army. Their function is to receive replacements, to arm them, to give them further individual and unit training, and to dispatch them to subordinate units or formations. Each army group normally includes one or two rifle regiments, one tank regiment, one artillery regiment, and one or two officer replacement regiments. The army field replacement regiment has two to three rifle battalions, one artillery battery, one noncommissioned officer school, one signal school company, and an engineer school company.

The army rifle replacement regiment consists of three rifle battalions, two rifle school battalions, one machine gun battalion, one antitank battery, one submachine gun battalion, one engineer company, one sniper company, and one antitank rifle company. Each tank army also has a tank replacement regiment. A small surplus is carried in smaller tank units and formations.

The officer replacement regiments are organized into battalions so that each battalion contains officers of the same rank. In one officer replacement regiment, for example, the 1st Battalion contained majors and captains who already had served as battalion commanders. The Second Battalion contained captains and lieutenants who already had served as company commanders. The Third Battalion contained platoon commanders. Generally, these battalions contained only officers. They perform all unit duties, including kitchen police.

In the zone of the interior, and in all field units down to the rifle division, the convalescent units at hospitals also operate as replacement pools.

3. FLOW OF REPLACEMENTS

Requisitions for personnel replacements are initiated at the lowest level of command, and are consolidated and forwarded upward through statistical control sections at each level of command.

a. Officer replacements. General officers are held in the Peoples' Commissariat of Defense pool for general officers, from which they are assigned individually and report directly for duty. The flow of general officers is automatic and continuous.

Field and political officers are assigned first by agencies in the zone of the interior to an army group. At army group, they are held in the field officer replacement unit, from which they are individually assigned. Requests for field officers are consolidated and filled periodically.

The flow of company grade officers from the zone of the interior to field unit assignments differs for the various arms and services. Infantry and artillery officers are assigned by agencies in the zone of the interior and are assigned directly to a specific army. There, they are assigned to specific field duties or to army group or army officer replacement units. Armored force officers are assigned to an army group by agencies in the zone of the interior. The army group assigns them to a tank army, army, or to a GHQ tank or mechanized formation, such as a tank or mechanized corps. These officers then are assigned individually to duty. The cavalry, air force, signal, engineer, and service force officers also are assigned to an army group by the zone of the interior. The army group then assigns them directly to the field units.

The requisitions for company grade officers are consolidated by statistical control periodically. Thus, company officer replacements reach the various levels of command periodically.

b. Enlisted replacements. Enlisted personnel are assigned by agencies in the zone of the interior. They are assigned to army group enlisted replacement units or to army enlisted replacement units. Both the army group and army then assign the enlisted personnel by military occupational specialty numbers to formation and unit replacement units. Requisitions for enlisted personnel are periodically consolidated by military occupational specialties. The flow of enlisted replacements to the field units is, therefore, also periodic.

54

4. REPLACEMENT OF PERSONNEL IN FIELD UNITS

In the Red Army, replacement units with field formations and units are held to minimum size. For example, the replacement company of a rifle division consists of only 100 officers and enlisted men. Losses in field units are replaced by direct dispatch of reserves to the unit, or the unit is withdrawn from action and refitted in the army or army group rear area. The latter method is preferred. But, when the number of field units is insufficient, or when the sector held by a unit is relatively quiet, the replacements are sent direct.

During the defensive battle of Stalingrad, when all fresh units were held for the planned offensive, and on the relatively quiet Finnish front, rifle units often were held in the line even though many were 50 percent understrength. Unit commanders systematically reduced the service overhead and weapons crews throughout all the subordinate units. Every effort was directed toward retaining as many men as possible in the forward line and toward leaving all subordinate units at the same level of efficiency. In such cases, little attention is paid to classification and military occupational specialties.

5. REPLACEMENTS FROM REOCCUPIED AREAS

When the Red Army advances into regions overrun by the enemy, a new organization, the Field Military *Rayon* is organized to call up men liable for military service in the reoccupied areas. Orders are issued for the enlistment of army personnel through depot and replacement units. The Field Military *Rayon* is authorized to follow closely behind the advancing front line and to recruit all males of military age and to send them to replacement regiments. It does not recruit engineers, miners, railway men, or, in some districts, metal workers. In practice, men often are dispatched directly to the army group or army replacement regiments and committed immediately to the front line, without training. Or, men may be enlisted directly by Commanders of units. In 1943, the members of the 1926 class, who had been drafted in the reoccupied areas in this manner and sent to the front line, were withdrawn by order of the Peoples' Commissariat of Defense and sent for 6 months' training with replacement regiments.

Section VII. DEMOBILIZATION SYSTEM

1. GENERAL

The same agencies that are responsible for conscription, mobilization, and replacement of personnel are responsible for demobilization. The demobilization of officers and enlisted men is the reverse procedure of that for mobilization. Each demobilized member of the Red Army reports back to the *Rayon* Military Commissar, or his deputy, to which he reported on mobilization. There he is given a medical examination, his Red Army Book is inspected, and he is given a Military Passport. He is enrolled immediately in the proper reserve category and is placed once again on the mobilization lists of that *Rayon*.

2. DEMOBILIZATION PLAN (1945–46)

The complete demobilization plan of the U. S. S. R. is not known. The demobilization law, to date, provides for two waves of demobilization: release from the armed forces of the 13 oldest classes in service, and the subsequent release of the next 10 oldest classes.

The demobilization of the first wave has been carried out in two echelons. In the first echelon, the 13 oldest classes from the field units were demobilized. This was followed by the demobilization of the 13 oldest classes from the zone of the interior.

The details of the demobilization of the second wave are not so well known. But, it is believed that the same priority has been applied.

3. DEMOBILIZATION LAW

The demobilization of the Red Army is administered according to the provisions of the Law for Demobilization of the Oldest Age Groups of the Active Red Army, passed by the Supreme Soviet of the U. S. S. R. on 23 June 1945.

The law provides for:

Demobilization of the 13 oldest age groups to be completed in the second half of 1945.

Transportation of demobilized personnel to their place of residence and maintenance on the journey at government expense.

A complete set of clothing for each demobilized veteran.

Lump sum money bonuses for each year of service during World War II, as follows:

Enlisted personnel of all arms and services—a year's salary for each year of service in World War II.

Enlisted personnel of special units, who receive a higher rate of pay—one-half year's pay for each year of service.

Noncommissioned personnel of all arms and services—one-half year's pay, not to exceed 900 rubles and not less than 300 rubles, for each year of service.

Officers, who have served during World II, to receive for—

> 1 year's service—2 months' pay
> 2 years' service—3 months' pay
> 3 years' service—4 months' pay
> 4 years' service—5 months' pay.

Assumption of responsibility by the Council of Peoples' Commissars of each Union Republic and Autonomous Republic, the Executive Committee of each *Krai* and *Oblast* Soviet of Deputy Workers, and Directors of all enterprises, institutions and organizations in urban areas, for furnishing work for all demobilized veterans within a month of their return home. Experience and new specialties acquired through service in the Red Army are to be given due consideration. Under no circumstances are lower positions to be furnished than those held prior to army service. Living quarters and heating facilities are to be furnished.

Assumption of responsibility by the Executive Committe of each *Rayon* and rural Soviet of Deputy Workers and by all Boards of Directors of collective farms for rendering all possible assistance to demobilized veterans returning to the villages for securing work and living quarters.

Assumption of responsibility by the Council of Peoples' Commissars of each Union Republic and Autonomous Republic and by the Executive Committee of each *Krai* and *Oblast* Soviet of Deputy Workers, in areas previously occupied by the Germans, for the furnishing of lumber for the repair and construction of living quarters for all persons demobilized from the Red Army.

Grants to demobilized veterans by the All-Union Bank, which finances communal and individual construction programs in areas formerly occupied by the Germans, of loans for the construction and repair of dwellings. Loans to be in sums of from 5,000 to 10,000 rubles for periods of from 5 to 10 years.

On 4 August 1945, the Council of Peoples' Commissars adopted a decree exempting all demobilized soldiers and their immediate families from taxes for 1 year.

On 7 September 1945, the Presidium of the Supreme Soviet authorized demobilization of the 13 oldest age groups serving with the Red Army in the Far East under the provisions of the demobilization law.

On 23 September 1945, the Presidium of the Supreme Soviet passed a decree for a second demobilization of Red Army personnel. This decree was to effect privates and noncommissioned personnel of the next 10 senior classes, except those in the Far East.

The second demobilization decree provided for:

Demobilization of the following categories of Red Army privates and noncommissioned officers:

> Graduates from middle agricultural and technical schools who possess special qualifications.
>
> Teachers who had taught in schools prior to joining the Red Army.
>
> Second year or senior students of all higher schools, including those taking correspondence courses, who had not finished their education because of their induction into the Red Army.
>
> Veterans who were wounded three or more times.
>
> Veterans who had been called into military service during or before 1938 or who have 7 or more years of continuous duty in the Red Army.
>
> All women privates and specialists other than volunteers for further duty.

Completion of demobilization in accordance with this decree by the end of 1945.

Extension of the social and welfare provisions of the Demobilization Law of 23 June 1945 to personnel demobilized in accordance with the decree of 25 September.

In an order of 10 October 1945, it was further directed that 10 percent of all dwellings must be set aside for demobilized soldiers, disabled veterans, and families of casualties.

4. DEMOBILIZATION PROCEDURE

It is believed that, while demobilization is not conducted individually according to any kind of point system, length of service, decorations, and age are taken into consideration. All 13 classes were not demobilized at one time under the first law. On the contrary, there is evidence that the oldest 5 of the 13 classes were demobilized first.

Demobilized personnel have been transported at Army expense to cities near to their point of recruitment. There they have been given a pass and provided with free entertainment for several days. They then have been transported to their places of call-up and officially separated from the Red Army.

5. DEMOBILIZATION OF OFFICERS

The release of officers of only the lower grades, up to and including major, is provided for by the demobilization decrees of 1945. The second decree does not provide for demobilization of officers.

PART III. PAY, ALLOWANCES, AND PENSIONS

Section I. PAY RATES

1. GENERAL

The special privileges, pay, and allowances granted to Red Army personnel attest to the importance Soviet law attaches to army service. Soviet propaganda stresses the esteem in which Red Army and Navy personnel are held, and Soviet law and practice support it.

Red Army personnel are tax exempt. They have special opportunities for education and careers, in a country in which these advantages are especially significant. Those holding decorations are given numerous small privileges, such as free theater tickets, free transportation in public conveyances,

Assignment	MOS	Pay	
		(Rubles)	Approximate equivalent in U. S. dollars
Supply and forage officer	4	9,000	1,800
Battalion adjutant	4	9,000	1,800
Chief of staff (rear echelon)	4	9,600	1,920
Chief of staff (statistical control)	4	9,600	1,920
Artillery supply officer	4	9,600	1,920
Infantry company commander	1	8,700	1,740
Machine gun company commander	2	9,600	1,920
Mortar company commander	2a	9,300	1,860
Howitzer battery commander	10	9,600	1,920

Figure 8. Variations in the pay of a Red Army captain.

Rank (U. S.)	Red Army pay (1943)		U. S. Army pay (1945) (in dollars)
	In rubles*	In dollars, approximate	
General of the Army	60,000	12,000	13,500
General	40,000	8,000	13,500
Lieutenant general	28,000	5,600	8,000
Major general	24,000	4,800	8,000
Brigadier general	19,000	3,840	6,000
Colonel	14,400	2,880	4,000
Lieutenant colonel	12,000	2,400	3,500
Major	10,200	2,040	3,000
Captain	9,000	1,800	2,400
First lieutenant	7,700	1,540	2,000
Master, or first sergeant	4,200	840	1,656
Staff sergeant	3,800	760	1,152
Sergeant	3,000	600	936
Corporal	2,000	400	792
Private first class	1,000	200	648
Private	600	120	600

*1 ruble=$0.20, approximately.

Figure 9. Comparison of annual base pay of U. S. and Red Armies.

one free round trip railroad ticket per year, and a small monthly pay increase in proportion to the rank of the decoration.

2. PAY RATES

Red Army personnel are paid according to rank, MOS, and type of duty. For example, a captain's pay varies between 8,700 rubles (approximately $1,740) and 9,600 rubles (approximately $1,920) per year as in Figure 8.

Red Army pay rates generally are lower than those of the U. S. Army. There also is greater variation between the lowest and highest grades.

Red air force personnel are paid approximately the same rates as corresponding ground force ranks. However, bonuses are given for each combat flight and parachute jump (25 rubles per jump).

In addition, there are various kinds of extra pay in the Red Army during war. Approximately 50 percent of the base pay of enlisted men is granted as extra field pay to combat troops and as extra arms pay to men in antitank, armored, and guard units.

Extra monthly pay for some of the decorations is as follows:

	Rubles
Order of Lenin	25
Order of the Red Banner	20
Order of the Red Star	15

Section II. PENSIONS, FAMILY ALLOWANCES, AND SPECIAL BENEFITS

1. WORKERS AND EMPLOYEES ORDERED TO ACTIVE DUTY

When a worker or employee is released for active military service, the management of the enterprise or institution releasing him must make a settlement in the form of full payment of wages, a separation allowance in the amount of the average sum for 2 weeks work, and a monetary compensation for unused leave. Reserve officers ordered to training periods are paid 50 percent of the wages they otherwise would earn.

2. ALLOWANCES TO FAMILIES OF ENLISTED MEN

Families of enlisted men called up from the reserves, families of volunteer enlisted men accepted by the field units of the Red Army, and families of enlisted men in the units of mobilized districts are authorized allowances by a decree of the Presidium of the Supreme Soviet dated 26 June 1941. Families of captains or higher do not receive allowances.

The families of enlisted men are paid additional allowances, by civilian agencies, if there is no one in the family who is able to work, if there is one member of the family who is able to work but three or more who are not, or if there is one member able to work but also two children under 16 years of age.

Individuals considered unable to work are as follows:

Children under 16.
Students under 18.

Brothers (when parents are not able-bodied).
Grown children, brothers, and sisters who are invalids and younger than 18.
Fathers over 60.
Mothers over 55.
Wife and parents who are invalids.

Individuals are regarded as dependents only when the serviceman has been the constant and major source of support.

Monthly allowances are as follows:

Single dependent unable to work, 100 rubles ($20 approximately). Two dependents unable to work, 150 rubles ($30 approximately).

Three or more dependents unable to work, 300 rubles ($60 approximately).

One member of family able to work and three or more unable to work, 150 rubles ($30 approximately).

One member of family able to work and two children under 16, 100 rubles ($20 approximately).

Enlisted men's families living in farming communities or in any way connected with agriculture receive only 50 percent of the above allowances.

3. PENSIONS FOR ENLISTED MEN AND THEIR FAMILIES

Pensions are assigned on the basis of a decree of the Council of Peoples' Commissars dated 16 July 1940. Servicemen who sustain wounds or incur diseases in combat, in active military service, or as a result of accidents not in line of duty are eligible for pensions.

The degree of disability determines the amount of the pension. The first category includes those with complete physical disability, and who require constant care. The second category includes those with complete physical disability, but who can take care of themselves. The third category includes those with partial disability who require special working conditions or training in less strenuous occupations.

Servicemen who become disabled in line of duty and who earned 400 rubles (approximately $80) per month or less in civilian life receive pensions as follows:

First category—100 percent of average monthly earnings.

Second category—75 percent of average monthly earnings.

Third category—50 percent of average monthly earnings.

Families of servicemen who are killed or reported missing in action and who earned 400 rubles or less per month in civilian life receive pensions as follows:

One person killed—35 percent of average monthly earnings.

Two persons killed—45 percent of average monthly earnings.

Three persons killed—60 percent of average monthly earnings.

Servicemen who become physically disabled as a result of accidents not directly in line of duty receive pensions as fixed by social insurance regulations for workmen and employees who are disabled by ordinary diseases. Military service is credited as worktime.

Disabled servicemen and families of deceased servicemen living in farming localities, or otherwise connected with agriculture, receive 50 percent of the above pensions.

The following dependent members of the families of deceased servicemen, if unable to work, have a right to a pension: children under 16 and students under 18; brothers and sisters under 16 and students under 18 if their parents are unable to work; children, brothers and sisters up to 18 who are unable to work; father over 60, mother over 55; disabled wife and parents of the first and second categories regardless of age.

4. PENSIONS FOR OFFICERS AND ENLISTED MEN ON VOLUNTARY EXTENDED SERVICE, AND THEIR FAMILIES

Pensions also are provided for intermediate, senior and higher officers, noncommissioned officers on re-enlistment service, and private-specialists on re-enlistment service. Their families are granted pensions, in case of death, by a decree of the Council of People's Commissars dated 5 July 1941.

Retirement pensions are granted for 25 or more years of enlisted and commissioned service. Credit for length of service is computed as follows:

Each month in the detachments of the Red Guards (7 Oct. 1917–23 Feb. 1918) counts as 4 months.

Each month in the Red Army in a theater of active operation, in the Red Army liquidating counter-revolutionary movements, or in the security forces or *Cheka* during the Revolution—3 months.

Each month in the Red Army in remote regions, in chemical units handling explosives, in border units, on submarines, and as divers—2 months.

Each month in a plague-infested region—3 months, if infected—15 months.

Pensions are paid as follows:

For 25 years service—50 percent pay.

For each year service in excess of 25—3 percent in addition.

For 35 or more years service—80 percent of pay.

Provisions were made in 1945 to grant generals and senior officers (colonels, lt. colonels, and majors) who have served 25 years or more and are on reserve status, or were retired because of age, increased pensions as follows:

Generals—90 percent of pay.

Senior officers—80 percent of pay (plus 3 percent for each year in excess of 25 years up to a maximum of 90 percent.)

A general or senior officer who becomes a civil employee after being placed in reserve status, or retired after 25 years of service, does not lose his right to full pension.

Physically disabled command personnel and re-enlisted noncommissioned officers and privates receive pensions as follows:

In line of duty:

First category—75 percent of pay.

Second category—55 percent of pay.

Third category—40 percent of pay.

Not in line of duty:

First category—60 percent of pay.

Second category—45 percent of pay.

Third category—30 percent of pay.

Increases up to 85, 65, and 45 percent respectively for each category are granted for length of service.

Families of command personnel and reenlisted noncommissioned officers and privates who die in line of duty receive monthly pension payments of 30 percent of pay if there is one person unable to work, 45 percent if there are two, and 60 percent if there are three or more. If death is not in line of duty, families receive 25, 35, and 45 percent of the pay respectively. Increases up to 35, 55, and 70 percent for deaths in line of duty and up to 30, 45, and 55 percent for deaths not in line of duty are granted for length of service.

5. BENEFITS FOR MILITARY PERSONNEL AND FAMILIES

In addition to pensions, disabled servicemen, members of their families who are unable to work, and members of families of deceased servicemen who receive pensions are furnished prosthetic and orthopedic devices at government expense.

With the high casualty rates of World War II, the families of casualties became the object of extreme solicitude on the part of the Communist Party and the Soviet government. Special departments were established to aid the families of servicemen. These departments organized food supplies, provided living quarters, and found jobs for dependents. Substantial concessions in taxes, in deliveries of agricultural products to the state, and in rent were granted to families of Red Army casualties. Special grants were awarded to families of men displaying heroism in battle.

Special provisions have been formulated for the training and employment of disabled veterans.

Preliminary short-term training, the character of which is selected in consultation with a Medical and Labor Expert Commission, is given at the medical institutions of the Red Army. Servicemen discharged as physically unsuitable for service report to the Medical and Labor Expert Commission, where their degree of disability is determined and an appropriate type of work is recommended.

The Department of Social Welfare of the *Rayon* Soviet secures employment for disabled veterans on the basis of the Commission's findings. Attempts are made to reinstate them in enterprises where they formerly were employed, or at least in the same type of work. Those not provided with work in government institutions and enterprises are sent to *Artels* (small cooperative light manufacturing enterprises) or to special cooperatives for the disabled, where those of the first and second categories are offered work at home. Disabled veterans may be sent to training institutions or to courses offered by various enterprises for general education or instruction in a new type of work.

Disabled veterans of the first and second categories, who do not receive proper care, may apply to the *Rayon* Department of Social Welfare for admittance to a home for invalids.

Command personnel, re-enlisted noncommissioned officers and privates who receive pensions, and their families receive free treatment in sanatoria and health resorts.

Concessions in the form of income tax exemption and exemption from obligatory deliveries to the government also are granted to disabled veterans.

PART IV. LEGAL AND SURVEILLANCE SYSTEMS

Section I. LEGAL SYSTEM

1. GENERAL

Supervision and control of Red Army personnel is divided among a number of administrative structures, whose representatives are found at all echelons of command. No single code of laws and regulations exists which cover all the crimes and misdemeanors of Red Army personnel. A sharp distinction in codes and enforcement machinery is made between military criminal law, army disciplinary regulations, political discipline, and the supervision

of personal loyalties to the Red Army and to the Soviet Union.

Military criminal law consists of a code of laws based on the civil laws of the Soviet Union, translated into terms applicable to military personnel and military conditions. It is developed by the Military Collegium of the Supreme Court and administered by the Main Administration of Military Tribunals of the Commissariat of Defense, through the system of Military Tribunals.

The disciplinary regulations of the Red Army cover offenses which have no analogy in civil law, and they are administered by Commanders at all echelons.

Disciplinary control of Communist Party members and of the political ideology of other members of the Red Army is combined with morale and propaganda as the special mission of the political apparatus, at all echelons, under control of the Main Political Administration of the Commissariat of Defense. Loyalty of personnel to the nation and to the regime (as distinct from party loyalty as it affects military security) is the responsibility of the Main Administration of Counterintelligence of the Commissariat of Defense, and of the offices and agencies under its control at all echelons.

The considerable difficulty which arises in exactly defining the jurisdiction of these four systems of supervision is obviated by close cooperation, particularly at Commissariat of Defense level. The exclusion of undesirable elements from the Red Army initially is charged to the Commissariat of Internal Affairs (NKVD) and its representatives, the local police. It is carried out by the Conscription Boards, of which one member is always a representative of the local NKVD force.

2. MILITARY PENAL SYSTEM

a. Military criminal law. The mission of Soviet military criminal law is identical with that of Soviet criminal law in general: "The legal defense of the socialist state of workers and peasants against socially dangerous actions which undermine its power or violate its established order." The basic purpose of criminal law as applied to the armed forces is to strengthen the defensive power of the U. S. S. R. and the military effectiveness of the armed forces of the Soviet state.

The existence of military criminal law as a special branch of criminal law is necessitated by the peculiarity of the activities of the Red Army and Navy as distinguished from other Soviet organizations. Certain crimes, such as the nonexecution of an order, desertion, spoilage, or loss of military equipment, violation of guard rules, etc., are purely military offenses and, thus, are covered specifically only by military criminal laws. Certain other crimes, such as insults and abuses of power, assume a special significance in military conditions and also demand special consideration in a separate military criminal code. Further, to eliminate mistrust and wavering in the execution of an order, the principle of absolute obedience is defined appropriately in military criminal law, which states: "An order of a commander is a law for his subordinates."

During World War II, all citizens other than those specifically excepted were made subject to military criminal law by decree of the State Defense Committee. Those classes of Red Army and other personnel normally subject to military criminal law are as follows:

> Persons undergoing pre-conscription training while participating in active field-training periods.
>
> Enlisted men on active duty, in the training periods required during extended furloughs, or on reserve status.
>
> Students in cadet and military schools.
>
> Officers on active duty, on detached service, in training periods required during extended leave, or on reserve status.

The soldier of the Red Army is obligated "to know thoroughly and execute unquestioningly the military oath, military regulations and instructions, and all orders and decrees of his superior and leaders; to observe strictly the established order in the Army, and to restrain others from its violation; to fulfill his service obligations conscientiously; to guard all military and state secrets; and, finally, to preserve military and state property to the best of his ability.

"With the taking of the military oath, the soldier pledges himself to defend his socialist fatherland with bravery and honor, if necessary, risking life itself in the achieving of complete victory over its enemies. Failure in these duties constitutes the commission of a military crime."

The decision as to whether a particular case is punishable under military criminal law or under the disciplinary regulations of the Red Army is made by the immediate commander of the offending party. There are certain crimes which automatically exclude the offender from the milder provisions of army discipline as, for example, espionage, desertion to the enemy, willful departure from the field of battle, and resistance to any person who is executing an order. Such acts, because they immediately are dangerous to the entire state, always involve trial and sentence under military criminal law.

On the other hand, offenses such as infringement

of uniform regulations and submitting complaints in a manner contrary to the regulations generally entail only disciplinary measures.

More complicated are those crimes which require disciplinary action in some circumstances and court action in others. Examples are absence without leave, breach of guard rules, and loss of military equipment. The determining factor is the degree of danger to society and to state involved in the crime.

Because Soviet military criminal law is directed mainly against "enemies of the people," such as traitors, spies, diversionists, and terrorists who may infiltrate into the Red Army to undermine its strength or to destroy its equipment, any crime of this nature, because it endangers the military security of the country, is tried under military criminal law, regardless of whether the offender has military status. In such cases, arrest may be made by officers of the state security forces or local police (NKVD, etc.). On the other hand, military personnel who commit crimes not covered by military criminal law are tried by civil or regular criminal courts.

b. The military court system. Violations of military criminal law are prosecuted by military Procurators and tried in Military Tribunals throughout the U. S. S. R. and at army group, army, mobile corps, and division headquarters. Centralized control over the system of Military Tribunals is exercised by the Main Administration of Military Tribunals and by the Military Collegium of the Supreme Court.

The Military Collegium is composed of a chairman, a vice-chairman, and four members, all of whom are appointed by the President of the Presidium of the Supreme Soviet. The chairman is a member of the plenary session of the Supreme Court.

The Military Collegium is charged with:

Supervision and control over all Military Tribunals.

Appointment and dismissal, with advice and consent of the Commissars of Defense and Navy, of all members of Tribunals.

Organization of new and abolition of old Tribunals upon request of the Commissars of Defense and Navy.

Review of all military cases.

Each Military Tribunals consists of a president, a vice-president, and two or more members. Attached are investigators and a secretariat (administrative section). The investigators and members of the secretariat are appointed by the president and approved by the Military Collegium and the Commissar of Defense or Navy.

Division and brigade Military Tribunals may try military personnel of rank no higher than major. Corps Tribunals may try personnel holding the rank of lieutenant colonel or below. Higher Tribunals may try persons of any rank, with the exception of army and army group Commanders and officers of the high command, who are tried only by the Military Collegium of the Supreme Court.

All sentences are imposed in the name of the U. S. S. R. All Military Tribunals inflicting capital punishment must notify the Military Collegium by telegraph within 24 hours after sentence is passed. If no reply is received within the succeeding 72 hours, the execution is carried out immediately.

There is a Military Procurator for every Military Tribunal, appointed by the Chief Procurator of the U. S. S. R. with the advice and consent of the Commissariat of Defense or Navy. The Chief Military Procurator is the senior Assistant Chief Procurator of the U. S. S. R. Procurators are charged with:

Supervision of the legality of the acts of all personnel and agencies of the military forces.

Prosecution of cases.

Review of cases by Tribunals at lower echelons.

Supervision over investigations.

Assurance of legality of arrests.

Assurance of the execution of sentences.

c. Disciplinary regulations and enforcement. Disciplinary penalties are imposed for offenses by military personnel on duty, or for the violation of an order common to all in the military service, including reserves, provided the offenses do not warrant reference to a Military Tribunal. The disciplinary regulations are applied only if "no intentional violation of directives and no consciously hostile intention against the Soviet state" are involved.

Disciplinary penalties are regarded as measures of education, and it is forbidden to complain about their severity. Military personnel may, however, submit through official channels formal complaints regarding illegal or unjust actions and orders of their commanders or any point of dissatisfaction.

A disciplinary penalty is a punishment applied to military personnel by an immediate or higher commander, to whom they are permanently or temporarily subordinated. Punishments are scaled in severity and may be imposed only in accordance with the rank and position of the offender and the commander concerned (fig. 10).

d. Comrades' Courts and Officers' Courts of Honor. Cases in which Red Army personnel have "disgraced the honorable name of 'soldier' by unworthy behavior" are handled by Comrades' Courts and by Officers' Courts of Honor. All units, formations, and higher headquarters organize such courts, independent of higher jurisdiction. The courts are designed to further the *esprit de corps* of units and to prosecute minor offenses. Neither type of court may invade the disciplinary jurisdiction of the commander or the criminal jurisdiction of the Military Tribunal.

The jurisdiction of Comrades' Courts extends to such offenses as drunkenness, disorderly conduct, insults to fellow soldiers, unbecoming behavior in public, and petty thefts among enlisted men. Sentences are determined in public sessions and are executed in public. Most penalties do not exceed reprimands or lectures to the offender before assembled personnel. Penalties may include, however, recommendations to the commander for demotions in rank or assignment.

The Officers' Courts of Honor are similarly designed, but uphold a quite different and higher standard of conduct (a significant indication of the still increasing social gap between enlisted and commissioned ranks and of the steady development of an officer corps). In addition to the types of offenses covered by the Comrades' Courts, the Officers' Courts may disapprove an officer's choice of wife, his cleanliness, his table manners, and other social matters of similar significance. Sentences are determined and imposed as in the Comrades' Courts.

e. Encouragements and rewards. Encouragements and rewards are as much a part of the disciplinary system of the Red Army as are disciplinary penalties. Encouragements and rewards

are bestowed on military personnel who conduct themselves conscientiously and assiduously in discharging their official obligations, who display care in the preservation of military equipment and property, and who show special success in political and combat preparation. Rewards and encouragements have been established as follows:

> Expressions of gratitude, personally or before the ranks.
> Expressions of gratitude in Red Army orders of the day.
> Granting of extra off-duty time.
> The bestowing of valuable gifts.
> Payment of monetary compensation.
> Withdrawal of disciplinary penalties (effected only by the commander who imposed the penalty).

Beyond these awards, there are the multifarious military decorations and awards established by the Supreme Soviet. Encouragements and rewards, like disciplinary penalties, may be granted in accordance with the rank of the individual bestowing them.

f. Absence without leave and desertion. Absence without leave and desertion are worthy of note, not only because they are among the most numerous of the serious offenses of Red Army personnel, but also because the history of their punishment illustrates the distinction between military criminal law and disciplinary regulations.

Willful and punishable absence without leave consists of the unauthorized departure of:

> Enlisted men, from their unit or its immediate area.
> Noncommissioned officers on voluntary extended duty, from the locality in which their unit or institution is stationed.
> Officers, from the locality in which their unit, institution, or office is stationed.
> Officers and enlisted men of the reserve, from their *Rayon* or *Oblast* without registering immediately with the *Rayon* or *Oblast* Military Commissar of the area to which they move.

Failure to report to the designated place in time of mobilization or for induction as a conscript and failure to perform service, through fraudulent allegations as to health, etc., also are punishable under provisions for absence without leave.

63

Type of Punishment	Squad Commander	Assistant Platoon Commander	First Commander	Platoon Commander	Company Commander	Battalion Commander	Regimental (or Ind Bn) Commander	Division (or Brigade) Commander	Corps Commander	Army (or Military District) Commander
Warning	All subordinates	Pvts only	Pvts and conscript NCOs	Pvts and conscript NCOs (except 1st Sgt)	All subordinates	All subordinates	All subordinates	All subordinates	All subordinates	All subordinates
Reprimand	All subordinates				All subordinates	All subordinates	All subordinates	All subordinates	All subordinates	All subordinates
Reprimand in ranks		Pvts	Pvts	Pvts	Pvts	Pvts	Pvts	Pvts		
Publish reprimand							Pvts, Conscript NCOs, & officers	Pvts, Conscript NCOs & officers	All subordinates	All subordinates
Delay discharge	1 wk for Pvts	2 wks for Pvts	3 wks for Pvts, 1 wk for Conscript NCOs	4 wks for Pvts, 2 wks for Conscript NCOs	6 wks for Pvts, 4 wks for Conscript NCOs	6 wks for Pvts, 4 wks for Conscript NCOs				
Extra fatigue duty	1 for Pvts	2 for Pvts	4 for Pvts, 2 for Conscript NCOs	6 for Pvts, 4 for Conscript NCOs	8 for Pvts, 4 for Conscript NCOs					
Arrest			3 da for Pvts	5 da for Pvts	10 da for Pvts, 5 da for Conscript NCOs	15 da for Pvts, 10 da for Conscript NCOs	20 da for Pvts & Conscript NCOs	20 da for Pvts & Conscript NCOs, 15 da & 25% of pay for time of arrest or 10 da & 50% of pay for Regular NCOs		
Report to Comrades' Court					Pvts and Conscript NCOs	Pvts and Conscript NCOs	Pvts and Conscript NCOs	Pvts and Conscript NCOs		
Forbid leave					3 da for all EM	5 da for all EM, 3 da for Plat Comdrs	10 da for all EM, 5 da for Co officers	15 da for all EM, 10 da for officers up thru Bn Comdrs	15 da for officers up thru Asst Regtl Comdrs	15 da for officers up thru Regtl Comdrs
Reduce in rank							Conscript NCOs	Conscript NCOs, 1 grade for Regular NCOs		
Transfer to reserves								Regular NCOs	Co officers	Co officers
Confine to quarters					3 da for all EM	5 da up thru Plat Comdrs	8 da up thru Co officers	10 da for Co officers, 5 da up thru Asst Regtl Comdrs	15 da for Co officers, 10 da up thru Asst Regtl Comdrs	15 da up thru Asst Regtl Comdrs
Relieve from command							Co officers in emergency	Up thru Bn Comdrs in emergency	Up thru Regtl Comdrs in emergency	Up thru Bn Comdrs normally, up thru Div Comdrs in emergency
Report to Officers' Court of Honor							Up thru Bn Comdrs	Up thru Asst Regtl Comdrs	Up thru Asst Regtl Comdrs	Up thru Regtl Comdrs
Fine								Co officers fogies for 3 mos.	Up thru Asst Regtl Comdrs fogies for 3 mos.	Up thru Asst Regtl Comdrs fogies for 6 mos.; up thru Regtl Comdrs fogies for 3 mos.
Delay promotion										Up thru Regtl Comdrs for 1 yr.

Figure 10. Persons entitled to impose disciplinary penalties.

Absence without leave is interpreted as a breach of disciplinary regulations or as desertion subject to military criminal law on the basis of duration of absence, evidence of willful desertion of duty, and the existence of a state of war or emergency. Normally, unwarranted absence of an enlisted man for more than 24 hours, or of an officer or noncommissioned officer on voluntary extended duty for more than 6 days, is termed desertion.

Punishments for absence without leave vary with the length of absence and with the degree of guilt of the offender. They are imposed by commanders as disciplinary measures. Desertion always is punished by Military Tribunals, as an offense against military criminal law.

Absence without leave and desertion are regarded as deliberate offenses and violations of regulations or law, regardless of the intent of the offender. Intention to desert, though forestalled by arrest, is punishable as is desertion. Railroad tickets and similar indications are accepted as evidence of intent.

Absence of enlisted men without leave is punished almost as severely in wartime as is desertion in time of peace in that it is always regarded as a violation of law. In the zone of combat, during war, any absence without leave, of whatever duration, is regarded as desertion.

Grade	Offense	Punishment	
		In peace	In war
Enlisted men..	Absence without leave as a disciplinary offense.	Consignment to Comrades' Court or punishment under disciplinary regulations.	
	Absence without leave as a military criminal offense.	Consignment to Penal Battalion, 6 to 24 months.	Imprisonment, 3 to 7 years.
	Desertion.................	Imprisonment, 5 to 10 years....	Death and confiscation of property.
Officers.......	Absence without leave as a military criminal offense.	2 or more years' imprisonment, with or without confiscation of property.	Death and confiscation of property.
	Desertion.................	2 or more years' imprisonment with confiscation of property.*	Death and confiscation of property.

*This provision was retained from an earlier code. Because it provides a milder punishment for desertion of officers than for enlisted men, courts are instructed to consider the offense in the light of other legal emphasis on the responsibility of officers.

Figure 11. Punishments for absence and desertion.

Section II. SURVEILLANCE SYSTEM

1. POLITICAL SUPERVISION IN RED ARMY

a. General. The functions of the political administrations, branches, sections, and offices of the Red Army are as follows:

Supervising of Communist Party and *Komsomol* members in the Red Army.

The bolstering of morale of all Red Army troops.

Indoctrination of Red Army personnel.

Political surveillance of commanders and staffs.

Propaganda against the enemy.

All of these functions or objectives are included in the term, "political work."

Although the position of Party representatives within the Army has undergone numerous changes, particularly in their relationship to military Commanders, the political machine always has been and still is an integral part of the Red Army and an important force within it. In October 1942, the military Commanders were freed of direct political control, but the actual influence of the Communist Party in the Red Army is still great, as it is in every phase of the Soviet system.

Party membership carries extra responsibilities in the demonstration of qualities of leadership, self-sacrifice, and heroism. From the point of view of officers, Party membership often eases the path to promotion and decorations. However, membership is not easily obtained and proof of genuine enthusiasm for the Communist ideology, reliability, and conscientiousness are required from candidates. Candidates must pass through a probationary period. Recruiting has been maintained at a high level. Since December 1941, entry to the Party has been made easier for members of the Red Army who have distinguished themselves in battle. Their three sponsors now need not have known them for an entire year as was required previously. Also, the probationary period is only 3 months, instead of a year.

Party members are expected to be exemplary soldiers. Whenever a military operation is planned, the political agency of each echelon involved is responsible that Party members are placed in responsible positions and that they know exactly what is expected of them. The instruction of Party members often takes the form of meetings, where lectures and discussions are used to coordinate their work. At higher levels, senior Party officials and agitators attend conferences in Moscow, where they are addressed by Party leaders on tactics and Party policy. Mobile Party commissions are attached to fronts. They carry libraries and offer expert advice on all phases of political work.

b. Propaganda and agitation. Propaganda addressed to officers and Communist Party members largely is concerned with Communist theory. Other ranks, who are not Party members, are instructed chiefly on the practical problems of the U. S. S. R. When training in the rear, units normally receive 2 hours of daily political instruction, by companies. Enemy atrocities and heroic deeds of Soviet personnel are frequent subjects.

c. Leisure and cultural activities. Each division and higher formation has a club, which includes a mobile motion picture unit and a cultural group. The cultural group arranges dances, concerts, and other forms of entertainment. Regiments have officers' clubs, where concerts and amateur theatricals are presented. A number of clubs for Red Army personnel are run by the Main Political Administration and by the Central Theater of the Red Army in Moscow.

d. Literature. Each battalion daily receives more than 100 papers for distribution, including *Pravda, Izvestia, Krasnaya Zveda* (Red Star), and the paper published by the army group or army. In addition, each division publishes a paper several times a week. Regiments and battalions publish weekly wall-newspapers. Radio news bulletins and orders of the day are duplicated and distributed to units. Much of this material is read aloud and discussed at meetings.

Libraries are found at company level, although they often are lost during marches. Divisions and higher formations publish a variety of pamphlets and posters. Division pamphlets containing both military instruction and general material, are designed to foster patriotism and to explain the principles the Red Army defends.

e. Motion pictures. Each division has a mobile motion picture unit, which is said to exert a powerful influence. In conformity with the general trend of Soviet internal propaganda, the films shown largely are of a historical-patriotic character, such as the films *Alexander Nevski, The Rainbow, Kutuzov,* etc. The Red Army also produces films. Its film studios process the material collected by Red Army cameramen attached to each army group.

f. Propaganda against the enemy. Propaganda against the enemy is conducted by means of leaflets and loudspeakers in all the languages used by troops fighting against the U. S. S. R. Advice to desert to the Red Army is the principal theme of the propaganda. On 11 June 1943, for example, the Red Army high command issued an order offering extra rations, accommodations in special camps in good climate, preferential treatment in the choice of an occupation, priority in forwarding of letters to Germany, and an early return to Germany or another selected country after the end of the war as special inducements to deserters. Another recurrent theme is the strength of the U. S. S. R. and her allies, the superiority of Red Army leadership and equipment over that of the enemy, the weaknesses of enemy strategy, enemy atrocities, and the strength and aims of U. S. S. R. political groups. German troops were supplied plentifully during World War II with information and propaganda concerning the League of German Officers and the Free Germany Committee organized under Soviet supervision.

g. Organization. Headquarters, at all levels down to division, include political offices as an integral part of the administrative machinery. Commanders of tank and mechanized corps and rifle divisions, as well as regiments, battalions, and other equivalent units, have assistants for political affairs. The subordination of political offices is similar to that of other sections of the head███████ ████ the Political Division at an army headquarters receives instructions concerning policy and technical guidance from the Political Administration at army group headquarters, although it is under the orders of the army commander and technically responsible to him.

One of the most important activities of the political system is its operation as a reporting channel. Complete and confidential information is collected concerning the political and ideological records of Party members, in particular, and of all command and staff personnel insofar as their actions can be given political interpretation.

MAIN POLITICAL ADMINISTRATION. The Main Political Administration of the Commissariat of Defense is both an offshoot of the Central Committee of the Communist Party and an agency within the Peoples' Commissariat of Defense. It is headed by a senior member of the Central Committee of the Communist Party. The following is an approximate list of the subdivisions of the Main Political Administration:

> Organization and Training Administration.
> Political Propaganda Administration, with branches for:
>> Propaganda and agitation in the Red Army.
>> Morale in the Red Army.
>> Psychological warfare.
>> Propaganda for Partisans and occupied territories.
>> Motion pictures.
>> Press (with printing facilities).
>> Supply of cultural and education material.
> Information Administration.
> Inspecting and reporting service (probable).
> *Komsomol* Administration.
> Party Administration, with branches for:
>> Personnel and recruiting.
>> Records.
>> Finance.

The Main Political Administration operates the Lenin Political War Academy for the training of senior political staff officers; operates a number of military-political schools, such as the Engels Military-Political School; and operates various exten-

███████d other courses. It also runs the Frunze Central House of the Red Army in Moscow.

ARMY GROUP POLITICAL ADMINISTRATION. Each army group has a Political Administration, which is part of front headquarters and is organized into branches similarly to the Administrations of the Main Political Administration. The Chief of the Political Administration, always a general officer of long party standing, is a deputy to the army group Commander for political matters. He also is a member of the Military Council. The deputy of the Chief of the Political Administration is the Chief of the Propaganda and Agitation Branch.

The function of the Political Administration is to issue general directives and to supervise all political work within the army group. This includes psychological warfare and political work among Partisans and the civil population in enemy-occupied areas. The Political Administration publishes pamphlets for the use of propagandists and agitators and of the individual newspaper of the army group.

Periodic reports are submitted by the Political Administration of each army group to the Main Political Administration of the Red Army.

The Political Administration has a pool of instructors for the training and guidance of unit and formation political workers. There are believed to be:

> Instructors for organization, whose primary duty is to advise political workers concerning their spheres of responsibility in relation to the unit or formation commander.
> Instructors for agitators, who instruct junior agitators and *Komsomol* agitators in their duties and hold meetings and demonstrations to raise morale and to instill "hatred of the enemy."
> Propaganda instructors, who instruct Party members, *Komsomols* and non-Party officers in the art of distributing propaganda to troops.
> Instructors for information, who probably are inspectors of the reporting system.

There also is a Party Commission for the army group, which supervises the work of all the Party organizations within the front, administers reprimands when necessary, and is generally responsible for Party discipline. Its members visit, in an advisory capacity, the formations of the army group.

The Party Commission is elected by the Party Conference of the army group, delegates to which are Party members from formations of the army group.

The Chief of Staff of the army group has a political deputy whose duty it is to mingle with and engage in political work among staff officers. They give lectures and provide general background on operations in other sectors of the front and on current events.

During World War II, the Communist Party systematically sent its best propagandists to army groups. Among the Communists who voluntarily entered this work were college instructors, professors, and scientists. They became staff lecturers, attached to the Political Division of an army.

With one army group for the first 6 months of 1945, the reports and lectures included, 152 on orders and speeches of Stalin, 150 on current events, 50 on the history of the Communist Party, 16 on philosophy, 27 on the experiences of the war, 10 on problems of military education, 4 on military history, 14 on the "heroic work on the home front", and 10 on bordering countries.

During this same period, lecturers of the Political Department of one army gave 98 lectures explaining Stalin's writings, 121 on the history of the Communist Party, 37 on philosophy, 144 on current events, and 76 on the work of the home front.

ARMY POLITICAL DIVISION. All the features of the Political Administration of an army group are incorporated, on a smaller scale, in the Political Division of an army. The Chief of the army Political Division normally is a major general, who is required to have a minimum of 5 years of Party membership.

LOWER ECHELONS. The limited and purely operational nature of the rifle corps headquarters, as illustrated by the skeleton strength and function of the corps Political Branch, scarcely is adequate for more than political work among headquarters personnel. Political Branches at mobile corps headquarters are somewhat stronger and are similar to the Political Section at division level.

The Deputy Commander for Political Affairs, who commands the Political Section of a division, has the same rank as the Deputy Commander for Operations, usually that of a lieutenant colonel. He must be a Party member of at least 3 years standing. The Political Section of a division consists of an as-sistant in charge of administration, Chief of the divisional Party organization, Chief of the division *Komsomol* organization, officer in charge of party records and accounts, Chief of Propaganda and Agitation, and a Chief of Psychological Warfare. At least two clerks, as well as division motion picture operators, also are provided.

The Political Section of a regiment consists of a Deputy Commander for Political Affairs (a captain or a major), a representative of the Communist Party, a representative of *Komsomols*, and a regimental agitator. The regimental Party organization is divided into approximately 16 cells (primary Party organizations).

The Deputy Commander for Political Affairs of a battalion, a captain, commands the battalion Party and *Komsomol* organizers, who are full-time workers and are exempt from military duties. There is no full-time agitator in the battalion. The battalion Party organizer is assisted by a bureau of five men, which meets weekly. It is responsible that every Communist in the battalion is an effective agitator and upholds the required military standard.

The company has no Deputy Commander for Political Affairs and no full-time political officers. The company Commander, though he need not be a member of the Communist Party, is required to give a certain amount of instruction and to supervise morale. In these matters, he is supervised by the battalion Deputy Commander for Political Affairs. Company Party meetings are held frequently. The Party leader of the company may hold any rank, and is most frequently a senior noncommissioned officer. He is required to fulfill normal military duties in addition to his political work. A *Komsomol* organizer also is appointed in each company.

2. COUNTERINTELLIGENCE SYSTEM

The Counterintelligence System of the Red Army was a branch of the Commissariat of Internal Affairs (NKVD) until 1943, when the NKVD personnel in the ranks of the Red Army were transferred from the jurisdiction of the NKVD to that of the Main Administration of Counterintelligence of the Commissariat of Defense. The administrations, branches, sections, and agents of the counterintelligence system at all echelons down to company level are responsible exclusively for the security and loyalty to the nation of all Red Army personnel and for the discovery of enemy elements which have infiltrated into the ranks or the area for which each headquarters is responsible.

The NKVD has not been excluded completely from Red Army affairs, however. It is responsible for screening persons due for conscription, but considered prejudicial to Army security because of their records with the local police (NKVD). It also is responsible for supplying full information about all inducted persons to the various agencies of personnel administration. The screening process is emphasized, particularly, in reoccupied areas of the U. S. S. R., where enemy agents are certain to report for conscription to the Field *Rayon* Military Commissar appointed by the army group.

In the combat zone, the Red Army's own counterintelligence services collaborate closely with the counterintelligence agents of the Commissariat of State Security (NKGB) in the apprehension of enemy agents outside the ranks of the Red Army.

PART V. TRAINING

Section I. OBJECTIVES AND METHODS

1. OBJECTIVES

The objectives of military training in the U. S. S. R. are to produce highly qualified permanent cadres and a large reserve for use in event of war. The professional cadre of officers and enlisted men is procured by a system of selection from a broad base, competitive examination at each level of training, and intensive programs for the improvement of the military and general educational level of all personnel. Thorough political indoctrination of all candidates for command positions in the Red Army, and constant political supervision over their activities are deemed essential.

Steady growth of a large body of reserve officers and enlisted men is assured by the universal military service law and by the automatic transfer to reserve status of all company grade officers who are not promoted to field grade by their fortieth birthday. Political indoctrination and surveillance of reserves is conducted during their period of active duty and after their transfer to reserve status.

2. BASIC PROBLEMS

The low educational average of U. S. S. R. population presents the most serious military training problem in the Red Army. Analysis of 2,300 Red Army pay books shows that the average is 4 years of school for privates, 7 years for noncommissioned officers, and 7 to 10 years for officers. This handicap is mitigated somewhat by the State Labor Reserve. Boys between 14 and 17 years of age are trained by the state for skilled trades. This provides a pool of 85,000 technicians annually which may be drawn upon by the Red Army.

Although very elaborate tests exist for qualifications for the various levels of officer and noncommissioned officer training, the demand for command personnel exceeds the supply to such an extent that the required qualifications practically are meaningless. All graduates of universities, and nearly all graduates of high schools and technical schools are given officer training.

Thus, in order to have sufficiently trained personnel to meet the requirements of modern warfare, the Red Army has to maintain an extensive educational program. Schools are established in every independent command and in every military district. Correspondence and night courses are offered to all officers.

Although the entrance requirements to schools for officers are of necessity low, admission to the higher branch schools and academies is progressively more difficult to obtain. Candidates for these institutions must improve their military and general education to a higher degree by taking advantage of the educational opportunities offered by the Red Army. The fact that higher education in the U. S. S. R. is difficult to obtain creates keen competition for assignments to the higher military schools. Thus, the average educational level of the Red Army is low, but that of the field and higher grade officers much higher.

World War II forced the Red Army to reduce considerably the length of training periods and time allotted to courses in army schools and academies. This did not, however, imply any serious lowering of the quality of instruction. The acceleration was achieved by greater condensation of courses, rather than by omission of important phases or subjects, particularly for the training of officers. The over-all improvement in the educational level of command personnel, which already was appreciable in the years before World War II, made it possible to eliminate a considerable amount of the general educational instruction which had previously been found necessary. Another ameliorating circumstance was a direct result of World War II itself. Battle experience soon indicated which elements of instruction required greater emphasis and which could be eliminated safely.

3. TRAINING METHODS

a. Characteristics. The Red Army training methods are characterized by thorough planning, realism, repetition, and constructive critiques at the end of each training period and each engagement. Thorough planning and preparation of training material is practiced at all levels from the Commissariat of Defense down to the individual training group. Examples of long-range training policies are the schedules for civilian and pre-conscriptive training; the courses of military schools and academies, which are planned for 2 or more years in advance, even in time of war; and the lists of subjects, published in advance, which are to be discussed by the publications of the arms and services. The training programs for fixed installations are prepared in great detail, leaving little to the initiative of the individual Commanders and instructors. Training in the field and replacement units, however, although governed in over-all scope by higher authority, is left largely to the initiative of the Commanders.

Realism in training is emphasized equally in time of peace and of war. It is achieved by conducting from 85 to 90 percent of all tactical training under field conditions. Training camps are so constructed that they may be moved by the unit training in the area. Such moves often are made during a tactical problem to simulate the confusion inherent to combat. The training in use of weapons, observation, control of fire, and staff work also is accomplished under field conditions. While the unit's rear installations are being set up, convoys move through the area and simulated enemy counterbattery fire is used to imitate combat confusion.

Repetition of a military technique until correct reaction to a given situation becomes automatic is another characteristic of Red Army training methods. A maneuver, whether by an individual of a small group, is repeated until the required technique is mastered. The maneuver is repeated under varied conditions. Basic and refresher training often is conducted on the front line during inactive periods.

A critique at the end of each training period is required. The critique, generally conducted by the officer in command of the exercise, assisted by the participants, covers the mission of the exercise, lessons learned, and the degree of proficiency attained.

b. Individual training. The teaching techniques by which the Red Army trains the individual soldier are the same as those used by teachers everywhere. Methods used include explanation, demonstration, imitation, repetition, and examination. Sometimes the best, and at other times the slowest, student is used as an example. The monitor system is also in extensive use.

In group instruction of the individual, and in small unit training, the over-all problem, as well as the problem of each individual or of an individual group within the unit, is explained to all participants. The critique of such a training problem includes the discussion of the detailed as well as the over-all problems.

Instruction in the use of a weapon includes its relation to the firepower of the unit, theoretical discussions of its trajectory and capabilities, actual firing (preceded by dry runs), maintenance, and emergency repair. Officer students of the technical arms and services are required to learn how to disassemble, repair, and assemble their particular pieces of equipment. For this purpose, training frequently is conducted in factories.

A feature of Soviet training technique is the attachment of students to field training units. Such students may not be used by the unit commanders as part of their complement of personnel. Their progress is checked by instructors, who similarly are attached. Officer students from the General Staff Academy and from the higher academies of the arms and services often are attached for training to field units in combat during war, and technical officers often are sent directly to factories.

At the end of such a tour of duty, each student is required to prepare a report. Some of these reports are used as a basis for reorganization of units, changes in tactical concepts, or rearrangement of assembly lines and other processes at industrial plants. Thus, the higher academies are responsible not only for training, but also for military research as an essential part of higher military training.

c. Unit training. Unit training in the zone of the interior and in the rear area of an army or an army group (front) compares closely with that instituted by an army group prior to a major operation, but is of suitably smaller scale and of longer duration. The conduct of unit training generally is the same regardless of the size of the unit. The preparation and execution of a problem or training maneuver by a formation or unit is organized so that every phase, including the preliminary planning, is a training exercise for appropriate personnel at every point in the process.

Unit training problems are supervised and directed by the most competent officers available, usually including the Commander or Chief of Staff. The planning of a training maneuver is a training process in itself. The staff is joined in this phase by the staffs or representatives of the staffs of all component units or elements, including officers from elements as much as four echelons below that of the highest staff concerned. The commanders of artillery regiments, for example, join an army group staff in planning training maneuvers involving the entire army group.

The organization, capabilities, and armament of each component are reviewed in great detail. The subject matter of such reviews is prescribed in advance and is as exhaustive as time permits. In this process, commanders are thoroughly familiarized with the capabilities of other arms and components as well as their own.

The group then studies the latest directives from higher echelons concerning the employment of arms, equipment, and elements, and the latest tactical doctrine. It then turns to the intelligence branch or section of the headquarters staff for a complete survey of the organization, equipment, and capabilities of the real or hypothetical enemy force. The latest trends in enemy tactical practice are discussed. The operations section or branch of the staff then reviews the basic training principles for all arms and ranks, as appropriate. This phase is followed, finally, by a careful detailed presentation of the particular maneuver. Detailed missions are defined for each operating component of the force, with particular emphasis on the coordination of the arms and serv-

ices. If the formation concerned is sufficiently large, the same procedure may be repeated at a lower echelon so as to include all the staff officers of each major component of the larger formation.

After the combined planning and instruction has been completed, the maneuver or exercise is conducted as planned.

The same groups of commanders and staffs join in critiques immediately after completion of the maneuver. Their findings become the basis for subsequent training plans or are applied directly in the next training problem.

d. Training prior to combat. Whenever possible, units and formations about to engage the enemy, whether in the line or in rear areas, conduct comprehensive battle rehearsals. The scope of the rehearsal and the period allowed for preparation and execution is determined by the Commander.

A whole army group (front) may be ordered to conduct extensive training, including intensive courses for officers in staff work, coordination, reconnaissance, and control of combat. Intensive basic training and training in the use of new weapons is conducted by all subordinate organizations. Assault groups rehearse their missions in terrain similar to that which is to be found in the actual operation. All training and rehearsals are carried out both in daylight and at night. The same procedure is executed by organizations down to combat patrols. Formations and units which already are in action conduct such training in shifts. On quiet sectors, some formations allot as much as 40 hours for training during a 2 weeks' period.

e. Training aids. The training aids used by the Red Army consist of those normally employed in conjunction with military training. They include sand tables, training films, obstacle courses, prepared assault houses, maps, charts, and training periodicals. Although the quantity of training aids at lower echelons is insufficient, it is believed to be adequate in officer and technical training schools.

Soviet training films are realistic and well-planned. Training films follow general instructional practice by presenting the over-all problem before describing the particular subject or phase of training.

The official journals of the General Staff, of the Inspector of Infantry, and of the arms and services, and the official newspaper of the Red Army, "Red

Star," all are used to raise the level of general and military education and to improve the training programs of the Red Army.

The "Journal of Military Thought," official journal of the General Staff, is intended for use by other military publications and commanders of formations. Its mission is to raise the military education of these officers, to present current military thought and ideology, and to publish interesting military developments of foreign countries. It is published once a month, with a circulation of 15,000 copies. This circulation is too small to permit the distribution of this journal to any but the highest staffs of the Red Army.

The "Military Bulletin," official journal of the Inspector of Infantry, is intended for the use of commanders of formations. Its mission is to discuss combat lessons learned during war, and to publish news of military developments in foreign countries. It is published twice a month, with a circulation of 50,000 copies.

"Red Star" is published daily, except on Sundays, by the Commissariat of Defense. It has a wide circulation, and is intended for use by all military personnel. "Red Star" contains articles of general interest, political indoctrination, combat lessons, accounts of exploits of Soviet arms, and current events. Promotions and decorations of Red Army personnel and official communiques and orders of the day are released through "Red Star."

The journals of the technical arms and services are intended primarily for the use of the commanders and staffs of the corresponding formations and units. Their content, scope, and missions are the same as those of the "Military Bulletin," but are limited to the special field concerned.

4. TRAINING INSTITUTIONS

Institutions of military study and training exist in large numbers, but they engage only in instruction of officers and officer candidates. Enlisted men train with units only. The pre-conscription training system supplies sufficient training for both infantrymen and technical personnel to eliminate the need for special institutions for basic or technical training of enlisted personnel.

Chief among the academic institutions operated exclusively by the Red Army are the Voroshilov (General Staff) and the Frunze Academies and the academies and officer schools of the arms. There are also a number of officer candidate schools not specialized as to arm, extension courses for officers of the arms and for command personnel whose training requires exhaustive knowledge of all arms and services, and a military-political academy and military-political schools. Special courses for the periodic training sessions of reserve officers are prescribed, but are given in units rather than in separate institutions.

Section II. PRE-CONSCRIPTION TRAINING

1. GENERAL

The expansion of the military training program for school-age youth represents an important development in the program of extending military preparation to increasingly larger segments of the Soviet population.

Military training for pupils in the last 3 years of secondary school was introduced first in 1929–30, but on a limited scale and chiefly as an experiment. The 1939 military service law, however, provided for the military education of students in all elementary and secondary schools and their equivalents, beginning with the fifth year of school and occupying 2 hours of school time per week. A detailed program of study was established. Instructors were provided from the ranks of the subordinate and junior officers of the reserves. During World War II, the Commissariat of Defense ordered this training extended to the first grade of elementary school and intensified at other levels.

Three distinct phases of pre-army training include military-physical for the first 4 years of elementary school, elementary military training for the fifth through the seventh years, and pre-conscription training proper for the last 3 years of secondary schools and *tekhnikums* (vocational training schools). Each stage of the training is planned and supervised carefully. Since August 1945 the military phase has started only with the seventh year. In the first through the sixth year, the program has become one of physical training and indoctrination.

The time allotted for the military preparation of the pupils at the various levels of elementary and secondary education during World War II is shown in Figure 12.

Class	Age at beginning of school year	Number of hours	
		Weekly	Yearly
I..................	7	1	33
II.................	8	1	33
III................	9	2	66
IV................	10	2	66
V.................	11	3	99
VI................	12	3	99
VII...............	13	3	99
VIII..............	14	4	252
IX................	15	4	*252
X.................	16	5	165
			1,164

*Includes 120 hours of instruction in summer camps.

Figure 12. Time allotted military preparation in Soviet schools.

As the student advances through the program, he undergoes increasingly complex training. The type of instruction in the final grade approaches that given in regular army camps. The program aims to train the student so that at completion of his secondary school education he is able to function as an individual soldier or, as a member of a squad or platoon, undertake further specialized training, or enter a school for noncommissioned officers. Girls are trained as sanitation workers, medical assistants, and as radio, telegraph, and telephone operators in a special program which begins in the fifth year of school. In the first four classes, girls receive the same training as boys.

2. MILITARY-PHYSICAL PREPARATION

The mission of the first stage in pre-conscription training is to instill a spirit of devotion to the motherland and the Soviet regime; to develop students physically; to inculcate courage, perseverance, group action, and a spirit of comradeship, and to teach military drill. In the first and second grades, 1 hour per week is allotted for this training. In the third and fourth years, 2 hours per week are allotted.

The discussions and readings on the Red Army for the first four grades cover the following subjects:

How the Red Army was born—Lenin and Stalin as the founders and organizers of the Red Army.
Stalin as Soviet Leader and Chief.
Leaders and heroes in the Civil War.
Heroes of World War II.
Young patriots in World War II.
Soviet Partisans in World War II.
Guards of the Red Army.

3. ELEMENTARY MILITARY TRAINING

The program for students in secondary schools is similar to that of the military-physical preparation program, with the addition of individual and unit training. The 3 hours per week allotted to military instruction are distributed as in Figure 14.

4. PRE-CONSCRIPTION TRAINING

Pre-conscription training in the eighth through tenth years of secondary school includes more advanced individual and unit training. In the eighth and ninth grades, 4 hours per week are devoted to this training; in the tenth year, the time is increased to 5 hours. The training is of five basic types as follows:

In-ranks training: Individual training in ranks with mock arms, manual of arms, formations and drill, military gymnastics

Subject	Hours of Training Per School Year				
	First grade	Second grade	Third grade	Fourth grade	Total
Training in ranks (formations, gymnastics and military games, skiing)............................	30	30	60	60	180
Use of gas masks..................................	1	1	1	1	4
Discussions and readings on the Red Army..............	2	2	5	5	14
Total........................	33	33	66	66	198

Figure 13. Time allotted military instruction in the first four grades.

73

Subject	Hours of Training Per School Year			
	Fifth grade	Sixth grade	Seventh grade	Totals
Training in ranks (drill in ranks without arms; drill with mock arms; gymnastics and military games; preparation for close combat; skiing)	52	52	48	152
Marksmanship	19	19	34	62
Tactical training (soldier as scout, lookout, messenger; reconnaissance patrols; soldier in the attack and on the defense; action against tanks)	15	16	16	47
Chemical defense	3	2	1	6
Acquaintance with the types of troops	5	5	5	15
Red Army and Russian military past history	5	5	5	15
Total	99	99	99	297

Figure 14. Time allotted military instruction in the 5th, 6th, and 7th grades.

and sports, grenade throwing, crawling, creeping, and jumping; obstacle courses; hand-to-hand combat; bicycling, motorcycling, and jumping from parachute towers.

Weapons training: Automatic rifle, pistol, anti-tank grenades, machine guns, mortars, dry run and firing of rifles, and sniper technique.

Tactical training: Squad and platoon in the attack, in defense, in reconnaissance, and on patrol; topography; orientation, use of entrenching tool; entrenchment; construction of trenches; camouflage; and orientation on basic type of troop types by means of tours to military schools, airdromes, and army units.

Chemical training: Chemical agents; individual chemical defense; gas mask drill.

Marching: Marches of from 5 to 12 miles.

In addition to study during the school terms, youths in the eight and nine grades and the equivalent first and second year in *tekhnikums* must spend 2 weeks in summer camps. Here, they undergo a special program of training in formations, topography, and tactics under field conditions. They fire standard rifles and perform practical work in field fortifications.

The 669 hours of military instruction given to pupils during the eighth, ninth, and tenth grades are distributed as shown in Figure 15.

5. MILITARY TRAINING FOR GIRLS

The training program for girls in the first four grades is the same as for boys. From the fifth through the seventh grades, sanitation and hygiene are added to unit training and the firing of small-caliber rifles. The curriculum for girls in the last 3 years of secondary schools and *tekhnikums* includes the training of sanitation workers; the elementary training of radio, telegraph, and telephone operators; small unit drill; gymnastics; and

Subject	Hours of Training					
	Eighth Grade or I Tekhnikum		Ninth Grade or II Tekhnikum		Tenth Grade or III Tekhnikum	Totals (for 3 years)
	School term	Summer camp	School term	Summer camp		
Tactical training	35	61	35	64	46	241
Firing	25	40	25	37	31	158
In-ranks training	45	15	45	15	60	180
Chemical training	4	4	4	4	5	21
Red Army regulations	3	0	3	0	3	9
Acquaintance with other types of troops	5	0	5	0	5	15
Red Army and Soviet military history	15	0	15	0	15	45
Total	132	120	132	120	165	669

Figure 15. Time allotted military instruction in 8th, 9th, and 10th grades.

the firing of small-caliber rifles. To facilitate the training of girls, coeducation above the fifth grade was abolished.

The military instruction given to girls during the fifth through the tenth grades is divided as in Figure 16.

Subject	Hours of Training			
	Fifth to seventh grades	Eighth and ninth grades and I, II Tekhnikums	Tenth grade and III Tekhnikum	Total (for 6 years)
Marksmanship........	48	30	15	93
Formations and gymnastics...........	165	104	52	321
Specialist training....	60	100	83	243
Chemical...........	9			
Red Army and Soviet military history....	15	30	15	60
Total........	297	264	165	726

Figure 16. Time allotted military instruction for girls.

Section III. CONSCRIPT TRAINING

1. GENERAL

Conscripts taken into the ranks of the active army are assimilated into regular tactical units and given their basic training at regular posts and stations. Periodic training at schools and at training centers for those on long-term furlough is conducted in separate training units, with the exception of trial mobilizations. In the latter case, the conscripts also are trained in regular tactical units.

In peacetime, basic training is conducted in two periods totaling 1 year, at the end of which the soldier is considered experienced. A second year was spent on advanced tactical problems in battalions and regiments. During World War II, the basic training period was reduced to 3 months.

2. PROCESSING OF CONSCRIPTS

Upon completion of physical examination and induction, recruits are issued equipment and are segregated for 10 days. During this period the soldier is familiarized with general regulations, studies the insignia of military and political officers of the Red Army and Navy, receives sanitation instruction, is trained in accordance with the schedule of the day, and in the care of uniforms and equipment. Then he is assigned to duty.

3. FIRST PERIOD OF TRAINING

The first period of unit training consists of: combat training, political training, physical training, administrative training, sanitation, and veterinary training. The soldier then takes the oath of allegiance, usually on the Red Army Day, May 1. Since February 1939, the oath has been taken and signed individually, instead of collectively, to increase the sense of responsibility of the citizen-soldier to his country. After taking the oath, the soldier is considered indoctrinated, whereas more reliance is placed on him, and he is given greater responsibilities as he passes into the second period of training.

4. SECOND PERIOD OF TRAINING

The second period includes, in addition to the above subjects, study and practice in guard duty, tactical training on sand tables, field practice in the problems of the individual soldier, and tactical training of small infantry units.

5. ADVANCED TRAINING

Advanced training is provided for soldiers in the technical arms and services. The experienced soldier studies combat training in companies, battalions, and regiments. There are tactical exercises, including combat practice firing, for units and elements. All enlisted men take examinations in combat training at the end of the course. Advanced training also includes political training, general education, disciplinary education, and participation in political activities.

Section IV. NONCOMMISSIONED OFFICER TRAINING

1. ORGANIZATION

The noncommissioned officer schools are, in general, similar to regimental noncommissioned officer schools of the U. S. Army.

The typical infantry noncommissioned officer school staff includes three senior lieutenants, one lieutenant, and one political officer. The 145 selected students are organized into three rifle platoons and one machinegun platoon. Three months of basic training and political reliability are prerequisites.

The students generally are selected from among volunteers. Because heavy demands are made on the trainees, and because noncommissioned officers are obligated to spend 3 years on active duty as against 2 years for privates, many do not wish to enter the school on a voluntary basis. Thus, selected privates frequently are required to attend. The school is segregated from the rest of the regiment and conditions in it are better than those for enlisted men in the rest of the unit.

2. INSTRUCTION

The noncommisioned officer training period before World War II was 9 months, divided into three equal periods. At the beginning of the war with Germany, the instruction was reduced to 3 months. The working day, however, was increased from 8 hours to between 10 and 12 hours; thus, the program of instruction remained substantially the same.

> Political training.
> Tactical training.
> Formations.
> Firing.
> General education.
> Engineering.
> Red Army regulations.
> Signal communications.
> Chemical defense.
> Aviation familiarization.
> Artillery.
> Medical.
> Accounting.
> Administration.

Tactical infantry training includes detailed instruction in individual offense, defense, and reconnaissance. The offensive problems are worked out by the Commander of the Section with every student individually. They include selection of cover; planning of routes for successive rushes to covered positions, camouflage, crawling, etc.; mutual fire support in combat; attacking enemy trenches; throwing hand grenades; bayonet training; consolidating of a position; and reconnaissance by observation of enemy fire. Training in defense consists of selection and organization of a firing position; visual reconnaissance and the preparation of reports; preparation of coordinated mortar fires; preparations for night harassing fires; preparation for the attack; disengagement maneuvers; defense of encircled

positions; and evacuation of casualties. Training of the individual soldier in reconnaissance includes preparation for reconnaissance missions, briefing, observation, action of patrols in contact with isolated enemy elements, methods of locating enemy firing positions, night patrolling, and the handling of prisoners.

All three of the above phases include instruction in gun and crew drill, sniper techniques, gunnery, and grenade throwing.

The Signal Communications Noncommissioned Officer School of each infantry division may be considered typical of noncommissioned schools of the arms. It is operated in conjunction with the division's independent Signal Communications Battalion. Its mission is to train radiomen, telephone personnel, aviation signalmen, and noncommissioned officers and specialists.

The school is staffed by enlisted men who have completed a minimum of 6 to 7 years of school. Particular care is exercised in the selection of radiomen, a specialty requiring good background and political reliability. The peacetime training term varies between 8 months and 1 year.

The training program includes the following subjects:

> Political indoctrination.
> Red Army regulations.
> Physical training.
> Drill.
> Topography.
> Weapons training.
> Engineering.
> Infantry training.
> Range firing.
> Chemical warfare training.
> Sanitary-medical training.
> Tactics.
> Special tactical training (technical radio; telegraphy; technical study of radio, telephone, telegraph and other apparatus, switch-boards, transmitters, and receivers, wiring diagrams of telephone network, etc.; study of documents, logs, etc.; practical work).
> Establishing communications lines.
> Construction.
> Aviation signal training.
> Signaling.

Section V. OFFICER TRAINING

1. GENERAL

The education system for officers of the Red Army is based largely upon academies, schools, and extension or correspondence courses. The Voroshilov, or General Staff, Academy is the highest of the institutions, followed by the Frunze Academy and the academies and schools of the arms and services. The courses offered at these institutions are supplemented by secondary school training in the Cadet Schools; by unit training, particularly in special officers' courses; by training period courses for the reserve; and by extension courses for commanders and specialist officers, given locally or by mail.

The officer training system is pyramidal and closely correlated with promotion scales. Initial opportunities are broad, but further advancement is highly competitive. Admission to officer candidate schools is open to men from 17 to 22 years of age who have completed 8 years of school and have passed entrance examinations. The examinations are waived when higher educational qualifications can be proven.

Commissions are also available to personnel from the ranks and to suitably qualified civilians, especially those with the technical training demanded by one of the arms.

2. MILITARY PREPARATORY SCHOOLS

Military training modeled on the pattern of the Czarist Cadet Corps recently was established in the U. S. S. R. The reconstruction decree of 22 August 1943 created a Section for Suvorov Military Schools in the Main Administration of Military Educational Institutions of the Red Army, and provided for the establishment of nine Suvorov schools (named after Alexander Suvorov, the Russian 18th century army leader) in the towns of regions and territories liberated from the Germans. There are now 12 such schools.

The Suvorov schools (and similar naval schools named for Admiral Nakhimov) have as their primary mission the training of young boys for service in the armed forces. Students successfully completing the course with excellent or good grades and with good conduct records may enter military schools for officers without entrance examinations. Graduates may, however, enter any higher institu-

tion of learning and prepare for whatever profession they choose.

The schools, each of which has an enrollment of 500, accept males 10 years of age or older, for a 7-year course. As an exception, in 1943, the Suvorov schools enrolled pupils from 8 to 13, inclusive. They are open to orphans of Red Army men and Partisans or to sons of veterans of the Soviet-German war. Many of the students themselves participated in Partisan warfare against the enemy.

The directors of the Suvorov Military Schools are major generals. Either lieutenant colonels or majors command the separate companies which compose each school. The students of each of the seven main classes are divided into four companies. Each company, in turn, consists of educational sections of 25 students each. At the head of each educational section is an officer-instructor, who accompanies the same group of students as it advances from one class to another until graduation. An experienced sergeant major assists the officer-instructor.

Along with general secondary school subjects, the students of the Suvorov schools study tactics, rifle training, the Soviet constitution, Red Army regulations, military history, drill, horsemanship, automobiles and motorcycle operation, gymnastics, fencing, swimming, skiing, music, and dancing. To graduate, each student must speak two foreign languages, English and either French or German. Neither smoking nor drinking is countenanced. Profanity and abusive speech are banned. Military discipline and courtesy are stressed.

During the summer months, the four senior classes are sent to outdoor camps for practical application of the military knowledge gained during the year.

The pupils of the Suvorov Military Schools wear special military uniforms and observe all military regulations. On their epaulets, they bear the initial letter of their school. Food is of the highest quality. The individual ration is even larger than that of adult workers.

Although the Suvorov and Nakhimov schools represent a new element in the preparatory training of officer candidates, they merely supplement other schools which serve a similar purpose. Since 1938, the Commissariat of Education of the Russian S. S. R. has operated special artillery and military aviation schools, which prepare candidates for enrollment in schools of the Red Army. These special secondary schools offer 3-year courses, upon completion of which the students go on to regular Red Army officer schools. The Commissariat of the Navy also maintains naval preparatory schools for youths from 15 to 16, which prepare them to enter a regular naval academy. Students in these schools live and study at state expense.

3. SCHOOLS OF THE ARMS

As of January 1944, there were 123 infantry schools, 22 machine gun and mortar schools, 38 armored force schools, 9 cavalry schools, 58 artillery schools, 7 chemical schools, 13 signal communications schools, and 13 political schools. In scope of instruction, these schools are a combination of the U. S. Army branch schools and the U. S. Military Academy. They are administered in a manner similar to that of the U. S. Military Academy and the status of the cadets is almost identical. Courses are of 2 years duration (lowered to 6 months during World War II) and graduates become junior lieutenants of their respective branches. Entrance requirements are general education equivalent at least to that of an eighth-grade class, mental and physical acceptability, single marital status, and, during World War II, age between 17 and 22.

Those desiring a commission may make application either to the commandant of the particular school desired or to the Military Commissar of the *Rayon* or *Oblast*. Noncommissioned officers in the army may apply to their commanders. Graduates are assigned to units for active duty. Further military education is highly selective.

4. ACADEMIES

Officers who have been commissioned for at least 4 years, who have been with troops at least 1 year, and who are not more than 35 years of age are eligible for appointment to the academy of their respective arm or service. The courses represent a combination of those of the U. S. Army advanced branch schools and the Command and General Staff School. In peacetime, they are of 3 years duration. Graduates are assigned as battalion or regimental commanders.

At the beginning of World War II, there were 16 military academies and 9 military faculties attached to civilian institutes, all operating under the direc-

Subject	Hours		
	First course	Second course	Total
Political subjects............	300	230	530
Tactics....................	300	380	680
Artillery....................	350	440	790
Topography................	200	140	340
Supply unit of artillery......	60	70	130
Communications............	30	50	80
Handling of arms..........	90	90	180
Military-engineer work......	30	40	70
Line preparation............	40	40	80
Physical preparation........	40	40	80
Artillery instrumental reconnaissance.................	20	20	40
Manuals...................	20	..	20
Use of autos and horses......	50	60	110
Chemical work.............	20	20	40
Individual arms............	30	40	70
Sanitation.................	10	..	10
Russian language...........	50	20	70
Mathematics...............	60	50	110
Physics and mechanics.......	30	20	50
Chemistry.................	30	20	50
Gunnery..................	40	40	80
	1,800	1,800	3,600
Reserve time........	32	32	64
	1,832	1,832	3,664

Figure 17. Distribution of study hours by subject at an artillery school.

tion of the Main Administration of Military Educational Institutions of the Commissariat of Defense. The academies were located as follows:

The Frunze Academy_____ Moscow
Lenin Military-Political Academy_____ Moscow
Dzerzhinski Artillery Academy_____ Moscow
Zhukovski Military Aviation_____ Moscow
Military Veterinary Academy_____ Moscow
Kuibishev Military Engineering Academy_____ Moscow
Flight Command Academy, Military Air Forces_ Moscow
Kirov Military Medical Academy_____ Leningrad
Military Medical Academy_____ Kuibishev
Stalin Military Academy of Mechanization and Motorization _____ Moscow
Higher Military Pedagogical Institute_____ Kalinin
Kaganovich Military Transport Academy_____ Leningrad
Voroshilov Academy of Chemical Defense_____ Moscow
Molotov Quartermaster Academy_____ Kharkov
Budenny Military Electrotechnical Academy____ Leningrad
Military Juridical Academy_____ Moscow

In addition to performing their primary task of training battalion and regimental commanders for the various arms and services, the military academies carry on research work in their various specialties. They assist in the development of new weapons, equipment, and tactics, and are responsible for the dissemination of the latest information to officers in the field. Of particular importance is their function of conducting and supervising the correspondence courses for officers on active duty. This has been of considerable significance in raising the standards of officers of the arms, large numbers of whom have received their training for higher command duties in such courses.

5. FRUNZE ACADEMY

The Frunze Academy is the oldest high-level military educational establishment of the U. S. S. R. It corresponds to the U. S. Command and General Staff School, and its graduates serve as regimental commanders and division or corps staff officers.

Officers over 35 years of age rarely are admitted. Officers are selected from all arms, and before World War II were required to have served 4 to 6 years with line units of the Red Army. Especially distinguished records in their regiments, a secondary school education, and a knowledge of either English, French, German, Polish, Japanese, Turkish or Persian are prerequisites.

Entrance examinations cover tactics, Red Army regulations, topography, and general education. They require from 1 to 2 years of thorough preparation. Candidates are granted from 1 to 2 months leave for final preparation. The first part of the examination is held at the military district headquarters in the presence of Academy representatives. It is both written and oral. Examination papers are sent to Moscow, where those qualified to take the second part of the examination are selected. The second examination is held at the Academy and lasts for about 1 month. In addition, candidates appear before a special commission which investigates their political background. After the second examination, candidates return to their units to await notification of acceptance.

Studies are pursued in the Academy under the direction of various departments, or "faculties," such as the physics and chemistry faculty, the military history faculty, the tactics faculty, the faculty of general military education, and the faculty of intelligence. The tactics faculty receives the greatest emphasis. Approximately 30 percent of the student's time is allotted to tactics. The first year deals largely with the tactics and techniques of the separate arms. The course offers all information required for the conduct of combined operations, including operations, supply, and advanced studies of logistics.

Academic instruction is supplemented not only by field exercises during summer months, but by realistic, simulated field conditions in classrooms of the Academy.

The Frunze Academy is equipped with more than 100 laboratories and indoor ranges. The laboratories include equipment for the study of aviation, chemistry, artillery tactics, strategy, military history, mechanization, motorization, camouflage, electronics, searchlights, and hydrotechnics. Indoor ranges include ranges for field artillery, antiaircraft artillery, machine guns, and aircraft armament.

The aviation laboratory includes much complex equipment. Elaborate command exercises are conducted in the central hall of the laboratory. The hall is equipped with air-to-air command posts suspended from the ceiling, with a moving landscape beneath them. Simulated speed and altitudes can be controlled. The officer practicing command must cope with the dictates of the changing situation depicted on the moving landscape.

During World War II, the program of the Academy was modified to meet the increased demand for graduates. The length of the course, and particularly of the training period, was reduced. Secondary subjects were dropped from the curriculum. Special attention was given to rapid orientation, to accurate but rapid evaluation of military situations and to operations against the enemy's flank and rear. Increased emphasis was placed on enemy tactics and on intelligence and reconnaissance methods. Tactics in confined sectors and encircled positions also received added emphasis. Student officers were taught to handle enemy as well as Soviet weapons.

Of the new students admitted during World War II, more than 70 percent had previously received university or higher technical education. The great majority was less than 35 years of age.

Since World War II, all students of the Frunze Academy have been taking part in research conducted by the instructors. The lessons of World War II are being analyzed and studied, and instruction is based largely on tactical lessons learned in combat. The Academy also issues a monthly information bulletin, in which combat experiences of the Red Army are developed and instructional notes and lessons are drawn from the experiences of foreign armies. Fifty instructors and an editorial staff are preparing an album and atlas describing the operations of 1941–1945. The Academy has a special room in which the history of World War II is displayed graphically. A series of bi-monthly conferences on major operations are conducted. The transition from defensive to offensive strategy and the pursuit, encirclement, and destruction of enemy forces, as illustrated in the campaigns of 1944, are under particularly close study in these conferences.

6. VOROSHILOV ACADEMY

The highest school for officers of the Red Army is the Voroshilov, or the General Staff, Academy, comparable to the War College of the U.S. Army. The academy prepares senior officers, usually general officers, for duty as division and higher commanders or as staff officers of armies or higher formations.

The basic course at the academy lasts for 2 years. One hundred students are enrolled in each class. In addition, 100 qualified officers are assigned each year to attend special classes designed to improve the general and military education of the general officers of the Red Army. Thus, 300 students are enrolled in this academy each year.

The content of courses at the Voroshilov Academy is prescribed by the Chief of the General Staff, and generally includes the tactical, operational, and strategic employment of large formations. In 1940, the Chief of the General Staff, Marshal Shaposhnikov, directed that the following subjects be emphasized in the Academy during the academic year of 1940–41:

> "Clear understanding of the nature of modern combat and employment of massed tanks, artillery, and aircraft; control of combat involving complicated maneuver; skill in preparing tactical and operational estimates; and mastery of staff techniques for large formations."

The course of the special class covers the same subjects as the regular course but it has fewer theoretical, and no field problems.

The methods of instruction employed at the academy are individual and group solution of assigned problems, lectures, panel discussions, and field exercises. The field exercises are conducted during the summer session. They consist of 〓〓〓〓〓 and

reconnaissance of terrain; the tactical or operational decision of the commander, and theoretical solutions of the resulting staff and logistical problems; and participation in command or staff functions during the fall exercises of the field units.

There is no age qualification for assignment to the Voroshilov Academy. The candidates for both the regular and special courses are appointed by the military districts according to the number of appointments allotted by the Main Personnel Administration of the Peoples' Commissariat of Defense. The assignments are approved by the Chief of Staff. The candidates for the regular course must be graduates of the Frunze Academy, or of the higher academies of the specialized arms and services. They must have had at least 2 years' experience as staff officers of large field formations, or in one of the administrations of the Commissariat of Defense. The candidates for the special course are selected from the commanders of divisions and higher formations. They need not be graduates of higher academies of the arms or of the Frunze Academy.

The graduates of the regular course are assigned as follows:

> Chiefs of staff of rifle corps.
> Chiefs of the Operations Division of the staff of military districts, armies, or army groups.
> Chiefs of the Intelligence Section of the above staffs.
> Chiefs of the Mobilization Administration or Chiefs of Signal Communications of the General Staff.
> Chiefs of the Operations or Intelligence Divisions of the General Staff.
> Instructors in tactics and operations of other academies.
> Military research with the Voroshilov Academy.

The graduates of the special course are assigned as commanders of divisions and higher formations.

In addition to its instructional functions, the Voroshilov Academy of the General Staff conducts extensive research on military subjects, which often results in recommendations for changes in the Field Service Regulations of the various arms and services of the Red Army. This research also forms the basis of articles published in the "Journal of Military Thought," the journal of the Academy.

CHAPTER III

FIELD ORGANIZATIONS

INTRODUCTION

1. PREWAR FIELD ORGANIZATIONS

Immediately prior to the outbreak of the war with Germany, the highest active field organization in the Red Army was the military district. Each military district was responsible for the administrative, mobilization, and command functions of its specific geographic area. The Finnish War, for example, was conducted by the Leningrad Military District.

The highest tactical organization of the military district was the corps. The rifle corps consisted of headquarters, three to four rifle divisions, one or two regiments of corps artillery, an antiaircraft artillery group, a signal battalion, a chemical warfare battalion, an air reconnaissance squadron, and various service units, all making a total of 60,000 to 65,000 men. The cavalry corps included headquarters, two to three cavalry divisions, a howitzer regiment, a mechanized brigade, an engineer and a signal battalion, and service troops, totaling about 20,000 men. The moto-mechanized corps, then still in the experimental stage, comprised headquarters, two mechanized brigades, a motorized infantry machine gun brigade, an engineer company, a chemical warfare company, a flight of reconnaissance aircraft, and minor service units, totaling about 12,000 troops.

The principal ground formations were the rifle, cavalry, and artillery divisions, and the moto-mechanized and the tank brigades. The rifle division consisted of headquarters, three rifle regiments, two artillery regiments (a mixed field artillery and a howitzer regiment), a reconnaissance, a light tank, an antitank, an engineer, a signal, and a medical battalion, an antiaircraft machine gun company, a field hospital, and services (figs. 1 and 2).

The cavalry division included headquarters, four horse cavalry regiments, one mechanized cavalry regiment, a mixed artillery regiment, an engineer squadron, a signal group, an air reconnaissance squadron, and service units. The strength of a cavalry division was 7,000 men. It had 64 light tanks and 16 armored cars. Its principal weapons consisted of sixteen 76-mm guns, eight 122-mm howitzers and sixteen 76-mm howitzers, and eight 45-mm and 37-mm antitank guns.

Four artillery divisions were reported. Their organization was believed to be as follows: headquarters, one light artillery regiment, two heavy artillery regiments, one antiaircraft artillery regiment, and various services.

The moto-mechanized brigade consisted of headquarters, three tank battalions, a reconnaissance battalion, an infantry battalion, a motorized artillery battalion, a troop transport battalion, special troops, and services. Its strength was 3,300 men. Is principal armament consisted of twelve 76-mm guns, one hundred and sixty light and medium (10-ton) tanks, nineteen tankettes, and tweny-four armored cars.

The tank brigade consisted of headquarters, three tank battalions of heavier tanks (T28 and T35), and a security battalion which was comprised of a signal company, an engineer company, an antiaircraft machine gun company, a traffic control company, and a brigade park.

2. UNDERLYING FACTORS IN MODIFICATION OF THE ORGANIZATION OF THE RED ARMY, 1941–44

The factors which influenced changes in organization of the Red Army units and formations included: combat lessons learned in the Finnish War and the war with Germany, initial weakness and subsequent growth of the officers' corps, necessity to halt the advance of the German Army, huge losses of personnel and matériel in 1941, decreased output of factories in the early years of the war, and subsequent abundance of matériel.

The war with Finland proved several things to the Soviet high command. It showed that the

Figure 1. Table of Organization and Equipment of the principal field units of the Red Army.

Unit	O & EM	7.62-mm SA R, R, & Cbn	7.62-mm SMG	7.62-mm LMG	7.62-mm HvMG	12.7-mm AAMG	14.5-mm ATR	50-mm Mort	82-mm Mort	120-mm Mort	37-mm AA G	45-mm or 57-mm AT G	76-mm G & How	85-mm AA G	122-mm How	122-mm G	152-mm How	152-mm G/How	132-mm RL	Flame Thrower	T-34/85 Tk	SU 85 (85-mm) SP (G)	SU 152 (152-mm) SP G/How	Armd C	Armd Pers Carr	Trac	Tlr	Trk	Sp Veh	H-dr Veh	H	Kl	Rad
R Corps	32,400	19,200	7,775	1,645	405	63	750	108	249	63		150	96		24		24								15	221	196	861	257	1,830	5,319	225	390
R Div	9,619	5,426	2,398	522	135	18	218	56	83	21		50	36		12											21	12	160	66	610	1,773	63	56
Tk Corps	17,964	7,180	2,963	415	47	55	217		52	42	16	46	48						8	10	200	20	20	31	43	41	24	1,336	241			78	470
Mecz Corps	17,457	10,098	4,900	731	109	9	375		100	54	16	52	64						8	10	192	20	20	48	35	25	24	1,878	217			100	525
Mtz R Brig	3,298	1,707	955	165	35	74	81		30	6		12	12								65			7	10	11		299	30			17	44
Tk Brig	1,306	692	300	25		44	24		6			4	4								83	20		3				115	21			9	93
Cav Corps	18,720	12,234	6,175	616	137	24	400	108	108	56	34	48	96	16		12	24	24	8							38	294	854	168	1,316	14,503	130	271
Arty Div	9,743	7,907	1,215	144	144	64	288			108	48		72		48	12										262	72	1,103	12			90	294
AAA Div	2,043	1,541	456			9																				16		278	50			11	41
L Arty Brig	2,063	1,772	255	36		3	72						72				24									18	136	280	36			25	82
L How Brig	2,242	1,892	362	36		9	72								48			24								158		214	18			24	78
Medium G Brig	2,128	1,396	308	18			36									12										86	76	191	35			17	66
120-mm Mort Brig	1,705	1,397	135	54		3	108			108																		268				16	52
Rkt Regt	808	656	104	15		6													24									110				4	20

Figure 2. Changes in strength and equipment of the Rifle Division 1939–1945.

Date	Off	EM	Total O & EM	7.62-mm SA R, R, & Cbn	7.62-mm SMG	7.62-mm LMG	7.62-mm HvMG	12.7-mm AAMG	14.5-mm ATR	50-mm Mort	82-mm Mort	107-mm Mort	120-mm Mort	37-mm AA G	45- or 57-mm AT G	76-mm G & How	76.2-mm AA G	122-mm How	132-mm How	RL	Flame Thrower	Rad	Mtrcl	Armd C	T-38 Tk	Trac	Trk	H-dr Veh	H	Kl
13 Sept 1939	650	18,191	18,841	17,713		578	162	33		81	18	12			54	42	4	28					145	12	38	92	725	2,177	6,208	140
5 Apr 1941	792	13,662	14,454	12,318	1,195	392	166	33		84	54		12		54	16	4	20	12		30		16	13	16	99	586	888	2,033	96
29 July 1941	465	10,225	10,790	10,201	162	162	108	9	60	54	18		6		18	16	4	8	12		30		4			5	200	797	2,468	57
6 Dec 1941	671	10,225	11,907	10,627	552	251	108	12	18	72	72		36		18	16		12			60		4			16	243	868	2,640	85
18 Mar 1942	729	11,236	12,813	8,875	639	352	114	9	81	76	76		18	4	30	20		12			60		4			15	154	729	1,858	81
28 July 1942		12,084	10,566	8,854	712	338	139		279	85	85		21	6	48	32		12				59	4			15	150	721	1,804	64
12 Dec 1942			9,447	8,491	2,200	512	135		228	56	83		24	6	50	32		12				71	4			15	167	642	1,840	56
12 Dec 1942 (Guards Div)			10,556	5,984	2,698	507	162		212	60	85			6	52	36		12		8		59	4			24	175	699	1,968	62
June 1944–May 1945			9,619	5,426	2,398	522	135	18	279	56	83		21		50	36		12					4			21	226	610	1,803	56

organization of higher tactical units was too un-wieldly, and that a generous allotment of armor, technical services, and arms to the rifle divisions often resulted in the needless dilution of these reinforcements. The dispersal of these special units along the entire front made difficult the concentration of armor, artillery, engineers and other technical arms and services in a decisive sector. Thus, the major changes in organization—such as the reduction in size of the rifle division, and the concentration of special and technical forces in GHQ units—were initiated in April 1941. Although these changes were retarded and modified by other factors, they were carried out during the first 2 years of the war with Germany.

As a result of rapid expansion of the field forces, and initial heavy losses of officer personnel, many Red Army formations in 1941 were commanded by officers inadequately trained to employ efficiently the many specialized arms, services, and heavy weapons assigned to their formations. The lack of a sufficient number of adequately trained officers necessitated the creation of manageable units which could be commanded by men of common sense and strong character, but lacking in highly specialized training.

The command of heavy weapons, for example, could not be entrusted to the officers then in command. As a result, most infantry heavy weapons, and many specialized arms and services from infantry, cavalry, and armored formations, were withdrawn and made independent. This reorganization not only placed specialized arms and services under competent leadership, but also effected considerable economy of equipment and personnel. Reduction in size of the field units, and simplification of their organization, simplified logistical problems and made these units more efficient even when commanded by inexperienced officers.

During the early years of the war, the Soviet high command was primarily concerned with halting the German advance. This necessitated the activation of new units and the reorganization of depleted units when sufficient time could not be allotted for the training of large formations. Simultaneously, Soviet industry was redeploying to the east, curtailing or stopping production of some items of armament and equipment. These factors resulted in the formation of a large number of rifle, tank, and mechanized brigades instead of divisions, and in the creation of emergency organizations such as the marine rifle brigades and workers brigades and battalions.

During the first year of the war, a great mixture of organizations existed. Side by side in the surviving regular divisions were reserve and emergency organizations of varying size and composition. Much of their armament was obsolete.

3. RESULTS OF REORGANIZATION

The developments in the organization of units were carried out logically, quickly, and thoroughly, as were all other combat lessons which the Russians learned, and adapted to their own use, during the war.

An increasing number of re-equipped, fully manned, and trained units appeared in the winter of 1942-43 and, especially, after July 1943. The outlines of a new Red Army organization, its basic doctrines of 1941 considerably modified by combat experience, were generally clear in the winter of 1943-44. Since 1941, the major modifications in ground organizations have been toward increasing the mobility and fire power of the rifle, cavalry, and armored units and formations; the centralizing of supporting arms and services, and their groupment into independent units. Basic units with standard Tables of Organization have become the foundation for a wide range of temporary combat groupings of basic and specialized arms and services, as prescribed by tactical requirements.

Army Groups (Fronts) have superseded the military districts as the main planning and administrative agencies under the Supreme Command. This change was anticipated in the Soviet theory and training doctrines as early as 1934. Military districts are maintained in rear areas only, where they perform the special missions of local security, troop mobilization and training, and control of traffic and supplies.

Armies superseded corps in controlling combined operations, handling administration for, and servicing their component formations and units.

The organization of rifle corps was changed several times. During the retreat of the Red Army, the rifle corps were eliminated. Armies controlled the rifle divisions directly. During subsequent offensive operations, the rifle corps reappeared as the forward headquarters for tactical control of rifle divisions. During the last year of the war, rifle corps became a more permanent organization. The rifle corps lost an antiaircraft artillery battalion and a chemical warfare company. It gained a tank destroyer artillery regiment and a rocket battalion or regiment.

The cavalry corps became a powerful, balanced team. Its light howitzer regiment was replaced by a more mobile heavy mortar regiment. It gained a self-propelled artillery regiment, an antiaircraft automatic weapons regiment, and a rocket battalion.

The moto-mechanized corps disappeared. In its place, two new organizations, the tank corps and the mechanized corps, were developed. The tank corps consists primarily of tanks supported by motorized infantry. The mechanized corps consists primarily of motorized infantry supported by tanks. Both the tank and the mechanized corps are supported by powerful organic artillery comprised of self-propelled, tank destroyer, mortar, antiaircraft, and rocket units.

Artillery corps, controlling several artillery divisions reinforced by independent brigades and regiments, appeared in 1944. Four artillery corps were identified in the spring of 1945.

The rifle division has been drastically reduced in strength. In April 1941, it was reduced from 18,841 to 14,454 officers and enlisted men. Its basic size of approximately 10,000 was determined in July 1941. The reduction in size was accomplished by eliminating the light tank battalion, the howitzer artillery regiment, and the mechanized reconnaissance elements, and by a reduction in the size of service units. The divisional hospital, for example, was taken over by the army. At the same time, the forward fire power of the rifle division has been increased by a generous allotment to the rifle regiments of submachine guns, machine guns, and mortars. Thus, the 1945 rifle division, as compared with the 1939 rifle division, has a reduced reconnaissance ability and weaker replacement capacity, but it has better tactical and strategic mobility. With normal artillery attachment, it has greater fire power.

Artillery divisions have greatly increased in number and size. They now include 24 to 30 firing battalions, organized into brigades and regiments. The number, type, and caliber of weapons in the component brigades and regiments are determined by the mission of the division.

Cavalry divisions lost a mechanized and a horse regiment. Mortars, submachine guns, and antitank rifles, however, have been introduced in large number, increasing the forward fire power of the division and improving its local antitank and antiaircraft defense.

The mechanized and motorized infantry machine gun brigades were discontinued. The mechanized brigade (formerly called moto-mechanized) tank strength has been reduced to 40 medium tanks, and its reconnaissance battalion to a company. It is now a balanced team of motorized infantry, tanks, and supporting artillery. The tank brigade has been better balanced. A great many artillery brigades, both independent and as parts of artillery divisions, have appeared.

4. PROBABLE FUTURE TRENDS

The indications of future trends discussed below are based on fragmentary information and represent possible developments. The speed with which these changes are likely to take place will vary considerably between the various arms and services.

Tactical units of the Red Army were evolved during the course of the war with Germany and have been proved in combat. Basic changes in the organization of infantry and cavalry divisions, and of tank and mechanized corps, are not expected. However, the development of new weapons, and improvements on existing models, will lead to adjustments within the frameworks of standard organizations. Some of the weapons which will influence changes in Tables of Organization of the Soviet ground formations include the new 100-mm high-velocity gun, the 160-mm heavy mortar, powerful light antitank and antiaircraft weapons for infantry and cavalry, and increases in caliber of self-propelled artillery, rockets, and guided missiles.

Reduction in the size of the army, elimination of combat losses of specialized equipment and personnel, plus ample time for production of necessary equipment and training of specialists, will make it possible to increase the quality of technicians within the standard units of the Red Army. An increase in the number of specialized GHQ units may also be expected. It is not expected that signal, ordnance, motor maintenance, medical, and engineer units will be larger. It is not anticipated that motorization will be effected in infantry and cavalry formations and units. There may be slight increase in the number of organic motor vehicles.

Although airborne troops were not used on a large scale during the war with Germany, it is expected that further development of this arm will be stressed. Together with the growth of the airborne arm, the Red Army will improve the training and equipment of airdrome engineers.

There is evidence that the engineer arm will become more independent, and that large engineer units such as divisions and brigades may be organized.

a. Infantry and cavalry. Future changes in over-all organization of infantry and cavalry units and formations will probably be conservative. However, certain changes within the larger framework may be expected. For example, persistent though unconfirmed reports in the winter of 1945–46 have mentioned motorized rifle divisions with tanks (in 1941 the Red Army had two motorized rifle divisions which were later disbanded). It is likely that the antitank rifle will be replaced by a light, powerful, rocket-type or recoilless weapon. Antiaircraft defense of front-line troops may be augmented by light rocket-firing devices. The fire power of the rifle battalion will be increased by substitution of 57-mm antitank guns for the 45-mm antitank guns and by increasing the number of battalion 82-mm mortars from nine to twelve. The 50-mm company mortar will be eliminated. Regimental artillery will probably undergo changes. The regimental 120-mm mortar battery may have four instead of seven mortars. The antitank battery may have six 76-mm guns instead of six 45-mm antitank guns. It is likely that the divisional artillery of both the rifle and the cavalry divisions will have a heavy mortar unit and a second 122-mm to 152-mm howitzer-artillery regiment, by attachment if not organically. The present artillery regiment already has been strengthened, and will be used in RCT role.

b. Artillery. There probably will be a marked difference between corps artillery and artillery of the higher formations (armies, Fronts, and GHQ) in type of weapons, and in their employment. Corps artillery probably will continue to be organized into brigades and regiments, and will absorb most of the light and medium artillery which is at present controlled by higher formations. It will be used for direct support of ground operations. Newly developed weapons, such as long-range rockets, guided missiles, super long-range guns, and the present heavy artillery (made for the most part self-propelled), will be organized into artillery corps, divisions, brigades, and independent regiments. Control of these units will be retained by the High Command, which will assign them to Fronts and armies for special long-range missions. The new 160-mm mortar gradually will replace the 120-mm mortar in mortar regiments and brigades. It is expected that tank destroyer artillery units will be

armed to an increasing extent with self-propelled weapons, probably the new 100-mm guns.

c. Tanks. At the end of the war with Germany, the proportion of heavy to medium tanks in the Red Army was approximately 1 to 5. It is believed that the intention is to increase the number of heavy tanks, and to manufacture light reconnaissance tanks so that the ratio of medium, heavy, and light tanks will be 4 to 3 to 1. In order to maintain such a ratio, and at the same time preserve logistical requirements of the present tank corps, some adjustment in the structure of the tank brigades will be necessary. A possible organization of the tank components of the tank corps will be as follows: reconnaissance battalion with 25 light tanks, and three tank brigades with four medium tank companies of 10 medium tanks each and four heavy tank companies of 5 heavy tanks each (plus 3 headquarters tanks). Such a tank corps would have a total of 214 tanks including 25 light, 60 heavy, and 129 medium tanks.

A possible organization of the tank components of a mechanized corps would include: a reconnaissance battalion with 25 light tanks, a tank brigade with 43 medium and 20 heavy tanks, and three mechanized brigades, each with a mixed tank regiment. The mixed tank regiment would have three medium tank companies with 10 medium tanks each and three heavy tank companies with 5 heavy tanks each (plus 3 medium tanks in headquarters). Such a mechanized corps would have 222 tanks including 25 light, 132 medium, and 65 heavy tanks. The ratio of the heavy to medium tanks in the above organizations is approximately 2 to 1. The remainder of the heavy tank strength probably will continue to be organized into independent heavy tank regiments of 20 tanks each.

Section I. ARMY GROUPS, ARMIES, AND CORPS

1. ARMY GROUP (FRONT)

The Army Group (Front) is the basic planning and administrative organization. The size of its sector is determined by lines of communication. It contains and allots tactical and service reserves. It services its combat components, operates the primary axis of supply and evacuation, and coordinates the supporting military districts. The development of the Front was largely governed by logistics. The lack of adequate roads and relative scarcity of railroads in the U. S. S. R. not only brought about a rigid centralized control of transportation, but even determined tactical capabilities. As a result, the basic planning and administrative organizations were delineated by routes of communication, rather than the political boundaries of the military districts.

An Army Group's strength is approximately 1,000,000 men. It is generally commanded by a marshal who is assisted by a military council and staff. The council, presided over by the commander of the front, has three other members. One represents combat arms and services; the second represents rear area services and administration; the third is an officer secretary of the council. If the Front is located within the political boundaries of the U. S. S. R., the secretary of the regional committee of the Communist Party acts as a liaison officer between the military and civil authorities. The military council determines basic policy on organization, training, and administration of the Front. It supervises the execution of the commander's orders. A member of the council countersigns field orders of the commander.

The staff of the Front, consisting of the forward and rear echelons, is controlled by the Chief of Staff. The forward echelon, during combat, includes the (Operations) Staff, the staffs of the Chiefs of Arms and Services, political administration, and the training and personnel departments. The rear echelon includes the service staff, controlled by the deputy commander for rear area, and consisting of chiefs of rear area services, administration for captured matériel, the field post office, and the judge advocates department.

A Front consists of a permanent headquarters, attached service troops, supply and administrative installations, and a variable number of combat formations with their supporting units. Variations in the number and type of major combat formations and supporting units are numerous. A typical active Front has the following major components: four or five infantry armies, one or two tank armies, one or two air armies (1,000 to 1,100 planes each), four artillery divisions, five antiaircraft divisions, five rocket brigades, two independent mortar brigades, four independent heavy artillery brigades, five tank destroyer brigades, two tank corps, one or two mechanized corps, and a cavalry corps.

In addition to the headquarters and staff, a Front has the following service units, whose number is commensurate with the number of the combat components of the Front: engineer construction brigades, bridging battalions, motor transport brigades, signal regiments, road repair regiments, signal intelligence battalions, security battalions, officer replacement regiments, infantry replacement regiments, penal battalions, and maintenance, ammunition, fuel rations, and forage depots.

2. ARMIES

Infantry, tank, shock, and cavalry armies are found in the Red Army. An army is the basic strategic organization of combined arms, including air. Although air divisions normally are not an organic part of the ground army, the artillery commander is responsible for the tactical coordination of the supporting aviation. The army plans, coordinates, and maintains all phases of a continuing operation.

An army consists of a large, permanent headquarters to which are allotted combat troops and services to execute a strategic mission. Theoretically, it is a task force, although in actual practice the major components have been increasingly stable. Considerable variation exists in the composition of the different armies, especially in the number of supporting armored and artillery units which may be allotted to them by the Army Group (Front). Every army consists of headquarters and at least the following service and administrative elements:

1 signal regiment.
1 replacement regiment.
2 engineer construction battalions.
1 flame thrower battalion.
1 chemical warfare battalion.
1 road maintenance battalion.
Field bakeries.
2 reconnaissance battalions.
2 to 4 motor transport battalions.
1 security battalion.
1 penal battalion.
1 ordnance battalion.
Quartermaster depots.
Work shops.

Medical resources of an army include field hospitals in proportion to the number of subordinate formations, two to three evacuation hospitals, three hospitals for slightly wounded, two hospitals for infectious diseases, two veterinary hospitals, and one or two veterinary evacuation hospitals. The service components of an army total 20,000 to 25,000 men.

Major combat components of a typical infantry army include three to four rifle corps, each with three to four rifle divisions; a brigade with 152-mm gun howitzers and 122-mm guns; a tank destroyer regiment; an antiaircraft artillery regiment; and a mortar regiment. Combat engineers are allotted to an army, from the reserve of the Army Group, at the rate of one battalion for each active division.

Tactical components of a tank army vary according to the terrain and the mission. The 3d Guards Tank Army, for example, consisted of two mechanized corps, a tank corps, one light artillery and two heavy gun-howitzer brigades, a tank destroyer brigade, two self-propelled artillery regiments, a rocket regiment, an antiaircraft artillery regiment, and an engineer brigade. Tank armies normally form part of the mobile reserve of the high command, and are committed at a decisive point during major operations. They are generally withdrawn after the operation.

Cavalry armies consisted of two cavalry corps, one mechanized corps, and the normal army troops. Cavalry armies, like the tank armies, constitute GHQ troops and are used to augment other mobile troops.

Shock armies are made up of picked tank and mechanized corps and rifle divisions. They are combined, according to their mission, with artillery, tank, and engineer units to form a powerful assault force which may be shifted from sector to sector for either offense or defense. These armies are retained in the reserve of the high command. Their composition varies not only from one army to another, but the composition of an individual shock army changes according to the situation.

Guards armies may be infantry, tank, cavalry, or shock. The title "Guards" is appended to any army which distinguishes itself in combat. Components of Guards armies are upgraded in personnel and equipment.

3. CORPS

There are two general types of corps in the Red Army, the operational control corps (rifle and artillery) and the mobile corps (tank, mechanized, and cavalry).

The rifle corps is primarily a forward headquarters, with attached supporting troops, for tactical control of two to four rifle divisions. The commander of a rifle corps has no military council. The forward echelon of a rifle corps headquarters consists of the operations, intelligence, signal communication, and penal sections, and artillery, engineer, and chemical warfare staffs. The rear echelon of the headquarters of the rifle corps is a skeleton organization which consolidates the reports and requisitions of the subordinate formations, and reinforces subordinate rear echelon staffs in critical situations. Normally, attached supporting troops of a rifle corps include a howitzer and a tank destroyer artillery regiment, a signal battalion, and an engineer construction battalion. The service elements of a rifle corps services only the corps headquarters and the attached corps troops.

The artillery corps is a forward artillery headquarters with a balanced staff. It controls two or more artillery divisions and other GHQ artillery units which are assigned to it for a specific operation, or series of operations. Because the artillery corps is primarily a task force, there is considerable variation between corps, and within the artillery corps itself. For example, the V Artillery Corps in the summer of 1944 consisted of three artillery divisions, a heavy howitzer brigade, a medium howitzer brigade, and a heavy mortar brigade. The VII Artillery Corps consisted only of three artillery divisions.

Several antiaircraft artillery corps were identified during the last year of the war with Germany. Each corps controlled two or three antiaircraft artillery divisions, and other GHQ antiaircraft artillery units.

Cavalry, tank, and mechanized corps, in contrast to the rifle corps, are permanent formations with standard Tables of Organization and Equipment.

Section II. ORGANIZATION OF THE GROUND ARMS

1. INTRODUCTION

The stable formations and units of the Red Army are made up of two types of standard organizational elements—the specialized and the interchangeable.

The specialized organizational elements are found in rifle and cavalry divisions. They are characterized by economy of personnel and by maximum cross-country mobility. For example, the engineer battalion of the rifle division has only 164 officers and enlisted men, as compared with 270 officers and enlisted men of the engineer battalion of the rifle and mobile corps.

The interchangeable organizational elements are common to several formations. For example, the motorized 120-mm mortar regiment is found in the tank and mechanized corps; in the artillery division; or it may be independent.

The specialized organizational elements are com-

87

posed of companies, batteries, or platoons which are identical to the corresponding companies, batteries, and platoons of the interchangeable organizational elements. For example, the battalions of the divisional artillery regiment are unique in that they consist of two batteries of 76-mm guns and one battery of 122-mm howitzers. The organization of each 122-mm howitzer battery is identical with the 122-mm howitzer battery of the howitzer regiment.

The employment of standard organizational elements facilitates rapid creation of temporary tactical groupings. (Temporary tactical groupings are discussed in Chapter V.) Standard organizational elements are as follows:

Formation (*Soyedineniye*). The Formation is a stable organization of combined arms and minimum services designed to execute one phase of a large operation such as a penetration, exploitation, delaying action, or counterattack. Rifle and cavalry divisions, tank and mechanized brigades are examples of a Formation.

Unit (*Chast*). The Unit is the basic organization of a single arm or service: it is the smallest organization with balanced staff and services. Its size varies from a brigade to a battalion. The term applies to an entire, large, secondary component of a Formation; for example, the artillery Unit of an infantry division includes not only divisional artillery, but all artillery in the division including heavy mortars and battalion guns.

Element (*Podrazdelenye*). The Element is a basic grouping of one arm or service lacking balanced staff and services. It varies from battalion to company size. The term is applied to lesser secondary components of a Formation; for example, the engineer or special-troops Element of an infantry division. It is also applied to the main tactical subdivisions of Units; for example, the battalions within an infantry or artillery regiment.

Group (*Gruppa*), and Detachment (*Otryad, Razezd*). The Group and Detachment are small, temporary organizations of mixed arms which are prescribed for given tactical missions. The composition of these special Groups or Detachments is loosely outlined in field service regulations. Some typical examples of such organizations are the reconnaissance Group or Detachment and a leading Group. A reconnaissance Group (Detachment) ranges in size from a company to a reinforced battalion, or two cavalry squadrons. It operates on a front 3 to 8 miles wide and 12 to 15 miles deep. A leading Group (Detachment) may be as large as a reinforced battalion. It is sent out by an advance guard of a rifle regiment and operates 1.5 to 2 miles in front of, or to the flank of, the parent body.

The following Tables of Organization and Equipment of the principal tactical units of the Red Army are believed to be correct in all major items of equipment and over-all strength. The allocation of small arms and submachine guns, and the distribution of headquarters troops, are, however, partly estimated. The description of units is confined to their primary mission and, when practicable, a comparison with a comparable U. S. unit. (The supply and resupply requirements, movement weight, maximum axle load, and limiting speed of the major units are listed in Chapter VII).

2. INFANTRY

a. Rifle division. The mission of the Red Army rifle division is close combat. It is characterized by a marked strength in automatic weapons, especially submachine guns, and heavy and medium mortars. These weapons compensate for relative weakness in field artillery. Although the personnel strength of the Red Army rifle division is 4,424 smaller than the U. S. infantry division, its combat strength is only 200 less. Its supporting and service elements make up only 26 and 12 percent of its total strength, respectively, as compared with 36 and 21 percent in the U. S. infantry division.

	U.S.S.R.	U.S.
Infantry	62%	53%
Supporting Arms	26%	36%
Services	12%	21%

With the exception of medium artillery, heavy mortars, and the artillery supply column (and the previously mentioned report of a possible increase in infantry motorization), the Red Army rifle division is horse drawn. Its tactical mobility is low, but it is not road bound. It is incapable of extended offensive effort because the capacity of its organic transport is low, and weapon crews are cut to a minimum. The replacement pool is small (100

Unit	O & EM	7.62-mm SAR, R, & Cbn	7.62-mm SMG	7.62-mm LMG	7.62-mm Hv-MG	12.7-mm AA-MG	14.5-mm ATR	50-mm Mort	82-mm Mort	120-mm Mort	45-mm ATG	76-mm How	76-mm G	122-mm How	Trac	Tlr	Trk	Sp Veh	H-dr Veh	H	Ki	Rad
Hq & Hq Co	117	110	6	1														5		25	1	2
Rcn Tr	74		68	6																80		2
Sig Co	130	90	40															2	20	29	1	7
Engr Bn	164	149	15														4		9	18	1	2
CWS Co	40	25	15														2		6	10		1
Div Arty Regt	998	738	206	18			36						24	12	21	12	10	17	99	587	11	16
AT Bn, Mtz	233	172	43	6			18				12						39				2	11
AAMG Co, Mtz	97	67	30			18											18					
Repl Co	100	75	25	5			2	2	2		2								5	10		
Med Bn	90	90															9		25	31	1	
Vet Hosp	11	11																	2	2		
Bkry	63	63															3					
Trans Co	80	80															54				1	
3 R Regts	7,422	3,756	1,950	486	135		162	54	81	21	36	12					21	42	444	981	45	15
Total	9,619	5,426	2,398	522	135	18	218	56	83	21	50	12	24	12	21	12	160	66	610	1,773	63	56

Figure 3. Table of Organization and Equipment: Rifle Division.

men). Even moderate numbers of casualties greatly reduce its effectiveness (fig. 3).

The Red Army rifle division can be completely motorized by the addition of 1,200 trucks. If horses of the division were left behind, only 825 trucks are needed, 110 of which operate supply lines and tow guns.

Divisional artillery consists of a mixed field artillery regiment, an antitank battalion, and an antiaircraft machine gun company. The mixed artillery regiment includes 998 officers and enlisted men (fig. 4). It is armed with 122-howitzers and 76-mm guns. With the exception of the 122-mm howitzers, which are tractor drawn, and ammunition trucks, the regiment is horse drawn. Thus, divisional artillery, although it is lighter than that of the U. S. infantry division, is capable of providing close support to the rifle regiments in varying terrain and weather.

The divisional antitank battalion consists of headquarters, headquarters battery, three firing batteries—each with four 45-mm antitank guns—and a small train (fig. 5). During the last year of the war with Germany, the 45-mm antitank guns of the antitank battalion were often replaced by 57-mm antitank or 76-mm guns. It is expected that, in the future, this unit will be armed with light self-propelled artillery.

The divisional antiaircraft machine gun company is armed with eighteen 12.7-mm antiaircraft machine guns. It was reintroduced into the rifle division during the summer of 1944.

Ammunition and fuel for the divisional artillery

Unit	Off	EM	Total O & EM	7.62-mm SAR, R, & Cbn	7.62-mm SMG	7.62-mm LMG	14.5-mm ATR	76-mm G	122-mm How	Trac	Tlr	Trk	Sp Veh	H-dr Veh	H	Ki	Rad
Hq & Opns Stf	9	2	11	11											9		
Political Stf	3		3	3											1		
Sup Stf	13	4	17	17											5		
Hq Btry																	
Hq Plat	2	7	9	6	3										3		
Rcn Plat	1	14	15		15										15		
Sig Plat	1	25	26	21	5									5	13		
Topo Plat	1	20	21	18	3									2	9		
Sup Sec		9	9	9										2	6		
3 Bns	81	738	819	585	180	18	36	24	12	21	12	9	15	66	480	9	12
Med Plat	3	8	11	11									2	2	7		
Vet Sec	2	6	8	8										2	5		
Ord Wk Shop	3	9	12	12								1					
QM Wk Shop		6	6	6													
Trans Plat	1	30	31	31										20	34	1	
Total	120	878	998	738	206	18	36	24	12	21	12	10	17	99	587	11	12

Figure 4. Table of Organization and Equipment: Division Artillery Regiment.

comprise more than 50 percent of the total supply requirement of the division.

Two variations of the standard rifle division exist in the Red Army: the Guards Rifle Division, and the reduced division. The Guards Rifle Division differs from the standard division in that its supporting and service elements are slightly larger. Each Guards rifle regiment has an extra submachine gun company and its replacement pool is twice as large.

Unit	Off	EM	Total O & EM	7.62-mm SAR, R, & Cbn	7.62-mm SMG	7.62-mm LMG	14.5-mm ATR	45- or 57-mm AT G	Trk	Ki	Rad
Hq & Hq Btry...	6	11	9	4	5	---	---	---	1		
Rcn Sec...		8	8	4	4	---	---	---	1		
Topo Sec...	1	9	10	8	2				1		2
Sig Plat...	1	17	18	12	6				2		9
3 Btrys...	15	96	111	93	18	6		12	24		
ATR Co...	4	57	61	36	7		18		4		
Am Plat...	1	7	8	7	1				5		
Sup Sec...		8	8	8					1	2	
Total...	28	213	233	172	43	6	18	12	39	2	11

Figure 5. Table of Organization and Equipment: 45- or 57-mm Antitank Gun Battalion.

The reduced rifle division is based on emergency flexible Tables of Organization and Equipment which were authorized by the high command in November 1943. The actual size of the division ranged from 5,000 to 8,000 officers and enlisted men. The size was determined by the commander of an Army Group (Front) or of an independent army. Reduction of over-all strength of the rifle division was accomplished by a proportional reduction of all components.

A few mountain infantry divisions existed during the early months of the war with Germany. Each consisted of four mountain rifle regiments, 2,200 men each, and the same supporting and service units as the standard division. Mountain artillery regiments of the mountain division had 1,500 officers and enlisted men, organized into two mountain artillery battalions. Each battalion contained two mountain howitzer batteries and one mountain mortar battery. The division had an antiaircraft battalion, and relatively large supporting and service elements. Its total strength was approximately 12,800 men.

b. The rifle brigade. A great number of rifle brigades were activated during the winter of 1941–42. The majority of these brigades were disbanded or upgraded to divisions during the following year, and at the end of the hostilities few rifle brigades existed. A rifle brigade consists of three to five rifle battalions. Each battalion included three rifle companies, a submachine gun company, 82-mm mortar battery, antitank rifle company, machine gun company, and engineer, medical. transport, and ampule-thrower* platoons. In addition to the rifle battalions, the brigade has submachine gun, machine gun, artillery, mortar, and antitank gun battalions, and reconnaissance, engineer, signal, medical, and transport companies. Its strength is approximately 5,400 officers and enlisted men. Marine rifle brigades and emergency workers brigades were organized, in the same manner as the rifle brigades, from surplus naval personnel and workers pools.

c. The rifle regiment. The Red Army rifle regiment is an organization which contains the arms and minimum services necessary for the execution of independent combat missions. It has 2,474 officers and enlisted men. In contrast with 3,257 officers and enlisted men of the U. S. infantry regiment, it appears small. The difference is due mainly to smaller weapons crews and service elements. The Red Army rifle regiment is stronger than the U. S. infantry regiment in automatic weapons, especially submachine guns, and in medium and heavy mortars. But it is weaker in regimental artillery and antitank guns (fig. 6). Outstanding feature of the organization of the rifle regiment is the submachine gun company of 100 men, all armed with submachine guns.

With the exception of heavy mortars and signal equipment, which are motorized, all of the regimental weapons and transport are horse drawn. The regiment is free to maneuver in all kinds of weather and terrain. It is not road bound. The regiment is, however, incapable of extended independent combat, because the supply and maintenance capabilities of its organic transport are low. Even moderate casualties greatly reduce its effectiveness. The regiment is easily maneuverable. It requires only three 50-car trains for movement by rail.

The artillery commander of a rifle regiment has considerable fire power at his disposal. By combining the resources of the battalion artillery and mortars with organic regimental artillery, he can concentrate the fire of 27 medium mortars. 6 heavy mortars, 12 antitank guns, and 4 regimental howitzers.

---

*A flat-trajectory mortar which propels an incendiary "ampule" against armored vehicles up to ranges of 300 yards. Used by the Red Army in 1942–43, it has since been discarded.

Unit	Off	EM	Total O & EM	7.62-mm Sniper's R	7.62-mm R & Cbn	7.62-mm SAR	7.62-mm SMG	7.62-mm LMG	7.62-mm HvMG	14.5-mm ATR	50-mm Mort	82-mm Mort	120-mm Mort	45-mm ATG	76-mm How	Sp Veh	H-dr Veh	H	Ki	Rad
Hq & Stf	29	13	42		4	7	4									7		8	2	
Rcn Co	3	34	37	2		15	20											12		
SMG Co	7	93	100				100													
ATR Co	6	67	73		20		26			27							3	6		
Sig Co	6	44	50		40		10									3	6	11		5
Engr Plat	1	19	20		1	10	9										1	2		
3 R Bns	114	1,743	1,857	54	387	495	435	162	45	27	18	27		6		3	81	129	9	
AT Btry	6	49	55		43		12							6			2	26		
How Btry	7	67	74		59		15								4		13	49	2	
Mort Btry	6	59	65		52		14						7			8				
Med & Vet Co	4	32	36		17												9	17	1	
Ord & QM Shop	2	12	14		5															
Trans Co	5	34	39		31		3										29	60	1	
CWS Plat	1	11	12		10		2										4	7		
Total	197	2,277	2,474	56	669	527	650	162	45	54	18	27	7	12	4	21	148	327	15	5

Figure 6. Table of Organization and Equipment: Rifle Regiment.

The Guards Rifle Regiment differs from the standard rifle regiment in that it is upgraded in personnel, and made stronger in light and heavy automatic weapons (fig. 7). It has two submachine gun companies. The machine gun companies of its battalions have 12 heavy machine guns, instead of the 9 in the company of a standard battalion. The antitank rifle platoon of the Guards Rifle Battalion has 16 antitank rifles, as compared with 9 of the standard battalion. Thus, a Guards Rifle Regiment is able to put more men in the forward lines, and is capable of more extended action than is the standard rifle regiment.

Unit	O & EM	7.62-mm SAR, R, & Cbn	7.62-mm SMG	7.62-mm LMG	7.62-mm HvMG	14.5-mm ATR	50-mm Mort	82-mm Mort	120-mm Mort	45-mm ATG	76-mm How	Trk	H-dr Veh	H	Ki	Rad
Hq & Stf	46	42	4									8		10	2	
Rcn Co	40	20	20											20		
2 SMG Co	200		200													
ATR Co	73	20	26			27							3	6		
Sig Co	55	40	15									4	6	11		5
Engr Co	27	18	9										2	4		
3 R Bns	1,981	1,179	548	162	54	48	18	27		6		3	90	156	9	
AT Btry	55	43	12							6			2	26		
How Btry	95	80	15								4		17	65	2	2
Mort Btry	70	54	16						8			8				1
Ord Shop	14	14														
QM Plat																
Med Co	34	34											9	18	1	
Vet Plat	3	3											1	1		
CWS Plat	12	10	2										4	7		
Trans Co	43	40	3										33	66	1	
Total	2,748	1,597	870	162	54	75	18	27	8	12	4	23	167	390	15	8

Figure 7. Table of Organization and Equipment: Guards Rifle Regiment.

d. Rifle battalion. Basic organizational element of the infantry arm is the rifle battalion. It consists of headquarters, three rifle companies, antitank rifle platoon, mortar company, machine gun company, antitank gun platoon, and a medical unit (fig. 8). Its strength is 619 officers and enlisted men. The battalion is the lowest administrative and housekeeping unit of the infantry arm maintaining a kitchen, a repair shop, a medical unit, and a pharmacy for its subordinate units. With its light transport, organic supporting mortars, and light artillery, it is well suited for outflanking and infiltrating tactics in any terrain.

In comparison with the U. S. infantry battalion, the Red Army rifle battalion is weaker in personnel and weapons, except light automatic weapons and medium mortars. The outstanding feature of the armament of the rifle battalion is its large number of submachine guns.

91

Unit	Off	EM	Total O & EM	7.62-mm Sniper's R	7.62-mm R	7.62-mm SAR	7.62-mm SMG	7.62-mm LMG	7.62-mm HvMG	14.5-mm ATR	50-mm Mort	82-mm Mort	45-mm ATG	Bcl	H-dr Veh	H	Ki
Hq	4		4				4										
Sig Plat	1	9	10		9		1							1	1	1	
3 R Cos	18	411	429	18	15	165	114	54	6		6				3	3	
MG Co	6	52	58		29		14		9						6	9	
ATR Plat	1	22	23		10		4			9					1	2	
Mort Co	6	55	61		41		5					9			9	9	
G Plat	1	16	17		12		3						2		2	4	
Med Plat		5	5		4										1	1	
Sup Plat	1	11	12		9										4	14	3
Total	38	581	619	18	129	165	145	54	15	9	6	9	2	1	27	43	3

Figure 8. Table of Organization and Equipment: Rifle Battalion.

Supply and maintenance capabilities of the rifle battalion are small. For more than a day of light combat it must be assisted by regimental or divisional services. A rifle battalion can be easily moved. One truck company (100 SIS–5 trucks) can carry a complete battalion with sufficient rations, forage, and ammunition for 7 to 8 days of heavy combat.

Two variations of the rifle battalion—the motorized rifle battalion and the motorized submachine gun battalion—constitute the infantry element of the motorized and the tank brigade respectively. The motorized rifle battalion differs from the standard battalion in that it has additional antitank rifle, antitank gun, and submachine gun platoons. It has six instead of nine 82-mm mortars. Its strength is 662 officers and enlisted men. The motorized submachine gun battalion, a part of the tank brigade, is smaller than the standard rifle battalion. It lacks the machine gun company, and has six instead of nine 82-mm mortars. But, like the motorized rifle battalion, it has additional antitank rifle and antitank gun platoons.

3. ARMORED AND MECHANIZED FORCES

a. Armored forces. Tactical units of the Red Army armored forces are organized into tank corps, tank brigades, and independent heavy tank regiments and battalions.

TANK CORPS. A tank corps usually forms a part of the mobile striking forces of the commander of a Front or an army. It is used to deliver a decisive blow on a narrow sector, and in cooperation with other arms to exploit a break-through. A tank corps is an example of a Soviet practice of building a formation from standard organizational elements. The tank corps consists of three tank brigades, one motorized rifle brigade, six artillery regiments of various calibers, and supporting arms and services (fig. 9). Tank corps may differ in the number of organic self-propelled artillery regiments. They may vary between one and four per tank corps.

Red Army tank corps are comparable in strength and armament with U. S. armored divisions. They have fewer tanks than the U. S. division (200 as compared with 272) and fewer self-propelled guns (40 compared with 62). However, many of the Soviet tanks and self-propelled mounts are heavier gunned than the corresponding weapons of a U. S. armored division. Organic artillery weapons, including medium and heavy mortars and rockets, of the tank corps outnumber those of the U. S. armored division by more than 2½ to 1.

Transport and ammunition companies of a tank corps carry two rations, two refills of fuel, and one-half unit of fire for all of its organic and attached units. It can maintain them for 5 or 6 days of moderate combat. Its maintenance and repair shops operate approximately 30 miles behind the front lines. Major repairs involving exchange of motors, gun tubes, welding of armor, and manufacturing and fitting some spare parts are effected in these shops.

TANK BRIGADE. The mission of a tank brigade is destruction of hostile infantry by means of fire and shock action. A tank brigade usually forms a part of a tank corps. In operations, it is supported by a portion of the tank corps' self-propelled artillery, and can be compared with a combat command of a U. S. armored division. A tank brigade is also built from standard organizational elements, including three tank battalions, a motorized submachine gun battalion, an antiaircraft machine gun company, and services (fig. 10). Maneuverability of a tank brigade is good. Although its service echelon is road bound, Soviet tanks with their wide tracks and high clearance can operate in difficult terrain. Without its support and service group, the tank brigade has limited supply capabilities. They are sufficient for only a few hours of operation. The service group extends these capabilities to a day or two of moderate combat. With corps resources, a tank brigade can be committed to moderate combat for 5 or 6 days.

A tank brigade has two recovery tractors and a mobile repair shop for effecting minor repairs as near the front lines as possible.

Motorized Rifle Brigade. The mission of the motorized rifle brigade is to support tanks in breakthrough or pursuit operations, to hold captured terrain objectives, and to protect the tanks from hostile infantry and antitank weapons. The motorized rifle brigade is, in fact, a reinforced rifle regiment, motorized. It consists of headquarters, three motorized rifle battalions, a powerful mechanized reconnaissance company, a mortar and a field artillery battalion, an antitank rifle, submachine gun, and antiaircraft machine gun companies, and services (fig. 11). The proportion of services to infantry and supporting arms in the motorized brigade is about twice as large as in the rifle regiment. An important feature of the organization of the motorized rifle brigade is the engineer mine company, whose mission is to establish offensive antitank minefields. The motorized rifle brigade is tactically mobile on roads and easy terrain, and is easily maneuverable.

Artillery of the Tank (and Mechanized) Corps. The artillery commander of the tank and mechanized corps has at his disposal six artillery units armed with a variety of weapons. The mission of this artillery is to support tanks and motorized infantry in mobile operations. The type and relative proportion of artillery weapons were selected so as to achieve maximum flexibility and shock power of artillery fire without impairing the mobility and maneuverability of the corps. The greater part of the tank and mechanized corps artillery consists of flat trajectory weapons. Their fire against hostile infantry and area targets is supplemented by heavy mortars and rockets. The 152-mm self-propelled gun-howitzer regiment executes long-range, as well as direct, support missions.

Unit	Total O & EM	7.62-mm SAR, R & Cbn	7.62-mm SMG	7.62-mm LMG	7.62-mm HvMG	12.7-mm AAMG	14.5-mm ATR	82-mm Mort	120-mm Mort	37-mm AA G	45-mm or 57-mm AT G	76-mm G	SU 85 (85-mm SP G)	SU 152 (152-mm SP G/How)	132-mm RL	Flame Thrower	T-34/85 Tk	Armd C	Armd Pers Carr	Trac	Tlr	Trk	Sp Veh	Mtrcl	Kl	Bkry	Rad
Corps Hq	130	82	72	4													3					10			1		
3 Tk Brigs	3, 918	2, 076	900	75	12	27	72	18			12	12					195	9		33		345	90	36	27		279
Mtz R Brig	3, 238	1, 707	955	165	35	9	81	30	6		12	12						7	10			299			17		44
85-mm SP Arty Regt (L)	440	150	240	11			18						20				1	1		2		42	2	7	2		27
152-mm SP Arty Regt (Hv)	476	162	270	11			18							20			1	1		2		47	2	7	2		31
76-mm TD Arty Regt	546	450	50	12								24									24	84	17		8		28
37-mm AAAW Regt	397	295	102			16				16												56			2		8
120-mm Mtz Mort Regt	489	395	37	18					36													72	9		5		16
Rkt Bn	213	190	23			3									8					4		9			1		4
Mtz AT Arty Bn	233	172	43	6			18				12											39			2		11
Rcn Bn	220	139	72	24							10							13	33			19		17	2		6
Mtrcl Bn	288	139	92	56				4								10						12		43	2		6
Sig Bn	250	200	50																			40	1		1		10
Engr Bn	290	225	50	24																		25			1		
Corps Serv	(836)	(798)	(31)	(9)																		270	(120)		5	2	
Total	11, 964	7, 180	2, 963	415	47	55	207	52	42	16	46	48	20	20	8	10	200	31	43	41	24	1, 369	241	110	78	2	470

Figures in parentheses are approximations.

Figure 9. Table of Organization and Equipment: Tank Corps.

Unit	O & EM	7.62-mm SAR, R, & Cbn	7.62-mm SMG	7.62-mm LMG	7.62-mm HvMG	14.5-mm ATR	12.7-mm AAMG	82-mm Mort	45-mm AT G	76-mm G	T-34/86 Tk	Armd C	Rad	Trac	Trk	Mtrcl	Sp Veh	Ki
Hq	22	8									2		2		1	3		
Hq Co																		
Rcn Plat	43	19	21	3								3	3		3	3		
Engr Plat	35	24	6	3												3		
CWS Plat	25	22	3												1	3		
Hq Plat	12	5	6	1												3		
Sup Sec	12	12													1			1
Sig Plat	30	15	5										5		2			
3 Tk Bns	441	130	90								63		72	6	15		18	3
Mtz SMG Bn	403	228	138	18	4	6			6	4			7		30			3
ATR Co	44	21	10			18							1		2			
AT Btry	52	42	10							4			1		4			1
AA Co	48	37	1				9						1		9			
Ord & Maint Co	125	115	10										1	5	42		12	1
Med Plat	14	14													2			
Total	1,306	692	300	25	4	24	9	6	4	4	65	3	93	11	115	12	30	9

Figure 10. Table of Organization and Equipment: Tank Brigade.

Including artillery and mortars of the tank and motorized brigades (except tank guns), the artillery commander of the tank corps has 232 pieces of artillery and 8 multiple rocket launchers at his disposal. The weight of a single salvo of these weapons is more than 5 tons, and if the fire of tank guns is included it is more than 7 tons.

Normally, two of the artillery regiments are self-propelled. These are a light 85-mm regiment and a heavy 152-mm gun-howitzer regiment (figs. 12 and 13). The mission of these regiments is close sup-port of tanks. Normally direct fire is used. However, both regiments have sufficient personnel and equipment to conduct indirect fire against distant targets.

The tank destroyer regiment is a part of the tank, mechanized, and cavalry corps. It also may be independent or a part of a tank destroyer brigade. It consists of headquarters, headquarters battery, five or six firing batteries, and regimental services (fig. 14). Each firing battery has four 76-mm guns. Some regiments, however, were encountered which

Unit	O & EM	7.62-mm SAR, R, & Cbn	7.62-mm SMG	7.62-mm LMG	7.62-mm HvMG	12.7-mm AAMG	14.5-mm ATR	82-mm Mort	120-mm Mort	45-mm AT G	76-mm G	Armd Veh	Armd Pers Carr	Trk	Ki	Rad
Brig Hq	69	69												7		
Hq Co																
Sig Plat	30	30												3		5
CWS Plat	11	11												1		
Hq Plat	25	16	7	2										2		
Serv Plat	7	7												1	1	
3 Mtz R Bns	1,986	807	723	135	27		54	18		12				129	9	21
Mort Bn	199	165	9					12	6					22	1	5
Arty Bn	224	134	63	12							12			27	3	6
ATR Co	60	27	6				27							3		1
SMG Co	94	1	93											5		1
Rcn Co	144	74	48	10	8							7	10	4		4
Ord & Maint Co	72	72												6		
Engr Mine Co	121	109	6	6										9	1	
Trans Co	109	109												66	1	
Med Plat	39	39												5	1	
AAMG Co	48	37				9								9		1
Total	3,238	1,707	955	165	35	9	81	30	6	12	12	7	10	299	17	44

Figure 11. Table of Organization and Equipment: Motorized Rifle Brigade.

Unit	O & EM	7.62-mm SAR, R, & Cbn	7.62-mm SMG	7.62-mm LMG	14.5-mm ATR	SU 85 (85-mm SP (G)	T-34/85 Tk	Armd C	Trac	Trk	Mtrcl	Sp Veh	Ki	Rad
Hq	20	13	7				1			5				2
Ren Plat	30	11	16	2				1		2				
Sig Plat	15	10	5							2				
Engr Plat	20	15	5							2				
4 SP Btrys	140		120			20					5			25
SMG Co	79		70	9						1	1			
ATR Co	61	36	7		18					2				
Ord & Maint Shop	30	20	10						2	2	1	2		
Am Plat	18	18								16				
Fuel Plat	10	10								7				
Sup Sec	10	10								2			2	
Med Plat	7	7								1				
Total	440	150	240	11	18	20	1	1	2	42	7	2	2	27

NOTE.—Antitank rifles, engineers, and submachine guns may be assigned from parent formations. The organic strength is, in that case, approximately 300.

Figure 12. *Table of Organization and Equipment: Self-Propelled Artillery Regiment.*

had six guns in each battery. This regiment is completely motorized. The ammunition columns of the tank, mechanized, and cavalry corps carry a full unit of fire for the tank destroyer artillery regiments, but only one-half a unit of fire for their other components.

The light antiaircraft artillery regiment may be a part of the tank and mechanized corps, antiaircraft artillery division, or may be independent. It consists of headquarters, headquarters battery, four firing batteries and regimental services (fig. 28). Its strength in armament and personnel is approximately half that of a U. S. antiaircraft automatic weapons mobile battalion.

The motorized mortar regiment may be a part of the tank and mechanized corps or the mortar artillery brigade, or it may be independent. It consists of headquarters and headquarters battery, two mortar battalions, and regimental services (fig. 26). Missions of heavy mortars are outlined in the discussion of the mortar brigade.

The rocket battalion is a part of a tank and mechanized corps, and a part of the rocket regiment. In the tank corps, the mission of the rocket battalion is to support the advance of tanks and motorized infantry. It generally engages area targets, employing HE projectiles against personnel, and incendiary projectiles against buildings and supply areas. The rocket battalion is highly maneuverable on roads and easy terrain.

Unit	O & EM	7.62-mm SAR, R, & Cbn	7.62-mm SMG	7.62-mm LMG	14.5-mm ATR	SU 100 or 152 (100-mm SP G or 152-mm SP G/How)	T 34/85 Tk	BA-64 Armd C	Trac	Trk	Mtrcl	Sp Veh	Ki	Rad
Hq	20	13	7				1			5				2
Hq Btry														
Ren Plat	34	11	16	2				1		2				
Sig Plat	15	10	5							2				
Engr Plat	20	15	5							2				
4 SP Btrys	160		140			20					5			29
SMG Co	79		79	9						1	1			
ATR Co	61	36	8		18					2				
Maint & Ord Plat	30	20	10						2	2	1	2		
Am Plat	30	30								21				
Fuel Plat	10	10								7				
Sup Plat	10	10								2			2	
Med Plat	7	7								1				
Total	476	162	270	11	18	20	1	1	2	47	7	2	2	31

Figure 13. *Table of Organization and Equipment: Heavy Self-Propelled Regiment.*

Unit	Off	EM	Total O & EM	7.62-mm SAR, R, & Cbn	7.62-mm SMG	7.62-mm LMG	76-mm G	Trac	Tlr	Trk	Sp Veh	Ki	Rad
Hq & Opns Stf	10	2	12	12						2			
Political Stf	3		3	3									
Sup Stf	7	8	15	15						2			
Hq Btry													
Hq Plat	1	7	8	4	4					1			
Rcn Plat	1	16	17	12	5					2			
Sig Plat	1	20	21	16	5					5			10
Sup Sec		7	7	7						1		1	
6 76-mm G Btrys	36	348	384	312	36	12	24		24	48		6	18
Med Plat	3	8	11	11						1	1		
Ord Wk Shop	3	9	12	12						1	1		
QM Wk Shop		7	7								1		
Trans Plat	2	44	46	46						20	14		
Sup Sec		3	3							1		1	
Total	67	479	546	450	50	12	24		24	84	17	8	28

Figure 14. Table of Organization and Equipment: Tank Destroyer Artillery Regiment (Towed).

The antitank gun battalion of the tank, mechanized, and cavalry corps is armed with twelve 45-mm antitank guns, eighteen antitank rifles, and other small arms (fig. 5). It is completely motorized. Its

Unit	O & EM	7.62-mm SAR, R, & Cbn	7.62-mm SMG	7.62-mm LMG	BA-10 Armd C	BA-64 Armd C	Trk	Mtrcl	Ki	Rad
Hq	8	5	3				2			
Hq Co.										
Sig Plat	20	10	5				2	2		3
Engr Sqd	11	15	5				2			
CWS Sqd	7	8	2				1			
Sup Sec	7	7					1		1	
Hq Plat	12	6	6	1		3				
2 Rcn Co	150	83	51	23	10		9	15	1	3
Sup Sec	5	5					2			
Total	220	139	72	24	10	3	*19	17	2	6

*Including ten armored personnel carriers.

Figure 15. Table of Organization and Equipment: Reconnaissance Battalion.

mission is to protect the headquarters and principal supply installations of the corps against infiltrating light armored vehicles. It is likely that the 45-mm antitank guns of this unit will be replaced by 57- or 76-mm guns, or by light self-propelled artillery.

Other supporting arms and services of the tank and mechanized corps consist of a reconnaissance battalion, motorcycle battalion, signal battalion, engineer battalion, chemical warfare company, water and fuel column, transport company, field bakery, and a medical battalion.

The reconnaissance battalion consists of headquarters and headquarters company, two mechanized reconnaissance companies, and a supply platoon (fig. 15). The motorcycle battalion (fig. 16) is the only organic unit of the Red Army field organization to contain flame throwers. Its missions are varied, including reinforcement of the reconnaissance battalion, flank security, protection of lines of communications, and reduction of small, bypassed enemy forces.

(Organization of the engineer, signal, medical, and other service units is described in Section III, Technical Services.)

b. Mechanized forces. In the Red Army the term, "mechanized," is applied to a team of motorized infantry, tanks, and artillery in which the infantry element predominates. There are two such formations in the Red Army: the mechanized corps, and the mechanized brigade.

MECHANIZED CORPS. A mechanized corps forms a part of a mobile reserve for the commander of a

Unit	O & EM	7.62-mm SAR, R, & Cbn	7.62-mm SMG	7.62-mm LMG	82-mm Mort	Flame Thrower	Trk	Mtrcl	Ki	Rad
Hq & Sig	8	5	3				1	1		2
Engr Sqd	7	5	2				1			
Serv & Trans Sqd	8	8					1		2	
2 Mtrcl Cos	146	48	64	48				42		2
Mtz Co	61	36	16	8			4			1
Flame Thrower Plat	22	10	2			10	2	2		
Mort Plat	36	27	5		4		4			1
Total	288	139	92	56	4	10	12	43	2	6

Figure 16. Table of Organization and Equipment: Motorcycle Battalion.

Front or an army. Its primary mission is to exploit a break-through, pursuit, or a counterattack. A mechanized corps is composed of organizational elements which include three mechanized brigades, one

96

tank brigade, six artillery regiments, and supporting arms and services (fig. 17). As in a tank corps, the number of self-propelled artillery regiments in a mechanized corps may vary between one and four. The calibers and types of artillery weapons also may vary. For example, the motorized heavy mortar regiment may be replaced by a 122-mm howitzer regiment. There is no organization in the U. S. Army which is comparable to the Red Army mechanized corps.

The artillery commander of a mechanized corps has 336 artillery pieces at his disposal. These pieces include the artillery and mortars of the mechanized and tank brigades, but exclude tank guns. The weight of a single salvo from these weapons is more than 6½ tons. If tank guns are included, it is more than 8½ tons. (For discussion of the supporting artillery units of the mechanized corps, see Artillery of the Tank Corps.)

Tactical mobility of a mechanized corps is good except in swamps, wooded terrain, deep snow, or during heavy thaws. A mechanized corps carries sufficient ammunition, rations, and fuel to sustain all of its components for 5 or 6 days of moderate combat. Transport and ammunition companies of the mechanized corps carry two rations, two refills of fuel, and one-half unit of fire for all its organic and attached units. As in the tank corps, its repair and maintenance shops operate approximately 30 miles behind the front lines. They are capable of effecting major repairs to vehicles and ordnance such as the replacing of motors and gun tubes, welding armor, and manufacturing and fitting some parts for vehicles and weapons.

MECHANIZED BRIGADE. A mechanized brigade, a part of a mechanized corps, consists of a motorized brigade (fig. 11), and a tank regiment (fig. 18). On roads or easy terrain, the mechanized brigade is extremely mobile, and capable of wide, bold maneuvers. Typically, it fights on or near roads. With organic transport and services alone, the supply and maintenance capabilities of the brigade is low. It has, however, two to four Type B mobile repair shops. The tank regiment has two recovery tanks which endeavor to repair slightly damaged tanks on the battlefield and tow more severely damaged ones under cover.

TANKS AND SELF-PROPELLED ARTILLERY. The basic organizational elements of the tank arm of the Red Army are the medium tank regiment, the

Unit	O & EM	7.62-mm SAR, R, & Cbn	7.62-mm SMG	7.62-mm LMG	7.62-mm HvMG	12.7-mm AAMG	14.5-mm ATR	82-mm Mort	120-mm Mort	37-mm AA G	45-mm or 57-mm AT G	76-mm G	SU 85 (85-mm SP G)	SU 152 (152-mm SP G/How)	RL M13	Flame Thrower	T-34/85 Tk	Armd C	Armd Pers Carr	Trac	Tlr	Trk	SP Veh	Mtrcl	Ki	Bkry	Rad
Corps Hq	130	82	48	4													3					10			1		
3 Mecz Brigs	11,343	6,009	3,492	531	105	27	297	90	18		36	36					123	30		6		1,038	36	36	57		284
Tk Brig	1,306	692	300	25	4	9	24	6			4	4	4				65	3		11		115	30	12	9		95
SP Arty Regt (M)	440	150	240	11			18						20				1	1		2		42	2	7	2		27
SP Arty Regt (Hv)	476	162	270	11			18							20				1		2		47	2	7	2		31
TD Arty Regt	546	450	50	12								24									24	84	17		8		28
AAAW Regt	397	295	102			16				16												56			2		8
Mtz Mort Regt	489	395	37	18					36													72	9		5		16
Rkt Bn	213	190	23			3									8					4		9			1		4
AT Arty Bn	233	172	43	6			18				12											39			2		11
Rcn Bn	220	139	72	24														13	35			19		17	2		6
Mtrcl Bn	288	139	92	56				4								10						12		43	2		6
Sig Bn	250	200	50																			40	1		1		10
Engr Bn	290	225	50	24																		25			1		
Corps Serv	836	798	31	9																		270	(120)		5	2	
Total	17,457	10,098	4,900	731	109	55	375	100	54	16	52	64	20	20	8	10	192	48	35	25	24	1,878	217	122	100	2	525

Figure 17. Table of Organization and Equipment: Mechanized Corps.

Unit	O & EM	7.62-mm SAR, R, & Cbn	7.62-mm SMG	7.62-mm LMG	14.5-mm ATR	T-34/85 Tk	BA-64 Armd C	Trac	Trk	Fuel Trk	Mtrcl	Sp Veh	Ki	Rad
Hq	12	7	5	1		1			2		5			1
Hq Co:														
Hq Plat	18	6	6								3			
Rcn Plat	31	10	16	2			3		2					1
Engr Plat	27	26	1											
Sig Plat	19	17	2						2					3
4 Tk Cos	168	80	88			40					4			44
SMG Co	75		66	9					1					1
ATR Co	61	28	15		18				1					
Trans & Maint Co	105	95	10					2	42	8		2		1
Sup Plat	20	20							3				2	
Med Plat	7	7							2					
Total	543	296	209	12	18	41	3	2	55	8	12	2	2	51

Figure 18. Table of Organization and Equipment: Tank Regiment.

heavy tank regiment, and the tank battalion. Regimental organizational elements are found in the mechanized brigade and as independent heavy tank regiments. The first type of regiment (approximately equivalent to the U. S. tank battalion) is a balanced organization with its own reconnaissance, engineer, signal, and maintenance units. A submachine gun company protects the tanks from hostile infantry. This tank regiment is organic to a mechanized brigade, thus completing the tank-infantry-artillery team of that organization.

The second type of Red Army tank regiment is the independent heavy tank regiment. Such regiments always are controlled by the commander of a Front or an army, and are allotted to subordinate formations according to their needs. A heavy tank regiment consists of four companies each with five heavy tanks, a submachine gun platoon for protection of the tanks from hostile infantry, a headquarters company, and relatively large supply and maintenance units. It is used to support infantry and medium tanks during attacks on heavily fortified positions, and as heavy artillery in support of mobile operations.

Initial supply requirement of a heavy tank regiment is 88 tons. Daily resupply requirement in heavy combat is 48 tons. Rail movement of a heavy tank regiment requires one 40-car train.

TANK BATTALIONS. Two types of tank battalions exist in the Red Army. They are the independent tank battalion and the tank battalion which is organic to a tank brigade. The independent tank battalions are few in number, and they are generally equipped with older model tanks. Their organization is not uniform. They differ from the organic tank battalions of a tank brigade in that in addition to the tank companies and ammunition platoons, they have engineer, smoke, medical, and service platoons. The independent tank battalions have the same mission as the independent tank regiments discussed above. It is believed that the latter have displaced the independent tank battalions in the Red Army organization.

Tank battalions which are organic to a tank brigade generally consist of two companies of medium tanks, a headquarters with one tank, and an ammunition platoon. Some battalions, however, have three companies. In that event, there are only two such battalions to a tank brigade.

In the Red Army, self-propelled artillery is a part of the tank and mechanized forces. Organization of the self-propelled artillery regiments reflects tank rather than artillery doctrine. In fact, the organization of the heavy tank regiment is the same as that of the heavy self-propelled artillery regiment (fig. 13). It has the same supply requirements and capabilities, and the same mobility. The medium self-propelled artillery regiment is a smaller version of the heavy regiment.

4. ARTILLERY

The artillery of the Red Army is organized into corps, divisions, brigades, regiments, and battalions. (The artillery corps was discussed in Section I, Corps.)

The artillery division is a base of fire for major offensive and counteroffensive operations. It is es-

Unit	O & EM	7.62-mm SAR, R, & Cbn	7.62-mm SMG	7.62-mm LMG	12.7-mm AAMG	14.5-mm ATR	120-mm Mort	76-mm G	122-mm How	122-mm G	152-mm How	152-mm G/How	Trac	Tlr	Trk	Sp Veh	Mtrcl	Ki	Rail
Hq & Hq Btry	(250)	200	(50)												35	5	5	1	
L Arty Brig	2,063	1,772	255	36	3	72		72					18	72	280	50		25	82
How Brig	2,242	1,892	362	36	9	72			48		24		158	136	214	36		24	78
MG Brig	2,128	1,396	308	18	9	36				12		24	86	76	191	18		17	66
Hv Mort Brig	1,705	1,397	135	54	3	108	108								268	35		16	52
Arty Obsn Bn	300	300													(25)	(15)		2	(6)
Sig Bn	255	200	(55)											(10)	(15)	(1)	(24)	1	(10)
Serv	(800)	750	(50)												(75)	(8)		4	
Total	9,743	7,907	1,215	144	24	288	108	72	48	12	24	24	262	294	1,103	168	29	90	294

Figures in parenthesis are approximations.

Figure 19. Table of Organization and Equipment: Artillery Division.

sentially a task force headquarters with permanent planning, fire control, reconnaissance, intelligence, and liaison staffs. It has adequate technical and service personnel for effective employment of 24 to 36 firing battalions. The number, type, and caliber of its component units depend primarily on its mission. It may be reinforced by GHQ heavy artillery regiments, aviation units, antiaircraft artillery and rocket regiments, army transport, and service units. A typical artillery division is shown in Figure 19.

Tactically and strategically, the artillery division is not highly mobile. It requires extensive engineer assistance for road and bridge maintenance, preparation of firing positions, camouflage, and constructions of shelters for personnel and equipment. Much of its equipment is tracked. Single units of this equipment weigh up to 35,000 pounds.

In addition to the artillery division described above, there are also the specialized weapons-artillery divisions, including the heavy gun division, and the antiaircraft artillery division. Little is known of the heavy gun divisions. Presumably they consist of several heavy artillery brigades.

The antiaircraft artillery division consists of three 37-mm antiaircraft automatic weapons regiments, an 85-mm gun regiment, and divisional troops (fig. 20). The 85-mm gun regiment is approximately equal in personnel and armament to the U. S. 90-mm gun battalion. The 37-mm antiaircraft automatic weapons regiment is approximately equal to half a U. S. antiaircraft automatic weapons battalion. Thus, the Red Army antiaircraft division corresponds roughly to a U. S. automatic antiaircraft weapons group. One antiaircraft artillery division is generally assigned to each operational army, and one or more to each Army Group (Front). In addition to their primary mission of antiaircraft defense of important installations and troop concentrations, antiaircraft artillery units are used for antitank defense, support of ground troops by direct fire against targets whose destruction requires high-velocity fire, and less often for indirect fire against general ground targets. An antiaircraft artillery

Unit	O & EM	7.62-mm SAR, R, & Cbn	7.62-mm SMG	12.7-mm AAMG	37-mm AA G	85-mm AA G	Trac	Trk	Sp Veh	Ki	Rail
Hq and Stf	60	40	20					6			
Hq Btry											
Rcn Plat	12		12					1			
Topo Plat	18	15	3					2			
Sig Plat	35	30	5					4			4
Sup Sec	7	7						1	1		
3 37-mm AAAW Regts	1,191	885	306	48	48			168	3	6	24
85-mm AAA Regt	620	464	110	16		16	16	68	2	3	13
Am Plat	45	45						22			
Fuel Plat	6	6							5		
Ord Wk Shop	15	15						1	1		
Mtr Wk Shop	10	10						1	1		
Sup Sec	10	10						2	1		
Med Plat	14	14						2			
Total	2,043	1,541	456	64	48	16	16	278	12	11	41

Figure 20. Table of Organization and Equipment: Antiaircraft Artillery Division.

division is completely motorized and has good strategic mobility.

a. Artillery brigades. An artillery brigade is a permanent tactical unit comprising a headquarters and a headquarters battery, two or three artillery regiments, and a service train. The headquarters battery has reconnaissance, survey, fire control, signal, and service platoons aggregating between 70 and 85 officers and enlisted men. The service train contains an ammunition platoon, ordnance and maintenance shops, fuel platoon, service and administrative platoon, and a small medical unit. An ar-

Unit	Off	EM	Total O & EM	7.62-mm SAR, R, & Cbn	7.62-mm SMG	7.62-mm LMG	12.7-mm AAMG	76-mm G	Trac	Tlr	Trk	Sp Veh	Ki	Rad
Hq & Opns Stf	20	5	25	25							4	2		
Political Stf	3		3	3								1		
Sup Stf	10	10	20	20							4	1		
Hq Btry:														
Hq Plat	1	11	12	6	6						1			
Rcn Plat	1	16	17	12	5						2			
Sig Plat	1	34	35	30	5						3			4
Topo Plat	1	20	21	16	5						3			
AA Plat	1	15	16	13	3		3				3			
Sup Sec		7	7	7							1		1	
3 76-mm G Regts	228	1,623	1,851	1,584	231	36		72	12	60	243	42	24	78
Med Plat	3	8	11	11							1	1		
Am Colm	1	20	21	21					6	12	12			
Wk Shops	6	18	24	24							3	3		
Total	276	1,787	2,063	1,772	255	36	3	72	18	72	280	50	25	82

Figure 21. Table of Organization and Equipment: Light Artillery Brigade, Motorized.

tillery brigade may be independent or a part of an artillery division.

LIGHT ARTILLERY BRIGADE. A light artillery brigade generally forms a part of an artillery division. It is armed with seventy-two 76-mm guns, which are characterized by good muzzle velocity and great maneuverability. It is employed in close support of infantry and tanks, especially for direct fire. Its primary missions are destruction of personnel, infantry and light artillery weapons, and light field fortifications. A light brigade consists of three light artillery regiments, and brigade troops (fig. 21). The independent tank destroyer brigade is a variation of the light artillery brigade in which the firing batteries are controlled by the regimental headquarters. Battalion headquarters are eliminated.

LIGHT HOWITZER BRIGADE. A light howitzer brigade may be either independent or a part of an artillery division. It is armed with 122-mm howitzers and their companion pieces, the 152-mm howitzers. The 122-mm howitzer is characterized by great flexibility in muzzle velocity and trajectory, effective burst, and good maneuverability. The 152-mm howitzer has a lower rate of fire, greater burst, and slightly greater range than the 122-mm howitzer.

The brigade may be used for any mission except destruction of strong fortifications, or long-range fire. Its primary missions include destruction of

Unit	Off	EM	Total O & EM	7.62-mm SAR, R, & Cbn	7.62-mm SMG	7.62-mm LMG	12.7-mm AAMG	122-mm How	152-mm How	Trac	Tlr	Trk	Sp Veh	Ki	Rad
Hq & Opns Stf	20	5	25	25									4	2		
Political Stf	3		3	3										1		
Sup Stf	10	10	20	20									3	1		
Hq Btry:																
Hq Plat	1	11	12	6	6								1			
Rcn Plat	1	15	16	11	5								2			
Sig Plat	1	24	25	20	5								3			4
Topo Plat	1	20	21	16	5								3			
AA Plat	1	15	16	13	3		3						3			
Sup Sec		7	7	7									1		1	
2 122-mm How Regts	212	1,820	2,032	1,706	338	36	6	48	24	146	112	176	28	22	74
Med Plat	3	8	11	11								1	1		
Am Plat	1	24	25	25							12	24	12			
Wk Shops	6	18	24	24									3	3		
Sup Sec		5	5	5									2		1	
Total	260	1,982	2,242	1,892	362	36	9	48	24	158	136	214	36	24	78

Figure 22. Table of Organization and Equipment: Light Howitzer Brigade.

Unit	Off	EM	Total O & EM	7.62-mm SAR, R, & Cbn	7.62-mm SMG	7.62-mm LMG	12.7-mm AAMG	122-mm G	152-mm G/How	Trac	Tlr	Trk	Sp Veh	Ki	Rad
Hq & Opns Stf	20	5	25	25								4	2		
Political Stf	3		3	3									1		
Sup Stf	10	10	20	20								4	1		
Hq Btry															
Hq Plat	1	11	12	6	6							1			
Rcn Plat	1	15	16	11	5							2			
Sig Plat	1	24	25	20	5							3			4
Topo Plat	1	20	21	16	5							3			
AAMG Plat	1	15	16	13	3		3					3			
Sup Sec		7	7	7								1		1	
2 Medium G Regts	226	1,692	1,918	1,210	284	18	6	12	24	74	52	152	10	16	62
Med Plat	3	8	11	11								1	1		
Am Plat	1	24	25	25						12	24	12			
Wk Shops	6	18	24	24								3	3		
Sup Sec		5	5	5								2			
Total	274	1,854	2,128	1,396	308	18	9	12	24	86	76	191	18	17	66

Figure 23. Table of Organization and Equipment: Medium Gun Brigade.

personnel in the open and in shelters; accompanying and antipersonnel barrages and concentrations; neutralization of light fortifications, mortars, and light artillery weapons; and fire reconnaissance. Additional missions include destruction of minefields, antitank ditches, and medium field fortifications. A light howitzer brigade consists of two howitzer regiments, and brigade troops (fig. 22).

MEDIUM GUN BRIGADE. The medium gun brigade consists of two medium gun regiments, and brigade troops (fig. 23). It is armed with 152-mm gun-howitzers and their companion pieces, the 122-mm guns. The 152-mm gun-howitzer is characterized by greater penetration, lower rate of fire, and, except with the self-propelled mount *KV*, considerably less maneuverability than the 152-mm howitzer. The 122-mm gun is characterized by high muzzle velocity, great penetration and range, good rate of fire, and only moderate maneuverability.

The brigade is used against targets which are beyond the range and capabilities of the light howitzer brigade. Its primary missions are destruction or neutralization of artillery and armored trains, neutralization or interdiction of distant targets, destruction of field fortifications, fire reconnaissance of important or exceptionally resistant targets, and destruction of distant minefields. It is likely that the new high-velocity 100-mm guns are replacing some of the 122-mm guns in the brigade.

HEAVY HOWITZER BRIGADE. The heavy howitzer, and possibly the heavy gun brigade, armed with 203-mm howitzers and 152-mm guns respectively, consist of brigade headquarters and headquarters battery, four firing battalions, and brigade services. The 203-mm howitzer is the most powerful piece habitually used by Soviet field artillery when great blast and penetration are required. Targets are carefully selected because of low rate of fire and great weight of ammunition. Primary missions of this brigade include destruction of permanent fortifications, bridges, railroads, and buildings. In tactical groupments, the 203-mm howitzer is combined with its companion piece, the 152-mm gun—a weapon which is characterized by great range, high muzzle velocity and penetration, low rate of fire, and poor maneuverability.

120-MM MORTAR BRIGADE. Every artillery division has a mortar brigade. Mortar brigades, however, also may be independent. A mortar brigade has good tactical and strategic mobility. It is armed with 108 120-mm mortars which are characterized by high rate of fire, great maneuverability, and good radius of burst. Primary missions of the mortar brigade include destruction of personnel in the open and in light shelters; destruction of light field fortifications and wire barriers; destruction or neutralization of artillery, mortar, and infantry firing positions; accompanying and defensive barrages and concentrations; and smoke screens. A heavy mortar brigade is especially useful in woods and swamps in direct support of infantry or cavalry. The brigade consists of three mortar regiments and brigade troops (fig. 24).

Unit	Off	EM	Total O & EM	7.62-mm SAR,R,& Cbn	7.62-mm SMG	7.62-mm LMG	12.7-mm AAMG	14.5-mm ATR	120-mm Mort	Trk	Sp Veh	Ki	Rad
Hq and Opns Stf	20	5	25	25						4	2		
Political Stf	3		3	3							1		
Sup Stf	10	10	20	20						2	1		
Hq Btry	5	119	124	98	24		3			12		1	4
3 120-mm Mort Regts	279	1,188	1,467	1,185	111	54		108	108	216	27	15	48
Med Plat	3	8	11	11						1	1		
Ord Wk Shops	6	18	24	24						3	3		
Am Plat	1	30	31	31						30			
Total	327	1,378	1,705	1,397	135	54	3	108	108	268	35	16	52

Figure 24. Table of Organization and Equipment: 120-mm Mortar Brigade.

b. Artillery regiments. Artillery regiments may be independent or may be parts of artillery brigades and artillery divisions, and organic to for-

Unit	Off	EM	Total O & EM	7.62-mm SAR, R, & Cbn	7.62-mm SMG	7.62-mm LMG	76-mm G	Trac	Tlr	Trk	Sp Veh	Ki	Rad
Hq & Opns Stf	7	2	9	9						1			
Political Stf	3		3	3									
Sup Stf	7	6	13	13						2			
Hq Btry													
Hq Plat	1	7	8	4	4					1			
Rcn Plat	1	10	11	6	5					2			
Sig Plat	1	23	24	19	5					3			4
Topo Plat	1	20	21	16	5					3			
Sup Sec		4	4	4						1		1	
2 76-mm G Bns	48	428	476	406	58	12	24	4	20	54	6	6	22
Med Plat	3	8	11	11						1	1		
Ord Wk Shop	3	9	12	12						1	1		
QM Wk Shop		5	5	5						1			
Trans Plat	1	16	17	17						11	5		
Sup Sec		3	3	3						1		1	
Total	76	541	617	528	77	12	24	4	20	81	14	8	26

Figure 25. Table of Organization and Equipment: 76-mm Gun Regiment, Motorized.

mations of combined arms. An artillery regiment generally consists of headquarters and headquarters battery aggregating between 75 and 100 officers and enlisted men, three firing battalions, and service troops. The headquarters battery has reconnaissance, topographic, signal, and headquarters platoons. Service troops consist of ammunition platoon, ordnance and motor work shops, supply train, and a small medical unit.

Independent artillery regiments carry a full unit of fire for their subordinate units. Regiments which are parts of larger artillery units or of formations of combined arms carry one-third of a unit of fire. Regiments are the lowest housekeeping and administrative units of the artillery arm.

Artillery regiments may be homogeneous or heterogeneous. (All units of homogeneous regiments are armed with the same weapon, whereas heterogeneous regiments are armed with two or more companion weapons.) Homogeneous regiments include the light artillery regiment (fig. 25), the mortar regiment (fig. 26), and the rocket regiment (fig. 27). A light artillery regiment generally forms a part of a light artillery brigade. It consists of headquarters and headquarters battery, two battalions with three firing batteries each, and services. This regiment is often combined with a tank destroyer regiment (fig. 14) to form an antitank groupment. Other missions of the light artillery regiment are outlined in the discussion of the light artillery brigade.

A heavy mortar regiment forms a part of a mortar brigade, or it may be independent. It consists of headquarters and headquarters battery, two firing battalions with 18 heavy mortars each, and regi-

Unit	Off	EM	Total O & EM	7.62-mm SAR, R, & Cbn	7.62-mm SMG	7.62-mm LMG	120-mm Mort	Trk	Sp Veh	Ki	Rad
Hq and Opns Stf	10	2	12	12					2			
Political Stf	3		3	3								
Sup Stf	7	8	15	15					2			
Hq Btry												
Hq Plat	1	7	8	4	4				1			
Rcn Plat	1	16	17	12	5				2			
Sig Plat	1	29	30	25	5				3			4
Topo Plat	1	25	26	21	5				3			
Sup Sec		7	7	7					1		1	
2 120-mm Mort Bns	60	258	318	243	18	18	36		44		4	12
Med Plat	3	8	11	11					1	1		
Ord Wk Shop	3	9	12	12					1	1		
QM Wk Shop		7	7	7					1			
Trans Plat	3	17	20	20					11	5		
Sup Sec		3	3	3					1	1		
Total	93	396	489	395	37	18	36		72	9	5	16

Figure 26. Table of Organization and Equipment: 120-mm Mortar Regiment

mental services. It is used for destruction of personnel and matériel in open positions and in open trenches, for destruction of wire entanglements, neu-

102

tralization of machine guns and mortars, and for the establishment of stationary and moving barrages. During artillery preparation for an offensive operation, the mortar regiment is often reinforced by a 122-mm howitzer regiment to form a countermortar groupment.

Unit	O & EM	7.62-mm SAR, R, & Cbn	7.62-mm SMG	7.62-mm LMG	7.62-mm Hv MG	12.7-mm AAMG	37-mm AA G	132-mm RL	Trac	Trk	Mtrcl	Ki	Rad
Hq & Stf	10									5			
Hq Plat	12	6	6	2						1			
Rcn Sqd	10	1	9	1						1			
Sig Sqd	15		10	5						2	2		6
Sup Sec	7	7								1		1	
3 Rkt Bns	639	570	69	12				24		48		3	14
AAAW Btry	62	35	15			6	6			12			
Trans Co	53	27								40			
Total	808	656	104	15		6	6	24		110	2	4	20

Figure 27. Table of Organization and Equipment: Rocket Regiment

The rocket regiment (M13) may be a part of a rocket brigade, or it may be independent. It has a balanced headquarters, three rocket battalions with two rocket batteries each, an antiaircraft machine gun company, and services. This regiment is used against area targets. Weight of metal of a single salvo from this unit is more than 7 tons.

Unit	O & EM	7.62-mm SAR, R, & Cbn	7.62-mm SMG	12.7-mm AAMG	37-mm AA G	Trk	Ki	Rad
Hq & Stf	11	4	7			1		
Sig Plat	21	14	7			4		3
Engr Plat	20	15	5			2		
Hq Plat	12	6	6			1		
Sup Sec	7	7				1	1	
4 37-mm Btrys	200	156	44		16	16		4
AAMG Co	90	57	33	16		16		1
Sup Plat	15	15				11	1	
Ord Shop	14	14				2		
Med Plat	7	7				2		
Total	397	295	102	16	16	56	2	

Figure 28. Table of Organization and Equipment: 37-mm Antiaircraft Automatic Weapons Regiment.

The medium and light antiaircraft artillery regiments are also homogeneous. (The light antiaircraft artillery regiment [antiaircraft automatic weapons regiment] is discussed under tank corps.) The medium antiaircraft artillery regiment is comparable to the U. S. antiaircraft artillery gun battalion. It may be a part of an antiaircraft artillery division, or it may be independent. It consists of headquarters and headquarters battery, four 4-piece firing bat-

teries, an antiaircraft machine gun company, and services (figs. 28 and 29). In addition to its primary mission of antiaircraft protection of ground troops and installations, it is employed for direct fire against ground fortifications, antitank defense, and, less often, for indirect fire against ground targets.

Heterogeneous artillery regiments include the divisional artillery regiment (fig. 4), the howitzer regiment (fig. 30), and the medium gun regiment (fig. 31). (Organization and missions of the divisional artillery regiment are outlined in the discussion of the rifle division.) The howitzer regiment consists of headquarters and headquarters battery, three firing battalions, and services. Its missions are outlined in the discussion of the howitzer brigade.

Unit	O & EM	7.62-mm SAR, R, & Cbn	7.62-mm SMG	12.7-mm AAMG	85-mm AA G	Trac	Trk	Sp Veh	Ki	Rad
Hq and Stf	26	15	11				2			
Hq Btry:										
Rcn Plat	12		12				1			
Topo Plat	12	9	3				1			
Sig Plat	35	30	5				4			4
Engr Plat	20	18	2				2			
Sup Sec	7	7					1		1	
4 Btrys	360	260	44		16	16	16			8
AAMG Btry	90	57	33	16			16			1
Am Plat	22	22					22			
Ord Wk Shop	8	8						1		
Mtr Wk Shop	10	10					1	1		
Sup Sec	11	11					1		2	
Med Plat	7	7					1			
Total	620	454	110	16	16	16	68	2	3	13

Figure 29. Table of Organization and Equipment: 85-mm Antiaircraft Artillery Regiment

The medium gun regiment consists of headquarters and headquarters battery, three battalions, and services. Two of the battalions are armed with 152-mm gun-howitzers, and the third with 122-mm guns. Missions of this regiment are the same as those of the medium gun brigade.

c. Artillery battalion. The basic organizational and tactical element of the artillery arm is the battalion. The artillery battalion generally consists of headquarters and headquarters battery, three firing batteries, and an ammunition train. The headquarters battery has reconnaissance, signal, topographic, and fire control units comprising between 50 to 65 officers and enlisted men. Independent artillery battalions have sufficient maintenance, repair, and service personnel to effect first and second echelon repairs and to carry one unit of fire and one refill of fuel for its subordinate units. Artillery battalions which form a part of larger artillery units

103

Unit	Off	EM	Total O & EM	7.62-mm SAR, R, & Cbn	7.62-mm SMG	7.62-mm LMG	12.7-mm AAMG	122-mm How	152-mm How	Trac	Tlr	Trk	Sp Veh	Ki	Rad
Hq and Opns Stf	11	2	13	13								2			
Political Stf	3		3	3											
Sup Stf	5	3	8	8								1			
Hq Btry:															
Hq Plat	1	9	10	6	4							1			
Rcn Plat	1	14	15	10	5							1			
Sig Plat	1	34	35	30	5							3			4
Topo Plat	1	20	21	16	5							2			
AA Plat	1	15	16	13	3		3					3			
Sup Sec		7	7	7								3		1	
2 122-mm Bns	48	482	530	436	98	12		24		48	36	38	6	6	22
1 152-mm Bn	24	254	278	231	49	6			12	24	18	19	3	3	11
Med Plat	3	9	12	12								1	1		
Ord Wk Shop	3	9	12	12									1		
QM Wk Shop		7	7	7									1		
Tech Plat	3	32	35	35						1	2	6	2		
Trans Plat	1	10	11	11								7			
Sup Sec		3	3	3								1		1	
Total	106	910	1,016	853	169	18	3	24	12	73	56	88	14	11	37

Figure 30. Table of Organization and Equipment: 122-mm Howitzer Regiment, Motorized.

(regiments and brigades) do not have maintenance and repair personnel. Their supply train carries one-half of a unit of fire. Artillery battalions which form a part of a formation of combined arms also have no service and maintenance personnel. Their ammunition platoon carries only one-third of a unit of fire.

There are two basic types of artillery battalions: the 12-piece (fig. 32), and the 6-piece battalion (fig. 33). The light guns and light and medium howitz-ers are organized into 12-piece battalions. The 122-mm and 152-mm motorized howitzer battalions differ from the 76-mm gun battalion (fig. 32) only in having greater personnel strength and the addition of 22 tractors and 16 trailers. The 122-mm howitzer battalion has 346 officers and enlisted men; the 152-mm howitzer battalion, 359. The medium guns, medium gun-howitzers, and heavy guns and howitzers are organized into six-piece battalions. The 122-mm gun battalion and 203-mm howitzer bat-

Unit	Off	EM	Total O & EM	7.62-mm SAR, R, & Cbn	7.62-mm SMG	7.62-mm LMG	12.7-mm AA MG	122-mm G	152-mm G/How	Trac	Tlr	Trk	Sp Veh	Ki	Rad
Hq & Opns Stf	11	2	13	13								2			
Political Stf	3		3												
Sup Stf	9	9	18	18								2			
Hq Btry															
Hq Plat	1	9	10	6	4							1			
Rcn Plat	1	18	19	14	5							2			
Topo Plat	1	20	21	16	5							2			
Sig Plat	1	34	35	30	5							3			4
AA Plat	1	15	16	13	3		3					3			
Sup Sec		7	7	7								1		1	
2 152-mm G/How Bns	50	464	514	228	80	6			12	24	16	30		4	18
1 122-mm G Bn	25	208	233	190	40	3		6		12	8	15		2	9
Med Plat	3	9	12	12								1	1		
Ord Wk Shop	3	9	12	12									1		
Qm Wk Shop		7	7	7									1		
Trans Plat	4	32	36	36						1	2	13	2		
Sup Sec		3	3	3								1		1	
Total	113	846	959	605	142	9	3	6	12	37	26	76	5	8	31

Figure 31. Table of Organization and Equipment: Medium Gun Regiment.

talion differ from the 152-mm gun-howitzer battalion (fig. 33) only in the size of the gun crews. Over-all strength of these battalions is 248 and 296 officers and enlisted men respectively.

Unit	Off	EM	Total O & EM	7.62-mm SAR, R, & Cbn	7.62-mm SMG	7.62-mm LMG	14.5-mm ATR	76-mm G	Trac	Tlr	Trk	Ki	Rad
Bn Hq & Stf	8	3	11	11							1		
Hq Btry													
Rcn Sec		8	8	4	4						1		2
Sig Sec		8	8	5	3						2		9
3 Btrys	15	168	183	159	18	6		12		6	18		
Am Plat	1	16	17	13	4				2	4	2		
Sup Sec		11	11	11							3	3	
Total	24	214	238	203	29	6		12	2	10	27	3	11

Figure 32. Table of Organization and Equipment: 76-mm Gun Battalion, Motorized.

The 12-piece battalion may be homogeneous or heterogeneous. The heterogeneous battalion has three batteries, two of which are armed with the same weapon, and the third with a companion piece to this weapon. Soviet artillery doctrine considers the following weapons to be supplementary or companion pieces:

76-mm gun and 122-mm howitzer.
122-mm howitzer and 152-mm howitzer.
152-mm gun-howitzer and 122-mm gun.
203-mm howitzer and 152-mm gun.

The last two pairs of companion pieces are not generally found in the same battalion. Rather, they are combined in mixed regiments.

Mortars and rockets are a part of the artillery arm. The heavy mortar battalion, a part of a mortar regiment, consists of headquarters and headquarters battery, which has the same organization as the headquarters battery of the artillery battalion, and three 6-piece firing batteries. Mortar battalions seldom have service troops. The provisional mortar battalion of the rifle division is formed from three heavy mortar batteries of the rifle regiments. The 82-mm mortars of the rifle battalions are organized into companies with nine medium mortars each.

The M-13 rocket battalion forms a part of the tank, mechanized, and cavalry corps, and of the

Unit	Off	EM	Total O & EM	7.62-mm SAR, R, & Cbn	7.62-mm SMG	7.62-mm LMG	152-mm G/How	Trac	Tlr	Trk	Sp Veh	Ki	Rad
Hq and Stf	9	2	11	11									
Hq Btry:													
Hq Sec	1	6	7	4	3					1			
Rcn Sec		6	6	3	3					1			
Topo Plat	1	18	19	14	5					2			
Sig Plat	1	29	30	25	5					3			3
Sup Sec		7	7	7						1		1	
3 Btrys	12	144	156	129	24	3	6	10	4	4			6
Am Plat	1	9	15	10				2	4	2			
Sup Sec		11	11	11						1		1	
Total	25	232	257	214	40	3	6	12	8	15		2	9

Figure 33. Table of Organization and Equipment: 152-mm Gun-Howitzer Battalion, Motorized.

rocket regiment. It is a balanced organization consisting of headquarters and headquarters company, two rocket batteries with four multiple launchers each, and ammunition and maintenance platoons.

Unit	O & EM	7.62-mm SAR, R, & Cbn	7.62-mm SMG	7.62-mm LMG	7.62-mm HvMG	12.7-mm AAMG	14.5-mm ATR	82-mm Mort	120-mm Mort	37-mm AA G	45-mm AT G	76-mm G & How	SU 85 (85-mm SP G)	M-13 RL	T-34/85 Tk	Armd Veh	Trac	Trk	H-dr Veh	H	Ki	Rad
Corps Hq	88	88																3	10	100	1	(10)
Rcn Bn	(300)	(65)	(235)	(28)							(14)							(8)			(2)	(10)
Sig Bn	(250)	(200)	(50)															(30)			(2)	(10)
Engr Bn	(290)	(225)	(50)	(24)														(16)	(20)	(25)	(2)	
2 Tk Regts	1,100	750	350	24			36						82	6	4		156				2	4
85-mm SP Arty Regt	270	40	225									20		1	1	2	38				2	6
Mort Regt (H-dr)	450	(400)	(50)					20										(50)		564	2	17
TD Arty Regt (Mtz)	496	286	210	12			24				24					30	39				2	14
AAAW Regt	397	295	102			16				16							56				2	8
Rkt bn	225	225					1							8		2	40				1	5
AT Bn	233	172	43	6			18			12							39				2	11
Maint Bn	(150)	(150)															12				1	
Trans Co	(150)	(137)	(6)	(3)			(4)										75				1	
CWS Co	63	55	(6)	(3)													(8)					
Fuel Colm	(30)	(30)															(20)					
Med Bn	(180)	(180)															(12)				3	
Vet Hosp	(50)	(50)																(8)	(15)			
Fd Bkry & Ldry	63	63															(2)	(10)	(20)			
3 Cav Divs	13,935	8,823	4,848	516	144	27	336	108	36	18	36	72					300	1,212	13,779	105	186	
Total	18,720	12,234	6,175	616	144	44	400	108	56	34	48	96	20	8	83	21	38	854	1,316	14,503	130	271

NOTE.—Figures in parenthesis are approximations.

Figure 34. Table of Organization and Equipment: Cavalry Corps.

It is likely that the organization of the heavy M–30 rocket battalion is similar to that of the M–13 rocket battalion.

5. CAVALRY

a. Cavalry corps. The cavalry corps is the normal operating cavalry formation which consists of three cavalry divisions, two to four tank regiments of 41 tanks each, a medium self-propelled artillery regiment, a motorized tank destroyer artillery regiment, a motorized heavy mortar regiment, a rocket battalion, and supporting arms and services (fig. 34). (Individual artillery units of the cavalry corps are discussed in conjunction with the artillery of the tank corps.)

The artillery commander of a cavalry corps has at his disposal five artillery regiments armed with a variety of weapons. The mission of this artillery is to support tanks and cavalry in mobile operations. The type and relative numbers of artillery weapons are selected so as to achieve maximum flexibility and shock power of fire without impairing the mobility of the corps. Including artillery and mortars of the cavalry divisions, the artillery commander of the cavalry corps has 346 pieces of artillery and 8 multiple rocket launchers at his disposal. The weight of metal of a single salvo of these weapons is more than 6 tons.

A cavalry corps has sufficient organic transport to maintain all of its components for 5 or 6 days of moderate combat.

b. Cavalry division. The cavalry division normally forms a part of a cavalry corps. It may also be independent. A cavalry division is a formation which is designed to perform one phase of an operation, such as an encirclement, pursuit, or a raid. A cavalry division consists of headquarters, three cavalry regiments, a mortar-artillery regiment, a light antiaircraft artillery battery, and supporting arms and services (fig. 35). It lacks the antitank battalion normally found in other formations of comparable size. Its mortar-artillery regiment is singular in that it has no battalion organization, and that it consists of three 76-mm batteries, and two 120-mm mortar batteries. Services of the cavalry division are small. Its maintenance and resupply facilities are sufficient to maintain it for only 1 to 2 days of moderate combat. It has no replacement pool.

c. Cavalry regiment. The cavalry regiment is normally a part of a cavalry division. However, cavalry regiments may be attached to other formations for reconnaissance, or they may act as independent units for specific missions such as night raids. A cavalry regiment consists of headquarters, four cavalry squadrons, and supporting arms and services (fig. 36). The proportion of cavalry proper to the supporting arms and services is less than 50 percent, a much smaller ratio than the proportion of infantry to other arms and services in a rifle regiment. A cavalry regiment is strong in automatic and antitank weapons. In comparison to a rifle regiment, it is weak in mortars.

Unit	O & EM	7.62-mm SAR, R, & Cbn	7.62-mm SMG	7.62-mm LMG	7.62-mm HvMG	12.7-mm AAMG	14.5-mm ATR	82-mm Mort	120-mm Mort	37-mm AAG	45-mm ATG	76-mm G & How	Trk	H-dr Veh	H	Ki	Rad
Div Hq	120	105	12	3										5	130	1	2
Rcn Sqd	110		110	9											110		
Sig Half-Sqd	53	48	5											12	65		5
Engr Sqd	70	58	12	6										12	65		1
AAAW Btry Mtz	80	68	12	6						6			6			1	1
Mort-Arty Regt H-dr	450	400	50	12			16		12			12			570	3	17
Servs:																	
CWS Sqd	64	55	6	3									4	8	35		
Am Colm	143	125	14	4									54			1	
Sup Colm	48	48											21			1	
Med Sqd	50	50											6	20	50	1	
Vet Hosp	25	25												2	25		
3 Cav Regts	3,432	1,959	1,395	129	48	9	96	36			12	12	9	345	3,543	27	36
Total	4,645	2,941	1,616	172	48	9	112	36	12	6	12	24	100	404	4,593	35	62

Figure 35. Table of Organization and Equipment: Cavalry Division.

Unit	O & EM	7.62-mm SAR, R, & Cbn	7.62-mm SMG	7.62-mm LMG	7.62-mm HvMG	12.7-mm AAMG	14.5-mm ATR	82-mm Mort	45-mm G	Trk	H-dr Veh	H	Ki	Rad
Regtl Hq	25	20	5	1							1	30	1	2
Rcn Sqd	(40)	5	35	4								40		
AA Plat	16	16				3				3				
Sig Plat	25	20	5	2							4	30		4
Engr Plat	18	11	5	2							2	20		
4 Cav Sqd	560	140	400	32			24				20	600	4	
HvMG Sqd	125	120			16						15	130	1	3
How Btry	86	81	5								10	65	2	3
Mort Bn	(80)	(80)						12			12	80	1	
AT Btry	55	55	6				8		4		10	70		
Servs														
Sup Plat	20	20									2	20		
Am Plat	(45)	(45)									30	60		
CWS Plat	12	9	2	1							1	8		
Med Plat	26	20	2	1							7	20		
Vet Plat	11	11									1	8		
Total	1,144	653	465	43	16	3	32	12	4	3	115	1,181	9	12

Figure 36. Table of Organization and Equipment: Calvary Regiment.

Section III. TECHNICAL SERVICES

1. INTRODUCTION

The allotment of technical services to field organizations is based on economy of personnel and equipment in the standard organizations, and on generous reserves of these services under the control of Army Group, army, and task force commanders. These principles were put into effect in April 1941, and resulted in the activation of many specialized units such as engineer brigades, signal regiments, and motor transport and road maintenance battalions. Specialized equipment is similarly concentrated in reserves for the commanders. Reserve signal equipment, for example, always is maintained under control of the signal officer of a unit or formation.

2. ENGINEER

Engineer units which form a part of formations of combined arms, such as rifle and cavalry divisions, were drastically reduced in size after the first few months of the war with Germany. The engineer battalion of the rifle division, for example, was reduced from 509 officers and enlisted men to 162. Not only was there a reduction in the size of the companies (the pioneer company had an aggregate of 170 just before the war, it now has 72), but also specialized units such as bridging, road repair, construction, and demolition platoons were taken away from the battalion. These specialized units were combined to form independent engineer battalions,

regiments, and brigades which are used to support corps, divisions, and armies. This reorganization of the engineer arm resulted in increasing specialization into combat engineers, ponton engineers, and construction engineers.

At present, the Soviet doctrine prescribes that each active rifle battalion must be supported by a platoon of engineers, and each active rifle regiment must be supported by a company. Therefore, each active rifle division must have an engineer battalion in addition to the organic allotment of engineers of the rifle regiments and the divisional engineer battalion.

The engineer platoon of the rifle regiment has 1 officer and 19 enlisted men. Its transport consists of one horse-drawn wagon. The engineer battalion of the rifle division has 16 officers and enlisted men organized into headquarters and headquarters company, two engineer companies of three platoons each and a transport platoon. Organic transport of the divisional engineer battalion consists of four trucks and nine horse-drawn wagons. Its total strength is approximately 178 officers and enlisted men.

Engineer mining companies are organized as supporting troops to tank and mechanized units. Their mission is to lay mines during offensive operations, to protect the flanks of a tank or mechanized unit during a break-through, and to secure captured positions against armored counterattacks. An engineer mining company consists of headquarters and three platoons. Each platoon has two trucks for personnel and one for antitank mines. The company carries

107

1,000 mines. Its strength is 121 officers and enlisted men.

Road construction engineers are organized into independent battalions, each consisting of two construction companies, a transport platoon, and a small overhead. Their strength is between 230 to 250 officers and enlisted men. Each road construction company has a strength of 100 officers and enlisted men, organized into three platoons of three 10-man sections, and a supply platoon. The mission of the road construction engineers is the maintenance and repair of existing roads, the construction of new dirt and corduroy roads, and the construction and repair of small bridges (up to 30 tons).

a. Bridging engineers. An independent light bridging battalion is capable of building a 200- to 250-foot ponton bridge of 5- to 14-ton capacity in 70 to 90 minutes. It consists of headquarters and headquarters company, three light bridging companies, and transport and service units. Each light bridging company has three platoons with 18 to 23 men in each. Strength of a light bridging battalion is approximately 250 officers and enlisted men.

The independent light (16T) bridging battalion is capable of constructing a 500-foot ponton bridge in 2 hours. It consists of three companies of four platoons each. Strength of this battalion is approximately 300 officers and enlisted men. Two such battalions may be combined to form a light bridging regiment capable of erecting a 1,350-foot ponton bridge in 2 hours. Strength of the light bridging regiment is approximately 750 officers and enlisted men.

The independent medium (30T) bridging battalion is capable of erecting a 325-foot ponton bridge in 2½ hours. It consists of two companies of four bridging platoons each. Its strength is approximately 300 officers and enlisted men. The engineer park of each tank and mechanized corps is allotted sufficient ponton materials to build a 30-ton bridge 300 feet long.

A heavy (60- to 100-ton) bridging regiment is capable of constructing a 340-foot ponton bridge in 3 hours. It consists of two heavy ponton battalions of four heavy ponton companies each. Its strength is approximately 700 officers and enlisted men.

3. SIGNAL

Allotment of signal personnel and equipment to the various organizations in the Red Army follows a definite pattern. In general, each unit and formation receives one telephone and telegraph team of three to seven men for each of its major subordinate units, one radio team, and one message center team. For example, a rifle regiment has a signal company of 50 officers and enlisted men. This company is organized into two telephone and telegraph platoons, and a radio platoon. The first telephone and telegraph platoon has three squads to establish wire communications with the rifle battalions. The second telegraph and telephone platoon establishes wire communications within the command, staff, and rear area installations of the regiment and maintains the message center. The radio platoon establishes and operates the radio nets of the regiment.

The signal company of the rifle division consists of the headquarters, a signal communications company, a signal construction company, a maintenance and repair platoon, and a supply section. Its strength is approximately 130 officers and enlisted men.

The independent signal battalion attached to the rifle, mechanized, tank, and cavalry corps consists of a headquarters company, a telephone company, a radio company, a signal construction company, a technical maintenance and repair platoon, and a supply section. Its strength is approximately 250 officers and enlisted men. The headquarters company of this battalion includes a telephone platoon which establishes and operates communications within the headquarters, a messenger platoon, and an air liaison platoon. The telephone company consists of three platoons each with 3 trucks, 9 telephones, and 15 miles of field cable. For extended operations (laterally and in depth) the signal battalion is reinforced with one or more telephone companies. The signal construction company is equipped with six cable-laying trucks. Its strength is approximately 30 officers and enlisted men.

The army signal regiment has between 700 and 800 officers and enlisted men. Its mission is to establish and maintain communications for the army headquarters, staff, and rear area installations. For communications with subordinate units and formations, it receives one additional telephone company for each corps. It consists of headquarters, telephone and telegraph battalion, a signal construction battalion, a signal intelligence company, and a service battalion.

The telephone and telegraph battalion includes a teletype and telephone exchange, a radio company, and a messenger company. The radio company has one transmitter for each subordinate formation, six semi-mobile transmitters, and five radio trucks. The messenger company has 50 officers and enlisted men, 12 staff cars, and 6 motorcycles. The signal construction battalion consists of two or more cable companies, each with six cable-laying trucks. The service battalion consists of a transportation company, maintenance company, and supply platoon.

4. CHEMICAL WARFARE SERVICE

The chemical warfare units of Red Army field formations are organized into companies and platoons. Chemical warfare units which are part of the technical reserves of the high command are organized into companies and battalions.

Each platoon consists of an antigas squad and a decontaminating squad. Its strength is 12 to 15 men. Fifty to sixty officers and enlisted men form the chemical warfare company. It is believed that each army has a gas defense battalion with the primary mission of conducting refresher and basic training for the gas defense personnel of subordinate formations and units.

Although platoons and companies are described as antigas units, their primary mission has been to facilitate the work of assault groups, to screen water-barrier crossings, and to lay smoke screens to cover the withdrawal of damaged tanks and self-propelled guns from the battlefield.

Flame thrower units belong to the Chemical Warfare Service. A flame thrower platoon with ten flame throwers is organic to the motorcycle battalion of the tank and mechanized corps. A flame thrower battalion is part of the supporting troops of the average army.

5. MAINTENANCE

The organizational element of ordnance and maintenance in the Red Army is the field work shop. Each work shop is operated by 8 to 10 technicians under the supervision of an ordnance officer. The number of work shops assigned to a unit or a formation depends on the armament and degree of motorization of the organization. The rifle division has one Type A work shop. The tank brigade has two Type A work shops, one Type B work shop, an air compressor, and three trucks. Three tractors with trailers, and 29 trucks are used to haul spare parts, fuel, rations, and ammunition for the tank brigade. The work shop company of the tank and mechanized corps has two Type A and two Type B work shops, electrical work shop, four to six special vehicles, and

five tractors with two trailers. It is believed that recovery tanks with heavy cranes have been added to the maintenance units of formations down to and including the tank and mechanized corps and, possibly, to the work shop company of the tank and mechanized brigades. Figure 37 shows the organization of maintenance facilities of the army, tank and mechanized corps, and tank and mechanized brigades.

6. MEDICAL AND VETERINARY SERVICE

Medical and veterinary units in the Red Army, like other special services, are organized on the principle that those medical and veterinary teams organic to field units and formations should be kept to a minimum size, and that the specialized units constituting part of the technical services reserve of the high command should be organized into teams with ample personnel and equipment.

Medical teams of the rifle battalion, rifle regiment, and tank and artillery regiments consist of from five to seven men. Their primary function is to render first aid and to evacuate wounded. Tank, motorized, and mechanized brigades have medical units of approximately 32 men. Larger formations, such as cavalry divisions and rifle brigades, have a medical company of approximately 60 officers and enlisted men. The rifle division, cavalry, tank, and mechanized corps each have a medical battalion capable of emergency surgery, but whose primary functions are sorting, dressing, and evacuating wounded. This battalion consists of a sorting unit, an ambulance platoon, a divisional (corps) aid station, a collecting company, and an epidemic control unit.

Medical services for the field units are concentrated at the army level (see Section I, Armies). The army medical battalion, which allots reinforcing elements to the divisions and mobile corps, is organized into surgical and hospital teams. The number of such teams corresponds generally to the number of subordinate rifle corps, rifle divisions, and mobile corps. The surgical team has a surgeon, three to five physicians, four to five surgical nurses, five to six orderlies, and a recorder. The functions of the members of this team are self-explanatory. The recorder keeps the administrative records of the hospital, and records each operation as it takes place.

The hospital team is organized into sections according to types of injury. Each section consists of a surgeon, a physician, two to three surgical nurses

Attached to—	Number	Designation	Equipment	Strength	Operational area	Mission
Armd Bn; SP Arty Regt; Arty Regt; R Div.	1	Mbl Rep Shop Type A	1 GAZ-AA trk or 3-ton trk ZIS-5 with a lathe, welding equipment and repair parts.	8 to 10 men (1 tech off, 5 locksmiths, 1 lathe operator, 1 welder).	On the battlefield.	Repair of slightly disabled tks (caterpillars, transmissions, welding jobs).
Tk Brig. Tk Regt. Mecz Brig.	1 to 2 2 to 4	Tech Sup Co with: Mbl Rep Shops Type A Mbl Rep Shops Type B	Same as above. Each Rep shop has 1 covered ZIS-6 trk with lathe, and tools, spare parts, crane and storage-battery charger. In addition: 1 Milling machine and welding equip. 2 to 3 "Stalinets" tracs. 6 to 8 Trks. 1 Passenger car.	Same as above. 9 men each.	2 to 5 km behind the front line.	(a) Hauling. (b) Current simple and medium repair of tks and mtr vehs. (For instance, replacement of engines and of other parts.)
Tk Corps. Mecz Corps.	2 8 to 10	Mbl Fld Rep Base or Rep Bn. Mbl Rep Shops Type A Mbl Rep Shops Type B	Same as above. Same as above. In addition: 10 Mtr vehs. 8 to 9 Tracs.	Approx. 200 specialists.	10 to 30 km behind the front line.	Same as above.
Army.	1	Large Mbl Rep Shop Type C and probably several Fld Rep Bases. Also a repair shop in a factory located in the army rear area.	5 to 6 RR cars. 2 Lathes, drilling, cutting, milling, and grinding machines. 2 Forgeries, 1 electric plant, electric welding equipment, repair parts. In addition: 7 1½-ton trks. 1 5-ton trk. 1 Passenger car. 4 to 5 Tracs.	1 Off; 1 Engr; 44 EM. In addition: 30 EM.	50 to 100 km behind the front line.	Major repairs, supply of spare parts, reserve pools of repair shops.
Army.		Assembly places for disabled tks and trks (SPAM).			Area of sup station.	Collection and probably some repair of tks and trks.

Figure 37. Red Army maintenance services.

110

and five to seven orderlies. The infectious diseases section of the hospital team consists of a physician, a nurse, three to four orderlies, and an X-ray and physiotherapy unit.

The army convalescent battalion is capable of caring for 1,000 cases. It is divided into four convalescent companies, a dental clinic, an infectious diseases ward, and a pharmacy. Each convalescent company has a dressing station manned by two physicians, three nurses, and three to four orderlies.

The veterinary units are organized according to the same principle as the medical units. Organic veterinary units of the horsedrawn field troops are very small. A rifle division, for example, which has approximately 1,700 horses, has a veterinary aid station with 11 officers and enlisted men. Like the medical services, the veterinary services are concentrated at the army level. Each army has two veterinary hospitals—each capable of caring for approximately 250 horses—and one or two veterinary evacuation hospitals.

APPENDIX

The abbreviations which are used in the Tables of Organization and Equipment are those authorized by TM 20–205. They are reproduced in the table below for the convenience of the reader.

AA—antiaircraft
AAA—antiaircraft artillery
AAAW—antiaircraft automatic weapon
AAMG—antiaircraft machine gun
Am—ammunition
Armd—armored
Armd C—armored car
Armd Pers Carr—armored personnel carrier
Arty—artillery
AT—antitank
ATR—antitank rifle
Auto R—automatic rifle
Bkry—bakery
Bcl—bicycle
Bn—battalion
Brig—brigade
Btry—battery
Carr—carrier
Cav—cavalry
Cbn—carbine
Co—company
Colm—column
CWS—Chemical Warfare Service
Div—division
Dr—drawn
EM—enlisted men
Engr—engineer
Fld—field
G—gun
H—horse

H-dr—horse-drawn
Hosp—hospital
How—howitzer
Hq—headquarters
Hv—heavy
HvMG—heavy machine gun
Ki—kitchen
L—light
Ldry—laundry
LMG—light machine gun
L-Tk—light tank
M—medium
Maint—maintenance
Mbl—mobile
Mecz—mechanized
Med—medical
MG—machine gun
mm—Millimeter
Mort—mortar
Mtr—motor
Mtrcl—motorcycle
Mtz—motorized
O and EM—officers and enlisted men
Obsn—observation
Off—officer
Opns—operations
Ord—ordnance
QM—quartermaster
Pers—personnel
Plat—platoon
R—rifle
Rad—radio
Rcn—reconnaissance
Regt—regiment
Regtl—regimental
Rep—repair
Repl—replacement
Rkt—rocket
RL—rocket launcher
SAR—semiautomatic rifle
Sec—section
Serv—service
Sig—signal
SMG—submachine gun
SP—self-propelled
Sp—special
Sqd—squad
Stf—staff
Sup—supply
TD—tank destroyer
Tech—technical
Tk—tank
Tlr—trailer
Topo—topographic
Tr—troop
Trac—tractor
Trans—transportation
Trk—truck
Trk-dr—truck-drawn
Veh—vehicle
Vet—veterinary
Wk—work

CHAPTER IV

SEMI-MILITARY ORGANIZATIONS

INTRODUCTION

1. GENERAL

One of the outstanding features of a totalitarian state is the facility with which governmental agencies can be applied to military effort. During World War II, all agencies of the U. S. S. R. and the Communist Party were devoted, in varying degree, to military purposes.

The transition of agencies and individuals between civil and military positions within the Soviet Union has always been extremely fluid. A number of semiofficial bodies, commissariats, and main administrations were, however, specifically brought into the military structure during World War II. These organizations included those temporarily incorporated into the Red Army or Navy, those given the status of armed forces, those legally militarized, and the Partisans.

2. AGENCIES INCORPORATED INTO ARMY AND NAVY

The most important agencies temporarily incorporated into the Red Army and Navy were the Main Administrations of the Civil Air Fleet, the Hydro-Meteorological Service, and the Northern Sea Route. In addition, the Main Administration for Universal Compulsory Military Training of the Citizens of the U. S. S. R. (*Vsevobuch*) was organized in 1941 to place the semiofficial and voluntary training activities carried on by the national Organization for the Defense of the Soviet Union and Defense against Air Raids and Chemical Attack (*Osoaviakhim*) under military control and on a compulsory basis.

3. AGENCIES GIVEN ARMED FORCE STATUS

Even before World War II, troops of the Peoples' Commissariat of Internal Affairs (NKVD) had the legal status of an armed force equivalent to the Red Army and Navy. Its authority was extensive. It maintained border guards and strategic security forces, controlled all local police and fire departments, conducted foreign espionage, and conducted counterespionage among the civil population and in the army and the navy.

The Soviet government carefully controlled the functions of the NKVD. The Army was made responsible for its own internal security in 1943. Secret domestic counterespionage and foreign espionage functions were given to the newly organized Peoples' Commissariat of State Security (NKGB). The NKGB also was given the status of an armed force.

4. AGENCIES LEGALLY MILITARIZED

Because the operation of transportation and signal communications systems had to be coordinated closely with the requirements of the Red Army and Navy, the Soviet government legally militarized the Commissariats of Signal Communications, Transportation, Waterways, and the Maritime Fleet. Repeated enemy attacks also necessitated their militarization. Personnel in these organizations were subjected to martial authority and, in most instances, were given army or navy ranks. They wore special uniforms.

5. PARTISANS

The organization of the Partisan movement in the areas of the U. S. S. R. occupied by the Germans and in other countries overrun by German forces is the only exception to the rule that the Communist Party does not maintain an armed force within the Soviet state.

Early in World War II, the Central Committee of the Communist Party directly commanded and administered all Partisan activities through the Commander in Chief of the Partisans. Operational coordination of Partisan activities was taken over by the General Headquarters and by army group (front) headquarters in the field as the Red Army assumed the offensive. Once an area was reoccupied, control over all Partisans was assumed by the Chief of Security Troops, who commanded all NKVD forces within each army group zone.

Occasionally, Partisans in reoccupied areas were organized into "destruction battalions" to assist in the mopping up of the remnants of German forces.

All Partisans, however, ultimately were disarmed and screened by the NKVD. Some were drafted into field replacement units. Some were given responsible local positions with the NKVD or civilian authorities, and some were sent to the rear as unreliable elements. The secret agents of the Occupied Territories Administration of the NKGB assisted the NKVD screen Partisans.

6. EFFECTIVENESS

Semi-military organizations generally proved to be of marked usefulness in the Soviet war effort. Partisans were of strategic importance in impeding German operations. The NKVD and NKGB consolidated the rear area of the Red Army and protected the zone of the interior. A considerable number of German remnants and isolated dissident groups were controlled so effectively that they never interfered seriously with military operations. The signal communications and transportation systems of the U. S. S. R. were able to accomplish their missions successfully despite a partial break-down in the winter and spring of 1942 and despite serious shortages.

In contrast, *Vsevobuch* achieved only limited results. The attempt to add training to the total productive effort of Soviet civilians required an impossibly great effort. Results were achieved only for a few critical months and in a few special fields.

One of the most significant aspects of the Soviet employment of semi-military organizations was the care exercised to insure effective coordination with the strictly military effort, to prevent the growth of a vast competing structure, and to avoid duplication of effort.

The State Defense Committee maintained control over all semi-military agencies, although the General Headquarters directed NKVD, NKGB, and Partisan operations. Each organization was charged with strictly delimited functions. In several instances, notably the NKVD, prewar functions were reduced. Thus the NKVD lost its control over army intelligence, counterintelligence, and secret operations. It consequently was denied conditions favorable for grandiose usurpation of the military effort, such as was exercised by the SS in Germany. The volunteer *Osoaviakhim* was relegated to a secondary role during World War II. It was supervised strictly by the Communist Party so as to prevent its operation as the nucleus of any dissident movement.

Most semi-military organizations resumed their civilian roles with the termination of martial law in October 1945. Signal communications and transportation no longer are militarized. Military training, other than regular recruit training, now is voluntary and semiofficial.

The NKVD and NKGB, however, are of even greater importance than during World War II. They are insuring the orderly demobilization of the army, the effective integration of dischargees into the civilian population, and the careful screening of the future peacetime army to guarantee its complete political reliability.

Section I. PEOPLES' COMMISSARIAT OF INTERNAL AFFAIRS

1. GENERAL

The Peoples' Commissariat of Internal Affairs (NKVD) is responsible for maintenance of the security of the Soviet Union.

It conducts frontier and coastal patrols, controls all local police and fire departments, maintains special mobile forces for use against sabotage or insurrection, and is in charge of all prisons.

The local police functions involve the NKVD in the maintenance of internal passport control, birth certificates, and other vital statistics. Its control over local fire departments gives it over-all control of passive antiaircraft defense in time of war. Finally, the control of prison labor involves the Commissariat in extensive construction, mining, and development projects. All roads and highways are responsibilities of the Commissariat.

The NKVD is a Union-Republican Commissariat and consequently has corresponding organizations in the republics. Not all of the main administrations of the Commissariat, however, have counterparts in the republics (fig. 1).

The Main Administration of Border Troops, for example, is organized directly into Border Guard Districts. Railroad troops and other interior troops remain mobile under central control. Although prisoners are controlled directly by the Main Administration of Labor and Prisoner-of-War Camps, their productive efforts normally are directed by special trusts such as *Dalstroi*, a trust for the economic development of the Kolyma area in the Far East.

Semi-military forces of the NKVD include Border Troops, Interior Troops, Signal Troops, Police Troops (militia), and Fire Defense Troops. The Commissariat's troops normally are selected from reliable Party members. Their great strength, at one

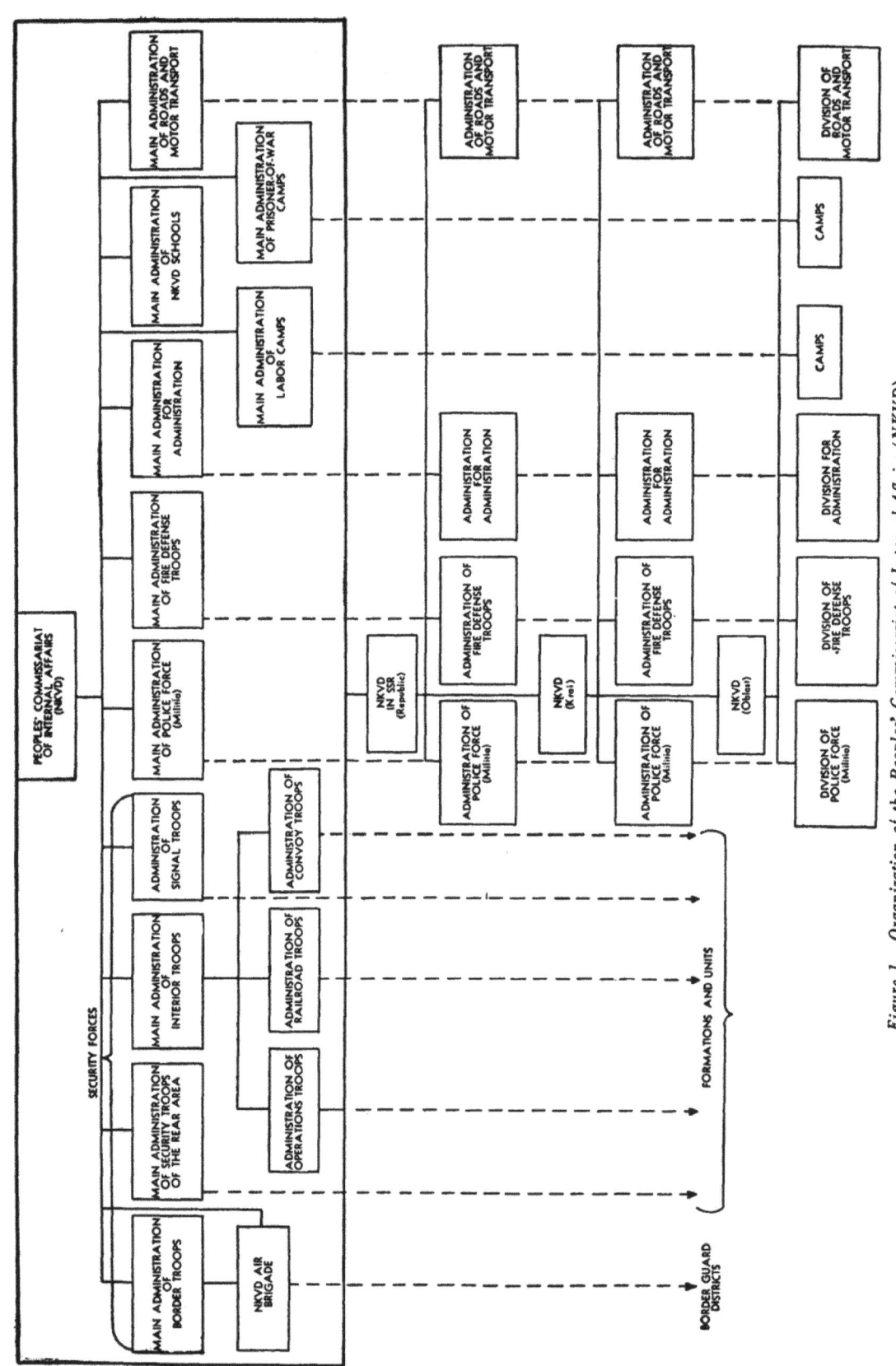

Figure 1. Organization of the Peoples' Commissariat of Internal Affairs (NKVD).

114

time well over half a million, attests to the importance of their activities during World War II.

2. BORDER AND SECURITY TROOPS

The Border Troops of the NKVD are charged with the supervision and security of the land and sea frontier. They are organized into Border Districts manned by Border Battalions (fig. 2), whose duties include border and coastal patrol, counterespionage and customs control. They do not garrison fortifications.

Border Battalions, averaging from 1,000 to 1,200 in strength, control the First, or Border, Zone of the U. S. S. R. The First Zone extends approximately 9 miles from the actual boundary. Only border troops and special construction units are permitted to enter the zone, except at control points. Every installation and road is guarded 24 hours a day. No movement is permitted at night, except mounted or foot patrols accompanied by dogs.

A Border Battalion's zone is approximately 60 miles wide, although it may be extended in areas of poor communications. Elements of the NKVD Air Brigade assist Border Battalions in difficult terrain. The Air Brigade is directly subordinate to the Peoples' Commissariat of Internal Affairs. It includes a number of air regiments and independent squadrons.

During World War II, the organization of Border Troops in theaters of operations was modified. The Border Troops were redesignated as Security Troops of the Rear Area of the Red Army. They were as-

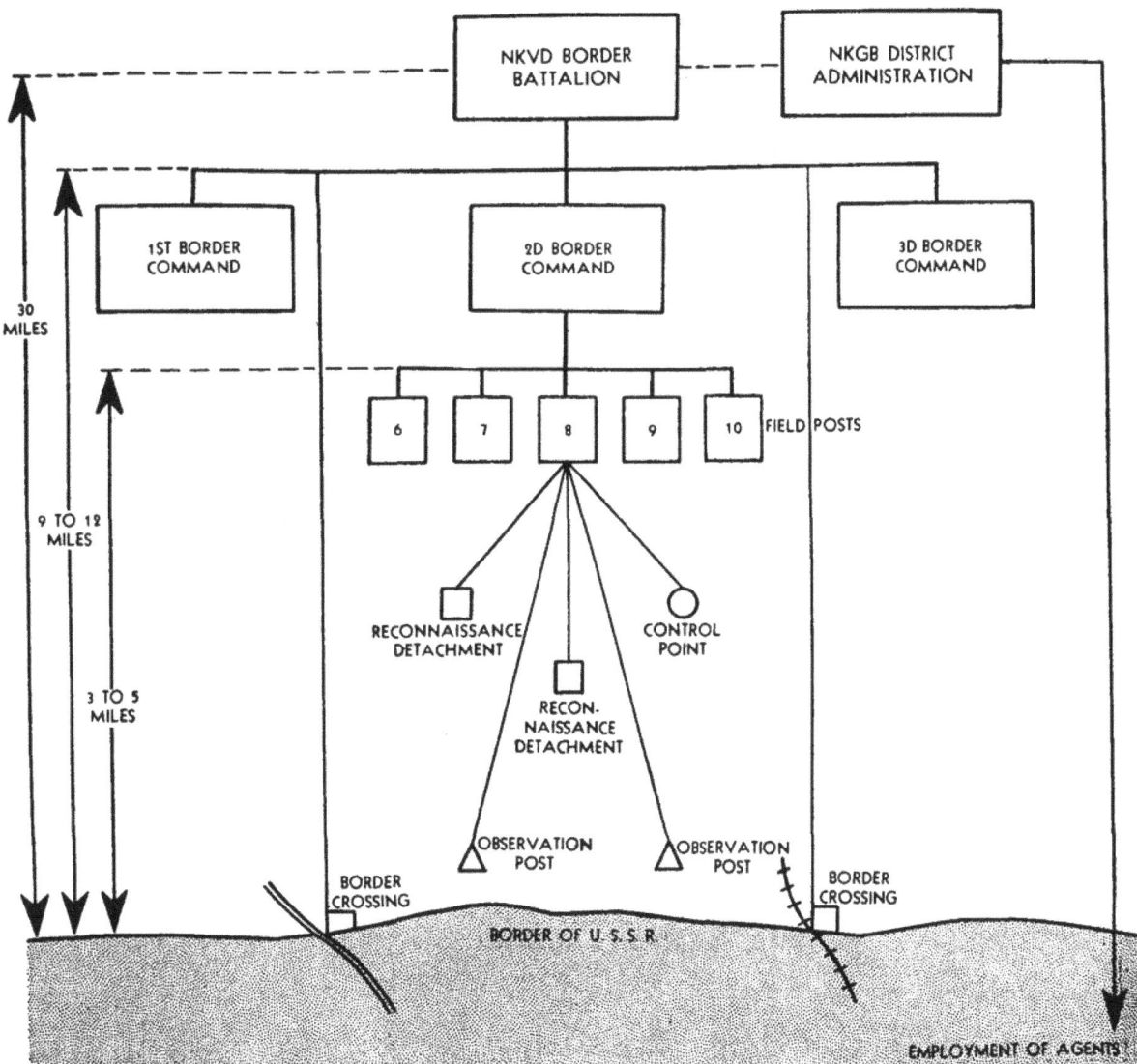

Figure 2. Organization and deployment of a NKVD border battalion.

signed the mission of apprehension of enemy agents, parachute troops, and Red Army stragglers or deserters. They also guarded rear area installations and maintained straggler lines. The Security Troops of the Rear Area of the Red Army were withdrawn from the Main Administration of Border Troops and placed under separate administrative control.

The former Border Battalions were organized into Security Regiments, subordinate to army groups (fronts) and commanded by the Chief of the Security Troops of the Rear Area.

Normally, one Security Regiment was assigned to the rear area of each army, and five to six regiments to the rear area of each army group.

Each Security Regiment consisted of three rifle battalions, a machine gun company, a reconnaissance company, a submachine gun company, a signal communications company, an antitank company, an engineer platoon, and maintenance, chemical warfare, and transport units. Artillery was attached as required. The strength of each regiment was approximately 1,650 officers and enlisted men.

3. INTERIOR TROOPS

The Interior Troops of the NKVD constitute mobile forces to insure the security of the state. They include Operational Troops, Railway Troops, Convoy Troops, and Factory Guards.

Operational Troops are charged with destruction of enemy elements in the interior and in the rear of the Red Army, suppression of insurrection, and protection of key installations and individuals. They also guard railroads and prisoners when necessary.

Their organization has been subject to several changes. Before World War II, they were organized into corps, regiments, battalions, and companies. The corps were reorganized into divisions of approximately eight regiments each early in the war. Approximately five of the regiments were similar to NKVD Security Regiments, organized from Border Battalions, one to two were motorized, and one was a cavalry regiment. By 1944, the divisions were being motorized, cavalry largely had been grouped into separate divisions, and brigades of two to three regiments and two to three separate battalions were being organized within each military district.

At present, the divisions are believed to be equipped with tanks and to approach the Red Army mechanized corps in size—approximately 15,000 officers and enlisted men—and in fire power. The brigades appear to be flexible semimobile organizations similar to the Security Regiments.

Missions of the divisions and brigades of the NKVD are different. The divisions provide a centralized mobile force for maintenance of state security. During the World War II, they were committed for operations, particularly anti-Partisan actions and mopping up of enemy remnants, in the rear of army groups under the army group Chief of Security Troops. The brigades, however, provide internal security within the military districts. Both conduct defensive operations against airborne forces.

The *Railway Troops* are charged with the defense of railroad lines. They employ armored trains and cooperate closely with Railroad Station Commandants of the Red Army, who are charged with the defense of terminals, stations, and depots. Railway Troops are organized into divisions, brigades, regiments, and separate battalions. Divisions in active operational zones have as many as 10 armored trains.

The *Convoy Troops* protect the movement of troops, supplies, and prisoners on the roads, railroads, and waterways. They also insure the uninterrupted movement of convoys. Although their major functions apply to the zone of the interior, their commitment extends to the rear areas of armies. Normally, they are concentrated in the zone of main effort. Convoy Troops are organized into divisions, each containing up to five regiments.

The *Factory Guards* provide local and interior protection for major industries.

4. SIGNAL TROOPS

The Signal Troops of the NKVD were organized in 1943 as a separate administration directly under the Commissariat to improve the communications security of the Red Army and of the Peoples' Commissariat of Signal Communications. Their mission includes monitoring of both friendly and enemy broadcasts, and the establishment, operation, and maintenance of signal communication systems for staffs and units of the NKVD.

One Signal Regiment is subordinate to the Chief of Security Troops of each army group. Each Signal Regiment includes three operating battalions and two signal construction companies. Its strength is approximately 1,000 officers and enlisted men.

5. POLICE TROOPS

The Police Troops (militia) of the NKVD are a uniformed force to suppress crime and control traffic. They also play a major role in state security through comprehensive control of passports and vital statistics. Police representation on all draft boards and in reception centers assures the political reliability of all inductees. All changes in residence, travel applications, births, and deaths must be reported to the police, normally within 24 hours.

Police control is especially stringent within the Second and Third Border Zones. The Second Zone extends approximately 60 miles in depth from the boundary. All inhabitants in it are examined carefully by the police to determine their political reliability. Unreliable elements are sent further into the interior. Travel within the Second Zone is permitted only with special passes.

The Third, or Alertness, Zone extends still deeper. The population in this Zone is supervised carefully and is specially indoctrinated to cooperate with the Police Troops and other agencies of the NKVD in the apprehension of suspicious characters. Travel in the Third Zone is controlled.

Police Troops are organized on a Union-Republican basis. Consequently, police headquarters are attached to all political subdivisions down to district or *Oblast* level. Police troops are organized into regiments, battalions, companies, and platoons. Each unit is much larger than corresponding units in the Red Army.

Service in the Police Troops was on a volunteer basis prior to 1941. Periods of enlistment were 2 years. Men who had served in the Red Army constituted the majority of personnel. Volunteers could join at 18. They could remain in the service and be exempt from military service if their performance was satisfactory. Women were recruited extensively for Police Troops during World War II.

6. FIRE DEFENSE TROOPS

The Main Administration of Fire Defense of the NKVD, assisted by the Central Research Institute of Fire Defense, controls the Fire Defense Troops. In time of peace, they are charged with local fire protection.

During World War II, the organization was changed into the Main Administration for Passive Antiaircraft Defense. The regional counterparts of the Main Administration controlled Passive Antiaircraft Defense Groups conscripted from local populations. They were responsible for preparatory measures against air raids, air-raid warning systems, camouflage, camouflage discipline, defense against chemical attack, damage control, and first aid.

The operations of the Main Administration for Antiaircraft Defense were integrated closely with those of the Main Administration of Antiaircraft Defense Forces (GUPVO) of the Red Army, with the *Osoaviakhim*, and with the Commissariats of Transportation and Signal Communications.

The Commander of the operational staff for Passive Antiaircraft Defense in each political subdivision was in direct communication with the GUPVO Commander, who was responsible for the active fighter and antiaircraft defense of the area. The visual observation systems of Passive Antiaircraft Defense were integrated fully with the observers and radar of the GUPVO.

Regional staffs of the Passive Antiaircraft Defense Main Administration controlled the passive defense of signal and railroad installations. Because such installations were major targets, they were provided with direct communications to the air warning center. Special damage repair brigades were provided for them.

Local air-raid defenses were based upon thorough preparation of shelters and full mobilization of the population. All air-raid shelters had to be approved by the local antiaircraft defense staff, a medical inspector, and construction organizations.

A Passive Antiaircraft Defense Group was organized in residences or apartments for every 200 to 500 population. One Group was organized for every 100 to 300 population in factories and other installations. All able-bodied men between 16 and 60 and all able-bodied women between 18 and 50 were subject to compulsory service in the Fire Defense forces. They served in both their place of residence and their place of work. The sole exceptions were persons on active duty with the Red Army or the NKVD.

Each Passive Antiaircraft Defense Group included a Commander, his deputy, and five detachments. Strengths of the detachments were as follows:

Detachment	Strength
Control and observation	6
Fire defense	9
Anti-chemical	5
Repair and damage control	7
Medical	4

Each Group maintained a reserve of not less than 25 percent of its strength.

The Main Administration for Passive Antiaircraft Defense shared the responsibility for civilian defense training with the *Osoaviakhim*, the nation-wide voluntary defense association of the U. S. S. R. Joint training regulations and a special 40-hour training program were prepared.

Fire Defense Troops were trained to form the nucleus of Partisan bands should their area be overrun by the enemy.

Section II. PEOPLES' COMMISSARIAT OF STATE SECURITY

1. GENERAL

The Peoples' Commissariat of State Security (NKGB) was organized in 1943 to assume the functions of counterespionage and strategic foreign espionage which had been handled by a special division of the Peoples' Commissariat of Internal Affairs.

Reconnaissance, tactical espionage, and counter-intelligence operations within the Red Army, however, were conducted by the Red Army itself. Overt surveillance of the civilian population and signal security remained functions of the NKVD.

The NKGB is a Union-Republican Commissariat, but counterparts of the national organization have been established in few of the republics and political subdivisions of the U. S. S. R.

2. ORGANIZATION

Functions of the Commissariat of State Security are performed by a number of administrations and divisions.

The *Foreign Countries Administration* organizes and conducts espionage outside of the U. S. S. R. It is believed to be composed of regional divisions. The Administration also is concerned with Soviet propaganda abroad.

The *Occupied Territories Administration* supervised and controlled Soviet nationals in enemy-occupied territory during World War II. It is not known whether this administration still exists. It may continue to conduct surveillance of Soviet nationals in areas outside direct Red Army control. It is believed that this administration was concerned primarily with political reliability and that it took little or no part in the conduct of Partisan operations.

The *Secret Political Administration* investigates anti-Soviet activities and organizations within the U. S. S. R. It maintains secret surveillance of the loyalty of Communist Party members.

The *Administration for Counterespionage in the Soviet Economy* is charged with the responsibility of preventing foreign economic espionage and sabo-

tage. It is charged with security control over industrial installations and output and over the fiscal position of the U. S. S. R.

The *Counterintelligence Administration* is concerned principally with control of the activities of foreigners in the U. S. S. R. It also watches Soviet citizens of foreign birth or suspected of foreign affiliations.

Other administrations and divisions of the Peoples' Commissariat of State Security are charged with mail censorship, telephone and telegraph communications, secret surveillance within prisons, etc.

The Commissariat of State Security, unlike the Commissariat of Internal Affairs, maintains no troops or armed forces of its own. It operates through small groups or individuals, largely under cover. It has, however, official militarized status. Its personnel are given military rank and the privileges of general officers.

Section III. PEOPLES' COMMISSARIAT OF SIGNAL COMMUNICATIONS

1. GENERAL

The Peoples' Commissariat of Signal Communications (NKS), a Union-Republican Commissariat, is responsible for the majority of Soviet signal communications systems. However, it is not responsible for combat zone communications, the internal communications of the Peoples' Commissariat of Internal Affairs, the railroad signal system, or the internal communications systems of the navy. It does include the postal, telephone, and telegraph services.

The Commissariat cooperates closely with both the Peoples' Commissariat of National Defense and the Peoples' Commissariat of Internal Affairs. Its personnel were placed under full military discipline during World War II.

The close relations between the Commissariats of Signal Communications and Defense during most of World War II were reinforced by the appointment of the Commissar of Signal Communications, Ivan T. Peresypkin, as Chief Marshal of Signal Troops and Chief of the Signal Division of the Red Army General Staff.

2. RESPONSIBILITY FOR ARMY COMMUNICATIONS

The Peoples' Commissariat of Signal Communications maintains and operates all communications in the area of army group (front) headquarters, except those direct to the GHQ. The Commissariat is responsible for the development, production, and initial supply of Red Army signal equipment, powerful radio stations, charging equipment, and other operations beyond the capabilities of Red Army signal troops.

3. ORGANIZATION

The Peoples' Commissariat of Signal Communications is known to include Main Administrations for the Postal Service, Signal Operations, and Signal Construction. It also includes a number of research and training institutes.

Coordination with the armed forces is the responsibility of the Central Military Administration of the Commissariat.

Section IV. PEOPLES' COMMISSARIAT OF TRANSPORTATION

1. GENERAL

The Peoples' Commissariat of Transportation (NKPS) is an All-Union Commissariat charged with the maintenance and operation of all railroads, including the Moscow subway.

Prior to 1931 the Commissariat controlled all types of transportation. During 1931, however, responsibility for all transportation other than rail was transferred to other commissariats. The Commissariat of Transportation was militarized in April 1943. Employees were compelled to remain on their jobs for the duration of the war. They were placed under the Red Army disciplinary code and were made subject to military tribunals. Special uniforms and military ranks were introduced in September 1943.

Thirty-nine railroad divisions have been identified. Generally, they correspond to the military districts.

Activities of the Peoples' Commissariat of Transportation are conducted through the following agencies:

> Departments:
>> Political.
>> Central Operating.
>> Central Locomotive.
>> Central Car.
>> Car and Track Maintenance.
>> Signal Communications.
>> New Railroad Construction.

> Central Sections:
>> Supply.
>> Economic Planning.
>> Finance.
>> Mobilization.
>> Lumber.
>> Electrification.
>> Personnel Training.
>> Sanitary.
>> Accounting.
>> Administration.
> Central Bureau for Foreign Relations.

2. COORDINATION

Coordination is effected between the Commissariat of Transportation and the Chief of the Rear Services of the Red Army, between the Chiefs of Railroad Divisions and the Chiefs of Transportation of the Rear Services of army groups (front), between the Chiefs of Railroad Divisions and the Chiefs of Transportation of military districts, and between the Transportation Commissariat Station Masters and the Railroad Station or Railhead Commandants.

3. MOVEMENTS

The planning and execution of major troop, supply, or evacuation movements by rail is the joint responsibility of the Peoples' Commissariat of Transportation and the Chief of Transportation of the Rear Services of the Red Army.

Major military movements normally must be planned 30 days in advance because of the demands made on the limited Soviet rail systems. The Transportation Commissariat must be prepared to inform the Red Army of its rolling stock and transport capabilities 25 days before the movement. Twenty-three days before the movement, the Chiefs of Transportation of the army groups and military districts involved must forward their estimated requirements for the movement to the Chief of Transportation of the Rear Services of the Red Army, who must submit his consolidated request to the Commissariat of Transportation.

Should the request exceed the estimated capabilities submitted by the Commissariat, the problem is referred to the Supreme Economic Council or to the State Defense Committee for adjudication. Adjudication must be completed and a joint Commissariat-Red Army plan must be transmitted to the Chiefs of Transportation of the army groups and military districts at least 13 days before the movement. The Chiefs of Transportation and the Railroad Divisions must have prepared their detailed joint plans and must have transmitted them as warning orders to military formations, railroad units, and industrial enterprises concerned at least 10 days before the movement.

4. RESPONSIBILITY

The maintenance of epidemiological and epizootic control on all railroads is a special responsibility of the Peoples' Commissariat of Transportation. The Commissariat maintains medical and veterinary inspectors on all trains and special infectious hospitals at major stations and all railheads. The Main Medical Administration and the Veterinary Administration of the Red Army share in this responsibility.

The Peoples' Commissariat of Transportation is responsible for the operation of all railroads up to army railheads. It is responsible for all permanent and heavy construction, even in advance of army railheads. The Railroad Construction Battalions of the Red Army are, however, responsible for initial mine clearance.

Coordination between the Chiefs of Railroad Divisions and the Chiefs of Transportation of military districts is limited to planning, epidemiological and epizootic control, and supervision of the Transportation Commissariat Station Masters and the Station Commandants.

Station masters have sole authority over the operations of railroad lines, rolling stock repair, rail line construction and repair, and railroad signal communications.

Station and railhead commandants of the Red Army are responsible for the orderly loading and unloading of troops, equipment, and supplies, the successful operation and maintenance of Red Army dumps and depots, and the active defense of stations. They exercise the disciplinary authority of garrison commanders over all troops and other personnel in transit or at stations. In defensive situations, it is believed that they have tactical command over all personnel in their sectors, including Transportation Commissariat Troops, Railroad and Convoy Troops, and the local Passive Antiaircraft Defense Groups (in the zone of interior).

Section V. SEMI-MILITARY TRAINING ORGANIZATIONS

1. GENERAL

Appreciation of the necessity for widespread interest and voluntary participation in military activities outside of the official organizations of the army dates from 1912, when a national society was organized for semi-military training. Following the Revolution, many Soviet citizens and the Communist Party realized the need for supplementing the limited conscript training of the Red Army of the early twenties. Consequently, various societies were formed to accomplish this function.

The societies were merged in 1926 into the Organization for the Defense of the Soviet Union and Defense against Air Raids and Chemical Attack (*Osoaviakhim*). The *Komsomol* (League of Communist Youth) and its children's affiliates, the *Pioneers* and the *Octobrists*, formed the core of *Osoaviakhim*. Defense training outside of the army became virtually compulsory for Soviet youth.

Although *Osoaviakhim*, and particularly its *Komsomol*, achieved considerable success, the status of universal military preparedness was not satisfactory at the beginning of the war with Germany. Consequently, military control and compulsory participation in prescribed training courses were instituted in 1941 with the organization of the Main Administration for Universal Compulsory Military Training of the Citizens of the U. S. S. R. (*Vsevobuch*) of the Peoples' Commissariat of Defense.

Osoaviakhim was relegated to a secondary and supplementary role for the duration of World War II. The State Defense Committee required the organization to turn its facilities over to the newly formed *Vsevobuch*. *Osoaviakhim* conducted passive antiaircraft and elementary aviation training, conducted war-bond drives, and assisted in mine clearance and collection of enemy weapons and equipment in recaptured areas. With the conclusion of the war and the termination of *Vsevobuch*, *Osoaviakhim* once more is the primary auxiliary military training organization of the U. S. S. R.

2. OSOAVIAKHIM AND KOMSOMOL

Osoaviakhim is comprised of a pyramidal series of local, *Oblast*, and republican organizations. It is directed by the All-Union Presidium.

The organization expanded rapidly following its formation. Its membership totaled 2,950,000 in October 1927 and reached 13,000,000 in 1941. As early as 1929, there were 47,200 organized groups for the study of military science. *Osoaviakhim* was actively engaged in aviation training. In 1931, it had 14 glider stations, 40 airfields, flying schools, model airplane shops, and centers for training aviation mechanics.

Although *Osoaviakhim* was designed to provide military and physical training for citizens of pre-conscript age, it also included former members of the Red Army who wished to study new technical developments in warfare. Its program, which centered about clubs and training centers, included virtually all types of military training.

Markedly close relations are maintained between *Osoaviakhim*, the state, the Communist Party, and the armed forces. The Soviet government has supported the organization strongly. It has authorized the use of army reserve personnel, giving them active pay duty.

The organization of *Osoaviakhim* has been changed for peacetime operations. The clubs have been replaced by military-type units, infantry or cavalry squads or platoons and detachments of specialists. The Communist Party supervises the selection of unit commanders, often reserve officers or noncommissioned officers on deferred status.

The *Komsomol* of the Communist Party specializes in tank, artillery, and marksmanship training. Red Army personnel on active duty often have served as its officers.

3. VSEVOBUCH

The Main Administration for Universal Compulsory Military Training of the Citizens of the U. S. S. R. (*Vsevobuch*), which existed between 1941 and 1945, had the mission of providing a reserve for the Red Army and for Partisan operations. It conducted training for all male citizens between the ages of 16 and 60.

A special 110-hour training program was given trainees during their off-duty hours, without interruption of production and without pay. Regulations provided that the program must be completed in not more than 5 months and that classes must meet at least twice a week. Instruction was presented by reserve officers and noncommissioned officers recruited from wounded Red Army personnel. Training was specialized by arm. Insofar as was practicable, the training organizations corresponded to units and elements of the Red Army, but had no military status.

The program achieved only partial success due to the inadequate supply of instructors and equipment. Best results appear to have been achieved in the initial training of specialists, such as signal men whose courses extended far beyond the initial 110 hours.

Section VI. PARTISANS

1. DEVELOPMENT AND MISSION

Partisan operations have always been an important factor in wars fought on Soviet territory. The large, inaccessible areas and the robustness of the Soviet population favor this type of operation.

The mission of Partisan warfare is to harass enemy forces, to cut their extended supply and communication lines, to assist Red Army operations, and to gather information about the enemy.

The Soviet government and the Communist Party, with the *Komsomol*, made preparations before World War II for the foundation of a Partisan movement. The *Osoaviakhim* and the Fire Defense Troops assisted in this preparation, and later in the actual organization of Partisan bands. *Vsevobuch* also assisted in the formation of Partisan bands after 1941.

During World War II, the development of Partisan bands was greatly facilitated by the German Army's inability to mop up the large territories captured during its rapid advance. Special recruiting agencies of the Communist Party in the rear of the enemy forces furnished the Partisans with a steady flow of replacements. It is estimated that more than 300,000 Partisans were operating behind German lines at the end of 1943.

The Soviet Partisan command also assisted Partisan bands in other countries under German occupation, such as Yugoslavia, Slovakia, and Poland.

2. HIGH COMMAND AND COORDINATION WITH RED ARMY

The Communist Party supervised and controlled the Partisans. The High Command of the Partisans was the Central Staff of the Partisan Movement, first under Marshal of the Soviet Union Voroshilov and later under *General Leitenant* Ponomarenko. The Staff is responsible directly to the Central Committee of the Communist Party.

The Central Staff of the Partisan Movement was represented in the General Headquarters and coordinated with the Operations and Intelligence Division of the Red Army to assure closest cooperation with the Red Army.

When the Red Army went on the offensive, much closer coordination was required. Special Partisan staffs were organized at army group (front) and army levels to achieve this coordination (fig. 3). The Operations Staff of the Partisan Movement in the Rear of the Enemy was organized in enemy-

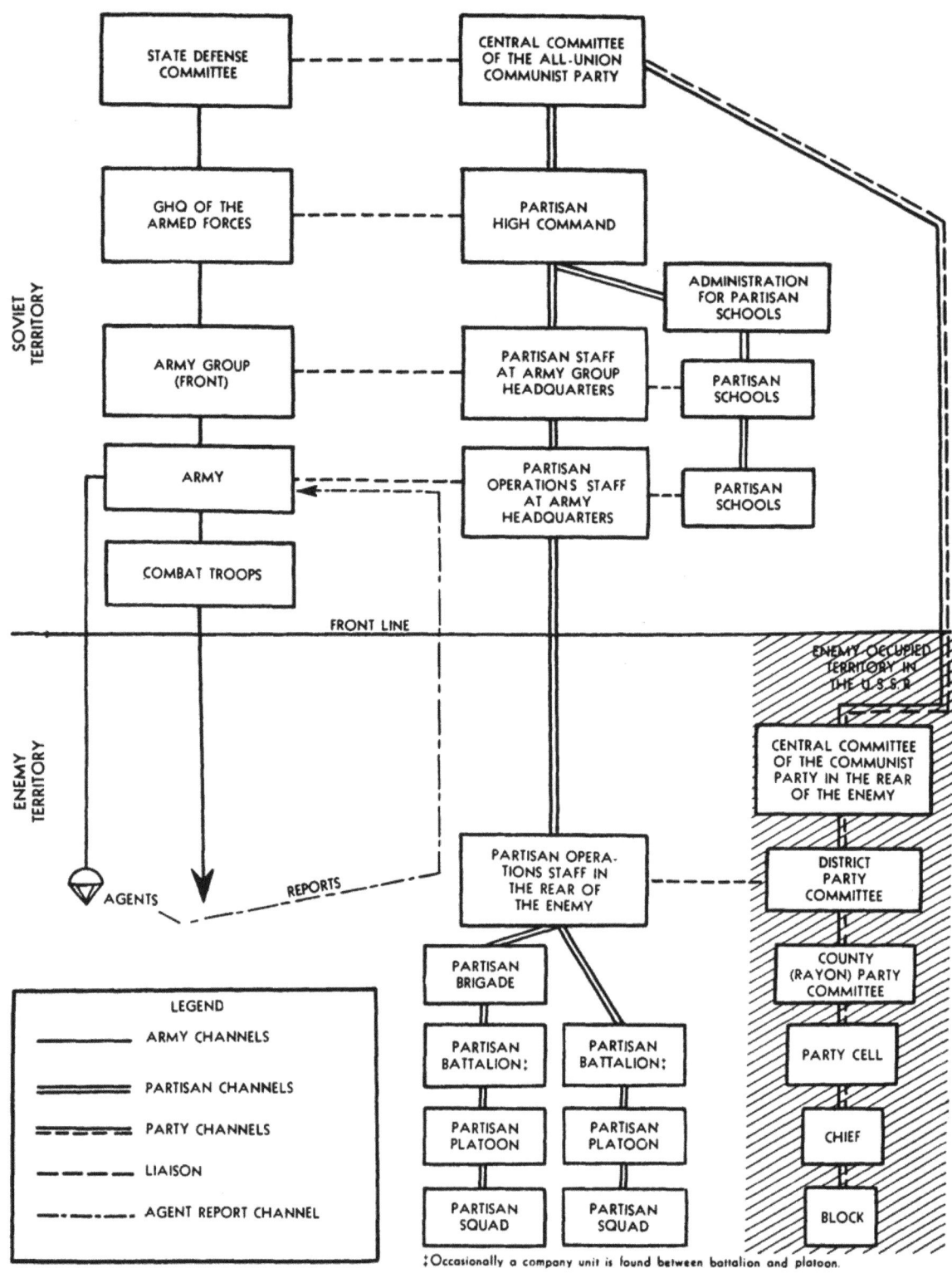

Figure 3. Structure and organization of Soviet Partisans, Communist Party control of Partisans, and lateral liaison with Red Army headquarters.

122

occupied territory to receive orders from the Partisan High Command and to assure the dissemination of orders to individual Partisan bands.

3. ORGANIZATION AND EQUIPMENT

The organization, equipment, and strength of Partisan bands varied greatly. They depended upon terrain conditions, density of the road net, and the strength of enemy forces.

The most commonly found unit was the Partisan battalion (*Otryad*), with 200 to 400 officers and enlisted men. In favorable terrain, battalions were often combined into brigades and, early in the war, into regiments (*Polk*). In very few instances, Partisan divisions (*Divisia*) were organized.

Partisan units were composed of personnel received from the Communist Party and semi-military organizations, of isolated Red Army soldiers, and of escaped prisoners of war.

The types and quantity of weapons, equipment, and supplies used by the Partisans, largely depended upon the initiative of the units and the success of Partisan raids on enemy supply depots and columns. Battlefields also were a source of supply.

Partisans normally did not receive supplies from the Red Army or the Soviet government, except for medical supplies usually delivered by air. When Partisan units were in contact with Red Army units, however, they were able to obtain equipment.

Most of the food for the Partisans was obtained from the local population and was supplemented by supplies seized from enemy dumps. They generally had sufficient supplies of weapons. Limited transportation was available to Partisans. It normally consisted of light horse-drawn carts.

4. TACTICS

In general, the Partisans operated on orders from the Partisan High Command to carry out specific operations. When the Red Army went on the offensive, Partisan units usually were confined to operations which gave direct assistance to the advance elements of Red Army assault forces. They also assisted the Red Army by gathering information about the enemy, often employing children, women, and the aged for these missions.

Surprise raids and ambushes were characteristic Partisan operations. They usually operated at night, often near woods and marshes. Partisan bands normally avoided engagements with strong enemy forces. After a successful raid, they returned to their bases by separate routes. They continually changed their positions, marching by night and hiding by day.

When Partisan units were surrounded, they broke up into small groups which attempted to pass through the enemy lines or hid in the surrounded area.

Partisan units employed a markedly effective security system of sentries, patrols, and advance observation posts. Roads leading to their camps normally were camouflaged and mined. Excellent communications were maintained by the use of radio and messengers.

CHAPTER V

TACTICS

INTRODUCTION

1. SOVIET TACTICS PRIOR TO 1942

At the beginning of the Russo-German War, June 1941, the Red Army tactical doctrines, which had developed from a mixture of Western European practice and original thinking, were still largely theoretical and untried. It is true that Red Army leaders had made careful studies of World War I, the Russian and Spanish Civil Wars, and the first year of World War II. As early as 1933, Red Army officers had formulated basic concepts of tank and moto-mechanized warfare. At Nomonhan and in the Finnish War, they gained experience in the strengths and weaknesses of armor. The critical importance of small-unit infantry tactics, the necessity of coordination and flexibility in maneuver and fire power, and the methods of artillery-infantry-tank rupture of a powerful fortified position also had been clarified in the Finnish War. But these lessons were not fully digested, even by higher officers. Rapid mobilization between 1937 and 1941 had brought great numbers of inexperienced leaders into service. The tactical modernization of the Red Army had just begun when the Germans invaded the U. S. S. R.

In 1941, command was concentrated in the infantry staff, although artillery was receiving continually increasing responsibility. The basic operational unit was the powerful infantry division, nearly 18,000 strong, with two regiments of artillery and a battalion of tanks. Except in the Far East, the corps was the highest organized command structure.

Full emphasis upon combat intelligence was not yet evident, although notable beginnings had been made in the development of aerial phototopography, special maps, and photographic ground reconnaissance; and sound ranging was in an advanced stage. Schemes of maneuver and combat dispositions in the offensive were conventional, featuring a predominance of frontal terrain objectives and deeply echeloned infantry assault forces.

Sound defensive doctrines existed. These showed thorough appreciation of the importance of depth, all-around security, successive obstacle systems covered by fire, and the employment of artillery in counterpreparation and antitank action. Staff work was detailed and slow, with written orders being employed as low as the regiment. Coordination presented a notable weakness; commanders overstressed personal leadership to the detriment of control. Supporting arms were not fully exploited. Signal planning and techniques—especially the employment of radio—were deficient.

In infantry tactics, the concepts of fire, maneuver, infiltration, and encirclement were beginning to crystallize. Mixed teams of infantry, engineers, and direct-fire artillery for special missions were not yet in evidence. However, rapidly prepared field fortifications, excellent camouflage, and the mass use of specialized snipers were standard practices.

Throughout the years prior to World War II, the Red Army concentrated attention on artillery tactics and techniques. By 1941, considerable progress had been made in analyzing artillery capabilities; developing observation and fire direction; employing destruction fire, barrages, and concentrations; and in handling artillery organizations. Four artillery divisions existed. The lack of heavy mortars and of massed mortar fire was an important deficiency.

Large-scale employment of armor was still in its infancy, with experimental tank divisions being the most powerful mechanized units. Technical equipment was not fully developed, while the roles of infantry, engineers, and supporting fire power in armored operations were incompletely understood. In contrast, large horse cavalry units had not been neglected; a powerful cavalry arm, coordinated with artillery and armor, existed at the beginning of the war.

The Finnish War provided excellent experience in winter operations and in the assault of fortified positions.

The first phase of the Russo-German War, June to November 1941, was a costly delaying action by the initial protective forces of the U. S. S. R. It revealed the tactical weaknesses of the prewar army; at the same time, new techniques were improvised. Deep obstacle systems justified themselves thoroughly, as did artillery—especially in the new role of direct fire. Combat in encirclement and partisan warfare proved effective.

By November 1941, the mobilized reserves of the U. S. S. R. were ready, and could be thrown in for powerful counterattacks at Tikhvin, Rostov, and Moscow. Between November 1941 and May 1942, the Russians engaged in a winter-spring offensive which nearly broke the German lines, but at great cost. The soundness of husbanding reserves for counteroperations at the critical time and the effectiveness of infiltrating ski units and large-scale cavalry raids were fully proved. Yet many weaknesses were evident. At Rostov (November 1941), the absence of motorized infantry, self-propelled artillery, and motorized bridging equipment prevented the Red Army from annihilating the encircled German forces. On the Central Front (January–April 1942), lack of air cover led to the destruction of the cavalry supply lines and nullified the offensive. At Kharkov (May 1942), inadequate flank protection for the advancing mechanized salient produced disaster.

2. NEW TACTICAL DOCTRINES

The High Command of the Red Army studied the reverses of 1941 and 1942 assiduously. By the autumn of 1942, it had assimilated the combat lessons of the war, formulated radically new combat regulations for the arms and the staffs, developed new organizations, and begun mass production of fully modern equipment.

As a result of this tactical evaluation, command responsibilities were specifically divided between the commander and staff of combined arms, and the chiefs of arms and services. The Commander became responsible for plans of maneuver and direct control of critical phases of an operation. His staff assumed the function of coordination, while the chiefs of arms and services were charged with detailed planning and control of their particular elements. The army became the basic planning and command group; army group and even several headquarters coordinated major operations. Uncompromising thoroughness of reconnaissance was required, both by combined and specialized arms.

Operation procedures were developed for systematically disseminating intelligence directly to using agencies. New tactical schemes were brought forward: converging double envelopment, parallel pursuit, and centralized and decentralized defense. The major development in staff work was the required employment of precise tables of combat coordination, which assured continuous, systematic cooperation of all arms. Such cooperation was further aided by advances in tactical signal communications, including the formation of special command, staff, cooperation, and other nets.

Reserves were committed in concentrated blows to exploit successes. The maneuverability of infantry was now organized and exploited to the utmost; the employment of small, mixed teams with heavy fire power facilitated infiltration, encirclement, and hasty defense. Deep echelon systems were replaced by wide frontal formations which promoted better lateral control and more flexible maneuverability. Artillery became the main striking force of the Red Army. The new concept of the "artillery and air offensive" embodied the responsibility of the artillery to coordinate *all* supporting fire power and to provide overwhelming fire power in anticipation of infantry requirements. To achieve this goal, large numbers of artillery organizations—artillery divisions, mortar divisions, antiaircraft artillery divisions, artillery brigades, etc—were formed. Direct fire became a normal function of all types of artillery. In general, artillery was used with great aggressiveness.

To implement deep mechanized operations, two basic types of mobile corps were created: the tank corps and the mechanized corps.* The tank corps, operating with infantry, had a high proportion of tanks and great shock power suitable for penetrations. The mechanized corps, with a large motorized infantry component and fewer tanks, was best fitted for exploitation. In addition, some ordinary infantry was motorized for special operations; shuttling by motor increased the mobility of still other units. The cavalry corps, aided by strong armor and artillery, retained a major role in special operations.

Engineers operated in immediate conjunction with assault waves, not only breaking gaps through minefields and obstacles, but also providing immediate

---

*The Red Army "tank corps" has no U. S. equivalent, but approximates a U. S. armored division. The "mechanized corps" resembles the German *Panzer Grenadier* Division and incorporates both armored and motorized infantry with tanks. (See ch. III.)

defense of newly won positions. Balanced, powerful tactical antiaircraft gun units (12.7-mm, 37-mm, and 85-mm), operating in close coordination with friendly fighter aircraft, helped prevent repetition of earlier disasters from hostile air action.

In special operations, the technique of river crossings especially was perfected. Crossings on a wide front, powerful artillery support, use of improvised as well as table-of-organization equipment, and rapid construction of timber bridges were characteristic. Tactical surprises such as underwater bridges were introduced. Defensive and offensive fighting in cities received careful attention. The Soviets clearly realized the importance of detailed reconnaissance, direct-fire artillery, and aggressive and rapid action by infantry well equipped with submachine guns and grenades.

3. TRENDS SINCE STALINGRAD

The basic tactics of the present Red Army were formulated in 1942 and were revealed for the first time in the victory of Stalingrad.

Following the Stalingrad campaign, modifications of Soviet tactics were governed by the need of destroying deep, bitterly defended German positions, and by the availability of increasing quantities of modern matériel and well trained officers. Consequently, heavy mine-clearing, bridging, and flame-throwing tanks have been introduced; assault engineer-pioneer brigades have been developed; artil-lery has been reinforced by superheavy equipment; and mobile corps have been provided with stronger echelons of self-propelled artillery, mortars, and rockets. As a result of these measures, operations even against powerful positions can progress rapidly. At the same time, mobility and flexibility of control have increased. Greater motorization and the use of ducks and amphibious tanks have speeded operations. Partial decentralization of control from army to infantry corps, has facilitated more rapid reactions to unexpected situations.

A number of future trends are foreseeable at present. Undoubtedly, the main patterns of current Soviet tactics will continue. But even more aggressive tactics may be promoted by light, powerful weapons for the infantry—particularly of the recoilless type—with such conservative motorization as will not reduce maneuverability. Also, improvements in engineer equipment may facilitate rapid exploitation by mechanized forces. The continuous dominating role of artillery will probably be maintained, especially by coordinated employment of very long range weapons (V-type) and self-propelled types. The trend toward decentralization of operating control to units of moderate size, such as corps, will probably continue. The tendency toward concentrating GHQ units (tanks, artillery, engineers, etc.) into large, specialized organizations for commitment in main efforts will, most likely, be maintained.

PART I. EXERCISE OF COMMAND: COMBINED ARMS

Section I. THE COMMANDER, THE STAFF, AND THE CHIEFS OF ARMS AND SERVICES

1. COMMAND

The command doctrine of the Red Army is characterized by specific definition of the responsibilities of the Commander of Combined Arms, his Chief of Staff, the staff, the chiefs of arms and services, and command liaison officers. The Commander of Combined Arms is the senior officer of the primary mobile arm—infantry, tanks, or cavalry—in the formation.* He is responsible not only for over-all success or failure, but also for direct personal control of reconnaissance and operations in critical areas and phases of combat. The initial scheme of maneuver and the employment of reserves are especially his responsibilities.

The Chief of Staff, second in command, is responsible for all secondary and routine operations. The staff assists him in over-all planning, reconnaissance, coordination, combat security, signal communications, and supply control of operations. The chiefs of arms and services are charged with the detailed planning and supervision of the operations of all elements of their arms or services within the combat team. They command those elements of their arms or services which are not attached to subordinate units.

Command liaison officers are senior officers, often members of the staff or chiefs of arms and services,

*The Red Army "formation" (*Soyedinenye*) has no exact U. S. equivalent but approximates a large-scale combat team, being a division, brigade, or comparable organization of normal, reduced, or reinforced strength. A stable, tactical grouping of necessary arms and minimum services, a Red Army formation is designed to execute one phase of a large operation, such as a penetration, an exploitation, a delaying action, or a counterattack. Hereafter "formation" is used in the Soviet sense.

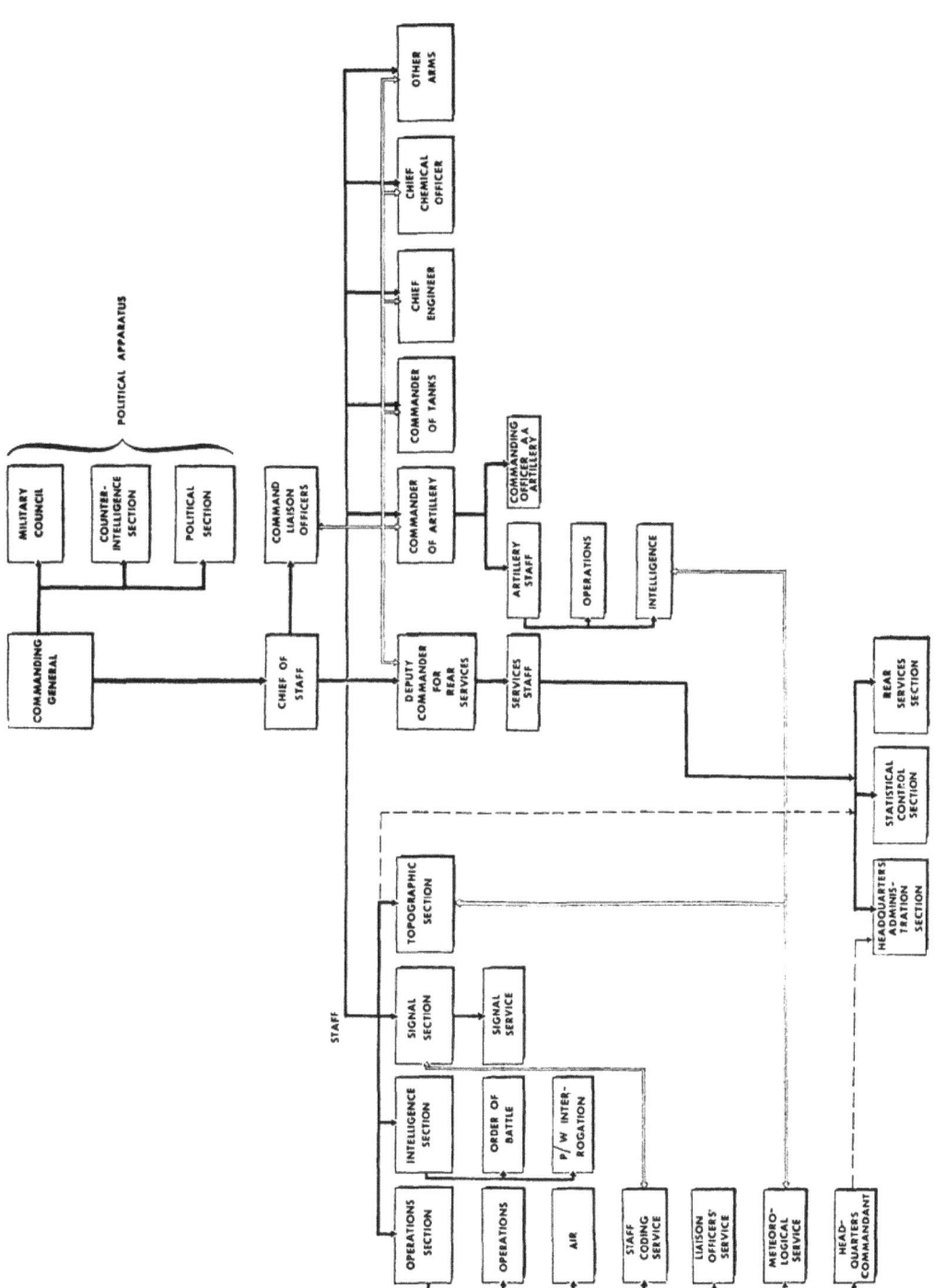

Figure 1. Channels of command and control, forces of combined arms

COMMAND CHANNEL
ALTERNATE COMMAND OR ATTACHMENT
COORDINATION

127

who represent the Commander in controlling operations along axes of secondary effort (fig. 1).

2. STAFF OPERATIONS

Contrary to U. S. practice, the staff in the Red Army is an advisory body to the Chief of Staff and not to the Commander. With data supplied by the staff, the Chief of Staff prepares the estimate of the situation and makes conclusions and recommendations for the approval of the Commander.

One of the fundamental functions of the staff, repeatedly stressed in Soviet doctrine, is to organize and assure uninterrupted coordination between all arms and services throughout all combat phases. The staff, chiefs of arms, and commanders of subordinate and reserve units participate in developing coordination, their basic objective being to provide continuous and effective artillery, mortar, aviation, engineer, and other support for the infantry and tanks.

The staff of a Red Army formation of combined arms, down to corps level, consists of the following sections: Operations, Intelligence, Signal Communications, Statistical Control, Rear Services, Topographic and Headquarters Administration. (No Topographic Section is found in the division.) Occasionally Training and other special sections are added.

a. Operations Section. The Operations Section is the senior section of the staff. Its chief is concurrently deputy to the Chief of Staff. He is fully informed of the situation at all times; he personally prepares field orders and the more important combat reports.

The Operations Section secures and compiles data on the situation, estimates the comparative strength of friendly and opposing forces, and prepares field orders, operations, summaries, and situation maps. It plans coordination between arms, and is therefore responsible for all liaison with other units, and for the coding service. It directs combat training. It is specifically charged with ensuring operational security by organizing antitank, antiaircraft, and antigas defense; traffic control and camouflage discipline; and defense of the rear echelon and the command post.

In the Operations Section, the first assistant is deputy to the chief of the section and is charged with controlling the operations of the subordinate units. The second assistant organizes coordination with higher headquarters and adjacent units, as well as within his own staff. The third assistant is responsible for all matters pertaining to combat security and training. In formations without a chief of the air arm, an air subsection is generally maintained in the Operations Section. A meteorological subsection may also be maintained.

The Operations Section directly controls the staff coding service and the headquarters commandant.

b. Intelligence Section. The Intelligence Section is charged with the planning and preparation of orders, and to some extent with the conduct of operations pertaining to the collection, evaluation, interpretation, and dissemination of information of the enemy. Its primary function is to keep the Commander, and all others concerned, informed regarding the enemy's situation and capabilities. It usually includes subsections or teams for order-of-battle studies and prisoner-of-war interrogation. All intelligence is reported by the chief of the section to the Chief of Staff and the Chief of the Operations Section.

c. Signal Section. The Signal Section organizes and maintains all necessary signal communications, and allots signal equipment to troops. It assigns radio frequencies and prescribes signal procedure. In cooperation with the Operations Section, it prepares radio-signal charts and systems of transmission, and organizes a time-signal service. It also plans, installs, and supervises the aircraft warning net; organizes postal and air mail services; and operates the message center. Furthermore, it conducts signal reconnaissance—particularly interception of communications and survey of locally available facilities. It submits signal summaries as necessary. The Chief of the Signal Section also commands the signal troops of the formation.

d. Topographic Section. The Topographic Section gathers and analyzes all terrain data. It organizes geodetic, topographic, and photogrammetric services, providing troops with maps and catalogues of benchmarks. The work of the Topographic Section is closely linked with the parallel duties of the artillery staff, which takes over all topographic functions on divisional and lower levels.

e. Rear Services. Since 1944, the Rear Services, Statistical Control, and Headquarters Administration Sections have normally been removed from the staff, and placed under the Deputy Commander for Rear Services.

The Rear Services Section organizes, maintains, and provides for the security of rear echelon installations and lines of supply and evacuation. It provides transportation facilities for the timely de-

128

livery of supplies in accordance with the policies of the Commander and instructions of the Chief of Staff. It coordinates transportation, supply, and evacuation requirements of the arms and services; prepares summaries; and regulates traffic. It requests from higher headquarters the additional facilities necessary for efficient operation of its installations, and allots these facilities to subordinate units as required.

The Statistical Control Section deals with personnel matters, tables of organization and equipment, strength reports, and replacements. It keeps records of all personnel, animals, equipment, casualties, captured equipment, and prisoners of war.

The Headquarters Administration Section keeps records, provides quarters and food for headquarters personnel, and controls military police and all administrative matters pertaining to the formation.

3. CHIEFS OF ARMS AND SERVICES

The chiefs of arms and services in a formation of combined arms have administrative and planning responsibility for all organic and attached units of their arms or services.

They command all such units not attached to subordinate organizations. As command liaison officers, they generally supervise the performance of key missions within the scope of their arm or service. As assistants to the Chief of Staff, they advise the Commander on matters pertaining to tactical and technical employment of the arms and services. Each chief of an arm or service develops operations, reconnaissance, and rear-area plans for his arm or service. In accordance with the requirements and within the limits set by the commander, each initiates requisitions for the procurement of equipment and supplies for his particular arm or service within the formation.

In addition to the responsibilities which are common to the chief of every arm or service, certain other responsibilities are specifically allocated. The Chief of Artillery is responsible for the organization of antitank and antiaircraft defense and for the procurement and distribution of all ammunition. The Chief of the Signal Service is responsible for the designation of coordination signals. Together with the Chief of Staff, he must be present at the announcement of the command decision. Together with the Chief of Artillery and the Chief of the Air Service, he establishes the aircraft warning service. The Chief of Engineers is responsible for camouflage and, together with the Chief of Artillery, for antitank de-

fense. The Chief Chemical Officer is responsible for the defense of the entire formation against chemical warfare.

4. LIAISON

Liaison is handled by the liaison officers' service organized by the Chief of Operations under instructions of the Chief of Staff. In divisional and corps headquarters, officer personnel of the Operations and the Intelligence Sections are as a rule assigned to this task. Liaison duties are divided between "command liaison officers" and "liaison officers."

a. Command liaison officer. A command liaison officer is dispatched from a higher commander of his headquarters to a subordinate unit. He must be a responsible senior officer (often the commander of an arm or a service) authorized by the Commander to supervise the execution of a combat mission. He is appointed and briefed personally by the Commander or the Chief of Staff.

The principal duties of a command liaison officer are to transmit his commander's orders to the subordinate unit, and to inform his commander of the actual situation, condition, and requirements of the unit. He must be thoroughly familiar with the mission and plan of operations and subsequent plans of his commander, which are fully described in the card given him personally by the Commander or the Chief of Staff.

Whenever necessary, the command liaison officer visits the troops to check on the execution of orders; he reports his findings both to his chief of staff and to the commander of the subordinate unit. If the decision of the subordinate commander is obviously inexpedient and threatens to disrupt the general plan of action, the command liaison officer must report this decision to his own commander before it is carried out.

b. Liaison officer. A liaison officer is an officer of a subordinate unit dispatched to a higher or a cooperating headquarters. He is dispatched by the Chief of the Operations Section, either for a definite period of time during a battle, for purposes of exchanging information and of intercommunication, or from time to time to carry out individual assignments. He remains with the Operations Section of the higher unit and is subordinate to its chief. He also reports to the Chief Signal Officer.

c. Lateral and support liaison. Liaison between adjacent units (lateral liaison) is maintained as a rule by direct communication. Between a battalion headquarters and a right flank battalion a direct telephone line is used, while contact with other battalions passes through the regimental headquarters.

Liaison between supporting and supported units, if established, is the function of the supporting unit. Field artillery habitually establishes liaison with supported units for the primary purpose of obtaining information as to the needs for supporting fire. For example, liaison is established by direct-support artillery battalions with the supported infantry battalions and also with the infantry regiment.

Section II. COMBAT INTELLIGENCE

1. OBJECTIVES

The elements of intelligence essential to a command decision in the offensive are, according to Red Army doctrine, the enemy combat dispositions and feasible approaches to the deep flanks and to the rear of the enemy main body. On the defensive, the Soviets consider it fundamentally vital to know the possible approaches to the main battle position, the direction of the enemy main effort, and the location and composition of his reserves. In every type of operation, precise determination of critical orientation points is essential for combat coordination.

2. RESPONSIBILITY

a. The Commander. On the basis of personal reconnaissance of the general situation, supported by information supplied by higher headquarters, the Commander initiates reconnaissance by advising his staff, through the Chief of Staff, as to what information is required, when it is desired, and what units may be employed. During the subsequent preparation for battle and during the course of battle, the Commander conducts command reconnaissance and gives additional missions to the reconnaissance agencies. The Commander is also responsible for the continuous training and coordinated employment of the Intelligence Staff and intelligence agencies, and for cooperation between staff sections.

b. The Chief of Staff. The Chief of Staff is responsible for carrying out the Commander's orders and for initiating necessary reconnaissance in the absence of instructions from the Commander. He develops the essential elements of information designated by the Commander, translates these into reconnaissance missions, combines these missions with the directives of the higher headquarters, and personally assigns them to the Chief of the Intelligence Section. The Chief of Staff designates time limits for reporting information. He insists on continuous exchange of information between Intelligence and other staff sections. All intelligence plans and summaries are signed by the Chief of Staff.

c. Chief of the Intelligence Section. The Chief of the Intelligence Section presents on demand the enemy situation, together with his evaluation of enemy capabilities and the validity of each source of information. He supervises the work and training of the Intelligence Staff. He is personally responsible for dissemination of intelligence to interested officers and headquarters, and for notifying the higher and neighboring headquarters of the composition, time schedules, and zones of action of his reconnaissance units. Jointly with the Chief Signal Officer, he prescribes the signal codes for reconnaissance units.

d. Intelligence Staff. The Intelligence Staff, under the supervision of the Chief of Intelligence, formulates the intelligence and observation plans, and evaluates, collates, and disseminates the resulting information in periodic and special intelligence summaries. The staff also insures maintenance of contact and exchange of information with subordinate units, and it is responsible, with the cooperation of the Operations Staff, for the establishment and functioning of observation and listening posts.

INTELLIGENCE PLANS. In drawing up all intelligence plans, the following general steps are applied:

> Determination of objectives which would yield required information.
>
> Disposition of reconnaissance units according to the principle of concentration of forces on salient problems.
>
> Assignment of single specific tasks to each reconnaissance unit (further tasks may be assigned after the completion of the initial one).
>
> Installation and maintenance of communications with the reconnaissance units.
>
> Maintenance of a reconnaissance reserve to replace missing units and to retain operational flexibility of the intelligence plan.

The intelligence plan, an operational document of headquarters, is approved by the Chief of Staff and is not disseminated. Intelligence plans of the specialized arms and services vary in detail. Every intelligence plan, however, must indicate the following:

The mission of the formation.

All available information on the enemy.

Nature, source, and schedule deadline of required information.

The composition of each reconnaissance unit, its mission, and its zone of action.

Time limits for reports, the route back, and the area where prisoners have to be captured.

Means of communication with reconnaissance units.

Order of relief of reconnaissance units.

The composition, strength, and possible tasks of the reconnaissance reserve.

The observation plan is prepared by the Operations and Intelligence Staffs. It shows the location of each observation post with the sector of responsibility and dead areas. In terrain and weather which are unfavorable for observation, the observation plan is augmented by a "listening plan."

The Intelligence Staff coordinates its combined intelligence plan and the intelligence plans of subordinate headquarters in accordance with directives from higher echelons. For example, the Intelligence Staff Section of an army coordinates the intelligence plan of the army and its subordinate units (infantry divisions and units of specialized arms and services attached to the army) with the intelligence plan of the army group. The chief of intelligence of each arm and service coordinates the intelligence plans of his own and all subordinate staffs with the plan of the formation of which he is a part, and with the directives of the next higher echelon of his arm or service. For example, the chief of intelligence of army engineers coordinates the intelligence plans of all engineer units of the army in accordance with the directives of the chief of engineer intelligence of the army group. This plan is then submitted to the Intelligence Staff of the army which modifies it in accordance with the combined intelligence plan (fig. 2).

COMMUNICATIONS. The establishment of signal communications with reconnaissance elements is the responsibility of intelligence staffs. Each intelligence observation post must have wire communications with the command post. Radio communications are established with mobile reconnaissance units. In the event of prolonged operations over a sector considerably removed from the command post, a forward information collection station is established, with reliable wire or radio communications with the command post. Wide use is made of intelligence liaison officers for the collection of information and control of reconnaissance patrols.

e. **Information collecting agencies.** Intelligence is obtained from higher echelons and from neighboring units; raw information is collected in the lower echelons through ground reconnaissance, air reconnaissance, technical reconnaissance, and special agents.

Ground reconnaissance is carried out by specially trained troops which are organic to all units down to regiments of combined and specialized arms. Air reconnaissance is carried out by observation squadrons and by combat aviation. Technical reconnaissance—such as sound and flash ranging, radio location, and ground photography—is carried out by technical troops and by specialized arms and services. Special agents, operating in rear areas of the enemy, are controlled by armies and higher echelons; these agents collect information which is usually related with strategic tasks.

In addition to collecting essential elements of information which are ordered by the Commander or the Chief of Staff, the agencies are continuously responsible for the following:

Location of concentration areas and the number and type of troops which occupy them.

Location of antitank and antipersonnel obstacles and minefields.

Location of firing points and sectors covered by them.

The system of defense.

Information on routes and system of supply and evacuation.

Location of flanks and weakly held sectors.

Capture of prisoners and documents disclosing the groupment and intentions of the enemy (sectors in which the prisoners are to be captured are often designated by the Commander).

Information on the condition of terrain and road nets which would influence the employment of technical equipment and armor.

Information indicating probable directions of attack, counterattack, and withdrawal.

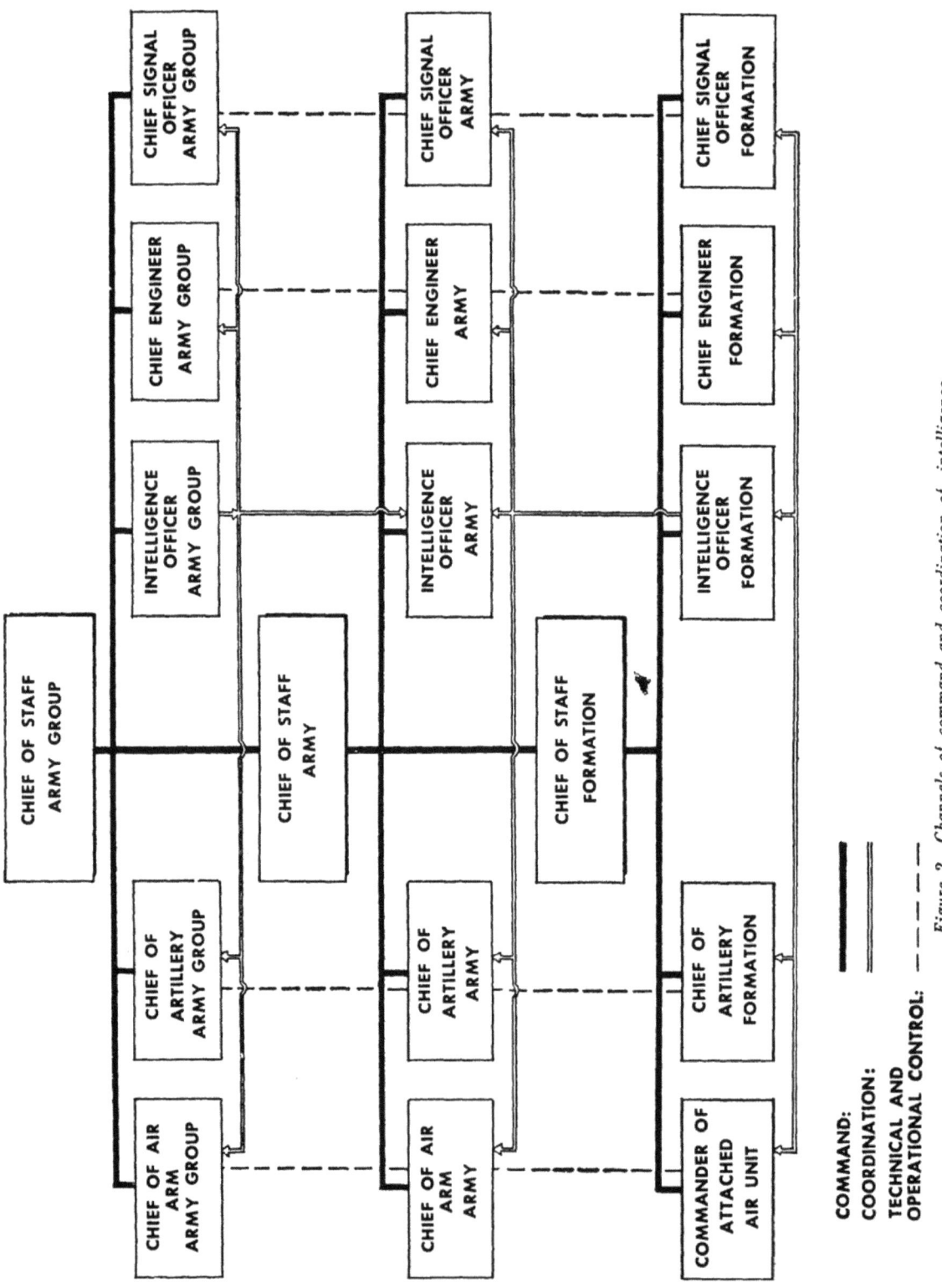

COMMAND:

COORDINATION:

TECHNICAL AND
OPERATIONAL CONTROL: ― ― ― ―

Figure 2. Channels of command and coordination of intelligence.

132

f. Chiefs of arms and services. In addition to the responsibility for the conduct of reconnaissance in their particular branch, the chiefs of arms and services are responsible for certain technical aid necessary for the over-all operation of intelligence. For example, the Chief of Artillery is responsible for the surveying of key observation posts and coordinating points, and for weather intelligence (Meteor-

3. RECONNAISSANCE AND OBSERVATION

The mission of reconnaissance in the Red Army is to obtain a complete and continuous picture of the enemy's capabilities and intentions, to be used as the basis for correct planning and retention of the initiative in the offensive. In order to accomplish this mission, reconnaissance must cover the entire front of a unit; must be carried out by units already

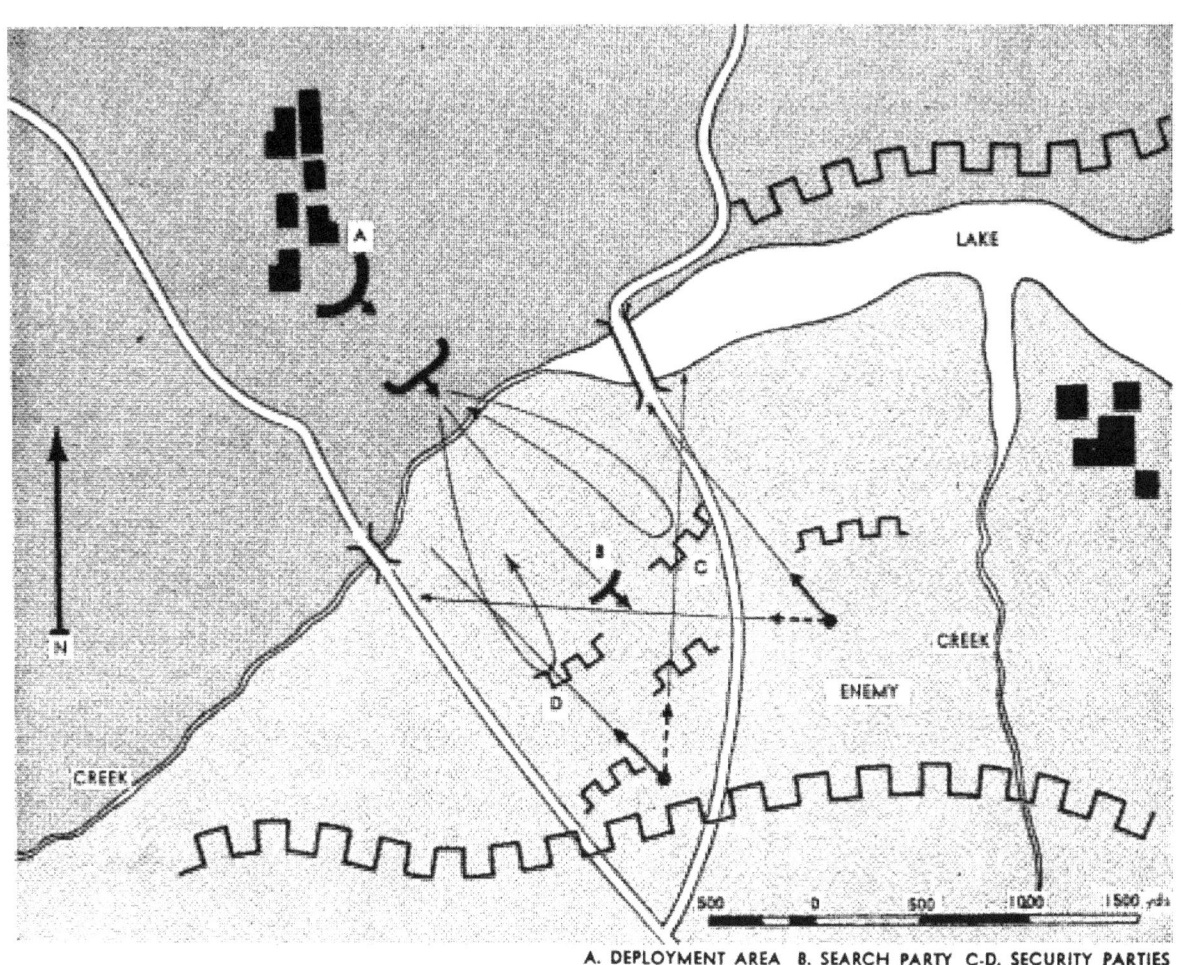

A. DEPLOYMENT AREA B. SEARCH PARTY C-D. SECURITY PARTIES

Figure 3.   Search plan.

ological Sections can also be attached to the Operations Sections of higher staffs). The Chief of the Air Arm is responsible for air observation and photography, and, jointly with the Topographic Service, for photo-interpretation. The Chiefs of Signal Communications, Engineers, and Chemical Warfare Service are responsible for supplying equipment and personnel of their branch to the reconnaissance units of combined arms.

in line; must be aided by the diverting reconnaissance of neighboring units; must be conducted without revealing the plan of attack; and must be concentrated on the specific problem at hand. Reconnaissance is carried out by specially trained detachments which are assigned to all major units.

The purpose of strategic reconnaissance is to secure all information for the use of staffs in planning and controlling operations. It is usually con-

133

ducted by staffs of an army or an army group. Its organs are aviation, mobile reconnaissance units, technical units, and special agents. Strategic reconnaissance is conducted to determine the following:

Disposition of enemy forces from the forward lines to strategic reserves.

Terrain occupied by the enemy.

Terrain which would have to be used by friendly troops for deployment and attack.

Terrain conditions, including roads and soil, of the region of prospective operations.

Technical reconnaissance is conducted by small, highly specialized units equipped with accurate optical, photographic, sound-ranging, meteorological, and radio-locator (radar and RDF) instruments. These technical units execute observation and reconnaissance beyond the technical capabilities of troop units. They are controlled by army and higher echelons.

a. Infantry reconnaissance. Tactical reconnaissance is usually organized and controlled by the commanders of formations. It attempts to determine the disposition of enemy units, fire positions, obstacles, and tactical reserves, and other factors (particularly terrain and routes of approach and withdrawal) which may affect the employment of troops in battle. Forms of tactical reconnaissance are raids, infiltration, and ambush (figs. 3 and 4). Stress is laid on careful preparation for each task, cooperation with supporting units, and skill of individual scouts. As a rule, a group charged with a particular task is supported by one or more security detachments.

The purpose of reconnaissance in force is to disclose the fire plan, scheme of defense, location of tactical reserves, and defensive installations of the enemy, and to capture prisoners. It is initiated by the commanders of divisions and regiments who also

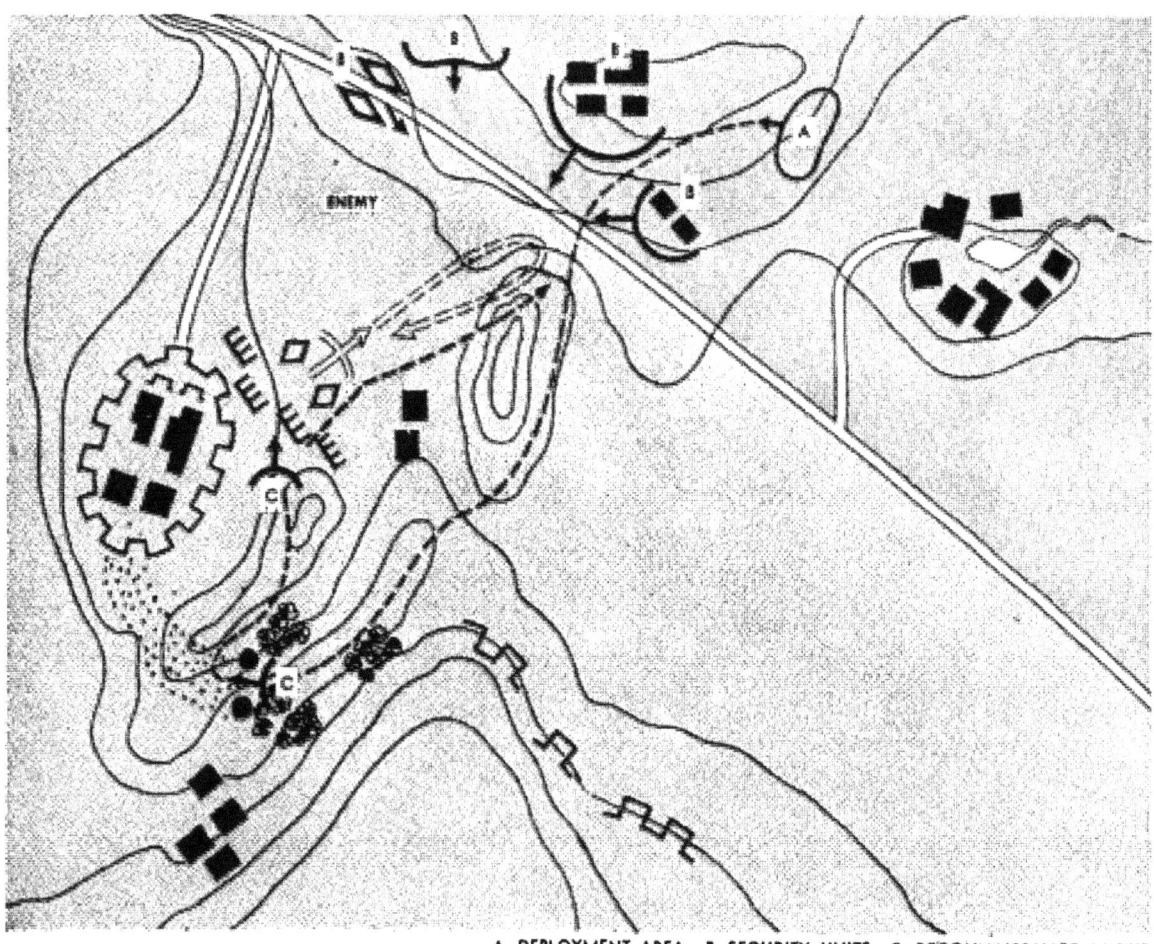

A. DEPLOYMENT AREA B. SECURITY UNITS C. RECONNAISSANCE GROUP

Figure 4. Reconnaissance plan.

134

determine the size of the reconnaissance and supporting units. Red Army doctrine emphasizes that in organizing reconnaissance in force too much importance cannot be given to the selection of personnel; to thorough planning and coordination of the operation; and to detailed rehearsal in daylight and at night under conditions similar to those of the

The establishment of continuous observation is a responsibility of all headquarters. During offensive operations and reconnaissance in force, command observation is mandatory. Observation posts must be selected by staff officers, and these posts must have independent wire communications with the command post. An observation diagram showing the

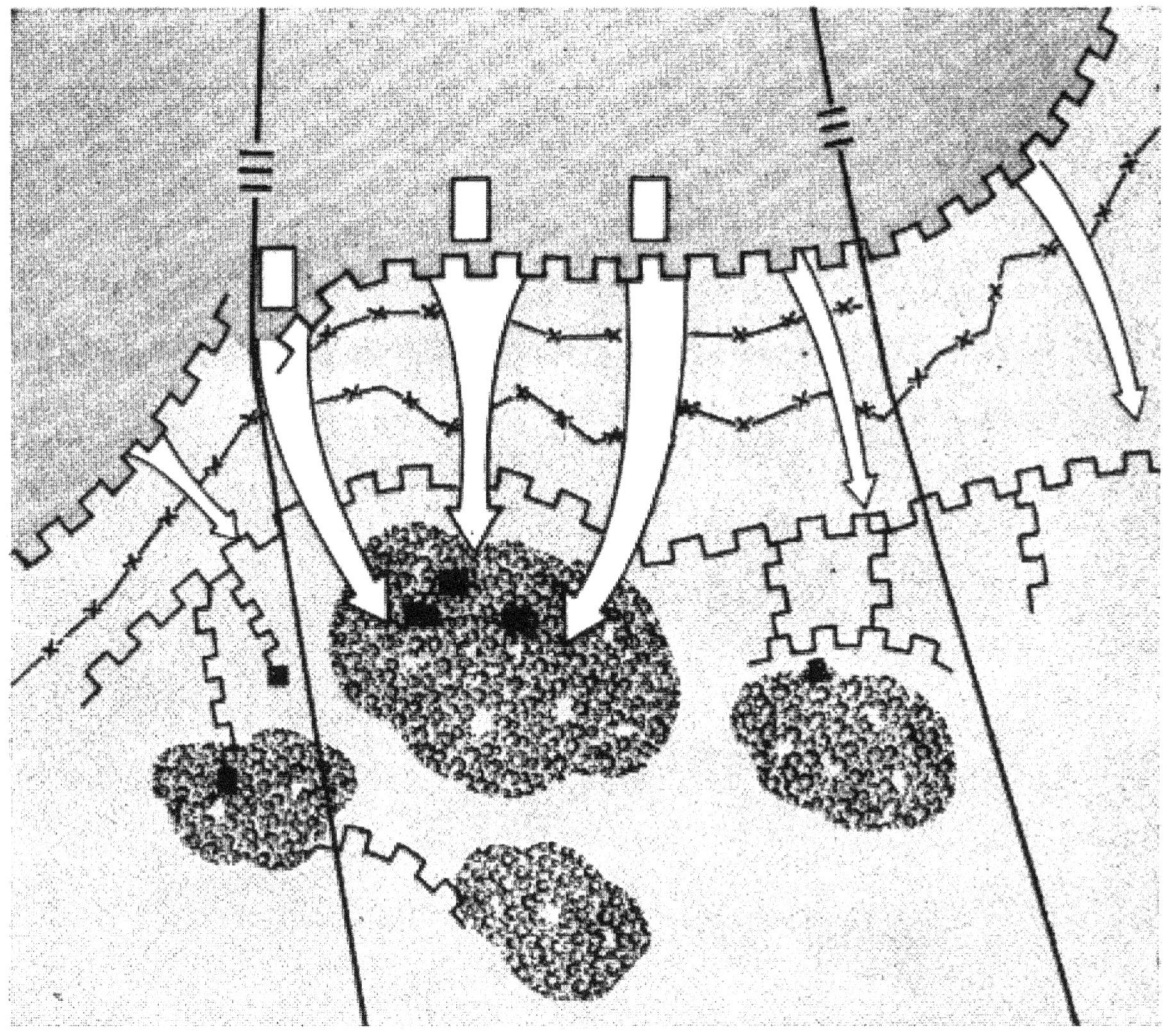

Figure 5. Plan of reconnaissance in force.

actual operation by both the reconnaissance and the supporting units. Reconnaissance in force must be undertaken only if other methods do not produce the required results. In addition, the terrain must be favorable for surprise, and sufficient time must be allowed for thorough preparation and rehearsal. Success depends on surprise and originality of action rather than on the number of troops employed (figs. 5 and 6).

location, sector of responsibility, and field of vision of each observation post is prepared jointly by the Intelligence and Operations Staffs. Each observation post is required to keep a journal and to submit an observation report (fig. 7).

At night and when the terrain and weather interfere with effective observation, observation reconnaissance is augmented by listening reconnaissance. Listening posts are selected as carefully as the obser-

135

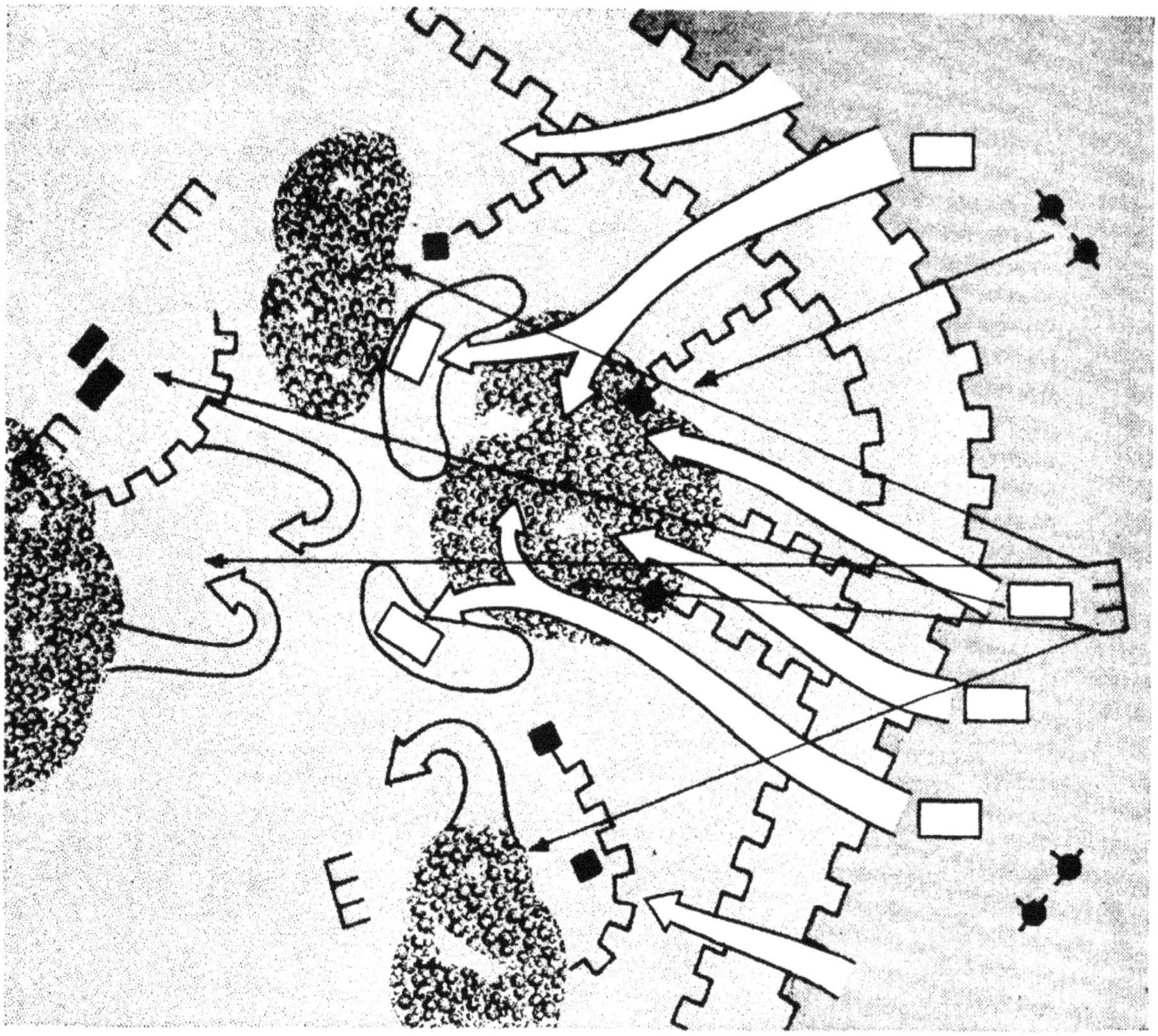

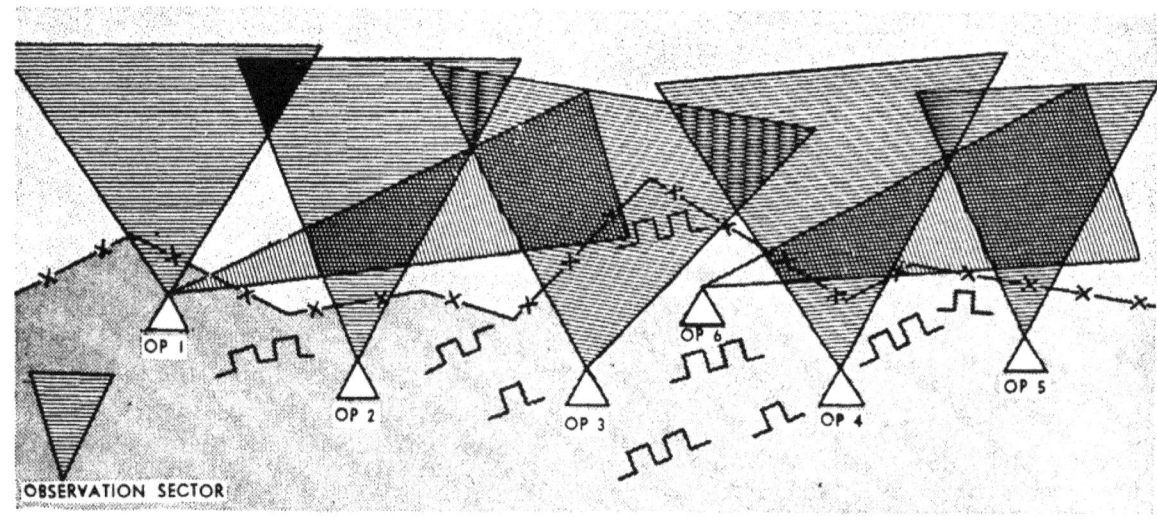

Figure 6. Execution of reconnaissance in force.

Figure 7. Observation plan.

136

vation posts. They are manned by trained personnel who are required to keep a journal and to submit a report at the end of their tour.

b. Reconnaissance by specialized arms and services. The general principles of infantry reconnaissance discussed above hold true for the intelligence and reconnaissance activity of the other arms and services. However, each arm and service has special forms and techniques of reconnaissance. Reconnaissance is initiated by the chiefs of branches, and coordinated and controlled by their intelligence staffs. Reconnaissance units of specialized arms and services operate either independently or with reconnaissance units of combined arms. Their objectives are to determine the quality and strength of the technical forces of the enemy, and the factors which may affect the employment of friendly technical troops.

ARTILLERY RECONNAISSANCE. Artillery reconnaissance is an integral and specialized part of combined reconnaissance. It demands exceptional accuracy, timeliness, and continuity. The objectives of artillery reconnaissance are the location and analysis of targets, evaluation of terrain, and the location and activity of friendly front lines. Artillery intelligence agencies are grouped into three categories: **troop,** instrumental, and air.

Troop reconnaissance is a primary responsibility of commanders and intelligence sections of artillery regiments, groupments, battalions, and batteries. Paired battalion observation posts are fully equipped with accurate optical instruments. When equipment is available, artillery observation posts augment their orientation and panoramic sketches with panoramic photographs. In addition to observation, artillery employs scouting parties which infiltrate behind enemy lines to observe targets and control fire.

Instrumental reconnaissance is conducted by a group of small, highly specialized units equipped with accurate optical, photographic, sound-ranging, meteorological, and other instruments. Sound-ranging batteries, normally operating in pairs, may be employed either in support of large artillery formations, or attached to counterbattery or countermortar groupments. One battery, deployed behind the firing line, reconnoiters targets such as medium and heavy mortars, and infantry and antitank guns. The other battery, deployed on the flanks of the firing positions, reconnoiters deep targets. The photogrammetric battery, attached to army and higher echelon artillery staffs, develops and interprets

aerial photographs and coordinates them with ground survey data. It controls friendly camouflage through photographic interpretation; takes, develops, and interprets ground photographs; and prepares and disseminates map substitutes. At least one artillery meteorological post is attached to each artillery regiment, groupment, separate battalion, and sound-ranging post. It provides the firing battalions and sound-ranging posts with current, local meteorological data by ground measurements and radiosonde.

Red Army artillery air reconnaissance closely approximates standard U. S. practice. Both artillery and combat aircraft are used. Outstanding emphasis is placed on comprehensive briefing of flying personnel, including visits to key ground observation posts, and on extensive use of air liaison officers.

ENGINEER RECONNAISSANCE. Staff procedure in the planning and conduct of engineer reconnaissance is the same as that for reconnaissance of combined arms except that the regimental engineer, rather than a staff officer, is personally responsible for the establishment of observation posts.

Engineer reconnaissance has a two-fold purpose: to reconnoiter terrain with a view to facilitating the movement and employment of friendly troops; and to determine the location and nature of enemy engineer construction, with a view to disclosing his system of defense. Specific objectives of the first task include the following:

> Quantity and condition of local resources available for use by engineers.
> Condition and capacity of roads and bridges.
> Supply of drinking water.
> Type of soil.
> Possible location of observation posts, defensive constructions, and means for camouflage.

Specific objectives of the second task include:

> The location, type, and camouflage of enemy defensive installation.
> Demolitions, antipersonnel, and antitank obstacles and minefields.
> Nature of engineer construction in progress.
> Safe avenues of approach to enemy positions.

Engineer reconnaissance is conducted by reconnaissance patrols, by observation, by interpretation of ground and air photographs, by study of topographic, geological, and hydrographic maps, and by interrogation of prisoners.

ARMORED AND MOTORIZED RECONNAISSANCE. In all armored and motorized units it is mandatory that command reconnaissance be made of all areas in which armor may be employed; also, a group of engineers must accompany each armored patrol. Because the employment of armored and motorized units is affected by terrain, especially in winter, the attention of intelligence staffs and reconnaissance units is concentrated on terrain, soil, roads, and bridges which are likely to be used during approach, deployment, and battle. In this connection, friendly as well as enemy minefields and antitank obstacles receive special attention. During the course of battle, or on the march, mobile observation posts are established with radio communications to the command post. Communications between the command posts and armored reconnaissance patrols are almost exclusively by radio. In preparation for a breakthrough of a fortified position, foot reconnaissance patrols of armored units operate independently or as parts of combined reconnaissance.

SIGNAL INTELLIGENCE. Signal intelligence is charged with gathering information about the enemy and about existing military or civil signal communications in the region of prospective operations. Signal headquarters of armies and higher echelons are provided with technical means for collecting signal intelligence of the enemy, including radio-intercept and radio-direction-finding units. In static situations, lower echelons monitor enemy radio nets, and signal patrols endeavor to tap enemy wire nets.

Utilization of local signal equipment is considered in every signal plan, and it is the responsibility of the intelligence section of the signal staff to organize reconnaissance of existing facilities for signal communications. Specific objectives of this type of reconnaissance are centers of communications, telephone and telegraph lines, and other equipment. Estimates are made of equipment and time needed to make it usable; extent of demolitions and sabotage are determined; and measures are formulated to protect signal equipment from enemy agents and the local population. In connection with signal liaison service, signal reconnaissance investigates the condition of existing landing strips and possible sites for new ones.

AIR RECONNAISSANCE. The two principal functions of air reconnaissance are aerial photography and observation. Air observation is carried out by special observation planes and by combat planes. It is organized by the air arm commander either independently or at the request of ground units. Observation missions are often coupled with photographic missions. Communications are established so that radio messages from air observers are received simultaneously by the air intelligence staff, the airdrome of the observation squadron, and headquarters of all supported formations down to and including corps. Some of the objectives of air observation include:

> Areas where the enemy is retreating.
> Directions of enemy attack or withdrawal.
> Phase lines reached by friendly troops.
> Signs of regrouping of the enemy in his rear areas.
> Control of friendly camouflage.

The work of air photoreconnaissance is closely integrated with photo-interpretation and topographic services. Results of photoreconnaissance are interpreted and entered on topographic maps at the headquarters of each reconnaissance squadron. This information is then sent to the topographic service of the army group, where it is evaluated and reproduced on maps and map substitutes for the use of ground formations and units. Special overlays containing a specific type of information—such as enemy defenses, artillery positions, or command posts—are prepared for the use of the general and special staffs. Ground photo-panoramas are supplemented with vertical and oblique stereopairs. Artillery units are given special distribution which, in major operations, includes firing battalions.

SPECIAL SERVICE RECONNAISSANCE. In addition to the reconnaissance agencies of the arms and services, the Red Army employs several specialized services which perform reconnaissance tasks beyond the scope of technical units of combat troops. The reconnaissance parties of these special services check existing topographical, hydrographical, geological, meteorological, and soil survey data with actual conditions; and prepare, reproduce, and disseminate the resulting intelligence by means of standard and special maps, studies, and surveys. For example, the photogrammetric service develops and interprets aerial photographs and coordinates them with ground survey data. The military topographic service prepares, reproduces, and disseminates standard and special maps such as tank, mortar, visibility, river-crossing, and mountain march maps. The hydro-meteorological service prepares hydrographic maps and long-range weather forecasts. The geological service makes soil surveys.

4. EXPLOITATION OF CAPTURED PERSONNEL AND MATERIEL

a. Prisoners of war. In Soviet reconnaissance, the capture of prisoners plays such a prominent part that commanders often specify in their reconnaissance directives the sectors from which prisoners are to be taken. Detailed instructions for processing prisoners are found in all handbooks issued to the various arms and services.

Standard operating procedure for handling prisoners of war is as follows: Prisoners are grouped according to their unit, officers being separated from enlisted men. Prisoners are conducted as soon as possible to the next higher headquarters, where each prisoner is interrogated alone; each echelon limits interrogations to subjects of immediate interest. Results of each interrogation are entered on a special form which accompanies each prisoner, and results of interrogations are forwarded to the next higher headquarters regardless of the final destination of the prisoners. Whenever possible, the interrogating officer is of the same arm or service as the prisoner; in regimental and higher echelons, prisoners of a particular arm or service are questioned by the chief of the intelligence section of the corresponding arm or service.

b. Captured documents. All Red Army reconnaissance personnel are impressed with the importance of documents found in areas occupied or recently vacated by the enemy. Document exploitation in the lower echelons follows the same procedure as that applied to the interrogation of prisoners. Each headquarters extracts applicable information immediately and then forwards the documents to the next higher echelon. At the army level and higher, thorough classification and study of the documents are made by a special staff of the Information Section of the Intelligence Staff.

c. Captured matériel. Captured enemy arms and equipment are collected by the headquarters section of the formation or by a special detail appointed by the Commander. The collected materiel is studied by the technical intelligence sections of the army and higher echelons. Primary tests, such as armor penetration, are undertaken in the forward area by locally available technical officers. All personnel are taught to report the performance and employment of new enemy weapons and equipment.

d. Reports. Reports from intelligence agencies are collected through the intelligence channels, but intelligence is generally disseminated through the operations sections of the various staffs.

Reconnaissance reports are submitted by each reconnaissance unit, and must indicate the following:

> Addressee (surname of the Commander only), location of the reconnaissance unit, and time of the message.
> Information on the strength, location, and activities of the enemy.
> Information on the terrain.
> Other pertinent information such as casualties and prisoners.
> Future action of the patrol, number of the message, and signature.

Observation reports are submitted by the commander of each observation post. They include the number of the post; names of the observers; and the time, date, azimuth, and range of each significant item observed. Reports may be given as a summary, as a plane or panoramic sketch, or as a combination of the two (figs. 8 and 9).

Intelligence summaries may be periodic or special. They are authenticated by the Intelligence Officer and by the Chief of Staff, and disseminated to the higher, subordinate, and neighboring headquarters. Intelligence summaries must include the following:

> General nature of enemy activities.
> Disposition of the enemy from right to left, accompanied by sources and time of the information.
> Enemy air activity.
> Information on the enemy rear areas as disclosed by air reconnaissance, prisoner-of-war statements, and other reports.
> Conclusions as to the significance of the enemy's actions.
> A list of items of information which should be verified or clarified, and the means by which this could be accomplished.

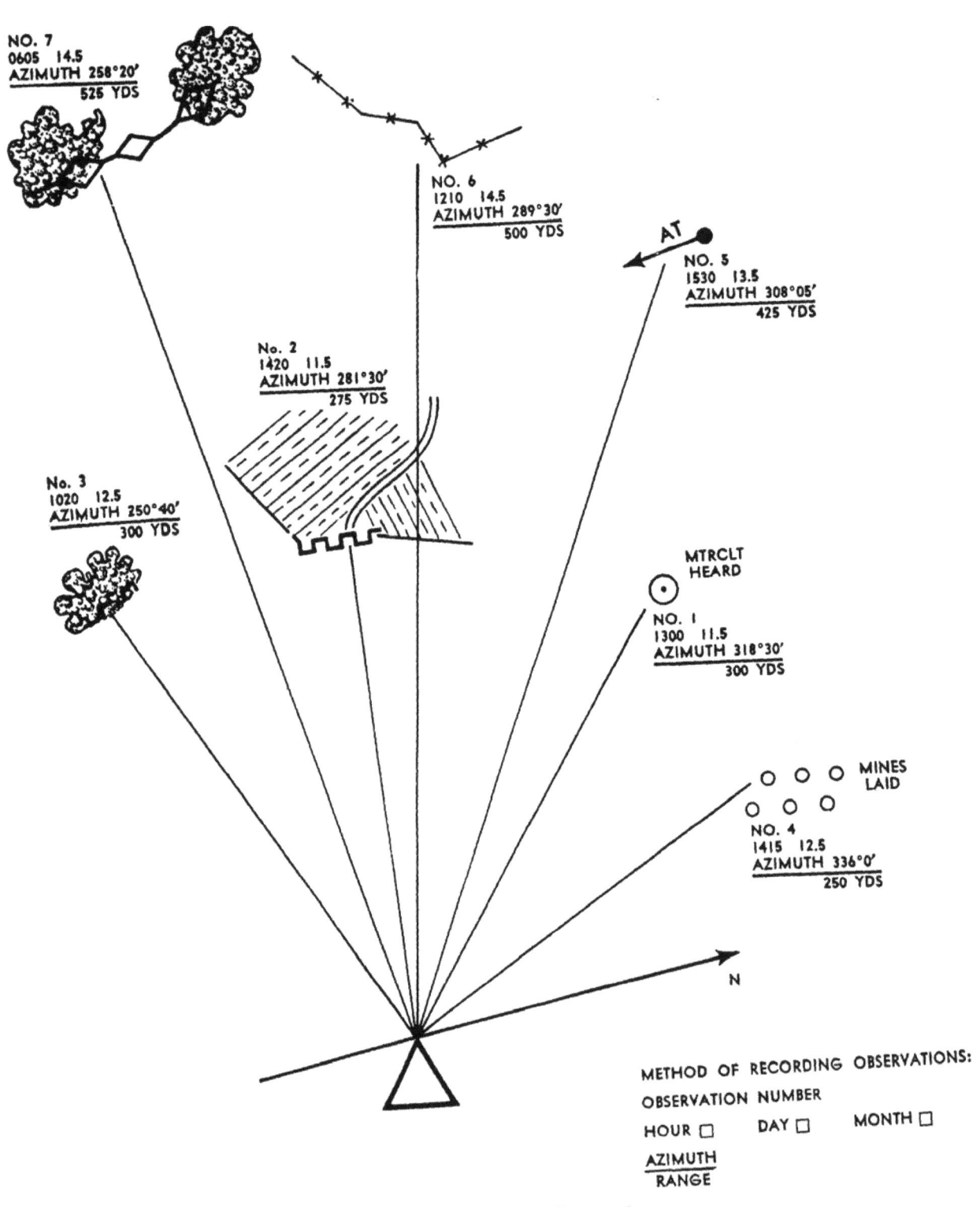

NO. 7
0605 14.5
AZIMUTH 258°20'
525 YDS

NO. 6
1210 14.5
AZIMUTH 289°30'
500 YDS

AT
NO. 5
1530 13.5
AZIMUTH 308°05'
425 YDS

No. 2
1420 11.5
AZIMUTH 281°30'
275 YDS

No. 3
1020 12.5
AZIMUTH 250°40'
300 YDS

MTRCLT
HEARD

NO. 1
1300 11.5
AZIMUTH 318°30'
300 YDS

MINES
LAID

NO. 4
1415 12.5
AZIMUTH 336°0'
250 YDS

N

METHOD OF RECORDING OBSERVATIONS:

OBSERVATION NUMBER

HOUR ☐   DAY ☐   MONTH ☐

AZIMUTH
RANGE

Figure 8. Observation report.

140

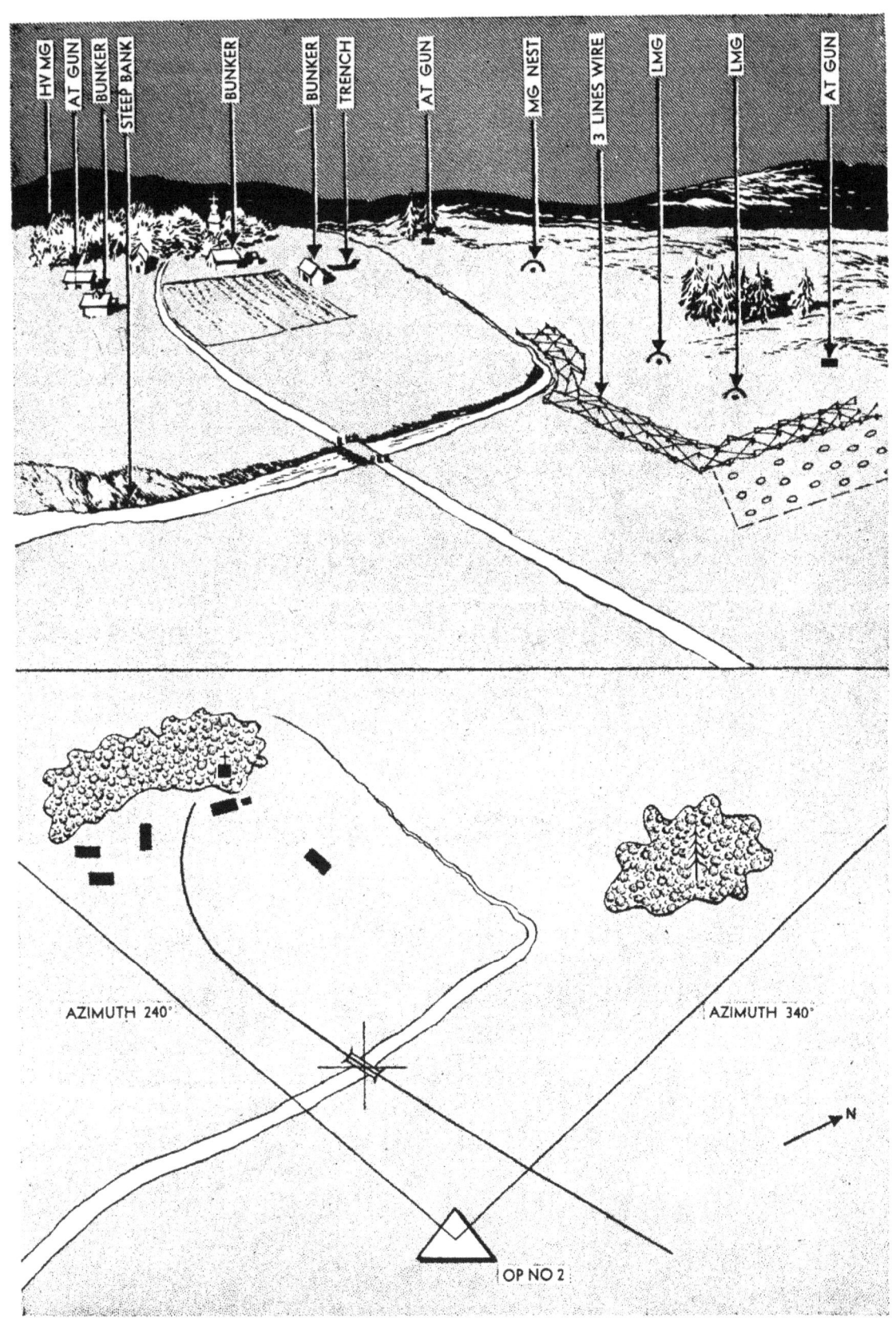

HV MG · AT GUN · BUNKER · STEEP BANK · BUNKER · BUNKER · TRENCH · AT GUN · MG NEST · 3 LINES WIRE · LMG · LMG · AT GUN

AZIMUTH 240°

AZIMUTH 340°

N

OP NO 2

Figure 9. Observation report combined with panoramic sketch.

141

Section III. BASIC TYPES OF TACTICAL PLANS

In Soviet practice, the forms of maneuver and organization of operations consistently follow a limited number of basic patterns: the infantry offensive, the tank and mechanized offensive, the meeting engagement, the pursuit, the centralized and decentralized defense, the mobile defense of mechanized forces, the withdrawal, and the disengagement from encirclement.

1. THE INFANTRY OFFENSIVE

The Soviet infantry offensive is made by infantry supported by artillery, tanks, engineers, and aviation as the situation demands. It is generally in the form of simultaneous attacks on a broad front with concentrations of artillery and, particularly, tanks in the break-through area. The attack seeks to penetrate the enemy defenses in two or more sectors and converge on a limited objective; its mission is to encircle or envelop enemy groupings and destroy them by simultaneous attacks from all directions. This scheme of maneuver is fundamental for the offensive operations of units of every size from the platoon to the army group.

A typical plan of attack (fig. 10) is formulated in the following manner:

> *Mission*: To destroy enemy forces which are guarding the approaches to communication center X.
>
> *Forces available*: Nth Infantry Division.
>
> *Enemy forces*: Two infantry regiments and two artillery regiments.
>
> *Plan of maneuver*: 1st Regiment to advance to Objective A through breach made by the neighboring division. 2d Regiment, using the same breach, to advance to Objective B, leaving one battalion to deal with points of resistance C and D. 1st Battalion, 3d Regiment to penetrate enemy defenses and join 2d Regiment at Objective C. Provide flank security for 2d Regiment. 3d Battalion, 3d Regiment to penetrate enemy defenses and join 2d Regiment at Objective E. 2d Battalion, 3d Regiment to penetrate enemy defenses and join 1st Regiment at Objective A.

Soviet offensive theory stresses the importance of combined or coordinated operations. Supporting arms are usually under the senior commander of that arm until such time as the predetermined phase in the combat plan directs subordination of the supporting arms directly under the command of the supported unit. Coordinated attacks are planned and rehearsed with the utmost care, and great attention is given to the smallest details. Daring and initiative on the part of smaller unit commanders is imperative.

In the offensive, a given situation may call for certain types of specially trained troops. In cases where columns of tanks make an assault of a fortified position, special detachments of combat engineers, thoroughly trained for their particular assignment, may be used to facilitate the assault or may even be assigned a combat mission such as seizing and securing bridges and water crossings.

Soviet tactical practice prescribes the use of line, wedge, inverted wedge, or echeloned arrangement of forces in the attack. Except for special operations, such as assault of a fortified position, columns will not be used. Normally, in preparation for a penetration, attacking forces are placed well forward, while mobile units used for the purpose of exploitation of a penetration are brought up from the rear.

To utilize maximum shock power, the Red Army normally limits the uncommitted reserves to one-ninth of the infantry combat strength. On difficult terrain this may be increased up to one-sixth.

Offensive operations are accomplished in five distinct phases:

a. Concentration of forces. This phase is characterized by intensive reconnaissance and observation, secret concentration and regroupment, elaborate rehearsals, and deception. Detailed reconnaissance is conducted by units which are already in line, and is combined with command reconnaissance by units designated for the break-through. In the final stages of preparation, reconnaissance in force is conducted in several sectors. At times, reconnaissance is staged to resemble a major offensive in order to deceive the enemy as to the real direction of attack and to throw him off balance.

Concentration and regroupment of forces is accomplished with great secrecy. Elaborate precautions are taken to prepare in advance camouflaged dispersal areas for troops, especially armor and artillery. Units are grouped according to the tactical plan, and further subdivided into teams, one team for each objective. These teams stage day and night rehearsals over ground which has been specially prepared to resemble that of the contemplated break-through. Artillery fire is rigidly controlled and is limited to the minimum consistent with antiaircraft

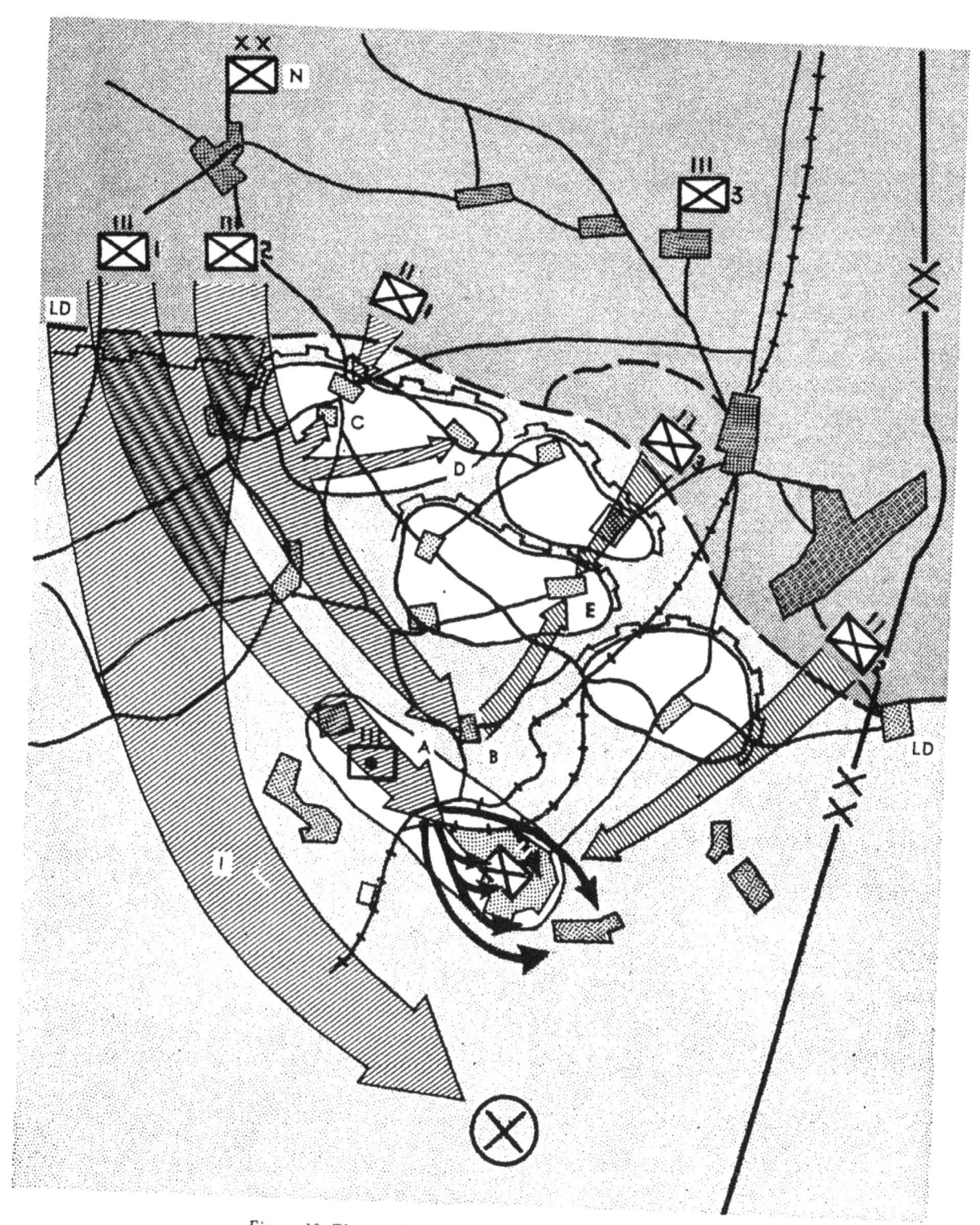

Figure 10. The coordinated attack—Soviet tactical concept.

and counterbattery defense requirements. Fire is conducted only by duty and roving batteries.

Meanwhile staffs, often augmented by special teams from General Headquarters (*Stavka Glavnogo Komanduishchego*), prepare field orders, artillery fire plans, tables of combat coordination, and other necessary papers. If the Commander judges that the troops and staffs are not sufficiently well prepared

143

for the operation, he prescribes a special training schedule which may extend over the preparatory period. Soviet preparation for an assault of prepared positions is deliberate, extending from several days to 6 or 10 weeks depending on the caliber of enemy resistance and the state of preparedness of the assault troops.

b. Fire preparation. In the second phase, the air forces seek to isolate the enemy by destroying his communication lines. Artillery undertakes the destruction of located fire positions. Finally, every available weapon, centralized under one command, concentrates a brief but extremely violent barrage immediately preceding the assault.

c. The assault. In the assault phase of the break-through or penetration, artillery is allotted to the various assault teams for direct support. Movement of units and fire of supporting arms are controlled on the initiative of local commanders. Artillery must observe the movement of supported units, executing firing missions on the request of assault team commanders or according to tables of combat coordination.

In order to maintain continuous control, the overall commander must observe the movement of units, especially in the decisive direction. Command liaison officers are delegated to supervise the execution of the assault in secondary directions and to transmit changes in combat plans which necessitate changes in tables of combat coordination.

d. Securing the offensive. After the objective in the enemy's rear has been reached, the attacking units consolidate their positions, secure their flanks against counterattacks, and prepare for the exploitation of the penetration. For example, in an attack made by tanks, combat engineers are used for the special purpose of protecting the tanks from counterattack by throwing out contact and controlled mines at the moment the assault is stalled or otherwise stopped for consolidation or regrouping. After regrouping or repelling a counterattack, the tanks continue the attack, passing over the areas covered by controlled mines. The mines are picked up and the operation is repeated at the next forward limit of the advance.

e. Exploitation. Mobile formations p a s s through the gap in parallel columns, pursuing the enemy. Motorized light artillery, engineers, and infantry from the assault units are attached to them as needed and available. The remaining infantry

units attack encircled enemy forces, continuing also to provide flank security. Air and artillery units reinforce the fire of self-propelled and mobile artillery on call from mobile formations striking in the enemy rear. On call from the infantry, they destroy encircled enemy remnants. Calculated risks are taken to secure bridgeheads and commanding terrain and to prevent the enemy from organizing a defense on intermediate positions.

2. THE TANK OFFENSIVE

A frontal attack by tank forces, normally a tank corps, differs from the coordinated assault of infantry with supporting arms. Tanks attack in deeply echeloned formation on a narrow sector, using their fire and shock power to achieve penetration. Resistance is by-passed in order to avoid full deployment and protracted local combat. Infantry and artillery mop up enemy strong points and provide flank security for the tank unit against enemy counterattack. The tank forces are assigned specific terrain objectives in the enemy rear rather than mission-type orders.

The tank forces themselves cannot hold territory, but must rely upon the following infantry and, sometimes, cavalry. Tank units destroy enemy rear installations and supply lines, and attempt to encircle and destroy the enemy by coordinating their penetration with adjacent units in a wide turning maneuver or by a double envelopment by two converging tank penetrations (fig. 11).

3. MEETING ENGAGEMENT

In general, Soviet and U. S. doctrines as to meeting engagements are virtually identical (fig. 12). Specifically, however, certain differences may be noted. According to Soviet doctrine, speed of maneuver, seizure of favorable terrain, and quick deployment of main forces and artillery upon contact are essential. Aggressive reconnaissance, ground and air, is continual throughout the operation. Usually, a strong advance guard is utilized. An attack upon the flank is sought. The fullest use of artillery at the earliest possible moment is made. The advance guard uses its organic artillery support to stall the forward movement of the enemy in order to enable the artillery of the main forces to be brought to bear on enemy firing positions. In one case in an operation northwest of Orel, artillery was brought into direct fire action from the march.

Soviet doctrine states that *the speed of deployment by artillery units decides the outcome of the battle.*

144

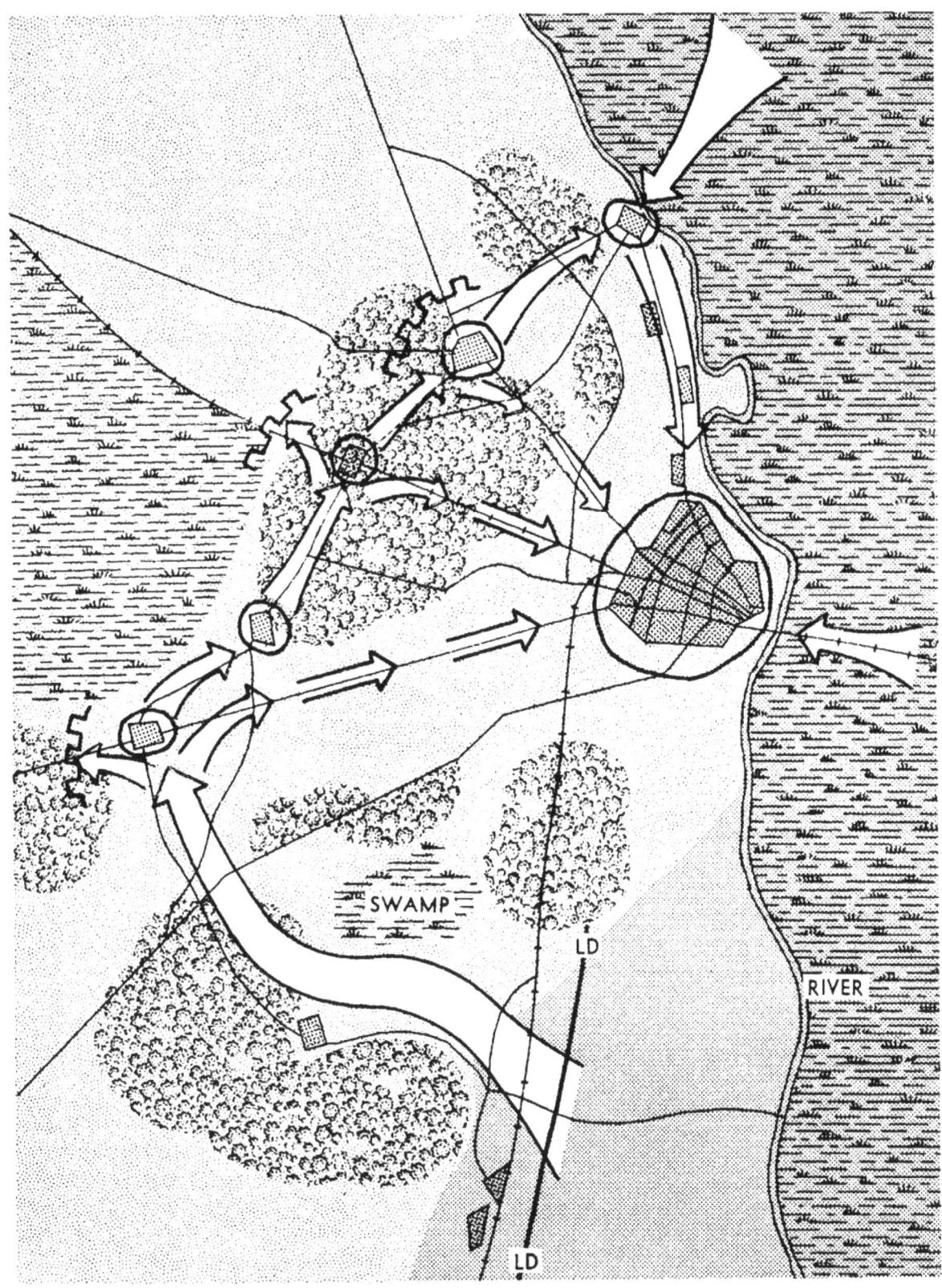

Figure 11. Bobruisk encirclement by large tank unit.

SWAMP

LD

RIVER

LD

145

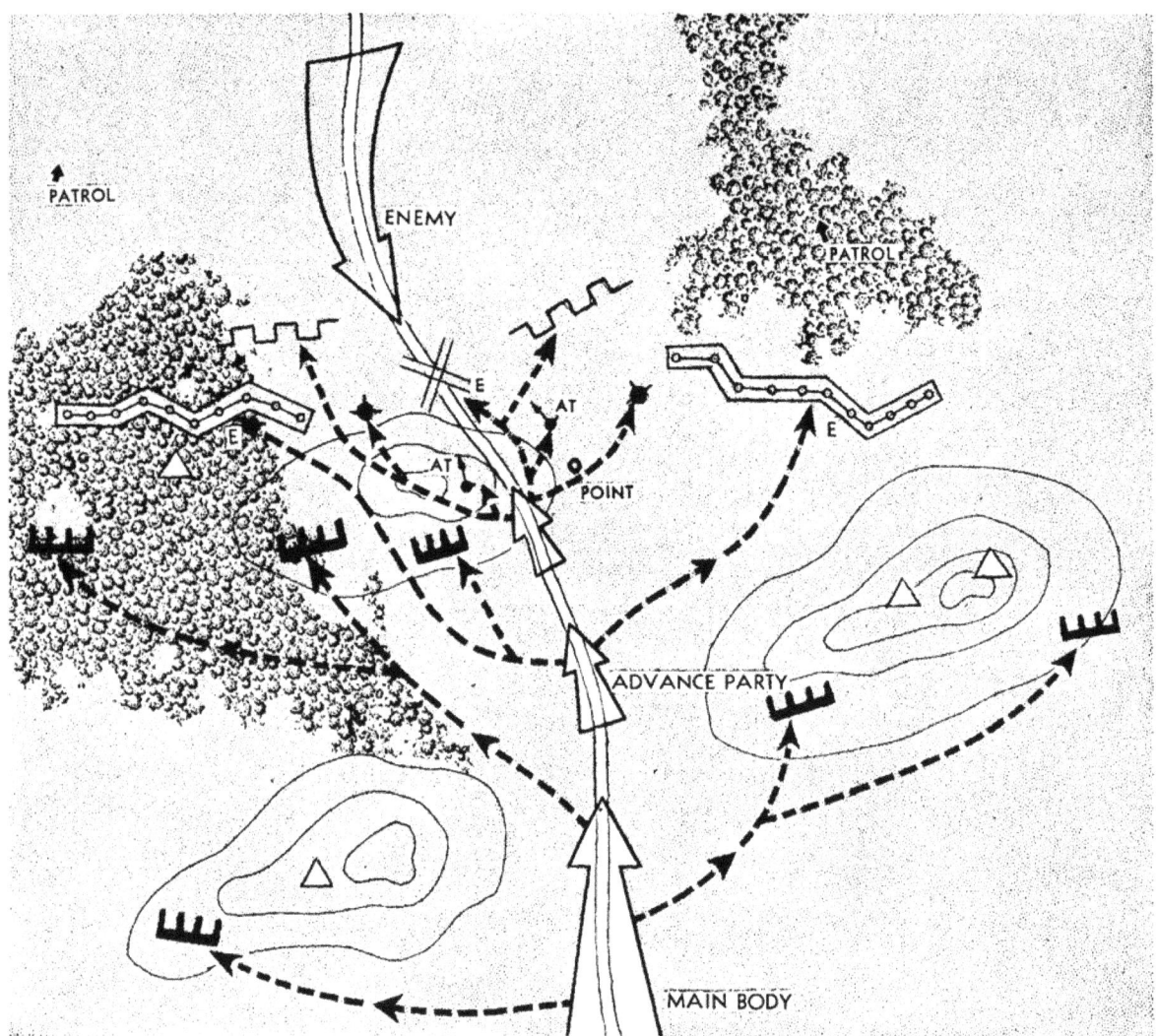

Figure 12. Meeting engagement, showing scheme of deployment of the point, advance party, and main body when contact with enemy occurs.

4. PURSUIT

The Red Army, as a general rule, pursues the enemy in a double parallel column, usually by mechanized units closely followed by infantry. Great care must be taken by the Commander in organizing for the pursuit; his planning should be detailed, but speed in this is essential.

A typical pursuit plan (fig. 13) includes the following elements:

> *Mission:* To destroy retreating groups and advancing reinforcements of the enemy, and to leave small groups to block avenues of escape of by-passed enemy garrisons.

> *Forces available:* Two tank brigades and one motorized brigade with supporting units.

> *Enemy forces:* Advancing reinforcements, retreating groups, and by-passed garrisons.

> *Plan of maneuver:* Group to advance in two parallel columns, a tank and a motorized brigade on the right, and a tank brigade on the left. Right column to exploit the break-through along the road T-R, to envelop S from south and southwest, to block advance of reinforcements from the north. Left column to exploit the break-through along the road I-L-S, to assist in the capture of S. The group to continue the advance to O.

The Soviets seek decisive combat with the main retreating forces, avoiding direct contact with enemy rear guards or other special units charged with the mission of slowing down the pursuit. When strong-

146

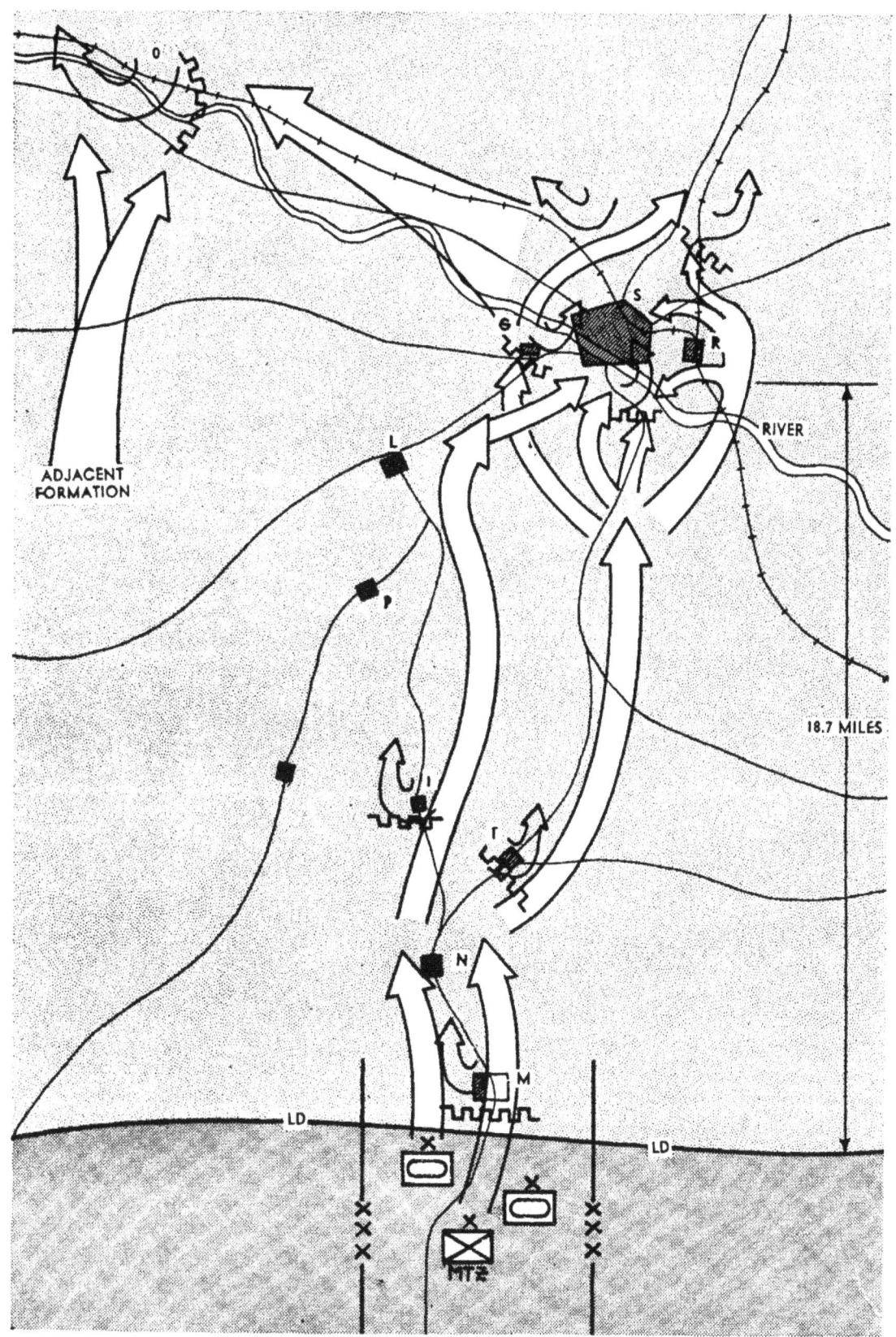

Figure 13. Pursuit.

points are found to be impeding forward progress of the pursuing forces, these points are by-passed and detachments of assault troops are assigned to surround and to destroy them.

Extensive use is made of engineers to facilitate the forward movement of the pursuing forces. Engineers clear enemy mines and other obstacles from the avenues of approach and mobilize the local population for constructing and rebuilding roads and bridges.

lery, and antiaircraft—so as to be able to withstand, absorb, or shatter mass attacks by enemy infantry supported by tanks, artillery, and aviation.

The use of reserves in the Soviet defense varies, depending on the type of defense, terrain, and objective. Usually the Soviets concentrate the overwhelming bulk of a unit's strength on the main line of resistance. The reserve is limited to approxi-

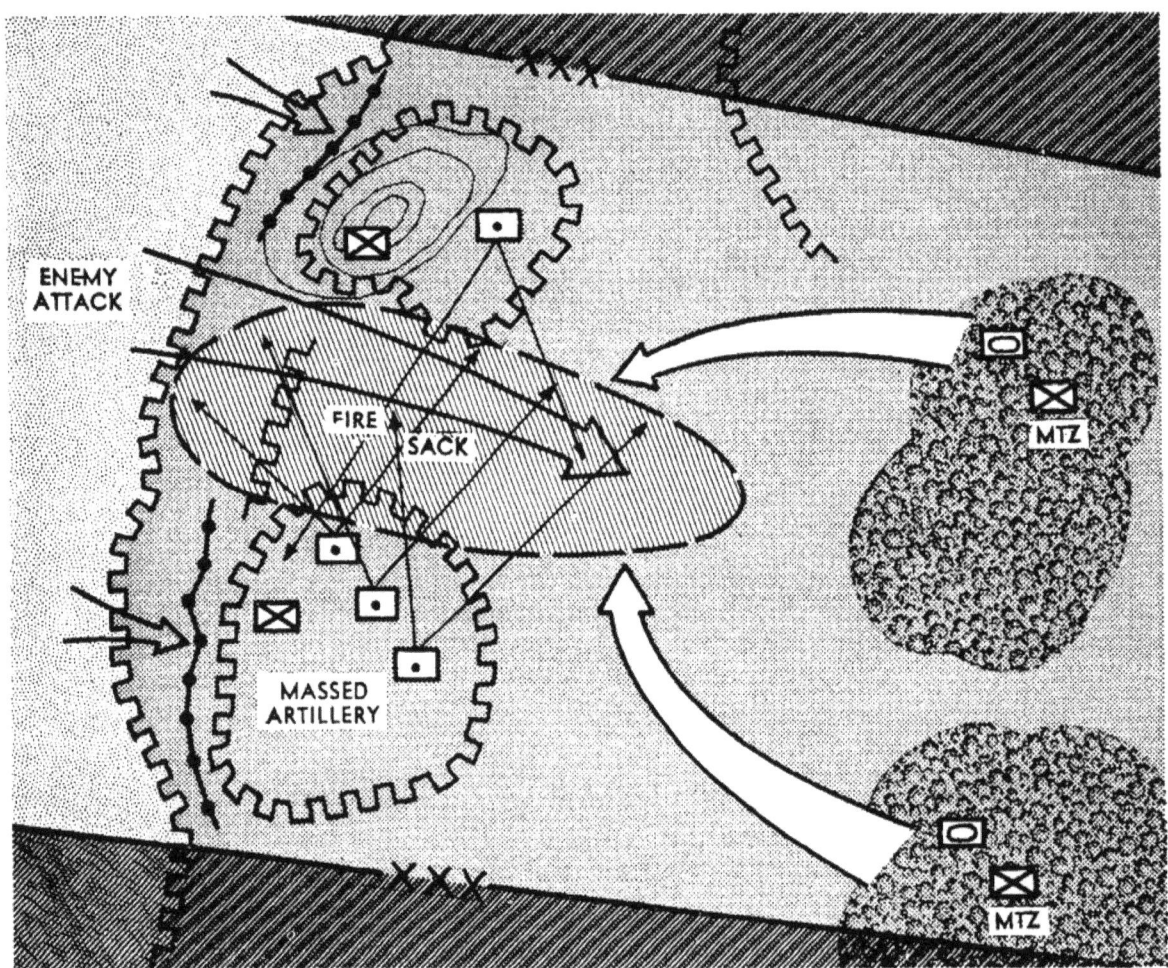

Figure 14. Centralized defense for destroying the attacking enemy, using massed artillery and counterattacks.

5. DEFENSE

The strength of Red Army defensive tactics lies in the determination of the troops, coordination of all types of fire with all systems of antitank and antipersonnel fortifications and obstacles, skillful organization of the ground, and decisive counterattacks.

The defense should be deep—antitank, antiartil-

mately one-ninth of the total combat strength. In certain situations, however, when decisive results can be gained, an extremely large mobile reserve is maintained. A tank corps, for instance, may act as a reserve for an infantry division. Such a tank unit is kept concealed well in the rear, with careful preparation made to facilitate its rapid commitment on the flank of the attacking force.

Depending on the situation, the Commander's objective, and available forces, the defense may be either centralized or decentralized.

148

a. Centralized defense. The centralized type of defense seeks, by employing obstacles or by maneuver, to channelize the enemy attack in a given direction in order to gain a more favorable position for a decisive counterattack with heavily armored units and concentrations of massed artillery (fig. 14). Dummy positions and false fortifications are

takes position for close all-around protection. Favorable terrain is sought for the development and fortification of strongpoints and islands of resistance. Each unit uses its assigned artillery and other organic weapons for its own protection. In decentralized defense, strongpoints and islands of resistance frequently will be surrounded or cut off from

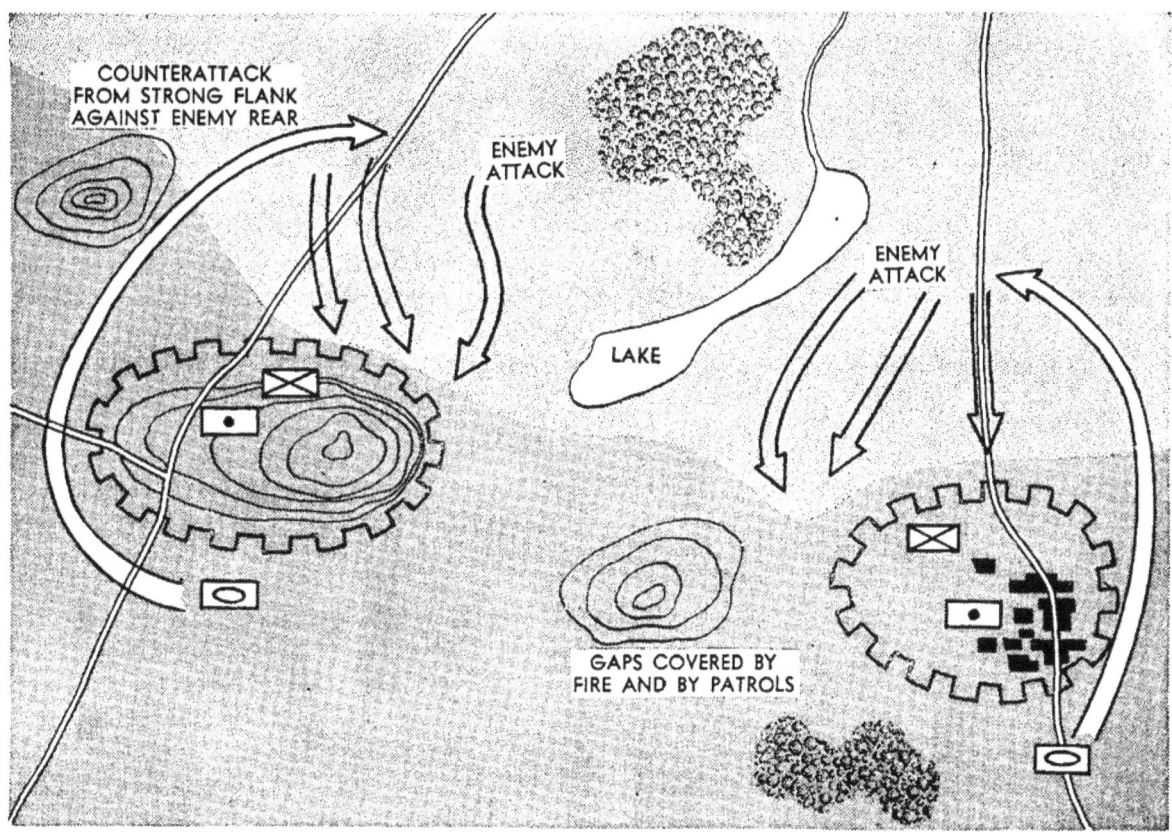

Figure 15. Decentralized defense for denying terrain to superior enemy forces by strongpoints with close-in, all-around defense.

used extensively. A favorite Soviet maneuver is to allow the enemy to penetrate deeply into the lines and trap him in a firesack. The counterattack takes the form of a large-scale ambush on the deep flank, the counterattacking units being supported by massed, registered artillery. The counterattack is under the direct control of the over-all troop commander. The mission of this type of defense is destruction of the enemy.

b. Decentralized defense. The objectives of decentralized defense are to deny the enemy use of terrain, to divide his attacking forces, and to destroy him by numerous local counterattacks on the initiative of the local ground commander (fig. 15). In this type of defense each unit down to the smallest

other friendly troops. Only on specific orders from the senior troop commander is the position abandoned. This particular type of defense is especially effective against tanks and mechanized units.

c. Defense by cavalry and mechanized forces. Mobile forces may assume either decentralized or centralized defensive positions. But, in order to retain the advantages of their mobility, they usually adopt more elastic tactics, particularly in terrain affording good concealment.

Avenues of approach are covered frontally by artillery and infantry (dismounted cavalry) road blocks. Other small groups, usually including self-propelled tank destroyers, prepare flanking positions to ambush enemy mechanized units. Finally, a powerful mobile reserve is held out with the mission of counterattacking the deep flank or rear of the forces stopped by the road block.

In general, this type of defense seeks to trap and destroy advancing enemy columns successively. In the face of a coordinated attack which threatens to destroy the road block and expose the rear of the mobile reserve, a withdrawal is executed to the next favorable position.

6. WITHDRAWALS

Retrograde movements are not heavily stressed in Red Army tactics; regulations state that a disengagement will be undertaken only on direct order from higher authority. The techniques of retrograde movement employed in day and night operations are virtually identical with those of the U. S. Army.

7. DISENGAGEMENT FROM ENCIRCLEMENT

In 1941 and 1942, the Red Army suffered heavy casualties due to encirclements of large units by German forces. As a result, specific procedures in disengagement from encirclement were incorporated in Red Army tactics.

When any unit is in danger of encirclement, the Commander designates troops to secure the flanks and rear, and then counterattacks in order to stall the enemy. Additional tactical measures to be taken include holding favorable terrain along the enemy approach routes, designating strong detachments with antitank weapons to threaten enemy flanks, coordinating his efforts with adjacent friendly units, closely supervising the expenditure of ammunition and other supplies, and locating and holding terrain favorable for supply by air.

When encircled, the Commander insures all-around defense, making especially sure that his forces are not under direct artillery fire. He is careful to conserve his strength, and makes sure that the hostile force does not destroy him by dividing his forces. He places the artillery at the most strategic positions, guarding approaches, vulnerable areas, and sectors of probable attacks. He insures signal communication with higher headquarters. The Soviets emphasize that even though a unit is encircled, the Commander is required to accomplish his mission. *The disengagement from encirclement is undertaken only on specific orders from higher authority.*

Disengagement from encirclement aims at the penetration of a given sector of the enemy circle and the retirement of the unit under great pressure from a numerically superior hostile force. Periods of impaired visibility—night, fog, rain, snowstorms—are the most favorable periods for this maneuver. Prior to undertaking the operation, the Commander should determine the general situation and disposition of neighboring friendly units and partisan detachments. By aggressive use of reconnaissance he determines enemy strength and groupings. He insures great secrecy in making preparations for the disengagement. Planning must be detailed and thorough, since disengagement from encirclement is considered the most difficult of operations. The more direct the maneuver, the fewer are the casualties.

The general rules for an assault are followed in a daytime attempt to break out of encirclement. Artillery fire in preparation for the assault is exceptionally heavy. At night, however, the technique differs. The advance to the line of departure is made under the strictest secrecy. A large portion of the artillery moves in the infantry column; the chief offensive weapons are the bayonet and hand grenades. Rifle fire is used only when resistance is encountered.

Having made the penetration, the general rules covering retirement prevail. Counterattacks by rear-guard units, security against parallel pursuit, and, if possible, tank attacks at the enemy rear, are prescribed.

The Soviets recognize that disengagements from encirclement are unsuccessful in many cases. When all hope of success has been abandoned, an order may be issued by competent authority to infiltrate through the enemy lines by small units, taking care that no matériel falls into enemy hands. Surrenders en masse or by individuals, except when wounded, are expressly forbidden. Infiltration parties are instructed to join or form partisan detachments in the enemy rear.

Section IV. TACTICAL STAFF DOCUMENTS

1. GENERAL

Translation of broad command decisions into specific, coordinated troop actions requires the preparation of a large series of staff documents. In Red Army practice, such paper work is concentrated primarily in the army; it is also especially necessary for the efficient performance of the technical arms and services, such as artillery (fig. 16). In con-

Figure 16. Artillery staff documents.

NO	TITLE OF DOCUMENT	ARTILLERY GROUPMENT STAFF					DIVISIONAL ARTILLERY STAFF					ARMY (CORPS) ARTILLERY STAFF				
		COMMANDER	CHIEF OF STAFF	OPERATIONS OFFICER	INTELLIGENCE OFFICER	SIGNAL OFFICER	COMMANDER	CHIEF OF STAFF	OPERATIONS OFFICER	INTELLIGENCE OFFICER	SIGNAL OFFICER	COMMANDER	CHIEF OF STAFF	OPERATIONS OFFICER	INTELLIGENCE OFFICER	SIGNAL OFFICER
1.	ARTILLERY FIELD ORDER		X					X					X			
2.	FIRING TABLE			X												
3.	FIRE PLAN		X	X				X					X			
4.	OPERATIONAL SUMMARY			X					X					X		
5.	INTELLIGENCE SUMMARY AND CHART				X					X					X	
6.	PLAN OF ORIENTATION CHECK POINTS			X					X						X	
7.	SIGNAL COMMUNICATION PLAN AND ORDER					X					X					X
8.	INTELLIGENCE PLAN				X					X					X	
9.	WORK MAP	X	X	X	X	X	X	X	X	X	X	X	X	X	X	X
10.	JOURNAL		X	X	X	X		X	X	X	X			X	X	X

151

trast, documentation in infantry and cavalry units is held to a minimum. Those arms never issue formal written orders below divisional level, but make maximum use of oral orders, overlays, and fragmentary orders.

Tactical field documents are divided into two classes: those disseminated for action or information, and those prepared for the use of the issuing headquarters only. The first class includes field orders, fragmentary and warning orders, administrative orders, summaries (intelligence, rear services, signal, operational), instructions, replies, and inquiries.

The second class includes orders and summaries of higher headquarters; general, special, and preliminary orders and directives pertaining to the work of the headquarters itself; copies of field orders and summaries of subordinate headquarters; and journals with attached documents and copies of conversations. A journal of field operations is kept separately.

2. FIELD ORDERS

U. S. Army and Soviet field orders are basically similar. The Soviet field order consists of the following:

> Disposition and activities of enemy forces.
>
> Missions of own unit and of adjoining units, and boundaries.
>
> Command decision.
>
> Special missions of principal subordinate units.
>
> Missions and attachments of arms, services, and special units which are controlled by the Commander.
>
> Location of the service area.
>
> Location and order of displacement of the command post, axis of signal communication.
>
> Time sequence of reports in relation to each phase of combat.

The field order is authenticated by the Chief of Staff and may be countersigned by the Commander.

Tables of combat coordination constitute the basic annexes to the Soviet field order. They contain time and space schedules for active cooperation between each arm during the various phases of combat operations; critical reference points for assembly areas and control of fire; schedules for forward displacement of artillery units; and coordination of

signal communications between the arms. For example, an offensive of an infantry division may be supported by additional artillery and tanks. The tables of combat coordination for such an operation would show which artillery and tank units would operate under centralized control and which would be attached to an infantry unit for direct support during the first and subsequent phases. The tables would indicate whether the phase lines are determined by time schedule or by terrain features, and would designate the signals to be used for the start of each phase.

The plan of coordination between artillery and aviation, one of the most important tables of combat coordination, anticipates immediate infantry requirements and includes the organization of a unified system of fire preparation, support, and security of infantry maneuver. The artillery-aviation plan is developed according to time, space, and targets by the staffs of artillery and aviation. It is signed by the Chief of Staff, Chief of Artillery, and Chief of the Air Arm, and is confirmed by the commanders of the cooperating units (fig. 17).

3. SPECIALIZED PLANS AND ORDERS

The staff of the chief of each arm prepares specific plans and field orders which are forwarded to the lower echelon of that arm, after approval by the Commander of Combined Arms.

The artillery order is based on the artillery fire plan developed under the direction of the highest artillery commander engaged in the offensive operation (army or army group). Consisting of a brief text and annexed operational documents, it includes:

> Information of the enemy.
>
> Missions and boundaries of neighboring units.
>
> Mission of the supported unit (infantry, tanks, etc.) and of cooperating units (air, engineers, etc.).
>
> Combat groupments of artillery, instrumental reconnaissance, and attached aviation (including missions, position areas and observation sectors, and primary and emergency sectors of fire).
>
> Time of readiness for opening fire.
>
> Duration of registration.
>
> Ammunition allowances.
>
> Location of command post and axis of signal communications.
>
> Location of supply points.

Confirmed by:
Commander
Air Force Unit Commander

Aviation Operations			Artillery Operations					
Time	Course	Ground Composition and Missions	Time	Missions	Assignment	Controls	Signal Comm.	AAA Mission
From: −2100 H To: −4 H	In accordance with air force staff plans.	1. Period of preparation on D−1. Course—In accordance with the plans of Air Force and Long-Range Artillery Staffs: Group "A"—200 sorties by long-range aviation "IL–2"; Group "B"—300 sorties by "IL–2." 2. Targets: For Group "A" Nos. 1, 3, 4; for Group "B" Nos. 2, 7, 9. Missions—Neutralization of artillery and mortar batteries, destruction of field fortifications and personnel.						Throughout all combat operations AAA supports aviation by AA barrages against enemy fighter aviation. Responsibility commander of "N" AA Division.
−3.30 H −3.00 H −2.30 H		2 "D" 9 Bombers on Target No. 1 same on Target No. 2 same on Target No. 1.	−3.35 H −3.05 H −2.35 H	Fire concentrations on AA batteries (targets Nos. 1565, 679, 186, 196, 102) on individual artillery pieces (Nos. 19, 301) and on newly spotted AA batteries.	The 7th battery of the army support group and one battalion in readiness to spot AA batteries. Responsibility of army support group commander.	Commander of artillery formation.	Wire signal communications and radio thru the O. P. of the commander of artillery formation.	

Signed by: Chief of Artillery
Artillery Chief of Staff
Air Force Chief of Staff

Special Remarks

1. Artillery fire on AA batteries must cease when air attacks begin.
2. During attacks by close-support aircraft, fire will be immediately directed against active enemy AAA batteries firing from positions outside of the area of air operations.
3. In the interval between air attacks, neutralization of enemy AA batteries shall be conducted on the individual initiative of the army group commanders.
4. As a safety measure when friendly aircraft appear artillery fire along the flight course will cease. Responsibility: Artillery corps commanders and army group commander.
5. Infantry units will mark their forward position by firing a series of red rockets.

Figure 17. Plan of coordination of artillery and aviation.

153

The engineer plan includes missions assigned to each unit during progressive combat phases; assignment of engineer personnel and allocation of matériel; time schedules; division of responsibilities; and individual missions executed by order of the chief engineer (army or army group).

4. FRAGMENTARY AND ORAL ORDERS

Fragmentary orders are used when speed in delivery and execution is imperative. These orders are issued successively as the situation develops. They consist of separate instructions to one or more subordinate units prescribing the task each is to accomplish in the operation or in the separate phases of the operation.

5. REPORTS AND SUMMARIES

Reports are classified as periodic reports and field reports. The schedule of reports, prepared by the Chief Signal Officer in cooperation with the Chief of Operations, is approved by the Chief of Staff.

Field reports are promptly submitted on the initiative of the subordinate commanders or of headquarters. Signed by the Commander and the Chief of Staff, they include:

> All operations taking place on the ground and in the air.
> Location and condition of the troops.
> Intensity and outcome of the engagement.
> New information about the enemy.
> Enemy strength, technical equipment, and activities.
> Decisions of the Commander with reference to the situation.

Summaries are submitted at fixed times and give an account of events which have occurred since the last summary was sent out. Summaries are classified as operations, intelligence, rear area, and signal summaries. The operations summary is prepared by the Operations Staff and is signed by the Chief of the Operations Section and by the Chief of Staff. It contains the following information:

> Ground and air operations and changes that have occurred in the situation since the last summary was forwarded.
> Nature of combat operations carried out by subordinate units.
> Condition of units, losses, and their present combat efficiency.
> Captured matériel.

> General nature of the situation and enemy action.
> Activities of Soviet air force.
> Soviet front line.
> Adjacent units and supporting troops.
> Communications, weather, visibility, and condition of roads.
> Location of command posts.

The intelligence summary is prepared by the Intelligence Section and is signed by the Chief of Staff and the Chief of the Intelligence Section.

Rear service summaries must give a clear account of the condition of the rear services. Signed by the Chief of Staff and the Chief of the Rear Services Section, they contain the following information:

> Location of supply stations.
> Transportation and evacuation roads (if changes have taken place).
> Status of transportation.
> Equipment shortages.
> Status of evacuation (men and animals).
> Amount of ammunition and fuel on hand.
> Food and fodder in daily rations, reserve supply on hand or in transit.
> Local resources and how they can be used.
> Medical and veterinary situation in rear districts.
> General conclusions.

Signal summaries are prepared by the Signal Section and are signed by the Chief of Staff and the Chief Signal Officers. They provide the following information:

> Equipment available.
> Types and requirements for signal communications between the command post, subordinate units, and the staff (commanders).
> Requirements for signal communications between chiefs of arms and the commanders of directly subordinated units.
> Requirements for signal communications for coordination between subordinated units and the various arms and between the second echelon of the staff, the command post, and rear units.
> Organization of the air warning system, with indications of the location of posts and the method of communication between them.
> Signal equipment reserve and its location.

Copies of summaries and reports are forwarded for the information of subordinate and adjoining units. In urgent cases, special conversations may be conducted over the telephone personally, or through liaison officers.

6. CODING SERVICE AND HANDLING OF DOCUMENTS

Responsibility for organization of the coding service in the field is assumed by the Commander and the Chief of Staff. The Chief of Staff organizes the coding service in the field through the Chief of the Operations Section. The latter selects the Commander's code keys, the conversation chart, map coding orientation points, and time of change. He controls the functioning of the coding service at his and subordinate headquarters.

Conversations concerning operations cannot be sent in the clear. Field orders and reports on decisions, from division and higher, may be transmitted by radio, in code, only if no other means of communication is possible. Violations may be made the basis of a court martial for disclosing military secrets. Clear text by radio is permitted in artillery to direct fire; in aviation, to transmit field orders in flight or, in case of forced landings, to report damage, when time does not permit use of code; and in the tank corps, to transmit field orders during combat. In all clear text messages, unit numbers are referred to by previously established code names.

Before opening a radio conversation, an officer must have at hand a coded situation map, a code conversation chart, radio-signal chart, pad of entry forms, pencil, compass, and watch. Conversation opens with the calling party stating his code name.

Field documents are divided into groups, based on urgency, as follows:

Group "G." Documents requiring immediate dispatch, urgent or operational priority. Field orders are always included in Group "G." The Commander and the Chief of Staff are the only persons who may classify documents as Group "G."

Group "K." Documents which are to be opened and read by the addressee only. Such documents are received and dispatched personally by the Commander and the Chief of Staff and are forwarded with the same priority as those in Group "G."

Group "B." All operational field documents, orders, and reports pertaining to combat organization and security. On these documents, group designation, time of delivery, and addressee are indicated.

Group "B" classification may be designated by all chiefs of sections at headquarters and the chiefs of arms and services.

All other documents bear no group designation and are forwarded by air and field mail.

Section V. COORDINATION AND CONTROL OF COMBAT

1. GENERAL

The Operations Section of the staff is responsible for the uninterrupted coordination of arms during combat, and for the organization of signal communications and liaison to insure this. Upon receipt of the mission, coordination of all arms is obtained by tables of combat coordination which are developed by the Operations Section together with the chiefs of arms. The main tactical controls—forward positions, artillery positions, line of departure, and barrage phase lines—are determined. The exact time schedule, missions, and areas of operation for each arm (artillery, tanks, aircraft, and chemical warfare) are established in accordance with the decision of the Commander.

Execution of coordination and adjustments in the tables of combat coordination are made possible by the direct control of the Commander, and by continuous intercommunication with subordinate units and between arms. The most important channels of intercommunication are through signal communications and liaison officers.

2. SIGNAL COMMUNICATIONS

The Chief Signal Officer is the immediate director of the Signal Service. He is fully responsible not only for the efficient and timely organization of signal communications and their uninterrupted operation, but also for the prompt transmission and delivery of all orders. Collaborating with the Chief of the Operations Section, on the basis of instructions received from the Chief of Staff and reconnaissance data, the Chief Signal Officer prepares a signal plan specifying the organization of communications throughout the projected operation. This plan is submitted to the Chief of Staff and issued with the field order.

a. Planning principles. Red Army signal communications systems are laid out in conformity with certain fixed principles. *Rigid centralization* and strict signal discipline are required to integrate the circuits of the various arms and subordinate units, eliminate unnecessary traffic, and maintain signal security. *Concentration* of signal equipment to facilitate execution of the main effort is achieved by ruthless economy in secondary sectors; service and administrative nets, except for ammunition supply, are virtually nonexistent. At the same time, *duplicate facilities* and *signal reserves* are always built up in critical areas. For instance, the passing of barrage phase lines by infantry is verified by radio voice, radio telegraph, and rocket as well as by observation from a dense network of infantry and artillery observation posts (fig. 18). To provide absolutely reliable communications with the artillery in support of the main effort, the normal artillery nets are split, with separate forward switchboards, double wire communications, and radio circuits being provided. The rest of the artillery uses the basic nets.

Similarly, 1.5 to 2 reserve battery sets must be maintained for each division or corps radio station, with 2.5 to 3 sets for each mobile detachment or flank unit. Two or three alternate channels must be provided for each major radio circuit. Reserve equipment for wire communications is similarly maintained.

Communications are established *down and to the left*, and supporting units are responsible for communications with the supported units. Liaison officers provide their own communications.

Another important factor is the timely organization of communication centers in the *progressive displacement* of the command and other staff posts. This is achieved by the echeloned forward movement of radio equipment according to a plan designating the order of setting up and closing down the specific radio stations; by the echeloned forward movement of wire circuits in coordination with the main phase lines; and by notifying all subordinate staffs as to the new main axis of communication and the location of forward message centers and secondary communication centers.

The full *utilization of captured signal equipment* (especially wire for duplicating lines) has become part of Soviet signal doctrine, and special reconnaissance groups are sent out on the personal initiative of the chief signal officers of regiments and higher units to collect usable equipment left by the enemy.

b. Signal nets. The signal doctrine of the Red Army stresses reliable and often duplicated communications, which are deemed necessary for operational control and coordination of combat units at the expense of administrative circuits. This is well illustrated by the types of signal nets which are habitually established in all formations of combined arms (fig. 19).

Two types of *command nets* are established. One command net connects the command observation post of the Commander of Combined Arms with the command post, the command observation posts of all immediately subordinate units, and those of the chiefs of arms. The second command net connects the command observation post of the chief of a particular arm with the chiefs of that arm in subordinate units. Both wire and radio are used. When radio is used, a set is assigned to each commander within the net and follows him wherever he may go. The establishment of the combined command net is often facilitated by the proximity of the principal command observation posts in units larger than the regiment. The command posts of regiments and higher units are often equipped with public address systems connected with the command net. This arrangement insures the dissemination of key decisions to all staff divisions, expedites transmissions of orders, saves time, and eliminates several circuits within the command post.

The *staff net* connects the command post of a formation with the command posts of immediately subordinate units. Staff nets are used for all routine staff operations. Wire, duplicated by radio, is used.

The *cooperation net* is established to insure synchronized action of all participating arms. Both wire and radio communications, supplemented by visual signals and liaison officers, are established through the forward message center to the command posts of the units participating in a given operation or in a phase of this operation.

The *artillery fire control net* is distinguished from the artillery command net in that, in addition to the command posts of each organic and attached artillery unit, it includes the command post of each supported unit, artillery forward and paired observation posts, and firing positions. Provisional mortar battalions (formed by grouping regimental mortar batteries) are included in the artillery fire control net. Wire communications are duplicated by radio, liaison officers, and messengers.

The *reconnaissance net* provides direct communication between each reconnaissance element and the command posts of the responsible headquarters. Dissemination of the results of reconnaissance is accomplished through the staff net. While radio is normally used, wire is often laid to forward information-collecting centers which are set up when recon-

156

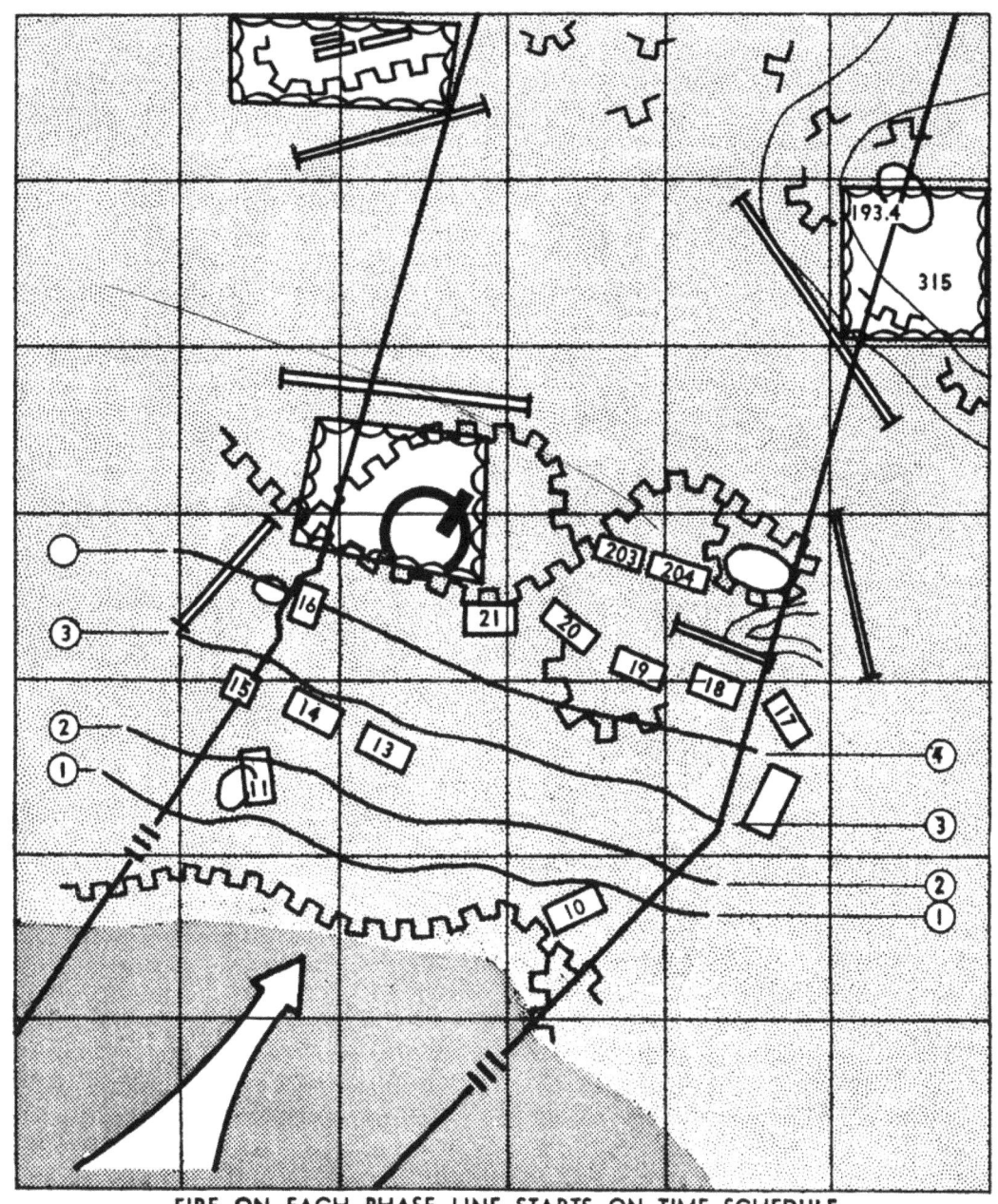

FIRE ON EACH PHASE LINE STARTS ON TIME SCHEDULE

LEGEND

SIGNALS FOR LIFTING FIRE:

1—1ST PHASE "EAGLE" YELLOW ROCKETS,
    RADIO 111

2—2D PHASE "LION" GREEN ROCKETS,
    RADIO 333

3—3D PHASE "TIGER" RED ROCKETS,
    RADIO 555

4—4TH PHASE "BAT" WHITE ROCKETS,
    RADIO 666

INTERDICTION FIRE BY CORPS
ARTILLERY

VOLLEY FROM ROCKETS

SPECIFIC TARGETS

Figure 18. Plan of coordination of artillery support of an infantry attack in depth.

157

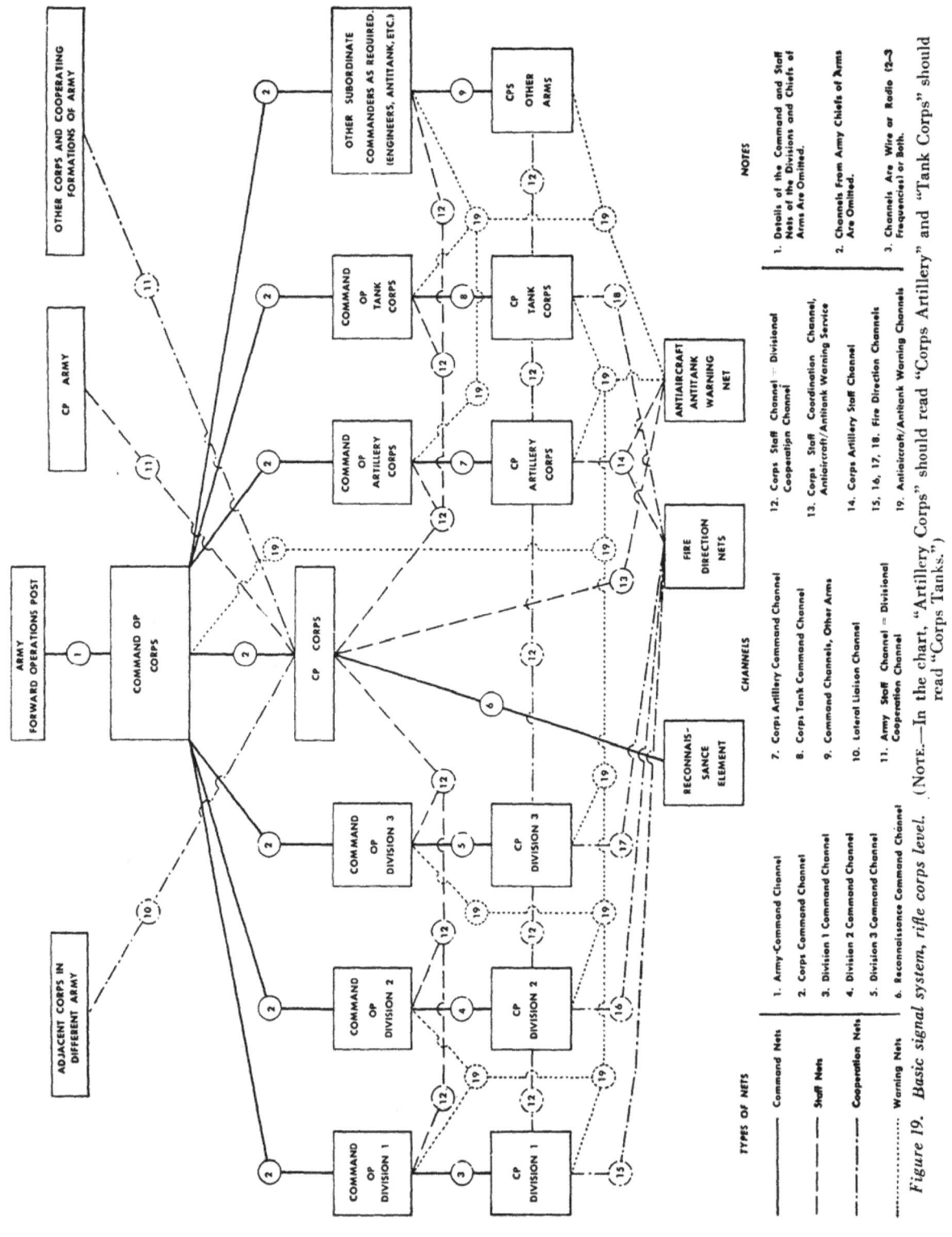

Figure 19. Basic signal system, rifle corps level. (Note.—In the chart, "Artillery Corps" should read "Corps Artillery" and "Tank Corps" should read "Corps Tanks.")

TYPES OF NETS

——————— Command Nets

—— · —— Staff Nets

— — — — Cooperation Nets

— ·· — ·· — Warning Nets

··········· Reconnaissance Command Channel

CHANNELS

1. Army-Command Channel
2. Corps Command Channel
3. Division 1 Command Channel
4. Division 2 Command Channel
5. Division 3 Command Channel
6. Reconnaissance Command Channel
7. Corps Artillery Command Channel
8. Corps Tank Command Channel
9. Command Channels, Other Arms
10. Lateral Liaison Channel
11. Army Staff Channel = Divisional Cooperation Channel
12. Corps Staff Channel = Divisional Cooperation Channel
13. Corps Staff Coordination Channel, Antiaircraft/Antitank Warning Service
14. Corps Artillery Staff Channel
15, 16, 17, 18. Fire Direction Channels
19. Antiaircraft/Antitank Warning Channels

NOTES

1. Details of the Command and Staff Nets of the Divisions and Chiefs of Arms Are Omitted.
2. Channels From Army Chiefs of Arms Are Omitted.
3. Channels Are Wire or Radio (2–3 Frequencies) or Both.

158

naissance elements operate for long periods at a considerable distance from their headquarters.

In large formations a distinct *antiaircraft and antitank warning net* is established. In smaller ones the air and tank raid warning net is superimposed on one of the other nets, with the highest priority being given to "flash" messages.

In armies and other formations which have organic air support, an *air liaison net* is set up. Wire, duplicated by radio, connects the headquarters of the formation of combined arms with the headquarters of the supporting air unit.

c. Signal elements. The communications system is organized according to the following elements:

Signal centers.

Primary and secondary axes of signal communications.

Intermediate stations.

Message centers.

Multiple-station and two-station radio nets.

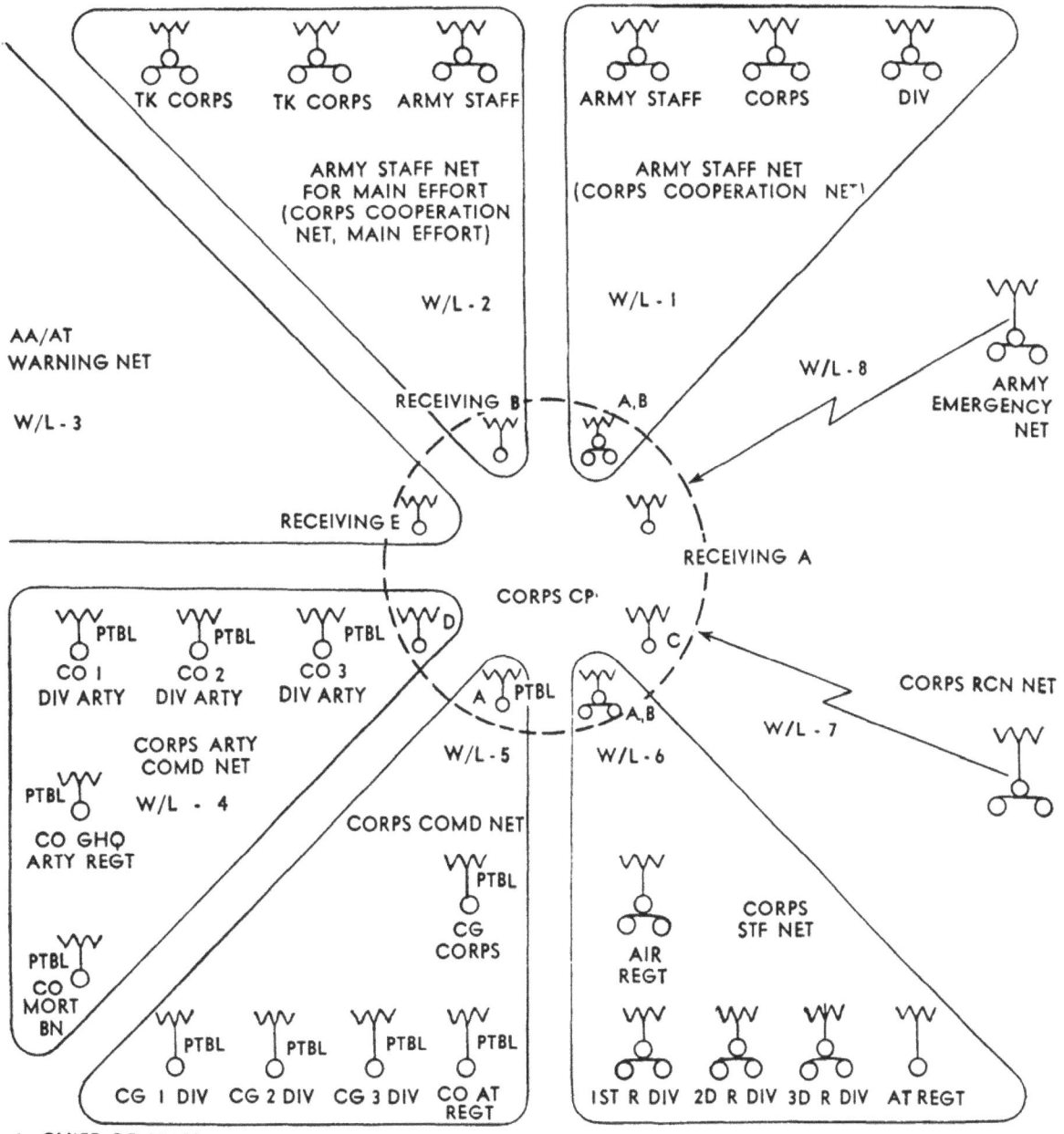

Figure 20. Rifle corps radio net (simplified).

159

The signal center is the point of concentration and intersection of primary and secondary axes of signal communications. The main centers are established at the command posts and provide staff and cooperation channels in all directions (fig. 20). Reserve signal centers are set up in the areas of reserve command posts, and maintain communication in the event of displacement of headquarters from the main to a reserve command post. Auxiliary centers are points where communication can be made with flanking communication lines. Artillery signal centers are also habitually established.

to enable the command to communicate with subordinate command posts, with the rear, with cooperating arms, with neighboring units, and with headquarters of reinforcing units.

Intermediate stations are established along primary and secondary axes of communication. The chief function of these stations is to maintain communications with separate units. Subordinate unit headquarters either utilize intermediate stations or connect these stations with their communication axes (fig. 21).

Message centers circulate necessary field docu-

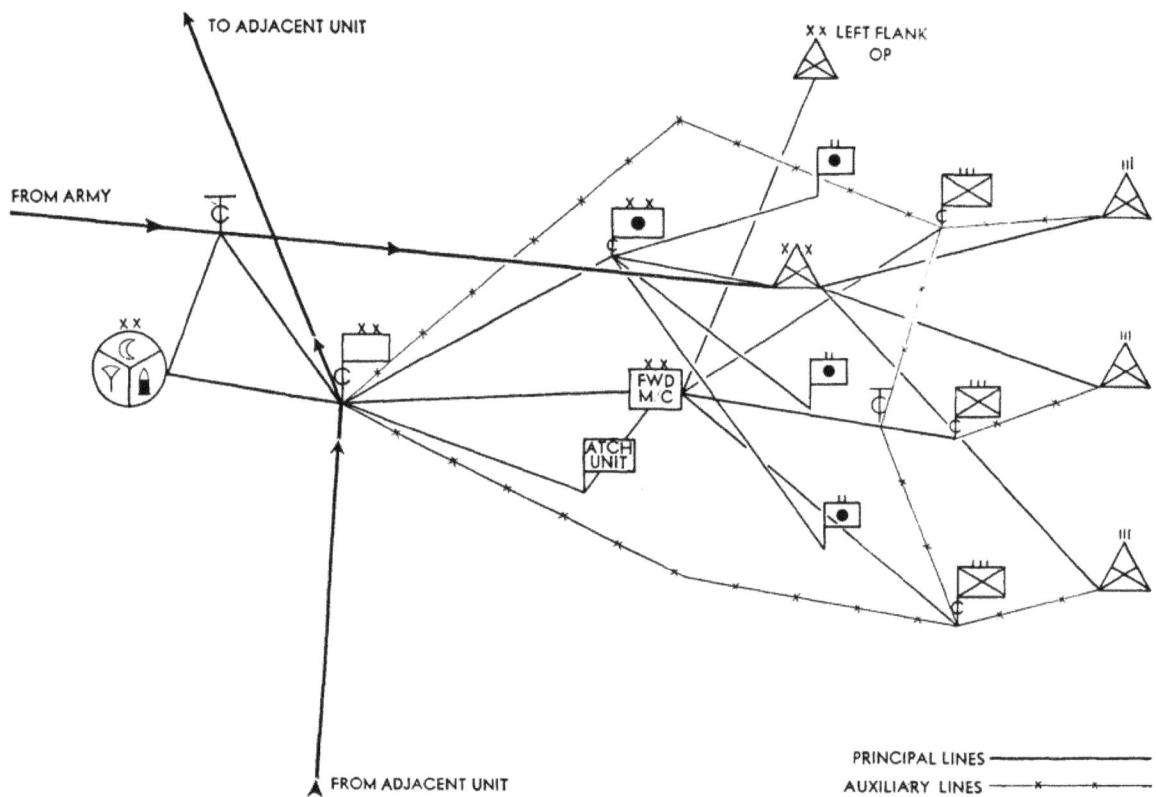

Figure 21. Rifle division wire net (simplified).

The primary axis of communications is the base for all other communication lines to subordinate and cooperating headquarters. Normally it consists of an all-wire circuit from the main switchboard at the command post to a forward switchboard near the command observation post; for emergencies, one or more switch lines provide alternate circuits. Primary axes provide a foundation for the entire Red Army communications system, especially during the displacement of command posts in the course of combat.

Secondary axes of communication are developed

ments among subordinate headquarters, and collect and deliver reports emanating from them.

A multiple radio net comprises a group of radio stations operating in accordance with general instructions concerning their employment. A two-station net constitutes two radio stations maintaining communications on a fixed wave length. This two-station net is used most frequently for command, reconnaissance, and lateral liaison circuits.

d. Equipment. In infantry units, wire is the primary means of signal communications in all except mobile situations. All-wire circuits are used for major circuits. Telegraph is used extensively for routine signal traffic at divisional and higher level, and teletype is used by armies and army groups. Except in extremely mobile situations, wire communications only are maintained with the rear services and installations.

While the organic wire facilities of the Soviet rifle division are only slightly greater than those of a U. S. infantry division, they are heavily reinforced for operations. In an offensive situation, 150 command and observation posts were set up in one rifle division sector by the division and supporting artillery. Approximately 30 switchboards were used to connect some 700 circuits joining the various command observation posts.

During the preparatory phase of an offensive, wire communications are established with the tank and mobile infantry units at their advance command posts (near the line of departure). Mobile observation posts maintain wire communications with the supporting artillery and mortar units.

The organic allotment of radios in a Soviet rifle division is a little over 10 percent of that of the U. S. infantry division; radio is used as an auxiliary to wire, principally in command and artillery fire control nets. In Soviet tank and mechanized units, however, the allotment of radios is about 30 percent of that of similar U. S. units. In special situations large quantities of additional radio equipment are furnished from higher echelon signal reserves. For example, 27,174 radios were used in the Belorussian operation in June–July 1944.

Centralized control of radio frequencies and grouping of available radios into radio nets insure efficient use of allotted equipment. Strict regulation of frequencies and economy of messages simplify technical employment of radios and also aid in maintaining signal security. The use of sky-waves even for short distances (up to 180 miles) reduces the number and types of radio sets necessary to maintain adequate communications. Radio centers at army and higher levels and allocation of priorities to messages reduce the number of necessary sending sets.

Auxiliary methods of signal communications are visual signals (rockets, blinkers), public address systems, liaison planes, and messengers.

e. Responsibilities of Commander, Staff, and Chiefs of Arms. During combat, the Commander must be at the command observation post, from which he can observe and control the main effort. In order to assign missions during the course of combat and to direct coordination between arms efficiently, he must have at all times complete knowledge of the capabilities of each arm and of the equipment and supplies available to both his own and enemy forces.

Normally, some members of the staff, the chiefs of the arms, and the Chief Signal Officer are with him. The staff at the command post maintains control over secondary operational areas and rear services. Liaison with neighboring and higher commands is continuous.

The tactical plan is prescribed in the field orders and annexed tables of combat coordination, issued by the Commander. Supplementing these are the orders and plans of the various arms (artillery, infantry, engineers, tanks, etc.), the primary responsibility for which rests with the chief of each arm.

It is the duty of the Commander, either by means of personal reconnaissance or through his staff, to check on the execution of these combat plans. During the course of operations, maneuvers may deviate from the preestablished tactical plans. Wide latitude is permitted subordinate commanders (of arms and lower units) to use their full initiative in attaining assigned missions. Over-all responsibility, however, remains with the Commander, who observes the progress of maneuvers, orders support, and commits reserves.

The appropriate staff sections conduct incessant observation and reconnaissance from ground and air, constantly collect and correlate incoming reconnaissance and observation reports from subordinate units, submit reports to the commander concerning front-line developments, suggest appropriate steps to be taken, and organize the coordination demanded by the development of new situations according to the commander's decisions.

When the Commander or Chief of Staff cannot personally control combat phases, command liaison officers (often the commanders of arms or services) are sent as his deputies to subordinate units.

If, on the basis of his personal observation, the Commander decides that alteration in the prescribed phase-lines with reference to time or space are necessary, he issues fragmentary orders amending the original orders. Fragmentary orders may also be issued on the basis of reports submitted by the chiefs of the various arms and by the numerous observers along the front.

Throughout the combat phases, the plans of the

arms are continuously coordinated and adjusted between the staffs of each arm, and also with the staff of the Commander. This cooperation insures the fulfillment of the prescribed time and space schedule, the maximum exploitation of tactical capabilities, and the maintenance of a joint system of combat security and camouflage discipline. Lateral adjustments may be made among the chiefs of the various arms (and lower units) as to the methods of attaining the phase-lines. The Commander is advised by signal (wire, radio, or rocket) as each phase-line is attained.

PART II. TACTICS OF GROUND ARMS

Section 1. INFANTRY

1. GENERAL

Soviet infantry units are characterized by great strength in automatic weapons and mortars. Their tactical mobility is low if they are equipped only with organic transport. Their moving weight is low, compared to similar U. S. units, and as a result their maneuverability is good. The rifle regiments (less their supply trains), rifle battalions, and rifle companies have horse transport only and can move across country even in difficult terrain. The supply capacity of Soviet rifle units is adequate even for heavy combat, but their maintenance facilities are inadequate and must be supplemented by army resources.

2. BASIC DOCTRINE

Soviet tactical employment of infantry is predicated on rapidity of maneuver of small groups, concentration of fire of automatic weapons, and shock action. In fluid situations, rapid deployment and immediate engagement with the enemy are the rule. In more stable situations, engagement with the enemy is generally preceded by thorough reconnaissance and planning, and detailed rehearsal of the contemplated maneuver, including even the tactics of the individual soldier. The objectives of infantry attack are to break the cohesive defense of the enemy, to divide him into small isolated groups, and then to destroy him. The plan of maneuver usually calls for an advance to the flanks of the enemy, culminating in a single or double envelopment. This plan may be varied to conform to the situation or to achieve surprise.

Soviet infantry units are deployed for combat similarly to the U. S. practice; that is, in line, wedge, inverted wedge, column, and echeloned to right or left (fig. 22). The size of the reserve is rigidly controlled. For example, if a regiment on the defensive occupies an interior position, the reserve consists of one rifle company, some antitank rifles, and the regimental antitank and howitzer batteries. In a similar situation, the battalion reserve will consist of one rifle platoon, one antitank rifle platoon, the battalion antitank guns, and several heavy machine guns.

A regiment generally attacks on a front 1,500 yards wide; an interior battalion on a front up to 700 yards; a company up to 350 yards; and a platoon up to 100 yards. On the defensive, a battalion occupies an area up to 2,000 yards wide and 1,500 to 2,000 yards deep; and a company occupies an area up to 700 yards wide and 700 yards deep.

To insure the success of its missions, the Red Army infantry regiment has at its disposal several specialized units: the reconnaissance company, the submachine gun company, the antitank rifle company, the heavy mortar battery, the antitank gun battery, and the regimental howitzer battery. The reconnaissance company executes normal reconnaissance and screening tasks. The submachine gun company is used for rapid flanking moves, infiltration, security of accompanying tanks, and as a mobile reserve. The antitank rifle company provides antitank security in all phases of combat. The antitank gun battery, together with battalion antitank guns, is used to repel tank attacks in especially vulnerable sectors. Regimental and battalion antitank guns, together with the regimental artillery, are used extensively for direct fire in support of river-crossing operations and assault of fortified positions. The heavy mortar battery is used under centralized control during artillery preparation on the offensive and for laying down barrages on the defensive. It is under control of supported units in the assault phase of the offense and in decentralized defense.

3. APPROACH MARCH

A Red Army infantry regiment, acting as an advance guard of a division, has the missions of overcoming the resistance of enemy outposts, occupying terrain favorable for deployment of the division, and organizing preliminary reconnaissance. To accomplish these missions, the regiment advances in the following order: advance guard preceded by reconnaissance elements, the main body, the flank guards, and the rear guard. The advance guard consists of an infantry battalion reinforced by artillery and engi-

an exposed flank, the flank guard on the exposed side is increased to approximately a battalion (fig. 23). Artillery elements which form parts of the main body must always be ready to support the advance guard. During long halts, artillery habitually deploys for action, while antitank units reconnoiter and deploy

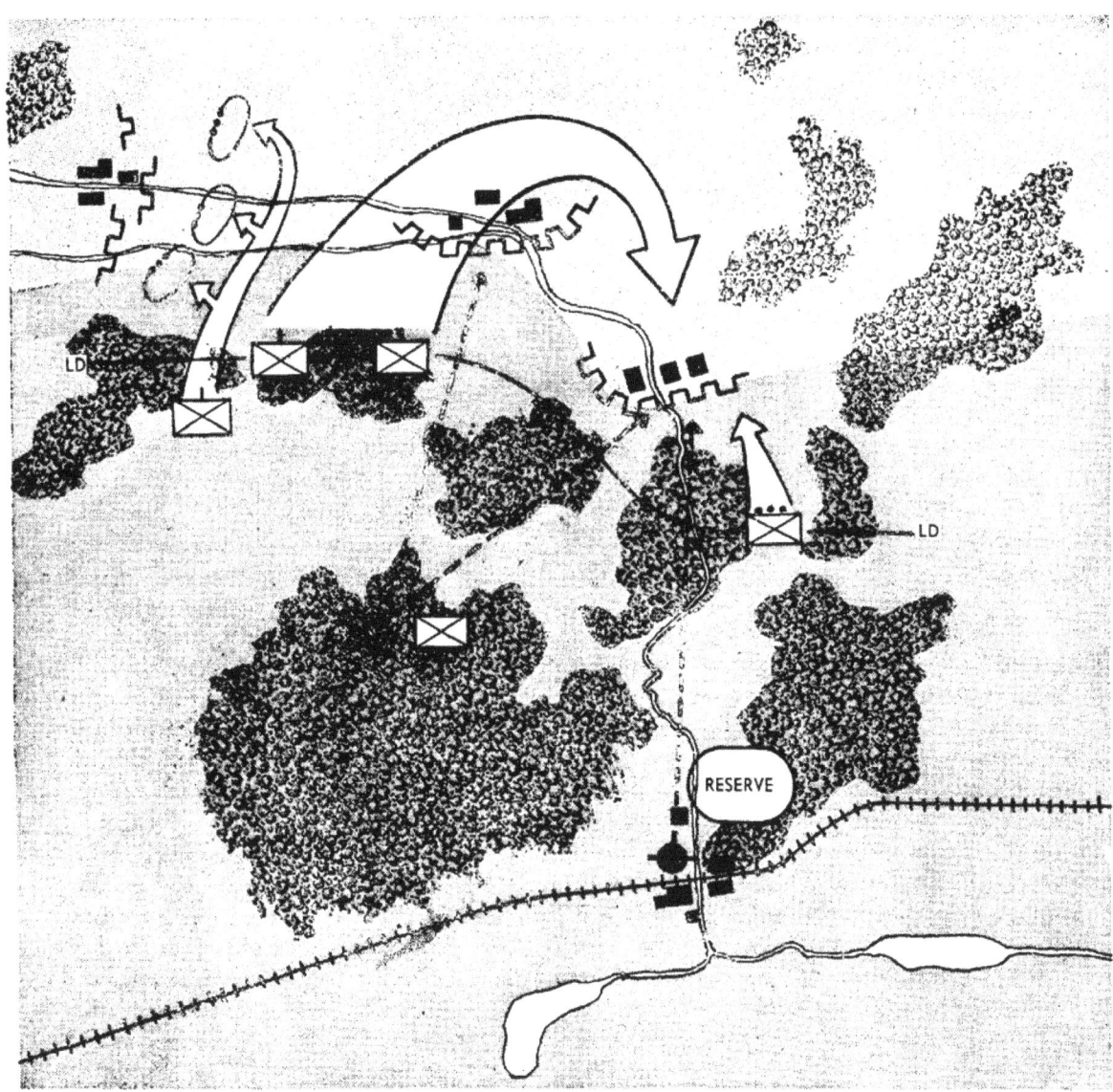

Figure 22. Plan of attack, rifle battalion echeloned to the left.

neers. The main body follows 1.2 to 1.8 miles behind the advance guard. It consists of several sections, each comprising a balanced fighting group of approximately battalion size. The main body is flanked by security groups consisting of rifle platoons reinforced with heavy machine guns and antitank rifles. The rear guard, likewise, consists of a reinforced rifle platoon. If the regiment advances along

in sectors considered especially vulnerable to attack by tanks.

If the advance guard encounters only disorganized resistance, it overpowers enemy rear guards while the main body continues advancing. If the advance guard encounters organized resistance at a well fortified position, the regiment deploys for action and endeavors to overpower the opposition by speed of

163

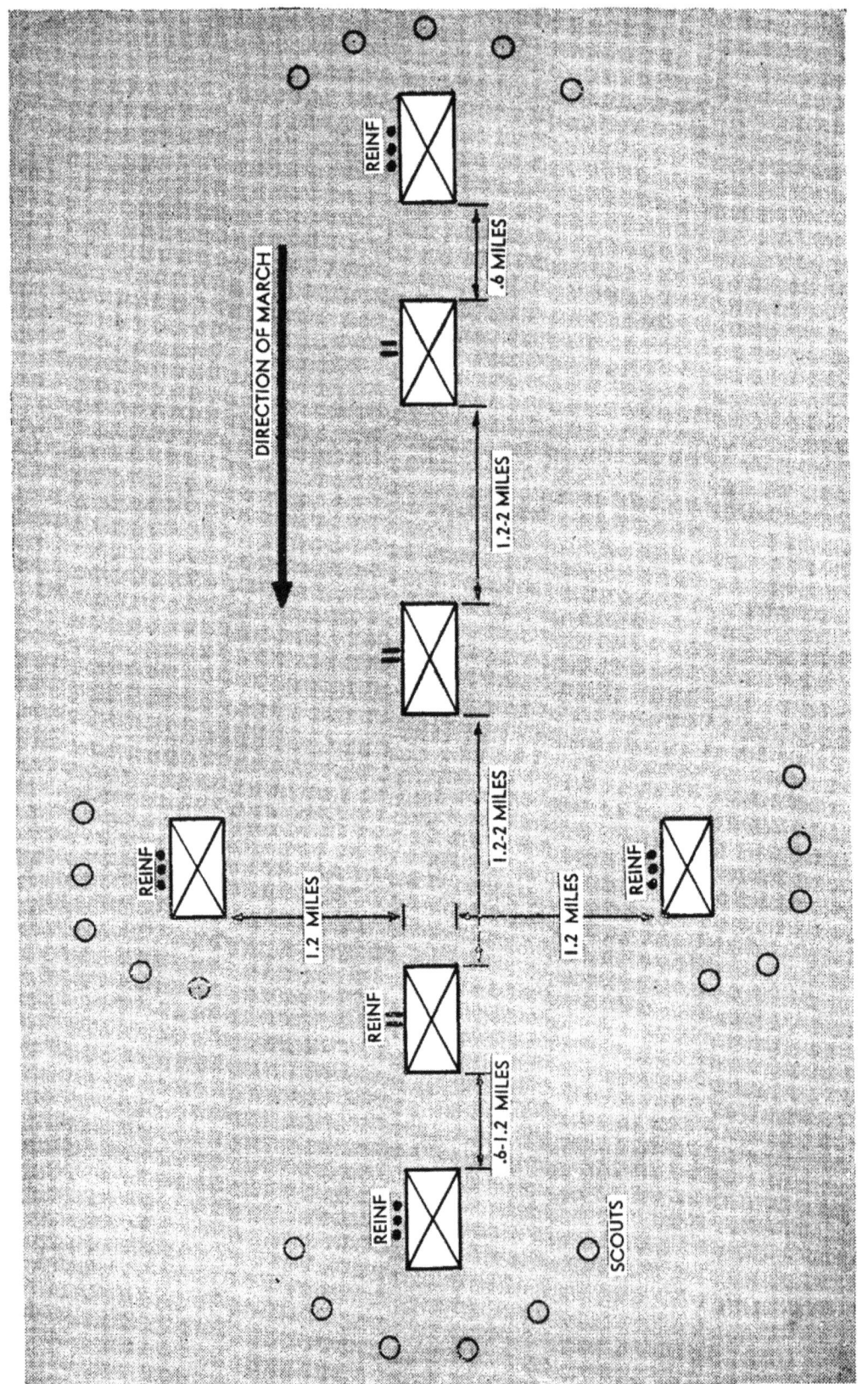

Figure 23. Infantry regiment in approach march formation.

164

maneuver and shock action. If the enemy is fully prepared to defend organized positions, the regiment secures advantageous ground for the deployment of the division and for organized intensive reconnaissance. During the advance the Commander retains his command post in the advance guard.

sion is determined by the over-all objective of the division. It generally consists of overcoming all enemy resistance in the assault sector including enemy artillery positions. Both the initial and the successive missions are designated in terms of space and time. The assault is conducted in three distinct

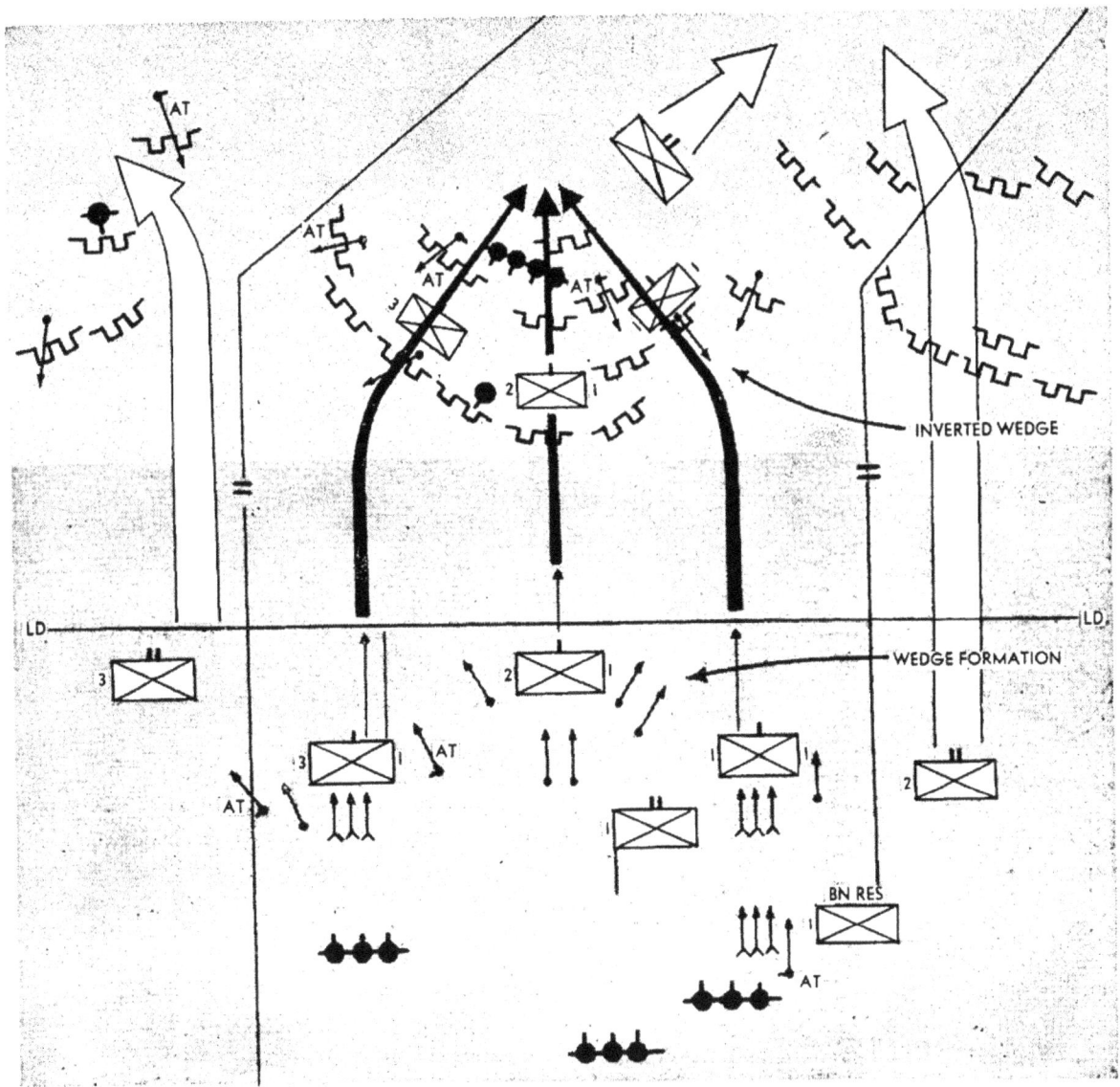

Figure 24. Example of infantry offensive, rifle battalion in double envelopment. Example of wedge and inverted wedge.

4. THE OFFENSIVE

In the offensive, infantry generally has two successive missions: First, it must break into the forward defense lines of the enemy in a particular sector and destroy or neutralize the system of infantry and anti-tank weapons. This mission is accomplished by the initial infantry assault groups. The subsequent mis-

phases: the preparation, the execution of the initial mission of the infantry groups, and the penetration of the enemy defenses in depth in the execution of the subsequent missions (fig. 24).

a. Preparation for the attack. The preparation phase includes command and staff reconnaissance; the command decision; formulation of the

165

operations, intelligence, signal, and rear area plans; and formulation of the tables of combat coordination. Upon receipt of their missions, subordinate commanders formulate their plans of maneuver and designate assault groups for the execution of specific tasks. A typical assault group consists of three to five engineers, a rifle platoon, and several antitank rifles.

Some battalion mortars and battalion guns are assigned to the various assault groups according to the general and partial fire plans. Heavy machine guns are either allotted to the assault groups, or retained under centralized control.

According to the demands of the situation, regimental and, less frequently, divisional specialized arms are distributed among the assault groups. If time permits, the assault groups rehearse the plan of maneuver both individually and as a whole. These rehearsals are generally conducted in daylight and at night over terrain similar to that of the contemplated operation and far enough removed from the enemy to escape his observation and interference. Before important operations it is not uncommon for Soviet troops to spend considerable time drilling in standard and specialized use of their weapons.

b. Conduct of the assault. During the assault, regimental and battalion commanders remain at their command observation posts. Only in exceptional circumstances may they leave their command posts to lead subordinate units in combat. It is considered imperative that the final artillery barrage be laid so that there is a minimum of time between it and the moment that the infantry reaches the forward defense lines of the enemy. Regimental and battalion antitank guns and mortars will continue to fire on their targets until the last possible moment. The infantry must be placed so as to reach the enemy forward lines from 1 to 2 minutes after the artillery barrage is lifted. Red Army regulations state that infantry can follow within 200 yards and 100 yards, respectively, of forward and flanking barrages of artillery firing at ranges of 2,000 to 3,000 yards. Infantry can follow within 150 to 200 yards behind the bursts of 82-mm mortars, and within 200 to 250 yards behind the bursts of 120-mm mortars.

During the assault, antitank guns and mortars revert to the control of the supported units. Regimental artillery supports the assault in depth and prepares to displace forward. Battalion commanders do not commit their units in extended fire duels with the enemy centers of resistance; instead, they move ahead, leaving small detachments to deal with the by-passed enemy.

When the infantry advance reaches the artillery positions of the enemy, widening of the breach, destruction of the by-passed centers of resistance, and exploitation of the break-through are achieved by the regimental reserve, assisted by some of the assault groups. The remainder of the assaulting force consolidates captured positions, prepares to repel counterattacks, or regroups and continues the advance.

If tanks accompany the infantry attack, regimental and battalion artillery concentrate fire on enemy antitank defenses. Infantry and engineers protect the tanks from hostile infantry, neutralize antitank minefields and other antitank obstacles, and help evacuate damaged tanks. Tanks must not outdistance their supporting infantry by more than 400 yards. Typical missions which may be assigned to accompanying tanks by an infantry commander include:

Determination of the location and number of breaches to be made in antipersonnel obstacles.

Firing positions of the enemy which are to be destroyed.

Sectors of responsibility for repelling counterattacks.

Assembly areas.

Subsequent missions of tanks.

5. THE ENCIRCLEMENT

The Soviet encirclement is carried out in two phases: the process of encircling an enemy force, and the destruction of the encircled force. Although under special circumstances a smaller force may encircle and destroy a larger one, normally a regiment is required for encircling and destroying a battalion.

In addition to problems which accompany frontal assault, combat for encirclement requires the maintenance of lines of supply and evacuation over longer routes, as well as protection of the exposed flanks and rear of an inverted front. Displacement of the service centers must be coordinated with the advance of the combat teams in order to utilize service personnel most efficiently. While the break-through sector is narrow, control of the service units must be centralized; that is, service elements of two battalions may be combined to render most effective aid to the encircling and security units. When the break-through sector becomes wider, these service elements revert to the control of the parent units (figs. 25 and 26).

Engineers must be allotted to the service elements in order to establish and maintain supply and evacuation routes, and to help the security units in the construction of defenses along the exposed flanks and rear. Infantry reinforced with antitank weapons must be made available to the commander of the rear echelon; these are assigned the tasks of clearing the break-through area of enemy stragglers, mop-

commander to initiate pursuit. Pursuit, once it is started, may be halted only by the senior commander. In order to prevent the enemy from withdrawing and forming march columns, infantry battalions increase pressure along the entire sector and the artillery and mortar batteries conduct interdictory fire on road junctions and assembly areas. The Commander moves his reserves forward, groups them into reinforced platoons, and deploys them for rapid advance in the direction of the main effort of the

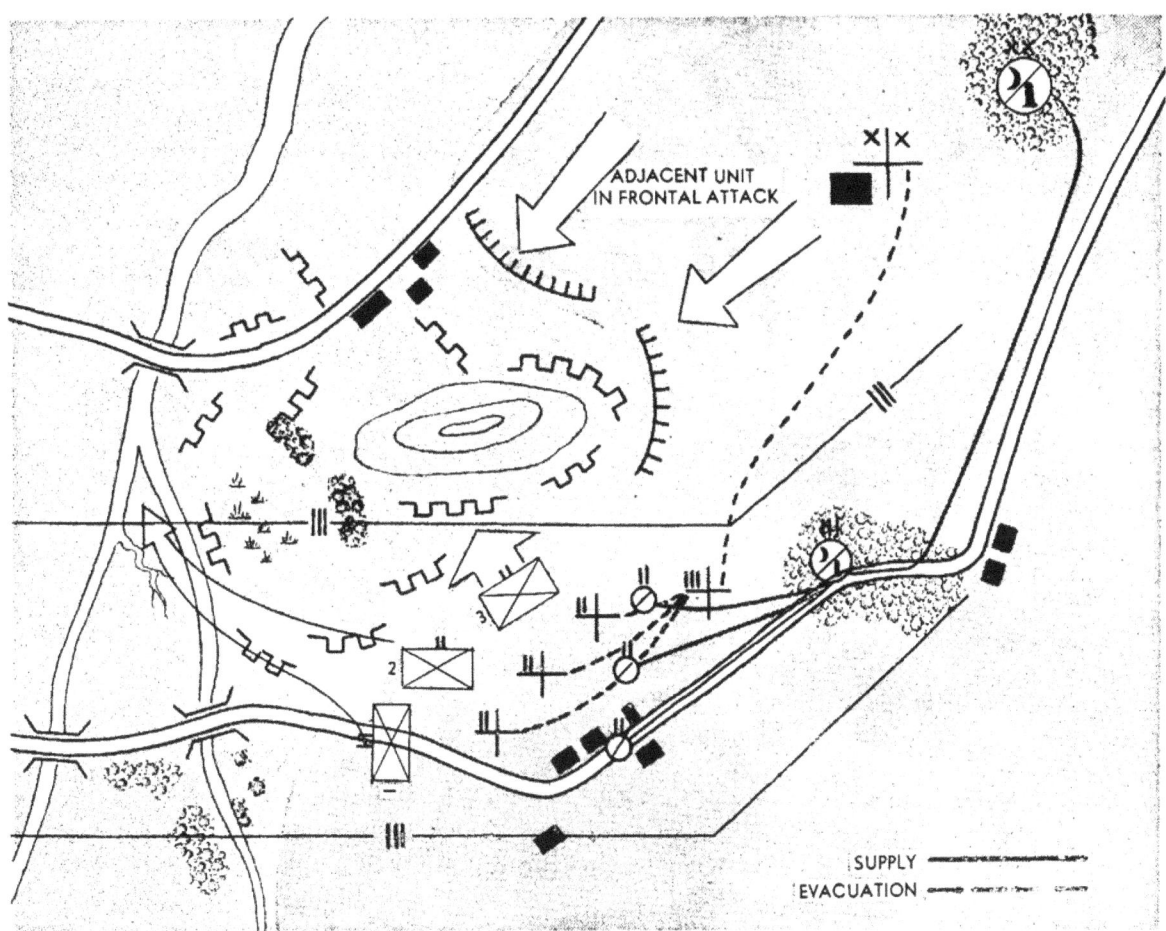

Figure 25. Organization of lines of supply and evacuation at the start of an encirclement.

ping up the by-passed centers of resistance, and defending the exposed rear and flanks of the inverted front. Medical elements of the encircling battalions must have additional personnel for evacuation of the wounded along longer than normal routes.

6. THE PURSUIT

The slightest indication of the enemy's intention to withdraw from combat is a signal for every Soviet

assaulting battalions. The submachine-gun company, grouped by platoons, infiltrates into the enemy's rear area, disrupting his lines of communication and control.

As the pursuit develops, artillery and mortars advance by bounds so that one echelon is ready to fire missions on request from the pursuing elements, while the other echelon displaces. The antitank-rifle company and the regimental antitank battery

167

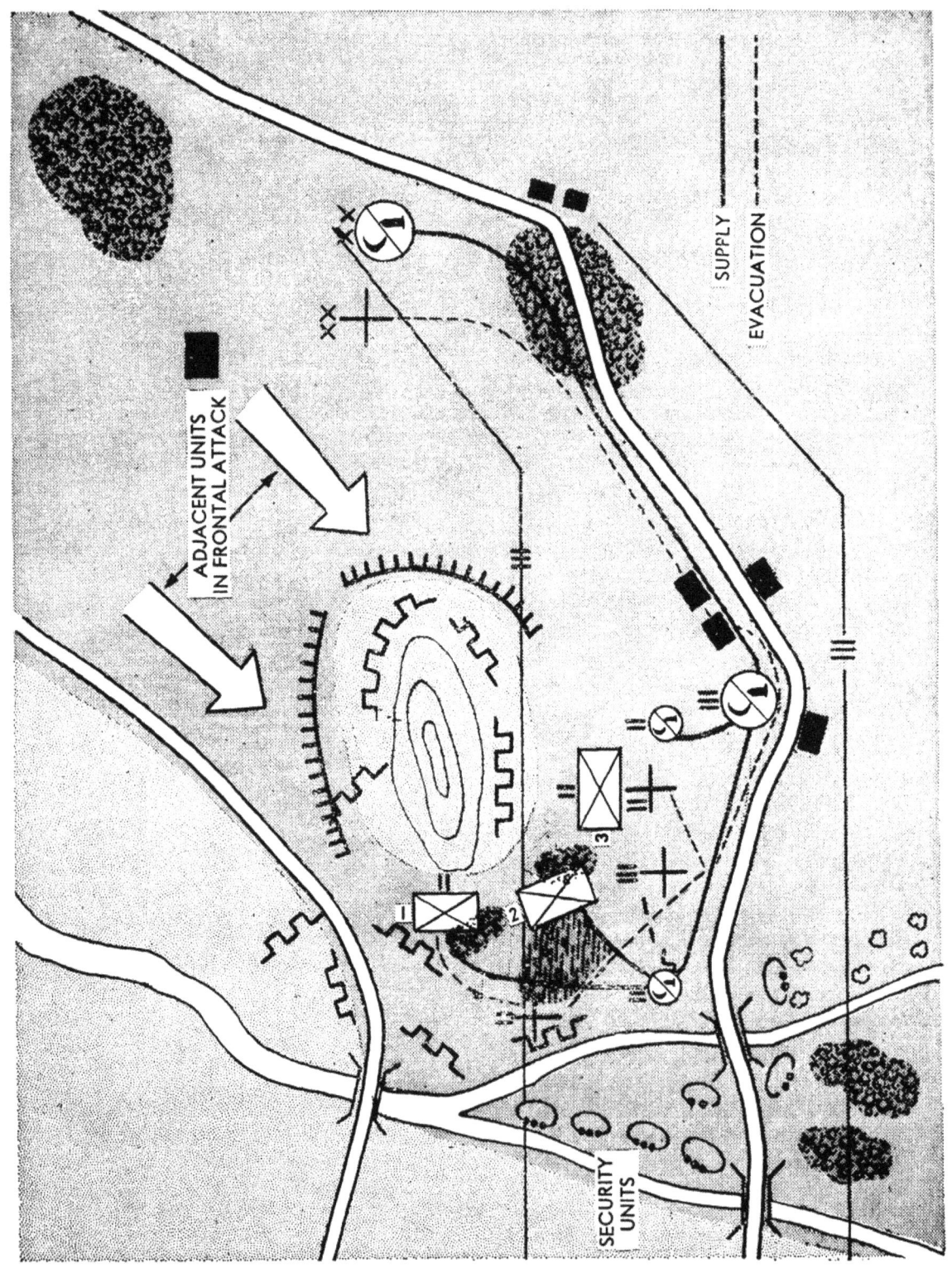

Figure 26. Organization of lines of supply and evacuation during an encirclement. Note that the supply and evacuation centers of the two encircling battalions have been combined.

168

organize protection of the flanks against counterattacks. Rear-area security groups keep the lines of supply clear of enemy stragglers. The engineer officer organizes obstacle-clearing detachments which march with the pursuing elements and facilitate the advance of artillery, mortars, tanks, and supply vehicles.

If motorized transport is available, pursuit detachments are organized and sent in parallel columns along secondary roads in order to overtake the enemy and strike him from the flanks and rear. A motorized pursuit group generally consists of a rifle company, a reconnaissance squad, a machine-gun platoon, an engineer squad, and an antitank-gun team. If possible, each pursuing vehicle is provided with an antiaircraft machine gun. If tanks are available for the pursuit, infantry riders are assigned from the battalions. Regimental mortars advance with the infantry, but if half-tracks or other suitable transport is available, mortars may be loaned to tank units for exploitation of the break-through. As the pursuing elements outdistance the original battalion assault teams, these teams are also organized into pursuit groups and sent on supplementary missions.

During the pursuit, the regimental staff organizes flank and rear security detachments, controls operations of the reconnaissance elements, organizes coordination between the pursuing groups and their supporting units, and provides for continuous supply of ammunition and fuel.

7. THE DEFENSIVE

The objectives stated in Red Army defensive doctrine are: hold important positions with small forces; utilize natural and artificial obstacles; inflict heavy losses on the enemy by an organized fire of all weapons, thus forcing him to abandon the attack; and finally, destroy him by a determined counterattack. Red Army doctrine for the organization of defensive positions prescribes the following requirements:

> The positions should be established in depth.
> Each defensive area and its parts should be capable of all-around defense.
> The defense should be supported by planned counterattacks.
> The fire plan should be designed to provide fire trap concentration on sectors subject to probable enemy attack.

In setting up defensive positions, all commanders are responsible for the construction of field fortifications, shelters, main and reserve command and observation posts, and main, alternate, and night firing positions for artillery and mortars. All defense installations and fields of fire are checked by the Commander and the Chief of Engineers. In the Red Army, lack of care and thoroughness in organizing and executing the construction of defense installations is considered one of the most serious of military offenses.

a. Centralized defense. Tactical doctrines of the Red Army define two types of defense: centralized and decentralized. Centralized defense is preferred. It is organized to hold the main approaches to important positions with a system of mutually supporting strongpoints. Secondary approaches are covered by fire and by a relatively large mobile reserve. In this type of defense, artillery is massed, counterattacks are initiated by the over-all commander, and supply installations are centrally located. Wire communications are established along the main defense axis.

b. Decentralized defense. Decentralized defense is undertaken when the forces available for defense of a sector are insufficient for the centralized type of defense. Decentralized defense consists of a series of self-sufficient islands of defense, each with a local commander, artillery, and supply installations. The reserve of the over-all commander is relatively small, and counterattacks are undertaken on the initiative of the local commanders. Communication is accomplished primarily by radio and visual signals.

c. Infantry division defense. In general, the defensive positions of an infantry division consist of an outpost line, a security line, and the main line of resistance.

OUTPOST LINE. The outpost line is designated by an army or divisional commander. It is sited 6 to 10 miles in front of the main line of resistance. The outpost line is intended to inflict losses on the enemy, to disrupt his attack groupments, and to gain time. It consists of forward and intermediate field positions manned by forward detachments.

SECURITY LINE. One-half to one mile in front of the main line of resistance, an infantry division forms a security line. The purpose of this line is to prevent surprise attacks and to form an anti-reconnaissance screen. It is established according to instructions of the divisional commander. The security line consists of a number of strongpoints manned by elements of the forward battalions and supported by their fire. Often, in order to deceive the enemy, the security line is made strong in front of dummy positions and weak in front of the main defensive positions.

MAIN DEFENSE LINE. The main defense line is intended to stop the attack of the hostile infantry and tanks, and to force the enemy to abandon the attack. The main line is divided into regimental sectors, which are in turn divided into battalion sectors and regimental reserve sectors.

Each regimental sector consists of several centers of resistance which integrate a system of strongpoints for all-around defense. The strongpoints con-

ASSIGNMENT OF MISSIONS. After personal reconnaissance of the terrain, the divisional commander assigns a defensive mission to the regiments. The regimental commander initiates command reconnaissance and issues preliminary instructions to his staff. These instructions include orientation points, boundary lines between battalions, and location of the outpost line, the security line, the main defense position, and the regimental reserve. The regimental commander sketches out the location of the principal antitank installations and specifies time limits for the completion of the various defense preparations. Instructions to the battalion commanders include

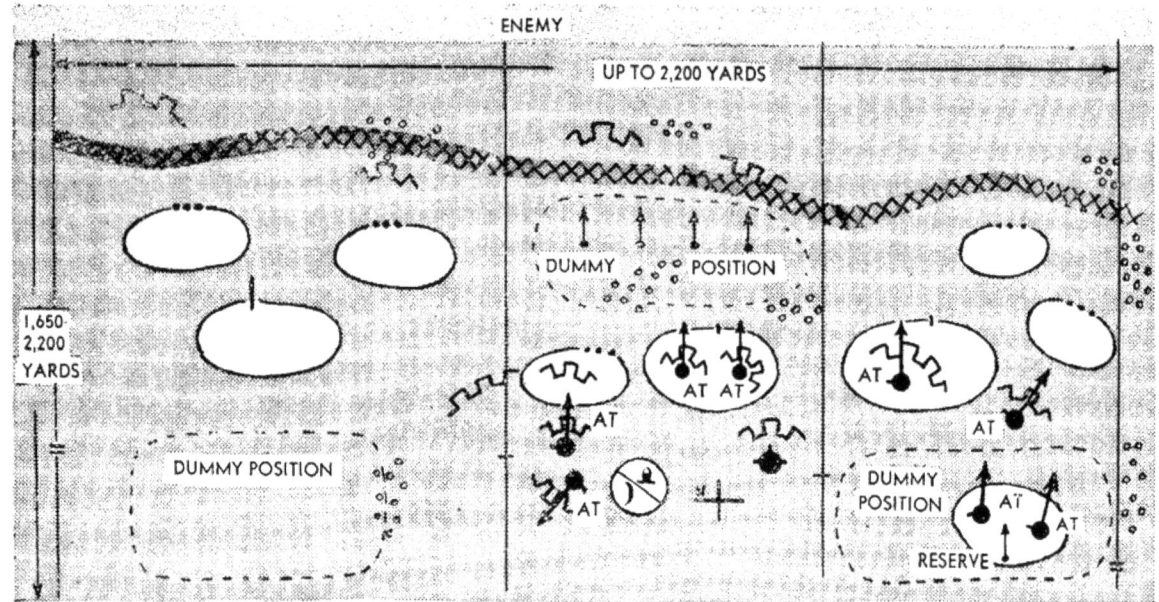

Figure 27. Reinforced battalion in defense.

sist of field and permanent fortifications connected by antitank and antipersonnel obstacles, minefields, and traps. The system of obstacles must contain gaps for use by counterattacking forces. These gaps must be arranged so that they may be quickly closed in the event of enemy penetration of the defenses. The strongpoints are manned either by specially designed garrisons or by elements of the forward battalions. In the former case, the forward battalions occupy positions defending approaches to the strongpoints and support them with fire. In defending a strong position, the regimental reserve may consist of a rifle battalion reinforced with artillery, antitank weapons, and tanks. The main line of defense may be abandoned only on orders of the commander of the next higher echelon.

boundaries of their sectors, antitank defenses for which they are responsible, plan of fire for long and intermediate ranges, and the composition and mission of the security line. The battalion commanders are told what fire support they may expect, and the probable direction and relative time of the regimental counterattack.

The regimental reserve is assigned its defense sector, probable direction of counterattacks, and a plan of fire within the defense positions (fig. 27).

ARTILLERY MISSIONS. In the defensive, regimental artillery and antitank weapons, together with allotted divisional weapons, are generally portioned out to the battalions according to the importance of their sectors. However, artillery fire is planned so that it can be shifted easily from de-

170

centralized to centralized control. The artillery fire is designed to support defensive operations of forward detachments. In particular, emphasis is placed on delaying enemy preparations for attack. The Soviet gunners attempt to cause casualties among enemy personnel and armor during deployment for the attack and to separate tanks from accompanying infantry, destroying the infantry with artillery and mortar fire and destroying the tanks which penetrate into the defensive positions with antitank weapons.

In organizing defensive positions, the formation of antitank centers of resistance is stressed. These centers, usually located in terrain inaccessible to tanks, consist of a rifle company with three to five antitank guns, one or two antitank rifle platoons, mortars, and heavy machine guns. Minefields are laid only on orders of the divisional commander.

The mission of the infantry is to keep enemy foot soldiers from destroying or neutralizing antitank obstacles. Antiaircraft positions are chosen in terrain inaccessible to tanks. Careful camouflage and camouflage discipline is emphasized. Defensive combat is controlled from a command post which must not be located within the artillery positions. Control of fire, timely commitment of battalion and regimental reserves, and avoidance of premature disclosure of positions and plan of defense are primary considerations in successful defensive combat. During the first stages of enemy attack, artillery fires from alternate positions.

8. WITHDRAWALS AND DELAYING ACTION

On receiving his mission, the regimental commander conducts command reconnaissance of the terrain and designates the first and subsequent defense lines. Sectors of responsibility of each battalion and of the reserve, and the composition of the supporting groups for each battalion, are determined for each defense line. The battalion commanders are given instructions concerning the relative time of their occupation and retreat from each defense line, and their responsibility for antitank defense. The reserve, approximately a battalion made up of rifle, submachine-gun, mortar, artillery, heavy-machine-gun, and antitank-rifle platoons, is instructed as to its sectors of responsibility and probable direction of counterattack from each position. The staff initiates reconnaissance in front of and on the flanks of the regimental sector, determines the axis of communications, provides for

flank and rear area security, and works out relative time schedules for the displacement of the command post and rear area installations.

Defense lines are so chosen that the enemy upon taking one line would have to displace his artillery and mortars in order to attack the next. Each successive position is strengthened with field fortifications and antitank and antipersonnel obstacles. The interval between strongpoints is covered by artillery and mortar fire. If terrain permits, ambushes are prepared in corridors between strongpoints. The location and composition of ambushes are designated by the regimental commander.

The regiment occupies two lines simultaneously: the first is occupied by the forward battalions and the second by the regimental reserve. When the enemy attacks, the forward battalions open fire at extreme ranges, forcing the enemy to deploy for battle, causing casualties, and delaying neutralization of obstacles. They do not engage the enemy, but on completing their delaying mission, retreat, covered by the fire of the reserve. The reserve counterattacks if the enemy succeeds in flanking one of the battalions or if the forward battalions are unable to disengage. The commander of the last battalion to occupy a defense line or, if the situation demands it, the regimental commander, orders demolition of bridges and roads.

Section II. ARTILLERY, MORTARS, AND ROCKETS

1. BASIC TACTICAL ROLE

Artillery is the basic striking force of the Red Army. Its mission is to neutralize and destroy the enemy system of fire throughout all operational phases, thus enabling Soviet infantry to encircle and destroy enemy personnel. To carry out this mission, the Red Army has used artillery on a much larger scale than any other modern army. In repeated offensive operations during World War II, the artillery density was 320 to 480 pieces per mile (200 to 300 pieces per kilometer). In certain operations the Soviets employed a total of more than 20,000 pieces, a number approaching the total quantity of artillery pieces used by all armies during World War I. This unprecedented mass employment of artillery required the development of large artillery units—such as artillery, mortar, and rocket divisions—to supplement organic artillery of the infantry division. To facilitate the commitment of such masses of artillery,

171

a highly developed system of artillery reconnaissance and artillery planning was essential.

2. TACTICAL EMPLOYMENT

The organization and tactical employment of Soviet artillery underwent continuous changes during the war. These changes were not always the result of newly formulated doctrines, but were often imposed upon the Red Army by specific strategic situations.

During the first period of the war, Soviet artillery was organized according to conventional conceptions. Only about 20 percent of the total artillery was in army artillery units (the Soviets had four artillery divisions, several independent artillery regiments, and a number of heavy artillery units), while the bulk was found organically in the rifle divisions or in corps artillery units. The major defeats suffered by the Soviet Union in 1941, which led to destruction of a great portion of its original number of artillery pieces, forced the Red Army to exploit the remaining artillery by increased centralization. Up to this time, the rifle division had two artillery regiments (one motorized and one horse-drawn regiment). The motorized artillery regiment was taken from the rifle division and organized in army artillery units. Within the rifle division, also, artillery and infantry heavy weapons were brought under centralized control.

Simultaneously with this reorganization, the production of artillery was given high priority. When newly produced weapons were made available to the Red Army, they were included in army artillery units. The great number of independent artillery regiments created a command and logistical problem, which the Red Army solved by forming larger artillery organizations such as brigades, divisions, and even corps. The great increase in the number of army artillery units also facilitated the organization of specialized units such as mortar regiments, mortar divisions, antitank divisions, antitank brigades, antiaircraft artillery divisions, and even superheavy artillery units. These new organizations were employed for the first time for large-scale operations at Stalingrad.

The steady growth of the army artillery made a reverse process possible, so that at the present time, army artillery regiments are attached to rifle divisions to increase the fire power of their direct support artillery.

a. Mortars and rockets. Mortars and rockets play a far greater tactical role in the Red Army than in any other army. The fundamental principle of mortar employment in the Red Army is the use of massed mortar fire as an independent striking weapon. Requirements are set by the infantry commander, while technical control and coordination are the responsibility of the artillery commander. Fundamentally, Soviet mortar units employ field artillery methods. The principle of rocket employment in the Red Army prescribes mass commitment at critical phases of an operation. Rocket units are normally coordinated in the general plan of artillery and mortars, and are under the control of corps artillery.

b. Self-propelled artillery. Soviet self-propelled artillery units are found either as organic parts of armored, mechanized, or cavalry corps or as independent regiments for employment in the main effort. Soviet self-propelled artillery is equipped with telescopic sights which permit indirect fire and employment for other than assault artillery missions, such as reinforcement of regular artillery units. Soviet doctrine prescribes that self-propelled artillery should be employed in batteries or larger units; for indirect fire it is centralized in regiments or brigades. When self-propelled artillery is committed in support of infantry, it is under the control of the infantry divisional (regimental) commander.

In the attack, self-propelled artillery is employed in the main effort to support infantry, tanks, or cavalry, with the primary mission of destroying unforeseen enemy centers of resistance at short range. It may also be used as the Commander's fire reserve for action against enemy counterattacks. When attacking on the move, self-propelled artillery goes into position on a broad front without echeloning in depth. In an attack on a fortified position, it is organized in depth. During the attack, self-propelled artillery provides continuous support for infantry and tanks by displacing forward and firing from concealed positions.

In the defense, self-propelled artillery regiments, as a rule, constitute the mobile fire reserve. This reserve is employed as support for counterattacking tanks and infantry, or as an antitank reserve. During retreat, it may be attached to the rear guards.

c. Division artillery. The artillery weapons and mortars of an infantry division are found in the field artillery regiment and in the infantry regiments. The field artillery regiments have three identically organized battalions. Each battalion consists of two batteries with 76.2-mm guns (four guns to a battery), and one 122-mm howitzer battery. The infantry regiment contains a howitzer battery with four 76.2-mm howitzers, and a heavy mortar battery with six 120-mm mortars. Each battalion also has nine 82-mm mortars. In stabilized situations, the 33 mortars of each regiment are organized, according to a definite standing operating procedure, into a provisional mortar battalion. The two 50-mm mortars of each company are for direct infantry support only. The antitank artillery pieces of an infantry division are found in the division antitank battalion and within each infantry regiment. The antitank artillery battalion has three batteries, each with four 45-mm or 57-mm antitank guns (a total of 12 pieces). The infantry regiment has four 45-mm antitank guns in its antitank battery and two 45-mm antitank guns in each infantry battalion.

Since the divisional artillery consists of only 36 artillery pieces, recent Soviet practice has been to reinforce the artillery by one to four battalions of 122-mm and 152-mm howitzers. The divisional artillery commander, however, is in control of all the artillery in the division including artillery reinforcement from higher echelons. He also exercises control of the over-all employment of the heavy mortar battery or provisional mortar battalion of each infantry regiment.

Organic artillery is employed on a regimental combat-team basis, but direct battery-infantry-battalion coordination is provided. In the regimental combat team, the field artillery battalion controls the provisional battalion that may be formed from the 120-mm mortar and the 82-mm mortar batteries.

76.2-MM GUNS. The tactical characteristics of the 76.2-mm guns (M1939 and 1942) are their high rate of fire, good muzzle velocity, and great maneuverability. These guns are employed in close support of infantry (tanks), and especially for direct fire. Their primary missions are destruction of personnel and neutralization of infantry weapons in the open; antipersonnel barrages; destruction of tanks, vehicles, embrasures, and dragon's teeth by direct fire; and harassing fire. Secondary missions are accompanying barrages and concentrations; neutralization of artillery and mortars; establishment of smoke screens; and destruction of wire. Exceptional missions are fire reconnaissance, destruction of light matériel with indirect fire, and destruction of minefields.

122-MM HOWITZERS. The characteristics of the other divisional artillery weapon, the 122-mm howitzer (M1938) which is the backbone of Soviet field artillery, are its great flexibility in muzzle velocity and trajectory, very effective burst, and good maneuverability. (A lighter model 1910/30 is employed when terrain prohibits the use of the M1938.) This weapon may be used for almost any mission except the destruction of strong positions or for distant fire. The primary missions are:

Destruction of personnel and neutralization of infantry weapons in the open and under cover.

Antipersonnel barrages, accompanying barrages, and concentrations.

Destruction of light field fortifications.

Neutralization or destruction of mortars.

Fire reconnaissance against camouflage and minefields or in conjunction with sound ranging.

Neutralization of artillery at medium ranges.

Establishment of smoke screens.

Harassing fire.

Secondary missions include antitank defensive barrages; destruction of artillery; attack on fortified houses; destruction of wire; and destruction of tanks, ordnance, embrasures, antitank escarpments, and dragon's teeth by direct fire. The destruction of minefields is an exceptional mission.

152-MM HOWITZERS. The 152-mm howitzers (M1938) differ from the 122-mm howitzers in their greater radius of burst, slightly longer range, lower rate of fire, and reduced maneuverability. Basically, they reinforce 122-mm howitzers or replace them against more resistant targets. Their primary missions are to furnish accompanying concentrations; to provide antitank defensive barrages; and to neutralize or destroy personnel, infantry weapons in the open or under cover, light and medium field fortifications (including fortified houses), antitank ditches, artillery and mortars, and minefields. Secondary missions are direct fire against very strong earth and timber fortifications; establishment of smoke screens; and reinforcement of antipersonnel and accompanying barrages. Exceptional missions are destruction of tanks and motor vehicles by direct fire, and harassing fire.

OTHER WEAPONS. The 76.2-mm howitzer is an organic weapon of the infantry regiment. Sometimes several 122-mm M10/30 howitzers are attached. Both weapons are excellent direct infantry support weapons because of their light weight. The 45-mm guns of the infantry regiment and battalion are employed for direct fire missions at ranges of about 1,000 yards.

The 120-mm and the 82-mm mortars compare in radius of burst with the 122-mm howitzer and the 76.2-mm gun, respectively. They are emplaced primarily against personnel, in concentrations or defensive barrages.

d. Organic artillery of armored formations and cavalry corps. The organic artillery of the mechanized, tank, and cavalry corps is highly mobile and possesses great fire power. The organization of the tank corps includes three self-propelled artillery regiments, one antitank artillery regiment, one antiaircraft artillery regiment, one mortar regiment, one rocket battalion, and one antitank battalion. The three tank brigades and the motorized brigades of the tank corps have additional artillery pieces, antitank guns, and, mortars. The mechanized and cavalry corps have only one or two self-propelled artillery regiments instead of three, while the other supporting components are about the same as in the tank corps.

Mobile formations are usually employed in the exploitation of a break-through to widen the gap and to pursue the enemy. Normally, they do not assist actively in the initial stage of the operation, although they may be employed for flank protection. In an extensive operation, the average distance of advance of such formations is about 200 miles. Their artillery is employed particularly for close support of infantry and tank elements, making large use of direct fire in the attack of organized positions. During the advance, the artillery is greatly decentralized. When, however, the formation establishes defensive positions far beyond the original line of departure, the artillery immediately converts to strictly centralized control. The formation possesses a sufficient amount of antitank and antiaircraft protection to enable it to hold out against enemy counterattacks until the arrival of the main forces.

e. Corps artillery. Artillery at corps level in the Red Army is of relatively less importance than in the U. S. Army, because the Red Army places greatest stress on artillery at army level. Corps artillery is normally in control of the artillery in sectors of secondary priority, while army artillery controls the artillery in the sector of main effort.

Artillery units at corps level include medium artillery brigades, antitank artillery regiments (towed tank destroyers with 76.2-mm guns), and rocket units. The weapons of the medium artillery brigade are the 122-mm guns and the 152-mm gun-howitzers.

122-MM GUNS. The 122-mm guns (M1931/37), the basic long-range weapons of Soviet field artillery, have high muzzle velocity, great penetration and range, good rate of fire, but only moderate maneuverability. (They are replaced by 107-mm guns, M1940 or 1910/30, in difficult terrain or when rapid movement is required.) The 122-mm guns are employed against distant targets and for destruction of matériel. Their primary missions are neutralization or destruction of artillery and armored trains; neutralization, interdiction, or harassment of distant targets; destruction of moderately strong permanent fortifications by flat-trajectory fire; and fire reconnaissance against distant targets. Secondary missions are destruction of tanks and vehicles by direct fire; destruction of elevated targets; and destruction or neutralization of field fortifications, mortars, infantry weapons, and infantry in the open. Exceptional missions are antipersonnel and accompanying barrages, and destruction of minefields.

152-MM GUN-HOWITZERS. The 152-mm gun-howitzers (M1931/37) have much greater range and penetration than the 152-mm howitzers, but a lower rate of fire and, except with the self-propelled KV mount, considerably less maneuverability. They are employed in conjunction with the 122-mm gun against targets beyond the range or capabilities of the 152-mm howitzer. Their most important missions are:

> Neutralization or destruction of artillery and armored trains.
> Neutralization or interdiction of distant targets.
> Destruction of strong field fortifications.
> Destruction of moderately strong permanent fortifications by flat-trajectory fire.
> Fire reconnaissance of exceptionally important or resistant targets.
> Destruction of distant minefields.

Secondary missions include destruction or neutralization of mortars, infantry weapons, and infantry in the open; and destruction of tanks, vehicles, armor, and concrete by direct fire. Reinforcement of antipersonnel fire and employment

174

in accompanying barrages and concentrations are exceptional missions.

ROCKET WEAPONS. Normally rocket units are not assigned to echelons lower than corps. Corps artillery control assures their centralized employment for intense, surprise shock actions during critical phases of offensive or defensive operations. Rockets are brought forward with great secrecy and are moved immediately after firing. They are committed against area targets, supplementing artillery preparations or counterpreparations, and are normally directed against enemy infantry concentrations.

f. Army artillery. The heaviest fire power of Soviet artillery is concentrated at army level. Great flexibility is the advantage of large artillery organizations. Soviet commanders are provided with the means to concentrate large artillery forces in the area of the main effort.

The artillery division of the Red Army includes in its organization a well balanced assortment of weapons which, as a rule, are employed together. The component parts of the artillery divisions are:

> One howitzer brigade with three regiments of 122-mm and 152-mm howitzers (M1938).
> One light artillery brigade with three regiments of 76.2-mm guns.
> One gun brigade with two regiments of 122-mm guns and 152-mm gun-howitzers.
> One mortar brigade with three regiments of 120-mm mortars.
> One observation battalion.

The fire power of the artillery division is reinforced as needed by additional brigades or regiments containing heavy, very heavy, or superheavy guns, howitzers, and motar-howitzers—such as 152-mm guns, 203-mm howitzers, 280-mm mortar-howitzers, 406-mm mortar-howitzers—and other superheavy caliber weapons.

The general characteristics of the guns are extremely great range, very high muzzle velocity and penetration, low rate of fire, and poor maneuverability. They are employed against extremely distant targets or, in conjunction with the heavy howitzers, for destruction or neutralization of exceptionally important and resistant targets. Heavy howitzers and mortar-howitzers are used by Soviet field artillery when exceptionally great blast and penetration are required. Targets for these weapons are carefully selected because of the low rate

of fire and great weight of ammunition. Typical targets are permanent fortifications (using either flat-trajectory or high-angle fire), bridges, railroads, and buildings. The mortar-howitzers are employed at moderate ranges. Normally, fire reconnaissance by lighter weapons precedes the employment of the reinforcing heavy-caliber weapons of the artillery division.

The mortar brigade of the artillery division composes the countermortar group which also may be reinforced by a 132-mm rocket regiment of 12 rocket installations or by a regiment of 122-mm howitzers.

Mortar divisions and brigades have been formed to support large-scale operations against strong enemy fortifications or powerful defenses at river lines. Mortar divisions contain rocket as well as mortar regiments. Rocket units of regimental size have also been organized. They employ mobile and stationary installations.

g. Artillery groupments. The outstanding organizational characteristic of Soviet artillery is the artillery groupments, which are the basic operating organizations of artillery. It is the responsibility of the artillery commander to form these groupments from artillery divisions, from units and elements of GHQ regiments, from infantry divisional artillery, and, to a limited extent, from regimental or even battalion mortars and cannon. These groupments are organized on the basis of a careful estimate of the special requirements for a specific operation.

TYPES. One infantry support groupment is set up for each regiment of infantry, divided into subgroupments for each battalion of infantry when three or more battalions of artillery are alloted to the groupment.

Countermortar groupments usually operate during the artillery preparation. They consist of 120-mm mortar and 122-mm howitzer units supported by sound-ranging or other instrumental reconnaissance elements. At the conclusion of their mission, the component elements are often attached to infantry support groupments.

Artillery destruction groupments normally consist of fire reconnaissance and destruction subgroupments. These groupments are often operative only during the preparation phase. The fire reconnaissance subgroupment and light guns from the destruction subgroupment are then attached to infantry support groupments, while heavy and very heavy artillery either reverts to the army artillery commander or is attached to the counterbattery or distant operations groupments.

Counterbattery groupments are maintained throughout the operation against deep defenses. When large quantities of artillery are available, separate distant-operations groupments are also formed.

Antiaircraft groupments initially protect the entire artillery and infantry deployment area. (An antiaircraft artillery division usually operates as the basis of such a groupment.) Upon displacement by light artillery and mortars, elements of the groupment are detached and placed under forward artillery or infantry control. Medium and heavy antiaircraft artillery remains in place to protect army artillery groupments and rear installations.

Roving batteries operate during the advance guard and screening phases of the operation only. They are then attached to infantry-support groupments.

Accompanying guns (direct fire weapons) are generally allotted and sited during the night preceding the artillery preparation. If they are allotted to artillery destruction groupments, they begin operations during the destruction phase of the artillery preparation. If they are allotted to infantry units (down to companies), they begin operations at the end of the preparation.

The number of groupments and subgroupments depends upon the expected difficulty and duration of the operation, the quantity of artillery, the width and the depth of the zone of operations, and possibilities for observation. A groupment may vary from one to nine battalions in size; a subgroupment from a battery to three battalions. A groupment or subgroupment must be provided with adequate fire control, signal communications, observation, and transport to execute its mission. The sector of fire varies with the range; it is usually divided into a primary and an emergency sector.

CONTROL. Groupments and subgroupments may be controlled by the army artillery commander, by an artillery division, by an infantry corps artillery commander, by an infantry division artillery commander, by a regimental artillery commander, or by an infantry commander (from corps to company). Control is determined by the phase of the operation, the scheme of maneuver, the width and depth of the firing sector of each groupment, and its position area.

In general, the divisional or regimental artillery commanders control artillery during the advance guard and covering phase. During *preparation*, control is highly centralized. The army (army group) artillery commander personally supervises fire against the most critical targets, regardless of their character. The artillery divisions control counterbattery, distant operations, antiaircraft, antitank, and sometimes countermortar and artillery destruction groupments. The divisional artillery commanders control infantry support and, normally, countermortar and artillery destruction groupments, as well as roving batteries and accompanying guns. Furthermore, the artillery commander at each level sets aside a portion of fire of one or more artillery units as command reserve for critical emergencies.

With the *assault*, control of accompanying guns and infantry support groupments passes to the infantry artillery divisions, to insure their most effective employment.

During *reorganization*, when the security of the assaulting troops is a paramount problem, the regimental and divisional artillery commanders control artillery in advanced positions, while the army artillery commander continues command of the artillery division.

In *exploitation*, control is increasingly assumed by infantry commanders, and artillery is decentralized to small units (even battalions or companies). Long-range artillery, however, remains under centralized control to give distant support to mobile troops.

The degree of centralized control varies with the tactical importance of each sector. In the zone of the main effort, the army artillery and artillery division commanders have primary responsibilities; in secondary sectors, the corps or the divisional artillery commanders. In operations on a wide front, the reinforcing artillery of secondary sectors may be controlled by infantry corps.

The width and the depth of the firing sector, and the position area of each groupment are determined by its mission. A countermortar groupment, for example, may operate on the front of two infantry divisions. An artillery destruction groupment may fire from firing positions of one division at targets in the sector of another. In such instances, control is assumed by the next higher echelon, corps or army, with subgroupments allotted to each division.

3. ARTILLERY AND AIR OFFENSIVE

a. Basic doctrine. The large-scale offensive use of artillery crystallized in 1942 into a Soviet tactical doctrine, "the artillery and air offensive." The fundamental element of this doctrine is the responsibility of the highest artillery commander, through the artillery chain of command, for the organization and execution of a unified system of fire preparation, support, and security for infantry maneuver. The operations of tactical air bombardment and other supporting fire power are coordinated with the basic artillery responsibility. The success of the doctrine can be judged from repeated operational examples: Orel, the crossing of the Dneiper River, Novogorod, the Karelian Isthmus, the Perekop Isthmus, and Sevastopol.

Most important in the execution of the artillery and air offensive are the following features:

INTELLIGENCE. A comprehensive intelligence system includes a thorough standing operating procedure for troop reconnaissance by batteries and battalions, and aggressive action by infantry and artillery patrols to push observation as far forward as needed. Specialized types of instrumental and air reconnaissance augment the results of troop reconnaissance. Extensive documentation and systematic analysis of information are required. Operational recommendations from lower echelons are combined directly with their intelligence reports. Higher echelons, particularly army, must disseminate all necessary intelligence directly and promptly to every operating level down to batteries.

PLANNING. Continuous comprehensive planning of fire is based upon a thoroughly developed firing technique. The requirements of fire against personnel, tanks and ordnance, field fortifications, permanent fortifications, minefields, wire and dragon's teeth, elevated targets, bridges, railroads, and highways have been well determined. Initial standards for the neutralization, destruction, interdiction, harassing, and fire reconnaissance of targets have been established. Beyond this, great attention is paid to secrecy and surprise, maneuver of fire, aggressive displacement, and variation of tactics. Planning develops from the combined scheme of maneuver and the detailed analysis of enemy capabilities by operational phases of time and space, starting with the initial concentration of forces through the destruction of the enemy defensive system and culminating with the exploitation in his deep rear. Neutralization of enemy capabilities must be effected within the time allotted, and with maximum economy of personnel, matériel, and ammunition.

After careful calculation of the requirements, the fire power, transportation, and signal systems of the entire task force (army, front or group of fronts) are reorganized accordingly. Flexibility to meet surprises or to exploit unexpected successes is provided by systematic duplication of material in critical areas (for example, radio duplicated by wire, mortars duplicated by rockets), and by allotment of reserves. Centralized reserves under the immediate control of the senior artillery commander are employed in mass for decisive results. Local reserves, particularly of ammunition, insure security.

COORDINATION. Coordination of time, space, and command is the basic concern of every artillery echelon. The following are mandatory: personal contact, exchange of liaison officers, multiple communications, unified code, and terrain reference systems within and between artillery units and with supported or cooperating arms. Survey is always initiated at the earliest possible moment; full survey is prescribed for all units in the main effort. Command and organizational groupments are changed as required with every new operational phase to support the infantry most closely and effectively.

b. Fire plan. Accurate, unceasing planning of fire is a mandatory function of artillery regimental and higher staffs. Advance planning, with suitable modifications during combat, alone can insure continuous, reliable, and close support of infantry (or tanks), as well as economy of ammunition and ordnance.

REQUIREMENTS. Primary responsibility for artillery fire plans rests with the highest artillery commander engaged in the operation (army, army group, or GHQ). The plan, based on the infantry (or tank) scheme of maneuver, must embrace the entire contemplated operation from advance guard action to completion of exploitation.

A correct plan is dependent upon continuously developing intelligence. Needed intelligence includes:

The forward line of enemy defenses, which determines the location of observation points and firing positions.

The grouping of enemy reserves, which determines the measures taken for their direct neutralization and for the interdiction of routes of communication.

The locations, numbers, and types of enemy artillery and mortars, which determine the composition, firing positions, and missions of counterbattery and countermortar groupments.

Detailed analysis of the enemy defensive system in the zone of main effort comprising the location of strongpoints and of firing and communications trenches.

Fields and densities of fire of automatic weapons, mortars, and infantry guns.

These factors determine the composition, firing positions, and missions of the infantry-support and artillery destruction groupments, as well as the allotment of weapons to infantry units. Basic factors of terrain, vegetation, and weather determine the systems of observation and fire control, and the capabilities of artillery displacement.

COORDINATION. The plan is initiated with the first warning order. It is continuously coordinated with the staff of combined arms, and with the staffs of other arms, to insure a common time and space schedule, a common system of essential signals and signal communication, maximum exploitation of tactical capabilities, joint combat security, and joint camouflage discipline. It is checked to the greatest practical degree by personal reconnaissance of the artillery commander and the commander of combined arms. It must be disseminated to lower echelons, in preliminary form, as early as possible; in final form, simultaneously with the field order.

The estimate of artillery fire allows for the neutralization of all probable enemy capabilities. Duplicate equipment must be provided for execution of the most important missions. Safety factors and reserves of ammunition and ordnance for unforeseen contingencies must be generous. Artillery must not hesitate to ask for fire by air, by mortars and rockets, by infantry, or by other weapons when more rapid, economical, and certain results can be achieved thereby.

The fire plan must provide maximum surprise and deception. Sudden concentrations, false transfers of fire, irregular periods of neutralization or interdiction, and employment of alternate firing positions or roving batteries—all are important methods which must be utilized to surprise and shock the enemy.

Soviet doctrine emphasizes the necessity for large-scale artillery support in offensive operations. An artillery groupment must be formed or activated for the execution of each major artillery mission, usually bringing the proportion of artillery to infantry to 2 to 1. Certain groupments are maintained throughout the operation; others, through one or more phases only.

USE OF THE PLAN. The artillery plan computes the necessary densities of fire and the capabilities of friendly artillery. In addition, it recommends army (front) and subordinate artillery groupments as well as the position areas and missions of army (front) artillery, and the missions of lower echelons of artillery. The plan computes the time necessary for artillery preparation and ammunition requirements; and it determines the time when the artillery will be ready for combat and the most effective methods for the support of infantry and tanks.

With the aid of this plan, the Commander of Combined Arms prescribes the following:

Attachment of army (army group) artillery to lower formations.

Composition of army (army group) groupments.

Priorities and system of deployment.

Time and duration of artillery preparation, infantry assault, and reorganization of assaulting forces.

Parallel regrouping of artillery.

Allotment of ammunition.

The Commander of Combined Arms checks the position areas or firing positions of army (army group) artillery groupments and assigns missions of the following types: counterbattery; neutralization of deep reserves; neutralization or destruction of supply installations; accompanying barrages and concentrations in the zone of the main effort; and destruction of strong permanent fortifications.

Control of the initial fire plan during combat is indispensable. The execution and effectiveness of firing missions must be continuously reported by lower echelons and checked by responsible staff officers. Estimates must be corrected to conform with actual expenditures of ammunition and ordnance. Groupments and missions must be modified with changes in enemy and friendly capabilities, with movement, with increasing intelligence, and with changes in weather and observation. *The objective of artillery at all times must be to anticipate the immediate requirements of the supported troops.*

DEVELOPMENT AND EXECUTION. The development and execution of fire plans is accomplished in six steps: The combined scheme of maneuver; analysis of targets and enemy capabilities; determination of objectives of fire; computation of artillery fire requirements; formation (or activation) of groupments and assignment of batteries, position areas, and mission; and control of operations.

The scheme of maneuver is normally divided into five phases of time and space: advance guard (covering forces) action and assembly of main forces; fire preparation; infantry (or tank) assault; reorganization and security of assaulting forces; and exploitation.

Known targets and suspected areas are plotted. Enemy capabilities of movement and employment of fixed installations, both for the known and the probable order of battle, are then calculated. The objectives of artillery fire against each group of targets in time and space are then prescribed.

During the first phase (advance guard action and assembly of main forces) normal objectives are neutralization of enemy artillery, interdiction of enemy attack, and fire reconnaissance.

During the fire preparation phase (subperiods: neutralization; registration, fire reconnaissance. and destruction; and neutralization) the normal objectives are:

Neutralization and destruction of enemy field and antiaircraft artillery.

Neutralization and destruction of enemy mortars.

Neutralization of observation and command posts, local reserves, and important centers of resistance in enemy rear areas.

Interdiction of main enemy routes of communication and fire reconnaissance.

Destruction of the most important fortifications, especially permanent ones of concrete and steel.

Break-through of gaps in obstacle systems (in conjunction with engineers and tanks).

Destruction of located flanking, firing points (machine guns and infantry and antitank guns) and neutralization of the automatic weapons defensive system.

Support of the infantry assault requires the following of artillery:

Continued neutralization of enemy artillery.

Interdiction of main enemy routes of communication.

Destruction of antitank guns, machine guns, and field fortifications in the zone of advance (especially by direct fire of accompanying weapons).

Neutralization of observation and command posts, local reserves, and important centers of resistance in enemy rear areas.

Accompaniment of infantry and tanks by fire and displacement.

Interdiction of enemy counterattacks.

Normal artillery objectives during the fourth phase (reorganization and security of assault forces) include neutralization of undamaged, newly found, and revived enemy batteries and centers of resistance; interdiction of enemy counterattacks and of the movement of tactical reserves; neutralization of rear installations.

The artillery's tasks during exploitation include support of mobile forces by displacement of light artillery and by long-distance fire from heavy artillery; destruction of remaining enemy centers of resistance; interdiction of enemy counterattacks, and movement of tactical or strategic reserves.

Computation of artillery fire requirements involves two problems: the expenditure of ammunition, and the types and quantities of artillery. Ammunition expenditures include the total required for all targets (with a safety factor in some cases); duplication of the most important missions; a command reserve for each echelon (to be utilized only by permission of the next higher commander); and an unallotted reserve. Requirements for each target are determined by: the nature and the size of the target; the accuracy of target location, registration, and survey; the range; and the objective of fire. (In neutralization and interdiction, the duration of fire is also a factor.) The range and the objective of fire are basic factors in the choice of weapons. The time allowed for the mission governs the needed quantity of artillery.

EXAMPLES. Figures 28 and 29 present an example of an artillery fire plan in the offensive in a secondary sector. Thus, corps rather than army, is in control. The field fortifications encountered require only a brief period of destruction fire.

Characteristic of the operation are the alternation of concentrations, destruction fire, and repeated false transfers. The duration of the preparation is 1 hour and 55 minutes. The plan for the artillery commitment after the assault phase is not detailed in this instance, but is of the general mission type.

179

GROUPS AND MISSIONS

PHASES OF ARTILLERY ATTACK	TIME IN MINUTES	INFANTRY WEAPONS	DIRECT FIRE ARTILLERY	ARTILLERY AND MORTARS (DIVISIONAL)	CORPS ARTILLERY	CORPS COUNTER-MORTAR GROUP	CORPS ROCKET GROUP	ARMY LONG-RANGE SUB-GROUPMENT
I. ARTILLERY PREPARATION:								
a. First concentration	5	At emplacements in first trench line (A–A).	.....	On first trench-line (A–A) and on communication trenches to second line (B–B).	On second and third trench-line (B–B, C–C); on an identified strongpoint in forward position (concentration 120); on communication trenches from second to third trench-line; and on CPs in forward position.	On mortar batteries identified in the forward position.	On an identified strongpoint in forward position (the same target as for corps artillery—concentration 120); Fire: one battalion concentration.	On identified artillery batteries behind the rear position; on reserves in the enemy's rear. (Nos. 390, 302, 320, 321, 322, 333, 331, 352, 353.)
b. Destruction	50	As in a.	.....	Divisional mission.	On selected trench sector in the second and third trench-lines (B–B, C–C).	Methodical fire on neutralized batteries; destruction fire on active mortars.	.....	Methodical fire on neutralized batteries and neutralization of active batteries.
c. Second concentration	5	As in a.	As directed.	As in a.	On first trench-line (D–D) and on an identified strongpoint in the rear position (concentration 201).	On active mortar batteries.	.....	On active batteries and signal centers.
d. First false transfer	5	As in a.	As directed.	On first trench-line of rear position (D–D) and on communication trenches to second trench-line (E–E).	Third trench-line of forward position (C–C) and on communication trenches from second to third trench-line.	As in a.	On an identified strongpoint in forward position (coordinates 38-49) Fire: One regimental concentration.	As in a. (Excluding 300 and 302.
e. Direct fire	15	.....	Division plan.	Methodical fire on destroyed trench sectors in second* line of trenches and deeper.	.....	.....	.....	Neutralization of active batteries.
f. Third concentration.	10	..	.....	As in a.	On target coordinate 38-49 strongpoint (concentration 120) on third trench-line of forward position (C–C).	As in c.	.....	On active batteries and signal centers.
g. Second false transfer.	10	.....	As directed	.....	On second and third trench-line of forward position (B–B, C–C) and on communication trenches from second to third trench-line.	As in a.	As in d. Fire: On battalion concentration.	On revived batteries and reserves near Height 191 (rear position) (concentration 200).
h. Fourth concentration.	15	As in a.	On previously destroyed targets.	As in a.	As in a.	As in c.	.....	On active batteries and reserves concentration 120.
II. ASSAULT	"H"	.....	.....	Support assault with double accompanying barrages. Transfer to first phase line. Transfer to second phase line under divisional artillery control. Further transfer to phase line (coordinates 37–49–51 under division control.	Transfer to second phase line under divisional artillery control.	As in 1e.	As in 1d	On active batteries.
III. COMBAT SECURITY PHASE:								
a. When infantry passes phase line coordinates 37–49—36–51.	.....	.....	.....	Prepared to neutralize enemy in area 191.2 and 35–49 with four battalions.	Prepared to neutralize enemy with concentrations 200, 201. Interdict counterattack with anti-personnel barrages M and N Interdict retreat from strongpoint Kamen (in rear position).	Special attention to southern reverse slopes. Height 191.2.	Prepared for full concentration on Height 191.3 and Kamen.	Neutralization of active batteries. Interdict approach of reserves from direction Height 193.4—Ustinovka.
b. When infantry passes phase line Ivanorka Maryv..ka.	.....	.....	.....	.....	Prepared to neutralize enemy areas, with concentrations 215 and 216. Interdict counterattack with anti-personnel barrages N and O. Cover commitment of second infantry division.	Neutralize active mortar batteries special attention to Height 193.4.	Prepared for regimental concentration.	

*Methodical fire is conducted for continuous neutralization and to prevent reoccupation of previously destroyed positions. Normally it is observed fire.

Figure 28. Extract from the plan for artillery offensive of the 1st Rifle Corps.

180

The plan covers the commitment of the following weapons, units, and formations in the corps sector with an approximate width of 1.5 miles: infantry weapons, mortars, and an organic field artillery regiment plus one howitzer regiment under division control; a medium gun brigade, a mortar regiment, a rocket regiment and probably one antitank regiment under corps control; and part of a heavy gun brigade and part of an antiaircraft artillery division under army control.

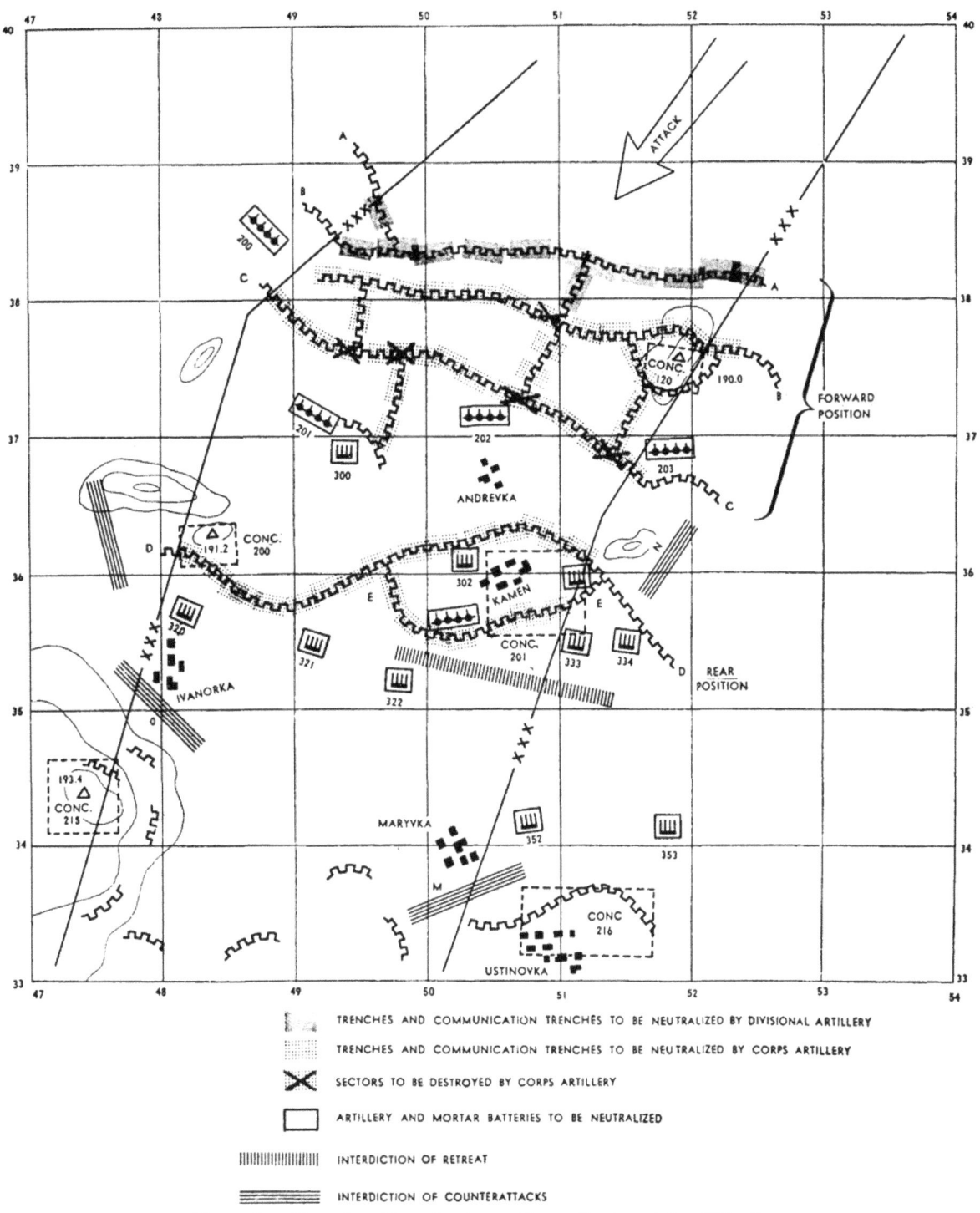

Figure 29. Plan of artillery fire for artillery offensive of 1st Rifle Corps.

TRENCHES AND COMMUNICATION TRENCHES TO BE NEUTRALIZED BY DIVISIONAL ARTILLERY

TRENCHES AND COMMUNICATION TRENCHES TO BE NEUTRALIZED BY CORPS ARTILLERY

SECTORS TO BE DESTROYED BY CORPS ARTILLERY

ARTILLERY AND MORTAR BATTERIES TO BE NEUTRALIZED

INTERDICTION OF RETREAT

INTERDICTION OF COUNTERATTACKS

Figures 30 and 31 are examples of the fire plan of a regimental infantry-support groupment in offensive operation in a moderately defended enemy sector. The infantry-support groupment in both examples comprised three artillery battalions (one battalion from the divisional artillery and two attached battalions) and a provisional mortar battalion temporarily organized from the infantry, regimental, and battalion mortar batteries.

Examples A and B present different methods employed by the infantry support groupment. In Example A, the artillery fires accompanying barrages which cover the entire width of the sector during the assault phase, while in Example B, the artillery supports the assault with accompanying concentrations on definite targets in each phase line.

c. Characteristics of artillery in the offensive. The location of firing positions is determined about 10 days before the attack by the comprehensive reconnaissance of assault unit and artillery commanders. About 2 to 3 days before the attack, the reinforcing artillery moves into prepared firing positions under the cover of night and noise created by mortar fire and planes. The newly arrived artillery immediately starts registration fire with single pieces from dummy and roving gun positions, making extensive use of the firing data available from the artillery already active in the sector.

As a rule, every battery has a main firing position and an alternate position to the front or rear of it. The main firing position is usually sufficiently far forward to facilitate effective fire into the depth of the enemy position. For the destruction or neutralization of individual strongpoints, firing positions are located far forward and prepared for single direct-fire artillery pieces. The most effective ranges for direct fire during short and intensive artillery preparations are 440 to 880 yards for 45-mm guns, 1,100 to 1,320 yards for 76.2-mm guns, and 1,650 to 2,200 yards for 122-mm and 152-mm artillery pieces.

The army or army group artillery commander controls registration when a large amount of artillery is committed. Plans for registration and deceptive registration are developed to assure secrecy.

During the course of the attack, Soviet artillery displaces forward as soon as the enemy main line of resistance is reached by friendly infantry, always keeping two-thirds of the artillery in firing position while the other third is on the move.

4. ARTILLERY IN DEFENSE

a. Basic doctrine. The Red Army considers its artillery as the main weapon of the defense. As previously described, Soviet tactics distinguish two basic systems of defense: decentralized and centralized. The artillery in decentralized defense is broken up, and its components are under the control of the individual strongpoint commanders. In the centralized system, the artillery remains under the control of the artillery commander.

The artillery missions, however, are the same for both defense systems:

> Fire against enemy march columns and troop concentrations.
> Support of the units in the forward positions.
> Interference with the deployment of the attacking enemy.
> Counterbattery and countermortar fire.
> Firing of smoke against enemy observation posts.
> Annihilation of the enemy infantry and tank attacks in front of the main line of resistance.
> Destruction of tanks which have penetrated through Soviet lines.
> Preparation fire for counterthrusts and counterattacks.

b. Concentration of artillery for defensive operations. Soviet artillery in the defensive is usually organized to facilitate the massing of fire in definite areas. For this purpose, artillery in a corps sector is normally divided into infantry-support groupments and artillery groupments for long-range counterbattery and countermortar missions.

Soviet tactical doctrine also prescribes the establishment of three firing positions for each battery, and emphasizes that the positions must be selected so that the bulk of the artillery can participate in the fire against enemy tanks which have penetrated the defenses. Emphasis is laid on the construction of alternate and dummy positions and the employment of roving guns and silent batteries to deceive the enemy as to the location of the real positions and artillery strength. The weapons are brought into position only when firing; the rest of the time they are kept to the rear in well camouflaged dugouts.

The artillery commander also develops a fire plan for each sector, considering all possible combat phases, including:

> Concentration by long-range artillery upon enemy artillery positions, approach routes,

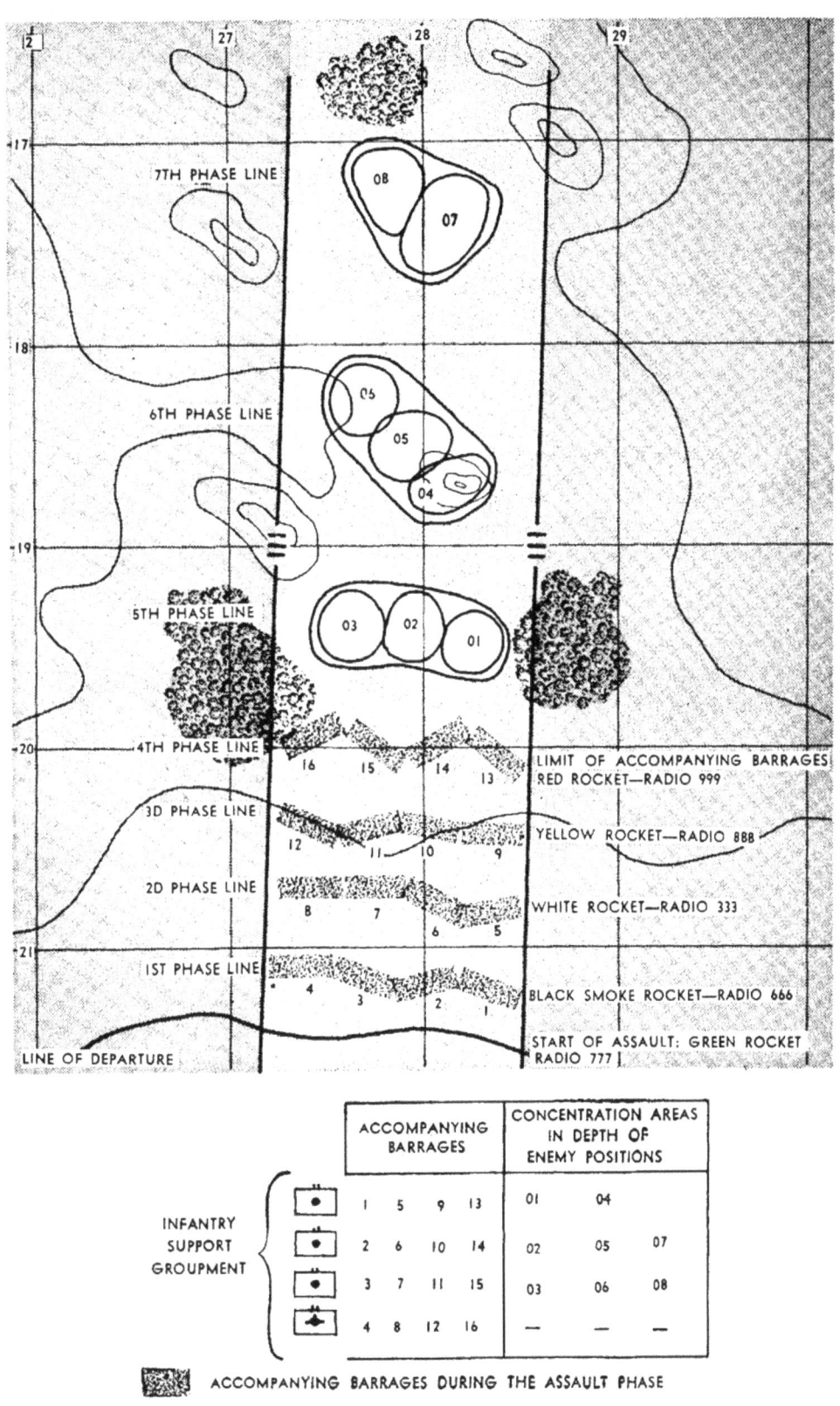

Figure 30. *Fire chart of regimental infantry support groupment during assault phase and the subsequent concentrations in the depth of the enemy position (example A).*

183

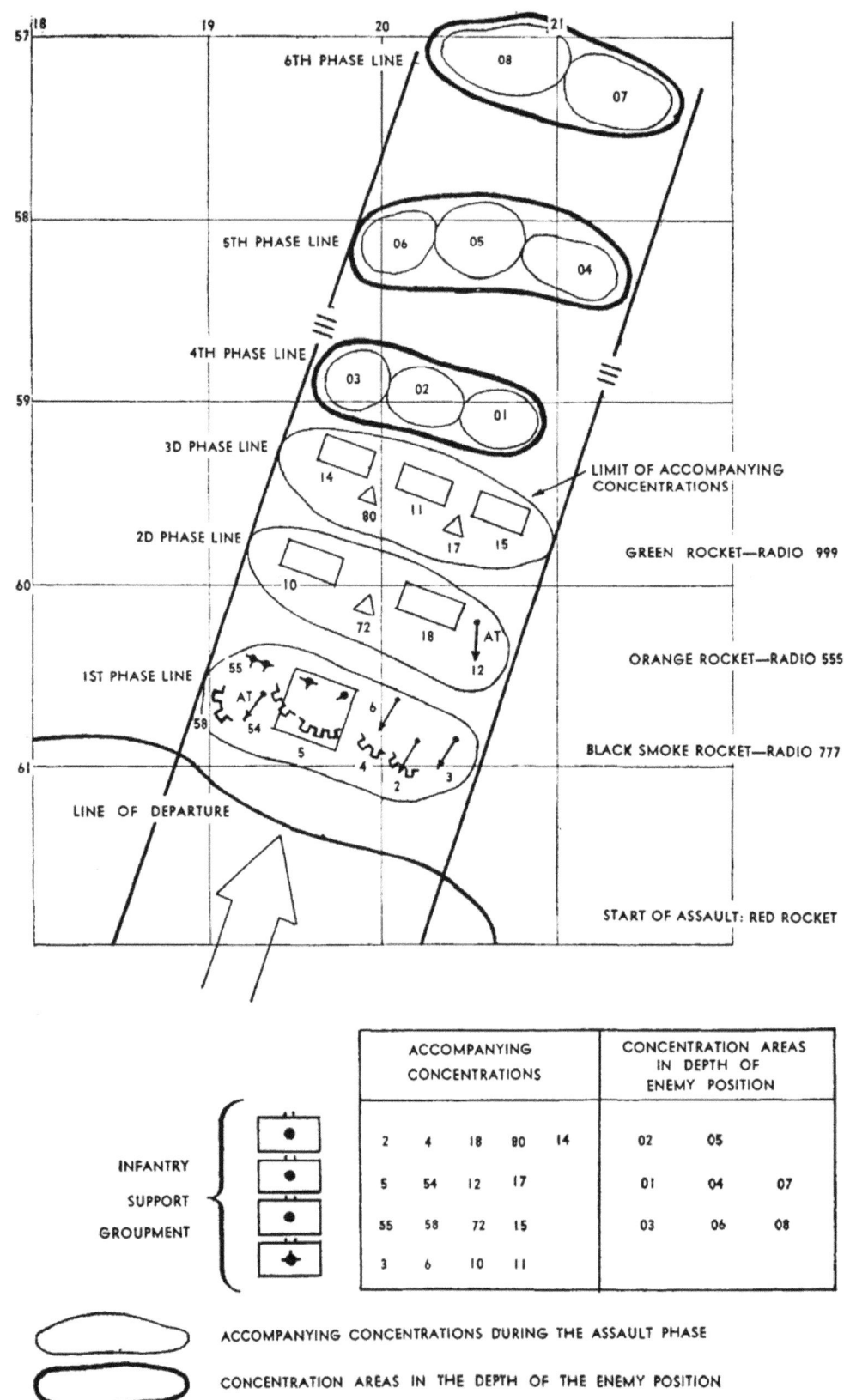

Figure 31. Fire chart of regimental infantry support groupment during assault phase and the subsequent concentrations in the depth of the enemy position (example B).

184

road crossings. and other important installations in the enemy rear.

Massed fire at enemy assembly areas. command posts, and observation posts.

The Red Army employs stationary antipersonnel and moving antitank defensive barrages. Antipersonnel barrages are the rule in the defense. All types of artillery weapons, mortars, and rockets are

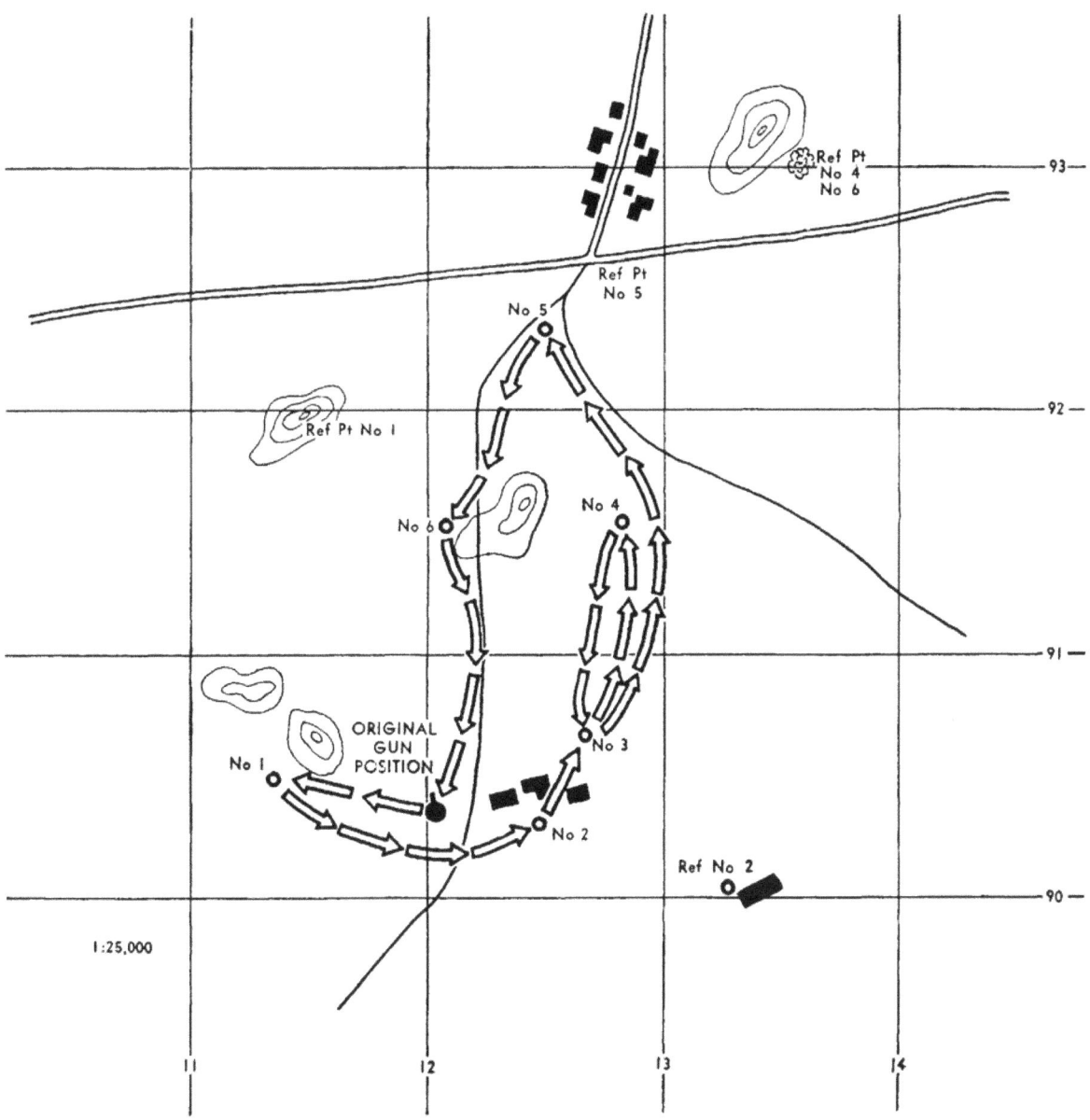

Figure 32. *Map for the chief of section of the roving gun.*

Box barrages against enemy tanks and large troop concentrations.

Direct fire against tanks which have penetrated.

Barrages in front of the main line of resistance and in the depth of the friendly main battle position.

coordinated for these barrages, which normally are about 330 yards in front of the friendly main line of resistance. The areas covered by the barrages are usually identified with names. Each artillery battalion is supposed to have not more than four barrage areas. about 440 yards wide and overlapping the barrage areas of adjacent artillery battal-

185

ions. Antitank barrages follow the enemy along his axis of approach to the friendly main line of resistance; however, these barrages find only limited employment due to gunnery difficulties.

The Red Army places great emphasis on the employment of roving guns in the defensive. They deceive the enemy as to the quantity and grouping of the friendly artillery and thereby force the enemy to disperse the fire of his supporting weapons.

Plans for the employment of roving guns are carefully worked out by the battalion commander of the firing platoon to achieve maximum effects. These plans include the march route of the gun, positions to be occupied and the reference points, firing positions to be used for effect, and deceptive firing positions. With the assistance of the topographical computation platoon of the battalion, the battalion commander also prepares a chart which contains: a description of the observation points and reference points; a description of the march route; target designation and firing data; and the number of rounds to be expended for each target and firing position. The firing platoon also is furnished with a small map which contains the march route, the firing positions (which are staked previously on the ground for easier identification), and the reference points (fig. 32).

c. **Artillery counterattack.** Soviet doctrine speaks of an "artillery counterattack," thus emphasizing the offensive character of the artillery in the defensive. The mission of the artillery is to crush an enemy attack in its initial phase. The artillery counterattack, controlled by a carefully prepared fire plan, commences when the enemy moves into his assembly position and begins his attack preparations. Soviet artillery relies on the observation battalions for firing data, to obtain complete surprise and abstain from using registration fire. The organization of artillery in the centralized defense facilitates the conduct of the artillery counterattack.

d. **Artillery in delaying action and retreat.** In delaying actions and retreats, the artillery is organized in depth. Firing positions and ammunition reserves are prepared in the rear to facilitate speedy retrograde displacement and to permit relatively large expenditure of ammunition by the covering forces. Single motorized batteries or battalions are subordinated to the rear guard covering the retreat of the infantry. Soviet artillery opens fire at great ranges to delay and disorganize the advancing enemy.

5. ATTACK OF TARGETS

The effectiveness of artillery fire, according to Red Army doctrines, depends upon correct determination of the nature and location of the target, correct choice of the objective of fire, and the mode of attack (including weapons, ammunition, fuze, charge, angle of impact, firing pattern, and expenditure of ammunition).

Accuracy of registration and constant correction of fire, as well as continuous, accurate planning are additional factors.

Surprise is of maximum importance in fire against personnel; prior adjustment directly on the target is permissible only in exceptional cases. Short bursts of sudden, massed fire at maximum rates produce the greatest physical and psychological effects. Methodical fire, with the observation and adjustment of each round, is most effective in the destruction of matériel.

Tabulated standards for neutralization or destruction of targets are only guides. In the destruction of point targets, direct fire is most rapid and economical; no expenditure of ammunition can replace accuracy in destruction fire. Direct fire, however, demands extremely careful preparation and camouflage to prevent excessive losses of personnel and matériel. All types of fire for effect must be employed until the required tactical results have been achieved.

The rate of fire should not exceed the technical capabilities of each weapon as designated in standard tables. With reduced charges in prolonged fire, increases up to 50 percent are permissible. The rate of fire must not be increased at the expense of accuracy. After prolonged or intense fighting, corrections for heating and other ballistic changes are essential.

a. **Types of targets.** From the standpoint of artillery fire, enemy operations and installations may be divided into seven general components, excluding aircraft: personnel (or animals); tanks, motor vehicles, and other ordnance; field fortifications, tank ditches, houses, and other structures of moderate strength; permanent fortifications and structures of great strength; minefields; wire, dragon's teeth, and similar resistant, small, but immobile, targets; and elevated targets, such as observation posts in high trees and observation balloons.

PERSONNEL. Personnel are the primary or secondary targets of all artillery fire. Fragmentation and incendiary projectiles are most effective against personnel in the open; heavy blast can often neutralize or destroy personnel under cover even in the absence of direct hits. Light and medium artillery may be usefully employed against personnel, although mortars and rockets of similar calibers are more effective. Surprise and quick action are mandatory.

Against moving infantry, cavalry, or motorized troops, shrapnel and high explosive shells with superquick, delayed (to produce ricochet), and time fuzes are employed. Fire is usually by battery, with a normal or concentrated sheaf, in rapid bursts of four to six volleys, at each sight adjustment. Whenever possible, fire is delayed until the approach of troops to a registered phase line. Concentrated fire begins with their arrival on the line of shorts. Against large or rapidly moving masses of infantry, zone fire by all available artillery produces decisive results. At long ranges, such fire should be adjusted by aerial observation whenever possible.

Against infantry in the open or troops in shallow trenches, ricochet fire, and fire with superquick fuze and minimum charge are most effective. HE with time or superquick fuze is employed against reverse slopes. In very broken terrain, high-angle fire is used with delayed fuze to get maximum vertical dispersion. The sheaf must be normal or concentrated to correspond to the width of the target. Bursts of three to six volleys alternate with methodical fire.

Several methods of fire may be employed against personnel in field fortifications. Small groups of observed or unobserved, but accurately located, targets may be grouped into target areas not exceeding 72,000 to 96,000 square yards, which are brought under fire by sudden concentrations of medium or heavy artillery (at least one battalion per 240 square yards) employing suitable zone fire, with HE and incendiary ammunition, quick fuze, and minimum charge. When targets are inaccurately located, the probable error in range and dispersion must be determined.

If the target is large, such as a battery position or a supply installation, fire is distributed uniformly. If the target is small, distribution of fire corresponds to the law of probabilities, with the heaviest concentration in the center of the area.

TANKS AND OTHER ORDNANCE. Projectiles which result in penetration, incendiary action, and strong blast are effective against tanks and other ordnance. Accompanying exposed personnel must always be attacked simultaneously—by fragmentation fire from other weapons, if necessary.

Distant firing missions against tanks, motor vehicles, artillery, and similar matériel are executed by the concentrated fire of medium or heavy guns, or heavy howitzers. Aerial observation and control, or precise registration, are essential to prevent excessive waste of ammunition. HE with superquick fuze, or concrete-piercing ammunition, are combined with incendiary shells for optimum results. Fire proceeds at maximum rates in bursts of 2 or 3 minutes, interrupted by periods of methodical fire and adjustment.

Firing missions against moving tanks at medium ranges (antitank defensive barrages) must be previously organized, with one or two battalions of medium artillery assigned to each probable tank approach, and with light artillery and mortars prepared to fire upon accompanying infantry. Phase lines are registered along these approaches at intervals of 330 to 440 yards, depending on the probable speed of the tanks. HE superquick-fuze ammunition is allotted and prepared at firing positions. As the head of the enemy tank column reaches each phase line, concentrated fire at maximum rates is conducted for 2 or 3 minutes. As soon as the main tank group has passed the point of concentration, fire is then laid down upon the next phase line. Antipersonnel fire may be continued on the first phase line to isolate the tanks from their infantry. The last phase line is within direct fire range.

The Red Army considers training in direct fire against tanks essential for all light and medium artillery. In massed tank attacks, fire must be opened at a maximum direct-fire range of 1,100 to 1,650 yards. To destroy single tanks or small units, the most effective ranges are 330 to 770 yards, depending on muzzle velocity. Maximum charges, with armor-piercing or concrete-piercing ammunition, are employed. In the absence of AP ammunition, HE with quick or superquick fuze may be used, especially against tankettes, armored cars, and other lightly armored vehicles.

FIELD FORTIFICATIONS. Field fortifications, tank ditches, houses, and similar structures present a variety of firing problems. Some of the more important variables to be considered are: hardness and texture of the ground; drainage and vegetation; presence of timber, brick, steel rails, or other reinforcements; surface and subsurface profiles; nature and degree of overhead cover; and the degree of compartmentation. Hasty defenses may sometimes be destroyed by light artillery and mortars, while developed systems often require prolonged operations by heavy artillery and direct cannon fire even for effective neutralization. The peculiarities in each case must be established by the most thorough reconnaissance possible.

Fire upon field fortifications is best initiated by surprise concentrations of medium howitzers, mortars, and rockets (high-angle fire, HE and incendiary shells, quick and superquick fuzes). In addition to the physical and psychological effects against personnel, such concentrations serve to remove camouflage, exposing armor or concrete, and reveal dummy positions or weak spots. Soviet artillery then initiates destruction fire. Compact groups of light fortifications may often be destroyed by several repeated concentrations, carefully observed and adjusted.

The destruction of strong and extensive field fortifications in this manner, however, is rarely feasible. In firing upon such systems, comprehensive reconnaissance must establish, as far as possible, the coordinated tactical grouping of the fortifications, differentiating occupied and alternate firing positions, observation posts, personnel shelters, communication trenches, barrier systems, and dummy installations. A definite firing plan must be developed for each strongpoint.

An artillery-destruction groupment or subgroupment is formed, and necessary types and numbers of weapons are allotted. Guns or howitzers are used for direct short-range fire at embrasures or vertical walls (using HE delayed fuze). Medium howitzers or heavy mortars with HE and quick or delayed fuze destroy and interdict communication or other trenches: in frontal fire, high-angle fire is used; in flanking fire, flat-trajectory. Personnel shelters and emplacements with good overhead cover must be destroyed by high-angle fire from heavy or very heavy howitzers using HE or incendiary shells and delayed fuze. Mortars, howitzers, or light guns may be used to neutralize other, lighter positions or to blind them with smoke. In all cases, fire must secure maximum accuracy. Observation is deployed as far forward as possible. No more weapons than necessary are employed, and every round must be observed.

Firing upon fortified houses is normally difficult and time consuming, because, in modern tactics, the main battle position is dug into the basement, with firing apertures broken through the wall. In the center of the basement, a personnel shelter is constructed, while a communication trench facilitates escape from one or more hidden exits. This position is not only given natural protection by the house foundations, walls, and floors, but it is also reinforced and fireproofed by the construction of barricades and blast walls, and the packing of earth on floors. The roof and upper stories are used for observation and harrassing fire.

There are two methods of artillery attack upon such a strongpoint. Heavy or very heavy howitzers may demolish the entire position. If these are not available, or if time and ammunition do not allow their extensive use, an entirely different technique must be employed. Destruction of the upper structure alone is not only futile, but it hampers subsequent artillery and infantry operations by limiting visibility in dust and smoke, and increasing protection and camouflage afforded by rubble. The most effective technique is neutralization of the windows and roofs with time fire or shrapnel; destruction of the forward and other edges of the basement with direct fire or flat trajectory (HE, delayed fuze) fire from medium howitzers or guns; and interdiction of possible exits with suitable zone fire (by howitzers or mortars). After the main battle position is thus destroyed or neutralized, the upper structure may be destroyed by using HE or incendiary projectiles, or it may be mopped up by infantry.

PERMANENT FORTIFICATIONS. Successful fire upon massive structures requires comprehensive visual and fire reconnaissance, employment of very heavy howitzers and medium guns, close range and continuous observation and adjustment, and, if possible, suitable firing positions not over 5 kilometers from the target. Under favorable circumstances fortified targets up to 10 kilometers distant may be destroyed; at greater ranges only neutralization is usually possible. Destruction can rarely be accomplished in less than several days' reconnaissance and a day's fire, or with the expenditure of less than several hundred rounds per target.

Permanent fortifications are destroyed by the flat trajectory fire of medium and heavy guns, and of very heavy howitzers, or by high-angle fire from very heavy howitzers. Such targets are neutralized by direct, short-range fire of light and medium guns at embrasures and armor. The angle of impact in all cases must not be less than 58 degrees. Flat-trajectory fire, and especially direct fire, must be

188

employed whenever possible, since these bring about an economy of 80 to 90 percent in time and ammunition. Care must be exercised, however, to conduct such fire against the actual wall of the position, rather than against a mask or exterior blast wall.

Red Army artillery missions against massive structures are divided into four phases: fire reconnaissance, selection of firing positions for very heavy artillery, registration, and destruction fire. To conduct such an attack, an artillery destruction groupment or subgroupment is formed. As far as is necessary, its operations must be protected against counterbattery fire by the neutralization of enemy artillery.

Fire reconnaissance is conducted by medium and heavy howitzers, and, to a lesser degree, by mortars and rockets. It must be closely coordinated with repeated aerial and ground photography, and with continuous optical observation. Fire on the suspected area seeks to strip away masks and camouflage, and to establish the presence and thickness of concrete or armor, the outlines of the fortified structures, the location and direction of embrasures, and the system of tactical coordination with other strongpoints. In fire reconnaissance, the presence of gray dust in a low, wide burst and a sharp reverberation indicate concrete; a very marked reverberation, and frequent, sudden ricochets indicate the presence of armor. Indisputable evidence of the presence of permanent fortifications is afforded by the gradual disclosure of angular outlines, embrasures, and cupolas. On the other hand, a dummy position is indicated if repeated hits develop a large, sagging depression not over 2 yards above ground level without revealing any indications of the presence of concrete or armor.

If fire reconnaissance discloses a field fortification within the capabilities of the artillery then firing, these guns continue fire until the target is destroyed. Once fire reconnaissance has definitely established the presence and character of permanent fortifications, firing positions for very heavy artillery are chosen. One to two pieces are assigned to each target. Whenever feasible, the positions should allow flat trajectory or very high-angle fire at ranges under 5,500 yards, provide reasonable cover from enemy fire, and coincide as closely as possible with the longitudinal axis of the targets. Suitable covered approaches must exist. Observation must be provided as far forward as possible, preferably within 550 yards of the target. In some instances,

local infantry attacks may be necessary to facilitate such observation. Observation posts are either single or in pairs. The single observation post must coincide as closely as possible with the gun-target line. In every case, exact survey is indispensable.

Soviet gun positions for direct fire against embrasures are also chosen with great care; they should be within 660 yards of the target and in direct line with embrasures, vertical walls, or other vulnerable parts of the target. Extremely careful camouflage must be maintained in occupying positions and prior to opening fire. Artillery which has a mission of destruction takes precedence over all other weapons in the occupation of suitable firing positions and observation posts.

Fire continues until the obvious collapse of the target, or until two or three complete penetrations have resulted. This requires from two to ten direct hits by heavy guns or very heavy howitzers, depending on the strength of the fortification and the power of the weapon. Approximate ammunition requirements for each hit may be calculated by the probability formula. When destruction has been completed, interdiction fire by light and medium artillery is essential to prevent reoccupation of the ruins.

MINEFIELDS. Establishing gaps through minefields involves two phases: fire reconnaissance and fire for destruction. In fire reconnaissance, a heavy battery combs the entire suspected area, employing a parallel sheaf and elevation changes of one probable error. (Combing fire is an observed barrage progressively covering an area with suspected, especially immobile, targets. As soon as results of fire confirm the location of the targets—by explosions, sudden ricochet, etc.—massed fire for effect is initiated.) HE, with quick fuze, is employed. Two battery salvos are fired at each sight setting, with careful observation for signs of sympathetic detonations.

Once the boundaries of the minefield and of the desired gaps have been determined, fire for effect is begun. If possible, heavy or very heavy howitzers are used. The sheaf is closed or concentrated to 11-yard intervals. Ricochet fire is employed, with the burst no higher than 11 yards above the ground. Fire is conducted at one sight setting, with observation of each salvo, until no evidence of sympathetic detonations can be seen or heard. If the probable error in range is small and the minefield deep, then the bombardment is repeated at the next sight elevation, until the gap has been completely cleared. In the absence of heavy or very heavy howitzers, the Red Army may use medium howitzers or light guns against minefields. HE with quick fuze is used. Large expenditures of ammunition are necessary, however, and results are not always certain.

WIRE. Against wire, dragon's teeth, and similar resistant, small, but immobile, targets, the Soviets employ frontal, flat-trajectory fire by light guns or, in some cases, medium howitzers. Protection of these weapons by other artillery fire is generally necessary. If more than one weapon is employed, calibration and ballistic corrections must be applied. Whenever possible, direct fire is used; in no case should the range exceed 3,300 yards.

Medium howitzers or light guns are employed, singly or in small units, to destroy wire. If the desired gap is 9 yards or less, a concentrated sheaf is used; otherwise, the sheaf corresponds to the desired width. HE ammunition is employed, with superquick fuze and the minimum possible charge (to produce the maximum angle of impact with least range dispersion). The forward edge of the wire serves as the aiming point; to secure the best results, one-third of the rounds should be shorts. Fire is continued until the gap is completely cleared. Requirements in time and ammunition vary greatly with the range and the depth of the wire barrier.

Dragon's teeth are attacked with short-range direct fire. Light guns with AP ammunition are employed against concrete and granite dragon's teeth; timber obstacles are destroyed by medium howitzers with HE fire and superquick fuze. Artillery fire is ineffective against heavy steel obstacles. In all cases, dragon's teeth and similar obstacles require the expenditure of much time and ammunition. Fire must be continued until the remnant stumps can be cleared by tanks.

b. Fire objectives. The objectives of Soviet of fire for effect are: neutralization, destruction, interdiction, or harassment. Fire reconnaissance is either an independent objective or a phase of observed fire for effect. Above all, choice depends on the targets' threat to the infantry (or tank) scheme of maneuver. Successive phases of an operation will often require different objectives in firing upon the same target: for example, neutralization during the artillery preparation, destruction during the assault, and interdiction of the ruins during exploitation. Other important factors are: firing capabilities of the artillery within the time and with the ammunition available; accuracy of target location and reg-

istration; size of the target and its resistance to fire; range; and meteorological and visibility conditions.

Neutralization is the normal objective of artillery fire; by employing surprise and intense fire, almost any target can be successfully neutralized. This condition is primarily psychological, and results normally from attacks on personnel that achieve 25 percent casualties, with accompanying shock and destruction. Neutralization is achieved by two or three repeated periods of concentrated fire, interrupted by periods of adjustment and methodical fire. Whenever possible, continuous observation must be maintained on neutralized targets. If signs of activity are observed, harassing fire should be employed; a major resurgence of activity should be neutralized by a new concentration of fire.

The annihilation of personnel or the certain destruction of matériel by artillery fire are possible only under favorable conditions. Direct fire at short ranges, as the most certain, rapid, and economical method, must be employed whenever possible. Flat-trajectory observed fire and high-angle observed fire by medium, heavy, and very heavy artillery demand successively greater accuracy in initial data and a greater expenditure of time and ammunition. Unobserved fire for destruction is practicable only with large masses of heavy and very heavy artillery and cannot be guaranteed against small, mobile, or very resistant targets. It should be utilized only in exceptional cases, against targets of the greatest importance. Fire for destruction by large masses of artillery is usually feasible only against personnel or light field fortifications. When more than one piece is employed for the destruction of a small resistant target, full ballastic preparation, precise registration, and continuous control of fire are indispensable.

Soviet artillery fire is widely employed to deny terrain to the enemy and to immobilize him undercover. The principal types of interdictory fire are antipersonnel and antitank defensive barrages, accompanying barrages, accompanying concentrations, and distant interdictory concentrations. All interdiction fire requires accurate registration on the target, and continual knowledge of the exact location of friendly troops. The battalion, or its equivalent, is usually the smallest unit to conduct interdiction fire. Often such types of fire are mixed: for example, an antipersonnel mortar barrage fired in conjunction with an antitank artillery barrage.

ANTIPERSONNEL DEFENSIVE BARRAGES. These are planned so as to lay down fire on registered and observed phase lines, screening friendly forces against infantry attacks or counterattacks. If the friendly troops are under cover, such barrages may be laid down not closer to them than 220 yards with frontal fire, and 110 yards with flanking fire. If the friendly troops are in the open, minimum distances for light or medium artillery are 440 yards with ricochet or superquick fuze, and 220 yards with quick fuze. The normal sheaf is employed in frontal fire; in flanking fire, platoon (two-gun) concentrations are separated by one sight setting for guns or two for howitzers. Fire is conducted at one sight setting only. At each piece, 10 or 12 rounds of fuzed ammunition are set aside; in firing, two or three rapid volleys are followed by methodical fire every 5 to 10 seconds. Registered ranges and deflections are noted prominently on each piece; care is taken to correct for decreases in range after prolonged fire and for other errors. Calls for antipersonnel defensive barrages take precedence over all other firing missions, which are immediately suspended.

ANTITANK DEFENSIVE BARRAGES. These have been described under attacks against tanks.

ACCOMPANYING BARRAGES. These are employed to support infantry and tanks through the main line of enemy resistance (1,650 to 2,200 yards) in the assault of organized positions. They consist of a rolling barrage by heavy mortars, medium howitzers, or light guns; direct fire through gaps in the infantry lines by light guns and howitzers; and accompanying concentrations against rear areas by heavier weapons. In organizing the rolling barrage, the zone of fire is divided into sectors by primary and intermediate phase lines. The first primary phase line is 220 to 275 yards from the line of departure. In the support of infantry, other primary phase lines are from 165 to 330 yards apart (usually on enemy trenches or on other lines of resistance or movement); in the support of light tanks, 275 to 440 yards; in the support of medium or heavy tanks, 440 to 880 yards. Intermediate phase lines for infantry are separated by 110 yards; for tanks by 220 yards.

The width of the sheaf varies from 40 to 80 percent of normal. Density of fire on each phase line varies from 6 to 18 rounds per 110 yards per minute, depending on the caliber (76.2- to 152-mm) of the weapon used. When exceptionally heavy resistance is expected, the barrage may be deepened—not thickened—by additional layers of medium or heavy artillery fire. HE with superquick or delayed (ricochet) fuzes and flat-trajectory fire are employed; also shrapnel and smoke shells under favorable circumstances.

The duration of fire on each primary and secondary phase line is determined by the speed of advance of the supported troops. Fire is lifted by signal from primary phase lines, and by schedule (not over 2 minutes) from intermediate phase lines. Accompanying barrages require exceptional safeguards: full ballistic preparation and precise registration, reliable multiple-signal systems, and continual observation of friendly troops from all possible points.

ACCOMPANYING CONCENTRATIONS. This type of fire, employing uniform zones, neutralizes suspected or active areas of enemy resistance. It is employed either as a part of an accompanying barrage or—if the resistance is moderate or when ammunition is insufficient for an accompanying barrage—independently. The concentrations may be fired on call or on a schedule. Generally, fire is lifted by signal.

INTERDICTION FIRE AT LONG RANGES. This is used to block communications. Employment of precise data is necessary to avoid excessive waste of ammunition. If the target is under observation, fire is begun at the approach of enemy vehicles or personnel; otherwise, an irregular schedule of harassing fire is maintained. The weapons and firing unit employed depend on the range and the size of the target.

Harassing fire, designed to reduce enemy efficiency and excite return fire, is conducted by roving batteries or from alternate positions. It may consist of sudden concentrations, or the more constant fire of a few guns. Intervals, expenditure of ammunition, and pattern of fire must be constantly varied to secure maximum effect. High explosive with delayed (ricochet) or superquick fuze and minimum charges are utilized.

Fire reconnaissance, conducted by roving batteries or by elements of an artillery destruction groupment, seeks to clarify the enemy situation and to permit the economical and effective use of heavy and very heavy artillery by provoking enemy fire or other noticeable activity; by stripping off camouflage, earth, and other cover from suspected permanent fortifications; by detonating mines, etc. Medium guns and howitzers are employed, with delayed (ricochet) or quick fuze, depending on the target. Observation, aerial photography, or sound ranging are indispensable. Against areas suspected of containing personnel, harassing or combing fire is most effective; against minefields, combing fire is required; against camouflage, combing or concentrated fire may be utilized.

c. Registration. The Soviets regard accurate registration as the indispensable foundation of their techniques of massed fire and fire on unobserved targets. The four elements of registration are: ballistic preparation; development of a network of registration check points; adjustment of fire; and transfer of fire to the target, or massing it on the target.

In massing large quantities of artillery, registration is limited to gain surprise and to avoid obscuring observation. Registration fire is usually conducted by one piece of each caliber and a model from each battalion or groupment, although the proportion may be as low as one piece every 4,400 to 5,500 yards. Ballistic preparation and survey must have been completed. The registration piece must be the best available, that is, have the lowest differential reduction of muzzle velocity, and be carefully calibrated, preferably by fire.

ADJUSTMENT TECHNIQUE. The primary technique of adjustment of fire is bracketing, controlled by a single axial or lateral observer. Whenever possible, shells from the same lot and of the same weight and fuze setting are employed both in adjustment and in fire for effect. For adjustment on an impact check point, at least four rounds are required; for adjustment on an air burst or sound ranging check point, from six to nine rounds.

Normally, adjustment is fired by a single piece, with corrections for range, deflection, and—in air burst or ricochet—elevation. When speed is desired, as in adjustment on personnel, or when adjustment is by sound ranging or aerial observation, battery or battalion salvos are employed.

OBSERVATION. Aerial observation is undertaken with the light, two-seater U-2 airplane, the slow but heavily armored Stormovik, or with an observation balloon. It is normally limited to ranges in excess of 5,500 yards or to areas inaccessible to ground observation. In every case, thorough briefing of the pilot and air observer in land marks, orientation points, and recognition signals is required to reduce time in the air and to obviate errors. Salvos are always concentrated. The fire of battery or battalion ladders is a common type of

control. In another method of correction, the observer drops a flare or a smoke bomb at a point visible to ground observers and adjusts fire in relation to this reference point.

When large numbers of guns are firing, identification of the correct bursts for adjustment is insured by checking the estimated time of flight with a stop watch.

Adjustment of fire by paired observers is undertaken to insure both greater accuracy and greater economy of ammunition than are possible with a single observer. This is the basic method for heavy artillery, and is utilized whenever time and terrain permit establishment of suitable observation points and signal communications. The angle of intersection between the observers' lines of sight and the target must always exceed 250 mils.

FIRE TRANSFER. Two techniques are employed for transfers of fire: K-transfer (computation of the coefficient between survey and registration distances, angle of site, drift, and necessary additional corrections for changes of ammunition) when survey has been completed; and direct transfer from a real or an arbitrary check point with or without survey. The first method is applicable to transfers up to 1,650 yards from the check point; the second, up to 330 yards, with a deflection not in excess of 300 mils.

Whenever possible, fire should be transferred immediately after adjustment on a check point. When this is impossible, the correction of two factors must be considered. Adjustments for meteorological conditions must be made within a maximum of 3 to 12 hours, depending inversely on the height of trajectory. Adjustments for change in range of the trajectory due to the heating of tubes and ammunition must be made after 20 to 30 minutes of steady fire. To compensate for this decrease in range, elevations should be raised by one or two sight graduations for ranges of 3 to 6 kilometers; by two to three graduations for longer ranges.

More accurate correction of the transfer results from re-registration executed by the original registration piece. If graphs of the lines of registration distances and deflections have been previously prepared, it is necessary only to fire one check point. The old data are then recomputed proportionally to the new correction. Such re-registration is especially important in unobserved fire.

6. ARTILLERY ANTITANK TACTICS

The destruction of tanks and self-propelled guns is the primary or secondary mission of all artillery, and Red Army crews on all types of artillery are trained in direct fire. The antitank defensive barrages of medium and heavy artillery have been described above under the discussion of types of targets. The primary tank-destroying weapons are, rifle corps and division commanders for the protection of primary sectors. Part of the antitank artillery must always be kept by the Commander of Combined Arms as a reserve. For example, one-fourth of the antitank guns of a rifle division, in-

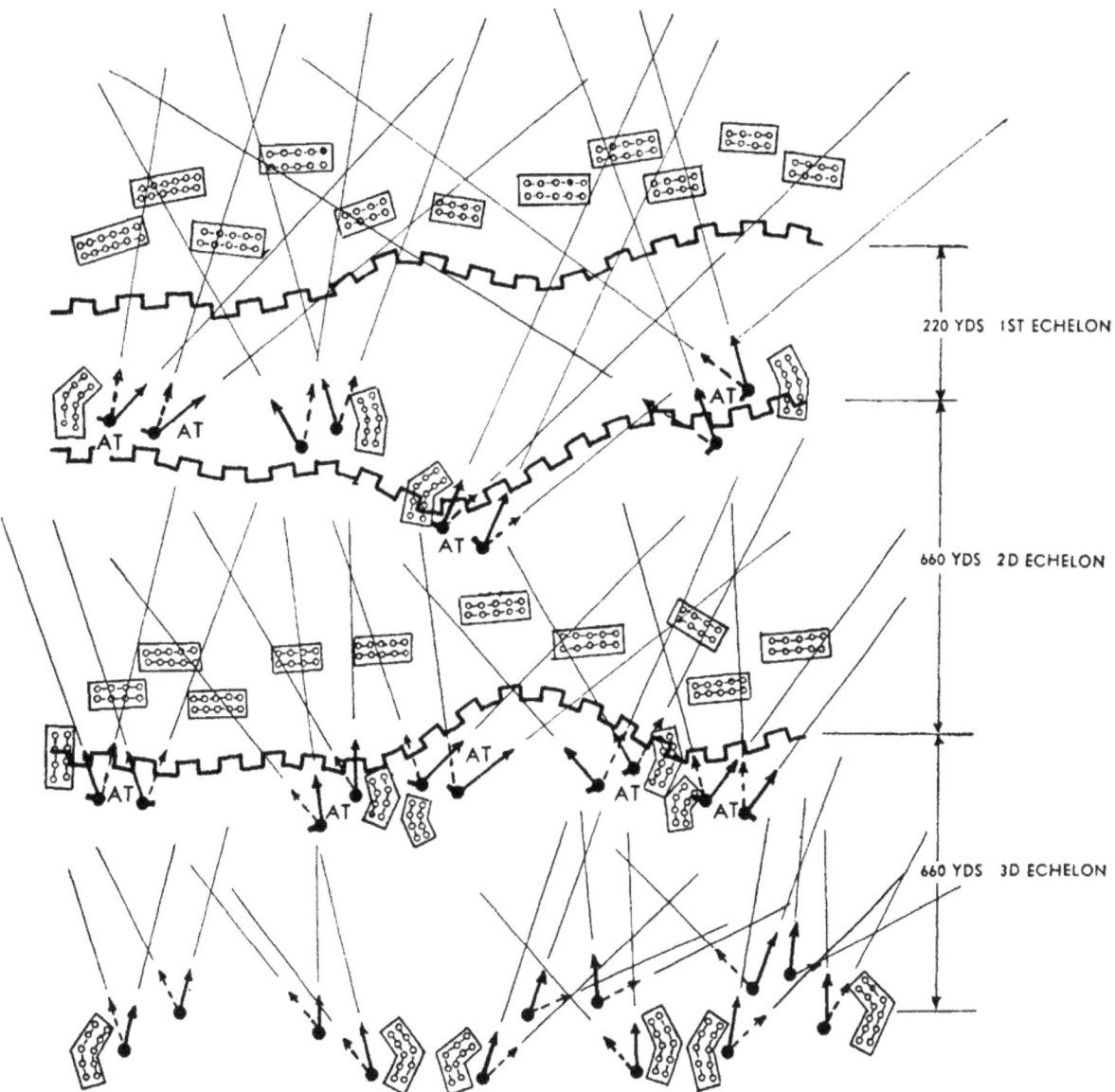

Figure 33. Antitank artillery supplemented by obstacles in a Soviet main battle position.

however, towed antitank guns: 45-mm, 57-mm, 76.2-mm, 85-mm, and 100-mm guns are found in organic and GHQ antitank artillery units. Self-propelled artillery often supports towed antitank guns, particularly in mobile corps; self-propelled artillery tactics are described under section III, Armored and Mechanized Forces.

Antitank artillery regiments are often attached to

cluding regimental and battalion weapons, are held in the mobile divisional antitank gun reserve.

Coordination between antitank artillery and other arms, especially field artillery, mortars, engineers, and infantry, is of prime importance. Antitank artillery regiments are also used as tank support in the area of the main effort.

193

Antitank artillery is usually employed in echelons, with weapons of varied caliber in each to insure equal distribution of fire power. Light and medium antitank artillery is supported as a rule by heavy antitank artillery, such as the newly developed 100-mm gun, for fire against heavy enemy tanks. Lighter guns are emplaced as far forward as practicable, although normally not before the second line of infantry trenches. Well dug-in and camouflaged positions, protected by infantry and antitank rifles, are mandatory. Each battery must have at least one alternate position. When this is occupied, the original position is maintained as a dummy position. Change of position usually takes place at night. Antitank guns in each position are placed in rhombus pattern to obtain all-around fields of fire.

The fire plan of Soviet antitank artillery is carefully worked out, with particular attention given to the natural tank approach routes. The fire of the antitank guns is usually coordinated with a system of ground obstacles erected under engineer control; constant liaison and coordination between antitank artillery and combat engineers is therefore mandatory. Also, minefields normally are laid to protect the gun position itself (fig. 33).

The Soviets compute the minimum required density of antitank weapons in defensive sectors on the basis of the suspected number of enemy tanks, the number and characteristics of tank approaches, and the average number of rounds necessary for a tank kill. On the basis of experience against enemy armor, the Red Army figures on six rounds of fire from 76.2-mm antitank guns, or 12 rounds from 45-mm antitank guns, for the destruction of one medium tank.

Antitank fire is directed not only against tanks, but also against accompanying infantry. Such antipersonnel fire is usually supported by mortar units and automatic weapons in coordination with the antitank artillery.

Antitank guns continue firing until overrun, since the Red Army considers that the destruction of a large number of enemy tanks represents the successful execution of the mission even when all of its own pieces are lost. The Soviets consider that each antitank gun is capable of destroying an average of 2 to 3 enemy tanks before it is put out of action.

As a rule, antitank guns fire at ranges of 550 to 660 yards in order to avoid revealing prematurely the location of positions. However, when a so-called "firesack" is prepared, a limited number of guns (usually flank pieces) open fire at the first enemy tank wave at 1,650- to 2,200 yard ranges, attempting to channelize the enemy tanks into the area of the prepared concentration. Reinforcing self-propelled artillery fires at the tanks from concealed positions; supporting artillery, such as 152-

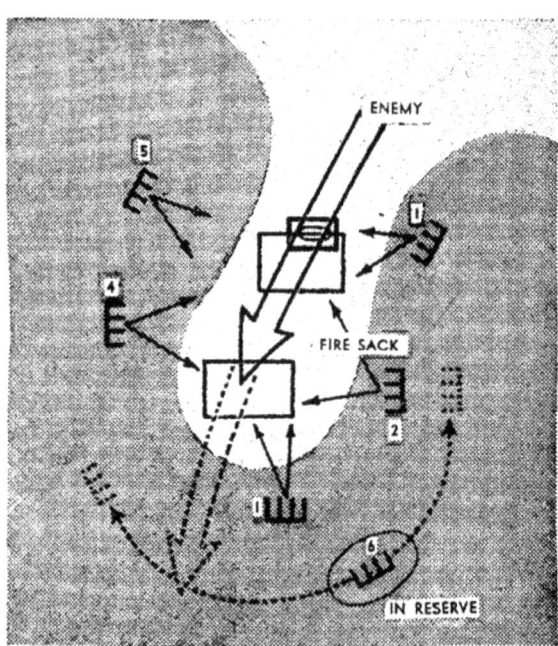

Figure 34. Organization of a firesack by an antitank artillery regiment.

mm howitzers, fires from positions to the rear and flanks of the antitank guns (fig. 34).

The mobile antitank artillery reserve usually consists of one battery from each regiment. It is located to the rear, in the center, and on the flanks of the defense sector under the centralized control of the Commander. Artillery reserves are committed by platoons against enemy tank attacks at the flanks. One platoon will open fire immediately while another moves to a more favorable position, pulled over short distances by the gun crew.

A secondary mission of antitank artillery is its employment in support of infantry and tank attacks, with the bulk of the antitank artillery committed in the first assault echelon (fig. 35).

194

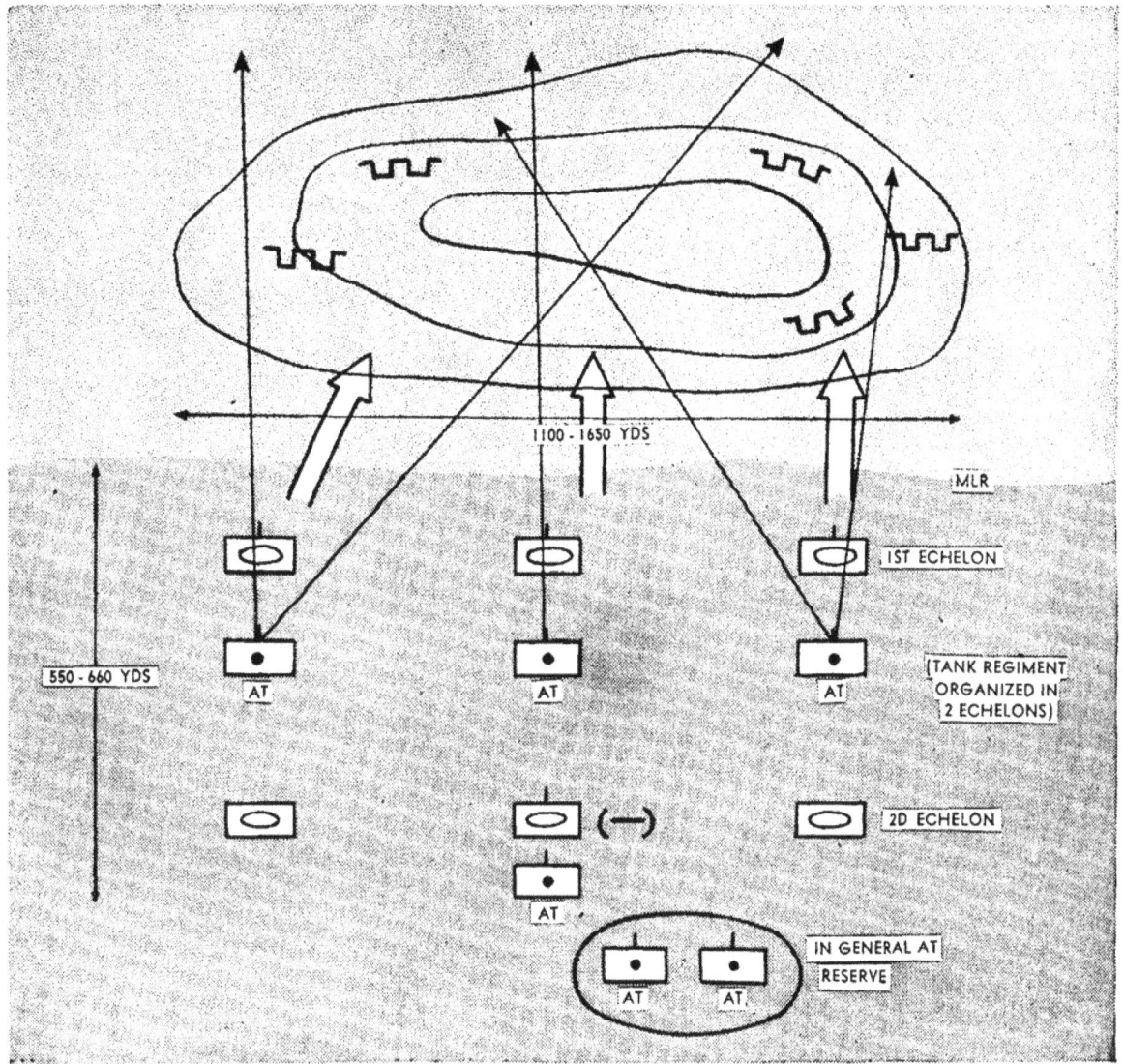

Figure 35. Antitank artillery regiment in support of a tank attack.

Section III. ARMORED AND MECHANIZED FORCES

1. COMBAT MISSIONS

The combat tasks of Soviet armored forces are to deliver decisive blows on a narrow sector, to wedge deeply in the enemy defensive system, and, in co-ordination with other arms, to envelop and destroy large hostile units. The paramount principles of Soviet tank tactics are the continuity of coopera-tion with other arms and full exploitation of tank mobility.

From late 1942 to the end of World War II was a period of definite change in Soviet employment of armor. Soviet strategists believed, in the early part of this period, that the main effort should be made primarily by infantry and that armor should be used in the exploitation of a break-through to develop a pursuit. This tactic, however, seldom was successful, since German defenses were progres-sively deepened to the point where resistance was never completely broken by a penetration of the main line of resistance.

As German defenses stiffened, Soviet armor was more extensively used to effect penetrations; and additional units of armor were used successively to effect exploitation, pursuit, and envelopment.

Current Soviet doctrine requires that all armor be given local protection by infantry, normally riding on the vehicle prior to deployment in order to com-

195

bat concealed infantry traps. Advance engineer detachments and engineer tank riders clear lanes in minefields. In addition, mine-clearing vehicles called "trawlers" (operating on the same principle as the British "Scorpion") have been developed to clear paths for tanks in the assault of strong defensive positions. The enormous depth of German defensive systems with continuous lines and centers of resistance made it necessary for Soviet tank formations to be reinforced by fully mobile infantry, artillery, and mortars in order to regain their momentum against continuous resistance. Self-propelled artillery could not be limited to the role of assault guns but had to be capable of centralized, massed indirect fire. Full-track carriers (Bren gun carriers and Weasels) proved most effective for the transportation of infantry and mortars.

2. ARMORED FORCES AND THEIR CAPABILITIES

Armored forces as large as "tank armies" are found within the Red Army, but the normal operating units are the tank corps and the mechanized corps. These units are usually part of the GHQ reserve to be used by the army or front commander as the situation may demand. They are well balanced units resembling our armored divisions in strength and organization. There are fewer tanks in the Soviet armored units but the medium and heavy tank components, compared to U. S. light and medium tanks, give more weight to the Red Army armored units. Similarly, the Soviet units have less self-propelled artillery but it is of greater caliber length, hence more powerful. The Soviet armored unit has a larger infantry component than the U. S. armored division and also contains heavy mortar units and a rocket battalion which are absent in the U. S. armored division.

The Soviets consider that armored forces are most effectively employed in the enemy operational depth. After intensive artillery preparation, the infantry assault penetrates into enemy defenses. Then, armored forces strike in the direction of the deepest infantry penetration on a narrow front from a concealed centralized position, develop the break-through, and strike at the enemy's rear to destroy him (figs. 36 and 37). The scale of operations may reach mammoth proportions as in the break-through of German defenses on the River Oder by some 4,000 tanks supported by 5,000 planes on a 50-mile front. Large Red Army armored forces advanced as far as 125 miles in 3 days under conditions of continuous and intensive combat against the German Army.

The maneuver of armored forces is limited by extreme terrain conditions such as swamps, thick woods, mountains, and deep snow, but they are not road bound and operate freely over difficult country. In a break-through sector a tank corps moves on a front not wider than 3 miles, but may spread out in the enemy operational depth depending upon the available road nets, terrain, enemy resistance, and assigned objectives.

Rapid transfers of Soviet armored units from one sector to another laterally have been executed on many occasions. These movements have been executed with secrecy and without disrupting the supply lines of units holding the area traversed. The Soviets emphasize that the duration of sustained combat depends upon resupply efficiency. Continuous fuel and ammunition supply can maintain armored units in action for several weeks, but Red Army doctrine prescribes that infantry units must consolidate and hold the territory penetrated by tanks. The cavalry-tank team can increase the tempo of the offensive from 1.5 miles per hour with infantry to 3.5 miles per hour with cavalry.

a. Tank corps. The mission of the tank corps is to destroy enemy infantry and firing positions throughout the depth of the defenses in the break-through sector. The tank corps has great fire and shock power for a frontal attack in a narrow sector, but coordinates its assault with infantry units in that sector. This infantry-tank assault team, aided by intensive artillery preparation, repeatedly spearheaded Soviet offensives.

The major corps units are the three tank brigades, and the motorized infantry brigade, supported by two self-propelled artillery regiments—one regiment each of 76.2-mm antitank artillery, antiaircraft artillery, and 120-mm mortars, a rocket battalion, and a 45-mm antitank battalion.

The tank brigades are the striking elements of the tank corps, and are reinforced by an attached heavy tank regiment when circumstances require maximum shock power. The tank brigade has a strength of about 1,200 men and consists of 65 tanks and a battalion of infantry with antitank rifles, antitank guns, and mortars.

b. Mechanized corps. The mechanized corps is very similar to the tank corps in composition except for its larger infantry component. Three motorized infantry brigades, one tank brigade, and one additional tank regiment give the mechanized corps a strength of 16,000 as compared with 10,300 in the tank corps. The tank corps has two self-pro-

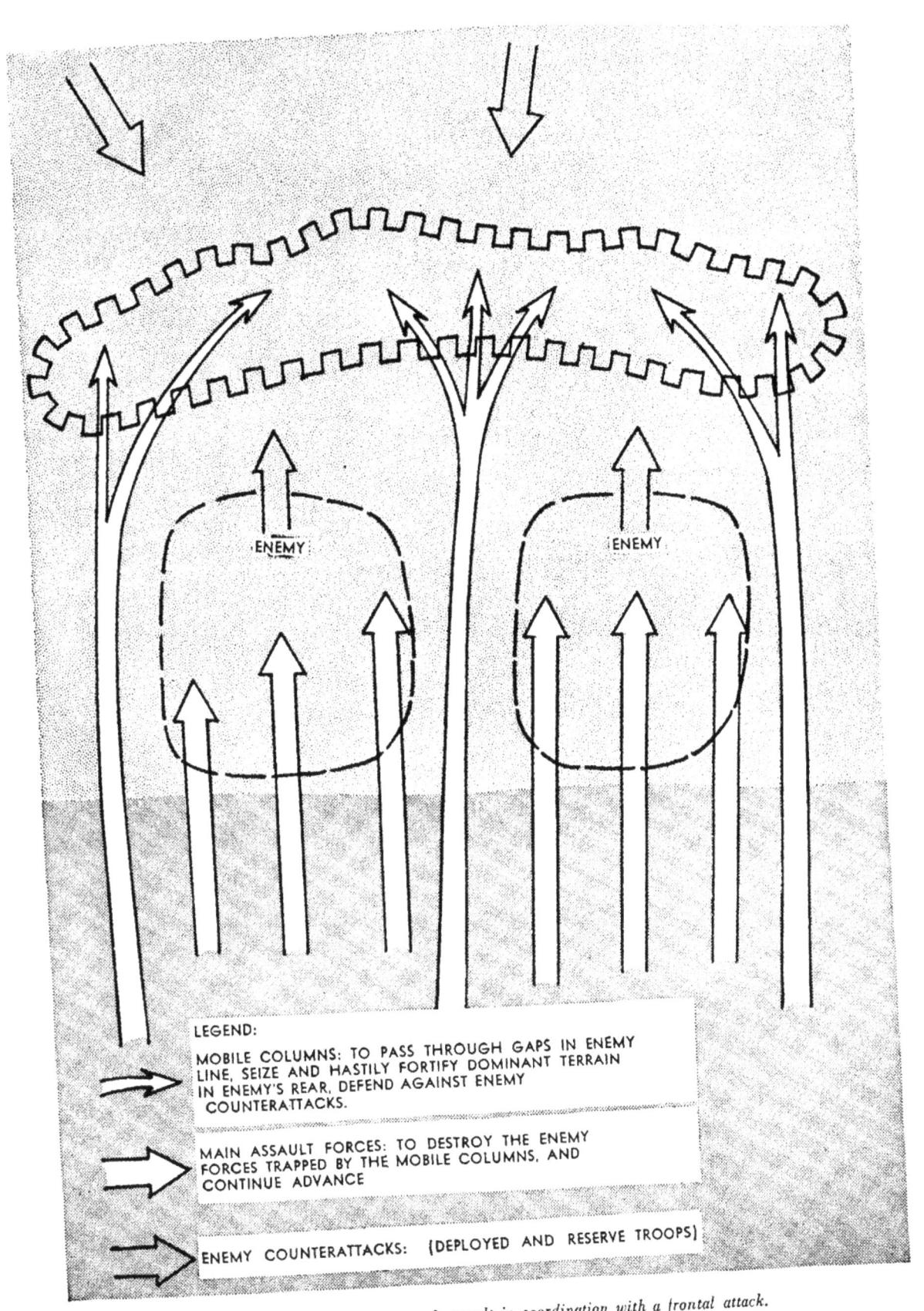

LEGEND:

MOBILE COLUMNS: TO PASS THROUGH GAPS IN ENEMY LINE, SEIZE AND HASTILY FORTIFY DOMINANT TERRAIN IN ENEMY'S REAR, DEFEND AGAINST ENEMY COUNTERATTACKS.

MAIN ASSAULT FORCES: TO DESTROY THE ENEMY FORCES TRAPPED BY THE MOBILE COLUMNS, AND CONTINUE ADVANCE

ENEMY COUNTERATTACKS: (DEPLOYED AND RESERVE TROOPS)

Figure 36. A typical armored assault in coordination with a frontal attack.

197

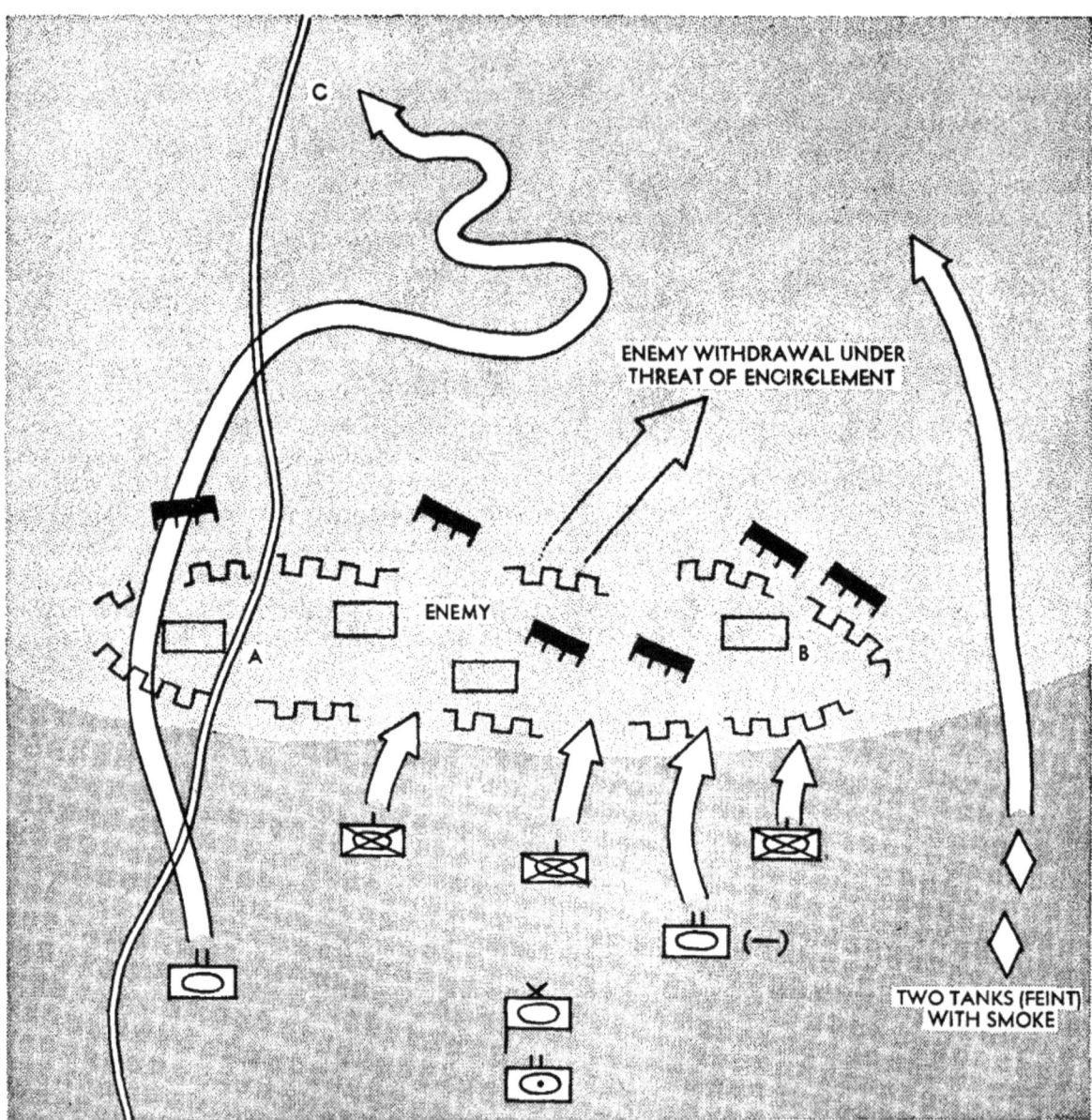

Figure 37. Tank brigade in a coordinated attack.

pelled artillery regiments; the mechanized corps has one.

A mechanized brigade consists of a motorized brigade and one tank regiment of 40 medium tanks. The mechanized corps centralizes control of the four tank regiments but may detach them to support the infantry elements. An additional heavy tank regiment is sometimes attached to the corps.

The mission of the mechanized corps is to exploit break-throughs in organized defenses rather than to accomplish the break-through. It is capable of greater independent action than the tank corps, be-

cause of its balanced strength of infantry and armor which resembles the U. S. combat command in tactical employment.

The average for mechanized corps operations in four major offensives during 1943–44 follows:

Continuous action	46 days
Period of concentration	4 days
In offensive operation	20 days
On defensive	22 days
Percentage of time on defensive	52 percent
Maximum penetration	228 miles
Depth of territory consolidated after counterattacks by enemy reserves	202 miles

198

c. Infantry-support armored units. Small GHQ units, such as the independent heavy tank regiments, are frequently attached to infantry units to support the infantry assault of strong defensive positions. The missions of these tank units are designated by the commander of the infantry unit to which the tanks are attached.

3. ROLES OF COMPONENT ARMS OF ARMORED FORCES

a. Medium tanks. In the Red Army, the medium tank is the basic shock and maneuvering element of all armor. Its primary mission is to assist the infantry in occupying enemy positions and destroying enemy personnel. This mission is usually accomplished by frontal penetration or deep outflanking of enemy positions. In frontal assaults, medium tanks advance on a broad front or in a wide wedge under cover of supporting weapons. They are preceded or closely followed by infantry or engineers who guard the flanks and rear, reconnoitering areas of suspicion. The tanks engage machine guns, infantry heavy weapons, and antitank guns with utmost vigor in order to force the enemy to disclose his entire system of defensive fire. Frontal tank attacks must always be deeply echeloned.

In operations against enemy armor, particularly against heavy tanks and assault guns, medium tanks made full use of their speed and maneuverability, attempting constantly to strike at flanks or rear. The use of medium tanks as tank destroyers from concealed positions is exceptional. Even in defense, tanks are used in a mobile role and particularly to support counterattacks.

b. Heavy tanks. Heavy tanks are used in mass in the direction of the main effort, and always in coordination with medium tanks which protect their flanks and rear. Medium tanks force commitment of enemy antitank weapons which are then destroyed by heavy tank fire. In operations against armor, particularly medium tanks, the heavy tanks attack frontally, while accompanying medium tanks envelop the enemy flanks and rear. Only in the support of assault groups destroying emplacements are heavy tanks used in small separate detachments of 2 or 3 tanks. Infantry must always support heavy tanks. When enemy opposition is severe, heavy tanks reinforce medium tanks by attacking heavy enemy tanks, self-propelled artillery, antitank and field artillery, and permanent fortifications. They depend primarily upon long-range, flat-trajectory, direct fire from short halts.

c. Self-propelled artillery. Self-propelled artillery provides security for tanks by protecting their flanks and rear against armored counterattacks. They operate from hull defilade or concealed positions, covering probable avenues of tank approach. Unlike towed antitank guns, which fire in place until either they or enemy tanks have been neutralized, Soviet self-propelled guns utilize their mobility and speed repeatedly to outflank attacking tanks. They must, however, be provided with automatic weapons and antitank rifle protection against enemy infantry. In frontal assaults, self-propelled guns follow tanks (at approximately 400 yards) by moving from cover to cover.

They also support infantry in the reduction of by-passed field or light permanent fortifications. Heavy self-propelled guns reinforce the fire of medium self-propelled howitzers and tank destroyers. Their heavier armor permits more aggressive tank-like tactics. Their great fire power makes them extremely effective against all armored vehicles, artillery, and permanent fortifications. Low rates of fire and limited ammunition capacity are their principal weaknesses.

d. Mine-clearing tanks. Flail-type mine clearing tanks are employed to clear lanes through enemy minefields as rapidly as possible in order to facilitate the uninterrupted forward progress of tanks and self-propelled guns. Mine-clearing tanks approach the line of departure from concealed positions during the artillery preparation phase and take lead positions in the infantry tank-support groups. Two or three mine-clearing tanks are used for clearing each lane. Close support by tanks, self-propelled guns, mortars, and pioneers (combat engineers) is always provided to protect the mine-clearing tanks from enemy fire covering the minefield. Assault tanks follow mine-clearing tanks within 60 yards. The pioneers from the first echelon of the tank support group move forward with the mine-clearing tanks, using visual signals for working with the tanks. The pioneers remove mines from sectors of the field inaccessible to mine-clearing tanks, remove tank obstacles, and assault prepared enemy engineer fortifications under fire cover of the mine-clearing tanks and assault tanks. After passing through a minefield, the mine-clearing tanks assemble in a concealed area to reorganize for succeeding missions, while the assault groups move forward.

e. Artillery and mortars. Close artillery support is delivered to tank formations at all times. Great flexibility in the control of artillery is normal when it moves forward into the penetration area. After the artillery preparation, which is the normal initial artillery mission for all artillery and mortars, long-range army artillery units continue to support the armored assault for depths up to 5 or 6 miles. Direct army artillery support of the armored unit ceases at this point, and other missions are executed—such as counterbattery fire against enemy positions on the flanks of the break-through area. The mobile artillery units continue to deliver fire against enemy strongpoints encountered in the penetration area and on the flanks, as directed by the supported armored unit commanders. One of the most important Soviet artillery missions is to combat counterattacking enemy tanks. Fire against strongpoints is delivered in short area concentrations. Not less than one unit of fire is allotted to artillery for the assault phase of the armored offensive. Approximately one brigade of artillery supports each tank brigade of the first corps echelon. The 152-mm gun-howitzers and the 122-mm guns are deemed especially effective in supporting tanks against strong resistance.

Heavy mortars are always employed in support of motorized infantry. The battery commanders' observation posts are well forward within $\frac{1}{2}$ to 1 mile of the advance units. Control is decentralized to battery commanders; larger concentrations are developed when enemy resistance slows down the advance. The heavy mortars are always used in supporting the independent operations of motorized infantry, as well as during the break-through phase.

f. Rocket units. The rocket battalion is under the control of the corps commander throughout the entire operation. Rocket units are used only at critical times. The launchers are brought to their firing positions secretly and are fired in sudden concentrations. Rocket units are used for independent operations of the armored corps, against enemy counterattacks, and during the general artillery preparation for the corps offensive.

g. Infantry component. The infantry component of the armored corps is not entirely concentrated in the motorized infantry brigades, but has infantry groups for local security of tanks and self-propelled guns. The motorized submachine-gun battalion of the tank brigade has a tank-riding company as well as a mortar, antitank gun, antitank rifle, and an automatic-weapons company. These infantrymen facilitate the advance of armor by neutralizing enemy infantry antitank weapons and traps; they

also organize small defensive positions against enemy counterattacks.

h. Engineer troops. Engineer troops of the armored corps are used especially in small units as tank riders and with the leading motorized elements. Their primary duties are to clear enemy mines and obstacles, to facilitate the advance of armored vehicles, and to assist in the reduction of strongpoints with demolitions, flame throwers, and other engineer assault equipment. In defending armor against counterattacks, special hasty mine-laying techniques are employed using both controlled and contact type mines. The corps engineer battalion is capable of other types of engineer support as well.

4. ARMORED AND MECHANIZED FORCES IN THE OFFENSIVE

The armored offensive differs from the infantry offensive in the following respects: The main effort of the armored offensive is made on a relatively narrow front by a deeply echeloned formation with the objective of completely breaking through enemy defensive positions and exploiting the break-through by attacking enemy rear installations, encircling and destroying enemy forces, and generally effecting deep penetrations. The break-through operation of large armored units passes through five distinct phases: Concentration of forces, fire preparation, the assault, securing the offensive, and exploitation (fig. 38).

a. Concentration phase. This phase involves movement of units, the dispersal of units, and very extensive planning of coordinated action of all arms for all phases of the offensive. Carefully planned lateral movements of armored units from adjacent sectors to the concentration area are executed at night for distances up to 60 miles. Special traffic controls insure regulated movement across the supply lines of adjacent front-line units with minimum interruption. Usually the armored formation moves in at least two columns, with tanks and self-propelled artillery to the front, and the remaining columns of wheeled vehicles and tank corps reserves moving on interior roads.

The concentration is usually 25 to 50 miles from the front lines (fig. 39). The concentration phase varies in duration from 3 to 8 days, during which time coordination of all arms is based on information obtained from reconnaissance units and observers. The reconnaissance group of the tank or mechanized corps, the various artillery observation and survey detachments, engineer reconnaissance

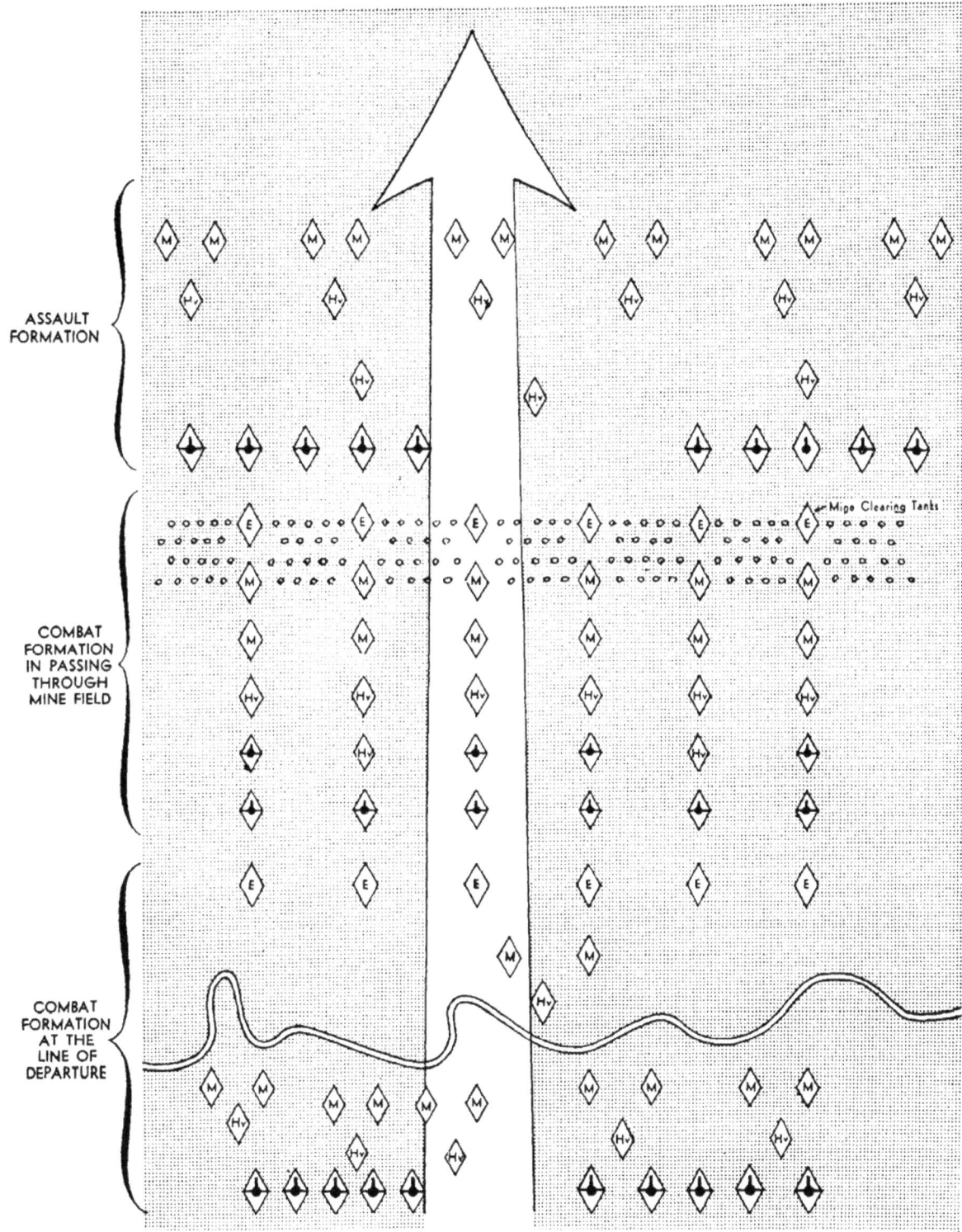

Figure 38. Tank brigade in break-through operations.

201

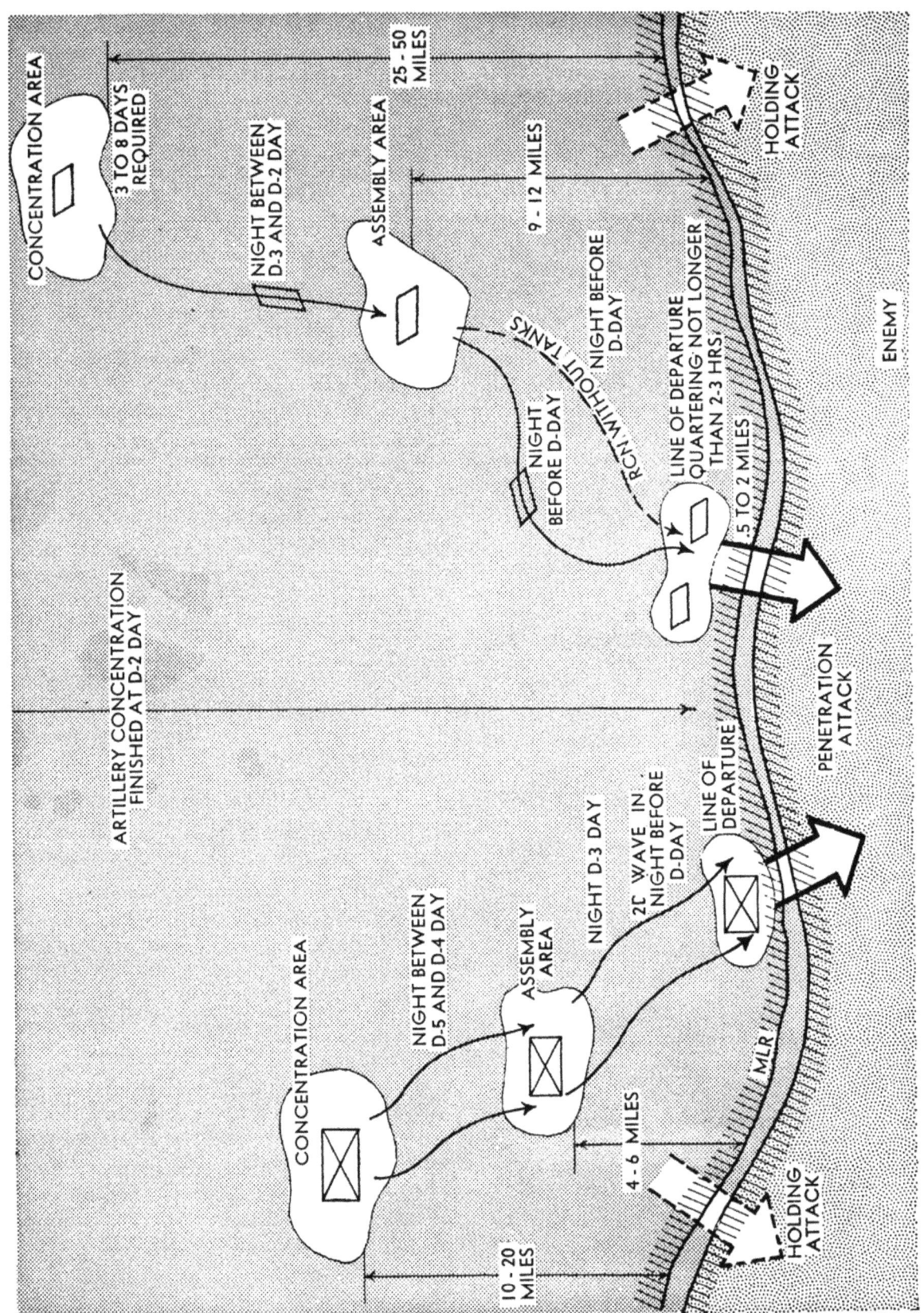

Figure 39. Concentration of armored forces and infantry for offensive operations.

202

units, and infantry patrols conduct intensive uninterrupted operations in the break-through sector. Specific information vital to the armored force offensive is obtained by ground observation of engineer and tank reconnaissance units. This information includes:

> Terrain throughout the enemy defensive depth with respect to the maneuver of armored units.
> Location and extent of the enemy fortifications strongpoints (especially antitank-gun emplacements) and troop dispositions.
> Routes of withdrawal available to the enemy.

Air reconnaissance supplements this information by determining the possible directions of enemy tank counterattacks, the location of tank reserves, and other pertinent data. The various artillery reconnaissance groups and observation posts determine the location of artillery targets and firing plan of the artillery offensive.

b. Fire preparation phase. This phase varies in duration from several hours to several days, depending entirely on the extent of the enemy defensive position. The tank corps attacks independently only in a sector where enemy defenses are relatively weak. Then a short intensive artillery preparation, immediately followed by the tank assault, combine the shock power and surprise necessary to achieve a break-through. Otherwise, an extended infantry-artillery attack is necessary to breach the enemy defensive position. Large armored formations move forward from the concentration area to the assembly area, which is 9 to 12 miles from the enemy front lines, prior to the period of artillery preparation. This movement is made by echelons during the night between D-minus 2 and D-minus 3 days.

c. Assault phase. During the period of artillery preparation on the night before D-day, the armored formation advances to its jump-off position, located from ½ to 2 miles from the enemy front line. Assault groups are organized from infantry, engineers, and tanks for infantry support. These groups vary in size from infantry companies to regiments and are supported by tanks from independent battalions, regiments, and brigades. Coordination between elements of the assault groups, the following echelons, and supporting artillery is worked out in detail. The mission of the assault group is to destroy enemy firing positions and fortifications which the

artillery preparation failed to neutralize, and to clear lanes in minefields.

The first echelon of medium tanks follows immediately behind the assault groups, together with mine-clearing tanks which clear lanes through minefields, and attacks enemy positions by direct fire and flank maneuvers. The first infantry echelon follows the tanks at a distance of 200 to 400 yards. The second echelon of tanks consists of heavy tanks and self-propelled artillery moving behind the infantry at a distance of 100 to 200 yards. These tanks and self-propelled artillery support both the infantry and the medium tanks of the first echelon. The artillery-support group and the second infantry echelon follow behind the heavy tanks (fig. 40).

Enemy defensive positions, 3 to 5 miles deep, often consist of multiple belts containing lines of trenches and numerous strongpoints. The immediate objective of the infantry-support tank group, together with the first infantry echelon and assault groups, is to seize the first two trench lines of the forward defense belt. The immediate objective of the infantry group (infantry strength of about one division) of the first corps echelon is to penetrate the entire forward defensive belt, including enemy battalion reserve positions and all strongpoints between the forward and the second defense belts. Successive missions of the group, reinforced by armor and infantry of the second corps echelon, are to penetrate the second and remaining enemy defensive belts. The assault of an armored corps takes place on a sector not less than 3 miles wide. Tanks in the first echelon move in bounds from phase line to phase line, from 1,000 to 2,000 yards apart.

d. Securing the offensive. The closest contact is maintained between combat arms of each echelon and with supporting echelons, in order that enemy counterattacks may be effectively repulsed by tanks and self-propelled artillery. The speed of the offensive is maintained by centralizing the control of self-propelled artillery in support of tank battalions when enemy counterattacks are imminent. Infantry with engineers, supported by mortars and artillery support groups, seize and fortify all vital positions on the flanks of the break-through area. Enemy firing positions on the flanks are neutralized, and hasty mine belts are placed across flank approaches. Flank security groups organize road blocks, covering the approaches by artillery and mortar fire.

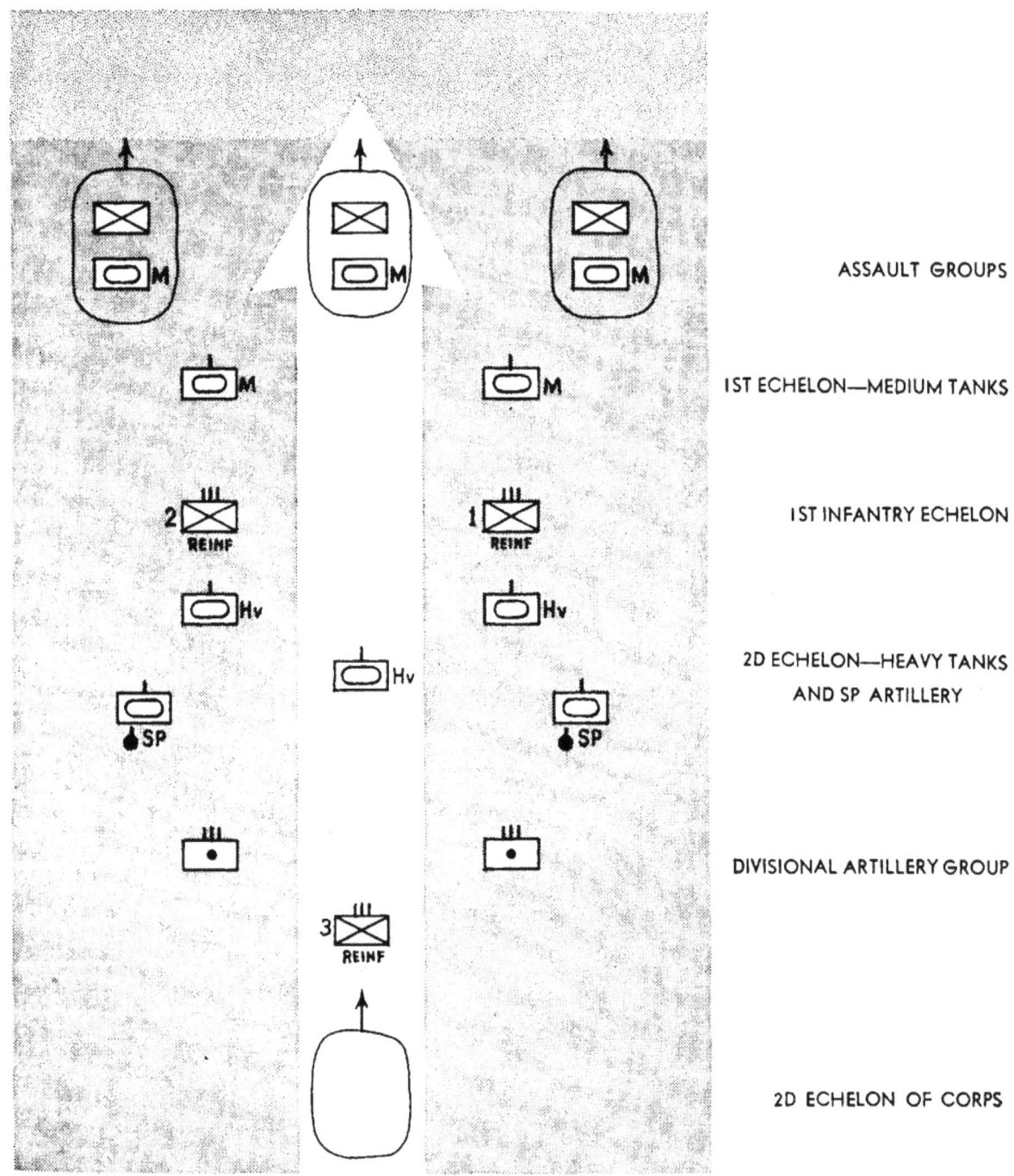

ASSAULT GROUPS

1ST ECHELON—MEDIUM TANKS

1ST INFANTRY ECHELON

2D ECHELON—HEAVY TANKS
AND SP ARTILLERY

DIVISIONAL ARTILLERY GROUP

2D ECHELON OF CORPS

Figure 40. Combat formation of tank-supported infantry in the first phase of break-through operations.

The second echelon of the tank or mechanized corps similarly organizes strong flank protection and may use rockets as well as mortars and artillery to repel enemy infantry attacks. As the offensive penetrates deeper into enemy defenses, screening groups supplement flank security groups to facilitate rapid forward movement of motorized infantry and supply trains (fig. 41).

e. **Exploitation.** The tank corps in exploitation advances rapidly toward a series of terrain objectives such as crossroads, bridges, and dominant terrain features. Enemy lines of communication are cut, supply dumps are seized, and the enemy is attacked on the flanks and rear with the intent of cutting enemy units into many segments which are encircled and destroyed. If several break-throughs

204

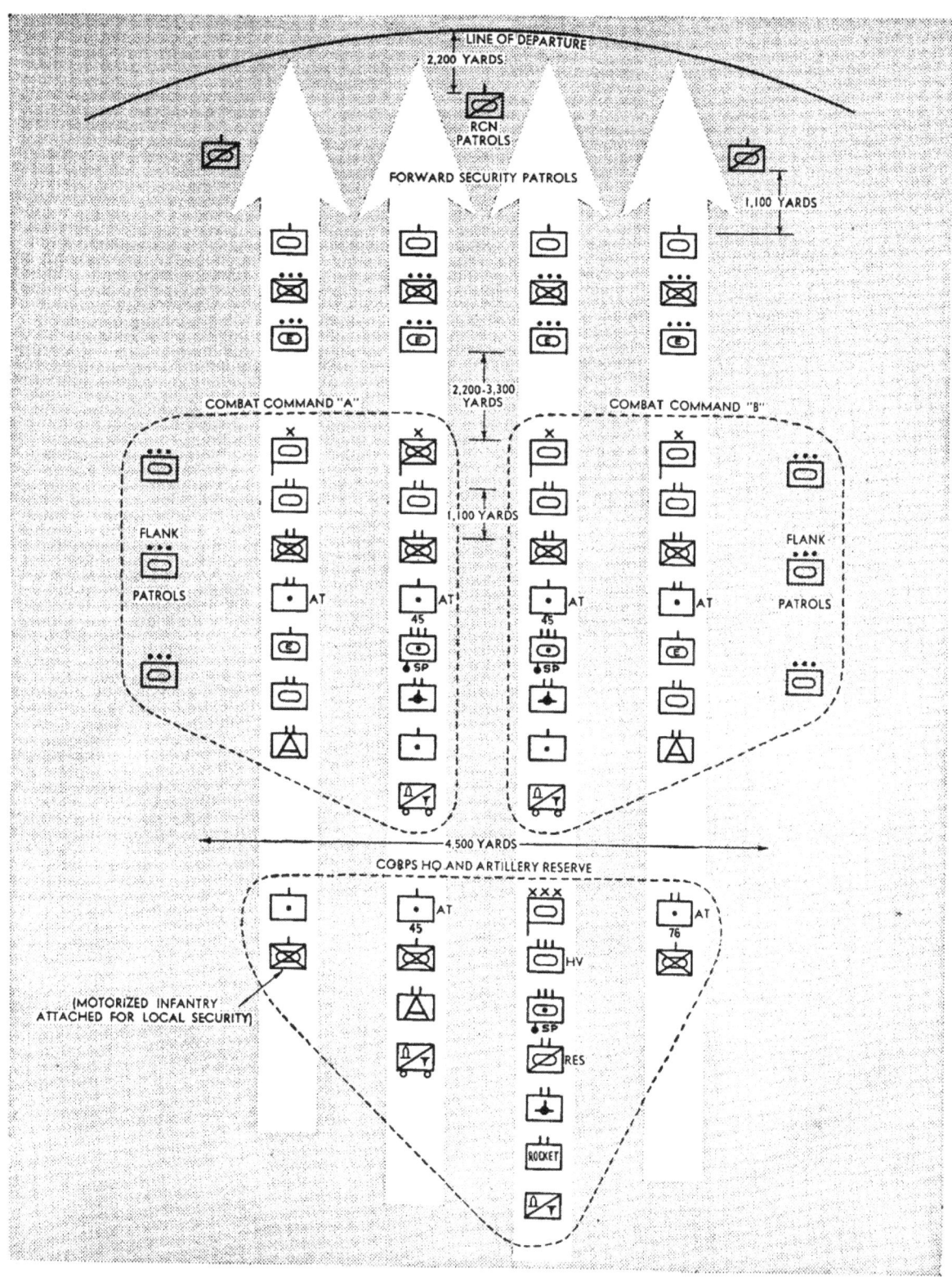

Figure 41. The corps organization in an approach march.

205

are made, the tank forces exploiting each converge in a double envelopment.

ADVANCE UNITS. In exploitation the tank corps sends forward the bulk of its tactical reconnaissance units, including the armored car reconnaissance battalion and the motorcycle battalion, often reinforced by a tank company. The group operates 10 to 15 miles in advance of the medium tanks in the first echelon. The security reconnaissance detachment of each tank brigade operates 6 to 9 miles in advance of the brigade and consists of motorcyclists, motorized infantry, armored cars, and a tank platoon sometimes reinforced by antitank guns. The reconnaissance detachment of the motorized infantry battalion operates 3 to 4 miles forward and consists of a squad of motorcyclists or motorized infantry. Flank security detachments, drawn from the reconnaissance reserves, are used for flank defense and to destroy by-passed strongpoints. They consist of a platoon of tanks, armored cars, and a squad of motorized infantry and engineers.

The mechanized corps has far greater capabilities for extensive exploitation than the tank corps, due to the powerful motorized infantry component which is added to its armored strength. The mechanized corps invariably has been employed in every major offensive operation, not only to exploit break-throughs but to develop the break-through into pursuit. Air support of armored units has progressively increased with Soviet air supremacy and the close coordination of these arms has resulted in more rapid penetration and encirclement of enemy positions.

EXPLOITATION OBJECTIVES. During the exploitation period, mechanized units encounter the enemy's tactical reserves and also rear reserves rushed up by motor, rail, or even air. Therefore, in the process of exploitation mechanized units have to carry out bitter actions, sometimes to defend themselves, sometimes to disengage themselves. All actions are carried out with the following goals in mind: to retain the initiative, to defeat the pursued enemy in detail, and to surround and destroy his reserves after cutting them off. The job of complete liquidation is left to regular front-line troops, while the mechanized units go on to exploit the new success.

PURSUIT. This strategy is organized in accordance with the possible routes of enemy withdrawal, the terrain features, and indications of enemy withdrawal prior to the disengagement of his main forces. Soviet units selected for pursuit are very mobile and capable of independent action. The basic composition of each detachment includes medium tanks, reinforced by assault troops with automatic weapons, motorcyclists, motorized infantry, artillery, and engineers. Parallel pursuit is emphasized in Soviet doctrine. Enemy rear guards and organized defensive positions try to turn parallel pursuit into a pursuit from the rear; thus parallel pursuit consists of a series of actions, partly frontal and partly flanking. Advanced detachments delay and hold up the enemy's withdrawal in order to give the main forces an opportunity to overtake and destroy him (fig. 42). At the same time, advanced troops, who have penetrated to the rear of the withdrawing enemy, attack command posts, destroy supplies, rupture communications, and create panic by surprise thrusts.

The main body operates on the flank of the withdrawing enemy or in the space between withdrawing columns. The combat formation of the main body covers the area of the main effort. Strong reserves, consisting of tanks, self-propelled artillery, and motorized infantry, are held in readiness to engage enemy reserves which may be committed. If separate strongpoints succeed in resisting direct assaults, the main body by-passes them, leaving motorized-infantry groups to cover such strongpoints until the arrival of troops following the mechanized corps.

Air support is considered vital to successful pursuit operations. Air action destroys enemy reserves advancing to engage the pursuing forces. Stormovik units are especially effective in giving close support to advance detachments. Pursuit must be maintained night and day, stopping only on orders of the Commander or when fuel supplies are exhausted. Every expedient is used to maintain supplies, including mobile corps supply units, air drops, and captured enemy supplies. Fresh troops from the armored corps reserve are held in readiness to be sent forward on combat reconnaissance missions.

5. MEETING ENGAGEMENT

The deployment of Red Army armored units in a meeting engagement varies greatly, depending upon enemy strength. During pursuit, counterattacking enemy rear guards are repulsed by combat reconnaissance groups reinforced by medium tanks, self-propelled artillery, mortars, rockets, and motorized infantry of the first echelon. The main body continues the pursuit without deploying its forces,

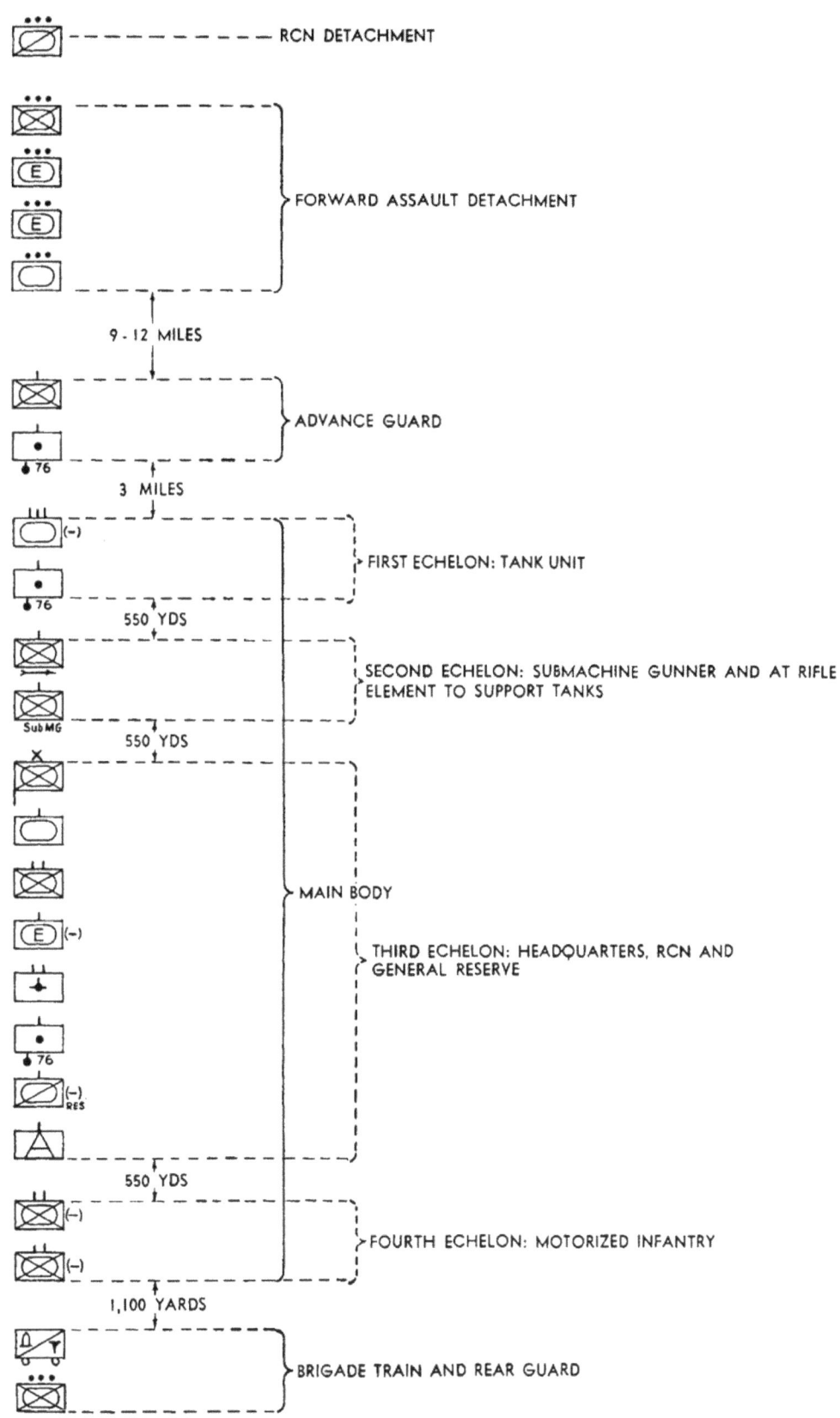

Figure 42. Mechanized brigade organization in pursuit.

207

although other combat reconnaissance units will be organized to replace the units detached.

When superior enemy forces are encountered, a powerful combat group of tanks and self-propelled artillery assaults the forward enemy elements in a short thrust designed to permit the mechanized corps to deploy in a favorable defensive position.

The corps deploys along a wide front with combat groups occupying separate, favorable terrain features. The groups are organized for hasty defense, with infantry supported by artillery, mortars, and self-propelled guns in the forward echelon, while the tanks are assigned to the second echelon as reserves and for defense of the rear. Motorized infantry occupies the gaps between strongpoints, which are also covered by artillery and mortar fire. The corps reserve deploys to the rear of the position, ready to move against any likely direction of enemy attack. Air reconnaissance and the advance reconnaissance group, 9 to 15 miles ahead of the advance guard, give armored formations timely information concerning enemy strength, movements, and dispositions. This information enables the formation to deploy to greatest advantage in the meeting engagement.

6. THE DEFENSIVE

In independent operations, the tank corps and the mechanized corps are frequently counterattacked by superior enemy forces, especially after deep penetrations following a break-through. The defensive mission generally is to hold seized territory against enemy counterattack until the combined forces following the armored units arrive to secure the area.

a. Tank corps. The tanks corps is limited in its capacity for protracted defense. The infantry component of the corps is relatively small, and tanks used in fixed positions are not as efficient as when their high mobility and shock power are fully employed. The self-propelled artillery, antitank guns, mortars, and rockets are the core of defensive strength; but superior enemy infantry units, supported by armor and artillery, can force the tank corps to withdraw by outflanking the defensive position. Soviet doctrine emphasizes the tank corps has not sufficient infantry to risk encirclement for any length of time. The mechanized corps, on the other hand, is well organized for independent action far forward of the advancing main forces and passes from the offensive to the defensive in every major operation involving deep offensive thrusts into enemy territory.

b. Mechanized Corps. The organization of defenses by the Soviet mechanized corps is as thorough as its combat potential, favorable terrain, the strength of enemy counterattacks, and time permit. Extensive mine belts and fields are laid by engineers; antitank gun positions and mortar positions are emplaced in a fire system integrated with self-propelled artillery and rocket launchers. All firing positions, infantry positions, and transport vehicles are camouflaged to the fullest degree. A second defensive position to the rear is developed as thoroughly as time permits, at the next tactically advantageous area.

The mechanized corps can resist enemy attacks from an encircled position for several days. If the position to be held is of great tactical value, the mechanized corps remains in position, permitting the enemy to effect an encirclement, rather than withdrawing. This is achieved with the expectation that advancing strong, friendly forces will relieve the mechanized corps within a reasonable time.

The defensive position consists of groups of motorized infantry in separate strongpoints located in advantageous terrain. Each group contains about a battalion of infantry supported by two or three batteries of antitank artillery, mortars, and self-propelled artillery and tanks. The self-propelled guns and tanks are distributed within the groups in accordance with the most likely avenues of enemy approach and the terrain cover available. Three tank reserve groups consisting of medium and heavy tanks are held in centralized, concealed areas. Their mission is to counterattack enemy forces which penetrate into the defenses through the gaps between the strongpoints. The gaps are held lightly by motorized infantry but are covered by artillery fire from adjacent strongpoints, as well as by the corps artillery group deployed to the rear of the tank reserve group. The corps reserve, together with all supply echelons, is in the rear area of the defensive position and is protected by the remaining tank units from flank and rear attacks. Forward defenses in two echelons are most effective, provided sufficient personnel strength is available. Successful defense is largely dependent upon the efficient operation of the tank reserve groups which cover a wider front than the first defense echelon and must be ready to attack enemy forces at all points of penetration (fig. 43).

The defensive strength of the mechanized corps is greatly increased by the attachment of a howitzer regiment. The strength of air support and expectations of supply by air greatly influence the corps commander's decision to hold a position or to withdraw. The antiaircraft regiment deploys its guns to protect the main body of the corps from hostile armored formation is held in a concealed centralized position 10 to 30 miles to the rear of the first infantry echelon. When the direction of the enemy main effort is determined, the armored formation

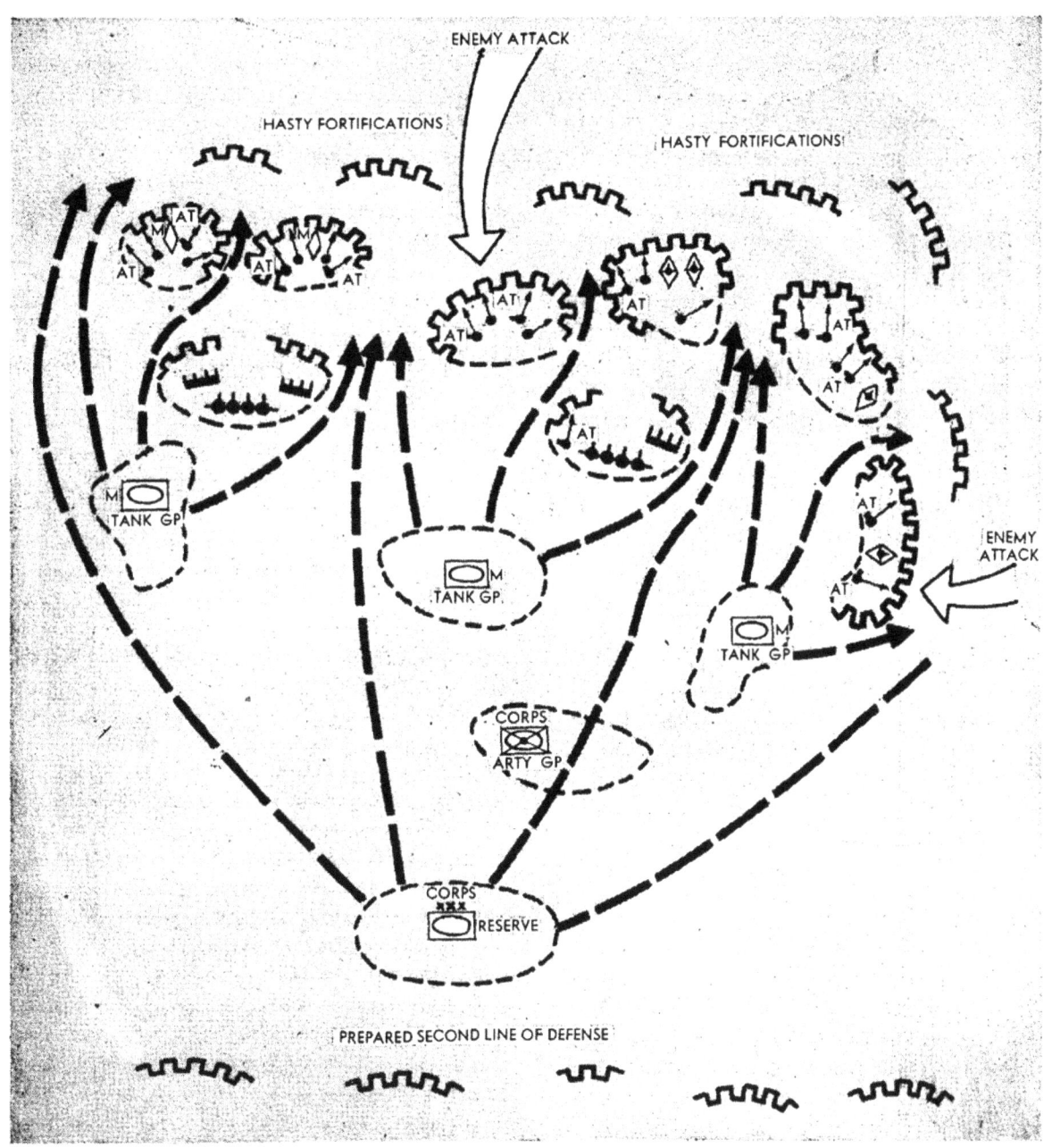

Figure 43. Defensive position of a mechanized corps.

air attack. Antiaircraft artillery is also given the role of covering the gaps between strongpoints where enemy ground forces are likely to penetrate.

c. Other defensive tactics. Armored units, supporting infantry in decentralized systems of defense, are used as mobile counterattack groups. The

moves forward in a wide flanking maneuver and attacks the enemy's flank and rear.

Another type of ambush defense is used when a fluid situation exists and defensive positions have not been firmly organized. Tank units concentrate in concealed areas adjacent to main approaches along which enemy forces are advancing. Terrain conditions determine whether two groups of tanks in flanking positions or one concentrated group is better suited to deliver sudden flank attacks against enemy assault spearheads. Tank-riding automatic riflemen and self-propelled guns support the tanks in destroying the enemy assault elements. The mission of armor in this type of Soviet defense is to protect infantry units withdrawing under enemy pressure, as well as to inflict the maximum losses on the enemy and thus disrupt his offensive operations.

7. WITHDRAWALS

If possible, withdrawals are executed at night, and to prepared positions. Daytime withdrawals are made under the cover of a smoke screen. Soviet daytime withdrawals often coincide with a sudden limited counterattack of a strong tank group, supported by self-propelled artillery, in the direction of the enemy main effort. Soviet doctrine prescribes that withdrawals be executed rapidly by echelons, without lessening normal artillery fire. Mobile armored groups cover the withdrawal by counterattacks if the enemy attempts to interfere.

Section IV. CAVALRY

1. CAVALRY MISSIONS AND CAPABILITIES

a. Basic doctrine. The Red Army has retained the cavalry arm for use as an independent striking force. The fundamental doctrine in the employment of cavalry stresses that cavalry is not a substitute for mechanized forces but is a powerful force for operations where motorized units are handicapped by impassable terrain. By Red Army definition, the cavalry is capable of independent operation, of taking part in every kind of engagement, and of carrying out actions in every kind of cooperation with other arms. A basic difference between Red Army cavalry tactics and U. S. cavalry doctrine is the stress placed by the Soviets on the employment of artillery with cavalry. Divisional artillery operating with cavalry is employed under centralized or decentralized control, depending on combat requirements. The primary mission of divisional artillery is the neutralization of enemy antitank guns, personnel, machine-gun positions, and similar ground targets.

The tactical employment of cavalry in night operations and in terrain impassable to motorized elements such as swamps, steppes, and deep snow was repeatedly and successfully carried out by the Red Army in World War II.

b. Capabilities. Cavalry averages 5 miles per hour over severe terrain. Small independent cavalry units cannot maintain continuous movement for more than 3 days under combat conditions. Large units with sizable supply trains and established resupply systems can operate for more than a month over distances of 100 miles. Whenever possible, cavalry forces attempt to strike the enemy flank or rear, and to encircle and destroy the main group in cooperation with the air forces, armored units, airborne units, and frontal assault groups. Other cavalry missions include: large-scale raids by cavalry divisions and corps, especially during the winter; the screening of troop movements of other arms; and the execution of counterattacks against the enemy flanks and rear from concealed areas in the rear of a defensive position.

Soviet cavalry raids extend to far greater depths and are made by larger forces than are envisioned by the definition of a raid in U. S. cavalry doctrine. For example, Lieutenant General Sokolov's VI Guard Cossack Cavalry Corps made a 135-day raid and fought behind the enemy lines most of the time.

c. Cavalry in auxiliary role. The tactical employment of small cavalry units for reconnaissance, counterreconnaissance, screening, and patrol missions is essentially the same in the Red Army as in other armies. Emphasizing the cavalry's surprise potential, however, the Soviet's place added significance on more extensive employment of night reconnaissance and night raiding parties, especially when terrain and weather are favorable to cavalry tactics. Assaults are generally made dismounted from all sides after rapid and secret flanking movements have been executed (fig. 44). Heavy machine guns—mounted on carts—light machine guns, and submachine guns constitute the greatest fire power of small cavalry units.

Normally, a cavalry regiment operates from 1 to 3 days in a local area up to 15 miles in depth. The objectives are local enemy command posts, artillery or antitank batteries, small relatively undefended garrisons in the enemy rear, and the capture of prisoners.

2. CAVALRY UNITS AND BASIC WEAPONS

Red Army cavalry was modified greatly before and during World War II. The cavalry divisions have shrunk to a strength of 4,645 officers and enlisted men, losing their mechanized regiment and one of

210

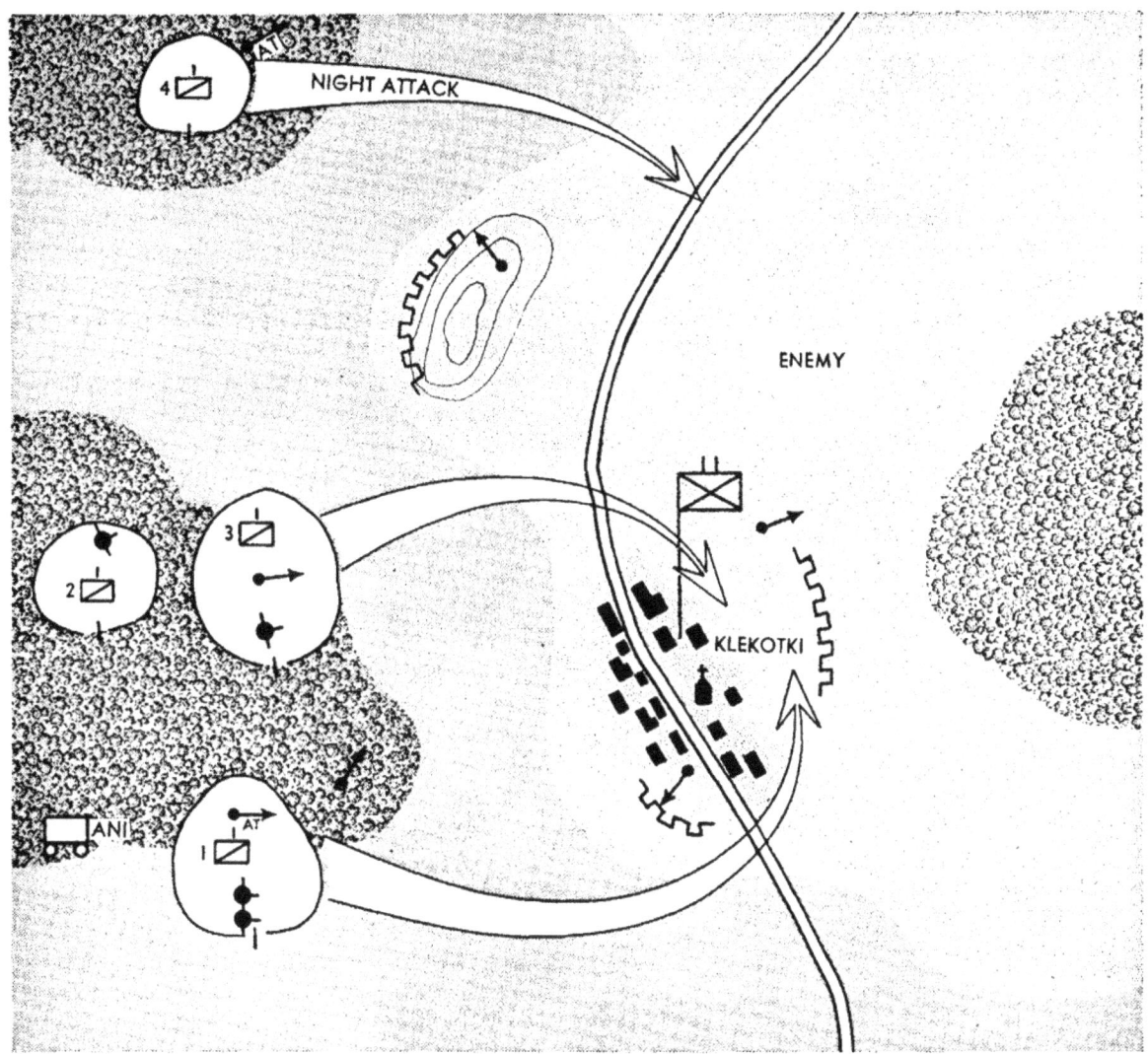

Figure 44. Cavalry regiment attack in winter.

their horse regiments. Medium and heavy mortars, and submachine guns have been introduced in large numbers. The number of antitank guns has been increased. The introduction of antitank rifles has further facilitated close antitank and antiaircraft defense. The normal operating unit is the cavalry corps, which consists of three cavalry divisions, two to four tank regiments of 41 tanks each, an antitank regiment, either a composite artillery regiment or a mortar regiment, and a rocket battalion. Additional tank reinforcements are normally added for large-scale operations.

Cavalry units are well equipped to protect themselves against enemy armored attacks, although their staying power under such circumstances is limited. The 14.5-mm long-barrelled antitank rifle carried by pack horse provides antitank protection within

the squadron. The horse-drawn 45-mm gun is the regimental antitank weapon, while the 76-mm field artillery pieces, as well as the 120-mm mortar batteries, are brought into play where necessary. The Corps has considerable protection against enemy armor in the 76-mm gun antitank regiment, the self-propelled artillery regiment, and the composite artillery and mortar regiment. The rocket battalion and the mortar units provide effective antipersonnel fire.

The vulnerability of cavalry to air attack is the greatest single weakness of cavalry units. To counteract this vulnerability, the cavalry division has been strengthened in antiaircraft fire power to nine multiple antiaircraft machine guns and six 37-mm antiaircraft guns, while the corps is reinforced by an antiaircraft artillery regiment in operation

211

where enemy air attacks are likely. As the relative strength of the Soviet Air Force increased, cavalry operations were given effective fighter support by the air forces of the army group. In some instances, supporting fighter units have been attached to the cavalry corps. In the first case, an aviation liaison officer maintains continuous liaison between the corps and the army group headquarters, whereas in the second case no such liaison exists. Night marches are stressed for cavalry, especially in winter, with movements planned to conceal the cavalry during the day in such covered or camouflaged areas as collective farms.

General Belov's cavalry corps inflicted great losses on superior enemy forces in the autumn of 1941 by moving at night and striking the enemy rear at dawn. Two German divisions were surrounded and partly destroyed by this corps in October 1941. During that winter, the cavalry corps engaged in extensive offensive operations under severe winter conditions of cold and deep snow, traveling 30 to 40 miles a day across enemy lines of communications. When necessary, dismounted combat against fortified positions was undertaken. Although at first the offensive succeeded in destroying many enemy positions, later large losses were suffered by the corps when it was itself encircled, primarily due to powerful enemy air attacks which destroyed the corps supplies and artillery positions.

This again stressed the vulnerability of cavalry to air attack, especially in winter.

3. COORDINATION WITH OTHER ARMS
Coordinated operations of cavalry forces with large tank units have been developed by the Red Army where the terrain and season are suitable. This cooperation may take different forms. In some instances these large units, while executing the complete mission by joint efforts, operate independently but coordinate their blows. In other cases the tank groups are attached to the large cavalry unit whose commander assigns missions to each tank group. Finally, a situation may occur when both types of cooperation, operational and tactical, takes place at the same time. A part of the tank forces execute their missions independently, while the balance is attached to and operates with the cavalry.

An outstanding operation in which cavalry and tank forces were employed successfully was the encirclement and capture of the German garrison at Taganrog in August 1943 (fig. 45). In this operation the cavalry units followed the tanks which had broken through the enemy lines. After entering the gap, the cavalry moved rapidly towards the Sea of Azov to encircle the enemy garrison at Taganrog. The tank units moved in two groups, covering the flanks of the cavalry against enemy counterattacks by mechanized German relief units as well as from the encircled enemy group. All other Soviet tanks were attached to the leading cavalry division; these tanks moved ahead of the cavalry and paved the way by overcoming scattered enemy detachments. Wherever enemy resistance was strong, cavalry units dismounted and attacked with close support of tanks.

The massed artillery fire of all cavalry artillery was effectively used against strong enemy positions. Enemy counterattacks were broken by artillery fire and by maneuvering cavalry-tank groups against the enemy flanks. Complete success was assured by uninterrupted contact between the cavalry division commanders and the tank group commanders, as well as by powerful air support which destroyed enemy artillery positions and armor and also provided cover against hostile air attacks (up to 1,200 sorties were flown daily).

Self-propelled artillery regiments work especially effectively with cavalry in deep penetrations and flank operations. Self-propelled artillery has supported cavalry in extensive Red Army maneuvers across swampy terrain, covering as many as 125 miles in 2 days. One of the most important tactical cavalry maneuvers is to establish and to hold road blocks on highways over which the supporting self-propelled artillery must pass. Cavalry executes wide outflanking maneuvers across swamps to attack enemy artillery from the rear; then the self-propelled guns advance over the secured highway. Cavalry moves on both sides of the artillery units for protection against possible flank attacks. Whenever enemy guns or small fortified areas are encountered, the self-propelled artillery quickly deploys and smashes the enemy with concentrated fire. Rapid transition from mounted to dismounted attack by cavalry units and uninterrupted liaison with self-propelled artillery are basic principles in effective pursuit operations. Attached engineer and ponton detachments greatly facilitate rapid movement of armor in such operations.

4. COORDINATED OFFENSIVE
a. Organization of attack. Cavalry is used to best advantage in coordination with infantry. In an offensive, the infantry holds the enemy with a frontal attack while the entire mass of cavalry and

212

tanks is thrown upon the flanks and rear of the enemy. The objective of cavalry is to strike at the enemy's flank and rear; disrupt his headquarters main force and the direction of his main effort. The cavalry corps must be reinforced by infantry, tanks, artillery, and mortars, and held in a centralized po-

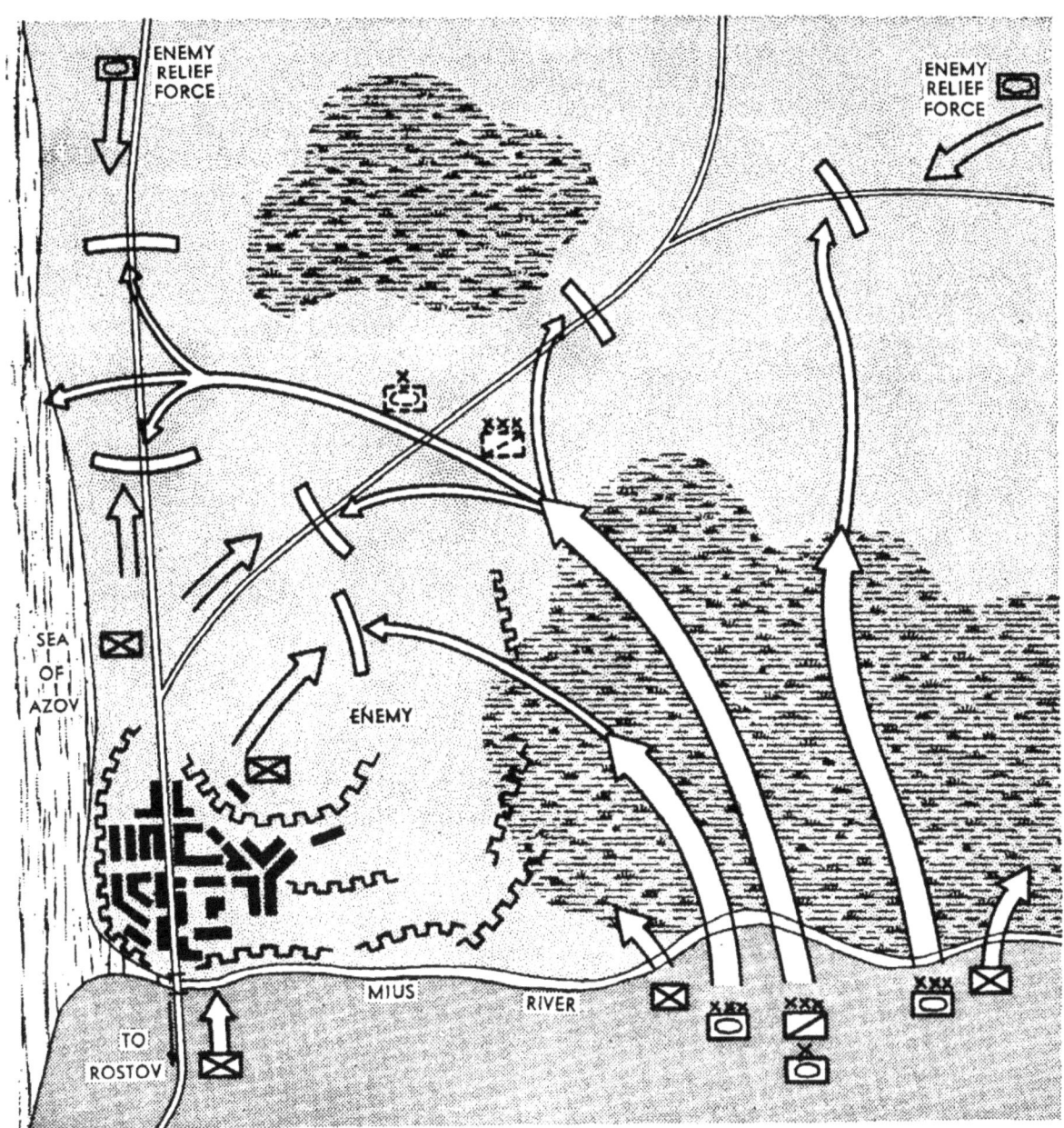

Figure 45. Cavalry-tank coordinated break-through to encircle enemy garrison at Taganrog.

and lines of communications; and encircle and destroy his main force. To accomplish this, the cavalry must utilize its mobility to the utmost. This is achieved by holding the enemy with a frontal attack by other arms; by restricting his maneuverability; and by determining the disposition of his sition from where it can attack the enemy's flanks. It is considered advisable to locate the cavalry on the enveloping flank of the main attacking force with the missions of reducing the enemy's flanks and destroying his communications. The success of a cavalry operation, especially when it has pene-

213

trated into the enemy's operational depth, is conditioned by continuous coordination with the combined arms and tanks attacking frontally.

Red Army doctrine maintains that the expedient moment to commit cavalry is when the enemy's defenses in depth have been penetrated by a frontal or enveloping assault. The enemy is then forced to bring up his reserves. He is in a state of fluid defense, has not had time to organize any defensive positions, and is most vulnerable to a cavalry attack.

A successful operation depends not only on a well executed initial phase but also on the successive

Cavalry formations advancing on the flank of an assault group may use two types of attack: the "open flank attack" and the "interior flank attack" (figs. 46 and 47). In an open flank attack, coordination and liaison with troops attacking frontally is maintained only on one side, while in an interior flank attack, liaison must be maintained with both flanks, permitting cavalry to pass through the secured corridor. Coordination with units of adjacent sectors is limited to the initial phase.

The Soviet disposition of troops will depend on whether the corps attacks in an open flank or in an

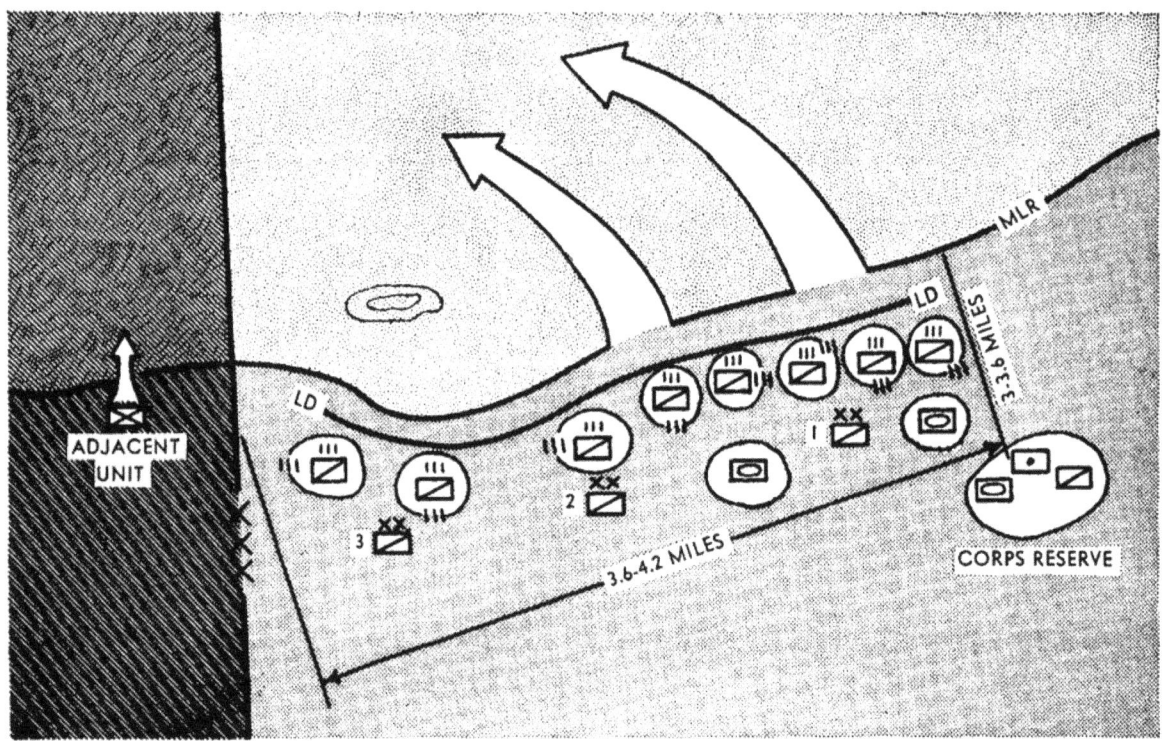

Figure 46. Cavalry corps attacking with an open flank.

phases. Cavalry units should not be restricted by boundary lines that reduce their mobility and force them into protracted combat for strongpoints. Therefore, in designating missions to the cavalry, the objective, the direction of the main effort, and time are indicated. The time factor is coordinated with the capabilities of units making the frontal assault, while the direction of the assault is aimed at operationally important objectives in the flanks, rear areas, and communication lines.

Essential considerations are air cover, liaison between army group and corps headquarters, secrecy of concentrations, thoroughness of reconnaissance, surprise, and continuous flow of supplies.

interior flank. In an open flank attack, the cavalry has more maneuverability during the initial phase and attacks on a wider front. The corps reserve is deployed on the open flank. In an interior flank attack, the corps attacks on a narrower front, is echeloned to a depth of 5 miles, and has a higher density of troop concentration. In this case the reserves will be used to augment the blow, and will be located to the rear of the main thrust.

b. Attack phases. COORDINATION AND PLANNING. A cavalry attack consists of several phases. During the initial or coordination and planning phase, the Soviet forces will secretly approach the assembly area. In this phase air cover must be

214

strong and is provided by the front and army fighter air units; one or two battalions of small-caliber antiaircraft artillery are attached for protection against hostile aircraft.

Concentration of cavalry takes place in areas 25 to 35 miles from the front lines, and should end 2 to 3 days before the start of the general offensive. Coordination with units attacking frontally, reconnaissance, line of departure, and engineer preparations are determined at this stage.

the corps is in the initial assembly area. Detailed and careful planning of coordination in this phase is the foundation of success in the initial assembly. Matters of supply are also determined during this initial phase. They assume particular importance since cavalry cannot depend on local supplies. In addition to ammunition, food, and fuel, cavalry requires large quantities of fodder. Any interruption in the supply of fodder will materially impair the mobility and combat value of cavalry. Both army

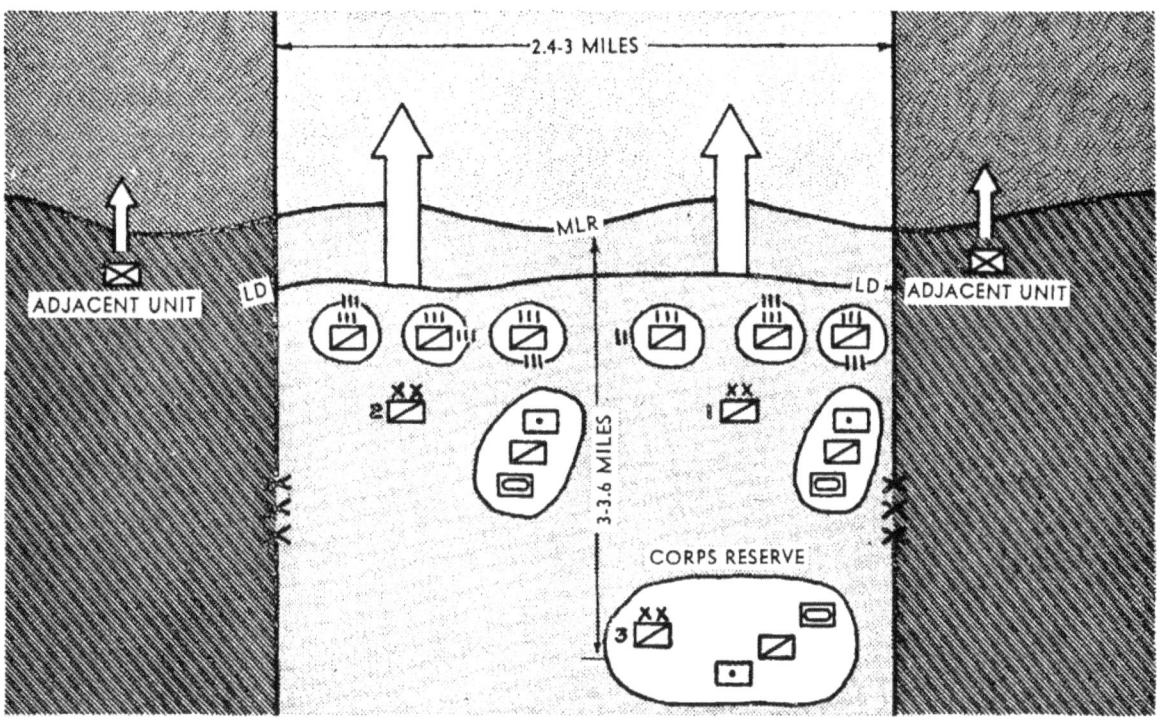

Figure 47. Cavalry corps attacking with covered flanks.

The corps commander must be acquainted with the following:

Initial and successive objectives of infantry and tank units attacking frontally.

Time of attack and boundaries, and direction of the main effort.

Location of command posts and their axis of displacement.

Methods of communication with command posts, and the signals to be used by units reaching designated phase lines.

Assembly area of tank units, particularly GHQ tanks.

The corps commander's field order includes the above information and is issued after coordination with the chiefs of supporting arms during the time

group and army transportation facilities are widely used to insure a regular flow of supplies.

MOVING TO THE ASSAULT. Movement to the main line of departure for the attack is the second phase of an operation. The main line of departure is usually selected beyond the range of enemy artillery and mortar fire, although this distance should not exceed 7 to 10 miles. The formation adopted depends on the decision of the corps commander and should permit deployment against hostile air and tank attacks. The open flank attack is on a front 4 to 5 miles wide with three cavalry divisions abreast and the corps reserve deployed toward the outside of the turning movement. In the attack where both flanks are covered, the front is reduced to from 2.5 to 3.5 miles with two cavalry divisions in assault and the third division with corps reserve echeloned to

215

the rear. From the beginning, special attention is paid to continuous mobility, freedom of movement, and combat preparedness. To protect the formation against enemy artillery and mortar flanking at-

tinuous coordination are essential for cooperation between the cavalry and units attacking frontally.

LAUNCHING THE ATTACK. The third phase of the operation is the actual execution of the basic mis-

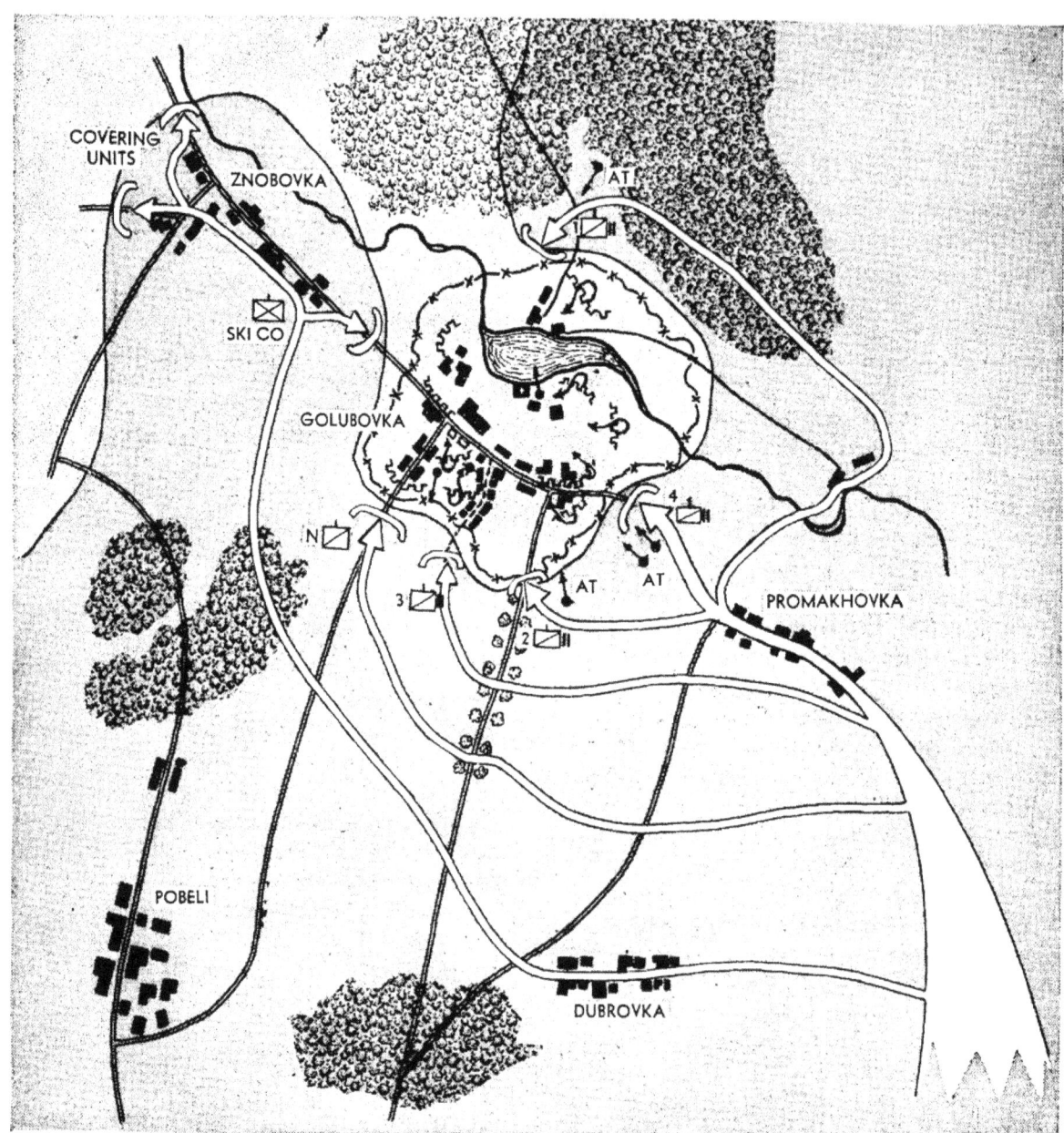

Figure 48. Reinforced cavalry regiment attack on a fortified town.

tacks, and also from infantry and tank counter-attacks, air cover is provided and artillery is detached to protect the flanks. These units move as far as 5 miles from the flanks. Consolidation of forces is the primary consideration of the second phase. Timely exchange of information and con-

sion. Cavalry detaches itself from the troops attacking frontally and loses direct tactical contact; however, coordination must not cease. The cavalry seizes positions to prevent the main enemy force from extricating itself from encirclement. Part of the cavalry cuts the enemy's route of retreat, while the main force, in coordination with units attacking frontally, encircles and destroys the enemy's principal units.

Liaison during the third phase of the attack is the responsibility of the army group command; without continuous liaison, coordinated action with cavalry is not possible.

5. CAVALRY IN PURSUIT

In exploiting a break-through, cavalry is well suited to execute parallel pursuit. Whenever enemy rear guards attempt to restrict cavalry activity to pursuit from the rear, wide outflanking maneuvers across swamps or rough country permit cavalry to strike at the flanks of the retreating enemy column or cut off his withdrawal by creating road blocks.

The supporting self-propelled artillery moves up to destroy enemy rear guard positions, while the cavalry seizes important tactical features in the enemy rear to secure highways over which the supporting Soviet artillery and other arms may advance more rapidly. Cavalry cannot hold terrain for long; therefore, motorized infantry and supporting arms must move forward rapidly to relieve cavalry units counterattacked by the enemy. The mobility and maneuverability of cavalry in sudden continuous flank attacks against withdrawing enemy are the basic elements of cavalry striking power. Mortars and machine guns mounted on horse-drawn carts supplement the automatic weapons carried by cavalry men. The striking power is considerable when tanks operate with cavalry. Artillery is the basic arm against enemy counterattacks, as well as in the assault of fortified positions and road blocks.

During pursuit operations, small cavalry units are detached to reduce important by-passed strong points—especially enemy supply centers—situated on vital lines of communication. Dismounted assaults are made simultaneously from all directions by squadrons reinforced by antitank guns, mortars, and automatic weapons (fig. 48). The assault group may be as large as a reinforced regiment to which self-propelled guns are attached to facilitate the destruction of enemy defensive positions. Sufficient striking power is given such assault units to clear the enemy from the position quickly, enabling the cavalry unit to rejoin the main body.

6. DEFENSIVE TACTICS

On the defense, cavalry covers withdrawals and protects the flanks and the gaps between units, inflicting losses on the enemy by sudden counterattacks upon the flanks of enemy salients. Under extreme conditions, cavalry engages in dismounted defensive combat as infantry. In a decentralized defensive position, care is always taken to conceal horses in a defiladed area for safety and to facilitate withdrawal. In the defense of road blocks or tactically important terrain, artillery and mortars are basic defensive weapons relied upon by Soviet cavalry.

Section V. ENGINEERS

1. BASIC DOCTRINE

Engineer work in the Red Army regularly proceeds under rapidly changing combat conditions and in the face of limitations in the quantity and types of engineer equipment available; this is especially true of heavy construction and bridge building materials. These conditions serve to emphasize the importance of combat engineers (pioneers) and to demand from them efficient and speedy performance of a great variety of engineer tasks. In addition, the Soviets place a premium on detailed calculation of engineer capabilities, full exploitation of available equipment, development and perfection of engineer techniques, and constant coordination between the engineer arm and other arms, especially artillery.

The primary mission of the Soviet pioneer battalion is identical with that of the U. S. engineer combat battalion: to increase the effectiveness of the division in all phases of combat by general engineer work and to hinder the movement of the enemy. Due to the nature of combat on the Eastern Front— frequent German counterattacks, lesser reliance on friendly air cover, pressure of time in executing engineer missions—greater emphasis fell on mine laying, both in the offense and in the defense, on construction of hasty field fortifications, and on camouflage.

The Soviet divisional pioneer battalion is less than one-fourth the size of our combat engineer battalion, comprising 164 to 170 men as compared with 637. Since it is not motorized, when rapid movement of engineers is required, units are attached to other troops such as tank units or motorized infantry which provide transportation. Standard equipment is similar to ours—wire-cutters, grapnels, mine-detectors, shovels, saws, demolition sets, flame throwers, etc.—but there is less power-driven and more hand equipment.

The pioneer battalion of the mechanized corps is approximately the same size as our armored division engineer battalion, and is motorized for movement into great depths in short periods of time. Each of the three motorized brigades in the mechanized corps has an engineer company of 121 men.

Specialized GHQ engineer units—independent battalions, regiments, and brigades—are used extensively in the Red Army for reinforcement, and particularly with infantry, for the assault of fortified positions. Light and heavy ponton regiments are respectively comparable to the U. S. engineer light ponton company, which may be attached down to divisional level when necessary, and to the heavy ponton battalion, which may be attached to corps or army. There also are other special GHQ units—such as camouflage—similar to ours in function.

The employment of army and corps construction engineers, operating to the rear of the infantry divisions and executing heavier and more complicated engineer work, is identical to ours. The use of local labor in construction work is common in rear areas.

2. OFFENSIVE OPERATIONS

a. Reconnaissance. Soviet doctrine stresses the importance of thoroughly planned and efficiently executed engineer reconnaissance. The organization of engineer reconnaissance varies, however, with combat conditions and with each specific situation. Thus, no Soviet organization can be considered typical. The following examples serve to indicate the saturation of elements for engineer reconnaissance and the importance attached to it, especially in the offensive (fig. 49):

During the period of preparation for a breakthrough of enemy defenses, partially located on the bank of a river, the engineer staff of a Soviet army group composed a plan of engineer reconnaissance and assigned to supervising staff officers missions and areas of responsibility. Reconnaissance objectives included enemy installations and obstacles on the front line, the presence of escarpment, and of breaks in the ice; the nature, extent, and areas of defensive constructions; sectors accessible to tanks, etc. It was conducted chiefly by observation. On a front of 8½ miles, 20 forward observation posts were operated, 10 of which were manned by engineer commanders.

A systematic reconnaissance of the ice in the areas of possible crossings was also undertaken; reconnaissance groups of six to seven men were sent out to discover mined sectors. Some minefields were located by interrogation of prisoners and by mine

tracers or indicator movements or sounds; the enemy defense system was photographed from the air. This was done three times during the period of preparation for attack so that changes in the arrangement of enemy defenses could be observed and provided for. During the period of movement through the defensive zone of the enemy, two mobile engineer posts with four men each were organized for the first echelon of each division. In several sectors special pioneer groups—each composed of six to eight men—were sent out for mine and obstacle reconnaissance. Two to three pioneers were also allotted to each reconnaissance group of combined arms. Reconnaissance in the second echelon of troops was conducted chiefly for the discovery of mine obstacles on the roads and road shoulders, and for providing passage for heavy tanks.

During the period of preparation for attack by another army group, engineer observation was conducted by regimental, divisional, and, partially, army reconnaissance units. In each divisional zone two to three engineer observation posts were set up in addition to command observation posts in the main operational sectors. The observation posts of other arms were used: about 40 percent were artillery observation posts, and 60 percent were combined-arms observation posts.

Mobile groups of combined arms, which conducted active day and night reconnaissance, were also allotted pioneers for mine and obstacle clearance.

In the advance, mobile engineer observation posts were formed from regimental and divisional pioneers (one to two posts per division), while army groups and army engineer reconnaissance platoons acted as mobile reconnaissance groups (one to two per divisional zone). Special groups were also organized for reconnaissance of specific centers of defense and for assisting tank and infantry units. Small engineer reconnaissance groups, which infiltrated through the front line of defense or were parachuted from airplanes, operated in the deep rear of the enemy.

In still another instance, the following elements were created for engineer reconnaissance during the period of preparation for the attack:

Two army group reconnaissance platoons, operating in the deep rear of the enemy.

Four army group reconnaissance groups, comprising part of the tank reconnaissance elements.

218

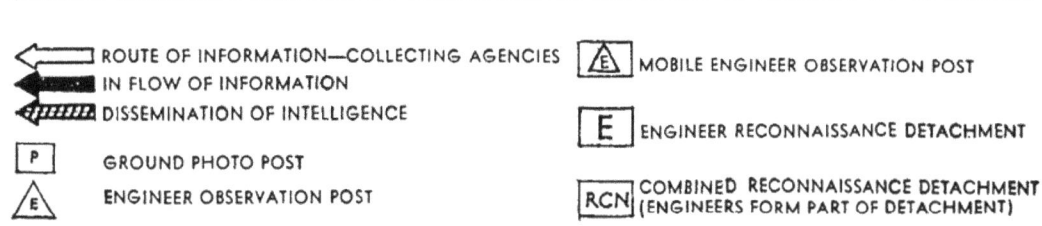

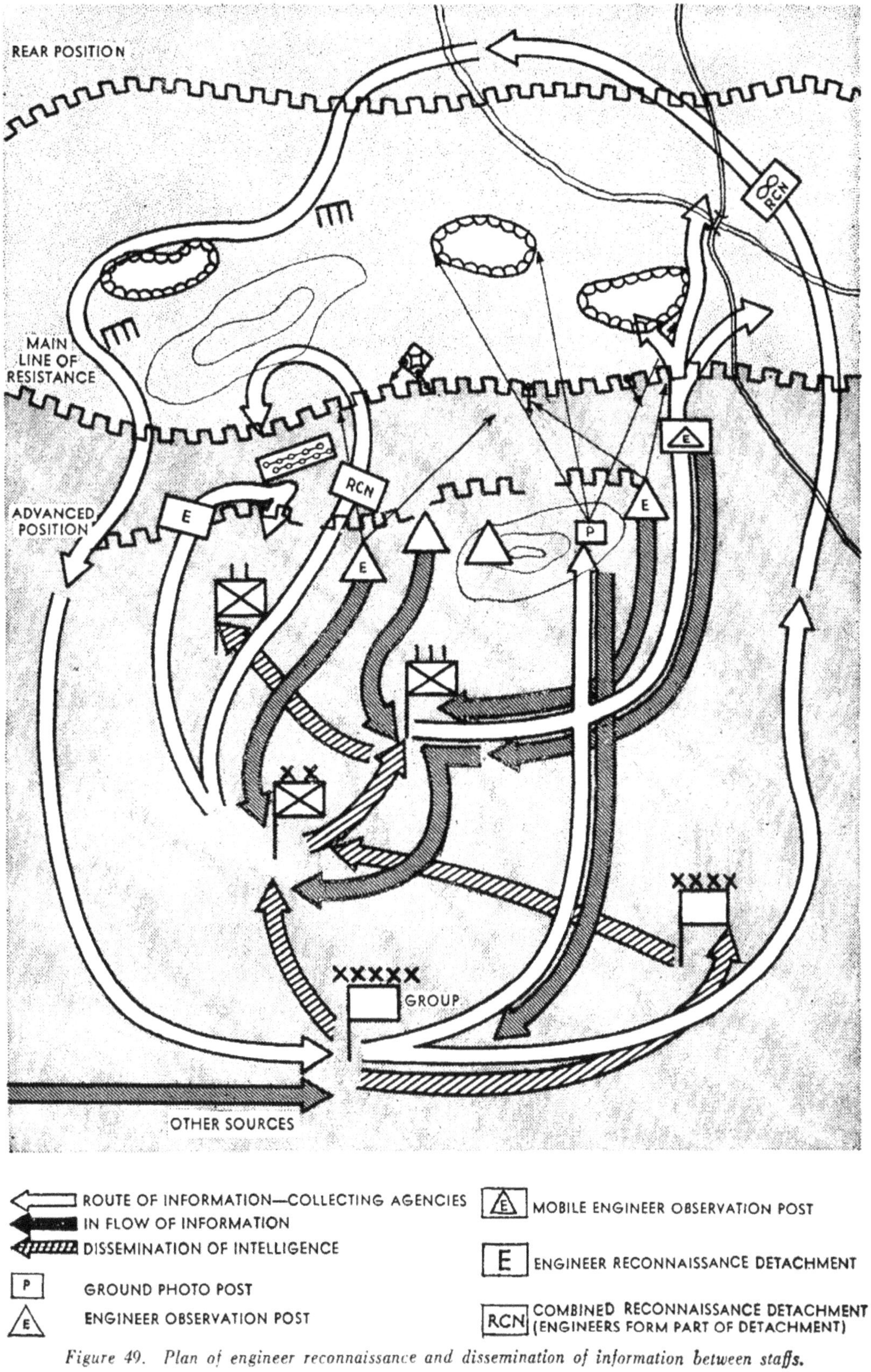

REAR POSITION

MAIN
LINE OF
RESISTANCE

ADVANCED
POSITION

RCN

E

E

P

E

E

XXXX

XXXXX
□ GROUP

OTHER SOURCES

⇦ ROUTE OF INFORMATION—COLLECTING AGENCIES
◆ IN FLOW OF INFORMATION
⇦ DISSEMINATION OF INTELLIGENCE

P GROUND PHOTO POST

△E ENGINEER OBSERVATION POST

△E MOBILE ENGINEER OBSERVATION POST

E ENGINEER RECONNAISSANCE DETACHMENT

RCN COMBINED RECONNAISSANCE DETACHMENT
(ENGINEERS FORM PART OF DETACHMENT)

Figure 49. Plan of engineer reconnaissance and dissemination of information between staffs.

Six army group reconnaissance platoons, operating in army zones of advance.

One engineer group operating within the army group reconnaissance organization of combined arms.

Three reserve platoons of the engineer staff.

Six army reconnaissance platoons, operating in army and divisional zones.

In addition, one or two squads in each divisional pioneer battalion were designated for engineer reconnaissance.

On the basis of collated and verified data from all sources, the Soviet engineer staff finally prepares an engineer situation map (showing the enemy defensive zone, the lines and centers of defense, and antitank and antipersonnel obstacles) and a detailed description of enemy installations, which aid in determining the areas most favorable for a breakthrough. In addition, situation maps are developed, showing water barriers, condition of line of communication, availability of water supply, and presence of local materials for construction of crossings and roads and for camouflage.

Simultaneously, the engineer staff must assemble complete data about its own engineer units to determine the quantity and condition of personnel and equipment, and to what extent reinforcements from the troops and higher engineer echelons will be needed.

b. Preparation for the attack. In preparation for the launching of an offensive operation, specific responsibilities are assumed by combat engineers. Troop concentrations at the line of departure and other installations are camouflaged. Dummy troop concentrations, artillery, tanks, fortifications, and roads are constructed. Provisions are made for water supply. The engineers repair roads and bridges, or construct new ones; they fortify observation and command posts.

Engineer work for clearing lanes through obstacles and minefields is organized. Trenches are dug—at least two to a company—to approach enemy positions as closely as possible. Small bridges are laid across communication trenches to permit passage of infantry—one bridge for each platoon. Two bridges per battalion are laid for passage of motor transport and artillery.

All preparatory work is executed as silently and as secretly as possible so that the direction of attack will not be disclosed to enemy ground or air observation.

During this period, the engineer staff organizes and supervises instruction of the troops in various engineer measures. In one army, for example, tank-borne companies in each infantry regiment were organized to force a water barrier independently and to secure the opposite shore. In addition, other detachments were organized in each infantry and artillery regiment and in each division to repair roads along the route of march and to clear mines. All army troops were instructed in the use of local materials for crossing a river.

c. Assault tactics. ASSAULT ENGINEER-PIONEER BRIGADE. The organic pioneers and engineers of infantry and tank formations must be reinforced by GHQ assault units in operations against strongly fortified positions. Assault engineer-pioneer brigades are the basic Soviet assault units. Normally, they are employed under centralized control in the zone of the main effort. In a typical successful operation, an assault brigade operated in the zone of an infantry corps and was subordinated to the corps commander. Units of the brigade, as part of assault groups, secured divisional operations and took part in the assault.

Assault engineer-pioneer brigades should never, the Soviets teach, be dispersed over a two- or three-army area with equal distribution of equipment along the entire front.

Brigades are employed in close coordination with the other arms; pioneers must at all times be supported by infantry, artillery, and tanks. Assault brigades and assault units should not be used as "armored infantry" operating to the front of the infantry or for pioneer-tank raids in breaking through strongly fortified positions.

In the break-through of strongly fortified positions, the brigade performs the following:

Conducts engineer reconnaissance.

Detaches mobile obstacle-clearing detachments.

Includes assault engineer-pioneer elements in corps and army antitank reserves for cooperation with antitank destroyer artillery regiments.

Repairs and constructs roads, bridges, and crossings and lays corduroy roads at the line of departure.

Clears lanes in minefields and other obstacles and organizes the passage of advancing units through them.

220

Participates in assault groups (detachments) for the destruction of timber-and-earth and concrete firing positions, and steel pillboxes.

Accompanies tanks and artillery and, together with infantry elements, assists in the displacement of guns and mortars attached to assault groups to new firing positions, and in equipping these firing positions.

Covers flanks and salients of advancing formations and secures seized areas by mines and other obstacles.

Clears routes of march and inhabited points used by troops of mines and obstacles.

MINE AND OBSTACLE CLEARANCE. In the offensive, pioneers move forward in front of the infantry, or with it, to clear lanes through minefields for infantry, tanks, and artillery. Primary march routes are cleared of mines first; the most experienced pioneers are assigned this task.

In the Stalingrad offensive, 85 groups of carefully selected pioneers, composed of from 10 to 25 men each, were designated to clear mines on the basic roads. They began work early in the morning and in 3½ hours had made 64 lanes and had rendered harmless more than 5,000 mines.

Security detachments are sent out to complete mine removal in abandoned houses, trenches, shelters, and mud huts, command posts and troop concentration areas, road gullies, enemy fortifications, etc., as the offensive develops.

Thirty-six obstacle-clearing groups may be organized from an assault engineer-pioneer battalion to clear 36 lanes for 12 to 18 infantry companies or 4 to 6 infantry battalions. An assault battalion can clear 18 to 36 lanes for tank platoons—fully servicing a tank brigade or two tank regiments.

DESTRUCTION OF PERMANENT FORTIFICATIONS. When earth and timber or concrete pillboxes, "crabs" (German mobile steel pillboxes), and concrete emplacements are expected, special assault groups must be formed by the infantry and pioneers. Each group contains from a section to a company of pioneers; consequently, 9 to 18 assault groups can be formed from one assault engineer-pioneer battalion. The infantry battalion or company, supported by the assault group, is usually commanded by an infantry officer, but sometimes by an experienced commander of an assault engineer-pioneer company or battalion.

The assault group is usually organized into the following subgroups (for an alternate, slightly stronger organization, see the assault regiment, paragraph 1b, section II, part III):

Demolition subgroups, composed of one to two infantry sections, one to two assault pioneer sections, and two to four flame-thrower operators.

Blocking subgroups, each composed of 1 to to 1½ infantry platoons with one to two heavy machine guns, a section of antitank rifles, a platoon of 50-mm mortars, two to four men with flame throwers, and up to a section of pioneers.

Reinforcing subgroups (fire subgroups), consisting of one to two antitank guns (45- or 57-mm), two to six flame throwers, and one to two heavy tanks. In addition, one to two 82-mm mortars and one to two 76-mm guns are often included. In the case of especially heavily fortified installations, a 122-mm howitzer is added.

The assault group must be covered by at least as many direct-support infantry guns and machine guns as there are enemy direct-support infantry guns and machine-gun embrasures.

The organization and preparation of assault groups proceed under the centralized direction of the staff of infantry units, with cooperation by commanders of engineer elements for both tactical and technical supervision of engineer maneuvers. Coordination of infantry, tanks, artillery, and assault engineers must be organized between elements within the assault group; between groups within an assault detachment; and also between the assault group, infantry elements, security group, and group of artillery support. At least two practice assaults are conducted to perfect coordination. Three to 4 hours, after receipt of the mission orders, must be allowed for daylight reconnaissance.

The assault of pillboxes, "crabs," and casemates, proceeds in the following order: The assault group moves out under cover of artillery fire (which continues throughout the assault), and of smoke screens. Fire cover for the attacked position is neutralized first. "Crabs" are assaulted next by groups of reduced strength. Antitank rifles conduct fire on the side and rear walls, while pioneers use hollow charges to blow up the roof.

221

The method of storming a timber-and-earth or a concrete pillbox is as follows: The reconnaissance and obstacle-clearing subgroup verifies the information obtained by engineer reconnaissance and especially notes any new firing installations that may have appeared on the flanks. The blocking and fire subgroups cover approaches to the firing position from the enemy side. Simultaneously, part of the reconnaissance and obstacle-clearing subgroup clears the way for passage of the demolition subgroup. Camouflaged pioneers with antitank rifles, using all available cover, move up to positions for firing on the pillbox embrasures and approaches; the assault group must first concentrate its full force on neutralization of the embrasures. Flame throwers blind and tanks destroy the embrasures. If tanks and flame throwers are not available, embrasures are blocked with bags of earth and sawdust. Then the demolition pioneers throw Molotov cocktails, incendiary bombs, or smoke hand grenades in any openings; or sear the interior of the pillbox with a flame thrower. Finally, they blow up the pillbox with explosive charges. After its seizure, the pillbox must be secured with the help of infantry regimental security groups (or battalion security groups).

d. Hasty defense in offensive operations. Red Army combat experience has demonstrated that captured enemy positions must be organized and prepared immediately against violent and repeated counterattacks, especially on flanks and salients. Hastily laid minefields are the primary methods of engineer support against such counterattacks, although mobile pillboxes and prepared obstacles are important supplements.

PLANNING THE DEFENSES. Sectors scheduled for fortification are chosen with a view to utilizing natural barriers which inherently, or with minimum adaptation, serve as effective obstacles to enemy advance. Inhabited points, forests, copses, and heights are especially favored. All enemy fortications, after being cleared of mines, are used. Camouflage concealing the system of fortifications is erected if time permits.

Mine laying is planned in detail by commanders of pioneer battalions or of regiments who are designated as chiefs of mine operations on a division or corps front. The plans are based on thorough reconnaissance and designate methods to be used, quantities of materials needed, and timing of demolition with troop movements. They are presented for the Commander's approval through the Chief Engineer. Chiefs of mining operations maintain communication with the Chief Engineer, by means of daily reports, and also with the over-all commanders of combat sectors with whom mine laying is constantly coordinated. This uninterrupted contact enables engineer units, with a minimum loss of time, to meet combat developments such as the necessity for securing a newly seized enemy position, combating a sudden enemy counterattack, or eliminating an unforeseen obstacle.

Coordination of pioneer maneuvers with antitank artillery in the laying of minefields is of special importance. Mines serve not only to destroy enemy tanks by their own action, but also to canalize tanks in minefields adequately covered by direct Soviet artillery fire. To acquaint artillerymen with possible areas of tank approaches within range of direct artillery fire, and with areas in which cover for pioneers laying minefields must be provided, engineer and artillery officers make a preliminary reconnaissance for strategic locations for minefields and firing positions. Artillerymen must be kept constantly informed of the limits of minefields and belts, and of any changes in them.

LAYING THE DEFENSES. The Red Army often attaches a pioneer platoon to an infantry company, or a pioneer company to an infantry battalion, for laying protective mine belts. An engineer unit assigned to an infantry company is held responsible for a sector not more than $\frac{1}{2}$ to 3 miles wide. A unit assigned to a battalion may cover a sector up to 5 to 6 miles in width. The depth in both cases is 3 to 4 miles. In one instance, the first belt was completed within 3 hours after assignment of the task, the second within 4 hours, and the third within 6 hours.

Mine and demolition equipment are brought forward on large sleds hauled by tanks and on hand sleds. The engineer troops are organized into small, mobile mine-laying units armed with automatic weapons and rifles. Such units are equipped with ten sleds, each loaded with six fragmentation mines improvised from captured 155-mm artillery shells; two prepared electrical circuits from the engineer demolition chest; 90 antitank mines; fifty 200-gram blasting caps, with fuzes; two mine detectors; six probes; five grapnels; and two machine guns. Controlled, electrically detonated mines in circuits are placed across main avenues of approach so that the offensive can be continued without waiting for the removal of minefields. Contact mines are used in large numbers, however, in order to install adequate defenses within the limited time available (fig. 50).

The time element is so important that mine laying is continued even under enemy artillery fire.

3. DELIBERATE DEFENSE AND WITHDRAWAL

Chief engineers of regiments and divisions are responsible for technical assistance to their commanders in organizing deliberate defenses. They participate in working out the plan of defense and all orders concerning the fortifying of defensive po-

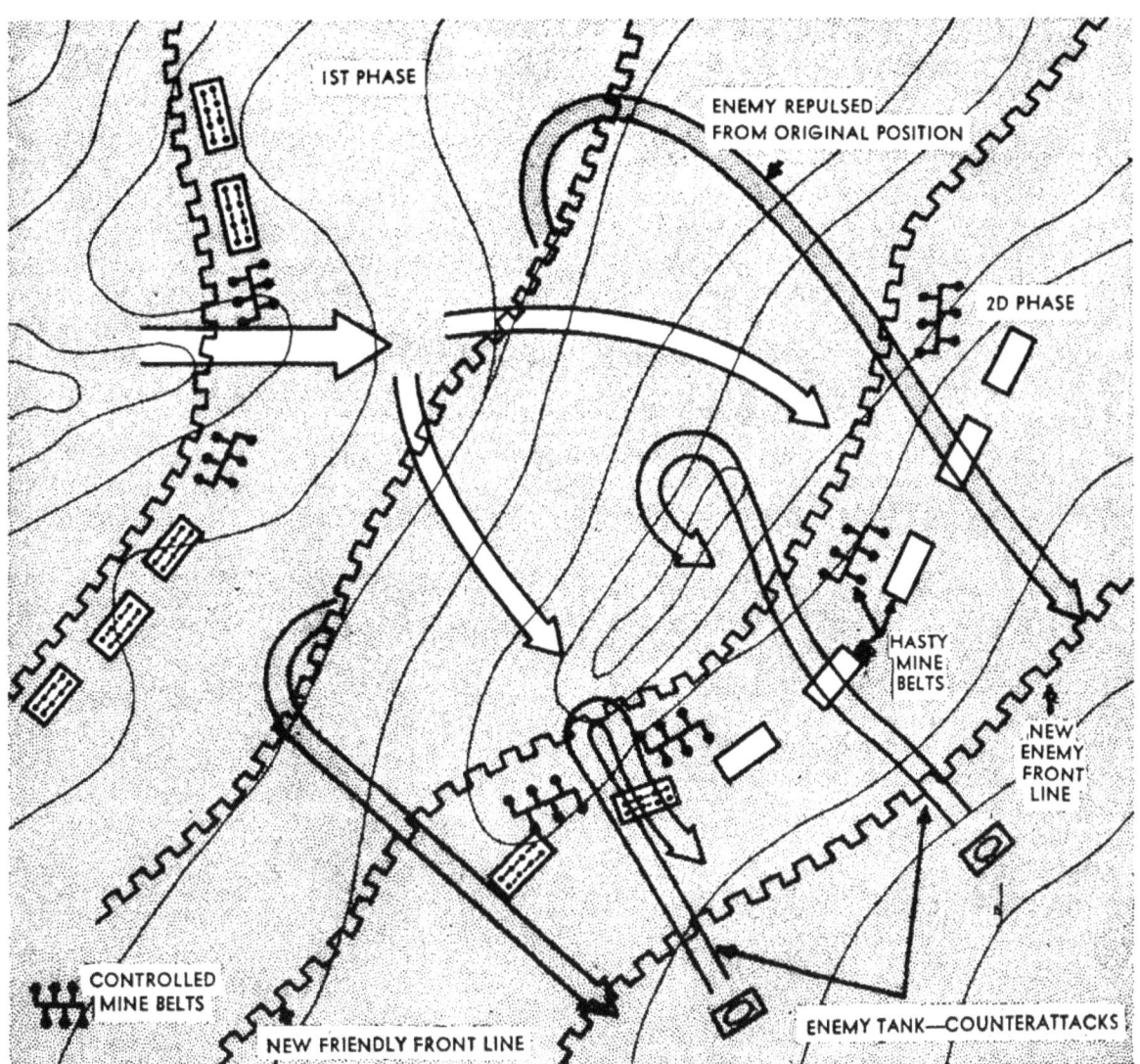

Figure 50. Hasty mine belts in an offensive operation.

Even though the enemy may observe some of the mine-laying activity, the prime Soviet consideration is to complete the system of defensive belts to the greatest possible degree. The necessity for rapid action may become so pressing that full completion of mine laying according to the planned pattern is left to the second echelon of pioneer units.

sitions. By authorization of the regimental (divisional) commander, they give orders to (company) battalion commanders concerning the priority of engineer work. Priority is determined by a careful evaluation of the nature of combat, character of the terrain, quantity of water supply. pressure of time, and availability of equipment and personnel.

223

The troops themselves, within the limitations of their organic equipment, fortify positions in their own particular sectors, under the direction of their commanders. Pioneers act as technical supervisors and instructors, themselves carrying out only the most complicated and difficult work. Under engineer leadership, communication trenches are dug; minefields are laid; machine-gun nests are dug in; mortar emplacements, command and observation posts, and troop shelters are constructed; obstacles are erected; and strongpoints are fortified.

For technical supervision of the fortifying of positions, the battalion commander has three to four pioneers at his disposal and up to a squad of regimental pioneer instructors. For more complicated work (mining, preparation of timber-and-earth firing positions, etc.), he will have in addition divisional pioneers—one to two platoons per regiment.

In the withdrawal, engineers are responsible for the destruction of all equipment, supplies, and munitions which cannot be transported with the troops.

4. CAMOUFLAGE

Engineer camouflage troops (army, army group, and GHQ) supervise the execution of strategic camouflage plans issued by the commander of combined arms. The practices of individual concealment, simple camouflage construction, and camouflage discipline are the responsibilities of the individual soldier. The engineer camouflage units advise, supervise, and instruct the troops in camouflage work and discipline, inspect camouflage work, assist in supply and preparation of camouflage materials, and themselves construct complicated, large-scale camouflage expedients.

American and Soviet camouflage doctrines are basically similar in purpose, fundamental principles, and methods employed. Camouflage by complete concealment, imitation, or disguise is used, depending on tactical desirability and physical practicability. Specific methods are influenced by the distance of enemy forces, the nature of enemy reconnaissance, available time and manpower, accessible materials for camouflage, season of the year, character of the terrain, and meteorological conditions. Emphasis in both American and Soviet doctrine is laid on utilization of natural and artificial materials, pattern painting, and dummy construction.

Soviet camouflage doctrine, because of a lesser reliance on friendly air power for protection, places heavy stress on camouflage discipline in eliminating tell-tale indications associated with location of bivouac areas, firing positions, command and observation posts, tanks, supply points, etc.

Bivouac areas are revealed by the regular, sharply defined borders of unit sectors and outlines of tents, by smoke from camp fires and kitchens, and by worn paths to and from water supply areas, kitchens, etc. Rigid Soviet camouflage discipline provides for the disposition of troops in small groups so as to disguise the strength of infantry forces, and for the pitching of tents in uneven rows using trees and bushes as natural camouflage. Campfires can be lit only with special permission. Smoke from kitchen fires must be controlled and dispersed and, if possible, kitchens are located in nearby inhabited areas and used only at night. Buildings are constructed along already existing roads; movement within bivouac areas takes place along paths discovered and marked by engineer patrols.

Similar camouflage discipline hinders enemy discovery of observation and command posts, artillery positions, and tanks. Activity in command and observation posts commences only after camouflage measures have been taken. They are approached and left only on designated roads. Exposed routes do not end at an artillery position but are extended to another logical termination. Tank tracks are camouflaged by brushing them out or by covering them with local materials. In all cases, camouflage materials must be prepared, under engineer supervision, at a distance from the position or installation to be camouflaged so that tell-tale indications of activity, such as trampled paths and uprooted vegetation, will not disclosed their true location.

Section VI. TACTICAL ANTI-AIRCRAFT ARTILLERY

1. MISSIONS

The primary mission of Red Army tactical antiaircraft artillery is to protect troop concentrations, forward and rear area installations, and forward lines of communications from hostile aircraft attacks. Antiaircraft artillery also conducts direct fire against land fortifications, attacks hostile infantry in assembly and deployment areas, assists in repelling attacks of enemy ground forces, and executes other firing missions which are normally assigned to light field artillery. Strategic antiaircraft artillery—with heavy, fixed, semimobile, and mobile guns, radar, searchlights, and barrage balloons—operates in close cooperation with interceptor aviation as an entirely separate arm beyond the scope of this discussion.

2. TYPES OF UNITS

Tactical antiaircraft artillery units consist of independent antiaircraft artillery divisions, and organic antiaircraft units of mobile formations. The antiaircraft division is the basic GHQ reserve antiaircraft artillery organization which is allotted to the various armies and army groups as required. An antiaircraft artillery division consists of an antiaircraft gun regiment and three antiaircraft automatic weapons regiments totaling sixteen 85-mm guns, forty-eight 37-mm guns, and sixty-four 12.7-mm antiaircraft machine guns. It can effectively protect an area 10,000 yards wide and 7,000 yards deep—that is, a deployment area for the main effort of a major infantry-artillery offensive (fig. 51). This tactical employment of antiaircraft artillery gives a powerful concentration of medium antiaircraft artillery in addition to a barrage of automatic weapons which is equivalent to that of U. S. practice.

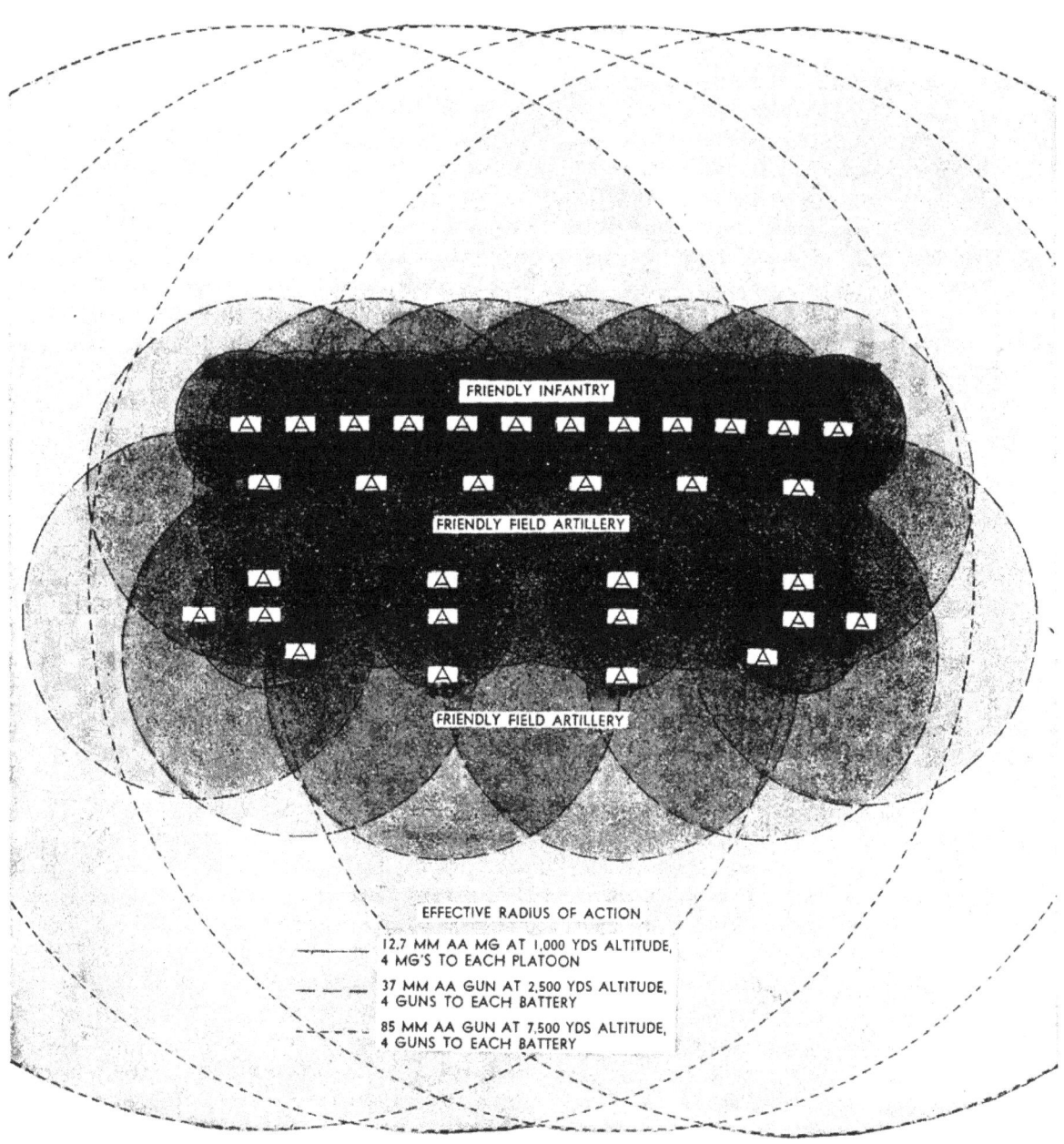

Figure 51. Antiaircraft artillery division in defense of an infantry offensive.

225

The organic antiaircraft artillery of the armored, mechanized, and cavalry corps consists of an antiaircraft artillery regiment plus the antiaircraft machine-gun companies of the component formations, comprising in all sixteen 37-mm guns, and fifty-two 12.7-mm antiaircraft machine guns. By U. S. standards, this allotment of organic antiaircraft artillery to the mobile corps is incapable of providing adequate antiaircraft protection over the entire corps deployment area in most situations. However, centralized control of the antiaircraft weapons makes up for some of their deficiency in numbers, and permits defense of vital installations. Combat troops employ their own 7.62-mm machine guns and 14.5-mm semiautomatic antitank rifles for local protection.

3. CONTROL

The commander of the antiaircraft artillery units of a Soviet combined-arms formation is subordinate to the artillery commander of the formation. The artillery commander is the only person who may change the missions of the antiaircraft artillery; only he may shift its effort from a primary to a secondary mission, and the reverse. The commander of the antiaircraft artillery must keep himself informed of the general situation and of the mission of the supported units. He maintains communications with the staff of the supported organization and with the artillery commander of that organization. Jointly with the signal officer he establishes antiaircraft warning service.

In support of ground operations, the commander of the antiaircraft artillery groups his batteries to give maximum support to units which are in a most advantageous position to develop the offensive. In a static situation he groups his batteries to achieve concentration of fire over important installations and assembly areas. The antiaircraft artillery commander must not allow his tactics to become stereotyped and passive; guided by reconnaissance reports and study of the tactics and habits of the enemy, he must maneuver his batteries, use ruses, and, in cooperation with interceptor aviation lead the enemy into firetraps.

4. DISPOSITION

Tactical antiaircraft artillery is used for the protection of deployment and assembly areas, forward and rear area installations such as supply dumps and artillery and mortar positions, and for the support of ground operations. In protecting troops deployed in forward areas, antiaircraft artillery is deployed linearly. The heavy machine guns are emplaced by platoons between 300 and 500 yards from the forward elements. Light antiaircraft guns are emplaced by batteries on a line 1,000 to 1,500 yards from the forward lines. The distance between batteries is between 1,000 and 2,000 yards, the distance between platoons is between 100 and 150 yards, and the distance between individual pieces is at least 30 yards. The medium antiaircraft guns are emplaced by batteries on a line approximately 2,000 to 3,000 yards from the forward lines. The distance between batteries is also between 2,000 and 3,000 yards, and the distance between individual pieces is at least 30 yards.

In protecting assembly areas and rear echelon installations, antiaircraft artillery is deployed in two concentric circles. The inner circle is located within the defended area; the outer circle is approximately 1,000 yards from the perimeter of the defended area. Distances between the batteries, platoons, and individual pieces are the same as those employed in linear defense.

Normally, medium antiaircraft batteries are emplaced approximately 2,000 yards apart in dug-in positions, and are camouflaged. Alternate and dummy positions are always prepared for the whole battery; if fire against land targets is anticipated, special dual-purpose emplacements are also prepared. The depth of emplacements is such that gun sights are protected from mortar fragments. The preparation of all types of emplacements and maneuver of batteries from one position to another are habitually accomplished at night.

Five types of fire control are used by Red Army medium antiaircraft artillery: tracking individual targets, moving barrage, stationary barrage, direct fire against land targets, and observed indirect fire against land targets. In tracking individual targets, a battery fires as a unit from data computed by a range finder and director, or by radar. In erecting moving and stationary barrages, a battalion or a larger groupment is a firing unit. These barrages are considered inefficient and wasteful of ammunition, and are used only when tracking is impossible due to meteorological conditions or other causes. In direct fire against land targets, fire is controlled by individual gun commanders against designated targets. When massed fire is desired, a battery may be used as a unit. Direct and indirect observed fire are used against land targets as parts of artillery preparations. Antiaircraft artillery guns are assigned targets whose destruction requires high velocity projectiles. Observed indirect fire is controlled in the same manner as that of light field artillery.

Light antiaircraft artillery is normally emplaced by platoons in dug-in and camouflaged positions. Emplacements are deep enough to protect gun sights from mortar fragments. Alternate positions for duty pieces and positions for fire against land targets are prepared with embrasures covering the sectors of responsibility for antitank defense. Light antiaircraft artillery employs direct fire only. The platoon is the firing unit. Effective range against approaching targets is 2,000 yards; against departing targets, 1,000 yards. In attacking ground targets, light antiaircraft guns are effective against embrasures of fortifications, personnel, observation posts, machine gun and antitank positions, and tanks.

5. SUPPORT OF GROUND OPERATIONS

In supporting ground operations, antiaircraft artillery has three functions: protection of march columns against air and land attacks; protection of personnel and matériel in assembly and deployment areas; and active support of the assault.

During the approach march, antiaircraft batteries are disposed throughout the column. Some light antiaircraft guns are emplaced in advance at points along the route where traffic may become channelized (narrow defiles, bridges, fords, or woods). Antiaircraft machine guns are dispersed along the column to protect the heavier antiaircraft weapons against attacks by low-flying planes and enemy ground forces. At night 50 percent of the machine guns must be ready to fire against ground targets.

Active support of ground operations is carried out in three phases. During the artillery preparation for the assault, antiaircraft artillery—in addition to its primary mission—is used in planned fire against enemy fortifications, firing positions, and observation posts. During the assault, light antiaircraft artillery guns and machine guns accompany the assault teams to protect them against air attacks and to assist supporting arms. As a rule antiaircraft weapons are concentrated in sectors where the assault is most successful, in order to assist in repulsing probable counterattacks and to maintain the momentum of the assault.

6. IMPROVISED ANTIAIRCRAFT DEFENSES

In addition to the antiaircraft weapons proper, the Red Army effectively uses light field artillery and semiautomatic antitank rifles against air targets. Field artillery batteries (76.2-mm guns and 122-mm howitzers) fire in volleys at predetermined ranges with pre-cut fuses. Gun emplacements are constructed so that trails can be lowered to increase the maximum elevation by 30 degrees. To facilitate control and to speed fire, orientation points are selected in directions of probable approach of enemy planes.

Three to five semiautomatic antitank rifles, firing on the same target, are used against low-level and dive-bombing attacks. They are considered effective at ranges up to 500 yards.

PART III. SPECIAL OPERATIONS

Section I. OPERATIONS IN LIMITED VISIBILITY

1. NIGHT OPERATIONS

The Red Army has been successful in both large- and small-scale operations at night. The Soviets consider that night operations are preferable when terrain, dense minefields, and other obstacles—combined with enemy preparedness—eliminate the possibility of surprise and make heavy casualties in daytime operations a probability.

Night raids, small-scale attacks, and reconnaissance in force are initiated to complete reconnaissance data, to force the enemy to disclose his plan of defense and plan of fire, to capture prisoners, to harass the enemy, and to divert his attention from other sectors of the front. During preparation for a major offensive, small-scale night operations are conducted in order to capture terrain favorable for observation of the enemy or suitable for deployment of the main force. All night operations are carefully planned and coordinated. For example, a typical small raid (figs. 52 and 53) was planned 6 days in advance and was preceded by careful observation of the enemy by members of the raiding party.

Order of advance of the reconnaissance party.	Cross the Vistula in a boat disembarking near a separate clump of bushes. Cross the trench and deploy in the rear of the heavy machine gun.
Objective.	Heavy machine gun in open firing position about 400 yards to the east of height 124.8.
Organization of the attack.	Reconnaissance party to consist of four men; Number 1 to guard the boat. Nos. 2 and 3, to attack the machine gun crew. No. 4 to throw a grenade into the shelter.
Fire support: Artillery.	Two batteries to lay interdictory barrage at A and B. One battery to fire interdictory mission in depth along the communication trench. 45-mm guns to fire in pairs on the enemy firing positions to the north and south of the objective.
Mortars.	To lay interdiction barrage at C.
Machine guns and antitank rifles.	To engage the same targets as 45-mm guns.
Coordination signals.	To call for artillery and mortar fire—one green rocket fired upstream. To call for a reserve boat—red light from a flashlight.
Order of withdrawal.	No. 4 to convoy the prisoner to the boat. Nos. 2 and 3 to cover No. 4, then Nos. 1 and 4 to cover Nos. 2 and 3.

Figure 52. Plan of a night raid across the Vistula, 16 November 1944

The success of night operations depends on careful reconnaissance, simplicity of maneuver, speed of execution, and surprise. The deployment area is occupied secretly during twilight hours so that the commanders of the assault teams may familiarize themselves with orientation points, phase lines, and avenues of approach. To achieve surprise, artillery preparation is often omitted during the initial assault. Two phase lines are selected. The first is located within the forward defense zone of the enemy. This position is used to regroup the assault teams and to establish coordination with the supporting artillery for the attack of the next objective. The second phase line is so selected that its capture would force the enemy to displace his artillery. To facilitate control of combat and designation of targets for the supporting artillery, the assault zone is divided into sectors. Orientation points for infantry and tanks are carefully designated. The assault is launched by a signal from the line of departure. Advance of the assault teams is marked by visual and auditory signals. In order to reduce the effectiveness of enemy mortar fire, infantry advances at a jog. Battalion commanders must continue the assault until the second phase line is reached. If the attack fails, it is often repeated in the same sector on the assumption that the enemy does not expect such a tactic. This is in contrast to U. S. doctrine.

The battalion attacks in a single wave preceded by a small advance guard. The rifle companies are deployed in line, each company in turn being deployed in a line of platoons. Individual riflemen wear white arm bands. Squads advance in wedge formation: riflemen to the right of the point fire ahead and to the right; those to the left of the point fire ahead and to the left. If the assault sector is narrow (400 to 500 yards), a rifle battalion may attack in two echelons. The second echelon then consists of a reinforced rifle company whose mission is to protect the flanks of the battalion. For raiding missions, a special detachment is formed to evacuate captured documents, equipment, and prisoners. The assault-team principle is followed in grouping elements of the rifle battalion; that is, riflemen are supplemented by company and battalion weapons and by engineers according to the mission of each assault team.

Tanks are frequently employed in support of infantry at night. Preliminary terrain reconnaissance, clear statement of tasks, clear definition of orientation points, and close cooperation with infantry are considered the salient points in successful use of tanks at night. Each tank is assigned its route, mission, and the infantry assault team which it supports. Several riflemen are assigned to each tank to aid its crew in locating antitank weapons and obstacles. When the situation permits, tank headlights are used to illuminate enemy firing points, to light the way for obstacle-clearing parties, and to blind the enemy. In street fighting at night, tanks often set fire to buildings in order to illuminate the enemy.

In a night tank-infantry attack on Kuestrin, Germany, the following action was reported: Retreating Germans prepared an ambush for the pursuing Red Army infantry and tanks in a town park. The lead Soviet tank stopped and fired a few rounds into the town hall, setting it on fire (fig. 54), while the remaining tanks and infantry deployed in a rough semicircle. German soldiers in ambush were

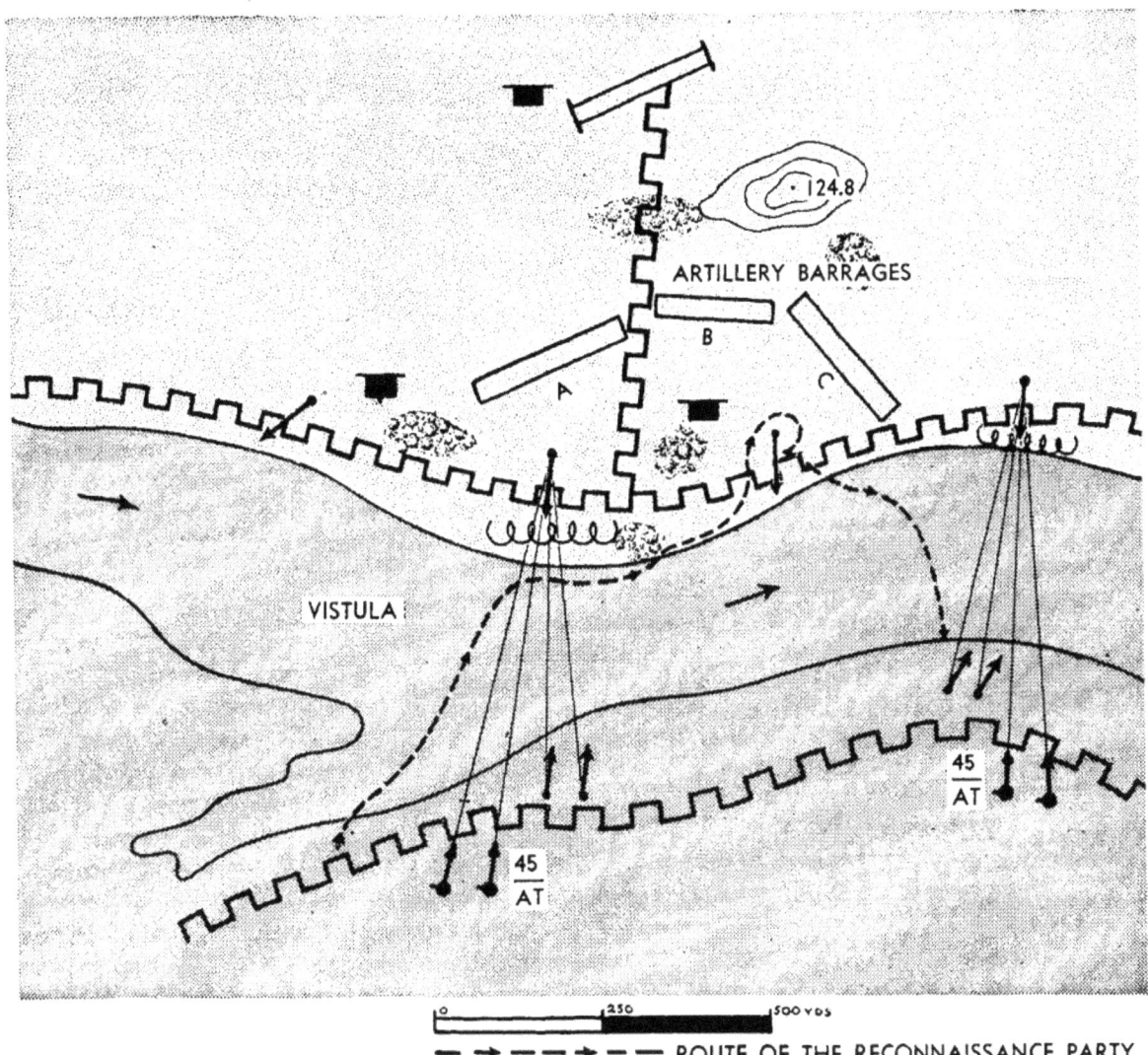

ROUTE OF THE RECONNAISSANCE PARTY

Figure 53. Sketch showing plan of a night raid across the Vistula, 16 November 1944.

silhouetted against the burning building and Soviet tommy-gunners who remained in the shadows made short work of the ambush.

Forcing of the Oder River line is an example of a large-scale night operation: 5,000 planes, 4,000 tanks, and over 22,000 pieces of artillery supported the infantry attack. A special feature of this operation was the use of massed searchlights. Over 200 searchlights were spaced about 200 yards apart to illuminate the path for Soviet tanks and blind the enemy. Surprise was achieved by launching the main attack along the entire front at night instead of at daybreak when it was expected.

2. USE OF SMOKE

Soviet tactical doctrine stresses the employment of smoke to cover friendly troops as much as to blind

enemy observation (fig. 55). Smoke is used to cover regroupment of forces, concentrations of troops, direction of the main effort, and all phases of large- and small-scale operations where the terrain affords little cover from enemy observation. It is also used to deceive the enemy by false smoke concentrations which cause him to waste ammunition and disclose his firing positions.

The Red Army uses smoke concentrations over large areas for extended periods to cover major attacks; to protect vital installations such as railroad bridges, assembly areas, and supply dumps from enemy aviation; to screen a counterattack; or to cover a withdrawal. The width of such a smoke screen varies from 2,500 to 3,500 yards. Roads leading to important locations and all orientation

229

points in the proximity of targets are also covered with smoke to make their detection more difficult.

Smoke, when used to cover a major attack, is coordinated with the principal phases of the assault. In the preparatory phase, smoke is used to cover the activities of the reconnaissance parties and obstacle-clearing detachments (fig. 56). During the assault phase, smoke is laid over the forward lines of the enemy (fig. 57). Care is taken not to blind friendly observation posts. In this phase, false con-

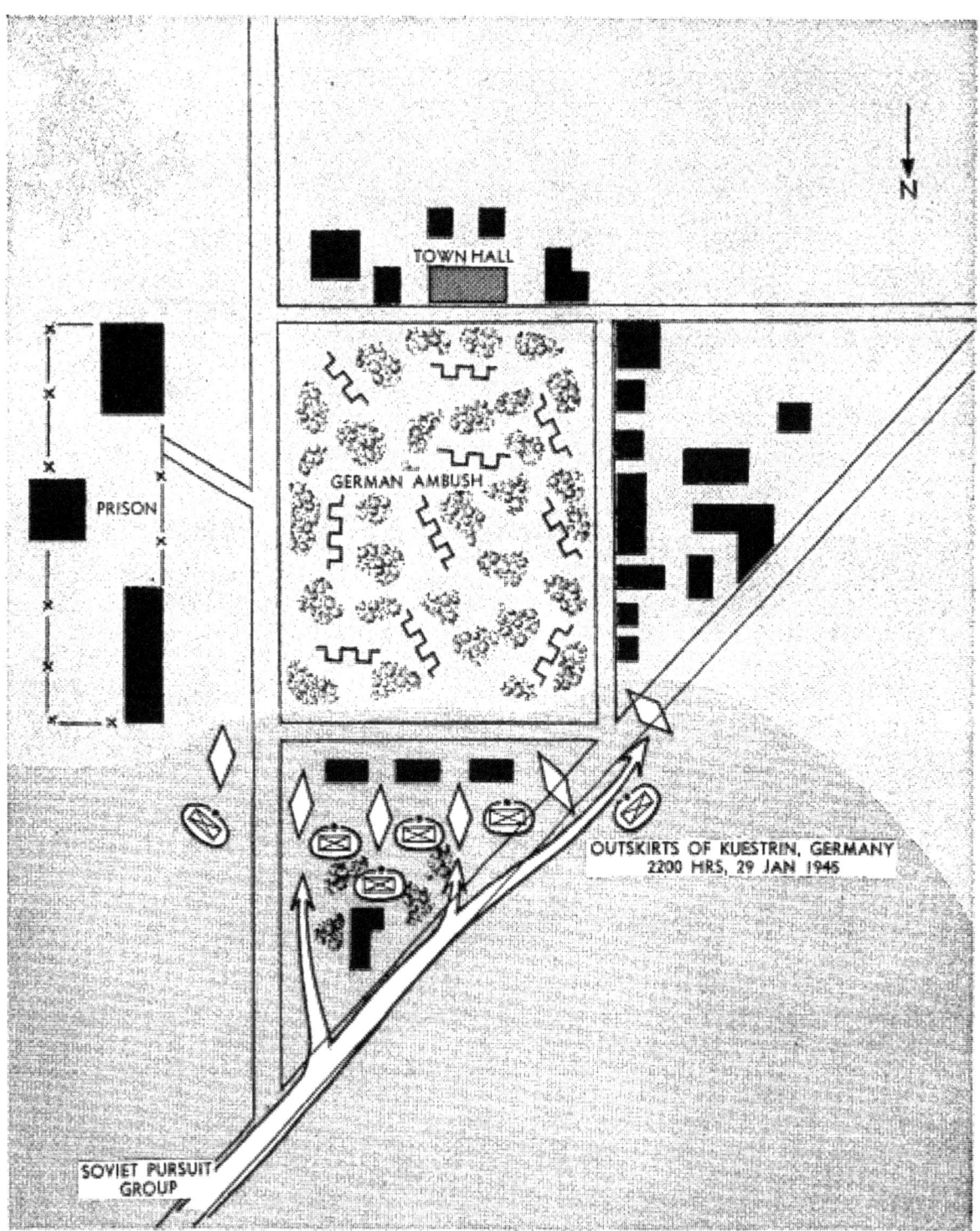

Figure 54. Armored attack on a town at night.

230

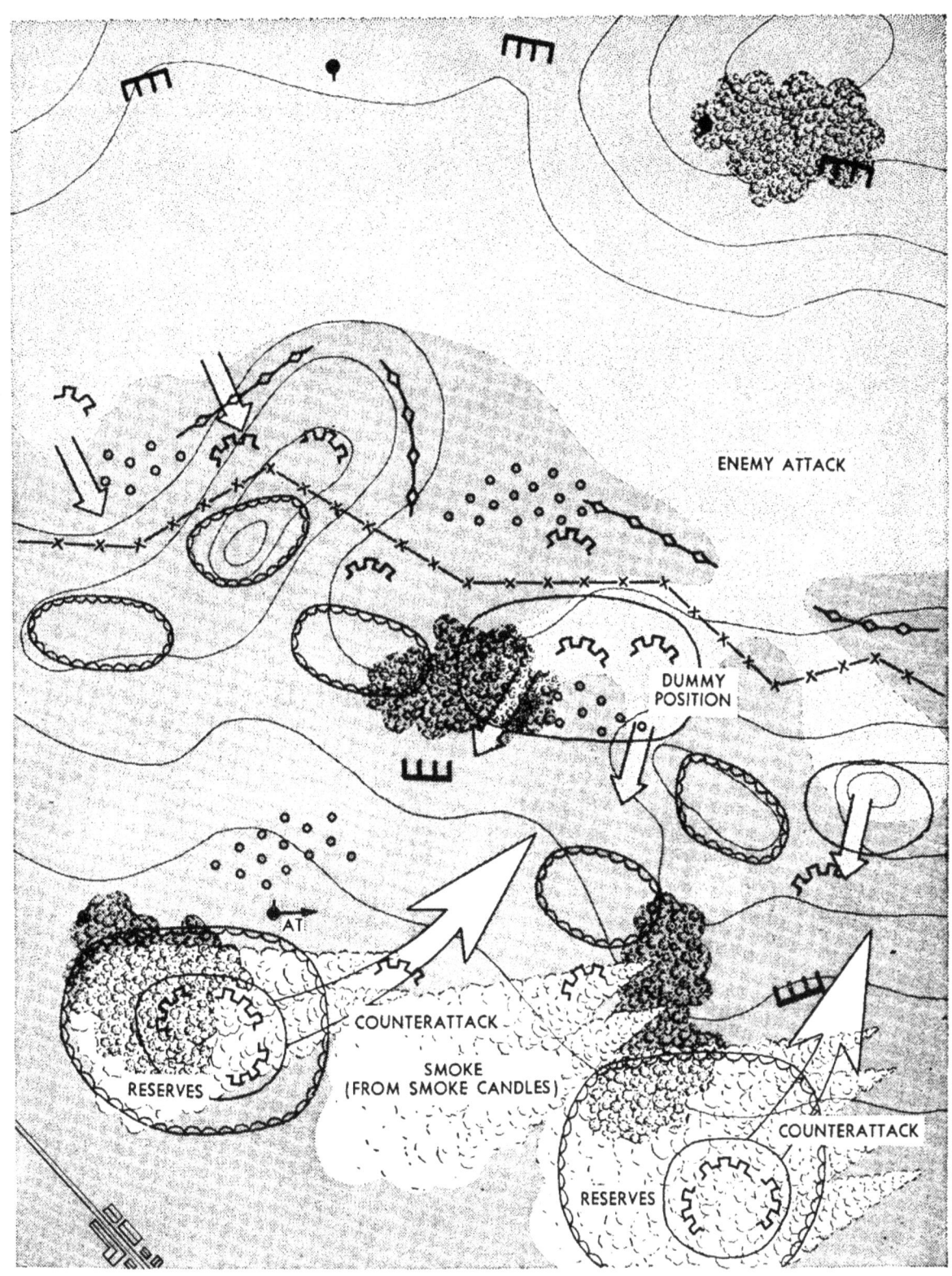

ENEMY ATTACK

DUMMY POSITION

AT

COUNTERATTACK

SMOKE
(FROM SMOKE CANDLES)

RESERVES

COUNTERATTACK

RESERVES

Figure 55. Smoke used to hide a counterattack. Note that smoke covers friendly rather than enemy troops.

231

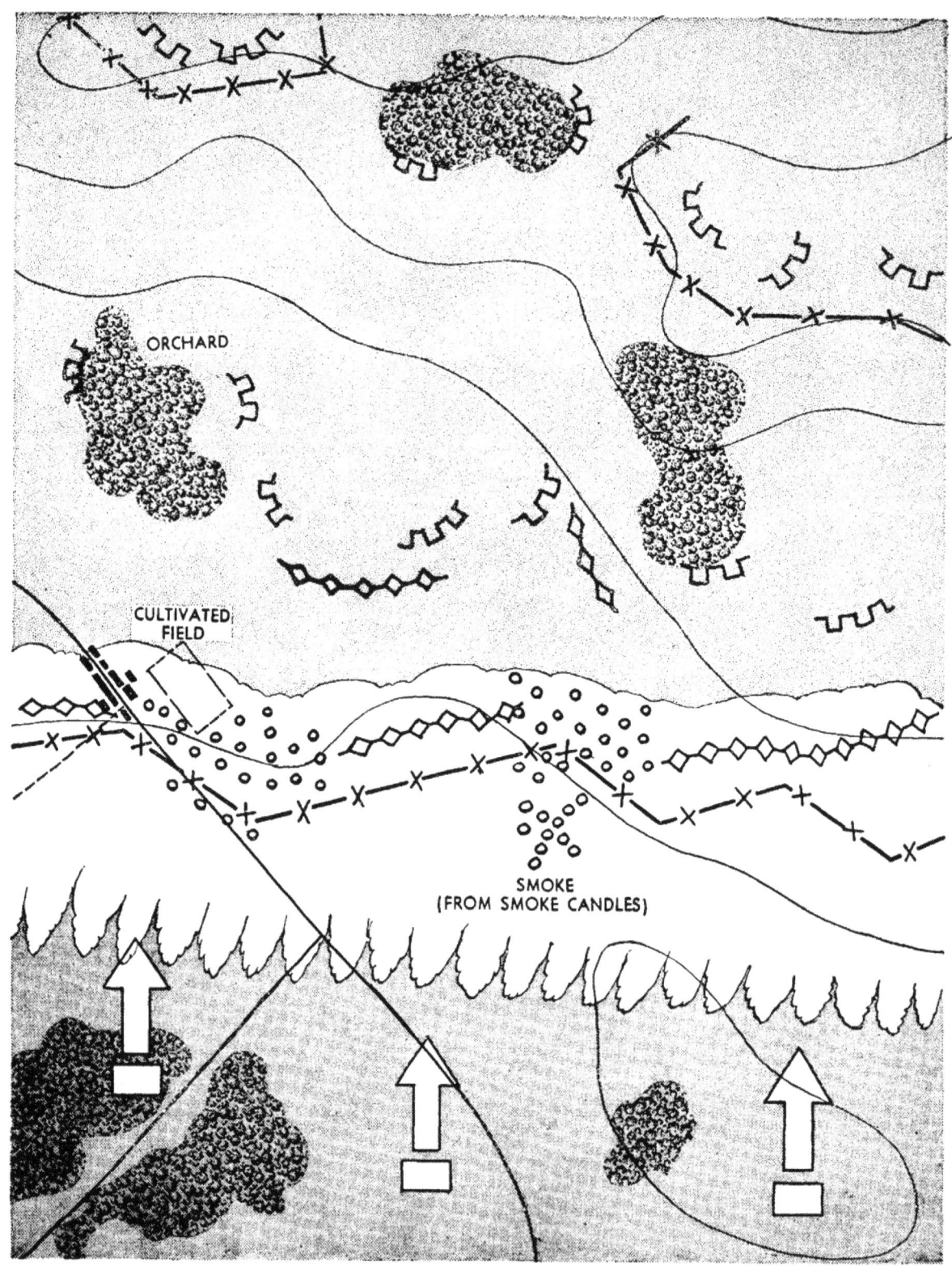

Figure 56. Use of smoke to cover removal of obstacles.

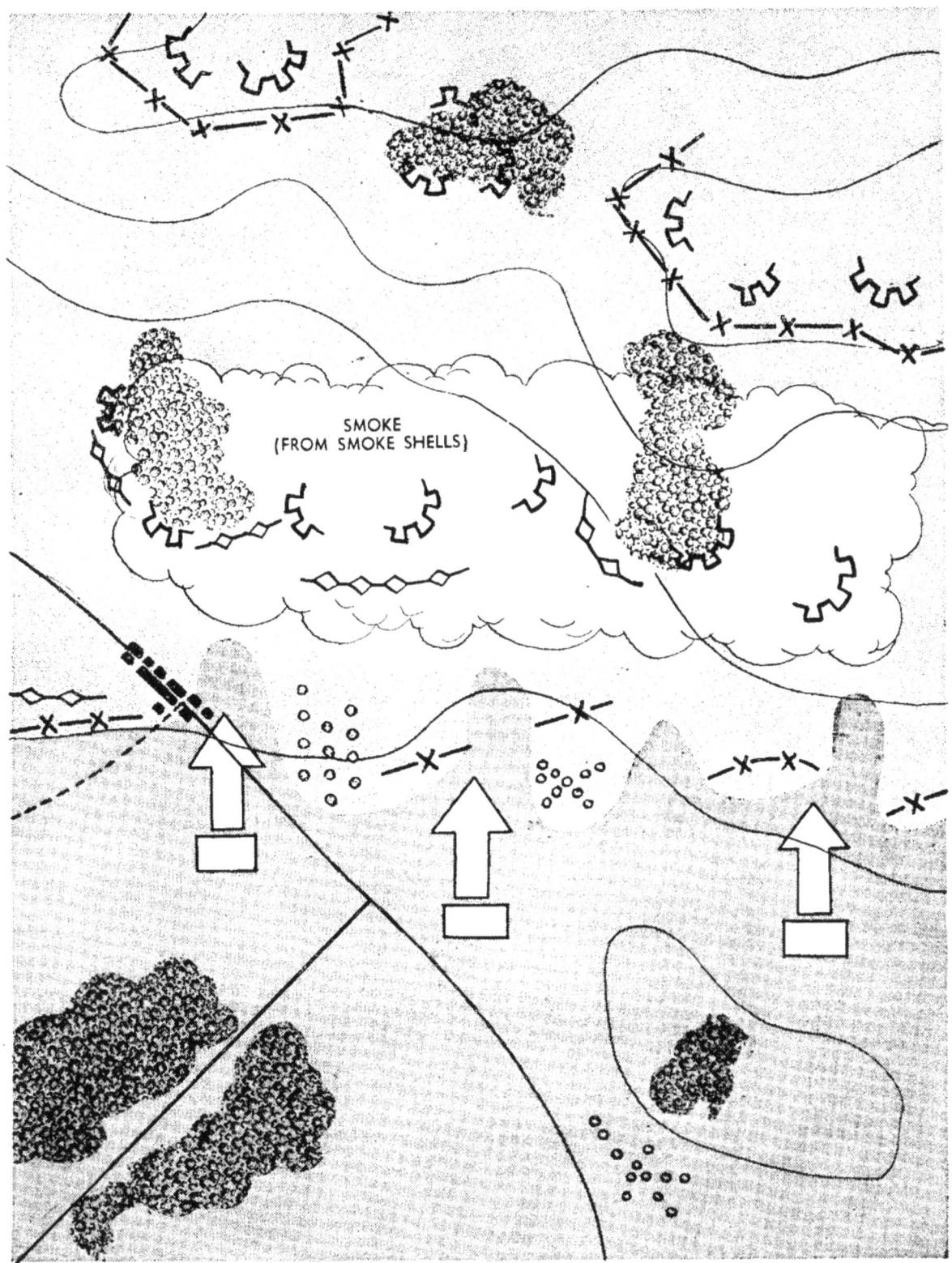

Figure 57. Smoke used to cover the initial objective of the assault.

233

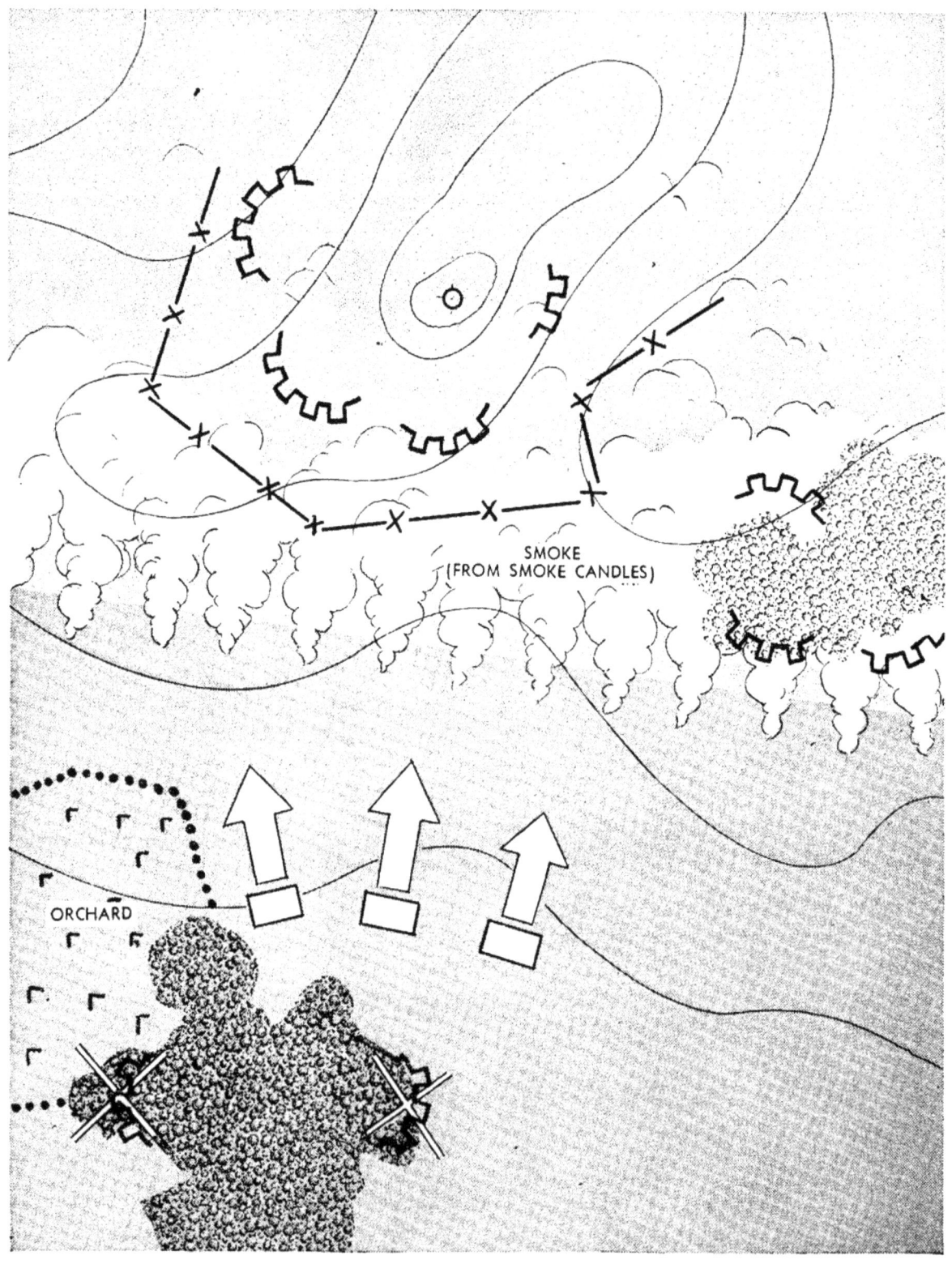

SMOKE
(FROM SMOKE CANDLES)

ORCHARD

Figure 58. Smoke used within the defensive positions of the enemy.

centrations of smoke are used to confuse the enemy as to the direction of the main effort. A smoke screen may be laid between the first and subsequent assault waves. During combat within the defense lines of the enemy, smoke is used to cover portions of the enemy positions, to blind by-passed centers of resistance, or to blind stubbornly defended areas (fig. 58).

Small-scale employment of smoke is an established practice in the Red Army. Smoke pots or smoke hand grenades are used to cover the actions of an individual soldier or a small unit, or to blind individual enemy observation posts or firing positions. Smoke is a valuable cover for individual riflemen or a small infantry unit during the advance toward enemy lines. Tank units use smoke not only to cover their advance from the assembly area to the deployment area and maneuvers within the enemy defense zone, but also for withdrawal from enemy fire. Smoke is also used to simulate tank losses, to screen the work of tank crews in repairing minor damage on the battlefield, and to facilitate the evacuation of damaged tanks under fire. Three to five smoke pots are used to screen the maneuvers of one tank.

Judicious use of smoke can nullify efforts of the enemy when he uses smoke shells for registration fire.

Section II. ASSAULT AND DEFENSE OF FORTIFIED ZONES

1. PLANNING AND ORGANIZING THE ASSAULT

The destruction of enemy forces in a fortified zone is accomplished by the complete break-through of all enemy defensive positions in the sector of the main effort, and subsequent flank attacks against adjacent sectors to clear the entire fortified zone. (See also sections II and V, part II.)

Fortified zones vary in defensive strength according to the extent of development, type of fortifications, terrain, strength of the defending personnel, and defensive fire power. The German fortified zones encountered by the Red Army were usually about 40 miles deep and extended up to 100 miles along the front. The outpost defense zone, 9 to 12 miles from the main defensive position, consisted of strong points at all dominating terrain features. The main defensive positions consisted of permanent steel and concrete emplacements organized as strong points, with numerous trenches and separate firing positions interlaced between

them. Switch positions, to prevent lateral movement if main defensive positions were breached, covered the 7- to 10-mile distance between the main defensive positions and the second defensive positions. The second defensive position was generally weaker than the main defensive position except that counterattacks were a constant threat to the assault groups, especially if strong units from the main defensive positions succeeded in falling back to the second line. This line was 2 to 3 miles deep; behind it was the rear defensive belt, generally of earth and timber construction, 1 to 2 miles in depth.

Soviet doctrine prescribes two possible types of assault, the accelerated attack and the progressive attack. The accelerated attack is used when enemy forces are disorganized and the fortified zone is not fully developed. Combat formations of combined arms and mobile troops reinforced by infantry, artillery, engineer units, and aviation are used to break through the fortified zone. The progressive attack is employed when considerable resistance from thoroughly developed fortifications is anticipated. Soviet doctrine stresses the intensive training of assault groups together with the supporting arms as the most important single factor in the successful assault of fortified zones. In many World War II operations, at least two rehearsals by assault groups and cooperating arms were held in rear areas prior to the actual assault.

The assault may be made with the main effort along a single front from 6 to 9 miles wide or in multiple thrusts each 2 miles in width. Holding attacks are made simultaneously for diversion and to seize isolated fortified positions. The basic mission is to destroy enemy forces within the defensive zone and in the rear. Great emphasis is made on attacks against the flanks of the penetration area. In mountains and swamps, assaults are generally made on a narrower front in successive stages.

2. COMBAT ORGANIZATIONS IN THE ASSAULT

Infantry assault groups must be of balanced composition to facilitate control under exacting conditions. The echeloning of troops must be organized to provide for the immediate replacement of losses in the leading assault groups, to increase the intensity of the attack into the enemy's defensive depth, and to develop the breach by attacking the enemy flanks. The organization of assault groups begins with the assault division; the basic combat element is the assault battalion. While some details of the

235

assault organization vary with the situation, the basic structure has been standardized since 1944.

a. Assault division. This consists of a Guards Rifle Division of 10,500 men, and strong tank, artillery, and engineer reinforcements which bring the total strength up to 16,000 men (fig. 59). The supporting armor normally consists of one regiment each of heavy and medium tanks, a regiment of 76.2-mm or 85-mm self-propelled artillery, and about a company of mine-clearing, flame-throwing, and bridging tanks. GHQ artillery includes a light artillery brigade, a mortar regiment, two to four battalions of 122-mm to 152-mm howitzers, a battalion of 203-mm howitzers, and a battery of superheavy artillery. The assault engineer-pioneer regiment includes flame-thrower operators and other special engineer troops.

The assault division forms three assault regiments. In addition, artillery groups and subgroups, the tank support group, the smoke-laying group, and the antitank reserve are constituted.

Four types of artillery operate under the control of the divisional artillery commander:

The divisional artillery support groupment (120-mm mortars, 122-mm howitzers, and 152-mm howitzers) is responsible for neutralization of at least the first two lines of trenches in the assault and for reinforcement of the regimental artillery groupment. Part of the artillery employs direct fire against enemy firing positions and obstacles.

The division is also allotted subgroupments from the corps countermortar (120-mm mortars and 122-mm howitzers) and destruction groupments (152-mm and 203-mm howitzers, superheavy artillery). The former subgroupment is assigned the mission of countermortar and counterrocket operation; the latter, the destruction of permanent fortifications.

Finally, the division maintains an artillery reserve, which is committed by the divisional commander as required.

The assault division is deployed in one or two echelons in accordance with the strength of enemy fortifications and the assigned missions. A general reserve and an antitank reserve must be provided. The divisional assault front in the main effort has a width of from 0.6 to 1.2 miles. In secondary efforts, and in mountain and swamp combat, the front is 2 to 2.5 miles wide.

b. Assault regiment. Each regiment of the basic rifle division employed in the assault is reinforced by the following:

Artillery (one battalion of the organic divisional artillery, one battery of the organic divisional antitank battalion, a GHQ mortar battalion, and a GHQ light gun battalion).

Armored vehicles (two companies of medium tanks, one company of heavy tanks, one battery of light or medium self-propelled guns, and about a platoon of mine-clearing tanks).

About a battalion of combat engineers (fig. 60).

The assault regiment resulting from these reinforcements forms two assault battalions. The third rifle battalion is utilized for the infantry component of the regimental assault group, the regimental obstacle-clearing group, and the regimental reserve. The regimental assault group is used in operations against forts and concrete casemates of great strength. In addition to a rifle company, it comprises a pioneer platoon, a heavy tank company, mine-clearing tanks, a self-propelled gun battery, and platoons of mortars and flame throwers. It is often supported by a smoke-laying group. The regimental obstacle-clearing groups clear passages through minefields and obstacles, prior to and during the infantry and tank assault, support the battalion obstacle-clearing groups in difficult operations, and enlarge gaps for the passage of succeeding echelons. The regimental reserves provide antitank and antipersonnel security, especially for the flanks and rear of the regiment; they also serve as a personnel and matériel replacement pool for the assault battalion and the regimental assault group.

The tank support group consists of two medium tank companies, each of which normally supports one assault battalion.

The regimental artillery groupment consists of one organic battalion of divisional artillery (regimental combat team), plus a battalion of heavy mortars. This groupment is under the control of the divisional artillery commander during the artillery preparation phase, but passes under the control of the regimental commander during the assault phase. This artillery fires from open as well as covered positions, supports the assault as directed by the regimental commander, and may be utilized to replace losses in the battalion direct-fire artillery groupment.

236

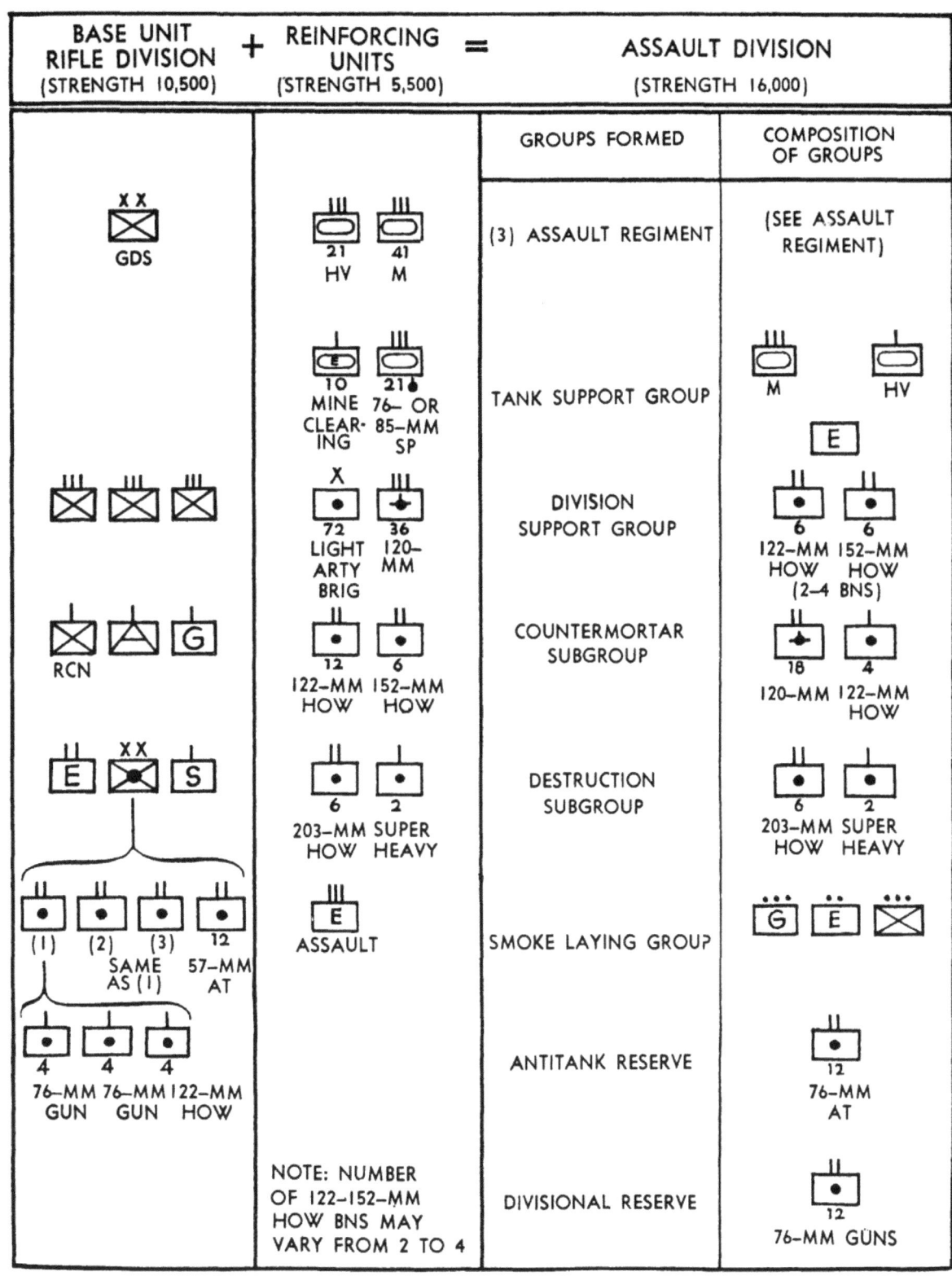

Figure 59. Organization of the assault division.

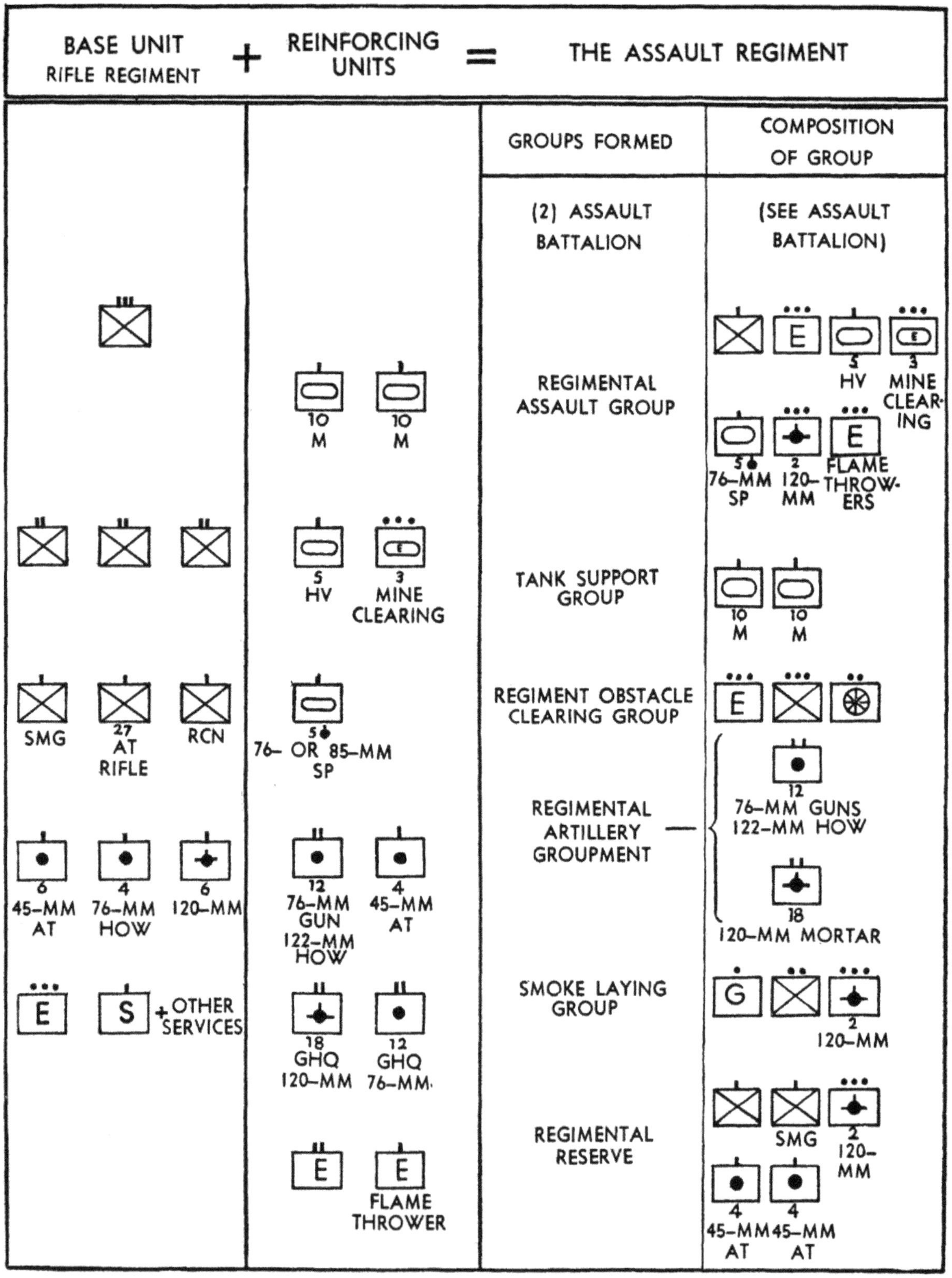

Figure 60. Organization of the assault regiment.

238

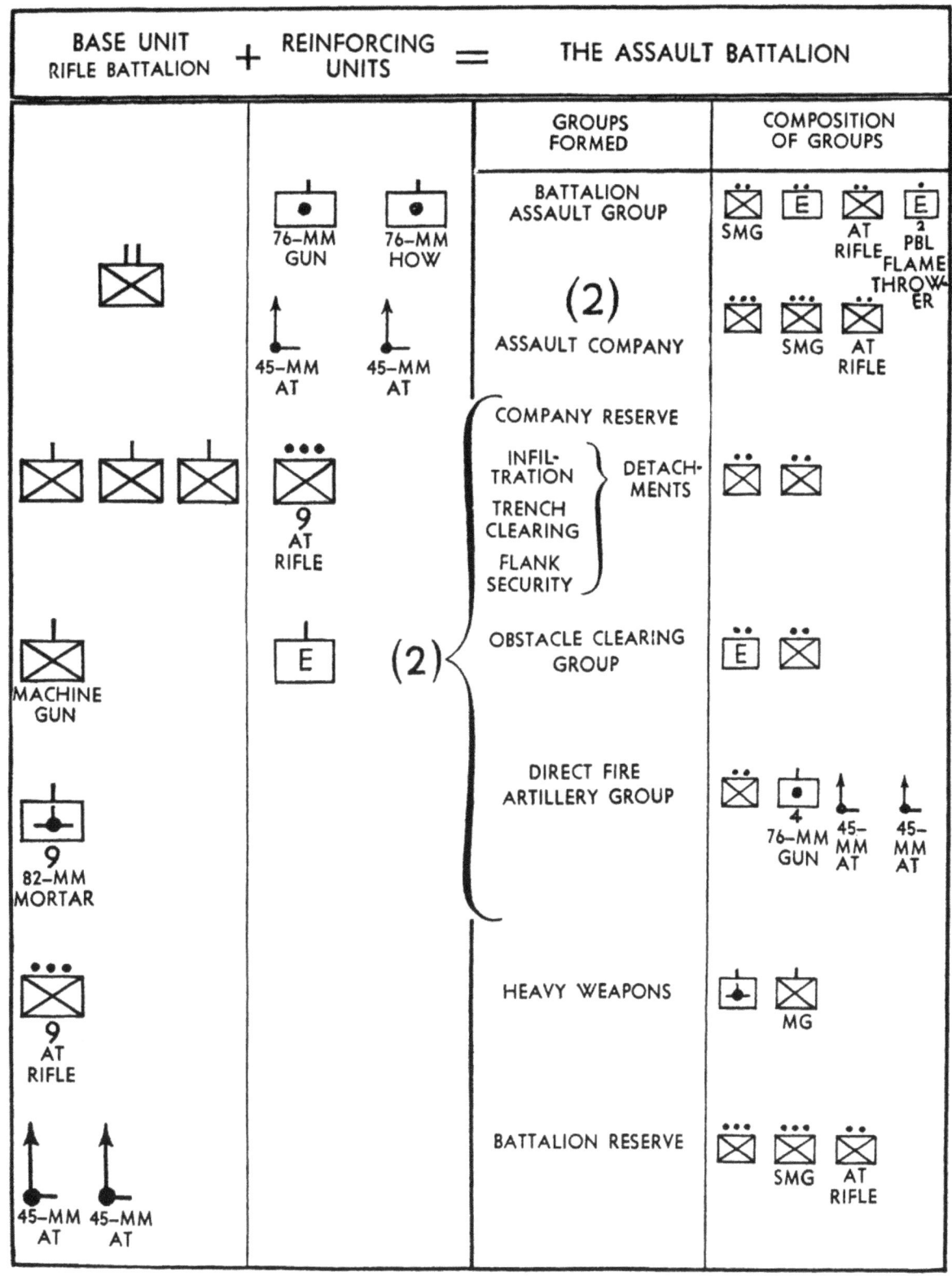

Figure 61. Organization of the assault battalion.

The assault regiment in the main effort deploys with assault battalions abreast or in column; its zone of action therefore varies from 550 to 1,100 yards.

c. Assault battalion. The assault battalion is the primary tactical unit employed in the assault of fortified positions. It consists of the rifle battalion reinforced by two batteries of 76.2-mm guns or infantry howitzers, two light antitank guns, a platoon of antitank riflemen, and a company of pioneers (fig. 61).

The assault battalion, like the assault regiment, forms but two assault companies, the third rifle company being allotted to the battalion assault group, the direct-fire artillery groups, and the battalion reserve. Each assault company deploys two platoons—one rifle and one submachine-gun platoon—abreast. Infiltration and trench-clearing teams, as well as personnel for flank security, are organized from the third platoon. Each company is reinforced by an obstacle-clearing group of one pioneer and one rifle section; and a direct-fire artillery group of 76.2-mm guns or a howitzer battery, two light antitank guns, and a rifle section for security (fig. 62). Direct-fire artillery does not participate in the artillery preparation.

For operations against pillboxes and concrete emplacements, an assault group is organized in the battalion. Its organization varies slightly in strength and capabilities in accordance with the resistance of the enemy position to be assaulted. Typically, it consists of a section of submachine gunners, a section of pioneers, a section of antitank riflemen, and two or three men with portable flame throwers.

The battalion mortars and heavy machine guns remain under centralized control. The battalion reserve consists of the balance of the third company (one rifle and one submachine-gun platoon) and an antitank rifle section.

The battalion deploys on a front of 550 yards and to a depth of 440 yards in one assault echelon. In mountain warfare and in swamps, the battalion deploys in two echelons.

3. PREPARATION OF THE ASSAULT

a. Organization of reconnaissance. The staff of the senior troop commander organizes the reconnaissance plan for the entire operation. Soviet practice prescribes mission-type and continuous reconnaissance by all reconnaissance units to make possible the proper command decision. A minimum

of three separate sets of aerial photographs is often prescribed to supplement ground reconnaissance. Extensive and uninterrupted ground observation during the preparation phase, as well as during combat, is one of the most important forms of reconnaissance. Day and night reconnaissance patrols determine specific enemy data. Complete information must be gained by means of combat reconnaissance. A combat reconnaissance group consists of a rifle battalion supported by two or three divisional artillery battalions and reinforced by GHQ artillery and tanks, mortar units, and aviation. During this operation, special artillery, tank, and engineer reconnaissance is conducted simultaneously with general troop reconnaissance. During combat reconnaissance, forward enemy firing positions and outposts may be assaulted and seized if the neutralization or capture of such positions will facilitate general assault.

All information of enemy installations and dispositions is recorded on large-scale maps and distributed down to battalion and company commanders several days prior to the assault.

b. Planning the assault. Assault group training is a fundamental requisite during the preparation phase. Thorough training in the proper employment of the individual weapon is followed by the training of assault groups in close coordination with all supporting arms. In many operations this type of training has taken place on a large scale in an area far to the rear, and has included practice assaults by the assault teams against reproduced enemy fortifications. Holding forces and reconnaissance units remained in contact with the enemy forward positions during this time.

The line of departure is far more elaborate in this type of operations than in the offensive where no heavily fortified zone is encountered. A forward trench position is constructed at a distance of 150 to 200 yards from the enemy outpost line, and is occupied by observers and security elements. Infantry units are deployed in several lines of trenches to the rear where elaborate shelters, dumps, and concealed gun positions are prepared. These trenches are 100 to 150 yards apart; they contain battalion and regimental reserves, dug-in direct-fire gun positions, mortar positions, command posts and medical stations, and ammunition and other supply dumps.

The topographic service produces maps (R. F. 1/2,000) in sufficient quantities for complete dis-

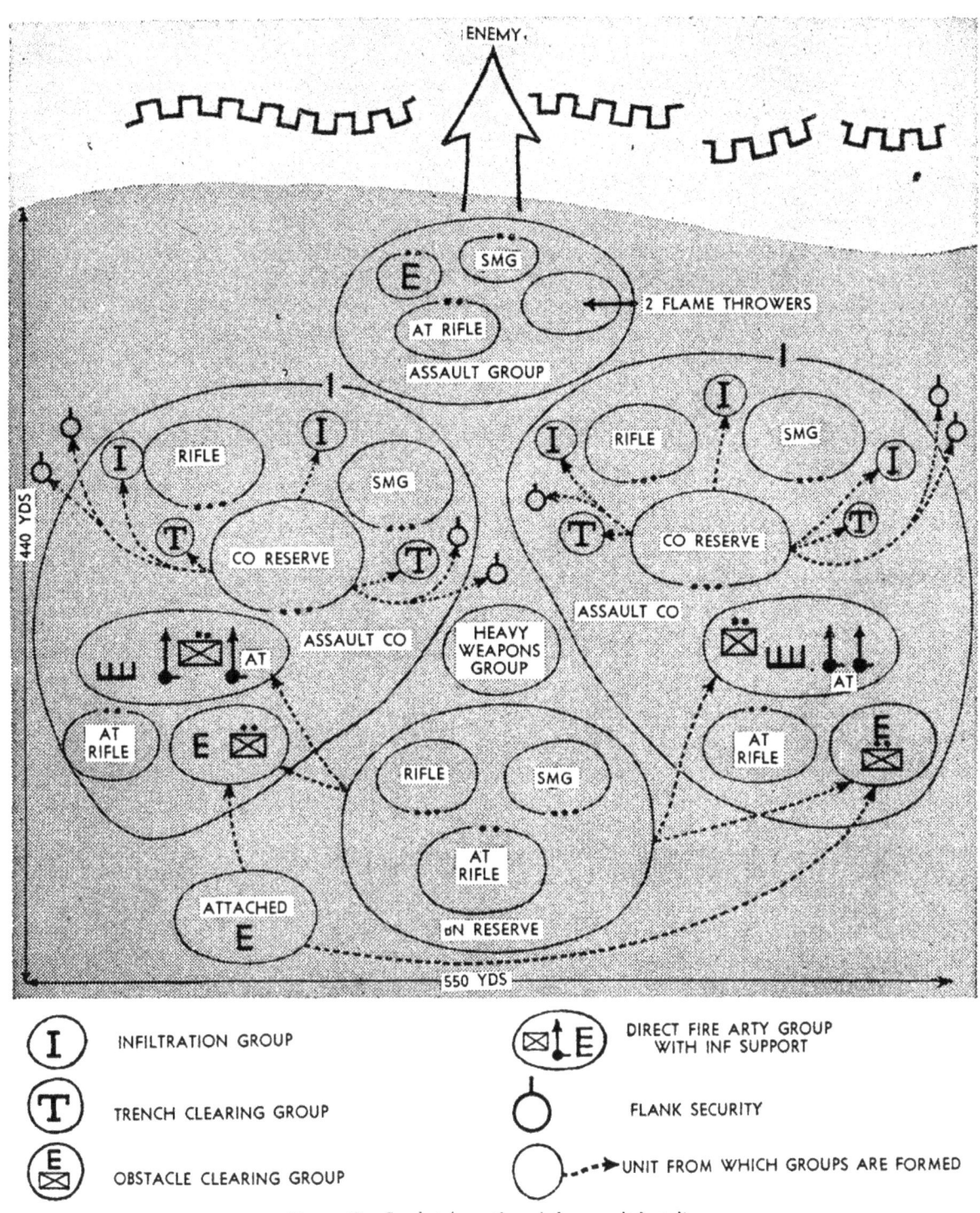

Figure 62. Combat formation of the assault battalion.

semination. The entire enemy fortified zone is indicated in the greatest possible detail. The combat coordination tables are worked out in complete detail with definite missions assigned to every assault group.

Troop concentration and redeployment prior to

the assault are carried out by night with great secrecy, using specially constructed communication trenches. Assault groups must occupy the line of departure trenches within one day of the assault. On the eve of the assault, ramps are dug and passages are cleared to facilitate movement forward of per-

241

sonnel, tanks, and guns from their entrenched positions.

4. CONDUCT OF THE ASSAULT

The artillery and aviation preparation has the mission of weakening enemy resistance to the greatest possible degree. Artillery and bombardment units attack all known enemy fortifications on a front wider than the main effort sector in order to neutralize enemy positions which can direct flanking fire on the penetration area. Stormovik formations attack enemy personnel in trenches, assembly areas, and rear areas as well as firing positions and targets of opportunity. Fighter groups provide cover against enemy air action throughout the entire operation. Artillery and close-support aviation continue to neutralize enemy positions throughout the entire assault phase by attacking successive enemy defensive lines and strongpoints impeding the progress of the assault groups. Particular attention is directed against concentrations of enemy infantry antitank guns and revived strongpoints, gun batteries, and mortars.

The obstacle clearing groups prepare lanes through minefields and wire entanglements on the eve of the assault and move forward during the artillery-aviation preparation phase to continue obstacle clearance.

Final assault group and tank preparations are completed during the artillery and air offensive, in accordance with the observed results of the preparation.

The assault begins at the moment tank units reach the line of departure. Artillery fire is transferred against enemy positions in depth and on the flanks of the assault sector. The assault must follow close behind the artillery barrage, to deny the enemy an opportunity to reorganize.

Infiltration units move forward prior to the assault in order to cover the assault units with submachine-gun fire directed against enemy infantry firing positions. Infantry and tank assault groups then pass through obstacles along prepared lanes, directing their fire on the first and second line of trenches. Upon reaching the first line of trenches, grenades are thrown and the group continues the offensive, keeping close to its supporting artillery and mortar barrage. Enemy personnel left behind in trenches are destroyed by the trench-clearance teams and units of the second echelon. The obstacle-clearing groups continue to remove mines and obstacles,

guide infantry and tanks through the gap, then follow them for further obstacle clearance. Automatic weapons and artillery fire at revived enemy firing positions to facilitate the forward advance of assault groups.

The offensive is intensified by feeding an increasing number of supporting troops into the penetration area to reinforce the break-through spearheads and to deliver strong flank attacks from the gap.

Those special fortification assault groups which have been assigned the specific mission of destroying known enemy fortifications are placed in the first echelon. Other special assault groups follow in the second echelon in readiness to assault new or revived casemates or strong points as directed by the battalion commander in that sector. The assault group commander determines the direction and mode of attack, taking into account the location of supporting enemy firing positions, their sectors of fire, the characteristics of the fortifications to be assaulted, and precautions against enemy counterattacks. The assault group sections operate as follows: Direct-fire artillery, machine-gun and tank sections fire on adjacent enemy firing positions and infantry protecting the fort or casemate. The obstacle-clearing section and the main body of the assault group advance through obstacles up to 100 yards of the casemate and cover the demolition section with submachine-gun fire and by grenades. The demolition section destroys the casemate in a single blast or piecemeal, depending on its size and strength. At the same time, charges are placed; grenade, flame-thrower and submachine gun attacks are directed against apertures. In some cases, embrasures are blocked by sand bags. (A detailed description is given in section V of part II.) After the assault is launched, artillery and machine-gun support is brought up behind the assault group to cover probable approaches of enemy counterattacking infantry.

Powerful forts are assaulted after the advancing echelons of infantry and tanks have isolated the fort from its supporting firing positions and enemy infantry. Smoke screens are often used to facilitate the assault on a powerful fort which has been bypassed and is isolated from enemy support.

After breaking through the main defensive position, the next positions are similarly assaulted but at a greater tempo. To facilitate the complete seizure of the fortified zone, every small breach in depth and on the flanks must be immediately exploited even though the breach may not be in the sector of the main effort.

Artillery and air bombardment in short concentrations support the deep penetration of the assault groups. Increasing numbers of supporting troops develop the penetration in depth and width. Every captured position is carefully secured against enemy counterattacks—by hasty minefields, firing positions, and wire obstacles placed by engineer groups of the second echelon. When enemy counterattacks are repulsed, the assault groups must follow on the heels of the withdrawing enemy for further exploitation.

5. DEFENSE OF FORTIFIED ZONES

The bases of organization of permanent fortified areas are battalion and regimental defensive positions. Special defensive battalions are often formed for this purpose, and equipped with a high proportion of automatic weapons, medium mortars, and antitank weapons. (For general discussion of defensive organization see chapter VI.)

a. Battalion defensive position. The infantry battalion can defend a forward position up to 1 mile in width. However, in strongly fortified zones the front width is narrowed to 500 yards or less, and the battalion is echeloned in depth in conformity with the lay-out of the strong point and prepared fortifications. The battalion must be prepared to organize the strong points for all-around defense, but defensive positions normally contain a "gorge" exposed to fire from rear positions. This prevents immediate utilization of the battalion position if captured by the enemy.

In occupying a prepared position, the battalion commander must analyze the defense plan which indicates the strength, equipment, and locations of individual fortifications, strong points, trenches, and concrete pillboxes to be manned by the battalion units, as well as the attached infantry support groups for each casemate. The system of fire, antitank defenses, camouflage requirements, engineer works, and minefields are also indicated. The first missions of the battalion commander are to supplement the existing system of fire with the battalion and attached weapons, and to continue the development of the position by the construction of supplementary communications trenches, personnel shelters, observation posts, and switch positions for personnel and weapons, especially mortars. All battalion, artillery, and attached mortars must be registered on avenues of approach, on outpost positions, and on obstacles. Alternate mortar positions, observation posts, and command posts are prepared, wired for signal communication, and registered on critical areas within the battalion fortified sector in order to destroy enemy forces in firesacks should the enemy penetrate into the battalion sector.

Artillery and mortars are organized for counterpreparation fire. During enemy artillery preparation, destructive enemy fire against fortifications and firing positions may be immunized by laying protective smoke screens. This is done on orders of the regimental commander. When firing positions are neutralized or destroyed, the system of fire is reorganized by moving forward machine guns and other weapons to reserve positions. When the assault phase begins, all destroyed weapons in firing positions must be replaced by reserve weapons. Soviet casemates are always provided with a rear exit and ramp to facilitate rapid movement of artillery in and out of the position.

During the assault, enemy penetrations are isolated by machine-gun and mortar fire from rear and flank positions; counterattacking groups then destroy the isolated enemy. Tanks are engaged by antitank guns, casemates, and open emplacements. When tanks break through the forward defensive position, they are destroyed at the next defensive position while mortar fire and automatic weapons separate enemy infantry and tanks by antipersonnel fire. Revived pillboxes are supported by artillery, mortar, and machine-gun fire while fortification support groups and tanks counterattack the enemy to reestablish the position. Deep enemy penetrations are resisted by maintaining heavy fire against the enemy flanks and preventing the isolation of individual strongpoints. Artillery fires from open positions when necessary, and all weapons deliver the maximum fire to restrict enemy movement and to enable regimental reserves to organize an effective counterattack.

b. Regimental defensive position. Although the battalion organizes strong points for all-around defense, the regiment is responsible for intermediate defensive positions and switch positions which may be occupied upon orders from the division commander. The regimental defensive position is characterized by extensive development of firesacks and ambushes, well camouflaged infantry positions, and highly maneuverable artillery and mortar fire. The regimental reserve consists of at least one infantry battalion, reinforced by tanks and artillery. The reserve is deployed to the rear of the battalion strong points with the missions of reinforcing the battalion positions by fire and counterattacking enemy assault forces which penetrate or by-pass the forward battalion positions. The regiment must be prepared for all-around defense if encircled. The regimental position has considerable defensive strength, due to minefields and intricate obstacles erected by the engineers. The regimental smoke-laying group is organized for screening the position from observed enemy artillery fire.

Counterpreparation fire by divisional and attached artillery has been a decisive factor in weakening large-scale enemy attacks on the fortified zone. Fortified zones are the key positions which deflect the attacking enemy into channelized sectors in which he may be isolated and destroyed. Massed artillery fire is concentrated on enemy forces which penetrate between strong points into a firesack. Then a powerful tank and infantry counterattack destroys the enemy salient. These tactics are characteristic of the centralized type of defense. A notable example of this was the destruction of German forces in their attempt to penetrate the fortified zone of the Kursk salient in 1943.

Section III. CITY WARFARE

1. OFFENSIVE OPERATIONS

Since the nature of city fighting gives an advantage to the defense, Soviet doctrine, like U. S. doctrine, favors isolating and by-passing cities rather than attacking them directly. Numerous large cities were encircled by the Red Army during the latter part of the war, thereby cutting off large enemy field forces defending them. The organized German defense of encircled cities continued when the battle lines of the front were 20 or more miles beyond them.

Soviet doctrine teaches that the rapid and economical assault of defended cities is achieved by thorough and continuous reconnaissance, and by isolation of centers of resistance which are reduced by infantry-artillery assault groups. The attack on a city may be compared to the assault of a fortified zone, but with certain advantages. The civilian population, particularly women and children, imposes a burden on the defending military forces with respect to food, water, health, and shelter, as well as providing a negative morale factor. The main disadvantages of defense derive from the inherent tactical weakness of city building. Streets constitute corridors which restrict movement and prevent the organization of a continuous system of defense. Buildings are not uniform in strength and size, and many are highly inflammable. In addition, they afford little opportunity for mutual fire support at close ranges, impose a perimeter type of defense in each structure, and can be used as shelters for attacking forces. Further disadvantages to defending forces are the restricted fields of fire and visibility.

On the other hand, the offense also encounters disadvantages in city warfare not found in open terrain. The extreme compartmentation horizontally and vertically makes progress slow and costly. The rubble of destroyed buildings affords the defenders easily adaptable defensive positions with excellent camouflage. The ease of mining, booby-trapping, and flooding by the defenders; the presence of traps for armor and artillery; the danger of collapsing structures—all these factors favor the defense and must be overcome by specially trained assault groups. The presence of unsuspected passages, such as subways and sewers, and the ease of interior communication facilitate infiltration counterattacks and breakout offensives by the defending forces. Offensive operations also involve difficult problems of direction and control.

Two basic types of attack are employed: the systematic attack against continuous defensive lines in depth, and the accelerated attack against weak sectors such as large city parks or open spaces. Seizure of the latter divides the defending forces into smaller pockets.

a. Reconnaissance. Detailed intelligence must be prepared concerning the enemy fire plan, the main fortified city zones, firing positions and principal weapons, and approaches affording the best cover. The deadly effect of hidden fire in city warfare makes location of enemy firing positions especially important.

In Red Army practice, combat reconnaissance is the chief means of obtaining information about the enemy in cities. In the assault of large cities, reconnaissance detachments of every arm and of the combined arms may operate for 6 days prior to assault. Combat reconnaissance continues during the assault to determine all new firing positions, especially on the flanks of the penetration. Combat reconnaissance is supplemented by other methods of obtaining data. City plans are studied in detail, particularly with regard to the location of utility systems, subways, sewers, and the like. Observers are located at posts which permit overlapping visibility; each observer is assigned a sector covering not more than 15° to 20° of vision. Special patrols are organized to capture prisoners for interrogation. These patrols consist of a seizure group of seven men and two support groups of six men, each armed with grenades and submachine guns. When full information cannot be obtained by other forms of reconnaissance, reconnaissance in force is conducted both day and night to draw enemy fire.

b. Assault formations. The basic operating unit in city warfare is the rifle battalion, reinforced with armor and antitank guns. When enemy resistance is intense, one city block is designated as the objective for each battalion. The variations in enemy defenses necessitate considerable flexibility in supporting artillery and armor.

The battalion is deployed for assault in column formation composed of four distinct groups (fig. 63). The advance guard or the infiltration group consists of a rifle company of two or three platoons and an antitank section. It is armed with automatic weapons, grenades, antitank rifles, and antitank rocket launchers. The second echelon or main body is the assault group, and is similar in strength and composition to the regimental assault group organized for the assault of fortified zones (see section II, part III). It consists of a rifle company, about half of the battalion heavy weapons, and a detachment of demolition engineers and smoke layers from the rifle regiment. Supporting weapons are two to three battalion or regimental direct-fire guns and a platoon of self-propelled guns. The third group is the support group which includes the balance of the battalion heavy weapons, three to four regimental or divisional direct-fire guns, and one platoon or medium tanks or self-propelled guns. The last group is the battalion reserve of one rifle company, which provides flank-security patrols.

Subgroups of varying size and composition are detached for separate assault missions on isolated structures. A typical subgroup consists of seven submachine gunners, five engineers, three to four heavy machine-gun crews, and two antitank riflemen. Two to four regimental or divisional guns may be placed in support of each subgroup.

c. Conduct of the assault. The two basic arms on which the burden of city warfare chiefly falls are the infantry and the artillery. Engineers supplement infantry combat by extensive de-mining work and by executing demolitions. Tanks use their mobile fire power to supplement artillery. Prior to every assault, coordination plans are developed between the rifle battalion commander and the commanders of artillery and tank support on the basis of their combined reconnaissance. Visual and radio signals are established to indicate when phase lines are reached and for the subordination of supporting artillery and tanks to small subgroups.

ASSAULT TECHNIQUES. Specific techniques have been developed by infantry and supporting arms in city warfare. In the assault of a strongly defended city block by a rifle battalion, the support group opens concentrated fire on the windows, doors, and along the flanks of the buildings. Mortar crews fire on intersections and areas to the rear of the block to prevent the enemy from organizing new firing positions. Automatic weapons direct their fire on the upper floors and roofs of buildings, while artillery fire is directed at the lower floors and cellars (fig. 64). Smoke-laying crews throw smoke grenades to cover the approach of tanks and self-propelled guns whose fire is directed toward the center of the block. As soon as a breach is made in the center of the block, the infiltration group dashes through the breach under cover of smoke. Small parties of the infiltration group expand their operations in all directions, taking positions inside the neutralized buildings to ward off counterattacks. Artillery fire shifts to the enemy position on the flanks. Tanks and self-propelled guns move into the neutralized sector out of the line of enemy direct fire, concentrating their attention on the corner buildings. The assault group, coordinating its operations with tanks and self-propelled guns, enters the remaining buildings in the block and destroys the enemy garrison.

An engineer mine-clearing company follows the rifle battalion into newly occupied positions. Each platoon consists of special mine-clearing subgroups organized as follows: a mine-reconnaissance section of five to six men, a mine-clearing section of eight to ten men, a mine-clearance checking section of four to five men, and a collecting and storing section of two to three men. The engineer company clears one to two large buildings or 20 to 30 small buildings per day. De-mining assignments are planned and controlled by the engineer staff of the formation in charge of the city sector. Tactically important buildings, streets, and blocks are given work-order priority. Trained engineer crews double-check all important areas, giving special attention to time bombs.

245

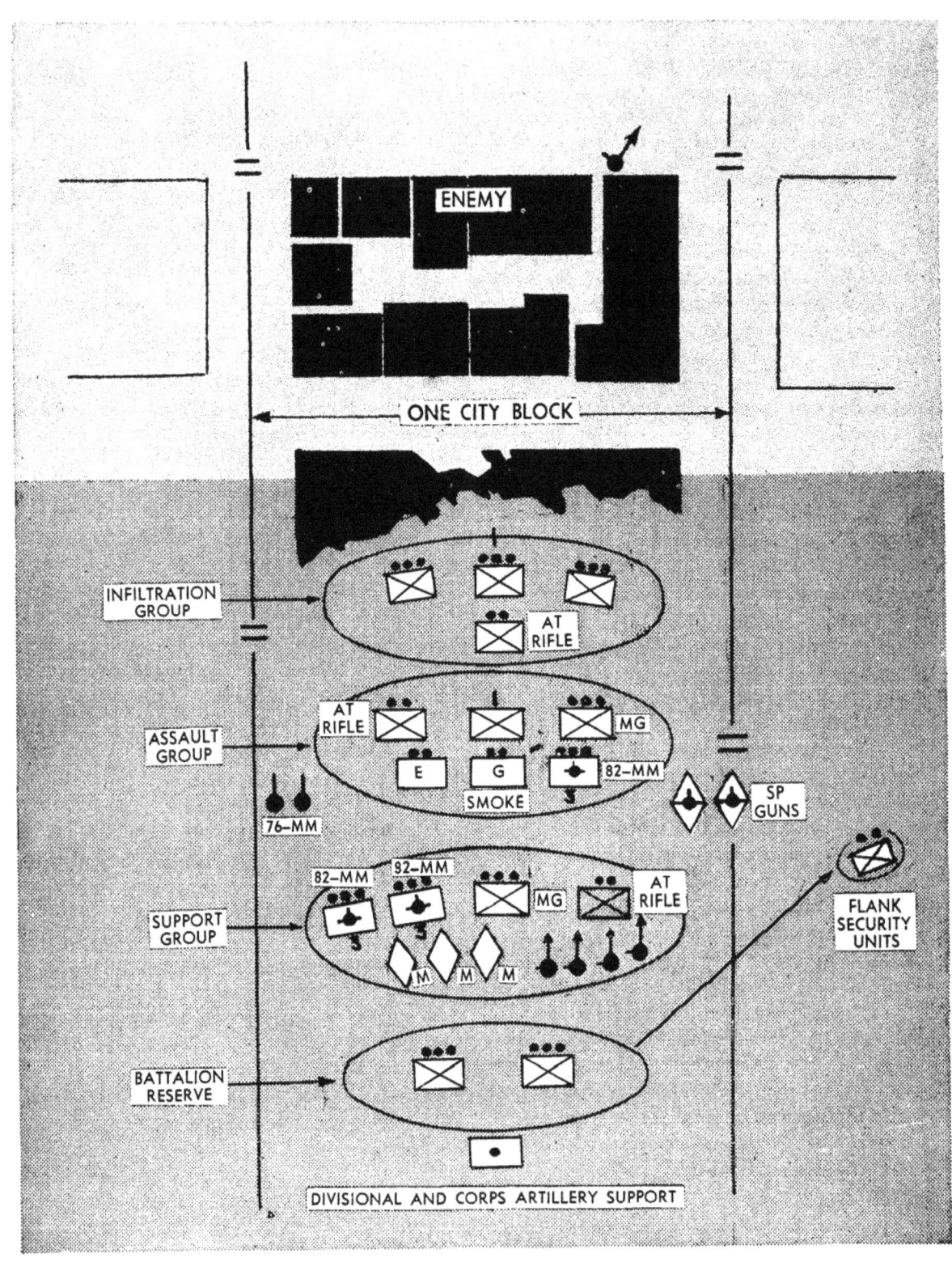

Figure 63. Combat formation of the rifle battalion for offensive operations in city warfare.

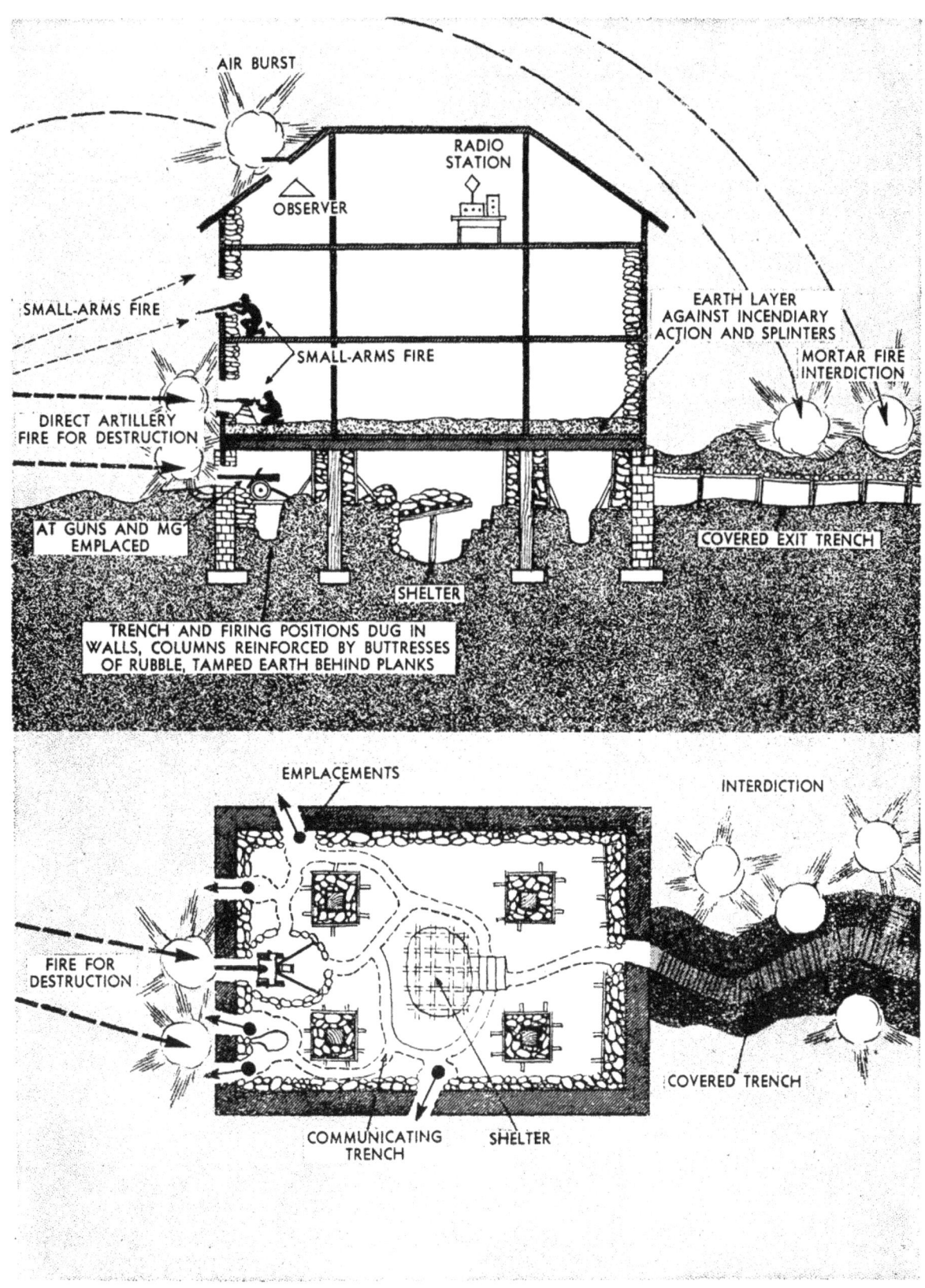

Figure 64. Fortification and fire attack of a building.

247

In the event that a block is neutralized and seized rapidly, the reserve is committed at once to consolidate the position and to carry the assault to the next block, denying the enemy time to reorganize his system of fire. The support group is displaced forward to engage new enemy firing positions, and the sequence of the operation is repeated. Tanks and self-propelled guns never move ahead of the infantry, to avoid entering firesacks or striking land mines. The signals of de-mining engineers and infantrymen guide the movements of armor.

ROLE OF ARTILLERY. The mission of light artillery is to destroy enemy firing positions by direct fire. In the assault of Berlin, up to 80 percent of all batteries attached to infantry units conducted direct fire from open positions. In Budapest, artillery ranging from 45-mm antitank guns to 203-mm howitzers fired directly at embrasures, windows, and every type of firing position. In addition to neutralizing enemy firing positions, direct fire is used to create breaches in buildings, walls, and barricades.

Guns are displaced forward alternately under heavy fire cover of other guns and infantry automatic weapons. Large-caliber howitzers, 152-mm and 203-mm, are used to destroy buildings completely. Tanks with large-caliber guns, self-propelled artillery, and large-caliber howitzers act as rams to make gaps in the enemy defenses.

Mortars of all calibers cover possible channels of enemy troop movements, such as street intersections, trenches, and alleys. Mortar firing positions are placed behind walls or inside buildings close to their objectives. Their mobility and effective fire from concealed positions provide strong fire support for the assault groups.

Artillery firing at high angles from concealed positions exercises great care in registration. The exact locations of friendly troops must be known, and each burst must be observed in firing for destruction. Registration shifts are made in two to four graduations from computed firing data, gradually approaching the target.

Rockets are used in closely congested building areas where direct artillery fire is restricted. The Soviets have used improvised launchers for firing rockets from the second and third floors of buildings.

The mission of the artillery reserve is counterbattery and countermortar fire. Massed fire from heavy batteries of the artillery reserve is used against citadels or other strong enemy fortified positions. Separate missions of the artillery reserve include interdiction and destruction of enemy supply dumps, headquarters, communication centers, and other important objectives. The artillery reserve is retained under centralized control under the corps and division artillery commanders.

COORDINATION. For effective coordination, the regimental command post is placed close to battalion command posts. Battalion combat formations become broken up to a great extent in city warfare. Staff officers are therefore given more authority to make decisions in areas under their control. Infantry units must be well trained in close-in combat, in the employment of grenades and demolitions, and particularly in coordinated fire and movement. To keep command posts constantly informed concerning the progress of local missions and troop dispositions, radio communication, signal flares, and messengers supplement and duplicate telephone systems which cannot be relied upon for uninterrupted operation.

Radio communication is often the only means of maintaining contact. Each battalion has one radio set; there are two in the regimental command post; two are located near the regimental Chief of Staff; and one set is kept in reserve. Stations are located on the top floors of buildings or in concealed, open areas to avoid the interference with transmission. Wire communication is maintained between the regimental command post and the battalions operating in the direction of the main effort. For close coordination, the regimental commander's observation post is at the forward battalion command post.

SECURITY. Convenient interior lines of communication give the defending forces the advantage of rapid troop concentration for counterattacks and particularly for large-scale break-out offensives. Large mobile reserves of infantry, artillery, and armor must be held in readiness to support any sector which may be assaulted by the enemy, especially the sectors in the direction of other enemy forces outside the encircled city. In local actions, every seized enemy building and block must be completely cleared of the enemy from cellar to roof, then fortified and protected against enemy counterattacks by automatic weapons, mines, and supporting fire. A specially trained security detachment in every assault group has the specific function of organizing defensive positions in newly captured buildings and block sectors. Mortar fire and self-propelled guns are particularly effective in repelling enemy counterattacks.

248

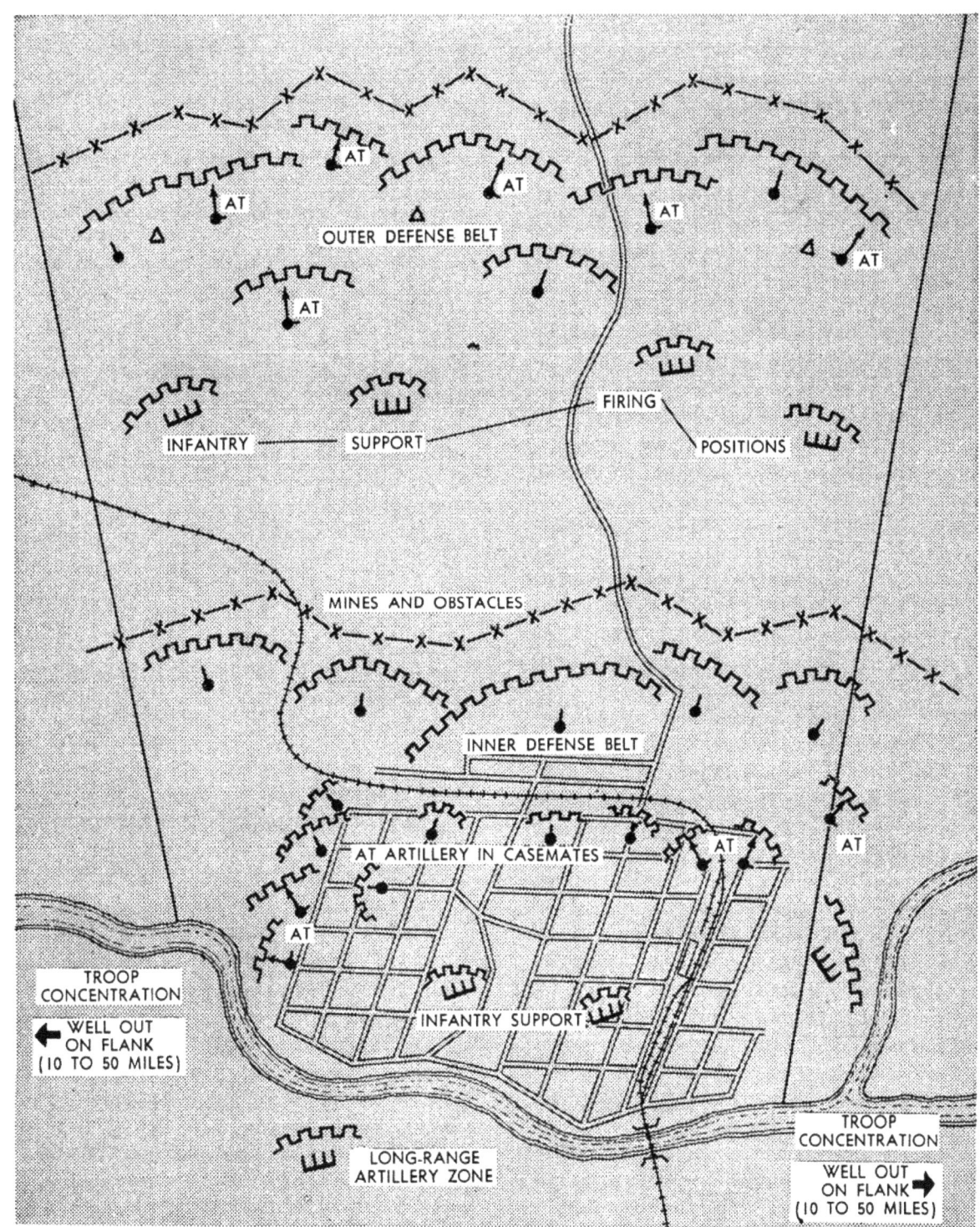

Figure 65. City defenses in depth.

2. DEFENSE OF CITIES

The Red Army has employed highly effective defensive tactics in the defense of cities. The strategically vital cities of Leningrad, Moscow, and Stalingrad were successfully defended despite full-scale enemy offensive operations. Leningrad was under heavy long-range artillery fire for 2½ years, while Stalingrad was completely destroyed but never fully occupied by the enemy.

a. Tactical doctrine. Basic principles characteristic of Red Army tactics in the defense of cities are the mobilization of the civilian population for defensive city combat, the development of deeply echeloned defenses extending far forward from the city, and the concentration of large bodies of troops on both flanks of the city (Figure 65).

The civilian population is politically indoctrinated to take part in the organized and active defense of the city. Civilian military training in elementary tactics, rifle marksmanship, and defense against air attack were organized in peacetime by the Ossoviahim Society and the Komosomol League. When the battle front approaches a city, the civilian population organized into combat and service units in accordance with individual ability, assists in the construction of field fortifications, street barricades, and shelters. Intensive counter-intelligence screening of all civilians prevents any subversive activities.

Defenses are organized in depth in order to resist effectively the enemy massed-tank attacks which follow extensive air bombardment and artillery preparation. Particular attention is directed to antitank defenses consisting of obstacles, traps, and numerous concealed antitank guns. Heavy losses are inflicted on the enemy by permitting his forces to penetrate between strong points and thereby channelizing his attack into firesacks. A destroyed city is even more suited to prolonged and stubborn defense than one with all its buildings intact, since the debris offers greater opportunities for camouflage, surprise, and ambush than do standing buildings. Furthermore, debris is not as likely to be affected by subsequent bombardments and is invulnerable to incendiary attack. Troops are taught to improvise fortified positions among ruins and charred remains of houses as quickly as possible, and to provide a number of switch positions which are interconnected by a system of deep trenches.

The primary mission of troop concentrations on both flanks of a defended city is to prevent encirclement of the city by reinforcing the flank fortifica-

tions. Soviet combat experience has demonstrated that an enemy brought to a halt when already deep into the city's defenses and forced to wage exhausting combat for a prolonged period is a ready target for encirclement and destruction by fresh, constantly reinforced flank forces.

b. Defensive technique. The conduct of defense in city warfare is similar to that of fortified zones. Emphasis is placed on applicable defensive techniques, such as the elimination of dead spaces by enfilade fire and mobile groups of submachine gunners, which operate from under improvised cover and attack enemy assault groups in the flank and rear. Large numbers of snipers are used with the special mission of picking off officers and noncommissioned officers. Evacuation to the rear, as well as forward movement of supplies, reinforcement, and replacements, takes place at night.

The principal defensive objective is to force the enemy to abandon large-scale armored attacks by making the penetration of the deep defensive positions too costly. Operations will then revert to intense house-to-house combat between relatively small infantry and engineer assault groups supported by direct-fire artillery, automatic weapons, demolitions, and flame throwers.

The transformation of individual houses into strong points involves the following measures:

> Digging firing, shelter, and communication trenches (including at least one hidden exit trench) in the basement.
> Breaking through firing embrasures.
> Reinforcing the foundations with earth-and-rubble filled buttresses behind chicken wire, or plank retaining walls.
> Constructing safety underpinning as required, and covering the floor of the first story with a foot of earth for fire- and splinter-proofing.

The upper stories are used for observations, radio communications and sniping.

Defensive warfare has two overlapping phases, each with its own system of organization. In the first phase, prepared defenses which extend throughout the city and its approaches are organized as in the defense of a fortified zone, with particular emphasis on all types of antitank weapons. As enemy artillery and air attacks destroy city structures, a progressive transition in the organization of the defense takes place until the city is a continuous mass of rubble. The defenses now consist of a complicated tangle of trenches, deep dugouts under blasted buildings. and strongholds in ruins or in remains of large and strongly reinforced concrete buildings such as abound in factory areas. Large quantities of direct-fire artillery are emplaced in hidden firing positions to limit the progress of enemy assault. Rear areas contain many batteries of heavy artillery which support the city defenses. The defensive system of Stalingrad was typical of such an organization and proved that the ruins of a city can constitute one of the most formidable types of fortifications in modern warfare.

Section IV. OPERATIONS AT RIVER LINES AND AMPHIBIOUS OPERATIONS

1. RIVER CROSSINGS

The Red Army crossed every major river in Europe between the Volga and the Elbe during the course of the war. Successive operations of many types resulted in improved techniques and new methods, such as the underwater bridge.

a. Basic doctrine. Soviet doctrine in river-crossing operations places great emphasis on certain tactical measures which differ from U. S. practice, although the general principles of river-crossing operations are basically identical. All of the most successful Soviet river assaults in World War II were carried out on broad fronts. By restricting the crossing area to a narrow front, the Red Army appreciates. surprise is lost and enemy forces concentrate in the selected area. Diversionary or feint crossings in considerable strength are normally made to provide alternate crossing sites to which the main forces can be diverted, should the main crossings fail or be held up. The planning of the operation is detailed and intricate, and orders are given in writing. Concealment of crossing equipment and troops is carried out under the strictest discipline. The greatest single difference between Soviet and Allied river-crossing operations. however, has been in large-scale employment by the Red Army of rafts, bridge sections, and boats or ferries to transport armor, artillery, and loaded vehicles across water; whereas Allied forces generally waited until bridges were built.

Because of its superior accuracy, the Red Army places far greater reliance on artillery fire than on air action in river-crossing operations. Considerable artillery strength is concentrated, ranging up

to 240 to 320 pieces of all calibers—including 120-mm mortars—per miles of front. The greatest emphasis is placed on the use of local materials for the construction of boats, rafts, and bridges. The tempo of river-crossing operations is highly variable, depending entirely on the tactical location of the river line with respect to the offensive operations. Major water barriers were often reached at the end of extensive advances; and long periods of preparation were required, due not so much to the lack of crossing capabilities as to the need for consolidating the newly won territory and for bringing up troops and supplies. Rivers within the range of offensive objectives constituted no serious obstacles and were usually taken in stride.

b. Role of various arms in river-crossing operations.

ENGINEERS. Engineers play the dominant role in river-crossing operations. There is no essential difference between U. S. and Red Army doctrines with respect to the command responsibility or the functions of the engineer arm in the organization, the assault, or the construction phases. As in the U. S. Army, the maintenance of bridges, traffic control, and forward displacement of engineer equipment are also engineer functions in the Red Army.

River crossings on broad fronts require the concentration of far more equipment than the organic engineer units of the formation and attached GHQ engineer units can provide from their organizational equipment. The Red Army engineers have the tremendous task of constructing crossing equipment, ranging from wooden boats to heavy bridge sections, out of local materials. For example, 10,000 wooden boats were built entirely of local materials, except for nails, in 10 days prior to the crossing of the Vistula. In such situations infantry units do the work under engineer supervision. In addition, the operation of signal stations and troop regulating points by Red Army engineers involves operational control of large bodies of troops and equipment on a broad front.

ARTILLERY. Artillery has three basic missions in river-crossing operations: to destroy enemy defenses, to cover the crossing of troops, and to transport the artillery across the river. In Red Army practice a river crossing requires the same amount of artillery as the assault of a fully developed defensive position. The density of artillery and 120-mm mortars required is 240 to 320 barrels per mile of front. To obtain this concentration, about 120 to 200 extra guns are usually required per mile of front. This presents the difficult problem of concentrating large artillery units and at the same time maintaining surprise. Usually a concentration point is selected 10 to 16 miles from the proposed firing positions of the guns. Routes to the firing positions are carefully planned and covered in several night practice marches by all battery commanders. Strict control of fire is enforced during the concentration phase by permitting only two batteries per corps to engage in counterbattery fire, by restricting antiaircraft artillery to a limited number of duty batteries, and by using roving guns for deception. Great importance is attached to direct artillery fire; 70 to 80 percent of the regimental artillery is used in direct fire. A considerable portion of the antitank and regimental guns designated for direct-fire missions are dug in by night close to the river bank, and completely concealed by masking with shrubbery or tarpaulins with sand cover.

The preliminary bombardment of enemy positions by air and artillery is directed against enemy defenses and firing positions which can interfere with crossing operations. The first assault echelon occupies the line of departure positions 3 to 4 hours before H-hour.

The full intensity of the bombardment is developed as the first echelon moves its assault boats to the river for embarkation under cover of direct-fire artillery. The fire density is two to three bursts per minute on a front of 10 to 15 yards, lasting from 10 to 20 minutes. This is followed by less intense bombardment for 30 to 40 minutes, during which time the first assault echelon crosses to the opposite bank. The creeping barrage begins on both visual and radio signals from the assaulting infantry; time systems are considered unreliable. Forward observers and artillery observation posts direct barrage lifts of from 50 to 100 yards. The barrage is held at main objectives, which are usually at about 500- to 700-yard intervals, until the advancing infantry is observed to be 200 to 250 yards from them; then the barrage creeps forward in short intermediate lifts to the next objective. Surprise night crossings are made without artillery preparation. All direct-fire guns are held in readiness in their firing positions to neutralize enemy weapons, should the crossing be discovered. Supporting medium and heavy artillery and 120-mm mortars are held in readiness to fire on previously registered enemy positions and assembly areas.

Infantry guns and mortars, as well as four additional antitank guns per battalion, are sent across with the first echelon. Artillery crews are reinforced by 50 percent personnel reserves.

Artillery crosses on ferries and improvised rafts until the floating bridges are in place, but no more than one-third of the artillery is ever in motion at one time. During a pursuit, the time element is considered to be of such vital importance that forward units never wait for the arrival of bridging equipment if there is a chance to seize a bridgehead. All artillery units are trained in ferrying their guns across rivers by various improvised methods using local materials.

ARMOR. Armored units carry bridging equipment adequate for crossing rivers up to 300 yards in width. The motorized infantry generally crosses first to establish a bridgehead. Tank units enlarge the bridgehead, and wait until the main forces have crossed before continuing offensive operations. Amphibious tanks and ducks accompany the first infantry assault wave. Tanks approach river lines on a wide front and avoid concentrations. Reconnaissance for fords and undamaged bridges is always carried out. On many occasions tank spearheads and advance reconnaissance detachments have seized bridges intact as the result of unexpected wide outflanking maneuvers.

ANTIAIRCRAFT ARTILLERY. During the assault phase, antiaircraft batteries protect the crossing area from the friendly side of the river; in some cases antiaircraft guns are mounted on rafts. As soon as possible, additional batteries are also emplaced on the far side of the river. Airborne troops have not been used on a large scale in any Red Army river-crossing operation. Parachute troops of battalion size are used against enemy communications 5 to 10 miles from the river to hamper enemy movements, or are given missions of destroying bridges, flood gates, locks, etc.

c. The preparation phase. Thorough ground reconnaissance is organized as soon as a river is reached. Aerial photographs are continuously made to supplement ground observation. Engineer reconnaissance gives particular attention to local material for use in the crossing; to the characteristics of the river, its banks, and most suitable approaches; and to enemy obstacles and defensive installations across the river. Artillery reconnaissance determines the location and strength of enemy firing positions and plans the artillery system of fire for the preparation and assault phases. Observation posts manned by officers are usually placed 1,000 yards apart with mobile observation posts covering intermediate positions. Patrols of specialist troops operate along the whole front on the enemy side of the river to gain

concentration of forces in the area selected for the assault. This concentration is never hurried, due to the extreme emphasis placed by the Soviets on very thorough concealment.

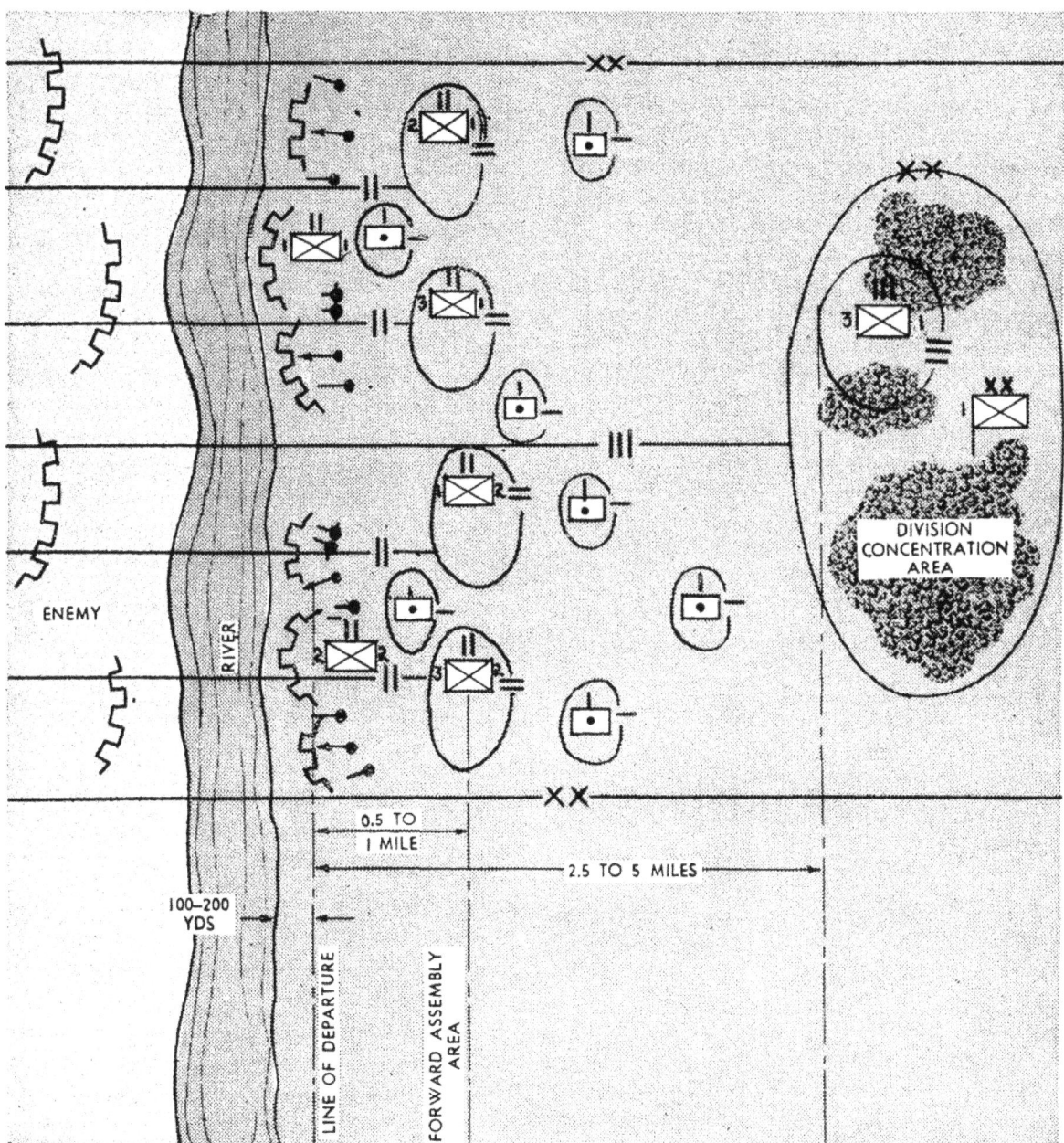

Figure 66. Deployment of troops prior to crossing operations.

further and more detailed information, and to remove underwater obstacles such as wire entanglements, posts, and mines.

During the preparatory stage, a period of at least 2 or 3 weeks is required to carry out the necessary

The organization of troops for the crossing operation follows a definite pattern (figs. 66 and 67). The division concentration areas lie from 2 to 5 miles from the river, wherever the greatest concealment is available. The forward assembly area is

253

situated from ⅔ to 1 mile from the river bank on a wide front. Thoroughly concealed dumps of medium and heavy pontons and bridging materials are placed from 300 to 900 yards from the river bank. Assault boats and spare equipment are con-

assistants are the chief engineers of subordinate units down to company level. The immediate responsibility of every engineer officer is that sector of the crossing operation to which his unit is assigned. Three categories of crossing points are

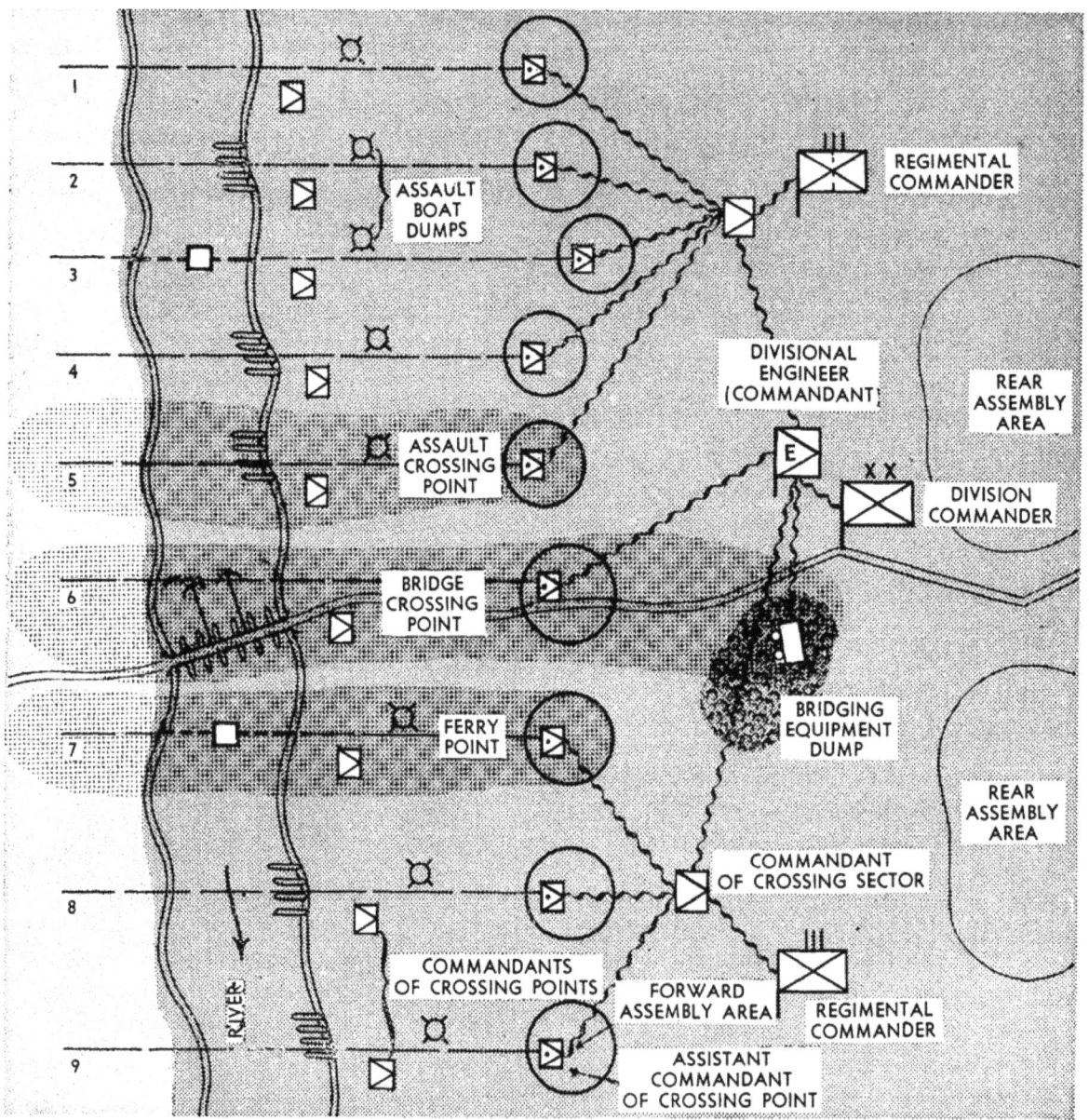

Figure 67. Organization of crossing control.

cealed under foliage or buried in sand in the forward zone 100 to 200 yards from the water (fig. 68).

The Commander of the entire river-crossing operation is the chief engineer of the formation. The Commander controls all troop movements from the forward assembly area to the opposite shore. His

organized within the general crossing area. These are the assault-boat crossing points, the ferrying points, and the bridge crossing points. Assault-boat equipment is concealed along a wide front, while ferrying and bridge equipment are concentrated further to the rear in concealed areas adjacent

254

to approach roads leading to the river (figs. 69 and 70).

d. Assault phase. The assault phase is usually launched at night, although daytime crossings under smoke cover have also taken place.

The rifle battalion is the basic unit for which assault-boat crossings are established. One or two crossing points are established per battalion as re-

where slit trenches are dug to conceal them. Trails marked by tape or wire lead to the assault boat dispersal area and thence to the line of embarkation. Signal points for regulating the troop movements from the assembly areas to the line of departure and to the loading line are operated by engineer personnel. Engineer guides and signal control stations regulate the movement of each wave in con-

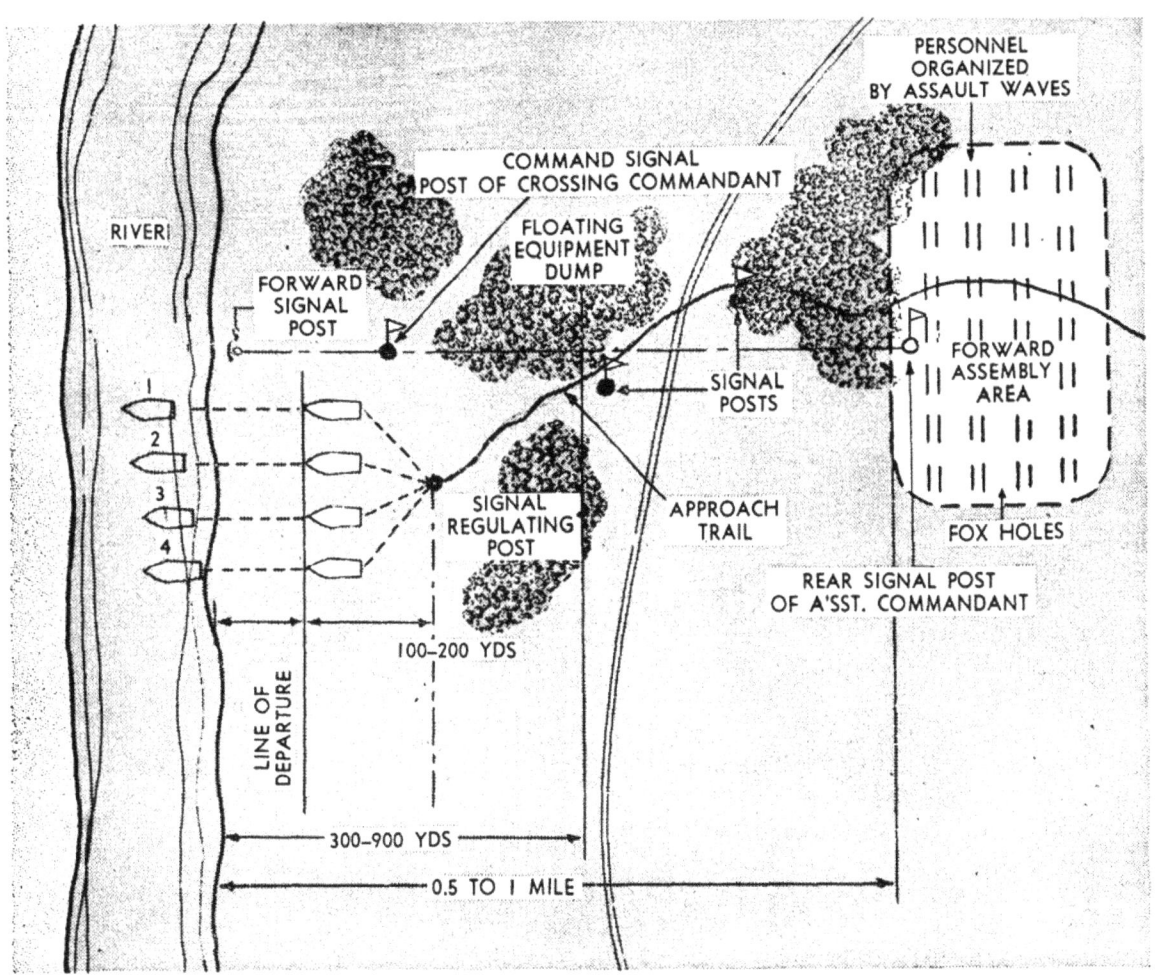

Figure 68. Assault-boat crossing point.

quired by the terrain and by tactical considerations. At the beginning of the assault, boats are placed at intervals of 15 to 30 yards along the line of embarkation, making the battalion front 200 to 550 yards wide. Equipment consists of organizational inflated rubber boats, pontons, and folding canvas boats; local fishing boats; or rafts and boats specially constructed to make up for deficiencies in requirements.

The organization of battalion personnel in assault waves is completed in the forward assembly area

formity with the established assault time schedule. The first wave loads into the boats which are manned by engineer crews. Artillery preparation against enemy defenses and firing positions usually precedes the assault, but on many occasions the element of surprise was considered to be sufficiently important to attempt silent crossings.

Machine guns, mortars, and light regimental artillery—as well as pioneers with a large supply of mines—accompany the first echelon. The pioneers clear minefields and wire obstacles, and lay their own mines in the most likely approaches for enemy counterattacks. Upon debarking, the infantry with their supporting weapons organize to attack the enemy screening forces. The artillery barrage across the river moves forward in jumps to support the assault.

Assault boats crossing a 500-foot river with average current make one round trip in 10 minutes, with oars; or one round trip in 6 minutes, with outboard motors. The number of boats required varies with the tactical decision concerning the

Use of fords is made wherever possible. Water depth, and not the character of the river bed, is the determining factor. If bundles of fascines and rock fills are not adequate to cover channels, holes, or soft spots at the proposed fording point, flexible wooden mats interwoven with rope are sunk in place by driving short piles along the edges or by weighting the mat down with rock.

e. Ferrying Phase. Ferrying operations begin after the assaulting infantry consolidates a small bridgehead—about 600 yards in depth—and con-

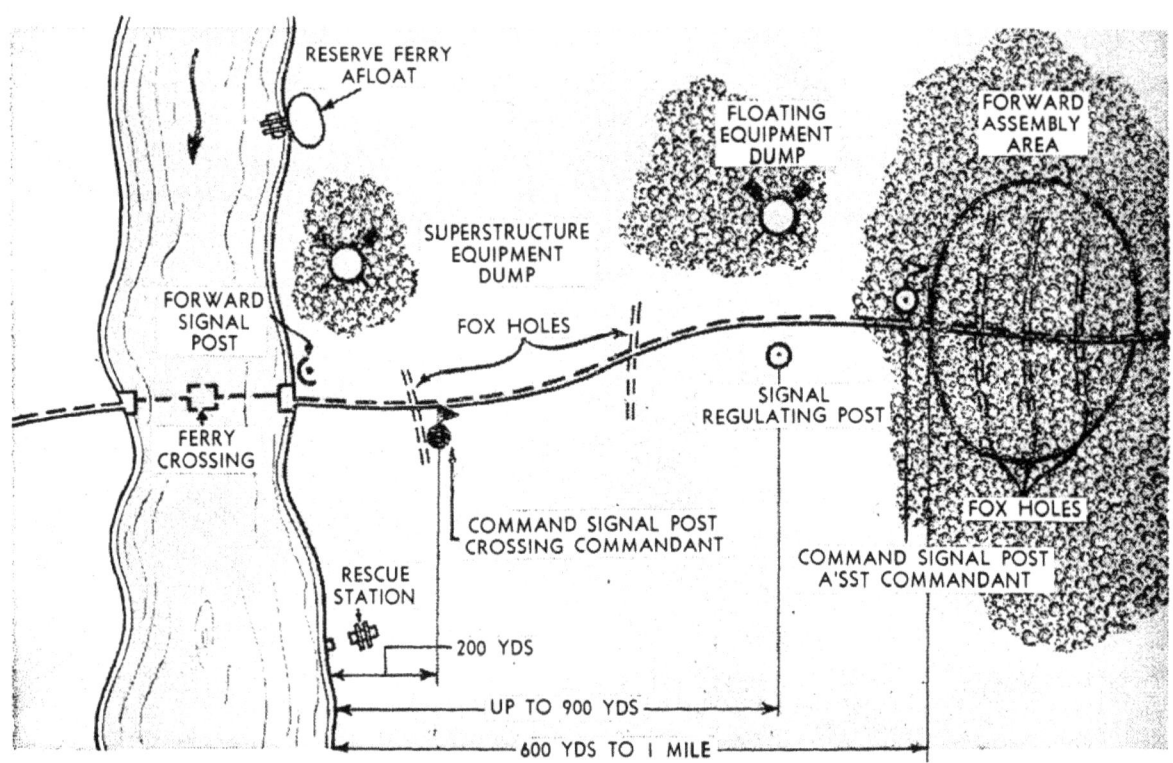

Figure 69. Ferry crossing point.

number of assault waves per battalion. The rifle battalion without its artillery (75-ton load) may cross in a single wave in 36 A-3 large pneumatic boats or light pontons, in 12 heavy pontons, or over 9-foot bridge sets of eight sections. The 10-foot footbridge section on four floats can carry 10 men; the light collapsible boats and pneumatic boats, 12 men; the light pontons, 25 men; and the heavy ponton sections, 50 men. Amphibious tanks and other amphibious vehicles accompany the first assault wave. In the crossing of the Svir River, U. S. lend-lease ducks were used effectively in the assault phase. Recent trends in river-crossing operations indicate an increased employment of amphibious vehicles.

tinue during all crossing phases, even after a secure bridgehead has been established and bridges are in operation. Ferries supplement bridges in transporting the maximum traffic across the river in the shortest time, and serve as reserve bridge sections in repairing combat damage. The ferry point is organized like the assault-boat crossing point.

The troop assembly area is located 500 yards to 1 mile from the river. A floating equipment dump is concealed about one-half mile from the river, and superstructure materials are hidden in a second dump about one-quarter of a mile from the river.

The approach road or trail to the ferry loading point is controlled by engineer signal control stations. An upstream ferry construction point is

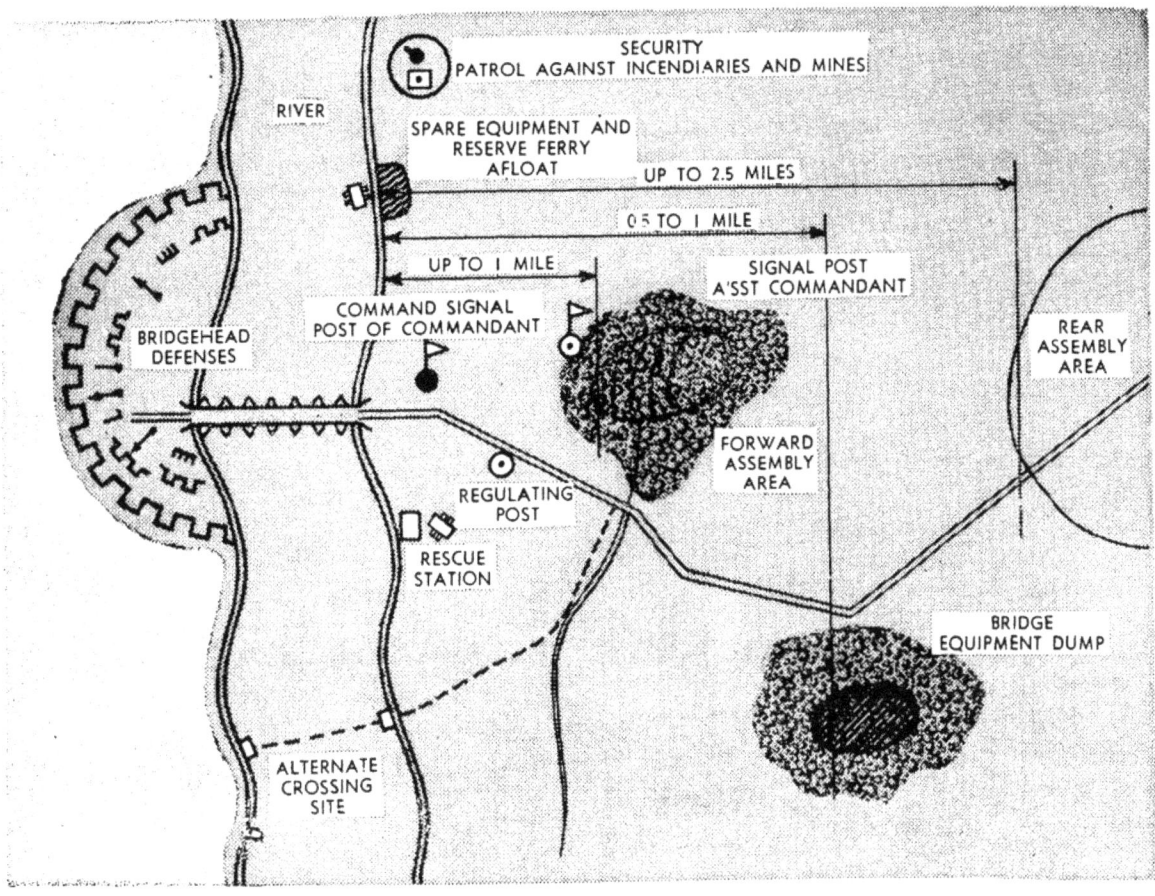

Figure 70. Ponton bridge crossing.

selected to supplement the crossing point, while a rescue station site is established downstream (fig. 69). Ferries constructed of organizational floating bridge sections carry from 5- to 16-ton loads for light ponton sections, and from 16 to 100 tons for heavy ponton sections. Carrying capacity is increased by adding additional pontons and by coupling two bridge sections. Two-lane coupled bridge sections on heavy pontons may carry four trucks or the equivalent weight of tanks or artillery pieces. Generally, two single-lane bridge sections carrying two vehicles are used in the initial phases to facilitate the rapid movement of ferries.

Small power launches, outboard motors, poles, or cables are employed in ferrying operations. Five round trips can be made per hour across a 500-foot river by a motor-drawn ferry as compared to two to three round trips without power. The greatest single factor in determining how rapidly a unit may be transported at any one ferry crossing is the ferry capacity. A rifle battalion with its com-

plete supply train may be loaded in 19 sixteen-ton ferry loads or 48 five-ton ferry loads. Using the larger ferries, in a single crossing, the battalion can cross a 500-foot river in 75 minutes, whereas using the smaller ferries over 3 hours are required. A rifle division generally crosses in two echelons, requiring 2 to 6 hours, depending on the number of ferry crossings and the size of ferries used. Ferries are assembled in 15 to 50 minutes depending on their size; docks are constructed in about 20 minutes, and unloading requires 10 to 15 minutes. As in the case of assault boats, extensive improvisation with local materials has taken place in the construction of ferries. Tables of buoyancy for all types of wood, barrels, drums, etc. are carried by engineers to facilitate rapid calculations in designing improvised ferries.

f. Bridging phase. The bridge crossing sector is identical in organization to the ferry point sector with the exception that bridging equipment is concealed farther from the river. The approach road

257

is capable of carrying heavy traffic, and runs from the rear assembly area of the main body (about 3 miles from the river) to the bridge site.

Bridging begins at the earliest possible opportunity, generally when the bridgehead is about 2 miles deep. Initially, the bridging is of light ponton construction to facilitate rapid passage of light equipment and infantry. Later, heavy ponton bridges or fixed wooden bridges are constructed by GHQ engineer troops. Large reserves of bridging equipment are at hand under the control of special repair units. Every precaution is taken to insure the continuous flow of troops and equipment across the river.

Strong mesh wire is hung upstream to stop floating mines; emergency and rescue stations are located down stream; look-out stations and flood-warning posts are placed upstream; alternate ferrying points and bridge sites are established and cables or hawsers are stretched across the river at various points to facilitate supplementary boat and raft crossings.

Upstream, an emergency patrol station, armed with machine guns and artillery, is on the alert for floating mines, floating incendiary materials, and enemy river gunboats. Camouflaged emergency floating bridge sections are anchored upstream, ready to replace a damaged bridge section. On the downstream side is located a rescue station, equipped with boats and rafts, as well as a reserve bridge crossing site. Floating bridge capacities range from 5 tons to 16 tons for light ponton bridges, and from 16 tons to 100 tons for heavy ponton bridges. Construction time varies from 75 minutes for a 450-foot, 5-ton bridge to 4 hours for a 100-ton bridge of the same length.

Construction time for floating bridges compares favorably with U. S. practice. Some categories of heavy ponton bridges are assembled in less time by the Red Army engineers than comparable U. S. floating bridges, with the notable exception of the treadway bridge of U. S. armored units. Red Army Engineer units use about 50 percent more men for assembling comparable floating bridges.

With the exception of bridge-laying tanks and the trestle spans of floating bridges, no prefabricated organizational fixed bridge equipment has been in evidence. The Red Army relies entirely on its highly developed technique of constructing wooden fixed bridges from materials brought forward, supplemented by lumber found locally. Six hours for the

construction of a two-lane, 430-foot, 60-ton capacity bridge is considered normal. The railroad bridge across the Dniepr at Kiev was built in 12 days, with 7,000 men and women engaged in the construction.

Red Army practice in wooden bridge construction is unique in its preference for wide piers. Rock-filled wooden cribs, piers formed by inclined trestle and pile bents, and square trestle piers are common (figs. 71 and 72). Piles are driven with heavy cross-lagging in temporary construction, and the unsupported span is strongly reinforced by inclined struts anchored on the piers (fig. 73).

g. Underwater bridges. Three types of underwater bridges have been developed by the Red Army engineers (fig. 74). In one case, four-pile bents at 15-foot spans were driven with muffled pile drivers and cut by special underwater saws 4 feet below the surface. Special caps with metal straps were then floated out and bolted to the piles. Log stringers and plank decking were easily bolted to the caps. All work was done at night so that the bridge was not discovered by the enemy. Underwater bridges of spans up to 36 feet are built on underwater rock-filled timber cribs anchored to corner piles. Steel I-beam stringers rest on the cup, to which the decking is securely fastened by bolts running through the guardrails. Short rail struts support a cable at the water surface to indicate the edges of the bridge. For shallow-river underwater bridges, short piles are driven for anchoring timber-grillage (cross layers of trimmed logs) piers to which stringers weighed down by rock are fastened.

At Voronezh, during the Red Army offensive in the spring of 1943, the underwater bridge served to deceive the enemy as to the offensive capabilities of forces in a relatively small bridgehead to which the bridge was secretly constructed. Large armored formations crossed the bridge at night, and surprised the enemy with a powerful and successful offensive.

h. Crossings of frozen rivers. The techniques for crossing frozen rivers have been thoroughly developed in the Red Army as the result of years of experimentation on the supporting strength of ice. Specific regulations are prescribed for allowable loads, spacing of vehicles, and the proper manner for placing plank roadways to distribute the load. Thin ice is crossed by infantry on long boards; loads on flat sleds are pulled across by ropes. For vehicles and artillery, bridges are quickly built by driving piles through the ice, using the ice to support the working crews. Such piles are almost

258

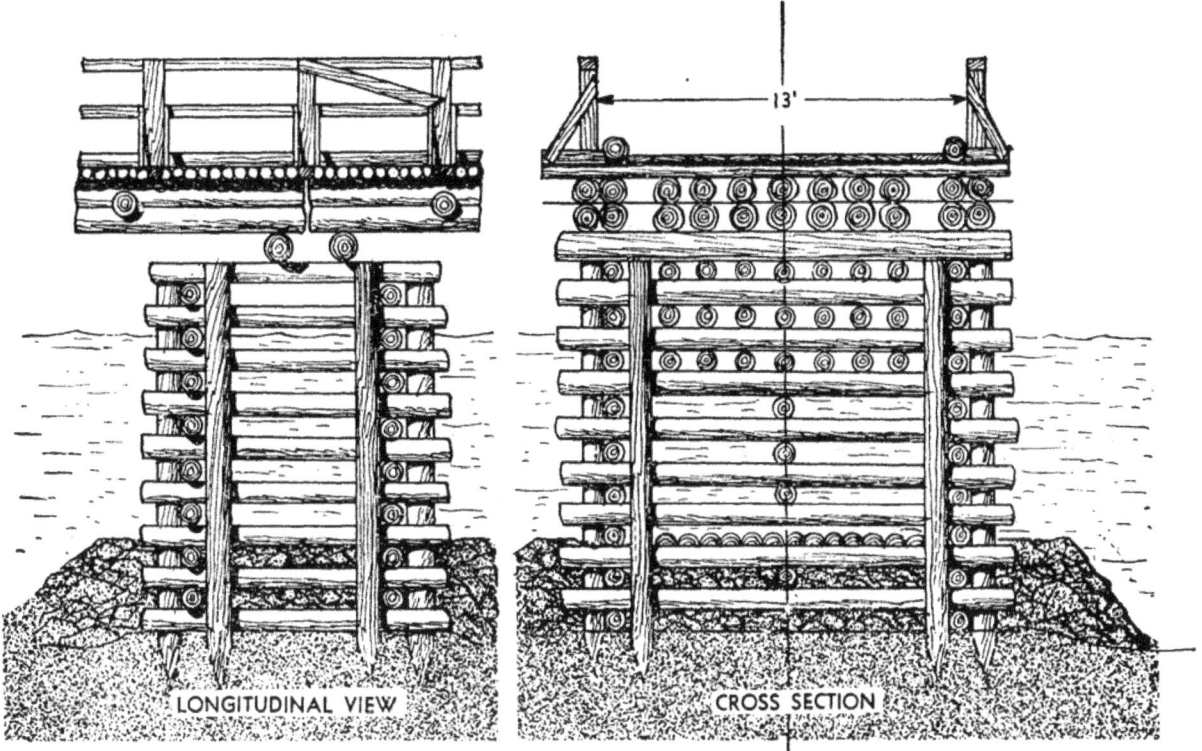

Figure 71. Grillage-type pier.

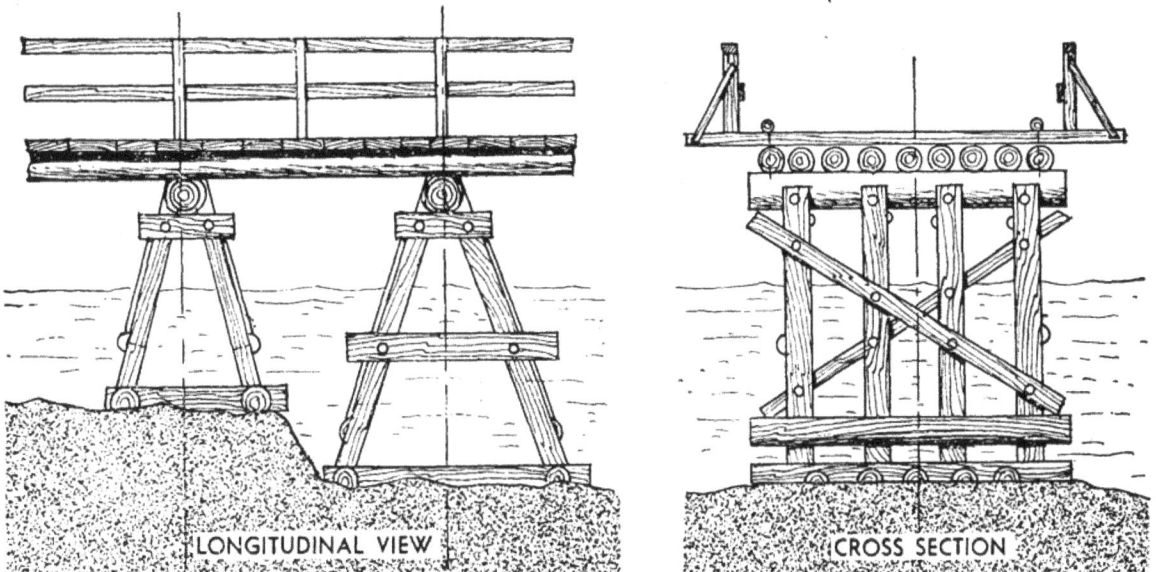

Figure 72. Inclined bent type of support.

always cross-lagged several feet above the point so that little settling will take place and driving can be done with large wooden mauls.

2. DEFENSE OF RIVER LINES

In the early years of the war, river lines constituted a vital part of the Red Army's defensive positions at the most important sectors of the front. The successful defense of the Voronezh positions along the upper Don prevented the enemy from outflanking Moscow from the south in August 1942. The historic defense of Stalingrad and the Volga River line for 106 days prevented the enemy from splitting the Red Army's continuous front in late 1942.

The outstanding tactical characteristic of the Red Army doctrine in the defense of river lines is that one or more powerful bridgeheads must be retained on the enemy side of the river. Such bridgeheads deny the enemy control of the river and restrict the maneuverability of enemy forces on their side of the river because of the constant threat of counterattacks from the bridgeheads. River gunboats supplement the defensive power of artillery and deny the enemy control of the river. Medium and heavy artillery support the bridgehead defenses across the river. The units defending the bridgehead have a large amount of direct-fire artillery as well as tank support. Replacements and supplies are brought across the river at night to maintain the maximum combat strength of the defensive position. Reten-

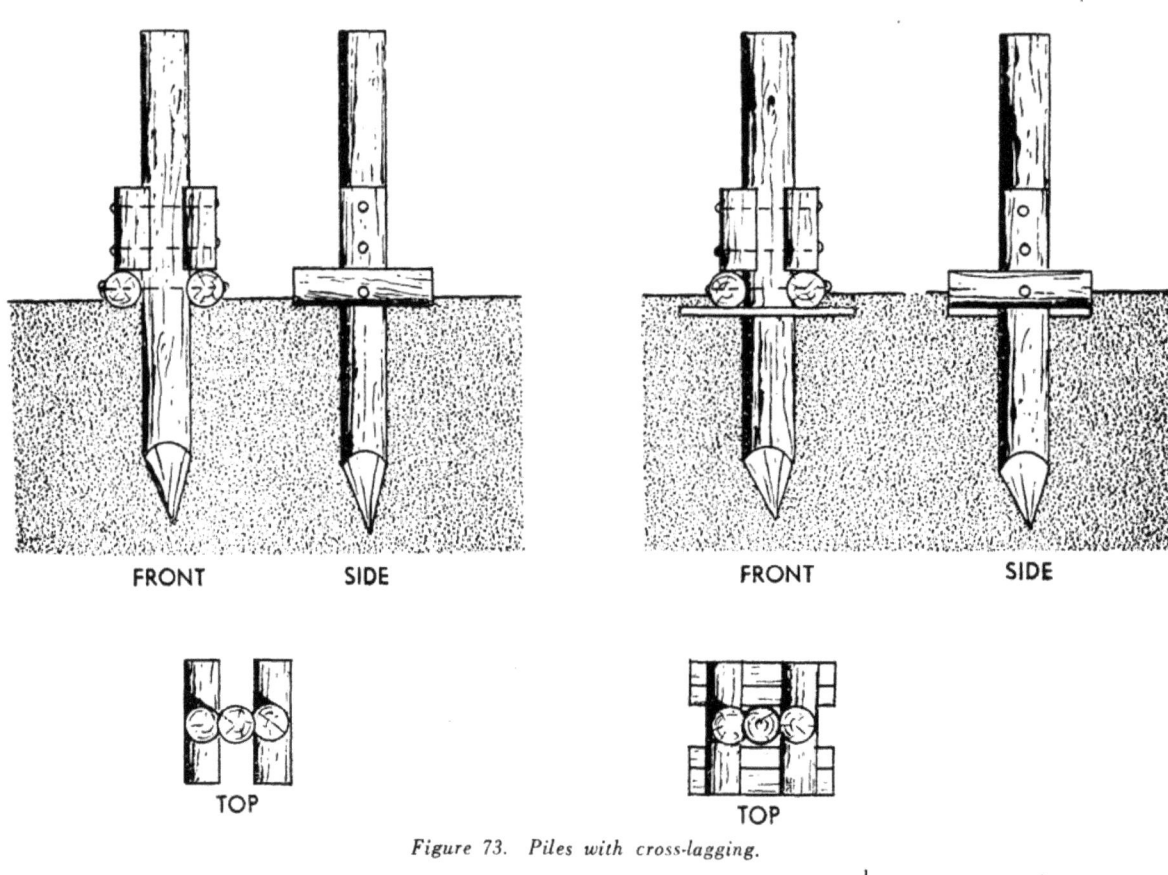

Figure 73. Piles with cross-lagging.

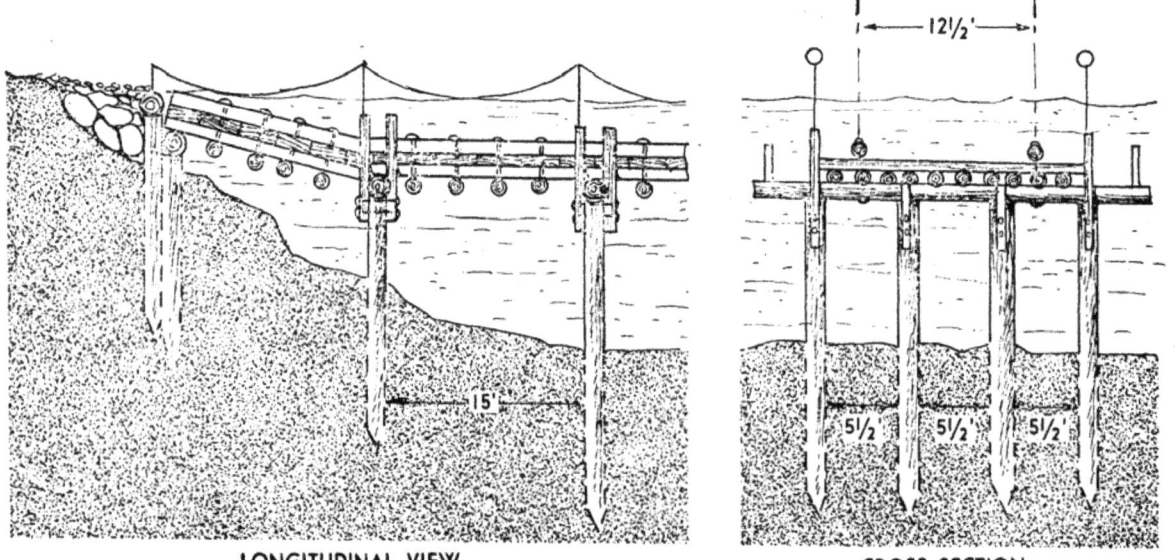

Figure 74. Underwater bridge on piles.

tion of the bridgeheads makes it possible to build up a concentration area from which offensive operations can be advantageously launched when the military situation warrants.

3. AMPHIBIOUS OPERATIONS

A number of medium-scale amphibious operations were successfully carried out by Soviet forces during the war. The outstanding tactical characteristic of every amphibious operation was coordination of the assault by sea with an offensive thrust on land converging on the same objective. The lack of strong naval support and armored landing craft for amphibious operation forced the Soviets into complete dependence on the element of surprise. In the capture of Petsamo, a sudden motor-torpedo-boat landing disrupted the shore defense system, permitting slower craft to land the main body of the assault units unmolested. The assaults on the Kerch Peninsular (1942–43) moved across a relatively narrow channel, facilitating surprise. The most extended amphibious operation took place in the capture of Constanza. In this operation, demoralized Rumanian units were in full retreat following a breakthrough of the Red Army on a wide front. The amphibious forces struck when enemy reserves were committed elsewhere and captured Constanza, thus outflanking the last defensive position available to the enemy.

Section V. OPERATIONS IN WOODS AND SWAMPS

1. GENERAL

Combat in wooded and swampy terrain is conducted by small self-sufficient Soviet units in a series of local actions. Tactical objectives are roads, clearings, road junctions, small woods, heights, and inhabited places. Engagements occur at short distances; visibility is limited; observation is difficult; and infiltration by small units is relatively easy. Movement of large forces is channelized; supply and evacuation must take place over the same routes. This necessitates strict control of road movements and careful planning. The effect of weather on road and ground conditions is magnified by the scarcity of roads and suitable deployment areas for heavy weapons. Combat in woods and swamps demands great physical effort from personnel and animals. The employment of motor vehicles for hauling supplies and pulling heavy equipment is limited to roads; elsewhere, horses and more frequently men have to carry extra loads and move heavy equipment.

Wire communications are used for all but mobile units. In forward areas whistles and signal lamps are also used. Because more time is required to string wire in woods and swamps than in open terrain, wire is not laid to the new position of a command or observation post prior to its displacement. Maintenance of wire communications is insured by frequently placed control stations and duplicate circuits. A signal construction platoon (28 men) can lay 3 to 4 miles of all-wire circuits per day.

2. USE OF WEAPONS

Combat in woods and swamps is conducted at short distances, which increases the importance of small arms and automatic weapons. As a rule, low-trajectory battalion and regimental weapons are assigned piecemeal to rifle companies, or even to rifle platoons. High-trajectory weapons—such as battalion and regimental mortars, and divisional howitzers—are retained under centralized control as much as possible. This is imperative not only because the fields of fire of low-trajectory weapons are so restricted that only high-trajectory weapons are capable of firing general support missions, but also because firing general missions requires a substantial expenditure of ammunition, which can at best be delivered to one or two places suitable for the deployment of massed artillery. The effectiveness of heavy weapons in woods and swamps depends not so much on their numbers as on uninterrupted supply of ammunition.

3. TACTICS OF SEPARATE ARMS

a. Infantry. Soviet infantry divisions with their light equipment, small daily tonnage requirements, horse-drawn transport, and readily available motive power (riflemen) are tactically mobile in woods and swamps. Infantry usually operates in small self-sufficient units, generally reinforced rifle companies. Rifle companies attack in a line of platoons. Reserves are drawn up close to the forward lines. Particular attention is directed toward the protection of flanks and lines of communications. Submachine-gun units are used in small groups (platoons or less) to infiltrate within the enemy lines, prepare ambushes, and counterattack. Antitank rifles and heavy machine guns, in addition to their normal employment, are used for sniping.

b. Cavalry. Cavalry is particularly adaptable to operations in difficult terrain, performing missions which in open country are generally assigned to motorized infantry. These missions include distant

261

reconnaissance, flank security, wide envelopment, pursuit, and raids.

c. Tanks. The Red Army considers that the effort expended in making possible a tank maneuver in apparently inaccessible terrain is fully recompensed by the surprise achieved by such a maneuver. After careful terrain and route reconnaissance, engineer and infantry detachments construct river and swamp bridges, fill holes, and, when necessary, lay corduroy roads. Tank units are assigned special engineer and infantry detachments which follow the tanks. A typical tank assault team consists of an engineer squad, a tank platoon (five light or three medium tanks), and from one to two rifle platoons. Such an assault team is followed by a second wave which, in addition to riflemen, engineers, and tanks, has light artillery or self-propelled guns.

4. IMPROVISATIONS

In crossing swamps the Red Army uses local resources as much as possible for the construction of improvised aids. Many improvisations devised in the early part of the war have been developed into standard methods. In crossing swamps the individual soldier uses short branches or bunches of twigs to make two mats about 2 yards long and 0.5 to 0.8 yards wide. He crosses the swamp by alternately placing one and carrying the other. A rifle squad uses two similar mats 3 to 4 yards long. Floating bridges are constructed from light logs and branches. A floating bridge made of 2- to 3-yard-long sections of woven fence will support horses and light antitank artillery when placed on large branches. Diagonally constructed floating corduroy roads 7 to 8 yards wide will support 8 to 10 tons. A similar floating bridge 2 to 3 yards wide can be used by a motorized column. For operations in the Pripet Marshes, Red Army riflemen were supplied with snow shoes.

5. DEFENSIVE USE OF SWAMPS

Small swamps are integrated into the system of defensive obstacles. Medium-sized swamps are used to cover frontal or flank approaches to the main defensive position. In this case, the line of outposts is placed within the swamp. Artificial islands of logs and branches are used to float security detachments and forward observation posts. Large swamps may be used in the same manner as medium-sized swamps, or the main defensive position may be established within the swamp area. From moss, turf, bushes, or branches, the Soviets construct corduroy communication roads and branch trails;

elevated gun, command post, and observation post positions; and communication trenches.

Section VI. WINTER WARFARE

1. GENERAL

The long and severe winters of the U. S. S. R. have compelled the Red Army to develop effective doctrines and techniques for winter operations.

The basic tactical principles for the employment of troops under winter conditions are the same as those developed for the conduct of operations in other seasons. However, low temperature, heavy snowfall, frozen ground, and changes in the relief and appearance of local objects create additional problems which the Red Army has successfully solved, and even capitalized, as testified to by the success of winter operations against the Germans.

The difficulties of winter conditions do not decrease the activity of the troops. On the contrary, the Soviets make skillful use of the cold weather and snow. Fortifications are built of snow and ice, and frozen rivers are used as airfields. The long nights in which snow lessens the degree of darkness are advantageously used for maneuvering and regrouping forces. The logistics—the movement of troops and supplies—is of greatest influence. The Red Army successfully employs tracked vehicles in snow, uses tractor-drawn sled trains and, for light operations and infiltrations, highly mobile motor sleds.

The Soviets are also well aware of the fact that winter climate increases the effectiveness of persistent chemical agents, keeping them active for several weeks.

Camouflage is of particular importance; all troops are issued white camouflage suits. All weapons are camouflaged either with white paint or by white tape to break the silhouettes. The concealment of tracks is particularly emphasized.

2. EMPLOYMENT OF ARMS

a. Coordination. Coordination of the various arms under winter conditions is complicated by the difficulties involved in the identification of landmarks and, in spite of the increased range of radio and wire communications in cold weather, in the utilization of communications equipment.

The rate of movement of tanks, infantry on skis, and cavalry is equalized to a considerable extent. As a rule, the maneuvering of troops is slowed up by the necessity of keeping to the roads.

The joint action of artillery with infantry is normally hindered by snow cover, in proportion to its depth and powdery condition. The cooperation of infantry with tanks is equally complicated. In pursuit of the enemy, the Soviets consider it is usually more advantageous to use infantry on skis than to employ cavalry. The necessity of careful use of camouflage often exerts retarding influences on the time factor of operations. In general, transportation, evacuation, and bringing up of supplies are associated with great difficulties.

The Soviets have found it necessary to make their operational plans for winter warfare flexible, providing alternatives to meet sudden changes in meteorological conditions. The operations culminating in the crossing of the Vistula in the winter of 1944–45 offer a good illustration of provisions made for possible changes in weather conditions. The Red Army developed two plans. One called predominantly for air support while the other depended mainly on artillery support. When the heavy overcast completely prevented the employment of aircraft, the second plan was available for successful execution.

b. Infantry (ski troops). Winter conditions not only restrict the movement of mechanized equipment, but also generally decrease the mobility of regular infantry troops. To overcome this difficulty, the Red Army equips part of its infantry with skis. The bulk of the infantry, however, is left without skis and depends on the use of good roads or sled transportation for mobility. A special adaptation of this principle of transportation is the use of tank-drawn armored sleds for infantry. Infantry on skis are found either in independent ski battalions or in ski units which are part of a rifle division. The normal armament of the ski battalions consists usually of rifles, submachine guns, light machine guns, and light mortars in the three rifle companies; heavy machine guns in the heavy-machine-gun company; and antitank rifles in the antitank-rifle platoon of the battalion. The lack of heavier mortars is explained by the tendency to keep the armament light in order to increase the mobility of this specialized unit. Depending on the particular mission and the combat situation, temporary ski formations of varying strengths are organized.

The use of skis greatly increases the mobility of the infantry. The individual skier can travel 4.2 to 7.2 miles per hour; small units can travel 2.4 to 5.4 miles per hour. The travel rate of a larger unit

usually does not exceed 3.6 miles per hour. Ski troops are also independent of the road net, a fact which makes ski troops well adapted for independent missions, such as penetrations to the rear of the enemy, destruction of installations, and cutting of communications.

As a rule the Soviets employ small groups of ski troops for reconnaissance, for raiding parties, for outflanking maneuvers, and for exploitation immediately after a break-through, when the regular infantry is limited to use of roads.

c. Motor-sled battalions. In addition to the ski battalions, the Red Army has organized numerous motor-sled battalions, some of which are combat battalions, while others are employed predominantly for transportation.

The combat motor-sled battalion is believed to be organized into three combat motor-sled companies, each with three platoons. One company has a total of ten sleds (three sleds per platoon and one for the company commander). The combat motor sled has one 7.62-mm machine gun "DT" as fixed armament. The battalion also has a supply company with ten transport sleds, three to four trucks, one tractor, and a maintenance platoon.

Combat motor-sled battalions stage surprise raids against enemy road columns or against an enemy who has no opportunity to deploy or to take up positions. They attack the flank or rear of deployed enemy troops and pursue the retreating enemy in cooperation with ski troops. They find employment as covering forces for troops dismounted from motorsleds, on open flanks of marching units of occupied islands and coastal sectors, and at the junctions of larger formations. Motor-sled battalions are used as reinforcements for motor-sled reconnaissance detachments; for reconnaissance in steppes, lakes, rivers, and coastal areas; and as lateral patrols behind their own defensive lines in a wide defensive sector to prevent the infiltration of enemy troops. In the defense they are committed in cooperation with infantry transported by sleds against enemy ski troops attempting outflanking maneuvers. They also maintain command communications and provide security for command posts. Their mobility makes them suitable for combat against enemy parachutists and for exploitation of a breakthrough in the enemy position, in close coordination with tanks, infantry, and ski troops.

Motor-sled transport battalions transport infantry cooperating with combat motor-sled units. They carry infantry to the rear of the enemy and also bring up replacements and supplies. The return trips are utilized for evacuation of casualties and captured matériel. The transport battalions transport machine-gun, ski, submachine-gun, and close antitank-combat troops; and provide transportation for the command personnel of larger formations. Finally, they are used as searching parties looking for damaged tanks and planes, and for bringing up maintenance crews and guards.

The Soviets give careful attention to a wide variety of factors when employing motor sleds. Motor-sled battalions must be employed either as a unit or in not less than company strength. Their employment requires thorough preparation and smooth coordination with infantry, tanks, aircraft, artillery, and engineers. Weather and terrain conditions have to be taken into account. Loose snow decreases the speed of motor sleds; low temperature makes the starting of the motors more difficult. At least 4 hours in daylight are required to prepare the sleds and crews for commitment. Ravines, woods, and brush land increase operating difficulties.

On the march, the Soviets employ unloaded sleds at the point of the column to make tracks and mark the path to be followed. The normal daily travel capacity of motor sleds is 60 to 72 miles on average terrain. Forced marches can achieve daily distances of 120 miles. The Soviets calculate on 12 to 15 miles per hour as an average speed when determining the time required for a given distance. Roads with two-way traffic may not be used by motor sleds, which are confined to parallel roads or to cross-country movement. The sleds must not be overloaded when transporting men and material. The normal load consists of four armed men plus the driver and 880 pounds of material. The greatest economy of fuel and oil is required. The fuel tanks should always be at least one-third full.

d. Artillery. The movement of horse-drawn and motorized artillery in snow more than 12 inches deep is usually confined to roads, even though the Soviet artillery is mounted on sleds. Occasionally the roads have to be specially prepared with mats and logs to secure movement of the artillery. Tractors are often equipped with grousers. Occasionally the infantry helps by hand to bring its supporting artillery into position.

In snow less than 12 inches deep, cross-country movement is possible, although engineers often have to break a path.

Mortars, rockets, and pack artillery pieces, having greater mobility than regular artillery, find extensive employment. Artillery observation is greatly influenced by the weather. Observation on clear days is normally good, while in a foggy haze the range of observation is greatly decreased. Ground bursts on forward slopes normally show up as black spots on snow background. Air bursts are barely visible. Smoke shells are frequently used for adjustment. Winter conditions usually create favorable conditions for the operation of sound ranging units which the Red Army freely employs to counteract, at least partly, the limitation of visual observation in foggy weather.

Whenever possible the Soviet troops clear the ground for their gun positions to avoid displacements when firing.

e. Tanks. Tanks and self-propelled artillery may, up to a certain degree, replace field artillery in supporting infantry because their maneuverability is less hindered by an equal amount of snow, although it is affected by the character of the snow. Ammunition supply, however, is a serious problem. Heavy and medium tanks are able to pass through snow 20 to 24 inches deep; equipped with grousers they can pass through a maximum of 28 inches. Light tanks can move through snow 12 to 14 inches deep. Soft snow does not impede tank movement seriously because it is compressed by the weight of the tank to below tank-clearance level. Hard snow breaks under the weight of the tracks, and following tanks are suspended without contact of the tracks with the ground. Thus, tank movement in column formation is impossible over deep, hard snow.

The Soviets equip tanks with grousers for movement over slippery terrain. In addition, special mats are used for movement over snow slopes.

Frozen rivers and lakes cease to be an obstacle for tanks when frozen to a certain thickness: 28 to 40 inches of ice can carry a heavy tank; 24 inches is necessary for a medium tank; and 12 inches for a light tank. Infantry can cross on ice 4 inches thick.

Since tank tracks are clearly visible in fresh snow, the Russians emphasize the movement of tanks in column, during the night, or in a snow storm. Often the last tank in the column will drag sleds or trees behind to erase the tracks and create the appearance of an ordinary trail.

When tanks reach an inhabited populated sector, they are always well dispersed and are brought into barns or destroyed buildings, or alongside walls of buildings. In the open they are covered with snow

264

or other natural camouflage material, depending on the locality. Efforts are made to make warm shelter available for the tanks. To assure constant combat readiness in wintertime, tank units are provided with water and oil heaters and other technical equipment.

f. Engineers. The work of the Soviet engineers becomes especially important in winter operations. They are responsible for road repair and construction; the erection of warm shelters for men, horses, and matériel; employment of special kinds of winter camouflage; and for other normal engineer responsibilities. One of the main tasks, however, is the construction of winter obstacles, using snow and ice. The procurement of drinking water, particularly for horses, occasionally presents difficulties.

g. Cavalry. Under winter conditions, the Soviets often encounter great difficulties in employing their cavalry units as prescribed by Red Army doctrine; that is, in combination with supporting tanks and artillery as an independent striking force in terrain not accessible to motorized equipment. In deep snow the mobility of cavalry is often reduced to 2.4 to 3 miles per hour; movement is often restricted to roads or to the tracks made by tanks. In snow up to 12 inches deep, cavalry attacks of brief duration are possible after thorough terrain reconnaissance. Successful operations have been conducted jointly by infantry on skis and cavalry.

The Soviets are well aware of the special care that horses require during winter operations. They therefore make as much use as possible of inhabited communities for bivouac. In uninhabited regions they construct protective shelters from local materials.

3. RECONNAISSANCE

Thorough ground reconnaissance, the Red Army teaches, is of the greatest importance for winter operations. Reconnaissance must, in addition to its normal missions, reconnoiter the terrain in regard to special weather and visibility conditions. The Soviets normally assign this mission to ski infantry units, although cavalry and motorized units may also be used when the terrain conditions permit. Cavalry and motorized units are usually limited to reconnaissance along roads.

Distances considered to be within the capabilities of units of varying strength assigned to reconnaissance missions are: 21 to 30 miles for a strong reconnaissance detachment of approximately battalion strength; 9 to 18 miles for reconnaissance companies; up to 6 miles for reconnaissance platoons; up to 1.8 to 3 miles for reconnaissance sections. In snowstorms, the distances are shortened by one-half because of the difficulties of observation and reporting.

Aerial reconnaissance in wintertime is considered extremely effective and furnishes valuable information as to the locations of enemy installations, obstacles, and troop concentration, and the enemy disposition on the front.

4. OFFENSIVE OPERATIONS

The objectives of offensive operations in winter remain the same as in other seasons, though the seizure of inhabited areas and road nets is of increased importance.

In the early part of the war the Soviets carried out attacks against the enemy lines of communication. This was facilitated by the German defense. Soviet infiltration in force by units up to a cavalry corps in size was possible through wide gaps between strongly fortified centers of defense. In the latter part of the war, when German defenses were organized in continuous lines of defensive positions built up in depth, the Red Army was forced to develop its offensives into operations of combined arms with all the characteristics of well planned and large-scale attacks.

The Soviets carefully time their offensive operations. They do not hesitate to conduct their attacks during blinding snowstorms which promote overwhelming surprise. In East Prussia, the Soviets outflanked the strongly fortified German position with large tank formations, which they moved across the ice during a heavy snowstorm, attacking the German position from the flank next to the sea, where they were least expected. In the interest of achieving surprise, the Soviets also do not hesitate to begin their attacks during the night.

Characteristic of Red Army winter offensives is the proximity of the line of departure to the front lines to avoid tiring the troops before contacting the enemy. Infantry on skis normally advances first, supported by heavy infantry weapons mounted on skis or sleds and by artillery and tanks which, however, are often limited in their advance to existing roads and sections of favorable terrain. Other ski units, cavalry, and tanks are used whenever possible for outflanking maneuvers, in order to block the exits of inhabited areas and thereby prevent the enemy from destroying bases useful for further operations by friendly main forces.

5. DEFENSIVE OPERATIONS

The same organization of stabilized defense is used throughout the year. However, extensive use of snow and ice obstacles is made in constructing defensive positions in wintertime. The selection of the defensive area is influenced by the location of inhabited areas, forests, and groves, which, with adaptations, may become important strong points. The Soviets also emphasize the necessity of adequate shelter for the troops to keep them warm and maintain their combat efficiency. They make extensive use of dummy installations, which they secure with mines and booby traps.

The Red Army prepares heavy weapons for unobserved fire into previously registered areas, covering the gaps between strongpoints to avoid successful enemy offensive operations during periods of limited observation. When the enemy succeeds in breaking into the Soviet defensive zone, with the intention of seizing built-up areas, the Soviets strive to halt him by previously adjusted artillery fire and by counterattacks.

During an enemy attack, artillery tries to slow his advance by forcing him off the roads and thus compelling him to advance crosscountry. Counterattacks are carried out in previously studied and prepared directions, usually on the flanks of the enemy units. Whenver possible, the Soviets counterattack with skiers, who move downhill, with the wind and sun in the face of the enemy. Counterattacks with shock troops without skis and supported by heavy infantry weapons and artillery, are carried out only for short distances.

When enemy pressure forces the Soviets to withdraw from action, they try to disengage themselves from the enemy during the night. In daytime they make extensive use of smoke. Ski troops are normally assigned as covering forces.

Section VII. MOUNTAIN OPERATIONS

1. BASIC PRINCIPLES

The tactical employment of troops, weapons, and equipment in mountain warfare is dictated by terrain and weather conditions, and the attendant logistical problems. Operations in the mountains impose great strain on men, animals, and materiel. Rapidly changing weather, road and soil conditions, and mountain altitudes necessitate the issuance of special equipment, additional clothing, and increased rations. Greater organizational weights and the decreased loads which can be carried by men and animals require larger unit trains. Whenever terrain conditions permit, narrow-gauge railroads are built for divisions and higher organizations. Tractors are assembled along the route to haul supplies over difficult areas. When other forms of transportation fail, air transport is used. Regimental and divisional supply and evacuation installations are placed closer to forward units. The divisional field hospital and service area must not be more than 2 hours' journey from the corresponding regimental installations. Contrary to normal Soviet practice, signal communications for the purpose of regulating traffic are established along supply routes in mountains.

Antiaircraft plays a prominent part in mountain operations. Both in the offensive and defensive, antiaircraft guns are placed at critical positions where traffic is channelized. Organic antiaircraft is supplemented by GHQ units which are assigned for duration of the mountain operations. Searchlight units are assigned for the defense of important railheads and supply dumps.

Mountain combat lacks the unity which characterizes combat on rolling terrain; the inaccessibility of certain areas and the lack of sufficient roads prevent the organization of continuous fronts. Combat in the mountains assumes a piecemeal character, resolving itself into separate, more-or-less isolated conflicts by small, self-sufficient units difficult to retain under centralized control. This necessitates initiative, within the expressed intentions of the higher command, on the part of subordinate commanders, as the appropriate actions of even individual units and elements often lead to decisive tactical success.

There are often gaps between friendly front sectors which may be occupied by the enemy. The appropriate disposition of second echelon and reserve troops is of utmost importance for coping with enemy attempts at envelopment, outflanking, and infiltration. Up to one-sixth of the entire infantry forces and up to one-fourth of cavalry should be designated for this purpose.

The abundance of dead spaces and areas of nonvisibility in the mountain lowers the effectiveness of arms for grazing fire at far and average distances, and gives added importance to high-trajectory weapons (howitzers and mortars). Snipers and submachine gunners play an important role in preparing ambushes and infiltrating through enemy lines. Direct fire, interdictory fire, bayonets, and hand grenades are used to great advantage.

266

2. CONTROL OF COMBAT

For uninterrupted control of combat in the mountains, command posts must be located closer to the troops. The security of command posts is provided for by advance and flank detachments which occupy heights commanding approaches to them.

In order for the commander to maintain constant contact with rapidly changing mountain combat conditions, he must not leave his command observation post unless under the severest necessity. For uninterrupted personal observation of battle progress, the commander moves forward to a new command observation post immediately after the seizure of crests and spurs obstructing his observation.

When direct communication between command posts and operating units is impossible, forward message centers are moved out along the axis of communications.

In spite of dead spaces and periodic bad reception due to mountain relief and atmospheric conditions, radio is the basic means of communication in the mountains, especially for communication with isolated units and aviation. The Red Army increases the employment and reliability of radio in mountain operations by careful training in the selection of frequencies, the siting of radios, and the adjustment of antennas. Visual signalling is also widely used because of the simplicity of setting up posts and stations. Liaison planes, foot and mounted messengers, and dogs (for communication over distances up to 1 to 2 miles) are also used. Use of wire is limited by such factors as time consumed in laying it (two times that on rolling terrain), possibilities of enemy tapping, damage to wire due to weather conditions, and difficulties of replacing damaged circuits.

3. THE OFFENSIVE

The offensive in mountains resolves itself into a series of attacks on successive objectives such as heights, ridges, passes, and valleys. The plan of maneuver generally consists of the isolation of separate tactical objectives and their annihilation by double or single envelopment; thus, the main effort must generally be supplemented by several secondary efforts. Successive displacement of supporting weapons between successive phase lines is imperative. In attacking enemy positions arranged in altitudinal levels, the fire of all weapons is first concentrated on the lowest level. While infantry attacks that level, artillery and mortars shift their fire to the firing positions of the next level.

The offensive in the mountains is conducted either along the mountain chain or across it.

An offensive along a ridge combines a breakthrough in the valley with an encircling maneuver over the mountains, and the seizure of commanding heights and road junctions in the enemy rear and flanks. The break-through is accomplished by a heavy concentration of artillery, tanks, and aviation. In the development of the break-through by mobile formations, the seizure of road junctions in the enemy rear may lead to the surrounding and defeat of his forces on important sectors of the front. In continuing the advance along a valley, friendly flanks and rear must be secured by airborne troops and mountain-infantry units who seize heights commanding the valley. Advancing troops must support flank security units by aerial attacks, artillery fire, and maneuvers into the rear of the enemy defending the heights; at the same time, these flank security units assist the advancing main body by fire and maneuver in the flank and rear of enemy units barricading the valley.

An offensive across a ridge is based on the possession of mountain passes. Mountain passes may be secured by the seizure of heights commanding them, by attacking the enemy's rear on the reverse side of the ridge in a rapid outflanking maneuver, by landing airborne troops in the rear of enemy units defending the pass, and, simultaneously with these actions, by launching an aggressive frontal assault, usually in coordination with aviation. Offensive operations assume the characteristics of close combat.

4. THE DEFENSE

Mountain terrain provides favorable locations for defensive positions while at the same time irregular relief, deep and hidden approaches, and the isolation of commanding heights and crests facilitate outflanking and enveloping maneuvers by the enemy. A successful defense depends on thorough reconnaissance, well organized outpost zone action, and timely and sudden counterattacks by second echelon and reserve troops to prevent these maneuvers.

Observation posts are established up to 9 to 12 miles from the defensive front line; communication with them is maintained by radio and visual signalling—relay points are established when necessary.

In the outpost zone, security elements cut off roads and approaches; secure flanks, intervals between defensive positions, and salients; and hold the enemy until the approach of support troops. Support troops in the outpost zone parry enemy outflanking maneuvers; destroy small groups attempting infiltration; and, when necessary, cover the withdrawal of friendly elements. In defense of the outpost zone, ambushes and flank fire barrages are used extensively.

The main defensive positions may be organized either along or across the mountain ridge; in either case the front line is situated on forward slopes, although a portion of the forces must be disposed on reverse slopes. Firing positions are echeloned vertically as well as in depth. In defending a mountain valley, strong points are echeloned on adjacent heights to cover the valley with cross fire. In wooded terrain, defensive positions are organized at the front edge of the woods or on commanding heights. In the latter case, the woods are used as a natural obstacle to trap the enemy. Elevated platforms are built in trees for heavy machine guns and observation posts. In all cases, antitank and antipersonnel mines, obstacles of all types, and artificial rock and landslides are widely employed.

The artillery and infantry antitank fire plan is developed to cover approaches to defensive positions and dead spaces by both frontal and flanking fire. Divisional artillery is always centralized when operating in broad valleys and foothills. It is partially centralized in support of the main defensive positions, and decentralized in support of secondary defensive positions. Submachine-gun teams are assigned to each artillery and mortar position for protection against infiltrating enemy units.

Even if the enemy succeeds in breaking into the defensive zone and begins developing his initial success, isolated heights must be firmly held. The second echelons of the army (corps) and divisional (brigade) reserves, in cooperation with tanks, then counterattacks to support threatened points as soon as the enemy drives over the crest; at this point his observation is limited and he is deprived of artillery support.

5. ROLES OF THE VARIOUS ARMS

a. **Infantry.** The infantry carries the chief weight of combat in the mountains. Under conditions where the support of other arms cannot always be relied upon, and where units often operate with open flanks and even without communication with adjacent units, unsupported infantry is best adapted to conduct successful mountain warfare. It is cap-

able of filtering independently through enemy defenses; reaching his flanks and rear from the most unexpected and weakly defended areas; and, by using bayonets, hand grenades, and point-blank fire, of destroying him.

To provide for uninterrupted artillery support when possible, the infantry must assist it in getting through inaccessible sectors and, by the seizure of heights, provide it with necessary observation.

For combat in high mountain sectors, where the relief is sharply cut and communications are unreliable, special mountain elements may be attached to regular infantry. Often, infantry units which have received special training—orientation in fog, night, and snow; camouflage techniques; construction of light defensive fortifications—and have special attached equipment are designated for combat in high mountain areas. If road conditions are bad, or roads are lacking altogether, infantry must be strongly reinforced with engineers and additional pack animals.

b. **Cavalry.** Cavalry is the mobile arm in mountain operations. It usually operates offensively, most often in meeting engagements and in attack. It often conducts mobile defense, using ambushes and surprise attacks, but is used only in special instances for stable defense.

Specifically, it is well adapted to surrounding enemy main groupings; developing a break-through made by the infantry by disrupting enemy attempts to stabilize the front; and pursuing the enemy with the intention of reaching rear areas and blocking his retreat. It is capable of supporting army operations by covering the concentration and deployment of forces; seizing and holding especially important tactical features before the approach of the main forces; securing flanks; covering retreat in the most threatened areas; and conducting reconnaissance and partisan activities in the enemy rear.

Cavalry divisions, assigned to armies or infantry corps, usually function independently for the execution of specific missions to which they are adapted. In sectors along wide valleys and in low mountains, larger cavalry units may be used. Cavalry is reinforced with tanks, infantry, artillery, and special units according to the mission assigned to it.

In areas in the enemy rear or where there are not sufficient roads, forage and provisions are supplied by air transport.

c. **Artillery.** Mountain relief restricts the movement of artillery and limits its flexibility of fire. Artillery is, therefore, attached directly to the individual units it is to support. Regimental anti-tank artillery and, in certain instances, divisional artillery guns are employed by platoon or even separate pieces in direct support of infantry groups. Infantry and pioneer commands are assigned to artillery units to secure their movement. Pack mountain batteries accompany infantry in high mountain areas.

An extensive network of vertical and lateral observation posts must be set up to ensure wide fields of observation. Command observation posts are moved out to forward units and located not only within their own sectors but, if necessary, also in adjacent sectors. Reserve observation posts are located in close proximity to the firing positions. Radio and visual signals are used for communication between observation posts and firing positions.

Mountain terrain and sharp changes in the direction and speed of wind hinder the use of artillery instrumental reconnaissance. Observation by paired observers is widely practised for determining the exact location of targets, and aviation is used for reconnaissance of enemy batteries and adjustment of fire.

The choice of firing positions for light field artillery batteries is governed not only by the minimum range of the guns but also by the fact that dead areas, abundant in mountain terrain, must be avoided as far as possible. Thus, firing positions are located on adjacent sectors and heights for flanking fire, and are moved back to use other trajectories.

Firing positions for high-trajectory guns (mortars and howitzers) may be located behind high natural covers and in deep valleys, thus bringing into range areas which are inaccessible to other batteries and permitting fire over the heads of advancing friendly infantry for longer periods. Firing positions and approaches to them should be carefully camouflaged by engineers.

Since the lower atmospheric pressure in high areas strongly affects the flight of shells, special auxiliary firing tables must be provided.

d. Tanks and armored cars. Tanks may operate in mountainous terrain if slopes do not exceed 30°. In areas not permitting the massing of tanks, they are distributed among infantry and cavalry units. The employment of tanks must be preceded by terrain and route reconnaissance. Special obstacle-clearing groups are assigned to each tank unit.

The basic mission of tanks in the mountains is the direct support of infantry. In close cooperation with infantry, and together with artillery and aviation, tanks operate as part of the main forces or on the flanks and in the rear of the enemy as part of outflanking units. Tanks also seize phase lines, inhabited points, defiles, road junctions, and passes; pursue the enemy; and cover the withdrawal of friendly units. Light tanks may be used in small independent groups.

One and one-half to two times the normal amount of fuel and lubricating oil is required in the mountains. Each tank must be provided with spare fuel drums; tractors are used to drag them on steep slopes and across wide passes to conserve fuel. Reserve spare parts must be provided. Two crews for each tank are necessary to eliminate overfatigue.

Armored cars are used on hard soil or wherever passable to them. They execute reconnaissance; seize inhabited points, narrow passes, road junctions, and crossings; and guard rear roads and communications.

e. Engineers. Each independent unit or element, regardless of its composition, must be reinforced with engineers for assistance in overcoming terrain obstacles, for building bridges, laying corduroy and other types of roads, forcing rivers, getting through swamps, conducting terrain reconnaissance, etc.

f. Airborne troops. Airborne troops (especially parachute troops) are used effectively for mountain operations in the enemy rear and on his flanks in coordination with land forces. Even small airborne groups equipped with automatic weapons and explosives can often decide the outcome of battle by seizing commanding heights and passes and disrupting the enemy system of communications.

Where level plateaus and valleys are not available for landing airborne troops of other types, parachutists are used. Landings must be preceded by careful and secret terrain reconnaissance.

Support aviation cooperates with airborne troops and parachute groups by bombing mountain roads and mobile enemy units.

Due to the lack of sufficient roads, combat with enemy airborne troops is chiefly the mission of support aviation, which destroys enemy equipment and personnel at their loading airdromes or attacks the enemy in the air before troops can land and disembark.

CHAPTER VI

FORTIFICATIONS

Section I. FORTIFICATIONS DOCTRINE

1. GENERAL

The length of the U. S. S. R.'s frontiers and the size of her territory have precluded the construction of a continuous, permanent system of frontier fortifications such as the Westwall or the Maginot Line.

to delay and channelize the enemy advance, thus facilitating destruction of the enemy by artillery and air counterpreparations and by counterattacks.

Properly sited and effectively developed systems of obstacles are the foundation of Soviet fortifications. These obstacles bar the enemy from access to tactical objectives. A system of fire is built up to defend the obstacles. Machine guns and individual anti-

Figure 1.—Organization of antitank defenses.

Shaped and developed by the impetus of modern armored and motorized warfare, the Soviet system of defense is primarily an antitank defense capable of rapid development. It is based on natural and artificial obstacles covered by and coordinated with an elaborate system of fire from field fortifications grouped into centers of resistance. Its purpose is

tank guns provide local cover. Artillery and mortar defensive barrages supplement the obstacles and interdict secondary approaches independently (figure 1).

With the development of the defensive system in depth, the obstacles form a more and more cellular system containing individual centers of resistance.

270

In planning the cellular system, it is essential that friendly counterattacks against terrain seized by the enemy not be impeded. As a result, the Soviets do not employ complete all-around defense of a strongpoint, but provide a lane through which supporting strongpoints can lay down fire on a lost strongpoint without endangering counterattacking friendly troops. Similarly, switch positions are designed for effective resistance in one direction only, when natural obstacles cover other approaches.

The Soviets stress the importance of providing an adequate reserve of fire in fortified areas. Key areas must be covered by several types of weapons—artillery, mortars, and automatic weapons. Local over-saturation of defensive weapons must, however, be carefully avoided since it discloses the system of defense, is vulnerable to artillery fire, and leads to unnecessary losses. On the other hand, a reserve of weapons in protected positions must be available to replace losses from enemy fire.

The construction of shelters, particularly of a permanent type, for large numbers of troops is contrary to Soviet doctrine. No more personnel is maintained within the defensive zone than is essential for the conduct of local defense. Mobile reserves are maintained under centralized control for general counterattacks supported by powerful artillery counterpreparations.

The Red Army also stresses the necessity for deception in a defensive system. Camouflage techniques and discipline have been highly developed. Dummy positions of the most elaborate description are often constructed and may be defended by small garrisons with equipment to simulate intensive fire. Generally, the dummy positions, particularly the dummy forward lines, are sited so as to induce enemy attack in a direction flanked by the actual positions. Forward slopes are often used for dummy positions, with the main positions on reverse slopes. Crests are frequently integrated within the boundaries of the main positions. Soviet communication trenches are usually covered; vertical masks provide concealment from ground observation.

The Soviets make extensive use of small concrete or steel pillboxes and emplacements, often prefabricated. These are used integrally with field fortifications, especially in key or exposed positions. Elaborate systems of permanent fortifications were originally constructed along parts of the 1939 U. S. S. R. boundary, but proved to be defensively inadequate. In general, heavy permanent works play a very minor role in Soviet fortifications doctrine at the present

time. Important strategic centers and naval bases are protected by forts, often old, with armored turrets housing heavy guns. These must be supported by field works and minefields to make possible their close-in defense.

Experience of the war has shown that populated centers, especially large cities, can be developed into extremely formidable fortifications (see City Warfare, chapter V). Houses provide excellent defensive positions, particularly in basements. Rubble serves for camouflage and protection against blast action. In addition, field fortifications of normal types are readily constructed in parks and streets. Sewers and subways afford unusual possibilities for unexpected counterattacks, shelter, and mining.

2. ORGANIZATION OF A DEFENSIVE SYSTEM

Soviet defensive positions are designed to stop the enemy in front of the main line of resistance, to localize the enemy's penetration, and to prevent his expansion frontally or in depth. The organization of defensive positions is ordinarily based on an interconnected system of defensive cells, often arranged in a staggered, checker-board pattern.

a. Army defensive zone. An army defensive zone (figure 2) includes an outpost zone; several zones echeloned in depth, of which the first is the main zone of defense; switch positions; and an obstacle system (minefields and antitank areas) to fill the gaps between individual defense zones and link them together into a single operational system. An Army defends a zone 18 to 30 miles deep and 30 to 50 miles wide. An infantry divisional defensive zone is 2½ to 3½ miles deep and 5 to 7 miles wide. Within the division, two regiments normally defend on line with three battalions abreast; the third regiment is held out as a mobile reserve or to man the rear defensive position, and to provide troops for the outpost zone of defense. Each battalion position is 1,500 to 2,000 yards deep and about as wide; of this area about half serves as a delaying position and about half as a center of resistance.

Greater depths and greater widths of defensive positions with relatively uniform distribution of strongpoints characterize the decentralized system of defense (see chapter V). Centralized defensive systems, on the other hand, are characterized by greater over-all density and by sharp contrasts in the distribution and concentrations of strongpoints and obstacles. Primary enemy approaches are heavily defended. Secondary approaches are covered chiefly by fire and mobile units.

271

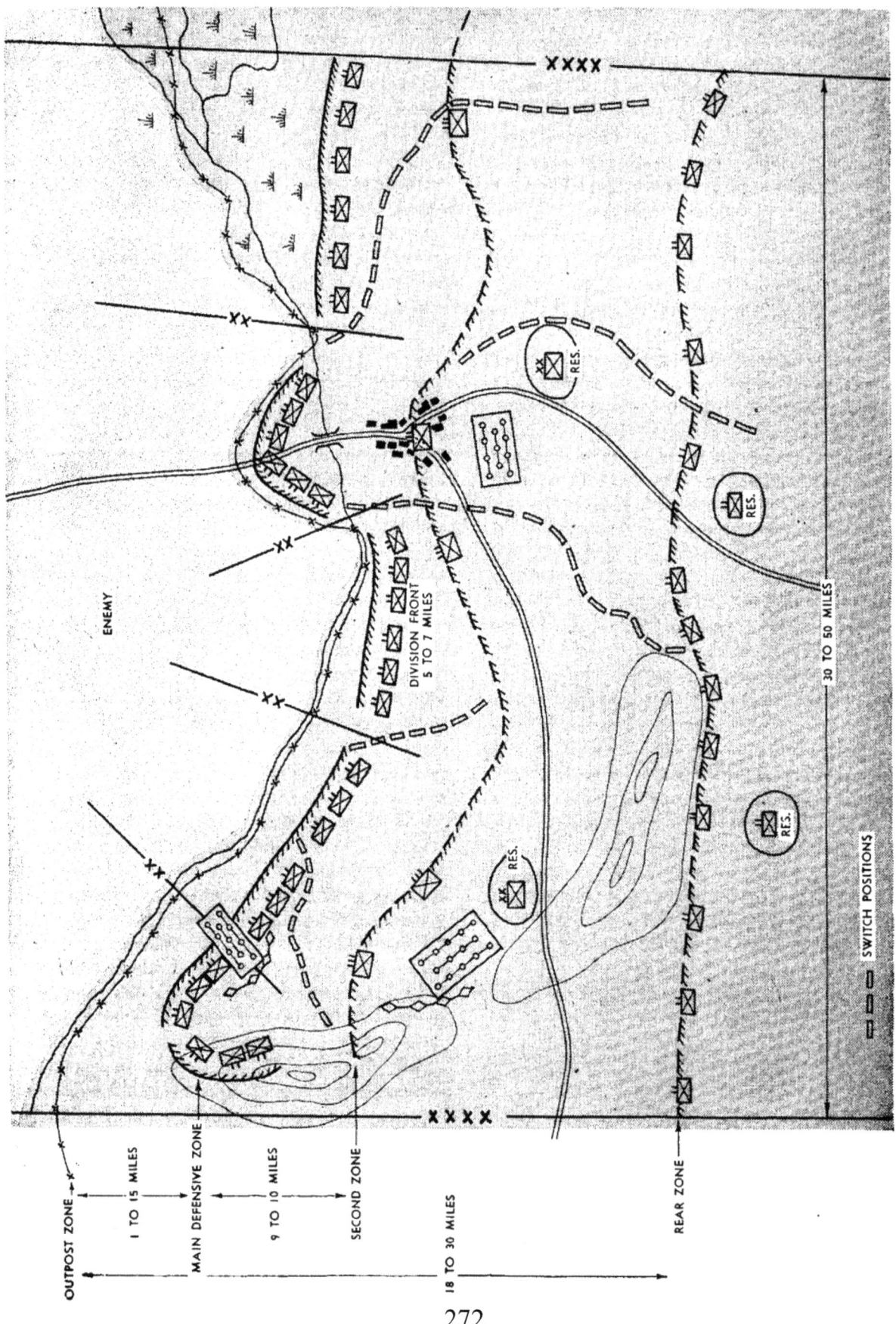

Figure 2.—*Organization of an army defensive zone.*

ENEMY

DIVISION FRONT 5 TO 7 MILES

RES.

RES.

RES.

RES.

RES.

30 TO 50 MILES

SWITCH POSITIONS

OUTPOST ZONE

1 TO 15 MILES

MAIN DEFENSIVE ZONE

9 TO 10 MILES

SECOND ZONE

18 TO 30 MILES

REAR ZONE

272

The flanks of strongpoints are often reinforced by emplacements for tanks and self-propelled guns which fire from concealed positions until the approach of the enemy forces their mobile action.

OUTPOST ZONE. The outpost zone must be organized before contact with the main enemy forces. Its missions are to facilitate observation and fire direction, to destroy small advance enemy elements, and to delay the advance of the enemy main body. It includes advanced and intermediate positions reinforced by obstacles blocking principal enemy approaches, especially for armor. The density of the obstacles increases toward the main zone of defense. The outpost zone ranges from 1 to 15 miles in depth, depending on terrain. Where surprise attacks by the enemy are likely, as in the mountains and in country accessible to armor, the outpost zone must be deep and capable of independent local action. Within the outpost zone a dummy forward edge for the main zone of resistance is often built.

MAIN ZONE OF RESISTANCE. The main zone of resistance is the basis of the defense system. Its forward edge is organized as the main line of resistance with a maximum concentration of fire and obstacles against the attacking forces. Provisions are made for the all-around defense of individual sectors of the main zone of resistance in the event of enemy penetrations. The zone consists of a series of battalion or, more rarely, regimental centers of resistance containing company and platoon strongpoints. The centers of resistance and strongpoints are so sited as to be protected by natural and artificial barriers, and to cover these barriers by fire. Trenches supplemented by pillboxes and open or covered artillery emplacements are the main types of strongpoint fortifications. Tactical intervals between strongpoints form pockets in which a penetrating enemy may be trapped under observed fire.

The relative strength of the main zone of defense depends upon the over-all tactical plan of centralized or decentralized defense. In centralized defense the bulk of the artillery remains massed behind the main defensive zone. The conduct of the defense is elastic. Secondary positions are abandoned under strong pressure. Chief emphasis is laid on maintaining a continuous defensive line and on channelizing the enemy attack in preparation for a decisive counterattack. In decentralized defense, artillery is assigned to individual centers of resistance and even company strongpoints. Consequently, a high density of direct fire exists, although

control of massed fire is rendered more difficult. Individual centers of resistance are held to the last.

SECOND ZONE. From 9 to 10 miles behind the forward edge of the main zone of resistance a second zone is organized, normally by the reserve regiment of each division in line. In general, the fortifications system of the second zone is similar to that of the main zone. Primary emphasis, however, is laid on the creation of obstacle systems and centers of resistance protecting principal enemy approaches, rather than on continuous lines of defense. The second zone of resistance is used as an assembly area for counterattacking forces, which employ centers of resistance and switch positions as lines of departure. Intervals between centers of resistance in the second zone and between the main and second zones are covered by switch positions and by anti-tank defensive areas at critical points. Care is taken in the disposition of switch positions and obstacles not to hamper the movement of counterattacking forces. If the enemy breaks through the main zone of resistance, a new main zone can be created from the second zone or from sections of the second zone in conjunction with switch positions. A third or fourth intermediate zone of defense may be created as dictated by terrain; for example, in the defense of mountain valleys.

REAR ZONE. The army rear zone of defense usually follows the second zone, although other intermediate zones may be present. Its mission is to contain the penetration of enemy armored spearheads, the main bodies of which are destroyed within the second zone. In case of a major rupture of the second zone, the rear zone conducts a delaying action (decentralized defense), permitting the army to regroup its reserves and launch a decisive counterattack or to form a new defensive zone based on the changed tactical situation. Fortifications are similar to those of the first zone rather than those of the second zone. The density of forces and fire power is lower, fewer reserves are available, and obstacles and field fortifications are less developed. In case of emergency, the rear zone serves as the main zone of defense.

SWITCH POSITIONS. Switch positions stretch to the rear from the main zone of resistance perpendicularly or at an angle. Their missions are to localize enemy penetrations to one sector and to prevent enemy outflanking operations along the rear of the defensive zone; to permit effective delaying action pending the arrival of reinforcements; to serve as transit positions from the main to second or rear

273

zones of resistance; and to serve as lines of departure for counterattacking forces.

Switch positions are classified as transverse or connecting. Transverse switch positions do not reach the second zone of defense. They serve to protect the main zone of resistance from enemy flanking attacks and to force the enemy to carry out deep enveloping movements. Connecting switch positions tie one defense zone with another and facilitate withdrawal of sectors adjacent to the areas of penetration, thus enabling the defending forces to limit the enemy advance and trap the enemy forces.

Army group switch positions are an integral part of the strategic defensive plan, and their layout, manning, and development are dictated by army group or higher headquarters. Army switch positions are designed particularly to cover lines of communication and service areas, as well as to facilitate the action of reserve divisions. Divisional switch positions are laid out, manned, and developed under divisional control for the primary purpose of facilitating the action of the reserve regiment.

Switch positions are normally designed for defense from one direction only, although the presence of other approaches, terrain conditions, and other special factors may dictate the construction of local all-around defenses. In open country, the defensive system of switch positions is mainly based on strongpoints and centers of resistance which are mutually visible and which sometimes support each other by fire. Intervals between strongpoints are mined. Emplacements are provided for armored and motorized equipment.

Antitank ditches and other elaborate systems of local defense are usually not provided for the protection of switch positions. Instead, mines and lines of tank traps are prepared in key sectors. These may be ultimately developed into complete obstacle systems.

b. Use of terrain. In general, Soviet doctrine governing the use of terrain for fortifications is identical to that of the U. S. Army. Primary stress is laid on the availability of natural or artificial obstacles, fields of fire, and observation. Other factors are secondary.

One special use of terrain by the Red Army has been the development of defenses in marshy regions. Such defenses are primarily designed against infantry and consist mostly of breastworks or, if the level of ground water permits, semisubterranean defenses. The breastworks stretch in line with distinct gaps for fire from rear positions. Parallel lines of breastworks are connected by camouflaged communication passages. Vertical masks of branches, twigs, and other natural materials are extensively used for camouflage. Artillery is emplaced on any available firm ground. Where ground water prevents deep digging, earth works are built above ground.

c. Fortifications in offensive combat. The Red Army emphasizes that the success of offensive operations depends, to a great extent, on the skillful employment of fortifications to reduce the danger of enemy counterattacks. Fortifications in offensive operations include the construction of defensive works in the assembly areas and along the line of departure, and the hasty fortification of seized areas. In the fortification of assembly areas, primary emphasis is on the development of peripheral positions to prevent enemy attacks against, or infiltration into, the assembly areas, and on expensive construction of dummy works to deceive the enemy regarding the sector and scope of the main effort.

In the assault of fortified positions, the construction of approach trenches and emplacements for direct-fire artillery as close as possible to the enemy is also stressed.

Hasty fortification during the course of the offensive must be undertaken with light equipment and with the greatest possible speed. Consequently, specialized materials must be provided, such as antitank and antipersonnel contact mines, concertina rolls, and wire and detonators for the construction of controlled antipersonnel mines from captured shells. These materials are brought up on tank-drawn or manhandled sleds or trailers by pioneers (combat engineers) immediately following the assault infantry. Hasty minefields are installed within 15 to 20 minutes after the capture of a position. Successive echelons carry forward prefabricated steel or concrete pillboxes on tank-drawn sleds or trailers; these are installed within a few hours after the seizure of a position. For maximum economy of matériel and transport, the obstacles and prefabricated pillboxes erected in rear positions are taken up as soon as they are no longer needed and are moved forward as required. Extensive use is also made of adaptable enemy defenses and of local terrain features, such as shell craters and the ruins of houses.

The purpose of such hasty fortifications is to delay enemy counterattacks and to permit the deployment of direct-fire artillery, which plays the primary role in covering the reorganization of infantry during operational pauses. Consequently, close liaison between fortifications pioneers and direct-fire artillery units is mandatory.

Section II. DELIBERATE CONSTRUCTION OF FORTIFICATIONS

1. ORGANIZATION OF A STRONGPOINT

Deliberate construction of fortifications is normally planned and carried out before contact is made with the enemy. During prolonged defensive operations, permanent defenses are developed from hasty fortifications. The nerve center of every defensive zone is the strongpoint, the effectiveness of which depends upon an adequate coordination of defense works with tactical requirements. The usual procedure is first to protect the positions against enemy tanks by mines and obstacles; then to provide fire protection for the obstacles; and finally to construct shelters for supplies and personnel (figure 3).

The Soviets stress camouflage of defensive positions as a principal requirement. The work of camouflaging is reduced by the concentrated form of Soviet strongpoints. Skillful use of dummy strongpoints helps to conceal the true positions from enemy observation. A few dummy defense works are sometimes scattered inside the actual strongpoints to distort its outlines.

The normal elements which constitute a strongpoint are trenches, machine-gun emplacements, mortar and antiaircraft emplacements, tank and self-propelled artillery emplacements, and antitank and antipersonnel obstacles and mines (figure 4).

a. Trenches. In selecting sites for trenches, chief consideration is given to fire and concealment. Clearly outlined landmarks are avoided. As a rule, trenches follow one elevation contour along gentle slopes. The Soviets cover trenches built near topographic crests. Occupation of reverse slopes for flanking and oblique fire is recommended in most cases.

Fire and communication trenches are built along the front and in the depth of strongpoints. The purpose of the trenches along the front is to connect separate firing positions and their elements (figure 5). If the strongpoint is small, fire trenches along its edge form practically one continuous line. Reserve fire trenches on or in front of the forward edge of the main line of resistance provide support in initial defensive action and during the repulse of attacks. Security of withdrawal from a strongpoint

is ensured by covered communication trenches and underground passages leading from the position to a concealed area in the rear. Communication trenches connect all fire trenches, gun emplacements, shelters, and observation posts to permit maneuverability within the strongpoint. For communication and maneuver along the forward edge of a strongpoint, a parallel trench is built which may also serve as a fire trench. Easy communication with the rear is organized. Tunnels are built if terrain conditions are favorable and sufficient time is available. A widened communication trench parallel to the front in the rear of a strongpoint is recommended to permit rapid transfer of units. This wider trench in the rear constitutes an additional antitank ditch. It may be built rectilinearly and is covered for camouflage.

Normally, a battalion defense zone has three lines of trenches and three communication trenches connecting the defensive zone with the rear. The first trench runs along the forward edge of platoon strongpoints. Usually it is not continuous and is sited on the military crest. The second, basic trench is, as a rule, continuous and follows the second line of platoon strongpoints and centers of resistance. The third, broken trench is dug on reverse slopes of elevations and runs along the third line of platoon strongpoints or along the rear boundary of the second line of platoon strongpoints. Sufficient space is left between the trenches for the organization of a dense fire system in front of the forward edge of the defensive position and for fire cover of obstacles. These distances are usually 650 to 1,300 feet between the first and second trench and 500 to 650 feet between the second and third trench.

Red Army trenches are deep and narrow. Stakes driven into the trench sides provide sortie steps at intervals of 25 to 30 feet. Exit to the rear is provided in trenches and communication passages by ramps or steps dug in the earth at intervals of 65 to 100 feet. On the average, trenches completed to a full profile are from 3.2 to 5.2 feet wide at the top and 1.6 to 2 feet at the bottom; their depth is 3.2 to 6.5 feet (figure 6). Fire pits for riflemen and machine-gun positions are built at close intervals—about 13 to 16 feet between riflemen and 65 to 130 feet between machine guns. Communication passages are of sufficient width (6 feet) for the transportation of heavy machine guns and, when necessary, antitank guns. Such wide communication passages are considered especially important between the main and reserve gun positions in open terrain.

275

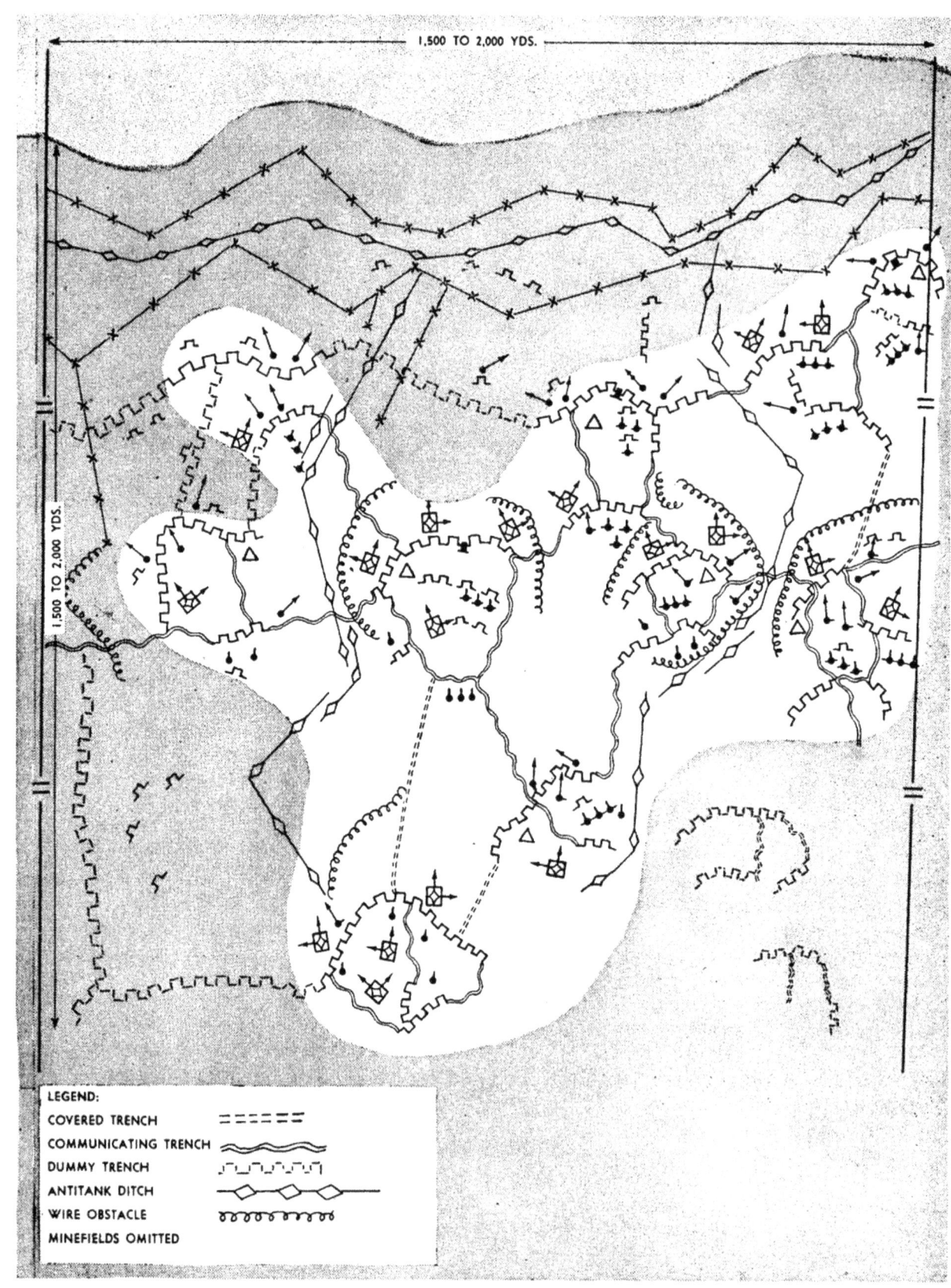

1,500 TO 2,000 YDS.

1,500 TO 2,000 YDS.

LEGEND:
COVERED TRENCH
COMMUNICATING TRENCH
DUMMY TRENCH
ANTITANK DITCH
WIRE OBSTACLE
MINEFIELDS OMITTED

Figure 3.—Fortification of a center of resistance.

276

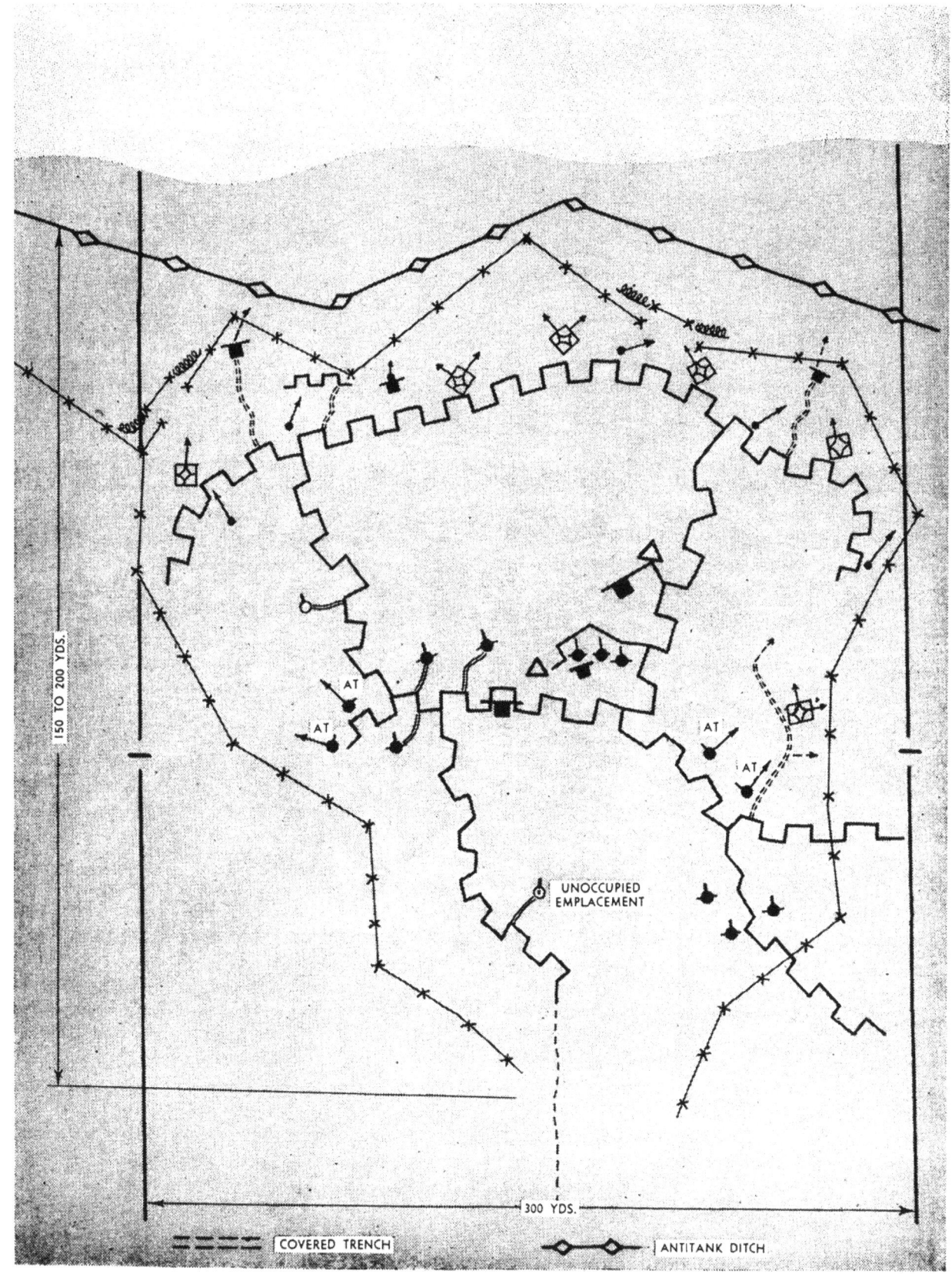

150 TO 200 YDS.

300 YDS.

UNOCCUPIED
EMPLACEMENT

AT AT AT AT

COVERED TRENCH   ANTITANK DITCH

Figure 4.—Fortification of a strongpoint.

277

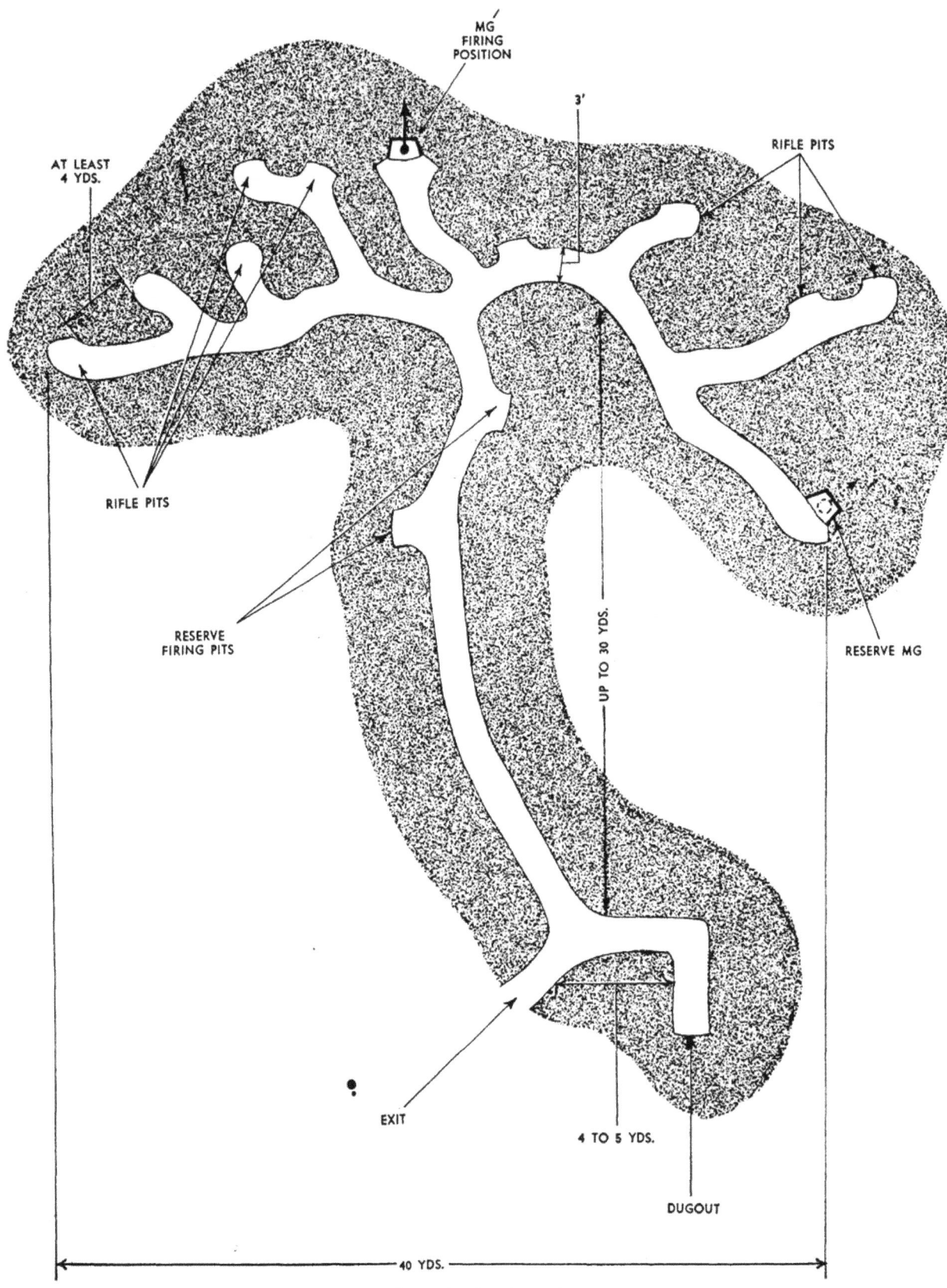

MG
FIRING
POSITION

3'

RIFLE PITS

AT LEAST
4 YDS.

RIFLE PITS

UP TO 30 YDS.

RESERVE
FIRING PITS

RESERVE MG

EXIT

4 TO 5 YDS.

DUGOUT

40 YDS.

Figure 5.—Squad trench.

278

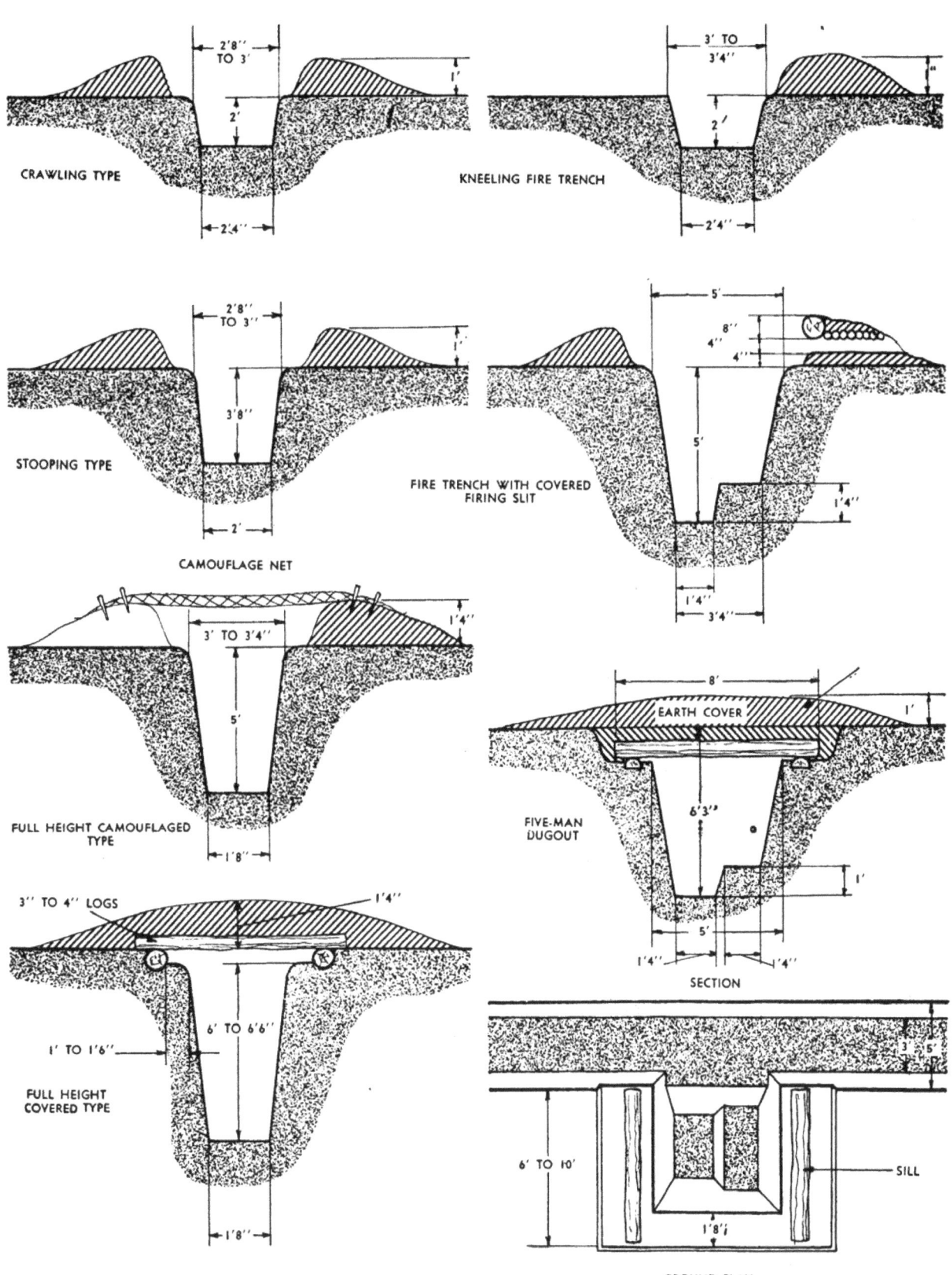

Figure 6.—*Standard trench profiles, showing development of a communication trench.*

Overhead cover of trenches consists of one or more layers of round logs with a layer of earth on top. Grass, bushes, or trees are planted on the cover for camouflage. In open, woodless terrain, flat overhead cover is used.

During prolonged periods of defensive warfare, trenches are further developed and improved. Recesses are built for men and supplies; light personnel shelters are constructed under the breastworks; provision is made for drainage; embrasures

Reserve and supplementary machine-gun emplacements are located close to the main firing positions. Their mission is to open fire on threatened areas in the event of enemy flanking attacks through gaps between strongpoints.

In the order of development, the known types of machine-gun emplacements include open machine-gun positions, covered machine-gun trenches, semi-covered timber-and-earth structures (*polukopanir*), covered timber-and-earth structures (*kopanir*), and

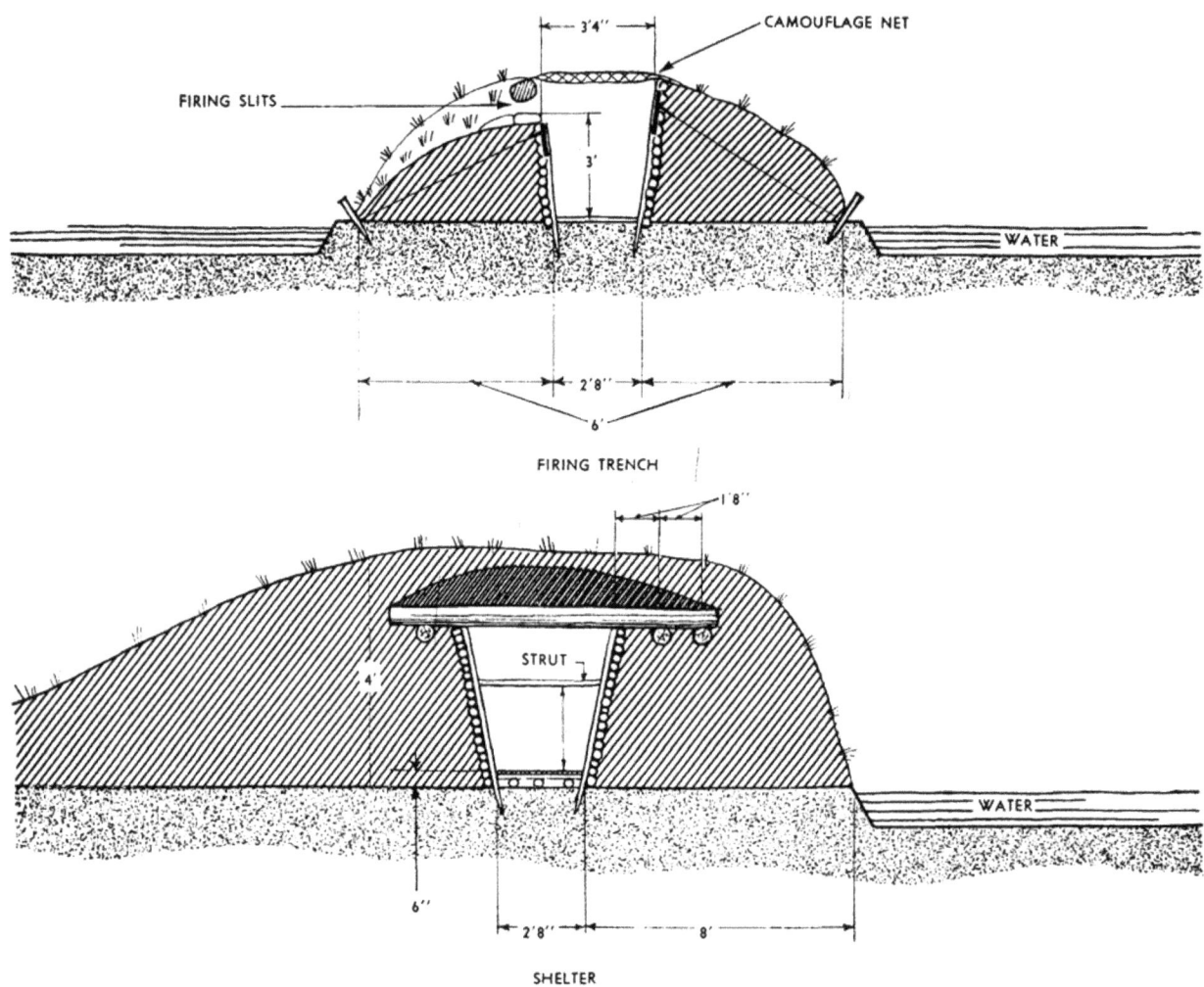

Figure 7.—Built-up fortifications in swampy terrain.

are provided; revetments are installed and overhead covers built (figure 7).

b. Machine-gun positions. To provide supplementary fire protection during initial action against separate, advancing enemy elements, machine-gun emplacements are built on, or in front of, the forward edge of the strongpoint. Flanking machine-gun nests are provided for converging, flanking, and oblique fire to repulse frontal attacks.

reinforced rock-fill wall and heavy concrete pillboxes (figures 8 and 9).

c. Personnel shelters. In the field, the Soviets provide shelter for about two-thirds of the personnel of a defensive position. In addition to recesses and light personnel shelters in trenches, separate shelters are built near firing positions, close to command and observation posts, and in the rear of defensive positions.

280

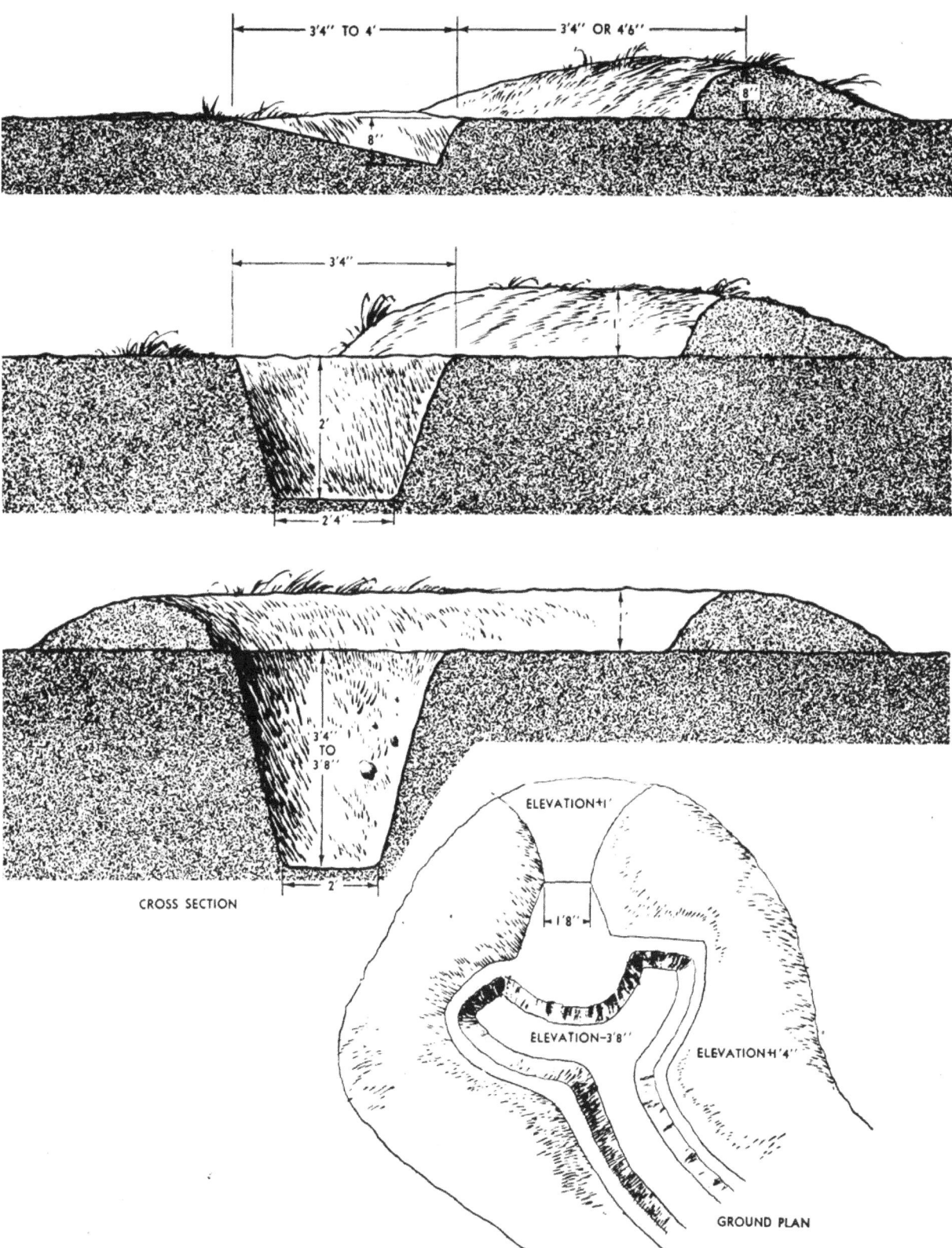

CROSS SECTION

ELEVATION+1'

ELEVATION-3'8''

ELEVATION+1'4''

GROUND PLAN

Figure 8.—Open machine-gun emplacements.

The most elementary type of shelter is a covered slit trench, which affords protection from air bursts and fragmentation. A slit trench is 6 to 6.5 feet deep and the space per man is computed at the rate

281

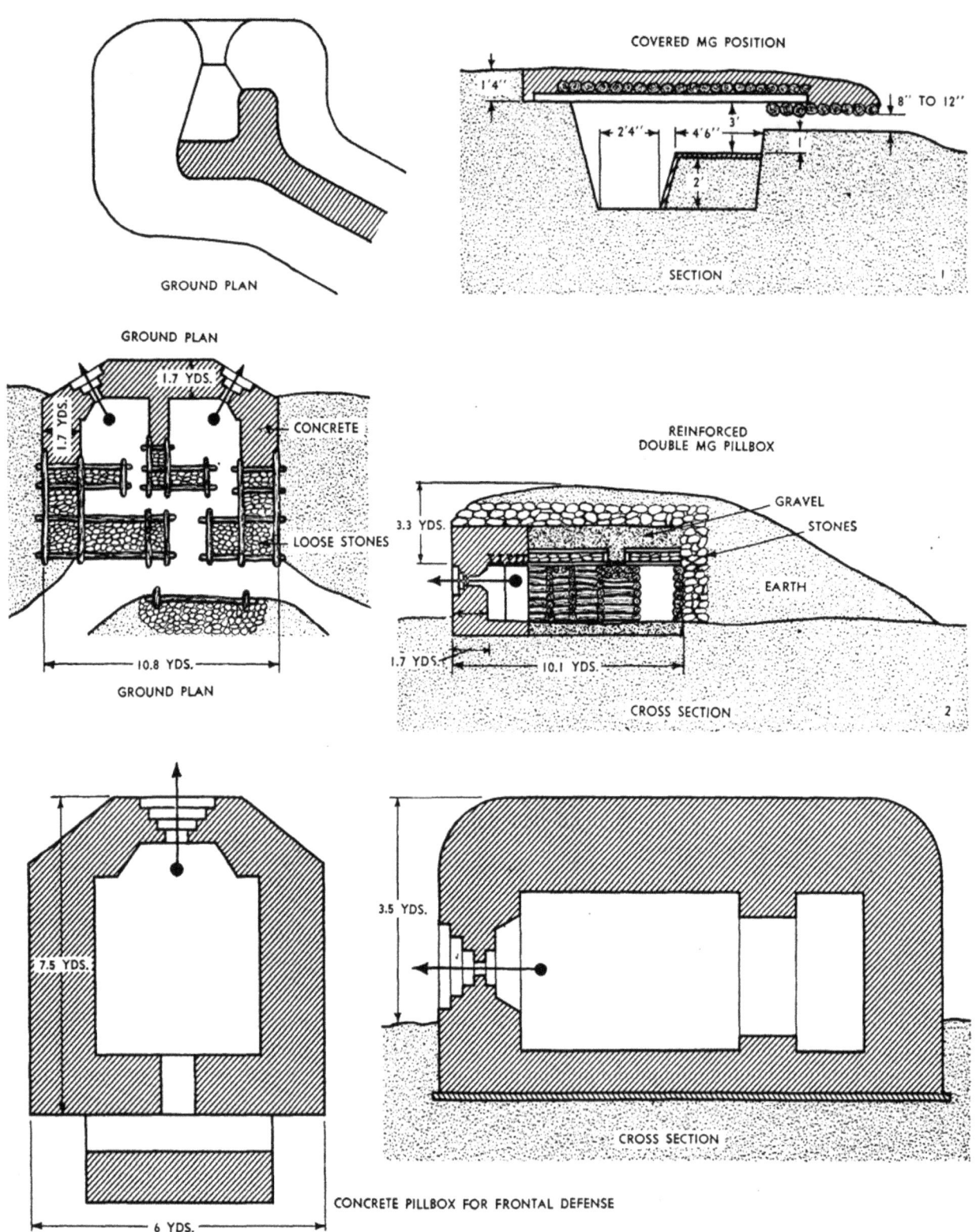

GROUND PLAN

COVERED MG POSITION

SECTION

GROUND PLAN

1.7 YDS.

1.7 YDS.

CONCRETE

LOOSE STONES

10.8 YDS.

GROUND PLAN

REINFORCED
DOUBLE MG PILLBOX

GRAVEL

STONES

EARTH

3.3 YDS.

1.7 YDS.

10.1 YDS.

CROSS SECTION

7.5 YDS.

6 YDS.

3.5 YDS.

CROSS SECTION

CONCRETE PILLBOX FOR FRONTAL DEFENSE

Figure 9.—Covered, reinforced, and concrete machine-gun emplacements.

of 2.3 to 3.2 feet in length. Slit trenches with double roofs resist the crushing effect of tanks (figure 10). Covered dugouts are built 32 to 65 feet from firing positions and observation posts for protection against aircraft machine-gun fire, aerial bombs, blast splinters, and artillery shells up to

282

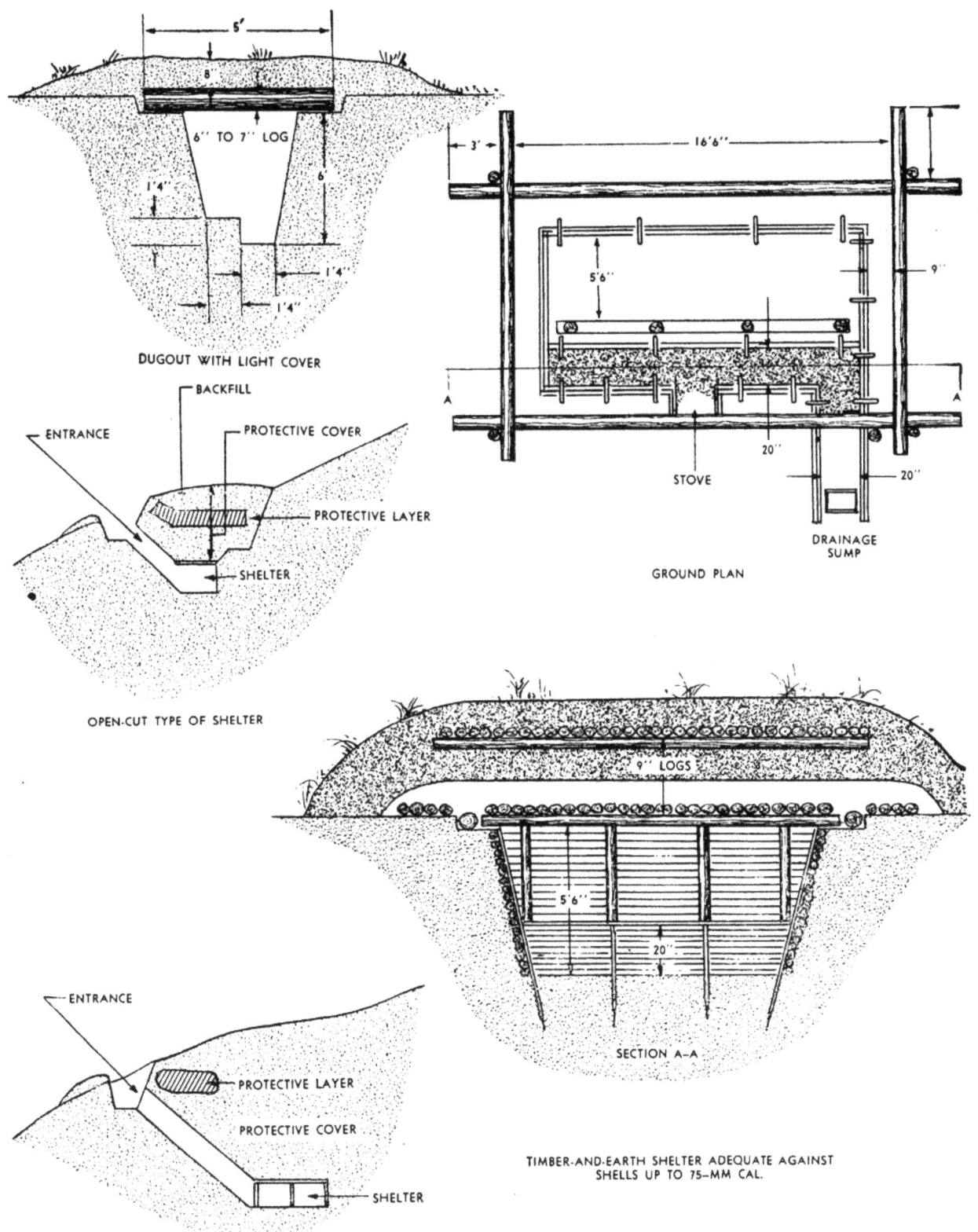

5'

8''

6'' TO 7'' LOG

6'

1'4''

1'4''

1'4''

DUGOUT WITH LIGHT COVER

3'

16'6''

5'6''

9'

20''

20''

STOVE

DRAINAGE
SUMP

GROUND PLAN

A

A

BACKFILL

ENTRANCE

PROTECTIVE COVER

PROTECTIVE LAYER

SHELTER

OPEN-CUT TYPE OF SHELTER

9'' LOGS

5'6''

20''

SECTION A–A

ENTRANCE

PROTECTIVE LAYER

PROTECTIVE COVER

SHELTER

EXCAVATED OR TUNNEL TYPE OF SHELTER

TIMBER-AND-EARTH SHELTER ADEQUATE AGAINST
SHELLS UP TO 75–MM CAL.

Figure 10a.—Development of personnel shelters.

283

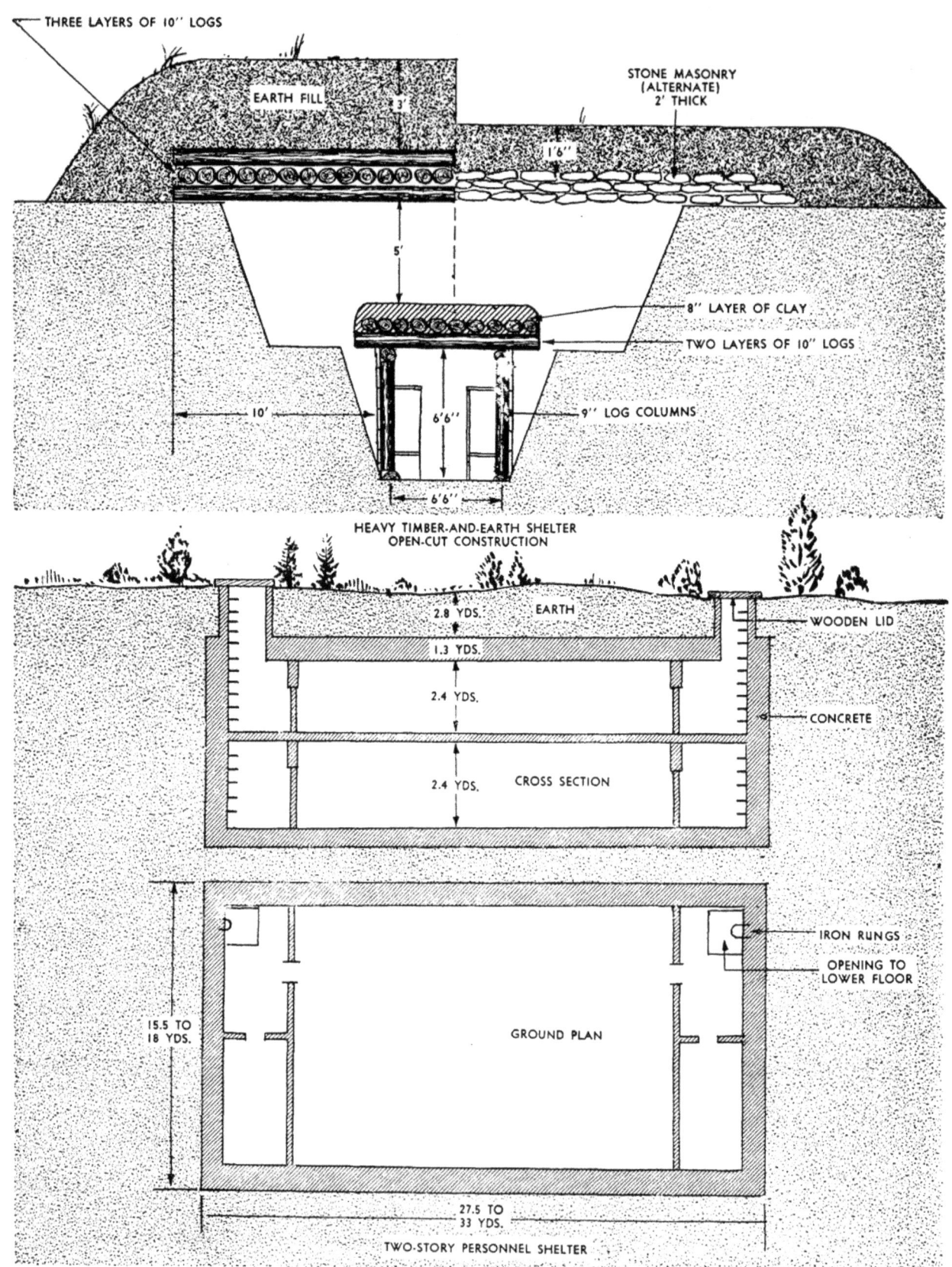

THREE LAYERS OF 10" LOGS

EARTH FILL

3'

STONE MASONRY
(ALTERNATE)
2' THICK

1'6"

5'

8" LAYER OF CLAY

TWO LAYERS OF 10" LOGS

10'

6'6"

9" LOG COLUMNS

6'6"

HEAVY TIMBER-AND-EARTH SHELTER
OPEN-CUT CONSTRUCTION

2.8 YDS.   EARTH

WOODEN LID

1.3 YDS.

2.4 YDS.

CONCRETE

2.4 YDS.   CROSS SECTION

IRON RUNGS

OPENING TO
LOWER FLOOR

15.5 TO
18 YDS.

GROUND PLAN

27.5 TO
33 YDS.

TWO-STORY PERSONNEL SHELTER

Figure 10b.—Development of personnel shelters.

284

75-mm. Reinforced shelters provide protection against shells of 75-mm guns and 122-mm howitzers. Heavy-type shelters provide protection against 105-mm gun and 155-mm howitzer shells and 110-pound aerial bombs. Staff and command posts housing about 10 men are built 13 to 16 feet underground depending on the level of the water table, with an overhead cover 8 to 10 feet thick. Superheavy two-story underground shelters, absolutely invisible on the surface, have entrances at opposite ends with flat wooden covers, and iron rungs set in concrete serving as steps. The arrangement of lower and upper floors is similar. The total height of the structure is about 33 feet. Individual compartments inside are about 7 feet high. The shelter has a surface of about 3,500 to 5,000 square feet.

Artillery and antiaircraft artillery observation posts are sited to permit good visibility of enemy positions or of the sky were desired. They are usually located on inconspicuous high ground, in ruins of inhabited places, or at the edge of a large forest. Locally available material is used for camouflage. The Soviets emphasize that observation posts should not be crowded into one area and that concentrations of men, horses or motorcycles, or any visible movement of messengers should not be permitted in the immediate area of an observation post. Observation posts for antitank defense are located behind natural or artificial obstacles (figure 11).

d. Supply shelters. Supply shelters provide protection for transport equipment and facilitate the distribution of ammunition to individual firing positions. To provide protection for transport against artillery fire, the Soviets build covered sheds on steep reverse slopes of elevations and gullies. The slopes are cut at nearly a right angle, and platforms are built for the transport equipment. A ditch above the shelter drains off rain water running down the slope. In open terrain, shelters for bulky transport are dug in at intervals of 100 to 200 feet.

Ammunition dugouts are usually placed 50 to 65 feet from the guns. They are built in communication trenches connected with the left side of gun emplacements.

e. Artillery emplacements. The primary mission of direct-fire artillery is to stop and destroy attacking enemy tanks. For this purpose, the artillery is massed in principal tank-endangered areas and is emplaced behind natural or artificial antitank obstacles. For concealment from enemy observation, artillery positions are sited on reverse slopes or in broken terrain covered with shrubbery and high vegetation. The basic artillery emplacement is sunken, with slit-trench shelters for the crew, ammunition recesses on both sides of the emplacement, and a ramp for the gun in the rear. The design undergoes minor variations in covered and reinforced structures (figure 12).

A sunken antitank-gun position for all-around fire consists of a gun platform connected with a shelter for the gun, a small slit trench for the crew on the right side, and one or two ammunition storage recesses. The depth of the slit trench is not less than 5 feet; its width is about 1.3 to 3.2 feet at the top; its length is 10 to 13 feet. Parapets about 1 foot high are built of spoil in front and to the rear of the slit trench. Approaches to the position, especially on the flanks and in the rear, are protected by antitank obstacles.

The gun emplacement for all-around fire is circular, with a diameter of 13 feet. It is dug in to a depth of about 1 foot. A ramp leads from the platform to the gun shelter. The shelter is square and about 3.5 feet deep. Along each side of the shelter special 3.2-by-1.6-foot steps are cut in the ground to support the gun wheels. Gun shelters are usually placed on the left side or in front of the platform. If the shelter is in front, the height of the front parapet does not exceed 8 inches. A space of about 1 foot 8 inches is left between the platform and the descent to the gun shelter to provide support for the trail spade.

If all-around fire is not required, platforms for antitank guns firing on a narrow sector are built as small as possible—about 10 feet long, 5 to 6.5 feet wide in front, and 10 feet wide in the rear.

Sunken emplacements for field-artillery guns consist of a gun platform dug in to a depth of about 2 feet and two small slit-trench shelters at the sides of the platform for the protection of commander and crew. The shelters are in line, the right one being at a small angle to the basic direction of fire to provide maximum protection for personnel against shells, grenades, and bombs exploding on the gun platform. A ramp for the gun is built in the rear of the emplacement. There is no parapet in front of the gun.

When time and materials are available, covered timber-and-earth artillery emplacements are built for protection against bullets and splinters. These emplacements are dug to a depth of about 2.5 feet. The walls are revetted with stakes. Ammunition storage recesses are built in the sides of the walls. The emplacement has a width of 6.5 feet in front and

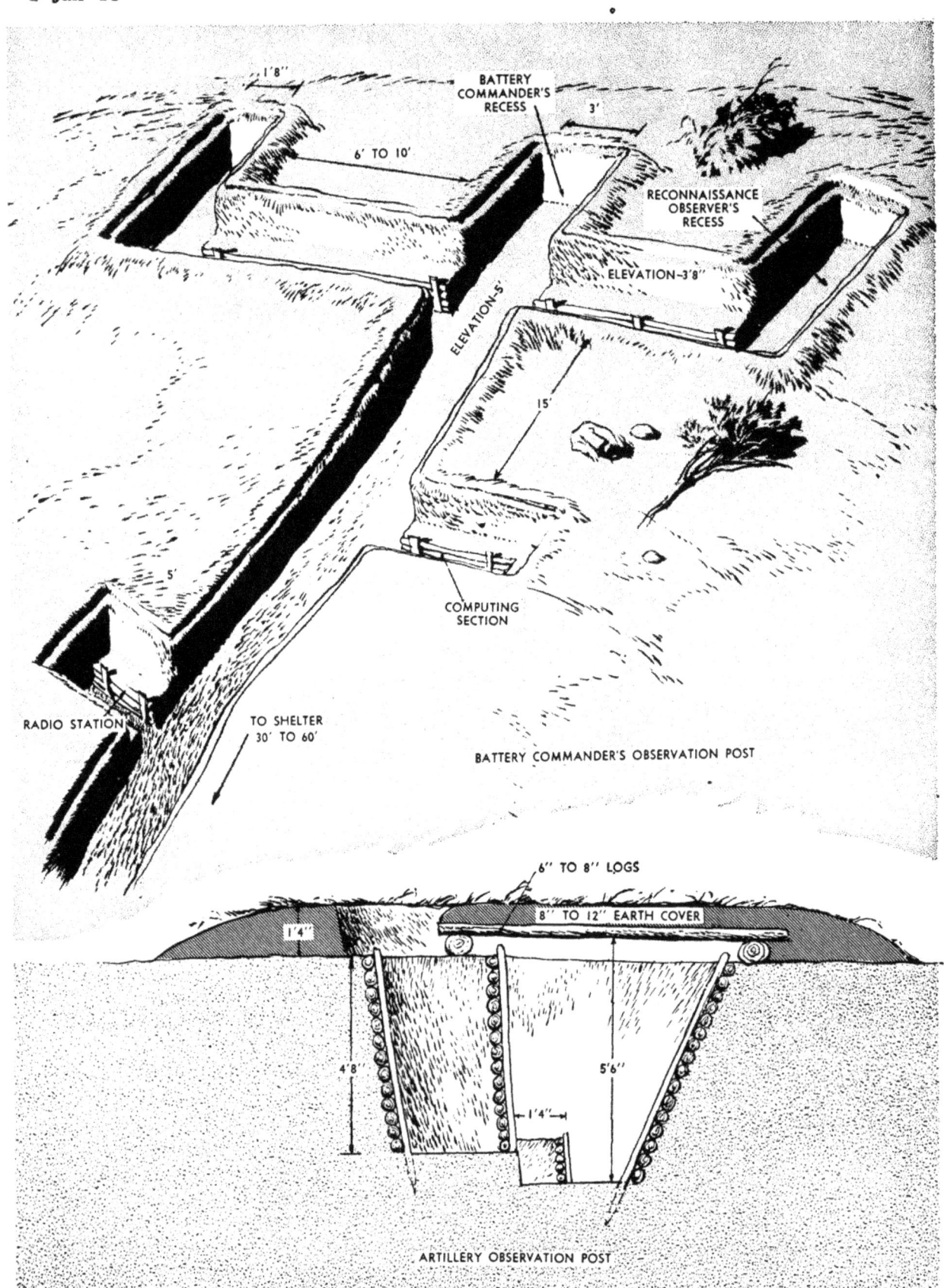

Figure 11.—Observation posts. Camouflage is not shown in upper drawing.

286

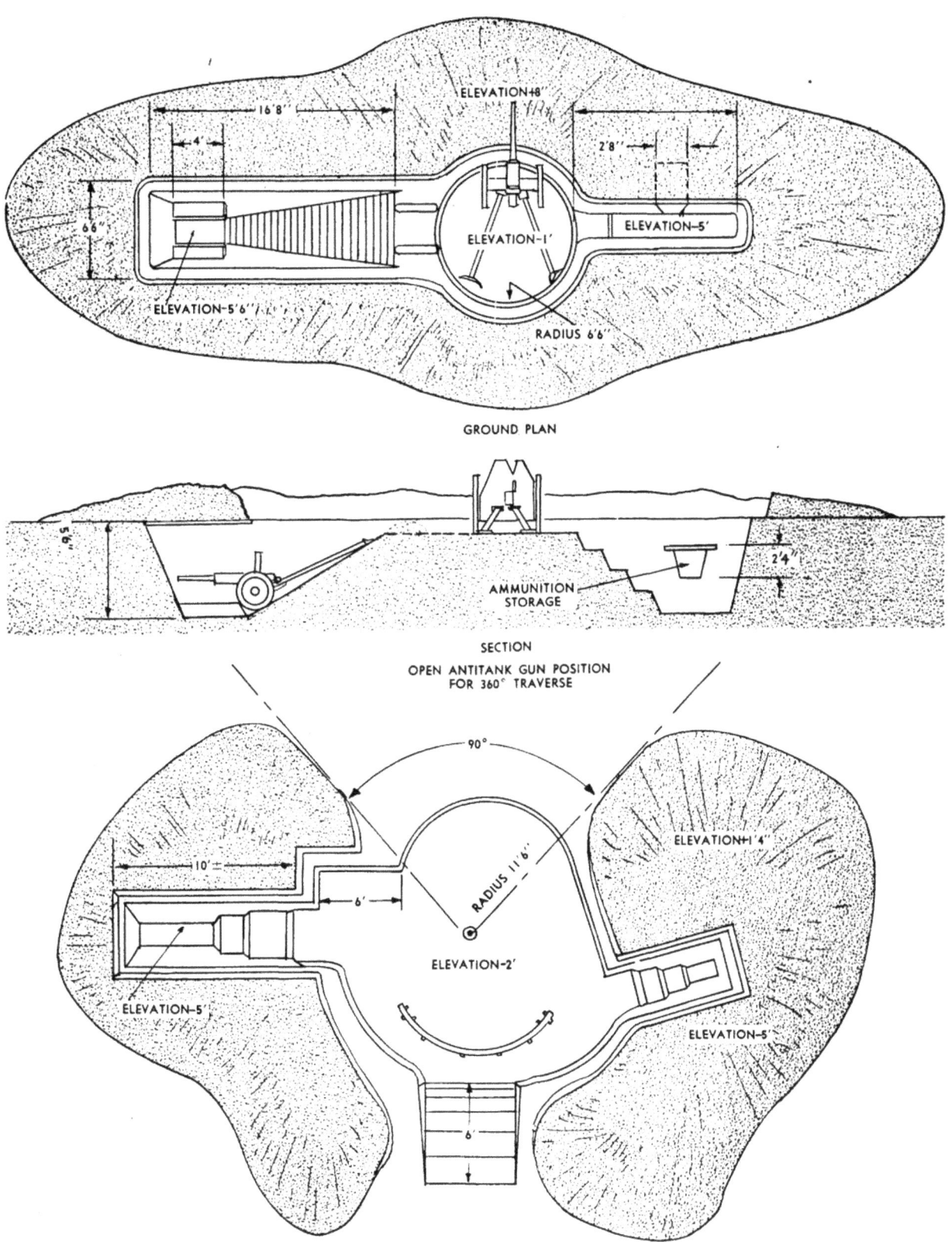

ELEVATION+8'

16'8'

4'

66"

ELEVATION-5'6"

2'8"

ELEVATION-5'

ELEVATION-1'

RADIUS 6'6"

GROUND PLAN

5'6"

AMMUNITION
STORAGE

2'4"

SECTION

OPEN ANTITANK GUN POSITION
FOR 360° TRAVERSE

90°

RADIUS 11'6"

ELEVATION+1'4'

10'±

6'

ELEVATION-2'

ELEVATION-5'

ELEVATION-5'

6'

76-MM GUN OPEN EMPLACEMENT

Figure 12a.—Development of artillery emplacements.

287

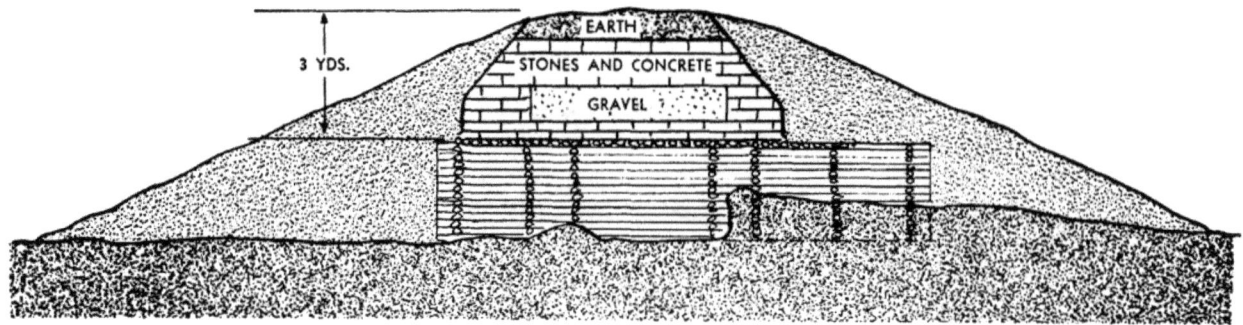

CROSS SECTION

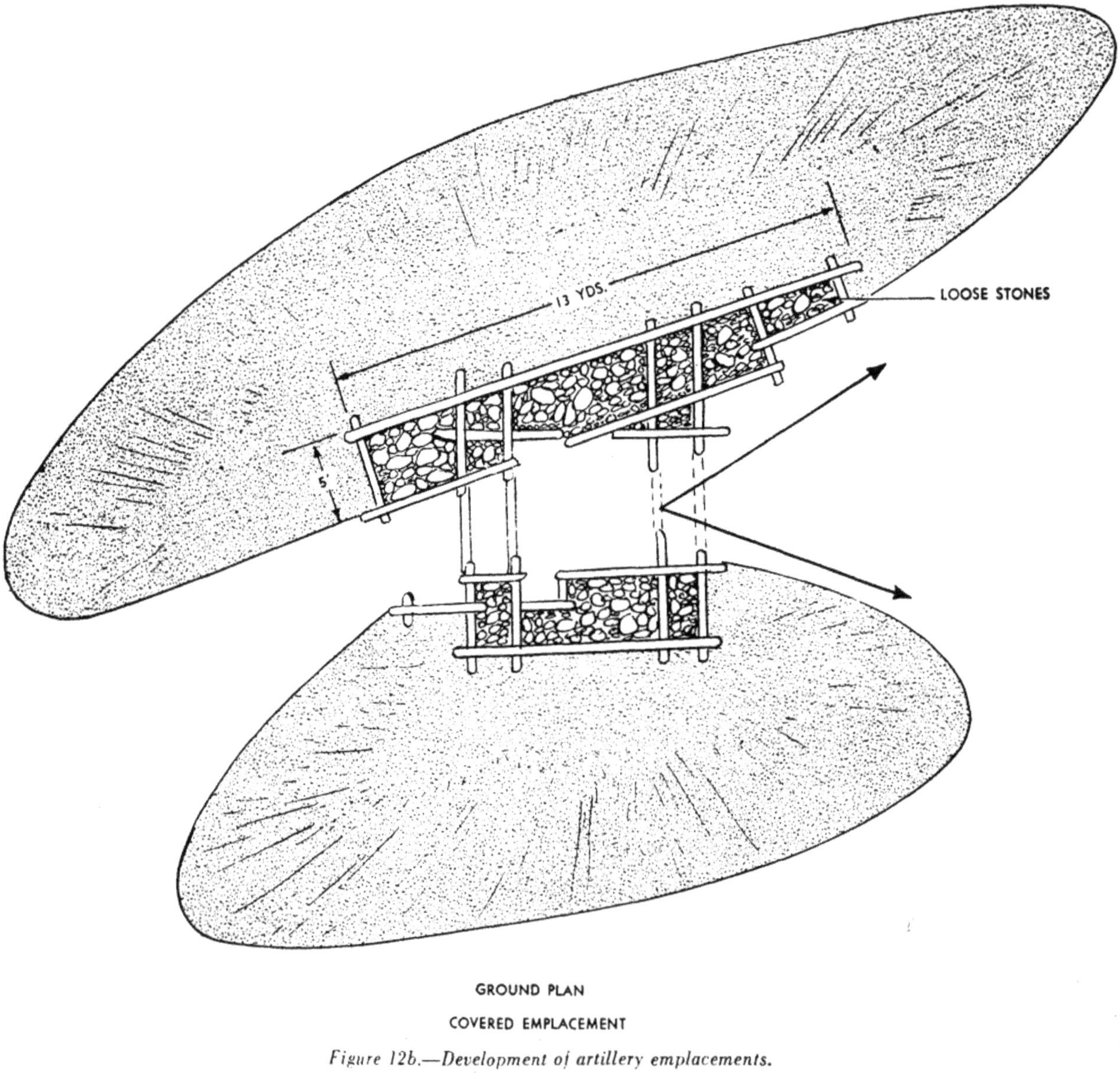

GROUND PLAN

COVERED EMPLACEMENT

Figure 12b.—Development of artillery emplacements.

11.5 feet in the rear; it is 15 feet long and at least 5.7 feet high inside. The front wall is revetted up to ground level, above which a firing embrasure allow-ing a traverse of 60 degrees is left open. A ramp is provided in the rear. The entire timber construc-tion is covered with earth and camouflaged.

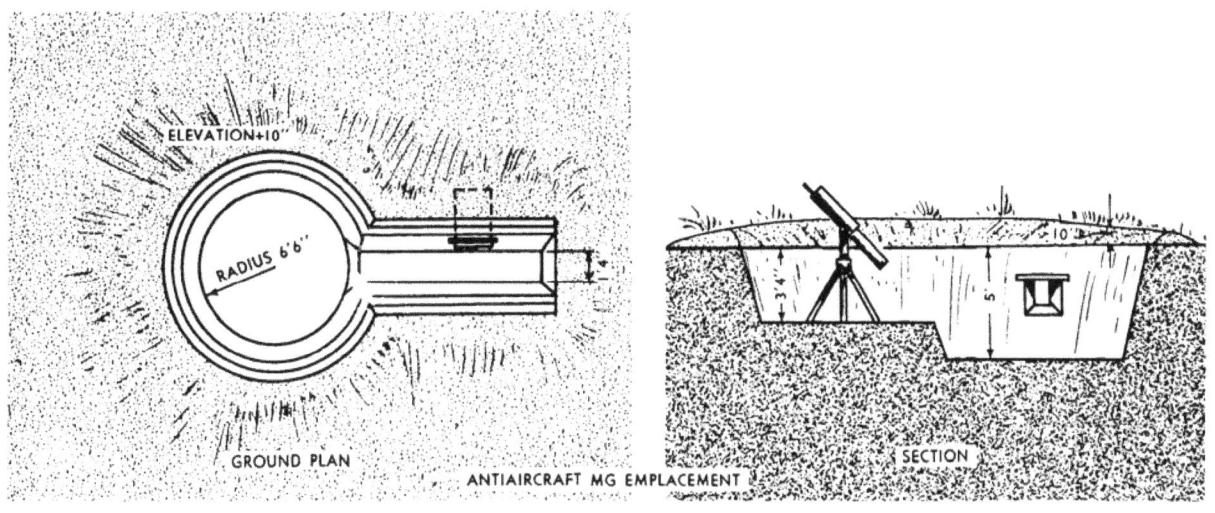

ELEVATION+10"

RADIUS 6'6"

3'4"

GROUND PLAN

ANTIAIRCRAFT MG EMPLACEMENT

10'

3'4"

5'

SECTION

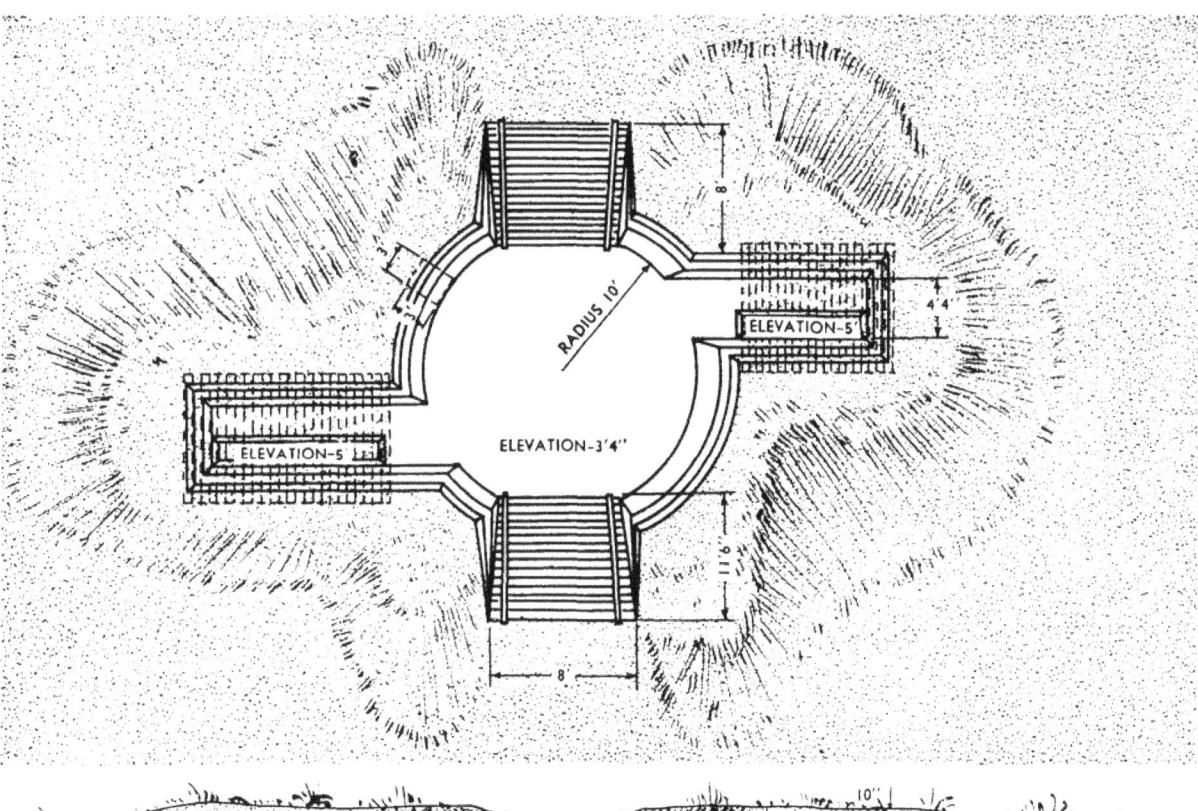

8'

RADIUS 10'

ELEVATION-5'

4'4"

ELEVATION-5'

ELEVATION-3'4"

11'6"

8'

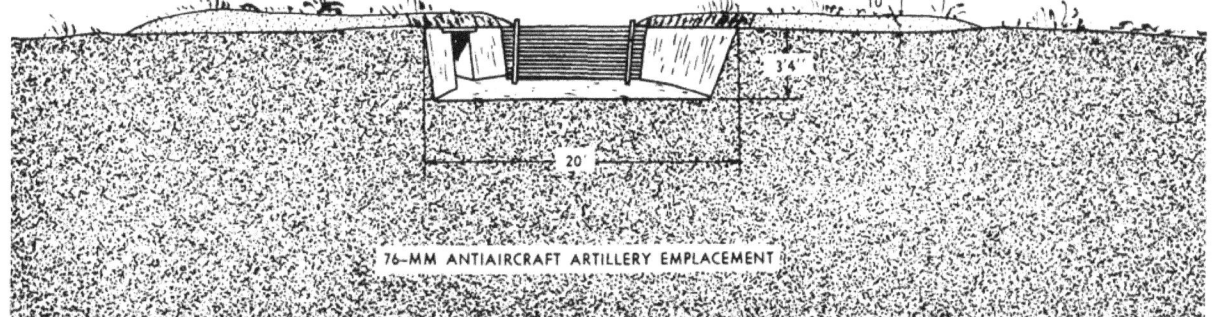

10'

3'4"

20'

76-MM ANTIAIRCRAFT ARTILLERY EMPLACEMENT

Figure 13.—Antiaircraft emplacements.

289

A further development of artillery emplacements are timber-and-rock fill structures, the design of which does not differ substantially from that of the timber-and-earth structures.

f. Mortar and antiaircraft-gun emplacements. Reverse slopes of elevations, deep undulations, gullies and ravines, glades, or far edges of groves are used as sites for mortar emplacements, since they provide natural concealment for weapon, crew, and flash. During combat, bomb craters, ditches, and defiles serve as emplacements. In popu-

Emplacements for antiaircraft artillery are provided with circular gun platforms. The platforms are surrounded by a parapet which is not over 10 inches high so as not to impede fire at ground targets. An exit for the gun is built in the rear. Two slit trenches with light overhead cover on both sides of the platform provide shelter for the crew. There are one or two recesses in the trench for ammunition storage (figure 13).

g. Emplacements for tanks and mechanized equipment. In the initial phases of defensive op-

Figure 14.—Tank emplacement with camouflage removed.

lated areas, mortars are sited in buildings, basements of ruined houses, debris, etc.

A full-profile trench emplacement for mortars has a depth of at least 3.6 feet. It is provided with a communication trench containing dugouts for crew and ammunition. Slit-trench shelters at the sides of mortar platforms and the communication trench of reinforced mortar emplacements are provided with timber-and-earth overhead cover.

Antiaircraft artillery positions are prepared for all-around fire and sited behind elevations or forests with a view to concealing the flash from enemy ground observation. Antiaircraft artillery must be prepared for defense against tanks and therefore is grouped primarily in antitank areas.

erations, tanks may be employed in the capacity of self-propelled artillery for mobile or stationary fire in cooperation with the infantry of the first echelon. Dug-in emplacements are provided for both tanks and self-propelled artillery (figure 14). Antitank strongpoints and flanks of switch positions are reinforced by entrenched tanks used as artillery. Camouflaged emplacements are provided for tanks protecting important approaches. Disabled tanks are also used as artillery in open, cemented emplacements, or are dug in and covered with earth and sod, leaving only the turret above ground.

h. Obstacles. In combating the German mechanized "blitz," the Soviets developed a great variety of highly effective antitank obstacles adapted to

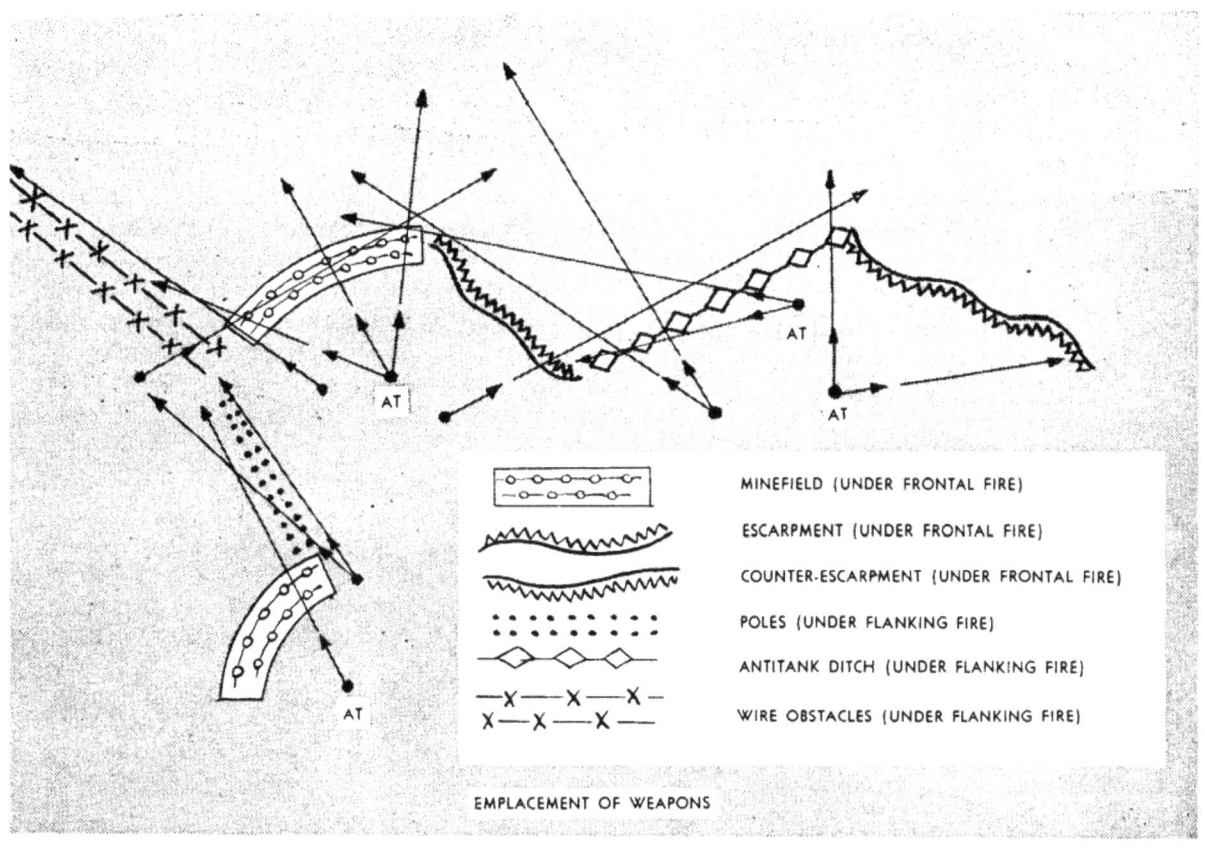

MINEFIELD (UNDER FRONTAL FIRE)

ESCARPMENT (UNDER FRONTAL FIRE)

COUNTER-ESCARPMENT (UNDER FRONTAL FIRE)

POLES (UNDER FLANKING FIRE)

ANTITANK DITCH (UNDER FLANKING FIRE)

WIRE OBSTACLES (UNDER FLANKING FIRE)

EMPLACEMENT OF WEAPONS

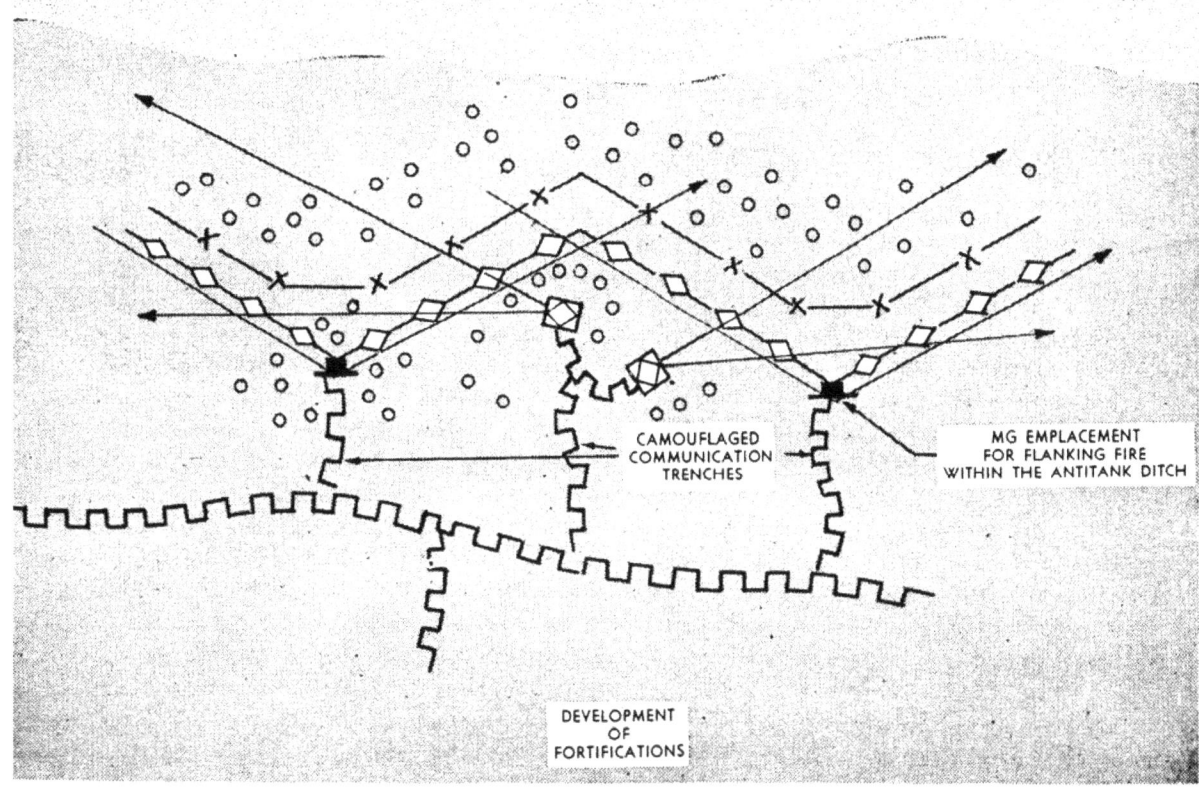

CAMOUFLAGED
COMMUNICATION
TRENCHES

MG EMPLACEMENT
FOR FLANKING FIRE
WITHIN THE ANTITANK DITCH

DEVELOPMENT
OF
FORTIFICATIONS

Figure 15.—Fire protection of obstacles.

conditions of terrain and availability of time and materials. Among their most effective types of antitank obstacles are ditches, escarpments, and counter escarpments, as a rule installed in front of the main line of resistance or used to protect the flanks and main approaches into the defensive depth. Locations and types of antitank obstacles are selected to ensure fire protection and the best possible vision and field of fire in front of the barriers as well as concealment from enemy observation (figure 15). In the event that fire protection for antitank obstacles is not practicable from the main firing positions, special firing positions are built for this purpose in the rear wall of an antitank ditch or escarpment (figure 16). To provide protection by flanking fire, the obstacles are built in a staggered (zigzag) pattern in single stretches up to 2,300 feet long.

Where natural water barriers do not exist, the Soviets build antitank ditches of various types (figure 17). Dimensions of antitank ditches may reach 10 feet in depth and 23 feet in width. Antitank barriers are built of various materials, such as earth, stones, trees, railroad ties, rails, and concrete. To reduce the dimensions of barriers, the Soviets recommend the construction in front of the barriers of speed-impeding ditches 3 feet deep (figure 18). Escarpments and counterescarpments are constructed in extensive stretches where terrain slopes are over 1: 5 (figure 19).

One type of barrier consists of tree trunks suspended horizontally between trees, high enough to deny cover to enemy infantry (figure 20). An effective obstacle in forested terrain is built of felled trees which are not detached from their stumps, making removal more difficult. The depth of such an abatis area is usually not less than 165 feet. It is frequently reinforced by mines and barbed wire. In thick forests, traps of fallen trees bar the advance of enemy columns. Iron hedgehogs are used either to reinforce other artificial or natural obstacles, or by themselves, arranged in three or four rows across secondary approaches and for rapid blocking of narrow gaps and defiles. In accordance with the character of terrain, the Red Army combines various types of obstacles. To protect possible tank.approaches in mountainous terrain, stone blocks, stone fields and stone slides are constructed (figure 21).

Antitank obstacles are frequently combined with antipersonnel obstacles. The principal types of Red Army antipersonnel obstacles consist of barbed wire

used with mines. When combined with antitank obstacles in front of the main line of resistance, antipersonnel obstacles may be either in front of or behind antitank obstacles. When placed in front,

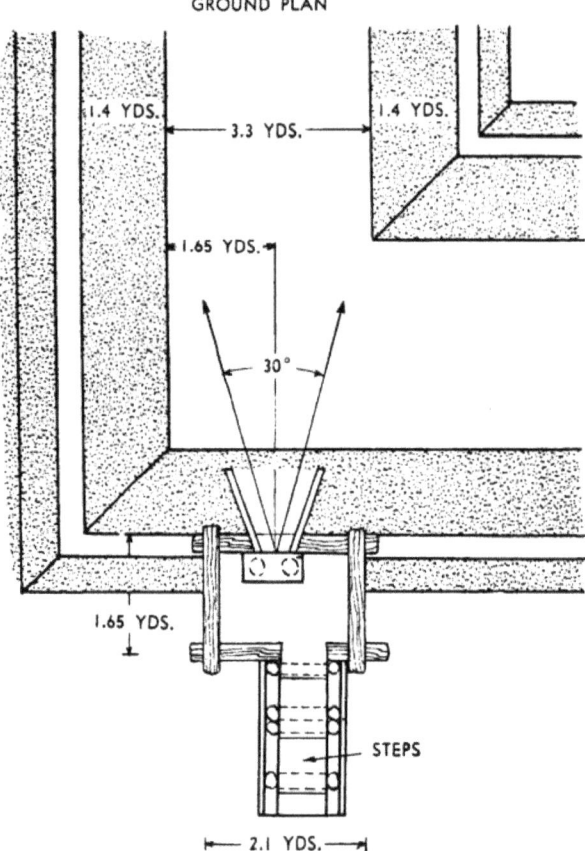

GROUND PLAN

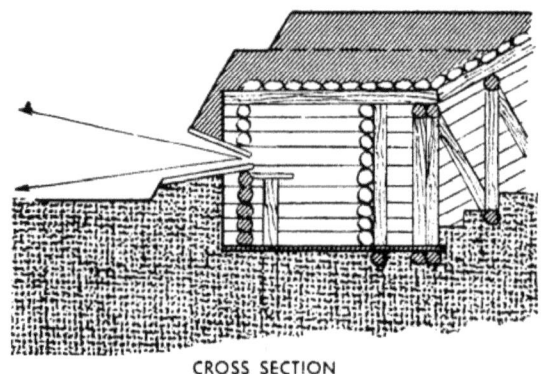

CROSS SECTION

Figure 16.—Machine-gun position covering an antitank ditch.

they are in the form of reinforced barbed-wire fences or concealed obstacles; when placed behind the antitank obstacles, they form the main barrier which

292

ESCARPMENT-TYPE ANTITANK TRAPS ON THE REVERSE SLOPE OF A HILL
(CAMOUFLAGE REMOVED)

Figure 17.—Antitank trap pattern.

consists of two or three belts of wire. If construction time is limited, antipersonnel obstacles on the flanks, in switch positions, and in the defensive depth are restricted to one row of barbed wire. The length of a barbed-wire fence section may reach 440 yards.

Protection of antipersonnel obstacles is provided by enfilade fire from positions of the main line of resistance or from special firing positions flanking the antitank obstacles. It is stressed that salients of antipersonnel obstacles should not coincide with salients of antitank obstacles. For rapid reinforcement of a position under enemy fire and replacement of destroyed obstacles, portable obstacles are used, such as "Bruno" (concertina) wire entanglements, "pioneer" wire nets, knife rests (*chevaux-de-frise*), hedgehogs, and combinations of these. Concealed

obstacles, including various types and patterns of trip wires, are used mainly in open country.

In forested terrain, in addition to barbed-wire entanglements, obstacles of felled trees, branches, and poles are constructed. In mountainous terrain, in addition to the obstacles already mentioned, stone slides, knife rests, and hedgehogs on escarpments are used.

i. Mines. Soviet antitank mines are considerably heavier than U. S. antitank mines. As a result, Red Army antitank minefields are less densely laid than U. S. minefields. On the other hand, Soviet antipersonnel mines weigh much less than U. S. antipersonnel mines, and the density of the Red Army antipersonnel minefield is higher (figure 22).

293

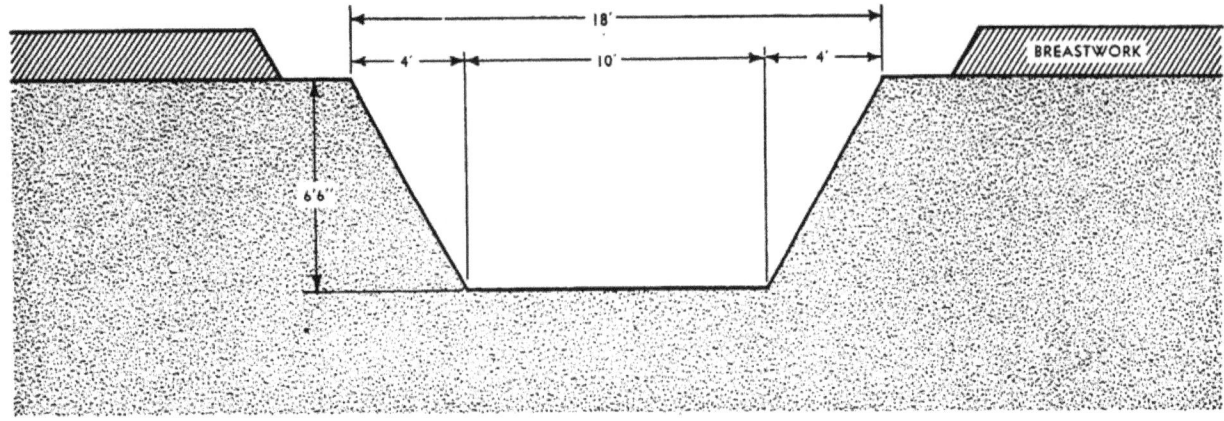

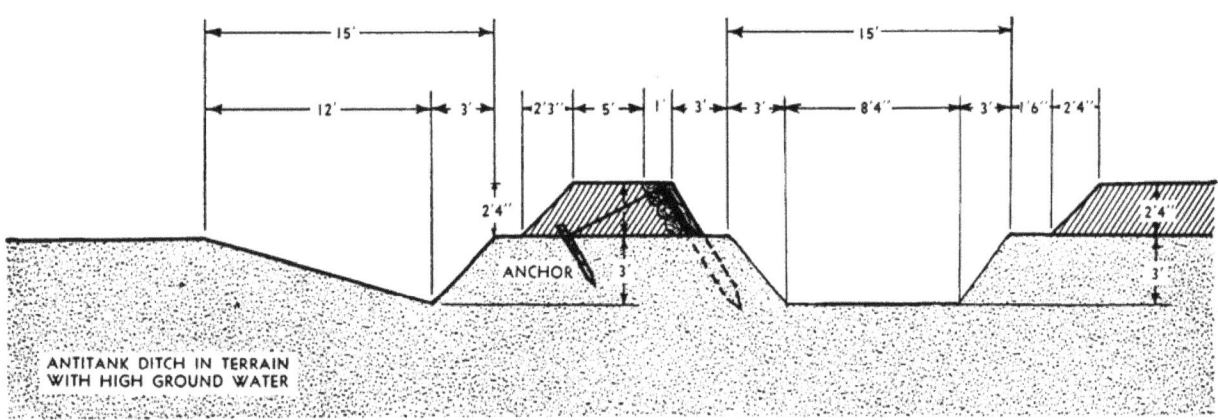

Figure 18.—Profiles of antitank ditches.

The basic type of antitank mine used is a simple wooden-box mine (*YaM-5*) which is difficult to detect. Antipersonnel mines are prewar types (*POMZ* and *PMD-6*), several modifications of which exist.

The enormous extent to which mines are used by the Red Army may be illustrated by the German claim of having cleared 137,000 mines during their attack on Sevastopol. The mines in this area were either dispersed or laid in irregular checkerboard pattern with 3 to 8 feet between mines. About 2,500 mines were cleared by the Germans in front of a regimental position in one day. Approximately 20,000 mines were located in front of a divisional zone.

Forward edges and flanks of defensive positions and gaps between strongpoints are protected from enemy tanks and infantry by deliberate minefields. In laying deliberate minefields, distances between mines are accurately measured and recorded. A special measuring cord marking spaces between mines is recommended for the mining of roads. This cord is used from one side of the road, with the cord's perpendiculars of varying length stretched at right angles across the roadbed. If an ordinary measuring cord is used, it is applied alternately on each side of the road.

Hasty minefields are largely used in offensive operations for the protection of flanks against enemy counterattacks. They are also laid in front of seized enemy positions and in the enemy's rear. Mines are used to disrupt enemy communications; broken road sections are mined to impede their reconstruction, and delayed-action mines further interrupt road traffic after repair. Hasty minefields are laid in somewhat irregular checkerboard patterns, mostly measured by pacing.

In mining roads, the dispersal of mines in space and time (delayed-action mines) is recommended. Antitank mines on roads are 30 to 80 feet apart; their density is one mine per yard of the road width. Thus, a 30-foot-wide road has ten mines on a stretch of 300 to 800 feet. Figures 23, 24, 25, and 26 represent patterns of hasty antipersonnel and antitank minefields and deliberately and hastily mined roads.

294

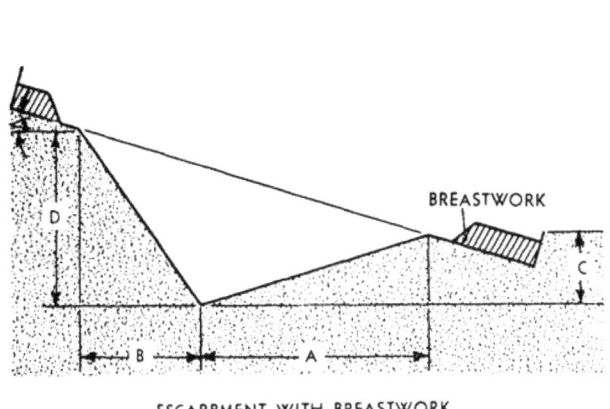

TABLE OF DIMENSIONS (in feet)

∡	A	B	C	D
10°	11	7	5	8
15°	11	6	3½	8½
20°	11½	5½	3	9
25°	14	7	2½	10½
30°	11½	8	1	12

ESCARPMENT WITH BREASTWORK
(USED ON SLOPES 10° TO 30°)

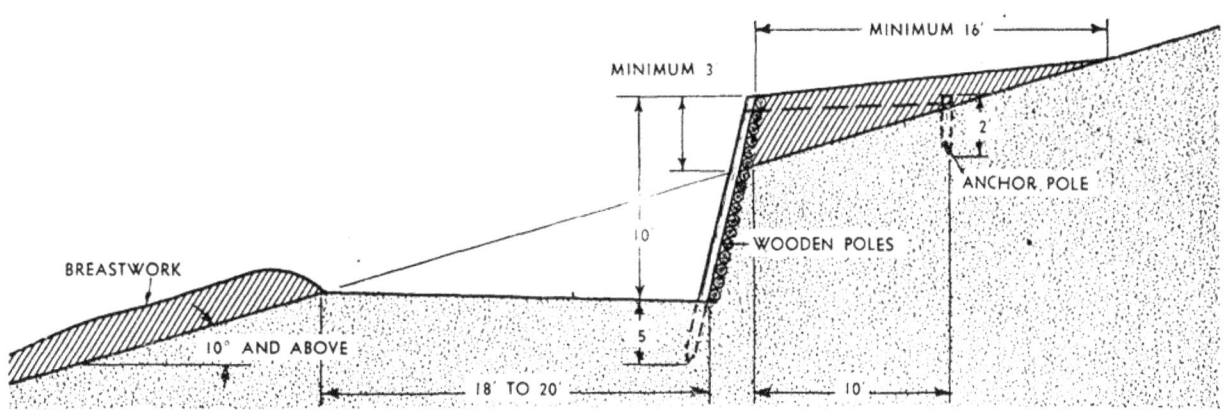

COUNTER-ESCARPMENT WITH BREASTWORK

Figure 19.—Escarpment and counterescarpment.

2. CONSTRUCTION STANDARDS

Russian field fortifications are classified, according to strength and material, as splinterproofs, light, reinforced, heavy, and superheavy.

a. Splinterproof construction. The splinterproof type is designed to afford protection against individual rifle bullets and splinters. This type of construction is primarily used in hasty fortification of localities during offensive operations and in defense. With the stabilization of a position, splinterproof constructions are gradually improved and reinforced to the strength of the light-construction type.

b. Light construction. Light construction includes the basic types of field fortifications affording protection from mass automatic fire of rifles, mortars, infantry antitank weapons, and machine guns. Light fortifications are designed to resist enemy infantry weapons, such as the German *MG–42* machine gun, the 7.92-mm antitank rifle

and the German 81-mm mortar. Walls consisting of tamped gravel or crushed rock placed tightly in a casing made of boards, with voids filled by sand, are considered by the Soviets to be very effective for light defense works. This type of construction has proved to be more resistant to concentrated machine-gun fire than reinforced concrete of the same thickness.

c. Reinforced construction. Reinforced structures are designed to resist direct hits by 105-mm howitzers, 120-mm mortars and six-barrel mortars. As a rule, fortified structures with walls which are vulnerable to direct hits of tank guns are built exclusively in mountainous or forested terrain, where tank maneuver is difficult and where only 75-mm infantry or mountain artillery, 105-mm mountain or field howitzers, and sometimes antitank guns may be used against fortified positions. Practice has shown that even without the use of concrete, walls

295

Figure 20.—Antitank log barrier.

of defense works can be secured against the effect of fire of all the above-mentioned artillery weapons, but afford no protection against direct hits of 75-mm antitank guns.

d. Heavy construction. Heavy construction affords protection against 75-mm and 88-mm tank guns with a muzzle velocity of 3,300 feet per second, and against 150-mm howitzers. Protection against direct hits from these weapons can be provided only by reinforced-concrete casemated works and underground shelters. Timber-and-earth constructions are vulnerable to hits of modern tank and antitank guns.

e. Superheavy construction. Specially reinforced heavy construction is used mainly for high command shelters and other buildings of similar importance.

3. PREFABRICATED PILLBOXES

The use of prefabricated material facilitates rapid construction in the field, decreases the number of qualified workmen necessary, raises the output of work by 500 to 600 percent, and materially lowers

the cost of construction due to economy in material, labor, and transportation.

a. Timber-and-earth structures. Individual parts of Soviet timber-and-earth structures are standardized and prefabricated. The weight and characteristics of each part are calculated to permit handling by one or two men and to permit its use under summer and winter conditions without any alterations. The elements of all types of structures include a frame, four shields, and a cover. The principal timber-and-earth structures are of the following types: emplacements for 50-mm, 82-mm, and 120-mm mortars; emplacements for 45-mm and 76-mm guns with sectors of fire of 100 degrees and 360 degrees; splinterproof pillboxes; antitank rifle positions; and antitank rifle shelters.

b. Concrete pillboxes. Prefabricated concrete pillboxes have an above-ground elevation of up to 8 feet. Pillboxes for machine guns have a circular shape; those for field guns are rectangular. The pillboxes for machine guns have two large em-

296

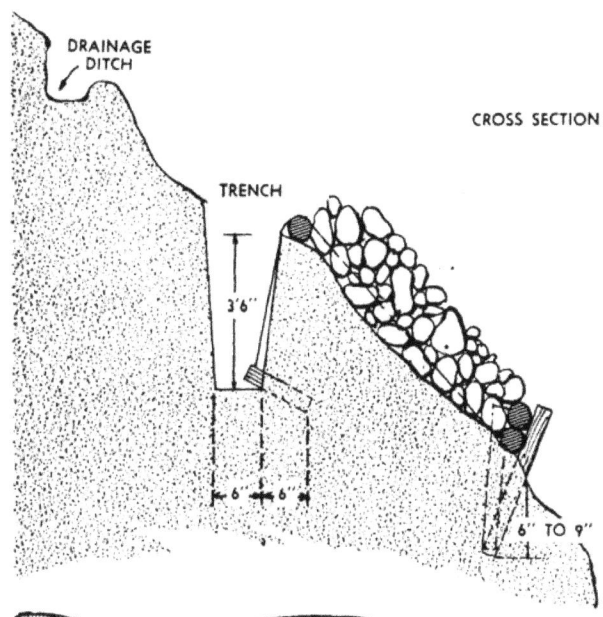

CROSS SECTION

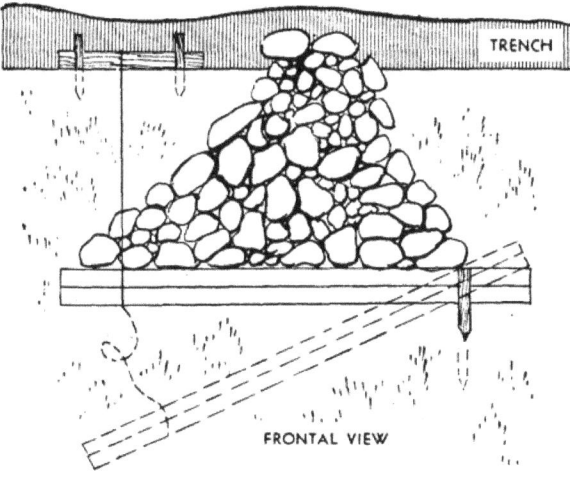

Figure 21.—Stone slide.

brasures which also serve as entrances. Those for artillery are provided with one embrasure which is protected by an overhang. The wall of the circular type usually consists of 16 reinforced concrete blocks. Each block weighs 33 pounds and has two openings

for anchor bolts by which four rows of blocks and the top cover are held together. The cement used to fasten the blocks forms vertical and horizontal seams 2½ inches thick. The cover of the circular pillbox is made of eight parts which are bolted to a special crossbeam and to the wall. The total weight of the cover is 1,302 pounds. All blocks are made of reinforced concrete. The reinforcing rods have a diameter of ¼ inch; spacing between rods is 2½ to 2¾ inches; percentage of metal is 1.1 percent. The total weight of the circular pillbox is 3,580 pounds. Total volume of concrete used for the circular type amounts to 1 cubic yard. This type of pillbox is installed on a special wooden frame. The concrete top of the pillbox is covered with a 1-foot layer of earth, then by a second layer of logs 10 to 12 inches in diameter, and a third 20-inch layer of rock which is camouflaged by a coat of earth. The walls of the pillbox are also protected by a 20-inch layer of rock covered with earth.

The Soviets used prefabricated concrete pillboxes principally in front of main lines of resistance and found their service satisfactory. Due to their comparatively light weight, the individual concrete blocks can be brought by hand to the place of installation and the construction work can proceed inconspicuously (fig. 28). These pillboxes are bulletproof and splinterproof and are not highly vulnerable to artillery fire. The main disadvantages of this type are the high elevation above ground, large embrasures, lack of blast walls, and the comparatively weak bond between blocks. The circular construction is more resistant than the angular.

4. PERMANENT FORTIFICATIONS

There appears to be no essential difference in the construction of Red Army permanent defense works and that of similar works in other countries. While one-story structures are most common, the Soviets also have two- and three-story pillboxes and casemates.

TYPE OF MINES	SPACING IN YDS.	DENSITY PER 1,000 YDS.	TIME IN HOURS TO LAY A 1,000-YD. MINEFIELD BY ONE ENGINEER COMPANY
ANTITANK MINES	6½ TO 11	1,000	3–6
ANTIPERSONNEL MINES	1 TO 2¼	2,000 TO 3,000	3–6

Note.—The density of American minefields equals 1½ mines per yard

Figure 22.—Density of minefields and time required to lay minefields.

297

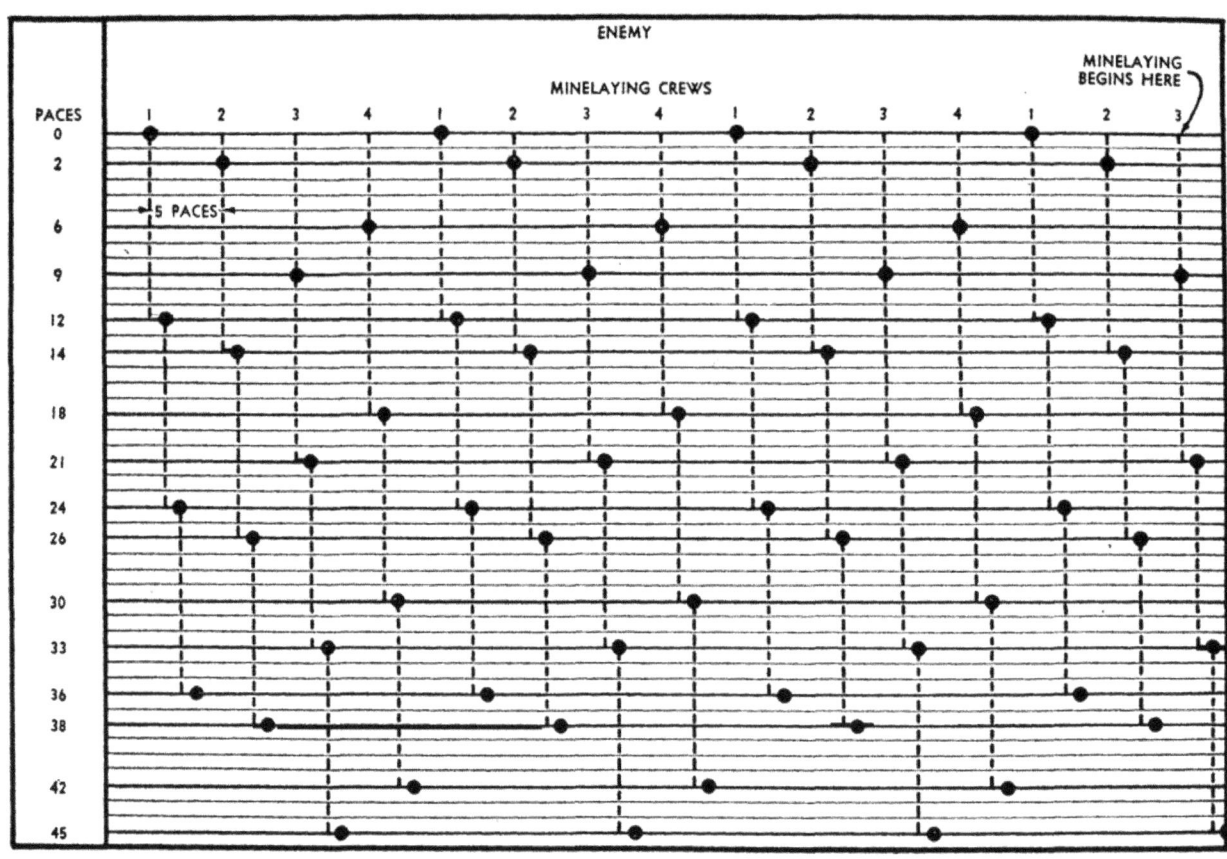

Figure 23.—Hasty antipersonnel minefield.

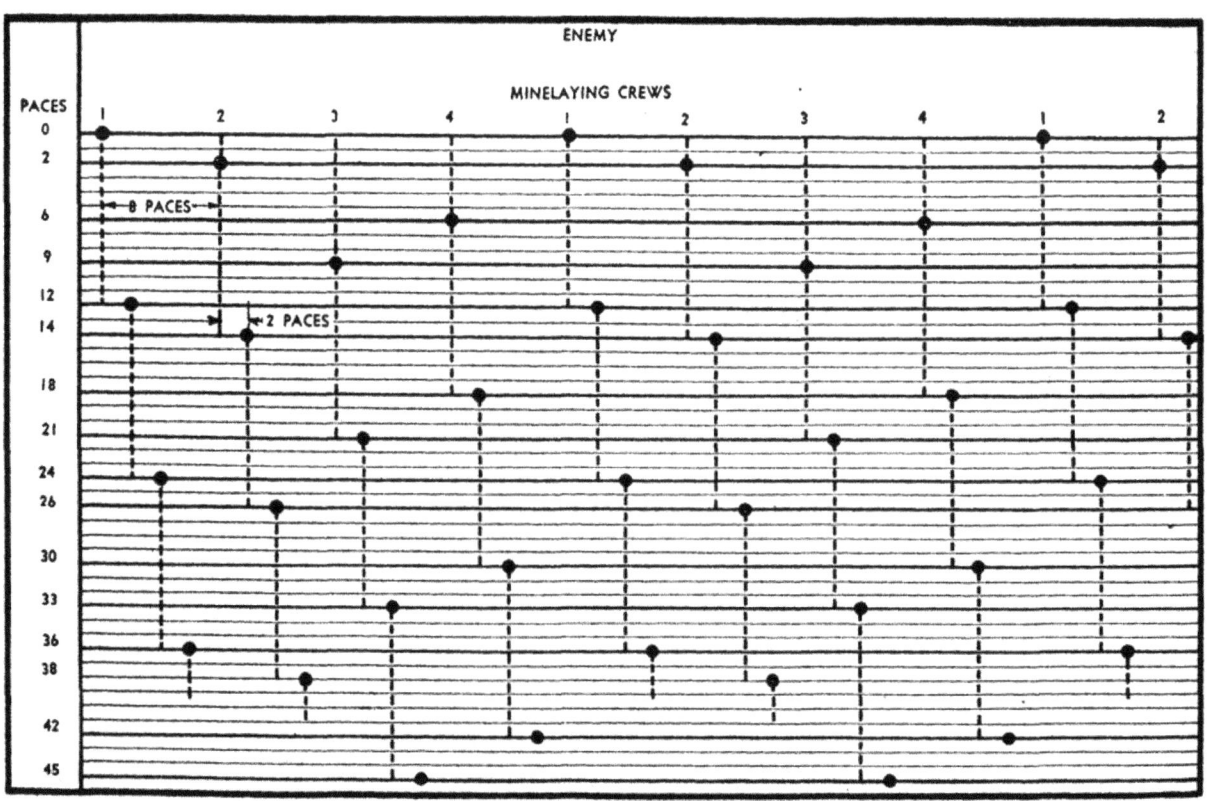

Figure 24.—Hasty antitank minefield.

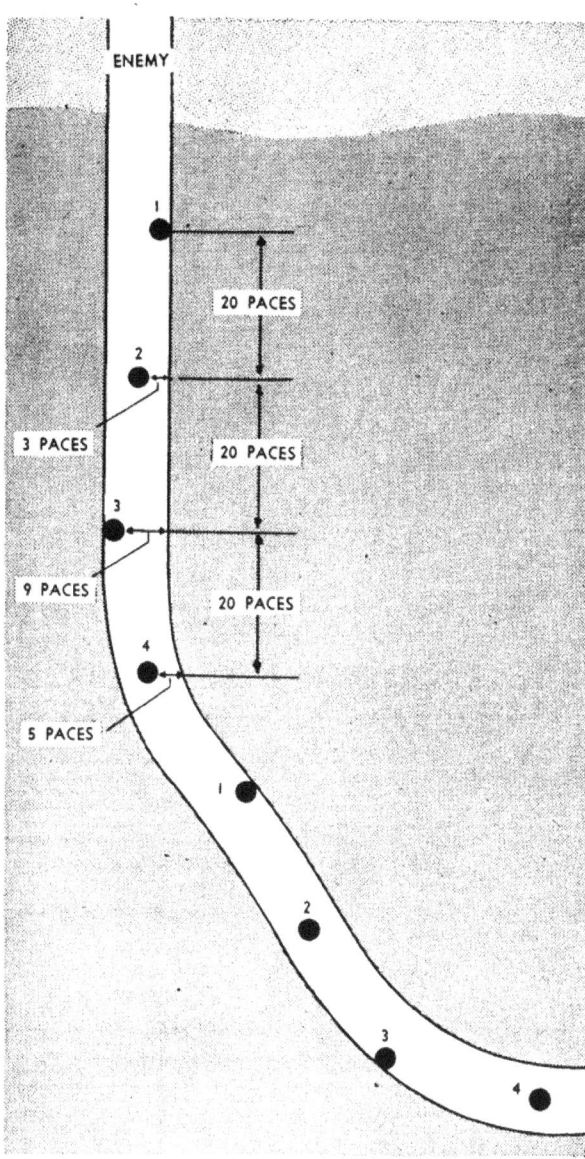

ENEMY

20 PACES

3 PACES

20 PACES

9 PACES

20 PACES

5 PACES

Figure 25.—Hasty mining of a road, ravine, or gully.

In general, quality of the Soviet concrete is good. Its resistance, however, is not very high, due to light reinforcing. The outer surface of ceilings and walls is usually more densely reinforced than the inner surface (figure 29). The following approximate thicknesses of concrete are used for various structural parts of defense works:

Ceilings	3.3 to 6.6 feet.
Front and side walls	2.3 to 7 feet.
Embrasures	4 to 6.6 feet.
Interior walls and ceilings	8 inches to 2.5 feet.

Rods for the reinforcement of concrete are about ¾ inch in diameter.

Turrets for machine guns and observation posts are not frequently used. Thickness of armor is from 5 to 7½ inches. Earth-covered walls of pillboxes usually have a protecting layer of loose rock or masonry under the earth cover which extends from the top of the structure to the ground level or deeper. The resistance of permanent works of a later date has been increased by adding burster layers about 3 feet thick of resilient asphalt. The asphalt is delivered in 2½-cubic-inch blocks which are melted for use.

Compartments in casemates are approximately 7 feet high or higher; in pillboxes, 6 to 7 feet high. Embrasures for artillery are either 6.6 by 4.6 feet or 4.6 by 2.6 feet. Embrasures are closed by sliding 4-inch steel plates measuring about 10 by 6.6 feet. Embrasures for heavy machine guns are rectangular in shape, tapering back from the outer to the inner face at varying angles in accordance with the field of fire of each machine gun. Outer dimensions of embrasures vary from 35 by 78 inches to 16 by 32 inches. Inner dimensions vary from 16 by 27 inches to 9 by 12 inches. Wall thicknesses are not less than 8 inches. Embrasures are closed by sliding steel plates 39 inches by 39 inches, at least 1¼ inches thick. Embrasures for light machine guns are approximately 5 by 20 inches or 8 by 16 inches. These embrasures are closed by sliding steel plates slightly smaller than those for heavy machine-gun embrasures.

From the outside, embrasures are covered with camouflaged wooden shutters which are either painted or covered with sod. As a rule, below the machine-gun embrasure there are two openings, 2⅜ to 2¾ inches in diameter, which serve as water and steam run-off drains. Machine guns are mounted on special fixed pedestals facing the embrasures. These pedestals are integral with the gunner's seat.

Normally, concrete pillboxes have only one entrance, shaped in a broken line. Slits about 8 to 20 inches wide and 80 inches high near the entrance facilitate natural ventilation. These slits may also be used for close combat. Some pillboxes have openings near the entrance for throwing out hand grenades. Doors are usually placed in the rear of pillboxes or, in some cases, in the side walls. Outer openings have either steel doors or iron gates about 5 to 6 feet high and 27 to 32 inches wide. Steel thicknesses vary from ⅞ to 1¼ inches, ⅞-inch iron bars having a spacing of 4½ inches. The entrance is protected by light machine guns which fire either through embrasures about 4 by 9 inches on both sides of the entrance door or through a

299

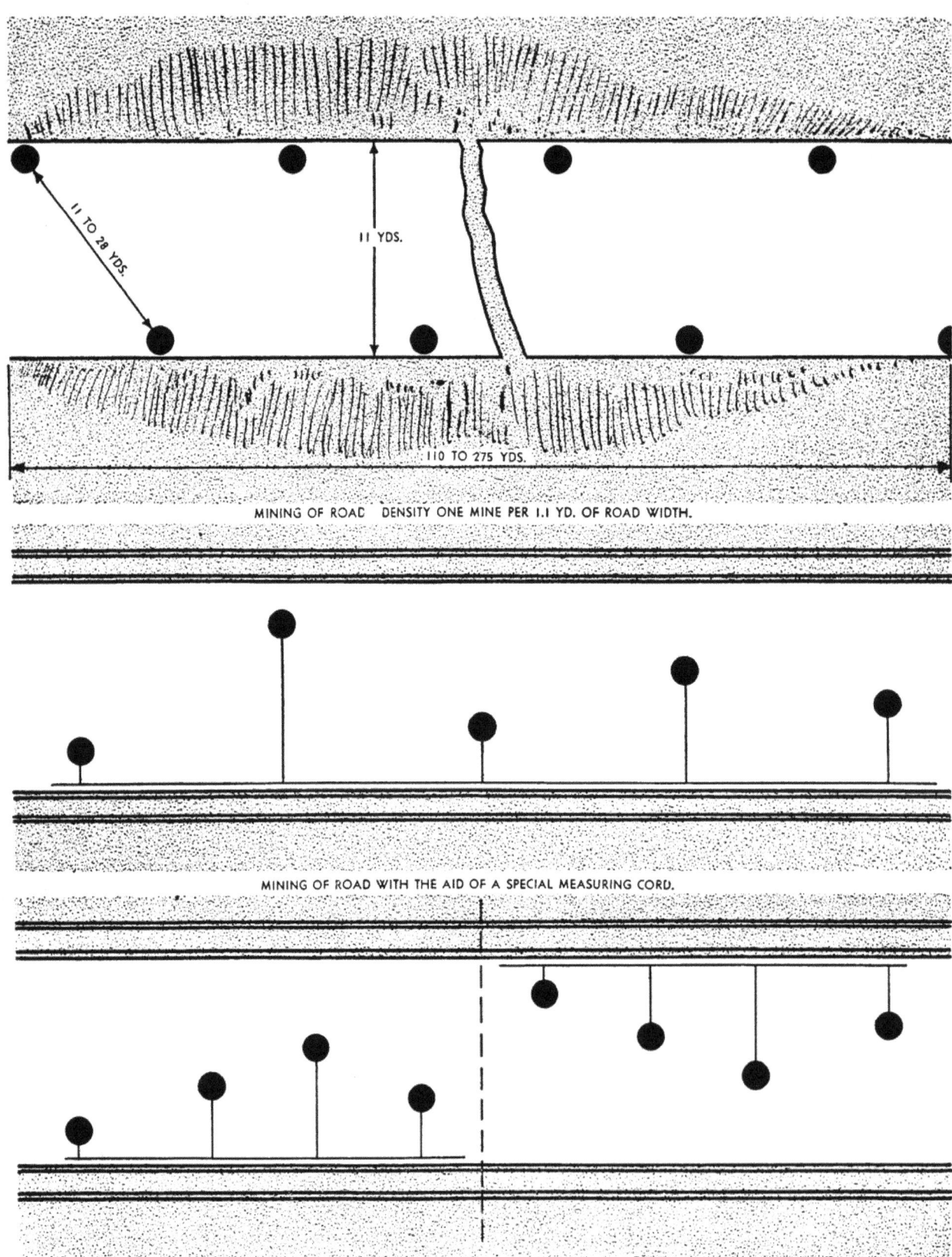

MINING OF ROAD DENSITY ONE MINE PER 1.1 YD. OF ROAD WIDTH.

11 TO 28 YDS.

11 YDS.

110 TO 275 YDS.

MINING OF ROAD WITH THE AID OF A SPECIAL MEASURING CORD.

MINING OF ROAD WITH THE AID OF AN ORDINARY MEASURING CORD.

Figure 26.—Deliberate mining of a road.

300

Type of construction	Span (feet)	Material	Thickness (inches)
Light construction Walls		Peat soil	82
		Clay or loose earth	47
		Sandy soil	35
		Tamped clay soil or black earth packed in a wooden casing.	16 to 20
		Tamped sand packed in a wooden casing	12
		Tamped gravel (crushed rock) with sand packed in wooden casing.	8
		Brick laid with cement	15
		Reinforced concrete	8
		Longitudinal layer of pin logs or boards	40
Overhead cover		Armor plate	3.5
Not vulnerable to crushing effect of tanks.	Up to 8	Logs, one layer	6 to 8
		Clay	4
		Soil	12
			22 to 24 Total
Vulnerable to crushing effect of tanks.	Up to 8	Woven brushwood	..
		Clay	4
		Soil	12
			16 Total
	Up to 6½	Fascines	10 to 12
		Clay	4
		Soil	12
			26 to 28 Total
Splinterproof Overhead	Up to 8	Poles, one layer	3 to 5
		Clay	8
		Soil	..
			11 to 13 Total
	Up to 6½	Boards	2
		Clay	..
		Soil	8
			10 Total
Reinforced construction Overhead cover for shelters	Up to 10	Logs, two layers	20
		Clay	4
		Earth	8
		Logs, four cross layers	40
		Soil	12
			84 Total
	Up to 8	Logs, one layer	10
		Clay	4
		Earth	20
		Rocks or brick, laid dry	24
		Soil	12
			70 Total
	Up to 8	Logs, one layer	10
		Clay	4
		Earth	20
		Reinforced concrete blocks	12
		Soil	12
			58 Total
Heavy construction Overhead cover for shelters		Logs, two layers	20
		Clay	4
		Earth	31
		Rocks or brick, laid dry	35
		Soil	12
			102 Total

Figure 27.—Protective thicknesses of various materials used in Soviet fortifications.

Type of construction	Span (feet)	Material	Thickness (inches)
Heavy construction—Continued. Overhead cover for shelters— Continued.		Logs, two layers	20
		Clay	4
		Earth	31
		Concrete blocks	18
		Soil	12
			85 Total
		Steel rails	6
		Clay	4
		Earth	20
		Concrete blocks	18
		Soil	12
			60 Total

Figure 27.—Protective thicknesses of various materials used in Soviet fortifications.—Continued.

Figure 28.—Prefabricated pillbox.

single embrasure located inside the pillbox opposite the entrance door, through which the entrance and adjacent corridor may be covered. Inner doors are gasproof and are made mostly of wood.

Pillboxes which have no entrance are connected by underground passages with adjacent structures. The cover of such passages is 3 to 10 feet thick and the walls are made of reinforced concrete, 8 inches to 1 foot thick. One floor of a multiple-story pillbox is connected with another by a ladder or through an opening. Normally, there are no stairs.

Pillboxes usually have camouflaged emergency exits immediately underneath or to one side of the entrance, from which a short tunnel leads to a con-

302

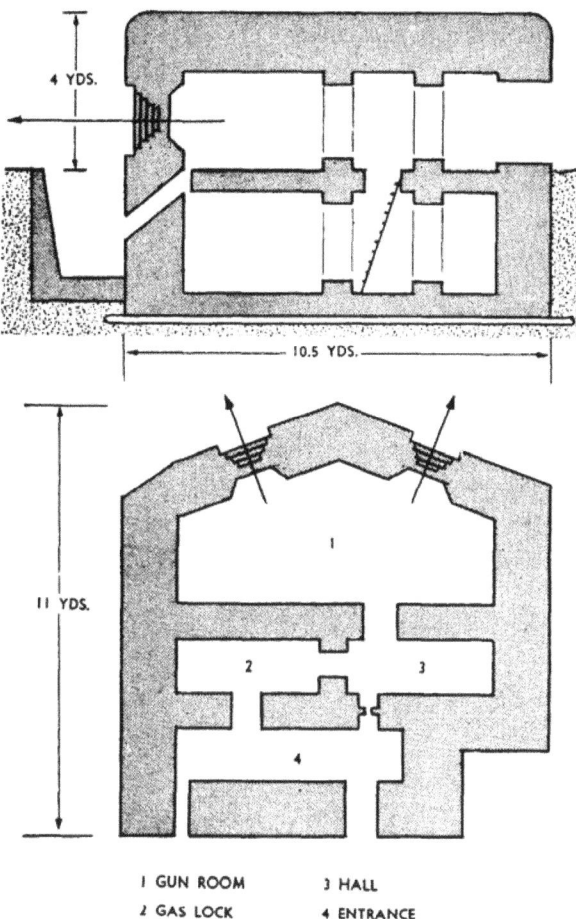

I GUN ROOM   3 HALL
2 GAS LOCK   4 ENTRANCE

Figure 29.—Typical permanent casemates.

cealed exit 35 to 165 feet from the pillbox. Electrically or hand-operated air pumps are provided for the ventilation of pillboxes. Higher air pressure inside the pillbox prevents penetration of chemical agents from the outside. Water is provided by wells or water pumps inside the structure. Pumps are electrically operated in structures which are connected with an electric plant. Electric lights, candles, or oil lamps are used for illumination. Small coke stoves are installed in niches with flues built in the concrete walls. Electric heaters are used in structures which are connected with an electric plant. Walls inside pillboxes and casemates are covered with wood or $\frac{3}{16}$-inch sheet iron. Telephone and radio connect command and observation posts with artillery and machine-gun emplacements. Observation is mostly by periscope through openings in the ceilings of pillboxes and observation shelters. Observation shelters may have two periscopes.

The armament of pillboxes ordinarily consists of a heavy machine gun, a 45-mm antitank gun, and usually a second heavy machine gun which fires through the same embrasure as the antitank gun. Cables for electricity and telephones are laid in wooden or concrete tubes having a diameter of about 8 inches. These tubes are placed in ditches about 6 feet deep, 20 inches wide at the bottom, and 40 inches wide at surface level. Near defense works, the depth of cable ditches increases to 10 to 13 feet.

Defense works are usually painted to match the color of the soil and are provided with an earth cover. Depending on surroundings, sod or plants are placed on top of the earth cover. Frequently the works are disguised as huts, sheds, stables, barns, and the like.

Concreted ditches built in front of some pillboxes afford defense against close attack. Such ditches are protected by hand grenades launched through special apertures of the pillbox.

Permanent works of an earlier date appear to be less resistant than the later structures built after the autumn of 1939. One-gun pillboxes for frontal defense are common. Their height above ground is 5 to 6.6 feet. Thickness of walls and ceilings averages from 3.3 to 5 feet. Embrasures are not armored and can be closed by 1½-inch steel plates. These pillboxes are equipped with periscopes, hand-operated ventilation devices, running water, and telephones. They are well camouflaged. Entrance is by wooden stairs.

5. ORGANIZATION AND PRIORITY OF FORTIFICATION WORK

Orders for the fortification of a position are issued by army or division staffs simultaneously with the order to defend a locality or zone, or, in offensive operations, at the time when an attack is halted.

The commanding personnel of individual army units are responsible for the fortification of defensive positions or of captured enemy positions by their troops. In the infantry, the company commander and his technical assistant, the regimental engineer, are in charge of defense work; in the artillery, this is the duty of the battery commander. Three to four pioneers and a section of regimental pioneer instructors assist the battalion commander in the supervision of fortification work. Complicated tasks, such as mining, construction of reinforced shelters and pillboxes, etc., are performed by divisional engineers, one or two platoons of which are attached to infantry regiments. Regimental and divisional engineers are technical advisors of regimental and divisional commanders.

303

CONSTRUCTION WORK FOR DEFENSE OF A STRONGPOINT	QUANTITY	LABOR		
		MAN-HOURS PER UNIT	TOTAL MAN-HOURS	
			FIRST PRIORITY	SECOND PRIORITY
TRENCHES, CAMOUFLAGED AND ADEQUATELY ORGANIZED				
FIRE TRENCHES	350 YDS.	2.7	640	320
COMMUNICATION TRENCHES [1]	770 YDS.	0.9	300	400
MACHINE-GUN NESTS	8	30	120	120
PILLBOXES, PARTLY COVERED	1	900		900
REINFORCED MACHINE-GUN EMPLACEMENTS	1	40		40
OPEN EMPLACEMENTS FOR AT RIFLES	9	8	72	
EMPLACEMENTS FOR 45-MM. AT GUNS	2	50	100	
OPEN OBSERVATION POSTS	2	7	14	
REINFORCED SHELTERS	2	1,500		3,000
DUGOUTS	2	40	80	
ANTITANK OBSTACLES [2]	175 YDS.			
ANTIPERSONNEL OBSTACLES [2]	950 YDS.			
CONCEALED PATHS	220 YDS.	0.5	110	

[1] Including widened communication trenches.
[2] Due to presence of natural obstacles, the number of mines and extension of artificial obstacles were reduced.

Note.—Labor required for the construction of artificial obstacles is not furnished by the garrison of the strongpoint, but by detailed engineers or by a special detachment from the rifle battalion.

Figure 30.—Time and labor required for the organization of a strongpoint.

They participate in the preparation of plans and orders issued in connection with the fortification of defensive positions, and are responsible for the supply of engineering materials and tools.

During the first 2 days' work on a position, troops use light entrenching tools. Regimental tools are usually distributed among machine-gun and mortar sections and the reserve units which are assigned to fortification work. At the end of the second day, all troops of the defensive positions must be supplied with heavy entrenching equipment from divisional and army dumps. Unit commanders decide on the type and priority of defense work to be executed. Their decision depends on the nature of operations, on local conditions of terrain, soil, and ground water, and on the availability of time and equipment. Hasty fortification of a position ordinarily takes 96 hours (4 days); deliberate fortification of a locality is carried out within 168 to 336 hours (7 to 14 days). The fortification of an army defense zone requires from 20 to 30 days (figure 30). Under conditions of mobile warfare, urgent fortification work is done as required. As a rule, fortification work is done by night; it begins at about 1900 or 2000 and is interrupted at daybreak.

The following order and priority of work is recommended: During the first day, trenches are dug for all sections garrisoning the defended area. Emplacements are prepared for machine guns, mortars, and artillery; command and observation posts are camouflaged and lightly covered; fire trenches are dug; light ammunition dumps and medical shelters are established. Reserve units construct the fortifications on the forward edge of the position, erect obstacles, clear fields of fire, and dig main communication trenches to secure ammunition supply. Highest priority is given to mining important approaches which may be threatened by tank attacks; this is done by regimental and divisional engineers.

During the second and third days, fortifications are developed and completed. At the end of the third day fire trenches including shelters and recesses must be completed. The fourth and subsequent days are mainly used for the development of obstacles and communication trenches and for the improvement of fire pits and trenches. Mining in front of the main line of resistance must be completed by regimental and divisional engineers.

On the fifth day, units commence construction of timber-and-earth works, erect prefabricated concrete pillboxes, and construct obstacles inside the defensive positions. They also begin the organization of fortified strongpoints. On the sixth day, reserve units are shifted to construction work on the second line of defense. By the end of the seventh day, the hasty fortification of the main and second lines of resistance must be completed. By the end of the fourteenth day, both lines of resistance must be fully equipped with defense works, command and observation shelters, and a system of covered communication trenches. Further improvements are dictated by combat conditions. However, fortification work in a defensive zone continues indefinitely without interruption.

Section III. WINTER FORTIFICATIONS

Winter conditions, which cause the transformation of many natural obstacles such as lakes, ponds, rivers, and swamps into dangerous approaches and render useless many artificial obstacles, create the necessity of adaptations in the organization of defensive positions. This involves, chiefly, the reorganization of antitank and antipersonnel obstacles, the subsequent readjustment of the fire system and of firing positions, the modification of existing works, and the construction of special winter defenses.

1. WINTER MODIFICATION OF FIELD FORTIFICATIONS

Existing structures may be adapted to winter conditions by various methods. The Soviets adapt splinterproof field works of the light type and specially prefabricated metal and concrete pillboxes by raising their zero or sighting line. To facilitate the use of fire trenches, observation posts, and machine-gun emplacements, the floors are raised by additional loose ground, sandbags, and available timber. This may be done gradually, as the snow cover increases in depth (figures 31 and 32).

For protection against snow, trenches are covered by special shields with spaces left open for observation, launching of grenades, and exit. Recesses in trenches, after necessary provisions for heating, are used as shelter for crews and weapons. At a distance of 10 to 16 feet from such shelters, one or two open machine-gun emplacements are provided for flanking and oblique fire. Low-set pillboxes, especially concrete or metal works with sufficiently high casemates, are adapted for winter conditions by raising the entire structure. Some gun emplacements used as shelter for weapons and crews are protected by one or two open firing positions usually built on the overhead cover of the structure and cut into its top layer. Such an arrangement provides flanking and oblique fire protection and facilitates rapid occupation of the firing position by the crew. The loose-earth cover of the construction affords protection against enemy frontal fire.

Trenches, gun emplacements, pillboxes, and observation posts which cannot be adapted to winter conditions and used for their normal function are converted into shelters. Embrasures and entrances of pillboxes are closed by shields or straw mats; doors or curtains are provided; bunks and tables made; heating arrangements installed; and all inside surfaces insulated with available material (straw, hay, canvas, blankets, etc.). Recesses and niches in trenches and such communication and fire trenches as are not used for their original function but utilized for shelter, are kept warm in a similar manner (figure 33).

Special attention is paid to the shape of overhead cover of defense works to avoid accumulations of drifting snow. Soviet experience has shown that the accumulation of drifting snow is encouraged by steep slopes, while surfaces with slopes of not over 1:4 do not obstruct the drift of air and therefore do not accumulate snow.

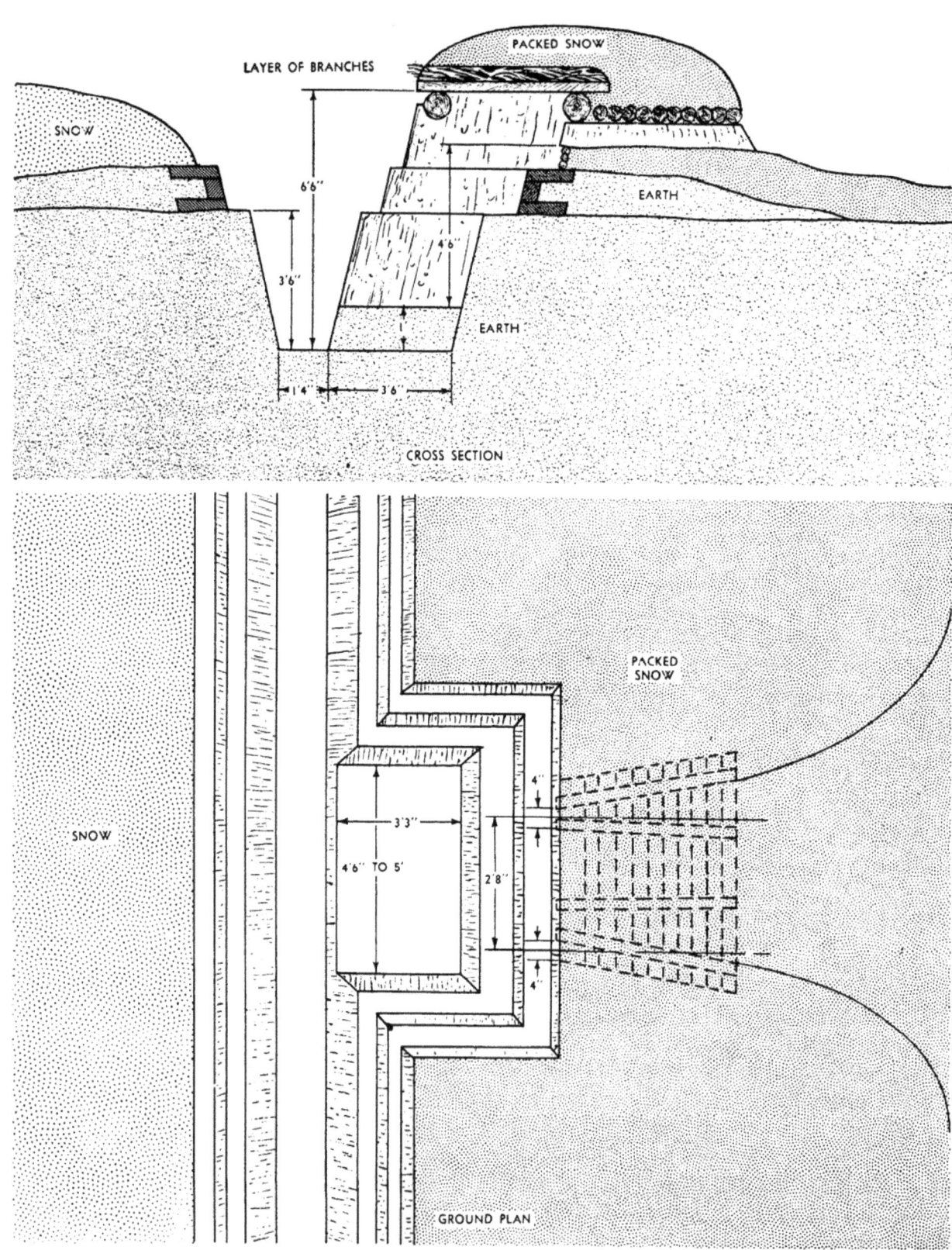

Figure 31.—*Winter modification of a firing position.*

306

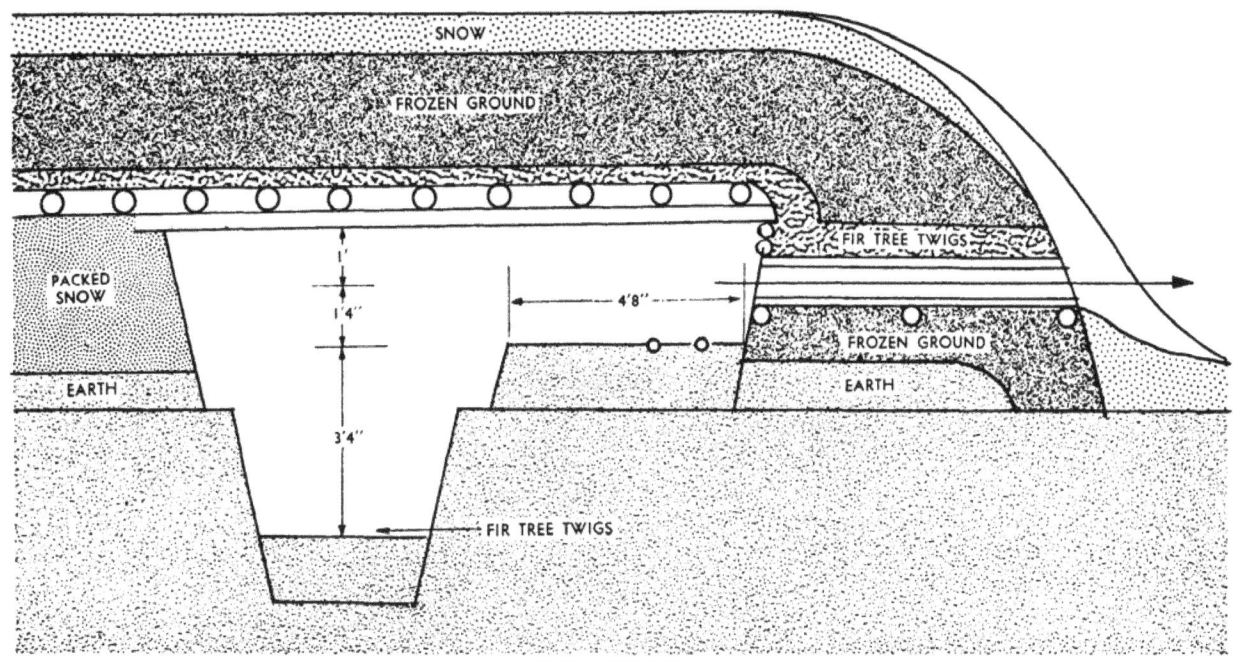

CROSS SECTION OF
A MG EMPLACEMENT

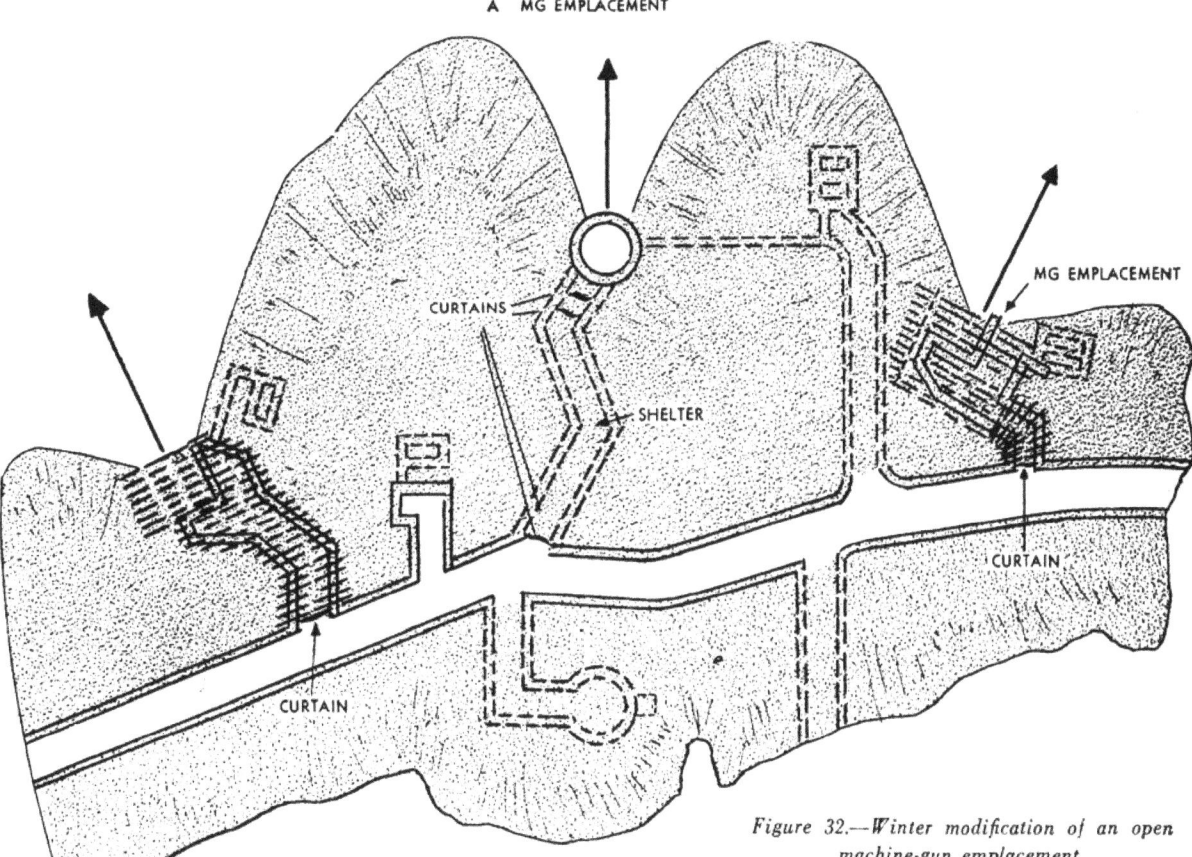

GROUND PLAN

Figure 32.—*Winter modification of an open machine-gun emplacement.*

2. EMPLOYMENT OF SNOW, ICE, AND FROZEN GROUND

a. Defensive work. Existing defense works modified for winter conditions are largely supplemented by special winter fortifications built of snow, ice, and blocks of frozen ground. Field works are reinforced with loose-snow covers, packed layer by layer, which afford protection against antitank

307

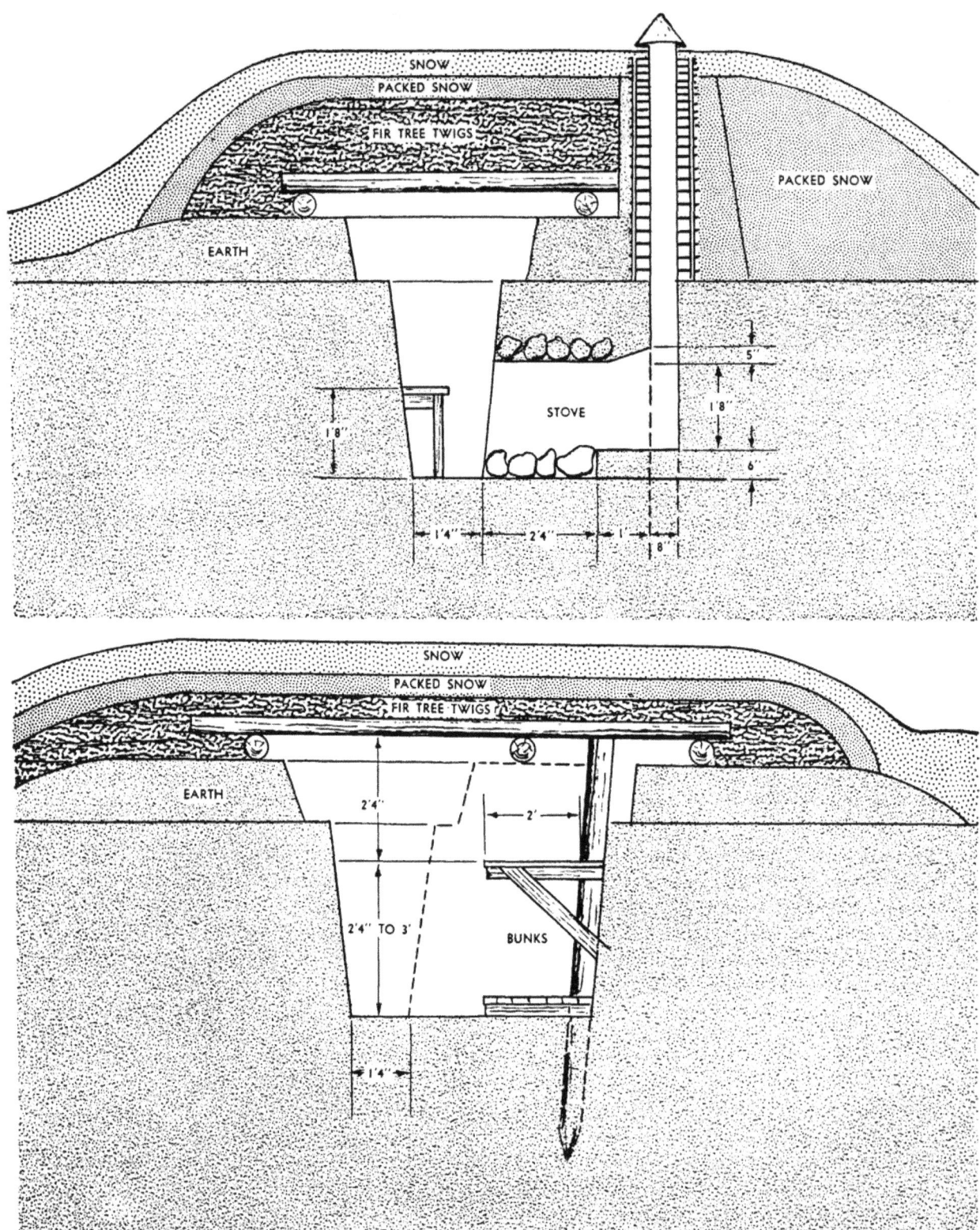

Figure 33.—Reconstruction of a trench into a shelter in winter.

grenades. When the snow cover is 4 inches deep or less, fire and communication trenches are dug to their full depth in the ground, and snow is used for camouflage. If the snow cover reaches a depth of

10 inches, fire and communication trenches are dug in the snow with only partial excavation of ground. When the snow is over 10 inches deep, fire and communication trenches are built entirely in the snow. Various available materials are used for revetment. A variety of shelters constructed of snow, or dug into ground frozen to sufficient depth, are built to meet the increased demand for shelter during winter. Observation posts are built of well-packed snow with walls 4 to 5 feet thick and a diameter of 3.3 feet. The false work inside, made of brushwood, is left in place to give additional protection from splinters. Such shelters resist penetration of ordinary and armor-piercing bullets.

Pillboxes for one machine gun are constructed of frozen blocks of sand and crushed stone. The wall blocks are fastened together with moistened snow. A 6-inch layer of logs supports the roof. Outside, the walls are covered with loose sand or packed layers of snow. This cover is 5 feet thick at the foundation, and 18 inches at the top. Individual blocks are carefully prepared, tamped until moisture appears on the surface, left in forms for a day, and then taken out at temperatures under 14 degrees F.

An effective antitank and antipersonnel obstacle used by the Soviets is an iced slope. The Red Army recommends the spraying of terrain having slopes up to 1:1½ when the ground is frozen but not yet covered with snow. The spray of water is directed from the top of the slope downwards, and kept as long as possible in the air. The preparation of an ice crust over snow requires a great amount of water and time. When the temperature is very low (5 degrees F.), it is preferable to pour water from buckets by hand. An ice surface of 7 to 9 square yards can be prepared by one man in 12 hours.

Excellent antitank obstacles are camouflaged openings, 13 to 22 feet wide, in frozen surfaces of rivers, lakes, and ponds. They are covered with insulating material to prevent their freezing over. A 6- to 7-inch layer of hay or straw, a 10-inch layer of fir branches, or a 10-inch layer of branches combined with a 4-inch layer of hay, provide such insulation which, in addition, is covered with loose snow. Traps of this kind are usually arranged in checker-board fashion along the near shore of frozen rivers, lakes, or ponds located in front of defensive positions. If an opening or thaw in the surface of a frozen water obstacle is covered by a 4-inch layer of ice, it can be maintained in this condition by an 8- to 10-inch cover of loose snow. A possible in-

crease in the thickness of ice of 1 to 2 inches will not prevent a tank from breaking through. Swamps are prevented from freezing in a similar manner.

Individual sectors in the rear of defensive positions, roads, and road sections are blocked by snow barriers formed by the placing of special snow fences against the wind. The use of several rows of snow fences permits formation of the desired wall width. Vertical and slanting snow fences are installed in various combinations in order to obtain the desired mass of snow. Such snow walls are used as a protection against tanks and mechanized vehicles.

The Soviets are very inventive in utilizing various materials for winter antipersonnel obstacles. Stockades 5 to 7 feet high made of poles 3 to 5 inches in diameter are set in ice in a checkerboard pattern inclined toward the enemy, with intervals of 10 to 12 inches along the front and of 12 to 16 inches in depth. Abatis of trees and branches attached to poles are also set in ice. Stumps of trees 8 to 16 inches in diameter, or logs, set in ice are found to be very effective. These types of obstacles on ice are also considered effective in preventing hostile aircraft from landing on frozen lakes or large rivers. When the ground is covered with loose and shallow snow, antitank mines are placed directly on the ground. If the depth of snow exceeds 10 inches, mines are installed on tamped snow or on pads made of boards or stakes at a depth of not over 4 to 6 inches from the surface of the snow.

b. Structural characteristics. If thoroughly protected by heat-insulating material of sufficient thickness, such as sawdust, wood shavings, peat moss, finely chopped fir twigs, dry conifer needles, and the like, structures of snow, ice, and frozen ground can remain structurally sound indefinitely at low temperatures. The principal advantages in the use of these materials for defense works lie in the general and immediate availability of the material, the comparative rapidity of construction, the facility with which such works can be repaired, the durability of such structures, and their noninflammability.

STRENGTH AND DURABILITY. Snow, ice, and frozen ground are highly plastic even when not under load. Continuous loading causes considerable and rapid deformation, especially at temperatures close to freezing. The strength of frozen ground to a great extent depends on the moisture content at the time of freezing and the cementing together of solid particles by ice. The low tensile strength of snow, ice, and frozen ground is given primary consideration in planning permanent structures. This applies particularly to overhead cover. Theoretical calculations, confirmed by practice, indicate that vaulted overhead cover is not subject to such effects and may stand indefinitely without suffering any deformation.

Snow. Flat overhead cover made of snow will not last long and is possible only if the span does not exceed 3 feet. Flat cover of ice and frozen ground with a span of 10 to 13 feet may last several months if the cover is not less than 2.3 feet thick and if its temperature can be maintained below freezing. Usually flat cover must be supported by a layer of logs or similar material.

The durability of dry, compact snow is materially increased by adding water up to 25 percent of the weight of the snow. This raises the compressive strength of frozen snow to 17 pounds per square foot. The accepted working strength of dry, compressed snow at 14 degrees F. is 10 to 16 pounds per square foot and that of frozen snow is 20 to 30 pounds per square foot. The allowable tensile strength in structures made of pressed snow is 0.2 to 0.4 pound per square foot; that of frozen snow, 1 to 2 pounds per square foot.

Ice. The structural strength of ice and frozen ground is much higher than that of snow. It increases with the decrease in temperature, especially within the range between freezing and 14 degrees F. when most of the mineral solutions contained between the particles of ice or frozen ground congeal. Salt-water ice is structurally weaker than fresh-water ice, but its elasticity is greater under continuous loading and it is less brittle. The compressive strength of fresh-water ice fluctuates between 30 and 125 pounds per square foot, with 60 pounds per square foot at 14 degrees F. The permissible tensile stress in ice structures is 4 to 6 pounds per square foot. A typical feature of ice in defense works is its high fragmentation in the event of direct hits or explosions.

Frozen ground. Frozen ground is three to five times stronger than ice. Its strength increases with decreasing temperatures. The resistance of frozen ground to blast action is greater than its resistance to continuous loading. The strength of frozen ground, like that of ice, depends not only on the quality of separate particles and crystals but also on the cohesion of ice crystals.

Sand and similar types of soil with a low moisture content are the most resistant and have high tensile and compressive strengths. The temporary compressive strength of such ground may reach 400 pounds per square foot and, in this respect, it equals good cement concrete or high grade brick.

Frozen clay is the weakest of all ground material, but while its temporary compressive strength is inferior to that of sand, it is not as fragile and is less subject to fragmentation by direct hits.

Ice concrete. Experiments carried out by Soviet specialists have shown that the compressive strength of ice concrete, a mixture of water and frozen sand, gravel, or crushed rock, equals the strength of good concrete or high grade brick, while its bending strength is from 2 to 4 times higher. The following table gives the average compressive strength of reinforced ice concrete:

Ice with dry sand------------ 300 pounds per square foot.

Ice with crushed rock-------- 350 pounds per square foot.

Ice with frozen sand---------- 270 pounds per square foot.

Ice with frozen crushed rock-- 210 pounds per square foot.

One and one-third cubic yards of ice concrete made with dry sand and crushed rock contains 1,540 pounds of sand, 375 pounds of water and 3,485 pounds of crushed rock. The bending strength of beams made of ice concrete with timber reinforcing was tested with a continuous load of 880 pounds, which equalled approximately one-third of the allowable load. With air temperature at 5 to 15 degrees F. for 72 hours, the deflection was 0.65 inch or 1/675 of the span. After a month under the same test load, deflection increased to 1.56 inch or 1/275 of the span.

The chief disadvantages of ice concrete are the comparatively complicated process of preparation and the necessity of using definite proportions of the aggregates in order to obtain a uniform mass. The strength of ice concrete does not differ much from that of frozen sand, and it takes less time to build defense works of frozen ground. The Soviets recommend the use of ice concrete for the construction of defense works only when sufficient time is available for its preparation, and when sand, crushed rock, or gravel is locally obtainable.

PROTECTIVE QUALITIES. Structures of ice, frozen ground, and ice concrete, due to their hardness, resist penetration of bullets and shell splinters, but their brittleness makes them vulnerable to blast. This is particularly true in regard to ice. For this reason ice is not used in the construction of pillboxes but may serve as material for obstacles.

Frozen sand or gravel and ice concrete are less brittle than ice. Soft frozen ground (clay, dry soil, or peat), though less hard than sandy ground or ice concrete, gives more resistance to blast action and fragmentation.

Fortifications of frozen ground and ice concrete must be provided with a protecting layer of brushwood, stakes, poles, or boards within the structure. Frozen ground should be reinforced with branches, straw, or similar material. The reinforcing must be placed in all directions and not in layers. Blast action causes fractures along planes of weakness in layer reinforcing, thus weakening the structure. Based on their experience, the Soviets list the effects of direct hits on various types of frozen ground as follows:

Frozen clay soil shows the best resistance to penetration (bullets and shell fragments) and blast.

Ice concrete with crushed rock offers better resistance to penetration than any other ice concrete. However, if it lacks vertical branch reinforcing, it is subject to destruction by blast and splits off along planes of weakness. A recommended composite ice concrete in which the inner layer is made of frozen ground, the intermediate layer of ice concrete, and the outside cover of loose frozen ground, reduces the destructive effect of bullets and blast to a minimum. An inner layer of dry branches, poles, or boards is used as protection against splinters. Loose frozen earth cover on concrete pillboxes considerably reduces the destructive effect of direct hits.

Frozen ground is recommended for splinterproof construction. Ice taken from water reservoirs does not resist penetration and therefore is not recommended for covered fortifications. Walls of winter structures are built of blocks of various types of frozen ground. Blocks of frozen sand, 39 inches thick, are composed of one part crushed rock and two and one-half parts sand. Blocks of frozen clay ground, 47 inches thick, are composed of one part clay and two parts sand.

The protective thickness of frozen materials against penetration of bullets varies:

Snow, loose	120 inches.
Snow, packed	80 inches.
Snow, with ice crust	40 to 60 inches.
Ice	28 inches.
Frozen ground	20 inches.
Ice concrete	12 inches.

c. Ground water and thawing problems.
Structures of snow, ice, and frozen ground which are planned to last until spring should be built on foundations not subject to thawing nor exposed to surface waters. The presence and level of underground water is given primary consideration, and sites with high ground-water tables are avoided. If conditions require the erection of defense works in areas with a high ground-water table, the process of freezing the structure is accelerated, or, if possible, dry earth is used as material. If time is available, acceleration of the freezing of the upper layers of the soil on which the structure is to be erected is recommended. For this purpose the snow is removed from the surface of a slightly larger sector than required for construction. With a temperature of 5 to 14 degrees F., 2 to 3 days are sufficient to freeze the base of the structure to protect it from the effects of high-level ground.

To protect ice or frozen-ground structures from melting during temperatures above the freezing point at the beginning of spring, the walls of such works are insulated with available material, such as peat, sawdust, straw, and fir twigs. Before insulating a snow, ice, or frozen-ground structure, thorough freezing should take place in order to increase its durability and thermic stability.

Peat is recommended as the best insulating material, since straw and hay are subject to decay with the resultant release of heat at temperatures above 50 degrees F. The best insulating effect is obtained when the insulating layer is moistened and thoroughly frozen. When the temperature is above freezing, the insulating material should be as dry as possible, and may be moistened when the temperature drops below freezing. By covering the insulating outside layer with 4 inches of snow, the effect of insulation will be increased. Surfaces inside a frozen-material structure should be insulated by dry material to protect them from the radiating warmth of stoves and human bodies. The thickness of insulating layers depends on the length of time the structure is to be used. An 8-inch layer is found sufficient for two or three weeks. The most effective insulation is afforded by interior walls made of stakes, poles, brushwood, canvas, bagging, etc., with an air space 4 to 8 inches wide between the inner wall and the frozen ground or snow structure. If no insulating material is available, the frozen structure should be covered with as thick a layer of snow as tactical conditions permit, although snow insulation will protect the structure from thawing for a few days only. Drainage must be provided for melting snow insulation.

CHAPTER VII

LOGISTICS

INTRODUCTION

1. GENERAL

The supply and transportation system of the Red Army is characterized by rigid adherence to several basic concepts. These include long-term planning, command position of the chiefs of rear services, grouping of supply and maintenance responsibilities according to arm, differences of supply systems between rifle and mobile formations, dependence on rail transportation, and priority of ammunition and fuel over all other classes of supplies.

The planning of supply and transportation requirements of the Red Army is coordinated with the production and delivery programs by the civilian commissariats. Specifications for civilian goods parallel specifications for military goods. Tractors, for example, which are manufactured for civilian use are built according to military specifications. They are included in the system for mobilization of the Red Army and are inspected periodically by representatives of the Red Army.

Key civilian commissariats, such as the Peoples' Commissariat of Transportation and the Peoples' Commissariat of Signal Communications, are organized along military lines. They are adaptable to military control.

2. RESPONSIBILITY

The Chief of the Rear Services of the Red Army is a deputy to the Peoples' Commissar of Defense. The chief of rear services, at each level of command, is a deputy to the over-all commander. He also may be referred to as the Deputy Commander for the Rear Services. Thus the rear services participate in the planning and coordination of all operations as well as in problems of transportation and supply.

Authority of the chiefs of rear services is second only to that of the over-all commanders and the chiefs of staff. Commanders of the rear area services are represented in the forward echelons of the staffs. They are required to assume the initiative in supply and evacuation problems.

Red Army field service regulations specifically designate the responsibility for supply and transportation. The design, development, and production of equipment for various arms and services are the responsibility of the arm or service concerned. The chiefs of arms and services are charged with the procurement and distribution of supplies for which their arm is responsible down to and including the army. Transportation for the delivery of all supplies is controlled by the chiefs of rear services.

3. SUPPLY AND EVACUATION

Supply and evacuation systems for mobile formations and units which normally form the mobile reserve of the over-all commander differ from those of rifle formations and units in order to provide maximum flexibility and to guarantee the flow of fuel, ammunition, and replacements under varied conditions.

The flow of supplies to the Red Army from production centers is dependent almost entirely upon rail transportation. Rail transportation, therefore, is a key factor in all major plans. It is extended as far forward as possible. Although rail transportation usually extends only to army railheads, numerous instances of railheads being established in the rear areas of rifle divisions have been reported.

Narrow gauge lines are constructed to serve troops operating in mountainous terrain.

To achieve maximum coordination of rail transportation with military requirements, the People's Commissariat of Transportation was militarized early in World War II.

Supply and evacuation schedules for personnel and matériel are determined by a rigid system of priorities, especially with regard to the flow of supplies to the front lines. The delivery of ammunition and fuel always takes precedence over all other classes of supplies.

Supply and evacuation systems of the Red Army were modified, developed, and supplemented during

312

World War II according to the dictates of combat experience and tactical requirements. All transportation was consolidated under a single command. Supply was transferred from a staff function to a command function. An echelon maintenance system was established. The utilization of local resources and captured equipment became standard procedure for all levels of command.

Evaluation of the supply and evacuation systems of the Red Army must take into account the critical shortage of equipment. The shortage of railroad tank cars, tank trucks, special evacuation equipment, and ambulances was especially acute. Military pipe lines were virtually non-existent.

4. FUTURE TRENDS

It is expected that the Red Army improvement of its supply system will be directed toward improvement in quality and quantity of equipment, military highways, and railroad nets.

Section I. ORGANIZATION OF REAR SERVICES

1. GENERAL

The Chief of the Rear Services controls all transportation other than air transport (see Chapter XI, Air Forces) and all supplies except weapons, ammunition, and technical equipment. He supervises medical and veterinary services, road maintenance, and other service agencies.

The Chief of Artillery controls the supply of weapons and ammunition from the factories to front-line units down to rifle regiments. A special organization exploits captured weapons and matériel. Technical equipment for armored troops, chemical warfare troops, engineers, and signal troops is controlled by their respective supply organizations. Transportation for supplies is furnished the supply organizations of the Chief of Artillery and the technical services by the Chief of the Rear Services.

Because of the number of agencies at each command level concerned with supply, close coordination and supervision of their activities by the Chief of the Rear Services is essential. This coordination is implemented by centralized control of transportation.

2. PEOPLES' COMMISSARIAT OF ARMED FORCES

a. **Chief of the Rear Services of the Red Army.** The Chief of the Rear Services is one of the members of the Peoples' Commissariat of Armed Forces (formerly Peoples' Commissariat of Defense). He serves as a deputy to the Commissar of Defense in supply matters. He is assisted by a staff and a personnel department. (For details of the structure of the high command, see Chapter I, National Defense System. For Red Army personnel and training agencies, see Chapter II, Personnel Administration.)

The following administrative offices are under the jurisdiction of the Chief of the Rear Services:

Main Administration of Army Transportation. This administration is responsible for the allocation of railroad rolling stock for army movements and for supplies.

Main Administration of Motor Transport. This administration was organized in January 1943 to increase control over available motor transport. It also took over from the main administrations of armored and motorized troops such duties as the control of schools, supply troops, technical services, and depots.

Main Administration of Roads.

Main Administration of Intendance. This administration is in charge of clothing, some individual equipment, laundries, and workshops.

Main Administration of Rations and Fodder. Attached to it is the Main Administration of Post Exchange Services, which is subordinate to the Peoples' Commissariat of Trade and which functions independently down to army level.

Main Administration of the Medical Service of the Red Army. This administration functions under the Chief of the Rear Services and also has its own service channels down to regimental level. Key personnel of the medical service also hold positions in the Peoples' Commissariat of Public Health, which has over-all responsibility for all medical matters. The same system applies to the veterinary service.

Administration of the Veterinary Service of the Red Army.

Motor Fuel and Lubricants Administration of the Red Army.

Finance Administration of the Red Army. Attached to it is an office of the State Bank of the Soviet Union, which has its own channels of communication down to regimental level.

Administration for Personnel Losses of Enlisted Men and Relief (pensions) for their Families. It is believed that this administration is responsible also for graves registration. Losses of commissioned personnel and pensions for their families probably are handled by the Chief of Personnel Administration of the Peoples' Commissariat of Armed Forces.

Administration for the Economic Management of the Peoples' Commissariat of Armed Forces.

Administration for the Economic Management of the Peoples' Commissariat of Armed Forces. Publication Office of the Journal, "Rear Services and Supply of the Red Army."

b. Schools of the rear services. The Chief of the Rear Services is responsible for the operation of schools to train officer specialists for the rear services. The Molotov Military Academy trains officers for the rear services and supply organizations of the Red Army. Kaganovich Military Academy trains officers for the transport service.

The Main Administration of the Medical Service of the Red Army and the Administration of the Veterinary Service of the Red Army are responsible for the Pirogov and Kirov military medical academies and the military veterinary academy.

c. Coordination of transportation. The Chief of the Rear Services coordinates transportation problems with the following members of the Peoples' Commissariat of Defense and their organizations responsible for supplying troops with technical equipment, weapons, and ammunition:

The Chief of Chemical Troops.
The Chief of Engineers.
The Chief of Signal Communications.
The Chief of Armored and Motorized Troops.
The Chief of Artillery.

The Chief of the Rear Services also coordinates with the Chief of Railroad Troops, who is directly responsible to the General Staff of the Red Army. The Chief of Railroad Troops commands a limited number of specialized railroad maintenance units and controls all personnel of the Peoples' Commissariat of Transportation operating trains for military supply or movements. It is believed that railroad troop commanders attached to army groups (fronts) function as deputies to the Chief of Railroad Troops.

d. Captured weapons. A Committee for Captured Weapons and its main administration are part of the Peoples' Commissariat of Defense. It is not under the jurisdiction of the Chief of the Rear Services. The Main Administration for Captured Weapons handles recovery, transportation, storage, and reconditioning of captured weapons. It has its own agencies down to division level and is responsible for the technical analysis of new enemy weapons. In addition, it is charged with the recovery of damaged Soviet weapons and equipment and their transportation to the rear. The Chief of the Main Administration of Army Transportation coordinates transportation requirements with the Committee for Captured Weapons. Captured air force equipment is handled by the air force.

e. Supply depots. Each main administration of the rear services and the main administrations of arms and technical services maintain a number of central depots or supply bases. These central depots or supply bases in the interior of the U. S. S. R. provide general reserves of all classes of supplies. From them come the replacement supplies for troop units and establishments of each military district or army, and the reserve supplies of each district command.

The artillery supply reserves of the Peoples' Commissariat of Armed Forces are stored in central artillery depots. Each category of artillery supplies is stored separately. Ammunition is segregated according to manufacturer, lot number, and year of manufacture. The splitting of an ammunition lot between warehouses is prohibited. Artillery reserve supplies are separated from artillery supplies for current requirements.

A supply depot includes headquarters, warehouses, workshops, and laboratories. Each supply depot is guarded by security and fire-defense (or passive antiaircraft defense) troops supplied by the NKVD.

Supply depots are located in compliance with instructions from the General Staff of the Red Army in accordance with operational and tactical requirements. Generally, they are located within a mile of railroads or highways. Many types of storage installations with widely varying capacities are used.

Each military district has from 15 to 50 supply depots. They include depots for artillery, ammunition, transport, fuel and lubricants, food, engineer supplies, medical supplies, and clothing. Some districts also have depots for chemical supplies, armored equipment, explosives, signal equipment, and other special supplies.

3. REAR SERVICES, ARMY GROUP AND ARMY LEVELS

a. General. The organization of rear services at army group (front) and army levels parallels the organization of the Peoples' Commissariat of Defense. There are administrations (army group level) or divisions (army level) for army transporta-

314

tion, motor transport, roads, intendance, rations and fodder, medical service, veterinary service, motor fuel and lubricants, finance, and personnel losses of enlisted men.

The army group (front) or army Chief of the Rear Services is the third ranking officer, ranked only by the Commander and the Chief of Staff. He also is a member of the Military Council, which formulates all administrative policies and effects civil-military coordination through attached political personnel, usually the secretary of the regional Communist Party.

Membership in the Military Council of the Chief of the Rear Services fosters cooperation in supply problems with the Chief of Armored Troops and the various technical services.

The Chief of the Rear Services also exercises strong influence on the supply administrations of the technical services, armored arms, and artillery. The supply administrations are located in the second echelon of the army group or the army headquarters, which are under the over-all jurisdiction of the Chief of the Rear Services. The Chief of the Rear Services also controls all transportation of supplies.

An army group (front) Chief of the Rear Services requests air transportation from the army group Commander, who issues orders to the Commander of the subordinate air force, usually an air army.

Supplies are delivered by air to support a tank or mechanized operation when forces outdistance ground communications. Supplies delivered by air usually are limited to ammunition and fuel.

b. Army group and army supply bases, depots, other installations. Large depots for all classes of supplies, except chemical agents, are maintained for army groups (fronts). They are located at suitable railroad stations or at unloading points behind the army group's rear boundary. Unloading points may be brought forward to within 95 to 125 miles from railheads.

Unloading points normally are located in rear of switching or regulating stations from which separate rail lines run to individual armies. Guard and labor units are assigned to army group depots. The individual supply depots and their administrations function under the army group (front) Chief of the Rear Services and the Chiefs of artillery, armored troops, and technical services.

Army supply bases are located near the regulating station in the rear of each army zone. One regulating station is established for each army. Should a single railroad serve several armies, they use a common regulating station.

The Chief of an army supply base is responsible to the army Chief of the Rear Services. Representatives of the artillery, fuel, and intendance supply sections act as his assistants.

Army field depots are established at railroad stations near the army regulating station. Depots handling inflammable supplies are located 1 to $1\frac{1}{2}$ miles from other depots or station buildings.

Depots usually are provided with special branch lines or sidings. Chiefs of field depots are responsible to the Chief of the Army Supply Base and to the Chiefs of artillery, armored troops, and technical services.

The permanent fixed reserves normally maintained at army field depots are as follows:

Ammunition_____ Up to 1 unit of fire.
Rations and fodder_____ 3 to 4 rations.
Fuel and lubricants_____ Up to 2 refills.

Reserves maintained of other supplies are governed by operational requirements.

The Commander of the army also may order the accumulation of the following mobile reserves:

Ammunition_____ Up to $\frac{1}{4}$ unit of fire.
Rations and fodder_____ Up to 2 rations.
Fuel and lubricants_____ Up to 1 refill.

Personnel of Army Field Depots

(Tank army):	Adminis-trative Officers	Personnel NCO's & EM
Type of depot:		
Rations and fodder_____	8	23
Medical _____	5	7
Automotive repair parts_____	2	2
Weapons and equipment_____	19	26
Fuel and lubricants_____	9	25
Advance fuel_____	9	29
Ammunition_____	41	72
Armor repair parts_____	3	19
Army clothing_____	?	?

(Personnel strength will vary according to the number of divisions in the army.)

Branches of army field depots are located within $1\frac{1}{2}$ to 3 miles of railheads, at connecting points between rail and road nets within the army's rear area. Normally, there is one railhead for each army. Each army includes from 6 to 10 rifle divisions.

Mechanized and cavalry units normally maintain their own supply depots at the railheads of the rifle units with which they are operating. Occasionally separate railheads are organized for individual mobile, mechanized, and cavalry corps.

In fluid situations, unloading stations (temporary railheads) are established instead of railheads. Supplies are shipped to them by rail for immediate delivery to troops. Forward elements of army field depots may be established at unloading stations. Should the distance between the railhead and troops exceed 95 miles, an advance army base is organized on the boundary between army and division rear areas.

Other installations found in army group (front) and army rear areas include collection points and repair shops for weapons and armored and motor vehicles, repair shops for technical equipment, repair and maintenance installations for quartermaster supplies, collection points for captured weapons and equipment, clearing stations, evacuation hospitals, field hospitals, veterinary evacuation hospitals, veterinary field hospitals, prisoner-of-war camps, and other installations necessary to maintain army group (front) and army personnel.

4. REAR SERVICES, RIFLE CORPS LEVEL

The rifle corps has limited control of supplies. Commanders of rifle corps are not assisted by military councils. The independent supply organizations of chemical, engineer, and signal troops end at army level. Supply in lower echelons is the responsibility of technical supply units under the Chiefs of the Rear Services, who are the deputy commanders for supply.

The rifle corps Chief of the Rear Services is assisted by a Chief of Staff of the Rear Services. The Chief of Staff of the Rear Services, in turn, is assisted by a deputy for each of the following activities: organization and planning, subsistence, intendance, fuel supply, requisitioning of motor transport, and technical equipment.

The corps medical officer and the corps veterinary officer are responsible directly to the Chief of the Rear Services.

A rifle corps maintains no supply depots or rear areas, and has only limited personnel to control supply.

5. REAR SERVICES, RIFLE DIVISION LEVEL

The strength of supply organizations at division level exceeds that of corps. Unlike corps, divisions have their own supply dumps.

The rear services at division level include the following groups:

Organization and Planning. The chief of this group is also the first deputy to the division Chief of the Rear Services.

Rations and Fodder. Also is in charge of the bakery.

Intendance. Controls the clothing depot, artisans, and laundries.

Fuel and Lubricants. Controls fuel and lubricants depots.

Motor Transport. Has one motor transport company.

Technical Equipment and Supplies.

Finance. An office of the State Bank is attached.

Division Medical Officer. Controls motor ambulances, medical battalions, collecting stations, divisional medical stations, pharmacy, and a delousing station.

Division Veterinary Officer. Controls a veterinary hospital, pharmacy, and motor vehicles to transport horses.

An artillery supply group functions under the Chief of Artillery. The chief of the artillery supply group controls a weapons, ammunition, and equipment depot, an armory, and a workshop. He depends upon the Chief of the Rear Services for transportation.

a. Division supply dumps and other installations. Division supply points normally are established near the boundary between division and regimental rear areas. Their location is governed by the decision of the division Commander.

The supply point in a division rear area includes an artillery dump, an ordnance workshop, a chemical equipment dump, a fuel dump, ration and fodder dumps, an assembly point for damaged vehicles, a clothing dump with a reserve of underwear and an intendance repair shop, and an assembly point for captured matériel. These dumps function under the chiefs of individual supply agencies controlled by the division Chief of the Rear Services and the Chief of Artillery. They are usually of a temporary nature.

To support an attack, division supply points are placed approximately 6 to 7 miles from the front line. During an operation, they may be left from 12 to 18 miles behind the front line without impeding the flow of supplies. Mobile divisional artillery supply units are moved forward within 2½ or 3½ miles from the battle front. The divisional Chief of Artillery Supply usually remains with this advance unit and has at his disposal two to four trucks to carry ammunition from the main dump to the troops.

The divisional medical station deploys 3½ to 6 miles from the battle front in regimental rear areas. In offensive operations, advance mobile supply units with ammunition and food follow the troops in 6- to

Supply	Total units carried	Distribution			
		With man, horse, gun, and machine	Carried by battalion or battery train	Carried by regimental train	Carried by division transport
Rifle Division:					
Ammunition (units of fire)	1. 5	0.5	0.25	0. 25	0.5.
Fuel (refills)	2. 0	1		. 5	0.5.
Food (rations)	5	1 (NZ)	1 (in kitchens)	1	2.
Grain feed (rations)	4	1–3 ¹		¹ 2	1.
Bulk feed (rations)	4	1–2–3 ²		2–³ 1	1.
GHQ Units:					
Ammunition (units of fire)	1. 5	0.5	0.5		In artillery train 0.5.
Fuel (refills)	2	1	0.5	. 5	
Food (rations)	4	1	1	2	

¹ For mounts, artillery and other draft animals—one ration; for remainder—three rations (after hauling). In the regiment's supply column—two rations for mounts, artillery and other draft animals.

² For mounts, artillery and other draft animals—one ration; for machine-gun-cart teams, medical, signal, and field kitchen animals—two rations; for remainder—three rations (after hauling).

³ For mounts, artillery and other draft animals—two rations. For machine-gun-cart teams, medical, signal, and field kitchen animals—one ration.

Figure 1. Basic supplies carried by a rifle division.

9-mile bounds, having at their disposal about 25 percent of all divisional motor vehicles. Dumps of the main supply point are moved forward in bounds of 9 to 15 miles.

Security of dumps at the division supply point usually is the responsibility of the motor transport company Commander and is provided by the personnel of the motor transport company and a special labor unit which performs loading and unloading operations at the main and advance supply points. The Chief of Artillery Supply, or an especially designated officer, is responsible for security of advance mobile supply units.

During rapidly developing offensive operations, division supply dumps are not deployed, but front-line troops are supplied by combined army and division transport. In mountain operations, division service areas are usually divided and separate supply points are established for units in isolated areas.

Each division normally is provided with five rations of food and fodder, two refills of fuel, and one and one-half units of fire for all subordinate and attached units (fig. 1).

6. REAR SERVICES, RIFLE REGIMENT LEVEL

The Commander of a rifle regiment is assisted by a deputy for supply, who controls the following supply units:

Rations and fodder (with ration dumps).
Intendance.
Technical equipment and supplies.
Horse-drawn transport company.
Finance officer (with State Bank agent).
Regimental medical officer.
Regimental veterinary officer.

The Chief of Artillery provides the rifle regiment with arms and ammunition from the artillery dump through the Chief of Artillery Supply. Supply transportation is requisitioned from the regimental Commander's deputy for supply.

Regimental ammunition dumps are located in the regimental rear area, 3 to 6 miles from the front line. Rations and fodder supply units remain near the rear boundary of the regimental rear area.

When a regiment is extended in mountain operations, regimental ammunition dumps usually are not deployed. Ammunition is delivered directly to battalion dumps by division transportation.

When companies become extended, the battalion ammunition supply section is divided among the companies and company ammunition dumps are serviced by regimental transportation.

7. REAR SERVICES OF MOBILE FORMATIONS

Mobile formations have no rear areas of their own. Their supply installations are established within the rear areas of the infantry formations they are supporting.

In addition to normal supply points, mobile corps and brigades are provided with service installations which include assembly points and mobile workshops for damaged vehicles, first aid stations, and a field bakery.

Mobile formations also have special mobile re-supply and evacuation groups. These groups are provided with special supply and evacuation equipment, such as recovery tanks and tractors and armored ammunition and fuel vehicles.

317

Section II. SUPPLY

1. GENERAL

The marked elasticity of the Russian supply system permits it to meet the rapidly changing requirements of mobile warfare. Although armies and divisions do have motor transport, it is impossible to define a definite constant range of division or army transport activity.

Army and division supply columns may be used separately to transport specific supply items, or they may be combined to expedite the uninterrupted delivery from distant depots to front-line units. The latter is especially true during offensive operations. This system has met transportation requirements satisfactorily despite persistent shortages of transport equipment.

Red Army supply is based on the principle of unit distribution, of "delivery forward," from the main supply administrations of the Chief of the Rear Services down to rifle battalions.

Rifle corps, being primarily tactical units, are not included in the chain of supply. No transportation is assigned to them for supply purposes.

2. REAR AREAS AND INSTALLATIONS

Headquarters, personnel, and supply installations servicing a unit are located in the rear area of that unit. The rear area of a regiment extends from 5 to 7 miles in depth; a division rear area from 18 to 22 miles. Combined regimental and division rear areas extend approximately 22 to 28 miles in depth. Army rear areas extend in depth from 95 to 125 miles, and the rear areas of army groups (fronts) extend from 185 to 250 miles in depth (fig. 2).

Armored, mechanized, and cavalry units establish their supply lines and installations within the rear areas of infantry formations (fig. 3).

Service organizations of rifle units and formations usually are established in rear of the combat line as follows (see fig. 4):

Organization:	Distance from combat line (miles)
Regimental ammunition dumps and artillery workshops.	3 to 6.
Regimental artillery supply dumps	3 to 6.
Regimental medical stations	1.5 to 3.
Regimental train, second echelon (including rations and fodder supply unit, transportation company equipment, veterinary aid station, and intendance workshop).	5 to 7.5.

Organization—Continued.	Distance from combat line (miles)
Division supply point	6 to 9.5.
Division medical station	3.5 to 6.
Field bakery and division veterinary hospital.	One day's march.
Division artillery supply installations.	In regimental rear area near boundary of division rear area.

There are two echelons of regimental and division services. The first echelon of regimental services includes ammunition supply and medical installations. The second echelon includes transport for rations, fodder, fuel, and other supplies, a veterinary aid station, and a quartermaster workshop.

The first echelon of division services is the division supply point (fig. 5). The second echelon includes a field bakery and a veterinary hospital. Usually, the division medical station is located in a regimental rear area along the axis of advance.

This pattern for the organization of rear areas may vary according to the dictates of operational requirements, terrain, weather conditions, and available transportation.

Rear area services of mobile units follow the above pattern down to brigade level. Brigade rear services also are divided into two echelons, but there are no organized rear areas for units or battle groups. Supplies from the brigade supply point are delivered directly to front-line units by armored supply vehicles.

Advance observation and communication posts for mobile formations are established from 1,000 to 1,500 yards in rear of the combat units. Special combat, supply, and evacuation groups are established from 500 to 800 yards in rear of the advance observation posts.

The advance echelons of the rear services, with collection points for damaged combat vehicles, are established from 2 to 2½ miles in rear of the re-supply and evacuation groups (fig. 3).

3. SUPPLY CHANNELS TO BATTLE FRONT

a. Factories to army group. The main administrations of individual classes of supplies, the Chief of Artillery, the Chief of Armored Troops, and the chiefs of the technical services in the Peoples' Commissariat of Armed Forces estimate their supply requirements as determined by demands sent through channels by lower echelons. Requirements must be approved by the Commissar of Defense.

318

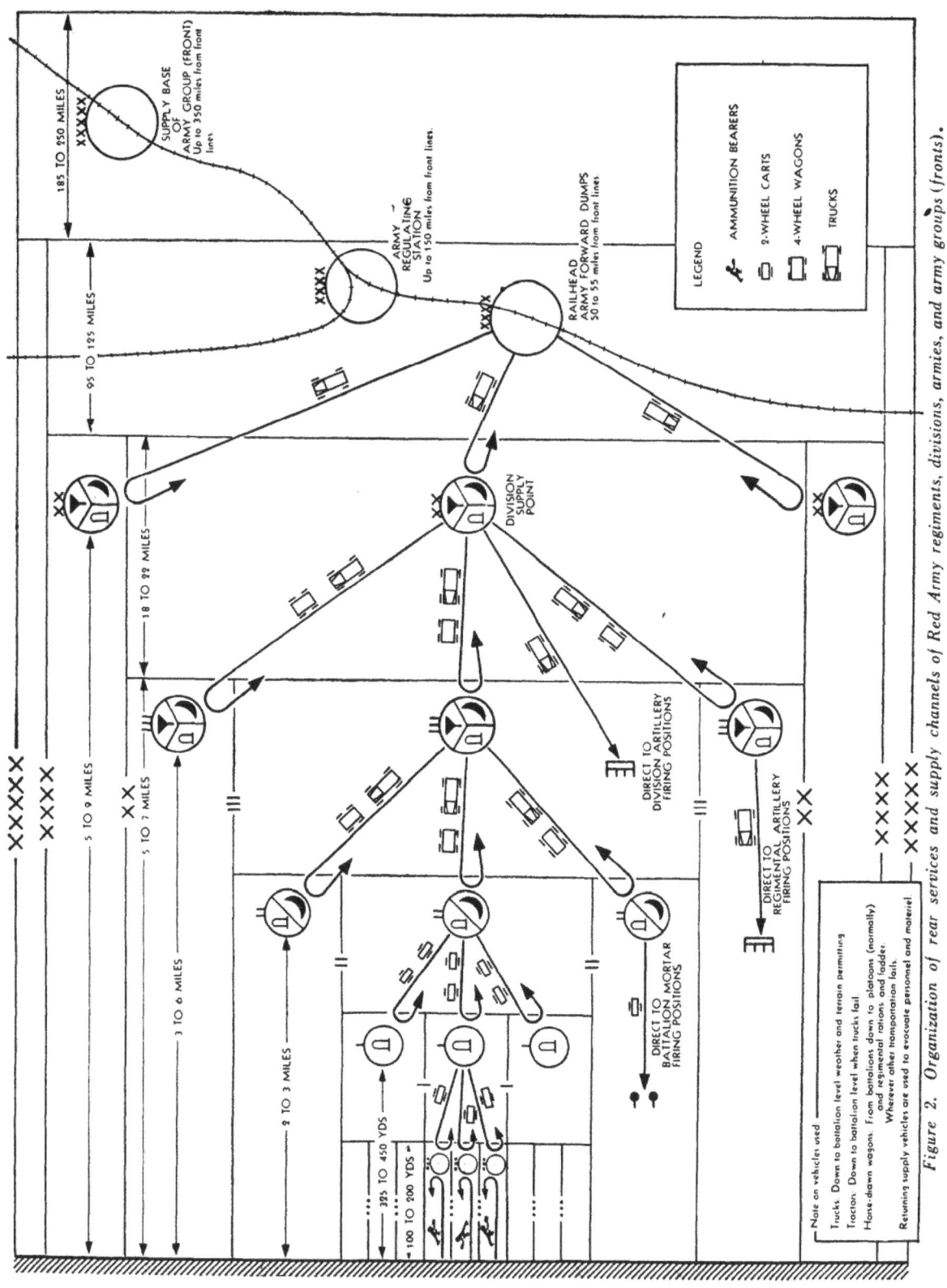

Figure 2. Organization of rear services and supply channels of Red Army regiments, divisions, armies, and army groups (fronts).

319

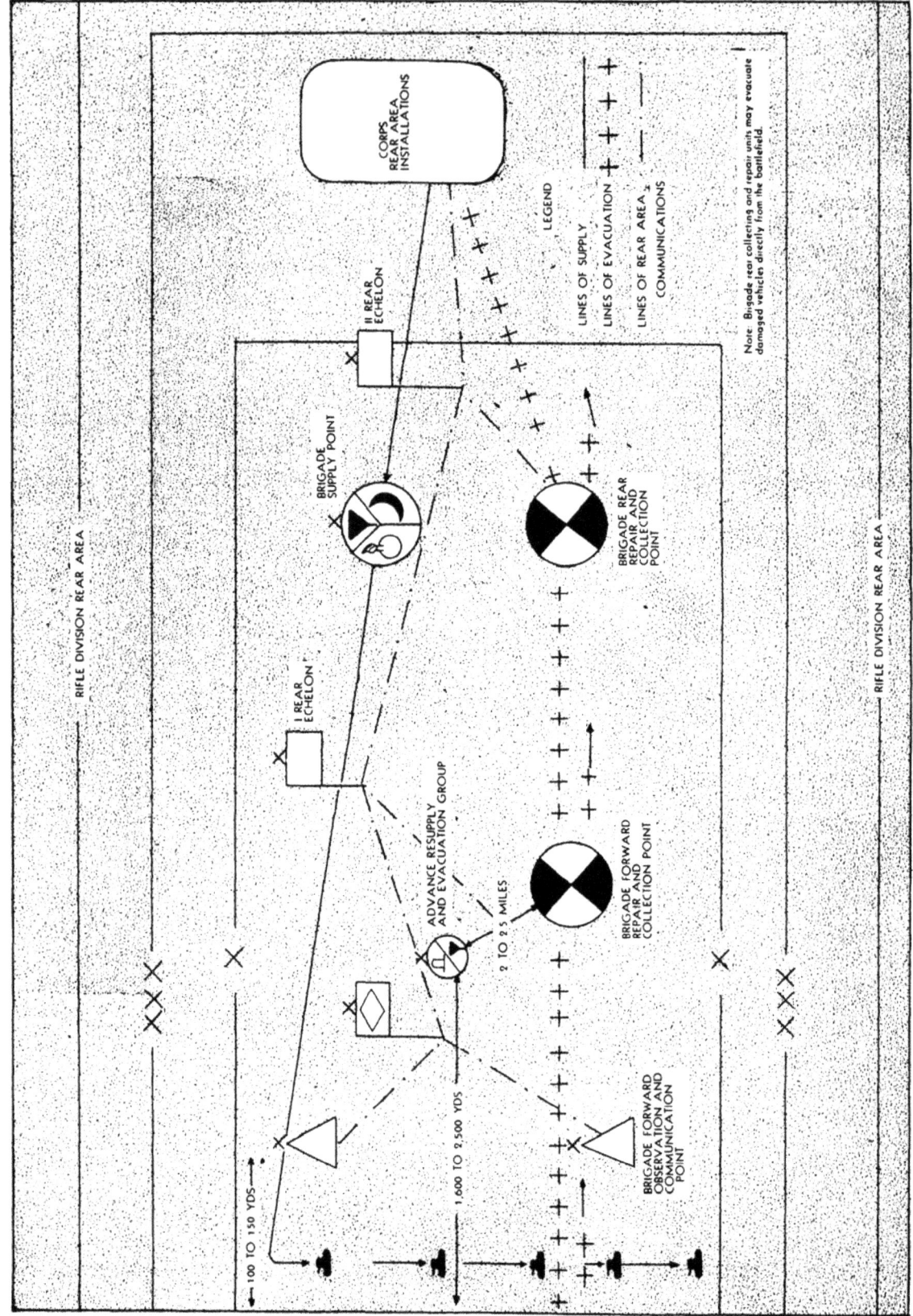

Figure 3. Channels of supply and evacuation for armored and mechanized units.

Installations	Distance from the front (miles)		Time (minutes)		Personnel
	On the offensive	On the defensive	Deployment	Reassembly	
Company ammunition dump.	0.3	0.3	5	3	Ammunition section of supply platoon of rifle battalion.
Battalion ammunition dump.	1 to 2	Up to 3	15	5	
Battalion quartermaster dump.	2 to 3	Up to 3	10 to 20	5	Quartermaster section of supply platoon of rifle battalion.
Battalion medical station	0.3 to 0.6	1.5	15	5	Battalion medical unit.
Regimental ammunition dump.[1]	3 to 3.5	5 to 6	45	20	First platoon of regimental transport company.
Regimental medical aid station.	1 to 3	2.5 to 3	45	20	Regimental medical unit.
Regimental veterinary hospital.	5 to 7.5	5 to 7.5	45	20	
Advance veterinary station.	1.8 to 4.3	1.8 to 4.3	15	10	Regimental veterinary hospital.
Second echelon of a regimental supply column.[2]	4.9 to 7.5	4.9 to 7.5	30	60	Second platoon of regimental transportation company.
Division supply point [3]	5 to 6	7.5 to 9	2.5 to 3 hrs		Division transport company.
Divisional veterinary hospital.	12 to 15.5	12 to 15.5	1 hr. 15 min	40	
Divisional field bakery.[4]	8.3 to 12	Up to 18	In summer 10 hrs. 5 hrs.[5] In winter 24 hrs. 3 hrs.[5]		

[1] The ammunition supply platoon of the regimental artillery and the ordnance workshop of the rifle regiment operates at the regimental ammunition dump.
[2] Includes quartermaster workshop.
[3] Includes ammunition dump, rations, fuel dump, collection point for damaged vehicles, and workshops.
[4] Bread ready for delivery 6 hours after deployment.
[5] Includes cooling of oven. Reassembly of bakery proper requires 1½ hours.

Figure 4. Time required for the deployment and reassembly of rear area installations.

Production orders then are issued to industrial commissariats, which distribute the orders to factories. Agents of individual supply administrations of the Peoples' Commissariat of Armed Forces at the various factories receive and check the supplies. They then direct them either to central depots of the Peoples' Commissariat of Armed Forces or to supply depots of military districts and supply bases of the army groups (fronts).

b. Army group to army bases and field depots. Supplies are shipped from army group (front) to army supply bases and field depots by rail. Chiefs of army transportation of the army groups are responsible that supplies are forwarded from the army group base to the army regulating station.

Regulating stations are important links in the supply chain. Supplies arriving from rear bases are distributed and forwarded toward the combat front from the regulating station. Wounded men and captured and damaged equipment are evacuated through them to the rear.

Only large railroad stations or groups of railroad stations are used as regulating stations. The commandants of these stations function under the army group Chief of Transportation, but also are responsible to the chief of the army base.

Part of the motor transport pool of the army group is held near the regulating station for emergency use. Station commandants share with railroad personnel responsibility for timely dispatching of trains and avoidance of delays. Commandants also are responsible for antiaircraft security and unloading by special labor units detailed for handling cargoes.

Regulating stations are linked with railroad sections of the army rear area, which are under the control of the army Chief of Transportation. Security of railroad sections in the army rear area is the responsibility of the railroad commandants appointed by the army Chief of Transportation.

A number of railheads are established in the rear area of an army. They are located near the boundaries of division rear areas. An air force railhead is established near the boundary of the army group (front) rear area. Army group and army Chiefs of Army Transportation are responsible for the shipment to air force railheads of supplies sent to regulating stations by order of the Chief of Air Force Supplies.

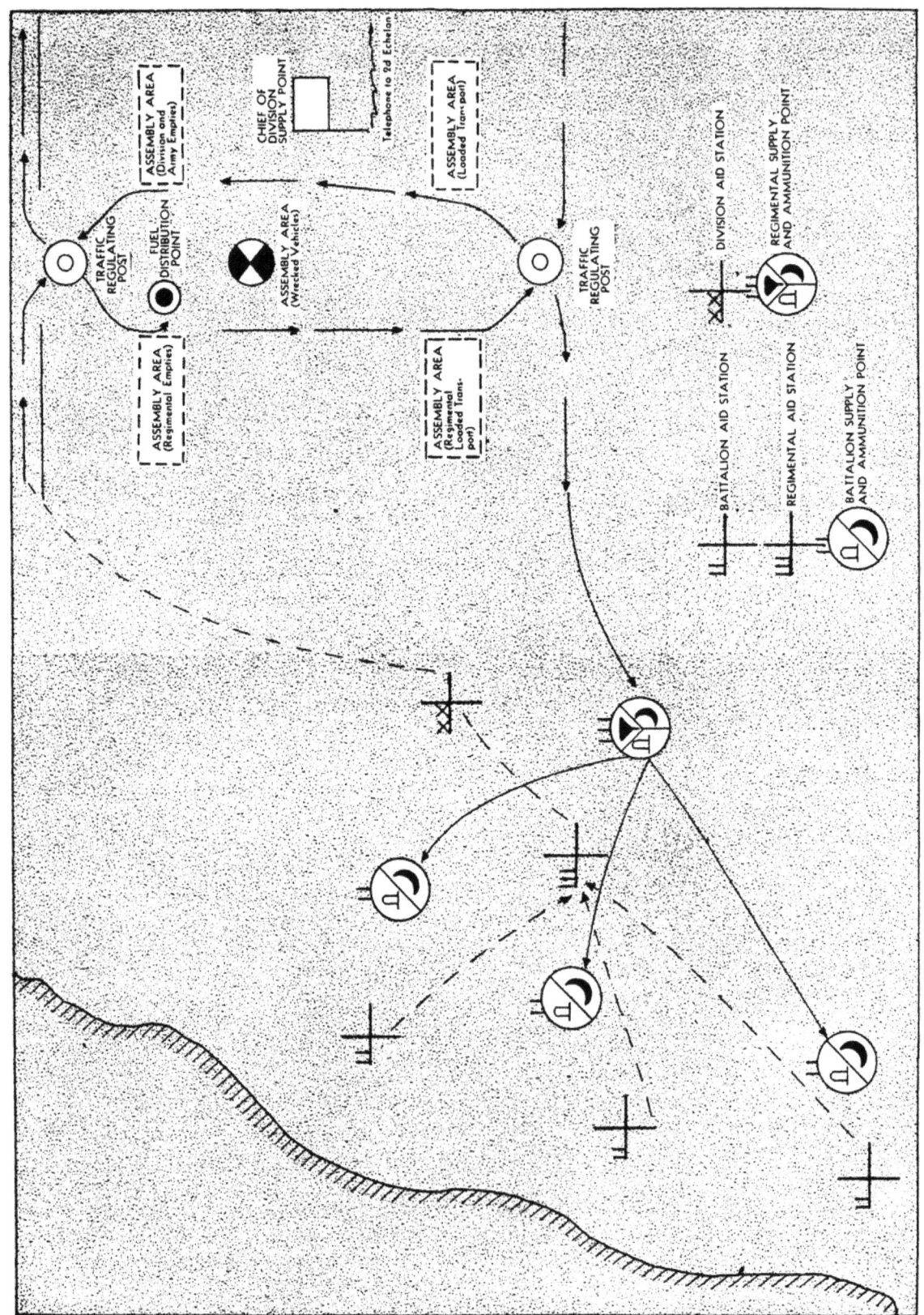

Figure 5. Organization of division supply point.

Should the railroad section's capacity prove insufficient, army group (front) or army chiefs of army transportation may order the shipment of supplies by truck.

Army supply bases and field depots located near regulating stations are provided with railroad sidings. A regulating station and an army supply base cover approximately 4 square miles. They contain individual supply depots, large repair shops, field and veterinary hospitals, and collecting points for damaged motor vehicles.

The regulating station is controlled by the chief of the army base, who functions under the army Chief of the Rear Services and who is responsible for the organization and security of loading and unloading operations. He provides assembly areas for waiting columns, determines routes of departure and arrival, and schedules loading and unloading operations.

c. Army supply base to front line. Motor transport battalions and companies move supplies forward from army supply bases.

Supply and evacuation roads to division supply points are constructed as necessary. These roads are divided into sections, each in charge of a military commandant. Road sections between army supply bases and division supply points are from 15 to 30 miles long. Should the distance between front-line units and the railhead exceed 95 miles, army truckheads are established on the boundary between army and division rear areas.

Should a railroad be rebuilt in a forward section during an advance, individual divisions are supplied by shuttle trains. Trucks are then used to move the supplies forward from these stations. Army as well as division trucks may be used.

Daily shipments of ammunition, food, and fodder are presumably forwarded to division supply points by army transport columns. These items constitute approximately 70 percent of the daily supply requirements. Division transport then carries ammunition to regimental ammunition dumps or directly to firing positions. Special artillery transport columns forward ammunition for artillery and technical units.

Normally, division transport carries food, fodder, and fuel to regimental second echelon supply points. However, horse-drawn columns of rifle regiments sometimes draw these items at the division supply points.

Fuel for divisions is supplied by armies. However, all motorized units have small tank-truck columns which draw their fuel at army depots.

All other supplies such as clothing, equipment for technical services, post exchange goods, and medical supplies are not furnished to division supply dumps. They are drawn at army depots by division and tank or mechanized corps transport columns.

This system reduces the volume of supplies handled by small units and, at the same time, limits the demand for army transport by restricting requirements to essential needs.

Attached artillery units use their own transport to draw all supplies from special depots located near division supply points. These supply points are serviced in the same manner as division supply points.

When the requirements of individual units during major operations cannot be satisfied by their own transport, combined division and army transport together with that of lower units transport ammunition directly from army supply bases to firing positions and other supplies directly to regimental supply points.

Tank and mechanized corps are equipped with transport columns capable of operating over distances up to 60 miles.

Supply of mobile units in break-through operations usually is effected by bulk employment of the army group motor transport reserve. Truckheads are established along the axis of advance in addition to the supply points provided for tank and mechanized corps. The distance between brigade supply points and the most advanced truckheads does not exceed 20 miles. The distance between truckheads does not exceed the length of a daily round trip for supply vehicles—from 40 to 50 miles. Truckheads maintain dumps for all classes of supplies.

Mobile supply reserves at corps command posts service mobile units which outdistance their supply lines or are cut off from them. These supply reserves contain only the most essential battle supplies, principally ammunition and fuel. They are handled by a forward supply staff detailed by the Chief of the Rear Services.

During mountain operations, division and attached army transport is used in the divisional rear area. Regimental transport may be reinforced by pack animals and porter commands of local civilians or enlisted men.

In mountainous terrain, the Red Army strives to guarantee that all sections of the supply chain are of equal capability in order to avoid bottlenecks in the movement of supplies. When sections of the supply chain become over-extended, it recommends the establishment of long round trips to avoid reloading operations.

4. ARTILLERY SUPPLY

In addition to meeting artillery requirements, the Administration of Artillery Supply provides weapons and ammunition for all units of the Red Army. The Administration is also charged with weapons repair and storage of ammunition. There is a Chief of Artillery Supply for each echelon down to and including the rifle regiment.

Estimated requirements of weapons and ammunition are based on General Staff plans for future operations. Preparations are then made to enable army group (front) and army rear services to supply divisions and forward units with the required supplies.

The Administration was relieved of the responsibility for battlefield recovery of weapons in April 1944. This responsibility was transferred to a special captured weapons and recovery service. The Administration of Artillery Supply is, however, responsible for the recovery and evacuation of cartridge cases.

The Chief of Artillery Supply at rifle regiment level is assisted by one clerk, two armorers, and one to two men in the artillery supply dump.

The Chief of Artillery Supply at rifle division level has one assistant, one clerk, and several men in supply dumps and workshops. His responsibilities include supply of ammunition to division units, replacement of weapons and associated equipment, storage and distribution of artillery supplies, coordination of ammunition transportation with the motor transport company, maintenance of daily records of ammunition expenditure and reserves, and evacuation of cartridge cases and weapons requiring repair.

When a major operation is projected, the Chief of Artillery Supply at division level, the Chief of Artillery, and the Chief of Staff prepare an estimate of weapons and ammunition requirements, prepare an ammunition supply plan, and issue an artillery supply order.

Rifle corps have a control agency headed by a Chief of Artillery Supply. He is assisted by a clerk, and receives copies of reports and requisitions submitted to the army supply division by divisional chiefs of artillery supply.

At army level, there is a division for artillery supply under the Chief of Artillery. The office of the Chief of Artillery Supply includes an inspection team of two artillery majors who inspect supply depots in subordinate echelons. The Chief of Artillery also controls an artillery supply depot and a repair shop. His responsibilities parallel those of the Chief of Artillery Supply at division level.

The artillery supply division at army level includes five groups:

Group One (Transportation) receives supplies, supervises storage, and issues ammunition. Transport is assigned to the transportation group by the army Chief of the Rear Services (motor transport division).

Group Two (Ammunition) receives daily reports from divisions on ammunition reserves. These reports are indorsed by the Chief of Artillery Supply, who indicates the amounts required for each division. The ammunition group provides division supply officers with a receiving certificate, which is submitted to the transportation group. The transportation group, in cooperation with the motor transport division of the Chief of the Rear Services, assigns the necessary transport. The depot then issues the required ammunition on the basis of the receiving certificate.

Group Three (Weapons and Equipment) functions similarly to the ammunition group.

Group Four (Repair) is charged with weapons repair.

Group Five (Prime mover) maintains, stores, and delivers prime movers.

When no special operations are projected, artillery ammunition depots maintain a supply of two to three units of fire (fig. 6). A day's consumption averages from .5 to .6 units of fire.

The Administration of Artillery Supply at army group (front) level follows the same basic pattern. The transportation group of the Administration depends upon the army group Chief of Army Transportation for rail transportation.

The prime mover group at army group (front) level is believed to be controlled by the Red Army Supply Administration of Tanks and Mechanized Troops instead of the Administration of Artillery Supply. This is the highest organization for the distribution of combat vehicles.

324

Weapon	Unit of fire		Rounds carried by—				
	Rounds per weapon	Weight (short tons)	Emergency reserve with weapons*	Btry, Co	Bn	Regt, Brig	Div; Tk, Mecz, Cav Corps
7.62-mm R	100	0.038	10	70	15	15	50
7.62-mm SAR	120	.046	....	90	15	15	60
7.62-mm SMG	300	.044	30	210	45	45	150
7.62-mm LMG	800	.27	98	98	490	212	400
7.62-mm HvMG	2,500	.1	500	1,500	500	500	1,250
7.62-mm Tk MG	3,000	.1	120	1,500	....	....	4,500
12.7-mm AAMG	2,000	.37	170	1,000	..	1,000	1,000
14.5-mm ATR	120	.16	10	50	35	35	60
50-mm Mort	120	.19	10	56	28	36	60
82-mm Mort	120	.51	10	40	40	40	60
120-mm Mort	80	2.2	5	20	30	30	48
160-mm Mort	...	...	...	...	...	...	...
37-mm AA G	200		15		115	85	100
45-mm AT G	200	.7	50	50	100	50	100
57-mm AT G	200	.69	25	50	100	50	100
76-mm How	140	.79	16	16	56	68	70
76-mm G	140	1.79	16	24	88	28	70
85-mm AA G	150	3.39	15		90	60	75
85-mm G (Tk)	48	1.1	6	48	....	....	48
100-mm G	...	...	...	...	...	...	...
122-mm How	80	2.99	8		36	36	40
122-mm G	80	3.66	6		40	40	40
152-mm How	60	6.33	4		30	30	30
152-mm G/How	60	3.95	4		34	26	30
152-mm G	40	3.56	4		22	18	20
203-mm How	40	5.85	2		22	18	20

*Included in total.

Figure 6. Units of fire for principal weapons and distribution of ammunition

Weapons and ammunition depots of the Peoples' Commissariat of Armed Forces are controlled by the Red Army Administration of Artillery Supply (fig. 7).

a. Army artillery supply during offense. The army Chief of Artillery Supply supervises the expenditure of ammunition and is responsible for the distribution of supplies available to him. He requisitions ammunition for projected operations on the basis of instructions and estimates received from the Army Chief of Artillery. In his requisition, he designates the units of fire and number of rounds required for each type of weapon, the permanent reserve which must be maintained at the end of the operation, amounts required to bring present stocks up to estimated requirements, and the schedule for delivery from army group (front) to army supply installations.

When his requisitions are changed at army group headquarters, the army Chief of Artillery revises his plan in accordance with the available ammunition supply.

The supply plan of the army Chief of Artillery Supply includes:

Ammunition requirements of individual units at beginning of operation.

Rate of ammunition expenditure for various phases of the operation.

Priority of units for ammunition supply.

The army Chief of Artillery Supply organizes the work of artillery supply agencies, issues instructions for the checking of weapons, prepares the necessary repair and evacuation facilities, and coordinates ammunition and damaged weapons evacuation transportation with the army Chief of Transportation.

Although the Chief of Artillery Supply is responsible for the delivery of ammunition to the troops, the agencies of the Chief of the Rear Services are responsible for furnishing the necessary transport.

The Chief of Artillery Supply is always informed of the situation at the battle front, the location of division supply points, and the expenditure and reserves of ammunition in the army. Ammunition expenditure is rigidly limited to the daily average planned for the operation.

The Soviets have prepared estimates of the ammunition requirements of an army at the beginning of an offensive operation (fig. 8). This estimate is considered sufficient to neutralize the entire tactical depth of the enemy's first defensive zone. To neutralize the second defensive zone, or to provide for a delay in the operation, it is estimated that ammunition expenditures will be increased 1 to 1½ times.

Ammunition issued to troops normally includes ammunition for the artillery preparation, ammunition for the following day, and the reserve carried by units (fig. 9). The remainder of the ammunition required for the operation is concentrated at the army supply base. The Soviets believe that the accumulation of large ammunition reserves at firing positions stimulates unnecessary expenditure.

Red Army doctrine emphasizes the necessity for close coordination of transportation and ammunition supply. The responsibility of the rear services normally is limited to the assigning of transport and general dispositions. The actual shipment of ammunition is handled by the artillery supply service. Ammunition supply normally requires up to 80 percent of an army's motor transport.

The Chief of Artillery Supply requisitions motor transport for ammunition delivery on specified days. He designates loading and delivery points and controls transportation through control officers stationed at designated control points.

The rear services are responsible for the timely arrival of transport at the loading points, supervise loading and unloading, prepare a march graph, and

325

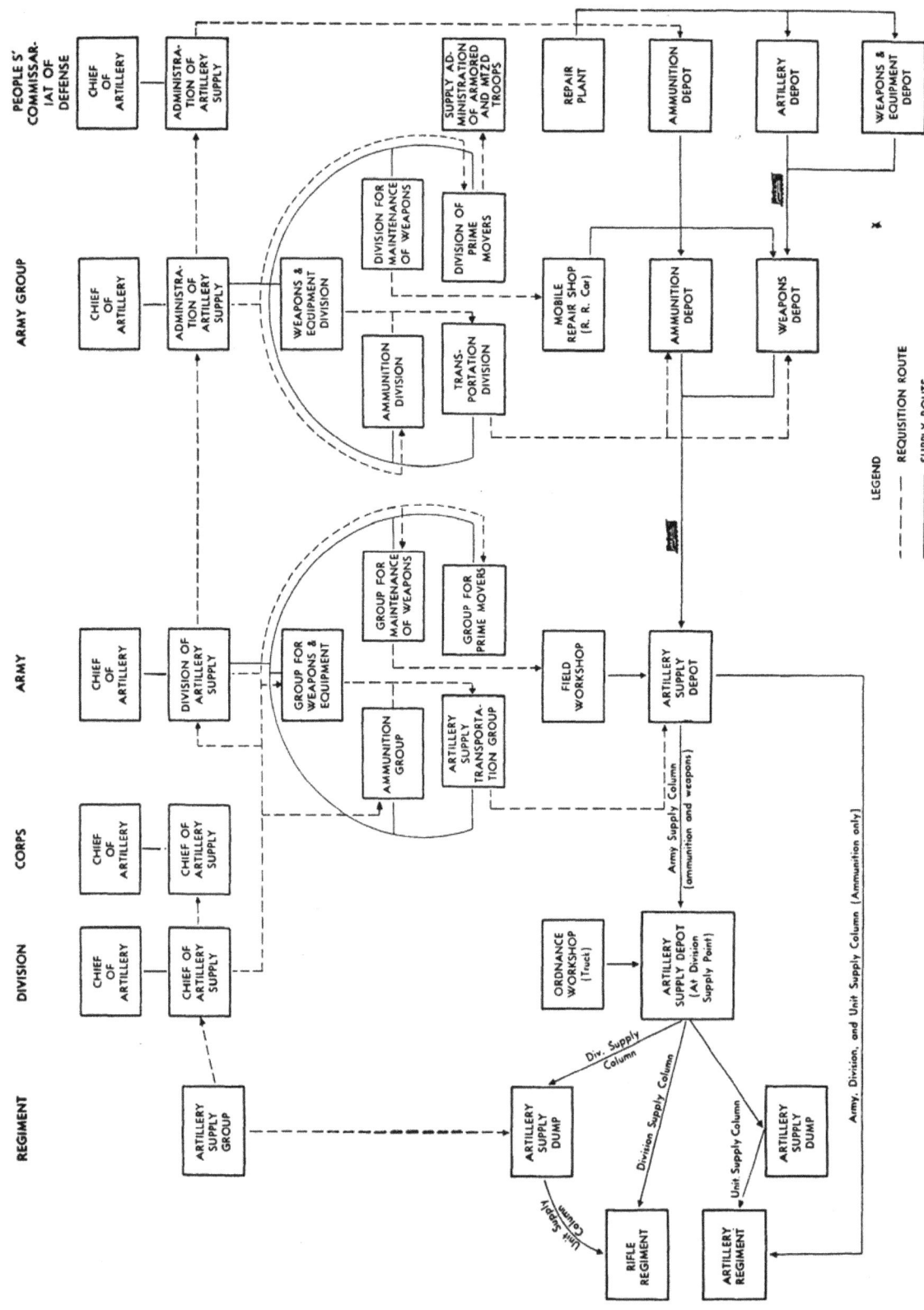

Figure 7. Channels of requisition and supply of artillery arm of the Red Army.

Type of ammunition	Units of fire		
	Operational requirements	Permanent reserve	Total
82-mm mortar	2.0	0.5	2.5 to 3.0
120-mm mortar	3.5	1.0	4.5 to 5.0
76-mm regimental and division artillery	3.0	1.0	4.0 to 4.5
122-mm howitzer and higher calibers	4.0	1.0	5.0 to 5.5
Rifle	.75	.75	1.5 to 1.75
Pistol	1.0	.75	1.75 to 2.00

Figure 8. Ammunition required by an army at the beginning of an offensive operation

Type of ammunition	Units of fire		
	At firing position	At division supply point	In advance ammunition dump
82-mm mortar	1.0	0.5	0.5
120-mm mortar	1.5	.75	.5
76-mm regimental and division artillery	1.5 to 1.75	.5	.5
122-mm howitzer and gun	2.0	.75	.75
152-mm howitzer and gun	2.0	.75	.75

Figure 9. Distribution of ammunition at the beginning of an offensive operation.

provide for repair facilities, refueling facilities, and timely return of vehicles.

When necessary, ammunition is delivered by army transport direct to division supply points or to the firing positions. These shipments are accompanied by guides from the combat units.

During offensive operations, the Chief of Artillery Supply usually remains at the first echelon command post. He is accompanied by the transportation and ammunition groups of his staff. The weapons, maintenance, and prime mover groups of his staff remain with the second echelon.

5. FUEL AND LUBRICANTS SUPPLY

Because day-to-day fuel and lubricants requirements of air forces and tank and mechanized units fluctuate markedly, the principle of unit distribution of fuel and lubricants is limited to rifle divisions (figs. 10 and 11).

Fuel and lubricants are delivered to division dumps by army supply agencies. Armored, mechanized, and motorized units are provided with their own fuel and lubricants vehicles, which draw from army fuel depots.

There is a shortage of railroad tank cars in the U. S. S. R. Railroad fuel bases seldom are used. Normally, fuel delivered to army supply bases is stored in barrels or in large, transportable containers.

6. RATIONS AND FODDER SUPPLY

The utilization of local resources to supply rations and fodder is widely practiced by the Red Army. Supply bases of the Peoples' Commissariat of Armed Forces provide army group (front) supply bases

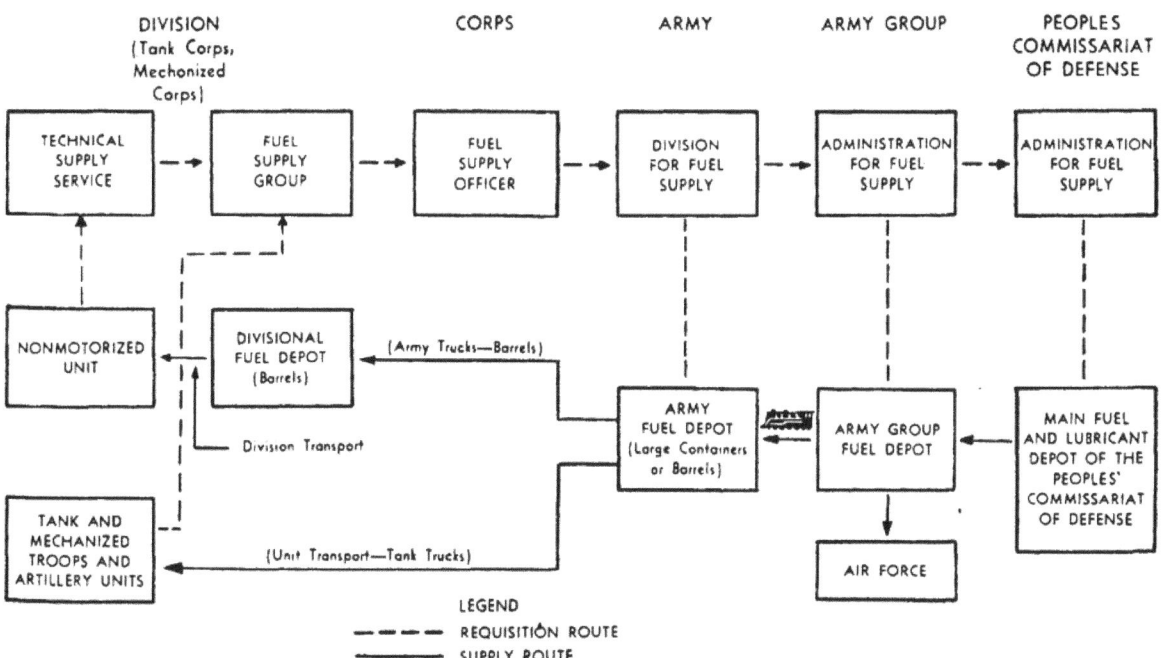

Figure 10. Channels of requisition and supply of fuel and lubricants in the Red Army.

Vehicle	Tank capacity		Fuel consumption (gallons per 100 miles)
	Gallons	Pounds	
Motorcycle with side-car	5.2	33	3.6
Motorcycle without side-car	3.7	24	3.2
Automobile pick-up	15.8	99	6.4
Automobile GAZ-A	10.5	66	5.4
Automobile GAZ-2A	11.6	72	9.4
Automobile GAZ-3A	11.6	72	12.9
Automobile ZiS-5	15.8	99	15.1
Automobile M-1	15.8	99	6.4
Automobile ZiS-101	22.4	141	11.6
Tractor STZ-5	47.5	329	7.6
Tractor CHTZ-65	74.2	580	7.6
Tractor *Voroshilovets*	145.2	965	14.1

NOTE.—Fuel consumption is based on movement over average dirt roads during dry summer weather. Consumption will be increased 1.2 times in mountainous terrain, 1.3 times in winter operations, and 1.4 times in operations over sandy terrain. Consumption of lubricants equals one-tenth the consumption of fuel.

Figure 11. Fuel capacity and consumption of Red Army motor vehicles.

only with unperishable staple commodities such as flour, canned foods, millet, sugar, etc.

Meat, vegetables, butter, and hay are obtained locally by the agricultural products procurement group of the army rations and fodder division. These supplies are sent to divisional food supply dumps.

Product	Allowance	
	Pounds	Ounces
Bread:		
October–March	1	15.5
April–September	1	12
Wheat flour of second grade		.7
Grits		4.9
Macaroni, vermicelli		1.05
Meat		5.25
Fish		3.5
Deodorized soy flour		.52
Fats		1.05
Vegetable oil		.7
Sugar		1.22
Tea		.035
Salt		1.05
Vegetables (regimental and division trains carry 5.74 ounces of grits instead of vegetables)	1	12.7
Tomato paste		.21
Bay leaf, pepper, vinegar, mustard powder		.098
Tobacco		.7
Totals:		
Winter:		
With vegetables	5	1.2
Without vegetables	3	10.24
Summer:		
With vegetables	4	13.7
Without vegetables	3	6.74
Additional monthly rations:		
Soap for toilet needs		7.0
Matches (boxes)		.105
Cigarette paper (booklets)		245

Figure 12. Break-down of individual ration.

Product	Quantity
	Ounces
Biscuits	17.5
Concentrates for the first course [1]	2.62
Concentrates for the second course	7.0
Smoked sausage [2]	3.5
Sugar	1.2
Tea	.07
Salt	.35
Total	32.24

[1] Instead of the two concentrates, 5.25 ounces biscuit and 2.80 ounces lard may be issued.
[2] Instead of smoke sausage, one of the following may be issued: 2.45 ounces hard smoke sausage, 2.45 ounces bacon, 2.45 ounces lard, or 5.25 ounces fish.

Figure 13. Break-down of individual emergency ration.

To economize transportation, grain is obtained from local collective farms whenever possible. Part of such grain is ground by hastily constructed division field mills and the flour furnished to division bakeries. Special military slaughter services are not organized in the field, but cattle procured locally are brought direct to regimental kitchens.

When a front becomes stabilized, the group for agriculture of the army ration and fodder division engages in farming activities and sends its products to the divisions.

Several types of rations are issued in the Red Army (figs. 12, 13, 14, and 15). Channels are prescribed for requisitions and routing of rations and fodder (fig. 16).

Post exchange services cooperate with the rations and fodder services, but are subordinate to the Peoples' Commissariat of Trade. Items stocked by the most important field exchanges include tooth paste, pocket mirrors, needles and thread, paper, and pencils. They also have tearooms and barber shops. Field exchanges are organized in the rear areas down to division level.

7. WATER SUPPLY

The organization of water supply in the field is based on plans carefully prepared by engineer units

Type of horse	Oats		Hay		Salt (ounces)	Total	
	Pounds	Ounces	Pounds	Ounces		Pounds	Ounces
Cavalry	8	12	10	15	0.5	19	11.5
Artillery	13	2	12	11	.5	25	13.5
Supply	7	10.5	13	2	.5	20	13

Figure 14. Break-down of individual fodder ration.

328

Requirements	Normal (gallons)	Reduced (gallons)	Minimum (gallons)
Individual:			
Drinking	0.9	0.7	
Cooking	1.0	.4	
Dish washing	.5	.1	
Washing face and hands	1.4	.1	
Laundry and shower	2.5		
Total	6.3	1.3	
Animal:			
Horse	12.3	7.4	5.0
Mule	5.4	3.4	2.5
Camel	14.8	7.4	5.0
Large livestock	12.3	7.4	3.7
Small livestock	2.5	1.3	.738
Dog	.7	.5	.5
Mechanical (one refill):			
Machine gun	.6		
Radiator:			
Automobile GAZ	3.0		
Automobile ZiS–5	6.4		
Tractor	11 to 17		
Tank	22		

Figure 15. Daily water requirements.

in cooperation with the medical service prior to offensive operations. A water supply plan includes the survey, a water supply chart, and a work schedule.

The survey establishes the location of existing water resources in the proposed zone of operations. The water supply chart organizes the basic decision for the utilization of existing wells, construction of new wells, deployment of water supply stations, etc.

The work schedule designates water points and other installations, specifies troop units assigned to water points, shows daily water requirements in cubic meters, daily capacities of water points, required work, available labor, available transport, necessary materials and equipment, schedule of operation, and a schedule of available water for various phases of the operation.

Special hydro-technical companies or combat engineers organize water supply points in the rear of army groups and armies. Water supply points for all other units, formations, and rear area establishments are organized by engineer units or by the troops themselves in accordance with plans prepared by the responsible Commander.

Daily water requirements are carefully computed (fig. 15).

The following table contains data on army water points:

	Regimental water point	Division water point	Army water point
Capacity per 24 hours (cubic feet)	140 to 280	210 to 700	350 to 3,500
Time required for deployment (hours)	1 to 4	4 to 12	6 to 72
Labor (men)	4 to 10	10 to 30	10 to 60
Number of water points in army zone	[1]25 to 35	7 to 10	4 to 8

[1] Bn points not included.

8. MOTOR AND ARMORED VEHICLE SUPPLY

Distribution and replacement of motor transport and armored vehicles in the Peoples' Commissariat of Armed Forces is the responsibility of the Main Administration of Motor Transport and the Main Administration of Armored Equipment. The armored equipment administration also handles prime movers and personnel carriers (fig. 17).

Transport and combat vehicles are handled at army group (front) and army levels by the Motor Transport Service, the Armored Equipment Service, and the Artillery Supply Service. The Motor Transport Service handles transport vehicles through the Administration of Motor Transport at army group (front) level and through the Motor Transport Division at army level. The Armored Equipment Supply Service handles combat vehicles and personnel carriers through the Supply Administration for armored troops at army group (front) level and through the Supply Division for armored troops at army level. The Artillery Supply Service handles artillery prime movers through the Prime Mover Division of the Administration of Artillery Supply at army group (front) level and the Artillery Supply Section at army level.

Tanks are delivered to their crews at the factories. They are shipped by rail to the army railhead, from which the crews drive the tanks to troop units. Few tank depots are known to exist in the U. S. S. R. There are no tank depots in army group (front) or army rear areas. Army group vehicle pools contain only supply vehicles and automotive equipment and tractors for armored and artillery supply units.

9. CLOTHING SUPPLY

Clothing and personal equipment are supplied to troops by the Intendance Service and its agencies in each echelon (fig. 18). The Red Army soldier receives a much smaller clothing and personal equipment issue than does the U. S. soldier (fig. 19).

329

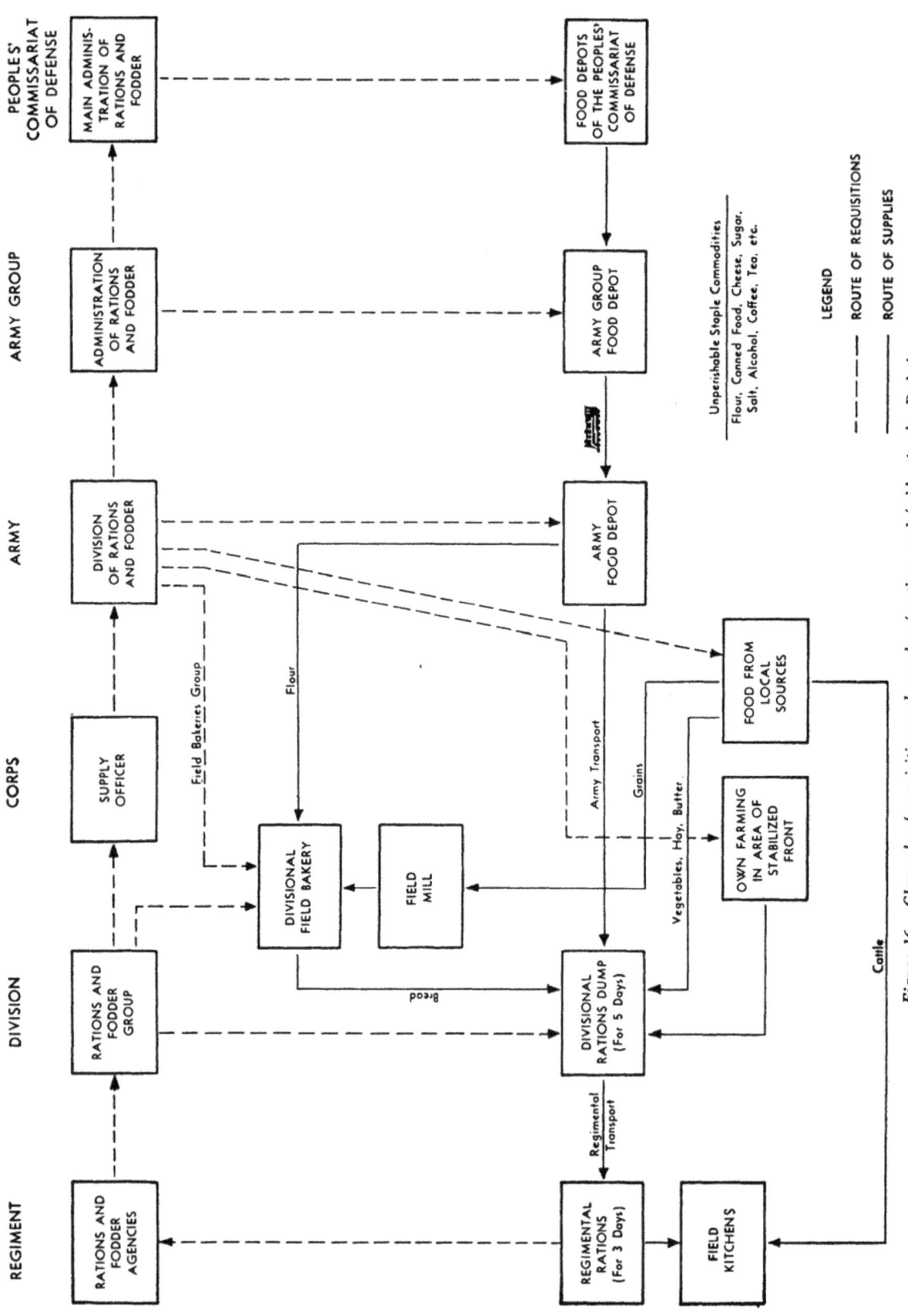

Figure 16. Channels of requisition and supply of rations and fodder in the Red Army.

330

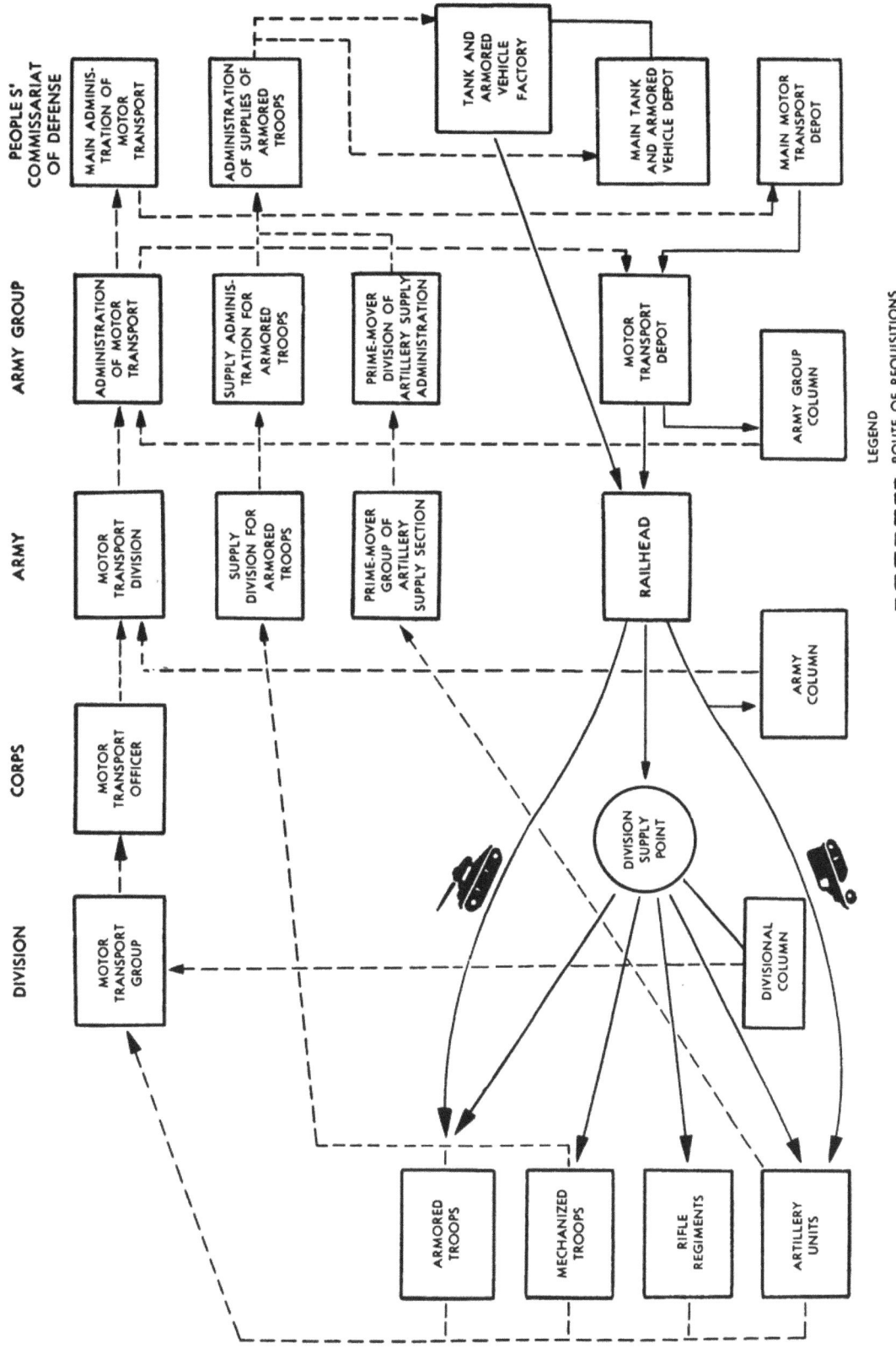

Figure 17. Channels of requisition and supply of motor transport and tanks in the Red Army.

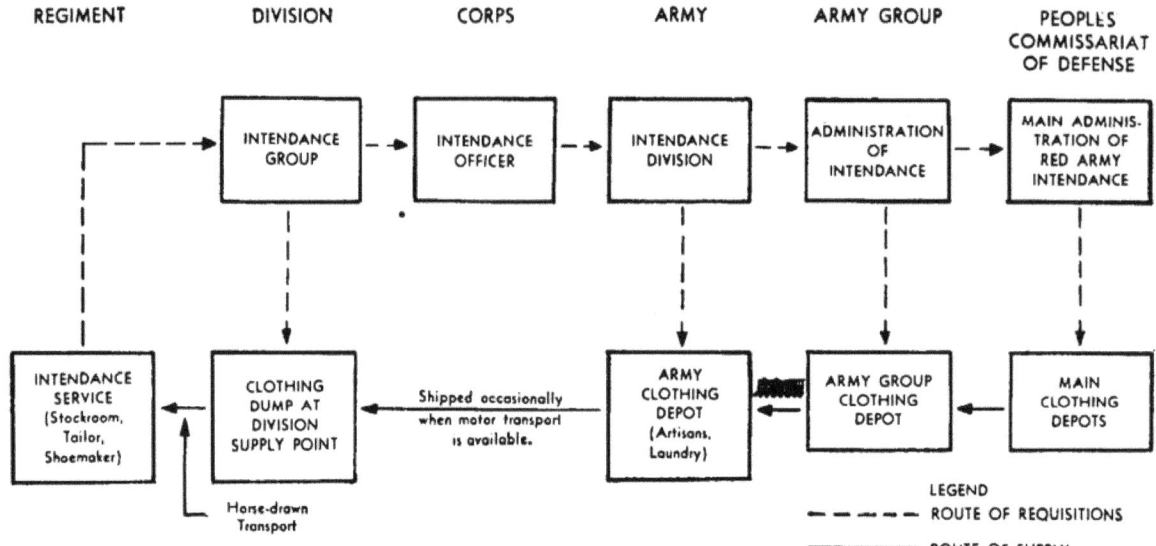

| REGIMENT | DIVISION | CORPS | ARMY | ARMY GROUP | PEOPLES COMMISSARIAT OF DEFENSE |

Figure 18. Channels of requisition and supply of clothing in the Red Army.

Section III. TRANSPORTATION

1. RAIL TRANSPORTATION

Red Army doctrine emphasizes the importance of delivery of supplies by railroad as close to front-line troops as possible. Movement of troops and supplies are carried out by agencies of the Peoples' Commissariat of Transportation (see Chapter IV). All railroads are militarized in time of war. Employees are uniformed and placed under military law, but technical operation by the Peoples' Commissariat of Transportation is continued.

The Red Army has no troop units to operate trains, except in combat areas where railroads are under construction. Rolling stock is kept at the disposal of the Main Administration of Army Transportation and its subordinate organizations. Transportation is conducted by civilian railroad officials in accordance with the plans of the Chief of the Rear Services.

Military commandants are placed in charge of sections of railroad lines and important stations. In military districts, the rear areas of army groups (fronts), and armies, railhead commandant supervise the loading, unloading, and timely dispatch of trains. They are responsible to military district, army group, and army Chiefs of Army Transportation.

Rail transportation of supplies ends normally in the rear areas of armies. Here, army railroad sections are established to ensure an uninterrupted flow of supplies to troops. Army railroad sections operate from regulating stations in rear of army group (front) and army zones to the most advanced railhead or unloading station.

Regulating stations are established at important rail junctions near the rear boundaries of armies. Two or three stations are combined into a regulating station where there is no rail junction. Supply and

| | | Quantity issued | |
Item [1]	Estimated serviceability [2]	First year	Second year
Cap, winter, pile	2 yrs	1	
Cap, service, cotton, wool trimmed	2 yrs	1	
Cap, garrison type	2 yrs	1	
Overcoat, woolen	2 yrs	1	
Jacket, cotton, padded	2 yrs	1	
Shelter, half-hooded cloak	4 yrs		
Blouse, wool	2 yrs	1	
Blouse, summer, cotton	6 mos	2	2
Trousers, (Breeches), woolen	1 yr	1	1
Trousers (Breeches), summer, cotton	1 yr	1	1
Trousers, cotton, padded	2 yrs	1	
Undershirt	6 mos	2	2
Underdrawers	4 mos	3	3
Towels	6 mos	2	2
Handkerchief	4 mos	3	3
Footwraps, summer, cotton flannel	4 mos	3	3
Coat, short, sheepskin	4 yrs	1	
Valenki (felt boots)	2 yrs	1	
Insoles	2 yrs	1	
Footwraps, winter wool	6 mos	2	2
Undershirt, warm, cotton flannel	2 yrs	1	
Underdrawers, warm, cotton flannel	2 yrs	1	
Mittens, trigger finger	1 yr	1	1
Toque	3 yrs	1	
Socks, wool	6 mos	2	2
Boots	8 mos	1	
Shoes, service	8 mos	1	1
Puttees, wrap	1 yr	1	1
Belt, trousers	2 yrs	1	
Pack	2 yrs	1	
Strap, overcoat (for making roll)	2 yrs	1	
Pouch, cartridge	10 yrs	2	
Belt, cartridge	2 yrs	1	
Mess kit	10 yrs	1	
Canteen	10 yrs	1	
Canteen cover	10 yrs	1	

[1] In January 1945, the issue of a Housewife, including needles, thread buttons, and hooks, was completed for all troops.
[2] Sixty percent of all winter clothing issued in the winter of 1944-45 was new. The remainder was renovated re-issue. All summer clothing, especially leather boots, is renovated during the winter months.

Figure 19. Estimated serviceability and basis of issue of clothing and individual equipment.

332

hospital trains consigned to an army are received at the regulating station. Arrangements are made for the unloading of supplies for the army base.

Commandants of regulating stations are controlled by the chief of the Army Base, who also commands the station garrison and is responsible for order and security.

Continuity of rail transportation in the combat zone is secured by railroad troops who are charged with hasty repair and reconstruction of damaged or destroyed sections of rail lines. Railroad troops, however, do not operate the trains, except on lines under construction in forward areas. Rail lines occasionally are projected as far forward as division rear areas.

a. Troop movements. The lack of railroad nets in the U. S. S. R. and their generally unsatisfactory condition are limiting factors in the movement of troops and supplies by rail.

U. S. S. R. railroads are of broad gauge. The capacity of a Soviet train, approximately 1,200 short tons, is more than twice the capacity of a comparable train of Western European cars. Soviet troop trains average from 12 to 15 miles per hour, or an average of from 125 to 185 miles per day.

For general logistical data on the principal Red Army units and formations, see Figure 20.

b. Organization, troop movements. Troops may be moved either in separate cars or in troop trains. A unit organized for movement and occupying at least 20 cars is called an "echelon." Each echelon is assigned a number by an agency of the Army Transportation Service. All troops must be familiar with their echelon number since several echelons may be moved on one train.

The unit commander designates a chief for each echelon. Each echelon chief is assisted by an assistant chief of echelon, a medical officer, and, when necessary, a veterinary officer.

The echelon chief reports to the station commandant a day prior to loading to receive a chart of the echelon and loading instructions. He examines loading facilities and reconnoiters routes to the station and to the assembly area. Units occupying assembly areas must comply with local security and camouflage regulations. The echelon chief also familiarizes himself with local antiaircraft regulations.

He then reports the results of his reconnaissance to the unit commander, prepares a loading plan for his echelon, schedules departure for station, and selects loading teams for the echelon.

Railroad cars containing inflammables or explosives are placed in the rear part of the train between two flatcars. Several cars containing explosives are separated by at least one car of safe cargo. They are separated from troop cars by at least 6 axles, from the forward locomotive by at least 12 axles, and from the rear locomotive by 6 axles.

Units are divided into two echelons for urgent movements. The first echelon contains combat troops, the second includes supplies and supply troops. To accelerate the movement of large numbers of troops, the Red Army uses "combined transport." Track-laying vehicles and the foot- and horse-drawn elements of infantry formations are moved by rail, while the motorized troops move on roads.

c. Railroad capacity. The average daily capacity of main U. S. S. R. double-track lines is from 30 to 40 trains. Single-track lines average from 15 to 20 trains daily.

To increase the capacity of railroad lines during operations, the Soviets operate lines one way only. Trains maintain visual distance. This method increases the capacity of even hastily repaired single-track lines to from 40 to 50 trains daily.

d. Military trains. Standard Russian military trains total 120 axles. However, trains on trunk lines may have from 166 to 172 axles. Cars are either 2- or 4-axle types, of 20- or 55- to 66-short ton capacities respectively. In logistical computations, one 4-axle car equals two 2-axle cars (fig. 20).

e. Loading. Box cars are used to transport personnel, 36 men to a 2-axle car and 72 men to a 4-axle car. These loadings are increased to 50 and 100 men for movements of less than 12 hours. Plank beds are installed for night movements, 36 planks in two tiers in 2-axle cars and 70 planks in three tiers in 4-axle cars.

Three trucks or staff cars are loaded on two flatcars to save space. The middle vehicle spans the gap between the cars. Five empty GAZ-AA 1½-ton trucks may be loaded on two flatcars. The front of the first truck is elevated and rests on a fixed support. The following vehicles are driven up ramps, and the front wheels of each rests in the body of the preceding truck. Wooden wedges are placed under the wheels and the vehicles are wired to each other and to the bed of the flatcar.

Capacities of U. S. S. R. railroad equipment are shown in Figures 21 and 22.

333

Formation	Strength	Supply requirements (short tons)				Resupply	Basic load	Transportation					
		Rations and fodder	Ammunition, 1 unit of fire	Fuel, 1 refill	Other supplies (5 percent of total)	1 ration, 1 unit of fire, 1 refill, and other supplies (short tons)	5 rations, 1½ units of fire, 3 refills, and others (short tons)	Number of vehicles		Limiting speed (m. p. h.)		Maximum axle load (short tons)	Rail movement requirements. Number of standard 120-axle trains*
								Horse-drawn	Motor	Cross country	Road		
R Div	9,619	43.5	303.6	11.3	17.9	376.3	742.3	610	226	2.5 to 3	2.5 to 3	1.5	12.0
R Regt	2,474	9.8	65.6	1.0	3.8	79.3	157.9	148	21	2.5 to 3	2.5 to 3	1.5	2.5
Tk Corps	11,964	29.9	797.6	197.4	51.3	1,076.2	2,035.0		1,756	9	18	10.0	30.0
Tk Brig	1,306	3.3	131.9	35.7	8.5	179.4	337.4		289	9	18	7.0	3.5
Mtz R Brig	3,238	8.1	81.6	20.1	5.5	115.3	234.4		333	9	30	1.5	5.5
Tk Regt	543	1.4	72.8	23.8	4.9	102.9	197.0		103	9	20	7.0	1.0
152-mm SP Arty Regt	476	1.2	37.9	25.3	3.2	67.6	145.6		72	6 to 8	18	10.0	1.5
Mecz Corps	17,457	43.6	908.0	239.2	59.5	1,250.3	2,412.5		2,470	9	18	10.0	38.5
Mecz Brig	3,781	9.5	154.4	43.9	10.4	218.2	431.3		436	9	20	7.0	6.0
Arty Div	9,743	24.4	798.5	134.3	47.8	1,005.0	1,808.7		1,623	9	15	7.85	25.0
AAA Div	2,043	3.9	112.0	19.0	6.7	141.6	256.7		306	9	25	4.7	4.5
Medium G Brig	2,128	5.3	153.8	32.8	9.6	201.5	373.4		312	6 to 8	15	7.85	5.0
L How Brig	2,242	5.6	250.0	55.2	15.5	326.3	597.0		420	6 to 8	18	1.62	7.0
L Arty Brig	2,063	5.2	140.5	22.3	8.4	176.4	318.6		373	9	25	1.23	6.0
Mort Brig	1,705	4.3	248.1	16.0	13.4	281.8	463.6		319	9	25	1.5	4.0
Rkt Regt	808	2.0	204.0	5.8	11.5	223.3	350.1		114	9	25	1.5	1.5
Cav Corps	18,210	205.7	712.7	99.6	50.9	1,068.9	2,516.1	1,316	883	3 to 5	3 to 5	7.0	50.5
Cav Div	4,645	62.1	128.6	5.0	9.8	205.5	544.3	404	100	3 to 5	3 to 5	1.5	12.0
Cav Regt	1,144	15.9	24.8		2.0	42.7	122.5	115	3	3 to 5	3 to 5	1.5	3.0

*The standard Soviet military train consists of railroad cars totaling 120 axles. These cars may be either 2- or 4-axle types (of approximately 20-ton or 50-ton capacities, respectively). In logistical computations, one 4-axle car is equal to two 2-axle cars.

Figure 20. Logistical data on principal Red Army field formations and units.

Loading and unloading time depend largely upon loading facilities and the type of transport. Unloading generally requires one-third to one-half of the time as loading (fig. 23).

In the absence of permanent loading ramps, the Red Army employs various types of portable ramps. Portable ramps require from 2¼ to 4½ hours for assembly. Hasty ramps are constructed when permanent or portable ramps are not available.

2. ROAD TRANSPORTATION

a. Supplies. The use of road transportation for the movement of supplies normally begins in army rear areas. Existing highways in the rear areas are organized into military automobile roads and supply and evacuation roads. Military automobile roads are organized in army rear areas from the supply base of the army to the rear areas of divisions. Army supply and evacuation roads are provided for the shipment of supplies from railheads or unloading stations to the boundary of division rear areas. Only army transport operates on military automobile roads. Army and divisional transport use army supply and evacuation roads.

Depending upon supply requirements, there may be motor transport battalions, regiments, and brigades attached to army groups (fronts) or armies.

Type	Capacity (short tons)	Length (feet)
Boxcar, 2-axle	16.5 to 22	21
Boxcar, 4-axle	55	43
Flatcar, 2-axle	18.5	28
Flatcar, 2-axle	22	29
Flatcar, 4-axle	55	43
Gondola, 4-axle	55 to 66	43
Tank car	44 to 55	(1)
Tank car	33	(2)
Tank car	Over 55	(2)

1 Most frequently used type.
2 Less frequently used type.

Figure 21. Capacities of U. S. S. R. railroad cars.

Type of load	Boxcars		Flatcars	
	2-axle	4-axle	2-axle	4-axle
Horses	8	14		
Personnel	36 to 40	72 to 80		
Field kitchens, in operation (1 for each 250 men)	1			
Field kitchens, idle			6	
Two-wheel carts			8	
Two-horse wagons			6	
Passenger motor cars			2	3
Tractors			2	3
Motor trucks			1.5	2.5
Reconnaissance tanks			2	3
Light tanks, T-70, or 76-mm SP guns			2	3
Medium tanks, T-34, or 85-mm SP guns			1	2
Heavy tanks, KV-85, or 152-mm SP guns				1
76-mm guns			3	
45-mm antitank guns			6	
122-mm howitzers			3	
107-mm guns			2	4
152-mm howitzers				2
Heavy artillery pieces				1
82- and 120-mm mortars with carts				6

Figure 22. Average capacities of Russian railroad cars by types of load.

334

Unit	Loading from—	
	Ramps	Platform or ground [1]
INFANTRY		
Rifle battalion without artillery or train	10 min	15 min.
Rifle battalion with regimental artillery or train	35 min	45 min.
Headquarters of rifle regiment with attached units	45 min	1 hr.
Headquarters of rifle division with attached units	45 min	1 hr.
Headquarters of rifle corps with attached units	45 min	1 hr.
CAVALRY		
Cavalry regiment or separate battalion without artillery or train	30 min	45 min.
ARTILLERY		
Battalion of division artillery	45 min	1 hr.
Battalion of corps artillery	1 hr	1½ hrs.
Battalion of heavy GHQ artillery	1 hr	2 hrs.
Battalion of GHQ howitzers	1 hr	2 hrs.
Battalion of antiaircraft artillery	1 hr	2 hrs.
ARMORED UNITS		
Company of armored cars, all types	1 hr	2 hrs.
Tank battalion, all types [2]	1 to 1½ hrs	2 to 3½ hrs.
TECHNICAL UNITS		
Engineer battalion with technical equipment and train	2 hrs	2½ hrs.
Ponton battalion with technical equipment and train	1½ hrs	2 hrs.
Road construction battalion with technical equipment and train	2 hrs	2½ hrs.
Signal regiment with train	1 hr	1½ hrs.
Chemical battalion with technical equipment and train	1 hr	1½ hrs.
Railroad battalion with technical equipment and trains	2 hrs	2½ hrs.
REAR SERVICES		
Artillery park	1½ hrs	2½ hrs.
Engineer park	1½ hrs	2½ hrs.
Medical installations	1 hr	1½ hrs.
Veterinary installations	1 hr	1½ hrs.
Motor transport battalion	1½ hrs	1½ hrs.
Horse-drawn transport battalion	1½ hrs	2½ hrs.
Tractor battalion	1½ hrs	2½ hrs.
Depots and bases	2 hrs	3 hrs.

[1] Time of loading from the ground includes the time required for the construction of loading facilities.
[2] Loading time depends on type of tanks.

Figure 23. Maximum permissible time for the loading of arms and services on trains.

The strength of motor transport units vary. A motor transport battalion normally has from 100 to 140 trucks and two workshop trucks. They are controlled by the motor transport administrations of army groups and the motor transport divisions of armies.

The following types of trucks are used by the Red Army (figs. 24, 25, and 26):

Type:	Capacity (Short tons)
Light truck, GAZ–AA	1.6
Heavy truck, ZiS–5, ZiS–6	2.7 to 3.3
Heavy truck, Studebaker, GMC, and other American models	3.7

ARMY GROUPS. Army groups have motor transport pools at their disposal for concentrated use

Type of ammunition	Average weight of box with ammunition (pounds)	Number of units in box	Loads (boxes)		
			Two-horse wagon	Truck	
				1½-ton	3-ton
Cartridges, rifle, without clips	57.2	880	18	52	100
Cartridges, rifle, in clips	47.3	600	22	60	120
Cartridges, revolver	70.4	2,184	14	40	80
Cartridges, submachine gun	66	2,304	15	42	84
Cartridges, 12.7-mm	61.6	170	16	46	90
Grenades, hand, RGD	116.6	50	8	22	47
Igniters for RGD grenades	9.3	104	4	12	24
Flares, signal and illuminating	88	400	12	30	63
Shell, mortar, 50-mm	40.5	14	25	66	140
Shell, mortar, 82-mm	110	10	9	24	50
Shell, mortar, 107-mm	110	4	9	24	50
Shell, mortar, 120-mm	110	2	9	24	50
Rounds, complete, 45-mm	79	10	13	36	72
Rounds, complete, 76-mm	154	6	6	18	36
Rounds, complete, 76-mm	206	8	5	13	27
Rounds, complete, 76-mm	127	5	8	22	45
Projectiles, 122-mm	154	2	6	18	36
Rounds, complete, 122-mm howitzer	193	3	4	12	24
Charges, propellant, 122-mm howitzer	121	12	1	3	6
Projectiles, 152-mm howitzer	129.8	1		21	43
Rounds, complete, 152-mm howitzer	205.6	2		12	24
Charges, propellant, 152-mm howitzer	136.4	8		3	6
Projectiles, 152-mm gun	165	1		17	34
Rounds, complete, 76-mm mountain howitzer	118.8	5	9	24	48
Rounds, complete, 76-mm mountain howitzer	184.8	8	5	15	30

Figure 24. Standard ammunition loads per transport unit.

Type of vehicle	Load capacity		
	Men	Pounds	Gallons
Packs:			
Horse		264	
Mule		176	
Camel		484	
Two-horse wagon	6	1,100	
Two-wheeled cart	4	484	
Horse-drawn medical wagon	2 lying or 4 sitting		
Two-wheeled horse-drawn medical cart	2 lying or 3 sitting		
Motorcycle without side car	1 to 2	176 to 330	
Motorcycle with side car	2 to 3	330 to 550	
Passenger car	4 to 6	770 to 1,000	
Truck, 1.5-ton	10 to 12	2,860	
Truck ZiS-5	16 to 20	5,500	
Truck ZiS-6	16 to 20	6,600	
Ambulance	4 lying or 9 sitting		
Veterinary ambulance	2 horses [1]		
Gas-tank truck ZiS-5			787.2
Gas-tank truck BZ ZiS-5			787.2
Water and oil tank truck ZiS-5:			
Capacity of water tank			270.6
Capacity of oil compartment			172.2
Tractor ZiS-3 and STZ-5, drawing strength on hook [2]		5,720	
Tractor CHTZ, drawing strength on hook [3]		1,210	

[1] Prostrate horses—one per vehicle.
[2] Two 2-ton trailers.
[3] Two 3- or 4-ton trailers.

Figure 25. Load capacities of U. S. S. R. transport units.

during major efforts. The size of the pools varies according to projected operations. During breakthroughs, they supply troops directly.

Type of supplies	Unit weight (pounds)	Load table			
		Two-horse cart		Trucks	
		Number of units	Weight (pounds)	1½-ton Number of units	3-ton Number of units
Biscuits	66.0	14	924	50	100
Flour	165	6	990	20	40
Grits	165	6	990	20	40
Rice	176	6	1,056	18	37
Baked bread	3.96	308	1,100	945	1,875
Macaroni	47.52	22	1,045	69	134
Sugar	180.4	6	990	18	36
Tea	99	10	990	26	36
Meat			990		
Canned meat	82.50	13	1,078	40	80
Sausage	111.32	9	1,056	30	60
Fish	550	2	1,000	6	
Potatoes			1,000		
Dried vegetables	89.10	12	1,078	37	74
Soap	132	8	1,056	25	50
Dry ration		400	1,012	1,300	2,600
Oats	110	9	990	30	60
Baled hay	74.8	14	1,056	43	82
Loose hay			726		
Rawhide	44	24	1,056	75	150

Figure 26. Food supplies carried by each unit of transport.

ARMIES. Armies normally have from two to three motor transport battalions. Their load capacity is from 385 to 550 short tons. Frequently, an army will have one motor transport battalion and several separate truck companies.

CORPS. Corps have no motor transport at their disposal.

RIFLE DIVISION. The rifle division is assigned a motor transport company. The company includes three transport platoons and an infantry squad. It has from 60 to 80 trucks, forty-five 1½-ton (GAZ-AA, Dodge, Ford) and fifteen to thirty 2½- to 3-ton trucks (Zis-5, GMC, Studebaker).

Rifle divisions requisition local oxen and horse-drawn wagons to supplement assigned motor transport in emergencies. Artillery horses and tractors may also be used for emergency supply purposes.

RIFLE REGIMENTS. Rifle regiments normally have no motor transport for supply. (Rifle regiments do have seven tanks, armed with 120-mm mortars, which transport their own ammunition.) Their transport companies each have 21 horse-drawn wagons. Twelve are used to transport rations and fodder from division; six transport quartermaster supplies (clothing); one is assigned to the finance section; and two are used by the staff.

MOTORIZED UNITS. Motorized units employ motor transport only. The motorized rifle brigade has approximately 27 supply trucks. Frequently, transport and repair organizations of motorized units are combined into a technical supply company. All motorized units have a special fuel and lubricants supply column, partially equipped with tank trucks.

ANTITANK AND FIELD ARTILLERY. Antitank and field artillery regiments have substantial supply columns. Frequently, they must draw their supplies at army field depots. Field artillery ammunition supply columns draw ammunition at division exchange points. Division artillery regiments are equipped with 30 ammunition trucks. The supply columns of all artillery units are capable of carrying one-half a unit of fire.

b. Troop movements. There are few hard-surface, two-way roads in the U. S. S. R. One four-lane highway does run from Gorkii to Minsk, via Moscow and Smolensk. One-way traffic is ordered on roads when they are used for troop movements. Divisions normally move over two or more parallel routes.

The average numbers of trucks required to move Red Army units are as follows:

Unit:	ZiS-5	GAZ-AA
Rifle battalion		100
Artillery battalion	180	250
Rifle regiment	550	700
Regimental howitzer battery		120

For movements of from 60 to 90 miles, rifle divisions are transported at reduced strength. They are not accompanied by horse-drawn trains. For movements in excess of 120 miles, rifle divisions are transported at full strength.

Distance between vehicles normally is 25 to 50 yards; interval between serials, 500 to 600 yards. Distance between vehicles is reduced to 20 to 30 yards for blackout driving. When columns are under enemy fire, or when roads are dusty, distance between vehicles is increased to 50 to 100 yards.

The prescribed interval between rifle battalions is from 500 to 600 yards, between rifle regiments 1,000 to 1,100 yards, and between tank and mechanized battalions and brigades 1,000 to 1,100 yards.

The rate of march is dependent upon the type of trucks, condition of roads, weather, and visibility. Motor columns average from 12 to 18 miles per hour on improved roads and may reach 20 to 25 miles per hour on asphalt highways. Averages of from 3 to 9 miles per hour are maintained in blackout driving on dirt roads.

Motor columns average 125 to 150 miles per day over highways or good dirt road; 180 to 250 miles per day on asphalt highways. A forced march covers 180 to 215 miles per day over average highways. With the use of relief drivers, they can attain 250 to 310 miles per day. On poor dirt roads, columns average 60 to 85 miles per day.

The following road spaces are estimated for principal Russian troop units:

Unit:	Road space
Rifle battalion	1,100 yards.
Rifle regiment	5,000 yards.
Rifle division	16.8 miles.
Artillery battalion	2,400 yards.
Artillery regiment	5.1 miles.
Artillery brigade	17.4 miles.
Tank battalion	2,100 yards.
Tank brigade	6.6 miles.
Tank corps	45 to 50 miles.
Mechanized brigade	12.6 miles.
Mechanized corps	65 to 75 miles.
Cavalry division	9.6 miles.
Cavalry corps	42 miles.

c. **Organization of road marches.** Army group (front) and army staffs normally organize road movements of troop formations (divisions, mobile corps). They issue movement orders to the commanders concerned. The orders include combat mission of unit or formation, purpose of movement, assembly area, loading zone, march schedule, unloading zone, and security instructions.

Commanders are provided with all available information on road conditions, loading and unloading zones, and speed limits for various road sections. Whenever possible, all necessary information is provided commanders 24 hours prior to movement. When roads organized by the army road administration and the motor transport service are to be used, 10 to 12 hours are allowed for the preparation and organization of the movement.

The unit commander, upon receipt of movement orders, promulgates policies regarding route reconnaissance, organization of the march, and loading and unloading zones. His staff and the staff of the motor transport unit organize route reconnaissance, assembly area, and loading and unloading zones. They schedule assembly of units, plan march organization, schedule loading and unloading, estimate transportation requirements, prepare security measures, prescribe march regulations, and assign loading and unloading teams and road and bridge maintenance teams. They prepare instructions for quartermaster, medical, and, if necessary, veterinary services. They issue orders to the commanders of reconnaissance units and the preliminary march

order. The staff of the motor transport unit also prepares plans for fuel supply, maintenance, and assembly of vehicles.

Loading and assembly areas are dispersed to avoid the bunching of vehicles. Battalion assembly areas and loading zones normally occupy 1 square mile, regiments up to 10 square miles, and rifle divisions up to 24 to 30 square miles.

Loading plans are based on the following daylight loading time requirements:

Loading unit:	Minutes
One truck with—	
Horses	5 to 7
Guns and lumber	25 to 30
Ammunition boxes	20 to 25
Carts	10 to 12
Rifle battalion	40 to 45
Artillery battalion	50 to 60

Regiments normally are divided into battalion echelons. Echelons are combined into columns which contain supply and maintenance units, to preserve the tactical independence of each echelon.

Traffic control is carried out by the road service administration through special traffic regulating units. Regulating units each have charge of a road section approximately 40 miles long. Regulating centers serve as temporary command posts for the marching formation. Regulating units also maintain mobile traffic control posts.

Liaison on the march is maintained through the communication net of the traffic regulating units, liaison officers, messenger cars, and personal contact of commanders during halts or on the march. Commanders also observe the movement of their units from liaison planes. To facilitate identification, two or three vehicles at the head and at the end of an echelon are marked with identification numbers. Special panels marked with echelon numbers are also used.

Unloading operations are scheduled so as to avoid delay and waiting. Normally not less than 3 hours is required to unload a regiment. Staffs meet their echelons as they approach the unloading zone and direct them to dispersed individual unloading points.

3. WATER TRANSPORTATION

Water transportation is of minor importance in the Red Army. Where adequate rail or road transportation is not available, waterways are used during the navigable seasons. Chiefs of army water sections are responsible to the Chief of Army Transportation of an army. The chief of an army water section

337

controls the commandants of landing places and forwarding points.

4. MAINTENANCE

a. Railroad maintenance. The railroad troops of the Red Army are under the control of the Commander of Railroad Troops who is responsible to the Chief of Staff. They are equipped for emergency construction only. Large-scale and special construction is handled by special units of the Peoples' Commissariat of Transportation.

There were at least 20 railroad brigades under the Commander of Railroad Troops in 1944. Each brigade included three railroad battalions, a bridge-building battalion, and 200 men to operate trains over advance sections under construction. Each railroad and bridge-building battalion consists of 3 companies, 200 men each, and a 40-truck motor column.

Railroad brigades cooperate with army group (front) Chiefs of Army Transportation who keep them informed of the clearance of the enemy from rail lines so that they may proceed with the repair work ordered by the Commander of Railroad Troops. The army group Chief of Army Transportation is informed of the progress of work and may request minor construction, such as ramps and sidings. Railroad bridge battalions are capable of constructing bridges up to 220 yards in length.

b. Road maintenance. The poor condition of U. S. S. R. roads requires constant attention by the road maintenance service. As mentioned in paragraph 2, roads in the rear areas of armies and front-line units are organized into military automobile roads and supply and evacuation roads.

Chiefs of military automobile roads are responsible to the chiefs of road administrations. Vehicles used for supply and evacuation on military automobile roads are under the operational control of the Chief of the Military Automobile Road.

Army supply and evacuation roads are organized according to the orders of the Chief of the Army Rear Services.

Supply roads in rear areas are divided into sections maintained by army road maintenance organizations, which are controlled by road section commandants. During major operations, these are reinforced by special units from the army group (front) rear area. The road construction units are included in the army group and army rear services.

An army group road administration has at its disposal one to two road construction regiments of two to three battalions each, one security and antiaircraft battalion, one traffic control company of women armed with submachine guns, and several labor battalions recruited from among local civilians.

Bridge construction brigades may be detailed to army groups (fronts) by the Main Administration of Roads of the Red Army for the construction of large bridges.

Army road sections are provided with two to three road construction battalions. They differ from the battalions of road construction regiments in that a traffic control company is attached to each battalion. Labor battalions are recruited locally as needed. Bridge construction battalions, capable of constructing bridges up to 110 yards in length, are attached as required.

In addition to their principal mission of maintaining and operating roads, road section commandants assist in the issue of winter clothing to passing troops (fur caps, mittens), supplementary food and fuel. They organize disinfection chambers, turkish baths, emergency medical-aid stations, and technical repair stations at traffic control posts. They also organize entrucking points for occasional evacuation of casualties in returning empty vehicles.

Section IV. MEDICAL AND VETERINARY SERVICES

1. ORGANIZATION AND EVACUATION

The Red Army medical service is well organized but poorly equipped. It is designed to bring medical aid as far forward as possible for early treatment and evacuation of casualties.

Higher units evacuate casualties from lower units. Stretcher teams evacuate casualties from the battlefield to aid stations. Unit commanders are responsible for evacuation from aid stations. Battalions evacuate casualties from company areas to battalion medical stations. Regiments evacuate casualties from battalion to regimental medical aid stations. Division transportation is employed for evacuation from regimental to division medical stations.

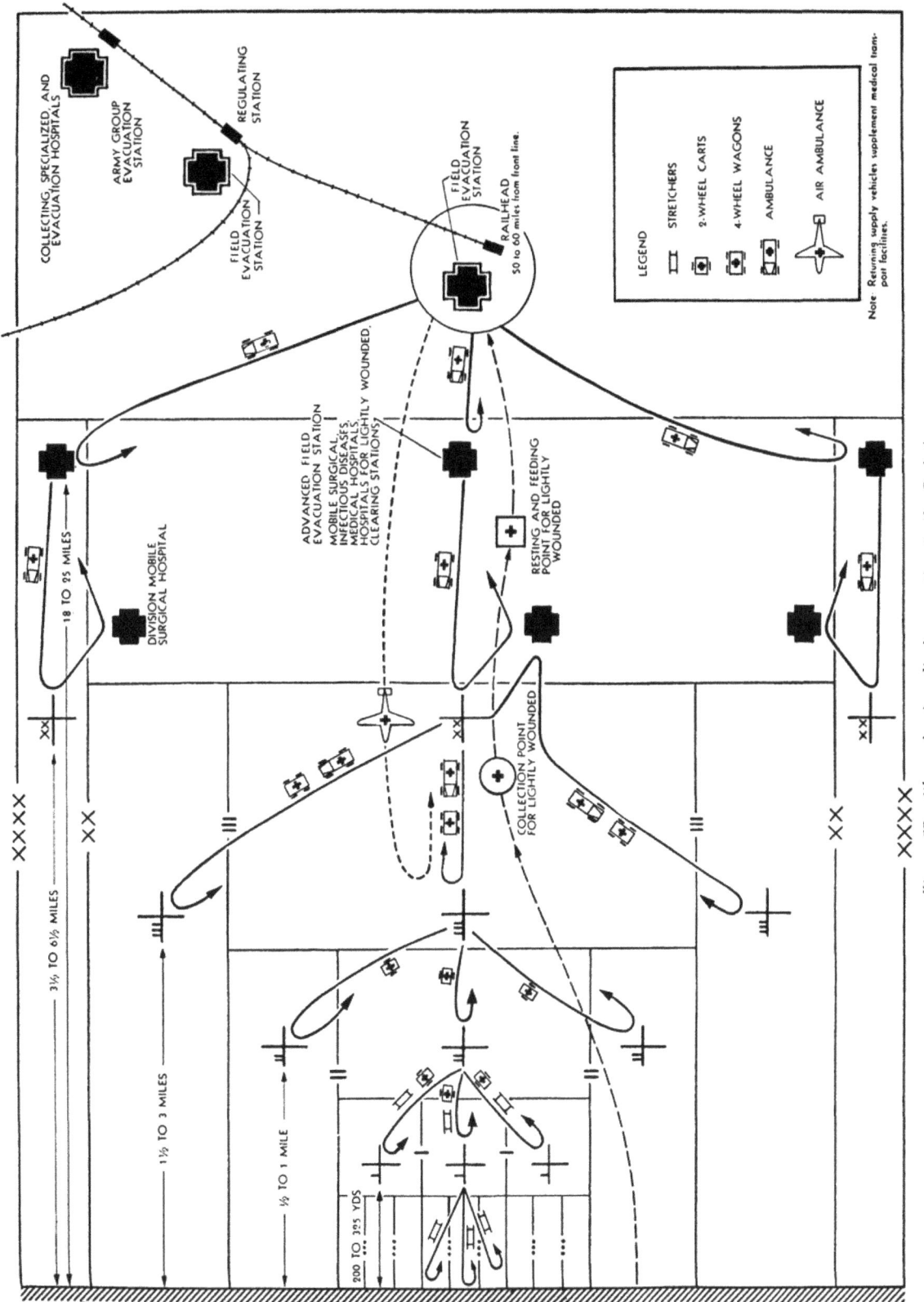

Figure 27. *Channels of medical evacuation in the Red Army.*

339

Specialized hospitals are established under the Red Army medical service in the following categories:

Orthopedic surgery.
Neuro surgery.
Plastic surgery.
Temporo-maxillary-mandibular surgery.
Thoracic surgery.
Venereal diseases.
Burns.
Psychiatry.

a. Channels of evacuation. (See Figure 27.) Normally, battalion aid stations are established within 1 mile of the battle front. Two medical officers are assigned to each active battalion whenever possible. One directs evacuation of rifle company casualties and administers first aid. The other operates the battalion aid station.

Rifle company casualties are evacuated by stretcher bearers. Approximately four stretcher bearers are attached to each company. Stretchers on wheels, dog carts and sleds, ski stretchers, and horse or motor ambulances are also used for battlefield evacuation. In mountain terrain, pack animals are used to evacuate casualties located by trained dogs. Ambulance planes are used when necessary.

Casualties normally receive medical attention within 1 hour after being wounded.

Regimental medical stations are established within 1½ to 3 miles from the front lines. A medical company is attached to each rifle regiment. It evacuates casualties from battalion aid stations to the regimental aid station. Empty battalion and regimental supply vehicles are used to evacuate casualties when the medical company's motor transport cannot reach battalion aid stations. Horse-drawn transport for evacuation is requisitioned locally, particularly in winter. The regimental aid station classifies and tags casualties, checks bandages, gives initial surgical treatment, and holds temporarily casualties who cannot be evacuated safely. Casualties are tagged with red or blue tags numbered "I" or "II," indicating the priority in which they are to receive medical treatment and are to be evacuated.

The division medical battalion establishes a division medical station from 3½ to 6 miles from the front lines, usually in a regimental rear area. It also evacuates casualties from regimental aid stations to division aid stations or to attached mobile surgical hospitals, approximately 18 miles behind the front line. It maintains a section in the divisional rear area for the lightly wounded and sick.

From division aid stations or attached mobile surgical hospitals, casualties are usually evacuated to army casualty clearing stations, which are normally established near roads or railheads.

From clearing stations, casualties are evacuated to army mobile surgical hospitals, to field hospitals attached to divisions, or to collecting hospitals in the army rear area. Contagious disease cases are segregated in special hospitals in division or army rear areas. Casualties whose condition is not critical and who can be returned to action soon and casualties whose condition precludes immediate evacuation are kept in hospitals in division or army rear areas. Casualties requiring prolonged hospitalization and those whose condition precludes return to active service are evacuated to civilian hospitals in the zone of interior for hospitalization and rehabilitation.

Hospitals for slightly wounded who are expected to return to duty within 10 to 15 days are established in division and army rear areas.

Army group evacuation stations, army evacuation stations, and advance field evacuation stations are established in army group and army rear areas to treat and evacuate casualties received from army casualty clearing stations or directly from division aid stations. Army group and army evacuation stations normally are established near army regulating stations. Advance field evacuation stations normally are located near railheads.

An army group or army evacuation station includes a headquarters, collecting and evacuation hospitals, a laundry and disinfecting section, a medical committee, and ambulance units.

An advance field evacuation station includes a headquarters, the army clearance station with a capacity of 500, and two to three mobile field hospitals.

Army group (front) Chiefs of Medical Service attach hospital trains to field evacuation stations. Many hospital trains are capable of functioning separately. They are shifted to areas where large numbers of casualties are anticipated.

The army Chief of the Medical Service plans army medical installations, evacuation, treatment of wounded, and prophylaxis in accordance with instructions of the army group (front) Chief of the Medical Service. The medical service at army level includes an epidemic control section to prevent and control epidemics. There are one to two special hospitals for contagious diseases in the rear area of each army. Special disinfecting companies are responsible for sanitary conditions.

Troop units and medical installations are supplied by medical field depots.

b. Medical service, offensive operations. Medical services during all phases of the planning and conducting of offensive operations are closely planned and supervised.

PRELIMINARY PLANNING. Prior to a projected operation, the medical service ascertains the number of beds which can be made available in the various types of hospitals established in army group (front) and army rear areas. All patients permanently disabled and those requiring prolonged treatment are evacuated to the rear.

An adequate reserve of field hospitals is provided by the army group (front) medical service. A portion of the available army field hospitals may be placed at the immediate disposal of the army group (front) Chief of the Medical Service and moved near the lines of communication to the rear area of the projected operation. Medical vehicles of armies not involved in the main operation may be placed in the transport reserve of the army group (front). Special attention is given hospital trains. Their distribution at railroad stations must be coordinated with the section of army transportation to ensure their movement at the beginning of operations.

PLAN OF OPERATION. The army group (front) Chief of Medical Service completes his plan when he receives detailed information on the projected operation from the Commander or Chief of Staff. He places special emphasis on the estimate of the number of mobile field hospitals required, the number of beds in army group (front) and army hospital bases, available transport of all types, available medical personnel, and epidemic control measures.

Mobile surgical field hospitals of the army group (front) reserve are distributed in army rear areas in accordance with the number of divisions included in each army and with casualty estimates. These hospitals are controlled by army Chiefs of the Medical Service during the operation. A number of mobile surgical field hospitals are kept in army group (front) reserve. The number held in reserve depends upon their availability, but normally it is felt that there should be at least two mobile surgical

field hospitals in army group reserve for each army engaged in the operation.

Each army also is provided with hospitals for slightly wounded, therapeutic hospitals, contagious disease hospitals, advance field evacuation stations with clearing stations, a collecting hospital, and a number of evacuation hospitals.

The Soviets estimate that 10 beds must be provided for each 100 men engaged in an operation. Fifty to sixty percent of the beds are in mobile field hospitals and hospitals for slightly wounded. The remainder are in evacuation hospitals. In addition, they estimate that 5 to 6 beds for every 100 men engaged in the operation will be required in the army group (front) hospital base, including evacuation hospitals, collecting hospitals, and hospitals for the slightly wounded. Should small railroad capacity impede evacuation from the area, the estimate of required beds is increased accordingly.

Requirements for medical motor transport depend largely upon the available road nets. The Soviets believe that each attacking army should be supported by a motor ambulance company, with an equal reserve at army group (front) headquarters. Horse-drawn vehicles normally are not used by army group or army medical services. However, it is considered advisable to include a horse-drawn reserve at army group medical service headquarters for concentrated evacuation in the immediate rear of front-line units during combat.

The requirements for hospital trains and railroad evacuation depend upon distances between loading and unloading stations and the time required for a round trip. Planes are frequently used at army group (front) and army level for the evacuation of serious casualties, particularly if ground evacuation is over long distances.

The army group (front) Chief of the Medical Service prepares the general plan for evacuation, hospitalization, epidemic control, sanitary measures, and distribution of medical units in accordance with the plan of operation (fig. 27).

Basic provisions of the medical service operation plan must be approved by the deputy of the army group (front) Commander for the Rear Services jointly with the political member of the Military Council in time to complete preparations prior to the projected operation.

CONTROL OF OPERATION. Successful functioning of the medical service during offensive operations, the Soviets emphasize, depends largely upon the control exercised by the army group (front) Chief of the Medical Service. He must be informed continually of the combat situation and must maintain close contact with the medical service of the army or armies engaged as well as with his own hospital base. For this reason, it is considered expedient for the army group (front) Chief of the Medical Service to remain with the first echelon, although existing regulations prescribe that his headquarters are included in the headquarters of the rear services and will remain with the second echelon of the army group command.

The medical operation group (within the first echelon), headed by the Chief of the Medical Service or his deputy, is charged with the obtaining of operational information. It is also responsible for liaison with and direction of the medical service of individual armies.

The army group (front) medical headquarters is responsible for the army group hospital base, railroad evacuation, and liaison with higher medical authorities. Special emphasis is placed on close coordination with railroad and motor transport agencies.

SERVICE DURING OFFENSIVE ACTION. During the operation, the army group medical service headquarters is also responsible for the shifting of medical installations to meet changes in operational requirements and for sanitation in occupied areas. Special emphasis is placed on the development of adequate army group and army hospital bases, and the timely evacuation from those hospitals by well-planned and regulated use of hospital trains and returning empty supply trains. Close and continuous contact with the army transportation service is mandatory.

The Soviets frequently shift medical installations to regulate the distribution of casualties to hospital bases. Thus the hospital bases of armies engaged in secondary operations and those of the army group which are located on secondary evacuation routes are utilized to the fullest extent.

While installations are being moved, steps are taken to receive casualties at the old location until deployment is completed. This is achieved by deployment from the rear. Part of the undeployed mobile surgical field hospitals are moved forward rapidly to follow advancing units. Evacuation hospitals from the army group (front) reserve join army hospital bases.

Timely reinforcement of army hospital bases with evacuation hospitals has proved effective. Consequently, the Russians recommend that armies engaged in the main effort should be reinforced by an adequate number of evacuation hospitals and that the army group Chief of the Medical Service should retain a number of undeployed evacuation hospitals at his disposal for use as the attack develops.

When a deep penetration into enemy territory is accomplished, part of the evacuation hospitals from the army group (front) and army hospitals bases are moved forward to the new army hospital base. The army group hospital base is then developed from the army hospital base evacuation hospitals remaining in the old army hospital base area. This method guarantees continuous treatment and evacuation.

The Soviets point out that successful maneuvering depends largely upon the capacity of army group (front) and army hospital bases and an adequate reserve of undeployed hospitals at the beginning of an operation.

2. VETERINARY SERVICE

Sick and wounded horses which do not require special treatment and are able to follow their units are not evacuated.

Regimental veterinary hospitals usually are established near the rear boundary of regimental rear areas. Divisional veterinary hospitals are established near the rear boundaries of division rear areas. Because 2 to 4 hours are required for a wounded horse to reach a regimental veterinary hospital, normally located from 5 to 7 miles from the battle line, the two echelons of the veterinary service have proved insufficient. The Russians recommend that advance veterinary aid stations be established by regimental veterinary hospitals. They are located on the line of evacuation nearest the main concentration of horses, normally near the regimental ammunition dump. To facilitate evacuation, division veterinary hospitals may detail evacuation sections which are located at the boundary of the regimental rear area.

From division veterinary hospitals, horses are evacuated to veterinary evacuation and field hospitals in army rear areas. The next echelon of evacuation is the army group (front) veterinary hospital bases.

Section V. MAINTENANCE AND MISCELLANEOUS SERVICES

1. MAINTENANCE

a. General. Maintenance in the Red Army is facilitated by standardization of types and models which enables individual depots to carry small stocks of parts. Maintenance facilities primarily handle three categories of matériel: automotive and armored vehicles, weapons and equipment, and clothing.

Modification of the maintenance service during the war resulted in an echelon system. Prior to 1943, all vehicular repair was controlled by the Main Administration of Armored Equipment. When the Main Administration of Motor Transport of the Red Army was organized under the Chief of the Rear Services of the Red Army, it also was charged with vehicular repair. Because the same workshops handle the repair of trucks, tanks, and tractors, it would appear that all repair of automotive and armored vehicles has been placed formally under the Main Administration of Motor Transport. It is presumed, however, that the Main Administration of Armored Equipment retains considerable control over the repair of its own matériel.

To simplify maintenance, the Red Army has developed two basic types of mobile unit repair shops. Type A is a GAZ–AA truck with a lathe, tools, welding equipment, and spare parts. Type B is a ZiS-6 truck with a lathe, tools, replacement parts, crane, and battery charger. Workshop companies are composed of varying numbers of these trucks.

b. Tank maintenance. Special attention is given the maintenance of medium and heavy tanks. Since 1941, the Red Army has been forced to increase its mobile maintenance and repair echelons six-fold. These echelons were able to handle approximately 50 percent of required services and repairs at the outbreak of the war. In 1945, they handled 92 percent. Previously, the Soviets depended primarily upon first echelon repairs, cannibalization, and improvisation in conjunction with major repairs at fixed bases. They now employ a complex system of maintenance and evacuation which places great emphasis upon unit replacement and subsequent specialized repair.

Tank companies (10 medium or 5 heavy tanks) are serviced by unit mechanic teams. Battalions (21 to 31 medium tanks) have workshop platoons. Brigades (63 medium tanks) and regiments (21 heavy tanks) are serviced by technical maintenance companies. Corps (200 to 250 mixed vehicles) are maintained by mobile repair bases. In addition, tank armies and corps groups have mobile plants for general and specialized work including electroplating, and motor, transmission, clutch, and electrical reconstruction.

The present routine of preventive maintenance for Red Army armored vehicles approximates U. S. practice. Outstanding differences are the comprehensiveness of Soviet first echelon inspection and the reduced intervals between second and third echelon services (25, 50, and 100 hours as compared with 50 and 100 hours in the U. S.). Overheating and winter maintenance are given special attention.

FIRST ECHELON MAINTENANCE. Tank crews conduct first echelon maintenance under supervision of platoon and company commanders. Maintenance includes check of ammunition, fuel, oil, and water and careful examination of vehicles. Check requires from 2 to 4 hours daily.

SECOND ECHELON MAINTENANCE. Second echelon maintenance is performed in the battalion, brigade, and regiment every 25 and 50 hours of operation. It includes cleaning of motors and other assemblies, refueling and lubricating, examination of all connections and regulating mechanisms, lubricating of all friction surfaces, cleaning all filters, and completion of a series of maintenance procedures. In combat under unfavorable climatic and terrain conditions, second echelon maintenance is performed as often as every 10 to 15 hours of operation.

THIRD ECHELON MAINTENANCE. Third echelon maintenance is performed in regiments, brigades, and corps every 90 to 100 hours of operation. It includes change of transmission lubricant, valve adjustment and a check of the fuel injection system.

Prior to extensive operations, thorough maintenance is carried out, including partial removal of hull armor and over-all checking and cleaning. All echelons cooperate in this check. Centralization by battalion is recommended. After a battalion has been serviced, its vehicles are given a 20-hour test run.

The Red Army has made careful provisions for winter operation of armored vehicles. Heating devices include auxiliary interior water heating. Dual kerosene lamps heat water coils, installed in the crew compartment, which are connected to the cooling system. Fixtures pre-heat the air for fuel injectors. All motors are pre-heated before starting.

Prior to movement over ice or snow, tracks are loosened and idlers and bogies are cleaned to avoid breaking of shoes. Grousers are used for movement over broken terrain.

c. Tank recovery. The maintenance service also recovers damaged armored vehicles. Recovery battalions recover disabled tanks and evacuate them to an assembly point at the army supply base. Vehicles are then sent to the zone of interior for major repairs or disposal as scrap.

Recovery battalions normally are equipped with 40 trucks and 100 tractors. Companies from recovery battalions are attached to armies. Concentrated employment of recovery units, controlled from special observation posts, results in rapid evacuation of disabled tanks. Premiums are paid for recovered tanks by the transport administration. Crews are punished for abandoning disabled tanks.

d. Weapons maintenance. The Chief of Artillery Supply is responsible for weapons maintenance and repair. Artillery weapons are repaired in army group, army, regimental, and battery workshops, which may work together or independently. An echelon system, similar to the automotive echelon repair system, exists.

Army groups (fronts) have repair shops on railroad cars at their disposal for medium repairs on infantry and artillery weapons. Weapons requiring major repairs are collected and forwarded by the Main Administration of Artillery to repair plants in the zone of interior. Weapons damaged beyond repair are sent to foundries for scrap.

In armies, a mobile repair shop functions under the weapons repair group of the artillery supply section. This shop consists of several light trucks, from 20 to 30 armorers, and 2 to 3 opticians.

Army repair shop functions include:

Replacement of major parts and assemblies.
Cannibalization of damaged weapons.
Re-riveting of fixed joints on a larger scale than can be done by regimental repair shops.
Lathe adjustments and manufacture of parts.
Electric welding.

In peacetime, regimental repair shops which have the necessary equipment may perform similar services.

Division artillery is provided with a divisional field workshop. It includes one truck with several armorers. Division workshops perform light repair and, when necessary, partial medium repair of weapons and equipment. Mobile repair shops may

perform emergency repairs on the battlefield. Normally division artillery and attached army workshops are located at division supply points.

Comparatively few technicians are assigned for the repair of infantry weapons. Two small arms armorers, two artillery armorers, and four technicians assigned to the ammunition depots of division supply points perform light repairs.

e. Clothing maintenance. Maintenance of clothing is handled by laundries and workshops of the intendance service. A shoemaker and a tailor under the regimental Chief of Intendance perform necessary repairs. Divisions have a laundry and larger workshops. Armies are provided with two laundries and workshops capable of large-scale repair. The intendance administration of an army group (front) and the main intendance administration of the Red Army send clothing and boots to factories in the zone of interior for repair.

2. CAPTURED WEAPONS

A special organization for the collection, repair, and transportation of captured weapons exists independently of the rear services. It is also responsible for the recovery of Soviet weapons. Its agencies operate at all levels of command.

Special commands for captured weapons are attached to regiments by divisional groups for captured enemy weapons. The collection and transportation of captured weapons are the responsibility of companies for captured weapons at army level. Battalions and brigades for captured weapons and evacuation companies and trains are attached to army groups (fronts) and armies.

Transportation for captured weapons and damaged Soviet matériel is provided by army group and army Chiefs of Army Transportation, who place returning empty rolling stock at the disposal of captured weapons units.

3. PRISONER-OF-WAR EVACUATION

Basic orders for the evacuation of prisoners of war were issued in January 1943. Prisoners are forwarded rapidly from lower units to army rear areas. Little time is allowed for interrogation in battalions, regiments, and divisions.

Prisoners normally are marched to army assembly stations. Occasionally empty trucks are used to transport them. Prisoners are turned over to the NKVD in army rear areas. The NKVD handles further evacuation with the cooperation of the Chief of Army Transportation.

344

4. POSTAL SERVICE

All Red Army mail was handled by the Peoples' Commissariat of Signal Communications until 1942, when it was subordinated to the main administration of the Chief of Signal Communications (Peoples' Commissariat of Defense).

The army postal service is also dependent upon the Formations Division of the General Staff for assignment of APO numbers and postal security measures.

Field post offices at army group (front), army, and division levels are assigned trucks to transport mail from railroad stations to units.

Section VI. ADMINISTRATIVE PROCEDURE

1. BASIC STAFF PROCEDURE

The basic documents through which administration of the rear services is carried out are the administrative estimate, the administrative order, and the periodic reports.

Upon receipt of preliminary instructions concerning a projected operation from the Chief of Staff of the next higher headquarters, the Chief of the Rear Services prepares an administrative estimate of all supplies required for the operation. Simultaneously, the Chief of Staff prepares an operations plan. Both make oral reports to the Commander.

When a final decision is reached by the Commander (or the Military Council of an army), the Commander and the Chief of Staff issue oral instructions to the Chief of the Rear Services and to the chiefs of artillery, armored troops, and technical services. Occasionally the instructions are issued only to the Chief of the Rear Services, who forwards them to the other services.

The Chief of the Rear Services and the chiefs of artillery, armored troops, and the technical services issue preliminary instructions to their subordinate organizations and installations.

Material for the administrative order and special instructions is prepared by the Chief of the Rear Services. The material is based partly on data furnished by the chiefs of the individual services.

The Commander, his Chief of Staff, and the Chief of the Rear Services sign the administrative order and special instructions. Army administrative orders are issued to rifle, tank, mechanized, and cavalry corps, the chiefs of artillery, armored troops, and technical services, adjacent armies, and army group

headquarters. The special instructions are issued to commandants of railroad supply stations, road maintenance divisions, motor transport units, motor transport divisions maintenance group, individual supply and medical organizations, and to local civil authorities.

Execution of the administrative order is supervised by the Chief of the Rear Services who receives copies of orders, requisitions, and reports of subordinate staffs and organizations.

Special attention is given to the rear services of tank, mechanized, and cavalry corps. Their rear services are coordinated with those of the formations in whose zones the mobile forces are operating. Consideration is given to their specialized supply requirements, and advance plans are made to guarantee the continuous flow of supplies to mobile formations after the break-through is accomplished.

2. ADMINISTRATIVE ESTIMATES AND SUPPLY PLAN

The administrative estimates of the Chief of the Rear Services normally are submitted to formation or unit commanders prior to the drafting of the Commander's administrative decision.

They include requirements and availability of basic supplies, schedule of issue for allotted matériel, possibility of utilizing local resources, delivery schedule for supplies and available transport, disposition of rear subdivisions, extension of rear area and daily assignment of supply bases, items to be evacuated, and security of the rear area.

The Chiefs of the Rear Services and Technical Deputy Commanders of tank and mechanized formations prepare their plans for the organization of the rear services. Their plans are based on the tactical and rear service decisions of the formation Commander. Preliminary work is carried out simultaneously with the preparation of the combat plan.

On the basis of available information, the Chief of the Rear Services issues preliminary instructions to his subordinate chiefs, notes data of the administrative order of higher headquarters on situation map, makes map reconnaissance for probable supply roads, determines tasks of rear services for each phase of operation, drafts a proposed decision for the commander on employment of rear services, prepares a report for the Commander and a draft of the administrative order, organizes necessary coordinations with the chief of the rear services of adja-

345

cent units. If necessary, he submits requisitions to higher headquarters for additional supplies.

The supply plan, which provides basic information for the administrative order, consists of a number of documents including a map of the rear area, a report to the Commander from the Chief of the Rear Services, a supply schedule, and a chart of planned displacement of rear area installations.

The supply plan includes the following:

Supply requirements for each phase.

Supplies to be carried by units.

Reserves to be accumulated for operation at supply base.

Supply routes.

Organization of transportation for each phase.

Displacement of rear services.

Security measure for communication routes and rear area installations.

Signal communication with the rear.

Axis of communication for the Chief of the Rear Services and the chiefs of services.

3. COMMAND DECISION

The Commander's decision for the employment of the rear services is based upon his estimate of the tactical situation, his Chief of Staff's tactical estimate, the administrative estimate, and information and recommendations of his Chief of the Rear Services. (When tank or mechanized formations are attached, the army Commander also receives information and an estimate from a deputy for those formations.)

He considers enemy capabilities and possible lines of action, effect of enemy fire or attack on rear area installations, probable matériel and personnel losses, ammunition and fuel requirements, availability and condition of transport and equipment, supply and evacuation road nets, security measures for lines of communication and the rear echelon, medical evacuation, priority of supply and maintenance, etc.

The Commander's decisions regarding the rear services include:

Organization of supply and evacuation roads.

Rates of expenditure of fuel and ammunition for each phase.

Supply requirements of break-through units.

Displacement of rear echelon units.

Supplies to be accumulated in units and supply points prior to operation.

Priority of supply and maintenance.

Refueling and evacuation of tanks for each phase.

Medical evacuation.

Organization of security for rear services and lines of communication.

Readiness deadlines.

4. ADMINISTRATIVE ORDERS

The administrative order, based upon the Commander's decisions and the supply plan of Chief of the Rear Services, is issued simultaneously with the combat order. It is drafted for the Commander by the Chief of the Rear Services and is checked by the Commander and his Chief of Staff. The administrative order is signed by the Commander, the Chief of Staff, and the Chief of the Rear Services.

The army administrative order includes:

Location and operation schedules for supply points and evacuation terminals.

Disposition of rear area installations.

Supply and evacuation routes.

Boundary lines of rear areas.

Division administrative orders also include:

Boundary lines of regimental rear areas.

Location of reinforcements.

Daily rates of expenditure for ammunition, fuel, rations, and fodder by unit.

Organization and schedule of supply.

Regimental administrative orders also include:

Distribution schedule for hot food.

Disposition of evacuation points.

Evacuation schedules for personnel, horses, and matériel.

Utilization of local resources.

Displacement plans for second echelon of headquarters.

Schedule of periodic reports.

Fragmentary orders or individual instructions may be issued instead of the full administrative order. The location of regimental ammunition dumps and division supply points are included in regimental combat orders.

An administrative order for mechanized formations engaged in break-through operations covers only the first phase of the operation, normally the first day. During the action, the Chief of the Rear Services issues separate instructions based on the general plan for organization of rear services as approved by the Commander of the mechanized formation.

The administrative order for a break-through operation includes:

> Location of supply installations.
> Amount of supplies to be issued.
> Supply issue schedule.
> Supply and evacuation routes.
> Organization of transportation.
> Supplies to be carried by units.
> Displacement of rear services.
> Rate of expenditure of ammunition and fuel.
> Resupply points and schedules.
> Priority of repair and evacuation of matériel.
> Repair deadlines.
> Organization of medical evacuation.
> Organization of collection of captured weapons and matériel.
> Combat disposition of second echelon of command.
> Schedule and content of periodic reports.

The administrative order as drafted by the Chief of the Rear Services of tank or mechanized corps is submitted to the Corps Commander in the presence of the Chief of Staff and the Commander's technical deputy.

The Soviets recommend that preliminary instructions be issued to the Chief of the Rear Services of subordinate units and the commanders of various rear service installations in addition to the administrative order.

Efficient operation of the rear services during combat is dependent upon close control. It is emphasized that a tank corps Chief of the Rear Services should remain with the corps' first echelon of command not only during the period of organizational operation, but also during the actual break-through operation. Liaison with army group (front) or army rear services and control of rear echelons behind infantry units can be maintained by the chief of one of the services, preferably the tank corps Chief of Intendance. All other personnel of the rear and technical services move through the breach with the corps.

Radio and armored cars are used to maintain liaison between tank or mechanized corps' first and second echelons during the first phase of break-through operations. Air liaison has been found most satisfactory during later phases. Flexibility of rear service operation during break-through operations is stressed.

5. PERIODIC REPORTS

Contents of periodic reports for a formation are determined by the higher headquarters.

Periodic reports normally include:

> Location of supply points and evacuation terminals (for divisions only).
> Supply and evacuation routes.
> Disposition and condition of transport.
> Disposition and condition of rear area units.
> Expenditure of ammunition and fuel.
> Matériel losses.
> Personnel and horse strength reports.
> Supply of ammunition, fuel, rations, and fodder.
> Utilization of local resources.
> Medical and veterinary situation.
> Security of the rear (for divisions only).
> General conclusions regarding supply and maintenance (for divisions only).

347

TECHNICAL MANUAL

HANDBOOK ON U. S. S. R. MILITARY FORCES

TM 30–430 is being published in installments to expedite dissemination to the field. This chapter should be inserted in the loose-leaf binder furnished with Chapter V, November 1945

WAR DEPARTMENT
WASHINGTON 25, D. C., 30 July 1946

TM 30–430, Handbook on U. S. S. R. Military Forces, is published for the information and guidance of all concerned.

[AG 300.7 (13 Mar 46)]

BY ORDER OF THE SECRETARY OF WAR:

OFFICIAL: DWIGHT D. EISENHOWER
    EDWARD F. WITSELL   *Chief of Staff*
    Major General
    The Adjutant General

DISTRIBUTION:
    AGF (80) ; ASF (2) ; T (10) ; Arm & Sv Bd (1) ; S Div ASF (1).
    Refer to FM 21–6 for explanation of distribution formula.

CHAPTER XI

AIR FORCES

PART I.   ORGANIZATION

Section I.   COMMAND ORGANIZATION

1. GENERAL

The air forces of the U. S. S. R. consist of separate forces, the most important of which are the Red Army Air Force and the Red Naval Air Force, integral parts of the Red Army and Navy. The Fighter Aviation of the Air Defense Forces of the Red Army, the Air Force of the NKVD, and the Civil Air Fleet are the remaining separate forces.

2. MAIN ADMINISTRATION OF THE RED ARMY AIR FORCE

a. General. The Main Administration of the Red Army Air Force, headed by commander of the Red Army Air Force, is the highest command and administrative organization of the Red Army Air Force. It is subordinate in technical and administrative matters to the Commissariat of the Armed Forces and, operationally, to the commander in chief and the General Headquarters.

Assisting the commander are a first deputy, a political deputy, various deputies and assistants, a Counterintelligence Division, a headquarters staff, and a military council.

b. Military council. The military council consists of the commander of the Red Army Air Force, the chief of staff, the chief of the Rear Services, the chief engineer, and the chief of the Political Administration. Its functions are the consideration of all policy matters pertaining to the Red Army Air Force and the appointment and dismissal of all senior air force personnel.

c. Staff of the Red Army Air Force. The staff of the Red Army Air Force, under the direction of the chief of staff, whose deputy is the chief of the operations section, acts as the operational center of the Main Administration of the Red Army Air Force. All sections of the staff of the Red Army Air Force work in close collaboration with and are limited in function by the corresponding divisions of the Red Army General Staff. The staff is composed of seven sections as follows:

OPERATIONS SECTION. The Operations Section, which prepares detailed plans for employment of units on the basis of information supplied by other sections of the staff, works closely with the Operations Division in the Red Army General Staff.

INTELLIGENCE SECTION. The Intelligence Section supervises all intelligence organizations of subordinate air staffs. It is the center for collation and distribution of reports from subordinate staffs, but the publishing of such reports is the responsibility of the corresponding Intelligence Division of the Red Army General Staff. Assignment of reconnaissance missions, in accordance with the orders of the Red Army General Staff, also is a function of the Intelligence Section.

ORGANIZATION SECTION. The Organization Section is responsible for tables of organization and equipment, and for statistical control of strengths of all Red Army Air Force units.

AIR TRANSPORT SECTION. The Air Transport Section is responsible for the planning and coordination of all air transport operations, including, in time of war, those of the Civil Air Fleet.

CIPHERS SECTION. The Ciphers Section distributes and supervises ciphers and codes used in the Red Army Air Force. The Operations Division of the Red Army General Staff supplies the ciphers and determines time of change.

METEOROLOGY SECTION. The Meteorology Section controls all meteorological services of the Red Army Air Force and works in close coordination with the main administration of the Hydro-Meteorological Service of the Red Army.

INTERNAL AFFAIRS SECTION. The Internal Affairs Section supervises such matters as pay, rations, equipment, clothing, and billeting for personnel of the Red Army Air Force headquarters. It also supervises the Red Army Air Force buildings in Moscow and vicinity.

d. The General Inspectorate. The General Inspectorate supervises and advises the individual branches of the Red Army Air Force through the fighter, ground attack, bomber, *Sturman* (navigation, bombing, and observation), and technical inspectors.

There also is a General Department and, probably, a Chemical Warfare Department.

Some inspectors, such as the inspectors of flying technique, are attached to front-line units in headquarters of air armies, corps, and divisions. Others are sent on inspection trips of front-line units to serve as advisors and to carry out the functions of the General Inspectorate, i. e., to maintain high standards of flying and navigation and to investigate existing problems. Dismissals and appointments of personnel, even of high-ranking officers, may be effected by these inspectors.

e. Main Administration of Airborne Forces. Although the position of the air-borne forces in the organization of the armed forces of the U. S. S. R. is not clearly established, it is believed that they are controlled by a branch of the Main Administration of the Red Army Air Force. It is probable that the Main Administration of the Airborne Forces includes a military council, an operational staff, and the following administrations: Artillery, Engineer, Chemical Warfare, Signal Communications, Flight Service, Parachutes, Rear Services, Personnel (officer personnel), Combat Training (enlisted replacements), Political, and Counterintelligence.

f. Main Administration of the Rear Services. This office is one of the most important branches of the Main Administration of the Red Army Air Force. It is responsible for supply of air armies and, through them, for supply of the regional commands of aviation ground services and the airfield servicing battalions with items peculiar to the air arm. It also coordinates the requirements of operational air units for all other items of supply with the Chief of Rear Services of the Red Army. Its organization is analogous to that of the Main Administration of the Red Army Air Force, of which it is a part, with a political and other deputies, a headquarters staff, and subordinate administrations. The Main Administration of the Rear Services contains four staff sections and six administrations as follows:

SECTION FOR REAR ORGANIZATION. The Section for Rear Organization is in charge of organization for supply and of setting up new ground organization units.

AIRCRAFT AND ENGINE ACCOUNTS SECTION. This section is a central bookkeeping agency for aircraft and engines in the Red Army Air Force. It maintains current strength records extracted from the reports of senior engineers of units, schools, and repair shops.

PERSONNEL SECTION. The Personnel Section is responsible for officer personnel matters.

INSPECTORATE. The Inspectorate serves as an advisory and inspection administration for units of the rear services.

ADMINISTRATION OF TECHNICAL SUPPLY. The Administration of Technical Supply performs its functions of requisition of materials and supervision of storage through the following departments:

> Technical Materials Department (glass, hardware, wood, etc., to be used for repair work).
>
> Special Materials Department (fabrics, chemicals, metals, etc., for repair work).
>
> Special Equipment Department (parachutes, cameras, etc.).
>
> Spare Parts Department (spare parts for aircraft and engines).
>
> Ammunition Department.
>
> Stock Control Department (supervises utilization of surplus goods and repaired captured matériel).
>
> Finance Department (settles accounts for supplies).

ADMINISTRATION OF FUEL AND LUBRICANTS. The Administration of Fuel and Lubricants receives requisitions for fuel and lubricants from Red Army Air Force units and insures distribution through a corresponding Fuel and Lubricants Administration of the Red Army. It operates through the following departments:

> Central Depot Department (plans distribution of aircraft gas and lubricants and directs their storage on the basis of detailed accounts of gas and lubricant supplies).
>
> Aircraft Gasoline and Lubricants Department (supervises distribution of aircraft gas and lubricants and directs shipments to air armies, replacement units, flying schools, and repair shops).

Automotive Gasoline and Lubricants Department (forwards requisitions for automotive gas and lubricants from all units and installations of the Red Army Air Force to the Administration of Fuel and Lubricants, which then insures distribution).

Diesel Fuel Department (functions in the same manner as the above department, but deals with fuel for Diesel motors and anti-freeze products).

Requisition Department (compiles statistics from requisitions received from all Red Army Air Force installations and forwards them to the Administration of Fuel and Lubricants of the Red Army, and effects contracts with the State Oil Marketing Cooperative for aircraft gasoline and lubricants).

Finance Department (handles accounts with the State Oil Marketing Cooperative).

Transport Department (insures the allocation of rail and motor transport for gasoline and lubricants).

ADMINISTRATION OF INTERNAL SUPPLY. The Administration of Internal Supply controls issue and consumption of rations, clothing, and equipment through the Rations Department and the Clothing and Equipment Department. The Clothing and Equipment Department corresponds in function to the Main Intendance Administration of the Red Army.

FINANCE ADMINISTRATION. The Finance Administration, corresponding to the Main Finance Administration of the Red Army, is responsible for pay and for the budget for supplies and materials for the Red Army Air Force.

ADMINISTRATION OF CAPTURED MATÉRIEL. This administration, upon orders from the Captured Matériel Committee of the Red Army, supervises the allocation of captured aircraft equipment.

ADMINISTRATION OF AIRFIELD SERVICING AND CONSTRUCTION. This administration is divided into the following departments:

Airfield Servicing Department (services ground organization formations).

Airfield Construction Department (responsible for equipment and technical supplies for construction and development of airfields).

g. **Main Administration of the Engineer Service.** The Main Administration of the Engineer Service is headed by the chief engineer of the Red Army Air Force, who also is a deputy of the commander of the Red Army Air Force and a member of the Military Council. His responsibilities include supervision of the activity of chief engineers of the air armies and air forces of the military districts. This main administration is responsible, in cooperation with the aircraft industry, for technical development of aircraft and equipment, aircraft repair methods, and airfield installations and equipment. The following administrations function under the Main Administration of the Engineer Service:

ADMINISTRATION OF TECHNICAL SERVICE. The Administration of Technical Service is the most vital part of the Main Administration of the Engineer Service. It controls, through the exercise of its inspectional function, the employment of aircraft, guns, and equipment and insures the serviceability of all aircraft stocks. Engineers of all air units and schools are under the supervision of the Administration of Technical Services. The administration also conducts close liaison with Red Army Air Force research institutes for improvement in aircraft design. It functions through five departments as follows:

Imported Aircraft and Equipment Department.
Fighter Aircraft Department.
Ground Attack Aircraft Department
Bomber Aircraft Department
Schools Department.

MAIN REQUISITION ADMINISTRATION. The Main Requisition Administration places orders for aircraft and parts, guns, and equipment. It operates through 11 departments as follows:

Special Materials Department.
Technical Materials Department.
Engines Department.
Fighter Aircraft Department.
Ground Attack Aircraft Department
Bomber Aircraft Department.
Spare Parts Department.
Automotive Department.
Electrical Armatures and Equipment Department.
Heating Department.

INVENTIONS ADMINISTRATION. This administration corresponds to the Inventions Division of the Affairs Administration of the Commissariat of the Armed Forces. It studies inventions, and maintains a construction bureau and experimental workshop for development work.

ADMINISTRATION OF REPAIR SERVICE. The Administration of Repair Service is divided into the following departments:

Field Repair Department.
Major Repairs Department.
Department for Installations, Repair Workshops, and Factories.
Department for Research and Introduction of New Repair Methods.

The Field Repair Department supervises all field repair shops and assigns them to air armies or military districts. The Major Repairs Department cooperates closely with the aircraft industry and the Main Administration of the Civil Air Fleet, whose repair shops effect the major repairs and overhauling of most Red Army Air Force aircraft. The department also exercises limited control over Red Army Air Force static repair shops. The Department for Installations, Repair Workshops, and Factories supplies machines and tools for repair work. The Department for Research and Introduction of New Repair Methods employs the Scientific Experimental Institute for Aircraft Repairs as a workshop to develop new repair methods.

ADMINISTRATION FOR MECHANIZATION OF AIRFIELD INSTALLATIONS AND EQUIPMENT. Responsibility of the Main Administration of the Engineer Service for airfield installations is discharged by this administration.

In addition to the above administrations, the Main Administration of the Engineer Service also maintains the following technical research institutes:

Scientific Research Institute of the Red Army Air Force. Research for development of new aircraft types and for improvement of existing types is conducted by this institute.
Scientific Research Institute for Aircraft Armament. This institute conducts research on aircraft armament and ammunition.
Scientific Research Institute for Aircraft Materials. This institute conducts research on materials employed in the manufacture of aircraft.

h. Main Administration of Replacement and Training. Although dealing with the same matters as the Main Administration for the Forma-

tion and Equipment of Units of the Red Army, this Main Administration of the Red Army Air Force differs in that its functions include training and replacement organization for officer personnel as well as for enlisted men. It is divided into two administrations as follows:

ADMINISTRATION OF SCHOOLS. The Administration of Schools controls all pregraduate air and ground crew training establishments of the Red Army Air Force. In this capacity it supervises training schedules and courses, and the procurement of instructors, equipment, and sites.

ADMINISTRATION FOR ORGANIZATION OF UNIT FORMATION AND TRAINING. The Administration for Organization of Unit Formation and Training is responsible for the operational training of air and ground crews sent from training establishments. It supervises replacements, reequipment, and activation of new units. Operationally subordinate to it are the replacement air brigades and the replacement air regiments.

i. Administration of Air Academies. The academies of the Red Army Air Force are supervised by the Administration of Air Academies, part of the Main Administration of the Red Army Air Force.

j. Sturman Administration. The *Sturman* Administration, whose chief is the assistant to the commander of the Red Army Air Force for *Sturman* (navigation, bombing, and observation) affairs, controls the *Sturman* service of all units and training institutions of the Red Army Air Force. The supervisory work of this administration includes improvement of navigation; operations and regrouping, insofar as *Sturman* regulations are affected; training of *Sturman* personnel in basic schools, replacement air regiments, and Air Force academies; operations of *Sturman* in air units; supply and improvement of navigational, bombing, and other *Sturman* equipment; and supply to the Red Army Air Force of visual beacon and radio equipment, maps obtained from Topographic Division of the Red Army General Staff, and literature on navigation, bombing, and other *Sturman* matters.

Subordinate to the chief of *Sturman* is the chief of the Aircraft Safety Service of the Red Army Air Force. He controls all aircraft safety personnel through the aircraft safety services in the air armies and air forces of military districts and through the reserve or special units of the Red Army Air Force Aircraft Safety Service. It is his duty to set up aircraft safety devices in rear and forward areas, to distribute information concerning aircraft safety devices and regulations, to inspect all aircraft safety stations, to supervise aircraft safety trainees, to maintain the distribution of aircraft safety devices, to coordinate types of equipment used by the Red Army Air Force with those used by various civil authorities, and to perfect new techniques for aircraft safety.

k. Administration of the Aerial Gunnery Service. The Administration of the Aerial Gunnery Service was created as a special administration in 1943. Its chief is the assistant to the commander of the Red Army Air Force in all matters pertaining to the Aerial Gunnery Service. The responsibility of this administration includes supervision of the training of flying personnel in the use of all aircraft armament in schools and front-line units as well as in replacement units, publication and supervision of regulations for the Aerial Gunnery Service, supervision of appointments of heads of the Aerial Gunnery Service within the Red Army Air Force, advising on aircraft armament for new aircraft, and initiating improved methods for effective use of aircraft armament.

l. Administration of Signal Communications. The Administration of Signal Communications formerly was part of the Ciphers Section of the Air Staff, under the general control of the Commissariat of Signal Communications. However, the introduction of radar and the increasing importance of radio communications resulted in the creation of signal units for the air forces warranting a separate administrative organization. The administration regulates tables of organization and equipment for signal units and supervises signal training programs, development of equipment, and new signal communications methods. It is subordinate technically and operationally to the Main Administration of Signal Troops of the Red Army and to the Signal Division of the General Staff. It maintains close liaison with scientific research institutes.

m. Personnel Administration. The Personnel Administration is responsible for appointments, promotions, decorations, and replacements of officer personnel in the Red Army Air Force. It maintains records of all officers, including those of the special services as well as flying personnel. It is probable that this administration also controls officer replacements in conjunction with the Administration for Organization of Unit Formation and Training. It does not supervise officers schools.

n. Administration of the Medical Service. The Administration of the Medical Service, headed by the chief medical officer of the Red Army Air Force, cooperates closely with the main administration of the Medical Service, which is subordinate to the chief of the Rear Services of the Red Army. The administration of the Medical Service supervises the general health of air force personnel and conducts physical examinations. Although it maintains its own sanatoria, convalescent homes, and hospitals, air force personnel usually are hospitalized in Red Army hospitals.

3. LONG RANGE FORCE

Until the end of 1944, the Long Range Force was a separate air force, subordinate to the Peoples' Commissariat of Defense. Its operational employment against targets of special importance or in front-line sectors of special effort was determined by the General Headquarters. Units committed to a front-line sector may have been placed under temporary operational control of the air army of the sector.

The Main Administration of the Long Range Force was headed by a marshal of aviation. He was assisted by a general deputy, a political deputy, and staff sections and administrations similar to those of the Main Administration of the Red Army Air Force. It maintained its own servicing and training establishments.

Late in 1944, the Long Range Force was converted into an air army. It is probable that its command organization has been retained intact within the Main Administration of the Red Army Air Force.

4. AIR DEFENSE FORCES

The Main Administration of the Air Defense Forces is subordinate directly to the Commander in Chief, to the General Headquarters, and to the Commissariat of Defense, as are the other main administrations of the arms and services. It controls the fighter units allotted to it, the antiaircraft and early warning components of the strategic air defense system, and the passive civil defense system organized locally by the Commissariat of Internal Affairs. It is believed that since 1944 the fighter aviation of the Air Defense Forces has assumed a position of predominance over the antiaircraft artillery component within the Air Defense Forces.

5. RED NAVAL AIR FORCE

During World War II, the Main Administration of the Red Naval Air Force was subordinate to the Commander in Chief of the Red Navy, to the Supreme Naval Council, and to the Commissariat of the Navy. However, since the reorganization of the Soviet armed forces in February 1946, the exact position of this branch is not clear.

The Main Administration of the Red Naval Air Force is believed to include staff sections and administrations similar to those of the Main Administration of the Red Army Air Force. The Red Naval Air Force has its own servicing and training organizations.

6. CIVIL AIR FLEET

The Civil Air Fleet is subordinate directly to the Council of Peoples' Commissars. During World War II, it was controlled operationally by the commanders of the Red Army Air Force and the Long Range Force.

The Main Administration of the Civil Air Fleet is known to include the following elements:

> Council (similar to the Military Councils).
> Director General.
> > Political Department.
> > Legal Department.
> > Medical Department.
> > Technical Department.
> > Construction Department.
> > Repair Department.
> > Personnel Department.
> > Publications Department.
> Inspectorate.

The main administration of the Civil Air Fleet also maintains a scientific research institute which is responsible for the following functions:

> Control of air routes, including planning and construction of new routes and fields;
> Supervision of registration of and permits for civil aircraft, flights outside the nation, and foreign air traffic;
> Direction of research for civil aviation and for new types of transport aircraft and equipment;
> Organization of fire-fighting and medical services;
> Organization of production of nonmilitary aircraft;

> Supervision of repair and servicing of all Civil Air Fleet aircraft;
> Supervision of training of Civil Air Fleet flying and ground personnel.

Operational control of the Civil Air Fleet by the Red Army Air Force and the Long Range Force during World War II included supervision of the following functions:

> Supply of Partisans and isolated ground force units;
> Movement of troops and wounded;
> Dropping of agents and paratroopers;
> Courier, transport, ferrying, and photographic missions.

It extended even to the promotion and decoration of Civil Air Fleet personnel employed in military operations. However, elements of the Civil Air Fleet employed in military operations remained under the administrative control of the Main Administration of the Civil Air Fleet.

The lower echelons of the Civil Air Fleet are divided into district commands, each of which is similar to the Main Administration of the Civil Air Fleet. The district commands are authorized to negotiate with the Soviet Republics and to supervise officers in command of units and airfields within the districts. Some Civil Air Fleet districts coincide with military districts of the Red Army. Civil Air Fleet branch offices are located in all other military districts where there is no Civil Air Fleet Administration.

7. AIR FORCE OF THE NKVD

The Administration of the Air Force of the Commissariat of Internal Affairs (NKVD) controls the air units of the NKVD. (For further details, see ch. IV.)

Section II. TACTICAL AIR FORCES

1. AIR ARMIES OF THE RED ARMY AIR FORCE

a. General. Air armies, which include both flying and servicing organizations, are the largest operational units of the Red Army Air Force. They are responsible for the conduct of aerial warfare for an Army group (front). The flying formations and service units are directed by the commander of the air army, his staff, and a military council (fig. 1).

The flying units of an air army include a variable number of air corps, independent air divisions, and a few independent regiments and squadrons. Usually included among the independent regiments and

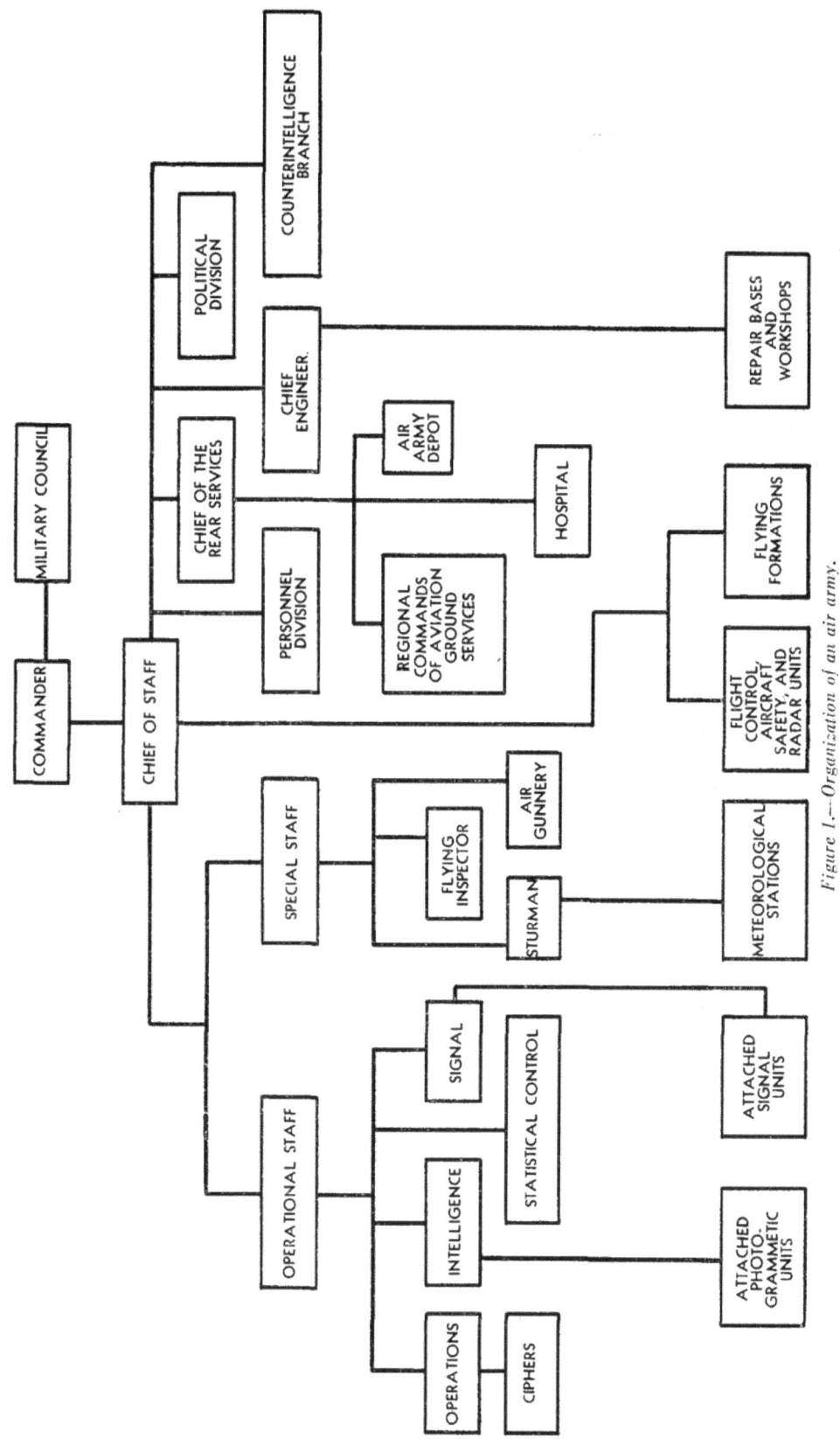

Figure 1.— Organization of an air army.

355

squadrons attached directly to an air army are reconnaissance regiments (both long and short range), several reconnaissance spotting regiments, and a liaison regiment or squadron from the Civil Air Fleet. During the early part of World War II, a demonstration and training regiment usually was attached to each air army, but these are believed to have been disbanded.

Most of the service units within the ground organization of the air army are grouped under regional commands of aviation ground services, which are subordinate to the chief of the rear services of the air army. Regional commands of aviation ground services are administrative organizations operating as headquarters of ground regions. The number of regions into which an air army is divided may vary. At the end of World War II, there was an average of five per air army. Subordinate to a regional command of aviation ground services are the following ground units:

Several airfield servicing battalions, each servicing one or, in exceptional cases, two to three air regiments.

An airfield engineer battalion.

Several airfield technical companies, one attached to each airfield servicing battalion.

One captured matériel company.

One to two independent motor transport battalions.

Several truck workshops for minor repairs, attached to the airfield servicing battalions.

Several independent signal companies, one attached to each regional command of aviation ground services and airfield servicing battalion.

One advanced supply depot.

Several airfield weather stations, attached to airfield servicing battalions.

Service units directly subordinate to members of

Components	Number per air army	Personnel per unit	Aircraft per unit	Trucks per unit	Total personnel	Total aircraft	Total trucks
Air army headquarters	1	500	(10)	....	500	(10)	....
Fighter corps	1	1,655	258	....	1,655	258	....
Ground attack corps	1	3,283	387	....	3,283	387	....
Bomber corps	1	2,278	198	....	2,278	198	....
Independent fighter division	1	790	129	....	790	129	....
Independent ground attack division	1	1,060	129	....	1,060	129	....
Long-range reconnaissance regiment	1	387	35	....	387	35	....
Short-range reconnaissance regiment	1	387	(35)	....	387	(35)	....
Reconnaissance spotting regiment	5	(300)	(35)	....	(1,500)	(175)	....
Liaison regiment	1	(300)	(35)	....	(300)	(35)	....
Liaison squadron	1	33	10	....	33	10	....
Regional command of aviation ground service	5	93	3	....	465	15	....
Airfield servicing battalion	30	270	....	70	8,100	....	2,100
Airfield engineer battalion	5	500	....	70	2,500	....	350
Airfield technical company	30	120	....	7	3,600	....	210
Independent truck battalion	5	200	....	80	1,000	....	400
Truck workshop (for minor repairs)	30	40	....	4	1,200	....	120
Signal regiment	1	1,136	....	....	1,136	....	....
Signal battalion	3	(400)	....	....	(1,200)	....	....
Signal company	39	150	....	....	5,850	....	....
Independent signal company	35	56	....	8	1,960	....	280
Air force weather station	30	8	....	2	240	....	60
Divisional weather station	9	7	....	....	63	....	....
Advanced supply depot	1	150	....	....	150	....	....
Air army depot	1	(100)	....	....	(100)	....	....
PARM-1	36	12	....	2	432	....	72
PARM-2-5	....	(30)	....	5	....	....	....
Static aircraft repair shop	1	(250)	....	....	(250)	....	....
Railway aircraft repair workshops	1	(250)	....	....	(250)	....	....
Static truck repair workshop	1	(250)	....	....	(250)	....	....
Aircraft safety station	....	....	....	....	....	....	....
Flight control unit	....	....	....	....	....	....	....
Radar unit	1	60	....	....	60	....	....
Total	....	....	....	....	40,977	1,416	3,592

NOTE.—Figures in parentheses are tentative.

Figure 2.--Estimated strength of an average air army.

356

the air army staff include: an air army depot, subordinate to the Chief of the Rear Services; several mobile aircraft repair bases (usually, one for each air division), their mobile aircraft repair shops as well as independent mobile aircraft repair shops, a static aircraft repair shop, a railway aircraft repair shop, all subordinate to the chief engineer; a possible static truck repair shop, the subordination of which is not known; an air signal regiment, subordinate to the Chief of the Signal Service; other signal units, attached to flying formations; aircraft safety stations, which probably are subordinate to the chief *Sturman*, but which also are subordinate to the Chief of the Signal Service for services involving the use of Red Army Air Force signal equipment; flight control and radar units, subordinate to the chief *Sturman*; and a photogrammetic company, subordinate to the Chief of the Intelligence Service.

The average air army is estimated to include 41,000 officers and enlisted men, 1,400 aircraft, and from 3,500 to 4,000 trucks (fig. 2). The large number of trucks is an indication of the high degree of mobility of the components of an air army.

b. Air corps. Air corps originally were formed in the latter part of 1942 as staffs controlling a number of divisions to facilitate the redeployment of units and the commitment of new units. The corps then became subordinate to the commander of the air army to which it was assigned temporarily. Whenever a mobile ground force formation was supported by an entire air corps, liaison personnel usually were assigned to the staff of the air corps.

By 1943 air corps were operating on a more permanent basis, and the corps staffs were assuming many of the operational and administrative functions of air army staffs. At the end of World War II, many corps had been subordinate to the same air armies for a sufficient length of time to warrant the assumption that they should no longer be considered a mobile reserve.

The staff of the air corps, although larger, is similar to that of an air division (fig. 3). It maintains operational and planning control over its subordinate divisions in a manner similar to that of an air army staff. Two, or occasionally three, air divisions normally are subordinate to an air corps. They all are of the same type, i. e., fighter, bomber, or ground attack. One fighter division occasionally is included in a ground attack corps to provide fighter protection. During World War II, there also were

some mixed air corps, but these were replaced gradually by homogeneous corps.

c. Air divisions. Air divisions, tactically subordinate to air armies or corps, initiate no independent decisions regarding operations, but operate only on orders from the staffs of the air armies or corps. The division commander determines which of the subordinate regiments shall be employed, and may even select the crews in critical situations.

Staff	Type of division	
	Fighter and ground attack	Bomber
Headquarters	3	3
Political division	6	6
Operations staff	19	24
Special staff	14	24
Engineer division	5	10
Rear services	2	4
Liaison flight	9	9
Total	58	80

Figure 3.—Personnel strengths for air division staffs.

Divisions and corps are designated, according to function, as fighter, bomber, or ground attack. Divisions usually contain three regiments of the same role, although four or more regiments occasionally have been identified with a division. By the end of World War II, most divisions were equipped with aircraft not only of the same role, but also of the same type. Ground attack divisions occasionally contained one fighter regiment, but by the end of the war most ground attack divisions also were completely homogeneous. As in the case of air corps, mixed divisions seem to have been discarded.

d. Air regiments. Air regiments are subordinate to air divisions, or are "independent" regiments directly subordinate to an air army or to the Red Army Air Force.

Regiments subordinate to an air division are assigned to operations by the division, usually for a period extending only for 24 hours. The commander of the regiment arranges the order of take-off, method of approach, and other operational details. Commanders of independent regiments assume more responsibility for planning and carrying out orders.

Air regiments are the fundamental Red Army Air Force units, having fixed tables of organization and equipment. At the beginning of World War II, all tactical regiments had 60 aircraft, but they were reduced to 20 planes per regiment after the tremendous losses of the first few weeks. By February 1943 the strength was increased to 32 aircraft. Present personnel and aircraft strengths for the principal types of air regiments of the Red Army Air Force are shown in figure 4. For break-down of personnel strengths of regiments and squadrons see figure 6.

Strength	Type of regiment		
	Fighter	Ground attack	Bomber
Number of squadrons............	3	3	3
Combat planes..................	36	36	27
Liaison and training planes........	2	2	2
Headquarters planes.............	4	4	3
Personnel.....................	244	337	342 [1]

[1] Varies slightly with type of bomber employed.

Figure 4.—Present personnel and aircraft strengths of Red Air Force regiments.

Independent regiments vary more in strength than regiments subordinate to divisions. Both long and short range reconnaissance regiments, usually subordinate to the Reconnaissance Section of the air army, have variable numbers of squadrons. Reconnaissance spotting regiments, operationally subordinate to army group artillery commanders, have 32 aircraft including 2 squadrons of 10 fighter aircraft, 1 squadron of 10 ground attack aircraft, and 2 liaison planes. Another special type of regiment, which, although not employed during most of World War II, may become more prominent in the future, is the weather reconnaissance regiment. In August

1944 the existence of an air reconnaissance regiment, subordinate to the Hydro-Meteorological Service and especially trained to make weather observation flights, was reported. It employed 20 light bomber aircraft.

e. Air squadrons. Air squadrons almost invariably function as elements of the regiment to which they are subordinate, rather than as independent units. During World War II, the trend was to eliminate independent squadrons attached to the headquarters of air corps or air divisions by incorporating them into independent regiments. By the end of the war, only communication and medical squadrons (elements of the Civil Air Fleet) remained independent in the Red Army Air Force, although a few independent liaison squadrons still may be attached directly to army group and army staffs.

Squadrons are divided into flights, usually three, of from three to four planes each, depending upon the role of the squadron. Aircraft and personnel strengths of various types of squadrons are shown in figure 5.

f. Regional commands of aviation ground services. The regional commands of aviation ground services, which are headquarters organiza-

Type squadron	Aircraft	Personnel
Fighter...............	3 flights of 4 planes...........	65
Ground attack...........	do........................	93
Bomber..............	3 flights of 3 planes...........	97
Reconnaissance..........	do........................	98
Liaison..............	do........................	33

Figure 5.—Aircraft and personnel strengths of squadrons.

	Fighter		Ground attack		Bomber		Reconnaissance		Liaison
	Regiment	Squadron	Regiment	Squadron	Regiment	Squadron	Regiment	Squadron	Squadron
Headquarters..................	3	4	3	4	3	4	3	4	2
Political division................	4	....	4	....	4	....	4	....	1
Operations staff................	12	....	12	....	15	1	49	2	3
Special staff...................	7	1	7	1	7	1	15	1	4
Engineer division...............	7	9	7	10	8	18	8	18	2
Headquarters flight..............	13	39	22	54	11	46	11	46	10
Liaison.......................	3	....	3	....	3	....	3	....	....
Total headquarters staff personnel..................	49	53	58	69	51	70	93	71	22
Flying personnel.................	....	12	....	24	....	27	....	27	11
Total squadron personnel..................	....	65	....	93	....	97	....	98	33
Total regimental personnel (on basis of headquarters staffs and 3 squadrons)....................	244	....	337	....	342	....	387	....	....

Figure 6.—Personnel strengths of air regiments and squadrons.

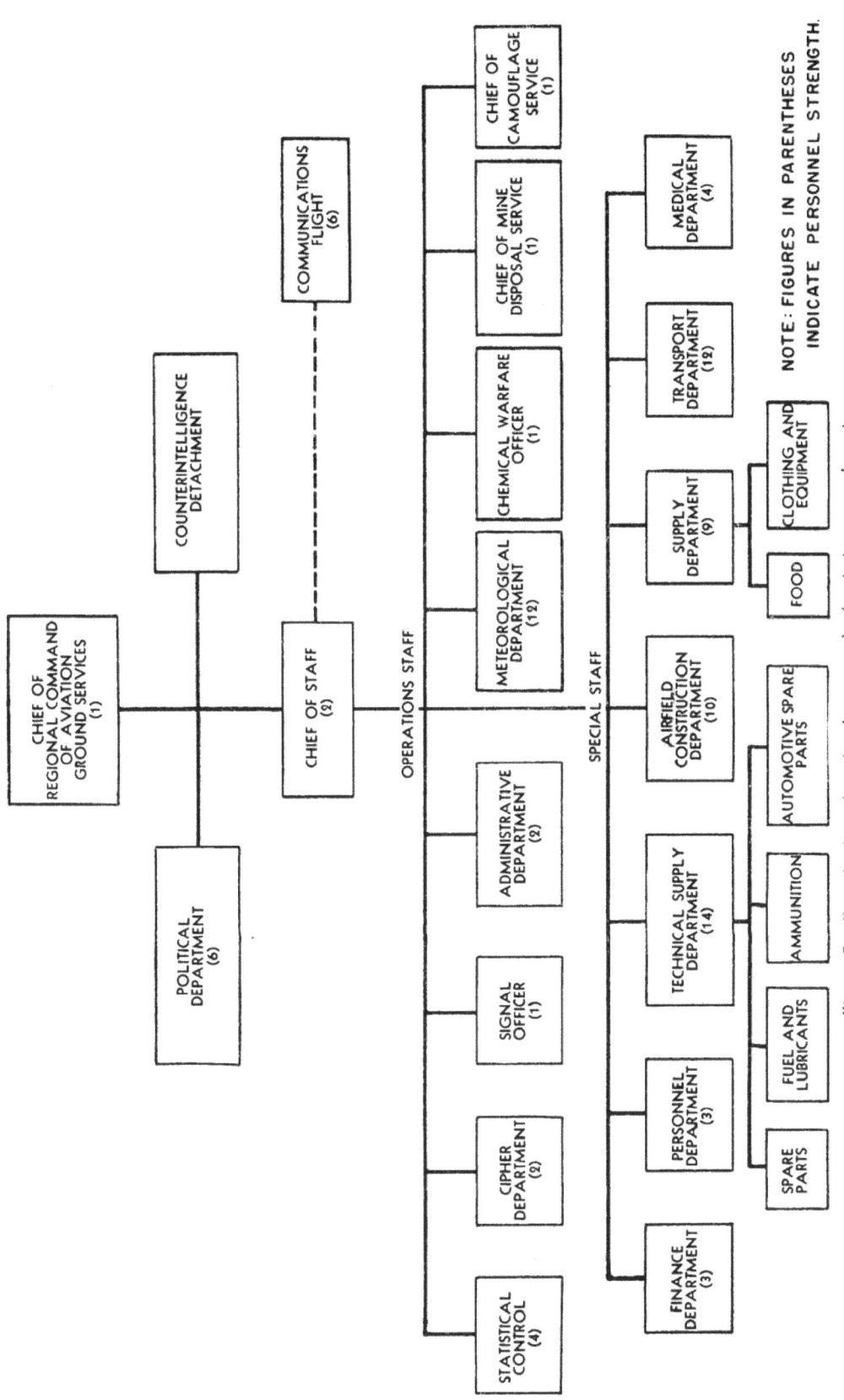

NOTE: FIGURES IN PARENTHESES
INDICATE PERSONNEL STRENGTH.

Figure 7.—Organization of regional command of aviation ground services.

tions for the main servicing units, are subordinate immediately to the Chiefs of the Rear Services of air armies or of air forces of military districts. They are subordinate only operationally to the air corps or divisions deployed within their regions, which may issue necessary orders for the proper functioning of their units. Functions of regional commands of aviation ground services include organization of unit movements, allocation of supplies, and control of operations of subordinate units according to instructions from the air armies. Staff organization of regional commands of aviation ground services is shown in figure 7.

AIRFIELD SERVICING BATTALION. The Airfield Servicing Battalion is subordinate operationally to the commander of the air regiment or regiments which it services, but otherwise to the regional command of aviation ground services. It includes a staff, an airfield company, a truck company, and a technical supply department, which is divided into sections for spare parts and engines, fuel and lubricants, and ammunition. Each airfield servicing battalion has approximately 270 personnel and 70 trucks. Each battalion normally services one air regiment, but in some cases may service two to three. If more than three regiments are serviced by a battalion, a subordinate headquarters is established at a subsidiary airfield.

The Airfield Servicing battalion normally is stationary. When a flying unit moves out of the area, it must be serviced by another battalion.

Services provided include upkeep of airfields (other than repair or large-scale work), guarding of airfields and installations, construction of take-off and landing equipment, transportation of fuel and ammunition to unit technical personnel, provision of transport for unit movements, removal of damaged aircraft, maintenance of weather service, and provision of rations, quarters, and medical service for unit personnel.

AIRFIELD ENGINEER BATTALION. There is at least one Airfield Engineer Battalion subordinate to the Airfield Construction Department of each regional Command of Aviation Ground Services. In addition, there are reserve battalions at the disposal of air armies. Each battalion includes three companies, a pioneer and truck squad, and one field truck repair shop. Personnel strength varies between 350 to 500, plus civilian recruits for manual labor. Approximately 70 vehicles, including tractors, are divided

among the companies. Tractors, fuel cars, and ambulances are assigned to the truck squad.

Building and repair of airfields is the responsibility of the airfield engineer battalion. Sites for new airfields are selected by detachments from the battalion and the airfield servicing battalion, under the direction of the regional command of aviation ground services.

AIRFIELD TECHNICAL COMPANY. The Airfield Technical Company is subordinate to the Airfield Servicing Battalion for operations, but is subject to the commander of the Regional Command of Aviation Ground Services for discipline and to the Airfield Construction Department of the regional command for technical matters.

Each company consists of three platoons. It has approximately 120 personnel and from 6 to 7 trucks. It is the responsibility of the airfield technical company to carry out maintenance of airfield installations and to complete new airfields laid out by the airfield engineer battalion.

INDEPENDENT MOTOR TRANSPORT BATTALION. Subordinate to each Regional Command of Aviation Ground Services is an independent motor transport battalion consisting of two transport truck companies and one special truck company of two platoons and a truck repair shop. Although each battalion originally was equipped with 250 vehicles, it is believed that the number has been reduced to 80, of which 20 are tank cars and 60 are trucks. It is believed that each battalion includes approximately 200 personnel.

Since routine transporting of supplies is one of the functions of the airfield servicing battalion, the independent motor transport battalion may be considered as a reserve for special tasks, such as large-scale movements and transfers.

INDEPENDENT CAPTURED MATÉRIEL COMPANY. Subordinate to each Regional Command of Aviation Ground Services is an independent captured matériel company, consisting of two platoons and a demolition unit. It is believed to include approximately 130 men and from 14 to 18 trucks.

INDEPENDENT SIGNAL COMPANY. An Independent Signal Company, consisting of a radio and a telephone platoon with a personnel strength of approximately 56 men and equipped with 8 trucks, usually is attached to each Regional Command of Aviation Ground Services and Airfield Servicing Battalion.

ADVANCED SUPPLY DEPOT. Supply units included in the ground organization of the Red Army Air

Force are under the ultimate authority of the main administration of the Rear Services. They include central supply depots in the rear areas, air army depots, and advanced supply depots.

The advanced supply depot is subordinate to the regional command of aviation ground services and consists of a clerical and accounting staff and sections responsible for different types of supplies. Personnel strength is approximately 150 men. The main function of the advanced supply depot is to provide the regional command with supplies for air units.

g. Specialized control units. The aircraft safety stations are subordinate to the Aircraft Safety Service, which is under the control of the *Sturman* Administration. They are controlled, in respect to services involving the use of Red Army Air Force signal equipment, by the chief signal officer of the air army.

h. Repair units. The following types of repair units, under the ultimate authority of the Main Administration of the Engineer Service, are employed in the ground organization of the Red Army Air Force: mobile aircraft repair shops, static aircraft repair shops, railway aircraft repair shops, mobile truck repair shops, and static truck repair shops.

There are five types of mobile aircraft repair shops (PARM's), ranging from PARM–1 to PARM–5, the figure indicating the number of repair trucks. PARM–1's are subordinate in disciplinary and technical matters to mobile aircraft repair bases, which serve as their administrative headquarters. One mobile aircraft repair base, controlling from three to five PARM–1's, usually is attached to each air division, although it is subordinate directly to the field repairs section under the chief engineer of the air army. Operationally, the PARM–1 is subordinate to the chief engineer of the air regiment to which it is attached. It depends upon the regional command of aviation ground services and its subordinate units for supplies, rations, and billeting.

A PARM–1 normally includes approximately 12 men, a repair truck, and 1 to 2 transport vehicles. Its chief function is the performance of minor repairs the air regiment technicians are unable to handle. PARM's–2 to –5 are subordinate to the section for major repairs under the chief engineers of air armies, and are employed on major repairs either in rear areas or as mobile reserves for front-line repair work.

Static aircraft repair shops also are subordinate to the section for major repairs under the chief engineers of air armies. There usually is one static aircraft repair shop, with a strength of several hundred men, for each air army. They repair aircraft which are too badly damaged to be repaired by PARM's, and assemble so-called "new" aircraft from parts of damaged planes or captured aircraft.

Railway aircraft repair shops are subordinated the same as the static aircraft repair shops. They include several hundred men and approximately 30 railway cars, outfitted as repair shops.

Mobile truck repair shops are believed to be attached to the airfield servicing battalions, and to be subordinate ultimately to the regional command of aviation ground services. There are believed to be two types of these repair shops. Type A repair shops handle simple truck repair work and have approximately 10 men per truck. Usually, from two to three trucks are attached to units which employ trucks. Type B repair shops are attached to transport units, and may include as many as 50 men.

There are very few static truck repair shops. They are designed for major repair of truck equipment and are believed to have a strength of several hundred men.

i. Air signal service. Senior signal officers commanding signal units are subordinate to the Administration of Signal Communications in the Main Administration of the Red Army Air Force. They receive orders to establish signal communications from the chief of staff or the operations department of the air unit to which the signal unit is attached. Operational signal units are divided into two main types. The so-called regular units function as organic parts of the air units. The independent signal units, although at the disposal of air units, have a more flexible organization (fig. 8).

The largest operational units of the Air Signal Service are air signal regiments, which serve air armies. Air signal battalions serve air corps, and air signal companies serve air divisions, regiments, regional command of aviation ground services, and airfield servicing battalions.

Personnel strength of an air signal regiment is approximately 1,136. Air signal companies vary between 100 to 200 men, depending on the type of air unit serviced. The air signal units maintain signal communications with subordinate staffs, with aircraft in flight, between air and ground units, and with the other air forces, such as the fighter aviation of the Air Defense Forces (PVO). In order to fulfill these tasks, the air signal units maintain the following establishments:

Signal traffic centers.
Telephone and telegraph links.
Radio nets and two-station links.

Signal traffic centers, consisting of a teletype station, a radio receiving and transmitting center, a message center, and a central telephone exchange are located near the staff command post of each air unit.

Telephone and telegraph contact with staffs of higher and lower formations, ground units, cooperating air units, the Aircraft Reporting Service of the Air Defense Forces, and with radio transmitting centers and nearby message centers of the Commissariat of Signal Communication (NKS) are maintained by the air signal units. Both the Red Army Air Force and the Red Army use the NKS network.

Radio is the most important means of communication. Radio contact is established by the air signal units with staffs of higher and lower formations, ground units, cooperating air units, planes in flight,

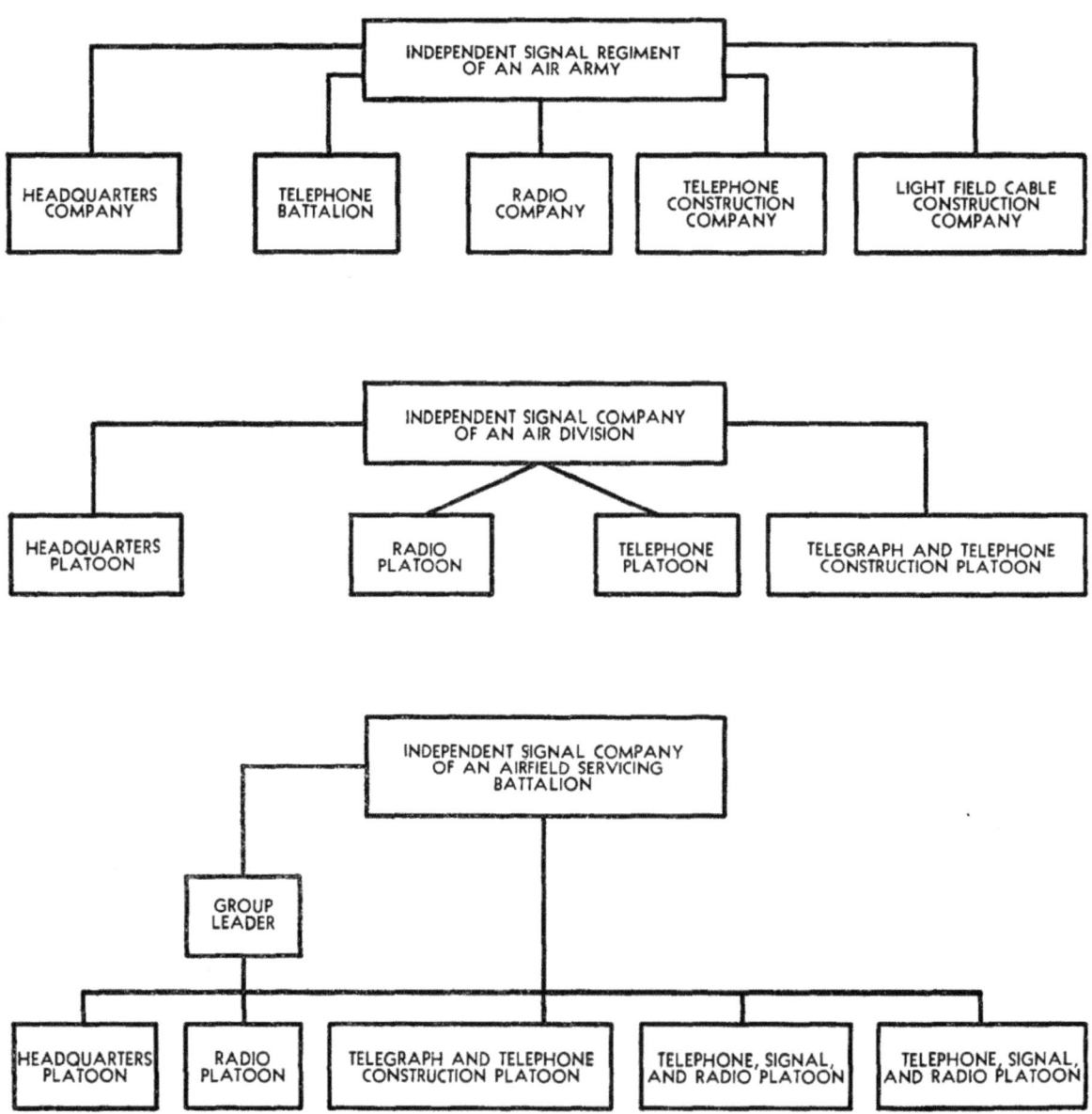

Figure 8.—Organization of independent air signal regiments and companies.

and for reception from air defense units. Air signal units also establish radio stations for the aircraft control and warning systems of the Air Observer Corps, for the command posts of air units, for service at points of concentration and those requiring fighter protection, and for all airfields.

j. Meteorological service. The chief of the weather service of an air army is subordinate to the chief *Sturman* of the air army. The weather service within the region of the air army consists of airfield weather stations, which provide weather information to air regiments, and of weather stations attached to operational staffs of air corps and divisions.

The airfield weather stations are subordinate to the commanders of Airfield Servicing Battalions for discipline, to the chiefs of the Meteorological Service of the Regional Commands of Aviation Ground Services for technical matters, and to the *Sturman* of the air regiments for operations. An airfield weather station normally includes eight men: the chief of the station, a senior meteorologist, two junior meteorologists, two wireless operators, and two observers. This group moves with its airfield servicing battalion and is equipped with two trucks. Divisional weather stations are believed to include seven men: chief of the station, an engineering meteorologist, a senior meteorologist, a junior meteorologist, two wireless operators, and one observer.

It is the task of each aviation weather station to provide weather information for flights within its own region to the *Sturman* of the air unit. If the air formation flies beyond the boundary of the region, its weather station must arrange for the information to be supplied by the weather stations through whose regions it passes. The reports of the aviation weather stations are based entirely on the forecasts of the Central Forecasting Institute at Moscow, and information only up to 6 hours in advance may be issued.

2. RED NAVAL AIR FORCE UNITS

a. Flying units of the naval air arm. Flying units of the naval air arm attached to the four fleets (Black Sea, Baltic Sea, Arctic, and Pacific) and a few units attached to the flotillas of the Red Navy consist of air divisions (formerly called brigades), with component regiments and squadrons. A few independent reconnaissance regiments and squadrons may have direct subordination to fleet command staffs. There are no naval air corps.

Naval air force divisions are designated according to role, as are those of the Red Army Air Force. They, also, contain from three to four regiments. In addition to the types of units found in the Red Army Air Force is the mining and torpedo division, which also may include bomber regiments. Personnel and aircraft establishments of naval air force regiments correspond closely to those of the Red Army Air Force.

Naval air force units are employed for attacks on ports, ships, harbor installations, and on enemy shipping. They also are used in reconnaissance activity, in support of amphibious operations, and in support of ground forces engaged in coastal areas.

b. Servicing units. The largest unit in the ground organization of the Red Naval Air Force is the naval air base. It includes departments for administering supply, equipment, spare parts, pay, rations and billeting, transfers, guarding of airfields, and minor repairs. The largest bases have a personnel strength of 650, and usually service an entire naval air division, administering as many as four airfields. Smaller bases, 400 men, service from one to two regiments and not more than two airfields.

All bases are assigned to a naval air division and are subordinate to the division commander. Subsidiary airfields and seaplane units are serviced by special detachments. Several small repair shops and a larger repair shop, which is not an integral part of the base but which is subordinate to the base commander, are assigned to each base. Subsidiary airfields and seaplane units are serviced by special detachments.

Section III. STRATEGIC AIR FORCES

1. LONG RANGE FORCE

a. Flying units. As originally constituted, the Long Range Force was organized into divisions and regiments. But by 1943 these were incorporated into corps. In December 1944 the Long Range Force was converted into the Eighteenth Air Army, but the division of component units into corps of two divisions each, three regiments per division, remained the same.

A long range bomber regiment consists of three squadrons, with a total of 381 officers and enlisted men. Personnel strength varies somewhat according to the type of aircraft employed. Division staff and regimental personnel strengths are shown in Figures 9 and 10.

	Staff	Squadron (each)
Headquarters	3	4
Political division	4	....
Operations staff	17	1
Special staff	8	1
Engineer division	9	20
Headquarters flight	13	46
Liaison flight	3	....
Staff total	57	72
Flying Personnel	....	36
Total squadron personnel	....	108
Total regimental personnel (staff and three squadrons)	381	

Figure 9.—Strength of long range bomber division staff.

Headquarters	3
Political division	6
Operations staff	33
Special staff	27
Engineer division	7
Rear services	12
Liaison flight	13
Total	101

Figure 10.—Strength of long range bomber regiments.

b. Servicing Units. The ground organization of the Long Range Force was, before its incorporation into the Red Army Air Force, completely independent. As in the fighter aviation of the Air Defense Forces, there were no regional commands of aviation ground services. But each air regiment had its own airfield servicing battalion which moved with the regiment. Airfield servicing battalions were subordinate to the division commander for discipline and to the divisional supply deputy for technical matters. Each battalion averaged approximately 250 officers and enlisted men and from 40 to 50 vehicles.

Just before the incorporation of the Long Range Force into the Red Army Air Force, it was reported that signal, antigas, and meteorological units were separated from the airfield servicing battalions and given independent status. All radio communications were controlled by the Long Range Force staff in Moscow, and each regiment maintained its own meteorological station.

For repair work, PARM's, from 10 to 12 men, were subordinated to each regiment. Supply was effected through special Long Range Force depots which were given the same designation (GAS) as those of the Red Army Air Force.

After the incorporation of the Long Range Force into the Red Army Air Force, it is probable that the Red Army Air Force servicing system was applied to Long Range units.

2. AIRBORNE FORCES OF THE RED ARMY AIR FORCE

a. Flying Units. Although the airborne forces have a small air force, it now consists only of training planes. They have no operational flying units. Units and aircraft for World War II operations were supplied by the Red Army Air Force (particularly by the Long Range Force) and by the Civil Air Fleet.

b. Tactical units. The basic tactical formation is the airborne brigade, with four airborne battalion landing teams each. Airborne corps served as operational headquarters for three or more brigades prior to 1943. Their existence after the reorganization at that time has not been confirmed. Guards airborne divisions have no connection with the airborne forces, but are rifle divisions made up in part of former airborne personnel.

The first battalion landing team of the airborne brigade is wholly parachuted, while the other teams are mixed.

Principal components of the airborne brigade are as follows:

Brigade headquarters (approximately 170 officers and enlisted men).
Signal company.
Chemical defense platoon.
Medical platoon.
Mobile reconnaissance company (approximately 120 officers and enlisted men).
Pioneer company (approximately 80 officers and enlisted men).
Rifle battalions (four) (approximately 690 officers and enlisted men each).
Headquarters.
Signal platoon.
Reconnaissance platoon.
Pioneer platoon.
Rifle companies (three per battalion) (three 50-mm mortars each).
Mortar company (six 82-mm mortars).
Machine gun company (twelve 7.62-mm heavy machine guns).
Antitank rifle company (twenty-seven 14.5-mm antitank rifles).
Medical platoon.
Supply platoon.

364

Artillery battalion (approximately 230 officers and enlisted men).

Howitzer batteries (two) (four 76-mm infantry howitzers each).

Mortar battery (four 120-mm mortars).

Antitank battalion (approximately 220 officers and enlisted men).

Antitank gun batteries (four) (four 45-mm antitank guns each).

Antitank rifle company (eighteen 14.5-mm antitank rifles).

Antiaircraft battalion (approximately 170 officers and enlisted men).

Gun platoon (four 37-mm automatic antiaircraft guns).

Antiaircraft machine gun companies (two) (twelve 12.7-mm antiaircraft machine guns each).

Brigade services.

Each brigade totals approximately 3,750 to 3,850 officers and enlisted men.

Weapons in the airborne brigade are as follows:

76-mm infantry howitzers	8
45-mm antitank guns	16
37-mm antiaircraft guns	4
120-mm mortars	4
82-mm mortars	24
50-mm mortars	36
12.7-mm antiaircraft machine guns	24
7.62-mm heavy machine guns	48
14.5-mm antitank rifles	126
7.62-mm light machine guns, rifles, and submachine guns	not known

In general, the airborne brigade is comparable in organization, strength, and armament to the rifle regiment, although it is somewhat larger and has greater fire power in all categories, especially antiaircraft weapons. There are a number of distinctive characteristics. These include the greater emphasis on light mortars, the concentration of all battalion heavy machine guns in one strong machine gun company and similar concentrations of antitank guns in the brigade antitank battalion and the difference in organization and proportion of howitzers and heavy mortars.

A few organizational trends have been established. Since 1942 increasing emphasis has been placed on antitank artillery and on antiaircraft weapons. Mortars have increased in caliber. In 1942 the 37-mm. mortar was the basic mortar for air-borne troops. It is believed that armored reconnaissance recently has been added to the airborne brigade.

Section IV. AIR FORCES OF THE ZONE OF THE INTERIOR

1. FIGHTER AVIATION OF THE AIR DEFENSE FORCES

a. Flying Units. The fighter aviation of the Air Defense Forces (PVO) consists of air corps, divisions, and regiments equipped with fighter aircraft. The tables of organization and equipment are similar to those of the air armies, although there probably is considerable variance depending upon the area of operations.

Air Defense Forces fighter corps were to be found, during World War II, in every part of the U. S. S. R. where concentrated fighter defense was necessary. Operationally, they were subordinate to the military district in which they were located. Corps near front line areas may have been subordinate operationally to air armies. After extension of the front line beyond the Soviet frontier, the fighter aviation of the Air Defense Forces defending areas close behind the front was divided into three sectors. Cooperation with the air armies at the front probably was maintained by Air Defense Forces fighter liaison officers.

b. Servicing units. The Air Defense Forces fighter force employs airfield servicing battalions but no regional commands of aviation ground services.

2. TRAINING AND REPLACEMENT UNITS

a. Flying units. Replacement units are organized into replacement brigades, regiments, and squadrons. Replacement brigades are subordinate to the Administration for Unit Formation and Training of the Main Administration of the Red Army Air Force. Each brigade probably deals with replacement and training for aircraft of a particular role, although they are not designated specifically as fighter, bomber, or ground attack. It is believed that there are from two to four regiments in each brigade. The replacement regiments usually contain from three to four squadrons, although there were more subordinate squadrons early in World War II. Each replacement air regiment includes from 140 to 180 officers and enlisted men and from 50 to 80 aircraft, depending upon the function of the regiment. The squadrons are divided into three flights, each training from 6 to 10 fighter or ground attack pilots or from 3 to 5 bomber crews.

The functions of replacement units include operational training of service school graduates as front line replacements, training of air-crew personnel for new types of aircraft, and ferrying of aircraft from factories either to operational units or to special storage depots near the front. Early in World War II, most of the replacement units were located near large aircraft factories. But by the middle of 1944, they began to move closer to the front.

From 1941 to 1942, the shortage of aircraft made it impossible for the replacement units to retrain and refit depleted units effectively. That function became the responsibility of newly created demonstration and training units, one of which usually was located at the rear of each air army. However, with the increase of aircraft production, the demonstration and training units gradually were disbanded.

b. Servicing units. Servicing of training establishments and replacement units is the responsibility of material-technical supplies battalions, similar to airfield servicing battalions, which are subordinate directly to the commander of the training school or the replacement regiment. Repair shops and radio stations are integral parts of the material-technical supplies battalions, but in other respects, their organization probably differs very little from that of the airfield servicing battalions.

3. CIVIL AIR FLEET UNITS

a. Flying units. During World War II, the Civil Air Fleet adopted a military organization of air divisions, regiments, and squadrons. The composition of divisions is believed to have been very flexible. The regiments are believed to have contained from 4 to 6 squadrons of from 18 to 20 aircraft each. Special liaison regiments were employed directly by Red Army staffs.

b. Servicing units. Civil Air Fleet units in the rear areas or those flying regular air routes use the ground services of the airfields from which they operate. When Civil Air Fleet units are employed in military work, they are assigned airfield servicing battalions and mobile aircraft repair shops. However, the units, even when tactically subordinate to the Red Army Air Force, continue to employ the independent Civil Air Fleet meteorological service.

4. NKVD AIR FORCE UNITS

The air force of the Peoples' Commissariat of Internal Affairs (NKVD) is organized into a brigade of three regiments, each having approximately two squadrons and five independent squadrons. In addition, there are a few other air regiments and squadrons. Each regiment probably has no more than 10 to 15 aircraft.

PART II. TACTICAL EMPLOYMENT

Section I. POLICY OF EMPLOYMENT

1. GENERAL

The geographical position and territorial expanse of the U. S. S. R. are factors from which has sprung a traditional and firmly established conviction that the sure defense of the U. S. S. R. lies with the Red Army. The years following World War I, although witnessing many new developments, did not produce anything which seriously shook this belief. The course of World War II tended to strengthen this conviction, with the result that the Red Army Air Force has developed into an arm which is, in the highest degree, specialized for the protection and support of the Red Army.

2. RED NAVAL AIR FORCE

The U. S. S. R., despite access to the Arctic and Pacific Oceans, always has been purely a land power. In comparison with the Red Army Air Force, the Red Naval Air Force is indeed small.

Before the outbreak of World War II, the Soviets attempted to equip the Red Naval Air Force with ship-borne aircraft and seaplanes. At the outset of the war, a considerable number of obsolete hydroplanes did exist. They were used by the fleet air arms chiefly for aerial reconnaissance. Ship-borne aircraft, on the other hand, were available only in very small numbers and were used as catapult aircraft on warships and icebreakers for reconnaissance.

Lack of aircraft carriers and the increasing demands of the Red Army Air Force during World War II caused the Soviets to discontinue production of naval aircraft. Consequently, with the exception of the obsolete models which existed before the war and the small number of PBY's received on lend-lease, the bulk of the Red Naval Air Force is land-based and is equipped with the same types of aircraft as the Red Army Air Force.

a. Missions of the naval air force. During the last year of World War II, the Red Naval Air Force engaged in attacks on enemy supply ports, disorganization of sea supply routes by attacks on enemy convoys and individual ships, convoy escort, defense of naval bases, reconnaissance for itself and for the fleets, support of ground forces during en-

gagements in coastal areas, and support of amphibious operations.

Some variations between the operations of the naval air arms of the various fleets have been noted.

BLACK SEA FLEET. The air arm of the Black Sea Fleet was engaged actively in attacks on sea targets during the mopping-up operations against German troops cut off in the Crimea. Previously, German convoy routes had been out of range of the Soviet air bases. After the fall of Sevastopol, the air arm played an active part in the defense of harbors in the area, particularly where units of the Red Navy were stationed. It also played an active part in supporting and protecting landings at Novorossisk and at Kerch. Reconnaissance flights over the coastal area were flown for both the fleet and for the army. Attacks were made on coastal fortifications and, to a lesser extent, on harbor installations. In a few cases, the air arm supported ground forces.

BALTIC SEA FLEET. At the beginning of World War II, the air arm of the Baltic fleet operated primarily in defense of strongpoints of the Baltic fleets, such as at Kronstadt. It also supported ground operations for the defense of Leningrad and, when the Red Army went over to the offensive, supported the drives up the Karelian Isthmus and toward Narva. Considerable reconnaissance activity was carried out over coastal areas and targets at sea. During the latter part of the war, the Baltic air arm was engaged actively in harassing the German withdrawal.

ARCTIC FLEET. The air arm of the Arctic Fleet was employed at the beginning of World War II in defense of Murmansk and Archangel. Later, it was used for defense of convoys, blockading of German fighter bases, and for attacks on German convoys and harbors in northern Norway. It also participated in attacks on German coastal batteries in addition to usual reconnaissance duties.

PACIFIC FLEET. It is believed that the functions and tasks of this air arm were essentially the same as for those air arms in the west.

b. Differences between Red Naval and Army Air Forces. There is a superficial similarity in the composition and organization of the Red Naval and Army Air Forces in that each employs the same aircraft establishments in the regiment, 42 aircraft in fighter and ground attack regiments, 32 aircraft in bomber regiments; in the grouping of regiments into divisions; in the grouping of divisions in fleet air arms; and in parallel composition of ground organization.

However, in addition to the omission of the corps from the Red Naval Air Force chain of command, there are a number of other essential differences.

In the Red Naval Air Force, operational specialization by regiments has been developed to a high degree. In some cases, there are even specialist divisions, such as mining and torpedo divisions. Regimental specialization is prescribed by the high command of Red Naval Air Force, whereas the high command of the Red Army Air Force has avoided specialization.

The different specialization policies affect the basing of air units. The Red Army Air Force seeks dispersion, while in the Red Naval Air Force an entire division usually is based on one airfield.

Naval bomber, ground attack, and fighter personnel are trained in essentially the same maner as those for the Red Army Air Force, with a relatively small amount of special naval training covering cooperation with naval units and conditions governing flights over the sea. Training of mining and torpedo crews is more extensive.

c. Conclusion. Several factors have a direct bearing on the strategic employment of the Red Naval Air Force and give rise to conditions affecting its future. First, it is to be noted that the aircraft types with which the Red Naval Air Force is equipped are the same as those used by the Red Army Air Force, with minor adaptations for specialized work. Secondly, the forces of the various air arms are interchangeable and can be moved from one fleet to another as strategic considerations dictate. Thirdly, the employment of the naval air arms to support ground forces in the performance of operations which normally would have been undertaken by the Air Army, was reported frequently during World War II.

3. LONG RANGE FORCE

The Long Range Force, alternatively described as the Long Range Bomber Force, is not designed as, nor has the capacities of a strategic bomber force, as understood by western nations. While independent in status and under independent command, it seldom operated against objectives beyond the short-term strategic demands of a specific ground offensive.

Strategic bombing was carried out against German towns from June to September 1941. Strategic bombing then was discontinued until the following July, when raids were continued until November, virtually marking the end of strategic bombing for World War II. In these attempts at strategic bombing, the performance of the Long Range Force was unimpressive in plan and execution.

From May 1942 until the end of 1944, intermittent strategic raids were carried out against German occupied towns.

In December 1944, the title of the Long Range Force was changed to Air Army. The implications of this change of title are not known precisely, but they are certain to extend beyond the mere change of name. For some time, the interests of the personnel of the Long Range Force had become increasingly detached from those of the air armies of the Red Army Air Force. Hostility consequently had arisen between the two air forces. It was detrimental to morale, and the Red Army Air Force obstructed Long Range Force administration, supply, and even, occasionally, operations. The change of title, it is believed, was designed primarily to overcome these difficulties, and may well have been only one part of a general adjustment of administrative machinery to produce closer cooperation between the two forces.

The great majority of Long Range Force operations were in direct and indirect support of a succession of ground offensives. As World War II progressed, its role became even more restricted. During the offensives of 1944 and 1945, its targets almost invariably were the railway facilities and rolling stock from 50 to 190 miles behind the enemy's defensive line.

Indications of the value placed by the Soviet high command on the Long Range Force presents much conflicting evidence. The growth of the Long Range Force during World War II indicates a considerable interest in its progress and confidence in its ultimate operational effectiveness. Personnel manning the force were selected carefully, and there were expectations of its emergence as an elite corps. There appears, however, evidence that the ostensible interest taken in the force exceeded the degree of priority given its demands on industry. The Long Range Force was badly equipped from the start. Also, its operational performance has been discreditable.

The Long Range Force was neglected over long periods in favor of the air armies. Its prominent position in Soviet propaganda probably was associated with Soviet appreciation of a world-wide knowledge of the power of the bomber forces of the Western Allies.

The Soviets well realize their shortcomings in strategic long-range bombing. The nucleus for the formation of such a force exists in the Long Range Force. However, much remains in the development of aircraft, equipment, and of operating doctrines before a thoroughly modern strategic force can be realized by the U. S. S. R.

4. FIGHTER AVIATION OF THE AIR DEFENSE FORCES

Fighter aviation of the Air Defense Forces is not believed to constitute a single integral force comparable to the Long Range Force or the Civil Air Fleet. It is comprised, in contrast, simply of Red Army Air Force units temporarily or permanently allotted to the Main Administration of the Air Defense Forces, to the commanders of air defense fronts, or to the air defense fronts, or to the air defense commanders of military districts.

It is under the operational control of the air defense commander of each defensive sector in the rear of the combat zone, and, is employed in conjunction with antiaircraft artillery, searchlights, barrage balloons, radar, visual and sound observation, and the passive defense forces of the NKVD. Over-all administrative and planning responsibilities for these allotted fighter units appears to be centralized in a low-ranking fighter force commander and staff in the headquarters of the Main Administration of the Air Defense Forces.

5. CIVIL AIR FLEET

The term "Civil Air Fleet," may refer generally to all nonmilitary aircraft, by whomever held, or in a restricted sense to those specifically controlled by the Main Administration of the Civil Air Fleet. Actually, no private persons or agencies hold title to aircraft in the U. S. S. R. Within the limitations imposed by public authority, however, nongovernmental users may direct the employment of aircraft. In addition to the Civil Air Fleet, the following agencies may operate nonmilitary aircraft:

> The Main Administration of the Northern Sea Route.

> Government departments, such as the various commissariats.
> Public organizations, such as *Osoaviakhim*.
> Private persons.

All of these, except the Main Administration of the Northern Sea Route, come under the policy-making authority of the Civil Air Fleet. All are subject to its inspections. The centralization of policymaking and inspection in the Civil Air Fleet indicates the existence of a coordinated plan of control not only for aircraft within the fleet itself but for all nonmilitary aircraft.

In peacetime, the Civil Air Fleet maintains passenger, mail, and cargo operations, and renders special services, such as aerial photography, sowing of seed, and spraying. During World War II, it furnished many units for operational use by the Red Army Air Force and provided air transport in the rear areas for both civil and military personnel.

a. Control by Red Army Air Force. Both before and during World War II, the Civil Air Fleet was subordinate directly to the Council of Peoples' Commissars. During the war, however, the fleet also was subject to a degree of control by the Red Army Air Force, and some fleet units were subordinated to it. The operations staff of the Civil Air Fleet, however, was responsible directly to the Council of Peoples' Commissars. Consequently, the exact limits of civil and military control are difficult to determine. However, it seems certain that the Red Army Air Force had plenary power over the military employment of the Civil Air Fleet. The Long Range Force had the authority to request flying personnel from the Civil Air Fleet and to make its own selections. The extent of Red Army Air Force influence in the civilian employment of the Civil Air Fleet is uncertain. It seems probable that the Red Army Air Force had paper authority to assign Civil Air Fleet equipment according to requirements and to control its activity, but that in practice only partial use was made of this authority and that the Civil Air Fleet retained freedom in matters not strictly military.

Elements of the Civil Air Fleet engaged in military operations continued to be designated as fleet units and were administered by the Main Administration of the Civil Air Fleet, even though they operated under Red Army Air Force directives. Civil Air Fleet divisions belonged to the rear areas and never appeared intact in the area of the front, although units as large as squadrons and regiments were so employed. Units operating at the front were at the disposal of army group or air army headquarters and were serviced by the air army ground organization. Subordination was limited to operations, however, and did not affect their status as Civil Air Fleet units. Except for units attached to the Main Administration of the Medical Service, the Civil Air Fleet had no specialized military assignments.

b. Missions. No hard and fast distinction can be drawn between the military and civil operations of the Civil Air Fleet. Even during World War II, air routes were operated in the rear areas with at least an outward preservation of their civilian character. Throughout the war, moreover, the Civil Air Fleet retained a fairly large stock of aircraft, some as organized transport units and some merely scattered over the civil airfields of the rear areas.

During World War II, the missions assigned to the Civil Air Fleet were divided into three general categories: those in the theater of operations, those in the zone of the interior, and those outside of the U. S. S. R.

In the theater of operations, the Civil Air Fleet transported supplies for ground forces (particularly isolated units), transported wounded personnel, transported combat troops, dropped paratroopers and agents, supplied partisans, and, in exceptional cases, flew night raids.

In the zone of the interior, the Civil Air Fleet maintained courier and transport service and, in emergencies, was used for the transfer of nonflying personnel of flight regiments. In addition the Civil Air Fleet performed special work for the Commissariats of Agriculture and Forestry.

Outside of the Soviet Union, the Civil Air Fleet maintained the U. S. S. R.'s foreign transport services and ferried imported foreign aircraft.

In peacetime, the scope of Civil Air Fleet activities is considerably narrower. It embraces air transport and courier services, flights connected with agriculture, forestry, and other branches of Soviet economy, scientific research in civil aviation, geodesy and aerial photography, medical service, and operations for cultural, educational, and recreational purposes.

c. Types of aircraft. The principal units of the Civil Air Fleet are equipped with the C–47 or its Soviet counterpart, the PS–84 (one version called the LI–2 when equipped with armament). In addition, captured German Ju–52's and some older Soviet bombers, such as the four-engine TB–3, also are

utilized. For training and courier service, the U–2 and R–5 (both similar to the U. S. Stearman PT–17) are used extensively. It has been noted recently that the Soviets are using a number of the more modern DB–3F (IL–4) twin-engine bombers for transport work, and it seems likely that the proportion of modern types will increase as the Civil Air Fleet continues to expand.

d. Operations. According to Soviet statements, the Civil Air Fleet flew 40,000 operational flights totaling more than 4,500,000 miles, and carried more than 2,300,000 passengers and 300,000 tons of cargo during World War II. These figures allegedly do not include nonmilitary air activity under control of the Main Administration of the Civil Air Fleet.

In civil operations, again according to Soviet statements, from 1923 to 1937, flights covered 142,-500,000 miles and carried 1,000,000 passengers and 110,600 tons of freight. By 1938, the combined length of Civil Air Fleet routes was 57,700 miles. While civil operations were restricted during the early part of World War II, it is known that by 1944 the Civil Air Fleet was flying not only a large network of air routes within the Soviet Union, but was extending into foreign countries.

At present, a consistent policy is being pursued of maintaining traffic connections beyond the frontiers with Civil Air Fleet aircraft and crews, rather than permitting foreign airlines to enter Soviet territory.

e. Conclusions. The Soviets appreciate the importance of air transport, as evidenced in the early and continuous attention given to the Civil Air Fleet, to its training program, and to the development of internal and external air routes. During World War II, it served as an important adjunct to the Red Army Air Force, and it is logical to assume that it will be expanded. In an Aviation Day address on 18 August 1945, Marshal Astakhov (Commander of the Civil Air Fleet) stated that Soviet economic development requires 8 to 10 times the volume of civil air transport as was carried prior to the war. This statement appears to be a significant indication of the importance attached to the future development of the Civil Air Fleet.

6. AIRBORNE FORCES

At the beginning of World War II, the U. S. S. R. was as well or better equipped with trained airborne troops as was any other nation. In contrast to other forces of the U. S. S. R., the airborne forces decreased in size during the war. Varying types of airborne operations were carried out in 1941, 1942, and 1943. It is possible that airborne operations also were attempted during the latter 2 years of the war, but they have not been reported.

Soviet airborne tactical doctrine embraces all the missions commonly accepted for parachute, glider, and transport-landed troops. Both large- and small-scale operations have been attempted. In large-scale operations during World War II, it is of interest to note that airborne troops generally were employed against critical enemy salients only when the denial of areas of supply or communications at the base of the salient would seriously cripple the enemy and losses to airborne forces would not be too severe. Landings generally were made in an area, in the rear of the enemy's salient, which would affect most seriously the coordination of the enemy's supply lines and, at the same time, avoid the enemy's front-line troops and make possible a break-through to friendly ground forces within a reasonable period. A landing area in the rear of the enemy salient and close to one of its flanks usually was selected. Airborne operations seldom succeeded in any more than the denial mission. The process of breaking out was accomplished only at a great cost in men, equipment, and time.

Small-scale operations during World War II consisted of cooperating with fast moving mobile forces on penetration or encirclement missions and of independent missions in the enemy's rear to raid headquarters, sabotage installations, and to reinforce active Partisan groups.

Section II. DOCTRINE OF EMPLOYMENT OF THE AIR ARMY

1. GENERAL

The employment of air armies, which constitute the tactical and operational forces of the Red Army Air Force, clearly exemplifies the role of aviation in support of the Red Army. Normally, each air army is assigned to an army group and operates under the orders of the army group commander. The employment of the air army is, therefore, governed primarily by the plans of the ground forces.

2. AIR-GROUND COORDINATION

a. **Responsibility.** Air-ground coordination is achieved by the Soviets through specific allocations of responsibilities to air and ground commanders participating in an operation.

DURING OFFENSIVE. In planning an offensive, responsibilities for successful air-ground coordination are prescribed as follows:

The army group commander must, in his over-all plan, stipulate the missions, types, and degree of air support required for the individual phases of the operation. In addition, it is his responsibility to specify the order in which the missions are to be executed by the air army in the event of break-through into the enemy defensive zone, the areas and sectors which must be covered by aerial reconnaissance, and the amount and type of support to be provided by the air army and ground units operating outside the zone of main effort. He also prescribes the assistance ground forces will render the air army in terrain reconnaissance, construction of airfields, and ground defense of air installations.

The army group staff works out the details of the field order, giving particular attention to the table of combat coordination (fig. 17, ch. V) for the projected operation. (In many instances, a detailed field order is prepared for only the first day of the ground offensive. Thereafter, fragmentary orders are more common.)

In conjunction with the tables of combat coordination, they determine lanes, front-line crossing points, bomb lines, and radio and supplementary signals for air-ground communications and target designation. The army group staff places particular stress upon effective air cover for artillery and mobile troops during all phases of combat. Stress similarly is placed upon effective support of air forces by counterbattery fire against enemy antiaircraft artillery and by ground-air-warning units. In addition, the staff also must prepare a detailed plan of the army group's aerial reconnaissance requirements.

Within the army group staff, the Chief of Staff personally is responsible for the establishment of air-ground signal communications. This specifically includes the determination of the axes of signal communication for all major ground and air components and the locations of their respective signal centers at various phases of the operation. In addition, he must issue instructions regarding the allocation of major stations, composition of key nets, and the tentative missions of signal reserves. The signal plan and detailed signal operating instructions are prepared by the army group signal officer.

The air army commander, in accordance with the over-all army group plan, is responsible for the specific assignment of air formations and units, including those to be retained under centralized control and those to be attached to mobile units during various phases of the operation. In addition, he assigns operational airfields to these units and issues general instructions relating to the preparation of navigation, ground control, and target designation signal networks.

The commander of the infantry army in the main effort and all other infantry army commanders to whom aircraft are attached, or who are to be supported directly by air units, must verify all aircraft lanes, front-line crossing points, and bomb lines by personal ground reconnaissance. They also must insure the full coordination of signal communications and space-time schedules.

The army artillery commanders, in conjunction with the commanders of supporting or attached air formations, are charged specifically with the detailed integration of artillery and air support fire plans. In addition, they must prepare a mutual support plan against enemy antiaircraft artillery and enemy aircraft. (For typical plan of air-artillery coordination, see fig. 17, ch. V.) They determine the exact distribution of targets as to space and time, manner in which targets are to be indicated or fire discontinued, and arrange for the exchange of information during the artillery and aviation preparations.

In all cases, the artillery must know the time, place, and altitude at which the friendly aviation will cross the front line and the signals for designating targets and for shifting or ceasing fire. When artillery and aviation are to attack the same target it is necessary to establish beforehand the order of attack, and both must operate upon a single plan. The altitude at which aircraft are to fly must be prescribed definitely in order to avoid the trajectories of artillery projectiles.

The commander of mobile troops (tanks, mechanized troops, and cavalry) must determine, in conjunction with the commanders of the air formations or units who will be attached or will support them, the specific plan of air cover and fire support for the mobile troops. They also must establish the detailed plan of maneuver, the space-time schedules, and the system of air-ground communications and liaison for the entire operation. A final responsibility of the mobile commander is to assist in terrain reconnaissance and construction of landing strips in areas captured during the operation.

DURING DEFENSIVE. In general the allocation of responsibilities closely approximates that for the offensive. The principal differences are the greater emphasis on reconnaissance and observation, by both ground and air forces, and the centralized employment of the air forces, which eliminates the necessity for detailed participation of subordinate ground components in the operating plan. Another specific difference is inherent in the phases of defensive combat as compared to offensive combat. In the defense, there generally are three main phases: combat for the outpost line of resistance, combat for the main line of resistance, and counteroffensive or withdrawal operations. Alternate plans must be prepared in accordance with the main alternatives of defensive action. Provisions for the ground defense of air installations, particularly against armored break-throughs, are of special importance. The air army commander, therefore, is responsible that the commanders of subordinate air units make specific local arrangements with ground troops for the security of air installations.

b. Coordination during combat. In theory, two types of coordination exist between air and ground forces: air units may be attached to, or may be in support of ground units. In actual Soviet operations, attachment of air units to ground echelons below army level is becoming increasingly rare.

During the air preparation and break-through phases of an offensive operation, air units never are attached to ground units, nor is attachment common in any type of defensive operation. When air units are attached to ground units, as in the security and exploitation phases of the offensive, the ground forces commander transmits his orders directly to the air unit commander, who either is physically present at the ground commander's forward operations post or who maintains a radio contact with the ground commander.

When air units support ground units, command is retained by the air forces. The ground commander transmits his requests for air support through the air liaison officer, who is stationed at the ground unit's command post.

In other respects, the procedure of air-ground coordination during combat is identical in both support and attachment. The principal procedures involved are the dispatching of air liaison sections to ground units, the mutual briefing and detailed discussions between air and ground staffs concerned, the establishment of control check points and ground control stations, and the mutual evaluation of operations in progress by the cooperating air and ground staffs.

AIR LIAISON SECTIONS. The composition of air liaison sections varies considerably in accordance with the importance of the headquarters to which they are dispatched. Air liaison sections with major headquarters, such as tank armies, consist of the chief and several senior officers of the operations section of the supporting air forces and officers from the intelligence, meteorological, and signal sections. At lower echelons, occasionally even tank or rifle battalions, single air liaison officers may suffice.

Air army and subordinate air staffs are responsible for the provision and maintenance of adequate signal communications for air liaison sections. These sections usually operate on two nets. One permits direct transmission of requests to air units in flight. This frequency also is used by the senior air commander from his ground command post to transmit orders in the event ground unit requests must be disregarded or current missions changed. The other net, wire and radio, connects the air liaison section directly with the commander of the air unit. When air and artillery are cooperating, the artillery commander receives on the frequency used by the air liaison officer to communicate with aircraft in flight.

During the initial phases of air preparation for all offensive and defensive operations, command of all units in flight is centralized directly at the air army command post. Communications between units in flight and air liaison officers are not maintained, except by special authority of the air army commander. Instead, all air liaison officers and the air army command post maintain a separate single intercommunication net. Thus, the air army is kept abreast of the needs of all ground units and also can relay to ground units such information concerning the massed employment of aviation as may be necessary.

The missions of air liaison sections include the relaying not only of requests for air support, but also of information to the cooperating commanders on major changes in the air and ground situations.

GROUND CONTROL STATIONS. All ground and air commanders share the responsibility for the establishment and proper operation of an adequate net of ground control stations. The primary missions of these stations are to control the flight of friendly aircraft, particularly with regard to air and ground safety; to inform them of major changes in the tactical situation; to retransmit requests and orders when necessary; and to warn both aircraft in flight and ground units of the approach of enemy aircraft.

Ground control stations may be classified as base and as auxiliary stations. Base stations are equipped with radar and are under the direct control of the senior commanders of air formations and units in an operation. From these base stations, senior commanders can change targets, regroup tactical formations, summon reinforcements, cancel attacks, or stipulate the number of attacks to be made. Auxiliary stations control aircraft only so far as is essential for air or ground safety. They generally are provided with visual and auditory observation facilities.

Each ground control station includes representatives of the operations section of the ground forces operating in the sector and an air staff, headed by a senior officer. The station consists of an air observation net, a signal and operations center, and an aircraft control check point, which is a terrain feature easily recognizable from the air. Ground staffs are responsible for providing adequate signal communications from ground control stations to ground units. Air staffs are responsible for communications to air units.

AIR WARNING. Throughout World War II, the Red Army maintained an efficient air observation and warning system. This function is one of the most important responsibilities of all operations staffs, at each level of command, for both ground and air forces. Although the facilities include army group and air army radar units, the air warning system is dependent fundamentally on a comprehensive net of visual and auditory observers from every military or civilian unit and installation. For example, during the war every group of 300 civilians was required to maintain a detachment of at least six observers.

Air warning reports are transmitted either directly to all headquarters over a reserved frequency to which all command posts constantly are tuned, or through control stations of the rear areas and the zone of the interior observation nets. Key observation posts are provided with duplicate radio and wire facilities. Reports of immediate value to aircraft in flight are relayed to them by the ground control stations. Aircraft in flight report the approach of enemy aircraft to the same stations, which immediately relay the information through air warning channels.

3. COMMAND OF AIR ARMY OPERATIONS

a. Air army staff procedure. The procedures of the air army staff briefly are as follows:

FORMULATION OF PLAN. The army group staff must give advance warning to the air army staff of the impending issue of combat orders for an operation and by what means they will be transmitted. Upon receipt of these warning orders, the operations duty officer reports immediately to the chief of staff and to the chief of the operations section. If the field order is to be transmitted by telephone, telegraph, or radio, the Chief of staff must insure that all channels involved in the transmission are ready. In addition, he alerts the chief of the Rear Services to assure an adequate supply of fuel, ammunition, and rations for the impending operation.

Upon receipt of the field order, the air army commander must make a personal study of his own forces and of the ground and air situation before making his decisions. To assist him, the chief of staff directs the chiefs of staff sections and services to prepare a short staff estimate. The short staff estimate consists of: an estimate of time available to the commander and his staff for making a decision, allowing a maximum of time for the transmission of orders and the preparation of the air army for the impending operation; information concerning the enemy, such as advanced ground troops, artillery, reserves, where, when, and by whom enemy antiaircraft artillery was observed, types and numbers of enemy planes noted and the character of their activity, system of antiaircraft defense on the front line and in the immediate rear; information concerning own troops, such as disposition, time schedules, objectives, and methods by which friendly aviation can assist; detailed combat missions of adjacent air armies, if available; status of personnel and matériel, such as number of units available for combat, number of aircraft available, condition of matériel, technical provisions; weather conditions at airfields and in the area of the intended operation, with a forecast for the duration of the operation; status of preparation of the aircraft for flight; and preliminary navigation and bombing charts, including distances to objectives, duration of flights, amount of fuel and lubricants needed for operations against

objectives, permissible loads of bombers, and types and calibers of bombs.

The work of individuals on the air army staff is as follows:

The *Chief of the Operations Section*, after issuing the warning orders to the air units, prepares the time schedules, information regarding units, and brings the situation map up to date.

The *Intelligence Officer* prepares a large-scale map of the enemy area and marks the objectives. He posts the latest information regarding the distribution and combat activities of enemy fighters, antiaircraft artillery, and other air defenses on the reconnaissance map and prepares the first paragraph (information concerning the enemy) of the field order. He dispatches orders to reconnaissance units.

The *Sturman* prepares the navigation chart, orders a weather forecast for the operation, and prepares preliminary navigation estimates for the operation.

The *Chief of Signal Communications*, on the basis of instructions received from the chief of the air staff, prepares the signal communications order (annex).

The *Chief of the Rear Services* prepares information regarding the requirements and reserves of fuel, ammunition, and rations needed for the operation and information regarding the drawing of supplies.

The *Chief of Staff*, with the assistance of his staff, prepares several alternate plans, if time permits, and submits them to the commander. In addition, he must be ready to advise the commander on the following: time remaining for the air army to prepare for the operation; time remaining for the air army commander to make his decision and to issue the order; contents of the field order received; objectives; aviation strength required; time of attack; number of air units available; description of objectives, accompanied by large-scale maps, photographs, or other means of identification; types and weights of bombs required to accomplish missions; anticipated countermeasures of the enemy air force in the area of operations; location of friendly front line and troops; condition and composition of own units; and preliminary estimate composed by the air staff.

THE FIELD ORDER. The field order is drawn up after the commander makes his decision. To expedite the preparation of the field order, the chief of staff and the responsible heads of sections and staff departments are present at the command post while the commander is making his decision. The operations officer takes down the verbal order of the commander. The assistant operations officer posts it on the map. The Chief of Staff instructs the operations officer in what sequence, to whom, and by what means the preliminary orders will be issued.

The Operations Officer then prepares a draft of the field order, a maneuver chart of the area of operation, coordinates all communications problems and a signal table with the Chief Signal Officer. The Intelligence Officer prepares the reconnaissance order and, after it is signed by the Chief of Staff, issues it to the subordinate staffs. The Chief Signal Officer prepares the signal order (annex). The *Sturman* prepares the navigation plan and, together with the Signal Officer, assists in the preparation of the signal order and the coded maps. Together with the Chief Engineer Officer, *Sturman* determines the most advantageous use of aircraft by types. With the Operations Officer, *Sturman* prepares the table for the coordination of the attack.

The Chief of the Rear Services, together with the Chief Engineer, estimates the requirements for fuel, lubricants, ammunition, and other supplies needed for the operation and submits it to the section for rear organization. In addition, he writes the field order (annex) for the rear organization and submits it to the commander and the chief of staff for signature. The Chief of Staff supervises, checks, and coordinates all documents and annexes, reports the draft of the field order and the order for the rear organization, approves instructions for the reconnaissance and navigation services, the signal annex, and the bombing table.

After the field order is signed by the air army commander, the operations officer dispatches copies and attached documents to the subordinate units and to commanders of all ground units directly concerned. Excerpts from the reconnaissance annex and instructions are dispatched by the intelligence officer to subordinate units, adjacent staffs, and to staffs of reconnaissance units.

The field order usually is transmitted by telephone and in written form. If time permits, the order may be issued through personal contact between the commander and subordinate commanders. Personal contact adds special importance to the missions assigned and allows for quick last-minute changes as the situation demands. Telephone, telegraph, and radio are used to report and receive instructions.

ASSIGNMENT OF MISSIONS. The assignment of combat missions to air units depends upon the types of missions, the time in which they are to be accomplished, and the number and location of units available for the operation. The air division usually is assigned missions requiring from 1 to 3 days to accomplish. However, it may be assigned missions requiring 1 day or even one flight.

b. Responsibilities of lower air staffs. Staffs of all subordinate air formations and units are charged specifically with insuring that all flight personnel are provided with adequate large-scale maps and aerial mosaics. They must check the familiarity of the air crews with the friendly and enemy situation in the zone of operations, with ground control stations, with established signal operating instructions (particularly for air-ground coordination), and with the major terrain features in the zone of projected operations. They are responsible for insuring direct staff discussions with the supported ground units and, when time permits, for personal ground reconnaissance (particularly to establish the locations of friendly and enemy front lines). If time is available, training exercises must be planned and executed in advance of the operation to insure precise time and space coordination with ground troops.

c. Control of staffs during combat. Because of the sudden change in tactical and meteorological conditions inherent in air operations, close command and staff control is essential during all phases of combat. Air army and subordinate staffs are manned adequately to provide alternate plans on short notice. Control of subordinate units is maintained through tours by commanders and staffs and through base ground control stations.

4. CONDUCT OF AIR ARMY OPERATIONS

a. The offensive. Offensive operations generally include four phases.

AIR PREPARATION. The duration of air operations in preparation for a ground offense may vary from several weeks to days, hours, or even minutes. Conditions which exclude the necessity of a long air preparation include: a stable front, complete air superiority, and comparative weakness of the enemy in reinforcements and supply. If a lengthy air preparation is necessary, the principal objectives are the physical exhaustion and lowering of the morale of enemy troops, disruption of enemy construction of defense positions, and the reduction of effectiveness of enemy weapons. These missions are accomplished by continuous and systematic action of the air force, both day and night, against combat formations, against the hostile main lines of resistance and positions deeper in the defensive zone, against fortifications and artillery positions, and against reserves.

Air activity is conducted over a wide front, to avoid disclosure of the direction of the main effort. Immediately before the launching of the ground offensive, the air preparation ends with a mass attack of large air formations in the direction of the main effort.

This mass attack can be conducted before, during, or after the main artillery preparation. In this phase, the entire air army is concentrated in the direction of the main effort, and has as its main objectives artillery and mortar positions, antitank guns, and tactical ground reserves. If the air preparation is conducted after the artillery preparation and immediately before the infantry assault, the main objectives of aviation are the destruction of personnel and firing positions in the enemy main line of resistance. This mass attack consists of a series of successive attacks at 5-, 10-, and 15-minute or, sometimes, less frequent intervals.

The saturation bombardment in the direction of the main effort may reach as high as 120 tons per 1,000 square yards marked for the break-through. The location, time, and height at which each attack wave is to cross the friendly front line must be communicated in advance to the artillery, which can then shift or cease fire as needed.

THE BREAK-THROUGH. Air support during the assault and break-through consists of periodic attacks on the enemy artillery positions, mortar batteries, and antitank weapons which are impeding the advance of friendly troops. It also serves to disorganize enemy counterattacks and to provide cover from enemy air action.

Covering aircraft must patrol constantly over the area of combat to observe changes in the ground situation. They must be ready to support ground troops by bombing and strafing on call. The action of aviation over the battlefield is continuous until the objective is taken and consolidated.

SECURING THE OFFENSIVE. During this phase, air operations continue substantially as in the break-through period. Certain complicating factors must, however, be taken into account. Ground maneuver deviates increasingly from the original plan. Consequently, the problem of identifying friendly units becomes increasingly important.

As ground forces advance deeper into enemy territory, active enemy antiaircraft weapons appear in large numbers. Long range counterbattery operations by the artillery are, therefore, of critical importance to avoid excessive losses of aircraft. In addition, enemy operational and strategic reserves, both ground and air, may be anticipated. As a result, strong air forces must be available on ground alert at nearby airfields to intervene in event of sudden changes in the situation. Coordination between advanced and succeeding echelons of ground forces and their supporting aircraft must be insured. Finally, the increasing dispersion of ground troops and the commitment of mobile forces necessitates increasing decentralization and partial change from direct support to attachment of air units to ground units.

EXPLOITATION. Exploitation of the break-through by the ground forces consists of the simultaneous pursuit of withdrawing enemy forces and the destruction of encircled remnants. In this complicated situation the air forces cannot be dispersed regardless of requests from ground commanders. All efforts must be directed to suport the main objective of the army group commander.

Normally this objective will be the continued advance of the mobile forces. To accomplish this, mass attacks are made on key enemy reserve positions, and, at the same time, air units provide continuous fighter cover for the mobile formations. Small groups of fighter or ground attack aircraft fly ahead of the mobile troops to reconnoiter, to neutralize enemy antitank defenses, and to provide continuous cover. Air-ground communications are maintained primarily by radio, in the clear, although signal rockets and other supplementary means also are employed.

In order to maintain the continuity of the air effort in the pursuit of retreating enemy forces, airfield construction battalions allocated by the air army advance with the second wave of mobile troops to prepare airfields as directed. The use of aviation against encircled enemy troops is a secondary mission in exploitation and is undertaken only when the encircled troops attempt to break out of the encirclement in conjunction with enemy counterattacks.

b. The defense. In the defense, all aviation is centralized fully under the air army commander.

Until the mass commitment of the air army is directed by the army group commander, the primary missions of the air forces include patrolling, observation, and harassment.

Aircraft must report the locations of important targets directly to artillery units. Massed aerial counterattacks are initiated either in conjunction with the artillery counterpreparation to destroy enemy fire, immediately before the enemy attack, or after the enemy break-through and just prior to the friendly counterattack. During air operations, the support of friendly antiaircraft artillery is vital.

During withdrawals, the air force's main mission is to cover ground formations. Special air formations are detailed, and may be attached to the rear guard ground commander. Because the ground situation is changing constantly in withdrawals and orders often are interrupted in transmission, mutual recognition and mutual target designation between air and ground units is of decisive importance. The air army commander personally is responsible for providing maximum support to rear guards. All aircraft of the air army, regardless of assigned missions, may be diverted to cover withdrawing ground forces.

Section III. FIGHTER METHODS AND TACTICS

1. GENERAL

Methods and tactics depend on a great number of variable factors. What is good today may be useless tomorrow. What is not warranted in the first phase of a war may find justification in a later stage. The methods and tactics presented emerged from World War II. Exactly what effect future developments in aircraft and equipment will have on them is not known at present.

2. RED ARMY AIR FORCE FIGHTERS

The missions of fighter units of the Red Army Air Force are to protect troops and installations from enemy air attack; to destroy enemy aircraft, both in the air and on airfields; to destroy enemy troops; to escort ground attack and bomber aircraft; to conduct aerial reconnaissance; and, as is true with all Soviet aviation, to support the Red Army in all operations.

a. Location of fighter bases. The Soviets advocate basing fighter units close to the front line. During an offensive operation, the main fighter concentration is based in a zone from 18 to 20 miles in depth running parallel to and 6 miles from the front line. Normally, one fighter regiment occupies one airfield. This method of dispersal may, of course, be abandoned in the event sufficient fighter fields are not available or bad weather results in poor airfield serviceability. As changes in the front line occur, fighter units are shifted accordingly.

In an offensive, airfield engineer battalions move with mobile formations. Many instances have been reported in which fighter units occupied airfields before the arrival of infantry. Protection for these units was provided by tank detachments until the infantry arrived. This factor, along with the small airfields from which Soviet fighters can operate, makes the fighter force outstandingly mobile.

During defensive operations, the main fighter concentration is dispersed on airfields distant from the front line. Small groups of fighters, however, are kept on forward bases for advance defensive patrols and interception. To minimize losses from enemy air attack, these small groups are shifted from one field to another, either early in the morning or late in the evening. Other forward bases also are maintained and, although not occupied, are available for projected operations. Supplies are brought in at night. Fighters move up from the rear to the forward bases, where they are refueled, and then take off against the enemy. In the event of a counterattack by the ground forces, the main fighter concentration is moved quickly from the rear area to the forward bases to provide immediate and direct support to the ground forces.

b. Tactical units. The basic tactical unit of any Soviet fighter formation is a *Para*, or element consisting of two aircraft (fig. 11).

A *Gruppa* is the largest tactical unit, and usually consists of from six to eight aircraft. The nucleus of a *Gruppa* is a *Zveno* (flight) of two *Paras* totaling four aircraft (fig. 12).

A *Gruppa* of six aircraft consists of one *Zveno* and one independent *Para*, but the eight-plane *Gruppa* is made up of two complete *Zvenos*.

Because the majority of Soviet fighter sorties are for escort or patrol duties, the formations for these operations may be considered typical. The main characteristics of these formations are greater spacing of *Paras*, both horizontally and in altitude, and the "stacking up" of subordinate aircraft in respect

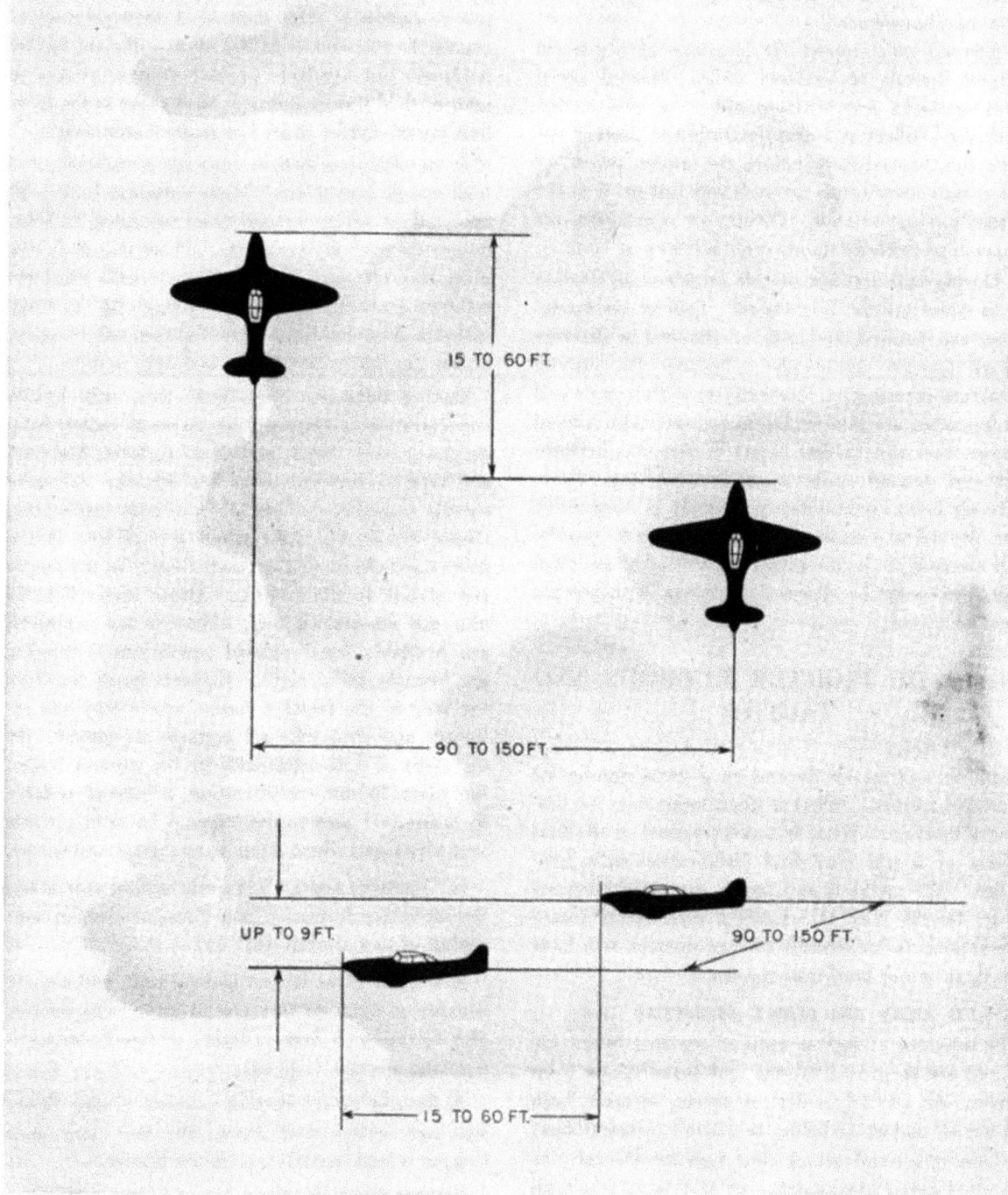

15 TO 60 FT

90 TO 150 FT

UP TO 9 FT.

90 TO 150 FT.

15 TO 60 FT.

Figure 11.—Typical Para formation.

378

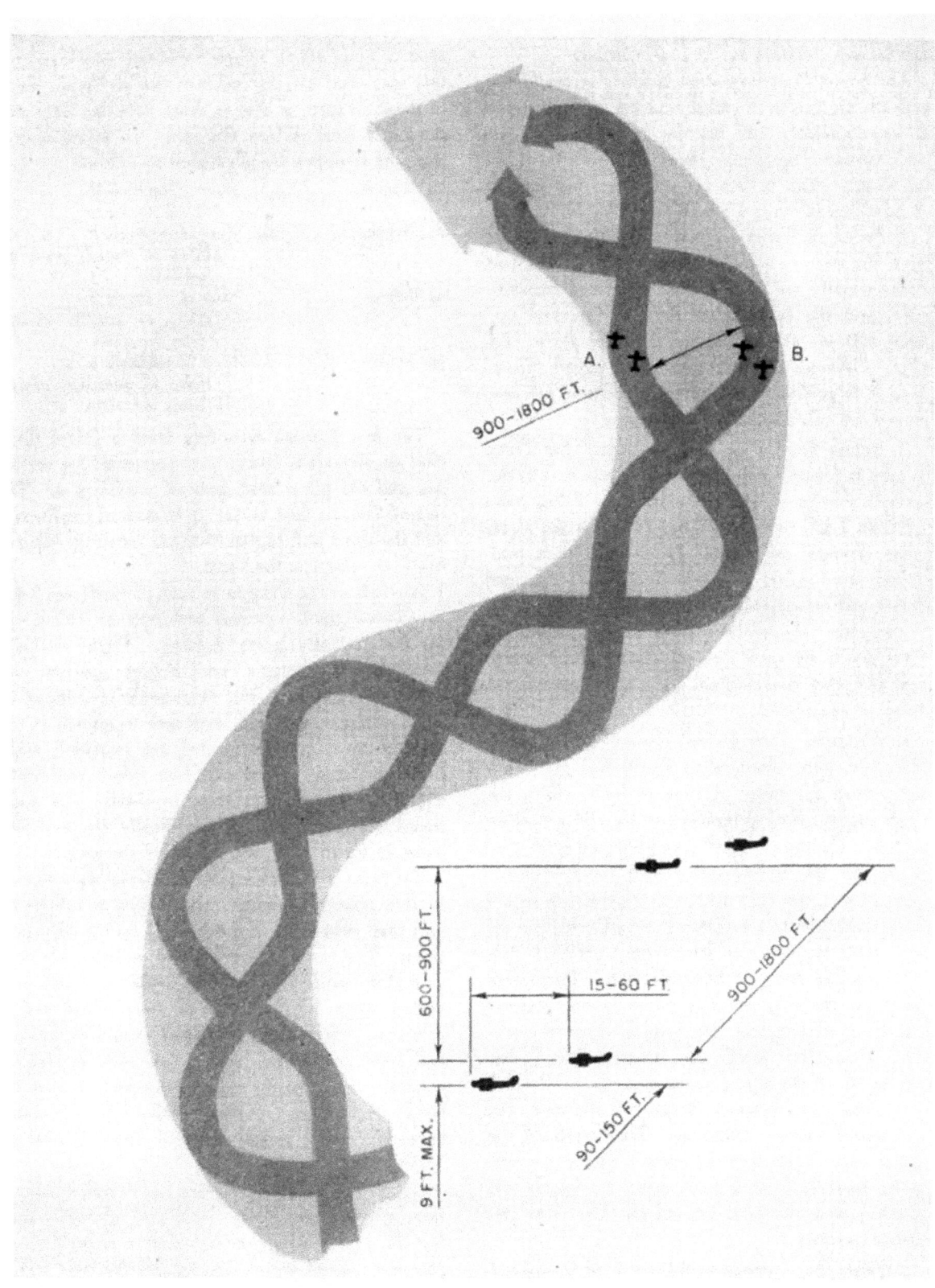

Figure 12.—Typical Zveno formation.

to the leader instead of "stacking down," as is the case in some western air force formations.

The Soviet *Para* formation is fairly conventional with the aircraft in the wing position out to the side at approximately 120 degrees in relation to the lead aircraft (fig. 11). However, the aircraft in the wing position is "stacked up" a few feet instead of down, as in many USAAF and RAF formations.

A *Zveno* in Soviet formations is quite different from the western conception of a flight. The two *Paras* usually are more widely separated horizontally, and the subordinate *Para* is "stacked up" from 600 to 900 feet above the lead *Para* (fig. 12). Although this is the standard patrol formation, it is probable that other formations are employed for other types of operations.

A fighter *Gruppa* in the Red Army Air Force usually is formed with one *Zveno* positioned as described above and with the extra *Para* flying from 1,200 to 2,400 feet above (fig. 13). In the eight-plane *Gruppa*, the second *Zveno* usually is positioned from 1,000 to 2,000 feet above the lead *Zveno* and presumably at a reasonable distance out to one side. As in the case of *Zveno* formations, there are many variations of this standard formation and other conventional types of formations for different operations.

c. Patrols. Four distinct types of patrol operations have been identified in World War II. They are patrols for cover of zone of main effort, advance patrols, tactical reserve patrols, and free lance patrols. During offensive operations, all four types of patrols are carried out almost simultaneously. In defensive operations, greater emphasis is placed on advanced patrols and free-lance patrols until the Red Army is capable of launching a counterattack.

COVER FOR ZONE OF MAIN EFFORT. To provide cover for the zone of main effort in an offensive operation, each fighter regiment is assigned a sector. The sector usually is assigned for 1 day. The width of the sector varies from 6 to 18 miles, depending upon weather, the ground situation, and anticipated enemy resistance. The depth of the sector varies from 6 to 12 miles. The sector normally extends from 2 to 3 miles inside friendly territory and continues beyond the front line into enemy territory.

Another characteristic sector is a circle from 3 to 6 miles in diameter. It is used when river crossings or other special operations are covered.

In order to provide a constant air cover over the zone of main effort, fighter regiments employed for this operation are divided into two sections. Each of these, in turn, is broken down into two *Gruppas*, making a total of four *Gruppas*. In actual operation, the *Gruppas* are alternated as follows:

1st *Gruppa*_____ State of readiness 1
(Flying mission.)
2d *Gruppa*_____ State of readiness 2
(Pilots in aircraft ready for take-off.)
3d *Gruppa*_____ State of readiness 3
(Pilots on airfield, aircraft fully serviced.)
4th *Gruppa*_____ State of readiness 4
(Pilots in barracks, aircraft being serviced.)

The first *Gruppa* returning from a patrol turns over its aircraft to the ground personnel for servicing and the pilots rest, state of readiness 4. The second *Gruppa* then moves up to state of readiness 1 and the third and fourth *Gruppas* move up accordingly, to complete the cycle.

Aircraft of the *Gruppa* in state of readiness 2 are considered reinforcements and may be called out for unexpectedly heavy fighting. Flight altitudes vary, depending upon cloud height, weather, and enemy air activity. For large-scale operations or when strong enemy air resistance or attack is expected, the sectors concerned are provided additional cover by *Gruppas* from other regiments, which are on constant stand-by duty. The additional *Gruppas* operate at specifically assigned altitudes to insure complete cover for the sector.

TACTICAL RESERVE PATROLS. *Gruppas* assigned to this mission operate only during an offensive, and then primarily at the critical points of operations. The normal patrol sector is twice as large as that normally assigned to a fighter regiment providing cover for the zone of main effort and is called an "air zone." Although these *Gruppas* patrol over the actual battle area, they engage in combat only when the enemy's superiority over the *Gruppas* covering the zone of main effort becomes apparent. The patrols operate from 17,000 to 18,000 feet.

ADVANCE PATROLS. During an offensive operation, advance patrols are employed especially during the period of preparations as a precautionary measure against enemy aircraft, particularly reconnaissance aircraft, penetrating to the zone of main effort. Advance patrol sectors are two to three

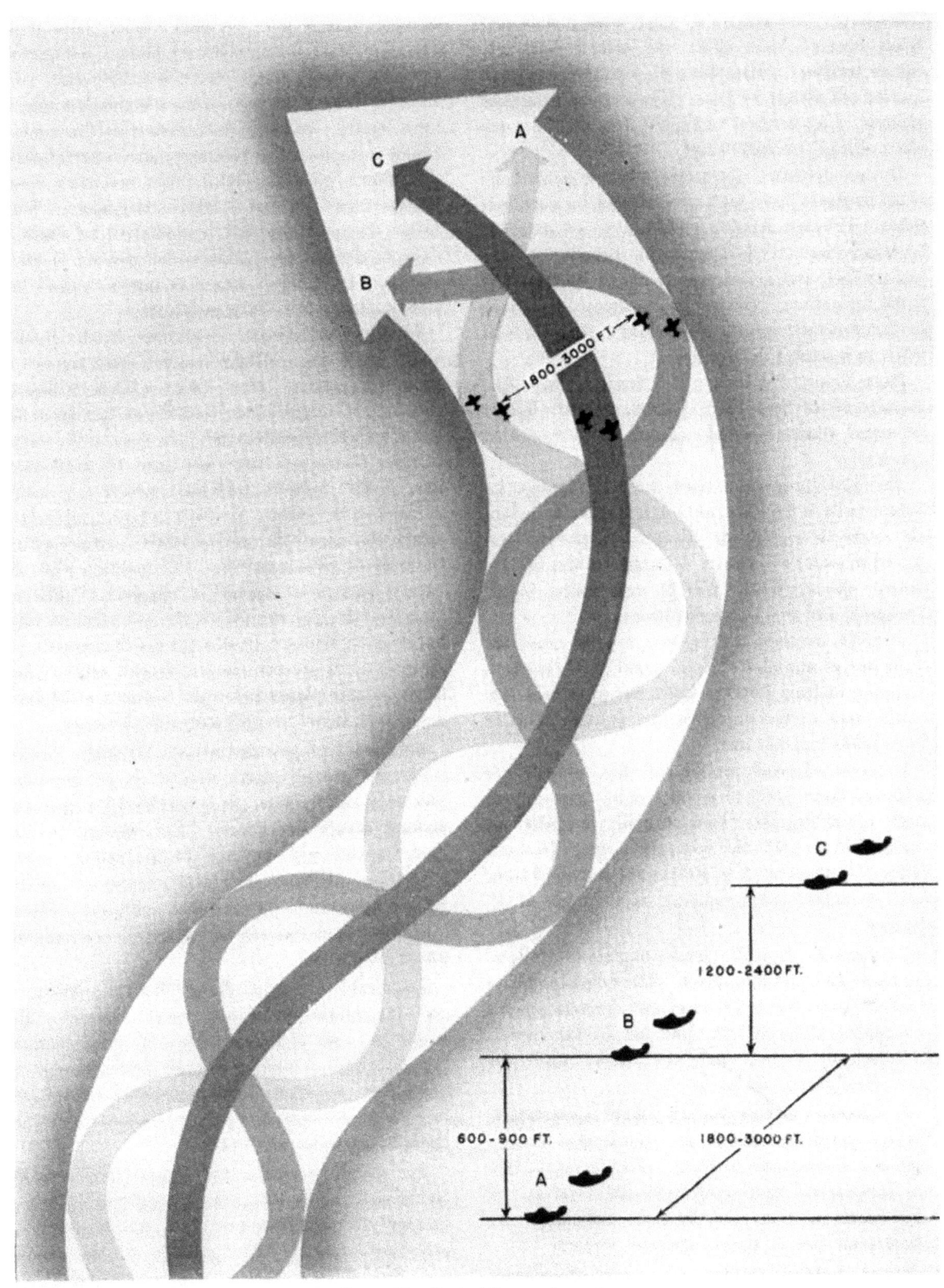

Figure 13.—Typical Gruppa formation.

times larger than sectors assigned to regiments covering zone of main effort and extend deep into enemy territory. Patrolling above these sectors is carried out mainly by *Para*. The average patrolling altitude is from 8,000 to 13,500 feet, with a maximum altitude of 20,000 feet.

During defensive operations advance patrols operate in *Paras* from well-camouflaged forward airfields. Primary mission on this type of patrol is reconnaissance to determine the direction of the main effort and to intercept aircraft, particularly small formations. Should large enemy formations be encountered, fighters are brought up from rear fields to intercept the enemy.

FREE LANCE PATROLS. The Soviets realize the importance of free lance patrolling. All fighter personnel receive special training in this type of operation.

The basic formation used for free lancing by fighter units is the *Para*, although on rare occasions the *Zveno* is employed. Targets usually are assigned in order of priority. Targets of the highest priority during World War II were trains, motor transport, and troop concentrations.

In clear weather, the fighters usually cross the front line at altitudes of from 6,000 to 12,000 feet, dropping to from 3,000 to 4,500 feet after crossing. In the area of the objective, the fighters drop to from 1,800 to 3,000 feet.

In areas of weak antiaircraft fire, attacks are delivered from 1,800 to 3,000 feet by diving at an angle of 30 degrees. Fire normally is opened at from 1,200 to 1,800 feet from the target. In areas of heavy antiaircraft fire, attacks are delivered from 4,500 to 6,000 feet by diving at an angle of 45 degrees.

In attack by *Para*, the leader signals the following plane and goes into attack. The following plane trails by from 600 to 900 feet and delivers attacks immediately following the pull out by the leader. In attack by *Zveno*, one *Para* attacks while the other *Para* flies cover above.

d. Combat tactics during patrol operations. Fighter patrol operations are coordinated closely with the antiaircraft artillery. Fighter personnel are familiarized thoroughly with the locations of antiaircraft positions and the zones and density of antiaircraft fire in their respective sectors.

Soviet fighters employ two basic maneuvers against enemy fighters. When outnumbered, they execute a turn into a closed circle. The radius increases with the number of planes, the interval between planes never exceeding 650 feet. The circling fighters attempt to draw the enemy aircraft over friendly territory into antiaircraft fire zones. Depending upon the situation, the Soviet fighters then either withdraw behind this protective screen or hover just outside to attack stragglers. When forces are equal, combat is conducted by *Paras* or *Zvenos*, the attacking planes endeavoring to maintain contact. Effort again is made to draw the enemy planes into antiaircraft fires.

In attacking bomber formations, Soviet fighters attack by diving on the formation from the sun or a cloud formation. Every effort is made to disperse the enemy formation so that *Paras* can press the attack on individual aircraft. As soon as the enemy bomber formation enters the zone of antiaircraft fire, Soviet fighters withdraw and fly a course parallel to the enemy aircraft, but gain altitude to attack the enemy formation when it comes out of the zone of antiaircraft fire. Frequently, when the enemy formations appear in elements at different altitudes, the fighters attack the top element while antiaircraft artillery attacks the lower elements. If an overcast is present, the antiaircraft artillery fires on the enemy planes below the overcast while fighters attack enemy aircraft above the overcast.

e. Escort of ground attack aircraft. Escort cover for ground attack aircraft is an important task of Soviet fighters. It is provided for nearly all ground attack operations. The strength of the escort varies with the size of the ground attack formation, distance to target, expected enemy fighter opposition, and weather conditions. However, the usual ratio is one fighter to one ground attack aircraft.

FORMATION. During World War II, fighter escort formations underwent several changes. But in the last year of the war, they fell into a definite system which remained in use until the end of hostilities. Escorting fighters are split equally into two parts: the immediate escort formation, and the assault formation (fig. 14).

The assault formation flies from 1,500 to 3,000 feet directly above the ground attack formation, or one-half to three-quarters of a mile ahead on a criss-cross course. The mission of the assault formation is to prevent enemy aircraft from reaching the ground attack formation. Frequently, one

382

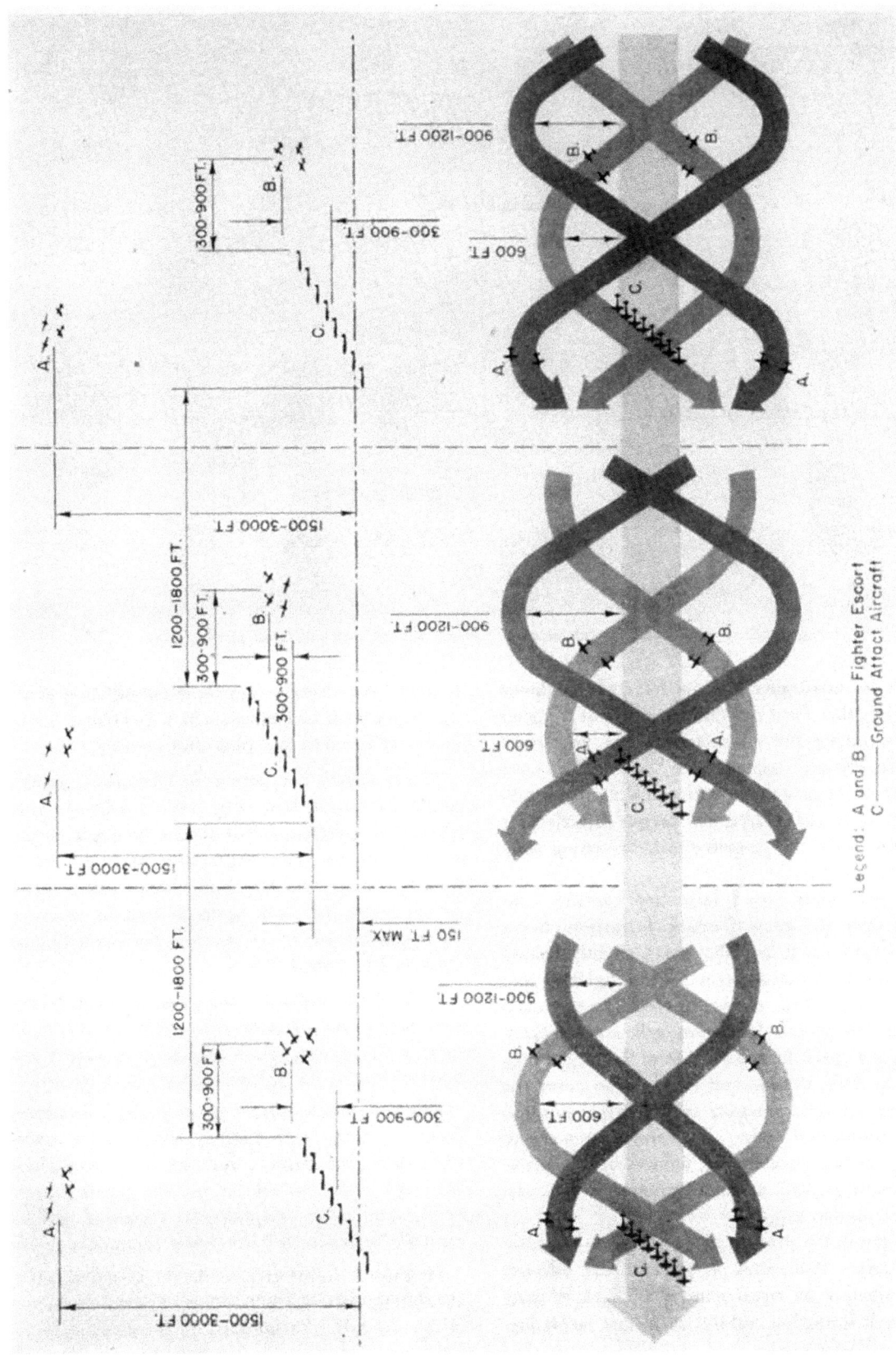

Legend: A and B —————— Fighter Escort
C —————— Ground Attack Aircraft

Figure 11.—Typical fighter escort formation for ground attack formation.

383

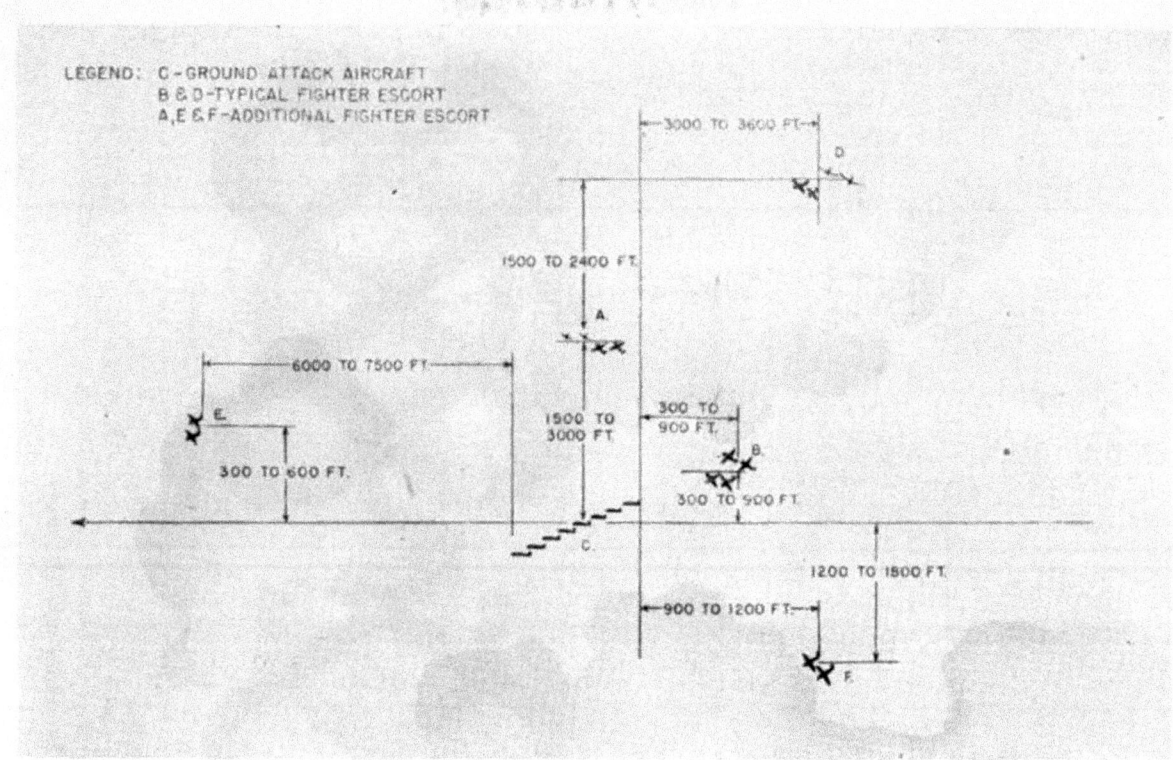

LEGEND: C-GROUND ATTACK AIRCRAFT
B & D-TYPICAL FIGHTER ESCORT
A, E & F-ADDITIONAL FIGHTER ESCORT

Figure 15.—Typical fighter escort for ground attack aircraft with additional escort fighters.

Para is far in advance to scout for enemy fighters, while the other *Para* remains in reserve at a higher altitude, taking full advantage of sun and cloud cover in event of contact with the enemy. Over the target, the assault formation maintains an altitude of up to 10,000 feet, and patrols directly over the target until the ground attack formation completes its mission.

The immediate escort formation remains constantly near the ground attack formation, flying from 300 to 1,000 feet above and slightly behind in continual criss-cross flight. These fighters enter combat only when enemy fighters have broken through the assault formation and are attacking the ground attack formation. Over the target, they maintain their altitude and stand by to cover the attacking aircraft, resuming their original position for the withdrawal flight. Frequently, when enemy fighters are not encountered, fighters of the immediate escort formation attack antiaircraft positions or other ground targets.

Changes in the strength of the escort do not alter the pattern. Reductions in strength are effected by eliminating an equal number of fighters from the assault formation and the immediate escort formation. An increase consists of the addition of one or more special formations, which fly behind, above, below, or ahead on sweeping missions (fig. 15).

When enemy air action is infrequent, ground attack formations frequently take off without escort. The main ground control station orders a formation of fighters flying patrol over the front line to pick up the ground attack formation and escort it to the target and back again to friendly territory. At the completion of the mission, the escort fighters resume their patrol duties.

Fighters do not leave the ground attack formation under any circumstance. Only a direct attack on the ground attack formation by enemy aircraft will cause the fighters to engage in combat.

When outnumbered, the ground attack formation forms a circle, as do fighters during patrol operations, with the fighters forming a similiar circle above the ground attack formation. Effort is made to draw the enemy aircraft into a zone of antiaircraft fire behind which the Soviet formations retire.

f. Escort of bomber aircraft. Escort of bombers differs slightly from the procedure for ground attack aircraft. In addition to the immediate es-

384

cort formation and assault formation. an independent combat formation is provided (fig. 16).

The immediate escort formation usually consists of from four to six aircraft and flies close to the bomber formation. Disposed in *Paras* on the flanks of the bomber formation, the immediate escort formation repels attacks of enemy aircraft on the bombers. Frequently, when six aircraft are employed, a *Para* of fighters flies below the bomber formation to cover the zone poorly protected by the bombers' guns. The immediate escort formation remains with the bomber formation, and at no time leaves the bombers to pursue the enemy.

The assault formation, following from 1,500 to 1,800 feet above the immediate escort formation, engages enemy aircraft in combat.

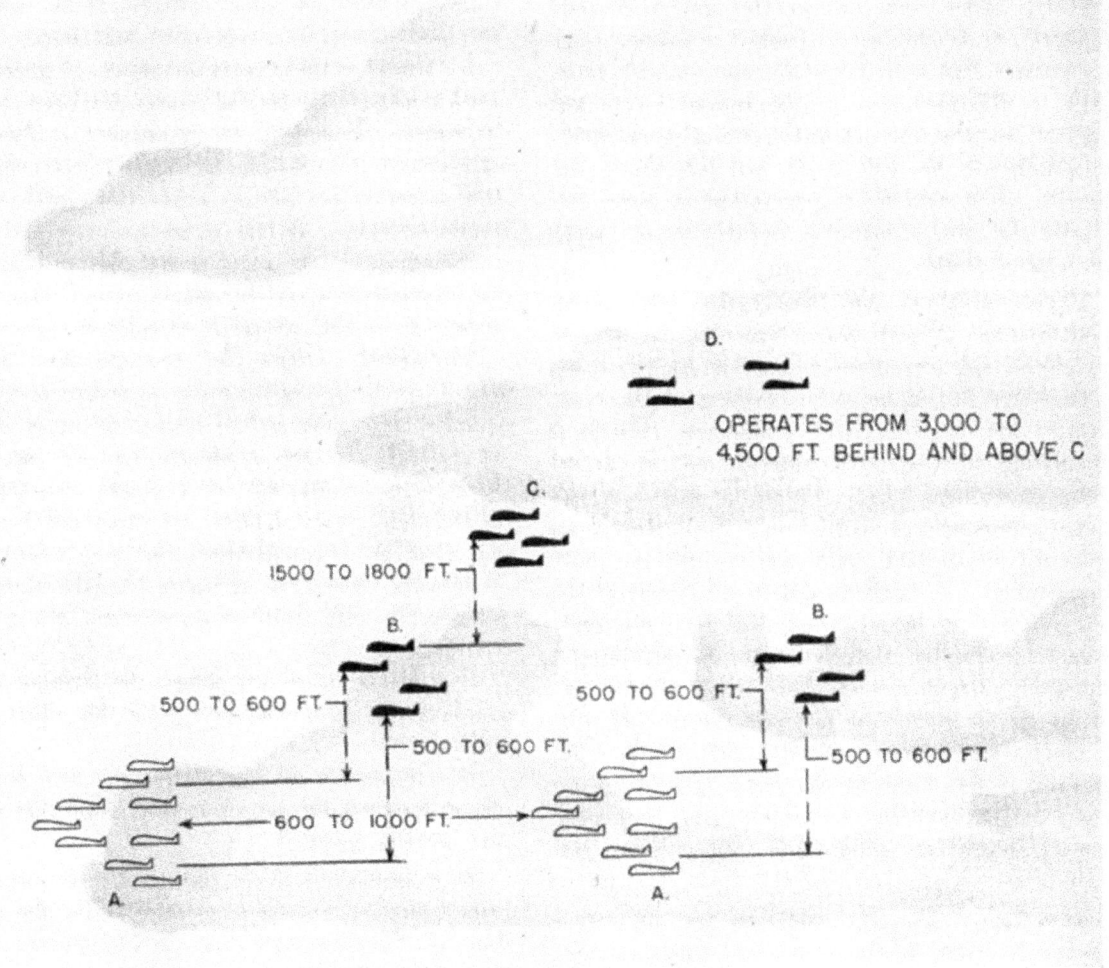

OPERATES FROM 3,000 TO
4,500 FT. BEHIND AND ABOVE C

1500 TO 1800 FT.

500 TO 600 FT.

500 TO 600 FT.

500 TO 600 FT.

500 TO 600 FT.

600 TO 1000 FT.

LEGEND: A—BOMBERS IN "V"
FORMATION
B—IMMEDIATE ESCORT
FORMATION (FIGHTERS)
C—ASSAULT FORMATION
(FIGHTERS)
D—INDEPENDENT COMBAT
FORMATION (FIGHTERS)

Figure 16.—Fighter escort for bombers.

385

The independent combat formation has a large degree of freedom of action. Upon nearing the target, this formation leaves the main formation to reach the target from 2 to 3 minutes before the bombers. The mission of the independent combat formation is to find and engage enemy planes. Upon the arrival of the main formation, the assault formation assists the independent combat formation.

g. Cooperation with ground forces. Frequently, aside from the general protection and support of ground forces, fighter regiments and, sometimes, fighter divisions are subordinated tactically to different arms of the ground forces and operate independently from the general coordinated operations of the Red Army and Red Army Air Force. This method of cooperation is used primarily for tank formations endeavoring to break through in depth.

RECONNAISSANCE AND PROTECTION FOR TANK FORMATIONS. Visual reconnaissance of the area in which the tank formation will operate usually is accomplished during the early morning or the evening by one or more *Para* of fighters. During a fluctuating situation, reconnaissance may be carried out several times a day. During the attack, a tank spearhead usually is escorted by a *Para* of fighters, who are in constant radio contact with the tank commander. The fighters report all phases of the development of the attack so that the tank commander is familiar at all times with the terrain and situation. Reconnaissance *Para* relieve one another in the air to provide the tank spearhead with continuous reconnaissance during the attack. The altitude of the reconnaissance *Para* may vary from low level to 7,000 feet, depending upon reconnaissance objectives, antiaircraft opposition, and visibility.

The fighter strength employed for protection varies according to the number of tanks, weather conditions, and the strength of enemy air opposition. Taking as an example a *Gruppa* of eight aircraft, the formation would be as follows:

Section 1—a *Para* ranging from 1,000 to 5,000 feet.

Section 2—a *Zveno* ranging from 6,000 to 10,000 feet.

Section 3—a *Para* ranging from 6,000 to 12,000 feet.

Sections 1 and 2 normally remain directly over the tank formation, while Section 3 covers the surrounding area in wide circles to intercept approaching enemy aircraft. If enemy aircraft are sighted, Section 3 directs the *Zveno* to the enemy by radio. Sections 1 and 3 remain in reserve. Should a large enemy air formation be encountered, Section 3 can call for reinforcements.

Cooperation of fighters with other arms of the ground forces, such as motorized units and infantry, follows the same pattern as the method described above for cooperation with tanks.

h. Other aerial reconnaissance. Fighters are used extensively in the Red Army Air Force reconnaissance. Normally, reconnaissance is flown in addition to other duties, and fighters are equipped with cameras for use in conjunction with visual reconnaissance. Aerial reconnaissance rarely is combined with free lance operations, and fighters on reconnaissance do not attack ground targets or engage in combat, except in extreme emergency.

PROCEDURE. Orders for reconnaissance flights usually reach the fighter units concerned from 2 to 3 hours before the actual mission is to be flown. In a fluid situation, missions often are assigned from 25 to 30 minutes before flight. Formations of two, four, or six fighters are employed, depending upon the reconnaissance objective, importance of mission, enemy air strength, strength of enemy antiaircraft, and depth of penetration into enemy territory.

In a formation of two planes, the leading plane conducts the reconnaissance while the other provides cover.

In a formation of four planes, the two leading planes conduct the reconnaissance while the other two provide cover.

In a formation of six planes, the two leading planes conduct the reconnaissance while the other four, in *Paras* on each side, provide cover.

i. Night fighter tactics. Night fighter operations are coordinated closely with antiaircraft artillery in the defense of important cities and other installations. The usual procedure is to defend the main target with a series of circular rings of antiaircraft weapons of all calibers, from 500 to 2,000 guns.

Fighters are assigned to regions, on the distant approaches to the target, outside the zone of antiaircraft fires. During World War II, these regions usually were marked by bonfires or other means of illumination on the ground.

Fighters are distributed at altitudes of from 6,500 to 20,000 feet, with a distance of 1,600 feet between planes at the same altitude. Thus, a large number of fighters can be put into the air, with minimum danger of collisions, to assure maximum protection from enemy aircraft.

Friendly aircraft are forbidden to fly over antiaircraft zones, and coordination of fighters and antiaircraft fires in the same zone at night is exceptional. The Soviets admit that this type of operation has not as yet been mastered fully.

SEARCH FOR ENEMY AIRCRAFT. Although Soviet operational documents stress that the basic method of directing friendly fighters against enemy aircraft is by radio used in conjunction with ground radar, the lack of radar equipment during World War II forced the Soviets to use many auxiliary methods. In addition to the basic method, fighter aircraft were aided by antiaircraft artillery batteries, which used target spotting station data to direct fighters toward the enemy aircraft. Upon receipt of this information, fighters flew lower than the enemy aircraft and searched every dark spot against the sky. Search tactics also included observation of antiaircraft shell bursts, bombs, and exhaust flames from the enemy planes. Ruses such as firing bursts, to obtain return fire from unseen enemy planes, were used successfully. Searchlights also were used, although prearranged zones were established so that the searching planes remained outside of the fields of antiaircraft artillery.

Whenever possible use was made of enemy flares, dropped on the approaches to intended targets, to spot enemy aircraft. In other cases, Soviet fighters dropped their own flares. Two or three fighters, flying from 1,500 to 3,000 feet above the anticipated height of the enemy aircraft, drop flares along the expected path of enemy flight. Two or three additional planes, normally from 1,500 to 3,000 feet above the flare-dropping fighters, fly into the illuminated zone to find and attack enemy aircraft.

NIGHT COMBAT. In night combat, the Soviets stress the importance of a sudden initial attack. This attack is made from 60 to 200 feet behind and below the aircraft at an angle of approximately 20 degrees. Careful aiming of the first burst is emphasized. After firing, the Soviet fighter with

draws downward to repeat the attack from another direction.

3. RED NAVAL AIR FORCE FIGHTERS

Generally, fighter tactics of the Red Naval Air Force are identical to those of the Red Army Air Force. Red Naval Air Force tactics are presented only for those operations in which an appreciable difference in formation or method has been discerned.

a. Escort of ground attack aircraft. Normally, the formation of the naval escort corresponds to the Red Army Air Force. However, this formation is altered in low level flights over the sea. The immediate escort formation and part of the assault formation fly on each side of the ground attack formation at almost the same altitude, to screen the presence of the main formation. One *Para* of the assault formation usually reconnoiters ahead of the entire formation.

b. Escort of torpedo aircraft. Escort fighters for this type of operation normally equal the number of torpedo aircraft, but if enemy fighters are unusually active, a ratio of 2 to 1 is used.

FORMATION. Normally, torpedo aircraft formations are divided into two or three subordinate groups of three, six, and, occasionally, nine aircraft. Torpedo aircraft formations approach targets at low level, with the fighters at the same altitude on both sides (fig. 17). "A" is the immediate escort formation. "B" is the assault formation. An additional *Para* of fighters, "C," included in the escort formation to take photographs, takes position as shown. Should fog over the water cause the torpedo aircraft to fly at higher altitudes, the immediate escort formation "A," remains with the torpedo aircraft, but the assault formation and the extra *Para*, "C," fly from 2,500 to 4,000 feet above the formation. If the entire flight is made at low level, the immediate escort formation, "A," climbs to from 500 to 1,500 feet when approaching the target to facilitate attack on antiaircraft batteries. The assault formation, "B," and *Para* "C" rise to from 5,000 to 6,500 feet and patrol the area while the attack is in progress. Frequently, if the exact location of the target is not known, *Para* "C" flies ahead, locates the target, and directs the torpedo aircraft formation by radio.

ACTIVITY OVER TARGET. Just before reaching the target, the immediate escort formation flies ahead to attack antiaircraft batteries. While the torpedo aircraft press home their attack, the immediate escort formation prepares to protect the assembly of the torpedo attack formation for withdrawal or for a second approach, if necessary.

If a second approach is made, the immediate escort formation again attacks the antiaircraft batteries and then covers the assembly of the torpedo aircraft. The assault group and the extra *Para,* "C," patrol the target area to intercept enemy fighters.

When the attack is completed, the torpedo aircraft with their immediate escort withdraw at low level. The assault formation covers the rear and then loses altitude to overtake the formation. *Para* "C" remains to take photographs, withdrawing when its mission is accomplished.

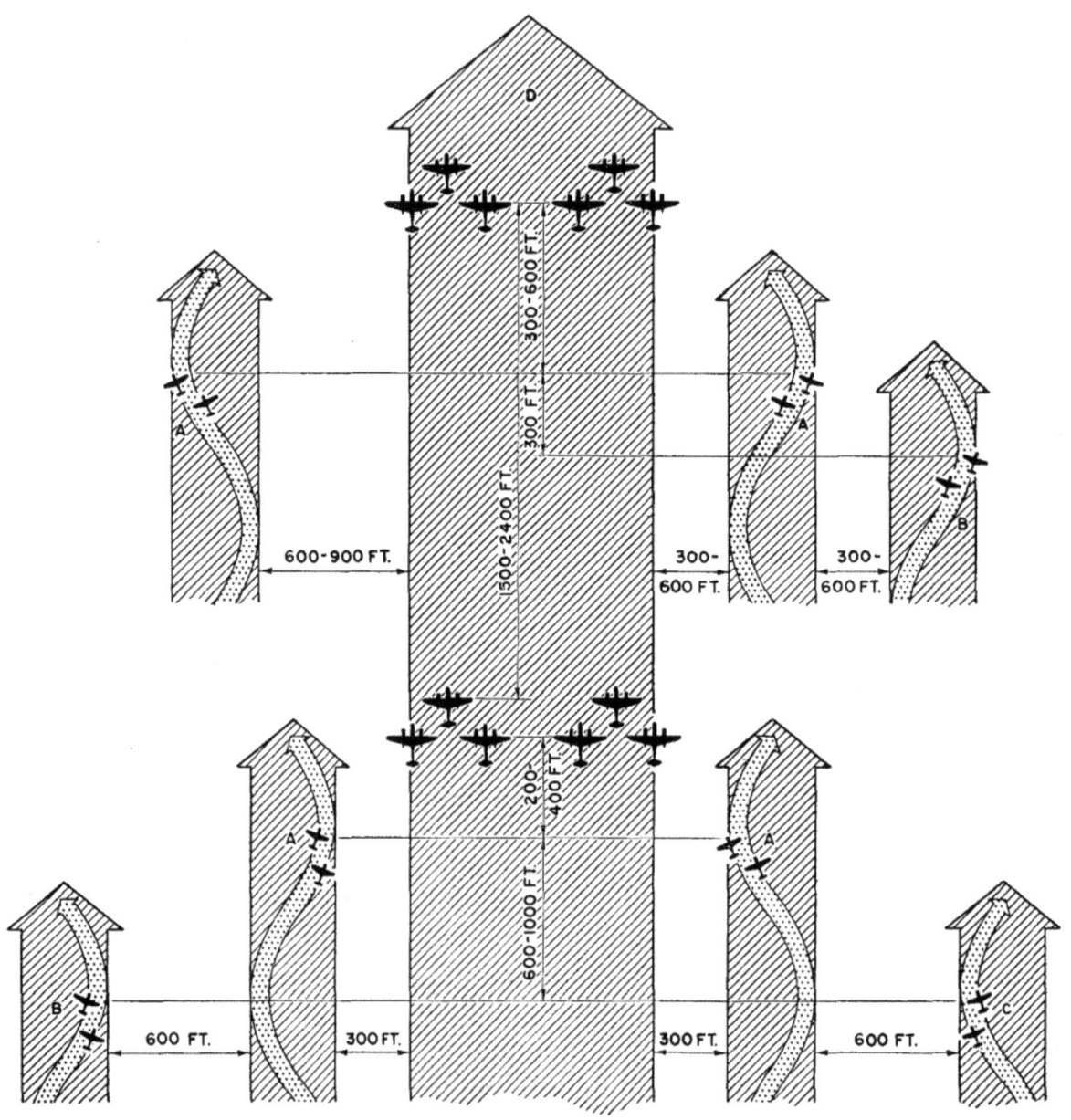

LEGEND: D- TORPEDO AIRCRAFT   A-B-C- FIGHTER ESCORT

Figure 17.—Fighter escort for torpedo aircraft of Red Naval Air Force.

Section IV. GROUND ATTACK METHODS AND TACTICS

1. GENERAL

The importance of ground attack aviation increased greatly during World War II, with the result that it ranks as one of the most important and effective air weapons of the U. S. S. R.

2. RED ARMY AIR FORCE

The primary mission of the ground attack aviation of the Red Army Air Force is to support the Red Army in all operations. It assists the artillery in the preparation for an offensive, supports the ground forces during the break-through, and covers them during disengaging operations by attacking enemy ground formations. In addition to this primary mission as "flying artillery" for the ground forces, it attacks enemy airfields, lines of communication, reserves, and performs reconnaissance.

a. Location of bases. During an offensive operation, the main concentration of ground attack regiments is located on airfields in a zone 30 miles in depth, parallel to and 15 miles from the front line. Units are not dispersed as widely as in the fighter force. Two or three ground attack regiments occupy the same airfield. Frequently, an airfield is occupied by a ground attack regiment and a fighter regiment for escort purposes.

In a defensive operation, small numbers of ground attack aircraft are based on forward fields for immediate support of ground forces. As is true with fighters, these planes are well camouflaged and are shifted from airfield to airfield. Supplies for the forward fields are moved in at night. For major operations, ground attack aircraft from rear fields are flown up to the forward bases, from which they operate to cover the disengagement of ground troops or to support counterattacks.

b. Operational technique. In World War II, ground attack aircraft operated under all types of weather conditions. Even in weather considered unsuitable for flight operation, ground attack missions were carried out without fighter escort. Only extremely unfavorable weather caused an interruption in operations.

Ground attack forces normally operated independently of other air arms, except for fighters which served principally as escort. The strength of formations, types of attack, number of attacks, target approach, and withdrawal were, as in any other air force, governed by operational necessity.

FORMATION AND STRENGTH. In World War II, the usual ground attack formations employed by the Soviets were right or left echelon or the conventional four-aircraft, unbalanced "V" used by the fighters of the Western Allies. Formations of right or left echelon were made up of from four to eight aircraft.

In a concentrated attack employing a large number of ground attack aircraft, a column of from four to eight aircraft in echelon, or a variation of this arrangement, is used (A and B, fig. 18). The echelon formation probably is assumed while maneuvering for, or just prior to the actual attack. The limitations of this formation in maneuverability, defense, and its excessive demands on the pilots made it seem improbable that it was employed during the entire mission.

The echelon formation immediately prior to the attack allows ground attack aircraft to form readily into either line abreast formation for an area target, or trail formation and then, possibly, a battle circle for pin point targets (fig. 19). It is possible that the arrangement of *Zvenos* in unbalanced "V's," (C, fig. 18), was used on the way to and from the target because of its defensive possibilities and maneuverability. Although there is little indication that this exact formation was used widely, it may be assumed that on long missions either the line abreast or some similar, relatively undemanding formation was used on the flight to and from the target.

The number of aircraft employed varies with the size of target and type of mission. During the assault by the ground forces on the enemy main defense line, simultaneous assaults were made by three or more formations of from 28 to 36 aircraft each, followed by similar waves spaced from 30 minutes to 2 hours apart.

In the support of the main effort, the density of attack by ground attack aircraft often reached five or six formations of from 28 to 36 aircraft, attacking at 5- to 15-minute intervals. Operations in secondary zones were supported by small formations of from four to six aircraft concurrently with the mass attacks in the zone of main effort.

In defensive operations, steady pressure was maintained by formations of from 4 to 20 aircraft attacking at frequent intervals. Attacks on the enemy's forward area were carried out usually by

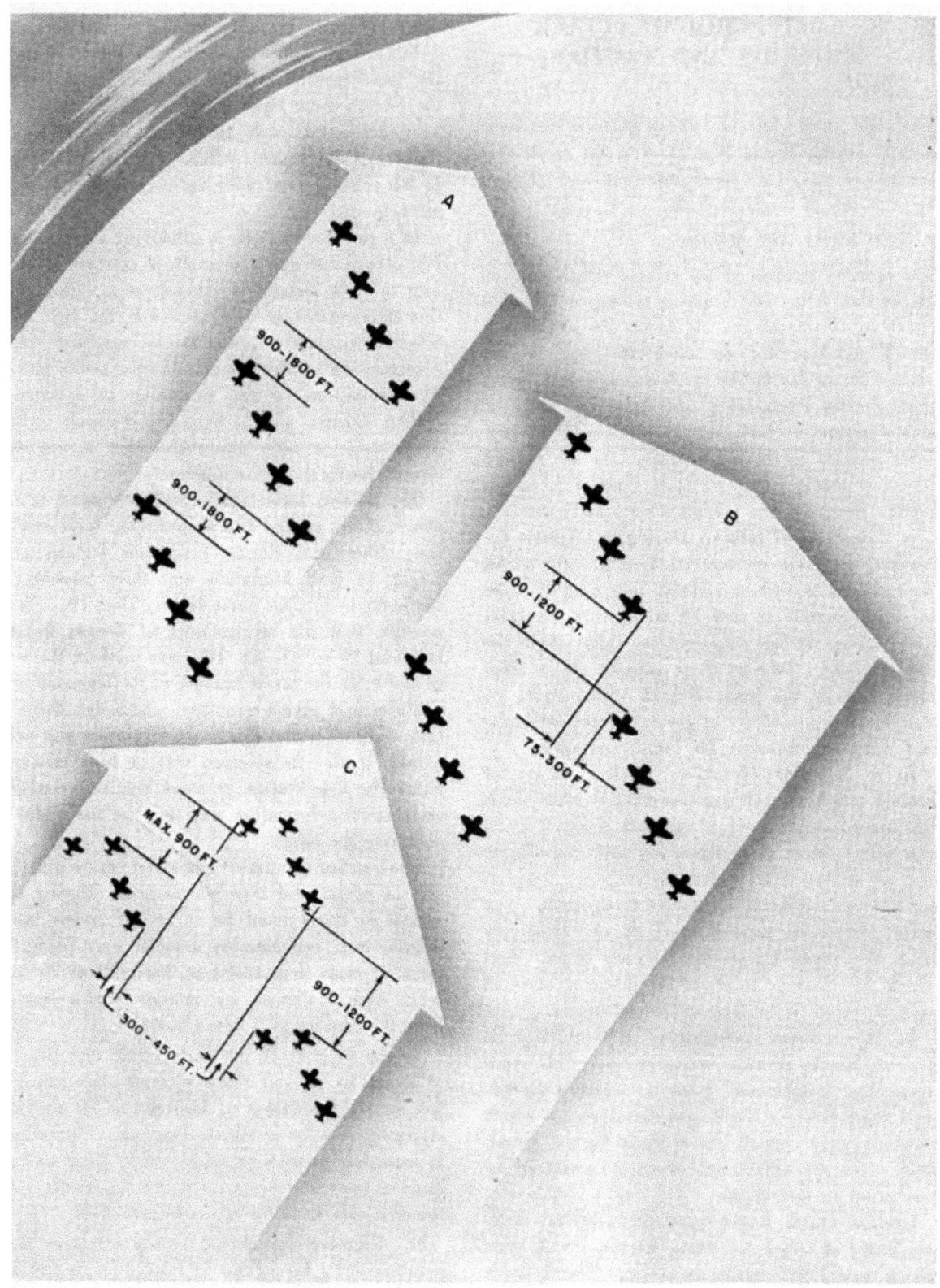

Figure 18.—*Typical ground attack formations.*

390

small formations of from 4 to 12 aircraft, normally striking beyond the range of friendly artillery. Enemy airfields were attacked by formations of from 16 to 32 aircraft, frequently followed by similar waves.

TARGET APPROACH. The Soviets advocate a low level approach for ground attack aircraft for greater protection against enemy fighters and to maintain the element of surprise. Low level flight is used particularly on free-lance missions against enemy fighters and to maintain the element of surprise. Low-level flight is used particularly on free-lance missions against ground targets with weak antiaircraft belts to attack roads and other special targets. However, in areas where intense antiaircraft fire was encountered, ground-attack aircraft frequently flew at altitudes ranging from 2,500 to 4,000 feet.

The direction of the approach usually was predetermined by previous reconnaissance. Full advantage was taken of sun, cloud cover, and terrain.

ATTACK ON FRONT LINES. In attacks on front-line targets, the time of arrival and time over target were prescribed strictly. Each wave of attacking aircraft covered its target in the time allotted, and then left to avoid interfering with the following wave.

For attacks on area targets, such as sectors of the front, the frontal run up is used, with each formation of from four to eight aircraft attacking in line abreast. Rockets are fired from 1,500 to 2,000 feet, in a 30- to 45-degree dive, followed almost immediately by release of bombs and fire from aircraft. When there is only one run on the target the entire bomb load is dropped. When several runs are made, bombs are dropped singly or in small salvos. In attacks on line or pin point targets the aircraft attack in trail with little interval or peel off from echelon formation into a battle circle (fig. 19). Aircraft guns are fired first and, if tracers show the aim to be accurate, the rockets are fired. Bombs are released after the rockets are fired.

Every wave of ground attack aircraft contains a formation whose primary mission is to neutralize enemy antiaircraft batteries. Usually, these aircraft remain behind the larger formation and wait until the enemy opens fire before launching the attack. If, however, the antiaircraft positions are known, the aircraft do not wait, but fly in ahead of the main formation to attack the antiaircraft batteries. If the antiaircraft batteries are neutralized on the first attack, the aircraft join in the attack on the target. When there is no air opposition, escort fighters assist in attacks on antiaircraft positions.

COORDINATION WITH ARTILLERY. Operations by large ground attack formations on the enemy front line are combined and coordinated with the artillery preparation during the break-through of the enemy's defenses. During the artillery preparation, ground attack aircraft attack targets which the artillery cannot cover adequately. In addition, they deliver a mass attack on the enemy's second defense line to neutralize it and to deny the enemy opportunity to consolidate forces withdrawing from the first line. When the first defense line is taken, artillery fire is shifted to the second line while the ground attack formations attack the third. The result is a rolling barrage of artillery fire and bombing, strafing, and rocket attacks on the entire enemy defense system.

In addition to these mass attacks on enemy defense lines, ground attack formations continually attack all enemy troops and matériel in the forward area to disorganize the retreat of the enemy, to impede the movement of enemy reserves, and to liquidate small pockets of enemy resistance.

COOPERATION WITH TANKS AND OTHER GROUND FORCES. Ground attack units also are attached to tank units effecting a deep penetration. When opposition is particularly heavy, ground attack aircraft fly continually above the tanks to attack enemy pockets of resistance which might impede tank movement. The flanks, in particular, are reconnoitered to prevent a surprise attack from these directions. When opposition is light, small numbers of ground attack aircraft normally escort tank units. The others remain in readiness on their airfields. They attack pockets of enemy resistance impeding the tank advance upon call from the tank spearhead commander. When the mission is completed, the aircraft return to base. Cooperation with infantry, motorized units, and other ground forces is generally similar.

ATTACKS ON TRAINS. To attack moving trains, aircraft approach from the front at an angle of from 15 to 20 degrees to the direction in which the train is going. Aircraft attack in pairs, one plane diving to the attack while the other provides cover and returns antiaircraft fire from the train.

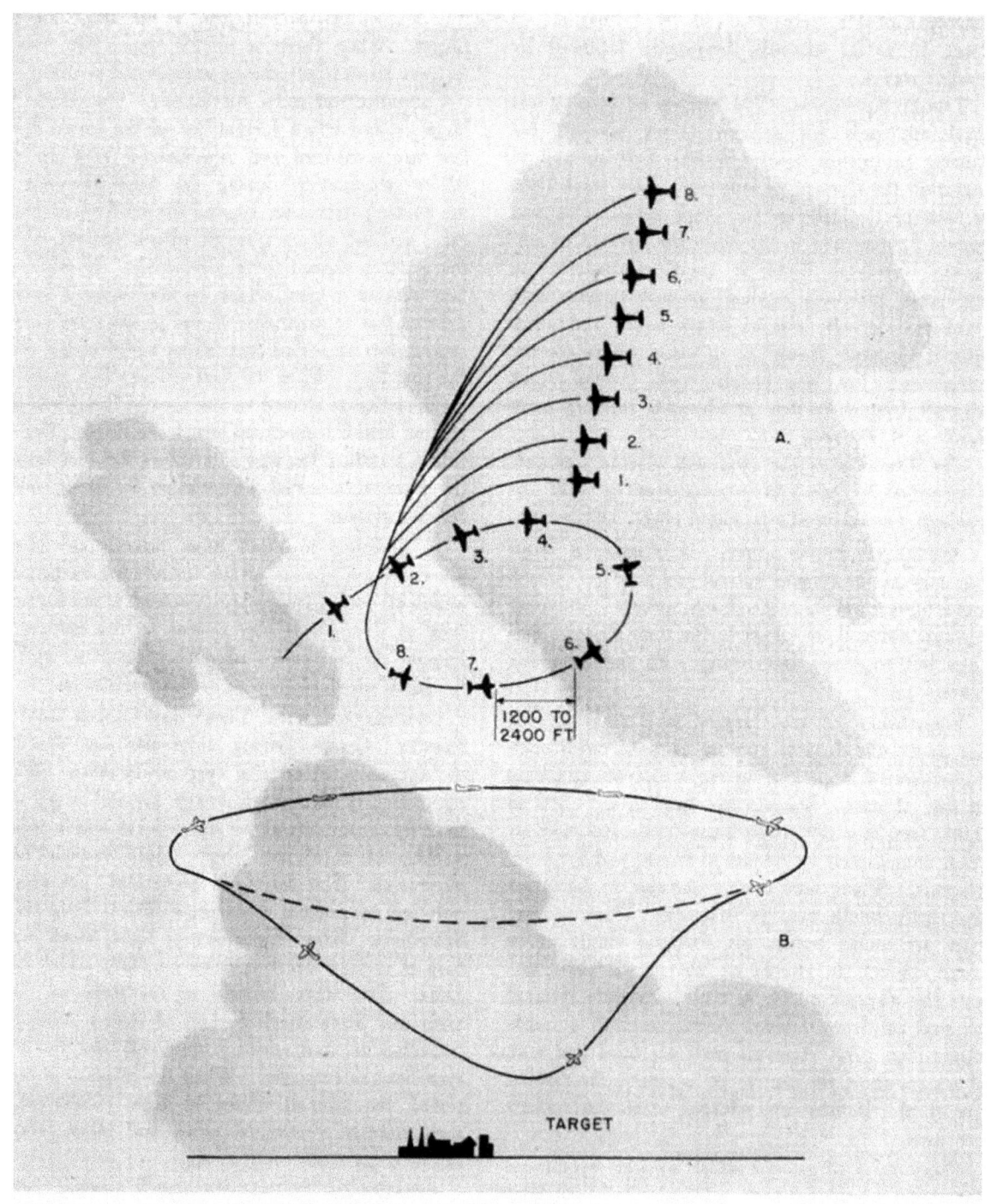

1200 TO 2400 FT

A.

B.

TARGET

Figure 19.—The battle circle.

Trains are attacked preferably in mountain passes or valleys to block traffic. Rail junctions and switch installations also are targets, and the attack is regarded as effective if trains are delayed for 5 hours or more.

To attack stationary trains, ground attack aircraft fly the "snake" pattern (fig. 20). The ground attack aircraft, in a distended echelon right or left formation, approach the target at an angle of from 5 to 10 degrees. Attack is delivered by single aircraft diving at the target and then making a small climbing turn to repeat the attack from the opposite end. Locomotives are attacked with rockets and aircraft guns. Bombs are dropped on railroad cars.

ATTACKS ON AIRFIELDS. Attacks on airfields usually are made by from 12 to 16 aircraft. The approach flight is made at low level only when antiaircraft positions and other ground defenses are well known. Even when low level flight is employed, the aircraft climb to an altitude of from 2,000 to 2,500 feet while 2 miles from the target to deliver the attack. In night and dawn attacks, ground attack aircraft endeavor to make a noiseless approach by gliding toward the target until antiaircraft fire is received. A specific target is assigned to each of the three to four attacking formations, four aircraft each. One formation attacks the antiaircraft artillery. Another formation prevents the aircraft on the field from taking off. The remaining one to two formations attack the parked planes. All attacking aircraft use rockets, bombs, and aircraft guns in the attack.

RECONNAISSANCE. Ground attack regiments also are called upon frequently to fly reconnaissance missions, weather reconnaissance included. Reconnaissance missions usually are flown by from four to six aircraft, without fighter escort. Ground attack aircraft always bomb and strafe the reconnaissance target.

DEFENSIVE MEASURES. Ground attack aircraft usually are provided fighter escort. (For defensive formation with fighter escort, see Fighter Methods and Tactics.) When enemy fighters are detected early enough, ground attack aircraft employ the "S" or "snake" pattern to withdraw to friendly lines, particularly to zones of friendly antiaircraft fire.

Evasive action against enemy antiaircraft fire consists of increasing the distance between individual aircraft and also between formations. Altitudes of formations also are changed continually during flight, and zones of antiaircraft fire and strong defensive areas are avoided when possible.

3. RED NAVAL AIR FORCE

During the first 2 years of World War II, the main mission of naval ground attack aircraft was to assist the Red Army Air Force in supporting ground operations. After this period, they were used chiefly against enemy convoys and harbor installations.

The tactics and formations employed by ground attack aviation of the Red Naval Air Force did not differ materially from those of the Red Army Air Force.

a. Attacks on convoys. Attacks on convoys are carried out by two types of formations. Ground attack aircraft, alone, or ground attack aircraft and bombers may be used. Even when both ground attack aircraft and bombers are used, the ground attack aircraft fly to the target independently with their escort, timing their arrival to coordinate the attack with the bombers assigned the same target.

STRENGTH AND FORMATIONS. When only ground attack aircraft are employed to attack a convoy, the formations vary from 12 aircraft to 2 regiments (60 aircraft), depending upon the size of the convoy, its importance and its fighter and antiaircraft defenses. Formations employed are the same as those of the Red Army Air Force, the smaller formations of from six to eight aircraft flying from 650 to 1,300 feet apart at right or left echelon in column or line. When two regiments participate in the attack, each regiment flies in the same manner, with one regiment from 150 to 700 feet above and from 2,000 to 2,500 feet away from the other.

In a combined attack with bombers, the number of ground attack aircraft rarely exceeds one regiment (32 aircraft).

EXECUTION OF ATTACK. The ground attack formation usually approaches a convoy at an altitude of from 2,000 to 3,000 feet. Sun and cloud cover are utilized for concealment. As with Red Army Air Force ground attack formations, certain formations are assigned the mission of neutralizing antiaircraft defenses. When the antiaircraft defenses are too strong to be neutralized successfully, or when there is strong fighter defense, the target is

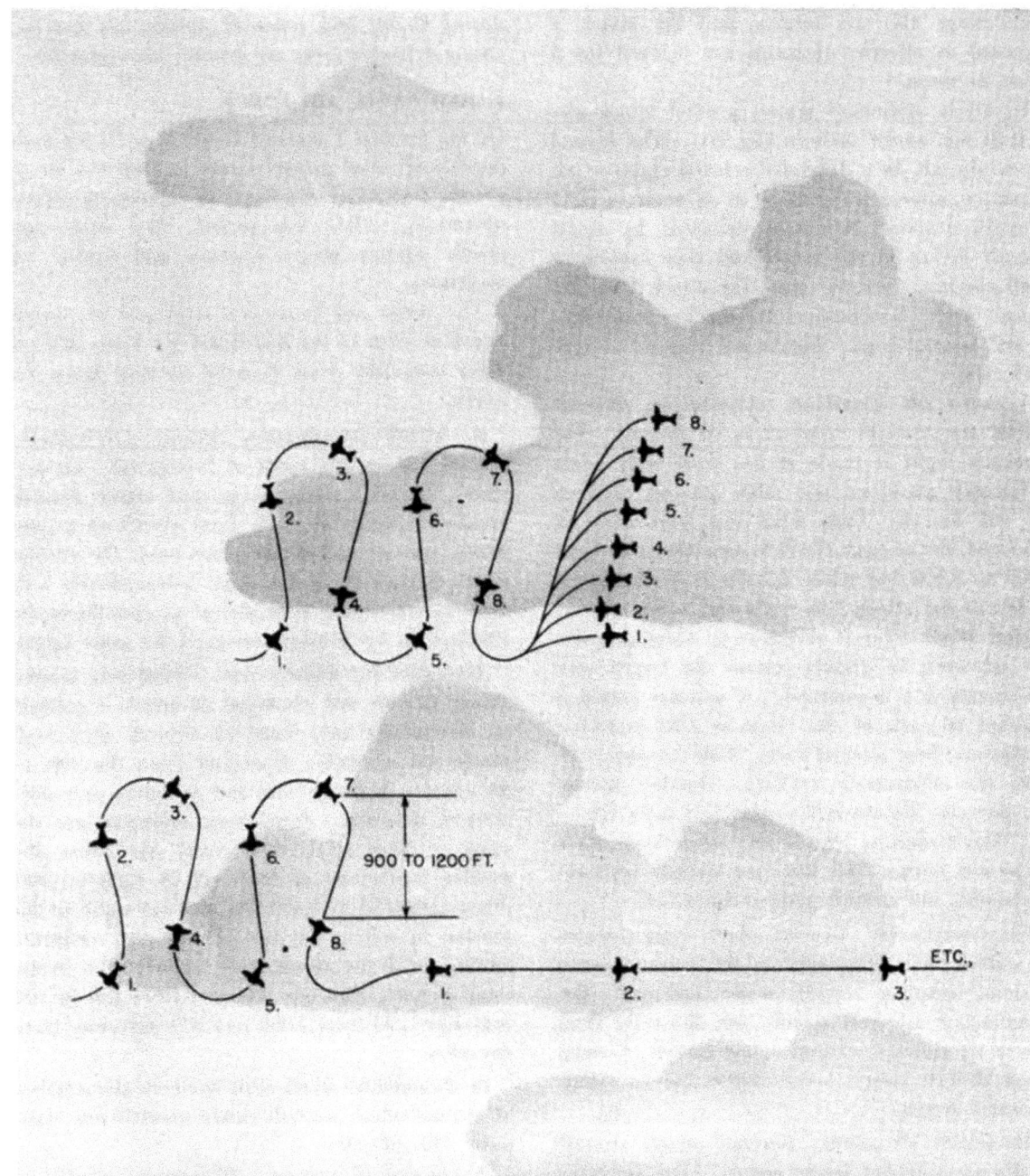

Figure 20.—The "snake" pattern.

attacked in one run by the entire formation. Bombs are dropped by the entire formation immediately after the formation leader drops his. When it is possible to neutralize the antiaircraft defenses and contain the enemy fighters, the subordinate formations of from six to eight aircraft are dispersed according to a prearranged plan. The first approach is made by the subordinate formations attacking successively in line abreast from different directions. The order in which subordinate formations attack is determined by the formation leader. Approaches are made next by individual aircraft attacking definite targets assigned them by the formation leader. Bombs are dropped singly from 1,200 to 2,500 feet, and bombing attacks are followed by low-level strafing.

In addition, several aircraft of the ground attack formation are assigned to bomb from mast height. The aircraft employed for this type of mission fly slightly in the rear of the ground attack formation while approaching the target. When at the proper range for attack, these planes dive sharply towards the target, level out at mast height, and drop their bombs at right angles to the length of the ship. Timing of these attacks is controlled by the formation leader. Usually, they follow the main bombing attack.

In the combined attack on convoys with bombers, ground attack formations are given a definite time attack. The method of attack does not vary from that of exclusively ground attack operations against convoys. As previously mentioned, the ground attack aircraft operate independently from the bombers. Upon completion of their attack, they make way for the bombers.

b. Attacks on harbors. Attacks on harbors are carried out by large mixed formations with all types of ground attack, bombers, torpedo, and fighter aircraft participating.

EXECUTION OF ATTACK. In attacks on harbors by large mixed formations, at least one ground attack regiment, and occasionally as many as two to three regiments, are used. Attacks are carried on a rigid timetable. Bombers attack the harbor installations. Torpedo aircraft attack shipping in the harbor. The ground attack formations attack the antiaircraft defenses. Escorting fighters protect the formations to which assigned. Other fighter formations blockade enemy airfields or intercept enemy fighters.

Each individual formation reaches the target at a different time and altitude and, except for the necessary coordination according to the timetable, completes its mission independently of the other formations. The usual procedure is for the ground attack formation to arrive before the bombers. After the first wave of bombers attack, some of the ground attack aircraft attack antiaircraft batteries on ships in the harbor to facilitate the approach of torpedo aircraft.

Following the torpedo attack, the ground attack aircraft usually are relieved over the target by other ground attack formations, which renew the attack on antiaircraft and other shore installations for the second wave of bombers and torpedo aircraft. Frequently, a third formation of ground attack aircraft arrives immediately after the departure of the second wave of bombers and torpedo aircraft to bomb and strafe any remaining targets.

Section V. SHORT RANGE BOMBER METHODS AND TACTICS

1. GENERAL

From the very beginning of World War II, the short range bomber force appears to have been neglected, particularly as to production, in favor of the fighter and ground attack forces. In contrast to the fighter and ground attack forces, the short range bomber force did not procure a sufficient number of planes until the war was drawing to a close, at which time there was a surplus of bombers. The short range bomber force did, however, have sufficient personnel. But, it was deficient in crew training. The lack of precision instruments for bombing and navigation, which were used as a matter of course by the Western Allies, had a particularly bad effect.

Toward the end of World War II, the Soviets tried to rectify their neglect of the short-range bomber force. This already was in evidence in the development of bombers and radar, bombing, and navigation equipment. However, these developments were not introduced generally before the end of hostilities. What effect these new or future developments will have on the methods and tactics of the short range bomber force is not known at present.

395

2. RED ARMY AIR FORCE SHORT RANGE BOMBERS

In World War II, short range bombers were employed almost exclusively for tactical bombing in support of ground operations. The principal missions assigned to short range bombers included destruction of enemy troops and matériel on the battle field, on the march, and in assembly areas; destruction of supply and communication lines; destruction of rail and other transport; destruction of enemy fuel, ammunition, and supply dumps; destruction of enemy airfields and installations and equipment thereon; and reconnaissance.

a. Location of bases. For an offensive operation short range bomber units are based in the same general area as ground attack aircraft. As are ground attack aircraft, two or three short range bomber regiments are based on the same field. Their fighter escort frequently is based with them.

In a defensive operation short range bombers are based on airfields from 100 to 150 miles from the front.

b. Operational technique. Bombing missions were carried out almost exclusively by day up to the end of World War II. Individual elite crews were sent out on night missions, in special emergencies, but these missions were rare. Weather also restricted daylight operations. Operations were not flown in an overcast because the short range bomber force was not adequately equipped with blind flying instruments.

FORMATIONS AND STRENGTH. Formation is flown in groups of nine aircraft of three flights of three aircraft each. Each flight and each group are arranged in "V" formation. The groups fly one behind the other at staggered altitudes. A loose formation is flown to the target. However, upon reaching the target area, the formation is closed up as closely as possible.

The srength employed varies with the importance and type of mission. Operations are carried out frequently by divisions, with each regiment supplying from two to three groups of aircraft.

BOMBING TECHNIQUE. Although a few regiments specialize in dive bombing, level flight bombardment is more common. Flights lose from 500 to 600 feet on the bomb run, with the result that bombs are dropped from a slight glide rather than from strictly level flight. Bombs are dropped usually by each flight of aircraft, with the wingmen releasing theirs immediately after the flight leader drops his.

The angle of dive never exceeds 60 degrees for the TU-2 in dive bombing. However, the PE-2 has better diving qualities and frequently dives at greater angles.

Occasionally a combination of both types of attack is employed, with a few aircraft attacking antiaircraft positions in a dive while the main body of bombers attack the target in level flight. Blind bombing is rare because of the lack of suitable equipment. On these rare occasions, the target is approached from a visible landmark and the bombs are dropped on an estimated time of arrival over target. This method is inadequate for precision bombing, and can be used only against large area targets.

Bombing altitudes always are specified in orders and vary according to the location of the targets. Targets in the enemy forward area are bombed from altitudes of from 2,500 to 6,000 feet. Those in the enemy rear areas are bombed from higher altitudes, ranging from 10,000 to 16,000 feet. For reasons of safety, the tendency prevailed during World War II to bomb from as high an altitude as possible. Lower altitudes were used only when necessitated by cloud cover.

DEFENSIVE MEASURES. Fighter escort is provided for short range bomber formations. For additional protection, routes are chosen carefully. Heavily defended areas are avoided whenever possible. Courses are changed frequently and the target approach is made to take full advantage of the sun and existing cloud cover. Evasive action against flak consists of variations in altitude and course. Evasive turns normally are limited to from 15 to 20 degrees.

c. Reconnaissance. Short range bombers usually carry out reconnaissance missions for their own benefit to locate suitable targets in absence of orders from higher headquarters, to determine the exact location of a specified target, to watch possible river crossing points for signs of enemy activity, or to determine exact weather conditions. The radius of action varies and depends upon the type of aircraft with which the particular regiment is equipped. Aircraft are sent out singly. When two are assigned to the same mission, there is an interval between their take offs, and each aircraft flies its mission independently. Altitudes range up

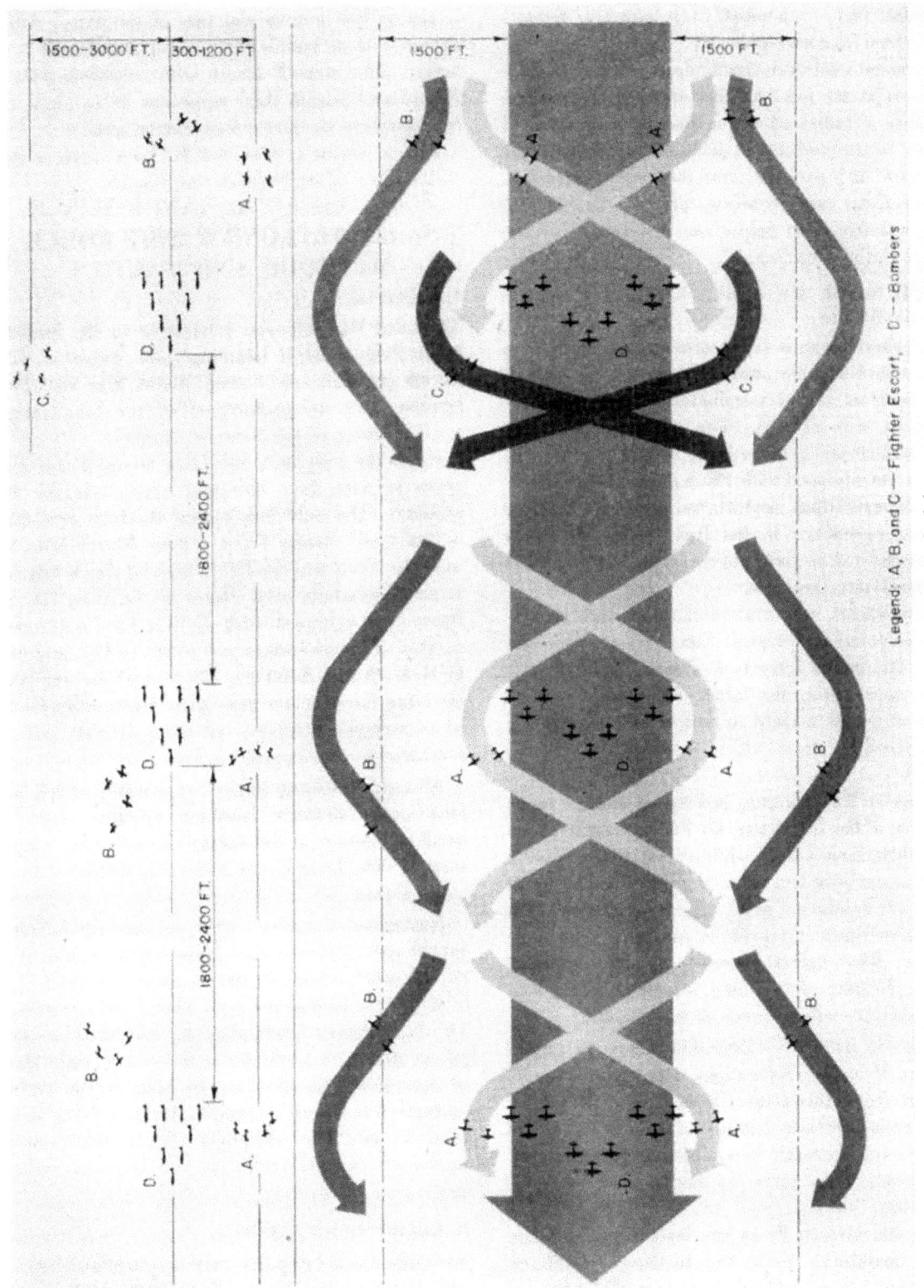

Figure 21.—*Typical bomber formation with fighter escort.*

Legend: A, B, and C — Fighter Escort.   D — Bombers

to 16,000 feet. An escort of at least four fighters is provided for each bomber.

In exceptional cases, particularly when reconnaissance units are not available or when the mission demands a radius of action greater than those of fighter or ground attack units, bomber units are required to perform reconnaissance missions. However, on rare occasions, they are carried out independently, with fighter escort governed by the fighter radius of action.

3. RED NAVAL AIR FORCE SHORT RANGE BOMBERS

Naval short range bomber units are equipped with PE-2's and operate principally against fixed targets, such as harbor installations, coastal artillery positions, and airfields. For attacks against convoys and shipping in harbors, special torpedo aircraft units equipped with PE-3 aircraft are used.

a. Operational technique. Short range bomber operations in the Red Naval Air Force are carried out by day, and then only when weather conditions are favorable.

FORMATIONS AND STRENGTH. Strength of formations varies. A typical formation of 27 bombers with fighter escort is shown in figure 21. Upon approaching the target, each group of nine bombers forms a right or left echelon depending upon direction from which attack was to be delivered.

BOMBING TECHNIQUE. In contrast to short range bombers of the Red Army Air Force, navy bombers drop their bombs only while diving. The dive is made from 5,000 feet at an angle of from 60 to 70 degrees. Bombers "peel off" from the echelon formation taken just prior to attack to drop their bombs. The fighter escort provides overhead cover. Results of bombing are photographed to determine the effectiveness of the attack.

TORPEDO ATTACKS. Depending upon the target, the size of torpedo formations varies from 6 to 27 aircraft flying in waves of from 3 to 9 aircraft in line abreast, with a distance of from 150 to 300 feet between aircraft. In some instances, each wave consists of from three to five aircraft in "V" formation.

Torpedo aircraft fly at low level throughout the entire operation. From two to three aircraft of each wave are armed with torpedoes, while the remainder carry bombs. The aircraft carrying bombs attack first, from low level and at right angles to the longitudinal axis of the ship. After dropping their bombs, they strafe antiaircraft batteries. The aircraft armed with torpedoes follow closely and launch their torpedoes at an angle of 60 degrees to the ship's longitudinal axis.

Fighter escort is provided for each wave as described in Fighter Methods and Tactics.

Section VI. LONG RANGE FORCE METHODS AND TACTICS

1. GENERAL

The Long Range Force, considered by the Soviets to be their strategic bombing force, failed to fulfill its intended role during World War II. The Soviets have no counterpart of the long range bomber forces of the Western Allies.

From the very first, the Long Range Force appears to have been equipped improperly for its mission. The only four-engine bombers available to the Long Range Force during World War II were the TB-3 and the PE-8, both of which existed in small numbers only. Most of the Long Range Force was equipped with IL-4's, LI-2's (armed version of Soviet counterpart of the C-47), and the U. S. B-25 and A-20 G. The end of the war saw the Long Range Force emerge as a composite force of twin-engine bombers, transport aircraft, and a few obsolete four-engine bombers.

Although the Long Range Force was intended for long range strategic bombing missions, only a small percentage of the operations were long range sorties. The Long Range Force was employed in a tactical role.

Numerous operations were carried out against supply and communication lines, repair and supply depots, and airfields in the enemy's rear zone (up to 200 miles behind the main enemy defense line). The Long Range Force also was employed against strong defensive positions in the enemy main line of resistance. In addition, the Long Range Force performed transport operations, such as flying supplies to the front, dropping agents over enemy territory, and supplying of guerrilla forces operating in the enemy rear area.

2. LOCATION OF BASES

Normally, each Long Range Force regiment occupies a static home base. The regimental bases of each division are grouped together to facilitate liaison. During World War II, however, units were moved frequently, particularly when providing direct support for the ground forces, to temporary bases from 100 to 120 miles from the front line.

3. CONTROL

Commitment of the Long Range Force is directed by the General Headquarters, through which all requests must pass. The commander of the Red Army Air Force is a member of the General Headquarters, and, thus, has considerable influence in the operational control. Administratively, however, the Long Range Force became a part of the Red Army Air Force in December 1944.

4. OPERATIONAL TECHNIQUE

The procedure for tactical and strategic operations is believed to be the same. The majority of the missions are carried out at night. However, it is believed that day missions also are undertaken, although their extent and procedure are not known.

a. Formations and Strength. On night missions, the Long Range Force used no special type of formation. The conventional bomber stream was formed automatically by the lapse of time between each aircraft taking off. Differences in speed of take off lengthened or shortened the bomber stream, which caused, among other difficulties, dispersion of effort. Efforts were made in 1944 to improve the situation, and aircraft were required to proceed to a general assembly area and then to fly in formation to the target. The number of aircraft employed varies with the target to be attacked. As many as 200 bombers have been employed on certain missions.

b. Procedure. Operational orders usually are received several hours in advance so that crews can be briefed. Take-off time varies according to the time of the year, to allow crossing of the front lines as soon as possible after dark.

At one time, the approach altitude was prescribed. However, this practice is believed to have been abandoned. The height of attack always was stipulated, and any infringement of this order was a punishable offense.

The height of attack varies according to the target to be attacked, anticipated antiaircraft defense, and the type of aircraft employed. Normally it is from 10.000 to 16,500 feet for targets in the enemy interior, and from 1,600 to 6,600 feet for objectives in the combat zone.

The attack on the target is made either by all aircraft from an exactly prescribed direction and height, or in a concentric form at different heights and from several directions. Bombs are dropped on the first run, a second run being exceptional.

After dropping its bombs each aircraft flies to a predetermined departure point and from there returns on a prescribed course to its home base. At least one alternate airfield is designated. Oral and written reports are made by each crew immediately after landing.

Although during World War II target marking had not been introduced generally, attempts were made to mark specific objectives by dropping flare cascades. Two or three aircraft of each regiment participating in the attack carried flares for this purpose. Different colored flares were used to confirm a correct cascade setting or to warn attacking aircraft that the cascade had been placed incorrectly.

c. Fighter escort and patrol regiments. No direct fighter escort was provided for bombers of the Long Range Force operating at night. In the spring of 1944, the Soviets introduced patrol regiments equipped with a night-fighter version of the U. S. A–20 G. They provide indirect protection for the Long Range units by attacking searchlights, antiaircraft batteries, and airfields in and around the target area. In addition, patrol regiments frequently attack railroads and roads to block and prevent dispersal of transport in the target area. For this type of mission, the A–20 G was armed with four 20-mm. cannon, four 12.7-mm. machine guns, and four rockets.

Section VII. RECONNAISSANCE METHODS AND TACTICS

1. GENERAL

During World War II, the Red Army Air Force emphasized reconnaissance. Specialized reconnaissance units included long range reconnaissance regiments, reconnaissance regiments of the air armies, and reconnaissance-spotting regiments under army group control. According to official Soviet data reconnaissance-spotting aviation, alone, increased 1,800 percent from January 1942 to January 1945. In addition to these specialized units all fighter, ground attack, short range bomber, and Long Range Force units performed reconnaissance missions.

The basic technique of reconnaissance in the Red Army Air Force is aerial photography supplemented by visual reconnaissance. From 50 to 70 percent of all reconnaissance missions performed by Soviet fighter aircraft in World War II were photographic missions. All ground attack aircraft employed on reconnaissance missions were equipped with cameras and few, if any, missions were flown for visual reconnaissance exclusively. Visual reconnaissance, supplementing aerial photography, is essential on all aerial reconnaissance missions. During defensive operations and for the adjustment of artillery fire visual reconnaissance alone often is used by the Soviets.

2. TACTICAL RECONNAISSANCE

Tactical reconnaissance is employed in direct support of ground forces and normally is limited to friendly assembly areas, the enemy main line of defense, and its immediate approaches. These general limits may be extended for tank and river-crossing operations.

a. Units. During World War II, tactical reconnaissance was flown primarily by reconnaissance-spotting regiments under army group control, and less commonly by reconnaissance regiments of the air armies. Frequently, fighter and ground attack units flew tactical reconnaissance in addition to their other missions.

b. Control. All units engaged in tactical reconnaissance are under the technical and administrative jurisdiction of the air army of each army group. Operationally, however, units employed for photo reconnaissance are attached to ground armies or more specifically to army artillery commanders, tank commanders, and, if a river crossing is to be undertaken, engineer commanders. Reconnaissance-spotting regiments, or other units used to adjust artillery fire, are attached to or support artillery divisions, and, sometimes, even brigades or regiments.

c. Procedure. Outstanding emphasis is placed on comprehensive briefing of air personnel and on limitation of aerial reconnaissance areas which cannot be observed from the ground. Prior to a mission, air personnel study all pertinent ground observation and intelligence documents, particularly photo panoramas, combined sketches of blind areas, and army intelligence maps. Air personnel also visit key ground observation posts to study the situation whenever practicable.

d. Photo reconnaissance. Requests for tactical reconnaissance normally originate with the commanders of the ground arms, especially artillery, and are coordinated by the army intelligence officer. For normal operations, requests are for verticals of approximately 1:15,000 scale, or sometimes larger scales for limited areas and pin-point targets. These verticals are gridded by the Topographic Service with the standard Soviet 1,000-meter grid. They are used as the basic map substitutes by all arms.

e. Adjustment of artillery fire. Artillery fire is adjusted from the light two-seater U–2, the slow but heavily armored IL–2, fighter, or from an observation balloon. The artillery battalion is the smallest unit for which air adjustment of fire is provided. Aerial observation is limited normally to ranges in excess of 5,500 yards or to areas which cannot be observed from the ground. Thorough briefing of the pilot and the observer on landmarks, orientation points, and recognition signals is required to reduce time in the air and to obviate errors.

Two methods are used by the Soviets to initiate the adjustment of fire. The first, and more common method, is the firing of battery or battalion ladders, a series of salvos fired at successive ranges on the same azimuth. In the second method, a flare or smoke bomb is dropped from the plane at a point visible to ground observers, and the air observer senses the flare or bomb. Ground observers combine the location of the flare or bomb and the air observer's sensing to compute initial data. The air observer then conducts fire in the normal manner.

3. OPERATIONAL RECONNAISSANCE

Operational reconnaissance covers areas up to 200 miles behind the enemy's front lines and has the primary mission of supporting the operations of army groups and their principal components, both ground and air. It embraces all coverage required for major offensive or defensive operations of the army group and for the fire plans of supporting artillery and air forces.

a. Units. Operational reconnaissance is carried out mainly by reconnaissance regiments of the air armies. When necessary, long-range reconnaissance units may be employed. Frequently, during World War II, bomber units flew operational reconnaissance in addition to their other missions.

b. Control. Control of reconnaissance regiments engaged in operational reconnaissance is the responsibility solely of the air army commander. Army group headquarters requests operational reconnaissance from the air army commander, who must meet the over-all requirements of the army group.

c. Procedure. Requests for operational reconnaissance missions originate with infantry, tank, artillery, or engineer commanders. They are forwarded to army group headquarters, where they are coordinated by the army group intelligence officer and forwarded to the air army commander. The air army commander then assigns missions to reconnaissance units or to any other units he deems necessary.

SUPPORT OF OFFENSIVE OPERATIONS. The principal mission of operational reconnaissance in the support of any offensive operation is the taking of aerial photographs for the correction of existing maps. From 160 to 180 square miles may be photographed for each rifle corps. The usual scale of photographs taken is from 1: 17,000 to 1: 20,000. On the first photo run for over-all coverage of the enemy defensive zone, photographs with a scale of from 1: 10,000 and 1: 8,000 are taken. On successive runs over important sectors, the scale is increased to from 1: 6,000 to 1: 3,000. The number of runs made depends upon the area covered and its importance. For an attack on a fortified position, at least three runs are mandatory.

Photo reconnaissance missions over the assembly area of friendly troops are flown to check the condition of all roads so that full utilization of the existing road net may be made. In the area of the line of departure, photo reconnaissance is flown to determine the areas invisible to the enemy, commanding heights, degree of cover from enemy aerial reconnaissance, and covered approaches. In the enemy defense zone, photo reconnaissance is carried out to locate areas invisible to friendly ground troops, enemy observation posts (particularly those which might be used by advancing friendly troops), tank obstacles, possible landing fields, roads, and passes. Photo reconnaissance of the enemy rear area is of assistance in developing a plan for pursuit of enemy forces should the offensive be successful. Great emphasis is placed on locating roads and, particularly, sectors where road blocks or other barriers might exist.

In addition to the basic mission of providing information for the correction of existing maps, photo missions are flown to provide special photomaps for tank units. These photomaps include enemy position areas, tank obstacles, orientation points, and areas not suited to tanks. For river crossings, special photo missions are flown and photomaps of 1: 10,000 scale are prepared of the approaches to both sides. Stereo pairs are indispensable and special attention is paid to shores, wooded areas, and roads.

SUPPORT OF DEFENSIVE OPERATIONS. Both photo reconnaissance and visual reconnaissance are employed in the support of a defensive operation. Priorities are placed on photographing of the friendly forward area and outpost line of resistance, and on visual reconnaissance of the rest of the zone of operations. Key reconnaissance objectives are natural obstacles, the condition of friendly and enemy roads and approaches, and observation posts available to the enemy. The main mission of this reconnaissance is to correct existing maps of 1: 50,000 scale. The average area covered is from 100 to 120 square miles for each rifle corps. In addition, a limited number of missions are executed to provide 1: 10,000 and 1: 15,000 photo maps of key defensive sectors and to check friendly camouflage.

d. Technique of aerial reconnaissance. Orders for tactical or operational aerial reconnaissance are transmitted to the regiments concerned the night before an operation whenever practicable. This allows time for the regimental commander to plan the number of sorties, take-off schedules, mission of each individual flight, and to arrange for fighter escort.

BRIEFING OF CREWS. The squadron Commander briefs the crews. The *Sturman* also is briefed in detail by the squadron *Sturman*, and the radio operators by the squadron signal officer. When the situation permits, flight crews are oriented on the front lines by the combat troops concerned.

For the briefing of crews engaged on operational reconnaissance, standard Soviet operational maps, 1: 200,000 particularly and 1: 500,000 less commonly, are used. For tactical reconnaissance, 1: 100,000 and 1: 50,000 maps are widely used and 1: 50,000 and 1: 25,000 maps and 1: 20,000 mosaics are used occasionally.

The line of battle, enemy airfields, and antiaircraft defenses are marked on the maps. The crews are supplied also with accurate information concerning changes in the enemy position. It is forbidden to make entries on the maps concerning Soviet positions, airfields, navigational aids, or unauthorized notes. For a pin-point photo reconnaissance mission, the *Sturman* is given a prepared section of a map with the objectives marked on it.

EXECUTION OF MISSION. The first reconnaissance aircraft takes off during the early morning hours and flies weather reconnaissance in addition to its other reconnaissance missions. The crews which take off later also forward weather reports if necessary, giving information concerning visibility, cloud cover, cloud base and ceiling, heights of clouds, and direction of cloud movement. Icing and direction and strength of wind allegedly are not reported.

Sorties are flown from dawn to dusk, with emphasis on the morning hours. Take-off times are changed daily as a counterintelligence measure. The crews select the route, never a straight line, and the altitudes at which the mission is to be flown. The front line is crossed at weakly defended points. Crossing points vary from day to day.

When there is little or no cloud cover, reconnaissance aircraft fly at 23,000 feet over enemy territory. Reconnaissance objectives behind the front lines are photographed from this altitude, and at such lower altitudes as are needed. Fortified positions along the front line are photographed from 10,000 feet or lower. The minimum altitude for aerial photography is 4,000 feet. Below 4,000 feet, all reconnaissance is visual. When enemy antiaircraft fire is weak, one aircraft will photograph two or three strips. When strong enemy defensive fire is expected, several aircraft are sent out in succession, or the same crew makes several flights, photographing one strip each time. Withdrawal always is flown over a different route. Visual reconnaissance is continued during the withdrawal.

FIGHTER ESCORT. There is a general order that fighter escort must be provided when the altitude for reconnaissance aircraft is less than 16,000 feet. In actual operations, the IL-2 reconnaissance aircraft usually fly without escort, unless the mission is especially important. Bomber aircraft, such as the PE-2, are provided with fighter escort of from four to six fighters, and more in special cases, when taking area photographs over the line of battle or directly behind it. The reconnaissance aircraft usually fly over the fighter airfield, where they are joined by the escorting fighters. Sometimes, if the fighter field is large enough, reconnaissance aircraft land on the fighter base and take off with the escort.

COMMUNICATION. Reconnaissance aircraft remain in constant contact with their own regiment and with units for which the reconnaissance is being conducted. Visual reconnaissance data is transmitted by voice in the clear, except for coded reference points. Weather reports are transmitted in code until the reconnaissance aircraft reach the front line. While over enemy territory, only important messages are transmitted. A short summary of reconnaissance results is transmitted when the reconnaissance aircraft cross the enemy front line on the return flight.

DAILY OPERATIONS REPORT. A full report is made by the crew upon landing. Important reconnaissance information is telephoned immediately to the headquarters concerned by the regimental intelligence officer. If exact details of especially important reconnaissance information is necessary, the *Sturman* of the crew are flown to air army or army group headquarters to make a personal report. At the end of each day of operations, the regimental operations officer assembles a daily reconnaissance report, which is sent to air army headquarters along with all air reports and interpretations of all photographs taken.

PART III.   TRAINING AND REPLACEMENT

Section I.   GENERAL

Training in the air forces of the U. S. S. R. is basically similar to the programs of the Western air forces. Students pass from one level of training to another through well-organized, and often highly specialized, schools. During World War II, the Soviet policy of "flexibility" permitted many emergency changes within this basic structure.

1. SEPARATE TRAINING PROGRAMS

The army, navy, and the Civil Air Fleet have separate air-training programs. The Long Range Force maintained special schools to supplement the standard Red Army Air Force training, and some of the Long Range Force flying personnel received their entire training in such schools. Although the Long Range Force is now an air army and no longer an independent arm, it is probable that its training system still exists. In addition, the Red Army Air Force has a few small, highly specialized schools, several for the training of command officers and one for the formation of elite regiments.

2. PREMILITARY TRAINING

A unique factor in Red Army Air Force training is the extensive premilitary training of civilians. During the decade preceding World War II, aviation clubs were giving both theoretical and practical training to thousands of Soviet youths. By drawing from this large pool of partially trained airmen, the Red Army Air Force simplified its wartime training problems.

3. SCOPE OF TRAINING

The doctrine that the Red Air Force is mainly an aid to the Red Army has affected the type of flying a pilot must be trained to perform. With ground attack operations and fighter patrols constituting a majority of the sorties, the Red Army Air Force can dispense with much training that is essential to a strategic force.

The usual Soviet mission is short and the formations participating are relatively small. Modern bomb sights, communications equipment, and navigation aids are not in widespread use. Therefore, navigation training can be limited, for the most part, to dead reckoning and contact flying. Mass formation and precision bombing techniques can be neglected. These factors permit earlier specialization. Consequently, a Soviet flyer can be sent into combat with few flying hours.

Section II.   RED ARMY AIR FORCE TRAINING

1. GENERAL

The Main Administration of Replacement and Training is part of the Main Administration of the Red Army Air Force. The Main Administration of Replacement and Training is subdivided into the Administration for Organization of Unit Formation and Training and the Administration of Schools. The Administration for Organization of Unit Formation and Training is responsible for the formation of regiments and for the training of all Red Army Air Force personnel after they have entered replacement flight regiments. The Administration of Schools is responsible for all training below the level of replacement flight regiments, including elementary flying schools, service schools, *Sturman* schools, and air force specialist schools.

The academies of the Red Army Air Force are under the Administration of Air Academies, part of the Main Administration of the Red Army Air Force. The Administration of Air Academies is on the same level as the Main Administration of Replacement and Training.

To receive specialist ratings, personnel of the Red Army Air Force must graduate from one of the following programs: ground crew, radio operation, an air force specialist school for aerial gunners, *Sturman* school. Pilots must pass through both elementary flying schools and service schools to obtain ratings.

In pilot schools, the flexibility of Red Army Air Force training is especially pronounced. A pilot trainee's progress through the various stages of training is governed by demonstrated proficiency, rather than by the completion of a fixed number of flying hours as in the Western air forces. Consequently, all flying schools after the elementary schools vary markedly in size and can have no fixed monthly quotas.

The first stage of postgraduate training is the replacement flight regiment. Newly graduated personnel from the various schools are assembled and trained in newly activated units. These units are sent intact to the front, or are disbanded and the personnel sent to operational units as replacements.

Trainees washed out of pilot training usually are sent to a *Sturman* school or to an air force specialist school for different air training. If this, in turn, proves unsatisfactory, the trainee is sent to a specialist school for ground crew training.

2. PILOT TRAINING AND REPLACEMENT

a. Elementary flying schools. Pilot trainees for all branches of the Red Army Air Force, including the Long Range Force, receive their first formal air training in elementary flying schools. These schools are equivalent to USAAF preflight and primary schools. In addition to elementary flying, a certain amount of basic theoretical instruction is given. The courses include practical maintenance, aerodynamics, navigation, political instruction, and general military training. The entire course at these schools usually lasts from 7 to 9 months. The first 4 months are devoted entirely to theoretical preflight instruction.

Flying training includes a minimum of from 30 to 50 hours, usually in UT–2's or similar aircraft. During this period, trainees are classified for future specialization.

Although the number of flying hours a student receives in an elementary flying school appears inadequate, there are other important considerations. Flying time is utilized to the utmost. In order to avoid explanations and delays during actual flight, the trainee takes a written examination on the exercise to be performed prior to take-off. Because the usual training flight averages from 10 to 15 minutes, a student executes a great many landings and take-offs during his course. Because of this intensive practice in basic flying, a trainee is able to solo a combat type aircraft after few flying hours.

b. Service schools. When students finish elementary flying school, they enter service schools to begin specialization. The level of training in these schools is similar to that of the USAAF advanced flying schools. Actually, it goes beyond USAAF advanced schools in that a large part of training in these schools is given in operational type aircraft.

There are three types of service schools, fighter, ground attack, and bomber. Each school trains students solely for one category of aircraft, with the exception of some fighter service schools which have one ground attack squadron to which students disqualified during fighter training are transferred.

Ground schools present training in signal communications, tactics, topography, meteorology, bombing, aerial gunnery, and radio navigation. Elementary flying school subjects also are continued.

Flying training in service schools includes approximately 70 hours, half of which are spent in operational aircraft. Approximately 10 hours are devoted to instrument flying. There is a limited amount of formation flying and aerial gunnery. Upon graduation, the student is a rated pilot eligible for a commission. Although he has considerable experience in first-line aircraft, he has had no real combat training.

c. Replacement air regiments. All ground and air crew personnel in the Red Army Air Force go to replacement air regiments after graduation from schools. Here, crews and units are formed and complete units are activated. All personnel receive from 6 to 10 weeks of intensive combat training.

During World War II, badly depleted units were reformed and reoutfitted in replacement air regiments. Individual replacements also are drawn from replacement air regiments. The replacement air regiments provide formal combat training and are similar to USAAF operational and replacement training units.

Most theoretical training is completed at this stage, unless a trainee fails to pass the ground school comprehensive examination. Actual flying usually includes from 20 to 30 hours of bombing, gunnery, formations, instruments, and simulated battle techniques. All replacement air regiment training is divided, as is service school training, into either fighter, ground attack, or bomber training.

A wartime function of the replacement air regiments that possibly may be discontinued is the storage of aircraft. Almost all the replacement regiments were based near aircraft factories and provided a reserve supply of first-line aircraft.

d. Demonstration and training regiments. Demonstration and training regiments were an emergency wartime measure to save time and to help relieve the replacement air regiments. They acted as field replacement regiments for the air armies and were responsible for the rapid reoutfitting and training of depleted front-line units. It is believed that they have been discontinued.

e. Advanced pilot training. Special schools for pilots and *Sturman,* called flying training establishments, give further specialized instruction to a limited number of carefully selected pilots. Although some exceptional students are accepted directly from service schools, the majority of trainees are chosen from operational units. The course includes approximately 100 hours of actual flying, and there is extensive practical and theoretical training. The graduates are considered qualified for assignment as flight or even squadron leaders. They usually are promoted.

SQUADRON LEADER COURSES. Special courses for squadron leaders are conducted for pilots from front-line regiments and, in some cases, for highly qualified replacement air regiment graduates. The course includes ground school and approximately 50 hours of flying, in which simulated combat with captured enemy aircraft formerly was an important part.

TRAINING OF "ACES." During World War II a school for the training of aces existed, and still may be in operation. The original plan was to train highly qualified pilots from operational units for the formation of elite fighter regiments. This never was accomplished during the war, but elite regiments may be established in peacetime. The school used the most modern equipment in the Red Army Air Force and gave the most intensive pilot training in U. S. S. R.

REPLACEMENT TRAINING. The highest level of training for the great majority of Soviet pilots is carried on in the operational units. As in the USAAF, new replacements are taken on practice missions and formation and gunnery training continues. During World War II, replacements flew wing positions on short, easy missions, until they were trained thoroughly.

AIR ACADEMIES. At present there are two air academies in the Red Army Air Force. The Technical Academy trains command and staff officers, who have good engineering qualifications, for responsible technical assignments.

The Operational and Navigational (or tactical) Academy is a war college for command and staff officers. Staff navigation officers, senior officers in the supply service, and unit commanders are trained. Qualifications and general educational standards are high, and the capacity of the academy is relatively small. Flying officers receive further air training to prepare them for command of large units. Ground tactics are studied with almost the same detail as air force tactics. Air-ground cooperation receives special emphasis.

3. AIR CREW TRAINING AND REPLACEMENT

a. *Sturman* training. The early part of the training at *Sturman* schools is devoted entirely to theory, after which ground and flying training are carried on simultaneously. Subjects include navigation, bombing, photographic reconnaissance, gunnery, radio, tactics, meteorology, and general military courses. Navigation is emphasized, but apparently only dead reckoning and radio navigation are taught. Air training usually consists of from 70 to 80 hours of flying for practice in navigation, bombing, gunnery, and aerial photography.

Upon graduation from a *Sturman* school, personnel proceed to replacement air regiments where crews are formed and trained as a unit before joining a front-line regiment.

b. Specialists schools. Before World War II, both radio operators and aerial gunners were given fairly extensive training in separate schools. During the war, all enlisted personnel were taught in the same specialist school. Aerial gunners and wireless operators were trained together and were almost interchangeable.

The 6-month course included training in armament, ballistics, theory of aerial gunnery, practice firing (air and ground targets), receiving and transmitting code, aircraft recognition, tactics, and general military subjects. Armament was emphasized because air crew personnel frequently perform ordnance and maintenance duties.

It is probable that wireless operator and aerial gunnery courses now are separate. Also, it is likely that both are more extensive than the hasty courses of World War II.

Upon graduation from a specialist school, air crew personnel proceed to replacement air regiments, where they are formed into crews and receive further training as a unit. A small percentage of wireless operators and aerial gunners are assigned to the Long Range Force, instead of replacement air regiments, and there receive further special training.

Also, a few exceptional radio operators are sent to more advanced schools for preparation for duties in aircraft-warning and navigational-aid stations.

4. GROUND CREW TRAINING AND REPLACEMENT

During World War II, training in an air force specialist school was flexible. The interchange of personnel after graduation was an accepted procedure. Not only did air crew members perform maintenance duties, but maintenance personnel were used as aerial gunners.

Probably the most detailed training given in a specialist school was that for "weapon specialists," who received more extensive armament maintenance training than was taught in the aerial gunnery course. The training of "engine maintenance" men was quite indefinite, and seemed to qualify the graduates only for cleaning and servicing aircraft.

All maintenance training was inadequate and rather informal during World War II. "Mechanics," who are the actual crew chiefs, were selected in the units from the "engine maintenance" men who had learned enough by practical experience or had special qualifications attained in civilian life. Of the "mechanics," the best qualified were sent to schools for aircraft technicians or were appointed "technicians" in the operational units. A "technician" is a commissioned officer comparable to the USAAF engineering officer. It is believed that this haphazard system was merely a wartime emergency measure, and that in time of peace efficient, well-organized schools will train maintenance personnel.

Special schools and promotions affect only a small minority of the Red Army Air Force ground personnel. Usually, graduates from air force specialist schools go to replacement air regiments for further limited training or go directly to front-line units, and never acquire special skill as mechanics.

5. LONG RANGE FORCE ADVANCED TRAINING

a. General. A portion of the Long Range Force's training was completely independent of the usual Red Army Air Force program. However, the basic training, up to the point of graduation, often was given by the Red Army Air Force prior to the trainee's assignment to the Long Range Force. Although the Long Range Force was changed from an independent organization into an air army in December 1944, it is likely that this training system still is in operation.

b. Pilot training. Pilots for the Long Range Force are trained by the Red Army Air Force through bomber service schools. Instead of going to replacement air regiments, they are assigned to the Long Range Force's "advanced officers schools for night crews," which are quite similar to replacement regiments in that all types of personnel are trained as a team.

In these schools, almost all pilot training consists of practical flying. There is great emphasis on night and instrument flying. The trainee receives approximately 100 hours in operational type aircraft.

c. *Sturman* training. All *Sturman* training for the Long Range Force is accomplished in special schools and is more advanced than standard Red Army Air Force training. There is special emphasis on night navigation, although bombing, gunnery, photography, and other standard subjects are included. The navigation training emphasizes radio navigation, but it is believed that celestial navigation is included.

Practical training consists of 100 hours of flying, of which 60 hours is at night. Upon graduation, *Sturman* enter "advanced officers schools for night crews," where they are assigned to air crews and receive further training.

d. Air crew training. The majority of its radio operators receive their entire air training from the Long Range Force. They are taught radio navigation and aerial gunnery in addition to the usual radio instruction. Most aerial gunners, however, receive their basic training in a standard Red Army Air Force specialist school. Both radio operators and aerial gunners, after completion of their training, are sent to "advanced officers schools for night crews" to receive further training with a complete air crew.

e. Ground crew training. Ground crew personnel of the Long Range Force, as well as aerial gunners, receive their pregraduate training in a standard air force specialist school. Upon assignment to the Long Range Force, some ground personnel receive further limited training. But, the majority are assigned directly to operational units.

f. Bomber crew training. All types of flying personnel of the Long Range Force assemble at "advanced officers schools for night crews," where complete crews are formed and trained as a unit. Practice missions are flown and further specialized ground school studies are continued.

406

During World War II, there was additional training for bomber crews when they joined operational units. They flew practice missions during relatively quiet periods. New crews were sent on short, easy missions under good weather conditions for their first combat experience. Progressively more difficult missions were flown until the new crew was indoctrinated thoroughly. On some of the first missions, it was often the practice to send an experienced *Sturman* with an inexperienced pilot or an experienced pilot with an inexperienced *Sturman*. It is highly probable that, in peacetime, training in operational units will continue and even increase.

6. AIR DEFENSE FORCES TRAINING

With the exception of practice in operational units, the Air Defense Forces have no special training system. During World War II, the pilots were drawn either from fighter service schools and replacement air regiments, or from pools of combat returnees, and sent to a replacement flight regiment for a short refresher course in first-line aircraft.

Although the Air Defense Forces did not get a good selection of pilots during World War II, it is probable that they now are receiving better pilots and are starting special ground-controlled interception training.

7. TRAINING OF AIRBORNE TROOPS

The system for training Soviet air-borne troops is similar to that of the Red Army infantry. Officers are trained at special officer schools, noncommissioned officers are trained in depot regiments, and enlisted men are trained directly in the brigades. Although slightly more specialized, the training, with the exception of jump training, corresponds to standard infantry training. Personnel are drawn from all possible sources, and new inductees are accepted as readily as personnel from the Navy, Air Force, and the Red Army.

Physical, political, and educational requirements are extremely high. Airborne troops are doubtless the most elite arm of the Red Army. A further indication of the special character of these units is that convalescent and disabled personnel are returned to airborne units for staff duties.

a. Enlisted training. Training of enlisted men is planned to cover a 4-month period. Often, during World War II, it was shortened considerably. Two hundred and sixty hours of training are scheduled

each month. Maneuvers are conducted by progressively larger units as the course continues.

During the first month, tactics, weapons, maneuvers, and map reading are studied. There also is a limited amount of specialized engineer training. Jump training starts during the second month, and combat signal communications are added to the curriculum. Maneuvers involving companies are conducted during the third month. The size of the operations is increased gradually until, at the end of the 4-month period, several brigades may participate in the combat exercises. Frequently, these final maneuvers are conducted in cooperation with armored and mechanized units and airborne troops are given practice in the employment of antitank weapons and light, airborne field pieces.

b. Officer training. Training for officers is conducted at special schools. The course is planned to cover from 5 to 6 months. Much of the curriculum is similar to that for the enlisted men, but the major emphasis is placed on the command responsibilities of orientation and coordination of units.

Section III. RED NAVAL AIR FORCE TRAINING

1. GENERAL

The Red Naval Air Force is considerably smaller than the Red Army Air Force. However, this is a distinct advantage in that selection may be more careful and standards more easily maintained. This was especially noticeable during World War II, when the Red Naval Air Force replacement situation was not so critical as that of the Red Army Air Force. Because of this, naval air training courses remained nearer the peacetime level, and naval air crew members almost always were trained more thoroughly than those of the Army.

Red Naval Air Force training is similar to the Red Army Air Force program. The training system and schools are almost identical to those of the Army, but the curriculum in some of the courses is quite different because of the special nature of certain naval missions.

2. TRAINING PROGRAM

Naval pilots start their formal training in elementary flying schools, which course is very similar to that in the Army schools. Upon completion of the course, students are sent to one of four naval flying training establishments for completion of pregraduate training.

The naval flying training establishments differ from the Red Army Air Force service schools in that most of them train air crew members as well as pilots. The First Naval Flying Training Establishment is the exception. It trains fighter pilots exclusively. The Second Naval Flying Training Establishment trains all naval bomber pilots and crews, the Third Naval Flying Training Establishment trains all ground attack pilots and crews. The Fourth Naval Flying Training Establishment trains pilots and crews for special torpedo bombing and mine-laying operations.

After graduating from these schools, pilots and crews formerly went to replacement air regiments for further training before assignment to an operational unit. This system, almost identical to the Army program, was discontinued in 1944 to save time. Pilots and crews were assigned directly to combat regiments for further training. However, in all probability, replacement air regiments again are operating as schools.

In addition, there are two small, special training schools. One is similar to the Red Army Air Force's special courses for squadron leaders, and performs an identical training function. The other school gives special transitional training in sea planes and flying boats.

The majority of naval fliers receive their most advanced training in a tactical regiment. This usually is more extensive than the regimental training in the Red Army Air Force, and is considered one of the most important stages of training in the Red Naval Air Force.

Section IV. CIVIL AIR FLEET TRAINING

1. WARTIME TRAINING

Independent Civil Air Fleet training was well established before World War II, but during the war this program suffered from its subordination to military needs and the many subsequent emergency changes. In the early part of the war, many Civil Air Fleet schools were taken over by the Red Army Air Force. Later, Civil Air Fleet personnel were subject to transfer to the Red Army Air Force and the Long Range Force. Also, it appears that the Civil Air Fleet training was shortened to 18 months, and the program became more similar to that of the Red Army Air Force, possibly to facilitate transfers of personnel to the latter. However, it is reasonable to suppose that Civil Air Fleet training has returned to the prewar program.

2. PREWAR TRAINING

Prior to World War II, the Civil Air Fleet was carrying out a fairly extensive training program. Physical and mental requirements for entrance were high and probably generally similar to peacetime military standards. Students who were being trained for foreign routes were given considerable language training. The duration of training was 2 years, but it is believed that an additional 2 years of apprenticeship and instruction, while serving as a copilot, was customary.

PART IV. LOGISTICS

Section I. REPAIR AND MAINTE-NANCE

1. RED ARMY AIR FORCE

a. History and development. In the early organization of the Red Army Air Force, the individual flying units had their own maintenance and repair equipment and technical ground personnel. This proved to be a cumbersome organization and limited the mobility of the flying unit.

In the general reorganization of the Red Army Air Force in 1927, an attempt was made to separate the ground service organizations from the flying units. Air parks were established. They varied in size and strength according to the type of unit they were designed to service. The largest air park, which serviced heavy bombers, included approximately 1,000 personnel. Its commander was assisted by a staff. The unit's functions were divided into two sections. The Technical Section was responsible for the supply of fuel, lubricants, ammunition, and technical personnel assigned to repair shops, garages, etc. The Administrative Section was responsible for rations, clothing, and equipment and performed the housekeeping duties of the unit. An airfield company, an antiaircraft defense company, a searchlight platoon, a chemical platoon, a weather station, and a fire prevention squad also were attached. Although the air park was an independent unit, it was attached to a flying unit and was subordinate to that flying unit.

In 1936 the air parks were reorganized into air bases. Internal organization remained about the same, but the air base was subordinate to the flying unit serviced only for operations. In all other respects, it was subordinate to the Chief of the Engineer Service of the Military District in which it was located.

It became evident by 1940 that the air bases did not meet the changing demands of modern aerial warfare, and the present system of regional commands of aviation ground services was put into effect. The Chief of the Main Administration of the Engineers directs the activities of the repair and maintenance organizations in the Red Army

Air Force. His only connection with the Regional Command of Aviation Ground Services is his dependency upon it for the spare parts and material needed by the small mobile aircraft repair shops (PARM–1) attached to the flying units.

b. Classification of repairs. There are four classifications of repair in the Red Army Air Force:

Minor—requiring up to 50 man-hours of labor.

Running—requiring up to 700 man-hours of labor.

Damage—requiring up to 1,250 man-hours of labor.

General (overhaul)—requiring more than 1,250 man-hours of labor.

Minor and running repairs are "field repairs" and usually are accomplished by the ground personnel of the air regiment and/or the mobile aircraft repair shop (PARM–1) attached to the air regiment.

Damage and general repairs are "major repairs." They are performed by the larger mobile aircraft repair shops (PARM–4 and 5) attached to an air army or a military district, by railway aircraft repair shops, and by static aircraft repair shops. There also are a number of repair shops within the aircraft industry, located in the rear areas, which are available to the Red Army Air Force for major repairs.

The removal of damaged aircraft is the duty of the nearest Airfield Servicing Battalion. Removal must be accomplished within 3 days of the report of damage.

Before an aircraft can be sent to one of the major repair units, permission must be obtained from the chief engineer of the air army to which the aircraft is assigned.

c. Types of repair organizations. The types of repair organizations include mobile aircraft repair shops (PARM), mobile aircraft repair bases, railway aircraft repair shops, static aircraft repair shops, and motor transport repair units.

Mobile aircraft repair shops are of several types, PARM–1 through PARM–5. The numeral indicates the number of repair trucks in the organization. PARM–1's are subordinate to mobile aircraft repair bases for administration, and to the Chief Engineer of the Air Regiment to which they are attached for operations. They perform minor and running repairs which cannot be handled by the ground personnel of the air regiment. PARM-2's to PARM-5's are under the jurisdiction of the major repairs department of the Chief of the Main Administration of the Engineer Service. They normally are located in rear areas for the performance of major repairs. But, they may be located near the front lines for the performance of mobile repair services.

Mobile aircraft repair bases are administrative organizations which operate under the direction of the field repair department of the Chief of the Main Administration of Engineer Service. They usually are attached to an air division, through which they control the PARM-1's attached to the air regiments.

Railway aircraft repair shops are large organizations consisting of approximately 30 railway cars fitted as workshops to perform high echelon repair. They operate under the immediate supervision of the major repairs department.

Static aircraft repair shops also are subordinate to the major repairs department, and are attached to an air army or a military district. They are large, permanently constructed shops equipped to perform the most difficult repairs.

Motor transport repair units include static motor transport repair shops, which perform major repair and overhaul on motor transport equipment, and mobile motor transport repair workshops, trucks equipped to perform minor repairs on motor transport vehicles.

d. Repair and maintenance of training organizations. Repair and maintenance service for schools, reserve air force regiments, etc., differs only in principle from that of the tactical units of the Red Army Air Force. In tactical organizations, the airfield servicing battalion is subordinate to the Commander of the Air Regiment to which it is attached for operational matters only, and otherwise is independent of his command. Maintenance and repair in a training organization is the responsibility of the Chief of Material-Technical Supplies who is subordinate to the Chief of the Training Organization and is his deputy for the maintenance

and supply of the training organization. His organization maintains its own workshops for field repairs.

2. LONG RANGE FORCE

Until December 1944, the Long Range Force was a bomber force entirely independent of the Red Army Air Force. In its ground service organizations, there was no system to correspond to the regional commands of aviation ground services of the Red Army Air Force. Each air regiment had an airfield servicing battalion attached, which performed all servicing and maintenance for the regiment and which moved with it when the regiment changed bases. High echelon repairs probably were made in the rear areas in workshops of the air industry or of the Civil Air Fleet.

In December 1944 the Long Range Force became an air army and was incorporated into the Red Army Air Force. It is probable that the system of repair and maintenance of the Red Army Air Force was adopted.

3. FIGHTER AVIATION OF AIR DEFENSE FORCES

It is believed that the ground organization of the fighter aviation of the Air Defense Forces parallels that of the Long Range Force prior to its incorporation into the Red Army Air Force.

4. CIVIL AIR FLEET

Civil Air Fleet units utilized for military duty are serviced by airfield servicing battalions and mobile aircraft repair shops (PARM). This repair and maintenance service corresponds to that of the Red Army Air Force. Major repairs and overhauls are accomplished by the workshops maintained by the Civil Air Fleet.

No servicing installations or organizations comparable to the airfield servicing battalion of the Red Army Air Force exist in the Civil Air Fleet for units operating on air routes or in rear areas. Each unit makes use of the maintenance and repair services at the various airports the Civil Air Fleet has at its disposal.

5. RED NAVAL AIR FORCE

Repairs are made by naval air bases, which are attached to the flying units at a division level. Each naval air base has several mobile aircraft repair shops (PARM), one of which is attached to each air regiment in the division. One large repair shop is located at the air base for higher echelon maintenance and repair.

Section II. SUPPLY

1. RED ARMY AIR FORCE

a. General. The Red Army Air Force is dependent upon the Red Army for all supplies not peculiar to air units. The chief of the Rear Services of the military district or army group supplies the air force with rations, clothing and equipment, fuel and lubricants, etc. He also is responsible for rail transportation of those supplies. Under this arrangement, the army central depots are closely associated with the air depots and the advanced supply depots of the Red Army Air Force.

Special air force depots are responsible for the supply of all specialized air force equipment, such as aircraft engines, plane and engine parts, ammunition, flying equipment, etc.

The delivery of all types of supplies from the air army depot or railhead to air units is a function of the airfield servicing battalions.

b. Supplies provided by the Red Army. General supplies common to all arms are provided by the Red Army for air units.

FUEL AND LUBRICANTS. A stock record is kept in each air unit of the amount of fuel and lubricants on hand, from which a daily report is made. This report passes through the airfield servicing battalion and the regional command of aviation ground services via air army Chief of the Rear Services to the Fuel and Lubricants Administration of the Main Administration of the Rear Services of Red Army Air Forces. The Fuel and Lubricants Administration prepares a requisition for the replenishment of stock and forwards it to the Red Army Fuel and Lubricants Administration. Fuel and lubricants are transported by rail from the main fuel and lubricants depot in the U. S. S. R. and issued to the various air ground units. Occasionally, the Fuel and Lubricants Administration requisitions from the same section of the forward staff (army group) which places orders for issue with the main Army fuel depots. The airfield servicing battalions and the independent motor transport battalions are responsible for the delivery of fuel and lubricants from the distributing stations to the air units (fig. 22).

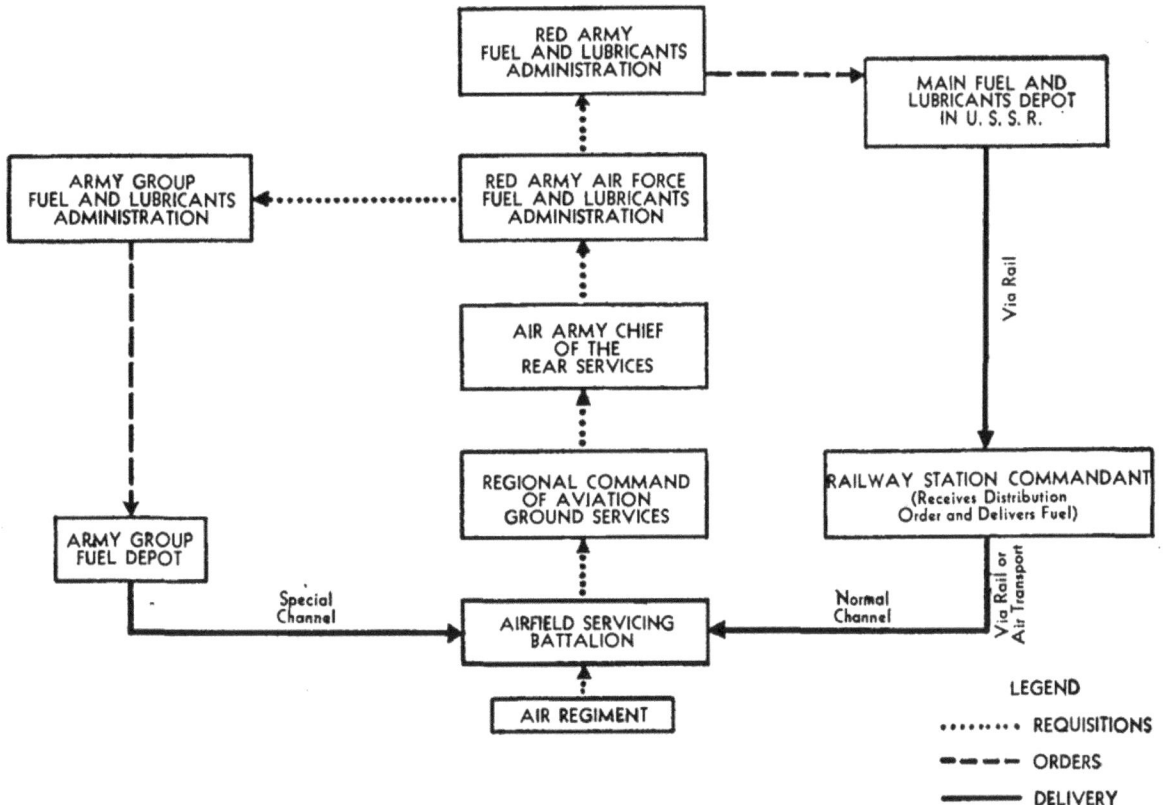

Figure 22.—*Channels of requisition and supply for fuel and lubricants.*

411

RATIONS, GENERAL ISSUE CLOTHING, AND INDI-
VIDUAL EQUIPMENT. Requisitions are forwarded
from the airfield servicing battalions through the
regional command of aviation ground services and
the supply section of the air army Chief of the Rear
Services to the army group Chief of the Rear Services
for approval. Supplies are furnished by the army
group depots to the air ground units. Transportation is furnished by the airfield servicing battalions
(fig. 23).

When transport planes are needed, they are requisitioned from the Air Transport Section of the Main
Administration of the Red Army Air Force (fig. 24).

SPARE PARTS, ETC. Requisitions for and the supply of spare parts, etc. to air units follow the same
channels as ammunition.

d. Transportation of supplies by air. When
the distances to be covered by motor transport are
excessive, when road conditions are unfavorable, or
when the supplies are needed urgently, delivery is

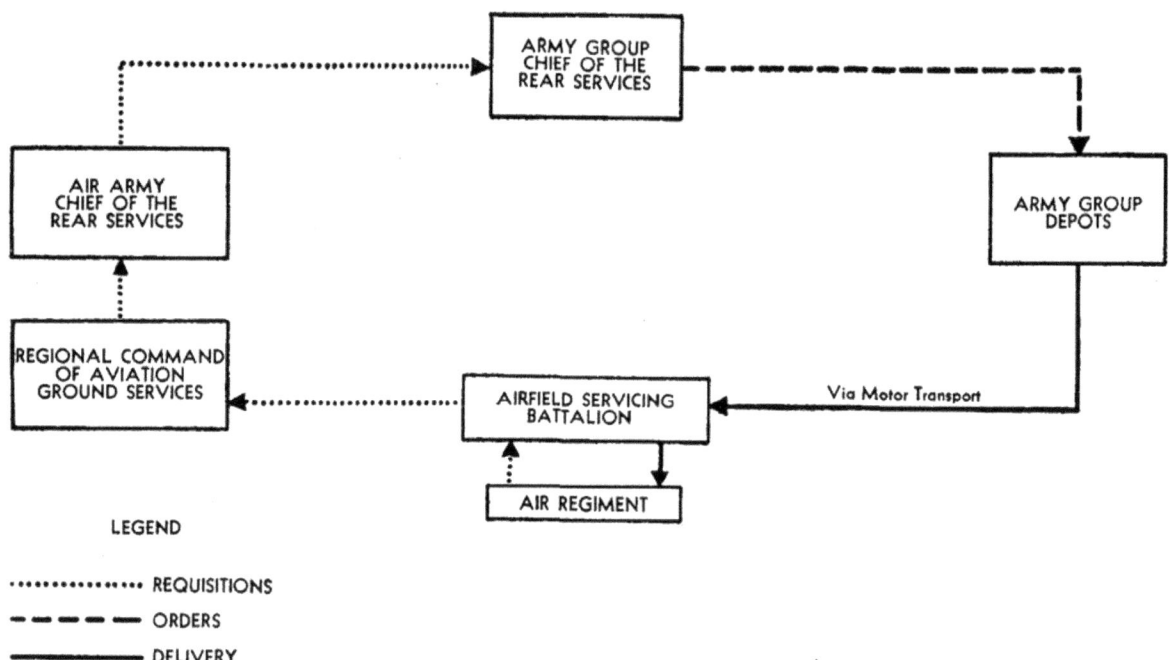

LEGEND

•••••••••••••• REQUISITIONS

— — — — ORDERS

———————— DELIVERY

Figure 23.—Channels of requisition and supply for rations, general issue clothing, and individual equipment.

c. Supplies provided by air force depots.

AMMUNITION. A stock record of ammunition and
bombs is maintained by the airfield servicing battalion, from which a daily report is prepared for
the regional command of aviation ground services.
If replacements are needed, a requisition is forwarded via air army Chief of the Rear Services to
the Administration of Technical Supply of the Main
Administration of the Rear Services of the Red Army
Air Force, which approves the requisition and orders the ammunition forwarded either from the main
depot or directly from the factory to the advanced
supply depot. It is delivered by the airfield servicing battalions or the independent motor transport
battalions. Delivery normally is made by truck.
But, if the distance exceeds 125 miles or road conditions are unsuitable, delivery may be made by air.

made by air transport. Transport aircraft are requisitioned from the Air Transport Section of the Main
Administration of the Red Army Air Force.

e. Supply of training organizations. The
supply system for schools, reserve air force regiments, etc., differs only in principle from that of
the Red Army Air Force. In tactical organizations, the airfield servicing battalions are subordinate to the commander of the air regiment to which
it is attached for operational matters only, and otherwise are independent of his command. The responsibility for supply in a training organization lies
with the Chief of Material-Technical Supplies, who
is the deputy for maintenance and supply of the
chief of training organizations.

**f. Estimated daily requirements of an air
force necessary to support one ground army.**

412

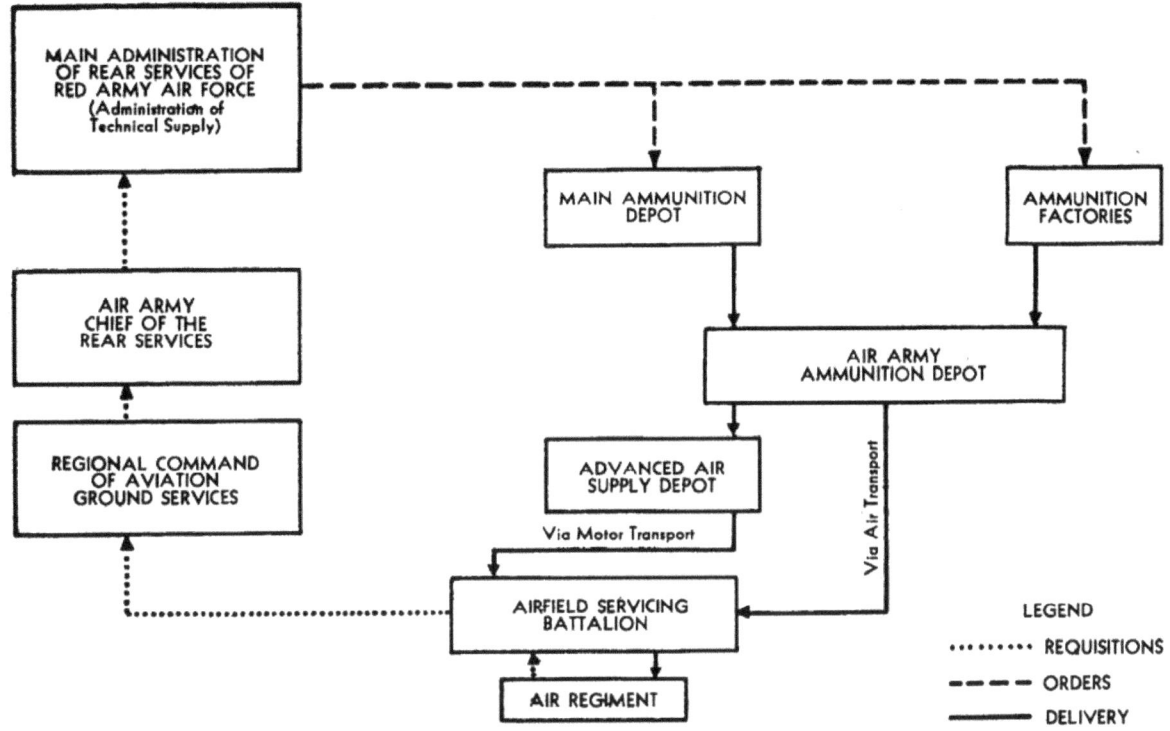

Figure 25.—Estimated daily supply requirements for an air force necessary to support one ground army.

Based on a general analysis of Red Army Air Force supply organization and equipment, it is believed that the organic transport of the ground establishments is adequate not only to supply a normal type of air effort, but also to allow an ample margin for the movement of airfield equipment and installations. However, the transportation facilities assigned to airfield servicing battalions must be augmented by vehicles from the army transportation pool to move airfield equipment and installations for ground attack and bomber regiments.

An estimate has been made of the daily supply requirements necessary for air units normally supporting a ground army (fig. 25). This estimate is based on Soviet practice on the Eastern Front during World War II of supporting each rifle division with approximately one air regiment. It is estimated that the normal supporting air force for a ground army consists of three fighter, two ground-attack, two short-range bomber, one reconnaissance, and one miscellaneous air regiments. Supporting ground units are estimated at one regional com-

Type of regiment	Strength			Requirements						
	Number of regiments	Personnel	Planes	Class I	Class II	Class III	Class IIIA	Class IV	Class V	Aggregate
				Short tons	Short tons	Short tons	Short tons	Short tons	Short tons	Short tons
Fighter	3	456	120	1.19	0.75	3.77	44.58	3.52	33.92	87.83
Ground attack	2	446	80	1.11	.74	1.84	29.72	1.72	111.78	146.91
Bombardment	2	560	60	1.4	.93	4.63	64.43	4.32	75.74	151.45
Reconnaissance	1	220	30	.55	.36	1.82	11.14	1.7	10.34	25.91
Miscellaneous	1	220	30	.55	.36	1.82	11.14	1.7	9.16	24.73
Total	9	1,902	320	4.8	3.14	13.88	161.01	12.96	240.94	436.73
Ground establishment	1	8,250	....	20.62	13.65	68.3	....	63.77	....	166.34
Aggregate	....	11,152	....	25.42	16.79	82.18	161.01	76.73	240.94	603.07

Figure 25.—Estimated daily supply requirements for an air force necessary to support one ground army.

413

mand of aviation ground services and nine airfield servicing battalions. Estimates for munitions, fuel, and lubricants are based upon the official Soviet-reported average of three sorties daily per each fighter and ground attack regiment and two sorties daily per each twin-engine bomber, reconnaissance, and miscellaneous air regiment.

The distances of the airfields from the front lines, the distances between the airfields and the unloading station, and the number of trucks required are presented in figure 26.

Regiments	Distance from front lines (miles)	Average hauling distance (miles)	Trucks required
3 fighter	20	115	30
2 ground attack	45	85	50
2 bomber	45	85	50
1 reconnaissance	20	115	9
1 miscellaneous	20	115	9

Figure 26.—Length of supply lines and number of trucks required to supply air regiments.

2. LONG RANGE FORCE

Until December 1944, the Long Range Force was a bomber force entirely independent of the Red Army Air Force. In its ground service organization, there was no system to correspond to the regional command of aviation ground services of the Red Army Air Force. Each air regiment was assigned an airfield servicing battalion, which handled all supply matters and which moved with the air regiment when it changed bases.

In December 1944 the Long Range Force became an air army and was incorporated into the Red Army Air Force. It is believed that its present supply system is the same as that of the Red Air Force.

3. FIGHTER AVIATION OF AIR DEFENSE FORCES

It is believed that the ground organization of fighter aviation of the Air Defense Forces parallels that of the Long Range Force prior to its incorporation into the Red Army Air Force.

4. CIVIL AIR FLEET

When the Civil Air Fleet is operating on air routes or in rear areas, it has no service organization comparable to that of the Red Army Air Force. Each unit makes use of the supply services available at the various airports at the disposal of the Civil Air Fleet.

Those units of the Civil Air Fleet which are engaged in military duty are assigned airfield serv-

icing battalions. It is believed that all systems of procuring supplies available to the Red Army Air Force also are available to these units of the Civil Air Fleet.

5. RED NAVAL AIR FORCE

As the Red Army Air Force is dependent upon the Red Army for general supplies, so is the Red Naval Air Force dependent upon the Red Navy for its general supplies. However, the Red Naval Air Force is believed to be independent of the fleet for its supply of fuel and lubricants. Aircraft engines, plane and engine parts, special equipment, fuel and lubricants, etc., are procured from special air depots. These special air depots include the central depot of the Red Naval Air Force and the Red Naval Air Force depots attached to the individual air fleets.

Section III. SUPPLY AND REPLACEMENT OF AIRCRAFT

1. GENERAL

The same systems of supply and replacement of aircraft (fig. 27) are used by all units of the Red Army Air Force, the Long Range Force, Fighter Aviation of the Air Defense Forces, and the Red Naval Air Force.

When aircraft production exceeded the immediate demands of the Soviet air forces toward the end of World War II, aircraft were sent from the factory to stored reserve or replacement air brigades and then to replacement air regiments, which delivered them to the flying units. This system was used chiefly for the replacement of air crews and aircraft. If aircraft replacements only were needed, delivery was made from the factory rear area stored reserve or replacement air brigades to the flying units in need of replacements.

In addition to the normal delivery systems, another method was used in 1944 for the re-equipping of flying units with new types of planes. This method, which was the delivery of aircraft directly to the flying regiment from the factory, or in a few instances through the replacement air regiments, was used only to supply a few front-line fighter and ground attack regiments with new type aircraft.

2. FERRY SYSTEM

Assembled aircraft at the factories are taken to factory airfields, test-flown, and delivered to the air force representative. When accepted, they are turned over to special ferrying squadrons, which

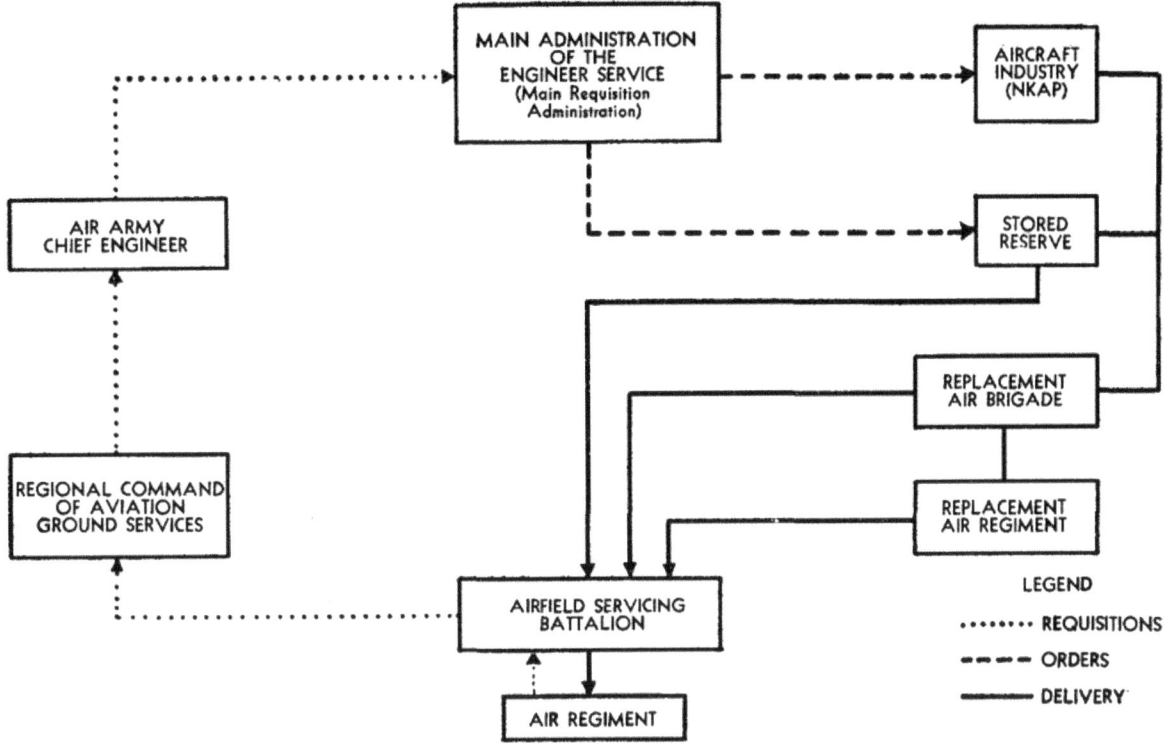

Figure 27.—Channels of requisition and supply for aircraft.

are a part of the replacement air brigades. The planes are flown from the factory airfield to those of the replacement air brigades. In 1943 new aircraft ordinarily went directly to the front. But, late in the year, when aircraft production began to exceed the demands of the air forces, planes went to reserves, from which they were delivered to units. Older series were delivered first, and the reserve was augmented constantly with new aircraft from the factories.

Toward the end of World War II, when flying units were being re-equipped with new types, aircraft were delivered by selected pilots of the units being re-equipped. Thus, the pilots gained experience with the new type plane. The flying units also picked up new type aircraft at the replacement air brigades and flew them to the front. This pick-up system was continued until a large part of the unit's crews were thoroughly familiar with the new plane. Thereafter, replacements were delivered through the usual channels.

3. TRANSPORTATION OF AIRCRAFT BY AIR AND RAIL

Ordinarily, aircraft are flown to front-line and reserve flying units. But, toward the end of World War II, many were delivered by rail. Light single-engined planes usually were delivered by rail when they were intended for reserve units behind the front.

Aircraft manufacturd at distant plants sometimes were shipped by rail to the replacement air brigades, where they were taken by the replacement air regiments and flown to the flying units.

When new aircraft were stored in reserve, they later were flown to airfields holding immediate reserves for the front. They usually were flown by ferry squadrons or, in cases of necessity, by crews of operational units in the area. Occasionally, they were shipped by rail to relieve the burden on the ferrying squadrons. From the reserve airfields immediately behind the front, the planes were flown to the operational units only by crews of the operational units.

Control of aircraft supply and replacement is a function of the Administration of Technical Supply. From mid-1944, the Technical Supply Administration concentrated a portion of the reserves in areas near the front line and turned them over to the air armies. The administration replenished these reserves in accordance with the general reserve policy.

415

Administration and distribution of these reserves were handled independently by the air armies.

4. MAINTENANCE OF AIRCRAFT STRENGTH

In 1943 air regiments which were to operate in sectors of the main effort were brought up to full strength and received reinforcements during operations. Replacements were furnished only at the end of operations, and badly depleted units were withdrawn from the front.

In 1944 an attempt was made to maintain the strength of all units by constant replenishment. By 1945 all regiments approached table of organization strength. Air regiments in active areas received additional reserves prior to the beginning of operations. Thus, in many instances, actual strength exceeded table of organization strength. Establishment of reserves close to the front permitted replacement of losses during large-scale operations.

In areas of main effort, immediate reserves were established still closer to the front. In 1945 aircraft reserves were so large that air regiments not only could replace losses, but could replace aircraft requiring repair.

While the first regiments to be equipped with a new type of plane received their aircraft in the rear areas one or more of the new type was furnished the flying unit to retrain its personnel during operations. This practice avoided the necessity of returning the flying unit to a rear area for re-equipping and training.

Re-equipment was carried out at all times, even during intense activity. One and one-half to three weeks was the average time required to re-equip the first regiment receiving a new type of aircraft in the rear areas. This time was shortened considerably by the practice of re-equipping flying units at the front.

5. SERVICE AND MAINTENANCE

a. Serviceability report. A daily report of the serviceability of aircraft on hand was made by all front-line air organizations throughout World War II. The reports included the following:

> Operational losses on the previous day.
> Nonoperational losses on the previous day.
> Number of aircraft to be withdrawn for periodic overhaul, to be overhauled, or to be written off.

Number of serviceable operational aircraft on hand.

b. Inspection of aircraft. The following regulations for inspection of aircraft were issued by the Main Administration of the Engineer Service.

PREFLIGHT INSPECTION. All aircraft are to be inspected before flight by the aircraft mechanic, technician, and crew. The flight technician is to examine at least two aircraft daily, chosen at random. The regimental engineer and the armament and special equipment engineer are to inspect 15 aircraft, chosen at random, each month.

PRESTART INSPECTION. In case of repeated operations, this is to be performed by the crew and ground technical personnel.

INSPECTION AFTER LANDING. This is considered the most important inspection since all deficiencies and damage occurring during the flight must be established. It is to be carried out by technical crew members and technical ground personnel, under the supervision of the squadron technical officer.

PERIODIC INSPECTION. This is to be carried out only in units in rear areas, in flying schools, and in training organizations. In front-line formations, only regulation jobs are to be done, the period of which is laid down in instructions for technical maintenance of the different types of aircraft.

INSPECTION OF AIRCRAFT AND ENGINES REACHING NORMAL LIMIT OF LIFE OR BECOMING DAMAGED. The purpose of this inspection is to determine whether the aircraft in question, on the basis of its actual condition, still is suitable for further use. The degree of repair required is to be established as well as the necessity for transfer to a maintenance unit. It is to be decided whether the aircraft can be written off as battle weary. For the purpose of such inspections a commission, with the regimental engineer as chairman, is established by regimental order. When the examination reveals that the aircraft, despite the completion of the regulation number of flying hours, still is not in need of repair, the commission has the authority to prolong the regulation overhaul period of the aircraft by 30 percent and of the engine by 20 percent. The decision, however, must be confirmed by the chief engineer of the air army. Aircraft which are worn out or are unfit for service because of damage can be written off by the commission, although the inspector of the air army must make an inspection and complete a confirmatory certificate. Only then is the aircraft struck off the unit's records.

The chief engineers of the air armies forward monthly reports to the chief engineer of the Red Army Air Force. Details of the aircraft and engines, whose period of service life has been extended, are given in full.

The purpose of these inspections is to control the operational serviceability of aircraft and to supervise the operation of all regulations for their servicing. Inspection can be ordered by divisions, by corps, by air armies, by the Chief Engineer of the Red Army Air Force, or by the Inspector General or the Commander of the Red Army Air Force.

PART V.   AIRFIELDS

Section I. ESTABLISHMENT OF AIRFIELDS

1. GENERAL

Permanent Soviet airports have hangars, underground fuel storage, asphalt or concrete runways, and paved parking ramps. They are similar generally to peacetime military airdromes of the Western air forces. During World War II, the rapidly advancing Red Army needed many quickly constructed, temporary airdromes as bases for thousands of tactical aircraft. Many details of wartime airdrome construction are not applicable to peacetime practice but policies and procedures of location, selection, construction, and winterization are of military importance.

Many factors affected Soviet airdromes during World War II. The Soviet doctrine that the air force is almost exclusively a ground support arm greatly affected the location of airdromes and the duration of their employment. Also, the characteristics of the aircraft employed dictated the quality of the landing surfaces, length of field, and consequently the number of personnel and time required for construction.

The Soviets constructed advanced bases for minimum requirements of the aircraft to be based on them, and in the shortest time possible. Shelter for personnel, supply stores, maintenance facilities, and many services considered necessary by other large air forces almost never were installed by the Soviets.

2. LOCATION

Probably the main consideration in the location of airdromes was proximity to the front. In all cases, Soviet units were stationed much closer to enemy territory than was customary with corresponding units of the Western air forces. This was due, in part, to the shorter range of Soviet aircraft and partly to pronounced Soviet emphasis on immediate ground support.

Fighter aircraft were based from 15 to 30 miles from the front line, and ground attack units usually were stationed only from 20 to 65 miles in the rear. Bases from 20 to 80 miles from the front were nor-

mal for twin-engine aircraft and tactical bombers. Aircraft of the Long Range Force were the only combat aircraft generally stationed more than 100 miles from the front line.

The Soviets almost invariably located their fields where little or no earth removal and leveling were required. The lack of heavy equipment and the demands of the rapidly advancing Red Army made such extensive construction impractical. In addition, an adequate supply of sand, rock, and gravel within 3 miles of the proposed site was considered indispensable.

The construction of airfields was affected by the activities on the front. The areas facing the greatest enemy resistance or behind an anticipated enemy or Soviet offensive contained many more airfields than a quiet sector.

The requirements for transportation appear to have been modest, and access to roads and railroads relatively unimportant. Whenever possible, the Soviets located their fields near a patch of forest for dispersion and concealment of aircraft, but this was only a minor consideration.

3. SELECTION

Reconnaissance and preliminary selection of airdromes was done by groups of from six to eight men in vehicles, who moved up rapidly behind the infantry into newly acquired territory. These special crews usually were detached from regional commands of aviation ground services, airfield engineer battalions, or, less frequently, from airfield servicing battalions. An additional inspection of proposed sites was made by specialists from an airfield detachment. In the final choice of a site, the headquarters of the flying unit involved usually was consulted.

4. FACILITIES

Compared to Western standards, Soviet tactical airdromes constructed during World War II were quite primitive. They were considerably smaller in all dimensions. The landing surfaces and taxiway systems were greatly inferior in quality.

The Soviets attempted to provide fields approxi-

418

mately 3,000 to 4,000 feet square for operational aircraft, but often they used a single strip for landing and take-off, frequently as narrow as 150 feet. Most of these temporary fields were fairly small, and usually only one regiment was stationed at each field. Liaison and hospital aircraft, however, often operated from fields offering a run as short as 1,000 feet. Parking areas and taxi ways were primitive, and all installations were cut to minimum requirements.

Night flying facilities for temporary airdromes were elementary. Most fields had no facilities at all. Those used as bases for night operations had only a flare path. The use of searchlights to illuminate the runway was exceptional.

5. CONSTRUCTION

Despite the lack of adequate equipment, temporary airdromes were constructed in an average of 3 days. A minimum of trained military personnel was employed. Many improvisations were used.

After evaluating the reconnaissance reports, the air army ordered the construction of the required airdromes. The actual construction then was undertaken and supervised by platoons or companies detached from airfield engineer battalions. However, most of the labor was accomplished by the local civilians drafted in the surrounding area. Personnel from the airfield engineer battalions usually limited their activities to supervision and highly specialized construction. When the field neared completion, the airfield engineer battalion detachment usually moved on, leaving approximately 20 men to supervise the completion of the field. Once the field was occupied by a flying unit, any further construction was accomplished by the airfield technical company, which was attached to the airfield servicing battalion.

Although the major part of the construction was accomplished by manual labor, the Soviets did have some specialized heavy equipment. There was a very limited supply of bulldozers and bucket type scrapers. In most cases, however, the only mechanized equipment consisted of tractors and rollers requisitioned from nearby collective farms.

Although large-scale removal of earth was avoided, bomb craters and ditches were filled in and slight ridges often were leveled off.

The surface of landing strips usually consisted of rolled earth with sand or gravel added to harden the surface and to facilitate drainage. Concrete was not used on temporary fields. The Soviets used steel plates and road metal on their strips only after 1944, and then on less than 10 percent of the fields. In the marshy areas of the northern U. S. S. R., runways often were constructed on a foundation of waste wood, brush, and sawdust.

Tactical airdromes in the forward areas were considered ready for use when a relatively safe strip had been completed. Hangars never were installed. Aircraft had to be sent to the rear for repairs beyond the second echelon level. Blast bays for aircraft were constructed only during the early part of World War II, when the German Air Force was an effective offensive force. Administration buildings and operations rooms were usually dugouts or small wooden huts. Personnel usually were billeted away from the field.

Roads to airdromes were provided whenever possible. Supplies of fuel, oil, bombs, and ammunition were brought in from rear depots by personnel from the airfield servicing battalions. Trucks and horse-drawn vehicles were employed whenever possible. Air transport was used only in critical situations. When extremely poor transportation conditions existed, supplies were packed in by large numbers of civilians under supervision of the airfield servicing battalions.

Section II. AIRFIELD MAINTENANCE

1. GENERAL

The main problem of Soviet airfield maintenance during World War II was the establishment of serviceable strips during spring thaws. Summer operations presented few problems. The use of sod kept dust at a minimum. Winter operations were more difficult, especially in the areas where intermittent snow storms and thaws occurred.

2. RESPONSIBILITY

Maintenance of airstrips was one of the duties of the airfield technical company stationed on a field. These units were attached to the airfield servicing battalions, and generally were charged with the maintenance of all installations. Large-scale snow removal usually was effected by the local civilian population under the direction of airfield technical company personnel. Equipment for winter maintenance consisted of a few tractors, used as prime movers for improvised plows, scrapers, and rollers. In rare cases, specialized graders and bulldozers were used.

3. WINTERIZATION

Two somewhat similar methods were used to winterize tactical airstrips. Both required almost continuous maintenance. The first method was to roll the snow into a firm surface shortly after it fell. Frequently, snowdrifts and ruts were leveled out just prior to rolling. The amount of snow removed usually was kept to a minimum. The second method was to scrape off nearly all the snow, leaving a surface of hard rolled snow less than 2 inches deep. The latter system generally was used where twin engine aircraft were expected to operate because a thick blanket of rolled snow often was too soft for heavy planes.

Whenever possible, the Soviets prepared both types of strips on the same field. The rolled-snow strip was used where light aircraft were stationed because of quicker and easier maintenance. The scraped strip generally was used during the short thaws in winter and during the initial stages of the spring thaw when the rolled strip became soft.

Once the spring thaw was well under way, a third strip usually was prepared. When both types of strips previously mentioned became unsafe, an unused area was cleared. The earth beneath newly removed snow was not frozen deeply. If more cold weather was expected, the strip was covered with straw or branches. Drainage was facilitated whenever possible. When the unused strip finally was needed, the insulating material was removed and mud holes were filled with sand, gravel, or cinders. In this way, operations were not halted completely by thaws, although they probably were impaired.

420

PART VI.   WEAPONS AND EQUIPMENT

Section I.   AIRCRAFT AND ENGINES

1. GENERAL

At the outbreak of the war with Germany, the Red Army Air Force was equipped largely with such aircraft as the I–15, I–16, and I–153. Although these planes already were obsolescent and definitely inferior to their German counterparts, the Soviets possessed them in large numbers and committed them to battle regardless of losses.

New designs soon were tested and ready for production. Although a great need existed for all types of aircraft, the Soviets were forced to concentrate primarily on fighters and ground attack aircraft to replace battle losses. Mass production of these types was initiated. Designers and manufacturers concentrated on production with little regard for improvements or modifications. This condition prevailed until the Soviets had achieved parity in numbers with the German Air Force.

At this stage, although the situation at the front had eased considerably, the designers yet were not able to stop production of existing types and to introduce newer and more effective combat planes. Consequently, they embarked on a program of improving and modifying existing models. This policy continued until the early part of 1944, when the Soviets had gained numerical superiority over the enemy. Only then did Soviet designers and manufacturers begin to concentrate on new types of aircraft. It is believed that Soviet aircraft designers now will make every effort to improve the quality and effectiveness of their air forces.

a. Prewar Soviet aircraft. Prewar types of Soviet aircraft compared unfavorably with corresponding types of the Western air forces. Generally, they were slower, less powerful, had less fire power, and were of inferior construction. Many were built of wood and covered with fabric. These were easy prey for the German Luftwaffe. As a result, the Soviets suffered tremendous losses, which they could afford only because they possessed large numbers of aircraft. The designs for new planes, however, were ready. Prototypes had been constructed and tested, and the manufacturers were ready to begin production.

b. Standardization. After Germany invaded the U. S. S. R., operational needs demanded concentration of all production on fighter and ground attack types. The urgency was so great that factories had to make deliveries without regard for improvements or modifications once the production of new aircraft types had begun. These planes, although still inferior, were more evenly matched with their German counterparts. At this stage, the Soviets were striving desperately to achieve at least numerical parity with the enemy, rather than technical superiority.

c. Improvement and modification of existing aircraft types. The effort to gain numerical equality with the enemy invited stagnation in technical development. After numerical parity had been reached, introduction of newer and more effective types of aircraft became advisable, but could be accomplished only by again losing numerical equality. Yet, technical improvement was mandatory. Because existing models had achieved comparative success, it was decided to concentrate all effort on the improvement of these aircraft. By this time, the difference in performance between the Soviet and German aircraft was not so great, and, more important, an uncontestable superiority over the enemy had been reached.

d. Present status and the future trends of Soviet aircraft. The policy of standardization on a few types of aircraft, and later a decision to concentrate on the development and technical improvement of those types, enabled the Soviets to gain numerical superiority over and technical comparability with the Luftwaffe in the early part of 1944. Soviet designers then were free to embark upon a program of developing new aircraft designs. A marked improvement in quality of both aircraft and equipment was noted almost immediately.

By the end of World War II, the striking power of the Red Army Air Force had risen considerably, and while not yet on an equal basis with Western air forces it was high above its prewar level. While working on new designs of their own, the Soviets devoted considerable time to the study of British and American planes obtained through lend-lease. Also, many of the latest German aircraft and equipment opened another source.

It is reasonable to assume that the most advanced improvements found in foreign aircraft will be incorporated, and perhaps improved, in future Soviet aircraft. Moreover, there are many indications that the Soviets have been experimenting with jet, rocket, and turbine development for some time.

2. AIRCRAFT DEVELOPMENT

a. Fighters. The Red Army Air Force had three basic fighter types at the outbreak of World War II, the I-15, I-16, and I-153. All had seen service in the Spanish Civil War. These obsolescent aircraft disappeared almost completely during the first few weeks of the war.

The LAGG-3 and MIG-3, the forerunners of modern Soviet fighters, were ready for production and reached operational units shortly thereafter. Somewhat later, the YAK-1 reached the production stage. Since a decision had been made to standardize aircraft types, the Soviets were confronted with the problems of deciding which of the three fighters was best adapted to the needs of the Red Army Air Force. The YAK-1 was selected and put into mass production immediately. There was a large reserve of YAK-7s, an advanced trainer, which was drawn upon. These advanced trainers were converted to fighters and met the requirements of the air force until the YAK-1 reached operational units.

In 1943, the YAK-9, of which there have been many derivatives, made its appearance. This was an improvement of the YAK-1, with little change in performance, but with better armament and improved rearward vision.

The YAK-3, a further development of the YAK-1 and YAK-9, made its appearance a short time later. The refinements of the YAK-9 were retained, weight was reduced, and there was an improvement in performance.

The Soviet counterpart of the FW-190 was put into action in 1943. This was the LA-5, a refinement of the discarded LAGG-3. Armament was increased, and speed and range were improved considerably.

In 1944, the LA-7, a development of the LA-5,

appeared in limited numbers. Weight was reduced by the more extensive use of light alloys, with the resulting improvement of maneuverability and rate of climb.

b. Bombers. At the outbreak of World War II, the Soviets had the AR-2, SB-2, SB-3, YAK-4, ER-2, DB-3, TB-3, and TB-7 bombers. These were obsolescent types which were destroyed largely in the first few weeks of operations. Only the DB-3, which was developed into the IL-4, and the TB-7, which later became the PE-8 and which was produced only in small numbers, became standard equipment.

The PE-2 was introduced in late 1941, and became one of the principal bombers of the Red Army Air Force.

The only new bomber of Soviet design to appear throughout World War II was the TU-2. It reached operational units late in 1944, but never in any large number. It was a greatly improved medium bomber, with heavier armament, a larger bomb load, and a better performance than any previous Soviet medium bomber.

The ER-4, an improvement of the ER-2, also appeared in 1944. It is a Diesel twin-engined bomber, with a normal bomb load of 4,000 pounds.

c. Ground attack. No specially designed aircraft for ground attack existed at the beginning of World War II. Until the IL-2 was developed, the light bomber SU-2, was used for such missions. The slow speed, poor maneuverability, and lack of rear guns of the first single-seat IL-2 Stormovik rendered it vulnerable to German fighters. In 1942 a second cockpit for a rear gunner was added.

Toward the end of the war, another version, the IL-10, began to appear in front-line units. It is an all-metal, lighter aircraft, powered with larger engines, and producing better performance.

Considerable use was made throughout World War II of the PO-2 (U-2) biplane trainer for low-level, precision, night bombing in close support of ground forces.

d. Naval aircraft. No new naval aircraft appeared during World War II. Naval aircraft include the obsolescent KOR-1, a single-engined, ship-borne floatplane; the obsolescent MBR-2, a single-engined flying boat; the GST; and the MDR-6. With the exception of these planes, standard equipment for the Red Naval Air Force is the same as that used by the Red Army Air Force, with minor adaptations for specialized naval work.

e. Lend-lease aircraft. The Soviet air forces received the following aircraft from the United States: P–39, P–47, and P–63 fighters; A–20, DB–7, and B–25 light and medium bombers; C–47 transports; and AT–6's and O–52's. The British delivered Spitfire, Hurricane, Mosquito, and Typhoon fighters; Albermarle and Hampden light and medium bombers; and Stirling and Lancaster heavy bombers.

f. Jet- and rocket-propelled aircraft. Since 1942 the scientific research institutes of the Soviet Union have devoted considerable time to the research and development of jet- and rocket-propelled aircraft. The Soviets have obtained complete details of German equipment in their possession, which probably will be incorporated or adapted for Soviet use.

g. Gliders. There are three known types of gliders in the Red Army Air Force: The small A–7, the G–11, which is a larger version of the A–7, and the KZ–20.

A–7. This small, high-wing monoplane was designed primarily for landing agents behind enemy lines. It is towed usually by an IL–4 or an SB–3.

CHARACTERISTICS

Span	59 feet.
Length	34 feet, 5 inches.
Weight (empty)	2,260 pounds.
Weight (loaded)	4,200 pounds.
Useful load	6 men or 1,870 pounds of freight.
Maximum speed (permissible)	185 m. p. h.
Gliding speed	90 m. p. h.
Landing speed	53 m. p. h.
Landing run (on wheels)	1,650 feet.
Length of tow rope	300 feet.

G–11. The G–11 is a modification of the A–7. It carries a useful load of 11 men or 2,640 pounds of freight.

KZ–20. The KZ–20 is a high wing monoplane for use as a troop and freight carrier. It is of wood and fabric construction, has a crew of two, and probably has a retractable landing gear and a skid for landing on rough terrain. It is towed by the IL–4 or SB–3. Span is estimated at 72 feet and length at 51 feet.

h. Helicopters. The twin-engined Omega helicopter, an original design by Bratukhin, is of all-metal construction and has a crew of two. It has a tricycle landing gear. Maximum horizontal speed is 112 miles per hour. Vertical climb is from 16 to 19 feet per second.

3. STANDARD AIRCRAFT

For details of standard Soviet aircraft, see the succeeding pages.

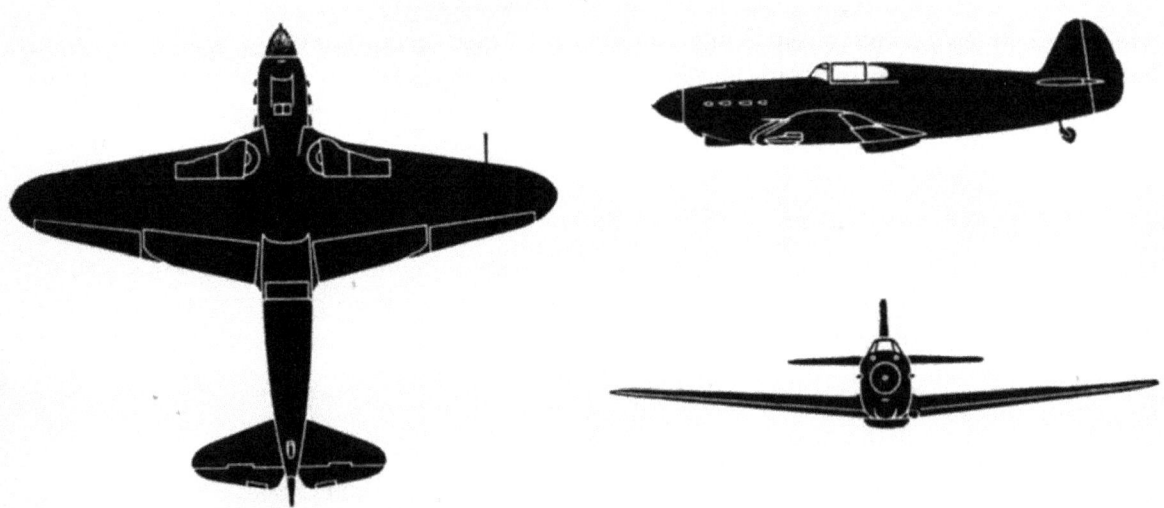

YAK–1 FIGHTER

Crew_____ 1.
Span_____ 32 feet, 10 inches.
Length_____ 27 feet, 11 inches.
Wing area_____ 188 square feet.

Maximum speed at altitude_____ 348 m. p. h./16,400 feet.
Range_____ 500 miles maximum.
Service ceiling_____ 33,000 feet.
Armament_____ 1 20-mm.
                                 2 7.62-mm.

Figure 28.

424

YAK–3 FIGHTER

Crew_____ 1.
Span_____ 32 feet, 10 inches.
Length_____ 27 feet, 11 inches.
Wing area_____ 188 square feet.

Maximum speed at altitude_____ 365 m. p. h./13,100 feet.
Range_____ 465 miles maximum.
Service ceiling_____ 35,000 feet.
Armament_____ 1 20-mm.
                                  2 12.7-mm.

Figure 29.

425

YAK–9 FIGHTER

Crew	1.	Maximum speed at altitude	348 m. p. h./16,400 feet.
Span	32 feet, 10 inches.	Range	465 miles maximum.
Length	27 feet, 11 inches.	Service ceiling	30,000 feet.
Wing area	188 square feet.	Armament	1 20-mm.
			1 12.7-mm.

Figure 30.

426

PE–2 LIGHT BOMBER

Crew	3.
Span	56 feet, 5 inches.
Length	41 feet, 6 inches.
Wing area	436 square feet.

Maximum speed at altitude	330 m. p. h./16,400 feet.
Range	930 miles (w/1,320 pounds of bombs).
Service ceiling	29,000 feet.
Armament	2 12.7-mm.
	3 7.62-mm.

Figure 31.

427

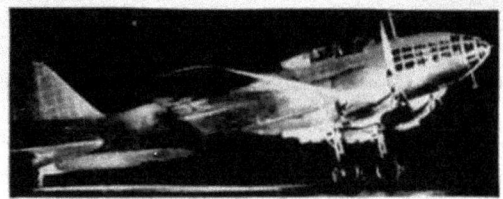

IL–4 MEDIUM BOMBER

Crew_____ 3.
Span_____ 70 feet, 3 inches.
Length_____ 48 feet, 6 inches.
Wing area_____ 715.8 square feet.

Maximum speed at altitude_____ 280 m. p. h./22,300 feet.
Range_____ 810 miles (w/6,600 pounds of bombs).
Service ceiling_____ 33,000 feet.
Armament_____ 2 7.62-mm.
1 12.7-mm.

Figure 32.

TU–2 MEDIUM BOMBER

Crew_____ 3 or 4.

Span_____ 61 feet, 10 inches (est.).

Length_____ 45 feet, 3 inches (est.).

Wing area_____ 615 square feet (est.).

Maximum speed at altitude___ 348 m. p h./19,000 feet.

Range_____ 1,550 miles (w/3,000 pound of bombs).

Service ceiling_____ 33,000 feet.

Armament_____ 2 20-mm.
3 12.7-mm.

Figure 33.

429

IL–2 STORMOVIK GROUND ATTACK

Crew	2.	Range	460 miles.
Span	47 feet, 9 inches.	Service ceiling	26,000 feet.
Length	38 feet, 1 inch.	Armament	2 7.62-mm.
Wing area	415 square feet.		2 20-mm
Maximum speed at altitude	250 m. p. h./7,000 feet.		1 12.7-mm.

Figure 34.

430

LI–2 (PS–84) TRANSPORT

Crew----------------------------- 5 or 6.
Span----------------------------- 94 feet, 6 inches.
Length--------------------------- 63 feet.
Wing area------------------------ 987 square feet.
Maximum speed at altitude------- 180 m. p. h./10,000 feet.

Range---------------------------- 310 miles (w/6,600 pounds).
Service ceiling------------------- 19,000 feet.
Armament------------------------- 1 12.7-mm.
                                                2 7.62-mm.

Figure 35.

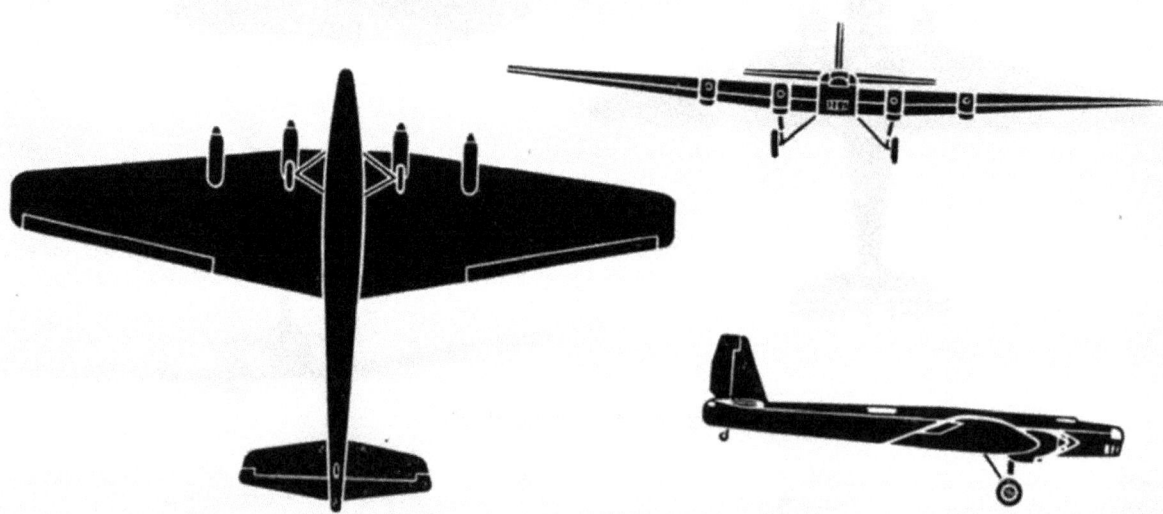

TB–3 TRANSPORT

Crew	8.	Maximum speed at altitude	160 m. p. h./15,800 feet.
Span	129 feet, 7 inches.	Range	1,430 miles.
Length	80 feet.	Service ceiling	25,200 feet.
Wing area	2,080 square feet.	Armament	4 7.62-mm.

Figure 36.

432

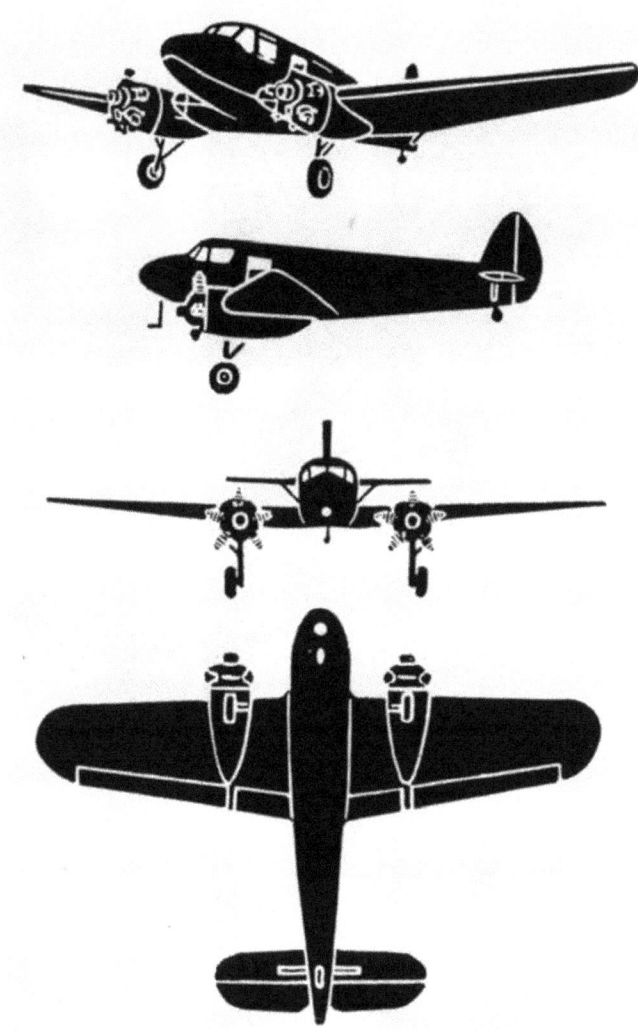

YAK–6 LIGHT TRANSPORT

Crew	2 or 3.	Maximum speed at altitude	135 m. p. h./sea level.
Span	46 feet.	Range	600 miles.
Length	36 feet.	Service ceiling	16,400 feet.
Wing area		Armament	1 12.7-mm.
			1 7.62-mm.

Figure 37.

433

PO–2 (U–2) PRIMARY TRAINER

Crew_____ 2.
Span_____
Length_____
Wing area_____

Maximum speed at altitude_____ 94 m. p. h./sea level.
Range_____ 310 miles.
Service ceiling_____ 12,500 feet.
Armament_____ 1 7.62-mm.

Figure 38.

UT–2 PRIMARY TRAINER

Crew	2.	Maximum speed at altitude	130 m. p. h./sea level.
Span	34 feet, 5 inches.	Range	360 miles.
Length	23 feet, 5 inches.	Service ceiling	15,500 feet.
Wing area	184 square feet.	Armament	

Figure 39.

YAK–7b ADVANCED TRAINER

Crew	1.	Maximum speed at altitude	348 m. p. h./13,100 feet.
Span	32 feet, 10 inches.	Range	465 miles.
Length	27 feet, 11 inches.	Service ceiling	30,200 feet.
Wing area	188 square feet.	Armament	1 20-mm.
			2 12.7-mm.

Figure 40.

436

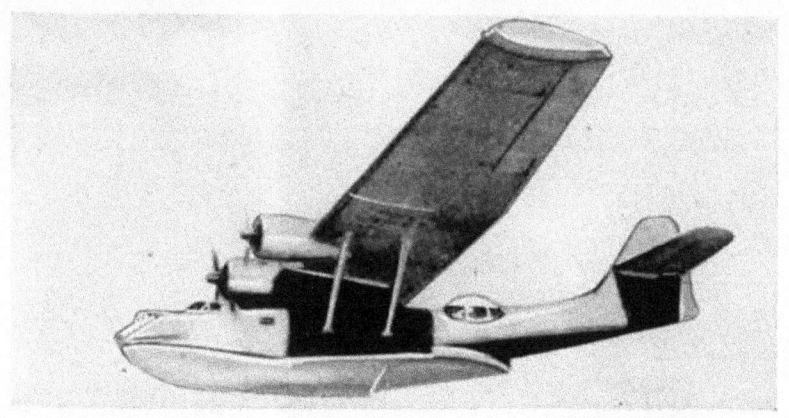

GST (U. S. "CATALINA") PATROL AND RECONNAISSANCE

Crew	7 to 9.	Maximum speed at altitude	175 m. p. h./9,000 feet.
Span	104 feet.	Range	2,900 miles.
Length	65 feet, 1 inch.	Service ceiling	23,000 feet.
Wing area	1,400 square feet.	Armament	4 to 6 7.62-mm.

Figure 41

437

MDR–6 PATROL AND RECONNAISSANCE

Crew	5 to 7.	Maximum speed at altitude	220 m. p. h./10,000 feet.
Span	66 feet.	Range	1,000 miles.
Length	49 feet, 3 inches.	Service ceiling	28,500 feet.
Wing area	700 square feet.	Armament	4 7.62-mm.

Figure 42.

438

4. CHARACTERISTICS AND PERFORMANCE OF SOVIET AIRCRAFT

For characteristics and performance of Soviet aircraft, see fig. 43.

5. AIRCRAFT ENGINES

Aircraft engine production in the Soviet Union has been based on four engines procured under licenses in the years 1930 to 1936, inclusive. They are the Wright Cyclone, the Gnome-Rhone 14K, the Hispano Suiza 12V, and the Bayerische Motorem Werke BMW–VI. A number of engines also were based on the Bristol Jupiter and Pratt and Whitney Wasp series. These basic types have been modified and developed by Soviet aeronautical engineers (figs. 44, 45, 46, 47, 48, 49, and 50).

In 1944 engine production was concentrated on the following types:

Air-cooled: M–88B, M–82, M–62IR, M–11.
Liquid-cooled: M–105PF, M–107, AM–38.

These engines usually are fitted with two-speed superchargers, providing a rated altitude of from 13,000 to 20,000 feet, except for the M–62IR and AM–38, which are designed for low-level operations and have single-speed superchargers. Some work has been done on a two-stage supercharger for the M–105PD engine. Except for its installation on the M–40F Diesel engine, the turbo-supercharger has not appeared in operational aircraft.

Section II. WEAPONS AND AMMUNITION

1. MACHINE GUNS AND CANNON

The standard light and heavy aircraft machine guns and cannon in the Soviet air forces are the SHKAS 7.62-mm., the BEREZIN BS 12.7-mm., the SCHVAK 20-mm., the V–YA 23-mm., and the NS 37-mm. (figs. 51 and 52). These guns are of a high standard in regard to rate of fire, method of operation, and general reliability. Gun mounts, however, some of which are similar in design to those used during World War I, fall far below the standards of a modern air force.

a. Reloading. The gas-operated principle of reloading is used in all light and heavy machine guns. The 23–mm. cannon uses the gas unlocking and recoil reloading method utilized in Hispano weapons. The 37-mm. cannon is entirely recoil-operated.

b. Types. All Soviet guns, with the exception of the 37-mm. cannon, are made in several types. The 7.62-mm. and 12.7-mm. machine gun can be mounted either fixed or free. Fixed guns can be synchronized.

c. Cocking. There are various methods of cocking 7.62-mm. guns. Mechanical cocking by hand always is provided. In addition, the newer types of guns have pneumatic or hydraulic cocking.

d. Feed systems. Rounds for 7.62-mm. machine guns and 20-mm. cannons are contained in disintegrating belts and are fed into a feed cage incorporated in the gun which breaks up the belt and feeds the rounds into the breach. The same method was tried on 12.7-mm. machine guns, but was not adopted. Disintegrating belts on 12.7-mm. machine guns and 23-mm. cannons feed directly into the guns.

e. Cannon installation. The 20-mm. cannon is installed usually as a fixed gun. But in the PE–8, obsolescent four-engined bomber, there is a 20-mm. SCHVAK installed in the rear gun turret. The 23-mm. cannonn always is fixed. Both guns can be mounted in the wing or engine.

2. AMMUNITION

a. General. The quality of Soviet aircraft ammunition is inferior to that of Soviet aircraft machine guns and cannon. Despite high muzzle velocity, 20-mm. and larger ammunition has poor armor penetration. The weight compares to that of the ammunition used by other first class air forces, except for the 20-mm. projectiles, which are lighter (fig. 53).

b. Special ammunition for SHKAS 7.62-mm. machine guns. AP/I round B-32 penetrates from 0.27 to 0.31 inch of cement at 656 feet and ignites combustibles behind the cement armor.

AP/Tracer round BV–46 penetrates 0.23 inch of armor plate at 656 feet and ignites combustibles behind the plate. It leaves a white trace for 2,297 feet.

Incendiary/Fragmentation round PS ignites fuel in tanks not protected by armor.

c. Special ammunition for 12.7-mm. machine guns. AP/I round B–22 penetrates 0.78 inch cement armor at 656 feet and ignites combustibles behind the cement armor.

AP/Phosphorous round BSF–46 penetrates 0.78 inch strong armor plate at 656 feet and ignites com-

Figure 45.—Soviet aircraft engines M–34 (top), M–34 RNA (lower left), and M–25 (lower right).

440

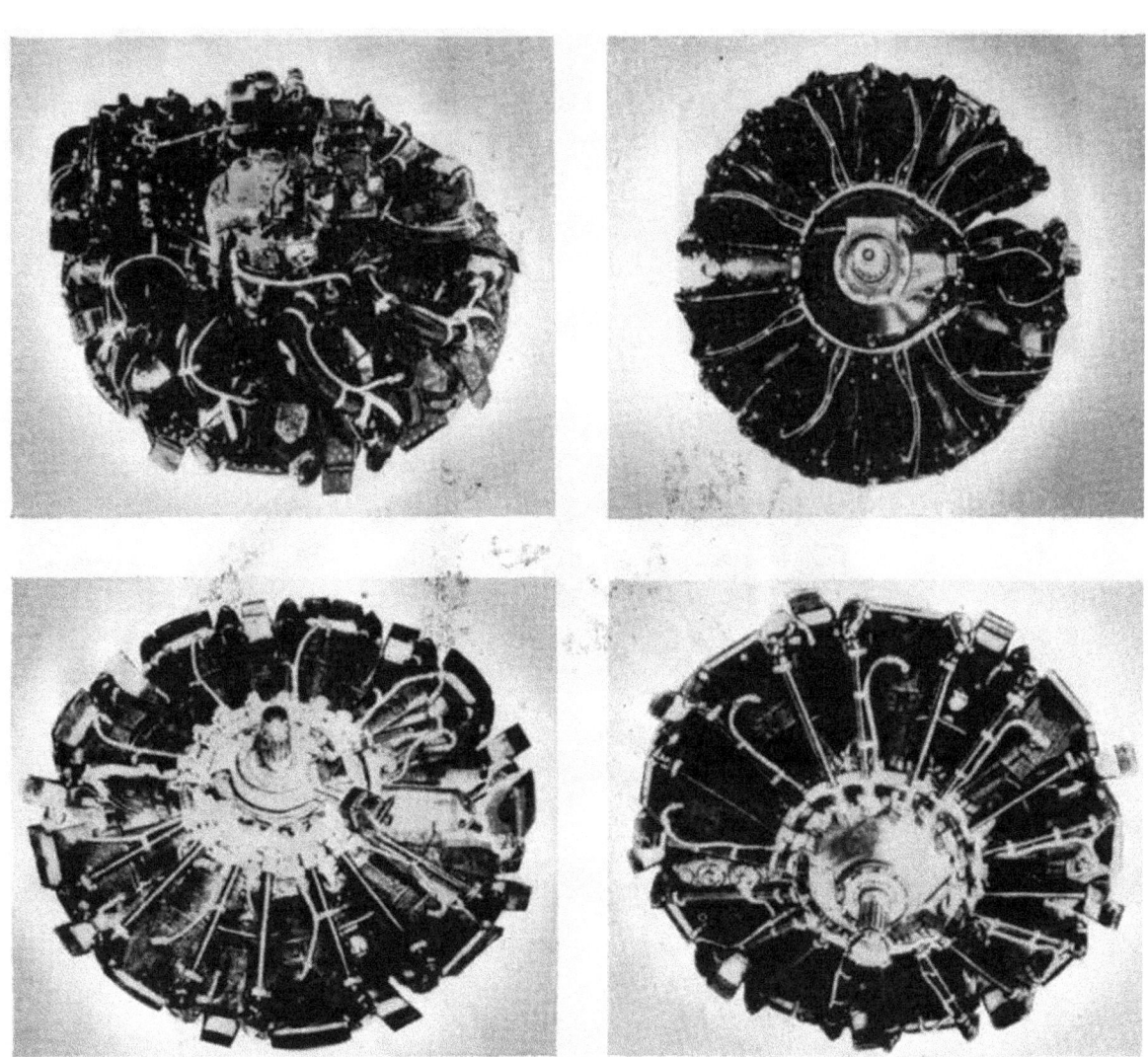

Figure 46.—Typical Soviet radial designs.

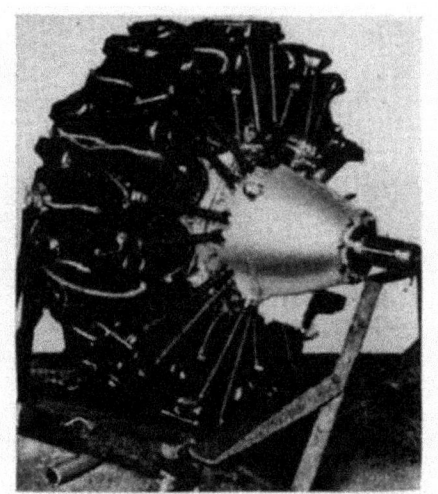

Figure 47.—Soviet aircraft engines M-71 (top left), M-82 (top right), and M-82 FNW (bottom).

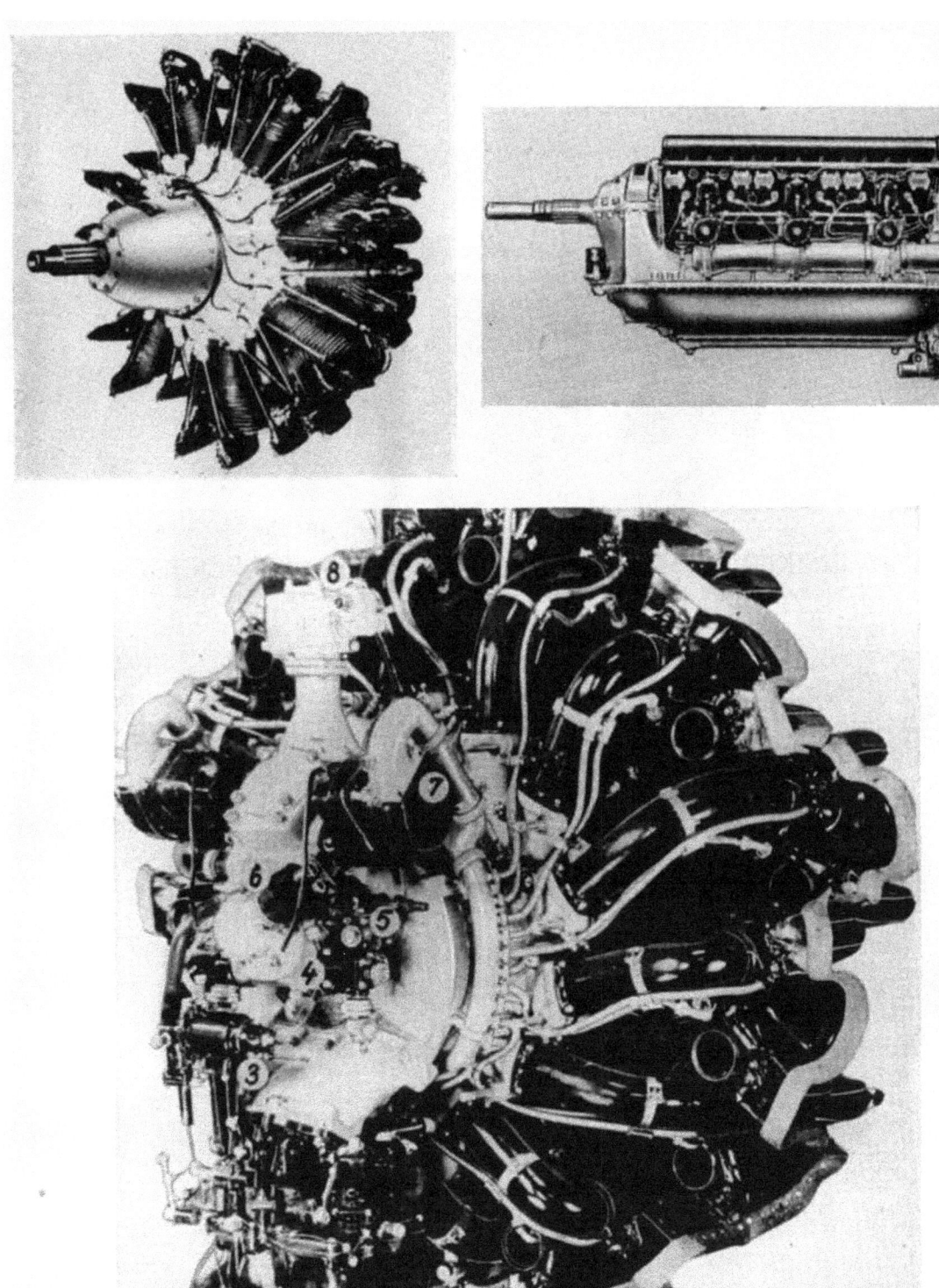

Figure 48.—Soviet aircraft engines M-85 (top left), M-100 (top right), and M 88B (bottom).

Figure 49.—M-105P (top) and M-105PF (bottom) aircraft engines.

444

Figure 50.—Typical Soviet liquid-cooled designs.

445

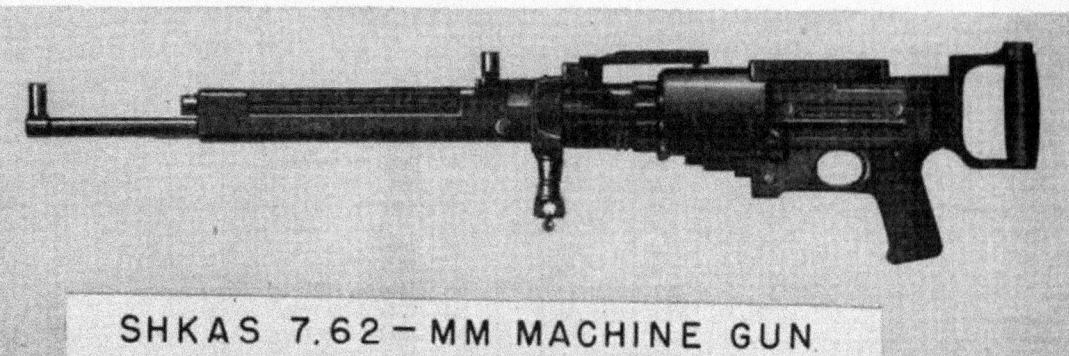

SHKAS 7.62—MM MACHINE GUN

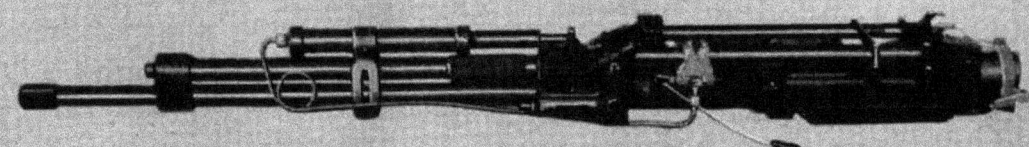

BEREZIN BS 12.7—MM MACHINE GUN

SCHVAK 20—MM CANNON

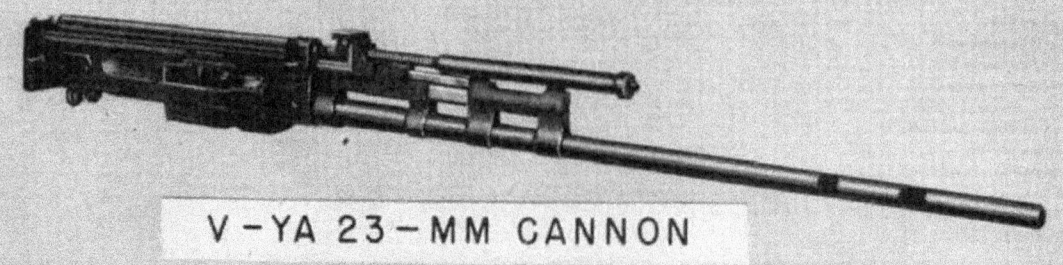

V-YA 23—MM CANNON

Figure 52. Aircraft machine guns and cannon.

Type	Caliber (mm.)	Weight of round	Weight of filler	Color of ogive	Color of band
		Grains	*Grains*		
Incendiary	7.62	152	49	Red tip, red ring	Red.
Tracer (day)	7.62	144	46	Green	Do.
Tracer/AP	7.62	150	49	Violet tip, red ring	Do.
HE/incendiary	7.62	152	47	Red	Do.
Ball (without groove)	7.62	149	49	None	Do.
Ball (with groove)	7.62	149	49	do	None.
Ball	7.62	182	47	Yellow	Do.
AP	7.62	168	47	Black	Do.
Incendiary	12.7		262	Black tip, yellow ring	
AP/tracer/incendiary	12.7	700	262	Violet tip, red ring	
AP/incendiary	12.7	740	262	Black tip, red ring	
		Ounces	*Ounces*		
AP/incendiary	20	3.42	0.60–0.63	do	
AP/HE	20	3.42	0.60–0.63	None	
AP/incendiary	23	6.9	2.2	do	
AP/HE	23	6.99	2.2	do	
AP/tracer	37	24.86			
HE/incendiary	37	24.93			
HE/tracer	37	24.15			
AP/tracer	37	26.52			

Figure 53.—Characteristics of aircraft ammunition.

bustibles behind the armor. It also ignites combustibles not protected by armor.

AP/Tracer round BST penetrates 0.59 inch armor at 656 feet and ignites combustibles behind plate. It leaves a red tracer up to 3,280 feet.

HE round MDS–46 ignites combustibles not protected by armor plate and covers an area 15.7 inches in diameter with splinters.

d. Special ammunition for SCHVAK 20-mm. cannon. Fragmentation round OS produces a hole 15.7 inches in diameter in skin of aircraft and ignites combustibles.

AP/I round BS penetrates 0.98 inch armor plate at 1,312 feet and ignites combustibles behind armor plate.

Section III. BOMBS

1. TYPES OF BOMBS

a. General. Soviet bombs usually are colored gray, although parts of bombs are not painted (fig. 54). Printed on the bomb body are the caliber, type of fuse, type of filler, and kind of detonator. On the tail are found the year of delivery, the delivery number, and the factory number.

b. High explosive. Both welded and forged high explosive bombs are manufactured (figs. 55, 56, 57, and 58). The explosive filler generally comprises from 45 to 50 percent of the total bomb weight. Depending upon the size of the bomb and type of filler, up to 20 exploder pellets, each weigh-

Type	Ogive	Neck	Band
HE			
AP		Yellow-red	
Fragmentation	Green	Blue	
Chemical warfare gas:			
HE/harassing gas	Green		Green-blue.
Persistent gases B	Red		Green.
Nonpersistent gases B	Green		Do.
AP or fragmentation gas	Yellow	Yellow-blue	
Toxic smoke			Yellow-green.
Incendiary (electron)	Yellow		Blue.
Flare	White		White.
Rocket		Blue	Black.
Practice	Red		White.

Figure 54.—Color of bomb markings.

	Welded HE bombs					Forged HE Bombs		
	FAB-1000	FAB-500	FAB-250	FAB-100	FAB-50	FAB-250	FAB-100	FAB-50
Maximum diameter (inches)	19.61	17.68	12.76	1.	9.43	12.77	10.72	8.6
Thickness of walls of cylindrical portion (inches)	0.51	0.35	0.23	0.54	0.35	0.43	0.35	0.31
Total length (inches)	140.37	94.75	84.88	41.46	37.21	70.15	41.14	37.09
Filler weight (pounds)	1,049.3	518	260.1	70.5	52.9	250.4	101.6	55.1
Percentage of total weight	46	46.3	47.5	31	48	48	47	41.5
Fuze (K-nose, H-tail)	KH	KH	KH	KH	K	KH	K	K
Terminal velocity from 9,600 feet (feet per second)	873	836	833	764	754			

Figure 55.—Characteristics of high explosive bombs—FAB.

Type	Fuze	Height of release (feet)	Penetration depth (feet)	Effect of blast (feet)	Size of crater (cubic yards)	Use
FAB-1000	APUV AV-1	3,280–1,312	34.4	183.7	483.9	Large important installations. Ships.
FAB-500	APUV AV-1	2,624–1,312	19.68	135.2	214.4	Important installations without special protection.
FAB-250	APUV AV-1	2,296–1,312	16.4	91.8	104.6	Industrial targets and heavy installations.
FAB-100	APUV AV-1	1,312	11.7	59	32.6	Difficult targets.
FAB-50	APUV AV-1	1,312	7.8	39.3	21.3	Village installations and tanks.

Figure 56.—Performance of high explosive bombs.—FAB.

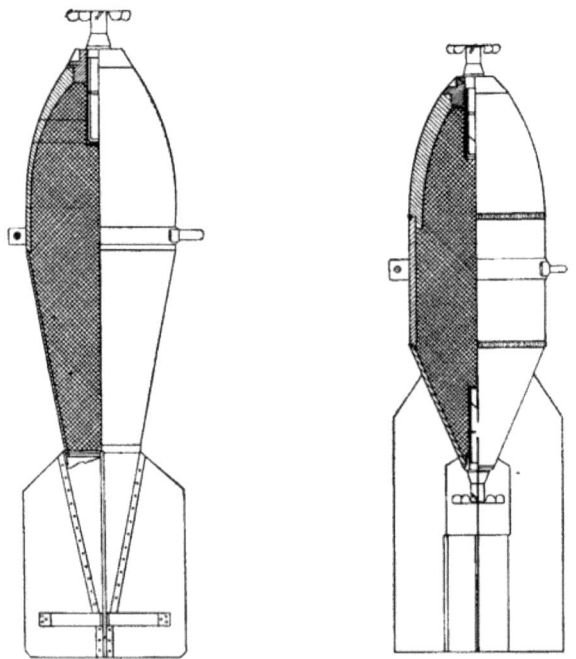

Figure 57.—High explosive bomb, FAB-50 (left) and FAB-100 (right).

448

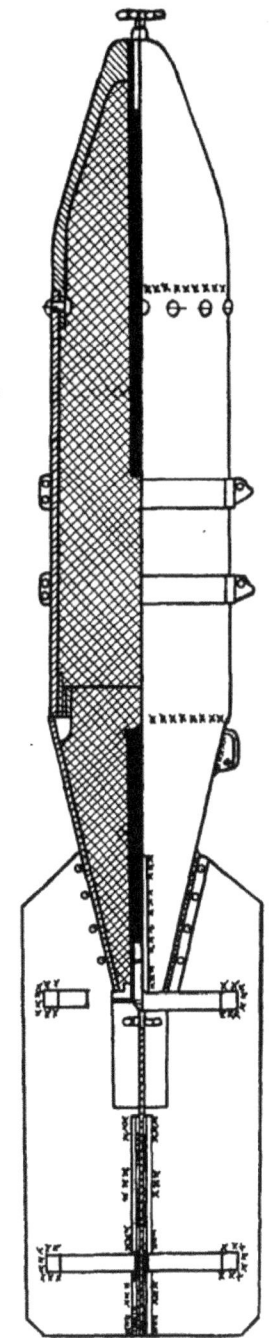

Figure 58.—*High explosive bomb FAB 1000.*

ing 2.99 ounces, can be inserted. Bombs up to 220 pounds are suspended for vertical and horizontal stowage by one lug. Larger bombs are suspended horizontally by two lugs. Nose fuzes are used on 110-pound and forged 220-pound bombs. All others are nose- and tail-fuzed. Types of fuzes include:

Time fuzes AGP and ADP.
Impact fuze AV–1 (with fixed delay action).
Variable delay fuze APUV (for large caliber, now obsolescent).

c. Armor-piercing. Armor-piercing heads are manufactured of cast iron and are screwed to the tail portion. The filler comprises from 16 to 25 percent of the total weight. Armor-piercing bombs are suspended horizontally by one or two lugs and are fuzed usually with the AM–1 impact fuze with delay action (figs. 59 and 60).

d. Fragmentation. There are approximately 20 different types of fragmentation bombs varying in weight from 5.5 to 110 pounds (figs. 61 and 62). The majority are modified artillery shells.

	BRAB–1000	BRAB–500	BRAB–220
Maximum diameter (inches)	18. 8	15. 7	10. 9
Total length (inches)	120. 8	93. 7	66
Filler weight (pounds)	457. 2	233. 6	83. 7
Percentage of total weight	21. 4	21	16
Total weight (pounds)	2, 127. 4	1, 104. 5	524. 6
Fuze	Tail	Tail	Tail

Figure 59.—*Characteristics of armor-piercing bombs—BRAB.*

Only four fragmentation bombs designed purely for aerial purposes are known, the 4.4-, 11-, 22-, and 33-pound bombs. These are made of cast iron. The filler normally comprises approximately 10 percent of the total weight. The 17.6, 22-, and 33-pound fragmentation bombs may be filled with gas. They then are designated AOKh–8, AOKh–10, and AOKh–15 (figs. 63 and 64).

Fragmentation bombs use impact fuzes AGM–1 (without delay), AGM–3, AM–4, AV–4, the time fuzes ADP and AGP, and the Universal variable delay fuze APUV. Nose fuzing is used almost exclusively.

e. Incendiary bombs. The Soviets have two thermite bombs and two bombs with a combustible

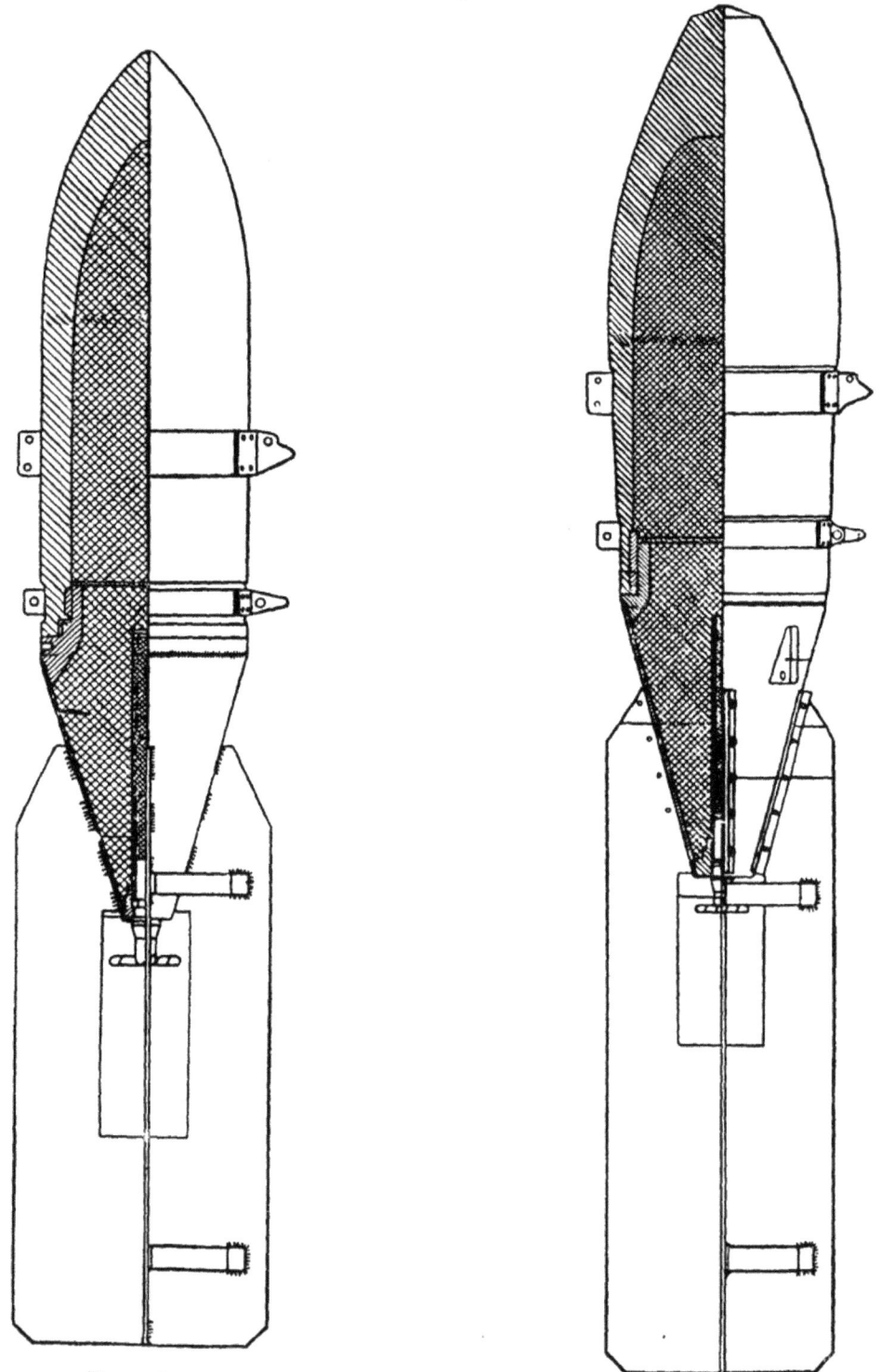

Figure 60.—Armor-piercing bombs BRAB-220 (left) and BRAB-500 (right).

450

Type	Maximum diameter (inches)	Total length (inches)	Weight of filler (pounds)	Total weight (pounds)	Fuze	Remarks
A02.5...............	1.7	8.21	0.22	5.29	AM-A, AGM-1...........	
A02.5...............	2.04	8.25	0.41	6.32	AM-A, AGM-1, AV-4.....	Cast iron.
A0-8M₂............	2.99	12.18	....	16.13	AM-A, AGM-1, AV-4.....	With fragments.
A0-8M₄............	2.94, 2.97	11.39	2.2	15.65	AGM-3.................	Two types.
A0-8M₈............	2.95, 2.99	12.18	....	....	AV-4, AM-A, AGM-1......	Do.
A0Kh-10...........	....	11.02	1.67	22.04	AV-4, AM-A, AGM-1......	Gas with fragments.
A0-10.............	3.53	11.39	1.89	20.96	AV-4, AM-A, AGM-1......	Cast iron.
A0Kh-15...........	4.2	9.43	2.53	32.76	AV-4, AM-A, AGM-1......	Gas with fragments.
A0-20M₁...........	4.16	18.82	4.93	45.98	AV-4, AM-A, AGM-1......	
A0-20M₂...........	4.51	13.24	....	37.98	AV-4, AM-A, AGM-1......	
A0-20M₃...........	4.71	15.91	6.61	46.36	AGM-3.................	Cast iron.
A0-25M₁...........	4.78	17.64	8	51.49	AM-A, AGM-1, AV-4......	
A0-25M₂...........	4.77	20.23	6.92	54.23	AV-4..................	
FAB-50M₂..........	5.91	22.38	15.21	92.59	ADP, ADS, APUV, AV-1....	
FAB-50M₃..........	5.94	23.77	15.12	88.18	ADP, ADS, APUV, AV-1....	
FAB-50M₄..........	5.97	23.65	15.14	96.38	AGP, AV-1, APUV.........	
FAB-50M₅..........	5.98	25.38	14.08	101.41	APUV.................	Two types.
FAB-50M₆..........	5.989	20.04	....	98.28	AGM-3.................	
FAB-50M₇..........	6.09	25.15	19.84	107.51	AGM-3.................	Picric acid filler.
FAB-50M₈..........	6.09	25.15	17.63	105.31	AGM-3.................	D-N napthalene and ammonium nitrate.

Figure 61.—Characteristics of fragmentation bombs.

Type	Fuze	Number of fragments	Effective area (square yards)	Use
AO2.5 (modified artillery projectile).	AM-A	70	211.69	Antipersonnel.
AO2.5 (HE).........	AM-A	148	845.57	Do.
AO-8.............	*AM-A	310	1,913.6	Do.
AO-10 (cast iron)....	AM-A	370	1,196	Do.
AO-15.............	AM-A	273	1,500.98	Do.
AO-20.............	AM-A	280	1,794	Moving targets, tanks, MT vehicles, and houses.
AO-25.............	AM-A	400	1,937.52	Do.
FAB-50............	AM-A	622	3,827.2	Do.

Figure 62.—Performance of some fragmentation bombs.

Type	Maximum diameter (inches)	Total length (inches)	Weight of filler (pounds)	Total weight (pounds)	Remarks
AOKh-8........	4.2	16.3–16.4	1.2 DA .... / 3.3 metal splinters........	17.6	
AOKh-10.......	4.2	23.7–24	1.1–1.8 DA, DM, or CN........ / 10.8 metal splinters.........	21.6	Scatters 225 fragments 0.25–1-inch over area 246 feet in diameter.
AOKh-15.......	4.1	24 –24.6	2.2 DA, DM, or CN........ / 2.5 HE	33	Wall is 0.75 inch thick.
AOKh-25.......	....	....	0.8 DA or DM..'....... / 3.3 HE	52	Weight of case is 39.6–41.8 pounds.

Figure 63.- Characteristics of gas/fragmentation bombs.

451

naphtha charge, which also contains a thermite composition (figs. 65, 66, 67, and 68). The incendiary composition comprises from 30 to 50 percent of the total bomb weight. The combustible naphtha

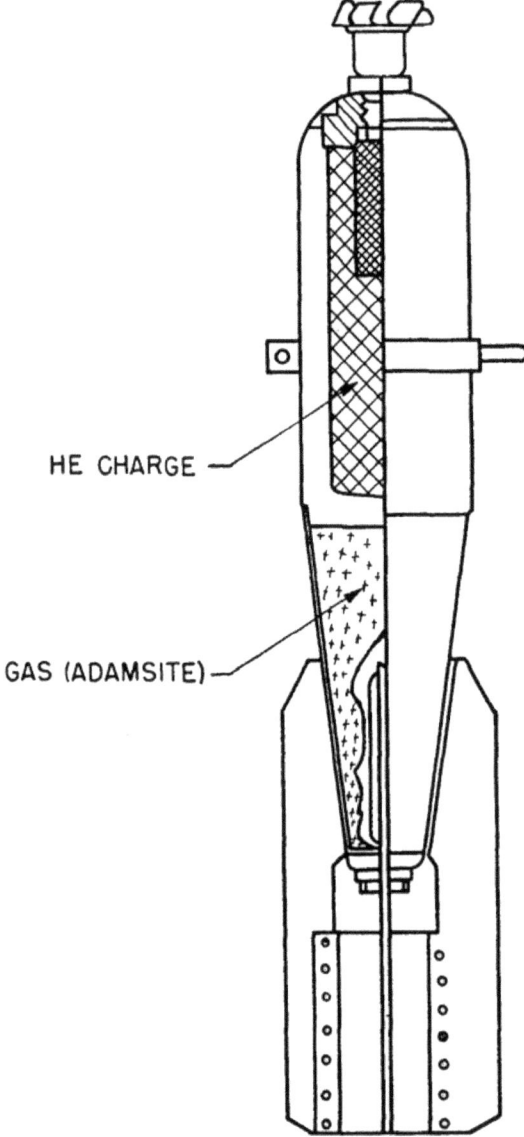

HE CHARGE

GAS (ADAMSITE)

Figure 64.—Gas/fragmentation bomb AOKh–15.

composition is mainly modified kerosene. The AGM–1 and AM–B impact fuzes are used.

An explosive incendiary bomb has been reported. It is similar in shape to a high explosive bomb, and weighs 231.5 pounds. It has a thin gage steel body and tail unit. The filler is a powdery explosive mixture, in the middle of which is a bundle of 10

thermite bombs, ZAB–2.5–T (without igniter or vanes). The bomb is reported to have the APUV fuze in its nose.

f. Cluster adapter bombs. The popular name for this type of bomb is the "Molotov Breadbasket." The bomb is in the form of a sheet iron container, divided into sectors, in which are stowed smaller bombs up to 55 pounds in weight (fragmentation, gas, and incendiary). There are three bombs, RRAB–1, RRAB–2, and RRAB–3 (figs. 69 and 70). Upon release from the aircraft, the angled tail fins of the adapters impart rotation. A special mechanism allows centrifugal force to disintegrate the adapter, scattering the bombs.

	ZAB–50TG	ZAB–10TG	ZAB–2.5	ZAB–1–E
Maximum diameter...(inches)..	7.97	4.2	2.35	2.35
Total length........(inches)..	38.86	23.97	14.42	14.42
Total weight........(pounds)..	105.6	22	5.5	3.3
Time of burning....(minutes)..	6	4	2.3	1.2
Weight of incendiary filler (pounds)..	57.3	11	2.79	1
Effective range of flame..(feet)..	16.4	6.5	0.65	0.65

Figure 65.—Characteristics and performance of incendiary bombs.

It has been reported that RRAB–1 can hold 1,064 2.2-pound ZAB–1 incendiary bombs or 240 AOKh–10 gas/fragmentation bombs. These numbers, which are at variance with the characteristics listed in figure 64, may possibly refer either to a larger modification of this cluster adapter or to a different model of the AOKh–10 bomb.

It also has been reported that the RRAB–3 can hold 240 ZAB–1 incendiary or 46 AOKh–25 gas/fragmentation bombs.

g. Chemical bombs. Chemical bombs include the KhAB and AOKh gas bombs and the KRAB–25 Y AD toxic smoke bomb (fig. 71). In addition to the previously discussed AOKh–8, AOKh–10, and AOKh–15, which are used either as gas or as fragmentation bombs, there are three different sizes of KhAB gas bombs (figs. 72 and 73). The gas filler is added immediately before use. Yperit and phosgene are the principal fillers. The marking "R–5" (*Rezept*–5) identifies Yperit, a blister gas. "R–YU" identifies phosgene. Gas bombs filled with persistent gas are fuzed with either the AGM–1 or the AMA fuze. Those containing non-persistent gas are fuzed

452

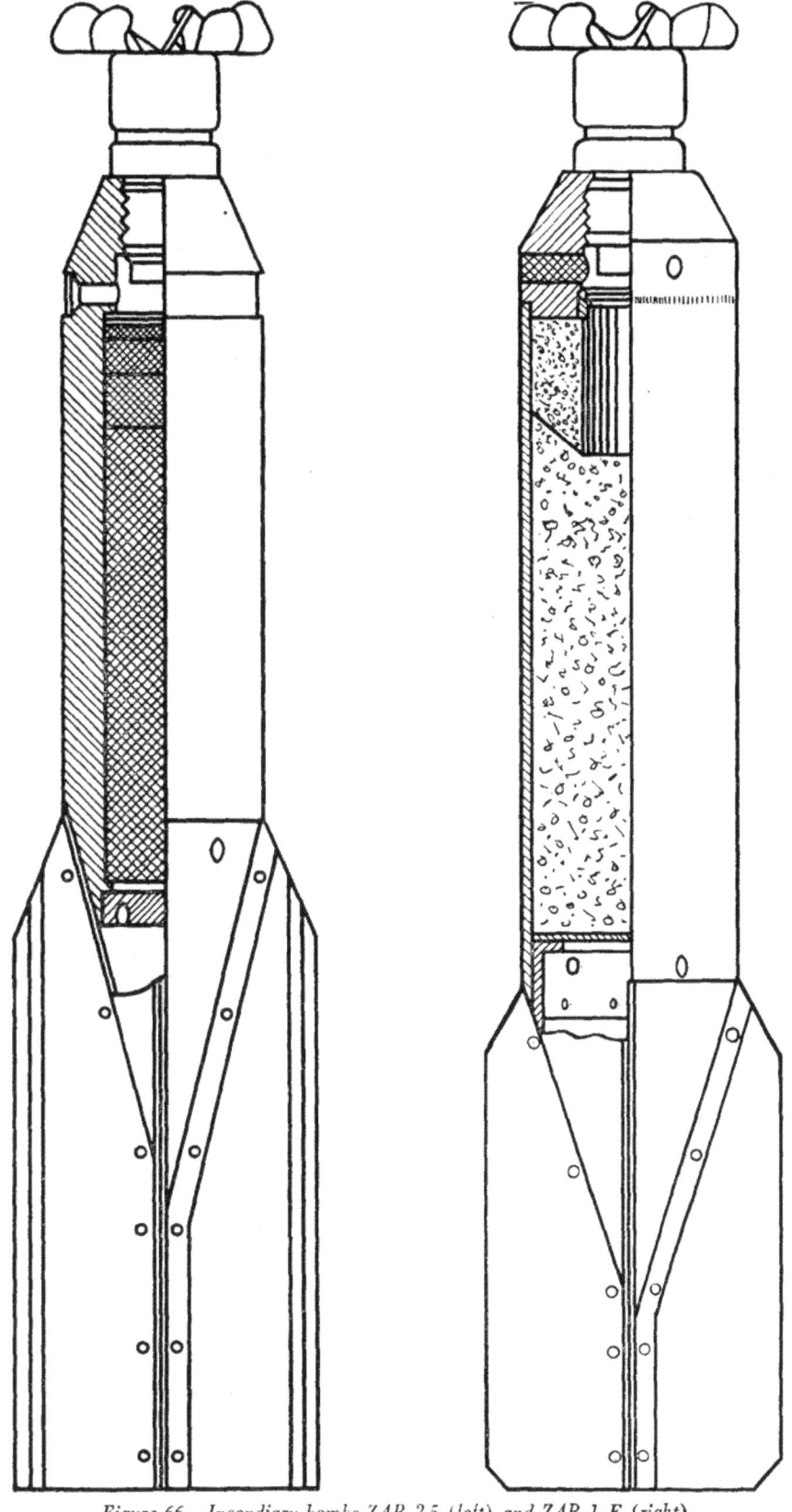

Figure 66.—Incendiary bombs ZAB-2.5 (left) and ZAB-1-E (right).

453

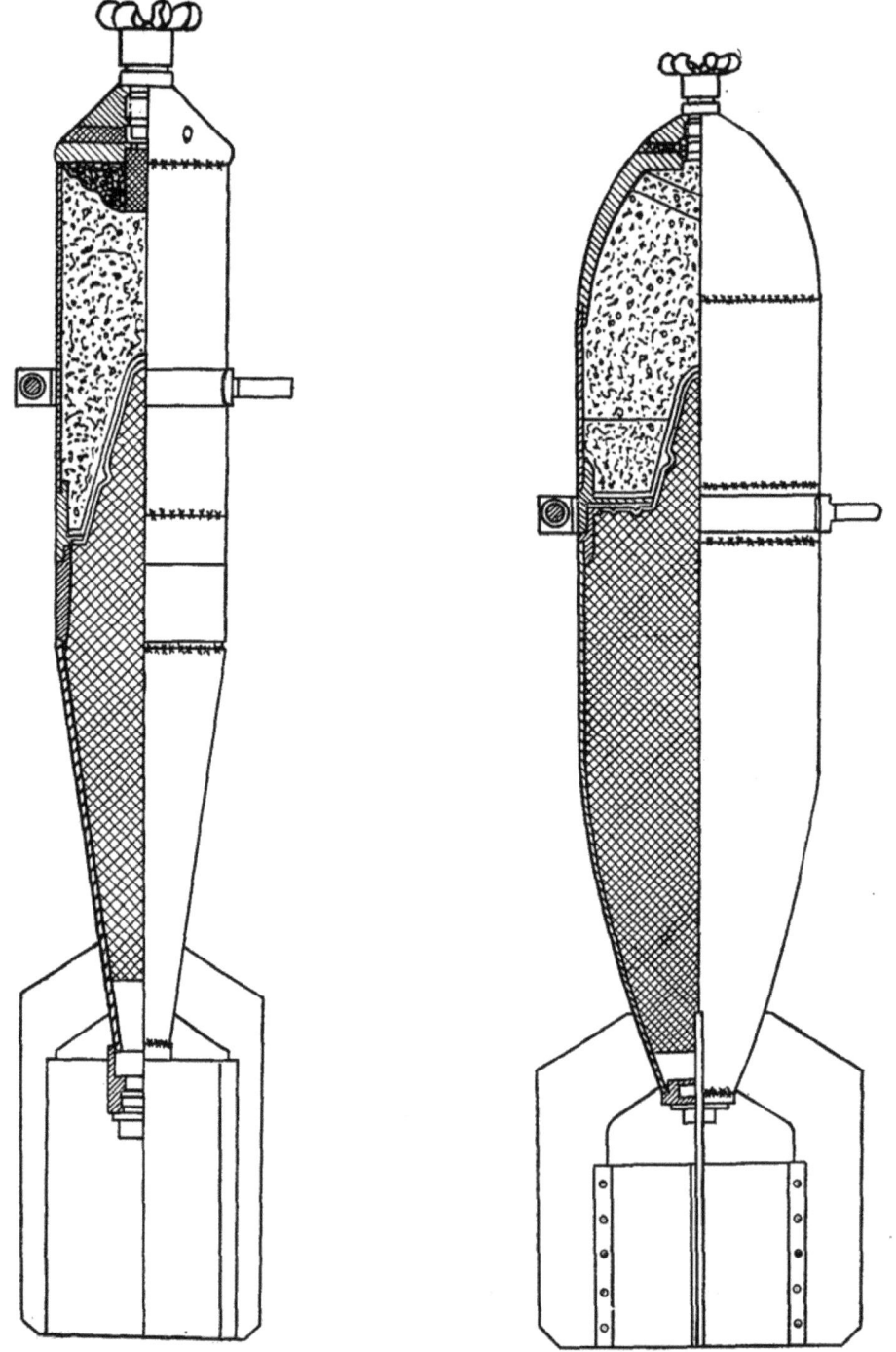

Figue 67.—Incendiary bombs ZAB–10TG (left) and ZAB–50TG (right).

with AGDT, the TM–4, or the TM–24 (for high altitudes).

The toxic smoke bomb, KRAB–25 YaD, is used to produce either smoke or a toxic smoke (fig. 72). Adamsite is used for toxic action. It is estimated that a toxic smoke bomb develops a cloud from 50 to 65 feet high and 620 feet wide. The AGM–1 fuze is inserted in the nose of the bomb.

Type	Total length (inches)	Maximum diameter (inches)	Total weight (pounds)	Number of thermite spheres in filler
ZAB–100 TSH	40.9–41.7	11	143	140–145
ZAB–500 TSH	82.7	17.7	600	775–785

Figure 68.—Characteristics of incendiary bombs with filler of thermite spheres.

Another gas bomb, KRAB–50, also containing adamsite, has been reported. Presumably this bomb weighs 110 pounds. It is filled with a screening smoke mixture, SIV, consisting of sulphur trioxide and chlorsulfonic acid.

h. Frangible sphere bombs. These consist of metal ball containers filled with fluid chemical agents. Frangible spheres are released from aircraft, and are used for disseminating incendiary materials or persistent gases.

CHARACTERISTICS

Maximum diameter	4.7 inches.
Capacity	1.06 quarts.
Weight (filled)	3 to 3.3 pounds.
Thickness of wall	0.014 to 0.02 inch.

The body of the frangible sphere is constructed in two sections, sealed together. One section is provided with four radial shear grooves. The other is fitted with a threaded filling plug. The grooved section of the sphere breaks into several pieces on impact and the filler is scattered.

The incendiary filler consists of 2.53 pounds of a liquid solution of phosphorus in sulphur and 0.22-pound of water. This filling ignites spontaneously on contract with air.

i. Flare bombs. The four known types of flare bombs include SAB–3, SAB–3M, SAB–15, and SAB–25 (figs. 74 and 75). The SAB–3 and SAB–3M differ very little. Flare bombs are suspended horizontally in the carrier ring. The time fuzes AGDT, TM–4, and TM–24 are installed.

j. Miscellaneous bombs. The navigation signal bomb, ANAB, is used as an air navigation aid (fig. 76). It is released over water, ignites on contact and burns from 5 to 10 minutes. At the time of burning a fluorescent patch is formed on the water which is visible for a considerable distance. The bomb weighs approximately 2.2 pounds. Prior to release, the sheet-metal cap over the nozzle is removed.

The propaganda bomb, AB, is used to distribute pamphlets from high altitudes. It is a wooden container which holds approximately 10,000 sheets of paper. The pamphlets are packed in rolls and are released by the AGDT time fuze at a pre-set altitude. Length of the bomb, without the fuze is 44.8 inches. It weighs 39.6 pounds.

k. Aerial torpedoes. There are two known types of torpedoes in the Soviet air forces, the

		BRAB–1	BRAB–2	BRAB–3
Maximum diameter	(inches)	28.29	23.58	20.43
Total weight	(pounds)	2,640	1,430	990
Total length	(inches)	152.09	128.7	89
Filler (number of bombs):				
Type AO–8		84–130	50–78	34
Type AO–10		100	66	25
Type AO–25		40	19	13
Type ZAB–2.5		580	260	116
Radius of scatter (feet):				
AO–8 from 6,561 feet		885.8–1,804.4	770.8–1,722.4	738.1–1,181
from 16,404 feet		1,000.6–2,296.5	869.4–1,842.8	820.2–1,640.4
AO–10 from 6,561 feet		1,374.3	2,165.3	1,099
from 16,404 feet		1,968.4	2,542.6	1,230.3
AO–25 from 6,561 feet		1,525.5	918.6	623.3
from 16,404 feet		1,788	1,345.1	1,115.4
ZAB–2.5 from 6,561 feet		2,591.8	3,116.7	2,181.7
from 16,404 feet		3,362.8	4,068.1	2,854.2

Figure 69.—Characteristics and performance of cluster adapter bombs.

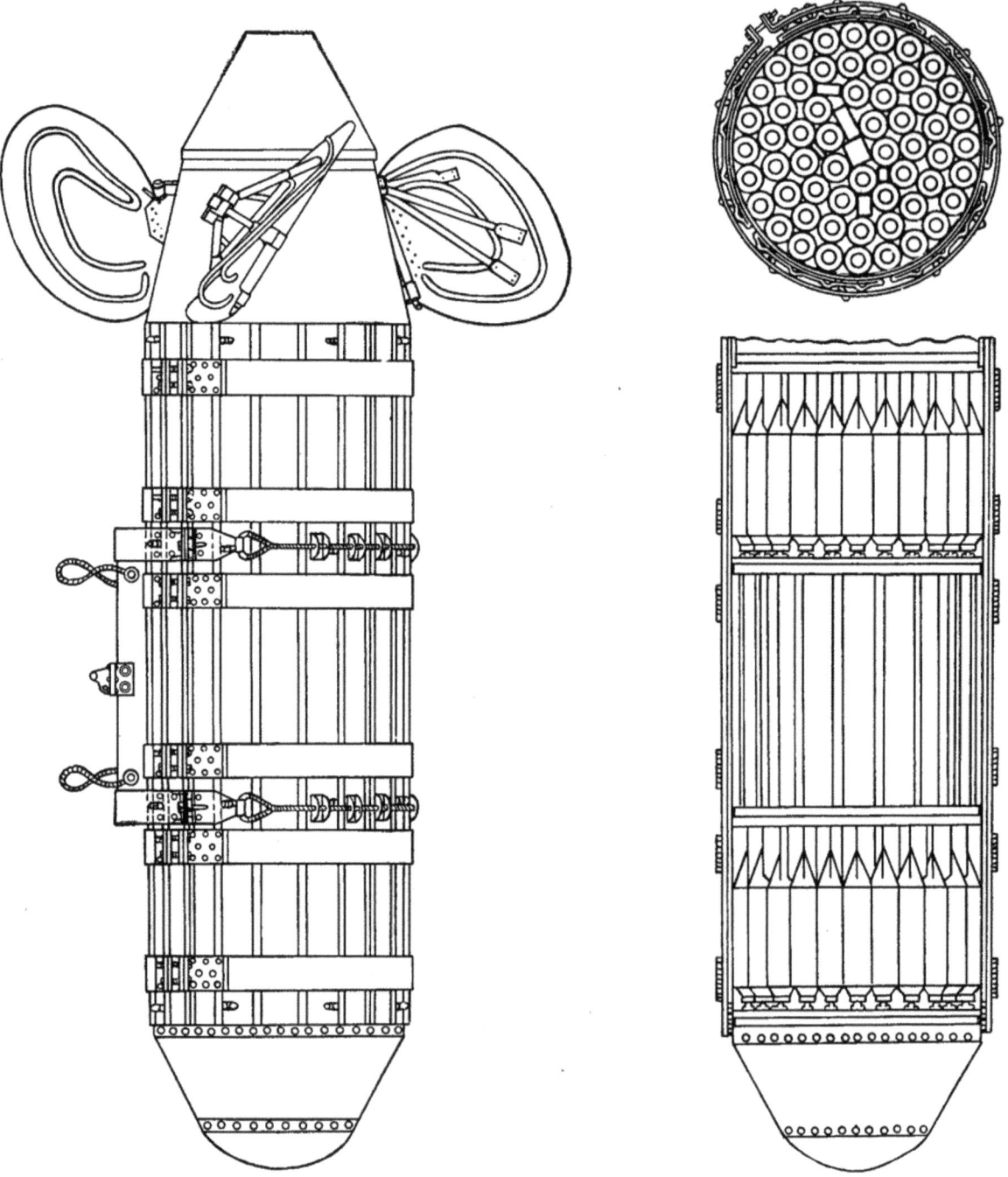

Figure 70.—RBAB–3 cluster adapter bomb.

	Gas bombs				Toxic smoke bombs
	KhAB-500	KhAB-200-R-5	KhAB-200-R-YU	KbAB-25	KRAB-25 YaD
Maximum diameter................................(inches)..	17.7	12.6	12.6	8	8
Total length....................................(inches)..	93.7-94.9	85.3	85.3		
Total weight...................................(pounds)..	600-690	354.2-363	378.4-418	34.6-34.8	33-34.5
Gas filler.....................................(pounds)..	374-407	171.6-183.7	193.6-202.4	57.2-61.6	66-75.9
Explosive filler................................(pounds)..	2.5-3.6	1.1-1.48	....	28.6	16.5-17.6
				0.9	5.7-5.9

Figure 71.—Characteristics of gas and smoke bombs.

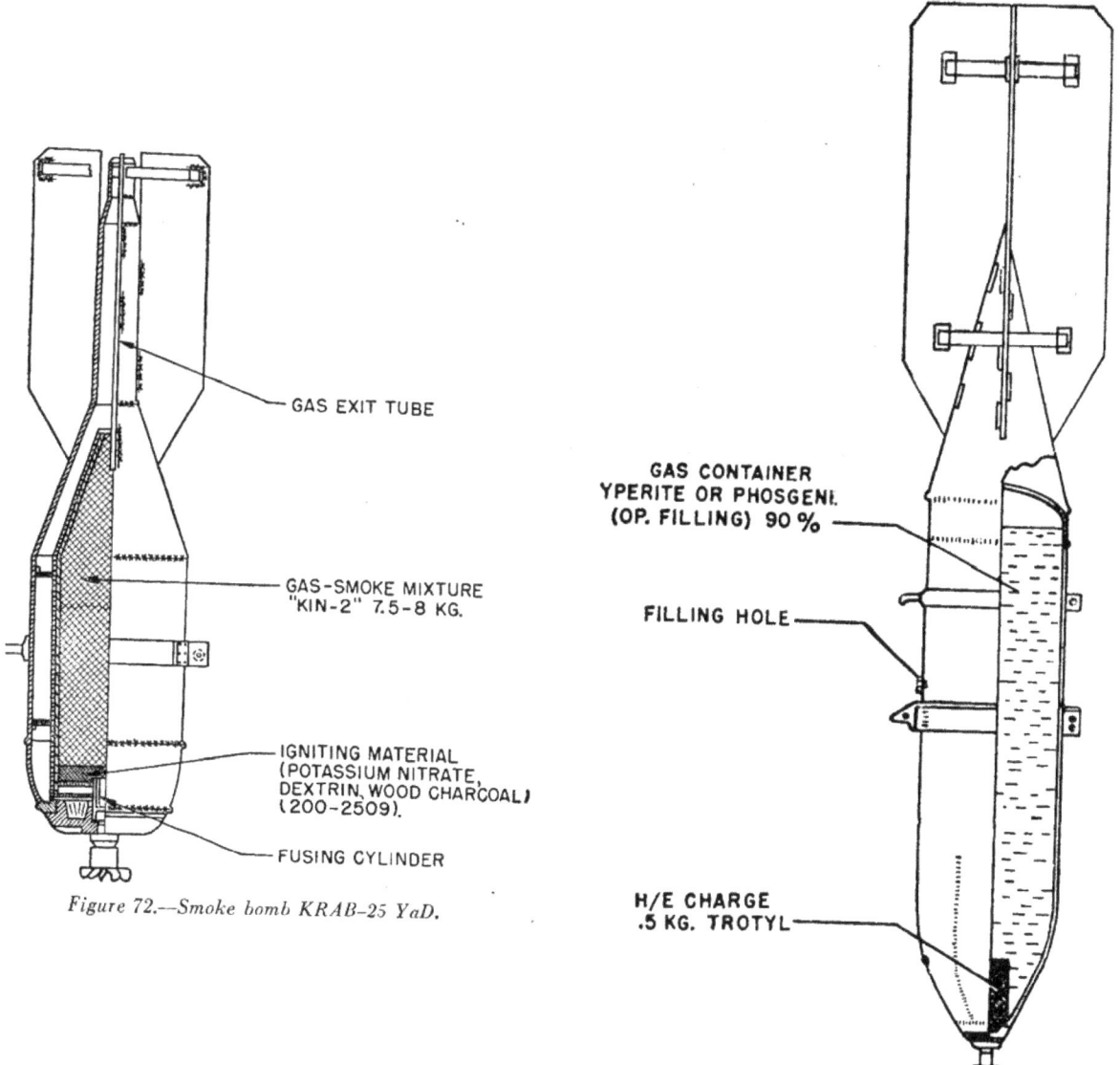

- GAS EXIT TUBE

- GAS-SMOKE MIXTURE "KIN-2" 7.5-8 KG.

- IGNITING MATERIAL (POTASSIUM NITRATE, DEXTRIN, WOOD CHARCOAL) (200-2509).

- FUSING CYLINDER

Figure 72.—Smoke bomb KRAB-25 YaD.

GAS CONTAINER YPERITE OR PHOSGENE (OP. FILLING) 90%

FILLING HOLE

H/E CHARGE .5 KG. TROTYL

Figure 73.—Gas bomb KhAB-200.

457

	SAB–25	SAB–15	SAB–3M	Photographic
Maximum diameter (inches)..	7.46	6.28	3.73	7.97.
Total length.....(inches)..	68.53	40.47	20.35	35.17.
Total weight....(pounds)..	51.5	31.7	8.8	77.1.
Time of burning (minutes)..	2.2	2.4	3.5	½ second.
Weight of filler..(pounds)..	26.4	21.2	4.8	44.
Candle power...........	700,000	500,000	22,000	230,000,000.
Rate of fall (feet per second)..	9.8	7.8	14.7	

Figure 74.—Characteristics and performance of flare bombs.

45–36–AN for release at low altitudes and 45–36–AV for release at higher altitudes. The first torpedo is released by the PTN–4 sighting gear. The second type is released by the normal bomb sight OPB–1. Each type weighs 2,068 pounds.

1. Rockets. For rocket projectiles, see chapter VIII.

2. BOMB FUZES

Soviet bomb fuzes are obsolete in comparison with United States and British fuzes, with inadequate detonating and safety features and with poor precision

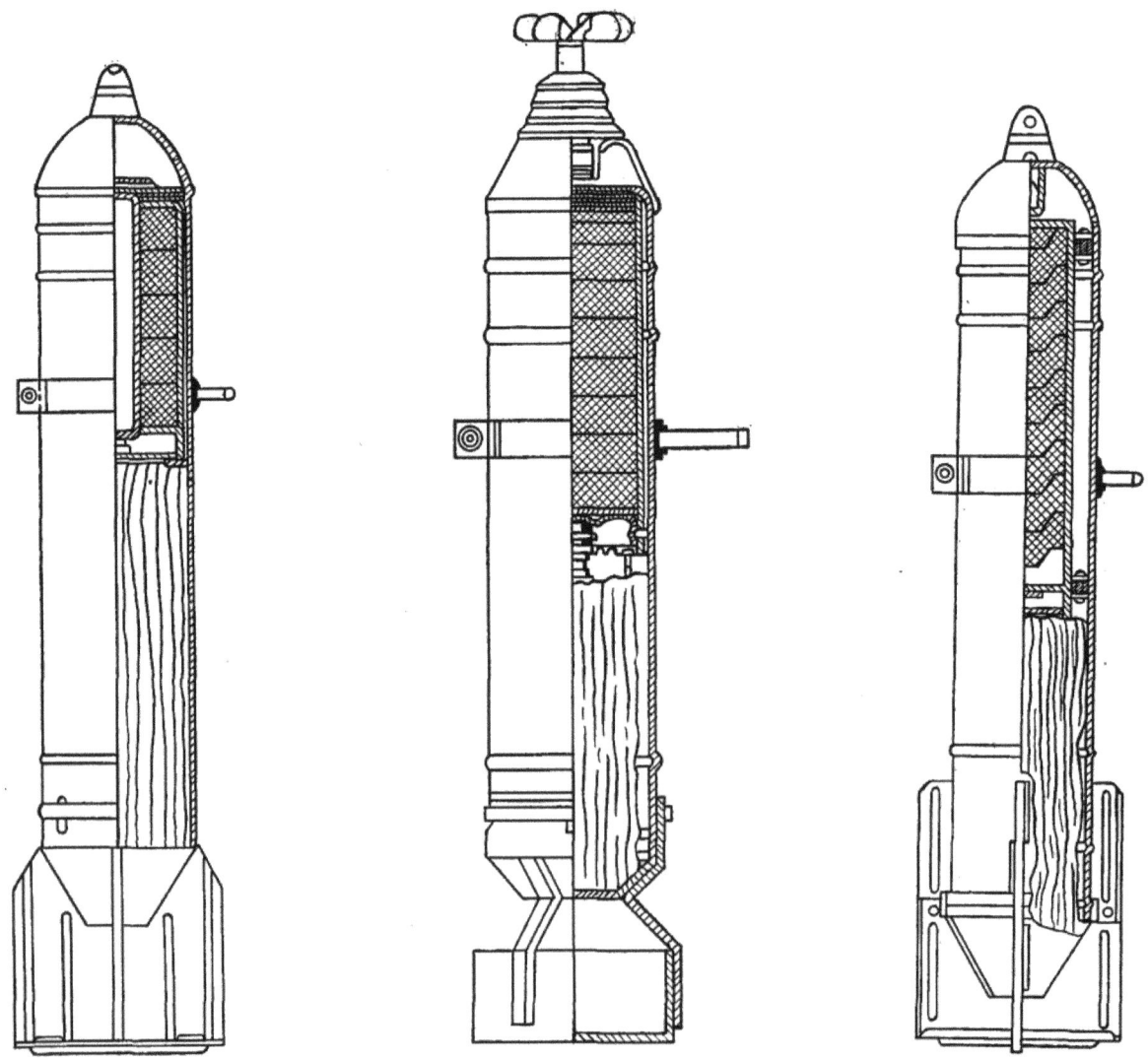

Figure 75.—Flare bombs (from left to right) SAB–25, SAB–3M, and SAB–15.

458

and time delay (fig. 77). They also lack suitable anti-disarming features. Development of bomb fuzes is far behind that of Soviet artillery fuzes.

a. Fuzes without delay. Several Soviet bomb fuzes do not contain delay features.

AV–4 Nose. The AV–4 is activated by the rotation of the arming vanes. The action appears to

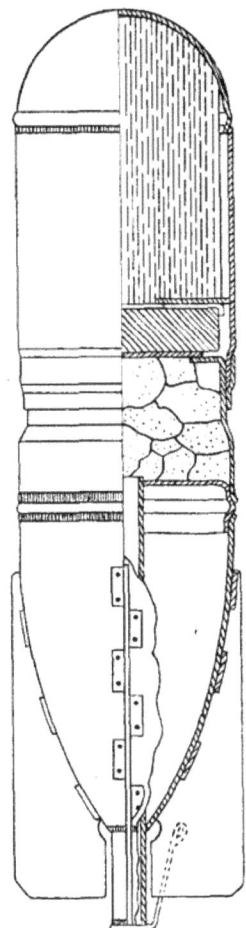

Figure 76.—Navigation signal bomb ANAB.

compress and heat the air in the fuze chamber which, in turn, ignites the detonator. Instantaneous action on impact may be effected by removing the side screw, which permits the flash of the igniter to pass through a flash tube to the booster. If the side screw is retained, a slight delay action results, because the flash must pass through an intermediate powder chamber before reaching the booster.

AM–A Plain Nose. This fuze is an inertia-type with a safety cap and arming vanes. The rotation

of the arming vanes apparently detaches the safety cap, which arms the fuze and the detonation occurs on the impact of the simple inertia striker against the igniter.

AM–B. The AM–B is similar to AM–A fuze, with a comparable inertia striker. It is fitted with a percussion primer rather than a detonator.

AM–Ab/v AND AM–Bb/v. These also are inertia fuzes. They differ from the AM–A in that the outer safety caps are removed by hand before use, rather than automatically in flight by arming vanes.

AGM–1 AND AGM–3. These are impact fuzes, provided with safety arms, and armed in flight by arming vanes. The rotation of the arming vanes forces out the safety arm, arming the fuze. On impact, the main spring is crushed and the striker is driven against the detonator. No delay is provided. These fuzes have a beveled, sliding collar in the head to insure detonation at varying angles of impact.

The AGM–1 appears to differ from the AGM–3, which has only a percussion primer, primarily in the construction of the detonator.

b. Fuzes with delay. The Soviets use several types of delay bomb fuzes.

AV–1 Nose AND Tail. The AV–1 is an always impact fuze, with arming vanes and a fixed delay of from 25 to 27 seconds.

ADSU. The ADSU probably replaced the APUV fuze. It is not an all-ways type. It has arming vanes, an inertia striker, and fixed delay.

ADS Tail. The ADS is believed to be obsolete. It has arming vanes and a fixed delay of from 0.15 to 0.3 second. A fuze similar to the ADS, designated ADSO, is considered obsolete and has no delay element.

Variable Delay Fuze APUV. This is suitable for nose and tail fuzing. It has arming vanes resembling the AV–4 in construction and in action, it is detonated by the increase of temperature caused by compression. By taking out the side screws, adjustment for delay and instantaneous action may be made. With screw "Z" removed, 0.1 second delay is effected. With screw "M" removed, no delay action is obtained. With both screws left in, 0.3 second delay is obtained. This fuze is used on high explosive bombs.

c. Time Fuzes. Seven different time fuzes are used.

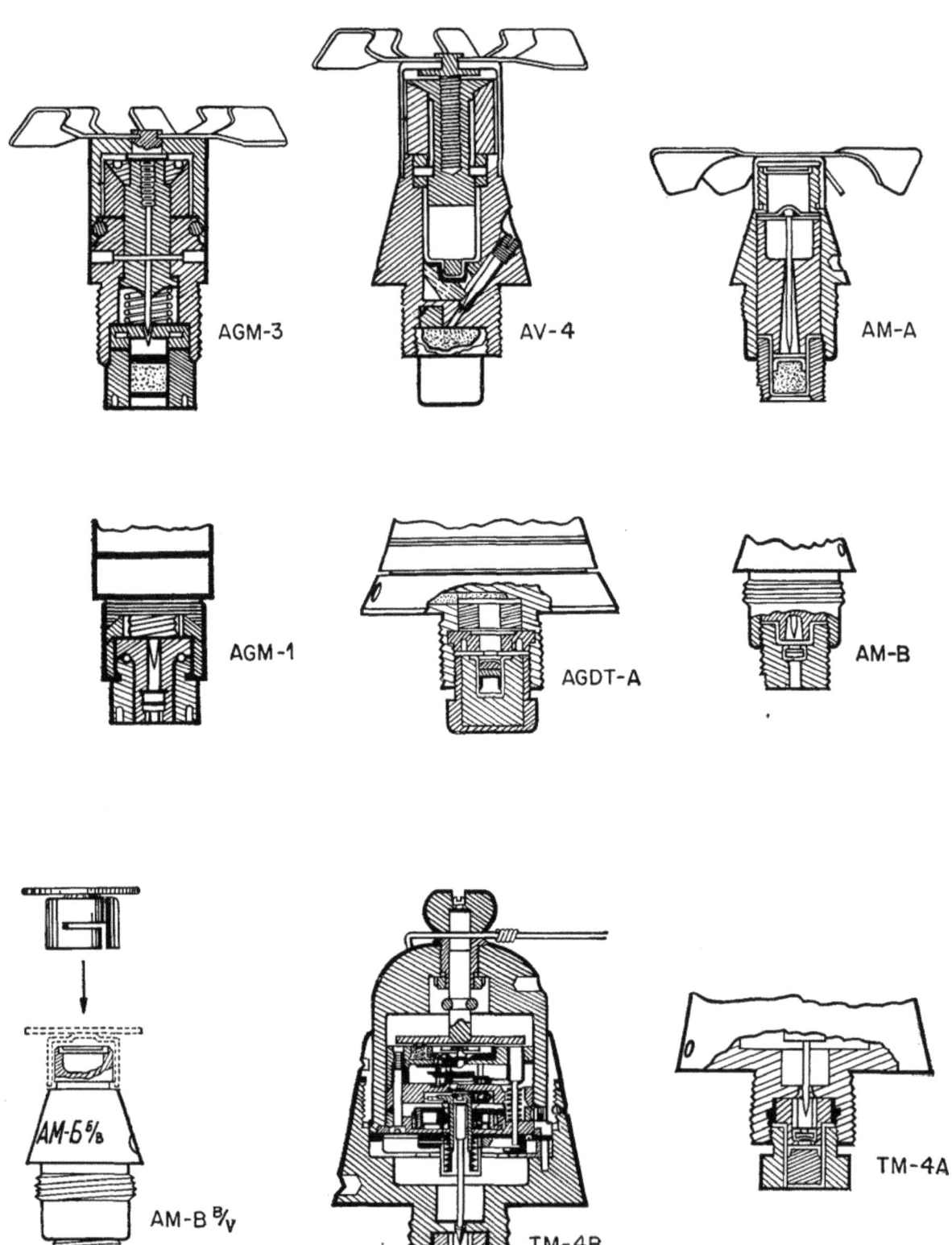

Figure 77.—Some Soviet bomb fuzes.

TM–4A. The TM–4A is operated by a mechanical time clock, which can be set at from 6 to 40 seconds. A wire release activates the clock when the bomb is released. The bomb is detonated above the ground. This type of fuze is used on fragmentation, gas, and photographic flash bombs.

TM–4B. The TM–4B is similar to the TM–4A. The mechanical time clock may be set from 2 to 40 seconds. It is used on flares and smoke bombs.

AGDT–A. The AGDT–A is a nose fuze to detonate bombs above ground. It has a selective time setting of from instantaneous to 5 seconds and 5 to 22 seconds, controlled by a powder train activated by pre-set arming vanes. It is used on fragmentation and flash bombs.

AGDT–B. The AGDT–B is similar to the AGDT–A. It has no special markings and is used for flares and gas and smoke bombs.

ADP TAIL. The ADP fuze has arming vanes, an inertia striker, and a variable powder train. The setting ring may be adjusted for from 0.01 to 0.05 second delay, from 0.05 to 0.15 second delay or from 5 to 22 seconds. It is used on high explosive bombs.

ADP. The ADP is the same as the ADP tail fuze, but is an older model. It resembles a projectile fuze in shape. It does not employ a safety pin.

AGP. The AGP is a nose, time impact fuze. It has arming vanes, adjustable delay, inertia striker, and rotatable pyrotechnic time ring. It can be adjusted for from 0.01 to 0.05 second, from 0.05 to 0.15 second, or from 22 to 35 seconds. It is used for fragmentation bombs dropped from more than 130 to 165 feet.

3. BOMB SHACKLES AND RELEASE GEAR

Soviet bombs usually are carried horizontally. In some of the older bombers, bombs weighing up to 220 pounds were carried vertically. Small bombs are attached by one lug. Those weighing more than 220 pounds are attached by two lugs. These lugs are made fast to the bands supporting the bombs. Vertically-carried bombs are supported under the tail. Release usually is effected by a cartridge fired by an electrically-heated filament. The resulting gases open the bomb slip. Electromagnetic release also is used occasionally. Emergency mechanical release is provided. Electrical bomb release is effected by the ESBR bomb distributor. Mechanical release is effected by the emergency gear ASBR.

Bombs may be dropped either armed or safe. When dropped armed, the safety pin on the arming vanes of the fuze is withdrawn mechanically. It is not withdrawn when bombs are dropped safe.

There are many models of bomb shackles, each adapted for the particular aircraft in which it is installed. Bombs weighing from 500 to 1,000 pounds are stowed internally and horizontally. Gas bombs

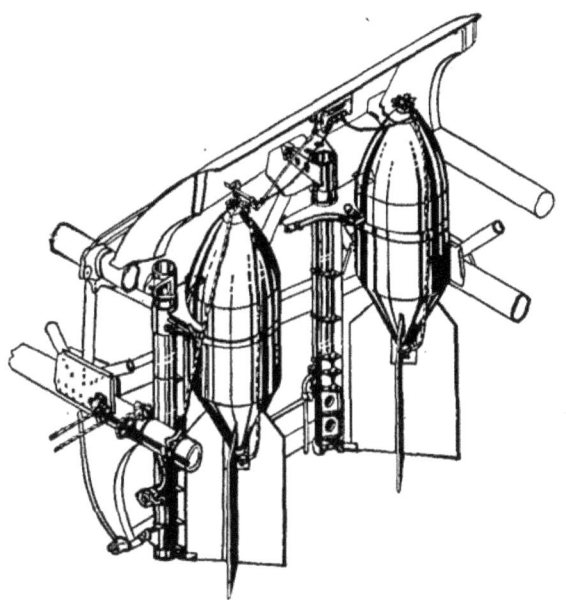

Figure 78.—Verticle bomb shackle DER–34.

are carried externally. In the TB–3F bomber, there are two fuselage bomb racks, each carrying five 220-pound bombs horizontally, one above the other. Under the fuselage are three bomb stations, the two outer station for 1,000-pound bombs and the middle station for 2,000-pound bombs.

The PE–2 bomber has stations in the fuselage, under the wings, and in the engine nacelles. There are interchangeable racks which can be installed in single-engined fighter-bombers for stowage of bombs weighing up to 200 pounds. Release is the same as for bombers, normally by an electrically-fired cartridge and in emergency mechanically. Some bombers have a permanently built-in hoisting winch for loading large bombs.

Bomb doors usually are opened and are closed mechanically by a hand ratchet.

a. Bomb shackles. Two types of bomb shackles used by the Soviets are the DER–34 and the DER–21.

VERTICAL BOMB SHACKLE DER–34. The DER–34 is used for the vertical stowage of one to two bombs, each weighing from 50 to 200 pounds

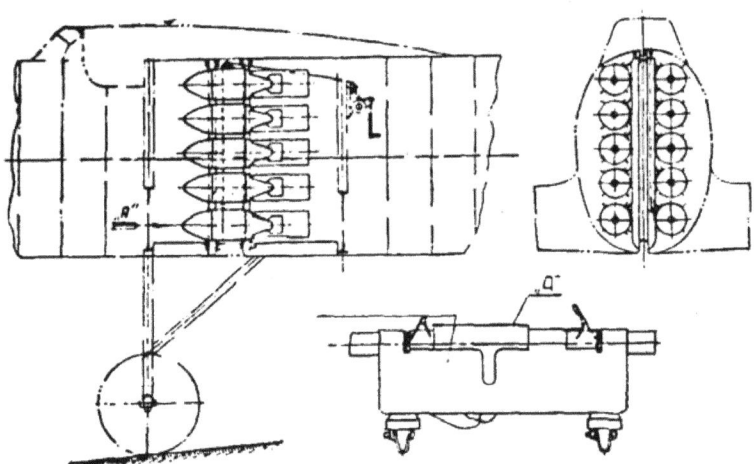

Figure 79.—Horizontal bomb shackle DER-21.

(fig. 78). The bombs are supported by a claw, which is attached under the tail and which is held by a band encircling the upper part of the bomb. Normal release is accomplished by an electrically-fired cartridge controlled by intervalometer ESBR. Emergency release is achieved mechanically by the ASBR-3 intervalometer.

HORIZONTAL BOMB SHACKLE DER-21. Two bomb stations are built inside the fuselage of the IL-4 (DB-3F) (fig. 79). They carry five bombs, weighing up to 220 pounds, horizontally, or an AK-2U container. Normal bomb release is achieved by an electrically-fired cartridge. Emergency release is mechanical. A bomb-hoisting winch is built into the aircraft. The shackle weighs 77 pounds, is 65.23 inches deep, 23.58 inches long, and 4.71 inches wide.

b. Intervalometers. Intervalometers are used to control the release of bombs.

ELECTRICAL BOMB INTERVALOMETER ESBR-2. The ESBR-2 intervalometer is fitted as standard equipment for bomb release in nearly all new Soviet aircraft. The ESBR-2 enables 20 bombs to be re-leased at time intervals or from 0.1 to 1.5 second, either singly or 2, 3, or 4 bombs simultaneously (fig. 80). The total number of bombs to be re-leased can be regulated by means of a selector.

The control panel of the intervalometer contains a selector switch to determine the total number of bombs to be dropped, a distributor switch to deter-mine the number of bombs to be dropped at each interval, and a time interval switch. Two indicator lamps, wired parallel, are provided for each bomb station, and are turned on by pressing down on the left-hand switch. The lamps are covered by red filters immediately upon release of the bombs.

The selector switch is located on the upper part of the panel. The total number of bombs to be dropped is set on the selector switch. It consists of a rotary contact knob and a contact track, with 20 contacts. The first contact is marked "salvo" for a single release. The second contact is marked "null" and returns the release gear to null.

To the left and below the selector is the distributor. The distributor determines the number of bombs to

462

Figure 80.—Electric bomb intervaltometer ESBR–2.

be dropped at each interval. It can be set for 1, 2, 3, or 4 bombs.

The time interval switch is on the right. It provides time intervals of from 0.1 to 1.5 second.

Thus, by setting the selector at 15, the distributor at 3, the time interval at 1, and pressing the release switches, 3 bombs will be dropped every second until a total of 15 have been dropped. By setting the selector at "salvo" and the distributor at 4, 4 bombs are released simultaneously.

The intervalometer weighs 13.2 pounds. It is electrically-heated and is protected by a felt and leather cover. It operates on the 24-volt aircraft electric system.

ELECTRICAL BOMB INTERVALOMETER ESBR–5. The ESBR–5 intervalometer is used in the TB–3 and TB–3F aircraft, each of which has two internal bomb racks built into the fuselage. Each rack carries five bombs stowed horizontally one above the other. It can be arranged for only two bombs to be released simultaneously. The ESBR–5 is similar to the ESBR–2 in construction, except for the bomb dis-

tributor switch, which allows the release of not more than two bombs simultaneously.

c. Frangible sphere release assemblies. Three models of release assemblies can be used for dropping frangible spheres. Model AVK–1 is adapted to small bombs as well as frangible spheres. Release assembly AK–2, and its smaller modifications AK–2u and AK–2uM, are designed for frangible spheres only.

AVK–1 RELEASE ASSEMBLY. The AVK–1 is a cylindrical metal container with a hemispherical lid at one end and a flat cover at the other. The containers can be suspended either vertically in the bomb rack or horizontally under the wings. Release is effected electro-pyrotechnically. Metal or wooden spacers are used to adapt the container to carry either frangible spheres or small size bombs.

CHARACTERISTICS

Total length_____ 42.8 inches.
Maximum diameter_____ 11.3 inches.
Weight (empty)_____ 42.9 pounds.
Capacity_____ 30 frangible spheres or 28 ZAB–1–E incendiaries.

463

AK–2 AND AK–2U RELEASE ASSEMBLIES. These are carried in the fuselage attached to the bomb rack. They consist of a frame work supporting sixteen vertically disposed duralumin tubes holding the frangible spheres (fig. 81). Each unit is fitted with four hinged lids at the bottom, each lid closing an outlet. Release is effected mechanically or electrically, the four lids of each unit being opened either consecutively or simultaneously. Four release assemblies can be carried by a four-engined bomber, while a two-engined aircraft can carry two of the shorter AK–2U model.

CHARACTERISTICS

	AK–2	AK–2U
Over-all length	76.9 inches	52.8 inches.
Cross section	45.4 x 7.9 inches	45.4 x 7.9 inches.
Weight (empty)	132 pounds	105.6 pounds.
Capacity	240 spheres	160 spheres.

Section IV. SIGHTS

1. GUN SIGHTS

a. Fixed. In the early part of World War II, an Aldis-type sight with an auxiliary ring-and-bead sight was installed. This type was replaced by a series of reflector sights. The PAK sight was equipped with a ring-and-bead sight and was used only as a gun sight, while the later models can be used as bomb sights. For example, the PBP sight can be used also as a rocket projectile and dive bombing sight.

b. Flexible. A sight of the "moving vane" type, with a relative speed ring rear sight, has been used. A more recent sight is the PMP, which has an automatic "own speed adjustment," and which, with additional apparatus, also can be used as a low-level bomb sight.

c. Types of gun sights. Several different types of gun sights are in use.

REFLECTOR SIGHT PAK–1. The PAK–1 is used for fixed guns. It has an auxiliary sight, consisting of a ring and bead, attached to its side. The PAK–1M and PAK–2 are modifications of the PAK–1.

CHARACTERISTICS

Aperture	4.32 inches.
Length	9.43 inches.
Width	4.71 inches.
Height	11.79 inches.
Weight	5.76 pounds.

REFLECTOR SIGHT PBP–1A. The PBP–1A is a dive-bombing sight and a fixed gun sight. It is used in the new single-seat fighters and in the PE bomber. A range adjustment, 20 degrees elevation and 5 degrees depression, is effected by tilting the reflector. It is illuminated by daylight or by an electric bulb. The reticle consists of two concentric circles and a cross with range graduations.

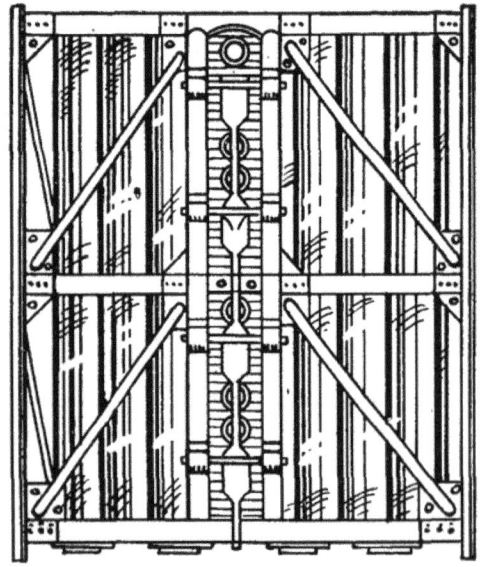
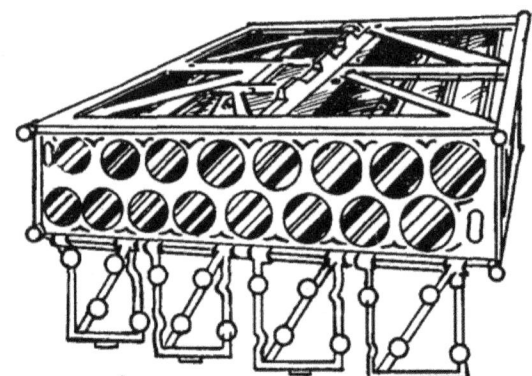

Figure 81.—AK–2 frangible sphere release assembly.

Focal length	2.39 inches.
Lens aperture	1.57 inches.
Angle formed by radius of small sighting ring	4 degrees.
Angle formed by radius of large sighting ring	6 degrees.
Limit of bombing angle	+ 20 degrees, − 5 degrees.
Height	6.28 inches.
Width	3.93 inches.
Depth (without illuminating installations)	4.32 inches.
Depth (with illuminating installations)	4.91 inches.
Weight	1.76 pounds.

REFLECTOR SIGHT PBP-1. The PBP-1 differs from the PBP-1A in that it is possible to put on a drift angle up to 20 degrees right or left. Weight is increased to 3.08 pounds.

REFLECTOR SIGHT PAN-23. The PAN-23 is similar to the PBP-1A in construction, and was developed along parallel lines. It has electrically illuminated reticles, which frame the target, for range computation. The reticles open to an angle of 17 degrees between the framing lines of the sight. It can be used as a gun sight for fixed or flexible guns and as a dive-bombing sight.

Depth	6.36 inches.
Width	3.45 inches.
Height	5.1 inches.
Focal length	2.63 inches.
Weight	1.85 pounds.

MECHANICAL GUN SIGHT PMP-3. The PMP-3 is designed for flexible machine guns. Lateral deflection correction, to compensate for the position of the target in relation to the axis of the gunner's plane, and vertical deflection correction are accomplished automatically.

It consists of a ring front sight and a bead rear sight. The distance between the two is adjustable, according to the speed of the gunner's aircraft. Corrections are effected by horizontal or vertical rotation of the ring, which is mounted on a ball and socket. Lateral deflection correction is accomplished by a cam rotated by a flexible shaft, which is actuated by a gear wheel on the turret ring. Vertical deflection correction is accomplished by a rod attached to the pivot point on the mount.

The sight is graduated for ranges up to 2,625 feet and air speeds up to 280 miles per hour.

Diameter of bead	0.1179 inch.
Diameter of rings	2.35, 1.17, and 0.27 inches.
Distance from ring to bead	5.3 to 8.96 inches.

MECHANICAL GUN SIGHT PMP-6, AUXILIARY APPARATUS PNB-2. The PMP-6 is a modification of the PMP-3. Distance from the ring to the bead is from 6.48 to 8.96 inches. For both sights, a special auxiliary PNB-2 is provided to adapt the sight for use as a bomb sight for horizontal flight. It is attached to the side of the sight.

The PNB-2 is graduated for 100- and 200-pound bombs, and for altitudes of from 165 to 2,300 feet. The gun is depressed below the longitudinal plane of the aircraft until an altitude reading corresponding to the altitude of the plane appears on a vertical sliding scale. This sets the proper dropping angle. Compensation for the different trajectories of the bombs is achieved by adjustments on a metal scale, which changes the dropping angle correspondingly. The bombardier then releases his bombs when the target appears in the ring and bead sight.

TELESCOPIC SIGHT OP-2L. This sight for fixed guns is used on a retractable mount in the belly of the fuselage of the PE-2 and IL-4. The line of sight is refracted 160 degrees forward to parallel the axis of the bore.

Length of eyepiece tube	14.14 inches.
Length of lens tube	9.9 inches.
External diameter of tube	1.92 inches.
Angle between lens tube and eyepiece tube	106 degrees.
Weight	6.6 pounds.
Magnification	None.
Field of Vision	40 to 42 degrees.
Aperture	0.7 to 0.78 inch.
Focal length	2.05 inches.

2. BOMB SIGHTS

a. General. The Goerz-Boykov optical sight was used for normal bombing in horizontal flight as early as 1941. The OPB-1, an obsolete model, was merely a telescopic sight for which the bombardier had to compute the dropping angle. In the OPB-2, computation of the dropping angle is determined automatically. The reflector sights PBP-1A and PBP-1 are used for dive bombing and firing of rocket projectiles. The NKPB-3 is a hand-operated, semiautomatic bomb sight.

b. Types of bomb sights. Three types of bomb sights are in general use.

BOMB SIGHT OPB–1. There are four models of this sight: the OPB–1, introduced in 1933; the OPB–1A, a shortened sight; the OPB–1M, introduced in 1939; and the OPB–1AM, a new shortened design. The later models are equipped with thermostatically-controlled electrical heating and are so designed that the telescope tube can be adjusted to the height of the bombardier's eyes.

The OBP–1, a copy of the Goerz-Boykov, is an optical sight. The dropping angle must be determined and then set on a scale. The telescope is housed in a ball joint to facilitate hand adjustment to center the bubble. The bearing ring is rotatable, to allow for the estimated drift angle. The vertical sighting angle may be adjusted by rotating a prism.

Ground speed is determined with the aid of a stop watch attached to the telescope. The time required to track an object directly beneath the plane through 45 degrees is measured. Ground speed then is computed. The dropping angle for the type of bomb, ground speed, and altitude is taken from tables. The dropping angle is set on the sight by means of an adjustable collar. The target is followed by rotating the sight angle knob. The bombs are released when the reticle intersects the target. Two buttons beside the release mechanism are used to guide the pilot to the right or to the left during the bomb run.

CHARACTERISTICS

	OPB–1M	OPB–1AM
Length	45.98 inches	38.51 inches.
Weight	13.2 pounds	12.12 pounds.
Magnification	1.2 x	1.35 x.
Field of vision	32 degrees	30 degrees.
Exit pupil	0.27 inch	0.31 inch.
Focal length	1.41 inches.	
Division of the Diopter scale	4.0 to −4.0.	
Diameter of the leveling bubble	0.13 to 0.21 inch.	
Diameter of the tube	1.96 inches.	
Sighting angle variation limits	−15 degrees to +75 degrees.	
Dropping angle variation limits	−5 degrees to +60 degrees.	
Smallest angular calibration	0.5 degree.	
Current consumption	24 V., 4.2 A.	
Base plate:		
Dimensions	8.13 x 4.32 x 4.48 inches.	
Weight	4.4 pounds.	

TELESCOPIC BOMB SIGHT OPB–2. The OPB–2, an adaptation of the Goerz-Boykov sight, was adopted in 1937 and has been used in recent bombers for bombing from horizontal flight. It is similar to the OPB–1, but is equipped with an automatic dropping angle computer, and may be used for both stationary and moving targets. The dropping-aiming computation procedure can be used in navigation for computing ground speed and drift. Ground speed is determined automatically and is applied by the computer during sighting. Readings can be taken from a dial on the computer.

After leveling the bomb sight, the bombardier sights the telescope on the target so that the level bubble and the reticle, coinciding with it, rest exactly on the target. The computer then is set in motion, and rotates the telescope vertically. The rate of rotation is controlled by the bombardier to hold the reticle on the target. He rotates a dial which changes the input rate of the computer by moving a gear over the surface of a rotating cone or spindle. The computer also moves the level bubble off the target as the telescope is rotated, and then on it again at the moment the bomb release point is reached. When the rotation of the telescope is synchronized with the speed of approach to the target, the computer is furnished with the target location and the ground speed of the plane. This data, together with the altitude, size of bomb, and drift settings, supplies the computer with all necessary information.

For navigation, the telescope also may be removed from its housing and fixed vertically for computation of ground speed and drift.

CHARACTERISTICS

Magnification	1.2 x.
Sighting angle	32 degrees.
Exit pupil	0.28 inch.
Adjustment of front sight	0.11 to 0.47 inch.
Sighting angle adjustment	90 degrees to 2 degrees 21 minutes.
Trail angle adjustment (automatic correction for drift)	0 to 12 degrees.
Drift adjustment	+ 20 degrees.
Maximum running time of clockwork mechanism	6 minutes.
Height scale range	3,280 to 39,396 feet.
Ground speed range	6.1 to 341.7 miles per hour.
Weight of footplate	40.56 pounds.
Length of telescope	42.44 inches.
Current (heating)	24 V, 6A.
Current (illuminating)	24 V, O2A.

BOMB SIGHT NKPB–3. This sight can be used only with a predetermined dropping angle.

	VAP-4M	VAP-6M	VAP-500	VAP-1000
Length .... (inches)..	64.8	44.4	103.1	133.62
Total capacity .... (gallons)..	21.7	11	92.5	186.3
Operational capacity. (gallons)..	20.3	10	83.2	177
Weight empty..... (pounds)..	42–46.4	22.4	188	275
Weight filled...... (pounds)..	264–275	136.6	1,089	2,191
Diameter of discharge opening............. (inches)..	5.1	4.7	7.9	....
Duration of spray release (seconds)..	3–6	3–4	3–9	6

Figure 82.– Characteristics and performance of nonpressure spray tanks.

The dropping angle is set on the dropping angle scale by turning a knurled knot. The target then is sighted through a Revi sight. By turning a knob on the left of the sight, the reticle cross is held on the target. A definitely perceptible resistance is felt when the preset dropping angle is reached, and a visual indication is provided in the graduated cross. In case of failure of electrical illumination, a mechanical auxiliary sight can be used. Leveling of sight is accomplished by means of longitudinal and horizontal segments and worm drives.

Allowance for drift can be made by rotating the sight in accordance with readings on a drift meter.

CHARACTERISTICS

Focal length_____ 1.9 inches.
Aperture_____ 1.72 inches.
Adjustment range of sighting angle_____ —15 to +85 degrees.
Adjustment range of dropping angle_____ —15 to +85 degrees.
Adjustment range of drift angle_ 30 degrees right or left.
Reticle arrangements_____ 2 course marks.
   Reticle cross with angle graduation (each graduation 0.5 degree).
Bombsight dimensions_____ 6.68 x 9.03 x 6.1 inches.
Base dimensions_____ 4.32 x 3.34 x 3.14 inches.
Bombsight weight_____ 6.6 pounds.
Base weight_____ 2.86 pounds.

Section V.. AIRPLANE SPRAY TANKS

1. GENERAL

Both pressure spray tanks and gravity-operated nonpressure spray tanks are used for disseminating chemical warfare agents from the air. These tanks are suspended under the wings or fuselage of the aircraft, attached to the bomb shackles. Spray release is effected mchanically or electrically over the bomb circuit. In emergency, full or empty tanks can be jettisoned.

2. NONPRESSURE SPRAY TANKS

Six models of nonpressure spray tanks, VAP, ranging in capacity from 11 to 185 gallons, are used (figs. 82, 83, 84, and 85). Two other models, VAP–200 and VAP–250, have been reported. They also can be adapted for scattering white phosphorous (fig. 83). This modification bears the designation ZAP.

The different models are identical functionally and are similar in design, consisting of a streamlined container with a discharge opening at the rear and an air intake in the front. When the lid sealing the discharge opening is lifted, the air intake opens automatically, admitting air, whch forces the contents out through the discharge opening.

The two smaller models of nonpressure tanks, having capacities of 11 and 22 gallons respectively, are fitted with an adjustable suspension bar, which makes it possible to install them in various slanting positions to help the flow within certain limits. The larger models lack this adjustment mechanism. All are identical in design, differing only in dimensions.

All nonpressure spray tanks have a relatively large opening and are characterized by a correspondingly high rate of flow.

When used as incendiary spray equipment, the tank is filled with 1.2- to 1.6-inch lumps of white phosphorus, which are kept moist by water or a calcium chloride solution. An auxiliary container is attached underneath the spray tank. It is filled

	ZAP-4	ZAP-6	ZAP-500
Total weight...(pounds)..	154	88	563.21
Weight WP filler..(pounds)..	66	31.9	264
Capacity auxiliary container:			
gallons..	1.12	1.12	6.7
pounds..	4.25	4.25	25.2
Weight filler in auxiliary container............................(pounds)..	15	15	88.7
Other characteristics...	See VAP-4M	See VAP-6M	See VAP-500

Figure 83.—Characteristics of nonpressure incendiary spray tanks.

467

with the smoke mixture, SIV, chlorosulfonic acid and sulphur trioxide. The spray tank and the auxiliary container are opened simultaneously. The phosphorus spray dries on contact with the smoke mixture and ignites in the air.

See figure 82, Characteristics of Nonpressure Spray Tanks, and figure 83, Characteristics of Nonpressure Incendiary Spray Tanks.

3. PRESSURE SPRAY TANKS

Airplane pressure spray tanks include the two models used for dissemination of smoke acid, DAP–100 and DAP–200, and the UKhAP–500 spray tank which can be used for dissemination of either war gases or smoke. All tanks are of a conventional design, consisting of a streamlined pressure container with a nozzle-tipped discharge pipe at the rear end of the tank. The filling is expelled by air pressure supplied by a compressed air cylinder in the plane.

Universal spray tank UKhAP–500 is a pressure spray tank of recent design that can be used for either war gas or smoke.

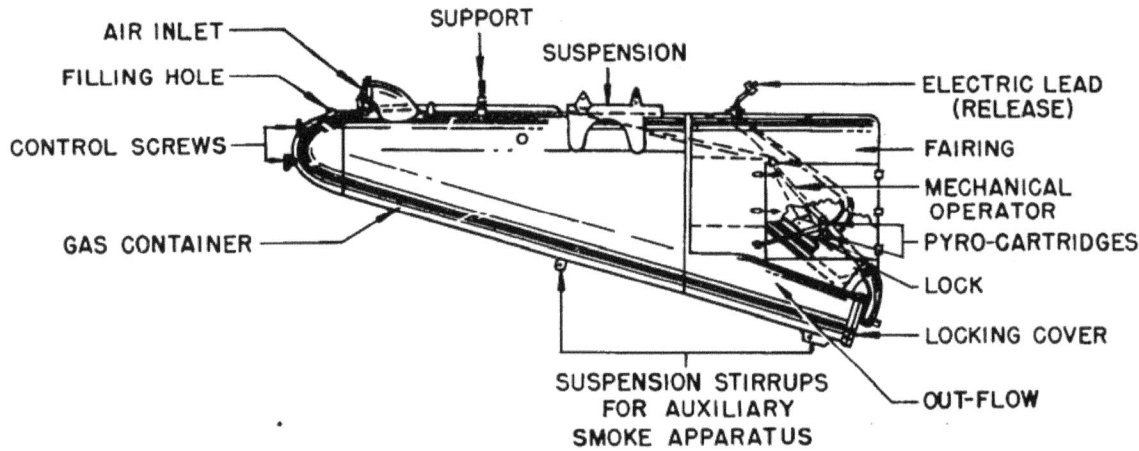

Figure 84.—Nonpressure spray tank VAP-500, VAP-1000.

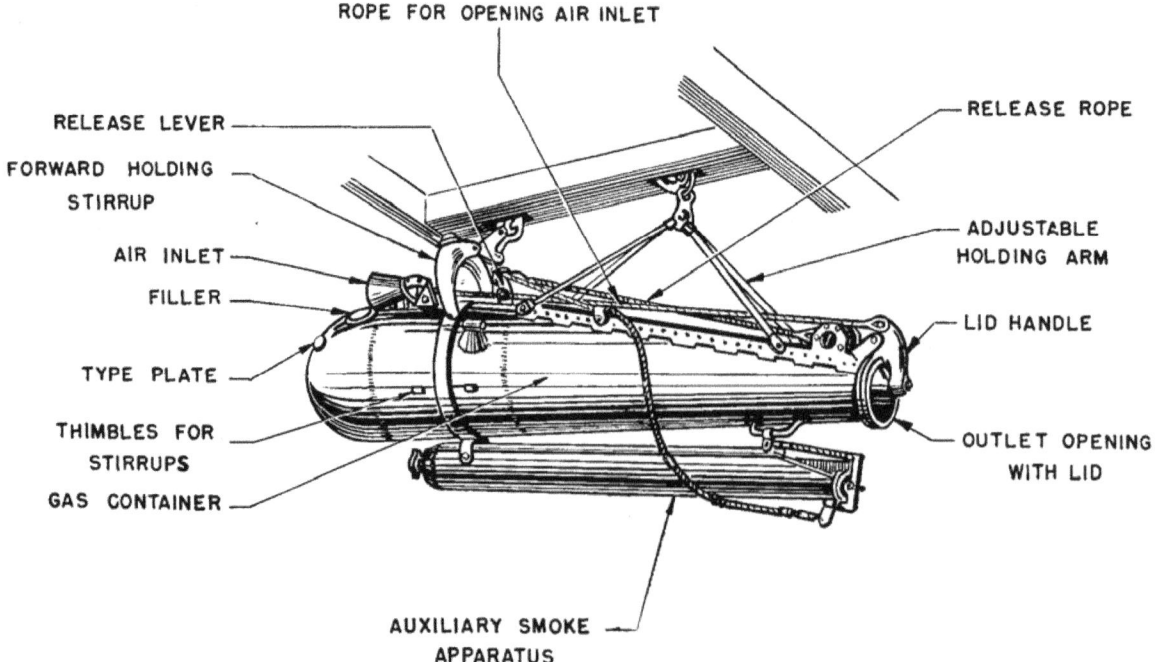

Figure 85.—Nonpressure spray tank VAP-6M with auxiliary smoke apparatus.

468

CHARACTERISTICS

Length	105.7 inches.
Operational capacity	81.6 gallons.
Weight empty	220 pounds.
Weight (filled with H)	1,100 pounds.
Weight (filled with smoke acid)	1,443.2 pounds.

Smoke spray tank DAP–100 has a total capacity of 26.4 gallons and an operational capacity of 22.4 gallons. With a 0.62-inch nozzle, the tank can be emptied in from 20 to 25 seconds. It is reported that this tank can lay a vertical smoke screen approximately 1,641 to 2,188 yards long, 55 to 82

Designation	Types of signals	Frequency (megacycles)	Transmitter power (watts)	Receiver sensitivity (microvolts)	Weight (pounds)	Power supply	Remarks
RSI–3 (transmitter)	Voice	3.5 to 5	3		4.4	Run 30 A	2 tubes; oscillator and modulator.
RSI–3 (receiver)	do	5 fixed frequencies 3.5, 3.8, 4.125, 4.25, 4.4.		60/10v	4.4	2.5-volt filament battery; 120-volt plate battery.	5 tube superheterodyne.
RSI–4 (receiver)	Voice, M. C. W.	3.7 to 6.05 (continuously tunable).		60/10v	4.4	RU. 11 A	6 tube superheterodyne.
RSWS–1		38 to 48					This V. H. F. appeared in 1941, but has not been reported operationally since.
RSI–6							
RSI–5							
RPD–35							
RSB–Bis (transmitter).	Voice, C. W.	2.5 to 4.05; 4.05 to 6.3; 6.3 to 9.5; 9.5 to 12.0.	13 to 36 (A1); 9 to 24 (A3)		29.7	RVK–300A	2-stage crystal-controlled transmitter; voice modulation without amplification.
US (receiver) (part of RSB–Bis).	do	0.175 to 0.350; 0.350 to 0.900; 0.900 to 2; 2.15 to 5; 5 to 12.		10/10v	12.1	RV–11A	8 valve superheterodyne; can be fitted with remote control by bowden cable.
US–3		0.625 to 3.75					
US–4		0.625 to 3.75					
RSR–1		2.5 to 6					
DVINA–Bis							
RSR							Old equipment similar to RSB–Bis for reconnaissance aircraft.
RES							
SRM							
RPK 2 radio compass	C. W., M. C. W., voice, visual indicators for D/F.	0.168 to 0.420; 0.420 to 1.		1/10v	22.8	RUN–10	This installation is a full radio compass with rotatable loop and remote controls.
RPK 10		0.270 to 0.850					This is a fixed loop homing set; reliability and accuracy is doubtful. 6 tube superheterodyne.
RPK–12 homing set							
RPK MN 26J homing set.							Reported to be an American equipment to replace the RPK 10; it is found on the latest Aircobras.
Notch I, blind landing.		29.6 to 43.9					
Blind landing set to replace Notch I.		59 to 96					
13 PS		0.275 to 0.550					Receiver only.
13 SK (transmitter)	Voice, C. W	2.5 to 4.48 in 2 bands.	40				
13 SK (receiver)		2.5 to 5					
14 SK (transmitter)	Voice, C. W	3.37 to 4.61	20				
14 SK (receiver)	do	3.37 to 5					
15 SK (transmitter)	C. W	4 to 5	20				

Figure 86.—Characteristics of Soviet airborne radio equipment.

469

yards in depth, which provides effective obscuration from 8 to 20 minutes under average conditions.

Section VI. RADIO AND ELECTRONIC EQUIPMENT

1. AIRBORNE RADIO

Soviet air-borne radio units (figs. 86 through 98) operate in the high frequency band. The fighter sets are small, lightweight, and of simple circuit design. This is characteristic of all Soviet airborne units, which are several years behind the communication sets built in the United States. For example, the RSI–3, which was used widely in 1945, employs a battery-pack power supply. By the end of the year, it was being replaced by RSI–4, which draws its cathode current from the plane's battery and its plate supply from a generator. Both sets have low receiver sensitivity (60 microvolt/10v.), and a transmitter output of only 3 watts, which indicates that they are used for short range work only.

A very high frequency set, the RSVS (33 to 42 megacycles) was used at later dates. It can be assumed that a set operating on such a narrow band would be impractical because of congestion of traffic.

R/T INSTALLATION, RSI–3. The RSI–3 is a R/T set with five fixed frequencies in the receiver. It is used in single-seat aircraft. The equipment is used for air-to-ground communication. Both transmitter and receiver have shock mounts.

TRANSMITTER RSI–3. See figure 88.

Circuit	Single-stage, self-excited.
Frequencies	3.5 to 5 mc/s.
Facility	Radiophone.
Power output	3 watts.
Tubes	2 Pentodes type 6P3. Oscillator and modulation amplifier.
Power supply	Dynamotor RUN30A.
Size	6.3 x 5.1 x 8.2 inches.
Weight	4.4 pounds.

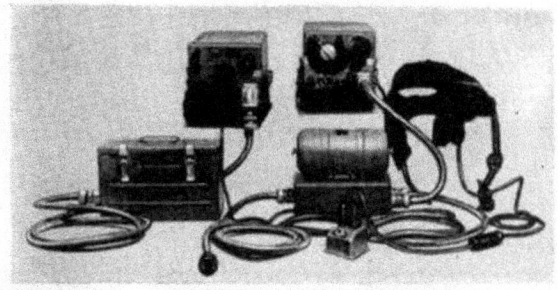

Figure 87.—R/T installation for RSI–3.

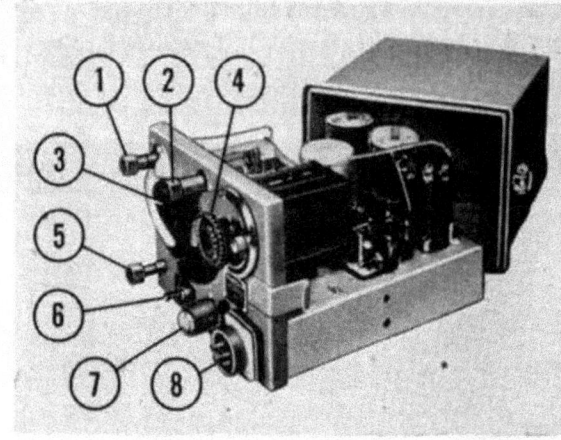

① Antenna post from receiver	⑤ Ground
② Antenna post	⑥ Switch for illumination
③ Primary tuner	⑦ Indicator in antenna circuit
④ Antenna tuning	⑧ Power plug

Figure 88.—Transmitter for RSI–3

RECEIVER RSI–3. See figure 89.

Circuit	5-tube, 7-stage superheterodyne.
Frequencies	Fixed frequency (3.5, 3.8 4.105, 4.25, 4.4 mc/s).
Facilities	Radiophone, MCW.
Sensitivity	60 microvolt/10v.
Tubes	1 Heptode SB242, 3HF Pentodes SO241.
Power supply	2.1v lead and cell.
Size	6.3 x 5.1 x 7 inches.
Weight	4.4 pounds.

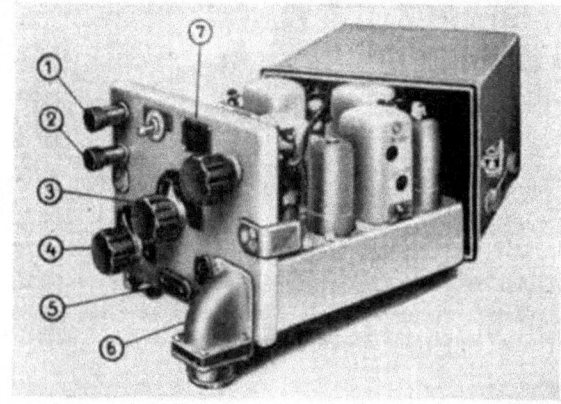

① Antenna post	④ Fine tuner
② Ground	⑤ Phone jack
③ Frequency selector switch	⑥ Power plug
	⑦ Volume control

Figure 89.—Receiver for RSI–3.

470

RECEIVER INSTALLATION RSI–4. The RSI–4 (fig. 90) is a continuously tunable R/T receiver for single-seat aircraft.

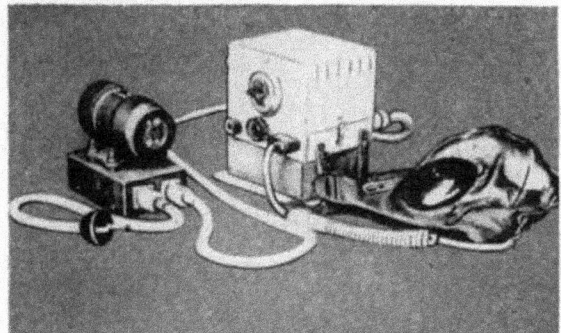

Figure 90.—Receiver installation for RSI–4.

RECEIVER RSI–4. See figure 91.

Circuit	6-tube, 9-stage superheterodyne.
Frequencies	3.7 to 6.05 mc/s.
Facilities	Radiophone, MCW.
Sensitivity	60 microvolt/10v.
Tubes	3 Pentodes 6K7, 1 Heptodes 6A8, 1 double diode triode 6G7, 1 output Pentode 6F6.
Power supply	Dynamotor RU–11A.
Size	5.9 x 5.9 x 4.7 inches.
Weight	4.4 pounds.

Figure 91.—Receiver RSI–4. Note that receiver also is used in tank mounted radio station 9–R.

AIRCRAFT UNIT RSB–BIS. For multi-seat aircraft air-to-air and air-to-ground communications. Box in upper left corner in figure 92 is dummy antenna for tuning transmitter.

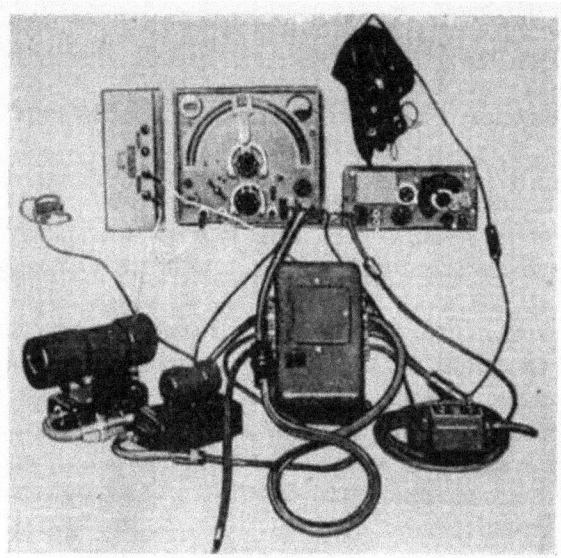

Figure 92.—Radio station RSB–bis.

TRANSMITTER RSB–BIS. A two-stage, crystal-controlled transmitter (fig. 93). Modulation during R/T is without amplification via microphone transformer on control grid of the output tube.

Frequencies	2.5 to 4.05 mc/s, 4.05 to 6.3 mc/s, 6.3 to 9.5 mc/s, and 9.5 to 12.0 mc/s.
Facilities	CW, radiophone.
Power	13 to 36 watts CW, 9 to 24 watts phone.
Tubes	Triode GU–4. Output Tetrode GKE–100.
Power supply	Dynamotor RVK–300A.
Size	13.8 x 12.6 x 7.9 inches.
Weight	29.7 pounds.

Figure 93.—Transmitter for RSB–bis.

471

RECEIVER US. See figure 94.

Frequencies................ 175 to 350 kc/s; 350 to 900
kc/s; 900 to 2,000 kc/s; 2.15
to 5 mc/s; 5 to 12 mc/s.
I. F. frequency............. 115 kc/s.
Sensitivity................ 10 microvolt/10V.
Tubes..................... 4 Pentodes 6K7, 1 Pentode 6J7,
1 Heptode 6L7, 1 double-diode
6K6, 1 Triode 6F5.
Power supply.............. Dynamotor RU-11A.
Size...................... 12.6 x 5.3 x 6.7 inches.
Weight.................... 12.5 pounds.

① Primary tuner   ⑥ Frequency switch
② Remote tuner connection ⑦ CW R/T switch
③ Fine tuner   ⑧ A. V. C. switch
④ Antenna plug   ⑨ Frequency chart
⑤ Volume   ⑩ Power cable

Figure 94.– Receiver US.

D/F RECEIVER UNIT RPK-2. Used for homing
with visual indicator, and for direction-finding. It
also can be used as a normal receiver for CW, MCW,
and radiophone. See figure 95.

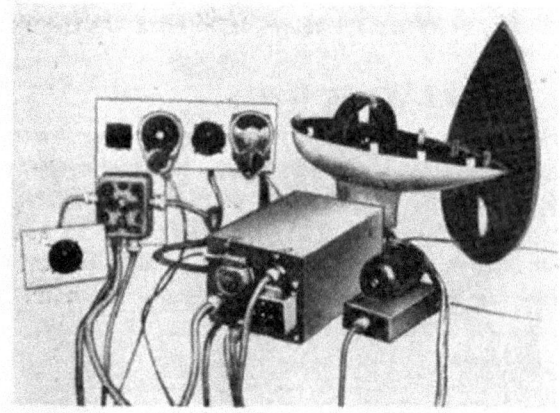

Figure 95.—D/F receiver unit for RPK-2.

RECEIVER RPK-2. This receiver (fig. 96) is
equipped with A. V. C. and uses U. S. type metal
tubes.

Frequencies................ 168 to 420 kc/s; 420 to 1,000
kc/s.
I. F. stages............... 112 kc/s.
Sensitivity................ 1 microvolt/10V.
Tubes..................... 1 Heptode 6A8, 1 Heptode 6L7,
1 Pentode 6K7, 1 Pentode
6F6, 3 Triodes 6C5, 3 double
diodes 6H6.
Power supply.............. Dynamotor RUN-10.
Size...................... 16.9 x 9.45 x 8.25 inches.
Weight.................... 22.8 pounds.

Figure 96.– Receiver for RPK-2.

INTERCOMMUNICATIONS UNIT SPU-3.

Amplifier.................. Single-stage, low-frequency.
Tube...................... Pentode 6F6.
Power supply.............. Dynamotor RUN 10–A.
Size...................... Amplifier and dynamotor unit
7.1 x 13.8 x 6.3 inches.
Weight.................... 20 pounds (less cables).

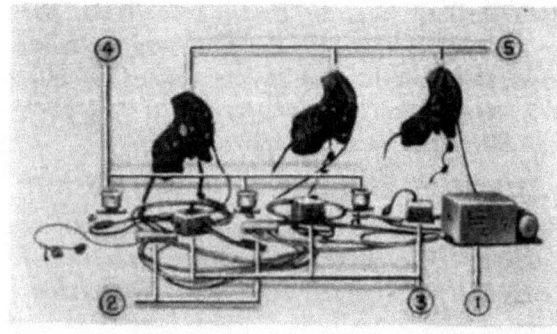

① Dynamotor and ampli-   ④ Buzzers and push but-
fier   tons
② Junction boxes   ⑤ Helmets (phone and
③ Individual control   throat mikes)
boxes

Figure 97.—Intercommunications unit for SPU-3.

472

Figure 98.—Aircraft battery 12A-10.

Aircraft Battery 12A-10. See figure 93.

Cells_____ 12 in felt-lined metal case.
Strength_____ 24V, 10 AMP.
Size_____ 9.85 x 8.66 x 7.48 inches.
Weight_____ 35.2 pounds.

2. AIRBORNE RADAR

The Soviet Union made little use of airborne radar of any type. A few ASV–MK II sets are used on sea-reconnaissance aircraft, and a small number of sets were obtained from the British. The latter, however, could not be used to full advantage due to lack of suitable aircraft. The Soviets received 620 SCR–695 sets on Lend-Lease, and employed them in the lead aircraft to facilitate ground control.

3. AIRBORNE ELECTRONIC NAVIGATION AIDS

No use of radar for navigational purposes has been reported. The Soviet D/F receivers are used in connection with ground radio nets. The principal receiver used is the RPK–2 which appears to be a copy of the Bendix radio compass, operating on frequencies of from 168 to 1,000 kilocycles. A fixed-loop homing set, the RPK–10, is used in a few day fighters and night fighters and in the lead aircraft of ground attack fighters. A RPK–12 was developed

to replace the RPK–2, but the performance was so poor that it became unpopular with the air crews. Production was discontinued.

Ground aids used with the above sets include the following:

CW transmitters which are within the frequency range of the air-borne receivers.

Radio transmitters in the 160 to 1,000-kilocycle band. These stations operate on a fixed frequency in rear areas, and change frequencies and identification approximately every 2 to 3 hours in the forward areas.

1,500-watt omni-directional beacons with a range of from 600 to 900 miles, used to mark turning point on the more important flight routes. These are supplemented by smaller (500 watt) beacons located near the airfields and between the more powerful transmitters and the flight routes. Identification, repeated from 2 to 3 times, is followed by a continuous note for approximately 20 seconds. Then the cycle is repeated.

Directional beacons. They transmit 16 letters on 32 compass segments by means of an array of 16 antennas. Range approximately 700 miles.

Ground radio D/F stations in the 3800–4150 kilocycle band, used to provide linear bearings on the home field. Located at airports, these transmitters operate only upon interrogation by aircraft.

Blind landing equipment is used. A few British SBA sets were purchased, but in insufficient quantity to have any influence on blind landing procedure in the Soviet Air Forces. The Soviet *Notch* I operates on the Loring principle in the 29.6–43.9 megacycles. A set operating on 59–86 megacycles also is reported.

4. PRIMARY POWER SUPPLY

Radio and radar dynamotors operate on power drawn from lead-acid type storage batteries consisting of 6 or 12 cells (12 volts or 24 volts). Known types are 55 amperes, 12 volt, and 5, 10, 15, 30, and 60 amperes, 24 volt. The 24-volt, 10-ampere battery (fig. 98) can be used as a basis for estimating sizes and weights of the other types. It measures 9.85 by 8.66 by 7.48 inches and weighs 35.2 pounds, including the metal felt-lined case. These batteries are charged by the plane's generator (fig. 99).

Type	Output (watts)	5-minute overload	Output (amps)	Volts	R. P. M.	Weight (pounds)	Length (inches)	Height (inches)	Diameter (inches)	Remarks
65–10–350	350	525	12.7	27.5	3,200–5,900	16.1	8.45	5.75	4.34	Can be turned either direction.
65–20–650	650	975	23.6	27.5	3,200–5,900	25.3	9.82	6.55	5.12	Do.
65–1000	1,000	1,500	37	27	3,200–5,900	31.7	11.97	6.70	5.04	Can be turned either direction. Control for common positive pole of armature and field.
DSF–500	350	....	29	13.5	1,600–3,200	26.4	12.40	....	5.04	

Figure 99.—Aircraft generators.

5. GROUND RADAR

The U. S. S. R. started production of an early warning type of radar in June 1941 and produced a few sets operating on approximately 400 megocycles. This set was entirely original in design and shows no influence from other nations. An RGO, used as a transmitter, produces an electro-magnetic field 60 miles long and 75 miles wide in opposing directions. Two receiver units, RPO, are set up at the ends of the range. As soon as a target crosses the 120 mile beam it becomes visible on a cathode ray tube.

A few gun-laying radar sets were manufactured by the Soviets and were used by the Red Navy. However, a large number of British gun-laying radar units were observed in the Moscow area, so it may be assumed that production on this type of equipment was stopped when British and United States units became available through lend-lease.

A Soviet set, RUS–2, is of British origin and is used for measuring altitude and range. This set is mounted on a truck, with a two-arm antenna mount extending through the roof. Three small antennas are at each end. Another set, the RUS–5, has slightly greater range, approximately 100 miles as contrasted with 75 miles of the RUS–2.

6. FUTURE TRENDS

The contacts which the Soviets have had with United States, British, and German equipment probably will result in positive advancement of Soviet equipment.

From the United States, the U. S. S. R. received the following air-borne units on lend-lease:

SCR–695 (I. F. F.)
SCR–718 (radar altimeter)
MN–267
AN/ARN–7 (radio compass)

Testing equipment	Communications equipment
TS–10/APN	BC–453
TS–16/APN	BC–454
IE–46	BC–455
IE–12	BC–456
RC–54	BC–457
RC–55	BC–458
	BC–696
	SCR–277

The Soviets are thought to have captured the files of the German Works Commissions of the Radar Committee, which examined all captured Allied radar equipment. The German research probably will be exploited.

Impeding progress in electronic development is the lack of sufficiently trained personnel to manufacture the equipment, and the greatly retarded development of the vacuum tube industry. Soviet tubes, at present, are limited in variety and are of poor quality. Characteristics vary so much in the same series of tubes that it is impossible to guarantee that any one tube will replace one of the same model. Unless the Soviet vacuum tube industry can widen its range and improve its product, radio and radar development will of necessity be slow and difficult.

Section VII. COLD WEATHER OPERATION

1. GENERAL

The Soviet air forces are able to conduct operations in the coldest weather. All aircraft, except for a few types which do not require them, may be fitted with skis. In most instances, the skis are retractable. Flying boats and float-planes are fitted with special skids for operations from ice.

2. CARE OF ENGINES

Oil is drained from United States engines, procured by the Soviet air forces through lend-lease, at the completion of operations. Hot oil is poured into the engines for starting. Oil is heated to 170° F.

Figure 100.— Starting an engine in extreme cold.

in a specially designed truck, equipped with an oil or wood-burning boiler. It then is pumped into the planes. This operation requires a minimum of time and does not delay take-off preparations.

Oil is not drained from Soviet aircraft. It has been reported that clearances in Soviet engines are much smaller than those of United States design and that Soviet aircraft, therefore, use a much thinner type of oil.

Heaters are installed and operate approximately 10 minutes, during which time American engines are filled with hot oil (fig. 100). Engine covers and heating equipment are removed, the propellers are turned at least four revolutions, and eight shots of primer are applied. Engines start, usually on the first attempt, in from 13 to 18 minutes from the beginning of starting operations. Engines are idled for approximately 10 minutes for thorough warm up. No difficulty seems to be encountered in fighter engines overheating when idling.

Soviet engines use
is attached for use as a reserve tank.

Engine covers are of quilted cotton approximately three-fourths inch thick. They fit closely and permit the propeller to turn. In liquid-cooled engines, the heating duct is introduced at the rear lower section of the engine.

During the warm-up, all traps are opened and drained to insure that there is no water in the traps and that none remains frozen. All traps are drained at the completion of operation.

In extremely cold weather, air-cooled engines are fitted with an aluminum baffle inside of the engine cowling. This baffle has sliding shutters, which are controlled mechanically from the cockpit. It is believed these are necessary both for warming up and to prevent freezing while gliding.

All tubing is wrapped first with paper, then with wool cloth, and finally with asbestos-covered, fireproof material. This is considered necessary at temperatures of −86° F. or less.

A 70–30-percent mixture of alcohol and glycerine by volume is used in hydraulic systems. This mixture will not freeze above −140° F.

Either "Prestone" or a Soviet antifreeze compound of ethyl-glyco is used in liquid-cooled engines.

On completion of each operation, a check is made to insure that brakes have been released completely to prevent their freezing in a locked position.

3. SPECIAL EQUIPMENT

a. PSE–1 Ignition Apparatus. THE PSE–1 special ignition apparatus produces a more intensive sparking than the starting magnetos. This device operates on the principle of battery ignition, although it is a part of airdrome equipment, it may be carried in aircraft. It is designed to give from 200 to 250 starts. The alkaline accumulators employed do not require special care, and are not sensitive to low temperatures.

The PSE–1 consists of a starting coil with vibrator, and alkaline 12-volt accumulator battery, and a starting push button. It is housed in a wooden case, divided into three parts by removable partitions. The largest compartment holds the battery, which is protected from cold by a felt layer 0.23 inch thick. The coil is fixed to the movable partition wall inside of the second compartment. The third compartment holds a reserve of electrical leads. On the

Page 129 and later pages missing.

CHAPTER XII

MAPS, CONVENTIONAL SIGNS, AND SYMBOLS

Section I. MAP SYSTEMS

1. INTRODUCTION

Soviet tactical signs and symbols have undergone considerable change, particularly since 1942. These changes have consisted largely of the simplification of complex signs by more abundant use of abbreviations and by the introduction of new signs for recently introduced weapons, such as self-propelled guns.

Soviet usage is not always consistent, even in official manuals. Different arms and services frequently use signs which vary from those used by other arms and services. This is particularly applicable to the signs for fortifications used by the engineers and by the infantry.

Tactical symbols representing friendly troops are red. Those for enemy troops are blue, the converse of United States usage. On black and white maps or charts, friendly troops are represented by solid heavy lines and enemy troops are indicated by lighter, double lines.

Soviet military abbreviations and conversion tables of the old Russian and metric systems of weights and measures are published in TM 30–544.

2. COORDINATE SYSTEM

The U. S. S. R. is divided into 28 map sectors, each 6° wide. The map sectors are divided by parallels, 4° apart into rows of coordinate zones. Coordinate zones are numbered consecutively from 1 to 32, starting at Greenwich and continuing east. Numbers for coordinate zones are derived from the numbers of the map sectors in which they fall. The number of a coordinate zone is determined by subtracting 30 from the number of the map sector in which it falls or by adding 30 if the map sector number is less than 30 (fig. 1).

A rectangular grid system is superimposed on each coordinate zone. The center of coordinates is established at the intersection of the equator and the central, or base, meridian of zone, that is, at the third, ninth, fifteenth etc., meridians. At the origin of this coordinate system, the value of the "X" coordinate is zero, and the value of "Y" coordinate is 500 kilometers. In the Soviet system the "X" coordinate is vertical, and the "Y" coordinate is horizontal because a large positive value is assigned to the "Y" coordinate, a value larger than half the width of a coordinate zone at the equator. The "Y" coordinate never becomes a negative value. The "X" coordinate, however, becomes negative in the southern hemisphere.

The length of a side of each grid square is equal to an even number of centimeters and represents an even number of kilometers on the ground. For example, the side of the grid square of a 1 : 25,000 map is 4 centimeters and represents 1 kilometer on the ground. The side of the grid square of 1 : 100,000 map is 2 centimeters, which represents 2 kilometers on the ground.

The full coordinate is written in the lower left corner of each sheet, the horizontal coordinate preceded by the number of the coordinate zone. The vertical or "X" coordinate indicates the distance in kilometers from the equator. The difference between the value of the horizontal or "Y" coordinate and 500 indicates the distance east of the base meridian of the coordinate zone if "Y" is greater than 500, and the distance in kilometers west of the base meridian if "Y" is less than 500. Thus, the numbers 5748 and 8690 locate the lower left corner of a map 5,748 kilometers north of the equator 190 kilometers east of the base meridian of the 8th zone. The full coordinate is printed only in the lower left corner of the map. Elsewhere only the last two numbers are given. In military communications, the "X" coordinate always is given first.

Although the decision to change from the old Russian system of weights and measures was made in the early 1920's, military maps employing the old

477

system still are in use. The old style military maps use the geographic coordinate system. The distances between consecutive vertical and horizontal lines are measured in *duims* (inches), which represent an even number of *versts* (0.663 miles) on the ground. For example, the size of a square on a 1: 84,000 map is 1 *duim*, which represents 1 *verst* on the ground. Prior to the adoption of the new system of coordinates, a metric grid was superimposed on the geographical grid of the old style maps.

3. TYPES AND CLASSIFICATION OF MAPS

Military maps of the U. S. S. R. are classified according to scale as strategic, operational, and tactical maps.

Maps of small scale are intended for general planning and strategic studies. In the Red Army, metric system maps 1: 500,000, 1: 1,000,000, and 1: 500,000,000 and old system maps 1: 1,680,000 and 1: 4,000,000 are utilized as strategic maps. These maps carry the usual geographic data.

Intermediate scale maps are intended for the planning of operations, for the scheduling of movements of large units and supplies, and for the selection of positions and communications systems. The operational maps generally include communications data classified according to the capacity and condition of roads, ridge lines, defiles, and other major terrain features and economic data. Operational maps of the new system include those of scales 1: 200,000 to 1: 1,050,000. The standard operational map of the Red Army is the new 1: 200,000 map. The collection of data for this map was started in 1925. Relief is shown by tinting and by contour lines. In the compilation of data for this map, particular attention was centered on strict classification of railroad and road nets and on population and population statistical data. In sparsely populated areas, this map also is intended for tactical use.

Three old style operational maps exist. The 1: 210,000 (1 *duim* equals 5 *versts*) map covers the Caucasus and the Turkmen S. S. R. The data on this map are old, and it is being replaced by the new 1: 200,000 map. The 1: 420,000 (1 *duim* equals 10 *versts*) map covers all the European S. S. R., neighboring western countries, Caucasus, Asia Minor, and

parts of Siberia. The 1: 1,050,000 (1 *duim* equals 25 *versts*) map covers all of the European S. S. R. and extends westward to Berlin, Prague, and the Adriatic. It is one of the oldest Russian military maps.

Maps of scale 1: 100,000 and larger are used as tactical maps. The new 1: 50,000, supplemented by 1: 25,000, is the basic tactical map. These maps include not only general topographic data, but also information regarding inhabitable localities, road nets, stream crossings and their condition, steep descents and ascents, classification of roads in terms of capacity, surface river system including speed of the current, and relief with emphasis on difficult terrain, orientation points, forests, and other vegetation by type.

On the 1: 25,000, 1: 50,000, and 1: 100,000 maps, relief is indicated by 5-, 10-, and 20-meter contour lines respectively. Hachure marks are used where relief cannot be adequately represented by contour lines. Prominent heights and depressions are indicated by a number which represents the difference in altitude between the top and the base, heights indicated by a plus sign and depressions by a minus sign. Supplementary tactical maps, 1: 10,000, are prepared as necessary during operations by the Military Topographic Service agencies in the field and by the Artillery Topographic Service.

In the old system the basic tactical map is 1: 42,000. Relief is shown by contours. Originally these maps were in black only, but later four colors were added, contours in black, water in blue, forests in green, and other terrain features in brown. The 1: 84,000 map of the western area also is used.

4. SPECIAL MAPS AND MAP SUBSTITUTES

Ground and air photomaps are used extensively to familiarize reconnaissance personnel with territory controlled by the enemy, to facilitate centralized fire control and target designation, to study defilades, and to facilitate coordination of infantry and artillery.

The Soviet photo-reconnaissance doctrines closely approximate standard United States practice. Air photographs, both oblique and vertical, are augmented by ground photo panoramas of critical sectors. In preparing photomaps for the use of tank and mechanized forces, in addition to appropriate marginal notes and contour lines, steep slopes are indicated by an arrow whose direction and length represent the direction and length of the slope. A fraction is placed near such an arrow, its numerator indicating degree of slope and denominator indicating the length of the slope in meters.

Stereoscopes are used extensively to facilitate tactical and operational·terrain map studies.

5. MAP INDEX SYSTEMS

Maps distributed by the Military Topographic Division of the General Staff of the Red Army are printed in sheets, the number of sheets for each map depending on the size of the area represented and the scale of the map. Index systems are necessary to catalog the sheets of each map. These systems consist of small schematic maps, which are divided by horizontal and vertical lines into rectangles or by meridians and parallels into trapezoids. Each rectangle or trapezoid represents a separate sheet of the map. Maps printed in the old measures are indexed in several systems. Maps printed in the metric system are all indexed in the same system.

a. Old Systems. There are two index systems for maps printed in the old measures. The first system used, if there are comparatively few sheets in a set, consists of numbering the sheets in sequence with Arabic or Roman numerals. With large-scale maps, this system becomes cumbersome. The second system consists of sheets arranged in horizontal rows, each row numbered with a Roman numeral. In each row, sheets are numbered in consecutive series of Arabic numerals, starting with "1." Thus, all sheets in the same vertical column have the same Arabic number. Each sheet of the map is designated by the Roman number of its row, and its Arabic number within that row.

b. Metric System. There is one index for all metric system maps. The basic map is the 1:1,000,000, which is divided into sectors and horizontal rows. Each row is designated by a Roman capital letter, starting with "A" at the equator. The height of each row is 4° of latitude. Thus, each sheet of the 1:1,000,000 map is 6° of longitude wide and 4° of latitude high. Each sheet is designated by naming its sector and its horizontal row. For example, the index number of the sheet which contains Smolensk is N–36 (fig. 1).

479

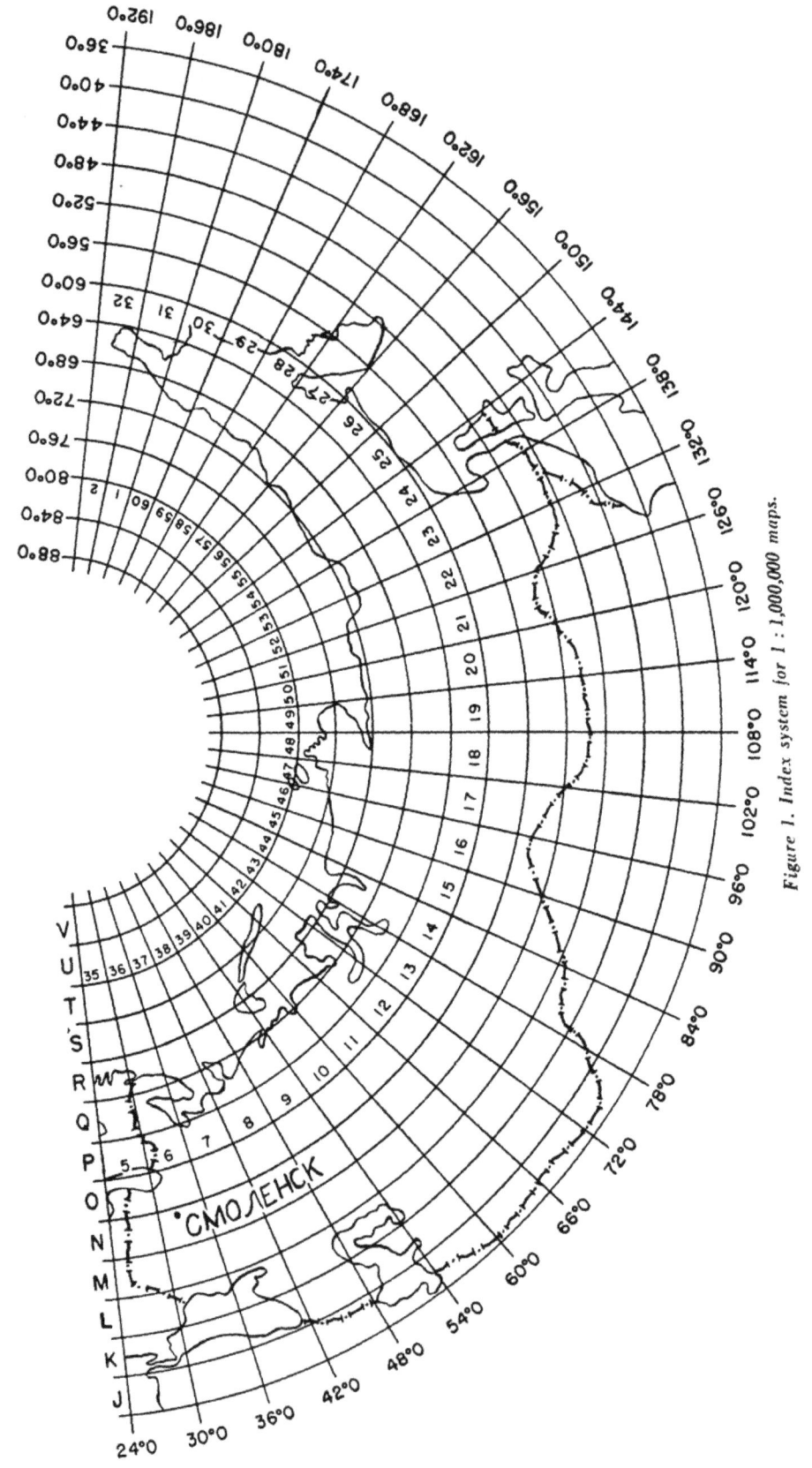

Figure 1. Index system for 1 : 1,000,000 maps.

480

Each sheet of the 1:1,000,000 map is divided for indexing larger-scale metric maps. A 1:1,000,000 sheet is divided into four 1:500,000 sheets, lettered А, Б, В, Г, (A, B, V, G). Thus, the sheet of the 1:500,000 map which contains Smolensk is designated by naming the sheet of the 1:1,000,000 map and by the appropriate letter, N–36–A (fig. 2).

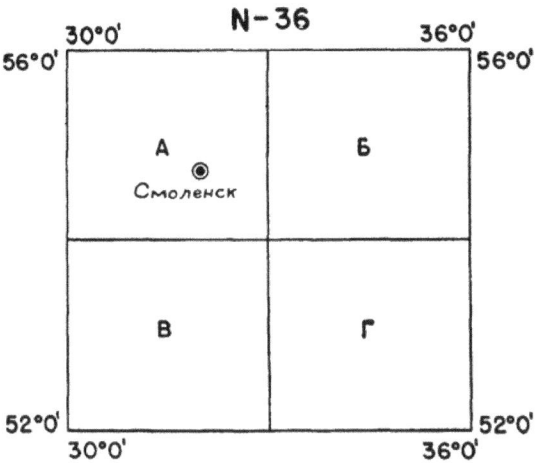

Figure 2. Index system for 1 : 500,000 maps.

Each 1:500,000 sheet is further divided into 18 1:200,000 sheets, each sheet designated by a Roman numeral, I through XVIII. The index number for the sheet of the 1:200,000 map which contains Smolensk is, for example, N–36–V (fig. 3).

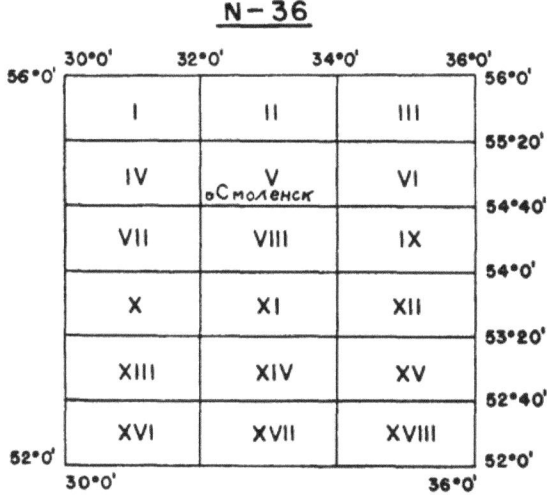

Figure 3. Index system for 1 : 200,000 maps.

Each 1:200,000 sheet is divided into 144 1:100,000 sheets. Each 1:100,000 sheet is numbered

with an Arabic numeral, 1 through 144. The index number for the sheet of the 1:100,000 map which contains Smolensk is N–36–41 (fig. 4).

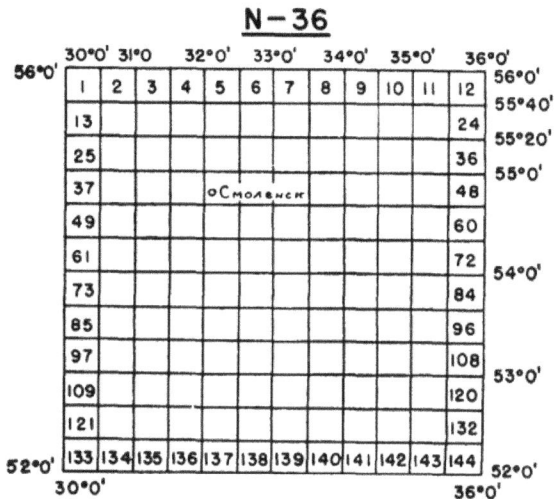

Figure 4. Index system for 1 : 100,000 maps.

Each sheet of the 1:100,000 map is divided into four 1:50,000 sheets, lettered А, Б, В, Г (A, B, V, G). Thus, the index number of the sheet of the 1:50,000 map which contains Smolensk is N–36–41–V (fig. 5). Each sheet of the 1:50,000 map is divided into four 1:25,000 sheets, lettered а, б, в, г (a, b, v, g). The

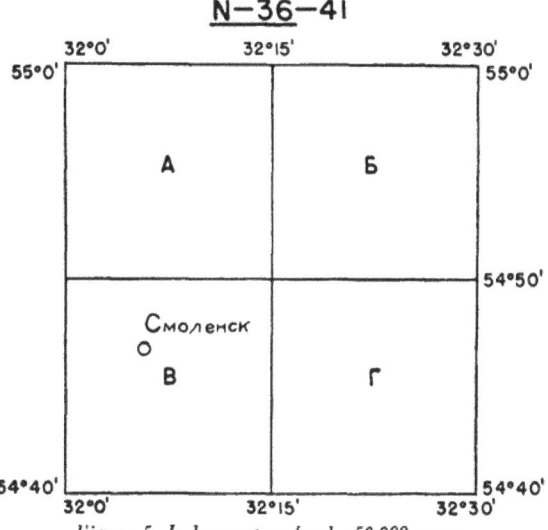

Figure 5. Index system for 1 : 50,000 maps.

index number of the sheet of the 1:25,000 map which contains Smolensk is N–36–41–B–a (fig. 6). Each sheet of the 1:25,000 map is divided into four 1:10,000 sheets, each designated by an Arabic number 1, 2, 3, or 4. Thus, the index number of the sheet of the 1:10,000 map which contains Gorki is N–36–41–B–g–3 (fig. 6).

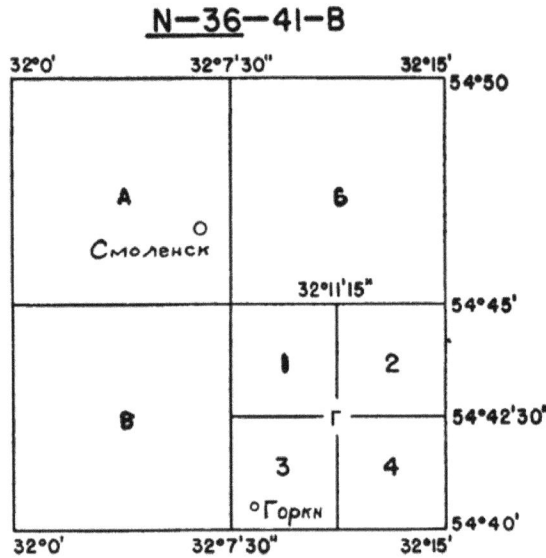

Figure 6. Index system for 1 : 25,000 and 1 : 10,000 maps.

6. SUPPLY OF MAPS

In peacetime, the Military Topographic Service of the General Staff of the Red Army is responsible for the distribution of regularly expendable maps for training and for general service purposes. Distribution is made on the basis of prescribed allotments.

The Military Topographic Service issues maps directly to the staffs of Military Districts, to independent armies, to the Main Administrations of the Peoples' Commissariat of Defense, to the Red Navy, and to the NKVD and the NKGB.

The Military Topographic Divisions of the staffs of military districts supply the other divisions of the staff and other organizations of the military district, including Red Army field units and formations, training installations, flotillas and training units of the Red Fleet, and NKVD and NKGB organizations.

The Chiefs of Staffs of military units and the Chiefs of Training Sections of military schools are responsible for initiation of requests for maps to Military Topographic Divisions of the staffs of military districts. They also are responsible for the distribution of maps within the units and the schools and for maintenance of topographic supply records.

The requisitions for maps by subordinate organizations are made on the basis of their allotments and on their programs for the year. These requisitions are consolidated annually by the military district and forwarded to the Military Topographic Division of the General Staff. Newly printed maps are distributed to the Peoples' Commissariat of Defense without formal requisition. Reproduction of maps without permission of the Military Topographical Service is prohibited.

The regularly expendable maps of peacetime must be replaced, corrected, or enlarged in time of war. Operational maps are drafted for use by the field army by the Topographic Service in accordance with the needs of constantly changing combat conditions. They are issued to designated units before or simultaneously with the preliminary orders of the Chief of Staff. New maps must be drafted as new terrain is encountered, and existing maps must be modified to meet requirements of varying types of combat.

Each unit maintains a supply of maps of the combat sector covering an area of 3 days' march forward and 2 days' march back from the current combat line.

The width of the sector covered by the map reserve of each unit encompasses its own front and those of its adjacent units. The quantity of each type of map issued for a given combat sector, as determined by army orders, usually is sufficient to supply each officer, each noncommissioned officer executing an independent mission, and each scout, sniper, and observer with a map.

Troops are supplied with maps from either stationary or mobile map depots by agencies of the Military Topographic Service of staffs of formations, or if such agencies are not included in the Tables of Organization, by the chiefs of the Operations Divisions of the staffs. Maps normally are supplied by the higher to the next lower echelon without special request. A regimental staff is supplied from the mobile division reserve. The division reserves are supplied by mobile corps reserves and the corps reserves are supplied by an army stationary map depot, or its mobile branch. Independent formations and units receive maps from the formation to which they are attached.

Section II. Soviet Tactical Symbols

1. SYMBOLS FOR HEADQUARTERS

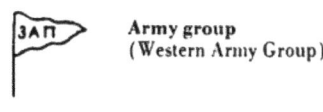

Army group
(Western Army Group)

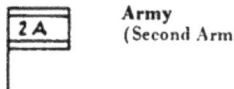

Army
(Second Army)

Corps
(II Rifle Corps)
ск —Rifle corps
тк —Tank corps or
кк —Cavalry corps

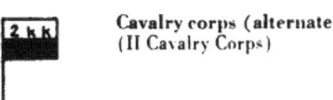

Cavalry corps (alternate)
(II Cavalry Corps)

Formation
(4th Rifle Division)
с д —Rifle division
сбр —Rifle brigade
тбр -Tank brigade
абр —Artillery brigade
исбр —Engineer-pioneer brigade
тпп —Heavy tank regiment
кд —Cavalry division

Cavalry division (alternate)
(5th Cavalry Division)

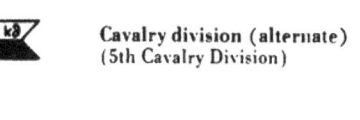

Unit
(10th Rifle Regiment)
сп —Rifle regiment
ап —Artillery regiment
шап —Ground-attack air regiment
тб —Tank battalion
ттр —Heavy tank company

Cavalry regiment (alternate)
(15th Cavalry Regiment)

Element
(3d Battalion, 10th Rifle Regiment)
сб —Rifle battalion
ад —Artillery battalion
тр —Tank company
вз — тт-Heavy tank platoon

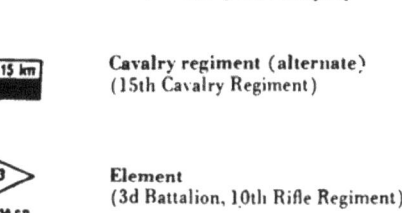

Command post
(Second Army)
(Flag and characters designate unit)

2. SYMBOLS FOR OPERATIONS

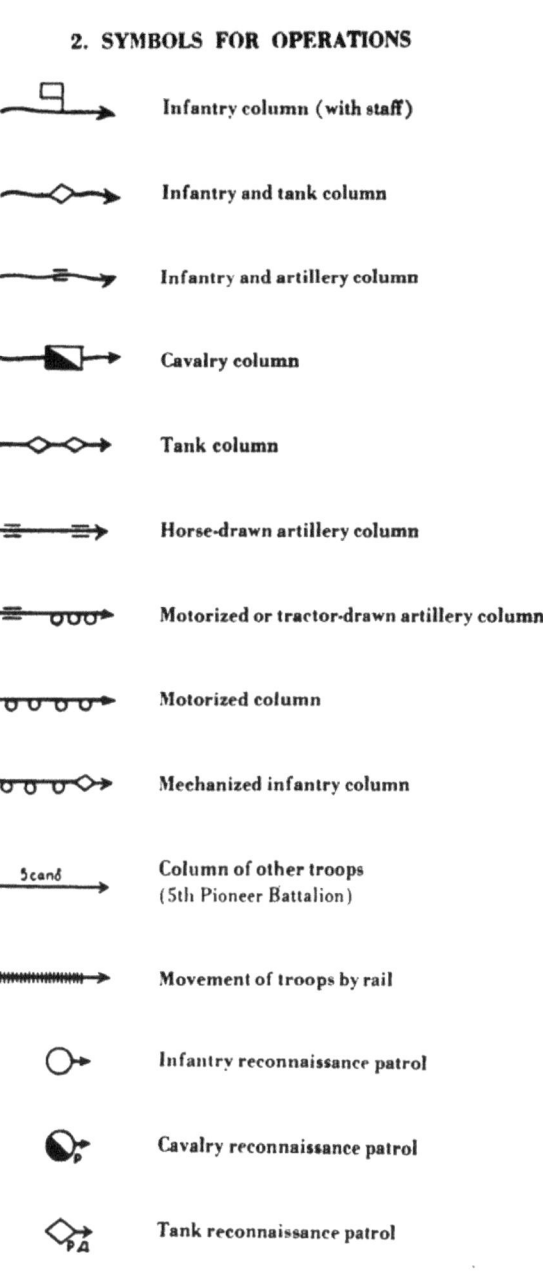

Infantry column (with staff)

Infantry and tank column

Infantry and artillery column

Cavalry column

Tank column

Horse-drawn artillery column

Motorized or tractor-drawn artillery column

Motorized column

Mechanized infantry column

Column of other troops
(5th Pioneer Battalion)

Movement of troops by rail

Infantry reconnaissance patrol

Cavalry reconnaissance patrol

Tank reconnaissance patrol

Tank reconnaissance group

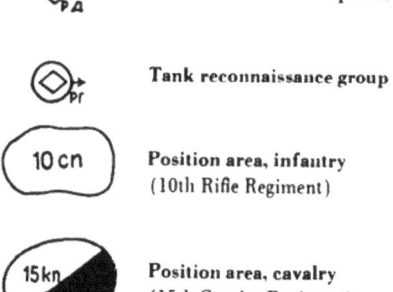

Position area, infantry
(10th Rifle Regiment)

Position area, cavalry
(15th Cavalry Regiment)

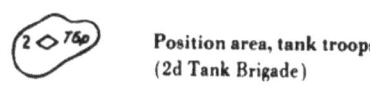

Position area, tank troops
(2d Tank Brigade)

483

	Position area, artillery (1st Artillery Regiment)		**3. INFANTRY SYMBOLS**
			Company position area
	Position area, special troops (6th Signal Battalion)		
			Platoon position area
	Position area to be occupied by infantry (10th Rifle Regiment)		
			Antitank rifle company
	Position area to be occupied by cavalry (15th Cavalry Regiment)		
			Antitank rifle platoon
	Position area to be occupied by tank troops (2d Tank Brigade)		
			120-mm mortar battery
	Combat sector occupied until a set time limit		
			120-mm mortar platoon
	Planned combat sector		
			82-mm mortar company
	Disposition of troops in defense		
			82-mm mortar platoon
	Disposition of troops in offense		
			50-mm mortar platoon
	Direction of attack		
			Four-piece machine gun battery
	Direction of main effort		
			Rifle company in offense (same for submachine gunners)
	Combat objectives		
			Machine gun platoon in offense
	Actual offensive		
			Submachine gun platoon in offense
	Withdrawal of troops		
			Rifle platoon deployed in line
	Withdrawal of troops after unsuccessful attack		
			Rifle platoon in offense
	Feint or dummy movement		
			Rifle squad in offense (same for submachine gunners)
	Boundary between formations		
			Rifle squad deployed in line (same for submachine gunners)
	Boundary between units		
			Submachine gun squad in defense
	Boundary between elements		
			Rifle squad in defense

484

Symbol	Description	Symbol	Description
	Company commander		Heavy machine gun (7.62-mm)
	Platoon commander		Heavy machine gun (12.7-mm)
	Squad commander		Light machine gun (automatic rifle)
	Observer		50-mm mortar
	Signalman		82-mm mortar
	Gun layer		120-mm mortar
	Sniper		Small-caliber (45- or 57-mm) antitank gun
	Submachine gunner		76-mm infantry howitzer
	Rifleman		
	Ammunition bearer		
	Loader		
	Pioneer		

4. ARTILLERY SYMBOLS

	Chemical man
	Horse driver
	Rider
	Mortar on cart
	Machine gun squad on cart
	Pack-loaded machine gun
	Pack horse
	Antitank rifle

	Battery in firing position (either 76-mm or unspecified)
	Planned position for medium gun battery
	Dummy battery
	Artillery battalion position area (group supporting 6th Rifle Regiment)
	Artillery position area (1st Battalion, 5th Artillery Regiment)
	Meteorological post
	Flash ranging or optical reconnaissance post
	Sound ranging post
	Observation post (approximate location)
	Observation post (surveyed location)

485

Reserve observation post
Д —Auxiliary observation post
Б —Flank observation post
П —Forward observation post

Topographic reconnaissance battery
computation post

Survey base or check point

Battery base piece (approximate location)

Battery base piece (surveyed location)

Accurately located target

Base direction of fire

Supplementary direction of fire

Concentration

Antipersonnel defensive barrage

Fire for destruction

Antitank defensive barrage

Accompanying barrage

Heavy gun (152 to 203 mm)

Medium gun (100 to 122 mm)

76-mm gun (or artillery in general)

76-mm mountain gun

Medium or heavy howitzer (152 mm up)

122-mm howitzer

Rocket launcher

5. TANK TROOP SYMBOLS

Light tank (or unspecified type)

Medium tank

Heavy tank

Self-propelled gun

Mine-clearance tank

Full-track personnel carrier

Light armored car

Heavy armored car

Armored half-track

Tanks in combat formation

Light or medium tank platoon in combat
formation

Light or medium tank company in combat
formation

Medium tank battalion in combat formation

Heavy tank company in combat formation

Heavy tank regiment in combat formation

Assembly area
К —Terminal
З -Reserve
П —Intermediate

Terrain barrier passable for tanks

486

−+−+− Axis of communication (for supply and replacement)

6. AIR FORCE SYMBOLS

Fighter squadron

Short range bomber squadron

Long range bomber squadron

Ground attack squadron

Long range fighter squadron

Short range reconnaissance squadron

Army reconnaissance squadron

Long range reconnaissance squadron

Liaison squadron

Medical evacuation squadron

Dive bomber regiment

Artillery spotter squadron

Air transport squadron

Fighter regiment

Ground attack regiment

Short range bomber regiment

Long range bomber regiment

Long range fighter regiment

Air reconnaissance regiment

Air transport regiment

Heavy air regiment

Tactical reserve air regiment

Air control post

Permanent airdrome

Airfield
З -Reserve
Л -Dummy
Landing field

Landing field for heavy aircraft

Landing field for fighters

Air photo reconnaissance

Air rendezvous (showing time and elevation)

Unit alerted for airborne flight

Patrol area

Ground-attack target (showing time)

Bomb target (showing time)

Landing site for airborne troops

Airborne landing

Parachuted air cargo

Air passage lanes (showing entrance and exit)

487

7. ANTIAIRCRAFT DEFENSE SYMBOLS

Antiaircraft artillery battery

Antiaircraft artillery battalion in firing position (showing effective zone)

Antiaircraft artillery battery on the march

Antiaircraft machine gun

Antiaircraft machine gun (double or quadruple mount)

Motorized antiaircraft machine gun

Small-caliber antiaircraft gun

Antiaircraft searchlight

Barrage balloon

Air observation and warning post

Air liaison post (for air warning at a ground CP)

8. CHEMICAL DEFENSE SYMBOLS

Contaminated area

Gas shelter

Meteorological station

Motorized decontaminator

Horse-drawn decontaminator

9. SIGNAL COMMUNICATIONS SYMBOLS

Signal battalion, company, or platoon (Right-hand letter indicates type of unit)

Radio battalion, company, or platoon (left-hand letter indicates size of unit)

Cavalry signal unit (telegraph squadron)

Radio direction finder company

Telegraph operating company

Telegraph construction company

Telephone line company

Telephone construction company

Cable construction company

Field post office

Message center

Telegraph

Central telegraph station

Sound-powered switchboard

Six-line switchboard (number of dots indicates number of lines)

Telephone testing station

Telephone control point (parallel connection)

Telephone control station (series connection)

Telephone

488

⌀~~~~	Sound-powered telephone	⊗↗	Engineer reconnaissance
—⑤—	Permanent telegraph line (five channels)	(Can)	Pioneer reconnaissance patrol
—376—	Permanent line	⊠	Pioneer (engineer) battalion
··—·—·.	Overhead telegraph line	▱	Ponton battalion
~~2~~	Cable (two-line)	⊠	Engineer dump
	Motorized radio direction finder station	⧄	Field power station
	Motorized radio	⊶⊷	Field power compressor
K	Radio receiver К –Testing С –Monitoring Д –Auxiliary		Rifle squad trench
	Radio beacon		Light machine gun trench (arrow shows direction of fire)
	Radio net		Heavy machine gun trench
λ₂	Wave length (wave length 1)		Mortar emplacement
	Radio communication		Antiaircraft machine gun emplacement
– – – – –	Messenger communication		Antitank gun emplacement
≫	Signal lamp communication		Artillery emplacement
	Signal flag communication		Reserve trench
	Signal rocket		Covered machine gun emplacement (general)

10. ENGINEER SYMBOLS
  a. Tactical positions and fortifications

	Antitank strongpoint		Splinter-proof machine gun emplacement
	Fire plan		Reinforced earth-and-timber machine gun emplacement
			Reinforced concrete machine gun emplacement
			Fort

489

Shelter (general)		Barbed wire fence (reinforced with stumps, bushes, etc.)
Light earthen shelter		Antitank ditch
Light shelter		Antitank escarpment
Reinforced shelter		Artificial ramparts
Heavy shelter		Rampart of snow
Reinforced concrete shelter		Dragons' teeth
Armored machine gun turret		Tank trap
Communications trench		Barrier of fallen timber
Concealed communications trench		Cut-off timber
Covered communications trench		Timber antitank barrier
Subterranean communications trench		Antipersonnel minefield

b. Obstacles

Barbed wire (one row)		Antitank minefield
Barbed wire (three rows)		Controlled demolitions
Barbed wire (ten rows)		Explosive charges
Low wire		Delayed-action mines
Concertina		Antipersonnel fragmentation mines
Inconspicuous obstacle		Booby trap
Removable obstacle (knife rest, etc.)		Unremovable mine
Electrified barbed wire fence		Antitank barrier (general)
		Inundation

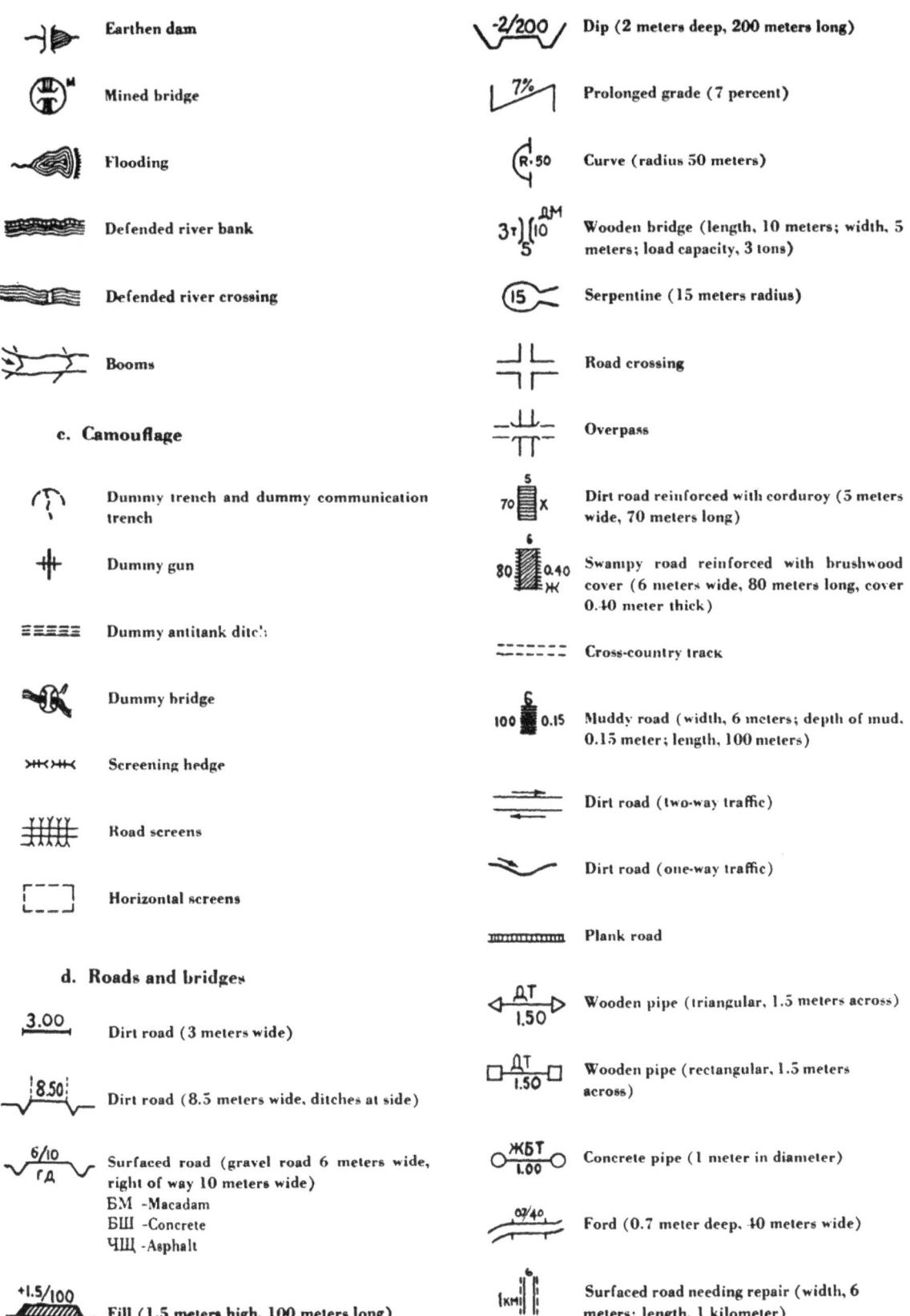

Earthen dam	Dip (2 meters deep, 200 meters long)
Mined bridge	Prolonged grade (7 percent)
Flooding	Curve (radius 50 meters)
Defended river bank	Wooden bridge (length, 10 meters; width, 5 meters; load capacity, 3 tons)
Defended river crossing	Serpentine (15 meters radius)
Booms	Road crossing

c. Camouflage

Dummy trench and dummy communication trench	Overpass
Dummy gun	Dirt road reinforced with corduroy (3 meters wide, 70 meters long)
Dummy antitank ditch	Swampy road reinforced with brushwood cover (6 meters wide, 80 meters long, cover 0.40 meter thick)
Dummy bridge	Cross-country track
Screening hedge	Muddy road (width, 6 meters; depth of mud, 0.15 meter; length, 100 meters)
Road screens	Dirt road (two-way traffic)
Horizontal screens	Dirt road (one-way traffic)

d. Roads and bridges

Dirt road (3 meters wide)	Plank road
Dirt road (8.5 meters wide, ditches at side)	Wooden pipe (triangular, 1.5 meters across)
Surfaced road (gravel road 6 meters wide, right of way 10 meters wide) БМ –Macadam БШ –Concrete ЧШ –Asphalt	Wooden pipe (rectangular, 1.5 meters across)
	Concrete pipe (1 meter in diameter)
	Ford (0.7 meter deep, 40 meters wide)
Fill (1.5 meters high, 100 meters long)	Surfaced road needing repair (width, 6 meters; length, 1 kilometer)

491

⦀⦀	Hard-surfaced road requiring major repair (width, 6 meters; length, 1.5 meters)		Logging area
³⁄₅ᴛ	3-ton wooden bridge (requiring reinforcement up to 5-ton capacity)		Gravel quarry
	Road in bad repair		Rock quarry (alternate symbol)
✗—✗—✗	Destroyed road		Boulders in field
	Dug-up and destroyed road		Sand quarry
	Detour		Clay quarry
	Mined road	♀30	Spring (flow, 30 liters per minute)
	Demolition charges on road	▬K	Open well
	Stone bridge	○	Piped well
	Destroyed bridge	◎	Field pumping station
	Bridge constructed from standard (T/E) equipment	◉ВП400	Water point (capacity of 400 liters of purified water per hour)
	Bridge (improvised construction)		

11. SYMBOLS FOR REAR SERVICES

	Steel bridge		Supply station
	Ferry crossing	⊠	Army supply depot (similarly, tank corps supply point)
	Ponton bridge		Hospital for infectious diseases
	Ice crossing		Field mobile hospital
•⁷⁄₂	Shell hole (7 meters in diameter, 2 meters deep)		Railhead field evacuation point

e. Local resources

			Army field veterinary hospital
	Sand deposit		

a. Divisional units

	Rock quarry	⊗	Divisional supply point (similarly, tank brigade supply point)

492

Divisional decontamination platoon	Ammunition platoon of an artillery battalion (horse-drawn)
Divisional portable artillery dump	Forward echelon of regimental rear services (second echelon bears No. 2)
Portable quartermaster dump	**c. Battalion, company, and battery installations**
Ammunition transport company (motorized)	Battalion ammunition supply point
Divisional fuel point	Battalion medical station
Divisional medical point	Battalion ration point
Collection and first-aid station for lightly wounded	Company ammunition point
Collection point for damaged motor vehicles	Platoon ammunition point
Corps or division veterinary hospital	First-aid post
Evacuation section of a corps or division veterinary hospital	**12. TRAFFIC SIGNS**
Motorized field bakery	Main traffic control post
Divisional sanitary battalion	Other traffic control posts
Divisional artillery workshop	Auxiliary traffic control post
Divisional livestock herd	Warning sign
b. Regimental installations	Road sign
Regimental ammunition point	Patrol
Ammunition transport platoon of the transport company	
Regimental medical station (similarly, tank brigade medical station)	
Forward veterinary station	
Regimental veterinary hospital	

Section III. CONVENTIONAL SOVIET SIGNS

(For Military Topographic Maps,
Scale 1:50,000)

1. TOPOGRAPHIC SIGNS

Cities

City-type and suburban settlements

Farmhouse-type settlement
(more than 100 households)

Farmhouse-type settlement
(less than 100 households)

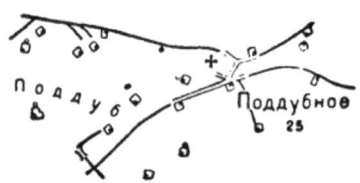

Separate farm households
(grouped under a single sign)

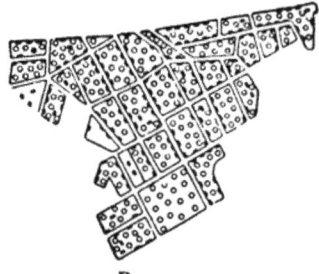

Resort

Barracks

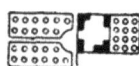

State farm

━ ∙ ━ ∙ ━ ∙ ━ ∙ ━ ∙ ━

National boundary

┣━┫ ∙ ┣━┫ ∘ ┣━┫ ∙ ┣━┫

Frontier marker

━ ━ ━ ━ ━ ━ ━ ━ ━ ━

Union-Republic boundary

━ ∙∙ ━ ∙∙ ━ ∙ ━ ∙∙ ━ ∙∙ ━

***Krai, Oblast,* and Autonomous Republic boundaries**

━ ∙ ━ ∙ ━ ∙ ━ ∙ ━ ∙ ━

Autonomous *Oblast* boundary
(and boundary of *Oblast* subordinate to *Krai*)

━ ━ ∙ ━ ━ ∙∼ ━∼

National and administrative district boundary

∙━∙∙━∙∙━∙∙━∙∙━∙

County (*Rayon*) boundary

494

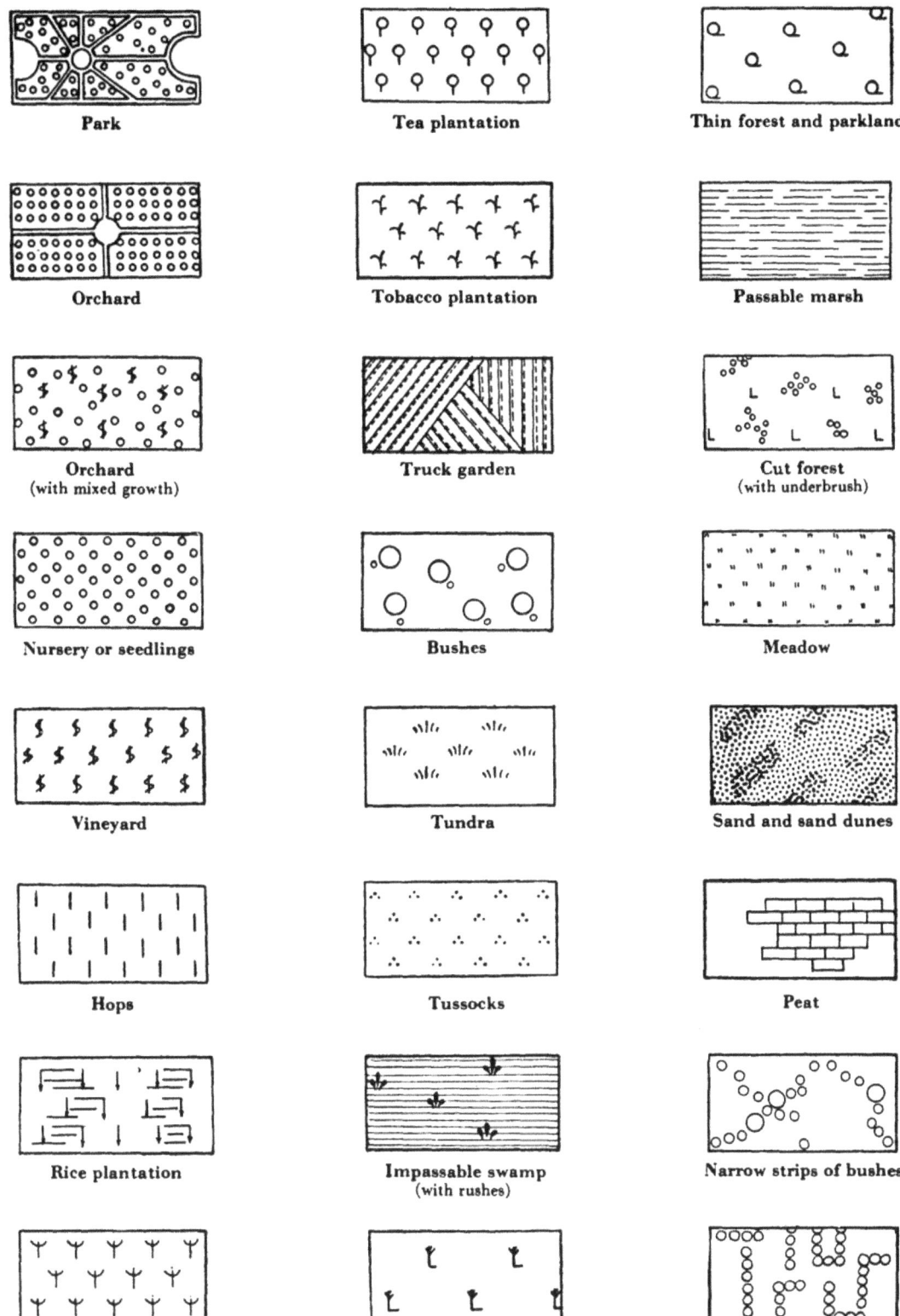

Park

Tea plantation

Thin forest and parkland

Orchard

Tobacco plantation

Passable marsh

Orchard
(with mixed growth)

Truck garden

Cut forest
(with underbrush)

Nursery or seedlings

Bushes

Meadow

Vineyard

Tundra

Sand and sand dunes

Hops

Tussocks

Peat

Rice plantation

Impassable swamp
(with rushes)

Narrow strips of bushes

Cotton plantation

Burned forest

Narrow strips of forest

495

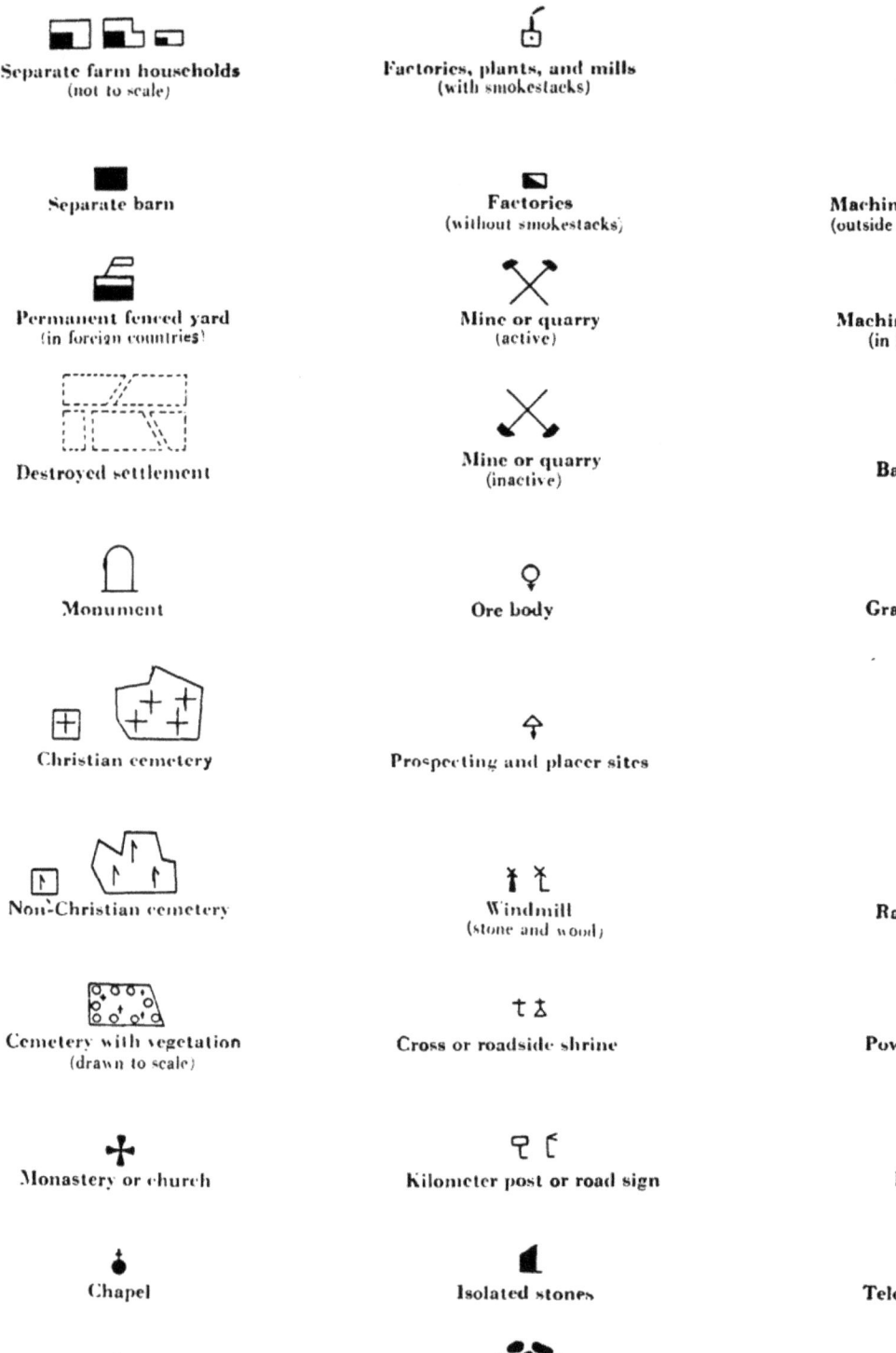

Separate farm households
(not to scale)

Separate barn

Permanent fenced yard
(in foreign countries)

Destroyed settlement

Monument

Christian cemetery

Non-Christian cemetery

Cemetery with vegetation
(drawn to scale)

Monastery or church

Chapel

Synagogue

Mosque

Factories, plants, and mills
(with smokestacks)

Factories
(without smokestacks)

Mine or quarry
(active)

Mine or quarry
(inactive)

Ore body

Prospecting and placer sites

Windmill
(stone and wood)

Cross or roadside shrine

Kilometer post or road sign

Isolated stones

Stones

Pit

Mounds

Machine-tractor station
(outside of inhabited place)

Machine-tractor station
(in inhabited place)

Base fuel depot

Grain elevator

Airbase

Radio station

Power station

Post office

Telegraph station

Postal and telegraph station

Central telephone station

496

Meteorological station	Stone quarry	Survey marker (on tree)
Telephone and telegraph lines	Oil seep	Survey marker (at crossroad)
High-tension power lines (elevated)	Isolated stand of trees (useful for orientation)	Underwater cable
Customs office	Evergreen tree (isolated)	Semaphore (useful for orientation)
Border-control station	Deciduous tree (isolated)	Livestock corral
Border-control outpost	Young trees (height more than 6 meters)	Rain pit (with brick superstructure)
Quarantine station	Mature trees (height less than 6 meters)	Pass
Observation points	Forester's house	Spring
Oil derrick	Marker (astronomically located)	Well
Fire lookout tower (with water supply)	Bench mark	Artesian well
Permanent apiary	Bench mark (on mound)	Well (with dipper)
Clay quarry	Elevation marker	Well (with windmill)
Sand quarry	Survey marker	Barbed wire fence

497

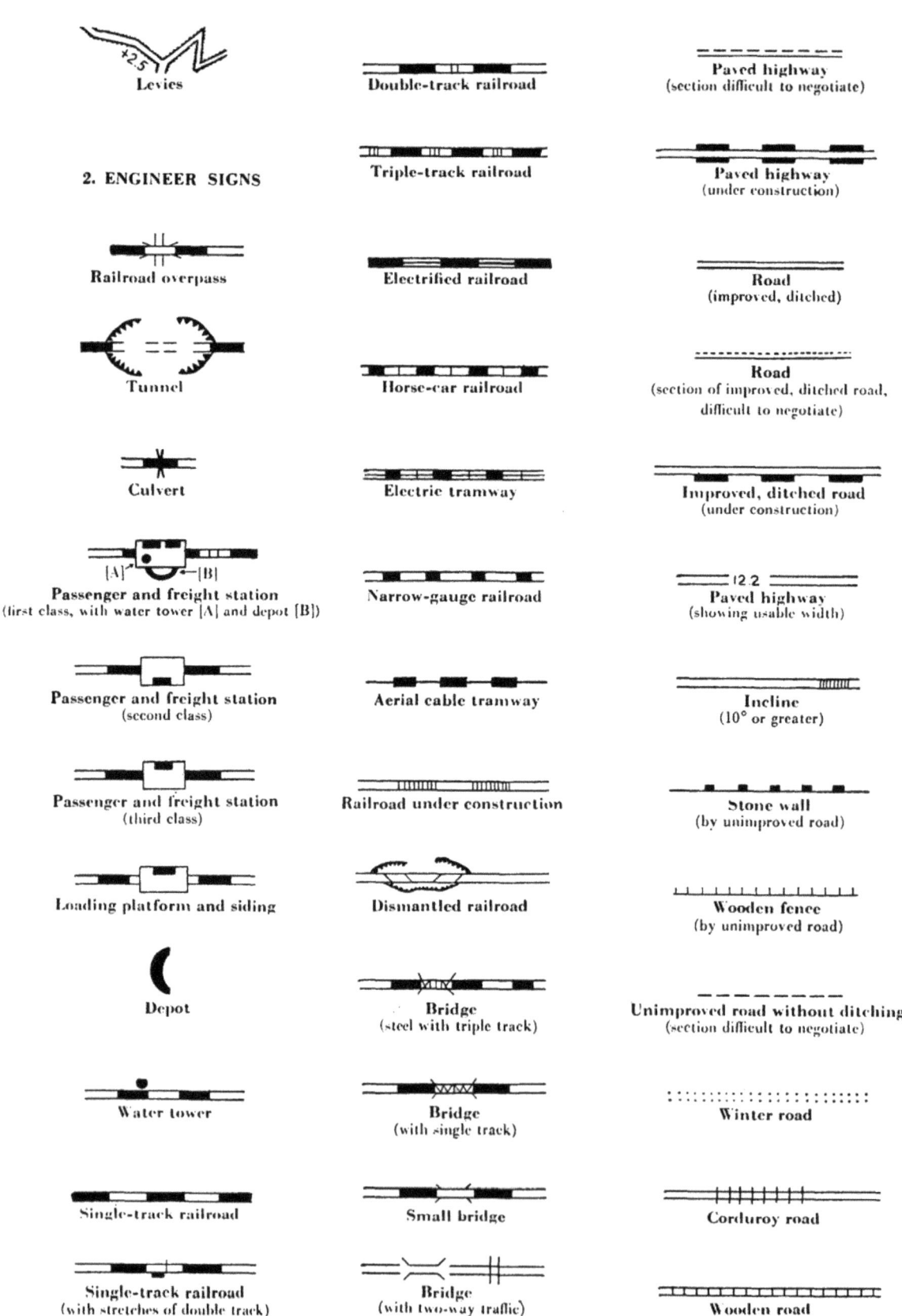

Levies

2. ENGINEER SIGNS

Railroad overpass

Tunnel

Culvert

Passenger and freight station
(first class, with water tower [A] and depot [B])

Passenger and freight station
(second class)

Passenger and freight station
(third class)

Loading platform and siding

Depot

Water tower

Single-track railroad

Single-track railroad
(with stretches of double track)

Double-track railroad

Triple-track railroad

Electrified railroad

Horse-car railroad

Electric tramway

Narrow-gauge railroad

Aerial cable tramway

Railroad under construction

Dismantled railroad

Bridge
(steel with triple track)

Bridge
(with single track)

Small bridge

Bridge
(with two-way traffic)

Paved highway
(section difficult to negotiate)

Paved highway
(under construction)

Road
(improved, ditched)

Road
(section of improved, ditched road,
difficult to negotiate)

Improved, ditched road
(under construction)

Paved highway
(showing usable width)

Incline
(10° or greater)

Stone wall
(by unimproved road)

Wooden fence
(by unimproved road)

Unimproved road without ditching
(section difficult to negotiate)

Winter road

Corduroy road

Wooden road

498

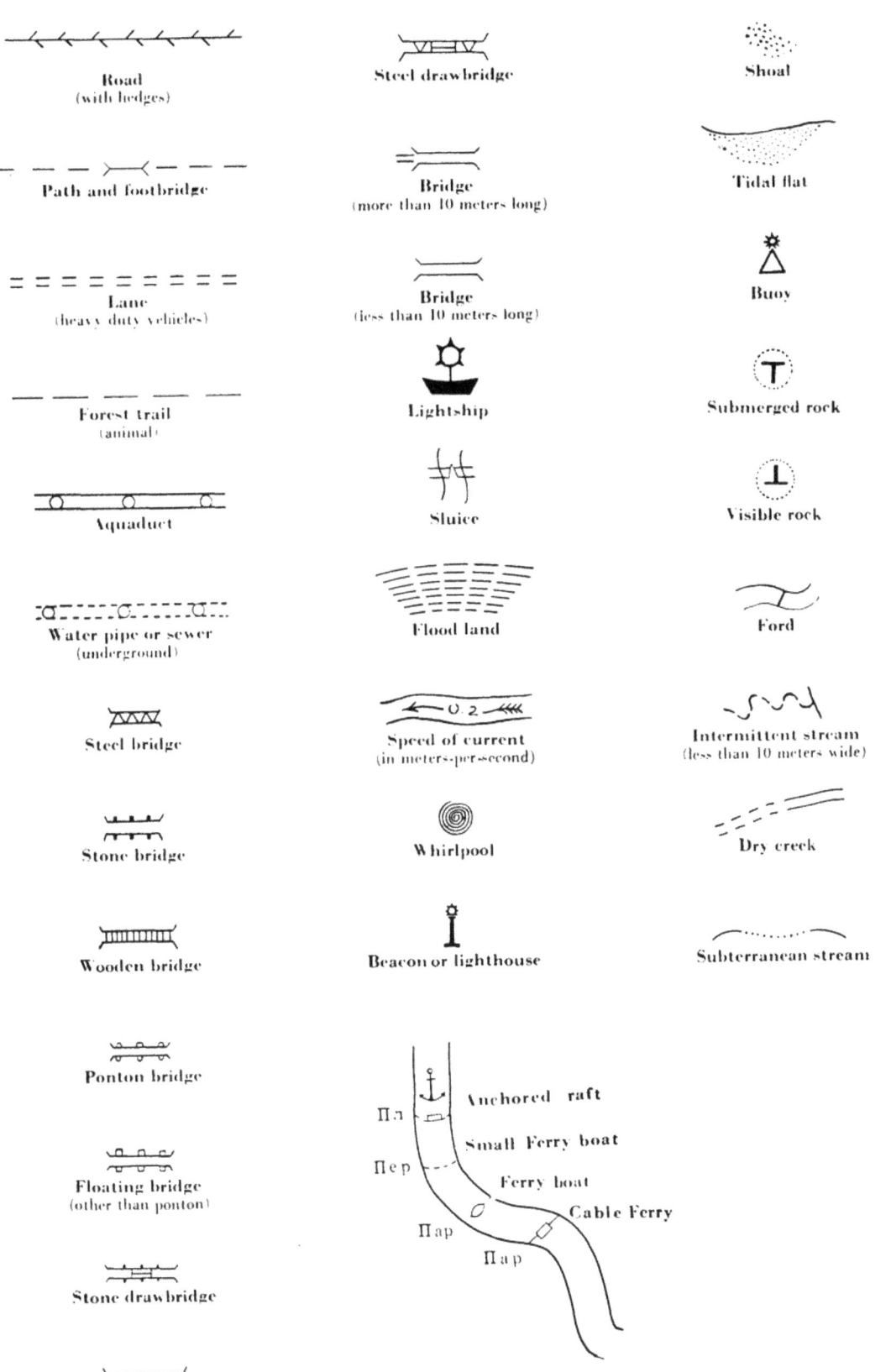

Road
(with hedges)

Path and footbridge

Lane
(heavy duty vehicles)

Forest trail
(animal)

Aquaduct

Water pipe or sewer
(underground)

Steel bridge

Stone bridge

Wooden bridge

Ponton bridge

Floating bridge
(other than ponton)

Stone drawbridge

Wooden drawbridge

Steel drawbridge

Bridge
(more than 10 meters long)

Bridge
(less than 10 meters long)

Lightship

Sluice

Flood land

Speed of current
(in meters-per-second)

Whirlpool

Beacon or lighthouse

Anchored raft

Small Ferry boat

Ferry boat

Cable Ferry

Shoal

Tidal flat

Buoy

Submerged rock

Visible rock

Ford

Intermittent stream
(less than 10 meters wide)

Dry creek

Subterranean stream

Lightning Source UK Ltd.
Milton Keynes UK
UKHW051821120120
356820UK00015B/215/P

9 781070 304458